CRIMINOLOGY REVIEW YEARBOOK

Volume 1

CRIMINOLOGY REVIEW YEARBOOK

Associate Editors

Volume 1

CRIMINOLOGY REVIEW YEARBOOK

Edited by
Sheldon L. Messinger
and
Egon Bittner

SAGE PUBLICATIONS   Beverly Hills   London

For information address:

SAGE PUBLICATIONS, INC.
275 South Beverly Drive
Beverly Hills, California 90212

SAGE PUBLICATIONS LTD
28 Banner Street
London EC1Y 8QE England

Printed in the United States of America

International Standard Book Number 0-8039-1062-2

International Standard Serial Number 0163-9056

FIRST PRINTING

CONTENTS

PREFACE

This is the first of a series of volumes designed to assist students of crime and crime control in staying abreast of their rapidly growing and changing field. We include among such students those interested in crime and crime control per se for intellectual or policy-related reasons, and those interested because the study of crime and crime control throws needed light on other phenomena of interest to them, such as social change and stability. These are not necessarily exclusive groups, of course. But to the extent that they are, we intend both to be served by this and succeeding volumes of the SAGE CRIMINOLOGY REVIEW YEARBOOK.

Each volume will contain specially prepared essays on emerging or controversial theories, perspectives, and issues in the study of crime and crime control; recently published materials dealing with these and additional themes; and a statistical appendix.

When we first discussed the series with the publisher, we thought the first volume might contain articles and book-segments of high quality published in the previous several years. We also wanted to be open to "fugitive" publications—those not reaching regular scholarly or commercial channels. Being aware that the study of crime and crime control was burgeoning, we believed that identifying, putting in one volume, and commenting on the "best" of this work would be useful. We did not expect that *selecting* materials of high quality would be a problem; we thought that *finding* them would be.

We were wrong. The flood of high quality materials that the recommendations of the associate editors, and our own reading, brought to attention was overwhelming. The large size of this volume reflects that fact. So, too, does the fact that most of the reprinted materials date from 1977 or 1978. Even so, we could not in one liftable or affordable volume contain all the high quality materials on crime and crime control printed (in regular channels, much less "fugitive" ones) in 1977 or 1978.

So we took another tack. Besides deciding to focus mainly on the most recent publications, we decided to "thematize" the volumes. Based on our reading, and conversations and correspondence with associate editors, we selected several themes and commissioned essays on them that would, in part, review the literature we could not reprint without devoting any given volume to a single theme. Selection of the three themes for the first volume was not difficult, although it was arbitrary to the extent that other, equally important themes might have been chosen. We are not troubled by this, caring less about what we have been unable to accomplish than the value of what has been done. We believe that any fair assessment of work on crime and crime control during the past few years would support our contention that, among the major developments to be considered, are the increasing attention of economists and historians to these phenomena, and the struggle, in theory and practice, to deal with "discretion." Other important paradigms, perspectives, and problems will be treated in later volumes.

To a lesser extent, however, some are treated in this volume too. In view of the complexity of the field, we decided not to limit any given volume to three themes, but to include materials on two or three more that seemed important, even though our resources would not permit commissioning essays on them. Thus, in this volume, we have included work on delinquency theory; organizational criminality; and prevention, treatment, and control. We have supplied some comments on these as well as the other themes in our introductory materials.

The statistical appendix is intended to enhance the use of each volume for reference purposes, as well as to provide some quantitative information to illustrate matters discussed in the preceding materials.

Decisions about the commissioning of essays and the statistical appendix and about the inclusion of papers were made, in the end, by the editors, and we accept full responsibility for them. We were ably assisted in coming to these decisions by the associate editors, and thank them warmly. We also want to thank Isaac Ehrlich, Michael S. Hindus, Arthur Rosett, Joseph G. Weis, and James Henney for preparing original materials for this volume; Lee S. Friedman, for permitting us to print this "fugitive" article on multiple regression analysis; and the many authors and publishers who gave us permission to reprint the many works included. We greatly profited from the assistance of Nancy Cushing Jones, of Sage Publications, Inc., and thank her too. Last but not least, Jean Collard gave able typing assistance: thanks.

INTRODUCTION

Many students of crime and crime control feel that their subject is no longer adequately described and analyzed in received terms. An era stretching back at least to the early part of this century appears to be passing away; a new era, requiring a changed vision, appears to be emerging. Whether the events engendering this feeling truly constitute or portend a new era, it is probably too early to say. It is not too early to suggest what some of these events have been.

I

The so-called "lawless years" of the Prohibition Era and the years of the Eisenhower presidency could be compared in all their important aspects on a number of dimensions. One can, of course, place the present and very recent past on this continuum, comparing rates of criminality, changes in the size of prison populations, variations in the number of executions, and the dollar losses due to crime. But none of these comparisons would reveal the critically new in the just past years.

None, for example, would show that in our times crime has been lifted from its traditional place in the scheme of things and shifted into the center of public attention as a political issue of first importance. The rise in the national significance of crime manifests itself in many ways, conspicuous being how references to rising crime rates and risks of criminal victimization have become an almost habitual part of public discourse in all parts of the country and in all segments of life. Polls, newspapers, and campaign oratory assure us that "the people" place "the crime problem" very high on the inventory of what is wrong with the country. Further, while this apprehension centers on what the F.B.I. inventories as "index crimes," it goes beyond them, and includes the perception of certain aspects of national politics as crime—especially, but not exclusively, expressions of popular protest.

It is not our view that these phenomena are unique in American history. Instead, we propose that the period between the mid-1960s and the mid-1970s was characterized by a public perception according to which the country was beset by a vast and growing outbreak of lawlessness in both the private and public spheres, and that the meaning of crime during this period must be understood in relationship to the elevation of crime to a matter of national importance and the criminalization of nation-wide political protest.

A refracted version of this perception characterizes criminological scholarship as well, and helps account for the decided sense that a new vision is needed. This new vision, hard in coming, is meant to apply to more than the present and future; it is meant to apply to the past as well. If crime has only recently become a subject for national political debate, the debate itself seems to have suggested that it may always have been a more important matter than commonly appreciated—or than realized by scholars. If political dissent has been criminalized, perhaps this, too, was true but insufficiently appreciated in the past.

II

Republican candidates in 1964 attacked the Democratic administration for taking—or at least abetting—a "soft attitude" toward crime and criminals. More specific targets of attack included the Supreme Court for shifting the balance of procedural advantage in the criminal process to defendants; trial judges for releasing convicted offenders faster than they could be arrested; and the correctional establishment for pursuing the elusive aim of rehabilitation of convicts. More generally, representatives of conventional liberalism were scored for attempting to give the underdog the jump in a dog-eat-dog world. Into this world conservatives sought to introduce, or reintroduce as they maintained, the principle of unaided competition. Liberal welfare programs aimed at abolishing conditions within which crime is known to thrive to get at the "roots of the crime problem" were held by conservatives to encourage the very predatory outlook underlying criminality. In a world of "no free lunches," the people who paid for theirs—even if aided by IRS subsidies—were certain that telling the sturdy rogue that he was the victim of past injustices virtually gave him a claim on something for nothing.

The Republican attack on liberal attitudes toward crime and on the programs designed to deal with it were reminiscent of accusations of being "soft on communism" in the heydays of the Cold War. We think this is no accident: criminals, overrepresented by members of minority groups unsatisfied with the status quo, bid fair to become an enemy within; proper subjects for a not-so-cold-war.

Conservatives were not the only persons crediting official misfeasance and official nonfeasance for crime. A related view was gaining strength on the liberal side. The old liberal dogma that crime must be fought by attacking its causes was replaced by the belief that existing programs based on such provisional identifications did more harm than good. Scepticism about the significance of what used to be referred to as the "causes of crime," and the shift of attention to the possibly criminogenic function of crime control activities was first expressed by Frank Tannenbaum (1938), later elaborated by Edwin M. Lemert (1951), and grew into a full-fledged school of thought commonly identified as "labeling theory." Thus, the idea that misguided government agencies entrusted with crime control contributed to criminality did not originate in Republican campaign rhetoric. It was Republican politics, however, rather than "labeling theory," that effectively demolished the house built around attempts to locate and dissipate "criminogenic factors."

Of course liberals and conservatives made different inferences from these similar insights. Where liberals saw the need for a reduction of official intervention by decriminalization and diversion, conservatives argued for creating an effective barrier between the community of law abiding citizens and the torrent of depredation that threatened to engulf it. In both cases, however, state action at the highest level was indicated: the liberals moving to provide incentives through government for government at lower levels to decriminalize and divert; the conservatives support for increased but more cost-effective crime control, primarily through the police.

In terms of popular sensibilities, the conservative definition of the meaning of crime carries the day; in our day the initiative has shifted to the side of crime control activism. In self-declared sober minds it takes the shape of views commending the resolute use of penal sanctions in a way likely to contribute maximally to the reduction of crime rates. And as a theme of political ideology the meaning of crime acquires a penumbra of connotations expressed in the form of analogies to the "decline and fall of the Roman Empire." When this attitude gains wide currency, talk of crime and dealings with it can no longer be freed of a sense of great urgency and of national importance: burglars become national enemies and their victims become witnesses to a higher cause. Such beliefs give rise to a rhetoric with an independent momentum that subsists and retains viability even when dissociated from reality. Thus the people, politicians, and media continue talking about "rising crime rates," quite unperturbed by the fact that these rates have recently been declining, even according to the F.B.I., which has never been accused of sympathies for the liberal cause. Talking about crime realistically becomes somehow subversive of the struggle against it; pointing to declining rates is perceived as raising captious and frivolous objections to a task of critical importance for the survival of the nation.

The zeal of condemnation of crime and the frantic urgency it evokes is only one part of the "crime issue" at the national level. Not only have we mobilized for a war against crime, but we have taken this war into areas involving matters other than criminality in the traditional sense. While the law enforcement institutions of the country were confronted with rapidly rising crime rates in the second half of the 1960s, they nevertheless accepted, eagerly it would seem, the added responsibility of controlling political protest related to the civil rights struggle and the war in Vietnam. The principal response of government to these activities was to brand them with the stamp of lawlessness and criminality. The justification was that while the right to orderly dissent was intact and remained available, persons who breached the norms regulating its expression forfeited the right to present their case for a fair hearing. Indeed, according to this view, the choice of methods deliberately or incidentally disrupting the convenience and decorum of urban life disqualified the dissenters from participation in the democratic process. Accordingly, government attention was directed not to the substance of the dissent, but to those external aspects of the dissenters' conduct that seemed to involve law-breaking in the ordinary sense. The choice to criminalize parts of political life, the attempt to dispose of opponents by defining them as merely peace-breakers, enriched the struggle against crime of the ordinary sort. The defense of "law and order" almost reached a siege state, clearly demanding measures of extreme condemnation and control.

We are quite prepared to admit that the criminalization of politics, like the politicization of crime, is not unprecedented in American life. What appears to be relatively new is that the "law and order" campaign against political dissidents was carried out with sustained vigor, and on a broad scale, despite the fact that many of the dissidents came from the upper-middle and upper strata of society.

There is an irony difficult to miss in the fact that the most outspoken advocates of using penal law against political opponents became themselves victims of this method of political struggle. Despite many differences, the trial of the Chicago Eight, the persecution of the Black Panthers, the mass arrests of war protesters, on the one hand, and the legal proceedings arising out of the Watergate Scandal including the impeachment hearings, on the other, spring from the same impulse.

In sum, the politicization of crime and the criminalization of politics are two critically important aspects in the meaning of crime in our times. Americans seem to perceive a far greater necessity for, and possibly have greater faith in the effectiveness of, the criminal justice process in the broadest sense, as a preferred method of social control, than in the years past. If one is to believe the polls, Americans have made the control of crime the first item on the agenda of the internal functions of government, and opinions concerning the relative importance of this task have become an important crystalization point for political partisanship. Further, Americans have seemingly accepted the desirability and feasibility of attacking political opponents by focusing on those aspects of their activities that are, or can be interpreted to be, violations of penal law. For this to be effective one cannot rely on the spontaneous lawlessness of the opponent; thus, it should come as no surprise that recent revelations strongly suggest the use of agent-provocateurs and of other instigations of lawless aspects of protest in the 1960s.

III

The appointment of the President's Commission on Law Enforcement and Administration of Justice, and to a lesser extent the creation of the National Commission on Civil Disorders and the National Commission on the Causes and Prevention of Violence, indicate the conspicuous rise of crime in the broadened sense into the sphere of national politics. The "Crime Commission," as the first of the three came to be called, is of special interest because its work sought to combine the old and the new.

Though clearly aware of the heightened significance of crime in national life, the Commission intoned its recommendations with controlled alarm and measured optimism. We may have fallen behind somewhat in dealing with criminals effectively, it said, but we were basically on the right track, and could and would catch up if we got better organized and more adequately financed. This is the essence of the seven principles to which the Commission boiled down its many reports. One would look in vain through the volumes the Commission produced for the kind of sober scepticism and matter-of-fact practicality that permeates Norval Morris and Gordon Hawkins' (1970) advice to honest politicians on crime and crime control. While the latter work always deals with matters involving crime in ways that address simultaneously the prevailing social and political interests in these matters, the Commission's utterances betrayed supreme indifference for the consequences of the national anxiety about crime. Thus, the Commission's work was mainly the last statement of a past era, comprising the highest level of its scholarship and the most eloquent expression of its ideology. If this kind of scholarship and this ideology are not yet exhausted, they have lost the dominant position they once occupied. The reorientation of policy that set in with the beginning of the Nixon presidency was soon joined by a turn to scepticism and pessimism in criminological scholarship about the prospects of rehabilitative correction or the promise of crime preventive service programs. The Commission's recommendations along these lines were, therefore, just an echo of the past, rather than an indication for the future.

IV

Like the rest of President Lyndon B. Johnson's quest for the Great Society, the work of the Crime Commission produced the typical outcome of harried liberalism—a federal agency. The Omnibus Crime Control and Safe Streets Act of 1968 established an agency whose very name echoes the New Deal—the Law Enforcement Assistance Administration (LEAA). Ten years later the agency has fallen into disfavor and legislative action has been initiated to replace it with a new governmental structure. It is fair to say that the 6 billion dollars the agency has infused into the struggle against crime have not been the best husbanded expenditure of modern government. And it is no doubt true that "a complex bureaucratic structure has enveloped the Federal effort, involving state and local law enforcement officials in excessive regulation, complexity and mountains of red tape—rather than providing them with needed financial and technical assistance," as President Carter stated in his message to the Congress. Still, there is little doubt that the LEAA will have made a significant and long lasting impact on American criminal justice administration, however inefficient and misguided some, many, or perhaps all its activities will be judged to have been.

That the LEAA and its arm, the National Institute of Law Enforcement and Criminal Justice, have been influential seems certain. Where its intended impact can be defined precisely, however, there is often a good deal of uncertainty that the changes introduced really took hold in the planned sense. For example, it is quite unclear what the effects of changes in urban police patrol practices really mean for the quality of policing. But there are few who would not agree that a new aspect has been added to what is going on in police departments, prosecutors' offices, and courtrooms. If this new aspect cannot easily be characterized, it is clearly due to the presence of the LEAA.

The LEAA provided impetus for a movement in the direction of synthesis and uniformity in American criminal justice. Its direct efforts to move along such lines may have been less effective than certain byproducts of the agency's activities. Wherever the agency brought local authorities into relationships with itself, it imposed upon them a degree of uniformity and pressed them to conform to certain universal standards. It initiated "requests for proposals," spelling out in detail the kinds of efforts deemed worthy of its support in the war against crime, as well as the forms that responses had to take. More diffuse but more important, as there developed a structure and lore around dealings with LEAA, local authorities found themselves trotting common paths. Even though the similarity of the paths was determined mainly by the circumstances of addressing federal largess, it resulted in a closer integration of parts of national law enforcement which in the past scarcely knew of each other's existence. All this was augmented by institutes, conferences, meetings, and the dissemination of information about research and development which contributed to bringing formerly autonomous elements together and creating a sense of community among them.

Relations with LEAA also inevitably forced local authorities to a higher level of bureaucratic formalism. Outside sponsored and financed activities called for more deliberate planning and more careful assessment of practices than was ordinary in American criminal justice administration. Police departments, court houses, and correctional institutions acquired advanced elements of public administration. With them came electronic technology and the technicians to run them. Last but certainly not least came a progressively more open and willing acceptance of research, experimentation, and innovation.

It is possible, of course, that the air of modernizing would have swept into the Halls of Justice without the LEAA. However, the vastly preponderant majority of these changes were introduced under LEAA aegis and scrutiny, and paid for with LEAA money. One is justly sceptical whether all those bright young women and men with degrees in political science or sociology would have had an opportunity to try to solve the eternal puzzles of justice with computers had it not been for LEAA. And one finds it very difficult to believe that their presence and its consequences for good or ill will not become an integral part of law enforcement in the United States.

We do not want to exaggerate the degree of national integration or modernization of American law enforcement and administration of justice. But there can be no doubt that whatever made it hidebound, inert, closed to outside influence, and otherwise intractible has given way to some extent. If nothing substantive has as yet changed to any significant degree, change seems far more likely today than it was ten years ago. In this the six billions of dollars and the sheer weight of the word from Washington have played a decisive role.

V

The shift of the crime problem to higher and more central levels of authority is also evident in the rise in the significance of offenses that cannot be handled adequately by most local jurisdictions. These offenses involve transgressions against administrative regulation of business, professional service, and various other practices. To the extent that many of these offenses are statutorily defined as criminal, they become the concern of the administration of criminal justice even if they are not part of the conventional criminal law. Many of these transgressions are committed by large-scale organizations, or by persons in connection with large-scale organizations. For the most part they are economic crimes of a very high level of complexity, and very often involve violations of federal law. In any case, this newly prominent form of criminality is typically dealt with least at the level of state prosecution and most often at the federal level. One should take note of the fact that this expansion of regulation by means of penal sanctions is taking place at the time when decriminalization of sumptuary offenses is urged from many quarters. Though there has been so far only a minimal response to these urgings to decriminalize, it is clear that the combination of these two trends represents a drift, even if not a drive, in the direction of centralization of crime control.

It should be noted in passing that such decriminalization as has taken place has resulted in the suspension of the use of penal sanctions, but it has not resulted in either the suspension or reduction of control by the state. This is most evident in those areas where diversionary programs have steered people away from the formal criminal process toward other remedies. In the area of juvenile justice, for example, the creation of categories of "Persons in Need of Service" redirected children from the more formal aspects of the process of delinquency determination into possibly more benign treatment settings. But the availability of more benign remedies permits casting a net wider and extending control to matters that in the past were left alone. Further, the new means of control often remained in the hands of government agencies, like probation departments. Similar consequences may not have resulted from the abolishment of the offense of public inebriation. The substitution of detoxification centers for drunk tanks may have brought about a general reduction of state intervention. In either case, however, diversion always means a turn to remedies that are in fact, or in pretense, more rational, more bureaucratically administered, and more morally neutral, than the sanctions administered under the auspices of the legal process. Advocates of diversion claim primarily technical effectiveness for it, rather than justice. That is not to say that they are not concerned with meeting standards of justice—or, at least, avoiding injustice—any more than it could be said that adherents of an unqualified principle of justice are uninterested in effectiveness, only that primacy is differently decided between the two.

The advocates of diversion from the criminal process to some form of therapeutic remedy are no longer contending with straightforward retributionists advocating penal sanctions, as their main adversaries. Many of those who argue in favor of punishing offenders do so not because they value punishment as a just response to transgression, but because they believe that the practice of punishing offenders is a cost-effective deterrent to further misdeeds. The punitive outlook has appropriated the criterion of effectiveness as its justification. It is important to emphasize that with regard to the moral problem of crime many partisans of punishment and many partisans of treatment are on the same side. They make the minimal ethical commitment to the prevention of unnecessary and preventable suffering. Beyond that they are interested solely in costs and outcomes. To be sure, the psychologically oriented partisans of treatment are often more strident in claiming humanistic motives, but the cost conscious partisans of punishment make up for it by rising in the defense of innocent victims of criminal predators. Neither of these avowals play much part in the determination of the programs of remedies they propose. The programs will stand and fall on demonstrable, practical effects.

VI

One could say that the present-day approach to crime across most of the range of its doctrinal variations proceeds from the productivity principle. There is a rise in the significance of calculable aspects of the criminal process, aspects making possible precise assessments of the relative value of alternative practices. Moreover, the business-like approach to the reduction of risks and to optimizing of outcomes is matched by pressures toward "Taylorization" of the criminal process. The efforts to limit, reduce, and eliminate as far as possible, the exercise of discretion by officials aim at the reduction of the function of these officials to strictly executory roles. For example, advocates of determinate sentencing would require judges to apply formulated criteria of judgment on the assumption that treating all offenders as if they were in all relevant aspects equal automatically serves the aims of justice. Now, although the efforts to limit discretion were undertaken to redress certain demonstrable wrongs in the decision-making process, standardization in the output of decisions was certainly not the only possible remedy for the sorry state of affairs. To hold that other alternatives to arbitrary and irresponsible decision-making are possible, however, would mean virtually to oppose the entire drift of secular civilization. Wherever decisions are made, efforts are mounted to develop explicit, precise, objective, and comprehensive norms, and rules, principles, or instruments to determine decisions. Everywhere the effort is to reduce the contribution of the decision-making official's unique wisdom, conscience, and experience. This and this alone, we feel, will defend us against sloth, folly, and corruption. Frederic Winslow Taylor argued in essentially the same terms when he prescribed "scientific management" for the factory floor. If referring to the recent arguments and changes as embracing a form of "Taylorism" implies an indictment, this should make us pause. Because while Taylor the prophet has been denied, his gospel has become the paradigm of practical wisdom wherever people are in a position to hold one another to account for what they do.

VII

We have used the term "practicality" in connection with the economic approach to crime and again in connection with the problem of discretion. The basic sense of the expression identifies regard for the contingent realities of human existence. A "practical" person is one who is alert to the dangers, risks, and opportunities concrete circumstances produce; his "practicality" is the ongoing compromise the free intellect strikes with material necessity. Recently, however, practicality has acquired an added aspect. The world to which the practical person must yield is no longer revealed to unarmed vision. Instead, the world he must let have its way is presented in the form of aggregates, graphs, models, facts, and theories, from which inferences can be drawn in fixed ways, of a kind that computers can do as well or better. Such considerations of practicality compel accepting the execution of a determinate sentence on the basis of the scientifically formulated expectation that it will prevent a crime between persons one does not even know exist, in a place one has never heard of, at a time too distant to matter.

Let us hasten to add that there is nothing objectionable in caring about people one never heard about. But there arises a hint of possible discomfort at the realization that the discernments contained in this model of caring and acting with care are the only admissible discernments. In this model every case weighs exactly as much as every other case like it—just as in a laboratory every properly bred white mouse is exhaustively interchangeable with every other. In this model hatred, spite, bigotry, fear, and cupidity are rendered impotent; but so are love, wisdom, pity, kinship, and the rest. And so we seem to be placing our faith once more in a notion of human existence in which the fate of people is predetermined, or, to put it in a more modern idiom, where things are planned so that, once the relevant "factors" are known, who will be saved and who will be damned no longer turns on an individual's wisdom or folly, virtue or vice; these could not possibly matter in the least.

This Kingdom of Heaven on Earth, the scientific-practices society, must have, of course, the highest degree of cultural universality. Movement toward it is, therefore, congruent with departure from localism, with increase in scale, and with national centralization, at least as a way station toward what Marshall McLuhan once called the "global village" of the future. In this connection it is of some interest to note that modern historiography, including the historiography of crime and criminal justice, is moving away from grand synthesis, from the general picture of the past, from studies of the main institutions conceived as epitomes of the past, to the recovery of small details, of the commonplace in human life, and to the grubby concreteness of everyday existence. This is true of both the work of the cliometricians who laboriously aggregate quantifiable data of past events, and of historians like Foucault who would not dream of sparing his reader a single detail of the village life in which a crime took place. Perhaps this is so because history has once more become the locus for nostalgia at the level of society as a whole.

REFERENCES

Congressional Record (1978). Vol. 124, No. 102, July 10, H. Doc. No. 95-365, p. H6323.
LEMERT, E. M. (1951). Social pathology. New York: McGraw-Hill.
MORRIS, N., and HAWKINS, G. (1970). The honest politician's guide to crime control. Chicago: University of Chicago Press.
TANNENBAUM, F. (1938). Crime and the community. New York: Ginn.

Part I:

THE ECONOMIC APPROACH TO CRIME

It has been a long time since any new idea has been advanced in criminology with as much vigor and conviction as the economic approach to crime. It has also been a while since any new development in the field has been greeted with so much alarm by insiders. And—we cannot refrain from observing—no record exists of any group of scholars as unprepared to settle for anything less than a totally enthusiastic acceptance of their work as the economists writing about crime.

Isaac Ehrlich, a leader in this work, responded to our invitation to explain the economic approach to crime with an essay of remarkable comprehensiveness and complexity. The essay does not require—indeed, it hardly permits—an advertisement. Nor is this the place to raise specific objections in a polemical way. Further, we are unable—and if able, would be unwilling—to express here any assessment of the specific contributions or general signficance of the economic approach to the development of criminology. But we are not forbearing enough to withhold all comments. We propose to raise three questions that, in our view, are worth keeping in mind while reading Ehrlich's essay and the other materials collected here. These questions attempt to identify some of the ways this work matters for scholars who are not engaged in it, but whose studies are potentially affected by the economic analysis of crime.

The first and in some ways most basic question outsiders will want to have answered is whether the findings the economists advance are true. Ehrlich is confident of their truth, and if this is so he has nothing to worry about. In the interest of peace of mind for the rest of us, however, he will have to put up with the scepticism of critics. At this time, questions about the validity of findings center around the deterrent effects of penal sanctions. As Ehrlich points out, these are by no means the only factual observations he and others have presented. But these have become the most contested. This, he says, is due to the fact that the affirmation of deterrence contravenes modern criminological orthodoxy. That seems certainly true. But the fact that controversy has been joined around this topic does not necessarily mean that studies of deterrence are the most fruitful or should remain the main concern of the economic approach to crime.

By this last we do not mean to suggest that the substantive matters to which the term "deterrence" refers will cease to be in the forefront of attention, but only that the conceptualization these matters have received thus far may not last. Our suspicion is based on the observation that the function of deterrence is now attributed to the law enforcement process as officially represented. And we know that there exist subterranean aspects of the dealings between offenders and officials that are pervasive and important, that are part of the lore that offenders share with officials, and that, accordingly, permeate crime and crime control. This complex includes collusive arrangements between informer-offenders and police officials; the whole area of charging and plea bargaining; and the anarchy of correctional decision-making. It is necessarily part of the incentive structure to which the term "deterrence" alludes. We do not think that a role has been assigned to this complex thus far in the work of the economists. Surely no economist would want to make statements about a commodity market on the basis of estimates achieved solely by considering overt transactions when he knew that a vast, linked black market existed. Thus, on the question of whether the economists are right in what they say about crime and crime control: we should keep in mind that while they are certainly right enough to be entitled to our most attentive consideration, their being right about questions as now formulated is not the only thing we ought to examine.

The next question outsiders should keep in mind and try to answer for themselves is whether they must accept what Ehrlich considers the fundamental hypothesis of the economic approach to crime—namely, the responsiveness of offenders to incentives. Clearly, every economist starts from this premise. Moreover, the hypothesis is entirely plausible; indeed, it strikes us as a truism. The economists' usage rescues the hypothesis from the status of a simple truism by the qualification of measurability. The point then is not that people respond to incentives, but that they respond specifically to specific incentives. In normally competent, wide awake adults the quantum of incentives regulates the expression of stable preferences for crime (the assumption of stable preferences for crime is questionable of course, but we are not questioning it now). But anyone who has gone thus far must also accept, as Ehrlich explains, that

> the analysis does not suggest, nor does it require, that pecuniary considerations are the sole, or even the predominant, motive in the decision to participate in crime. The latter decision is viewed as being affected by both pecuniary and non-pecuniary or psychological considerations, including the capacity to tolerate risk. For methodological convenience, and in order to stress the distinct role played by attitudes toward risk, all other psychic costs and benefits may be defined in terms of monetary equivalents.

The last-mentioned expedient lends to incentives their measurable and, thereby, specific character. Now it is possible that for economists this creates no problems. They may, indeed, think of responsiveness to incentives in more or less the same "as if" way in which, as Ehrlich puts it, "offenders are assumed to behave as if they seek to maximize their *expected utility*." But if the "as if" must be excluded, then we find it difficult to imagine the monetary equivalent for the incentives needed in the following case. Indeed, we find it difficult to use the term "incentive" in any ordinary sense in connection with such a case.

There is the familiar story of the snarling young tough who, after having been caught committing a heinous crime, jeeringly tells his captors, "there is nothing you can do to me; I am a juvenile." According to its intended sense, and the sense in which it is ordinarily perceived, the expression means that he cannot be punished by death, or protracted imprisonment, or any other punishment commensurate with his crime, because of the immunity age gives him. But the "objective" truth of the statement is something altogether different. Though it is probably an exaggeration to say that nothing at all can be done to him, the truth is that what can be done to him is at most marginally worse than what his life is anyway. He would prefer to stay out of jail, but not to finish school, to have a family, to earn a steady income, to gain respect. He is so bereft of hope of attaining such objectives that he does not even avail himself of highly advantageous opportunities to pursue them. If we understand the language of the economic approach to crime, his resources to meet the costs of committing crimes are limitless; he can afford to pay any price put on them.

We do not think our example speaks of a person who is a captive of his natural or institutional environment in any deterministic sense. We think we are speaking of a person whose circumstances and choices are not well enough understood to be expressed in terms of monetary equivalents. In all this we do not mean to imply that our case involves a person beyond the reach of influence, but we do think that the nature of such influence transcends what is included in "incentives" in the ordinary sense. Now there are matters in criminology that probably stand entirely under the sway of the notion of "responsiveness to incentives"; especially, a good many of those transgressions commonly called "economic crimes." We merely raise the question whether all crime and crime control must be founded on a presumption that holds well for some of it, not so well for other parts, and probably not at all for the rest. And our question is not particularly directed at "crimes of passion."

The last question concerns the existence of an implicit "market" for criminal activities, and the conception of crime as the imposition of costs on society in excess of those borne by the perpetrator. It is our understanding that both of these assumptions are needed to make feasible the quantitative analyses of crime undertaken by economists. Yet their significance goes beyond that. We would like to know in substantive detail just what it means to say that acting criminally and reacting to it are in some ways analogous to the events of high finance or the stock exchange. We think that we should be told, again as concretely as possible, how engaging in criminal activities is to be distinguished, if at all, from receiving an education or marching in a parade. In close connection, though on a different plane of concern (one from which social scientists often feel absolved in their professional work), we should like to know something of the long range implications of considering criminality essentially the same kind of behavior as any other. We wonder what we are committed to when accepting the maxim that "*optimal* enforcement will not be compatible with the elimination of all crime," as Ehrlich suggests (emphasis added). Our question is not whether we must be resigned to accepting a certain irreducible amount of crime; we understand why this is urged on us at this time. None of these formulations alone, but all of them together bring up the question of whether we are being urged to be practical in following through the implications of the moral definitions of crime, or whether we are being urged to put considerations of practicality in place of considerations of morality.

The three papers by Ann Bartel, Isaac Ehrlich, and William M. Landes represent prominent illustrations of the economic approach to crime. Lee S. Friedman's previously unpublished paper makes clear the logic and limitations of multiple regression analysis—MRA—a centrally important tool of statistical analysis used in studies of crime by economists. The Summary of the Report of the National Academy of Science's Panel on Research on Deterrence and Incapacitative Effects contains a short version of the views of a group of scholars brought together to judge some aspects of the work of economists and others on these topics. We hope that the Summary will move readers to examine the entire Report. The last paper, by Sandra E. Gleason, examines what would have to be regarded as business activity within the world of crime, or rather within the world of punishment. We are not certain whether these forms of entrepreneurship merit the specific technical analysis of economists, but we think that they merit the attention of all scholars interested in prison life.

1

THE ECONOMIC APPROACH TO CRIME
A Preliminary Assessment

ISAAC EHRLICH

Does punishment deter crime? Can the behavior of offenders be altered through the effect of positive incentives? Is criminal behavior an expression of biological aberrations or "social ills," or is it to a significant degree a matter of individual choice? And what is the optimal social policy in connection with crime and punishment? Is the main role of punishment to incapacitate, reform, deter, or compensate? Should a greater emphasis be placed on the severity or the certainty of punishment? What is the proper balance among different instruments of law enforcement and "positive" means of crime control?

These and related issues have been of paramount importance to students of crime and social policy ever since the emergence of organized legal systems. The central thesis of this essay is that a better understanding of these fundamental issues can be achieved by applying to the study of criminality a body of general principles pertaining to all human conduct. Such principles are embodied, I believe, in economic theory. So far, economic theory has been applied and tested mainly in connection with legitimate human endeavors. As the essay will suggest, this situation is changing.

The fundamental hypothesis in the economic approach to crime is that offenders and those who attempt to control crime on the whole respond to measurable opportunities, or incentives. It is the verification and estimation of the extent of offenders' responsiveness to, and the cost of producing and meting out, such incentives that are posed as central targets of scientific investigation. Knowledge of these matters is shown, in this approach, to be important for determining the optimal enforcement of various laws, and for making reasoned choices among specific deterrence instruments and alternative incentives. Such knowledge has implications for selection among means of enforcement that differentially affect the probability versus the severity of punishment, the risk of apprehension relative to that of conviction, and the deterrence of potential

AUTHOR'S NOTE: Space limitations require focus on a selected set of theoretical and empirical investigations which set out and implement the basic economic approach to crime. Many fine contributions by both economists and other social scientists could not be surveyed.

offenders relative to the rehabilitation or incapacitation of known offenders. More generally, knowledge of offenders' responsiveness to different incentives and of the cost of producing a subset of the latter is important not only for designing resource allocation among various law enforcement agencies, but also for making the choice between private and public enforcement or protection. Even the determination of the subset of private endeavors society renders illegal, thus subject to public intervention, can be influenced by such knowledge.

The controversy surrounding many of these issues dates back to ancient times. But scholarly investigation into the causes and consequences of criminal behavior and means of crime control took a new turn in the past decade with the revival of scientific interest in the classical deterrence hypothesis. This renewed interest has cut across all disciplines of the social sciences, but has been particularly significant in the field of economics, where no systematic investigation into illegitimate behavior or illegal markets had been conducted since the early part of the 19th century. The works of Fleisher (1966), Becker (1968), Tullock (1969), Stigler (1974), and this author (1970, 1974, 1975, 1977a), among others, have provided a link to a neglected branch of classical economic thought. Further, they have challenged earlier approaches in criminology that have dominated the thinking of social scientists on matters of crime and punishment throughout this century. The new analytical and empirical work, despite numerous limitations of data and techniques, have appeared, on the whole, consistent with the implications of the economic approach to crime. They have also generated a great deal of debate and some misrepresentation as well.

This essay provides a short overview of the economic approach to crime, as reflected in basic work by economists. A preliminary assessment is made of the empirical findings, limitations, and overall potential of this approach. The following aspects of the developing research are discussed:

(1) the "deterrence hypothesis" as defined in the current work by economists;
(2) the link between current work on crime and earlier economic thought;
(3) the limitations of previous evidence on deterrence as developed in the conventional criminological literature;
(4) the assumptions, basic analytical components, and some of the basic behavioral propositions of the economic approach;
(5) an alternative hypothesis;
(6) methods, major findings, and limitations of empirical implementations; and
(7) criticism and additional evidence.

THE DETERRENCE HYPOTHESIS

In both its utilitarian, or classical, and modern versions, the "economic" approach to crime is heavily predicated on the "deterrence hypothesis." By its direct connotation the latter expression conveys the belief that the threat of a criminal sanction, or any other form of punishment, has some moderating or restraining effect on the willingness of actual or potential offenders to engage in criminal activity. But, to interpret this hypothesis so narrowly runs the risk of missing the basic idea on which it is founded, for the basic idea has to do with the moderating effect on criminal behavior of *all* commonly recognized incentives, *positive* as well as negative. Properly construed, the hypothesis is that *all potential offenders—even the perpetrators of "crimes of passion"—on the whole respond to costs and gains, prices and rewards, in much the same way, although not necessarily to the same extent, as do individuals who pursue legitimate or socially approved acitivities.*

This hypothesis, which seems largely compatible with common sense, derives from a particular view of man. That view is that man is not a *captive* of his natural or institutional environment, but is born with a capacity to shape his destiny through rational and enterprising utilization of his resources and opportunities for gains—opportunities which are partly determined by the natural and social environments and by purposive investments as well.

This has been the view shared by leaders of economic thought since Adam Smith.[1] Translated in the context of illegitimate behavior, the idea is that man is endowed with a capacity of both good and evil, and that his decisions to pursue one or both will be influenced by the opportunities associated with each type of behavior. Indeed, whether derived through Bentham's felicific calculus of pain and pleasure or from the expected utility formulations of contemporary economists, the deterrence hypothesis finds natural expression in economics, for its presumption of man's responsiveness to incentives mirrors the basic laws of the economic theory of choice: price deters demand, and profit motivates supply.

The basic proposition then is that the offender, even a perpetrator of high crimes, is a member of the human race who, like participants in legitimate endeavors, will attempt to maximize his well being. Thus, it is inferred that the general economic approach to the study of presumably legitimate behavior provides a unifying analytical framework for the study of all human behavior, illegitimate as well as legitimate. Even in connection with so-called "crimes of passion," responsiveness to incentives cannot be ruled out on a priori grounds. For why should emotional or passionate activities, even preference for risk and penchant for violence, rule out the ability to make self-serving choices? Given the same punishment for assault, those with a knack for violence may indeed be expected to manifest malevolent feelings via assault more frequently than would less passionate individuals. But, when the criminal sanction carried out against those convicted of assault is increased, it is not implausible to expect that all those contemplating assault will modify their behavior toward alternative pursuits, in the same way that individuals would be expected to intensify their assaultive behavior when social tolerance toward such crime becomes manifestly greater.

Not only does this proposition mean that offenders are not doomed to a life of crime independently of the opportunities provided through private and public reaction to the risk of crime; the proposition also implies that there is no need to treat offenders inhumanely. Indeed, the deterrence hypothesis as formulated by Beccaria, Bentham, and other utilitarians of the late 18th century was largely a reaction to what they considered excessively severe punishments throughout Europe at that time. The logic of the principle of proportion between crimes and punishment proposed at that time was the imposition of cost just sufficient to deter crimes of different severity. If *cost* or price is the instrument of deterrence, it need not involve cruel, debasing, or even incapacitiating punishment, nor should it exceed a level of severity commensurate with 'the greatest good to the greatest number.' It is no coincidence that Becarria (and even Bentham late in his career) called for the abolition of capital punishment largely in the name of the deterrence theory. Cesare Lombrose and other proponenets of the "biological school" in criminology, on the other hand, advocated castration as a remedy to sex offenses and other crimes as well.[2]

THE LINK WITH EARLIER ECONOMIC THOUGHT

To what extent was this hypothesis shared by economists of past generations? Even a superficial examination of the literature would reveal that economists of the classical period accepted with apparent unanimity the basic tenets of the deterrence theory. While the classical school of thought on crime is quite properly associated with the detailed writings of Beccaria and Bentham,[3] other major figures in economics—Adam Smith, William Paley, Robert Malthus, Edwin Chadwick, James Mill, and John Stuart Mill—each demonstrate a fundamental acceptance of the proposition that potential offenders respond to incentives and the corollary propostion that an optimal social policy in connection with certainty and severity of punishment must be predicated on the deterrence theory, with due recognition of the costs and gains involved.

Of particular interest may be William Paley's *Principles of Moral and Political Philosophy* (1822), first published in 1785. Here Paley presents a brilliant analysis of the determinants of the socially optimal magnitudes of probability and severity of punishment that contains virtually all the propositions that have been derived in the more recent contributions mentioned in my introduction without resort to a single graph or equation. Basing his analysis on the presumed power of the threat of punishment to alter behavior, Paley view optimal sanctions, or the degree of their enforcement, to be variables depending upon "exogenous" factors. Among such factors he notes the intrinsic severity of the offense, the facility of its commission, the likelihood of its detection, the difficulty of apprehending and convicting the perpetrator, and the availability of less expensive means of affecting behavior. He says (1822:360): "crimes are not by any government punished in proportion to their guilt, nor in all cases ought to be so, but in proportion to the difficulty and necessity of preventing them." And since punishment is "an evil . . . necessary to the prevention of a greater" evil, it need not be utilized "when the public may be defended from the effects of crime by any other expedient" (1822:361).

This is not the appropriate place to elaborate on Paley's or others' penetrating analyses of the principles of crime and punishment. Let me merely suggest that none would dispute the crucial role Adam Smith (1977:133-134) assigns to punishment:

> Nature has implanted in the human breast that consciousness of ill-desert, those terrors of merited punishment . . . as the great safeguards of the association of mankind, to protect the weak, to curb the violent, and to chastise the guilty.

Nor would they deny his symmetrical assertion that the phenomenon of crime can be controlled through the impact of "positive" incentives, for "nobody will be so mad as to expose himself upon the highway, when he can make better bread in an honest and industrious manner (Smith, 1896:149).

Karl Marx seems the only prominent economist of the classical period (roughly defined from Adam Smith through John Stuart Mill) to deny the deterrence propositon in connection with either the capital sanction or punishment in general.

> It would be very difficult, it not impossible to establish any principle upon which the justice or expediencey of captial punishement could be founded . . . punishment in general has been defended as a means either of ameliorating or of intimidating. Now what right have you to punish me for the amelioration or intimidation of others? And besides, there is history, there is such a thing as statistics which prove with the most complete evidence that since Cain the world has been neither intimidated nor ameliorated by punishment. Quite the contrary.[4]

Insofar as the moral right to depreciate, even destroy, the well being of one person for the future benefit of others is concerned, Marx's argument is wanting not only because it is imbalanced—after all, punishment is imposed as a consequence of malfeasance—but also because it is so grossly imcompatible with the Marxist justification of the forced abolition of private property and the redistribution of personal wealth in the name of social justice. From the standpoint of economic methodology, I find Marx's casual empiricism in his denial of the deterrence hypothesis even more unfortunate, however, because he mistakenly attributes to the deterrence theory the expectation that crime in the aggregate will be nil if some, even severe, punishment is enforced. Preceding the marginal revolution in economics of some years later, Marx does not recognize the potential influence of punishment as a check against additional crime on the margin. For example, would society's experience with murder have remained unchanged had Cain been rewarded for his crime? Marx also does not consider the role of certainty of punishment in modifying the deterrent effect of its prescribed severity. Indeed, his reasoning is equivalent to contending that the aggregate quantity demanded of a good be zero if its listed price is positive.

In the latter part of the 19th century, the classical approach to crime was supplanted in academic thought, if not in law, by a variety of alternatives known collectively as the positivist approach, which in its various forms was strongly deterministic in philosophy and methodology. The various strands of positivist thought provided the foundation for the establishment of criminology as a new academic discipline with its own schools and specialists. I shall not go here into a discussion of the challenge presented by the positivists to the classical approach or of the reasons why neoclassical economists seem to have conceded the field of criminology to other social scientists.[5] I wish to note only that I am unaware of any systematic work by an economist either in the classical or the neoclassical tradition that has directly challenged the deterrence hypothesis. Perhaps the narrowing of the scope of political economy during the 19th century, by dealing almost exclusively with the business sector of the economy, was necessary for the professionalization of economics as a science and the development of the tools necessary for systematic understanding of the laws of market equilibrium in production, investment, and distribution. By 1910, however, came Wicksteed's forceful reminder that economics is first and foremost a social science dedicated to the study of human conduct. Although Wicksteed does not mention criminal behavior specifically, his thesis is clearly compatible with the classical Benthamian notion that economic analysis (for Bentham, the calculus of pain and pleasure) is applicable in studying *all* human behavior.

> [I]t is time frankly and decisively to abandon all attempts to . . . establish any distinction whatever between the ultimate motives by which a man is actuated in business and those by which he is actuated in domestic or public life.

> [T]he general principles which regulate our conduct in business are identical with those which regulate our deliberations, our reflections between alternatives, and our decisions in all other branches of life. [Wicksteed, 1910:6-7.]

PAST EVIDENCE ON DETERRENCE

As compelling as the a priori logic of deterrence was to most economists, some criminologists were fully persuaded to the contrary.[6] Whether punishment deters, and criminal behavior generally is responsive to incentives, ultimately must be established on empirical grounds in the same way that the responsiveness of other types of human behavior has been tested. Indeed, the deterrent efficacy of punishment, in particular, had repeatedly been subjected to empirical investigations by notable criminologists in the past. It is crucial to point out in this context, however, that a meaningful and effective empirical test, short of a perfectly controlled experiment, cannot be developed without thorough consideration of the particular ramifications of the hypothesis to be tested. The basic issue in testing the deterrence hypothesis is not whether some data can be found which fail to reveal a deterrent effect of a particular punishment on a particular crime, but whether the nature of the data examined, the "model" implemented, the empirical measures used, the statistical specification and "controls" employed, and the pattern of findings obtained are sufficient to reject the (null) hypothesis of no-deterence. In the absence of such systematic considerations, failure or success in rejecting the null hypothesis cannot be considered meaningful.

The focus of much of the past criminological work on deterrence in both the 19th and the 20th century has been the deterrent efficacy of the death penalty; almost no attention was paid to the deterrent value of other sanctions by the 20th-century criminologists. The historical interest in the death penalty, while largely due to its political, philosophical, and moral significance, seems also to have been prompted by the unique opportunity to test the deterrence theory in connection with what most people would consider the most extreme sanction. As one researcher puts it (Schuessler, 1952:54), "since people fear death more than anything else, the death penalty is the most effective deterrent, so runs the [deterrence] argument."

The overall impression one obtains from reviewing the 20th-century literature is that the penalty had no effect whatsoever on the incidence of capital crimes. More than 40 years of intermittant empirical analysis of varying scope yielded remarkable agreement among researchers who uniformly concluded that the death penalty is inconsequential; they differed only in the definiteness with which this general conclusion was expressed. So great was the impact of this research that the issue of deterrence was considered by criminologists and other social scientists as closed (Tittle and Logan, 1973:371).

My main conclusion after surveying the past literature on the relation between capital punishment and capital crimes is twofold. In the first place, it turns out that in the 19th century investigations were conducted on the same issue, using techniques that are similar to those used by the 20th-century researchers, but which provided far more diverse results on the efficacy of punishment than those reported in the subsequent 20th-century research.[7] More important, most of the popular 20th-century studies did not perform tests capable of rejecting the hypothesis of no-deterrence. The principal short-coming of the work by Sellin[8] and others using his methodology is that the approach taken and the methods applied do not permit a systematic examination of the main implications emanating from the general theory of deterrence. The shortcoming is basic, because the implications following from the general deterrence hypothesis are what Sellin was challenging. Yet his work neither develops nor tests the full range of implications following from the theory he attempts to reject; nor does he develop or test a competing theory. In addition, to my knowledge, Sellin never reported in any of his studies the results of any systematic (parametric or nonparametric) statistical tests that could justify his strong and unqualified inferences.[9]

Two examples may illustrate this conclusion. Sellin has compared homicide rates in bordering "abolitionist" and "retentionist" states as defined by the legal status of the death penalty, but he never accounts for the extent of the actual *enforcement* of the penalty in retentionist states. Yet, by his own judgment the relevant variable is the *risk* of execution, not merely its legal status; as he himself puts it (1959:20), "where the death penalty is present in the law alone it would be completely robbed of its threat." The point is far from subtle. In a number of "retentionist" states whose homicide rates are compared to "abolitionist" states the execution risk was negligible throughout the period of comparison. This methodological shortcoming borders on the absurd in later studies by others following Sellin's approach, who have compared murder rates in abolition and death penalty states over the 1960s when no single execution has taken place in the so-called retentionist states being compared.[10] More generally, a prerequisite for any meaningful statistical test of the deterrence hypothesis that utilizes observational statistics is that measures of execution risk, if appropriate, would exhibit a minimum degree of genuine variability in the true risks across the observations being compared. If such variability is not present in the data, the hypothesis of no-deterrence cannot, of course, be rejected.[11]

Another fundamental shortcoming of Sellin's studies is their failure to account systematically for other factors that are expected by the deterrence hypothesis to affect the frequency of murder in the population, apart from the relevant risk of execution. These are variables such as the probability of apprehension, the conditional probability of conviction given apprehension, the severity of alternative punishments for murder, the distribution of income, the probability of unemployment, and other indicators of differential gains from criminal activities occurring jointly with murder. Since, as I shall argue later, some of these variables are expected to be highly correlated with the conditional probability of execution given conviction of murder, their exclusion from the statistical analysis can seriously bias estimates of the partial deterrent effect of capital punishment. Aware of the problem, Sellin attempted to compare states that are as alike as possible in all other respects. However, his "matching procedure," based on the assumption that neighboring states can satisfy such prerequisites without any explicit standardization, is simply insufficient for any valid inferences. Pairs of states, such as New York and Rhode Island, Massachusetts and Maine, or Illinois and Wisconsin all included in his comparisons, differ in their economic and demographic characteristics, in their law enforcement activities, and in the opportunities they provide for the commission of other crimes. Moreover, the direction of the *causal* relationship between the murder rate and the overall risk of punishment —be it the death penalty or any other sanction—is not self-evident because, for example, states with high murder rates are expected to and, in fact, do devote more resources to apprehend, convict, and execute offenders than do states with lower rates. Specifically, variations in the legal or practical status of the death penalty occasionally may be the result of, rather than the cause for, changes in the murder rate, and thus may give rise to an apparent positive association between these two variables. The same general point applies in connection with the identification of the effect of any other variable which is a product of law enforcement activity or private protection against crime. For these reasons, the true deterrent effect of a sanction such as the death penalty cannot be readily inferred from simple comparisons of the sort performed by Sellin.

This very brief overview of past literature was intended to give an idea of the methodology upon which previous conclusions have been based. More important, the argument I have attempted to develop is this: to derive an adequate procedure for testing the deterrence hypothesis, one must test the full set of implications emanating from the deterrence theory rather than view separately and in isolation particular associations between specific variables of interest. While the existence of deterrent or reinforcing effects of specific incentives on criminal behavior ultimately are empirical matters, they cannot be studied effectively without thorough consideration of both the relevant theoretical specification and its proper empirical implementation. An adequate analytical framework should recognize, for example, that if capital punishment deters potential murderers, then surely alternative punishments, such as imprisonment, are also expected to impart deterrent effects, and their influence on the rate of murder must be properly accounted for in the context of the statistical analysis. The converse follows a fortiori: if investigations indicate that probability and length of imprisonment do impart significant deterrent effects, then failure of the research to demonstrate specifically the deterrent efficacy of capital punishment may be taken more as evidence for shortcomings in the research design and methodology or in the measures of the theoretically relevant variables used than as a reflection on the validity of the deterrence theory itself. Also, one cannot expect sanctions imposed only rarely and with much delay to affect offenders' behavior as they would if imposed with greater frequency and swiftness.

There is an additional point worth stressing. Even if punishment by execution or imprisonment does not have any *deterrent* effect, surely it must exert some incapacitative effect on punished offenders by reducing or eliminating the possibility of recidivism on their part. The insistence of past researchers on *no* apparent restraining effect of punishment on crime appears to be incompatible with the deterrence hypothesis as well as the alternative hypothesis of no-deterrence. An adequate research design should attempt to isolate the deterrent from the incapacitating effects of criminal sanctions. Also, the direction of the observed causal relationship between the rate of crime and the levels of certainty and severity of punishment must be identified through proper statistical techniques. All these considerations must be taken into account before any systematic considerations can be drawn about the deterrence hypothesis.

THE ECONOMIC MODEL: OFFENSE AND DEFENSE

Assumptions

To provide a methodology more appropriate for studying the issues raised in the preceding analysis, recent work by economists has developed in broad outlines a model of crime and the criminal justice system that applies the basic principles of supply and demand analysis in explaining "equilibrium" in the criminal sector of the economy. Underlying the model are five basic assumptions.[12]

1. Maximizing Behavior. Offenders, actual and potential, are assumed to behave as if they are interested in maximizing their personal welfare, or preferences, subject to the opportunities available to them in alternative legitimate and illegitimate pursuits. More formally, because crime is committed under conditions of uncertainty regarding potential sanctions and rewards, offenders are assumed to behave as if they seek to maximize their *expected utility.*[13] Analogous welfare-maximizing assumptions are invoked in connection with the behavior of potential victims and law enforcement authorities in so far as defense against crime is concerned. This maximizing-behavior postulate may be contrasted with a alternative perception of crime as *involuntary* behavior due either to uncontrollable physiological and mental aberrations or to irrationality and errors of judgment. Not that the latter can be rejected as contributing factors in specific cases involving decisions by both offenders and law enforcers. But, on the whole, the view of criminal behavior as involuntary has the obvious weakness of being irrefutable: it may explain everthing *ex-post* but hardly anything *ex-ante* because it lacks a theory capable of forecasting the relevant biological aberrations or erratic choices. In particular, it cannot explain or predict the systematic, and often considerable, variations in the volume of specific crimes that are observed across different places and over time. In contrast, for the maximizing behavior postulate to be useful in explaining or predicting these variations systematically, it is sufficient that it apply only on average or even just for the "marginal" group of offenders.

2. Stable Preferences. While the maximizing-behavior postulate is a necessary aspect of the economic approach, it is not sufficient to accord it the desired explanatory power in empirical contexts. Recall that maximizing behavior is achieved by balancing individual preferences with objective opportunities. Thus, it can change as a result of shifts in either opportunities or preferences. Because the latter are not directly observable and economic theory does not incorporate a theory of the formation of preferences, however, the economic approach to crime—or any competing approach—may become entirely tautological should it rely on changes in "preferences for crime" to explain changes in the actual volume of crime. The assumption that lends the economic approach its explanatory or predictive power, therefore, is that the distribution of individual preferences for crime—penchant for violence, preference for risk, benevolence, malevolence, or envy, to mention a few— is, to a significant degree, stable across different communties at a point in time or in a given community over reasonable periods of time. At the very minimum, the assumption is that changes in preferences for crime are uncorrelated with the observed changes in measurable opportunities for criminal endeavors.

3. Unbiased Expectations. Because criminal decisions are made under uncertainty, maximizing behavior involves the assessment of probability of "success." Such assessment is subjective to the offender, however, whereas the risk measures utilized in empirical research are based on objective observations. To provide a link between subjective and objective assessments, the economic approach implicitly assumes that, on average, the two tend to be identical or, at least, systematically related. This assumption can be defended in large measure by the basic maximizing-behavior postulate discussed above. Although information pertaining to criminal sanctions or probabilities of their imposition is incomplete, in the same way that information pertaining to government taxes, probabilities of employment in specific industries, or the supply of money is not fully available, and assumptions of unbiased (or "rational") expectations concerning the actual magnitudes of these variables is justifiable on the ground that any systematic gaps between perception and reality would generate incentives to revise the former in the direction of the latter. The incentives would be paricularly strong when the consequences of misperception would be quite costly to the actor, as may be the case in connection with most felonies.

4. *Market Equilibrium.* The economic approach is based on the assumption that an implicit "market" for criminal activity exists, that coordinates the behavior of offenders, potential victims, and law enforcement authorities, and makes it mutually consistent through the effect of explicit prices (as in some illegal transactions) and implicit, or "shadow," prices (as in most law enforcement and private protection activities), and that the ensuing market equilibrium is stable. In principle, equilibrium in this broadly defined criminal market is determined simultaneously with equilibrium in all other sectors of the economy. If one were to pursue a Walrasian approach to general equilibrium, and view the equilibria in all sectors of the political economy as jointly determined, the analysis would become rather intractable and costly to implement empirically. Quite plausibly, however, some endeavors are more interdependent than others: while it would generally be unsatisfactory to treat the supply of burglars independently of the allocation of public resources to law enforcement activities directed against burglary, equilibrium in the market for trucking services may, for practical reasons, be taken to be determined independently of the equilibrium in the burglary market. The assumption invoked in most studies pursuing the economic approach to crime has been that equilibrium in the general labor and capital markets of the economy can be viewed as "exogenous" to that in the markets for specific offenses.

5. *The Concept of Crime.* Whereas the concept of crime relevant for the theoretical analysis of offenders' behavior can be defined as any unlawful activity punishable by a legal sanction, in the theoretical analysis of the demand for public enforcement crime is defined as an activity that imposes external diseconomies in either wealth or utility. External diseconomies (or negative externalities) are said to arise in all those circumstances where an activity by one person imposes costs on other persons, for which it is not feasible to make him compensate them—an activity which cannot be controlled

through voluntary exchanges between the parties involved. An illegal activity is thus conceived of in the analysis as one which imposes costs on society in excess of the direct costs borne by the perpetrator.

These assumptions have provided the foundation for the development of a simultaneous equation model of crime and defense against crime. The basic components of the model are defined below.

Basic Components of the Model

The Supply of Offenses.   Central to the economic approach is the assumption that despite the diversity of activities defined as illegal, all such activities share some common characteristics, which form the basis for a general analysis of individual participation in crime. Any violation of the law can be conceived of as yielding a potential increase in the offender's pecuniary wealth, his psychic well being, or both. In violating the law one also risks a reduction in one's pecuniary and nonpecuniary well being: conviction entails paying a penalty (a monetary fine, probation, the discounted value of time spent in prison, and related psychic disadvantages, net of any direct benefits received by the offender), acquiring a criminal record (and thus losing earning opportunities in legitimate activities), and other disadvantages. As an alternative to violating a specific law one could violate another, or participate in an alternative legitimate (wealth or consumption generating) activity, which may also be subject to specific hazards.

The model of participation in illegitimate activities[14] proceeds in this general context of decision making under uncertainty by treating the offender's relevant choice as one that involves the optimal allocation of time and other resources to competing legal and illegal activities. The factors identified as the basic determinants of that choice are the marginal probabilities of punishment for the relevant set of crimes, the discounted real value of the marginal penalties imposed upon conviction, the marginal "wage rates" in the competing illegitimate and legitimate activities, the probability of unemployment in the legitimate labor market, and the value of individual assets net of current earnings. Note that the analysis does not suggest, nor does it require, that pecuniary considerations are the sole or even the predominant motive in the decision to participate in crime. The latter decision is viewed as being affected by both pecuniary and nonpecuniary or psychological considerations, including the capacity to tolerate risk. For methodological convenience, and in order to stress the distinct role played by attitudes toward risk, all other psychic costs and benefits may be defined in terms of monetary equivalents and incorporated in the definitions of the marginal costs and gain variables discussed above.

The analysis indicates that when real earnings in both legitimate and illegitimate activities are not subject to strong time-dependencies due to continuous investments in on-the-job training, and returns from illegitimate activities are relatively safe, many offenders who are averse to risk have an incentive to participate in both types of activities, partly to hedge against the relatively greater risk in full-time pursuit of a criminal activity. Others, whose relative opportunities or psychic preferences lean strongly in favor of crime, or who are risk preferrers, have an incentive to specialize in criminal activity. The essential result of the analysis is that the *extent* of individual participation in crime, as well as the decision to enter criminal activity, is a continuous variable that reflects in large measure the maximizing-behavior equilibrium of people who differ in their earnings opportunities and in their preferences for risk.

An intriguing implication of this "equilibrium" analysis concerns the phenomenon of recidivism. The high frequency of recidivism among known offenders is often interpreted erroneously as proof of irrationality or deviance because, having been caught and punished, they still do not seem to be "learning their lesson" and reform their behavior. Consider, alternatively, the proposition of the economic analysis, that crime is the result of an optimizing behavior that assigns unbiased probabilities to the prospect of both success and failure. Then apprehension and punishment per se should not have systematic bearing on subsequent decisions to participate in crime any more than do other professional hazards or continued involvement in hazardous legitimate oc-cupations. For example, football players, professional soldiers, or miners are not expected to switch occupations just because they suffer occasional remedial injuries. The phenomenon of recidivism may very well corroborate rather than contradict the economic approach to crime (Ehrlich, 1974).

Of central importance from the viewpoint of the positive analysis are the behavioral implications of the model concerning the effects of specific incentives on the decision to participate in specific crimes. An increase in the probability and severity of the marginal punishment for any offense—be it larceny or assault, hijacking or industrial collusion to fix prices—is expected to lower the incentive to enter a criminal activity unambiguously, and generally also the frequency of offenders' participation in that activity.[15] In contrast, an increase in the absolute "wage differential" between an illegitimate activity and its immediate legitimate substitute would, by the same analysis, increase the incentive to enter, and the intensity of participation in, that illegitimate activity. The extent of offenders' responsiveness to changes in these incentives need not be the same in all criminal activities, however, and would depend, in part, on the availability of alternative activities that yield comparable returns. The practical existence of such alternatives points to the potential existence of cross effects of penalties or specific criminal returns on the incentive to participate in a set of interrelated crimes as well as in any one specific crime. For example, an increase in the punishment imposed for burglary alone may increase the incentive to participate in larceny if the latter were, on average, a close "substitute" to burglary (Ehrlich, 1974:n. 52, 1977).

Since information about the magnitude of criminal "wages" in comparison to wages in alternative legitimate activites is not readily available to the objective spectator, the model's implications concerning the role of positive incentives in affecting criminal behavior must often be tested indirectly. It can be shown that under some plausible assumptions concerning the degree of skill required for participation in most crimes against property, the level of personal income and the relative inequality in the distribution of personal income in the community can serve as useful proxies for the average differential return from criminal over legitimate activity—the latter variable because it indicates the relative disparity between the earning opportunities available to persons with low legitimate skills, and the former variable, because it indicates the average value of property that can be acquired in the community via crime. This analysis suggests that "affluence" and rapid economic growth that is not accompanied by a reduction in the extent of inequality in the distribution of earning opportunities may encourage a rise in the frequency of crimes against property—and in "complementary" crimes against persons as well—not because of any "pure" effect of income on criminal propensities, but because it represents an increase in the potential gains from crime obtainable by persons with low legitimate skills.

Perhaps the sharpest set of empirically refutable propositions that follow from the economic analysis of the supply of offenses concerns the relative magnitudes of the effects of key deterrence instruments: The model predicts that the elasticity of the supply of a crime of a given type with respect to the risk of apprehension for that crime (i.e., the percentage reduction in offenses due to a 1% rise in the probability of apprehension) will exceed the supply elasticity of the crime with respect to the conditional risk of conviction given apprehension, which, in turn, will exceed the corresponding elasticity with respect to the conditional risk of punishment through one *specific* sanction out of several that can be imposed upon conviction of that crime. Stated differently, the proposition is that the more general the event giving rise to adverse consequences to the offender, the greater the deterrent effect associated with its probability.[16] Specifically, the analysis shows that the deterrent effect associated with the output of police work (apprehensions) is expected to be greater than that associated with prosecution activity (convictions) and that prosecution, or court work, in turn, is expected to exert a greater deterrent effect than that associated with the degree of enforcement of a specific sanction. Thus, while an increase in the conditional risk of execution given conviction for murder is expected to deter the frequency of murder, an increase in the conditional risk of apprehension and conviction will generate an even greater discouraging effect on the incentive to commit murder. As to the issue of whether probability or severity of punishment for any given crime would be more effective in terms of controlling the level of that crime—an issue which has received frequent attention in past criminological literature—the model indicates that the answer depends, at least in part, on offenders' attitude toward risk. If, on average, robbers were risk preferrers, they might be more deterred by a 1% increase in probability relative to severity of punishment for robbery, but the converse would hold if they were risk averters, as most tax evaders probably are.[17] Of course, the determination of a socially optimal set of deterrence instruments depends not only on the effectiveness of the instruments in terms of crime prevention, but also on the social costs involved in their production and imposition.

Although the basic model of participation in illegitimate activity is formulated at the individual level of the analysis, its behavioral propositions apply at the aggregate level as well. The response of the aggregate supply of offenses to the various incentives elaborated upon in the preceding discussion can be shown to depend, however, not only on the extent of responsiveness of individual offenders, but also on the homogeneity of potential offenders insofar as criminal proclivities and abilities to generate returns from crime is concerned. The more homogeneous offenders are, the greater the elasticity of the aggregate supply of offenses to changes in specific incentives, the vice versa (Ehrlich, 1974). Unlike the classical or utilitarian approach to crime, which did not allow for individual differences in propensity or motivation, or in the degree of individual responsiveness to incentives in its analysis of crime and the criminal justice system (Radzinowitz, 1966:13), the economic model of the supply of offenses makes explicit allowances for such differences both theoretically and in empirical implementation. The recognition of individual differences in propensity and motivation, bounded within the general assumptions invoked in the previous section, is found to be a source of richness in the analysis of criminal behavior that has important implications for the determination of optimal punishments for different offenders, as discussed in the following analysis of optimal defense against crime.

The Demand for Protection and Law Enforcement.   Because criminal behavior results in losses to victims which, by a social consensus, are larger than the gains to offenders, potential victims have an incentive to protect themselves against the risk of victimization both privately and collectively. Private protection involves expenditures of resources on locks, guards, watchdogs, safes, burglar alarm systems, and a myraid of other precautionary steps which generally aim at reducing the probability of victimization (self-protection), the private loss if victimized (self-insurance), or both. In addition, there is the incentive to buy insurance against theft and other losses in the conventional market for insurance. As was the assumption for potential offenders, potential victims are assumed to choose an optimal mix of market insurance, self-insurance, and self-protection by maximizing their expected utility from protection, subject to their private opportunities.[18]

Private protection against crime has direct relevance for the analysis of "equilibrium" in the general criminal sector because it imposes limits on the profitability of criminal activity to offenders. By limiting the opportunities for profitable targets, raising the cost of successfully carrying out an offense, and increasing the likelihood that an offender will be apprehended and punished through the reporting of a crime and collaborating with enforcement agencies, potential victims help modify the net returns from crime to offenders in a fashion similar to that of public protection. Moreover, an increase in the threat of victimization is likely to increase the incentive to provide private protection against crime. This expectations is shown below to apply to public defense against crime as well.

If private protection and its effects on security were free of any externalities or "public goods" aspects, all protection against crime would be provided through private endeavors, including the enforcement of criminal laws. Indeed, prior to the 19th century, this was the prevailing method in England (Landes and Posner, 1975). Since the 19th century, however, public enforcement of laws constitutes the lion's share of all enforcement and protective activities in society—a fact suggesting that private protection alone would have resulted in a socially suboptimal level of criminal activity. The aim of public enforcement can be understood as effecting a socially optimal level of crime prevention through provision of optimal criminal rules and procedures, penal policy, law enforcement, and the general administration of justice.

In its essential form the economic model of optimal public defense agaist crime, as developed by Becker (1968), abstracts from any consideration of vengeance, moral "justice," or any distributional aspects of law enforcement and criminal penalties.[19] Instead, it seeks to explain the behavior of the relevant authorities as an implicit attempt to minimize the total losses to society due to crime. Social losses, measured in terms of potential aggregate wealth foregone, are present even in cases of thefts involving a pure transfer of property from victim to offender where no destruction of property or loss of efficiency in the utilization of property takes place, because the real resource devoted by offenders to carry out crimes represent a pure loss of resources from a social point of view—resources that could be utilized to increase society's potential product. Society is assumed to set up an optimal criminal justice system that would maximize that product.

More specifically, the aggregate social loss functions from crime are defined to incorporate three principal sources. The first is the net harm to victims, including the cost of private protection, minus the net gain to offenders from committing crimes. Both the average and the marginal net social loss arising from these activities are assumed to increase with the aggregate level of crime. The second source of social losses is the expenditure of real resources on apprehending, charging, and prosecuting suspected offenders. The third source incorporates the net social loss resulting from the impositon of criminal sanctions on all convicted offenders—guilty, as well as innocent (Ehrlich, 1975:403). Counted here are both the private losses to the offenders' net of gains to society if any exist, and the cost of meting out and administering the penalties. By this formulation gains and losses to both victims and offenders are assigned equal weight in calculating the social losses from crime.

An important implication arising from this formulation of the social welfare function underlying public defense against crime concerns the relative costliness of punishments such as execution, corporal punishment, and imprisonment, relative to monetary fines and other direct compensations that do not impose severe physical restrictions on offenders' freedom of movement. The former type of sanction amounts to a nontransferrable price from a social point of view: the "price" paid by the offender is not received by any other members of society since the offender's loss of potential earnings due to his incarceration or physical incapacitation reduces the potential social product by an equal amount. Furthermore, punishment by imprisonment entails direct resource costs to society due to the costs of guarding and maintaining prisons and the prison population. In contrast, fines amount essentially to transfer payments since the cost to the offender in terms of lost command over resources is fully received by other members of society and the only real costs to society from fines are the costs of "collecting," or administering the transfers. Of course, the latter may not be trivial when the optimal magnitude of fines is high enough to exhaust an offender's effective wealth constraint, which is, perhaps, one reason why the use of monetary fines as sanctions in criminal cases have so far been negligible in practice. The fact that society has tended to make relatively little and highly restrictive use of a sanction like execution, even in connection with conviction of the crime of murder, attests, however, to the validity of the assumption that the welfare costs to the offender from punishment as well as the welfare losses to society from crime itself are generally accounted for in the determination of the aggregate social losses corresponding to various policy options.

What is the socially optimal level of public law enforcement? In terms of the social optimization rule defined above, optimal enforcement occurs at the point where the reduced social income due to the cost of additional enforcement equals the increased social income due to the resulting decrease in crime: social policy is assumed to be conducted according to the basic proposition that severity and certainty of sanctions deter crime. Since the marginal social costs of enforcement are assumed to rise with the level of enforcement and its marginal social benefit is expected to fall as the frequency of victimization declines, however, optimal enforcement will not be compatible with the elimination of all crime. Put differently, it would be optimal for society to allow some crime to take place not because crime itself serves any useful social function, but because the additional costs of combatting crime beyond a certain finite level exceed the resulting additional benefits to society. In fact, because public enforcement is an activity organized through an effective state *monopoly,* its actual level may be expected to be lower than the level that might have been produced under a competitive market for enforcement free of any externalities or other imperfections due to the public good aspects inherent in specific law enforcement activities.

The same analysis leads to specific propositions concerning the optimal certainty and severity of punishment for specific crimes. Optimal sanctions require a measure of "proportionality" between crime and punishment not because abstract justice requires that the more serious crimes be more seriously avenged, but because the more "serious" crimes inflict greater social damages. Aside from consideration of the potential damages to society from crime, however, optimal penalties must also be determined in view of their effectiveness in moderating the level of the criminal activity itself; that is, in view of the expected responsiveness of prospective offenders to changes in penalties. For example, if crime is committed by various groups of offenders, optimal penal policy would require that punishment will be used in greater moderation when imposed on members of groups whose responsiveness to incentives is believed to be relatively low. This particular implication of the analysis is analogous to the optimal pricing rule for a discriminating monopoly in factor markets which sets lower prices and hires lower quantities of given factors of production in segmented factor markets where the supply elasticities of factors are relatively low. Note that the optimality of "price discrimination," or differential treatment of different offenders, is justified strictly on the assumption that the target of optimal social policy is to maximize potential social income. If other targets are introduced, such as equity in the treatment of equally guilty offenders under the law, these results and some of the other principles for governing optimal penal policy would necessarily require some modification.

Two behavioral propositions of the analysis of optimal public defense are particularly important in so far as testing the general economic approach is concerned. First, it can be shown that optimal defense requires that the magnitudes of the probabilites of apprehension, conviction, and punishment through one specific sanction say, execution for murder, be set so that the elasticity of crime with respect to the probability of apprehension and conviction exceed that with respect to the conditional probability of punishment through a specific sanction. Since this is precisely the same implication derived from the analysis of the "optimal" supply of offenses (see the discussion in the first part of this section), the economic model of the supply and demand for offenses provides a sharp test of its validity through systematic empirical investigation. Second, the analysis shows that as the frequency of offenses rises due to factors exogenous to the public defense system, the optimal social response would be to raise the level of social defense: not only does the analysis require that expenditures on enforcement and protection rise to meet the challenge of additional crime, but the magnitudes of the deterrence instruments themselves—probability and severity of punishment—must rise as well (Ehrlich and Gibbons, 1977:49). This result has a special significance in the context of an empirical implementation of the economic model of crime, because it exposes the analysis of the relationship between crime and punishment to the classical problem of "identification" in economics: whereas the supply of offenses is predicted to fall with an endogenous rise in punishment, the "demand" for punishment is expected to rise as a consequence of an externally induced rise in crime.

The Production of Means of Public Protection from Crime.   Imbedded in the analysis of the optimal demand for law enforcement and public protection are technical production functions which link any allocation of resources to a specific law enforcement activity with the instruments of deterrence or incapacitation it is intended to provide. Such technical production relations apply separately in each stage of the legal enforcement process: the production of the risk of apprehension, once the knowledge of crime becomes available; the determination of the risk of conviction, once a suspected offender is charged with crime; and so forth. The production relations span the operation of different agencies within the general enforcement system: police, prosecution, and courts. However, the behavior of these agencies is interdependent by virtue of the assumption that they all serve the common target of the public enforcement system.[20]

Technically each production function can be defined as an increasing and concave function of the level of real resources utilized in the production process: manpower of various degrees of specialization, professional equipment, and laboratory or research services. As long as the relative prices of these factors and the underlying production frontier are constant, all these separate factors may be combined into an overall "composite" factor of production represented by the total expenditures on these factors. This then, is the basic argument in each of the relevant production functions. It is also plausible to assume, however, that the productivity of the resources allocated to specific enforcement functions will be adversely affected by the "case load" spanning that function. The reason is that given, say, the number of man-hours allocated to police activity in a given area, a rise in the volume of offenses committed in that area due to reasons beyond the control of police would lower the probability that any single offense committed within the same period might be "cleared" by the manpower available.

Note, however, that the situation of a constant allocation of resources to enforcement in the face of a persistently higher level of crime is socially suboptimal. Although an increase in crime due to exogenous factors may temporarily depress the observed levels of deterrence variables, it is not expected to lower the magnitude of the latter variable once the optimal adjustments in enforcement activities are made to ensure a new equilibrium between crime and punishment, as the analysis of optimal social defense has shown. In particular, the associations between crime and punishment variables as reflected in cross-sectional samples of state data are not likely to reflect the involuntary discouraging or "crowding" effect of crime on punishment due to the technical production constraints discussed.

Market Equilibrium. In equilibrium, the quantity supplied of any object of choice equals the quantity demanded. Likewise in the general equilibrium pertaining to the criminal sector in society: the frequency of offenses supplied at an average net return from crime to offenders equals the quantity "demanded" by society as determined by private and public defense against crime. Because optimal private and public protection from crime is expected to rise with an exogenous increase in offenses, and because these activities lower the net returns to offenders from crime, the effective "demand" by society for crime will be negatively associated with the net return from crime to offenders.[21] In contrast, the supply of offenses is generally expected to be positively associated with an offender's net return from crime. These responses by offenders and by society act as stabilizing factors in the general criminal market because they are crucial in ensuring the stability of the equilibrium attained in this market.[22]

The expectation of a stable equilibrium in the criminal sector of society, as deduced through economic analysis, is compatible with Durkheim's (1958:1-15) assertion that crime is a normal "social fact." It goes beyond Durkheim's theory, however, in that it provides a systematic framework for identifying the basic determinants of equilibrium, for predicting displacement in equilibrium as a result of shifts in these determinants, and even for evaluating the deviations from equilibrium of public efforts at law enforcement and crime control in particular instances. Take, for example, the issue of whether society "should" devote additional resources to law enforcement and related programs of crime control. The central question in this connection is whether additional expenditures to effect specific means of deterrence or incapacitation, or a specific legal procedure, would result in social benefits greater than the additional costs of enforcement. The answer cannot be inferred simply from knowledge that a given instrument of deterrence, say, a sanction, lowers the frequency of offenses. It depends on the extent of the deterrent effect of the sanction and the marginal cost of its production.[23] In addition, an evaluation of the efficiency of a given sanction generally requires a simultaneous assessment of the relative efficiency of alternative sanctions, which jointly determine the frequency of crime in society.

Finally, a crucial lesson to be learned from the preceding equilibrium analysis in the context of an empirical implementation of the economic model of crime concerns the simultaneity relations between offense, defense, and the production of means of enforcement and crime prevention. The analysis emphasizes that while the crime rate depends, in part, on probability and severity of punishment, both the production and social demand for the latter may be affected by the level of crime itself. In addition, arbitrary changes in specific deterrence variables—such as the severity of a sanction—may lead to opposite modifications in the level of substitutable means of enforcement, such as the probability of apprehension and conviction.[24] Proper statistical testing of any of the basic propositions of the model therefore requires that the empirical analysis account for the multiple set of theoretically relevant variables, and that appropriate simultaneous equation estimation techniques be employed to "identify" the relevant causal relationship underlying the observed association between crime and punishment in specific samples.

An Alternative Hypothesis.   Another desirable principle of systematic empirical work concerns the explicit formulation of an alternative hypothesis relative to which the validity of a proposed theory can be evaluated. While economists have not devoted nearly as much attention to this issue as they did to the development and formulation of the economic approach itself, at least one alternative hypothesis has been addressed systematically from the outset. It concerns the hypothetical restraining effect of punishment on crime due merely to the incapacitation of known offenders, as distinct from deterrence of potential offenders. To the extent that offenders have a positive probability of recidivism once free to commit crimes outside of prisons, and if incarceration per se does not enhance that probability considerably, imprisonment or execution might reduce the actual rate of crime not because of their deterrent values, but because they are presumed to reduce the supply of potential offenders.

The basic strategy developed to distinguish the pure deterrent from the incapacitative effect of specific criminal sanctions has been to estimate an upper limit of the incapacitative effect of these sanctions which could then be compared with the overall restraining effects of the sanctions on the actual volume of crime, as inferred from systematic empirical investigations. The development of such upper limit estimates of the incapacitative effect of sanctions is theoretically possible if one assumed that all crimes were committed by persons who do not respond to incentives, and who would continue to participate in crime at a constant intensity as long as they remained free to do so.[25] Not surprisingly, even the upper bound estimates of the incapacitative value of currently imposed sanctions is found to be quite low in practice because of the low probability that any potential offender will be apprehended and convicted of crime in any recent period.

Empirical Implementation.   Studies implementing the economic analysis of the supply-of-offenses, demand-for-enforcement, or production-of-means-of-enforcement have relied with virtually no exception on regression analysis to provide quantitative estimates of the relations of interest. Regression analysis, which represents a statistical assessment of well specified dependence relationships, including a systematic evaluation of the properties of the estimated quantitative parameters, has been the standard tool in econometrics for estimating demand, supply, production, or investment relationships at both the micro and macro levels of analysis. It has become a standard econometric procedure because economic theory generally allows for the development of well specified dependence relationships between sets of "dependent" and explanatory variables, and because extensive methodological developments in econometrics in recent decades have allowed researchers to implement systematically not only the simple linear regression model, but also a number of more complex statistical models involving departures from the restrictive set of assumptions underlying the simple regression model. As hinted at the conclusion of the preceding sections, the economic model of offense and defense against crime translates into statistical dependence relations that in a number of ways may deviate from the relations underlying a simple regression model. The statistical problems encountered as a result, however, are quite similar to those encountered in implementations of any partial equilibrium analysis in economics. Therefore, a set of well developed econometric techniques could be deployed in the implementation of the economic model of crime as well. In the discussion below I shall first briefly mention the major special statistical problems encountered in the econometric work on crime and the main statistical methods used to confront these problems, and then turn to summarize the key findings.[26]

1. Errors of Measurement. Virtually all empirical measures of theoretically relevant variables are subject to random errors of measurement. This may be paricularly true in the case of crime-related variables. "Errors[11] in the recorded volume of the offenses examined in empirical investigations arise from several sources: stochastic errors in the reporting of crime, including systematic underreporting of crimes of specific categories; errors in identifying or classifying reported offenses into somewhat arbitrary categories; and errors due to the stochastic nature of the dependence relationship (the supply-of-offenses function) itself. Similarly, errors in the empirical measures of the risks of apprehension or the conditional risks of punishment are due to errors in both individual perceptions of the true magnitudes of these variables, and in the variables used to compute the objective risks: the actual number of apprehensions and conviction relative to the *potential* (maximum) number of such apprehensions and convictions, adjusted for random fluctuations. Although "errors of measurement" are for the most part assumed to be stochastic variates, distributed independently of other variables in the regression equation, the errors in some of the empirical measures of probability of punishment may be correlated with the errors in the reported crime rates themselves—this would be the case if the latter are used to compute the denominators of the risk of punishment measures. Ordinary least squares estimates of the regression coefficient measuring the association between the crime rate and such probability of punishment measures might then be biased in the direction of minus one.[27]

2. "Identification" Problems. Because of the simultaneous relations between offense, defense, and production of law enforcement measures, the statistical analysis must address the problem of "identifying" the structural equation of interest to assure that the regression equation estimated does not confound different structural relations. Put differently, the estimation procedure must assure the unbiasedness and consistency of the estimated regression coefficients in each relation.

3. Heteroscedasticity and Serial Correlation. Because the crime rate measures used as dependent variables in supply-of-offenses equations denote the *mean* frequencies of offenses in communities of varying population sizes (e.g., states), the distributions of the disturbance terms in the various linear regression models estimated can be shown to have

variances that are negatively correlated with the respective (state) populations: a typical case of "heteroscedasticity." The problem of heteroscedasticity may be particularly severe in cross-sectional studies using data from populations of widely varying sizes. In time series investigations of crime movements in a given population the distributions of the disturbance terms may be subject to yet another departure from the normal conditions of the simple regression model due to serial correlation in these terms. Both heteroscedasticity and serial correlations in the residual terms of specific regressions must be addressed to assure the efficiency of the regression estimates.

4. Interrelationships Among Regression Equations. If separate supply of offenses or production functions involving different instuments of law enforcement are interrelated in the sense of being "substitutable" or "complementary" activities, the disturbance terms of the separate equations themselves may be interrelated. An explicit recognition of the structure of correlated residuals would further assure the efficiency of the estimated regressions.

5. Regression Format. The theoretical analysis provides little clue as to the exact mathematical form of the linear regression model to be "fitted" to the relevant empirical data. An inefficient specification might distort the true values of the regression relations of interest.

The statistical methods most often used in the published studies pursuing the economic approach in order to account for the statistical problems just summarized include a combination of conventional and more advanced estimation techniques as follows:

a. Ordinary (or classical) least squares techniques in those situations where the disturbance terms of the regression models could be assumed to satisfy all the normal assumptions of the simple regression model.

b. Standard simultaneous equation estimation techniques to account for potential simultaneous equation or "identification" biases. Models using these techniques—mainly two-stage-least squares—have generally specified current values of crime rates, probabilities of apprehension, conviction and specific sanctions, and expenditures on law enforcement activities by police and courts as *endogenous* variables, while specifying variables related to the economy as a whole, or to the legitimate labor market, demographic variables, and lagged values of selected endogenous variables as predetermined or *exogenous* to the "market" for offenses. It is noteworthy that when the two-stage-least-squares technique is used to "identify" the supply of offenses equation, the (endogenous) probabilities of punishment variables are replaced by a linear combination of instrumental variables that do not include current measures of the corresponding crime rate. Estimates of the association between the crime and probability of punishment variables are then expected to be free of biases due to errors of measurement in the crime rates discussed at point 1 above, especially when the analysis also accounts for a potential serial correlation in these errors.

c. Generalized-least-squares techniques—mainly various "weighting" procedures—to account for potential inefficiencies in regression estimates due to heteroscedasticity. These are applied in conjunction with both ordinary least squares and simultaneous equation estimation procedures.

d. A nonlinear, three-round estimation procedure proposed by R.C. Fair (1970) to account for both the simultaneous relations between the crime and punishment variables and a potential serial correlation in disturbance terms in studies relying on time series data.

e. "Seemingly unrelated" estimation techniques proposed by Zellner (1962) to improve upon the efficiency of regression estimates through a joint estimation of interrelated sets of crime.

f. Maximum likelihood techniques proposed by Box and Cox (1964) to search for an optimal specification of the format of the linear models used for estimating supply-of-offenses functions. The techniques provide for a systematic comparison of the efficiency of alternative specifications, including the logarithmic, semilogarithmic, and simple linear transformations of variables of interest as well as of the regression results based on these transformations.

Apart from these formal procedures, the stability of various regression estimates and their sensitivity of "missing" variables have been examined through examination of comparable estimates based of differerent time periods, geographical units, and population aggregates (e.g., state and national populations). The major findings can be summarized as follows:[28]

1. Practically all studies applying the economic approach systematically to data on recorded offenses indicate that probability and severity of punishment by imprisonment exert statistically significant restraining effects on the incidence of crime in the population. These results emerge from studies focusing on different crime categories: murder and assault, as well as hijacking; robbery and burglary, as well as auto theft; subsets of crimes against persons and property and the set of all felony crimes.[29] Similar results are obtained in studies focusing on the criminal behavior of different groups: women and men; blacks and whites (Bartel, 1979; Ehrlich, 1970). They are corroborated in studies using aggregate statistics for the United States as well as in studies using cross-state, cross-metropolitan, and cross-county data (Vandaele, 1975; Ehrlich, 1975; Sjoquist, 1973; Phillips and Votey, 1975). They further appear to emerge in studies using both English and American data (Carr-Hill and Stern, 1973; Wolpin, 1978a).

2. The absolute magnitudes of the coefficients indicating the responsiveness of specific crime rates to the probability and severity of imprisonment are generally consistent with the hypothesis that sanctions and law enforcement impart a pure deterrent effect on offenders, not simply an incapacitative effect on convicted offenders (Ehrlich, 1974, 1975; Wolpin, 1978a).

3. This inference is compatible with additional findings concerning the effect of "positive" incentives. Analyses of cross-sectional data indicate that the incidence of most felonies is positively and significantly associated with indicators of both affluence (average wealth) and income inequality in the poplulation. Analyses of time series data further indicate that the probability of unemployment in legitimate occupations acts as an incentive to participate in criminal activities (Ehrlich, 1974, 1975; Vandaele, 1975).

4. The responsiveness of offenses to changes in probability and severity of the imprisonment sanction in categories of crimes against the person is not, on average, found to be lower in magnitude than the responsiveness of offenses in categories of crimes against property (Ehrlich, 1974).

5. The evidence developed in connection with the deterrent efficacy of capital punishment represents a serious challenge to the strong and unequivocal inferences of earlier studies denying the existence of any deterrent or incapacitative effects of the capital sanction. In addition to the original time series study by this author, which presented evidence consistent with the deterrence hypothesis, and which provoked a great deal of debate, a number of more recent studies using independent statistics from both the United States and England have produced evidence which generally corroborates the original findings (Barnett, 1978; Ehrlich, 1977; Cloninger, 1977). Even some recent studies denying the deterrent value of capital punishment report evidence consistent with the deterrent efficacy of imprisonment in connection with the crime of murder (Passel, 1975; Forst, 1977).

6. More important, some time series and cross-sectional investigations have produced evidence consistent with a sharp test of the deterrence hypothesis. The elasticity of specific crimes with respect to the probabilty of apprehension is found to exceed that with respect to the conditional probability of conviction given apprehension, which, in turn, exceeds the elasticity with respect to the conditional probability of a specific punishment (Ehrlich, 1975, 1977; Wolpin, 1978b).

7. Although most of the estimates of "supply-of-offenses functions" have relied on data on recorded offenses, some preliminary investigations using victimization survey data report results that are compatible with the economic approach in general and the deterrence hypothesis in particular (see, for example, Goldberg, 1977).

8. A few studies present evidence in support of the specific implications of the model concerning the production of means of deterrence or incapacitation at different stages of the enforcement process (Landes, 1974; Ehrlich, 1974; Phillips and Votey, 1975).

9. Some effort at the empirical implementation of the economic analysis of private protection against crime also present evidence generally compatible with the basic propositions concerning optimal private protection (Bartel, 1975; Komesar, 1973).

10. Statistics concerning the magnitude of different sanctions and the probability of their enforcement by type of crime in both the United States and England are compatible with the general implications of optimal public protection and enforcement of criminal laws (Becker, 1968; Wolpin, 1978b).

11. As for whether crime "pays" in expected monetary terms alone, the answer depends, in principle, on the importance of psychic payoffs to crime as perceived by offenders and, in particular, on their attitutdes toward risk. Some findings indicate that at least insofar as certain crimes against property are concerned, crime may pay (Ehrlich, 1974: App. 2, section IV; Krohm, 1975).

Clearly, the results summarized above are subject to important limitations, largely due to data exigencies that also have restricted the utilization of econometric techniques required for a comprehensive implementation of the analysis. For example, only modest progress has so far been made in studying those structural relations in the model concerning demand for and production of specific means of law enforcement activity, or the interaction between private and public protection from crime. Little knowledge has been acquired as to how well the economic model could explain international variations in crime or individual participation in illegitimate activities. Furthermore, the economic approach has not so far been implemented in a systematic analysis of the role of rehabilitation, incapacitation, and deterrence as competing instruments of crime control. All these are obvious tasks for future investigations.

Criticism and Further Evidence. The development and empirical implementation of the economic approach to crime has presented a serious challenge to dominant notions in criminology concerning criminal behavior and the role of the criminal sanction. The thrust of the work by economists has also been interpreted as having unequivocal policy recommendations that run contrary to popular sentiments in academic circles for rehabilitation, prison reform, and abolition of the death penalty, although, to my knowledge, none of the work by economists has actually derived any clear cut policy recommendations regarding these programs. Underlying the perceived challenge to some modern currents in criminological thought may be the very revival of the classical or liberal position which emphasizes the role of individual choice, and which may be contrasted with deterministic positions in modern criminology stressing the role of the organization and structure of economic production, or of the political and social institutions in dictating individual behavior in general. As asserted by one noted sociologist some time ago, the view of the potential offender being guided by the pursuit of personal gratification is objectionable because such "psychological hedonism . . . is not in accord with modern psychology and sociology, which see human behavior as largely unplanned and habitual rather than calculated and voluntary (Schuessler, 1952:55).

Given this background, it may not be surprising that the economic approach has spawned intense controversy and quite an extenisve critical literature. The latter has been directed mainly against findings concerning the deterrent efficacy of the death penalty. Findings such as the positive relationship between crime and the inequality in the distribution of income or the probability of unemployment in legitimate markets, and even the role of "affluence," have not been challenged. More important, hardly any criticism has been advanced against the formal economic model itself, nor have the critics offered an alternative theory capable of explaining systematically the amalgam of empirical findings developed from independent samples in connection with the effects of the death penalty, other sanctions, and other incentives on crime.

The criticism itself has been multifarious, centering first on issues such as the replicability of the results on capital punishment developed from time series data for the United States,[30] and whether regression analysis, despite its complexity and claim to scientific rigor, is really more satisfactory than the primitive "matching" procedure used by Sellin in his studies of the deterrent efficacy of the death penalty (Baldus and Cole, 1975). Also advanced initially was the bizarre proposition that the time-series regression results on the efficacy of capital punishment, even if valid, could be interpreted on strictly technical grounds as showing that an increase in the number of executions would lead to an actual increase in the frequency of murder in the population.[31] More substantive comments have referred to the alleged sensitivity of the regression results concerning the efficacy of capital punishment to exclusion of observations from the 1960s from the time series sample, first reported in Ehrlich (1973, 1975:413), to changes in the regression format, to fortuitous errors of measurement in the execution risk variables and, perhaps, other deterrence variables as well, and to omission of potentially relevant explanatory variables such as the deterioration of societal morals and values during the 1960s, and the increased "availability" of handguns.[32] Research on the deterrent efficacy of other sanctions is criticized essentially on the ground that it may have identified the production function of law enforcement instruments because of the crowding effect of crime on the production of certainty and severity of punishment, rather than a suppy-of-offenses function exhibiting the effect of the punishment variables on the incidence of crime.[33]

The reader may note that some of these issues, such as the measurement errors and identification problems, have been addressed in the economic literature from the outset and that careful implementation of the economic analysis has utilized the conventional econometric procedures to remedy and minimize whatever biases might have been imparted on the regression estimates due to these problems. Unfortunately, the critiques often ignore these facts and argue for the hypothetical existence of biases regardless of the methodologies used.[34] More important, in advancing their critical comments authors often fail to take account of the full implications of the equilibrium model of offense and defense, or to test systematically the validity of the criticism, even in those cases where a complete survey of the results easily contradicts the thrust of the criticism.[35] A number of crititques demonstrate technical errors.[36] Since these issues have already been discussed in the published literature, I shall not proceed to evaluate them in detail. Instead, I shall comment generally on some of the criticism contained in the "Report of the Panel on Research on Deterrent and Incapacitative Effects" (Blumstein et al., 1978), the summary of which is included in this volume.

Despite its own recognition that the evidence from the empirical studies of the deterrence hypothesis "certainly favors a proposition supporting deterrence more that it favors one asserting that deterrence is absent," the panel admits its reluctance to "assert that the evidence warrants an affirmative conclusion regarding deterrence."[37] That results based on observational statistics, as opposed to truly "controlled" experiments, cannot constitute a proof for any proposition is, of course, well recognized in statistical literature as well as in careful studies of the deterrence hypothesis. Hardly any empirical study in the behavioral sciences is immune to this basic limitation. However, the panel's reticence in properly recognizing the preponderance of the accumulated evidence derives primarily not from this constraint, but from one-sided and sheerly speculative analysis, assisted by the lack of any representation of the economic approach on the panel by a practitioner of this approach, whose familiarity with the economic model could have provided the much needed critical evaluation of some commissioned papers.

Two examples may highlight the nature of the criticism adopted in the panel's report. The panel accepts without criticism the speculation that most studies by economists may have identified a "production function of law enforcement instruments" (probability and severity of punishment) in which the negative association between crime and the punishment variables is due to the "case load," or "crowding" effect (see the discussion above), rather than a supply-of-offenses function in which the negative association between these variables is due to the deterrent effect of the punishment variables. Tha panel has failed to note, however, that

(a) Being aware of this problem, some of the studies evaluated used standard econometric procedures to ensure the identification of the supply-of-offenses function.

(b) A study commissioned by the panel itself (Vandaele, 1978) showed the robustness of the estimated supply-of-offenses functions to numerous modifications in identification restrictions.

(c) More important, the panel ignored the implications of the economic model that had been implemented in these studies in favor of speculative interpretations of the findings. Specifically, as the analysis above indicates, optimal behavior on the part of law enforcement authorities is expected to give rise to a *positive* association between crime and punishment once expenditures on law enforcement activity adjust to an autonomous increase in the threat of crime to society. At least in the cross-sectional investigations examined, the likelihood of such adjustment is quite high because of the *persistent* pattern of crime and enforcement activity across different states: If state A has a persistently higher crime level than state B due to factors outside the control of law enforcement agencies, then both the expenditures on law enforcement and the magnitudes of deterrence variables in state A would have ample opportunity to adjust to their socially optimal magnitudes. Thus, the more likely identification problem in cross-sectional investigations is that of confounding the supply-of-offenses function with a demand-for-enforcement function exhibiting a positive association between crime and deterrence variables, and not that of confounding the former with a production function of deterrence instruments. Because the report authors do not consider the theoretical predictions of the economic model in a systematic manner, they are led to stress the speculation that the magnitudes of the estimated deterrent effects they examined may be overstated, while ignoring cogent considerations pointing to an even greater possibility that they might be understated.

(d) The report authors do not explore seriously the implications of their own speculation that the estimate deterrent effects examined are essentially due to "crowding effects." A detailed examination of the complete set of results reported in the literature would reveal this speculation to be without basis in fact. If the "crowding effect" were the dominant factor underlying the estimated negative association between crime and punishment, then such effects would be much more pronounced in connection with less serious than more serious crimes, since prison authorities faced with temporary shortage of space would tend to release the petty offenders before releasing the more serious felons. For the same reason, the estimated effects should be more pronounced in years of high rather than low frequency of offenses. Time served in prison should also fluctuate significantly between years of high and low crime rates. None of these implications is compatible with the observed evidence.

A second example concerns the paradoxical argument made by Passel and Taylor (1975, 1977) and Friedman (1976, published in this volume), which was mentioned earlier, that the results of the time series investigation into murder and the death penalty, showing evidence for a deterrent effect of execution risk on the murder rate, actually mean that an increase in the frequency of execution would increase the frequency of murder in the population. This argument is repeated in the body of the report without criticism. Closer examination shows this argument to be completely false and the result of inappropriate application of basic principles of price theory.[38] Yet it has become part of the information disseminated through the report to the general public.

Not that the investigations into the deterrent effects of specific sanctions, or the effect of unemployment on crime for that matter, are necessarily free from any distortions due to inaccuracies in the crime and punishment measures, missing variables, or "identification" problems. However, the methods utilized in much of the recent econometric research into crime are, after all, the same methods used in econometric studies of the legitimate sector of the economy, where similar statistical problems are prevalent, and on which much economic wisdom rests. Moreover, the extent to which estimates are free of systematic biases ultimately must be judged by examining the consistency of the results with detailed theoretical predictions. On this criterion the econometric findings summarized earlier do fare quite well. Furthermore, evidence published since the panel's survey has further corroborated earlier findings concerning the deterrent effects of both imprisonment and the death penalty. The new studies by Bartel (1979), Landes (1978) and Wolpin (1978b) corroborate earlier findings on the effects of probabilities and severity of imprisonment and of income and labor force variables by examining, respectively, independent data on crimes by women, hijacking in the United States, and major felonies in Great Britain. New studies into the deterrent effect of capital punishment by Cloninger (1977), Ehrlich (1977a), Barnett (1978), and Wolpin (1978a), using cross-sectional data in the United States and time series data from Great Britian, generally corroborate the finding of deterrent effects. It is ultimately this array of empirical evidence from different time periods, states, and countries that militates strongly against the allegation that the results developed through applications of the economic approach are spurious.

CONCLUSION

It appears from this limited survey of the economic approach to crime that both economic reasoning and an extensive body of recently developed evidence based on this reasoning are compatible with the hypothesis that potential offenders respond to incentives—both positive and negative, that law enforcement authorities react to the threat of crime on the basis of this hypothesis, and that equilibrium analysis is a potentially powerful tool for analyzing and predicting movements in the frequency of various illegitimate activities at different times and places. The propostion that the probability and severity of criminal sanctions exert pure deterrent effects, independent of any incapacitative effects of specific sanctions, should not be confused, however, with any necessary recommendation for either greater or lesser emphasis on their utilization as instruments of crime control. The desirability of specific law enforcement activities at the margin is determined not only by their relative efficacy, but also by the relative cost of their production. The fact that capital punishment may be the most effective deterrent does not necessarily imply that it is the most desirable means of deterring murder: it is also the most costly means of deterrence in social terms and the desirability of its enforcement must be determined not only on the basis of the tradeoff between the life lost and the potential lives saved through deterrence of potential murders, but also on the basis of whether other incentives are being utilized optimally, because changes in the risk of victimization from murder may change the relative desirability of the death penalty. Indeed, the dramatic focus on capital punishment as the indispensable backbone of the criminal justice system really misses the point of the death penalty being just one element of a system in which, in principle, alternative mechanisms are available. By the same token, the desirability of positive incentives as a means of crime control cannot be determined simply from knowledge of their efficacy.

The basic conclusions in reference to the magnitudes of offenders' responsiveness to various incentives cannot of course be regarded as final. They are based on the broadest and most comprehensive body of systematic evidence we have, but that body of evidence leaves a lot to be desired.

One thing is, however, clear. The established views in past criminological research on the effects of deterrents and other incentives on criminal behavior—including the effect of capital punishment—are contradicted by at least one extensive body of empirical evidence relating to different crimes, different places, and different time periods. I know of no coherent body of evidence justifying them. They seem at this point part of criminological mythology, not the demonstrated conclusions of logical analysis, systematic quantitative studies, or common sense. Yet they have exerted immense influence on academic thinking in the past. Future advance in knowledge concerning this topic will require, at the very least, willingness on the part of researchers to confront the substantive issues with sufficient openness, free of institutional pressures.

NOTES

1. Adam Smith (1937:15) said that "[t]he difference between the most dissimilar characters, between a philosopher and a common street porter for example, seems to arise not so much from nature as from habit, custom, and education."
2. See Radzinowitz (1966:55).
3. Cesare Beccaria's "Dei Delitti E Delle Pene," initially published in 1764, is his singular work in this area (see the Farrer (1880) English translation). The major relevant works by Jeremy

Bentham are his "Introduction to the Principles of Morals and Legislation," "Principles of Penal Law," and "The Rationale of Reward," all contained in Bowering (1843).

4. Karl Marx, "Capital Punishment," reprinted from New York Daily News (February 18, 1853) in T.B. Bottomore and Maximilian Rubel (1956).

5. For some elaboration, see Isaac Ehrlich and Randall Mark, 1978:164-176.

6. "No man . . . can doubt for a moment," wrote Malthus (1798:259), "that if every murder in Italy had been invariably punished, the use of the stiletto in transports of passion would have been comparatively but little known." By contrast, Ferri (1917:214) wrote: "punishments, in which until now . . . the best remedies against crime have possibly been seen, have none of the efficacy attributed to them."

7. For some detail, see Isaac Ehrlich and Randall Mark, 1978:164-176.

8. See, in particular, Thorsten Sellin (1959), (1961), and (1967). Also see the references to other research following Sellin's in Ehrlich and Mark (1978).

9. As stated by Sellin (1959:34), "The conclusion is inevitable that the presence of the death penalty—either in law or in practice—does not influence homicide death rates." This conclusion was repeated in Sellin, 1967:138.

10. See, for example, the studies by William J. Bowers (1974) referred to in Ehrlich and Mark (1978).

11. The considerations apparently have been overlooked in some of the more recent research that attempts to test the economic approach in connection with the capital sanction. For example, the analyses by Peter Passel (1975) and Brian E. Forst (1977), based on cross-sectional data relating to homicides and executions in 1960 and 1970, depend entirely on the presumed distribution of execution risk measures in these years. However, no meaningful distributions of execution risk are available in these years because there were no executions in 1970, and in 1960 in 12 out of 20 "executing" states for which complete data are available, only a single exectuion occurred, with the trend in all such states clearly leading toward a practical abolition of the penalty. At such small levels of execution in each state and with an attenuated distribution, the effects of errors in the measures are likely to dominate the comparisons across states both in a given year and for changes over time. For a meaningful test of the hypothesis of no-deterrence, one must be careful to analyze those situations in which it conceivably can be rejected. To do otherwise would amount to searching for the lost coin not under the streetlight, but with the light out.

12. For a related analysis concerning other applications of economic analysis, see Becker (1976).

13. For a discussion of the axiomatic framework underlying this decision rule, see Von Neumann and Morgenstern (1947) and Arrow (1965). Note that the emphasis on the qualification "as if" is not accidental: the positive economic methodology does not assume that decision makers necessarily arrive at their choices through a conscious calculus of maximization or that they even rationalize their actual choices in this explicit manner. All that is required is that maximizing behavior be the principle (conscious or subconscious) that best describes the systematic pattern of decision makers' choices from an objective point of view. This important distinction is a central theme in Friedman (1953).

14. See, for example, Ehrlich (1974) for a formal exposition of the model within a one-period decision-making context.

15. For an exceptional case where an increase in severity of punishment may not deter actual offenders with a strong preference for risk, see Ehrlich (1974:78). These predictions relate to the *partial* effects of the theoretical measures of probability and severity of marginal penalties, defined to incorporate both monetary and psychic components, given that all other similarly defined indicators of marginal returns and costs from participation in crime are "held constant." (This restriction is misconstrued in Block and Heineke, 1975). The analysis of the partial effect of severity and certainty of the marginal penalties or other incentives can also be worked out with all incentives defined to incorporate only pecuniary componenets, in which case the predictions discussed in this section would hold unambiguously for "compensated" changes in sanctions or

other incentives that left the offender's relevant income or wealth position unchanged. This qualification is not unique to the analysis of crime, but applies in connection with any general price effects in economic theory. Thus, even if participation in criminal activity per se is an "inferior good" to the professional offender, a compensated increase in the magnitude of the fine he must pay upon apprehension and conviction would unambiguously reduce the extent of his criminal involvement. In the empirical implementations of the model via regression analysis, the introduction of measures of the level and distribution of income in the community go some way toward separating the theoretical pure income and relative price effects associated with changes in measurable sanctions.

16. The theorem is derived in Ehrlich (1975).

17. These results are discussed in Becker (1968) and Ehrlich (1974).

18. A formal model which analyzes this choice is proposed in Ehrlich and Becker (1972). Bartel (1975) applies this analysis to protection against crime by private businesses, and Komesar (1973) presents evidence bearing on self-protection against crime by private individuals.

19. An attempt to integrate some distributional elements in the analysis of optimal public defense against crime is reported in Ehrlich (1977).

20. For a separate analysis of the courts, see Landes (1974).

21. Although society, acting as a monopoly, does not have conventional "demand curve" for offenses, since it cannot take the net gain available to offenders from crime as given, the public reaction curve to exogenous shifts in the supply of offenses can be thought of as an "ex-post" demand curve for crime.

22. This analysis abstracts from any explicit discussion of the equilibria pertaining to additional submarkets within the general "market" for offenses, such as the submarket for stolen goods, or the market for lawyers. A schematic analysis of some of these additional markets is offered in Vandaele (1975). Pashigian (1977) provides a systematic analysis of the market for lawyers.

23. For an illustrative calculation that indicates that the level of expenditures on law enforcement by police and courts in 1965 may have been less than optimal, see Ehrlich, 1974:107-110. In contrast, Landes (1978) calculates the total expenditures on hijacking during the period 1973-1976 to have been in excess of the socially optimal amount, although the calculation does not evaluate the optimality of the actual resource allocation to hijacking prevention on the margin.

24. For an elaborate analysis, see Ehrlich and Gibbons (1977).

25. See the analysis in Ehrlich, 1974:83-85, and 1975:413. For an alternative method of estimating the incapacitative effect of punishment on the basis of a more restrictive set of statistical assumptions, see Wolpin (1978b).

26. For the definition and detailed analysis for any of the statistical issues mentioned in the following discussion, see, e.g., Madalla (1977).

27. An elaborate analysis of this problem is given in Ehrlich (1974:App. 1, section IV).

28. The list of studies mentioned here is by no means complete. The studies mentioned are mainly those which attempted to implement the economic approach under study.

29. See, e.g., Ehrlich (1974, 1975, 1977a), Landes (1978), Vandaele (1975) for studies using American data.

30. The allegation that the reported findings could not be reproduced was made by Bowers and Pierce (1975) and Passel and Taylor (1975). More recently, the results have been replicated to within rounding errors by Klein, Forst and Filatov (1978).

31. This patently paradoxical argument appears in Passel and Taylor (1975, 1977) and also in the paper by L.S. Friedman (1976), published in this volume. I shall briefly comment on the argument below.

32. Not all the critiques argued for overstated deterrent effects. Yunker (1976) argues that the estimated effect of risk of executions reported in Ehrlich (1975) is understated.

33. These issues are raised in Bowers and Pierce (1975), Passel and Taylor (1975, 1977), Klein, Forst and Filatov (1978), and Fisher and Nagin (1978). Also see the critical evaluation of the alleged biases in Ehrlich (1975a, 1977b, 1977c).

34. See, for example, the analysis by Klein et al. (1978) of the effects of errors of measurement and its critical evaluation in Ehrlich (1977c:298-299).

35. See the discussion of the identification problem by Fisher and Nagin (1978) and the response in Ehrlich (1977c:303-306).

36. For example, both Bowers and Pierce (1975) and Passel and Taylor (1977) use erroneous statistical tests when they infer that regression results based on post-1960 murder statistics are significantly different from those based on pre-1960 data. Their errors have been pointed out in Ehrlich, 1975a and 1977b, respectively. Klein et al. (1978) present a number of exercises with errors of measurement which are irrelevant for any valid inferences regarding the importance of errors of measurement in explaining the estimated deterrent effect of execution risk from the time series sample used in Ehrlich (1975). For a discussion, see Ehrlich (1977c:298-301).

37. This discussion is based on the material included in Ehrlich (1977c), which also contains detailed references to the report itself.

38. For a complete analysis, see Ehrlich and Gibbons (1977).

REFERENCES

ARROW, K.J. (1965).Aspects of the theory of risk bearing. Helsinki: Yrgö Johnssonin Stäätio.

BAILEY, W.C. (1975). "Murder and capital punishment: Some further evidence." American Journal of Orthopsychiatry, 45 (July).

BALDUS, D.C., and COLE, K.W.L. (1975). "A comparison of the work of Thorsten Sellin and Isaac Ehrlich on the deterrent effect of capital punishment." Yale Law Journal, 85 (December).

BARNETT, A. (1978). "The deterrent effect of capital punishment: Still another view." Unpublished manuscript, Sloan School of Management, Massachusetts Institute of Technology.

BARTEL, A.P. (1975). "An analysis of firm demand for protection against crime." Journal of Legal Studies, 4(2): June.

_____ (1979). "Women and crime: An economic analysis." Economic Inquiry.

BECCARIA, C. (1880). "Crimes and punishments." In J.A. Farrer (ed.), Crimes and Punishments. London: Clatoo and Windus.

BECKER, G.S. (1968). "Crime and Punishment: An economic approach." Journal of Political Economy, 78 (March/April).

_____ (1976). The economic approach to human behavior. Chicago: University of Chicago Press.

BLOCK, M., and HEINEKE, J. (1975). "A labor theoretic analysis of the criminal choice." American Economic Review, 65 (June).

BLUMSTEIN, J., COHEN, J., and NAGIN, D. (eds.) (1978). Deterrence and incapacitation: Estimating the effects of criminal sanctions on crime rates. Washington, D.C.: NAS.

BOWERS, W.J. (1974). Executions in America. Lexington, Mass.: D.C. Heath.

BOWERS, W.J., and PIERCE, G.L. (1975). "The illusion of deterrence in Isaac Ehrlich's work on the deterrent effect of capital punishment." Yale Law Journal 85 (December).

BOX, G.E.P., and COX, D.R. (1964). "An analysis of transformations." Journal of the Royal Statistical Association, 25 Ser. B.

CARR-HILL, R.A., and STERN, N.H. (1973). "An econometric model of the supply and control of recorded offenses in England and Wales." Journal of Public Economics, 2 (November).

CLONINGER, D.O. (1977). "Deterrence and the death penalty: A cross sectional analysis." Journal of Behavioral Economics, 6 (Summer and Winter).

DURKHEIM, E. (1958). The rules of sociological method. 8th ed. New York: Free Press.

EHRLICH, I. (1970). "Participation in illegitimate activities: An economic analysis." Ph.D. Dissertation, Columbia University.

_____ (1973). Working Paper No. 18, National Bureau of Economics Research.

_____ (1974). In G.S. Becker and W.M. Landes (eds.), Essays in the economics of crime and punishment. New York: Columbia University Press.

_____ (1975). "The deterrent effect of capital punishment: A question of life and death." American Economic Review, 65 (June).

_____ (1975a). "Deterrence: Evidence and inference." Yale Law Journal, 85 (December).

_____ (1977a). "Capital punishment and deterrence: Some further thoughts and additional evidence." Journal of Political Economy, 85(4): August.

_____ (1977b). "The deterrent effect of capital punishment-reply." American Economic Review, 67 (June).

_____ (1977c). "Fear of deterrence: A critical evaluation of the report of the Panel on 'Research on Deterrent and Incapacitiative Effects.' " Journal of Legal Studies, 6(2): June.

_____ and BECKER, G.S. (1972). "Market insurance, self-insurance and self-protection." Journal of Political Economy, 80(4): July/August.

EHRLICH I., and GIBBONS, J. (1977). "On the measurement of the deterrent effect of capital punishment and the theory of deterrence." Journal of Legal Studies, 6(1): January.

EHRLICH, I., and MARK, R. (1978). "Deterrence and economics: A perspective on theory and evidence." In J.M. Yinger and S.J. Cutler (eds.), Major social issues. New York: Free Press.

FAIR, R.C. (1970). "The estimation of simultaneous equation models with lagged endogenous variables and first order serially correlated errors." Econometrica, 38 (May): 507-516.

FERRI, E. (1917). Criminal sociology. Boston: Little, Brown.

FISHER, F.M., and NAGIN, D. (1978). "On the feasibility of identifying the crime function in a simultaneous model of crime rates and sanction levels." In Blumstein et al. (eds.), Deterrence and incapacitation: Estimating the effects of criminal sanctions on crime rates. Washington, D.C.: NAS.

FLEISHER, B.M. (1966). The economics of delinquency. Chicago: Quadrangle.

FORST, B.E. (1977). "The deterrent effect of capital punishment: A cross-state analysis of the 1960's." Minnesota Law Review, 61.

FRIEDMAN, B.E. (1977). "The methodology of positive economics." In M. Friedman (ed.), Essays in positive economics. Chicago: University of Chicago Press.

FRIEDMAN, L.S. (1976). "The use of multiple regression analysis to test for a deterrent effect of capital punishment: Prospects and problems." Department of Economics, Universtiy of California at Berkeley, Working Paper No. 3 (Rev.), January.

GOLDBERG, I. (1977). "True crime rates: The deterrence hypothesis revisited." Unpublished, Hoover Institution, Stanford University, October.

KLEIN, L.R., FORST, B., and FILATOV, V. (1978). "The deterrent effect of capital punishment: An assessment of the estimates." In Blumstein et al. (eds.), Deterrence and incapacitation: Estimating the effects of criminal sanctions on crime rates. Washington, D.C.: NAS.

KOMESAR, N.K. (1973). "A theoretical and empirical study of victims of crime." Journal of Legal Studies, 2.

KROHM, G. (1975). "The pecuniary incentives of property crime." In S. Rottenberg (ed.), The economics of crime and punishment. Washington, D.C.: American Enterprise Institute.

LANDES, W.M. (1974). "An economic analysis of the courts." In G.S. Becker and W.M. Landes (eds.), Essays in the economics of crime and punishment. New York: Columbia University Press.

_____ (1978). "An economic study of U.S. aircraft hijacking." Journal of Law and Economics.

_____ and POSNER, R.A. (1975). "The private enforcement of law." Journal of Legal Studies, 4(1): January.

MADALLA, G.S. (1977). Econometrics. New York: McGraw-Hill.

MALTHUS, R. (1798). An essay on the principle of population as it affects the improvement of society. London: J. Johnson.

MARX, K. (1956). "Capital punishment." In T.B. Bottomore and M. Rubel (eds.), Karl Marx, Selected writings in sociology and social philosophy. London: C.A. Watts.

PALEY, W. (1822). The principles of moral and political philosophy. London: T. Davidson, Whitefriars.

PASHIGIAN, P. (1977). "The market for lawyers: The determinants of the demand for and supply of lawyers." Journal of Law and Economics, 20(1): April.

PASSEL, P. (1975). "The deterrent effect of capital punishment: A statistical test." Stanford Law Review, 61.

_____ and TAYLOR, J. (1975). "The deterrent effect of capital punishment: Another view." Department of Economics, Columbia University, unpublished discussion paper No. 75-7509.

_____ (1977). American Economic Review, 67 (June).

PHILLIPS, L., and VOTEY, H.L. (1975). "Crime control in California." Journal of Legal Studies, 4(2): June.

RADZINOWITZ, L. (1966). Ideology and crime. New York: Columbia University Press.

SCHUESSLER, K. (1952). "The deterrent influence of the death penalty." Annals of the American Academy of Political and Social Science, 284 (November).

SELLIN, T. (1959). The death penalty. Philadelphia: American Law Institute.

_____ (1961). "Capital punishment." Federal Probation, 25 (September).

_____ (1967). Capital punishment. New York: Harper and Row.

SJOQUIST, D.L. (1973). "Property crime and economic behavior: Some empirical results." American Economic Review, June.

SMITH, A. (1896). Lecture on justice, police, revenue and arms, E. Canaan (ed.). Oxford: Clarendon.

_____ (1937). The wealth of nations. New York: Random House.

_____ (1977). The theory of moral sentiments. 6th ed. Dublin: J. Beatty and C. Jackson.

STIGLER, G. (1974). "The optimum enforcement of laws." In G.S. Becker and W.M. Landes (eds.), Essays in the economics of crime and punishment. New York: Columbia University Press.

TITTLE, C.R., and LOGAN, C.H. (1973). "Sanctions and deviance." Law and Society Review, 7 (Spring).

TULLOCK, G. (1969). "An economic approach to crime." Social Science Quarterly, 50.

VANDAELE, W. (1975). "The economics of crime: An econometric investigation of auto theft in the United States." Ph.D. Dissertaion, University of Chicago.

_____ (1978). "Participation in illegitimate activities: Ehrlich revisited." In Blumstein et al. (eds.), Deterrence and incapacitation: Estimating the effects of criminal sanctions on crime rates. Washington, D.C.: NAS.

VON NEUMANN, J., and MORGENSTERN, O. (1947). Theory of Games and Economic Behavior, Princeton: Princeton University Press.

WICKSTEED, P.H. (1910). The common sense of political economy. London: Macmillan.

WOLPIN, K. (1978a). "Capital punishment and homicide in England: A summary of results." American Economic Review, 62(2): May.

_____ (1978b). "An economic analysis of crime and punishment in England and Wales: 1894-1967." Journal of Political Economy.

YUNKER, J.A. (1976). "Is the death penalty a deterrent to homicide? Some time series evidence." Journal of Behavioral Economics, 5 (Summer).

ZELLER, A. (1962). "An efficient method of estimating seemingly unrelated regressions and tests for a regression bias." Journal of the American Statistical Association, 57 (June).

2

THE USE OF MULTIPLE REGRESSION ANALYSIS TO TEST FOR A DETERRENT EFFECT OF CAPITAL PUNISHMENT
Prospects and Problems

LEE S. FRIEDMAN

RENEWED INTEREST IN THE POSSIBLE DETERRENT EFFECTS OF CAPITAL PUNISHMENT

Recently, there has been renewed interest among social scientists in the possibility of testing whether or not capital punishment deters murder. This interest has followed naturally from a reexamination of crime deterrence in general, which itself has probably been stimulated by the continuing problem of crime and acknowledged failure of corrections to correct.[1] While the vast bulk of the literature suggests that crime deterrence through public law enforcement procedures is either nonexistent or of only slight effect, the empirical evidence offered is usually derived by methodologically flawed analyses.[2] In opposition to the empirical findings of these earlier studies, several economists have recently presented new analyses. Based on econometric techniques involving multiple regression analysis, they claim to isolate and identify general deterrent effects of law enforcement activity.[3] In a paper published in the June 1975 *American Economic Review*, Isaac Ehrlich reported an extension of earlier research results to include a specific test for the presence of a deterrent effect of capital punishment.[4] This study, which claimed to identify a significant reduction in the murder rate due to the use of capital punishment, was filed (in its preliminary and more detailed version) with the United States Supreme Court in the case of *Fowler v. North Carolina*.[5] The case concerned the constitutionality of the death penalty.

In a previous decision, *Furman v. Georgia* 408 U.S. 238 (1972), the Supreme Court invalidated most capital punishment laws then in effect. The central issue was whether or not the decision to impose the death penalty was cruel and unusual punishment in violation of the eighth and fourteenth amendments. Only Justices Brennan and Marshall held that capital punishment per se violates the constitution, while the others of the majority (Justices Douglas, White, and Stewart) made the narrower ruling that jury-discretionary capital punishment violates the constitution.[6]

From Lee S. Friedman, "The Use of Multiple Regression Analysis To Test for a Deterrent Effect of Capital Punishment: Prospects and Problems." Unpublished manuscript, 1976.

While the arguments made to support these opinions follow a number of strands, particularly that capital punishment is used arbitrarily and discriminatorily, this article is especially relevant to one component of the majority reasoning: that capital punishment as administered did not seem to provide any deterrent effect greater than that which could be achieved through imprisonment. The death penalty is therefore excessive, and violates the eighth amendment. Support for this reasoning was based in part on empirical social science investigations of deterrence.[7]

After the *Furman* decision, most states passed so-called "mandatory" capital punishment laws, intended to remove the discretion which caused the previous laws to be held unconstitutional. The *Fowler* case challenged the notion that the new laws (specifically that of North Carolina) are able to remove sufficient discretion to render the death penalty constitutional. How then can the deterrence issue again be raised, this time in support of capital punishment? It is not to argue that there is significantly greater deterrence under the new laws. The broader argument is made that all the prior studies are wrong and the new study by Ehrlich shows that there always has been a significant deterrent effect from capital punishment. Note that this entire social science debate does not concern the question of whether capital punishment, if administered very differently than has been the case in modern society, would have a deterrent effect. The question is whether or not capital punishment, as it has been actually used, has had a measurable deterrent effect.

This paper is intended to make the work of Ehrlich and others using similar statistical techniques accessible to a broad audience of scholars. More specifically, this paper is intended to explain in nontechnical language the hope for new knowledge that underlies work using multiple regression analysis in this area, and to delineate a number of barriers which must be overcome for this type of analysis to be persuasive. In this regard, frequent reference will be made to the Ehrlich paper in order to assess its contributions and pitfalls.

The paper is organized in the following manner: First, a brief explanation of how multiple regression analysis might be used to test for a deterrent effect of capital punishment is presented. Then, the barriers to making a persuasive test are discussed. These barriers are divided into three general categories: (1) matching theory and hypotheses to available data; (2) making statistical inferences from a particular body of data; and (3) drawing appropriate conclusions, including policy implications, from the statistical inferences.

THE HOPE FOR MULTIPLE REGRESSION ANALYSIS

Professor Black's Bleak and Correct Assertion

In a recent and excellent book by Charles Black, professor of law at the Yale Law School, it was asserted about capital punishment:

> After all possible inquiry, including the probing of all possible methods of inquiry, we do not know, and for systematic and clearly visible reasons *cannot know*, what

the truth about this "deterrent" effect may be. . . . The general problem . . . is that no adequately controlled experiment or observation is possible. . . . We have to use uncontrolled data from society itself. . . . When we do that, there are two basic modes of procedure. One can compare, say, homicide statistics in states, that, respectively, have or do not have capital punishment, over the same period of time. Or one can compare homicide rates in the same state, before and after the abolition or reinstitution of capital punishment.

The *inescapable flaw* is, of course, that social conditions in any state are not constant through time, and that social conditions are not the same in any two states. If an effect were observed . . . then one could not at all tell whether any of this effect is attributed to the presence or absence of capital punishment . . . *no methodological path out of this tangle suggests itself.*[8] [All italics added for emphasis.]

Professor Black's Seeming Omission of Multiple Regression Analysis

Professor Black's assertion seems to ignore the possibility that, through the use of multiple regression analysis (henceforth MRA), the effects of factors other than capital punishment can be statistically controlled. This omission may have been intentional, based on the correct proposition that, using this technique, one can never know with certainty that one has isolated a true causal effect of a particular factor.

But we cannot dismiss so easily the possibilities of learning from this technique or of making policy decision based on it. At least under certain conditions, some results of studies using MRA are accepted by both social scientists and the courts. These occasions are not exceptions to Professor Black's observation: *MRA can never provide absolute proof that one factor causes another, though it may provide reasonable circumstantial evidence of causality when (1) a statistical relationship is persuasively documented, and (2) all plausible theoretical explanations which purport to explain the relationship are consistent with respect to the direction of cause and effect between the two factors.* An example satisfying these conditions is discussed below. However later sections will argue that, in regard to MRA of the deterrent effect of capital punishment, we have not yet fulfilled the first condition, and may never fulfill the second.

Consider the economic proposition that the demand for a commodity will fall as its price rises, other things being equal. Economists think that other factors besides a commodity's own price might affect the demand (e.g., the price of substitute commodities, the general level of income), so they empirically test their proposition using MRA to control statistically for the effects of the other factors. Among economists, no single study is taken as "the" convincing proof of this fundamental proposition. But because thousands of such analyses have been done independently, on hundreds of commodities and in hundreds of different communities—and because these studies uniformly find that demand falls as price rises—economists agree that the basic proposition is correct.

Furthermore, evidence on the effects of particular price changes estimated through MRA is routinely considered by the courts in situations where the claimed effect is argued to be relevant to the legal decision. This occurs commonly in cases involving disputes between regulatory agencies and the firms they are regulating, as well as in anti-trust cases. For example, in the case of *Cargill, Inc. v. Hardin* 406 U.S. 932 (1972), the Department of Agriculture submitted an MRA to show that the price of wheat during a certain period was not "artificially" depressed as the respondents argued, but was determined by the usual demand and supply factors. The court cited this analysis in upholding the decision of the regulatory agency.[9]

The point of this economic example is to demonstrate that, despite the lack of *absolute* proof of an assertion supported by MRA, under certain conditions (1) a near consensus among experts can be reached on an effect of some factor (in this case, the factors determining the wheat price), making the claimed effect more *persuasive* than if there did not exist near consensus; and (2) the courts have been willing to consider the results of MRA as pertinent to their own determination in each case.

There is an additional element in the above example which is important to bring out—the implicit role of the known consensus among economists in the court's decision. Two different arguments were presented to explain the wheat price in the period considered. One was that the price was "artificially" depressed; the other was that it was determined by the "usual" demand and supply factors. The Department of Agriculture had to undertake an MRA to show that the price was *consistent* with the "usual" theory of price. This analysis did not prove the "usual" theory; perhaps the "usual" theory is not the true explanation and the "artificial" depression is correct. However, the strong consensus among experts concerning the "usual" determinants of price created a presumption in favor of accepting the "usual" theory rather than an alternative one as long as the data were consistent with the "usual" theory. *It did not matter if the data were also consistent with an "unusual" theory because the plausibility of the "unusual" theory was not accepted.* The consensus among experts served as an implicit guide for the court's decision. This is not to suggest that a court should always accept the usual theory; it may be possible in some cases to establish greater plausibility for an unusual theory (or perhaps alternatively, reasonable doubt about the applicability of the usual theory).

Having established that in *some* cases it seems reasonable to give weight to arguments based on MRA, we shall consider whether it is reasonable in the specific case regarding the deterrent effect of capital punishment. Then the critical role of combining theory building with the MRA technique, in order to establish a consensus among experts, is explained. This will not only serve the function of aiding those unfamiliar with this methodology, but will also attempt to establish the important proposition that, in some cases, the court should be quite reluctant to give much weight to results based on MRA.

An Extremely Brief Exposition of MRA

We attempt to develop here an intuitive understanding of the way in which MRA controls for the effects of several factors which operate simultaneously in the actual world, in order to derive estimates of their independent effects. It will be shown, through a simple example, that the process of "controlling" does *not* necessarily require *statistical* procedures; it does involve the establishment of a precise numerical relationship among the several factors.[10] Then it will be shown how statistical procedures like MRA can help find these numerical relationships when they are imprecise. Finally, the use of statistical tests as a way of measuring confidence in the established numerical relationship (i.e., does it really closely describe the observed behavior) is discussed. The following section will emphasize that even the confident establishment of a numerical relationship does not imply any *causal* relation; inferences about causality can at best be suggested by a theory which is *consistent* with the relationship. However, there are often different theories of causal relations consistent with an established numerical relationship.

Suppose we lived in a world where an *exact* linear mathematical relationship existed among three factors: the height of an avocado plant, the average temperature in which it grows, and the diameter of the pot in which it is planted. We are asked what the effect will be of transplanting a 17-inch avocado plant, in a temperature of 70° and currently in a pot with a 5-inch diameter, into a 6-inch pot. We also know that the height of another avocado, in a 4-inch pot and at a temperature of 60°, is 14 inches.

We might observe that the plant in the 5-inch pot is 3 inches taller than the plant in the 4-inch pot, and naively conclude that increasing the diameter 1 inch results in 3 inches of plant growth. By this reasoning, we would predict that putting the plant in the 6-inch pot will result in a 20-inch plant.

This type of reasoning is subject to the methodological flaw pointed out by Professor Black: *in making the deduction, we are not controlling for other factors (temperature) which explain why one plant that we observed is 14 inches tall and the other 17 inches.*

However, in this artificial case, we can solve the problem because the numerical relationship is exact. We know that plant height (H) is a precise linear function of the average temperature (T) and the diameter of the pot (D):

$$H = a_1 T + a_2 D$$

where a_1 and a_2 are the unknown parameters, or coefficients, of this relationship.[11] Furthermore, we know that this relationship always holds precisely; it must hold for the two plants about which we have full information:

$$17 = a_1 (70) + a_2 (5)$$
$$14 = a_1 (60) + a_2 (4)$$

But this is simply two equations in two unknowns, and can be solved by regular algebra. The solution is $a_1 = .1$ and $a_2 = 2$, or put differently, the "true" relationship (in this artificial world) is precisely:

$$H = .1 \ (T) + 2 \ (D)$$

By solving for the unknown coefficients, we have established the numerical relationship among the three factors.

The answer to our question, then, is that the plant will grow 2 inches to reach a height of 19 inches. That is, *controlling for temperature,* the effect of increasing the pot diameter by 1 inch is to increase the plant height by 2 inches. An equivalent way of expressing this is: *other things being equal,* the effect of increasing the pot diameter by 1 inch is to increase the plant height by 2 inches.

In the above example, notice that we did not require the use of MRA or, in fact, any statistical techniques at all. This is because we specified an artifical example where the relationship is always precise—so that no matter how many different avocado plants we observed, the specified relationship would always hold exactly. In the actual world, relationships are usually less precise.

To explain MRA, let us suppose the above relationship is basically true, but that any particular plant may deviate from its *expected* height (based on pot diameter and temperature) by a small random fluctuation. We could take two plants as before, *assume* that the random fluctuations are zero, and compute (with some uncertainty, this time) an *estimate* of the true relationship by making the same kind of calculation as above. This time, if we looked at a third plant, it would probably not fit this estimated relationship precisely. Suppose the estimated relationship "predicted" a higher height than the third plant had actually achieved. Then we might want to "adjust downward" the coefficients of the estimated relationship, so that the estimated relationship makes "predictions" off a little bit on all three observed plants, but not too far off from any single observation. As we added observations, we might continually adjust the coefficients so that the bulk of the predicted values were "close" to the actual observed ones. *All MRA does is to identify the coefficients, based on the observations you have, which minimize the sum of the squared amount by which each predicted height misses the actual height.*

Nothing in the MRA procedure can guarantee that the squared amounts (or errors) will be small—that depends on how well the actual observations "fit" the relationship with the best coefficients. If in truth the pot size and the temperature have nothing to do with the height of avocado plants, then one would not expect a very good fit. Fortunately, there are statistical tests which tell us how good a fit there is between the actual observations and the estimated relationship. Perhaps it will suffice here to suggest that when estimated relationships pass the tests, we gain confidence that we have estimated a reasonable approximation to a true numerical relationship. These tests can be used not only on the estimated relation as a whole, but also on each of the coefficients individually. We can statistically test, for example, the coefficient on the temperature factor to see if it is "significantly" different from a coefficient of zero. If the temperature factor is not really related to plant height, there is a high probability it would fail the test.[12] The test is carried out by finding the best estimated relationship when you force (constrain) the temperature coefficient to be zero, and then comparing the sum of the squared errors using the constrained relationship with the sum using the unconstrained one. If there is only a "small" difference between the two sums, then we conclude that not much "explanation" is added by the temperature factor, or that its coefficient is not "significantly" different from zero.

We now turn to the final section dealing with the use of MRA generally.

The Importance of Theory to the Fruitful Use of MRA

This section will attempt to establish the conditions under which a court should be reluctant to give much weight to an MRA, even when the analysis itself is technically sound. There are two key questions the court must consider. First, what is the degree of *statistical consensus* among experts that the estimated numerical relationship does, in fact, approximate reality? This concerns the statistical confidence in the estimated coefficients as an approximation to a true equation relating the factors. If there is sharp general disagreement among experts, the court cannot give much weight to the analysis. If there is a reasonable degree of statistical consensus, the court then must ask the second question: What is the degree of *theoretical consensus concerning the causal relations* among the factors in the established relationship? Without consensus on what the relevant causal variables are, the court must show great reluctance in accepting the conclusions based upon a particular causal interpretation. This is true even where there is high confidence that the established statistical relationship is accurate. The importance of theory in guiding both the selection of variables to be included in the analysis, and the selection of tests to be made on the estimated relationship, is discussed as a way of suggesting a causal interpretation about which consensus might form.

Let us continue with the avocado plant example from the last section. Suppose an MRA was done to estimate the relationship between plant height, pot diameter, and temperature. One of the factors, plant height, is specified as the dependent variable (the factor we are trying to explain or predict) and the others are referred to as the independent variables (the factors which "explain" the dependent variable). The coefficients are reported as statistically significant. A conclusion is drawn from the study that, other things being equal, an increase of one inch in pot diameter causes a two-inch growth in plant height. Should this conclusion be accepted?

The first question to consider is the degree of *statistical consensus* among experts concerning the estimated numerical relationship. Have there been any computational errors, or does an independent replication of the MRA (using the same data and making the same statistical tests) show results identical to the original study? Are the statistical procedures used the appropriate ones, e.g., if a coefficient is reported "significantly" different from zero, was the correct test for this proposition in fact made? Aside from features internal to the particular study, does the estimated relationship appear to be close to what other independent studies have found? If different observations were used in doing the MRA (i.e., different avocado plants comprising the sample data), would the results still be approximately the same? It should be clear that inability to replicate, the use of correct statistical procedures, parameter (coefficient) estimates quite different from other similar studies, and results sensitive to the particular observations used, all decrease confidence that the estimated relationship is close to the actual relationship. Only the third factor—parameter estimates quite different from other similar studies—has the possibility for being taken as an improvement over prior beliefs. That is, it is possible that previous studies have been wrong and that the new study offers a better estimate of the true relationship. However, this judgment would require consensus that the procedures used in the new study are superior to the ones used in other studies. Further support should then come over time as other independent studies using the superior procedures verify the new findings.

Assuming there is a reasonable degree of statistical consensus, one still must question the causal relations implied by the conclusion drawn in the study. For example, suppose plant height causes change in pot diameter (i.e., people buy bigger pots for their plants when they reach a certain size in the current pot). If the observations for the study were randomly selected, then some of the plants would have just been repotted and others just ready for repotting—so that in only a few cases would the maximum height have been attained. Recognition of this additional causal element in the process suggests that our coefficient estimates represent confounded effects: they are a mixture of the plant-growth effects and of consumer pot-purchasing behavior. If this is the "true" theory or causal structure that explains our observations, then the coefficients as estimated cannot be given a clear interpretation without additional information. It is sometimes possible, with additional information, to untangle these separate but simultaneous influences. Whether or not this is possible is referred to as the *identification problem*. Because this is a complex problem, a detailed explanation will not be offered here.[13]

The point so far is simple: In order to give an interpretation of the estimated numerical relationship, one has to specify a particular causal structure. If there is not a consensus on the causal relations, then there will generally not be a consensus on the meaning of the estimated coefficients. The above example, only about avocado heights, may fail to convey the possible significance of alternative causal structures relating the same factors. Suppose, however, we are trying to explain the murder rate over time. Assume there is statistical consensus (in fact, there is not) that the execution rate, as a factor in an MRA purporting to explain the murder rate over time, has a negative coefficient and that all relevant factors have been statistically controlled. This would mean that, other things being equal, the murder rate is inversely related to the execution rate (e.g., increases in the murder rate above and beyond those explained by other factors in the analysis are associated with decreases in executions). One might suggest the causal interpretation that capital punishment deters murder. However, that causal interpretation could be completely wrong. An alternative causal interpretation, consistent with the same empirical analysis, could be that the lower murder rate last year caused the decline in executions this year. The MRA, by itself, does not address this critically important issue of causality.

The examples above only deal with causal suggestions limited to the factors included in the MRA. However, *the problems become even more serious if the true causal structure includes a factor omitted from the MRA.* In this case, the coefficients on the included variables may be *biased* (bias will exist if the omitted variable is correlated with any of the included variables).

To go back to the avocado example, the independent variables included in the MRA were pot diameter and average temperature. However, most experts would agree that (at least) soil quality, sunlight, and amount of water are also important factors which explain plant height. By omitting them, the estimated relationship becomes invalid. At the risk of oversimplifying, suppose just one factor from the true relationship was omitted. Let that factor be S, the hours of direct sunlight the plant gets per day. Assume the true relationship happens to be:

$$H = .05(T) + .5(D) + 1(S)$$

Observe the differences between the above relationship and the one estimated earlier:

$$H = .1(T) + 2(D)$$

If the researcher had known to ask, he would have found out how much direct sunlight each of his observation plants received, and included this data in the MRA (e.g., that the 17-inch plant got an average of 10 hours of direct sunlight, and the 14-inch plant only 9 hours, etc.). But because he omitted this factor, he *overestimated* the true coefficient of temperature by 100% of its true value, and *overestimated* the coefficient on size of pot by 400% of its true value. (Omitted variables can lead to underestimation as well.) The truth is that, other things being equal, an increase of one inch in the diameter of the pot only leads to .5 inches of new growth (rather than the 2 inches suggested by the incorrect model).

This leads us to an interesting observation: The very methodological flaws which Professor Black cites for the state comparison type of analysis (sometimes referred to as the matching method) appear in MRA as well. That is, the problem with, say, comparing two states where one has capital punishment and the other does not, is that other factors (besides capital punishment) which affect the murder rate *may* be at different levels in the two states. If so, then the actual comparison made has not controlled for these other factors and the conclusions drawn may be incorrect. Similarly, if one omits factors that affect the murder rate in performing an MRA, then the estimated relationship is invalid because it has not controlled the relevant factors, and conclusions should not be drawn from it. In the state matching case, one tries to minimize this effect by matching states that are as similar as possible with respect to other factors thought important. While this does not control perfectly, it has the advantage of perhaps inadvertently controlling for factors which do affect the murder rate but which researchers do not know about. In the case of MRA, one tries to minimize the chance of seriously biasing the estimated coefficients by including directly all the factors which are thought to be relevant. MRA has the advantage of controlling more precisely for the factors suspected to be relevant, but has the disadvantage of possible serious error if an important factor is not explicitly included.[14]

What does this discussion about the importance of causal relationships imply about how much confidence to have in conclusions based on a MRA study? *If there is no theoretical consensus on the underlying causal relationships, then one must be very reluctant to accept a conclusion based on a particular (implicit or explicit) causal interpretation. MRA findings are particularly suspect when there is no general agreement on what explanatory factors to include in the analysis, and a substantial sentiment that some important factor or factors have been omitted.*

The challenge of achieving a theoretical consensus would seem like a very difficult one to overcome, particularly for problems as thorny as explaining the causes of the variations in the rate of murder. This is why *the importance of theory construction in guiding the use of MRA* cannot be overstated. It is really the only hope there is for achieving consensus among experts. When a specific theory of causal relations is hypothesized, efforts can be made to subject the theory to empirical testing. These efforts involve deriving implications of the theory which can be factually examined to test their validity. In this sense, the theory can either be found to be consistent with the data (facts) or inconsistent with the data. If it is inconsistent with the data, new theories must be generated and tested. Even if it is consistent with the data, one must ask if there is any alternative theory that also may be consistent with the data. If so, more work must be done (e.g., finding additional implications of each theory to test) to try to rule out all the competing theories but the correct one. If this sounds tedious and difficult, it is well to remember that such is the lot not only of those hoping to make progress through the use of MRA techniques, but of all science.

The Relevancy for Studies of Capital Punishment

The main points of the previous sections bear directly on the capital punishment issue. The task of those hoping to learn the true effect of capital punishment on the murder rate, through MRA techniques, is an arduous one. One must not only achieve a *statistical* consensus, a problem whose difficulties have barely been touched on so far. One must also achieve a *theoretical* consensus about the causal relations determining the murder rate, or the estimated effects may be subject to a wide variety of interpretations with no basis to choose one from among them.

The development of either consensus is made particularly difficult by the broad range of factors (psychological, social, economic, and political) which researchers in various disciplines suggest are important. For example, experiences during the developmental years of childhood, exposure to violent behavior on television, high unemployment rates, or the availability of guns, all might influence the overall murder rate. In order to achieve a statistical consensus about the relationship between murder rates and executions, one has to persuade the experts that other possible causal factors have been adequately controlled in the MRA. In order to achieve a theoretical consensus about the cause of a relationship between murder rates and executions, one first has to secure agreement on the statistical question of whether, other things being equal, the murder rate is positively or negatively related to executions (if it is related at all). The problems caused by the multiplicity of factors are compounded by the nature of the data available for use in empirical testing by MRA, which makes one skeptical that these issues can be resolved solely through this method.

Fortunately, social science inquiry is hardly limited to MRA methods. In trying to reach a consensus one should consider all the evidence. Thus, it is certainly relevant to the issue at hand that virtually all studies using non-MRA methods have found no deterrent effect of capital punishment as used in the past.[15] *Unless independent MRA studies show a persistent tendency to identify an inverse relationship between executions and murder rates, it would appear the current near consensus among social scientists that there is no discernible relationship would be maintained.* Furthermore, since no one has suggested a plausible theory which would maintain that a significant deterrent effect exists despite persuasive empirical evidence that the factors are not related, then a sufficient degree of theoretical consensus would exist to allow some confidence in the inference that capital punishment as it has been used does not measurably deter murder.

We now turn to a discussion of specific barriers which researchers using MRA in this area must handle.

BARRIERS TO THE SUCCESSFUL USE OF MRA TO TEST FOR A DETERRENT EFFECT OF CAPITAL PUNISHMENT

It will be useful to begin with the results of the study done by Ehrlich. That study claimed to identify a statistically significant deterrent effect of capital punishment. Reporting in the *American Economic Review* (p. 398), Ehrlich states that "the empirical analysis suggests that on the average the trade-off between the execution of an offender and the lives of potential victims it might have saved was of the order of magnitude of 1 for 8 for the period 1933-67 in the United States." This claim is derived from the results of an MRA analysis, using United States aggregate data for this time period, where Ehrlich estimated the following relationship (referred to as the supply of offenses equation) between the murder rate and eight explanatory factors:[16]

$$(Q/N) = K \ P_a^{a_1} \ P_{c/a}^{\alpha_2} \ P_{e/c}^{\alpha_3} \ U^{B_1} \ L^{B_2} \ V_p^{B_3} \ A^{B_4} \ (\exp)^{B_5 T} \ (\exp)^V$$
$$ {-1.512} \ {-0.424} \ {-0.059} \ {0.064} \ {-1.368} \ {1.455} \ {0.485} \ {-0.050}$$

where the numbers below the equation are estimated parameters (the α's and B's) and:

Q/N = the number of murders and nonnegligent manslaughters reported by the police per 1000 civilian population

P_a = the probability of arrest as measured by the national clearance rates (the percentage of all murders cleared by the arrest of a suspect)

$P_{c/a}$ = the conditional probability of conviction (the percent of those charged who were convicted of murder)

$P_{e/c}$ = the conditional probability of execution (the number of executions in year T as a percent of the total number of convictions in year $T-1$)

U = unemployment rate

L = labor force participation (fraction of the civilian population in the labor force)

Y_p = real permanent income per capita in dollars

A = fraction of the residential population in the age group 14-24

T = chronological time in years

V = a disturbance term

The discussion below will raise a number of specific issues that Ehrlich had to face, and that other researchers have to face, in the attempt to do a persuasive study.[17]

From Theory and Hypotheses to Data

This section will identify five barriers which researchers using MRA methods face in the early stages of their research, involving the construction of theories with testable implications and the identification of a reliable data set on which to test their theories. These barriers may be summarized as: (1) proper use of the implications of the hypothesized causal relations; (2) proper linking of the psychological influences on individual behavior (described in the theory) to geographic data; (3) avoiding aggregation bias in the choice of the unit of analysis from alternative geographic levels; (4) avoiding problems which might be expected from the use of any time-series or cross-sectional data; and (5) avoiding problems caused by various types of measurement error in the data. While the Ehrlich study is subject to criticism on all these grounds, it is doubtful that other researchers could avoid most of the problems encountered.

1. We have already seen the importance of specifying a theory of the causal relations between the factors hypothesized to be related to the murder rate. The Ehrlich study is unusually strong in deriving testable implications of the specified causal relations. For example, Ehrlich theorizes that potential murderers are rational in the sense that they weigh the benefits to them of committing murder against the expected costs (the probability of punishment and its severity). While it is too complicated to derive here, a theoretical implication that follows directly from breaking down the expected probability of punishment into its components of arrest, conviction, and sentencing—the three P variables in his equation—is that the coefficient (α_1) on P_a should be greater (in absolute value) than the coefficient (α_2) on $P_{c/a}$, which in turn should be greater than the coefficient (α_3) on $P_{e/c}$. Notice this is a purely theoretical implication which can be checked against the empirical estimates derived through MRA. According to his history, $/\alpha_1/>/\alpha_2/>/\alpha_3/$. If this is not empirically true, then there is probably something wrong with the theory. However, one can see from the estimates that $/\alpha_1/ = 1.512 >/\alpha_2/ = 0.424 > /\alpha_3 = 0.059$, as the theory predicted. Implications like this that can be derived and tested against data provide support for a theory. The more of these tests that the theory can pass, the more persuasive is the argument that the theory is correct.

A very important problem with the Ehrlich analysis is that it does not carry the theoretical implications far enough. For example, it does not include mathematically the implication that the *net* impact of executions on murders depends on another parameter which he does not estimate, and that the net impact may be to increase murder. His verbal theory suggests a causal relation where the probability of conviction is affected inversely by changes in the execution rate.[18] The hypothesized causal links can be shown in Figure 1.

In the diagram, the increase in executions is hypothesized to have two effects: a decrease in murders through the rise in the conditional probability of execution, but an increase in murders through the fall in the probability of conviction (because juries will be less likely to convict when execution is the result). Thus the net effect of increased executions, may be either to increase executions, according to Ehrlich's theory, may be either to increase or decrease murders, depending on how big a change in the probability of conviction results from a change in the execution rate. But *Ehrlich only empirically estimated that part of the causal chain which acts to reduce*

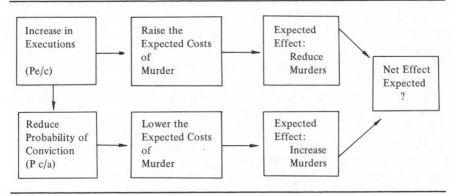

Figure 1: The Effect of Increases in Executions on Murders According to Ehrlich

murders. He omitted estimating the part of the theory which suggested that executions, through their effect on probability of conviction, cause murders.

An important general problem in this category is the *identification* problem referred to earlier. Ehrlich's theory includes not only the "supply of offenses" equation, but a "demand for offenses" equation which together simultaneously determine the observed values of some of the model variables. This is analogous to the avocado example where pot-purchasing is a response to plant growth, and at the same time plant growth arises due to pot-purchasing. In a deterrence theory represented by a simultaneous equation system, the independent deterrent effect of capital punishment on murders can only be untangled from the other effects if the theoretical structure is one which "identifies" its parameter. The Ehrlich study did not offer an explanation to persuade readers that the capital punishment parameter is correctly identified. One detailed critique of Ehrlich has argued that plausible assumptions about the underlying theoretical structure suggest that Ehrlich's estimates reflect the response of the criminal justice system to murder, and not the other way around.[19] Furthermore, this alternative interpretation leads to the same expected signs and relative sizes of the coefficients, though for reasons completely different than those offered by Ehrlich. *Because the truth concerning the identification of the parameter cannot be proven or tested, there is great uncertainty in interpreting the estimate as the claimed deterrent effect.*

2. Most theories of criminal deterrence, including the theory used by Ehrlich, hypothesize that individuals are deterred by their perceptions of both the probability of being punished and the severity of punishment. Presumably then, one would want to test this by seeing if individuals who perceive either a higher probability or a greater severity of punishment, other things being equal, are more deterred. Furthermore, it would seem important to learn the determinants of those perceptions, if one had hopes of altering them.

However, for the case of murder, the theory requires knowledge about these perceptions *at the time* of the decision to commit (or not to commit) murder. The collection of such data is impossible.

Therefore, one might try to fall back, as Ehrlich does, on what he calls the "objective" probability of punishment: for example, the ratio of arrests for murder to the reported number of murders in some geographic unit. There are two conceptual problems with this. First of all, the perceptions of individuals (and murderers, in particular) may not be related to this "objective" probability. In Ehrlich's sample, the average probability of arrest in two-thirds of the years was between .87 and .93. Is it really plausible that individuals would perceive such small variations in the "objective" probability? Second, even if individual perceptions were related to some "objective" measure, what geographic area would it encompass? Surely the national probability of arrest, which Ehrlich uses, is irrelevant to the calculating murderer in Phoenix, Arizona. For both these reasons, it makes interpretation of the negative coefficient (signifying in inverse relation between the murder rate and the probability of arrest) estimated for the probability of arrest unclear. While it is "consistent" with the theory, it is also consistent with the trivial mathematical fact of life that a number like Q/N (the murder rate) will have a strong tendency to be inversely related to another number A/Q (the ratio of arrests to murder or P_a) since Q appears in the numerator of one and the denominator of the other. That is, it is of little surprise that as one goes up, the other goes down.

Finally, if the probability measure used is not an acceptable proxy for variations in individuals' perceptions, then a variable of theoretical importance has been omitted from the MRA and the included coefficients may be biased.

Unfortunately, it is not obvious how to solve this problem. *It would seem to make testing on the smallest geographic units possible a desirable factor. On that score, the Ehrlich study could be improved upon.*

3. There is a potential problem of *aggregation bias* when a theory about individual behavior is tested using data on groups of individuals. The direction and extent of the bias on each coefficient caused by the aggregation problem can be different and is a function of essentially arbitrary factors.

The problem can be illustrated with a very simple example. Suppose that there are only two states in the country, and that in each state the true cause (and only cause) of changes in the number of murders is capital punishment. In state A, each execution in a given year causes an increase of 4 murders in that year above a constant base level of 80. In state B, each execution causes an increase of 40 murders above a base level of 0. In a two-year period, we might observe the data in Table 1.

Table 1: STATE DATA

		Murders (M)	Executions (E)
State A			
	Year 1	100	5
	Year 2	84	1
State B			
	Year 1	40	1
	Year 2	80	2

Suppose a researcher wants to know if capital punishment deters crime, and looks at data for the country as a whole in Table 2.

Table 2: COUNTRY DATA

	Murders (M)	Executions (E)
Year 1	140	6
Year 2	164	3

He assumes that the true relationship has a linear form:

$$M = A_0 + A_1 E$$

where A_0 and A_1 are the unknown parameters (coefficients) to be estimated. A_1 will be the estimated deterrence effect (which we know to be positive—an inducement effect—in both states). Fitting the data to the hypothesized relation:

$$\text{Year 1:} \quad 140 = A_0 + A_1 (6)$$
$$\text{Year 2:} \quad 164 = A_0 + A_1 (3)$$
$$\text{or} \quad -24 = A_1 (3) \text{ by subtraction}$$
$$\text{or} \quad A_1 = -8$$
$$A_0 = 180$$

The researcher has estimated that on average in the country each execution deters 8 murders! But the truth is that in state A each execution *adds* 4 murders, and in state B each execution *adds* 400 murders. Clearly there is something wrong with this researcher's analysis.

It can be shown that the estimated coefficient A_1 is a weighted function of the true state coefficients where the weights are arbitrary and can be of any magnitude, even negative—the weight for any state is the ratio of the change in the number of state executions over the change in the number of executions nationwide. But these are changes that bear no relation to the average "deterrent" effect, so it is not surprising that they cause perverse results.

Aggregation bias will exist if some sub-group of the aggregated group has a true coefficient different from the rest of the group. If all individuals were homogeneous, there would be no aggregation bias. In the case of the Ehrlich study, there would be aggregation bias if people in one region behave, on average, differently from those in other regions. However, the magnitude and direction of this possible bias on estimated coefficients cannot be determined. The way to minimize possible aggregation bias is to perform the MRA on the smallest geographic units possible.[20]

4. It is not always clear whether time-series data or cross-sectional data is appropriate for the testing of theories. One important criterion is whether the behavioral response in the unit of analysis can be expected to be constant for the sample. That is, if one had yearly observations of the same state, it is important that the average response of the people in the state to a particular factor be constant over the period of analysis. If teenagers in the state are violence-prone in 1935, they should be equally violence-prone in 1965 (all other things being equal). Similarly in a cross-section analysis, if teenagers are violence-prone in New York, then they should be equally violence-prone in Nebraska (all other things being equal). If this assumption, known as *structural homogeneity*, is violated, then the estimates will be biased (unless corrective statistical procedures are introduced).

To illustrate this, we can extend our earlier two state example (which "explained" murder rates) to three states and include a new factor, the number of guns per capita, in our model. Remember this is purely hypothetical and for illustrative purposes. The truth in this hypothetical world is that people in each state respond differently to executions, but the same to the availability of guns per capita. What we can show is that the estimate (made under the assumption of structural homogeneity) of the effect of guns is not only incorrect but can have the wrong sign.

Specifically, assume the true relationship between murders (M), executions (E), and guns per capita (G) is as follows for each state:

	True Relation	M	E	G
State A:	$M = 80 + 4E + G$	102	5	2
State B:	$M = \quad 40E + G$	42	1	2
State C:	$M = 40 + 20E + G$	60	1	0

If one made the assumption of structural homogeneity, or that in each state

$$M = a_0 + a_1 E + a_2 G$$

and used the data to estimate this (misspecified) relation:

$$102 = a_0 + 5a_1 + 2a_2$$
$$42 = a_0 + a_1 + 2a_2$$
$$60 = a_0 + a_1$$

Then a little algebra will show:

$$a_0 = 45$$
$$a_1 = 15$$
$$a_2 = -9$$

That is, the (incorrectly) estimated effect of gun availability is that each gun per capita reduces murders by 9, while we know the "truth" is that each gun per capita causes 1 murder.

The point of this is to suggest that *violations of the structural homogeneity assumption can lead to serious biases in the estimates of every parameter.* Fortunately, there are statistical tests which one may make to see whether the assumption is violated.

Ehrlich did not perform any tests for structural homogeneity. However, Passell and Taylor[21] did perform such a test on Ehrlich's data and found that the structure was not constant. *Ehrlich's time series was from 1933 to 1969, but the test results indicated that the structure shifted significantly starting in the early 1960s.*

Even more startling are the independent replications reported by Passell and Taylor and Bowers and Pierce.[22] *Both find that for the temporally stable period the estimated coefficient on the execution rate is insignificant and/or positive (i.e., there is no evidence of a deterrent effect of capital punishment).* Put differently, Ehrlich's results may be just an artifact of the structural change that occurred in the 1960s (in much the same way that our hypothetical estimate of -9 for the effect of guns per capita was an artifact of the structural differences in the three states).

While these findings make us skeptical about the specific estimates of Ehrlich, they do not resolve the question about the kind of data set which would be most appropriate for testing. The discussion of previous barriers indicated that smaller geographic units of analysis would be desirable, which suggests cross-sectional data by state.[23] Passell has recently completed such an analysis—relying on the same theory and essentially the same factors as Ehrlich—*and finds no evidence of a deterrent effect of capital punishment.*[24] Passell's analysis was done across 41 states for the year 1950 and 44 states for the year 1960. Of course, the Passell study does not resolve the issue of whether or not capital punishment as practiced deters murder; it does, however, suggest that MRA studies will not show a persistent tendency to find a deterrent effect.

5. The last set of barriers to be discussed in this section concerns measurement error: When the actual data are suspected to be contaminated and composed of two elements, the true value of the variable and some measurement error.

When the measurement errors are random, it can be shown that they cause a downward bias in the absolute value of the estimated coefficients: Whether or not the true coefficient is positive or negative, the estimated coefficient will be closer to zero than the true coefficient. Fortunately, this type of problem results in conservative estimates of the coefficients.

However, if the errors are not random, they may introduce a bias of either direction into the estimates. Sometimes even random errors may introduce a systematic bias. For example, the early data (before 1947) on criminal statistics were subject to measurement errors due to lack of complete geographical coverage. Consider the effect of any measurement error in the murder rate. If overestimated, it makes the clearance rate look lower than the true clearance rate (because the number of murders is in its denominator)—so by measurement error, an inaccurately high murder rate is being associated with an inaccurately low clearance rate. If the measurement error is to underestimate the murder rate, then the clearance rate gets overestimated. This time, an inaccurately low number of murders is associated with an inaccurately high clearance rate. Therefore, *either type of measurement error in the murder rate creates artifactual support for a deterrence theory!*

Again, one way to improve the MRA is to avoid choosing a data set where relatively large errors in the murder rate might be expected. For example, Bowers and Pierce suggest that the Census Bureau's causes-of-death statistics might provide a more reliable measure of homicides than the FBI data used in the Ehrlich study.[25]

From Data to Statistical Inference Using MRA

This section will discuss a number of barriers which have been or might be encountered in attempting to use a theory and a body of data in order to derive valid statistical inferences based on MRA. The validity of the inferences will be shown to depend on (1) replicability, (2) proper choice of functional form, (3) procedures used for handling missing data, (4) the appropriateness of approximate statistical tests, and (5) the inclusion of all relevant variables. This is by no means a complete list, but simply consists of potential barriers which seem particularly relevant to the problem at hand.

1. If the statistical results of a study cannot be replicated through independent analyses, then its claimed inferences become suspect. An exact replication, i.e., using the same data and making the same statistical tests, is the best way to ensure against computational errors. Two independent attempts to replicate the Ehrlich study failed. This probably occurred not because of computational error (through some of these were found), but because a precise specification of the data Ehrlich used was not available at the time. Such a specification is now available, and presumably would allow exact replication.

Through these attempts to duplicate Ehrlich's work exactly, something else important was learned: Ehrlich's results seemed to be extremely sensitive to very minor variations in the data. That is, the attempts at exact replication produced estimates substantially different than those Ehrlich reported. If an estimated relationship is very sensitive to only minor changes in the data, then one cannot have much confidence in the validity of those estimates. This "sensitivity analysis" is a second type of replicability study which is useful to perform.

A third type of replicability study moves away from the original data set, in order to see if the basic results hold in other samples thought at least as appropriate. With regard to the Ehrlich study, this type of replication has been done by Passell.[26] While Ehrlich's original test was based on time series data for the United States as a whole, Passell's study was cross-sectional using each state as an observation. The Passell study, however, found results opposite to that of Ehrlich; Passell found no effect of capital punishment on the murder rate.

2. In all the examples used so far in this paper, the estimated relationships were always (for simplicity) assumed to be *linear*. For example:

$$H = a_1T + a_2D \text{ (linear)}$$

However, the true functional relationship might be of a more complicated form, like:

$$H = a_0T^{a_1}D^{a_1} \text{ (log-linear)}$$
$$\text{or } H = a_1T + a_2T^2 + a_3D \text{ (curvilinear)}$$

Before an MRA can be performed, some functional form must be explicitly chosen. Once it is specified, MRA will identify the best coefficients for that functional form, given the data. However, how does one know which functional form to specify?

Essentially, there are two rationales for selecting a functional form. One is if the theory underlying the research implies a particular functional form, or rules out particular forms. For example, if one wants to estimate the relationship between the two inputs and one output of a certain production process, and it is known that both inputs must be used jointly to produce some output (e.g., seeds and farm labor), then one would rule out the simple linear form because that would imply some positive output could be obtained with only one factor.

However, there is no agreed-upon theory which implies the correct functional form for the case of explaining murder rates. Therefore, one must fall back on the second and more common rationale: Choose the functional form which fits the data best.

In the Ehrlich study, an inappropriate functional form may have been specified. In the version of the study submitted to the court,[27] Ehrlich reports that there is no substantial difference in the estimated relationships when the natural values of the variables are used (i.e., the linear form) as compared with the estimates using the logarithmic form (the latter results are the only ones presented). However, both Bowers and Pierce and Passell and Taylor independently report that their replications indicate that the coefficient on the execution rate using the linear form is either positive or insignificant or both, i.e., that the estimated linear relationship shows no evidence that capital punishment deters murder. Furthermore, both types of functional forms fit the data equally well. If there is no persuasive reason why one form is more appropriate than the other, then both sets of results should have been reported in the original study. While this would have weakened the claim that the results indicate a deterrent effect of capital punishment, it would have reflected the research effort more accurately.[28]

3. Missing data is an errors-in-variables problem which might cause a bias in the estimated coefficients if the missing values are not random. Ehrlich uses appropriate procedures to estimate the missing data. However, there is a second problem associated with approximating values for missing observations: correcting the usual tests for the significance of the estimated coefficients. It should be intuitively clear that if the usual tests give an accurate expression of statistical confidence when the data are composed of actual observations, the insertion of artificial data ought to lessen confidence in the estimated relationship. While this may not be serious if only one or two observations are missing in a large data set, it becomes more problematic when as many as 10 observations in a series of 35 are missing, as is the case in the Ehrlich study. Appropriate adjustments, not made by Ehrlich, are suggested in Dagenois.[29] These adjustments would tend to reduce the significance levels of the estimated coefficients.

4. In performing the MRA, Ehrlich used a statistical procedure designed to take account of a problem known as serial correlation (which would otherwise probably lead to serious underestimates of the sampling variances, and thus overstate significance levels). However, the procedure he used was designed by Fair[30] for large samples, and the Ehrlich analysis was based on only 35 observations. It is not clear how this affects the estimated significance levels. However, because the true degree of serial correlation is unknown, one must use an approximation to the approximation, which Fair reports will result in overstating the true significance levels.[31]

5. The problems caused by omitting factors from an MRA have been discussed previously: It can impart serious bias, in various directions, to the estimated coefficients of the included variables. The direction of the bias on a particular included variable depends on its correlation with the excluded factors and the true coefficients of the excluded factors.[32]

In the Ehrlich study, several variables thought to influence the murder rate were omitted: the average length of sentence for murder, the number of handguns in the population, the general crime rate, and the degree of income inequality. It is ironic that Ehrlich included the first and last two factors in an earlier study reporting on the general deterrent effect of law enforcement activity.[33] The second factor, handguns, was found to be a significant factor in an MRA study by Phillips, Votey, and Howell, and is generally thought to be a factor in determining murder rates.[34]

Let us consider the expected effects of each of these omitted variables. First, the average length of sentence is suspected to be declining over the time period of the Ehrlich study, so it would be *positively correlated* with the trend in the execution rate (also declining). The *expected coefficient* on length of sentence, according to the theory, should be *negative*: the longer the average sentence, other things being equal, the fewer murders. Since *the direction of the expected bias is given by the sign of the product of these two elements, which is negative, the omission of this factor tends to make the coefficient on executions actually estimated to be lower (more negative) than the true coefficient.* In other words, the omission of this factor acts to create the appearance of a deterrent effect of executions. The true effect of the omitted variable, length of sentence, is incorrectly attributed to the included variable, probability of execution, making the latter seem more important than it really is.

The other three omitted variables are expected to have *positive* coefficients: the more of them, the greater number of murders. Handguns and the general crime rate both would be *negatively* correlated with the execution rate, since they have been rising while the latter has been declining. Both of these factors, then, also impart a negative bias on the coefficient on executions. The degree of income inequality has remained fairly constant over this period, and is probably uncorrelated with the execution rate, thus not imparting any strong bias in either direction.

In short, the net effect of the omitted factors known or expected to influence the murder rate is to bias the coefficient on the execution rate toward creating the appearance of a deterrent effect.

From Statistical Inference to Policy

This section will consider briefly whether judicial inferences could be made based on the results of an MRA like the one Ehrlich attempted but which was thought statistically valid. Three questions will be treated: (1) did Ehrlich infer the correct marginal trade-offs based on his supply of offenses equation; (2) does the partial elasticity from the supply of offenses equation have any policy implications in light of the acknowleged simultaneity implied by the theory guiding the research; and (3) does this analysis offer an inference about the effect on murders of abolishing capital punishment? The obvious question of whether other alternatives (e.g., lengthier sentences) provide more effective deterrents will not be addressed here.

1. In the Ehrlich model, the coefficient estimated for the effect of the probability of execution on the murder rate (α_3), is interpreted as a partial elasticity—the percentage effect of a one percent increase in the execution rate on the murder rate, other things being equal. Ehrlich estimates this elasticity at about $-.06$. However, when Ehrlich attempts to derive the marginal trade-off

in terms of the number of murders deterred per execution, he (perhaps inadvertently) makes an assumption which may be incorrect.

The problem is how to hold the probability of arrest constant in this model. In this case, the model must maintain an identity, a relationship which holds true by definition at all times, which affects the "other things being equal" calculation. This identity is simply that the (true) probability of arrest equals the (true) number of arrests for murder over the (true) number of murders. This follows from the link implied by Ehrlich in treating the probabilities potential murderers perceive as equal to the objective probabilities constructed from the aggregate data he used. This in turn implies that the number of murders appears both on the left hand side of the supply of offenses equation (as the numerator of the murder rate, the dependent variable) and on the right side (in the denominator of the probability of arrest). Thus the effect of a change in the number of executions causes Q (murders) to change "twice": directly through the change in executions E, and indirectly through the resulting change in probability of arrest—all the time holding other factors constant. Unless some additional change is allowed to force the probability of arrest to be constant, this can be shown to imply that $\Delta Q/\Delta E$, the marginal trade-off is not equal to

$$\alpha_e \ (Q/E) \ \text{as Ehrlich assumes}$$

but equals

$$(\alpha_3/1 + \alpha_a) \ (Q/E)$$

Because Ehrlich has estimated that α_1 is about -1.5, this would imply that the marginal trade-off *has the opposite sign* from that reported by Ehrlich. Thus each execution, if the parameter estimates were correct and arrests were held constant, would not on average reduce the number of murders by 8, but would increase the number of murders by 14! However, we know for reasons stated previously the parameter estimates are of questionable reliability; additionally, the reasonable person would not expect arrests to remain constant.

The important point of this example is to draw out the hidden implication in treating the *probability* of arrest as constant, which my calculation does not do. Holding the probability of arrest constant when its denominator changes implies a particular change in the numerator, and there is absolutely nothing in the theory which would generate that particular change. For Ehrlich's calculation of the marginal trade-off to be correct, the necessary theoretical specification is to have the elasticity of arrests with respect to murders constantly equal to one—a very arbitrary assumption. There is no inherent reason why this elasticity value must be determined by assumption; future research may allow its empirical estimation.

2. Even if the marginal trade-offs could be estimated precisely and correctly, they in no way represent the net impact of a change in executions on the number of murders. This is because of the simultaneity issue raised before:

e.g., that changes in execution rates would *cause* (inverse) changes in the probability of conviction, which in turn would cause changes in the murder rate (in the same direction as the change in executions). There are other causal links that one would have to trace before an estimate of the net impact is derived. One would have to take account of the entire simultaneous structure, including the "demand for offenses" equation which is not estimated.

What is important here is that if policy in regard to capital punishment is concerned with any impact, it is the *net* impact and certainly not the partial ("other things being equal") impact.

3. The actual policy question at hand concerns the abolishment of capital punishment. It occurs at a time when actual executions have not occurred for a number of years. The relevance of any deterrent effect to this decision would then seem to be whether the threat of a highly unlikely possibility of being executed deters. The Ehrlich model, due to its functional form, is not suited to estimate any loss in deterrent effect from the current policy posture to the proposed abolition (where Ehrlich's equations are not defined).

Two MRA studies which are more relevant to this point are Passell and Robbins and Strasser.[35] Both the studies use cross-sectional analysis with the states as the units of observation, and relied on theory similar to that of Ehrlich. Robbins and Strasser estimate their model for the year 1969, when there were no executions but some states had the threat of capital punishment while others did not. The Robbins and Strasser analysis found no evidence that the threat of execution deterred murders. The Passell analysis, making estimates for the years 1950 and 1960, also found that, other things being equal, states without capital punishment had no higher incidence of murder than other states.

CONCLUSION

There is no need to belabor the points of this analysis. The use of multiple regression analysis to test for the deterrent effect of capital punishment can help the cause of learning. It is doubtful that results from these analyses will, by themselves, create a consensus about the effects of capital punishment. They are subject to the same type of methodological flaw found in the more traditional matching method—not controlling properly for the relevant factors.

However, there is a consensus among virtually all of the studies of all methodologies that there is no evidence of any measurable deterrent effect. The only major exception to this consensus is the Ehrlich study, which has been demonstrated to depend on a myriad of assumptions, many of them convenient to the generation of an estimate that appears to indicate a deterrent effect. It remains true that among all the social science inquiries made to investigate this matter, no one has yet turned up persuasive evidence that a deterrent effect of capital punishment as practiced exists.

Policy decisions with regard to the abolishment of capital punishment can best be made, then, by focusing on other criteria besides deterrence. In particular, the Supreme Court should concentrate on whether the existing laws make the imposition of capital punishment significantly less arbitrary than the laws it found unconstitutional in *Furman*.

AUTHOR'S NOTES: This paper contains minor changes in the text from the version circulated in January 1976. Since the writing of the paper, much new evidence has been published on the issue of whether capital punishment deters murder. I have not attempted to review the new evidence here. Since the primary purpose of this paper is to make the deterrence literature accessible to a broader audience, I hope that interested readers will pursue the newer literature on their own. The citations in this paper have been updated from the earlier version to show the published location of references.

I would like to thank Eugene Bardach, Diana Dutton, Richard Gould, Robert Hartment, Adele Hayutin, David Kirp, and Frank Levy for their helpful comments and criticisms. The presentation of this work at a faculty seminar of the Graduate School of Public Policy also provided valuable feedback. The author takes full responsibility for any remaining errors.

NOTES

1. See, for example, R. Martinson, "What Works? Questions and Answers about Prison Reform," The Public Interest 35, 23 (1974); and G. Tullock, "Does Punishment Deter Crime?" The Public Interest 36, 103 (1974).

2. For an excellent review and discussion, see F. Zimring and G. Hawkins, Deterrence: The Legal Threat in Crime Control (1973).

3. See, for example, I. Ehrlich, "Participation in Illegitimate Activities: A Theoretical and Empirical Investigation," 81 Journal of Political Economy 521 (1973); R.A. Carr-Hill and N.H. Stern, "An Econometric Model of the Supply and Control of Recorded Offenses in England and Wales," 2 Journal of Public Economics 289 (1973); and H. Votey and L. Phillips, Economic Crimes: Their Generation, Deterrence and Control (U.S. Clearinghouse for Federal Scientific and Technical Information, 1969). For a discussion of this research, see L. Friedman, The Economics of Crime and Justice (University Program Module, General Learning Press, 1976).

4. I. Ehrlich, "The Deterrent Effect of Capital Punishment: A Question of Life and Death," 65 American Economic Review 397 (1975) [hereinafter cited Ehrlich (AER)].

5. The preliminary version is I. Ehrlich, "The Deterrent Effect of Capital Punishment: A Question of Life and Death" (National Bureau of Economic Research Working Paper No. 18, November 1973) [hereinafter cited Ehrlich (NBER)]. The study was filed on March 7, 1975, as part of an Amicus Curiae brief submitted by the Solicitor General of the United States. According to an article in *Business Week* (September 15, 1973, p. 97), this unpublished version was submitted without Professor Ehrlich's permission after he refused "to submit a working draft for their presentation which in effect argued for the death penalty before the Supreme Court in Fowler v. North Carolina."

6. For a review of this decision focusing on the role of social science, see W. White, "The Role of the Social Sciences in Determining the Constitutionality of Capital Punishment," 13 Duquesne Law Review 279 (1974) [hereinafter cited White].

7. For example, T. Sellin, The Death Penalty, A Report for the Modern Penal Code Project of the American Law Institute (1959).

8. C. Black, Capital Punishment: The Inevitability of Caprice and Mistake 25-26 (1974).

9. For further discussion of the use of MRA in regulatory hearings and the courts, see M. Finkelstein, "Regression Models in Administrative Proceedings," 86 Harvard Law Review 1442 (1973).

10. We are only considering the nonexperimental setting. In an experimental setting, control of several factors can be achieved through the use of a control group.

11. I plead guilty to omitting a constant term from this example, in order to keep it as simple as possible. The force of this omission is to constrain the avocado plant to be of zero height when there is no pot for it and the temperature is 32° below freezing, an assumption for which I hope even the most ardent avocado supporters will not take offense.

12. The exact probability of failing the test, given there is no relation between temperature and plant height, is determined by the level of the test chosen by the researcher. In an exploratory analysis, one might perform a less stringent test than in an analysis which attempts to confirm exploratory results.

13. Many other examples of this type could be given where it may be impossible to interpret the estimated coefficients in a meaningful way. For example, in economics, researchers must specify a theoretical structure that identifies the demand relationship and the supply relationship—both relating price and quantity—since only the interaction of the two relationships is actually observed. However, it may be that the most plausible theoretical structure suggests that the influences explaining the observations simply cannot be identified, and therefore the coefficients of the structure cannot be estimated. See, generally, Studies in Econometric Method (W. Hood and T. Koopmans, eds., 1953).

14. For a more extensive discussion comparing MRA to matching methods in the attempt to discover the effects of capital punishment, see D. Baldus and J. Cole, "A Comparative Analysis of the Empirical Work of T. Sellin and I. Ehrlich as a Basis for Inferring a Causal Relationship Between Capital Punishment and the Murder Rate in the United States, 85 Yale Law Journal 170 (1975) [hereinafter cited Baldus and Cole].

15. For a review of these studies, see W. Bailey, "Murder and Capital Punishment: Some Further Evidence," 45 American Journal of Orthopsychiatry 669 (1975).

16. The parameter estimates are those reported in Table 3, equation 6 of Ehrlich (AER). The estimates are also presented in Table 4, equation 6 of Ehrlich (NBER). While Ehrlich presented a number of slightly different estimates for the effects of these factors on the murder rate, we discuss one representative equation for expositional ease.

17. It is substantially harder to secure agreement among experts about the magnitude of a particular parameter than it is to secure agreement about a predicted level of a variable. The Ehrlich study attempts the harder task.

18. Ehrlich (AER), 405.

19. Steven A. Hoenack, Robert T. Kurdle, and David L. Sjoquist, "Some Difficulties in the Estimation of the Deterrent Effect of Capital Punishment," Policy Analysis, forthcoming 1978.

20. There can be an aggregation bias even when there are no regional effects. Under a convergence rationale, it is sometimes argued that differences in individual behavior do not cause aggregation bias if the groups are composed of random samples. That is, if individuals in the population are normally distributed, and if the grouped observations are composed of random samples from the general population, then as the sample size is increased, the size of the aggregation bias tends toward zero. However, one further assumption is needed to make this argument correct: that, within any group, the size of the factors affecting each individual must not be correlated with the individual's propensity to react to those factors. For example, suppose we are considering the effect of the level of permanent income on the murder rate (according to Ehrlich's estimates, $1 decrease in permanent income per capita deters 12 or 13 murders). Assume that there is no reason to believe people in one region behave, on average, differently from people in another region in their responses to changes in permanent income. Then "convergence theorists" might argue it is acceptable to use aggregate (national) data. However, if *richer* people respond differently than poorer people, there will still be aggregation bias. For more extensive discussion of this problem, see H. Theil, Principles of Econometrics, 560-562, 570-572 (1971).

21. P. Passell and J. Taylor, "The Deterrent Effect of Capital Punishment: Another View," 67 American Economic Review 445 (1977) [herinafter cited Passell and Taylor]. This paper has been filed as Appendix E of the reply brief for petitioner in the *Fowler* case.

22. W. Bowers and G. Pierce, "Deterrence, Brutalization, or Nonsense: A Critique of Isaac Ehrlich's Research on Capital Punishment, 85 Yale Law Journal 187 (1976) [hereinafter cited Bowers and Pierce].

23. Peck has also suggested testing on state units. See J. Peck, "The Deterrent Effect of Capital Punishment: A Comment, 85 Yale Law Journal 359 (1976) [hereinafter cited Peck].

24. P. Passell, "The Deterrent Effect of the Death Penalty: A Statistical Test," 28 Stanford Law Review 61 (1976) [hereinafter cited Passell].

25. See note 22.

26. See note 24.

27. Ehrlich (NBER), 36-37.

28. There are reasons to suggest that neither the linear nor the logarithmic forms are appropriate for testing this model. The logarithmic form may exaggerate the importance of the very low number of annual executions occurring in the United States in the 1960s (Bowers and Pierce), and, in several years, the number of executions was zero, where the logarithms are mathematically undefined (Passell and Taylor). Peck suggests that the linear form, in this case, violates a necessary statistical assumption for regression in that the endogenous variables are bounded below by zero. In the Passell study mentioned earlier, functional forms that were neither linear nor logarithmic were tested, and produced no evidence of any deterrent effect of execution.

29. M. Dagenois, "The Use of Incomplete Observations in Multiple Regression Analysis," 1 Journal of Econometrics 317 (1973).

30. R. Fair, "The Estimation of Simultaneous Equation Models with Lagged Endogenous Variables and First Order Serially Correlated Errors," 38 Econometrica 507 (1970).

31. This point was made in Baldus and Cole.

32. See J. Johnston, Econometric Methods 169 (1972).

33. See note 3.

34. L. Phillips, H. Votey, Jr., and J. Howell, "Handguns and Homicide: Minimizing Losses and the Costs of Control," 5 Journal of Legal Studies 463 (1976). Also see G. Newton and F. Zimring, "Firearms and Violence in American Life," A Staff Report to the National Commission on the Causes and Prevention of Violence (1969).

35. L. Robbins and A. Strasser, "An Economic Analysis of Crime with Application to Capital Punishment," unpublished, Charles H. Dickerman Prize Senior Essay, Yale University (1974).

3

WOMEN AND CRIME
An Economic Analysis

ANN P. BARTEL

In the period 1960-1974, the number of offenses reported to the police grew by 200% while the per capita crime rate grew by 157%.[1] While these figures in and of themselves are of great importance, another interesting phenomenon took place during the same period. Table 1 documents the fact that between 1960 and 1974, female participation in criminal activities rose at three times the rate which male criminal activities increased.[2] In 1960, females accounted for 11% of the total number of people arrested, while in 1974, 20% of those arrested were females. Females could account for even more than 20% of the current criminal population if the probability of being arrested is less for female criminals than for male criminals. As Table 1 indicates, most of the females arrested in each of the two time periods were charged with larceny, which in most cases means shoplifting; however, the number of females arrested for this crime grew by 400% between 1960 and 1974.[3] Perhaps what is even

*Columbia University Graduate School of Business. I would like to thank an anonymous referee of this journal as well as participants in the University of Chicago Workshop in Law and Economics for helpful comments on a previous draft of this paper.

1. Federal Bureau of Investigation, *Crime in the United States*, 1974 Uniform Crime Reports, Table 2.

2. The figures in Table 1 may overestimate the true rise in female criminal activities, if, in the period 1960-1974, police officers became more willing to arrest female suspects. This change in police attitudes, however, would serve as proof of increased female participation in criminal activities, since police officers were obviously responding to the fact that women were likely suspects.

3. The larceny arrest statistics in Table 1 pertain to *all* larceny arrests regardless of the size of the loss experienced in the larcenies. Prior to 1973, only those larcenies "$50 and over" were included in the Crime Index even though the FBI collected data on all larcenies. In 1973, all larcenies became a part of the Crime Index and published data for earlier time periods were revised to give an accurate time series picture. Thus, it can not be argued that the observed increase in female arrests for larceny is merely due to inflation.

From Ann P. Bartel, "Women and Crime: An Economic Analysis," XVII (1) *Economic Inquiry* 29-51 (January 1979). Copyright 1979 by the Western Economic Association.

TABLE 1

Arrest Trends by Sex, 1960-74[a]

	MALE			FEMALE		
	1960	1974	Percent Change	1960	1974	Percent Change
TOTAL	305,732	648,933	112.3	36,855	158,879	331.1
Property Crime	268,495	562,890	109.6	30,539	144,218	372.2
Burglary	85,188	175,689	106.2	2,952	10,212	245.9
Larceny	118,916	262,949	121.1	24,769	124,838	404.0
Robbery	23,933	65,214	172.5	1,247	5,059	305.7
Auto Theft	40,458	59,038	45.9	1,571	4,109	161.6
Personal Crime	37,228	86,048	131.1	6,316	14,661	132.1
Murder and Nonneg. Mansl.	2,910	6,917	137.7	577	1,247	116.1
Assault	34,318	79,126	130.6	5,739	13,414	133.7

Source: *Crime in the United States*, 1974 Uniform Crime Reports, Table 32.

[a] These figures were compiled from agencies representing about one-third of the 1974 population. Although agencies representing about 80% of the population reported arrest data for 1974, only 40% of these agencies reported the data in 1960.

more striking about the data in Table 1 is that, for *every* category of property crime, the number of females arrested grew at a much faster rate than the number of males arrested. In the case of crimes against the person, however, we observe no difference between the percentage change in female arrests and the percentage change in male arrests. This distinction between the trends in female property and female personal crime is important since it invalidates a popular impression that in recent years women have been committing crimes of *violence* at a much higher rate relative to men than they have in the past.

Given that females are becoming a much more significant part of the population that commits property crimes, several interesting questions arise: 1) Is this new group of criminals as equally deterred by increases in penalties and conviction probabilities as the male criminal? 2) Are inferior legal opportunities responsible for the female's interest in criminal activities? 3) What is the relationship between the rise in the female labor force participation rate and the rise in the female crime rate? This paper attempts to answer these questions by analyzing the determinants of female participation in criminal activities through an economic model of crime.[4] In Part I, the theoretical framework is outlined. Part II

4. For some work by criminologists on female crime, see Adler (1975) and Simon (1975).

indicates how this model can be empirically specified for an interstate analysis of female crime. In Part III, the results of estimating a female crime equation are examined. Part IV compares these results with those obtained from a male crime equation and an equation that pools both males and females. Part V summarizes the findings of this study.

I. THEORETICAL FRAMEWORK

Isaac Ehrlich has developed a model of the optimal allocation of time and resources to competing legal and illegal activities.[5] He derives behavioral implications from a version of the model in which consumption time is fixed and from a version in which consumption time is endogenous. It is clear that an analysis of female participation in criminal activities requires a model that considers not only the optimal allocation of time between legal and illegal activities but also the optimal allocation of time between household and work activities (legal and illegal). In what follows, I outline the version of the Ehrlich model that assumes consumption time is endogenous, summarize the behavioral predictions analyzed by Ehrlich, and discuss some additional behavioral implications that result when the model is applied to women.

A. *The Ehrlich Model.* The individual is assumed to have the following expected utility function:

$$(1) \qquad E(U) = (1 - p)U(X_1, t_c) + pU(X_2, t_c)$$

where X_1 = income when not apprehended,

X_2 = income when apprehended and punished,

t_c = consumption (or household) time,

and p = the probability of being apprehended and convicted.

Let T be the total amount of time available to the individual and t_m be time spent in work activities where $T = t_m + t_c$: Also, X_1 and X_2 can be written as:

$$(2) \qquad X_1 = W_i(t_i) + W_l(t_l) + W_o$$

$$(3) \qquad X_2 = W_i(t_i) + W_l(t_l) - F_i(t_i) + W_o$$

where t_l = time spent in legal market activities,

t_i = time spent in illegal market activities,

---

5. See Ehrlich (1974).

$W_i(t_i)$ = returns from illegal activities,

$W_l(t_l)$ = returns from legal activities,

$F_i(t_i)$ = the discounted value of the penalty,

and W_o = other income.

Let $t_i = kt_m$ and $t_l = (1 - k)t_m$ where

k = the fraction of work time that is spent in illegal activities.

The individual then determines the optimal allocation of his time between legal work, illegal work, and consumption by maximizing the expected utility function in (1) with respect to k and t_c. The resulting first order conditions are:

(4) $\qquad (1 - p)U_1'/pU_2' = -(w_i - w_l - f_i)/(w_i - w_l)$

(5) $\qquad [(1 - p)U'_1 + pU'_2][w_i k + w_l(1 - k)] - pU'_2 f_i k = U'_{tc}$

where $w_i = \partial W_i/\partial t_i, f_i = \partial F_i/\partial t_i$ and $w_l = \partial W_l/\partial t_l$.

Equation (4) states that the optimal allocation of market time between legal and illegal activities is found by equating the rate at which income can be transferred between the two states of the world with the rate at which the individual is willing to make the transfer. Equation (5) states that the optimal amount of consumption time is found by equating the marginal utility of work time with the marginal utility of consumption time.

Assuming that the relative allocation of work time between i and l is independent of the scale of work time itself, Ehrlich shows that an increase in the probability of apprehension and conviction results in an unambiguous decline in t_i while an increase in the average penalty decreases t_i if the utility function exhibits constant or diminishing marginal utility. Moreover, an increase in the marginal return from illegal activities unambiguously increases t_i while an increase in the marginal return from legal activities causes a substitution towards more work but a redistribution of work time away from illegal activities, thus resulting in an ambiguous effect on illegal time.

B. Predictions for Female Participation in Criminal Activities. When the Ehrlich model is applied to women, some additional implications can be derived. Marital status itself should affect the amount of time a woman spends in illegal activities. Suppose we do not have perfect information on a woman's legal market wage but we do know her marital status. Since married women work intermittently throughout their lives while single women work regularly, a married woman, at any moment in time, has lower legal opportunities than a single woman, everything else held constant. This occurs because of less human capital investment by both the married woman and by her employer.[6] This would imply that married women would allocate a greater proportion of their non-household time to illegal activities than would single women if investment in skills was more important for legal activities than for illegal activities. This argument would appear to be viable for certain crimes, e.g. larceny, but may be questionable for others, e.g. burglary. Even if there is a positive substitution effect towards more crime, whether a married woman would spend a greater amount of time (in absolute terms) in illegal activities than a single woman is ambiguous because her total working time is less. The presence of children and market goods bought with the husband's income would result in a married woman having a higher marginal utility of time at home (U'_{tc}) than a single woman, thus producing a negative scale effect on work time. In other words, an inverse relationship between k and t_m would be observed. Whether the substitution effect outweighs the scale effect and married women do in fact commit more crime can only be resolved through empirical analysis. One factor might, however, reduce the theoretical ambiguity. It is possible to view certain criminal activities and certain household activities as joint, rather than competing activities. For example, while a woman is doing the shopping for the family, she can simultaneously be shoplifting. This argument implies that a certain proportion of a married woman's household time is really time spent in illegal activities. It may be possible, therefore, to observe married women committing more of certain crimes than single women even if the substitution effect is outweighed by the scale effect.

Criminologists have argued that the rise in female crime is due to the increase in female labor force participation.[7] The economic model of crime shows, however, that the relationship between criminal participation and labor force participation is ambiguous. The lower the woman's price of time at home (i.e., U'_{tc}), the more time she will spend in the market and, since k is held constant, the more time she will spend in illegal activities. Thus, the positive scale effect would produce a positive relationship between labor force status and criminal activities, everything else held constant. On the other hand, a woman may be in the labor force not because she has a lower price of time at home than another woman, but rather because she has a higher legal wage. In other words, if we did not have perfect information on legal wage rates, labor force participation would signal an increase in the legal wage; this higher legal wage would produce substitution and scale effects that have opposite effects on illegal time. Thus, as with marital status, the true relationship

6. See Polachek (1975) for an analysis of the optimal human capital investment of females and Landes (1974) for an analysis of employer investment in females.

7. See Adler (1975) and Simon (1975).

between labor force status and criminal activities becomes an empirical question.

An additional implication of the economic model of female crime is the following. Since an increase in U'_{t_c} results in a decrease in both forms of work time, it can be predicted that an increase in the number of children, particularly preschool children, would result in a decrease in the amount of time spent in illegal activities.

II. EMPIRICAL SPECIFICATION OF THE MODEL

A. Supply of Offenses Equation. The theoretical framework discussed above suggests the following supply equation for female criminal activities:

$$(6) \qquad \overline{Q} = Q(p, F, w_i, w_t, X)$$

where $\overline{Q}$ is the number of crimes committed by the average female in a community,

p is the probability of apprehension and conviction,

F is the average penalty,

w_i is the marginal return from illegal activities,

w_t is the marginal return from legal activities,

and X is a vector of variables such as marital status, labor force status, number of children, age, race, etc.

B. A Simultaneous-Equation Model of Crime and Law Enforcement. Equation (6) defines the female crime rate as a function of a set of socioeconomic variables and two law enforcement variables, p and F. One problem with equation (6) is that the probability of apprehension and conviction is likely to be jointly determined with the level of crime itself.[8] For example, holding police protection expenditures constant, an increase in the crime rate will result in a decrease in p. The simultaneity problem can be handled by adding the following two equations to the model outlined in equation (6):

$$(7) \qquad p = p(E/N, \overline{Q}, Z)$$

$$(8) \qquad E/N = E((E/N)_{-1}, \overline{Q}_{-1})$$

where E/N is per capita expenditures on police protection and Z is a

---

8. Ehrlich (1974) provides evidence that the severity of punishment, F, is probably unaffected by the joint determination of the crime rate and the probability of punishment.

vector of exogenous variables which may include some of the variables in X.

Equation (7) states that the probability of apprehending and convicting a female is a function of the level of per capita police protection expenditures, the female crime rate (and perhaps, the male crime rate as well), and a set of exogenous variables. Equation (8) states that police protection expenditures in this period are determined by last period's expenditures and last period's crime rate. Equations (6), (7) and (8) form the structure of a simultaneous-equation model of crime and law enforcement.

C. Variables. In order to test the behavioral function in (6), and the simultaneous-equation model in equations (6), (7), and (8), it is necessary to devise empirical counterparts for the variables. The two models are used to analyze the variation in female crime across states in the United States in 1970;[9] $\bar{Q}$ therefore refers to the number of offenses committed by the average female in the state. The crime figures published by the Federal Bureau of Investigation are number of crimes reported to the police; whether or not these crimes were committed by women is unknown until the criminal is apprehended. One way to measure female crime, however, is to utilize the number of females arrested.

For example, let Q/N measure the number of crimes committed by females divided by the number of females in the state, A/N measure the number of females arrested divided by the number of females in the state, A/Q measure the proportion of female crimes cleared by the arrest of a female and C/Q measure the proportion of female crimes cleared by the arrest and conviction of a female. Assuming a multiplicative form for equation (6) and including the probability of arrest as an additional independent variable results in:

$$(9) \qquad\qquad Q/N = B^{b_0}(A/Q)^{b_1}(C/Q)^{b_2}$$

where B is assumed to include all the other independent variables in equation (6).[10] Since data on Q/N are unavailable but data on A/N are available, equation (9) can be rewritten in terms of the female arrest rate by multiplying both sides of the equation by A/Q. This results in:

$$(10) \qquad\qquad A/N = B^{b_0}(A/Q)^{1+b_1}(C/Q)^{b_2}.$$

According to equation (10), the female arrest rate will be a function of

9. 1970 was chosen because it is the most recent Census year, and it is therefore possible to utilize several socioeconomic variables from the Census to proxy the theoretical variables.

10. Note that C/Q can be written as $(A/Q)(C/A)$, i.e. the product of the arrest probability and the conditional probability of conviction. Then equation (9) would be rewritten as:

$$(9') \qquad\qquad Q/N = B^{b_0}(A/Q)^{b_1+b_2}(C/A)^{b_2}.$$

the same variables as the female crime rate. The only difference between equations (9) and (10) is that the effect of the probability of arrest in equation (10) will be positive if the elasticity of the true crime rate with respect to A/Q is less than unity. The true elasticity could of course be calculated from equation (10). All the other independent variables in equation will have the same coefficients as in equation (9).

Empirical estimation of equation (10), therefore, requires data on A/N, A/Q and C/Q for females. The crimes included in this study are murder and non-negligent manslaughter, robbery, assault, burglary, larceny and auto theft. A/N is then calculated by using the number of female arrests for these crimes in the state divided by the number of females in the state. A/Q cannot be calculated separately for females since it is impossible to know the sex of a non-apprehended offender; instead it is estimated by the total number of individuals arrested in the state divided by the number of crimes reported to the police in that state *(ARREST)*. The assumption is that the probability of apprehending a female criminal equals the probability of apprehending a male criminal, or at least, that these probabilities do not differ systematically across states.[11] Similarly, C/Q, the probability of apprehension and conviction, is calculated by the number of individuals (male and female) committed to state prison for the particular offense divided by the number of such offenses reported to the police *(PRCONV)*. The coefficient on this variable is also an estimate of the deterrent effect of the probability of being convicted given apprehension (see footnote 10). Finally, the penalty F in equation (6) is measured by the average time served by offenders (male-female) in state prison for that crime before their first release *(SENT)*. Note that *PRCONV* and *SENT* refer to all offenders, male and female, since it is impossible to obtain data on convictions and time served broken down by sex.[12] A problem exists if female criminals do, in fact, experience lower penalties and conviction probabilities than male criminals.[13] If equation (6) is estimated in log-linear form, however, the coefficients on *PRCONV* and *SENT* would estimate the true deterrent effects for females if the female conviction probabilities and penalties differ from the male probabilities and penalties by a fairly constant percentage across states.

Marginal returns to legal and illegal activities are measured in the manner utilized by Ehrlich (1974). Payoffs to criminal activities are assumed to be determined by the opportunities provided by potential victims of crime which are, in turn, measured by the state's median

---

11. Even if this condition is satisfied, the ratio of number of people arrested to number of crimes reported is not a perfect measure of the probability of any criminal being apprehended since there is still the problem of multiple-crime criminals and multiple-criminal crimes.

12. Only one state, California, maintains this type of data broken down by sex, but will no longer release the data.

13. See Simon (1975) for some evidence from California.

family income *(INC)*. Returns to legal activities are proxied by the percentage of families with incomes below one-half the state's median *(PCENT)*. This variable is used because individuals in a state with legitimate returns well below the illegitimate return (i.e. median family income) would have a greater incentive to participate in criminal activities, relative to those with incomes well above the median.[14]

The theoretical discussion in Part I suggested the importance of several socioeconomic variables in explaining female crime. The variables that are used in the empirical analysis are as follows:

MAR — percentage of females aged 16 and over who are married with spouse present

LF — percentage of females aged 16 and over who are in the civilian labor force

LFPSG — percentage of single females aged 16 and over who are in the civilian labor force

LFPMAR — percentage of married spouse present females aged 16 and over who are in the civilian labor force

AGE — median age of the female population

NW — percentage of females who are nonwhite

UNEMP — unemployment rate of females aged 35-39

TEENUN — unemployment rate of females aged 16-19

CHF6 — average number of children under 6 in female-headed families

CHF17 — average number of children aged 6-17 in female-headed families

CHHW6 — average number of children under 6 in husband-wife families

CHHW17 — average number of children aged 6-17 in husband-wife families.

Finally, some additional variables are defined in order to estimate the simultaneous-equation model in equations (6), (7) and (8). They are as follows:

EXPEND — per capita police protection expenditures by the state and local governments in 1969

---

14. It might be argued that legal returns should be measured by using average female earnings. The problem with this variable is that it is very highly correlated with median family income and it becomes difficult to estimate separate effects for the two variables.

CRIMPC — the number of crimes (only those used in this study) per capita reported to the police in 1969 (note that these crimes can not be broken down by the sex of the offender)

PCURB — percentage of the population that lives in an urban area

EDUC — median education of the population aged 25 and over.

III. RESULTS OF TESTING THE ECONOMIC MODEL OF FEMALE CRIME ON INTERSTATE DATA

The empirical framework developed in Part II is applied here in a regression analysis of variations of female crime across states in 1970. Note that although the dependent variable is female arrests, the effects of the independent variables can be viewed as effects on *crime* rates since the probability of arrest is held constant (see equations (9) and (10)). Weighted regressions are utilized because the equation is formulated in terms of the average female in the state; the weighting variable is the square root of the female population in the state. The regression equation used is in natural logarithmic form and the coefficients can therefore be interpreted as elasticities. The sample size is 33; seventeen states were deleted because they did not report the information needed to estimate the penalties and conviction probabilities. The data in Table 2 show, however, that the means and standard deviations of the dependent variables are virtually the same for the included and deleted states.[15] Since most female crime is property-related (see Table 1), the regressions are run separately for property and personal crimes. Table 3 contains regressions where the dependent variable includes property crime arrests (burglary, robbery, larceny, and auto theft), and in Table 4, the dependent variable refers to personal crime arrests (murder, non-negligent manslaughter and assault). Tables 3 and 4 show the results of estimating equation (6) by ordinary least squares and by two-stage least squares using the model contained in equations (6), (7) and (8).[16]

A. Arrest Probability, Conviction Probability and Penalty. The probability of arrest *(ARREST)* has a negative and significant effect on female property crime with an elasticity of approximately −.6; in other words, a 10 percent increase in the probability of arrest for a property crime would reduce female property crime by 6 percent. (Recall that this elasticity is calculated by subtracting one from the coefficient on *ARREST*.) The probability of conviction, *PRCONV*, also has a significant deterrent effect on female property crime with an elasticity of approxi-

15. The deleted states were Florida, North Carolina, Virginia, Alabama, Arkansas, Louisiana, Texas, Alaska, Oregon, Nebraska, Iowa, Wisconsin, Michigan, Indiana, Pennsylvania, New Jersey, and Rhode Island.

16. The instruments used for *PRCONV* in the two-stage least squares analysis are all the variables in equation (6) except *PRCONV*, as well as *EXPEND, CRIMPC, PCURB* and *EDUC.*

TABLE 2

Means and Standard Deviations of Arrest Variables for
Included and Deleted States
(Arrests are expressed per thousand of population)

Variables	Included States N = 33		Deleted States N = 17	
	Mean	Std. Dev.	Mean	Std. Dev.
FAPC	2.02	1.15	2.03	.85
FPROP	1.90	1.11	1.89	.83
FPERS	.12	.08	.14	.11
MAPC	9.57	3.85	9.27	2.76
MPROP	8.60	3.50	8.24	2.56
MPERS	.97	.52	1.03	.53

FAPC   = female arrests per capita
FPROP = female property crime arrests per capita
FPERS = female personal crime arrests per capita
MAPC   = male arrests per capita
MPROP = male property crime arrests per capita
MPERS = male personal crime arrests per capita

mately $-.3$ from the *OLS* equations and $-.8$ from the *TSLS* equations. It can be shown that the coefficients on *ARREST* and *PRCONV* imply that the elasticity of the crime rate with respect to the probability of arrest holding constant the *conditional* probability of conviction, exceeds the elasticity with respect to the *conditional* probability of conviction, holding constant the arrest probability.[17] This result is consistent with the strong test of the deterrence hypothesis developed by Ehrlich (1975). The average penalty, *SENT*, also has a deterrent effect on female property crime which approaches significance in the equation estimated through two-stage least squares.

Since most female property crime is larceny, it is interesting to compare the deterrent effects for larceny and other property crimes. In regressions 3.5 and 3.6, significant deterrent effects of *ARREST* and *PRCONV* are observed for burglary, robbery and auto theft with much weaker negative effects for larceny. Moreover, *SENT* has a negative

17. From footnote 10, the elasticity of the crime rate with respect to the probability of arrest, holding constant the conditional probability of conviction is given by the sum of the coefficient on *PRCONV* and the coefficient on *ARREST* minus one, since the dependent variable is arrests per capita. The elasticity with respect to the conditional probability of conviction, holding constant the arrest probability, is given by the coefficient on *PRCONV*. Therefore, the first elasticity must exceed the second elasticity according to the coefficients in Table 3.

TABLE 3

Weighted Regressions on Female Property Crime Arrests Per Capita

$N = 33$

	3.1[a]		3.2[a]		3.3[b]		3.4[a]		3.5[a,c]		3.6[a,d]	
	b	t	b	t	b	t	b	t	b	t	b	t
PRCONV	-.268	(-1.86)	-.297	(-2.28)	-.811	(-2.31)	-.331	(-2.52)	-.349	(-1.93)	-.131	(-1.28)
SENT	.048	(.30)	-.077	(-.51)	-.394	(-1.41)	-.097	(-.73)	-.242	(-1.18)	-.001	(-.03)
ARREST	.440	(2.01)	.341	(1.70)	.329	(1.20)	.390	(2.08)	.722	(2.81)	.240	(1.28)
INC	1.991	(1.71)	-.347	(-.25)	-3.311	(-1.26)	-.822	(-.72)	3.302	(1.82)	-.323	(-.20)
PCENT	1.749	(1.47)	1.450	(1.35)	-.076	(-.04)	.512	(.48)	4.499	(3.04)	1.549	(1.37)
MAR	7.893	(3.22)	8.457	(3.83)	20.238	(3.24)	4.430	(1.70)	3.255	(1.19)	8.964	(3.82)
LF	2.086	(2.48)										
LFPMAR			-.343	(-.45)	-.178	(-.17)	-.883	(-1.15)	.160	(.15)	-.610	(-.73)
LFPSG			4.600	(2.99)	5.083	(2.37)	4.242	(2.92)	4.236	(2.01)	4.914	(2.83)
AGE	-.140	(-.13)	-.099	(-.10)	1.290	(.82)	-5.677	(-1.71)	.225	(.17)	-.608	(-.57)
NW	.127	(1.40)	.158	(1.93)	.336	(2.18)	.068	(.88)	.039	(.34)	.117	(1.45)
UNEMP	.169	(.35)	.460	(1.03)	.862	(1.31)	.505	(1.30)	-.458	(-.77)	.652	(1.28)
TEENUN	.037	(.08)	-.099	(-.24)	-.418	(-.69)	-.829	(-1.95)	.610	(1.11)	-.213	(-.46)
CHF6							.271	(.35)				
CHF17							.781	(.53)				
CHHW6							-4.901	(-2.18)				
CHHW17							.218	(.32)				
R²	.85		.89		.79		.94		.87		.87	

[a]Estimated via ordinary least squares

[b]Estimated via two-stage least squares

[c]Refers to burglary, robbery and auto theft only

[d]Refers to larceny only

TABLE 4

Weighted Regressions on Female Personal Crime Arrests Per Capita

$N = 33$

	4.1[a]		4.2[a]		4.3[b]		4.4[a]	
	b	t	b	t	b	t	b	t
PRCONV	.150	(.40)	.474	(1.33)	.743	(.80)	.557	(1.26)
SENT	−.129	(−.41)	−.161	(−.57)	−.054	(−.12)	−.029	(−.09)
ARREST	.500	(1.35)	.474	(1.44)	.432	(1.20)	.699	(1.72)
INC	3.563	(1.84)	.105	(.05)	.433	(.18)	1.668	(.72)
PCENT	3.884	(1.71)	3.981	(1.97)	4.572	(1.65)	3.363	(1.35)
MAR	.329	(.09)	−.798	(−.26)	−2.261	(−.37)	−4.921	(−.85)
LF	1.323	(.81)						
LFPMAR			−2.611	(−1.67)	−3.118	(−1.38)	−1.533	(−.74)
LFPSG			7.782	(2.69)	8.447	(2.34)	4.627	(1.28)
AGE	2.929	(1.56)	3.167	(1.88)	3.248	(1.89)	2.348	(.31)
NW	.420	(2.75)	.402	(2.95)	.364	(1.98)	.309	(1.73)
UNEMP	.345	(.40)	.769	(.99)	.826	(1.02)	.488	(.57)
TEENUN	.356	(.44)	.405	(.57)	.443	(.60)	.033	(.03)
CHF6							−.806	(−.48)
CHF17							3.174	(.97)
CHHW6							−3.696	(−.68)
CHHW17							2.118	(1.23)
R^2	.78		.83		.83		.83	

[a]Estimated via ordinary least squares

[b]Estimated via two-stage least squares

effect only on burglary, robbery, and auto theft. It therefore appears that law enforcement activity has a weak deterrent effect on larceny, the most important female crime, but the results are still consistent with the deterrence test discussed above. Finally, female personal crimes are found to be only weakly deterred by the arrest probability and not at all affected by the conviction probability or the sentence.

B. *Returns to Legal and Illegal Activities.* PCENT, the proxy for legal opportunities, has a positive and significant effect on personal crimes and on burglary, robbery and auto theft; the greater the percentage of families with incomes below one-half the median income in the state (i.e. the greater the degree of income inequality) the higher the level of these female crimes. It is interesting that this effect holds for personal crimes even though they are often not considered to be economically motivated. The fact that PCENT has an insignificant effect on larceny may be evidence of the widely held belief that shoplifting has become prevalent among middle class and upper class women. *INC*, the proxy for illegal opportunities, also has a positive and significant effect on burglary, robbery and auto theft.

C. Socio-Economic Variables. The theoretical framework developed in Part I showed that competing substitution and scale effects would produce an ambiguous effect of marital status on female crime. The results in Tables 3 and 4 indicate that married women are more likely to commit property crimes than single women, but marital status has no influence on the incidence of personal crime. It is also of interest that the coefficient on *MAR* is almost *three* times as large in the larceny regression as it is in the "other property crime" regression. The analysis in Part I provided two reasons for this striking difference: 1) Experience may be just as important for crimes like burglary, robbery and auto theft as it is for legal market work, and there would thus be no positive substitution effect for these crimes and 2) Larceny (shoplifting) and household activities (shopping) may be joint, rather than competing, uses of time.[18]

In Part I, it was argued that competing substitution and scale effects made the relationship between criminal participation and labor force participation ambiguous. From regression 3.1, however, it can be observed that women in the labor force *(LF)* are more likely to commit property crimes than women who are not in the labor force. This result could indicate that the rise in female labor force participation in recent years may have resulted in increased female crime because women who are out of the home have greater opportunities to commit crime, i.e. there is a strong positive scale effect. The results in regression 3.2, however, show that this conclusion is unwarranted. While an increase in the labor force participation rate of single women *(LFPSG)* has a positive effect on property crime, the labor force participation rate of married women *(LFPMAR)* has no effect. It appears therefore that the scale effect dominates for the single women while it is offset for married women by the substitution effect. In other words, the substitution effect is relatively stronger for married women.[19] When the children variables are added to the regression, *LFPMAR* becomes much more negative. This happens because the children variables hold constant the woman's price of time at home and *LFPMAR* then measures the effect of an increase in the legal market wage (see the discussion in Part I).

The fact that *LFPMAR* does not have a positive effect on female

---

18. A variable measuring the percentage of women aged 16 and over who are divorced was also added to the regressions in Tables 3 and 4. The results indicated a positive but insignificant effect of this variable on the rate of female property crime. In addition, the magnitude of the coefficient was quite small.

19. In Part I it was argued that labor force participation can be viewed as a measure of the woman's legal wage. An implication of the economic model of crime (see Ehrlich (1974)) is that changes in legitimate employment opportunities will have larger effects on offenders who engage in crime on a part-time basis than on those who specialize in it. Thus married women, who are likely to be part-time offenders, would reduce their participation in crime in response to an increase in the legal wage to a greater extent than would single women.

property crime is an important finding. Criminologists have argued that the recent dramatic rise in female crime is due to the increase in the rate at which women are participating in the labor force (see references in footnote 7). The sharp increase in total female labor force participation, however, has been due only to the increase in the labor force participation of *married* women. During the period 1960-1974, the labor force participation rate of married women rose by 40% while the labor force participation rate of other women rose by only 7.8%.[20] If the cross-sectional coefficients are accurate indicators of time-series coefficients,[21] then the results in Table 3 show that the recent dramatic increase in female crime can not be explained by the increase in female labor force participation; the increase in the non-married labor force participation rate would only have produced a 30% increase in female crime.

An increase in the unemployment rate of women aged 35-39 *(UNEMP)*, leads to an increase in female property crime, but this effect is not significant. This age group was chosen because it has a relatively high labor force participation rate compared to other age groups in the post-childbearing years. In order to correctly measure the demand for female labor, one would want to use an unemployment rate that abstracts from the effects of intermittent female labor force participation. The positive, but insignificant coefficient on *UNEMP* is weak evidence of the fact that as opportunities in the legal sector diminish, women turn to property crime.

The percentage of females in the population who are nonwhite *(NW)* has a positive and significant effect on the amount of female crime because nonwhites tend to have inferior legal opportunities. This racial differential in legal earnings would not be captured by *PCENT* since the latter is calculated over all families in the state.

A very interesting result emerges when the children variables are added to the female crime regressions. It can be seen that an increase in the average number of preschool children in husband-wife families *(CHHW6)* leads to a significant decrease in female property crime. Preschool children serve as a proxy for the housewife's price of time; the economic model of crime developed in Part I showed that an increase in the woman's value of time at home would produce a negative scale effect on both legal *and* illegal work time. This explains why the coefficient of *LFPMAR* becomes much more negative when *CHHW6* is held constant. What is important about the results in regression 3.4 is the

20. Calculated from *1960 U.S. Census of Population Detailed Characteristics*, Table 196 and from the *1975 Manpower Report of the President*, Table B-2. These figures refer only to women 16 years of age and over.

21. Over time, changes in the labor force participation rate may better measure changes in relative market opportunities than they would in the cross section; see Ehrlich (1975). It is therefore possible that the increase over time in the labor force participation of women may account for some of their increased participation in crime if the scale effect has dominated the substitution effect.

size of the elasticity of the crime rate with respect to the number of preschool children. Note that a *one* percent decrease in the average number of preschool children in husband-wife families leads to a *five* percent increase in the rate of female property crime. If the cross-sectional coefficients are accurate indicators of time-series coefficients, then this result implies that the decrease in the average number of preschool children per husband-wife family that took place between 1960 and 1970 would have resulted in an increase of 138% in the rate of female property crime or 58% of the actual 1960-1970 increase.[22] While the negative relationship between number of preschool children and women's labor force participation has been documented in several studies,[23] this appears to be the first evidence that a negative relationship also exists for female *criminal* participation.

IV. COMPARISON WITH MALE REGRESSIONS

In this part, the results from the female arrest regressions are compared with the results from weighted male arrest regressions (the weighting variable is the square root of the male population) which are shown in Tables 5 (property crime) and 6 (personal crime). The importance of estimating separate female and male regressions is discussed in section D where the results from estimating a pooled regression are analyzed.

A. Arrest Probability, Conviction Probability and Penalty. The deterrent effects of *PRCONV* and *SENT* in the male OLS property crime regressions are quite similar to those observed in the female property crime regressions. The coefficient of *PRCONV* in regression 5.2 is −.29, which is almost identical to the coefficient in regression 3.2. It might appear from a comparison of regressions 3.2 and 5.2 that males are deterred by an increase in the penalty while females are not. This conclusion would be unwarranted as can be seen by a comparison of the coefficients on *SENT* in regressions 3.5, 3.6, 5.5 and 5.6. Note that males and females are deterred almost equally by an increase in the penalty for burglary, robbery and auto theft, although the male coefficient is more significant. An increase in the penalty for larceny, however, does not have a significant effect on either males or females. While the probability of arrest *(ARREST)* has a negative and significant effect on male property crime, the elasticity is only −.3 which is fifty percent smaller than the corresponding female elasticity. Females, therefore, appear to be more strongly deterred than males by increases in the probability of arrest. Note, however, that the male results are still consistent with the strong test of the deterrence hypothesis discussed in Part III.

22. The average number of preschool children in husband-wife families decreased by 28% between 1960 and 1970. (Source: 1960 Census of Population, "Families," PC(2)-4A, Table 4 and 1970 Census of Population, "Family Composition," PC(2)-4A, Table 5).

23. See Mincer (1962) and Leibowitz (1975).

TABLE 5

Weighted Regressions on Male Property Crime Arrests Per Capita
$N = 33$

	5.1[a]		5.2[a]		5.3[b]		5.4[a]		5.5[a,c]		5.6[a,d]	
	b	t	b	t	b	t	b	t	b	t	b	t
PRCONV	−.200	(−1.65)	−.287	(−2.37)	−1.211	(−2.41)	−.365	(−2.92)	−.309	(−2.16)	−.102	(−1.12)
SENT	−.240	(−1.85)	−.222	(−1.83)	−.681	(−2.10)	−.233	(−1.94)	−.228	(−1.65)	.016	(.14)
ARREST	.696	(4.64)	.686	(4.92)	.831	(2.93)	.783	(5.22)	.779	(4.62)	.603	(4.67)
INC	3.284	(3.56)	2.974	(3.39)	−.732	(−.30)	2.491	(2.72)	3.334	(3.22)	2.644	(2.97)
PCENT	2.121	(2.05)	2.684	(2.66)	1.431	(.69)	1.937	(1.79)	3.183	(2.67)	1.801	(1.72)
MAR	3.749	(1.64)	5.857	(2.85)	14.234	(2.49)	4.842	(2.02)	5.375	(2.31)	6.014	(2.70)
LF	.215	(.12)										
LFPMAR			5.743	(1.85)	13.231	(1.87)	5.939	(1.55)	6.034	(1.64)	5.317	(1.63)
LFPSG			−.757	(−1.43)	−1.796	(−1.55)	−1.268	(−.82)	−.743	(−1.17)	−.970	(−1.74)
AGE	−1.493	(−1.34)	−.662	(−.59)	1.478	(.61)	−2.366	(−1.27)	−.584	(−.44)	−1.172	(−.99)
NW	.097	(1.15)	.069	(.86)	.310	(1.58)	.055	(.69)	.081	(.86)	.013	(.16)
UNEMP	.032	(.10)	.253	(.82)	.280	(.46)	.185	(.56)	.358	(.97)	.149	(.45)
TEENUN	.084	(.18)	−.131	(−.30)	−.271	(−.31)	−.119	(−.27)	−.490	(−.94)	.332	(.70)
CHHW6							−.702	(−.45)				
CHH17							−1.114	(−1.00)				
R^2	.83		.86		.44		.88		.85		.82	

[a] Estimated via ordinary least squares

[b] Estimated via two-stage least squares

[c] Refers to burglary, robbery and auto theft only

[d] Refers to larceny only

TABLE 6

Weighted Regressions on Male Personal Crime Arrests Per Capita

$N = 33$

	6.1[a]		6.2[a]		6.3[b]		6.4[a]	
	b	t	b	t	b	t	b	t
PRCONV	−.157	(−.56)	−.170	(−.58)	.314	(.31)	−.349	(−1.25)
SENT	−.393	(−1.81)	−.401	(−1.80)	−.217	(−.50)	−.388	(−1.97)
ARREST	.654	(2.22)	.637	(2.11)	.592	(1.77)	.632	(2.34)
INC	3.364	(2.18)	3.457	(2.18)	4.303	(1.82)	2.452	(1.69)
PCENT	3.888	(2.33)	3.849	(2.11)	4.727	(1.82)	1.926	(1.08)
MAR	4.486	(1.34)	5.304	(1.76)	4.432	(1.22)	4.066	(1.11)
LF	1.898	(.60)						
LFPMAR			1.009	(.19)	−.056	(−.01)	−.296	(−.06)
LFPSG			.345	(.34)	.991	(.59)	.494	(.17)
AGE	−1.810	(−.96)	−1.913	(−.95)	−1.698	(−.77)	−5.123	(−1.68)
NW	.247	(2.06)	.249	(1.87)	.221	(1.46)	.205	(1.72)
UNEMP	.460	(.82)	.491	(.82)	.471	(.74)	.390	(.66)
TEENUN	−.493	(−.56)	−.570	(−.62)	−.260	(−.23)	−.495	(−.56)
CHHW6							.457	(.17)
CHHW17							−3.894	(−2.31)
R²	.76		.76		.73		.83	

[a]Estimated via ordinary least squares

[b]Estimated via two-stage least squares

In the personal crime regressions there are noticeable differences between males and females in the effects of the law enforcement variables. An increase in the penalty has a negative and significant effect on male personal crime while no deterrent effect was observed for the females. Although the coefficients on *PRCONV* in Table 6 are not significant, their signs are negative as predicted; recall that in the female personal crime regressions these signs were positive. As with the property crime equations, the probability of arrest has a weaker effect for males than for females.

B. Returns to Legal and Illegal Activities. PCENT, the proxy for legal opportunities, and *INC,* the proxy for illegal opportunities, are positive and significant in all of the ordinary least squares regressions in Tables 5 and 6. Increases in illegal returns and decreases in legal returns lead to increases in both male property crimes and male personal crimes. Recall that for females these variables were significant except in the case of larceny.

C. Socio-Economic Variables. Marital status has a positive and significant effect on male property crime. The economic model of crime suggests that this positive effect is the result of competing substitution and scale effects: 1) Married men have higher legal wages than single men because of their closer attachment to the labor force[24] and therefore they should devote a larger percentage of each hour of work to legal work and 2) Since married men spend more time in the labor market than single men,[25] there should be a positive scale effect resulting in more crime. While the positive scale effect dominates, it is interesting to note that the elasticity of *MAR* in Table 5 is only two-thirds the size of the *MAR* elasticity for female property crime. Note also that the positive effect of *MAR* in the female equations was due to a positive substitution effect outweighing a negative scale effect.

The labor force variables have effects that are opposite in sign to those observed for females. Table 5 shows that married men who are in the labor force are more likely to commit property crimes than married men who are not in the labor force. This result may reflect the fact that married men who are not in the labor force are probably disabled (or retired) and would therefore be unable to commit crimes. For single men, however, labor force participation appears to be a weak substitute for criminal participation. Neither of the unemployment rate variables has an effect on male crime although some weak positive relationships were observed in the case of female crime.

D. Results from Pooled Regressions. In order to determine whether the same structure applies to female and to male crime, a property crime regression and a personal crime regression were estimated in which the female and male samples were pooled. The coefficients from these pooled regressions are shown in Table 7; it is worthwhile noting that the coefficients essentially average out the diverse effects that were observed for some of the variables in the separate male and female regressions. Applying Chow's test of equality to the full set of coefficients results in $F_{15, 36} = 1.70$ for property crime and $F_{15, 36} = 2.28$ for personal crime. The first statistic is almost significant at the 5 percent level while the second statistic is significant at that level. It can therefore be concluded that the structure underlying female personal crime differs significantly from that underlying male personal crime while the overall structures are also likely to differ in the case of property crime.

Further analysis of the structural differences between female and male crime is obtained by restricting subsets of the regression coefficients. For example, the hypothesis of the equality across samples of the coefficients on the labor force variables *(LFPMAR* and *LFPSG)* is rejected at

24. Borjas (1975) presents evidence of this wage-differential in the National Longitudinal Survey data.

25. In March 1975, the labor force participation rate was 84% for married men and 67% for non-married men. (Source: 1976 Manpower Report of the President, Table B-2). Grossman and Benham (1975) present evidence that married men work more weeks per year than non-married men.

TABLE 7

Weighted Pooled Regressions
$N = 66$

	7.1 Property Crime		7.2 Personal Crime	
	b	t	b	t
PRCONV	−.305	(−3.44)	−.229	(−.94)
SENT	−.104	(−1.14)	−.266	(−1.38)
ARREST	.672	(5.54)	.633	(2.66)
INC	2.608	(3.82)	2.092	(1.66)
PCENT	1.471	(1.95)	2.883	(1.88)
MAR	3.380	(2.39)	.830	(.30)
LFPMAR	1.162	(6.37)	2.302	(6.44)
LFPSG	.300	(.62)	.987	(.96)
AGE	−4.312	(−3.41)	−2.087	(−.82)
NW	.060	(1.06)	.269	(2.55)
UNEMP	−.098	(−.49)	.049	(.12)
TEENUN	.055	(.24)	.033	(.07)
CHHW6	−2.927	(−2.58)	−.859	(−.36)
CHHW17	−.042	(−.05)	−2.751	(−1.60)
R^2	.96		.91	

the 5 percent level for both property and personal crime. The coefficients on the set of law enforcement variables *(PRCONV, SENT* and *ARREST)* are significantly different across samples at the 5 percent level for property crime, but not for personal crime. A strong difference between males and females in the case of personal crime is in the effect of the constant term; a dummy variable indicating the male sample is statistically significant for this type of crime. In other words, while the set of law enforcement and socioeconomic variables used in this analysis is a good predictor of the differences underlying male and female *property* crime, the structural differences between male and female personal crime are, in part, explained by factors not accounted for directly in the regression analysis.

V. SUMMARY AND CONCLUSIONS

This paper has analyzed the determinants of female participation in criminal activities through the use of an economic model of crime. The model predicted that women's labor force participation and marital status would have ambiguous effects on female criminal activities as a result of competing substitution and scale effects, while the presence of preschool children would reduce female crime. Although the model was tested empirically using 1970 state data on female arrests, it was shown that the coefficients on all of the independent variables except the probability of arrest in fact measured the effects of these variables on the female *crime* rate. The major empirical findings are as follows:

1) The probability of conviction and the probability of arrest have significant deterrent effects on female property crime and the magnitude of these effects are consistent with the deterrence hypothesis. The average penalty has a negative but insignificant effect on female participation in burglary, robbery and auto theft. It is of interest to note that for larceny, the most important female crime, no significant deterrent effect of law enforcement activity is observed.

2) Married women (with spouse present) are more likely to commit property crimes, especially larceny. It was argued that this positive relationship is due to the married woman's inferior opportunities in the legal sector as well as the possible complementarity between certain household activities and certain criminal activities.

3) An important finding is that the labor force participation rate of married women has no effect on the rate of female crime; in other words, the substitution and scale effects offset one another. Criminologists have been arguing that the recent rise in female crime is due to the rise in the female labor force participation rate. To the extent that the cross-sectional parameters estimated in this paper are indicative of time-series coefficients, we see that the criminologists' hypothesis must be rejected.

4) The average number of preschool children in husband-wife families has a negative and significant effect on female property crime since this variable is a proxy for the married woman's price of time at home. Utilizing the estimated coefficient on this variable, it was shown that the decrease in the average number of preschool children per husband-wife family that took place between 1960 and 1970 could have accounted for 58% of the increase in the female crime rate that occurred during that period.

5) The need for analyzing female crime separately from male crime was shown through a test of the equality across samples of the coefficients. The structure underlying female crime is significantly different from that underlying male crime.

This paper has studied the determinants of female crime using the powerful tools of economic theory. The empirical results were generally consistent with the theoretical predictions and a popular hypothesis about the positive relationship between female labor force participation and female crime was rejected by the data. Rather, this paper has shown that what the female criminal participation rate and the female labor force participation rate have in common is that they are negatively and significantly related to the woman's price of time at home, as measured by the average number of preschool children per family. Once the number of preschool children is held constant, the partial effect of labor force participation on female crime is negative. The recent dramatic rise in female crime would therefore appear not to be due to the increase in female opportunities in the labor market but rather to the sharp decrease in the woman's value of time at home.

APPENDIX: DATA SOURCES

I. Crime Data

The number of female arrests and the number of male arrests for each state are taken from unpublished FBI data. The probability of arrest *(ARREST)* is calculated by taking the ratio of the total number of people arrested to the total number of crimes reported to the police. The latter data are available in the 1970 Uniform Crime Reports. The crime data used for the two-stage least squares model *(CRIMPC)* are taken from the 1969 Uniform Crime Reports.

II. Probability of Conviction and Average Sentence

The number of people committed to state prisons for various crimes (used to calculate *PRCONV*) is taken from "National Prisoner Statistics, State Prisoners: Admissions and Releases, 1970." The average sentence served by those first released is available in the same publication.

· III. Police Protection Expenditures

Per capita police protection expenditures are taken from "Government Finances in 1968-69" and "Government Finances in 1969-70." By averaging the data reported for these two time periods, an estimate is obtained for expenditures in 1969.

IV. Other Variables

All the other variables were taken from various tables in the state volumes of The 1970 Census of Population:
1. Median family income *(INC)* — Table 198
2. Percent of families with incomes equal to less than half the median *(PCENT)* — Table 198
3. Labor force participation rates *(LF, LFPMAR, LFPSG)* — Table 165
4. Percent married *(MAR)* — Table 165
5. Unemployment rates *(UNEMP, TEENUN)* — Table 164
6. Percent nonwhite *(NW)* — Table 48
7. Median age *(AGE)* — Table 48
8. Children variables *(CHF6, CHF17, CHHW6, CHHW17)* — Table 22
9. Median education *(EDUC)* — Table 51
10. Percent in urban areas *(PCURB)* — Table 48

REFERENCES

Adler, Freda, *Sisters in Crime*, McGraw-Hill, 1975.

Borjas, George, "Job Investment, Labor Mobility and Earnings," unpublished Ph.D. dissertation, Columbia University, 1975.

Chow, Gregory, "Tests of Equality Between Sets of Coefficients in Two Linear Regressions," *Econometrica*, 1960.

Ehrlich, Isaac, "Participation in Illegitimate Activities: A Theoretical and Empirical Investigation," in Becker, G. and Landes, W., eds., *Essays in the Economics of Crime and Punishment*, NBER, 1974.

––––––––––––– , "The Deterrent Effect of Capital Punishment: A Question of Life and Death," *American Economic Review*, June 1975.

Grossman, Michael and Benham, Lee, "Health, Hours and Wages," in M. Perlman, ed., *The Economics of Health and Medical Care*, 1974.

Landes, Elisabeth, "Male-Female Differences in Wages and Employment: A Specific Human Capital Model," NBER Working Paper No. 29, 1974.

Leibowitz, Arleen, "Education and the Allocation of Women's Time," in Juster, F. T., ed., *Education, Income and Human Behavior*, McGraw-Hill, 1975.

Mincer, Jacob, "Labor Force Participation of Married Women," in *Aspects of Labor Economics*, NBER, 1962.

Polachek, Solomon, "Differences in Expected Post-School Investment as a Determinant of Market Wage Differentials," *International Economic Review*, June 1975.

Simon, Rita, "The Contemporary Woman and Crime," National Institute of Mental Health, 1975.

U.S. Department of Commerce, Bureau of the Census, *Census of Population: 1960 Subject Reports*, "Families" PC(2) — 4A, US Government Printing Office, 1963.

U.S. Department of Commerce, Bureau of the Census, *Census of Population: 1970 Characteristics of the Population*, US Government Printing Office, 1973.

U.S. Department of Commerce, Bureau of the Census, *Census of Population: 1970 Subject Reports*, "Family Composition," PC(2) — 4A, US Government Printing Office, 1973.

U.S. Department of Commerce, Bureau of the Census, "Government Finances in 1968-69, 1969-70," US Government Printing Office, 1970, 1971.

U.S. Department of Justice, Bureau of Prisons, "National Prisoner Statistics, State Prisoners: Admissions and Releases, 1970," US Government Printing Office, 1972.

U.S. Department of Justice, Federal Bureau of Investigation, *Crime in the United States* (Uniform Crime Reports) 1969, 1970, 1974, US Government Printing Office.

U.S. President, *Manpower Report of the President*, 1975, 1976, US Government Printing Office.

4

AN ECONOMIC STUDY OF
U.S. AIRCRAFT HIJACKING, 1961-1976

WILLIAM M. LANDES

"Well, I could stop hi-jackers tomorrow . . . if everyone was allowed to carry guns them hi-jackers wouldn't have no superiority. All you gotta do is arm all the passengers, then no hi-jacker would risk pullin' a rod." Archie, "All in the Family."

I. INTRODUCTION

O_N May 1, 1961 a National Airlines aircraft en route from Miami to Key West was successfully hijacked and diverted to Cuba. Although aircraft hijackings had occurred in Eastern Europe and Cuba prior to that date, this was the first recorded hijacking of a U.S. registered aircraft.[1] Seven more U.S. hijackings took place between 1961 and 1967 (see Table 1), followed by an unprecedented increase in the next five years. Between 1968 and 1972, 124 hijackings occurred, leading some observers to proclaim that hijacking had become a national epidemic.[2] This surge of hijacking, however, came to an abrupt halt in 1973—one hijacking took place in that year and only ten more occurred in the next three years. A similar pattern of hijackings is

* I would like to thank Robert Sherwin for helpful comments and valuable research assistance and Elisabeth Landes, Fred Nolde, Richard Posner, members of the Industrial Organization and Law and Economics Workshops at the University of Chicago, and participants in a seminar at the Hoover Institution for helpful comments on an earlier draft. I also thank Ann Bowler, Thomas McKim, and Louis Salinas for their research assistance. Financial support was provided by the National Science Foundation through a grant to the National Bureau of Economic Research to support research in law and economics and by the Law and Economics Program of the University of Chicago Law School. This is not an official National Bureau paper because it has not undergone the full critical review accorded Bureau studies, including approval by the Bureau's Board of Directors.

[1] In this paper the term "hijacking" refers to air carriers and excludes the category of general aviation (for example, small aircraft such as Pipers, Cessnas, and so forth). Note also that the Federal Aviation Administration (FAA) defines a hijacking to include one in which the offender is unsuccessful (for example, he is captured before gaining control of the aircraft). Thus, the number of hijackings per year in my study includes both actual and attempted hijackings.

[2] Even during the peak year 1969, however, the probability that an aircraft would be hijacked on any given day in the United States was negligible (= .70 10^{-5}). Yet this was more than 30 times greater than the probability that an individual would be murdered on a given day (= .20 10^{-6}).

From William M. Landes, "An Economic Study of U.S. Aircraft Hijacking, 1961-1976," 21(1) *The Journal of Law and Economics* 1-31 (April 1978). Copyright 1978 by the University of Chicago Law School.

found outside the United States—relatively few incidents (19) between 1961 and 1967, a sharp increase (174) from 1968 to 1972, and a decline (56) thereafter.

What accounts for the dramatic reduction in U.S. hijacking after 1972, and how does one explain the pattern of hijackings in general? Is deterrence—measured by rates of apprehension, the likelihood of incarceration, and the severity of sanctions—an important explanation of the time series behavior of aircraft hijackings? Did the security measures introduced in the 1970s, in particular, mandatory preboard screening of passengers and carryon luggage, lead to significantly fewer hijackings? What were the costs of these security measures relative to the number of hijackings prevented? Alternatively, was hijacking simply a fad that would have lost momentum and sharply declined after 1972 without the imposition of elaborate security measures? The present study attempts to answer these and other questions, focusing mainly on U.S. aircraft hijacking.

Table 1 suggests that deterrence may be an important explanation of hijackings in the United States. Between 1961 and 1965, the proportion of offenders apprehended (within one year of the hijacking) was .80 and the rate of hijacking was low.[3] During the peak years, 1968-1972, the proportion apprehended declined to a low of .15 in 1968 then rose steadily to .60 in 1972. By contrast, all offenders were apprehended from 1973 to 1976, and the number of hijackings substantially declined. The broad pattern of sentencing is also consistent with the view that deterrence matters. Sentences were relatively low and variable to those convicted through.1971. But in the years 1972 to 1974—when nearly 50 per cent of apprehended hijackers were sentenced—the sentences meted out were severe, averaging almost 30 years per convicted offender.[4] Hijacking also imposes another significant risk on the offender—the chance of being shot and killed during the attempt. No offenders were killed until the third quarter of 1971, but since then more than 10 per cent (7 of 68) were killed during attempted hijackings.

The implementation of several security measures aimed at reducing the incidence of hijacking coincides with increases in the probability of apprehension. For example, in 1970 the major airlines began to use weapon-screening devices on passengers meeting a behavioral profile of a hijacker.[5]

---

[3] Unless stated otherwise, apprehensions always refer to offenders apprehended within a year of the hijacking. Note that 84% of all apprehensions occurred within a year of the hijacking. See Federal Aviation Administration–Civil Aviation Security Service, Chronology of Hijackings of U.S. Registered Aircraft and Current Legal Status of Hijackers, as of July 1, 1976 (mimeo).

[4] Statutory changes, however, do not appear responsible for the observed increase in sentences. The only congressional enactment dealing with sentences is the 1961 amendment to the Federal Aviation Act of 1958, 49 U.S.C. § 1472 (1961) that made aircraft hijacking a federal crime punishable by death with a minimum sentence of 20 years.

[5] The profile consists of a list of about a dozen characteristics. Although the airlines and the

TABLE 1
DOMESTIC AND FOREIGN AIRCRAFT HIJACKINGS

	1930–1960	1961–1965	1966–1967	1968	1969	1970	1971	1972	1973	1974	1975	1976[4]	Total 1961–1976[4]
U.S. Air Carrier Aircraft[1]													
Hijackings		8	0	16	38	20	23	27	1	3	6	1	143
Offenders		10	0	26	52	22	28	40	1	3	6	5	193
Proportion of offenders apprehended within 12 months		.80	—	.15	.29	.41	.50	.68	1.0	1.0	1.0	1.0	
Proportion of offenders who attempted to go to Cuba[2]		.60	—	.92	.96	.73	.64	.25	0	0	.17	0	
Average sentence (in years) during time interval[3]		16.3	4	1.5	10	21	6.8	32.1	23	41.7	13.3	14.3	
Number of persons sentenced to prison		3	2	1	2	7	6	12	10	3	6	4	56
U.S. General Aviation													
Hijackings		2	1	4	0	2	2	4	1	4	6	1	27
Offenders		4	1	4	—	3	3	6	1	6	9	1	38
Proportion of offenders apprehended within 12 months		.50	0	.75	—	.33	.67	.33	1.0	.83	.89	1.0	
World (excluding U.S.)													
Hijackings (excluding general aviation)	44	11	8	12	46	54	32	30	20	17	13	6	249
Offenders		45	47	23	129	152	60	79	45	27	19	17	643
Proportion of offenders apprehended within 12 months		.40	.50	.22	.27	.31	.62	.67	.53	.56	.68	.87	

Notes:

[1] Our definition of a domestic hijacking excludes hijackings of U.S. registered aircraft in foreign countries. The FAA's Civil Aviation Security Service includes these hijackings (of which there have been 11 since 1961) in their enumeration of domestic hijackings.

[2] If Cuba was one of several stated destinations and the hijacking was not completed, this was included in the Cuba class.

[3] Life imprisonment defined as 50 years for the purpose of computing average sentences.

[4] As of July 1, 1976.

Source: Federal Aviation Administration, Civil Aviation Security Service, Chronology of Hijackings of U.S. Registered Aircraft and Current Legal Status of Hijackers, as of July 1, 1976; Federal Aviation Administration, Civil Aviation Security Service, Domestic and Foreign Aircraft Hijackings as of July 1, 1976.

And beginning in the fourth quarter of 1970, air marshals, who numbered about 1,200 at their peak, were riding shotgun on selected flights.[6] The most significant security measure was the executive order requiring all the nation's airlines by January 5, 1973 to search electronically carryon luggage and passengers for possession of weapons. From that day on, all hijackers were apprehended. In addition to these explicit security measures, the United States and Cuba entered into a treaty on February 15, 1973, calling for both nations to extradite or punish hijackers. Since Cuba had been the principal destination of U.S. hijackers, at least through 1971 (see Table 1), the enforcement of this treaty meant that the probability of apprehension would be near unity for an aircraft successfully diverted to Cuba.

A preliminary discussion of deterrence would be incomplete without some mention of the types of hijackers. Until 1972 the primary objective of hijackers was to obtain "free" transportation to Cuba, in some cases for political purposes and in others to avoid prosecution for crimes in the United States. The Cuban connection began to taper off in 1970 (for example, 96 per cent of the offenders in 1969 attempted to reach Cuba compared to 73, 64, and 25 per cent in the next three years) as information on the treatment of hijackers in Cuba became available in the United States, partly from hijackers who had voluntarily returned.

A new breed of hijackers, known as parajackers, appeared in late 1971. A parajacker demanded both ransom money and a parachute to escape from the seized aircraft. The first such individual, the alias "D. B. Cooper," parachuted en route to Reno with $200,000. Neither Cooper nor the ransom money has ever been found. This was followed by seventeen more attempts in which ransom demands averaged over $300,000. None were successful—five offenders were apprehended after their jumps, three were shot and killed, another was shot and captured, and eight more were captured. Of the eleven sentenced to prison (three others were committed to mental institutions), the average sentence was forty-three years. This was indeed a risky activity—one success in eighteen tries with severe penalties for failure—and by the end of 1972 the expected returns were sufficiently low to discourage any further attempts.[7]

FAA have attempted to keep the contents of the profile secret, some of the identifying characteristics have been published. These characteristics include males between the ages of 15 and 55, purchasers of one-way tickets, and persons paying in cash. See Douglas M. Kraus, Searching for Hijackers: Constitutionality, Costs, and Alternatives, 40 U. Chi. L. Rev. 383 (1973) for a discussion of the various security measures.

[6] The number of sky marshals today is less than 100, and only on rare occasions do they ride shotgun (see Trained and Ready: The Air Marshals Carry On, 6 FAA World 8 (1976)).

[7] All parachute jumps were from Boeing 727s and DC 9s. A modification on the rear door of these planes prevented their opening during flight. This greatly increased the risk of a jump and reduced the offender's expected return since he was likely to be hit by the plane as he exited

Finally, one might speculate on the sanity of hijackers in recent years in view of the low probabilities of success and the severe sanctions. To be sure, a substantial number of lunatics have engaged in this activity. Of the approximately seventy-two offenders apprehended (excluding seven juveniles), roughly one-quarter were sent to mental institutions (seventeen of seventy-two offenders). Yet the proportion committed to mental institutions is not very different in the period before 1973, when about 40 per cent of hijackers were apprehended, compared to the 1973-1976 period when all were apprehended. Two of twelve offenders in 1973-1976 were committed to mental institutions compared to fifteen of sixty in the earlier period, suggesting that lunatics are no less deterred by a high probability than other potential offenders.

The organization of the paper is as follows. Part II sets out the underlying deterrence model of the hijacking offense function. Part III describes the variables used in the study and presents several estimates of the offense function. Part III also attempts to distinguish between the deterrence and "fad" hypotheses as explanations of the time series behavior of hijacking. Part IV contains estimates both of the number of hijackings deterred since 1972 by the use of mandatory searches at airports and of the net costs of this security procedure relative to its benefits. Part V presents a summary of the results and concluding remarks. An appendix contains an empirical analysis of the determinants of the probability of apprehension and the severity of sanctions.

II. The Basic Deterrence Model

The economic approach to criminal behavior, which has been developed in the pioneering works of Becker[8] and Ehrlich,[9] assumes that persons choose between legal and illegal activities on the basis of expected utility maximization. Adapting this model to hijacking, I write the potential offender's expected utility from hijacking an aircraft from country i to j (i may be identical to j) as

$$\bar{U} = (1 - P_a)U(W_j) + P_a P_c U(W_i - S) + P_a(1 - P_c)U(W_j - C), \quad (1)$$

where P_a equals the offender's estimate of the probability of apprehension

---

from a forward door. Note that I have excluded from the class of parajackers offenders who had demanded ransom and a parachute but chose instead to divert the aircraft to Cuba or another country.

[8] See Gary S. Becker, Crime and Punishment: An Economic Approach, 76 J. Pol. Econ. 169 (1968).

[9] See Isaac Ehrlich, Participation in Illegitimate Activities: A Theoretical and Empirical Investigation, 81 J. Pol. Econ. 521 (1973).

(assumed to occur in i), P_c is the conditional probability (given apprehension) of conviction and incarceration, W_j and W_i the offender's wealth (including the monetary equivalent of nonpecuniary income) in country j and i respectively, S the monetary equivalent of the sentence in i, and C the monetary equivalent of the costs associated with apprehension when the offender is not sentenced (for example, detention awaiting trial, costs of probation, lawyer's fees). Letting $U = U(W_i)$ denote the utility from not attempting to seize an aircraft, the potential offender will commit or refrain from committing the offense depending on whether $\bar{U} \gtrless U$. Note that a necessary condition for $\bar{U} > U$ is that the offender's full wealth in j must be greater than in i (that is, $W_j > W_i$).[10]

Equation (1) implies that the greater P_a, P_c, S, and C, and the smaller the differential between W_j and $W_i (W_j > W_i)$, the lower $\bar{U}$ is and the less likely the offender is to attempt to hijack an aircraft. Aggregating among potential offenders, one can write the aggregate offense function in time t as

$$O = O(\bar{P}_a, \bar{P}_c, \bar{S}, \bar{C}, \bar{Z}, \bar{X}), \tag{2}$$

where $\bar{P}_a$, $\bar{P}_c$, $\bar{S}$, and $\bar{C}$ are the average values in period of t of the variables specified in equation (1), $\bar{Z}$ is a vector of variables denoting the average wealth differential between country j and i in period t, and $\bar{X}$ denotes the combined effect of other variables. The analysis predicts that the level of offenses in period t will be negatively related to the values of $\bar{P}_a$, $\bar{P}_c$, $\bar{S}$, and $\bar{C}$, and positively related to $\bar{Z}$.[11]

---

[10] To simplify the presentation I have assumed only two adverse outcomes: a sentence S if one is convicted, and costs C if one is apprehended but not convicted. Actually there are multiple adverse outcomes: the offender may be killed in the attempt; there may be a variety of sentences, including commitment to a mental institution; and the sentence may differ depending on the type of hijacking and the time the offender is apprehended. Further, the offender may be apprehended in country j and extradited to i for sentencing, or he may be both apprehended and sentenced in country j, contrary to our simplifying assumption that he is apprehended and convicted in country i. Moreover, there may be many possible wealth outcomes in j, not a single outcome. One could incorporate this feature into the analysis by substituting $(1 - P_a) \Sigma \pi_j U(W_j)$ in equation (1) where π_j denotes the probability of the jth outcome. This points out that *ex post* the offender may be worse off in j than i (for example, the offender's wealth in Cuba was less than expected) and yet *ex ante* the expected wealth in j was sufficiently greater than in i to make $\bar{U} > U$.

[11] A central feature of Ehrlich's analysis, the simultaneity between offenses and the probabilities of apprehension, conviction, and so forth, has not been used in this paper. In Ehrlich's analysis, for example, $\bar{P}_a$ is an endogenous variable that depends, in part, on the level of offenses. That is, given the level of law enforcement, an increase in offenses lowers the probability of apprehension since fewer resources are spent in attempting to apprehend the average offender. A priori the simultaneity problem does not appear important in this study. Two hijackings have never taken place at the same airport on the same day. Moreover, except on two occasions, hijackings have taken place on different days. Given the standby enforcement capability, the observed rate of hijacking (even at peak periods) would seem insufficient to strain the enforcement capacity and make the probability of apprehension a negative function of

III. EMPIRICAL ANALYSIS OF HIJACKING

A. *Discussion of Variables*

The major difficulty in estimating the aggregate offense function is the limited number of observations in the hijacking sample. Since an annual time series analysis would contain at most sixteen observations (1961-1976), I have chosen the following alternatives to annual data.

1. *Quarterly Hijackings (HJK)*. Although a quarterly time series substantially expands the number of observations to more than sixty, no hijackings took place in about half the quarters. It would be misleading to delete these quarters because the fact that no hijacking occurred is valuable information for a deterrence study. But since these quarters have no offenders, there is no direct information on the probability of apprehension and conditional probability of conviction. To deal with this problem, I have estimated quarterly regressions on the probability of apprehension and conditional probability of incarceration, filling in the missing quarters with the predicted values from the regression equation. A similar problem of missing observations arises in assigning sentences to each quarter. Data are available on the sentences of only fifty-six offenders in twenty-seven quarters. However, by approximating the anticipated sentence in a quarter as an average of four past quarters, sentence estimates for most quarters can be obtained. A second problem with quarterly data is that quarterly changes in the deterrence variables may contain a relatively large random component, tending to bias the regression coefficients toward zero. To reduce the error component and increase the reliability of the results, I have used moving averages of the deterrence variables.[12]

2. *Time Interval (TINT)*. An alternative method of estimating the frequency of hijacking is to order the 143 incidents according to the date of their occurrence and compute the time interval (in days) between successive hijackings. Since the reciprocal of the interval is an estimate of the probability of a hijacking on a given day,[13] one would predict this probability to fall

---

the rate of hijacking. One could plausibly argue the reverse. A larger number of offenses in a period would increase the precautionary measures undertaken by airport guards, ticket agents, pilots, attendants, and so forth in *that* period, tending to increase $\bar{P}_a$ in periods of peak hijackings. This in turn would bias downward estimates of deterrence effects. I have attempted to deal with this problem by utilizing lagged values of deterrence variables in the regression analysis.

[12] I also tested the possibility of a systematic seasonal factor in hijacking by including a set of dummy variables to denote the quarter. The dummy variables were insignificant (individually and taken as a set) and had negligible effects on the other independent variables. The reported regressions exclude the dummy seasonal variables.

[13] Let p = the daily probability of a hijacking, then the expected duration between two successive hijackings is

and the time interval between observations to lengthen in response to increases in the levels of deterrence.[14] The principal advantages of this approach are the expansion in the number of observations in the regression analysis and the availability of information on the apprehension and incarceration of the individuals involved. The disadvantage is that the more successful deterrence is, the smaller is the proportion of observations available to measure the response of offenders to deterrence. Imagine little change in the probability of apprehension prior to 1973 but a large increase that substantially eliminated hijackings after 1973. In this case, there would be relatively few observations with high probabilities of apprehension, making it difficult to observe a significant deterrent effect. In the limit, if deterrence fully eliminated hijacking, there would be no observation in the sample measuring this phenomenon. In contrast, a quarterly time series would still contain a large number of observations with both zero hijacking and a high estimated probability of apprehension.

3. *Flight Interval (FINT)*. A variant of the time interval is the number of air carrier flights between successive hijackings. Since the expected value of the latter interval equals the reciprocal of the probability a flight is hijacked, one expects a lengthening in the flight interval in response to an increase in the level of the deterrence variables. The number of flights between successive hijackings can be estimated from monthly data on air carrier flight operations, assuming a uniform monthly distribution of operations. Note that a flight operation is defined as either a takeoff or landing, and hence the number of flights is one-half the number of operations.

A discussion of the independent variables used to estimate the hijacking offense function is presented below. For convenience I have included Table 2, which presents a brief description of the variables in the empirical analysis.

3. *Probability of Apprehension $(P_a{}^h, P_a{}^o)$*. The following estimates of the offender's forecast of the probability of apprehension in quarter t were utilized:[15] (1) a moving average $(P_a{}^h)$ of the proportion of hijackings in which

---

$$E(TINT) = p(1) + (1 - p)p(2) + (1 - p)^2 p(3) + \ldots + (1 - p)^{n-1} p(n)$$
$$= p\, \partial[(1 - p)/p]/\partial(1 - p) = 1/p.$$

[14] Richard Quandt in two statistical studies of aircraft hijacking (see Richard E. Quandt, Some Statistical Characterizations of Aircraft Hijacking, 6 Accid. Anal. & Prev. 115 (1975); and Der-Ann Hsu & Richard E. Quandt, Statistical Analyses of Aircraft Hijacking and Political Assassinations (1976) (mimeo, Econometric Research Program, Princeton U.) used the time interval between successive hijackings (also called the interoccurrence time) to test and reject the hypothesis that the pattern of U.S. aircraft hijackings was generated by a homogeneous Poisson process. In the second paper, Quandt allowed the Poisson intensity period parameter to vary for each hijacking occurrence and speculated on reasons (for example, differences in deterrence) for variations in this parameter, but he did not systematically test the effects of deterrence or other variables.

[15] All estimates first require a continuous quarterly series on the probability of apprehension.

TABLE 2
DEFINITION OF VARIABLES

Variable Name	Definition	Mean	Standard Deviation
HJK	number of domestic hijackings per quarter	2.27	3.43
TINT	time interval (days) between successive hijackings	40.0	147.9
FINT	number of flights between successive hijackings (thousands)	486	1614
$P_a{}^h$, $\hat{P}_a{}^h$, $P_a{}^o$, $\hat{P}_a{}^o$	probability of apprehension within 4 quarters—hijacking (h), offenders (o), and predicted $(\hat{\ })$	.607 (h) .627 $(\hat{h})$ .590 (o) .608 $(\hat{o})$	.240 .212 .245 .218
P_c, $\hat{P}_c$	conditional probability of incarceration (*i.e.*, prison and mental institution)—predicted $(\hat{\ })$	.782 .793 $(\hat{\ })$	.141 .080
S, $\hat{S}$	average sentence of persons sentenced in 4 prior quarters (S) and predicted sentence in current quarter $(\hat{S})$	16.22 (S) 16.13 $(\hat{S})$	10.04
P_k	proportion of offenders killed in 3 prior quarters	.084	.231
OPER	air carrier flight operations per quarter (thousands)	2237	327
U	quarterly unemployment rate of civilian labor force, seasonally adjusted	5.29	1.36
POP	quarterly population (millions)	201	9.57
Y	quarterly per capita personal consumption expenditures—1972 dollars (thousands)	3.14	.393
FHJK	number of foreign hijackings per quarter	3.95	4.96
TIME	time in quarters		

Note: Means and standard deviations refer to quarterly values of variables 1st quarter 1961–3d quarter 1976, except for *TINT* and *FINT* variables.

Sources:

(1) Federal Aviation Administration (FAA), Civil Aviation Security Service, Domestic and Foreign Hijackings, as of July 1, 1976 (mimeo)—all variables except *OPER, U, POP, Y.*

(2) Monthly and quarterly data on *OPER* provided by *FAA.*

(3) *U* from U.S. Dep't of Labor, Monthly Labor Review (1962-76).

(4) *POP* from various vols. of Bureau of the Census, Current Population Reports (1961-76).

(5) *Y* from various years of the Economic Report of the President (1963-77).

offenders were apprehended in quarters $t-1$, $t-2$, and $t-3$; (2) a moving average $(P_a{}^o)$ of the proportion of offenders apprehended in quarters $t-1$, $t-2$, and $t-3$;[16] (3) the predicted value $(\hat{P}_a{}^h)$ estimated from a linear regres-

---

Missing quarters were estimated from a regression on the probability of apprehension with the following independent variables: the number of offenders per hijacking, the size of the flight crew, age and age-squared of offenders, flight operations, dummy variables for the period when air marshals were riding shotgun and for the period when mandatory searches were required, and time. Missing values were then filled in by using the mean values for offenders, flight crew, age, age square, and the actual values for the two dummy variables. For further discussion see the Appendix.

[16] To illustrate the difference between estimates (1) and (2), consider the following example. Suppose two hijackings occur in quarter t and there is one offender in the first not apprehended

sion of $P_a{}^h$ in t on the probabilities in the three previous quarters; and (4) the predicted value $(\hat{P}_a{}^g)$ estimated as in (3). In addition, when (3) and (4) are utilized, I tested the hypothesis that the residual from the actual probability in period t is unanticipated and, therefore, has no deterrent effect.

4. *Conditional Probability of Incarceration* $(P_c, \hat{P}_c)$. This is defined as the proportion of offenders apprehended (excluding those killed) who were either sentenced to prison or committed to a mental institution.[17] Two estimates of the conditional probability in quarter t were utilized. P_c is a moving average of the conditional probabilities in quarters $t-1$, $t-2$, and $t-3$, and $\hat{P}_c$ is the predicted value of the conditional probability from a regression of the conditional probability in quarter t on the three previous quarters.

5. *Sentence* $(S, \hat{S})$. The average sentence expected by the potential hijacker in quarter t is approximated either by the average sentence (S) of all persons sentenced in the four quarters prior to t or by the predicted sentences $(\hat{S})$ from a simple regression of S in the current quarter on its value in the previous quarter. Observe that persons sentenced in quarter t may have committed offenses in any of the previous quarters. The most extreme example is the first offender (May 1961), who was arrested fourteen years later in 1975 and sentenced to twenty years. His twenty-year sentence is included in the first quarter of 1976 for purposes of computing the average sentence.[18] Note that the theoretically correct variable is the actual time served, not the sentence. Since data on actual time served are unavailable because of recent long sentences, one must use sentences, implicitly assuming they are proportional to time served.

6. *Conditional Probability of Death* (P_k). I indicated earlier that offend-

---

and three offenders in the second all apprehended. The proportion of offenders apprehended (estimate (2)) equals .75 while the proportion of hijackings in which offenders are apprehended (estimate (1)) equals .50. A priori it is not clear which method is preferable. One could argue that as a first approximation there would be no difference between the two in equilibrium because, if there was, potential offenders would adjust the number involved in a given hijacking. If the full costs of planning a multiple-offender hijacking were greater, then the equilibrium probability would tend to vary negatively with the number of offenders. We take up this question in the Appendix. Fortunately, the offender and hijacking apprehension probabilities are highly correlated (about .99) and the results are generally unaffected by which of the two sets of estimates are included in the offense function.

[17] Since observations on the conditional probability are available for only 27 quarters, values for the missing quarters were estimated using the coefficients from a regression on the conditional probability in the 27 quarters with data. Unfortunately, with the exception of time, the variables in this regression (number of offenders, degree of success of the hijacking, race and age of offender, presence of extortion, and apprehension outside the United States) all require data that are obviously not available for the missing quarters. Thus, missing values were estimated using the constant, time, and the mean values of the remaining variables. Therefore, my estimates of the conditional probability are probably subject to sizable error.

[18] When the date of arrest is given but not the date of sentence, I assumed that the offender was sentenced in the quarter following his arrest. This assumption corresponds to the typical lag between arrest and sentencing when information on both is available.

ers, at least after 1971, faced non-negligible probabilities of being shot and killed during the attempted hijacking. To the extent that this event is anticipated, it would reduce the expected gains and hence the incentive to commit hijacking. One can test this hypothesis by including in the offense function a variable measuring the conditional risk of death in each quarter (P_k). The latter is approximated by the ratio of offenders killed to the number apprehended in the prior three quarters.[19]

7. *Flight Operations (OPER)*. In order to standardize for the opportunities to hijack an airplane or alternatively for the number of potential "victims," I included in the offense function the number of air carrier operations per quarter. Other things constant, the greater the opportunities, the greater the number of hijackings. The potential importance of distinguishing opportunities from deterrence is illustrated by the fact that flight operations were sharply cut back beginning in the fall of 1973 (which coincided with increases in the probability of apprehension) in response to the oil price rise and the economic recession.

8. *Population (POP)*. Just as flight operations measure changes in the supply of potential "victims," one would also like to include an estimate of changes in the supply of potential offenders. Quarterly estimates of the population were included in the offense function to approximate changes in the underlying supply of offenders.[20]

9. *Economic Variables (U, Y)*. The theoretical analysis predicts that the incentive to engage in illegal relative to legal activities depends on the differential returns between the two. Although direct observations on the differential are not available, unemployment (U) and per capita personal consumption expenditures (Y) in the United States may roughly measure this differential. Other things constant, a reduction in U and an increase in Y would indicate improved legal opportunities and should reduce the number of hijackings. Two obvious problems, however, are associated with these measures. Changes in U and Y in the United States may be correlated with similar changes outside the United States. Thus, persons planning to leave the United States would be unresponsive to changes in U and Y. Secondly, changes in U reflect mainly cyclical, not permanent or long-run, changes in economic conditions, whereas the theoretical analysis stresses permanent changes. This is particularly important since a decision to seize an aircraft and leave the country often means a permanent and irreversible wealth

[19] Thus, P_k is zero for all quarters through the third quarter of 1971, in which the first hijacker was shot and killed.

[20] A better measure of potential hijackers is males over eighteen years of age since hijackers are primarily from this subgroup. Quarterly data on this subgroup are not available, although one can approximate quarterly values from quarterly data on the entire population. Although there is little gain from this approach, I experimented with it in several regressions and found negligible differences compared to the *POP* variable.

change. In contrast, other illegal activities within the United States may be highly responsive to cyclical changes since one can exit and enter the legal market as economic conditions change. For this reason I used consumption expenditures instead of current income as a rough measure of permanent income.

B. *Quarterly Results*

Table 3 presents estimates of linear regressions on the number of U.S. hijackings per quarter from 1961 to 1976.[21] Equations (1) and (4)-(6) are modified first differences, estimated via the Cochrane-Orcutt technique, and for comparative purposes I include a first-difference (eq. (2)) and a level (eq. (3)) equation.

Despite obvious shortcomings in the data (for example, the use of quarterly changes and missing quarterly values of deterrence variables), the findings strongly support the deterrence hypothesis. The probability of apprehension ($P_a{}^h$, $P_a{}^o$, $\hat{P}_a{}^h$, and $\hat{P}_a{}^o$) has a negative and highly significant effect in all equations. Moreover, the magnitude of this effect is substantial. To illustrate, an increase in the probability from .75 to .95, which corresponds approximately to the observed increase from 1972 to 1973-1976, is associated with 1.1 to 2.2 fewer hijackings per quarter in Table 3. The regression coefficients on the conditional probability of incarceration (P_c and $\hat{P}_c$) are also negative but generally less significant (as expected in view of the relatively small variation in this variable).[22] Here an increase of .10 in the conditional probability reduces the number of hijackers between .5 and 1.3 per quarter. Similarly, an increase in the sentence is associated with a statistically significant reduction in the number of offenses. For example, a ten-year increase leads to .8 to 1.6 fewer offenses per quarter. Although the conditional probability of being shot and killed (P_k) has a negative effect in all equations, it is at best marginally significant. The lack of significance may be due to probable errors in estimating P_k that arise, in part, from the circumstances surrounding the killing of offenders. An analysis of the seven offenders killed reveals that four were involved in shoot-outs with law enforcement authorities in which other persons were either wounded or killed. Possibly, these offenders could have avoided being killed if they had chosen

[21] A logarithmic transformation of the variables is typically used in other empirical estimates of offense functions (see Isaac Ehrlich, *supra* note 9). I have not used it here because of the large number (32) of quarters in which there were zero hijackings. The latter suggests that a Tobit analysis, where one estimates both the probability of a hijacking occurring and the frequency of hijackings, would have been appropriate for the quarterly hijacking data. However, I have not estimated any offense functions using the Tobit method.

[22] The small variation (for example, the coefficient of variation averages about .2) is due to the method of estimating values for missing quarters where the only source of variation was time (see note 17 *supra*).

TABLE 3

QUARTERLY HIJACKINGS (HJK), FOURTH QUARTER 1961–THIRD QUARTER 1976,
MODIFIED FIRST DIFFERENCES, FIRST DIFFERENCES AND LEVELS
(t-values in parentheses)

Independent Variables	(1) CORC ($\hat{\rho} = .589$)	(2) OLS ($\hat{\rho} = 1$)	(3) OLS ($\hat{\rho} = 0$)	(4) CORC ($\hat{\rho} = .577$)	(5) CORC ($\hat{\rho} = .659$)	(6) CORC ($\hat{\rho} = .642$)
P_a^h	−11.110 (3.040)	−9.708 (2.327)	−10.958 (2.961)			
P_a^o				−10.743 (3.112)		
$\hat{P}_a^h$					−5.783 (2.010)	
$\hat{P}_a^o$						−5.374 (2.074)
P_c	−6.867 (1.518)	−7.654 (1.762)	−4.742 (.998)	−6.424 (1.442)		
$\hat{P}_c$					−12.730 (2.334)	−10.867 (1.986)
S	−.129 (2.265)	−.163 (2.609)	−.082 (1.580)	−.139 (2.446)		
$\hat{S}$					−.140 (2.075)	−.147 (2.184)
P_k	−1.319 (.812)	−1.288 (.826)	−2.347 (1.212)	−1.490 (.917)	−1.430 (.887)	−1.481 (.915)
OPER	−.002 (.802)	−.004 (1.228)	.0002 (.061)	−.003 (.850)	−.001 (.363)	−.001 (.327)
POP	1.333 (1.142)	.822 (.354)	.870 (1.210)	1.141 (.986)	1.837 (1.433)	1.805 (1.452)
U	1.177 (1.456)	1.204 (1.252)	1.204 (2.056)	1.155 (1.444)	1.091 (1.285)	1.152 (1.373)
Y	10.684 (.979)	11.859 (.986)	9.717 (1.136)	8.700 (.799)	11.079 (.992)	10.778 (.970)
TIME	−.685 (.989)		−.480 (1.028)	−.553 (.797)	−1.007 (1.374)	−.999 (1.398)
Constant	−264.2 (1.181)	−.514 (.388)	−182.9 (1.309)	−223.7 (1.006)	−357.4 (1.966)	−352.7 (1.490)
R^2			.56			
D.W.	1.84	2.16	.96	1.82	1.83	1.84
Number of Observations	59	59	60	59	59	59

Note: For equations (1), (4), (5), and (6) all variables (X) are of the form $X_t - \hat{\rho} X_{t-1}$, where $\hat{\rho}$ is estimated via the Cochrane-Orcutt iterative procedure (CORC).

not to engage in a gun battle. This suggests that the observation that prior offenders were killed (which determines the estimated value P_k) would not necessarily increase the current offender's estimate of P_k, providing he chose not to engage in a gun battle. Finally, observe that the elasticities, computed at the mean values, of the deterrence variables (with the exception of P_k) are relatively large—1.4 to 3.0 for P_a, 1.6 to 4.5 (the latter for the $\hat{P}_c$ estimate), and .6 to 1.2 for the sentence.

As a further test of the deterrence hypothesis, I reestimated equations (5) and (6) entering the residuals (that is, the actual minus the predicted values of $\hat{P}_a$, $\hat{P}_c$, and $\hat{S}$) of the deterrence variables as independent variables. Since one can interpret the residuals as the unsystematic or nonforecasted component, I would not expect them to have any significant deterrent effect. Not only was each residual insignificant but jointly they were also insignificant.

In contrast to the findings on deterrence, the nondeterrence variables have no highly significant effects on the number of quarterly hijackings. The regression coefficients on population (POP) and unemployment (U) are in the predicted direction and sometimes marginally significant. The coefficients on flight operations ($OPER$) are negative in five equations and insignificant in all six. Per capita consumption (Y) is positive but always insignificant. The time trend variable is negative but never significant.

C. Time Interval Results

Table 4 presents regression equations on the natural logarithm of both the time interval (equations (1) and (2)) and flight interval (equations (3) and (4)) between successive hijackings. The effects of the deterrence variables in these equations are similar to their effects on quarterly hijackings. Increases in the probability of apprehension, the conditional probability of incarceration, and sentence are generally associated with statistically significant increases in the time and flight intervals between successive offenses,[23] which in turn translates into a reduction in the number of hijackings per time period.[24] To illustrate, an increase in the probability of apprehension of .2 lengthens the time interval (at its mean value) from 40 days to between 58 and 66 days—which is equivalent to a .7 to .9 decline in hijackings per quarter (that is, from about 2.3 to between 1.6 and 1.4). This compares to the 1.1 and 2.2 reduction estimated from the quarterly regressions of Table 3. Similarly, a ten-year increase in the average sentence is associated with a .6 reduction in hijackings per quarter (from 2.3 to 1.7), compared to a .8 to 1.6 estimated reduction in Table 3. The remaining deterrence variable, the conditional probability of being killed, is insignificant in all regressions in Table 4.

All the other variables in Table 4 are significant except flight operations.[25]

[23] To economize on space, Table 4 does not contain results on the alternative measure of the probability of apprehension ($P_a{}''$ and $\hat{P}_a{}''$) used in Table 3. The results on $P_a{}''$ and $\hat{P}_a{}''$, however, are virtually identical to those on $P_a{}^h$ and $\hat{P}_a{}^h$.

[24] It also follows, therefore, that an increase in the deterrence variables reduces the probability of a hijacking on both a given day and flight (see note 13 *supra*).

[25] Flight operations are not included as an independent variable in the flight interval analysis since the flight interval equals *TINT* multiplied by the average number of daily flights during the time interval.

TABLE 4
Time Interval (*TINT*) and Flight Interval (*FINT*) Between Successive
Hijackings: OLS Regressions, Fourth Quarter 1961–Third Quarter 1976
(*t*-values in parentheses)

Independent Variables	TINT		FINT	
	(1)	(2)	(3)	(4)
P_a^h	3.309		3.348	
	(3.779)		(4.120)	
$\hat{P}_a^h$		2.262		2.412
		(2.678)		(3.010)
P_c	2.647		2.634	
	(1.989)		(1.995)	
$\hat{P}_c$		4.259		4.203
		(2.381)		(2.355)
S	.033		.034	
	(1.789)		(1.927)	
$\hat{S}$		.033		.037
		(1.582)		(1.794)
P_k	−.700	.103	−.523	.450
	(.373)	(.054)	(.286)	(.241)
OPER	−.002	−.003		
	(.697)	(1.131)		
POP	−.740	−.830	−.750	−.860
	(3.160)	(3.352)	(3.340)	(3.580)
U	−.760	−.603	−.740	−.541
	(3.487)	(2.679)	(3.790)	(2.704)
Y	−10.073	−9.861	−9.955	−9.420
	(3.077)	(2.979)	(3.147)	(2.934)
TIME	.180	.195	.180	.193
	(4.067)	(4.300)	(4.078)	(4.280)
Constant	168.0	183.4	177.4	194.7
	(3.839)	(3.999)	(4.130)	(4.297)
R^2	.31	.30	.29	.28
D.W.	1.80	1.80	1.80	1.81
Number of Observations	140	140	140	140

Notes: (1) *TINT* and *FINT* in natural logarithms.
(2) Independent variables estimated for the quarter in which the hijacking occurred.

Increases in unemployment, which roughly measures a reduction in current legal opportunities, and population, which approximates an increase in potential offenders, reduce the time and flight intervals between successive hijackings. Increases in time (the time trend variable) lengthen the time and flight intervals over time. These results are consistent with the quarterly results on unemployment, population, and time though the coefficients in Table 3 were not significant. Per capita consumption, which has positive effects on the time and flight intervals, is the only variable in Table 4 whose results differ significantly from the predictions of the theoretical analysis.

D. *The Fad Hypothesis*

It is claimed that the pattern of aircraft hijacking in both the United States and abroad can only be understood as a manifestation of a world-wide fad. According to this hypothesis, the concentration of more than 75 per cent of world hijackings since 1961 in the 1968-to-1972 period resulted from a shift in preferences in 1968 in which hijacking became a fashionable form of behavior among a certain class of individuals. Since fads tend to be of short duration as preferences shift, the subsequent decline in hijacking after 1972 is viewed as further evidence to support the fad hypothesis.[26] Implicitly, this approach rejects or greatly discounts the importance of changes in the probability of apprehension and other measures of deterrence to explain the hijacking time series. Thus, the fad hypothesis would interpret the negative association between deterrence variables and hijackings in Tables 3 and 4 as due to a coincidence between changes in deterrence levels and the intensity of the hijacking fad. Although the reliance on fad to interpret hijacking is tautological (that is, when hijacking rises it is fashionable and when it falls it is unfashionable) and a concession that the phenomenon defies rational explanation, it is possible nevertheless to develop an independent estimate of the intensity of this fad. This estimate can then be incorporated into the preceding empirical analysis to differentiate between the deterrence and fad hypotheses.

Suppose the number of hijackings *outside* the United States is included as an independent variable in the U.S. quarterly regressions. On the assumption that hijacking was a world-wide fad, the number of foreign hijackings would approximate variations in the intensity of this fad: that is, when foreign hijackings increased (decreased) the fad was gaining (losing) momentum. Therefore, by holding constant foreign hijackings in the U.S. regressions, one would be able to estimate deterrence effects not confounded by a fad effect. There is, however, an obvious difficulty with this approach. To the extent that U.S. and foreign deterrence levels are positively correlated, variations in foreign hijackings due to changes in deterrence levels in foreign countries would imply similar changes in U.S. deterrence levels. This positive correlation, in turn, would tend to weaken and possibly eliminate the significance of the U.S. deterrence variables.[27]

[26] For an alternative analysis of faddish behavior that assumes unchanging preferences, see George J. Stigler & Gary S. Becker, De Gustibus Non Est Disputandum, 67 Am. Econ. Rev. 76 (1977).

[27] There is evidence of a positive correlation between U.S. and foreign deterrence levels. For example, screening of passengers and searching carryon baggage was instituted in both the United States and some foreign countries in the 1970s, and multi-country treaties were entered into that call for the extradition of hijackers. Further, the correlation between the probability of apprehension in the United States and the rest of the world is about .4 for the quarters between 1961 and 1976.

An alternative test of the fad hypothesis is to substitute foreign for domestic hijackings as the *dependent variable* in the regressions of Table 3. If hijacking is a world-wide fad, and thus the observed negative relationship between deterrence variables and U.S. hijackings is largely coincidental, one should find that the U.S. deterrence variables have about the same impact and degree of significance on the foreign variable as they do on U.S. hijackings. If so, this would suggest that the original deterrence findings in Table 3 are spurious (ignoring the positive correlation between U.S. and foreign deterrence variables). On the other hand, the deterrence hypothesis asserts that the deterrence variables would have their main impact on U.S. hijackings and a substantially weaker impact on foreign hijackings.[28]

Table 5 presents the results of these two tests of the fad hypothesis. The most striking finding of equations (1) and (2), which include foreign hijack-

TABLE 5
QUARTERLY REGRESSIONS WITH FOREIGN HIJACKING (*FHJK*) VARIABLE
MODIFIED FIRST DIFFERENCE AND LEVELS
(*t*-values in parentheses)

| Independent Variables | U.S. Hijacking (*HJK*) | | Foreign Hijacking (*FHJK*) |
	CORC ($\hat{\rho} = .549$) (1)	OLS (2)	OLS (3)
$P_a{}^h$	−9.770	−11.140	.684
	(2.904)	(3.309)	(.113)
P_c	−2.654	−5.153	1.546
	(.606)	(1.192)	(.199)
S	−.099	−.081	−.004
	(1.888)	(1.715)	(.047)
P_k	−1.592	−1.909	−1.649
	(1.055)	(1.081)	(.519)
FHJK	.216	.265	
	(3.150)	(3.381)	
R^2		.64	.43
D.W.	1.67	.98	1.74
Number of Observations	59	60	60

Note: All regressions also include as independent variables *OPER, POP, U, Y,* and *TIME.* To simplify the tables, these coefficients are not presented.

[28] Two other possibilities must be considered. First one might still find significant effects of U.S. deterrence variables on foreign hijackings if U.S. and foreign deterrence levels are strongly correlated. Second, substitution between U.S. and foreign hijacking may take place. For example, an increase in the level of deterrence in the United States might induce persons to switch to the hijacking of aircraft in foreign countries. Thus, the net effect of U.S. deterrence variables on foreign hijackings depends on the relative strength of two offsetting effects. The fad hypothesis, however, predicts a negative effect, given that one has already observed a negative effect in the U.S. regressions of Table 3.

ings (denoted by *FHJK*) as an independent variable, is that the magnitude and significance of the deterrence variables, with the exception of the conditional probability of incarceration (P_c), are comparable to their values when the *FHJK* variable is excluded from the analysis (compare equations (1) and (2) in Table 5 to equations (1) and (2) in Table 3). Although *FHJK* is positive and highly significant in Table 5, its interpretation remains ambiguous.[29] Assuming, however, that the coefficient on *FHJK* reflects the existence of a world-wide fad, one can then compare the relative magnitude of the fad and deterrence effects as follows. The coefficients of the *FHJK* variable indicate, for example, that if the intensity of the fad had been reduced by half during the peak years 1968 to 1972 (that is, if foreign hijackings had been 87 instead of 174), there would have been between 19 and 23 fewer hijackings in the United States or approximately a 15 to 19 per cent reduction. In contrast, if the probability of apprehension had been equal to .8 throughout this five-year period instead of its average value of .45, there would have been between 68 and 78 fewer domestic hijackings or a reduction of between 55 and 63 per cent. This comparison suggests that the initial findings on the importance of deterrence in explaining aircraft hijacking is still correct.

Of further interest is regression equation (3) of Table 5 in which *FHJK* is the dependent variable. The fad hypothesis implies that one should find significant negative effects of U.S. deterrence variables on *FHJK* since the relationship between U.S. hijackings and deterrence is alleged to be spurious. This prediction is strongly rejected since two of the four regression coefficients on the deterrence variables are positive and none are statistically significant.[30]

---

[29] The positive regression coefficient on *FHJK* may reflect a fad or an unmeasured component of deterrence in the United States due to the positive correlation between levels of deterrence in the United States and foreign countries.

[30] I have not experimented with testing the fad hypothesis on the time interval analysis because of the difficulty of defining the relevant foreign hijacking variable. I also performed one additional test on the foreign hijacking variable. Although it is not possible to estimate a complete equation on foreign hijackings—because foreign data on both the deterrence variables (for example, sentence, incarceration, and so forth) and other variables used in the U.S. offense function are not available—one can estimate foreign hijackings as a function of the foreign probability of apprehension and time. The CORC regression estimates for 63 quarters from 1961-1976 are as follows

$$FHJK = 4.533 - 5.297 FP_a{}^h + .086\ TIME \qquad D.W. = 2.24\ n = 62$$
$$(1.690)\quad (1.940)\qquad\ (1.761)$$

$$FHJK = 4.966 - 6.334\ FP_a{}^o + .082\ TIME \qquad D.W. = 2.21\ n = 62$$
$$(2.072)\quad (2.661)\qquad\ (1.710)$$

where $FP_a{}^h$ and $FP_a{}^o$ are respectively the moving averages (prior three quarters) of the probability of apprehension for hijacking and offenders respectively. The above results indicate a significant negative effect of the probability of apprehension on foreign hijackings.

IV. ANTIHIJACKING MEASURES: COSTS AND BENEFITS

The apparent success of public and private policies in drastically reducing the number of hijackings since 1973, the first year of mandatory preboarding searches of all passengers and carryon luggage, raises the questions of how many hijackings were deterred and at what cost?

Before turning to the empirical analysis of these questions, it is useful to consider first the relationship between deterrence and security measures.

A. *Ex Ante and Ex Post Deterrence*

There are two interrelated ways in which security measures deter offenders—for convenience I label them *ex ante* and *ex post* deterrence. Screening passengers at airports for weapons is an example of *ex ante* deterrence. Effective screening means that some potential hijackers are apprehended prior to boarding an aircraft. Therefore, screening lowers the expected returns from hijacking and, other things constant, reduces the number of these offenses.[31] If some offenders are able to avoid detection at the screening stage, however, the subsequent probability of apprehension, which is the probability observed in the hijacking sample, might not be any higher than prior to the imposition of screening. One might observe, for example, a large decline in hijackings (due to mandatory screening) without any increase in the measured probability of apprehension. If this were the case, a finding of no significant effect of the probability of apprehension in the earlier regression analysis need not imply rejection of the deterrence hypothesis. A significant number of prospective offenders might still have been deterred by the unobserved increase in the probability of apprehension at the screening stage.[32]

Ex post deterrence refers to the response of potential offenders to an increase in the probability of apprehension during or after the commission of

[31] Note that the deterrence hypothesis predicts that the total reduction in hijackings due to screening would be a multiple of the number of hijackings aborted at this stage; otherwise, the behavior of potential offenders would be unresponsive to the increase in expected costs from screening. That is, if the total reduction in offenses were identical to the number aborted at the screening stage, then the hypothesis that potential offenders are deterred by higher expected costs would be rejected.

[32] To illustrate, let the number of hijackings be a negative function of the probability of apprehension (P^h) defined as

$$P^h = P_{ms}{}^h + (1 - P_{ms}{}^h) P_a{}^h,$$

where $P_{ms}{}^h$ is the probability of apprehension at the mandatory screening stage and $P_a{}^h$ is the probability of apprehension once the hijacking is in progress (usually when the hijacker is aboard the aircraft). Obviously, P^h will rise and hijackings will fall when $P_{ms}{}^h$ increases while $P_a{}^h$ remains constant (or even falls slightly). $P_{ms}{}^h$, however, is not directly observable. The probability of apprehension utilized in the empirical analysis is $P_a{}^h$ because an offense is only recorded as a hijacking if the offender avoids detection at the mandatory screening stage.

the hijacking. High *ex post* deterrence is associated, for example, with sky marshals trained to apprehend hijackers once the offense is in progress, or with the treaty between the United States and Cuba in which persons successfully diverting an aircraft to Cuba are now apprehended and returned to the United States. In both instances, the measured probability of apprehension would increase ($P_a{}^h$ in footnote 32), and the deterrence hypothesis would predict a decline in offenses. Mandatory screening, however, is also likely to affect *ex post* deterrence because the credibility of an offender's threat to harm hostages, and so forth during an attempted hijacking will be weakened by the prospect that he is bluffing and has no effective means to carry out his threat (if he did, how would he have gotten through the screening procedure?).[33]

One can attempt to sort out the *ex post* and *ex ante* deterrent effects by reestimating regressions on a subsample of observations ending in the fourth quarter of 1972. Since this subsample excludes the mandatory screening period, the estimated effects of the deterrent variables are not confounded with the effects of the electronic screening procedure. Put differently, the measured response of potential offenders to a change in the probability of apprehension in the sample period ending in 1972 is net of any increment in *ex ante* deterrence associated with mandatory screening.[34]

Table 6 contains regression equations for the period prior to mandatory screening. Equations (1) and (2) are quarterly time series estimates and should be compared to equation (1) in Tables 3 and 5 that are estimated over the entire sample period ending in 1976. Equations (3) and (4) utilize the time and flight interval variables respectively and should be compared to equations (1) and (3) in Table 4. The relevant comparisons indicate that both the magnitude and statistical significance of the regression coefficients of the various deterrence variables in Table 6 are nearly identical to the estimates

[33] Some casual evidence on this phenomenon can be extracted from the hijacking incidents that took place after the screening procedure went into effect in 1973. In two of the ten recorded hijackings, the offenders were armed but boarded out-of-service aircraft without going through the screening procedure. In another there was a gun battle in the terminal prior to the screening and the offender subsequently boarded the aircraft. Of the remaining seven, all involving persons claiming to be armed, five had no weapons when they were apprehended. This is in sharp contrast to the 27 hijackings in 1972 in which there is no evidence that any of the offenders were not armed. See Federal Aviation Administration–Civil Aviation Security Service, Chronology of Hijackings of U.S. Registered Aircraft and Current Legal Status of Hijackers, as of July 1, 1976 (mimeo). Note that a possible offset to the claim that screening raises the measured probability of apprehension ($P_a{}^h$) is that only the more skillful offender is able to avoid being detected at the time of screening. Therefore, one would have a biased sample of offenders after screening was imposed—that is, offenders whose measured probability of apprehension was lower than that of the average offender.

[34] *Ex ante* deterrence was still a factor before the imposition of mandatory screening procedures. For example, passengers meeting a behavioral profile of a hijacker were searched beginning in 1970, and some airlines searched all passengers and carryon luggage.

TABLE 6

QUARTERLY HIJACKINGS (*HJK*), TIME INTERVAL (*TINT*)
AND FLIGHT INTERVAL (*FINT*) REGRESSIONS
FOURTH QUARTER 1961–FOURTH QUARTER 1972

Independent Variables	HJK		TINT	FINT
	(1) $(\hat\rho = .468)$	(2) $(\hat\rho = .464)$	(3) OLS	(4) OLS
$P_a{}^h$	−12.021	−10.517	3.388	3.422
	(2.896)	(2.616)	(3.766)	(4.042)
P_c	−6.406	−3.054	2.661	2.641
	(1.203)	(.574)	(2.040)	(2.041)
S	−.204	−.155	.041	.042
	(2.381)	(1.823)	(2.020)	(2.122)
$FHJK$		.198		
		(2.119)		
R^2	—	—	.20	.20
$D.W.$	1.76	1.61	1.86	1.86
$S.E.$	2.290	2.184	1.109	1.104
n	44	44	129	129

Note: Equations (1)-(4) also include the following independent variables: *UNEM, Y, POP, OPER* (excluded from equation (4)), and *TIME, TINT,* and *FINT* variables are in natural logarithms.

based on the full sample.[35] This shows (somewhat surprisingly) that the earlier findings on the significance of deterrence variables are not sensitive to the exclusion of the 1973-to-1976 period.[36]

One can use the regression coefficients of Table 6 to forecast the number of additional hijackings that would have taken place between 1973 and 1976 if (a) mandatory screening of passengers and carryon baggage had not been in force, and (b) the probability of apprehension had not increased after 1972 but instead had remained equal to its 1972 level of .81 (in part, due to the assumed absence of screening). Estimates of the number of additional hijackings, presented in column (1) of Table 7, range from 41 to 60 or an average of 2.7 to 4.0 more offenses per quarter during the 1973-to-1976 period.[37] That is, absent mandatory screening and assuming that the proba-

[35] I have also reestimated equations for the 1961-1972 period using alternative measures of the probability of apprehension, sentence, and so forth that were presented in earlier tables. These measures are not presented here because the regression coefficients and *t*-values were nearly identical to the estimates based on the full sample period. Note that the conditional probability of being killed (the P_k variable) is not included in the 1961-1972 equations because no one was killed until the third quarter of 1971.

[36] One might have expected the deletion of the 1973-1976 period to weaken greatly the effect of the deterrence variables because this period was one of few hijackings and relatively high values of the probability of apprehension.

[37] To compute the predicted values I used the 1961-1972 regression coefficients and the actual 1973-to-1976 quarterly values of all variables except the probability of apprehension. The latter is set equal to its 1972 value of .81. The actual number of hijackings that occurred in each

TABLE 7
PREDICTED NUMBER OF ADDITIONAL HIJACKINGS
FIRST QUARTER 1973–THIRD QUARTER 1976

| | Additional Hijackings, Probability of Apprehension 1972 Level | Probability of Apprehension = Estimated Values '73-'76 | | Probability of Apprehension = .98 in '73-'76 | |
| | | *Ex Ante* Deterrence | *Ex Post* Deterrence | *Ex Ante* Deterrence | *Ex Post* Deterrence |
Regression	(1)	(2)	(3)	(4)	(5)
OLS	60	41	19	33	27
CORC	67	46	21	37	30
OLS (foreign hijackings included)	41	21	20	12	29
CORC (foreign hijackings included)	50	32	18	24	26

Notes: 1. Estimates based on quarterly hijacking regressions from fourth quarter 1961–fourth quarter 1972. Note that the OLS coefficients on the deterrence variables were nearly identical to the CORC coefficients in Table 6 though the significant levels of the former were slightly lower.
2. The 1972 value of the probability of apprehension $(P_a{}^h)$ equals .81.

bility of apprehension remained at its 1972 level, total hijackings in the United States would have been between 52 and 71 compared to the 11 hijackings that actually occurred between 1973 and the third quarter of 1976. As expected, the lower range of estimates (41 and 50) in column (1) of Table 7 occur when foreign hijackings is included as an independent variable in the regression equation. Since the regression coefficient of the foreign hijacking variable is positive (Table 6) and the hijacking fad, measured by foreign hijackings, diminished after 1973 compared to the 1968-to-1972 period, the predicted number of hijackings after 1973 tends to fall when foreign hijackings is included in the U.S. hijacking regressions.[38]

Previously, I discussed the distinction between *ex ante* and *ex post* deterrence. *Ex ante* is primarily associated with screening procedures and *ex post* with measures that increase the likelihood of apprehension once the hijacking is in progress. One can partition the estimated reduction in hijackings

quarter from 1973 to 1976 is then subtracted from the predicted number to estimate the number of additional hijackings that would have taken place absent screening and assuming a probability of apprehension of .81.

[38] By including foreign hijacking in the regression equation, however, one probably understates the number of additional U.S. hijackings that would have taken place after 1972. Foreign hijackings declined, in part, between 1973 and 1976 because of an increase in the probability of apprehension abroad. But this increase is positively correlated with an increase in the probability of apprehension in the United States. Thus, foreign hijacking picks up the effect of an increased probability of apprehension in the United States, violating the assumption of a constant probability of apprehension between 1973 and 1976 equal to its 1972 value.

(column (1) of Table 7) into its *ex ante* and *ex post* components by predicting, as before, the number of offenses per quarter beginning in 1973 but letting the probability of apprehension take its actual value in each quarter, not its 1972 value. The differences between the predicted and actual hijackings now measures the reduction *not* explained by the subsequent increase in the probability of apprehension between 1972 and 1973-1976. Column (2) of Table 7 contains these estimates of *ex ante* deterrence. *Ex post* deterrence (column (3)) is simply the difference between the estimates in columns (1) and (2).[39] For purposes of comparison I also computed an upper limit of the importance of *ex post* deterrence by assuming that the offender's estimate of the probability of apprehension equaled .98 in all quarters beginning in 1973.[40] This modification produces an increase in *ex post* deterrence of about nine hijackings (compare columns (3) and (5) of Table 7).

Overall, the impact of *ex ante* deterrence on reducing the number of hijackings since 1973 appears to be greater than that of *ex post* deterrence; the former accounting for about 55 per cent of the number of hijackings deterred in the 1973 to 1976 period. (The one exception is the estimate in row 3 of columns (4) and (5) of Table 7.) This result is not surprising because of the already high (.81) probability of apprehension in 1972. Thus increases in the probability, even with a relatively large response by potential offenders, would at most reduce the number of offenses by three per quarter. Of further interest is the relative importance of the treaty with Cuba. If the treaty were the sole cause of the increased probability of apprehension between 1973 and 1976, then columns (3) and (5) would measure the treaty's impact. Surely, this would overstate the impact since the increased probability in 1973 to 1976 was in part due to the greater likelihood that offenders were unarmed (that is, the screening effect). There is another reason, however, for believing the *ex post* estimates in columns (3) and (5) exceed the effect of the treaty: the number of offenders attempting to reach Cuba had sharply fallen between 1969 and 1972 (from more than 95 per cent to 25 per cent). Assuming that the latter proportion would have persisted through 1976, then about 75 per cent of *ex post* deterrence would be unrelated to the treaty.[41]

[39] Alternatively, the estimates in column (3) can be derived by summing $\beta_1 (P_a{}^h \text{(actual)} - P_a{}^h \text{(1972)})$ for the 1973-1976 quarters where β_1 is the regression coefficient on the probability of apprehension, "actual" denotes the values of $P_a{}^h$ in 1973-1976, and "1972" denotes the 1972 value.

[40] Note that .98 represents only a small increase over the moving average estimates between 1973 and 1976 (which is the basis of column (3)). The latter estimates contain probabilities of less than .98 because quarters prior to 1973 are averaged in the 1973 estimates and some missing quarters (that is, no hijackings) were assigned probability estimates less than .98.

[41] A final issue concerns the interpretation of *ex ante* deterrence. There is no way to be sure that the numbers in this category in Table 7 represent deterrence in the sense of potential offenders substituting away from an activity in response to a reduction in the probability of

B. *The Costs and Benefits of Mandatory Screening*

Data on the costs of operating the mandatory screening program are available only for 1974. In 1974, U.S. air carriers and airports spent approximately $71.56 million to screen passengers enplaned in the United States.[42] Assuming identical real expenditures in 1973, 1975, and 1976 and adding $1.97 million of federal government expenditures on magnetic equipment to screen passengers, total expenditures (in 1974 dollars) from 1973 through the third quarter of 1976 on mandatory screening would equal $270.32 million.[43] This figure, however, probably overstates the net increase in direct security costs from 1973 to 1976 compared to the years prior to mandatory screening because no allowance is made for a reduction in other security

---

success. It is conceivable that all of the 12-to-46 reduction in hijacking in the *ex ante* category represents persons apprehended at the screening stage who are not deterred in the above sense. The Federal Aviation Administration's Semi-Annual Report to Congress on the Effectiveness of the Civil Aviation Security Program contains data on the number of persons screened and weapons (by type) detected. To illustrate, in 1975 more than 200 million persons were screened at airports, 4,783 firearms and 46,318 knives were detected, and 2,464 persons were arrested for various offenses such as weapons violations, giving false information, narcotics, and immigration violations. The number of firearms detected, persons arrested, and so forth at the preboarding stage greatly exceeds the number of hijackings that took place in the years before 1973. Thus, one could not utilize such information on firearms to estimate directly the number of would-be hijackers apprehended at the screening stage. The FAA, however, also reports on various incidents at airports that might have involved potential hijackers. In 1975 the FAA estimates that there were 35 such incidents. This number, however, is greater than my estimate for 1975 of *ex ante* and *ex post* deterrence combined. Therefore, it does not appear feasible to use the FAA data to estimate the number of hijackings prevented at the preboarding stage, which would then be subtracted from my estimates of *ex ante* deterrence to compute a corrected *ex ante* deterrence measure.

[42] Expenditures on the screening program for 1974 are contained in the Dep't of Transportation and Related Agencies Appropriations for 1976, Hearings Before a Subcommittee of the Committee on Appropriations, House of Representatives, 94th Congress, 1st Session, pt. 5, 955-59 [hereinafter cited as Hearings]. These expenditures include both the costs of labor services (for example, screening personnel, armed guards) and some capital services (for example, depreciation of X-ray equipment used for baggage inspection). Note that these expenditures are defined as the "incremental" security costs of the mandatory screening program and thus represent the amount the airlines are entitled to recover via a fare increase. (See C.A.B., Docket 25315, Airport Security Charges Proposed by Various Scheduled Air Carriers, June 4, 1974 and Sept. 23, 1974.) Finally note that total screening expenditures in 1974 were actually $75.45 million not $71.56 million as given in the text. The former figure includes expenditures by U.S. air carriers on passengers enplaned outside the United States (about 5% of passengers carried by U.S. carriers). These expenditures are excluded from my estimate of screening costs by assuming that the ratio of screening expenditures of U.S. enplaned to total enplaned passengers on U.S. carriers is proportional to the ratio of passengers enplaned in the United States (including Puerto Rico, the Virgin Islands, Guam, and American Samoa) to the total number of enplaned passengers on U.S. carriers.

[43] In December 1972, $2.5 million was appropriated by the federal government to purchase metal detection devices (see Hearings, *supra* note 42, at 952). Assuming a five-year useful life (which is the life allowed for X-ray equipment) and adjusting for inflation in 1973, this amounts to $2.63 million in 1974 dollars of which $1.97 million is the share for the 15 quarters between 1972 and 1976.

costs. In particular, federal government expenditures (in current dollars) on civilian aviation security positions (for example, air marshals and other security personnel) declined from an average of $28.45 million per year in the two years prior to mandatory screening to an average of $12.58 million per year in the 1973-1976 period. Adjusting for this factor yields an estimate of the net increase in costs of the mandatory screening program of $194.24 million (in 1974 dollars).[44] Note that this estimate ignores an important element of security costs, the additional time and inconvenience to passengers resulting from screening. Unfortunately, I have no information on these indirect costs and thus the analysis that follows only considers the net increase in monetary costs of the screening program.[45]

Data on the increase in security costs due to mandatory screening can now be combined with the hijacking projections of Table 7 to obtain several estimates of the average costs of deterring a single hijacking between 1973 and 1976.[46] If one assumes initially that mandatory screening is responsible for deterring all the additional hijackings that would have occurred between 1973 and 1976 in the absence of both screening and an increase in the probability of apprehension (that is, the estimates in column (1) of Table 7), the average costs of preventing a *single* hijacking range from $3.24 to $4.74 million depending on whether foreign hijacking is included as an independent variable in the U.S. regressions.[47] This range of estimates is likely to understate the true costs because it assumes no deterrent effect of the treaty

---

[44] Federal expenditures on civilian aircraft security positions and the amounts deducted from the costs of the screening program are contained in the table below.

| | | | MILLIONS OF DOLLARS[1] | | | | |
	1971	1972	1973	1974	1975	1976	Total
Current dollars	28.0	28.9	27.4	12.3	4.9	5.7	
1974 dollars	33.95	33.64	30.15	12.3	4.48	4.96	
Amount[2] deducted			3.65	21.5	29.32	28.84[3]	76.08

[1] Data obtained from Mr. Henry D. Williams of the FAA. The figures refer to funding for civil aviation security positions that include deputy U.S. marshals, customs security officers, personnel from the office of the secretary of transportation and the FAA, and in 1971 some military personnel.

[2] Amounts deducted based on the difference between average expenditures 1971-72 and actual expenditures 1973-76 (all in 1974 dollars).

[3] In 1976 I deducted .75 of $28.84 million to correspond with the projections that end with the third quarter of 1976.

[45] These indirect costs may exceed the direct monetary cost of the screening program since the latter is less than 50 cents per enplaned passenger.

[46] The average cost of deterring a single hijacking equals the net increase in security costs between 1973 and 1976 (=$194.25 million) divided by the number of hijackings prevented (see Table 7).

[47] Only the OLS estimates of Table 7 are used in these calculations.

with Cuba. Alternatively, if one assumes that all *ex post* deterrence in Table 7 is due to the treaty (which overstates the treaty's impact because it ignores the screening effect on *ex post* deterrence), the average costs of deterring a *single* hijacking rise to between $4.74 and $9.25 million.

What the above estimates make clear are the substantial costs allocated to deterring a single hijacking. I have not attempted to weigh these costs against the dollar value of the benefits because that would require estimates of the monetary equivalent of the added time and inconvenience costs to hijacked passengers, the dollar value of any additional risk of death and injury, fuel costs, the user cost of the airplane, labor costs, and so forth.[48] Nevertheless, some insight can be gained into the magnitude of the benefit that would be required to justify the relatively large security expenditure by posing the following hypothetical question. What would the dollar costs to a hijacked passenger have to equal to make the reduction in expected costs from being hijacked equal to the increase in security costs associated with the mandatory screening program? Mandatory screening has led to a .000003449 to .000001207 estimated reduction in the probability of a flight being hijacked at a net increase in security costs to an enplaned passenger in the United States of approximately 26.46 cents.[49] This change in probability, in turn, would justify an expenditure of 26.46 cents if the monetary equivalent of the costs of being hijacked to the average passenger were in the range of $76,718 to $219,221 (see Table 8). Put differently, if one were risk neutral, he would he willing to spend 26.46 cents on security providing the dollar equivalent of the hijacking loss was in the range of $76,718 to $219,221.[50]

V.   CONCLUDING REMARKS

The present study of U.S. aircraft hijacking can be viewed as a contribution to the rapidly growing literature on the economics of deterrence.[51]

---

[48] A further benefit from mandatory screening, which should be included in any cost-benefit calculation, is the reduction in *other* crimes resulting from screening (for example, the detection of narcotics).

[49] In 1974 the number of enplaned passengers in the United States was 195,756,000 (see Hearings, *supra* note 42, at 944-59) and the net increase in costs of the screening program for a single year equals $51.8 million ($194.25 million times 4/15). The average cost per enplaned passenger during the entire 1973-1976 period is then estimated to equal $.2646 (=$51.8/ 195.756). Note that I am ignoring the distributive consequences of the screening program (financed by passengers, air carriers, and airports) compared to prescreening security program (financed by tax revenues).

[50] If the indirect costs of the mandatory screening program (that is, time costs of screened passengers) were included, the estimate of the dollar equivalent of the hijacking loss would of course rise.

[51] A useful though somewhat outdated summary of the economic literature is contained in Gordon Tullock, Does Punishment Deter Crime?, Public Interest, Summer 1974, at 103. The most

TABLE 8

PROJECTED HIJACKING LOSSES OF A SINGLE PASSENGER, 1973–1976

Quarterly Regression (see Table 7)	Change in Probability of Flight Being Hijacked		Dollar Losses Assuming Risk Neutrality	
	Mandatory Screening Deters all Projected Hijackings (1)	Hijacking Deterred by Mandatory Screening = Ex Ante Deterrence (2)	(3) = .2646/(1)	(4) = .2646/(2)
OLS	.000003449	.000002357	$76,718	$112,261
OLS (foreign hijackings included)	.000002357	.000001207	112,261	219,221

Note: The following example illustrates the method of calculating the change in probability of being hijacked. Between 1973 and the third quarter of 1976 there were approximately 17,397,838 U.S. air carrier flights (= air carrier operations ÷ 2). If 60 hijackings were deterred by mandatory screening (column (1) of Table 7), the reduction in the probability of a flight being hijacked equals 60/17,397,838 (= .00000349).

Although the basic approach and empirical findings of this study are similar to the many other economic studies of deterrence, which typically find significant deterrent effects of conviction rates and sanctions on the amount of crime, it differs from these studies in several respects. I have focused on a narrowly defined type of offense that experienced an unprecedented increase in the 1968-to-1972 period followed by a dramatic decline thereafter. In contrast, other studies usually analyze broadly defined crimes that have increased throughout the 1960s and 1970s. I have utilized data on individual offenses, measured by time and flight intervals between successive hijackings, in addition to quarterly data to estimate offense functions. Other studies employ either aggregate cross-sectional or time series observations to estimate deterrence effects. Finally, I have attempted to measure the benefits attributable to the rapid introduction in 1973 of a new and important security procedure, the mandatory screening of passengers and carryon luggage. No comparable innovation in security has been introduced to deter other types of crime.

The main findings of this paper can be summarized as follows.

1. Increases in the probability of apprehension, the conditional probability of incarceration, and the sentence are associated with significant reductions in aircraft hijackings in the 1961-to-1976 time period. These findings are based on two methods of estimating the rate of hijackings, a quarterly time series and the time or flight intervals between successive hijackings, and alternative estimates of the deterrence variables.

2. To test an alternative explanation of hijackings, which I term the "fad" hypothesis, I included foreign hijackings as an independent variable in regressions on U.S. hijackings. Since the number of foreign hijackings coincide with variations in the intensity of the worldwide hijacking fad, the inclusion of this variable allows one to differentiate between deterrence and fad effects. Although foreign and U.S. hijackings are positively correlated, the deterrence variables remain highly significant and appear to be the relatively more important determinants of U.S. hijackings.

3. Regression estimates from the sample period ending in 1972 were used to forecast the number of additional hijackings that would have taken place between 1973 and 1976 if (a) mandatory screening had not been instituted and (b) the probability of apprehension (once the hijacking is attempted) had remained constant and equal to its 1972 value. Under these assumptions,

---

significant recent contributions are two papers by Isaac Ehrlich on capital punishment (see The Deterrent Effect of Capital Punishment: A Question of Life and Death, 65 Am. Econ. Rev. 397 (1975); and Capital Punishment and Deterrence: Some Further Thoughts and Additional Evidence, 85 J. Pol. Econ. 741 (1977)). For a critical review of the economic literature see Daniel Nagin, General Deterrence: A Review of the Empirical Evidence, in Deterrence and Incapacitation: Estimating the Effects of Criminal Sanctions on Crime Rates 95 (Alfred Blumstein, Jacqueline Cohen, & Daniel Nagin eds. 1978) (Nat'l Acad. Sci.).

there would have been between 41 and 67 additional hijackings compared to the 11 that actually occurred in the 1973 to 1976 period.

4. Although the mandatory screening program is highly effective in terms of the number of hijackings prevented, its costs appear enormous. The estimated net increase in security costs due to the screening program (which does not include the time and inconvenience costs to persons searched) is $194.24 million over the 1973-to-1976 period. This, in turn, translates into a $3.24-to-$9.25 million expenditure to deter a single hijacking. Put differently, if the dollar equivalent of the loss to an individual hijacked passenger were in the range of $76,718 to $219,221, then the costs of screening would just offset the expected hijacking losses.

APPENDIX

PROBABILITY OF APPREHENSION

Table A1 presents a least squares estimate of the probability of apprehension (P_a) for 154 hijackings.[52] The dependent variable, P_a, is a dummy variable that equals 1 if the offender is apprehended (within 12 months of the hijacking) and 0 otherwise.[53] The independent variables included in the linear probability function and their predicted effects are as follows:

1. *Flight Crew Members (FLCR)*. An increase in the number of flight crew members on the hijacked aircraft is equivalent to an increase in the quantity of resources available to protect the aircraft. Thus, an increase in *FLCR* should increase the difficulty of a successful hijacking and raise the probability of apprehension.[54]

2. *Offenders per Hijacking (OFD)*. Suppose planning and coordination costs increase with the number of offenders involved in a hijacking. Since a higher expected return would be required to offset these added costs, one expects a negative effect of *OFD* on the probability of apprehension.

3. *Age of Offenders (AGE)*. In the human capital literature, there are offsetting effects of age on earnings, which are estimated by including age and age-squared variables in an earnings function. Age is initially associated with higher earnings as

[52] The number of observations here differs from the number (143) in the text because the probability estimates were computed prior to adjusting the domestic hijacking data for hijackings of U.S. registered aircraft in foreign countries (see note 1 of Table 1, *supra* .

[53] In multiple-offender hijackings, all offenders were either apprehended or not. Hence P_a is either 0 or 1 in multiple-offender hijackings. Logit or probit techniques are more appropriate than ordinary least squares when dealing with a dichotomous dependent variable. I fitted some probability functions using logit analysis and the resulting estimates were similar to ordinary least squares. Only the latter results are presented in the Appendix.

[54] There is a possible selection bias, however, in that the size of the flight crew is a variable of choice in the offender's hijacking decision. He can, for example, reduce the flight crew by selecting a smaller aircraft. This implies that there may be other advantages to the offender of a larger aircraft (for example, greater range) which affect the probability, so that on balance the probability does not rise with an increase in the flight crew.

the positive effect of experience dominates, and subsequently with a decline in earnings as depreciation of skills offsets the effects of greater experience. One might expect similar effects on the probability of apprehension for hijackings (or crime in general)—a negative sign on age and a positive sign on age-squared.

4. *Aircraft Security Measures (SKY, SEARCH)*. I use two dummy variables to denote periods in which security was intensified. *SKY* takes the value of 1 (and 0 otherwise) for hijackings that occurred between 1970 (fourth quarter) and 1972 (fourth quarter), the period where sky marshals were flying on selected flights and informal screening was used by several airlines. Since this denotes a greater allocation of resources to deterrence, one predicts a positive impact of *SKY* on the probability of apprehension. *SEARCH* equals 1 (and 0 otherwise) for hijackings that occurred after mandatory screening was introduced in 1973. Given the added deterrence of screening, one expects a positive coefficient on this variable.

5. *Flight Operations (OPER)*. One would predict that the greater the number of flight operations during the quarter in which a hijacking took place, the smaller the amount of airport and aircraft security per flight, and hence the lower the probability of apprehension.

TABLE A1
PROBABILITY OF APPREHENSION, 154 HIJACKINGS

	Regression Coefficients (and t-statistics)								
CONSTANT	FLCR	OFD	AGE	$(AGE)^2$	SKY	SEARCH	OPER	R^2	D.W.
2.197	−.174	−.162	−.021	.00028	.201	.490	−.001	.26	1.90
(3.93)	(1.74)	(3.84)	(1.31)	(1.27)	(2.50)	(3.32)	(1.44)		

All variables in Table A1, except for *FLCR*, are in the predicted direction and are either significant or marginally significant. *OFD, AGE,* and *OPER* reduce the probability of apprehension, whereas $(AGE)^2$, *SKY,* and *SEARCH* raise this probability. The coefficients of *AGE* and $(AGE)^2$ indicate, for example, that the probability of apprehension is lowest for an offender who is 37.5 years of age.[55] Of further interest is that the mandatory search variable has a significantly greater impact on the probability of apprehension than the sky marshal variable.[56] As indicated in the text, this increase in deterrence is produced only by a substantial increase in expenditures on deterrence. The negative sign of *FLCR* may be due to the positive correlation between the size of the aircraft and the number of flight crew members. Since a larger aircraft has a greater range, this reduces the number of refueling points (possibly to zero), which in turn may reduce the likelihood that the hijacker is overpowered prior to reaching his destination.

[55] The joint effect of *AGE* and $(AGE)^2$ is not statistically significant.

[56] The results of the *SKY* and *SEARCH* variables are sensitive to the inclusion of a time trend variable. When time is entered, these coefficients become insignificant, whereas time is positive and marginally significant. The explanation for this result is that the two dummy security variables are highly correlated with time.

As noted in the text, quarterly estimates of the probability of apprehension were utilized to fill in missing quarter values of the probability of apprehension (see note 15 *supra*). The average quarterly values of the variables included in Table A1 plus a time trend variable were used in the quarterly probability estimate. The results are quite similar to the regression on the individual observations.

Sentence

The results of the sentence regression is presented in Table A2. The variables included in this regression, in addition to *OFD* and *AGE,* are a set of variables measuring a variety of factors that are likely to bear on the defendant's sentence. These include a foreign variable (*FOR*) that equals 1 if the offender is sentenced in a foreign country; a race variable (*WHITE*) that equals 1 if the offender is white (and 0 if he is black or Spanish); an extortion variable (*EXT*) that equals 1 if the offender attempted to extort money from the airline; a time variable (*DTS*) that equals the quarter in which the defendant is sentenced; and two dummy variables (*INC* and *SUC*) that denote the point during the hijacking in which the offender is apprehended. Specifically, in an incomplete (*INC*) hijacking the offender gains control of the aircraft but does not reach his destination. In a successful (*SUC*) hijacking the offender reaches his destination but is subsequently apprehended and sentenced. The omitted variable is an unsuccessful hijacking in which the offender is apprehended prior to gaining control of the aircraft (for example, he is apprehended on the ground prior to takeoff). If marginal deterrence is operating, the coefficients on both *INC* and *SUC* should be positive, and the coefficient on *SUC* should be greater than on *INC*.

TABLE A2
SENTENCE (IN YEARS) OF 56 OFFENDERS

	Regression Coefficients (and *t*-statistics)								
CONSTANT	*FOR*	*EXT*	*WHITE*	*AGE*	*OFD*	*INC*	*SUC*	*DTS*	R^2
22.42	−24.34	23.23	−6.41	.139	−3.04	6.10	13.63	−.225	.58
(2.34)	(4.78)	(6.12)	(1.62)	(.844)	(1.39)	(1.28)	(2.80)	(1.62)	

Although there is little theory to support the specification of the sentence function, the results are nevertheless interesting. Apprehension and sentencing in a foreign country lead to a significantly lower sentence while extortion leads to a significantly higher sentence. Marginal deterrence is observed since the sentence increases as one moves from unsuccessful to incomplete (though the coefficient on *INC* is only marginally significant) to successful hijacking. Of the remaining variables, one observes negative effects of the race and offender variables and no significant effects of the age and time of sentence variables.

5

CAPITAL PUNISHMENT AND DETERRENCE
Some Further Thoughts and Additional Evidence

ISAAC EHRLICH

Investigation of the deterrent effect of capital punishment has implications far beyond the propriety of execution as punishment since it concerns the general question of offenders' responsiveness to incentives. This study challenges popular allegations by earlier researchers denying the deterrence hypothesis. The empirical analysis based on cross-sectional data from the U.S. corroborates my earlier analysis of the time series. Findings indicate a substantial deterrent effect of punishment on murder and related violent crimes and support the economic and econometric models used in investigations of other crimes. Distinctions between classes of executing and nonexecuting states are also examined in light of theory and evidence.

The importance of determining the deterrent effect on crime of various punishments is one of the few issues concerning deterrence that is not controversial. The problem of deterrence is encountered in all socially disapproved behavior, but it has a natural and dramatic significance with respect to the crime of murder. The present essay will examine the evidence on the cross-sectional patterns of murder and execution in 1940 and 1950, both as an illuminating source of information on the problem

I am indebted to my colleagues Lawrence Fisher, Ronald Gallant, James Heckman, Sam Peltzman, George Stigler, and to two anonymous referees for numerous comments and suggestions. I am particularly grateful to Randall Mark for his general research assistance and suggestions and to Joel Gibbons for useful comments on a previous draft. I also wish to acknowledge the competent computational assistance of Linda Moy and Vasant Sukhatme. I am also indebted to Kenneth R. Brimmer of the National Prisoner Statistics of the Bureau of the Census for his help in obtaining execution data for the years 1936–40. I alone am responsible for errors. Financial assistance for this study has been provided by a grant from the National Science Foundation to the National Bureau of Economic Research for research in law and economics. The financial support of the Charles C. Walgreen Foundation is also gratefully acknowledged. The paper is not an official NBER publication.

of deterrence and as a supplement to my earlier study of the time series.[1] The cross-sectional studies on balance reinforce the findings of the substantial restraining effect on murders of punishment in general and capital punishment in particular. The specific results obtained are consistent with sharp predictions emanating from the deterrence theory.

I deal here with the relationship between estimates of the murder rate and the conditional probability of execution, but the present investigation explores more fully than the previous study the nature of deterrence. The time-series analysis was based on a small number of observations, whereas the present analysis uses a larger body of independent, cross-sectional data relating to different states in the United States. The cross-sectional data include estimates of severity of imprisonment for murder and other crimes, missing from the time series, and provide useful information on additional relevant variables. While the time-series analysis deals with aggregate data relating to both executing and nonexecuting states, the cross-sectional statistics allow separate investigation of the subsets of executing and nonexecuting states and other groupings. The more complete data on punishments imposed for other crimes also permit a partial investigation of the interaction between murder and related violent crimes and thus provide for a somewhat more complete assessment of specific deterrent effects. The cross-sectional data from 1940 and 1950 are advantageous also because they relate to years in which the level of enforcement of capital punishment in executing states appears to have been sufficiently high and variable to permit a meaningful statistical test of the hypothesis of no deterrence. And the general uniformity in the reporting of crime rates in 1940 and 1950 permits some testing of temporal as well as cross-sectional homogeneity. In contrast, however, data exigencies unique to the cross-sectional samples have at this stage precluded utilization of the relatively more sophisticated estimation techniques employed in my earlier investigations.

Some economists may feel that a study of murder is of little relevance for the purpose of testing the economic approach to criminality. Indeed, my main concern is the general question of offenders' responsiveness to incentives, an issue I have investigated in earlier studies by stressing other crimes and different punishments (see Ehrlich 1974). I return to the seemingly narrower study of murder both because of the presumed relative superiority of murder statistics and because I find no compelling reason to expect perpetrators of crimes of passion necessarily to be less responsive to incentives than perpetrators of crimes involving material gains only. Those with a greater proclivity or "taste" for violence are indeed more likely to commit assault or murder than others, given the

[1] Ehrlich (1975a, 1975b). A more complete critical review of the literature on the deterrent effect of capital punishment will be included in a forthcoming monograph on the topic.

same objective motives and equal prospects of punishment. However, they need not be less responsive to *changes* in these factors. Inelasticity of demand is not necessarily an increasing function of the extent of demand at given income and prices. Being emotional does not preclude the ability to make self-serving choices. Even if control over actions is foregone temporarily during the commission of crime, the prospect of punishment through public or private sanctions still may prevail upon individuals to avoid situations in which "loss of control" is likely to occur. And if rational people fear death more than other punishment, the death penalty should have the greatest deterrent effect. Conclusions reached in research concerning the abhorrent crime of murder, which some criminologists consider a special form of deviance, thus can shed important light on the relevance of the economic approach to crime and to human behavior in general.

The plan of the paper is as follows: Section I discusses some analytical issues unique to this study. Section II presents an econometric investigation of cross-state variations in murder and related crimes and analyzes the results. Section III examines data on differences in offense rates, conviction risks, and sanction levels across executing and non-executing states and analyzes these data in light of a model of optimal demand for public law enforcement. A brief comparison with previous findings is offered in the concluding section.

I. Analytical Considerations

The general model underlying the research into punishment and deterrence continued in this paper concerns three major structural relations comprising a system of crime and law enforcement: supply of offenses, demand for enforcement activities, and production of means of deterrence and prevention. Data exigencies and other related problems sharply limit at this point the opportunities for an effective investigation of this general system. As did the preceding time-series study of murder, the present investigation focuses on analysis of supply of offenses. The discussion in this section sets the stage for the pursuant empirical investigation. Considerations relevant to demand for enforcement, including imposition of the death penalty, are briefly discussed in Section III.

A. Deterrence Variables as "Prices"

If the decision to commit murder and other related crimes is considered to be the result of an independent either/or choice among alternative actions by a potential offender in a given period, then murder would be expected to occur if the expected utility from committing murder to that person U_m^* exceeds the expected utility from alternative pursuits. Let the outcome of murder consist of the three consumption prospects $C(o)$, $C(m)$, and $C(d)$ relating to three mutually exclusive states of the world: no punishment, entailing no imposed costs; imprisonment, entailing the (discounted) cost of m "dollars"; and execution, entailing the larger cost of d.[2] Assuming that the utility function is bounded, the expected utility from murder to the perpetrator is then given by

$$U_m^* = (1 - Pc)\,U[C(o)] + (Pc - Pe)\,U[C(m)] + Pe\,U[C(d)], \quad (1)$$

where $Pc - Pe \equiv Pm \equiv Pc(1 - Pe|c)$ and $Pe \equiv Pc\,Pe|c$ define, respectively, the conditional probabilities of imprisonment and execution (given crime), and $Pe|c$ defines the conditional probability of execution, given conviction. Equation (1) establishes the role of the exhaustive set of deterrence variables Pm, Pe, m, and d, or alternatively, Pc, Pe, m, and d as "prices" or negative rewards for murder. The latter set of prices is of particular interest in this analysis, since the effect of an increase in Pe given Pc measures the differential impact of execution relative to imprisonment rather than that of execution relative to no punishment. Moreover, one may infer not only the signs but also the ranking of the partial elasticities of U_m^* with respect to the *independent* components of Pc and Pe:[3]

$$\varepsilon_{Pc \cdot Pe|c} > \varepsilon_{Pe|c \cdot Pc} \equiv \varepsilon_{Pe \cdot Pc} > 0; \qquad \varepsilon_m > 0, \quad (2)$$

where $\varepsilon_{i \cdot j} \equiv -(\partial U_m^*/\partial i)(i/U_m^*)$, with j and the remaining relevant deterrence variables held constant.[4]

The decision to commit murder may be affected, however, not only by own "prices" but also by the costs and rewards associated with related

[2] Two additional basic hazards should be recognized in connection with murder and other related crimes. One is death through legal intervention by police. The other involves similar detriments through private sanctions such as lynchings. Incorporation of these events formally in equation (1) would not affect the implications stated in equation (2) if the additional events are defined to be independent of events originally summarized in equation (1). Empirically it may be important, however, to control for the probabilities of these other events if their levels are systematically related to those of deterrence and other explanatory variables. While the annual number of reported lynchings in the United States declined to negligible magnitudes after 1935 (see the *Historical Statistics of the United States from Colonial Times to 1957* [U.S. Bureau of the Census 1960, p. 218]), the total number of annual homicides inflicted through police intervention has exceeded that of executions in recent decades (282 homicides relative to 81 executions in 1950; 412 homicides relative to no executions in 1971; see *Vital Statistics of the United States* [U.S. Department of Health, Education, and Welfare 1953, 1975]). However, such homicide data are not classified by the type of crime leading to their perpetration, nor are any statewide data available prior to 1949. A test I have conducted in connection with the effect of a measure of the risk of death through police intervention on the rate of violent crimes in 1950 is briefly discussed in Section II (see n. 24).

[3] Focusing on the role of the independent components of deterrence variables has an analytical advantage in that these are produced separately through distinct law enforcement activities. They may thus be thought of as the relevant objects of choice from the viewpoint of the demand for optimal enforcement (see Section III).

[4] The identity $\varepsilon_{Pe|c \cdot Pc} \equiv \varepsilon_{Pe \cdot Pc}$ follows from the definition of Pe as a product of Pc and $Pe|c$. For this reason the theory also implies that $\varepsilon_{Pc \cdot Pe|c} \equiv \varepsilon_{Pc \cdot Pe} + \varepsilon_{Pe \cdot Pc}$.

crimes such as aggravated assault and robbery. These related crimes could be either "substitutes" or "complements" with murder. It is conceivable that an intended act of robbery or assault may result in, and thus be classified as, murder in the event the victim is fatally injured. Let μ be the probability that an intended robbery results in murder and assume, for methodological simplicity, that an offender guilty of murder cannot be convicted of a lesser offense. The expected utility from robbery is then

$$
\begin{aligned}
U_R^* = {}& \mu(1 - Pc^{rm})U[C^{rm}(o)] + (1 - \mu)(1 - Pc^r)U[C^r(o)] \\
&+ (1 - \mu)Pc^r U[C^r(r)] + \mu Pm^{rm}U[C^{rm}(m)] + \mu Pe^{rm}U[C^{rm}(d)].
\end{aligned}
\tag{3}
$$

In equation (3) $Pm^{rm} \equiv Pc^{rm}(1 - P^{rm}e|c)$, and $Pe^{rm} \equiv Pc^{rm}Pe|c^{rm}$, denote the probabilities that a robber guilty of robbery-murder will be punished through imprisonment or execution, respectively; Pc^r denotes the probability of conviction of "simple" robbery, for which imprisonment (r) is the only penalty; and C^{mr} and C^r designate the consumption prospects in case robbery results in murder or in a simple robbery only. If μ were fixed by nature and if robbery were not a close alternative to murder as an expression of malevolence, then robbery and murder would be "complements" in the sense that an increase in the set of prices for murder including the risk of execution would have similar deterrent effects on robbery as well.[5] Similarly, an increase in deterrence variables for murder, or a decrease in relative financial gains from robbery, would "deter" robbery. Like considerations apply in connection with assault.

But substitutability relations among murder and robbery or assault can also be predicted on theoretical grounds. Assault may be the closest alternative to murder as an act of malice. To the extent that the two activities are independent ("μ" is subject to control), an increase in the own price of murder might enhance the incentive to "produce" assault. A similar consideration applies in connection with a potential trade-off between the commission of robbery-murder as opposed to a simple robbery. The net effect of a change in, say, the risk of execution for murder on the frequency of robbery and assault must therefore be settled on empirical grounds.

B. The Effects of Other Variables

Whether the expected utility from crime exceeds that from the relevant alternative depends upon the relative rewards as well as the relative prices. In most cases of murder the rewards are expected to be largely psychic, depending on such intangibles as hate or the degree of social interaction (see Ehrlich 1975a, pp. 399, 412). By contrast, the cost of

[5] The elasticities of U_R^* with respect to Pc^{rm} and $Pe|c^{rm}$ will be "weighted," however, by μ.

imprisonment would be an increasing function of the opportunity cost of time which, for most potential offenders, is derived from legitimate earning opportunities. Moreover, relative legitimate and illegitimate opportunities may affect even the frequencies of murder and assault because of the interdependencies between these crimes and robbery or other crimes against property. Indirect proxies for such economic variables—the level and distribution of income—which were developed and tested in previous investigations (Ehrlich 1974, 1975a) will be examined in this analysis as well.

The interdependencies among murder, assault, and robbery are determined not only through the effects of prices and relative rewards, however, but also through the influence of medical technology and the cost of saving lives as well as the technology and cost of deadly weapons. These factors are relevant because they can influence the probability that a murderous attack such as aggravated assault results in the death of a victim. The probability of nonsurvival thus determines in large measure the probability that aggravated assault results in murder (the analogue of μ in eq. [3]). That the effect of medical technology on the incidence of murder in different areas over the period under investigation may be significant relative to advances in the technology of deadly weapons is indicated by significant and systematic variations in the ratio of murders to the sum of aggravated assaults and murders $\mu = M/(M + A)$, which is a rough indicator of nonsurvival risks in murderous attacks. The ratio of murders relative to all aggravated assaults and robberies also is presented. Table 1 shows that all rates have decreased between 1940 and 1970 and that nonsurvival risks in urban areas are lower than those in rural areas, although the differences have narrowed over time possibly because of the trends toward equalization of medical and hospital care (see Pashigian 1973). This analysis provides an independent justification for introduction of family income, indicators of relative poverty, and even the degree of urbanization among the set of variables accounting for state-wide variations in murder rates. Clearly, the quality and extent of utilization of medical and hospital care are functions of income and vary systematically across urban and rural areas and different racial groups (see, e.g., Aday and Anderson 1975).

C. *The Empirical Supply-of-Offenses Function*

The model presented in Part A of this section does not yield definitive implications concerning the form of the individual supply-of-offenses function. The form of the aggregate function, in turn, depends on that of individual functions as well as on the personal distribution of psychic returns for crime if the magnitudes of deterrence variables and other determinants of pecuniary net rewards were perceived to be the same by all persons. Several considerations imply, however, that for the purpose

TABLE 1

ESTIMATES OF NONSURVIVAL RISKS IN MURDEROUS ATTACKS
BY POPULATION GROUPS, 1940–70

	1940*		1950†		1960‡		1970§	
POPULATION GROUP	$\dfrac{M}{M+A}$	$\dfrac{M}{M+A+R}$	$\dfrac{M}{M+A}$	$\dfrac{M}{M+A+R}$	$\dfrac{M}{M+A}$	$\dfrac{M}{M+A+R}$	$\dfrac{M}{M+A}$	$\dfrac{M}{M+A+R}$
Total cities....	.105	.052	.065	.040	.050	.030	.044	.0195
Cities over 50,000......	.103	.049	.062	.037	.046	.027	.047	.0193
Cities under 50,000......	.113	.064	.076	.053	.070	.048	.030	.0207
Rural areas‖ .	.163	.108	.138	.098	.134	.105	.066	.058

SOURCES.—U.S. Department of Justice, *Uniform Crime Reports* (1940, no. 4, tables 76 and 85; 1950, no. 2, table 31; 1951, no. 2, p. 49; 1960, tables 1 and 6; 1970, tables 1 and 9).
* Total cities' crimes based on 2,001 cities with population of 65,128,946; rural crimes as reported by 1,016 sheriffs, nine state police organizations, and 66 village officers.
† Total cities' crimes based on 2,297 cities with population of 69,643,614; rural crimes as reported by 1,621 sheriffs, 162 rural village officers, and 11 state organizations representing a rural population of 42,433,145.
‡ Total cities' crimes based on 3,366 cities with population of 96,678,066; rural crimes are estimated totals in the U.S. rural population of 41,832,427.
§ Total cities' crimes based on 4,481 cities with population of 121,254,000; rural crimes are estimated totals in the U.S. rural population of 38,865,034.
‖ Statistics on rural crimes in 1970 and 1960 may not be fully comparable to those in 1950 and 1940. The latter may have been limited in some instances only to cases in which arrests were made.

of a simple empirical formulation a linear specification in the logarithms of the dependent and basic independent variables is superior to a linear specification in the natural values of these variables. In the first place, the theory identifies the basic deterrence variables in the murder equation to include the *unconditional* probabilities of conviction and execution which are functionally dependent via a multiplicative relationship $Pe \equiv Pc\,Pe|c$. Introduction of natural values of these variables in a regression analysis is then likely to produce imprecise estimates of their independent effects. The effect of the independent variable $Pe|c$, in turn, depends on the level of Pe in the same way that the effect of an ad valorem tax rate depends on the level of the unit price. A linear specification in Pc and $Pe|c$ is disadvantageous since it does not control directly for the level of the basic price Pe. In contrast, a linear specification in the logarithms[6] permits an equally effective estimation of the deterrent effects of interest via the following equation:

$$\ln q = \alpha - \beta_1 \ln Pc - \beta_2 \ln Pe|c \ldots , \qquad (4)$$

[6] The partial elasticities of the expected utility from crime of an average potential offender, U^*, with respect to Pc and $Pe|c$, for example, can be shown to be an increasing function of these variables. However, the supply of offenses relates to the average flow of crimes in the population, q, rather than to U^*; the latter two variables are monotonically, but not necessarily proportionally, related. Formally, given that $dq/dU^* > 0$, the effects of deterrence variables on q may be summarized by $e_p = e_{qU^*}e_p$, where $e_p = -(\partial q/\partial p)(p/q)$, $e_{qU^*} = (dq/dU^*)(U^*/q)$, $\varepsilon_p = -(\partial U^*/\partial p)(p/U^*)$, and p stands for Pc or $Pe|c$. Clearly, the value of $\partial e_p/\partial p$ cannot be inferred directly from that of $\partial \varepsilon_p/\partial p$, since the theory does not provide clear insights as to the way e_{qU^*} changes with U^*. The assumption that the relevant e's are constant can thus be taken as a useful first approximation. Also see Becker (1968, p. 209).

or the statistically identical form

$$\ln q = \alpha - \gamma \ln Pc - \beta_2 \ln Pe, \qquad (4a)$$

where $\gamma = \beta_1 - \beta_2$.[7] The logarithmic specification thus controls for the magnitudes of the basic prices Pc and Pe and at the same time eliminates their functional interdependence and permits an efficient test of the hypotheses summarized in equation (2).

Furthermore, the logarithmic form is a superior specification when the magnitudes of errors in the dependent variable are thought to be proportional to its level. It would be rather implausible to assume that the magnitudes of underreported and misreported crimes are independent of the level of reported crimes. It would be more plausible to expect a proportional relationship between the two. Similar considerations also apply to the observed values of deterrence variables (see Appendix B). This assumed proportionality of errors to levels of corresponding variables implies that the logarithmic specification is at least tractable in terms of an analysis of expected biases (see Ehrlich 1974, appendix I in his section IV).

These arguments can be evaluated systematically by application of a test of functional specification devised by Box and Cox (1964). The test provides a systematic method of determining an optimal transformation of the dependent variable or the entire set of variables entering a regression equation (X_i) of the form $(X_i^\lambda - 1)/\lambda$. This class of transformations is directly applicable in the present context, in that $\lambda = 0$ defines the logarithmic transformation and $\lambda = 1$ corresponds to the simple-linear specification. A related class of transformations permits a comparison between the logarithmic and the semilogarithmic functional forms. The assumption underlying Box and Cox's analysis is that some transformation λ exists such that the transformed observations satisfy the full normal theory assumptions and are linearly related to their determinants. The procedure then permits selection of an optimal transformation and testing of hypotheses concerning alternative values of λ as optimal transformations. A comprehensive application of this procedure is reported in Section IIB2 and Appendix A.

II. Empirical Implementation

A. Introduction

The supply-of-offenses functions relating to murder and other crimes are estimated in this investigation using cross-state data from 1940 and 1950. These years are chosen because the level of enforcement of capital

[7] This result, which is "forced" by the logarithmic specification, is, of course, consistent with the theoretical analysis itself (see n. 4 above).

punishment in individual executing states appears to have been sufficiently high and variable to permit a meaningful test of the hypothesis of no deterrence. Due to data exigencies, the parameters of the supply functions are estimated via classical least-squares and seemingly unrelated simultaneous-equations techniques rather than the two-stage least-squares procedure employed in my related works. Because the preferred regression format is found to be logarithmic and the estimated levels of conditional risks of execution in nonexecuting states are "zero," supply-of-offenses functions are estimated separately in executing states as well as in the full samples comprised of executing and nonexecuting states. In the full-sample regressions estimated via the approximate logarithmic transformation, statistical considerations dictate allowance for separate constant terms in each class of states. Following tests for homoscedasticity, generalized least-squares estimates are achieved by weighting all variables by the square roots of either urban, state, or (when available) the relevant sample populations. A detailed discussion of the estimation procedure and the variables used in the regression analysis is included in Appendix B. A list of·the variables used is given in table 2.

B. Analysis of Regression Results

1. Analysis of FBI (UCR) Data

FBI statistics on murder and other felonies are available in 1940 and 1950 only as crime rates in samples of urban areas covering, on average, 49 percent of the states' residential population in 1940 and 45 percent in 1950 (see U.S. Department of Justice, *Uniform Crime Reports*, 1940, 1950–51, 1960, 1970). Crime statistics are based on complaints of crime, subject to police verification procedures, and are recorded according to *Uniform Crime Reports* (*UCR*) classifications. The category "murder" refers to all willful felonious homicides.

a) *Subsets of states with positive executions.*—The basic regression model used in the analysis is linear in the logarithms of all relevant variables:[8]

$$E(\ln q^o) = a + b_1 \ln T + b_2 \ln P^o c + b_3 \ln P^o e | c + b_4 \ln NW$$
$$+ b_5 \ln X + b_6 \ln W + b_7 \ln AGE + b_8 \ln URB, \tag{5}$$

---

[8] The set of variables included in equation (5) generally yielded consistent and significant results in the different regressions performed. Other variables tested are measures of unemployment and labor-force participation rates. As in my previous cross-sectional investigations, these variables have not been found to have a systematic impact on the extent of crime rates across states, although both variables did appear to have such effects in my related time-series analysis (see the discussion in Ehrlich [1975a]). Their exclusion from the regression equations did not have any significant impact on the regression results reported here.

TABLE 2

LIST OF VARIABLES USED IN THE REGRESSION ANALYSIS

q_i^o = urban crime rate (per 100,000 population) for offense category i, based on UCR samples;

h^o = homicide rate (per 100,000 population), based on VS data;

$P^o{}_{c_i} = \dfrac{C_i^o}{Q_i^o}$ = estimate of probability of conviction: the ratio of prisoners received in state prisons to the estimated (state) total numbers of offenses in category i;

$P^h{}_c = \dfrac{C^o}{H^o}$ = corresponding estimate of probability of conviction for murder using VS data on the number of homicides in a state;

T_i† = median time spent in state prisons by offenders prior to first release;

$PX5 = \dfrac{\sum_{j=0}^{4} E_{t-j}^o/5}{C_t^o}$ = the ratio of the average number of executions in years t to $t - j$ to the estimated number of convictions for murder in sample year t;

$$PX4 = \frac{\sum_{j=0}^{3} E_{t-j}^o/4}{C_t} \qquad PXQ1 = \frac{E_{t+1}^o}{C_t^o} \qquad PXQ2 = \frac{E_t^o}{C_t^o} \qquad PXA = \frac{E_{t+1}^o + E_t^o/2}{C_t}$$

$PXQ1Q - PX5Q$‡ = same as the preceding ratios but with E_t^o defined to include only executions for murders;

W§ = median income of families in year $t - 1$: a census estimate:

X = percentage of families with income below one-half of W:

NW = percent of nonwhites in the population;

AGE = percent of population in the age group 15–24;

A_{25-34} = percent of population in the age group 25–34;

URB = percent of urban population in the total state population;

$EPOS$ = a dummy variable distinguishing executing states (1) from states (0) with $P^o e \,|\, c = 0$;

N_s = state population in 100,000s;

N_{URB} = urban population in 100,000s;

N_{REP} = size of population (in 100,000s) in UCR samples reporting q_i^o in 1951;

NOTE.—Due to data exigencies, UCR murder regressions omit from the full samples in 1940 and 1950 the following states: 1940—Georgia, Maine, Mississippi, Nevada, and Vermont; 1950—Georgia, Michigan, North Dakota, and Vermont.
† In the 1940 regressions data exigencies dictated the use of the corresponding variable from 1950 (T_{50}). The actual data are for prisoners released in 1951 (1952 for T_{MUR} in Idaho, Michigan, Rhode Island, South Dakota, and Vermont) because 1950 figures are not available.
‡ In 1940 $PX5Q$ cannot be computed because execution data for 1936 are not available by crime category.
§ In 1940 available only as median earnings of a sample of wage and salary workers.

with all variables weighted by the weighting factors discussed in Appendix B.[9] Table 3 presents estimates of regression coefficients and the ratios of these coefficients to their standard errors. Magnitudes of the "R^2"

[9] According to the discussion in Section IIA and Appendix B, weighted regressions are performed to derive generalized-least-squares (GLS) estimates of equation (5). Indeed, the standard errors of regression estimates derived from weighted regressions are virtually with no exception lower than the standard errors of corresponding unweighted regressions, a sample of which is given in table 3. The fact that weighted regressions using the square roots of urban and reporting populations as weighting factors are found to be somewhat more efficient than those derived from regressions weighted by the square root of the state population also is consistent with the heteroscedasticity argument, since the dependent variables are estimates of urban crime rates.

statistics reported in connection with weighted regressions are the conventional R^2 measures obtained after multiplying the variables in equation (5) by a weighting factor. These "R^2" measures thus may serve merely as indicators of goodness of fit in the transformed regression equations.

Results obtained in connection with the three deterrence variables, T, P^oc, and measures of $P^oe|c$, exhibit a consistent pattern throughout the regression analysis. The estimated regression coefficients associated with these variables are all negative, with magnitudes generally well above twice the values of corresponding standard errors. More important, with no exception, the estimated elasticities of the murder rate, with respect to the probability of conviction (P^oc), exceed those with respect to the conditional probability of execution, given conviction $(P^oe|c)$. In all of the cases reported in tables 3 and 4, the differences between the magnitudes of the latter elasticities are significant at the 5 percent level for a two-tail test.[10] As for the effect of T, it should be recalled that the variable used in both the 1940 and the 1950 regressions is the median length of time served by those released from prisons in 1951. In spite of potential biases which may be injected into regression estimates in 1940 as a result, estimates of deterrence effects are statistically indistinguishable across different regressions and do not depend on the inclusion of T_{50} in the 1940 regressions (see Part 5 below).

In contrast to time-series estimates of the simple correlation between measures of the murder rate and the conditional probability of execution, these simple correlations are found to be negative in all the relevant subsets of executing states.[11] In addition, estimates of deterrent effects derived from regressions in which only the three deterrence variables, T, P^oc, and $P^oe|c$, served as regressors show similar qualitative results, with estimates of deterrent effects actually larger in absolute magnitudes.

Except for estimates derived from unweighted regressions in 1950, virtually all 95 percent confidence intervals associated with the estimated

---

[10] All tests of significance reported in this investigation are conditional on the assumption that the error terms satisfy all the standard conditions of the regression model.

[11] The simple (unweighted) correlation coefficients between natural values of q^o and the measures of the conditional risk of execution listed below are:

1940	1950
$PXQ_1 = -.13697$	$PXQ_1 = -.11230$
$PXQ_2 = -.27668$	$PXQ_2 = -.17299$
$PX5 \ = -.18251$	$PX5 \ = -.00605$
$PX4Q = -.24158$	$PX5Q = -.10576$

The simple regression coefficients associated with these same measures of execution risk in weighted logarithmic regressions were always negative, and higher in absolute value than the coefficients reported in table 3 and n. 12. Note that the cross-state measures of the risk of execution given conviction of murder are based on independently reported conviction (prison commitments for both imprisonment and execution) data, which do not depend on the FBI estimates of murder rates.

TABLE 3

MURDER SUPPLY FUNCTIONS: GLS (Weighted) AND OLS REGRESSIONS, LOGARITHMIC FORM

Eq.	Year	N	"R^2"	Constant	T	P_c^o	$P^o{}_{e|c}$	NW	X	W	AGE	URB
Weight = $\sqrt{N_{\text{URB}}}$:												
1	1940	33	.9539	7.372 (1.89)	−0.292 (−2.35)	−0.673 (−4.70)	*PX5* −0.339 (−3.48)	0.508 (7.26)	⋯	0.436 (1.21)	−2.101 (−2.23)	−0.982 (−4.43)
2	1940	33	.9565	5.466 (1.44)	−0.232 (−1.93)	−0.709 (−4.99)	*PX4Q* −0.389 (−3.79)	0.468 (6.58)	⋯	0.505 (1.44)	−1.741 (−1.92)	−0.993 (−4.63)
Weight = $\sqrt{N_t}$:												
3	1940	33	.9518	5.757 (1.37)	−0.320 (−2.45)	−0.682 (−4.44)	*PX5* −0.366 (−3.46)	0.487 (6.20)	⋯	0.480 (1.26)	−1.691 (−1.58)	−0.928 (−4.01)
4	1940	33	.9585	4.259 (1.09)	−0.249 (−2.03)	−0.725 (−5.07)	*PX4Q* −0.430 (−4.23)	0.438 (5.79)	⋯	0.469 (1.33)	−1.393 (−1.41)	−0.882 (−4.08)
Weight = $\sqrt{N_{\text{REP}}}$:												
5	1950	35	.9581	−4.622 (−1.17)	−0.459 (−3.59)	−0.687 (−5.23)	*PX5* −0.272 (−4.74)	0.496 (7.13)	1.200 (2.22)	1.226 (2.65)	0.274 (0.44)	−0.742 (−2.08)

	Year	N	R²									
6..........	1950	35	.9588	−4.690 (−1.20)	−0.422 (−3.35)	−0.670 (−5.15)	*PX5Q* −0.270 (−4.81)	0.487 (7.01)	1.143 (2.12)	1.256 (2.74)	0.177 (0.29)	−0.783 (−2.21)
Weight = $\sqrt{N_i}$:												
7..........	1950	35	.9503	−3.024 (−0.84)	−0.507 (−3.87)	−0.719 (−5.30)	*PX5* −0.324 (−5.04)	0.468 (6.23)	0.904 (1.52)	0.921 (1.99)	0.374 (0.63)	−0.703 (−1.94)
8..........	1950	35	.9512	−3.101 (−0.87)	−0.460 (−3.53)	−0.694 (−5.18)	*PX5Q* −0.324 (−5.13)	0.456 (6.13)	0.834 (1.41)	0.940 (2.06)	0.282 (0.48)	−0.738 (−2.05)
Unweighted:												
9..........	1940	33	.9087	5.633 (1.19)	−0.152 (−0.98)	−0.792 (−6.11)	*PX4Q* −0.509 (−5.48)	0.312 (4.89)	...	−0.064 (−0.18)	−1.062 (−0.80)	−0.705 (−2.79)
10..........	1950	35	.8394	−2.201 (−0.50)	−0.490 (−2.39)	−0.595 (−3.33)	*PX5Q* −0.145 (−1.38)	0.460 (4.40)	0.945 (1.07)	0.793 (1.32)	0.192 (0.37)	−0.364 (−0.74)

NOTE.—$\hat{\beta}/S_{\hat{\beta}}$ in parentheses.

elasticities of the murder rate with respect to alternative measures of the conditional risk of execution include only negative values. Nevertheless, the quantitative differences observed among the point estimates of elasticities associated with other measures of $P^o e|c$ (not reported here due to lack of space) indicate the inherent limitations of these measures, resulting from the rather sizable relative fluctuations in the small numbers of executions carried out in a given state over successive years.[12] Indeed, the reported measures of $P^o e|c$ based on 4- or 5-year averages of the yearly number of executions generally yield more consistent and pronounced results across the 1940 and 1950 samples. The apparent superiority of $PX4Q$, $PX5Q$, and $PX5$ as measures of execution risk may also be due to the fact that the regressions utilizing these variables include a larger number of observations. Thus the results are based on a larger number of degrees of freedom.

The estimated effects of measures of income (W) and income inequality (X) may reflect the influence of different and possibly even conflicting factors.[13] The variables W and X may serve as indicators of the potential gains and the differential gains from property crimes relative to legitimate earning activities (see Ehrlich [1974, section IIIB] and the results in connection with robbery and assault in tables 6 and 7). The generally positive effects of these variables on the murder rate may be due to the fact that murder is often a by-product of these crimes. The direct partial effects of W and X on the incentive to commit acts of malice are more ambiguous, however (see Ehrlich 1975a). Presumably, the incentive effects of wealth on crime outweigh the effect of medical care available to victims of aggravated assault. Note, however, that the observed positive effects of X and NW on q^o may partly be due to the effect of inferior medical care services available to relatively low-income persons.

The percent of urban population in the total state population (URB)

[12] A sample of results associated with alternative measures of $P^o e|c$ defined in table 2 substituted for the measures used in equations 1–2 and 5–6 in table 3 relating to 1940 and 1950, respectively, is as follows ($\hat{\beta}/S_{\hat{\beta}}$ in parentheses):

Measure	PXQ_1	PXQ_2	PXA	PXQ_1Q	PXQ_2Q	$PXAQ$
1940 (set 1–2)	− .132	− .212	− .160	− .118	− .267	(− .151)
	(−2.42)	(−3.36)	(−2.62)	(−2.02)	(−4.03)	(−2.39)
1950 (set 5–6)	− .152	− .335	− .332	− .177	− .327	− .340
	(−2.05)	(−2.92)	(−4.50)	(−2.25)	(−2.25)	(−4.70)

The magnitudes of estimates of other deterrence variables do not change appreciably and remain statistically significant as alternative estimates of $P^o e|c$ are substituted. However, standard errors tend to be lowest with the measures presented in table 3.

[13] In the 1940 regressions, X_{40} yielded insignificant and inconsistent results across equations including a different measure of $P^o e|c$. However, both W_{40} and X_{40} are based on a sample of employed wage and salary workers with positive earnings in 1939 rather than on a sample of family income in 1949, including families with no income, from which W_{50} and X_{50} are computed. The exclusion of X_{40} from the regression equations had little impact on the estimated magnitudes of other regressors.

is found to be negatively associated with the (urban) murder rate in both 1940 and 1950. The result might suggest that the magnitudes of some explanatory variables computed from statistics relating to the entire state population differ by constant proportions across urban and rural areas, and, consequently, that URB serves as a "correcting factor." The net effect of URB then would not be clear a priori since it would depend on the direction of specific differences. Alternatively, the degree of urbanization of a state may serve as a proxy for other relevant factors, such as access to relevant medical services, the partial effect of which on the murder rate is expected to be negative.[14]

The percent of young age groups (15–24) in the state population (AGE) is not always found to have a systematic association with the murder rate, whereas the effect of the percent of nonwhites in the population (NW) is generally positive and significant in all regressions. As in the case of URB, AGE may perform the role of a "correcting factor" which allows derivation of unbiased estimates of the effects of deterrence variables. Presumably, magnitudes of these variables differ across different age brackets because of the differential treatment of young offenders under the law. While this consideration alone might lead to the expectation that q^o and AGE would be positively correlated, other differences in determinants of murder and acts of malice across different age groups may give rise to different associations. According to information compiled from the *Vital Statistics of the United States* (see Klebba 1975), the homicide victimization rate for nonwhites and for the total population has tended to peak at the age group 25–34 (A_{25-34}) in the period under study. Indeed, estimates of equation (5) with A_{25-34} replacing AGE reveal a positive association between A_{25-34} and the murder rate, especially in 1950, contrary to the inconclusive effect of AGE in these regressions. Generally, estimates of deterrent effects in (5) obtained with A_{25-34} as a measure of age composition did not differ markedly from the estimates discussed in the preceding analysis: the effects of $P^o c$ and $P^o e|c$ were found somewhat higher in absolute values, and that of T somewhat lower. The main change was observed in 1950 regressions in connection with the effect of the percent of nonwhites in the population, which decreased in magnitude although it remained statistically significant.[15] It thus appears that the

[14] This tentative interpretation is not incompatible with the fact that URB is found to be negatively associated also with a total homicide measure based on state statistics, especially in 1940 (see table 5). Differences in availability of medical services across urbanized and less-urbanized states may have been particularly high in 1940.

[15] For example, when A_{25-34} replaces AGE in equation 7 of table 3, the nonwhite coefficient drops by nearly half and the effect of W becomes insignificant. However, substituting A_{25-34} for AGE in the 1940 murder regressions does not have any marked effects on other variables' coefficients. Using A_{25-34} in the murder regressions yields somewhat higher "R^2" values than AGE in 1950 and slightly lower ones in 1940. Also, substituting A_{25-34} in the 1950 robbery and assault regressions (e.g., eqq. 2 and 3 of table 6 and in table 7) hardly affects the robbery regression, while the assault equation is affected much the same way as were the (1950) murder regressions.

positive and significant association of NW and q^o may be, at least in part, the result of its relatively high partial correlation with A_{25-34}. However, homicide victimization data reveal that nonwhites face a much higher risk of victimization than do their white counterparts in all age and sex groups. This evidence is not inconsistent with the hypothesis that the higher frequency of murder among nonwhites is the result of relatively low general (and age-specific) earning opportunities which reduce potential incarceration costs and access to relevant medical services at all ages.[16]

b) Full-sample results.—The basic regression equation estimated using the full set of observations available in 1940 and 1950 is a modified version of the regression model specified in equation (5),

$$E[q^{o(\lambda)}] = a + b_1 T^{(\lambda)} + \cdots + b_8 \text{URB}^{(\lambda)} + b_9 \text{EPOS}, \qquad (6)$$

where EPOS is a dummy variable distinguishing the relevant executing (1) and nonexecuting (0) states, and the transformation (λ) is defined in Section IC. Because the values of measured execution risks in nonexecuting states are zero, the log-linear regression format specified in equation (5) is here approximated by setting $\lambda = 0.001$. The results for the simple linear and the approximate log-linear transformations are reported in equations 1b, 1c, 2b, and 2c in table 4, parts A and B.

The full-sample results which allow for separate constant terms in executing and nonexecuting states via EPOS, especially those derived through the approximate logarithmic transformation, are essentially the same as the corresponding results based on subsamples of executing states. The point estimates of the elasticity of the murder rate with respect to estimates of $P^o e|c$ are virtually identical. More important, application of Chow's test of equality between the comparable regression coefficients associated with variables entering the approximate logarithmic analog of equation (5) in executing and nonexecuting states, except for the constant terms of the separate equations, shows that the hypothesis of equality for that set of regression coefficients cannot be rejected at the 5 percent, and generally much higher, level of significance. This is evident in tests relating to both the 1940, 1950, and pooled samples (see below) and for regressions using alternative measures of execution risk or different weighting factors.[17]

The effect of the dummy variable EPOS, in turn, is found to be significant in all the regressions using the approximate logarithmic trans-

---

[16] For some initial attempts to arrive at a methodology for testing for racial differences in criminal activity see Ehrlich (1970). A fuller investigation requires data concerning the level of law enforcement activity directed against specific groups in connection with crimes against the person and efficient measures of group-specific earning (and medical care) opportunities.

[17] For example, the F-statistics based on the sum of squared residuals estimated from equations 1 and 2 in table 8 (with $\lambda = 0.001$), its counterpart in nonexecuting states, and equation 4 in table 8 are $F_{5,74} = 0.686$ and $F_{6,72} = 1.260$, respectively.

formation and in the weighted regressions using the simple linear specifications. Indeed, the elimination of EPOS from the regression equation is found to have a drastic effect on the standard error and even the sign of the coefficient associated with $P^o e|c$ measures. In the approximate log specification of equation (6) the signs of the latter are positive and sometimes significant with magnitudes very nearly zero, whereas in the simple linear specification the coefficients have the expected negative sign and are occasionally significant as well.[18] The technical explanation is straightforward: EPOS is very highly correlated with $P^o e|c$, extremely so in the approximate logarithmic versions of equation (6). Thus, its absence from the regression equation produces the expected "specification bias" resulting from a missing variable, and the magnitude of the quantitative change in the coefficient associated with $P^o e|c^{(\lambda)}$ is expected to equal the product of the true partial regression coefficient associated with EPOS and the relevant partial regression coefficient relating EPOS to $P^o e|c^{(\lambda)}$. Indeed, it is estimated that the extent of "specification bias" resulting from the omission of EPOS is likely to outweigh the magnitude of the true partial coefficient associated with measures of $P^o e|c^{(\lambda)}$ in the approximate logarithmic regressions but not in most of the simple linear runs.[19] It is important to stress, however, that the *magnitude* of the coefficient associated with EPOS is an arbitrary number by definition. It is but an artifact of two related factors: the transformation applied to the dependent and independent variables in the regression and the range of the dummy variable measuring EPOS. If the value of EPOS is transformed, for example, by the same value of λ (0.001) used to transform all other variables in the approximate logarithmic regressions, then the quantitative magnitude of the coefficient associated with EPOS in these regressions would be reduced by precisely 1,000-fold. The only valid inference to be drawn from the estimated effect of EPOS is that it indicates the existence of a statistically significant difference between the mean rates of murder in executing and nonexecuting states after the effects of other variables entering equation (6) have been accounted for. This does

[18] Estimates of the elasticity of the murder rate with respect to measures of execution risk in equations 1b, 1c, 2b, and 2c in table 4, parts A and B, which were estimated without introducing EPOS in the regression equation $(\hat{b}_e)$, are reported in their respective order: 1940: 0.0003 (2.28), −4.491 (−0.88), 0.0006 (3.23), −6.963 (−1.84); 1950: 0.0003 (1.11), −17.35 (−2.58), 0.0001 (0.59), 3.124 (0.49). The numbers in parentheses are the ratios of the coefficients to their respective standard errors.

[19] The estimated regression coefficient associated with $P^o e|c$ in the regressions excluding EPOS $\hat{b}_e$ would be given by plim $(\hat{b}_e) = b_3 + b_9 b_{93}\ldots$ where b_3 and b_9 are the partial (population) regression coefficients associated with $P^o e|c$ and EPOS in equation (6) and $b_{93}\ldots$ is the partial (population) regression coefficient associated with $P^o e|c$ in a regression of EPOS on $P^o e|c$ and all other regressors entering (6). Since b_3 is expected to be negative, and b_3 and $b_{93}\ldots$ are found to be positive, the sign of plim $(\hat{b}_e)$ would reverse in those transformations where the term $b_9 b_{93}\ldots$ outweighs the absolute magnitude of b_3. Indeed, LS estimates of $b_{93}\ldots$ verify that $\hat{b}_9 \hat{b}_{93}\ldots$ tends to exceed $|\hat{b}_3|$ in the approximate log-linear transformations but that it falls short of $|\hat{b}_3|$ in the simple linear transformations, with $\hat{b}_3 + \hat{b}_9 \hat{b}_{93}\ldots$ virtually identical to $\hat{b}_e$.

TABLE 4

A. MURDER SUPPLY FUNCTIONS: 1940, 43 STATES

Eq.	λ	$L(\lambda)$*	Constant	T	P°_c	$P_{e\|c}$	NW	W	AGE	URB	EPOS
						$\overline{PX5}$					
1a......	$0.100 = \hat{\lambda}$	−5.0524	0.918 (0.268)	−0.231 (−3.026)	−0.885 (−5.645)	−0.481 (−3.920)	0.531 (9.332)	0.370 (2.032)	−1.510 (−2.057)	−0.756 (−5.212)	4.217 (4.257)
1b......	0.001	−6.2315	−331.71	−0.324 (−3.014)	−0.664 (−5.482)	−0.338 (−3.764)	0.535 (9.367)	0.635 (2.030)	−1.888 (−2.160)	−0.963 (−5.032)	337.16
1c......	1.0	−47.1601	−10.22 (−0.806)	−0.017 (−1.742)	−13.184 (−2.898)	−9.992 (−1.888)	0.314 (3.880)	−0.002 (−0.365)	−0.011 (−0.022)	−0.083 (−2.252)	3.313 (2.421)
						$\overline{PX4Q}$					
2a......	$0.175 = \hat{\lambda}$	−13.6604	−3.538 (−0.700)	−0.149 (−1.805)	−1.013 (−5.285)	−0.777 (−4.470)	0.391 (5.643)	0.138 (0.849)	−0.046 (−0.044)	−0.414 (−2.602)	3.680 (5.333)
2b......	0.001	−15.4821	−426.98	−0.254 (−1.665)	−0.624 (−4.994)	−0.429 (−4.106)	0.358 (5.304)	0.212 (0.535)	−0.192 (−0.130)	−0.529 (−2.121)	428.44 (4.112)
2c......	1.0	−46.9512	−12.76 (−0.933)	−0.019 (−1.892)	−9.272 (−2.949)	−9.363 (−2.628)	0.265 (2.949)	−0.002 (−0.426)	0.310 (0.453)	−0.068 (−1.502)	4.246 (2.820)

B. Murder Supply Functions: 1950, 44 States

Eq.	λ	$L(\lambda)^*$	Constant	T	P^c	$P^{e|c}$	NW	X	W	AGE	URB	EPOS
						$\overline{PX5}$						
1a........	$0.225 = \hat\lambda$	−2.3101	−5.088 (−1.722)	−0.149 (−2.790)	−0.975 (−4.792)	−0.776 (−4.849)	0.410 (6.405)	2.905 (2.689)	0.193 (1.708)	0.726 (1.623)	−0.151 (−0.878)	2.285 (5.009)
1b........	0.001	−4.5945	−278.12 (−4.421)	−0.294 (−2.439)	−0.538 (−4.588)	−0.274 (−4.309)	0.445 (6.118)	1.545 (2.711)	0.881 (1.811)	0.853 (1.374)	−0.342 (−1.020)	273.11 (4.313)
1c........	1.0	−25.3507	−4.491 (−0.291)	−0.013 (−2.419)	−7.475 (−3.017)	−25.780 (−3.903)	0.207 (4.287)	41.665 (2.234)	0.001 (0.466)	0.485 (1.703)	0.014 (0.444)	3.292 (3.119)
						$\overline{PX5Q}$						
2a........	$0.15 = \hat\lambda$	−12.5914	−1.481 (−0.386)	−0.152 (−1.412)	−0.568 (−2.885)	−0.268 (−1.289)	0.381 (3.893)	1.969 (1.387)	0.151 (0.645)	0.375 (0.850)	−0.022 (−0.084)	1.334 (1.421)
2b........	0.001	−13.2404	−157.87 (−1.358)	−0.239 (−1.299)	−0.401 (−2.941)	−0.158 (−1.364)	0.375 (3.759)	1.280 (1.432)	0.264 (0.451)	0.403 (0.753)	−0.004 (−0.011)	157.57 (1.365)
2c........	1.0	−32.9919	27.257 (1.192)	−0.015 (−2.109)	−4.298 (−1.763)	0.478 (0.069)	0.147 (2.336)	40.613 (1.264)	0.000 (0.071)	0.301 (1.188)	0.030 (0.721)	1.238 (0.996)

Note.—GLS and OLS regressions, selected transformations of linear form, results from Box and Cox tests on full observation set ($\hat\beta/S_{\hat\beta}$ in parentheses). Eqq. 1a–1c in part A are weighted by $\sqrt{N_{URB}}$; eqq. 1a–1c in part B are weighted by $\sqrt{N_{REP}}$; eqq. 2a–2c are unweighted throughout.

* $L(\lambda)$ is the magnitude of the estimated log-likelihood function at the given value of λ, as defined in eqq. (A2) and (A4) in Appendix A.

not mean, necessarily, that the mean rate of murder in nonexecuting states is lower than the rate in executing states where the level of $P^o e|c$ is lowest. More important, as the analysis in Appendix B indicates, it cannot be determined whether the observed significant difference between the estimated constant terms in equations relating to executing and nonexecuting states is the result of "missing variables" that differ significantly across these subsets of states or because of the arbitrary values assigned to measures of the perceived risk of execution in nonexecuting states: if the true risks were higher than "zero" in these states, then the assignment of zero values to estimates of $Pe|c$ will necessarily bias the constant terms of the corresponding regression equations toward negative values, especially in the approximate logarithmic format. That the effect of EPOS sometimes is found to be statistically insignificant in regressions based on the simple linear specification indicates the relative importance of this consideration (see also n. 27).

2. Box and Cox Tests for Optimal Transformations

Although the qualitative results derived through the GLS estimation procedure are found to be robust with respect to functional specification (see table 4, parts A and B), the Box and Cox tests for optimal transformations reported in Appendix A unambiguously establish the relative superiority of the logarithmic specification. In virtually all tests conducted, the logarithmic specifications cannot be rejected as optimal within the classes of power transformations considered. In contrast, the simple linear transformations and the semilogarithmic transformation considered are rejected as optimal in all cases. These results are consistent with the analytical considerations raised in Section IC and lend support to the results on deterrence derived through the logarithmic specification in earlier studies (Ehrlich 1974, 1975a). Moreover, the GLS results obtained through the *optimal* transformations $(\hat{\lambda})$ selected by the Box and Cox procedure are without exception compatible with the basic deterrence hypotheses concerning the effects of the probability of conviction, the conditional probability of execution, and the severity of imprisonment.

3. Vital Statistics Data on Homicide

The *Vital Statistics of the United States* (*VS*) (U.S. Bureau of the Census 1943; U.S. Department of Health, Education, and Welfare 1953) provides alternative data on homicides. For the purpose of an empirical implementation of the theory, however, the FBI data are conceptually superior to the *Vital Statistics* series because the latter includes justifiable and excusable homicides, whereas the FBI murder category is defined to include only willful felonious homicides.[20] The *VS* data may also understate the true number of homicides, because death certificates on which these statistics are based sometimes reflect classification of death by medical causes alone, especially in those instances when death from homicidal assaults lags the actual time of assault. The cross-sectional information in the *Vital Statistics* in 1950 is also somewhat noncomparable because in 1940 homicide statistics are reported by the place of the occurrence of homicide, which is the desired statistic, whereas in 1950 these statistics are reported by the place of the victim's residence. Also, only the 1950 data permit homicides caused by the legal intervention of police to be separated from the total homicide counts. One clear advantage of the *VS* data over the *UCR* statistics, however, is that the *VS* information is based on a count of homicides in the entire state, whereas the FBI data are based on samples of urban areas.

The regression models applied to the *VS* data are the models summarized in equations (5) and (6) with the following modifications: the dependent variable now is the homicide rate defined as $h^o = (H^o/N_S)$, where H^o stands for the *VS* total homicide counts[21] and N_S is the state population. The conviction risk is now defined as $P^h{}_c = (C^o/H^o)$. A sample of the regression results is summarized in table 5.

The results are qualitatively the same as those discussed in connection with the FBI data. The quantitative results differ mainly in connection with the estimated deterrent effect of the probability of conviction measures used in the separate analyses which is here smaller in magnitude and less precise. This result is not entirely surprising given that the *VS* data on homicide may not be as clearly related to the relevant concept of murder as are the FBI statistics. It indicates that the efficiency of empirical measures of conviction risk depend heavily on the relevance of the crime statistics used in their construction.

The pattern of results reported in table 5 generally is quite consistent with the pattern observed in the analysis of the FBI data. Weighted regressions, here executed only with $\sqrt{N_S}$ as a weighting factor, yield regression coefficients with lower standard errors than unweighted regressions in both 1940 and 1950. Furthermore, the log-linear regression format is found to be decisively superior to the simple linear format. A Box and Cox test performed on the full observation set in 1940, for example, shows that the approximate logarithmic transformation, unlike

---

[20] For an elaboration of this point see Ehrlich (1975*b*, pp. 212–13). The conceptual superiority of police-gathered data is generally recognized in the criminology literature; see, e.g., Wolfgang (1961, p. 49).

[21] Legal executions are excluded as are, in 1950 only, homicides through legal intervention of police.

TABLE 5

HOMICIDE SUPPLY FUNCTIONS: 1940 AND 1950, GLS REGRESSIONS

Eq.	Year	N	"R^2"	Constant	T	$P^k{}_c$	$P^o{}_{e|c}$	NW	X	W	AGE	URB	EPOS
Results from subsets of states with positive executions:*													
1........	1940	33	.9527	9.036 (2.42)	−0.226 (−2.07)	−0.562 (−4.26)	$\overline{PX4Q}$ −0.341 (−3.54)	0.432 (6.73)	...	0.262 (0.82)	−2.446 (−2.69)	−0.877 (−4.56)	...
2........	1950	36	.9555	−2.106 (−0.71)	−0.271 (−2.15)	−0.253 (−1.45)	$\underline{PX5Q}$ −0.196 (−3.21)	0.401 (6.68)	1.617 (2.92)	0.827 (2.14)	0.098 (0.20)	−0.284 (−0.85)	...
Results from full-observation set:†													
3........	1940	44	.9526	−326.5 (−3.45)	−0.276 (−2.73)	−0.551 (−4.60)	$\overline{PX4Q}$ −0.333 (−3.56)	0.467 (8.51)	...	0.483 (1.59)	−2.098 (−2.37)	−0.818 (−4.41)	333.0 (3.57)
4........	1950	46	.9523	−194.8 (−2.95)	−0.154 (−1.36)	−0.211 (−1.52)	$\underline{PX5Q}$ −0.194 (−2.94)	0.335 (5.38)	1.982 (3.51)	0.348 (0.86)	0.303 (0.59)	0.236 (0.82)	194.0 (2.94)

NOTE.—All eqq. are weighted by $\sqrt{N_s}$.
* All variables measured in natural logarithms.
† All variables except EPOS transformed via $x^* = (x^\lambda - 1/\lambda)$, where x denotes the natural value of a variable and $\lambda = 0.001$.

the simple linear transformation, cannot be rejected as an optimal regression form.

4. Murder, Aggravated Assault, and Robbery—
Further Analysis of FBI Data

A complete implementation of the analysis of interrelationships among murder, aggravated assault, and robbery developed in Section IA could not be pursued because of the absence of published data on all the specific conditional probabilities and severities of punishment entering equation (3). Introduction in the regression analysis of deterrence variables associated with a specific crime $(P^o c_i, T_i)$ along with corresponding variables associated with interrelated crimes $(P^o c_j, T_j, j \neq i)$ generally has been found to yield insignificant estimates of the effects of $P^o c_j$ and T_j on q^o_i, possibly because the latter are not efficient measures of the relevant conditional probabilities or due to a high degree of partial correlation between estimates of probability and severity of imprisonment for different crimes. Only the murder equations reported in table 6, lines 4 and 5, show some evidence for complementarity relations. The bulk of the analysis on interdependencies among these crimes has been conducted through implementation of the restricted model:

$$ q_i^{o(\lambda)} = a + b_{i1} T_i^{(\lambda)} + b_{i2} P^o c_i^{(\lambda)} + b_{i3} P^o e | c^{(\lambda)} + \cdots, \qquad (7) $$

where i = assault and robbery, $P^o e | c$ is the conditional probability of execution for murder, and the remaining relevant variables are those introduced in equations (5) or (6). In this model all the relevant probabilities and severities of punishment for related crimes (j) are identified with, or assumed to be proportionally related to, $P^o c_i$ and T_i, and the coefficient b_3 indicates the direction of interdependencies between murder and robbery or assault. In analyses of subsets of executing states the transformation employed in estimating equation (7) is logarithmic. The results are reported in table 6, equations 1–3. (The murder regression is shown for comparison.) Difficulties in the estimation of cross-deterrence effects of probability and severity of punishment notwithstanding the interdependencies among the three crimes examined may still be reflected in systematic correlations among the residual terms associated with each crime. Indeed, analysis of residuals estimated from the single equations reveals sizable *positive* correlations[22] indicating complementary effects. To take account of these correlations in deriving efficient estimates

---

[22] The correlation matrix of residuals associated with murder, robbery, and assault shows that the correlation coefficients between paired crimes range between +.35 and +.5.

TABLE 6

Interrelated Crimes: Selected Results for 1950 Single Equations, Logarithmic Form

Eq.	Dependent Variable	N	"R^2"	Constant	T_i	P^c_i	$P^e_{\|c}$	NW	X	W	AGE	URB
1	$q^o_{(murder)}$*	35	.9581	−4.622 3.950 (−1.17)	T_{MUR} −0.459 0.128 (−3.59)	P^o_{MUR} −0.687 0.131 (−5.23)	$PX5$ −0.272 0.057 (−4.74)	0.497 0.070 (7.13)	1.200 0.541 (2.22)	1.226 0.463 (2.65)	0.274 0.623 (0.44)	−0.742 0.357 (−2.08)
2	$q^o_{(assault)}$	35	.9818	−5.854 5.707 (−1.03)	T_{ASS} −0.416 0.209 (−2.00)	P^o_{ASS} −0.429 0.098 (−4.37)	$PX5$ −0.024 0.108 (−0.22)	0.761 0.110 (6.89)	0.175 0.879 (0.20)	1.694 0.701 (2.42)	−0.173 0.889 (−0.19)	−1.160 0.507 (−2.29)
3	$q^o_{(robbery)}$	35	.9819	−6.534 5.672 (−1.15)	T_{ROB} −0.570 0.219 (−2.60)	P^o_{ROB} −0.887 0.123 (−7.20)	$PX5$ −0.146 0.091 (−1.61)	0.266 0.105 (2.54)	0.932 0.746 (1.25)	1.309 0.772 (1.69)	−0.593 0.868 (−0.68)	0.439 0.519 (0.85)
4	$q^o_{(murder)}$	35	.9633	−3.013 (−0.75)	T_{MUR} −0.424 (−3.43)	P^o_{MUR} −0.640 (−4.92)	$PX5Q$ −0.204 (−2.99)	0.466 (6.25)	0.854 (1.35)	1.062 (2.29)	0.093 (0.15)	−0.841 (−2.33)
5	$q^o_{(murder)}$	35	.9671	−3.777 (−1.01)	T_{MUR} −0.398 (−3.20)	P^o_{MUR} −0.670 (−4.86)	$PX5Q$ −0.224 (−3.98)	0.515 (7.63)	0.822 (1.59)	1.073 (2.11)	0.192 (0.33)	−0.730 (−1.92)

Additional variables:

For Eq. 4:
T_{ASS}	P^o_{ASS}
−0.063 (−0.45)	−0.098 (−1.55)

For Eq. 5:
T_{ROB}	P^o_{ROB}
−0.189 (−1.25)	−0.167 (−2.13)

Note.—All eqq. are weighted by $\sqrt{N_{REP}}$; reported statistics are $\hat{\beta}$, $S_{\hat{\beta}}$, and $\hat{\beta}/S_{\hat{\beta}}$ in parentheses.
* From table 3, line 5.

165

of the interrelated regressions, both the subsets of executing states and the full observation sets have been estimated simultaneously via Zellner's seemingly unrelated regression method (SUR). The results are reported in table 7.[23]

The regression results are highly consistent with previously reported findings. The main novel finding is that the elasticities of robbery and aggravated assault, as well as of murder, with respect to measures of the conditional risk of execution are negative. Execution risk has the most sizable effect on the murder rate and the least sizable effect on the frequency of assault. The interpretation may be that aggravated assault is more of a "substitute" for murder than is robbery. This pattern of the results is seen more convincingly in the results derived from the application of the SUR method. The standard errors of SUR estimates of regression coefficients, without exception, are lower than the corresponding estimates derived from application of the single-equation least-squares procedure.[24]

5. Pooling of the Cross-Section Samples and Tests of Homogeneity

Not only do the results from 1940 and 1950 independently confirm the basic hypotheses of the model, but the results appear strikingly similar. Combining the two samples permits further testing of the hypothesized effects and allows for systematic examination of the homogeneity of the populations underlying different subsamples. Due to exclusion of the income variables and potential data exigencies, a dummy variable, D_{40}

[23] The results reported in tables 6 and 7 are derived from analysis of 1950 data, since in 1940 the application of the SUR analysis was difficult because of the small and variable sample sizes of executing states for which a complete set of data on specific variables is available. The results obtained from application of single-equation least-squares procedures to data from 1940 are qualitatively similar to those reported in connection with the corresponding regressions using 1950 data, but the standard errors of the estimated coefficients associated with $P^o e | c$ in assault and robbery regressions were relatively more sizable.

[24] Vital statistics data on the number of homicides occurring in 1950 through legal intervention by police have also permitted an examination of the effect of a measure of the risk of death from police intervention on the frequency of violent crimes. This was achieved by introducing in a regression equation combining murder, robbery, and assault the natural logarithm of the ratio of homicides through police intervention to the estimated total number of murders, robberies, and assaults ($P^o d$) as an additional explanatory variable in the context of the model specified in equation (5). The results, based upon the 27 states with both $PX5Q$ and $P^o d$ positive, indicate the existence of a negative but weak association between $P^o d$ and the rate of violent crimes with the estimated elasticity associated with $P^o d$ being -0.225 and its standard error 0.14. The introduction of $P^o d$ in the regression analysis did not have any significant effects on the coefficients associated with $PX5Q$ (which is found to be negative and significant) or the other deterrence variables entering the regression equation. Similar results are obtained when $P^o d$ is introduced as an additional explanatory variable in regressions relating to the crime of murder alone.

TABLE 7

INTERRELATED CRIMES: 1950, SIMULTANEOUS ESTIMATION SEEMINGLY UNRELATED REGRESSIONS

Subset of 35 states with $P^o_{e|c} > 0$; logarithmic form†

Eq.	Dependent Variable	Constant	T_i	$P^o_{c_i}$	$P^o_{e\|c}$	NW	X	W	AGE	URB	EPOS*
			T_{MUR}	P^o_{MUR}	$PX5$						
1a.........	q^o_{MUR}	-4.378 3.882 (-1.13)	-0.467 0.108 (-4.31)	-0.660 0.113 (-5.85)	-0.273 0.057 (-4.76)	0.494 0.069 (7.13)	1.192 0.522 (2.28)	1.213 0.462 (2.63)	0.255 0.615 (0.42)	-0.748 0.349 (-2.14)	::: :::
			T_{ASS}	P^o_{ASS}	$PX5$						
1b.........	q^o_{ASS}	-6.995 5.662 (-1.24)	-0.375 0.184 (-2.03)	-0.355 0.087 (-4.09)	-0.078 0.103 (-0.76)	0.778 0.109 (7.16)	-0.404 0.843 (0.48)	1.819 0.697 (2.61)	-0.090 0.885 (-0.10)	-1.103 0.502 (-2.19)	::: :::
			T_{ROB}	P^o_{ROB}	$PX5$						
1c.........	q^o_{ROB}	-7.211 5.631 (-1.28)	-0.413 0.195 (-2.12)	-0.780 0.109 (-7.14)	-0.176 0.089 (-1.97)	0.246 0.104 (2.36)	1.183 0.735 (1.61)	1.383 0.755 (1.83)	-0.564 0.868 (-0.65)	0.458 0.512 (0.89)	::: :::

Full observation set (44 states); approximate logarithmic form‡

2a q^o_{MUR}

		T_{MUR}	P^o_{MUR}	$PX5Q$						
	−281.85	−0.300	−0.541	−0.278	0.431	1.389	0.897	0.710	−0.416	399.75
	60.00	0.101	0.100	0.061	0.071	0.551	0.477	0.609	0.329	88.46
	(−4.62)	(−2.96)	(−5.43)	(−4.51)	(6.04)	(2.52)	(1.88)	(1.17)	(−1.27)	(4.52)

2b q^o_{ASS}

		T_{ASS}	P^o_{ASS}	$PX5Q$						
	−107.6	−0.393	−0.351	−0.101	0.733	0.315	1.543	0.163	−0.915	145.71
	94.66	0.169	0.079	0.094	0.096	0.778	0.635	0.789	0.429	135.95
	(−1.13)	(−2.32)	(−4.46)	(−1.07)	(7.64)	(0.41)	(2.43)	(0.21)	(−2.13)	(1.07)

2c q^o_{ROB}

		T_{ROB}	P^o_{ROB}	$PX5Q$						
	−166.77	−0.433	−0.831	−0.160	0.261	0.922	1.420	−0.588	0.338	229.78
	81.19	0.175	0.100	0.081	0.090	0.677	0.660	0.755	0.426	117.10
	(−2.05)	(−2.48)	(−8.31)	(−1.96)	(2.89)	(1.36)	(2.15)	(−0.78)	(0.79)	(1.96)

NOTE.—All eqq. weighted by $\sqrt{N_{EEP}}$; reported statistics are $\hat{\beta}$, $S\hat{\beta}$, and $\hat{\beta}/S\hat{\beta}$ in parentheses.
* EPOS is defined here as (2) in executing states and (1) in states where $Pe_{|c} = 0$.
† All variables measured in natural logarithms.
‡ All variables (here including EPOS) transformed as follows: $x^\bullet = (x^\lambda - 1/\lambda)$, where x denotes the natural value of a variable and $\lambda = 0.001$.

(1940 = 1), has been added to the regressions reported in table 8.[25]

The results are rather decisive in that they show that the restricted estimation via the pooled samples greatly improves the efficiency of the point estimates of all the deterrence variables. Indeed, the pooled sample results provide, perhaps, the strongest evidence for the deterrence hypothesis. Estimates of the elasticity associated with $P^o e|c$ are nearly the same as corresponding estimates reported in table 3, but their confidence intervals are markedly narrower. Point estimates of comparable deterrent effects are found to be statistically indistinguishable in regressions using the full observation set and the subset of executing states, which is consistent with the results reported in Part 2 of this subsection. Moreover, the differences between the estimated elasticities associated with $P^o c$ and $P^o e|c$ are statistically significant even at the 1 percent level in all the regressions but the southern subset. The analysis also indicates remarkable stability in the basic regression results derived from the 1940 and the 1950 samples. The only apparent difference between the 1940 and 1950 regression estimates reported in table 8 concerns the constant terms of the regressions, as indicated by the effect of the dummy variable.[26] The effect of D_{40} seems to be due to data differences and changes in the relevant income-distribution measures (see n. 25). It is also possible that the general downward trend in murder rates between 1940 and 1950 is partly due to the effect of improved medical technology—a factor which is not accounted for directly in the regression analysis. Application of Chow's test of equality between all other regression coefficients entering equations 1 and 3 in table 8 for 1940 and

[25] Because of substantial differences in the definitions of W and X between years, these variables are excluded in the regressions below. Curiously, however, when

$$\begin{pmatrix} X_{40} \\ X_{50} \end{pmatrix} \quad \text{and} \quad \begin{pmatrix} W_{40} \\ W_{50} \end{pmatrix},$$

along with D_{40}, are introduced into the pooled regressions as nondifferentiated vectors, both variables are found to have the expected positive and statistically significant effects, although the effects of the other variables in equations 2 and 4 of table 8 remain virtually unchanged. Moreover, the standard errors of the coefficients associated with the three deterrence variables and NW are reduced and the inferences concerning tests of homogeneity remain unchanged. Similar findings are obtained in less restricted regressions allowing the coefficients associated with X_{40} and W_{40} to differ from those associated with X_{50} and W_{50}, with the exceptions that the effects of X_{40} and, more notably, D_{40}, become insignificant. Detailed results are omitted here due to lack of space. To achieve greater comparability in variable definitions, the urbanization measure relating to the 1950 sample is defined in all the pooled regressions by the Bureau of the Census's "old," i.e., 1940 definition ($URBO_{50}$), rather than by the "new" definition used in the preceding 1950 regressions. Remaining potential data differences concern the variable T_{50}, used in both years, and UCR definitions of "urban areas" from which samples of the dependent variables are taken.

[26] It should be pointed out that there is a high degree of competition between D_{40} and AGE in the pooled regressions; the simple correlation between these two variables is about .8. Evidently, the percent of the age group 15–24 in the population of most states was systematically lower in 1950 than in 1940. Hence the sensitivity of the effect of AGE to inclusion of D_{40} in equations 2 and 4 in table 8.

TABLE 8

MURDER SUPPLY FUNCTIONS: POOLED 1940–50 SAMPLE

Eq.	Set	N	"R²"	Constant	T	P^c	$P^e{}_{|c}$	NW	AGE	URB	EPOS	D_{40}
							PX4Q					
1*	Full	87	.9271	−270.8 (−5.183)	−0.304 (−3.599)	−0.616 (−6.828)	−0.270 (−5.206)	0.443 (9.634)	1.252 (5.120)	−0.455 (−3.672)	269.6 (5.212)	...
2*	Full	87	.9337	−301.0 (−5.863)	−0.340 (−4.143)	−0.635 (−7.308)	−0.304 (−5.927)	0.460 (10.318)	0.043 (0.087)	−0.562 (−4.491)	303.5 (5.933)	0.362 (2.773)
3†	$P^e{}_{|c} > 0$	67	.9145	−0.939 (−0.716)	−0.346 (−3.552)	−0.654 (−6.173)	−0.269 (−4.898)	0.431 (−7.947)	1.226 (4.421)	−0.454 (−3.199)	...	...
4†	$P^e{}_{|c} > 0$	67	.9279	3.847 (2.038)	−0.394 (−4.314)	−0.700 (−6.985)	−0.311 (−5.939)	0.453 (8.950)	−0.347 (−0.643)	−0.607 (−4.358)	...	0.469 (3.311)
5*	North (full)	58	.9201	−266.3 (−4.270)	−0.222 (−1.590)	−0.635 (−5.910)	−0.269 (−4.312)	0.551 (8.839)	0.368 (0.541)	−0.887 (−4.682)	268.6 (4.316)	0.328 (1.823)
6*	South (full)	29	.9502	−442.0 (−3.667)	−0.425 (−3.534)	−0.587 (−3.900)	−0.444 (−3.689)	0.456 (4.215)	0.581 (0.487)	−0.485 (−1.823)	442.7 (3.688)	0.171 (0.790)
7†	North ($P^e{}_{|c} > 0$)	39	.9341	4.087 (1.810)	−0.251 (−1.498)	−0.687 (−5.236)	−0.285 (−4.594)	0.602 (8.060)	−0.013 (−0.018)	−1.080 (−4.893)	...	0.488 (2.538)
8†	South ($P^e{}_{|c} > 0$)	28	.9447	0.695 (0.166)	−0.426 (−3.530)	−0.584 (−3.895)	−0.442 (−3.686)	0.457 (4.214)	0.589 (0.492)	−0.484 (−1.813)	...	0.169 (0.782)

Eq.	Set	N	"R²"	Constant	ΔP^c	$\Delta P^e{}_{|c}$	ΔNW	ΔAGE	ΔURB
						PX4Q			
9‡	$P^e{}_{|c} > 0$ in 1940 and 1950	28	.7504	0.389 (2.597)	−0.642 (−5.919)	−0.256 (−4.682)	0.007 (0.026)	−0.422 (−0.720)	−0.048 (−0.098)

Note.—GLS regressions, selected transformations of linear form. $\hat{\beta}$'s $\hat{t}$ in parentheses. Eqq. 1–8 weighted by $\sqrt{N_{URB}}$. For comparability, URB in 1950 is defined as URBO (see n. 25).

* All variables, except EPOS and D_{40}, transformed via $X^* = (X^\lambda - 1/\lambda)$, where X denotes the natural value of a variable and $\lambda = 0.001$.

† All variables measured in natural logarithms.

‡ All variables measured as $X^* = \ln (X_{50}) - \ln (X_{40})$, where X denotes the natural value of a variable, and are weighted by $\sqrt{(N_{URB_{40}} + N_{URB_{50}})/2}$.

1950 produces decisive results: the relevant F-statistics are $F_{7,71} = 1.50$ and $F_{6,53} = 1.804$, respectively. Clearly, then, the hypothesis of no significant differences cannot be rejected at the 5 percent level of significance. Similar results are obtained through regression analyses based on alternative weighting factors and alternative execution risk measures. Results concerning tests of equality between coefficients associated with deterrence variables only are even sharper.

The homogeneity of populations pooled in the regression analysis performed in this study has also been tested across the North and South regions.[27] The results are found to be highly consistent. Comprehensive tests of equality between all the regression coefficients associated with northern and southern samples indicate that the hypothesis of equality cannot be rejected at the 5 percent level of significance. These results are corroborated across samples from 1940 and 1950 as well as the pooled sample (see, for example, eqq. 5 and 6 in table 8). The apparent homogeneity indicates that the regression results reported are not an artifact of *geographically* specific factors unaccounted for in the regression analysis.

In principle, the sharp set of results summarized in equations 1–8 in table 8 may be due to the fact that the 1940 and the 1950 samples are "identical" or that the vectors of variables are strictly proportional, in which case an apparent improvement of regression results is expected on spurious grounds. Examination of the distributions of the key deterrence variables reveals, however, considerable changes in the relative distributions. A stronger confirmation of the technical independence of the samples is provided through regressions based on differences in the values of the relevant variables within the same states between 1940 and 1950. The results, illustrated in equation (9) for the set of consistently executing states, are highly compatible with all previously reported results, as are other results not included here because of lack of space. The effects of deterrence variables are found to be quite similar to those estimated in the cross-sectional analysis, but the effects of demographic variables are considerably less pronounced, presumably because of the relatively

---

[27] States designated South in the 1940 and 1950 samples (constrained by data availability) include Alabama, Arkansas, Delaware, Florida, Kentucky, Louisiana, Maryland, Mississippi, North Carolina, Oklahoma, South Carolina, Tennessee, Texas, Virginia, and West Virginia. The same designation is applied in 1940 and 1950 with the exception that Mississippi is not included in the 1940 sample. Note that the introduction of EPOS in the southern subset (eq. 6 in table 8) is due to the fact that for only one state, Delaware, $PX4Q$ is zero in 1950. In related regressions using $PX5$ as the conditional risk of execution measure, all southern states, including Delaware, are classified as executing states. The results, nevertheless, are highly consistent with those reported in equations 6 and 8. The fact that EPOS has the usual positive and statistically significant effect even in equation 6 therefore underscores the argument that the appearance of significant differences between constant terms in "executing" and "nonexecuting" states is largely due to the assignment of inappropriate values to measures of $Pe|c$ in such states. Conceivably, the constant term in the regression equation associated with Delaware is estimated to be lower than in other states because the true level of execution risk in Delaware had been positive, not zero as equation 6 implies.

smaller changes in the relative distributions of these variables. The "disappearance" of the effect of *NW* in these regressions is compatible, however, with the results from the time-series investigation (Ehrlich 1975a, p. 412). It suggests that the significant effect of this variable in the cross-sectional investigations may largely reflect the effects associated with relatively low earning opportunities for nonwhites that are not captured by *W* and *X*. Over time, these opportunities have improved. The main contribution of the regression analysis of murder changes is its compatibility with the theorized predictions concerning the signs and relative magnitudes of the elasticities of the murder rate with respect to $P^o c$ and $P^o e|c$ and its consistency with the cross-sectional results on deterrence. It clearly suggests that the strong results derived from the pooled samples are not artifacts of "sample duplications."

III. Executing and Nonexecuting States

The murder rate has been shown to depend, in part, on the risks of conviction and execution and on the severity of imprisonment for murder, each of which, in turn, is subject to the control of public authorities. As is pointed out in Appendix B1, however, the magnitudes of these variables may be the result, rather than the cause, of the relevant crime rates. In particular, the tendency of state courts, juries, and other relevant authorities to retain or impose the death penalty is expected to be responsive to the perceived social costs of capital crimes. The purpose of this section is to compare some crime and punishment data across executing and nonexecuting states in light of theoretical expectations.

In the analysis of optimal defense against crime, law enforcement agencies are assumed to behave in accordance with the expectation that certainty and severity of imprisonment and the risk of execution have restraining (i.e., deterrent and incapacitating) effects on the frequency of crime. The agencies are assumed to set optimal penalties and produce optimal values of the probability of conviction and the conditional probabilities of specific penalties so as to minimize the net per capita social losses from crime, including the costs of all law enforcement activities. The components of the social loss function are identified in equation (8) below:[28]

$$L = D(q) + C(q, Pc) + \gamma_1 Pc \, Pe|c \, qd + \gamma_2 Pc(1 - Pe|c)m. \quad (8)$$

[28] In a more general formulation of the model, one may wish to define q as a vector of interrelated crimes such as murder, robbery, and assault. Similarly, Pc, m, and $Pe|c$ could be defined as vectors of corresponding deterrence variables. Such generalization would complicate the derivations of the basic behavioral implications discussed but would not change their basic thrust. Behavioral implications following from the formulation adopted in equation (8) are formally developed in the mathematical Appendix to this paper, omitted here for lack of space. One important implication of that model, which is compatible with the empirical findings reported in Section II, is that the elasticity of the murder rate with respect to Pc exceeds the corresponding elasticities with respect to both $Pe|c$ and the cost of imprisonment m, or $e_{Pe|c} < e_{Pc} > e_m$.

In equation (8) q is the crime rate, $D(q)$ designates the net direct social damage from crime, $C(q, Pc)$ represents the costs of apprehending and convicting offenders, and the last two terms represent the social costs associated with executing and incarcerating convicted persons, respectively. The terms d (treated as a parameter at a point in time) and m measure the discounted value of the private costs of execution and imprisonment per convict, and γ_1 and γ_2 are positive coefficients "translating" private into social (deadweight) costs and augmenting the relevant public expenditures in administering penalties. Both $D(q)$ and $C(q, Pc)$ are assumed to be convex functions.

In terms of the social loss function introduced in equation (8), optimal (cost-minimizing) values of the risk or status of execution as well as the other deterrence variables must equate the marginal cost of deterrence with the marginal revenue from the expected decrease in crime levels. An important implication of the optimality conditions is that the optimal risk of execution could be considerably below unity even if on the margin the death penalty has a differential restraining impact on murder over and above that of imprisonment because executions entail a larger deadweight loss on society (the difference between $\gamma_1 d$ and $\gamma_2 m$ is assumed positive). Variations in the enforcement level of capital punishment, including its abolition, as well as changes in the magnitudes of other deterrence variables generally can be explained as a consequence of shifts in three basic sets of parameters: the level of the marginal harm from murder and related crimes, the social cost of capital punishment relative to other sanctions, and the technology of producing means of deterrence and incapacitation. The first two sets of factors appear to be especially relevant for analysis of data relating to the classes of executing and nonexecuting states.

A central behavioral implication of the model is that the optimal magnitudes of all three deterrence variables generally must rise as a result of an increase in the marginal social damages from crime due to exogenous factors. Since stability conditions for optimal law enforcement are satisfied if, among other related conditions, the marginal damages from crime are monotonically related to the rate of crime in the population,[29] an increase in the crime rate due to exogenous factors would

---

[29] This assumption can be justified partly on the grounds that the resource costs expended by offenders in the course of their criminal activity rise with the frequency of crime committed (especially by new "entrants") and because the marginal costs of apprehending and convicting offenders are expected to be an increasing function of the frequency of offenses committed (both C_{qq} and C_{qPc} are positive). Indeed, it can be shown that if both the production function of law enforcement activity implicit in $C(q, Pc)$ and the supply-of-offenses function are of the Cobb-Douglas variety, then an exogenous increase in q will necessarily lead to an increase in the magnitudes of severity and certainty of punishment even if $D_{qq} = 0$. Of course, the marginal social valuation of the human and nonhuman assets destroyed through crime must eventually rise as their "stocks" are depleted with more crimes committed at a point in time.

require that the optimal values of deterrence variables be increased. A decrease in the crime rate then would have the reverse effects. While the theory does not predict that each of the three deterrence variables would be reduced as a consequence, it suggests that both certainty of conviction and severity of punishment would tend to decline if "punishment" were defined as a single-choice variable. More generally, $Pe|c$ and m always are expected to move in the same direction if γ_1 and γ_2 remain constant. In particular, it follows that those states where murder rates have traditionally been exceptionally low due to factors exogenous to the law enforcement system (such as demographic and general economic variables) are more likely to minimize the application of, or abolish, the death penalty either legally or in practice. These states also are expected to impose relatively short imprisonment terms and possibly to have relatively low conviction risks.

The theory allows for corner solutions in the risk of execution across states to occur not only, however, as a consequence of autonomous changes in the crime rate, but also as a result of changes in factors determining the "social cost" of execution. For example, changes in political factors strengthening the influence of groups interested in greater emphasis on rehabilitation or reformation of offenders, federal judicial or administrative rulings, or increased social aversion toward harsh punishments would either raise the magnitude of the coefficient γ_1 in equation (8) or might lead directly to a decrease in the magnitude of $Pe|c$. Under such circumstances, if a corner solution occurs so that execution is abolished de facto, the theory predicts that either the probability of conviction or the severity of punishment by imprisonment or both will be increased. The intuitive reason is that to the extent that cessation of execution is not motivated by a low level of crime, relinquishing the practice of execution must be "compensated" through greater reliance on alternative instruments of law enforcement in order to bring about an optimal level of deterrence and incapacitation.

Both predictions appear to be compatible with data on the mean value of crime and deterrence variables across various subsets of executing and nonexecuting states in 1940, 1950, and 1960. As table 9 demonstrates, in all 3 years analyzed, the murder rate is found to be lowest in states which abolish the death penalty in law, somewhat higher in states which persistently refrain from enforcing the death penalty, and is even higher in states which only intermittently refrain from executing convicts. In addition, the murder rate is always higher in the corresponding subsets of executing states which complement the three subsets of legally or practically nonexecuting states discussed above. Moreover, subsets of abolition states having exceptionally low murder rates not only choose to refrain from using the death penalty, they also tend to set somewhat lower

TABLE 9

MEANS OF ESTIMATED CRIME RATES, PROBABILITIES OF CONVICTION, AND IMPRISONMENT TERMS IN EXECUTING AND NONEXECUTING STATES, 1940–60

SUBSETS COMPARED BY YEAR AND MEAN*	EXECUTION STATUS IN t		EXECUTION STATUS IN 5 YEARS		LEGAL STATUS OF DEATH PENALTY	
	$E_t > 0$ (1)	$E_t = 0$ (2)	$\sum_{j=0}^{4} E_{t-j} > 0$ (3)	$\sum_{j=0}^{4} E_{t-j} = 0$ (4)	Legal (5)	Illegal (6)
1940:						
$q°$ (murder)	9.9069	2.0947	8.5583	1.5833	7.6048	1.2833
$P°_c$ (murder)†	0.2074	0.3438	0.2338	0.3523	0.2597	0.2739
T_{50} (murder)	119.759	158.105	130.222	149.083	135.143	133.500
$q°$ (assault)	87.0034	17.6421	75.0028	13.1833	66.0595	13.9667
$q°$ (robbery)	60.0414	29.0737	55.6083	24.3083	51.0309	25.0500
$PX5$‡	...	...	0.1552	...	...	...
No. of states	29	19	36	12	42	6
1950:						
$q°$ (murder)	8.5291	2.3752	6.3541	1.8591	5.8679	1.5167
$P°_c$ (murder)§	0.2324	0.3106	0.2595	0.3183	0.2735	0.2514
T (murder)	117.696	150.800	135.676	132.445	135.143	133.500
$q°$ (assault)	105.004	27.0960	76.0486	25.3363	69.8405	26.5333
$q°$ (robbery)	49.6522	31.1000	43.1378	29.4000	42.3809	23.2500
$PX5'$	...	...	0.0809	...	...	...
No. of states	23	25	37	11	42	6

175

1960:**

q^o (murder)	7.1050	3.3857	6.2492	2.2750	5.3397	2.3857
P^o_c (murder)††	0.4548	0.4830	0.4542	0.5034	0.4776	0.4330
T (murder)††	134.890	169.104	131.361	199.642	144.277	213.214
q^o (assault)	71.9200	40.7849	69.8000	21.7875	58.6103	25.4428
q^o (robbery)	40.1300	33.2727	43.4018	21.7875	38.1927	24.4857
$PX5$‡‡	....	....	0.0195	....	....	....
No. of states	20	28	32	16	41	7

* Simple means of the state statistics; number of states compared dictated by the availability of relevant data.
† Cols. 1 and 3 exclude Georgia, Mississippi, and Nevada; cols. 2 and 4 exclude Maine and Vermont; cols. 3 and 5 exclude Georgia, Mississippi, Nevada, and Vermont; col. 6 excludes Maine.
‡ Col. 3 estimate excludes Georgia and Mississippi.
§ Col. 1 excludes Georgia; col. 2 excludes North Dakota, Michigan, and Vermont; cols. 3 and 5 exclude Georgia and Vermont; cols. 4 and 6 exclude Michigan and North Dakota.
‖ Col. 3 estimate excludes Georgia.
** Data for 1960 exclude Alaska and Hawaii. The data for 1960 are not comparable to the 1940 and 1950 data due to the following differences: (1) In 1960 q^o is based on total reported crimes in each state, whereas q^o in 1940 and 1950 is based on a state sample of urban areas. (2) Commitments to state prisons in 1960 are convicts of homicide whereas in 1940 and 1950 commitments are for murder convicts. Commitments in 1960 include only convicts with definite sentences. To estimate convictions, F_{60} is added to commitments. Also, P^o_c in 1960 is based on total reported crimes, Q^o, whereas in 1940 and 1950 P^o_c is based on $Q^o = q^o \times N_s$. (3) T in 1960 is average time served whereas median time served measures T in 1950.
†† Cols. 2, 3 and 5 exclude New Jersey.
‡‡ Col. 3 estimate excludes New Jersey.

values of conviction risks and imprisonment terms.[30] Indeed, there is a strong indication—apart from the regression results in Section II—that the relatively low magnitudes of the execution risk variables in these subsets are the result rather than the cause of low murder rates. As table 9 shows, the subsets of persistently nonexecuting states are characterized by much lower frequencies of assault and robbery relative to the corresponding executing or retentionist states in all 3 years considered. Given the regression results, the differences between the crime levels in the two classes of states may be ascribed, in part, to the substantial differences in demographic variables, such as the percentage of nonwhites, and possibly to other "missing" or misspecified factors.[31] To some extent, the relatively low frequencies of assault and robbery may even be contributing causes for the legal or practical abolition of the death penalty, because murder is often a by-product of assault and robbery and the enforcement of capital punishment may have restraining effects on these crimes as well (see Section II). Thus the incentive to enforce the death penalty might be monotonically related to the frequencies of assault and robbery as well as of murder. Again, there is some evidence that at least severity of imprisonment for assault and robbery tends to be lower in abolitionist than in retentionist states.

At the same time, table 9 reveals that in the set of states which refrain from enforcing the death penalty in a given year, but not necessarily over a greater period, and in which murder rates are found to be higher than in the relatively smaller subset of persistently nonexecuting states, both probability and severity of imprisonment for murder appear to be higher than in the complementary set of executing states. This is the case in all 3 years considered. Furthermore, in 1960 even the set of persistently nonexecuting states, considerably larger in 1960 than in 1950, is characterized by higher values of probability and severity of imprisonment for murder relative to the complementary set of executing states.[32] This

[30] Due to the small number of states included in the subsets of states where execution is illegal, the means of the state statistics based on single-years data must be viewed with caution. (See also n. 32 below.)

[31] The simple mean levels of NW in executing (cols. 3 and 5 in table 9) and nonexecuting (cols. 4 and 6 in table 9) subsets are 12.3 and 11.0 as against 2.0 and 2.2 in 1950, and 12.9 and 11.4 as against 2.2 and 1.6 in 1940, respectively. The corresponding mean levels of A_{25-34} also are slightly lower in nonexecuting states in both years. It also seems that abolitionist states tend to be more urbanized than retentionist states in both 1940 and 1950. Other variables examined in the regression analysis do not differ markedly between the two subsets.

[32] Average and median imprisonment terms served for murder in nonexecuting states may be higher than those in executing states simply because murder convicts liable for capital punishment receive long prison sentences in the former class. That this technical consideration may not provide the main explanation for the observed differences in actual imprisonment terms between executing and nonexecuting states is apparent from the fact that states where the death penalty was illegal in 1950 did not have a higher median imprisonment term than states which still retained the death penalty in that year.

tendency for greater reliance on certainty and severity of imprisonment in specific subsets of nonexecuting states, especially in more recent years, is compatible with the theoretical expectation that reductions in execution risk prompted by an increase in the social cost of execution and related exogenous factors would result in compensatory changes in certainty and severity of alternative punishments. The existence of such a tendency is not inconsistent with the hypothesis that capital punishment and other penalties do exert a restraining effect on the murder rate. It is at least compatible with the assumption that law enforcement bodies behave in accordance with that hypothesis. [33]

IV. Summary and Conclusion

Contrary to strong inferences of many death-penalty researchers who interpreted their evidence as a categorical denial of the deterrence hypothesis, this study as well as a related analysis based on time-series data develop evidence not inconsistent with that hypothesis. The case for the deterrence theory is based, in part, on a critical evaluation of earlier works (see n. 1). In the main, the case is based on new empirical findings and their compatibility with a set of predictions derived from the theory.

Before summarizing the main findings of the empirical investigation, some of its inherent limitations must be stressed. The present analysis does not account systematically for potential simultaneity relations between crime rates and deterrence variables—especially the risks of execution and conviction. Although the simple remedies to the problem invoked here may lead to an understatement of the true effect of execution risk, the net direction of the bias cannot be ascertained with confidence because the estimates of effects associated with other deterrence variables may not be statistically consistent. There are many imperfections associated with measures of the probabilities of conviction and execution and the severity of imprisonment as viewed by potential offenders. The regression equations do not include estimates of the extent and quality of medical services available across states, and the interdependencies among murder, robbery, and aggravated assault are dealt with only in a partial manner. While the present investigation deals with the choice of an optimal regression format, it does so only in the context of restricted families of "power transformations." All the statistical tests conducted are conditional upon the validity of the assumptions concerning disturbance terms.

[33] Although this analysis of optimal law enforcement against murder has been applied here in explanation of changes in execution status across different states, it also can be applied in explanation of trends in the enforcement and status of capital punishment in connection with murder and other "capital crimes" over time. An attempt along these lines is included in a related unpublished paper where the social loss from offenses is generalized to incorporate a criterion of "equity" in addition to that of efficiency.

At the same time the consistency and stability in the results obtained upon application of efficient estimation procedures, given the sample limitations, and their consistency with specific theoretical predictions and previous findings seem remarkable. Indeed, it is noteworthy that all the deterrence variables examined in this analysis yield the expected results in connection with murder and other crimes, and that the coefficients associated with explanatory variables other than constant terms appear statistically indistinguishable across different samples as well as across subsets of executing and nonexecuting states. In particular, the subsets based on data from executing states indicate that when enforced the death penalty exerts a restraining effect on the frequency of murder and possibly robbery as well. The investigation shows the existence of distinct execution and imprisonment effects: both $P^o e|c$ and T appear to exert a deterrent effect on murder. Indeed, because the effect of imprisonment is accounted for explicitly in the analysis, this investigation, more directly than the earlier time-series study, indicates that capital punishment has a differential deterrent effect over and above the actually enforced imprisonment terms. The effects of execution risk and other deterrence variables are largely unaffected by the introduction of additional explanatory variables, including the "prices" associated with related crimes and other indicators of relative rewards. Even introduction of risk of death through police intervention (see n. 24) does not affect the regression results. Moreover, as predicted by the theory, the estimated elasticities of murder rates with respect to measures of conviction risk are significantly larger than the estimated elasticities associated with measures of the conditional risk of execution. Also, that the estimated elasticity of the murder rate with respect to conviction risk exceeds the corresponding elasticity with respect to imprisonment severity is not inconsistent with the analysis of optimal public defense against murder (see n. 28). The joint estimation of "supply functions" associated with murder, robbery, and aggravated assault, as well as the pooling of the 1940 and the 1950 samples, narrow the confidence intervals associated with point estimates. Furthermore, the analysis of changes in murder rates within states between 1940 and 1950 produces results which corroborate the general cross-sectional findings.

More important, the basic set of results derived in this cross-sectional investigation is in essence the same as that derived from analysis of time-series data on murder, although the results have been obtained through different estimation procedures and although the time-series analysis did not account for possible variations in imprisonment severity and other relevant variables. The corroborating independent evidence from the 1940 and the 1950 cross sections does not support the proposition that the time-series results on deterrence are merely artifacts of the 1960s or the result of "missing factors" such as the Vietnam War or the proliferation of handguns. Despite statistical differences, point estimates of the elasticity of the murder rate with respect to measures of unconditional probabilities of conviction in the time-series and cross-section analyses lie within each other's confidence intervals (compare, e.g., the results in Ehrlich [1973, table 7] and the results reported above in tables 3, 4, and 8). The larger point estimates of the effect of the unconditional risk of execution on the extent of the murder rate in the cross-sectional analysis may be the result of the fact that the data permit the estimation of such an effect within the set of states with positive executions, whereas the aggregate data used in the time-series analysis have not allowed for a separate estimation of deterrence effects within strictly execution states.[34] Tentative estimates of the average trade-offs between executions and murders computed via the method employed in the time-series study (Ehrlich 1975a, section IIIB) on the basis of the GLS results reported in equations 1–4 in table 8, for example, range between 20 and 24 murders for one execution. It is important to stress that these estimates are based upon regression coefficients derived through the GLS estimation procedure which does not insure consistent estimates. They also are conditional upon specific data limitations.[35]

One of the conspicuous results of the cross-sectional investigation is the strong statistical association between crime rates, especially murder and assault, and the percent of nonwhites in the population. However, the NW effect may, in part, reflect the roles of other demographic variables not fully analyzed in this paper. Its magnitude is reduced when A_{25-34} replaces the usual AGE (15–24) variable. The NW effect in the cross section may largely reflect the effect of low earnings opportunities, specific to nonwhites, which are not accounted for directly in this analysis. The relevance of the latter factor is indicated by the fact that both my time-series analysis and the examination of murder changes between 1940 and 1950 fail to uncover any significant association between NW and murder over time.

---

[34] See the discussion in Ehrlich (1975a, p. 408). It is possible that the cross-sectional elasticities are biased upward relative to the time-series results due to "spillover effects" (see Ehrlich 1974, n. 25) that result from interstate movements of offenders in response to interstate variations in deterrence variables. However, the results show that the estimated elasticities associated with conviction risk are much more similar across the time-series and the cross-section analysis. More generally, it seems unlikely that "spillover effects" would be empirically important in connection with crimes against the person. It should be pointed out that the estimated elasticity of the murder rate with respect to $Pe|c$, in principle, includes both deterrent and incapacitation effects. An estimate of the latter derived through a procedure similar to that used in Ehrlich (1975a, p. 413) indicates that the magnitude of the incapacitation effect is at most 0.08, much lower than the estimated elasticities.

[35] It should be emphasized that in 1940 and 1950 there do not exist estimates of the total number of murders within individual states so that even tentative tradeoffs cannot be calculated without additional assumptions. The numbers mentioned above are implied by the relevant elasticities associated with measures of execution risk on the assumption that urban and rural murder rates were identical in the states included in the general sample underlying table 8.

Another intriguing issue concerns interdependencies between levels of crime rates and deterrence measures in executing and nonexecuting states. Consistent with analysis of optimal social defense against crime, the persistently nonexecuting states face substantially lower risks of victimization through murder and related crimes than do the persistently executing states. The low crime levels in the former class of states, in turn, can be partly attributed to factors whose influence is reflected by the percentage of nonwhites in the population and related demographic variables. Some of the apparent differences in crime levels across the two classes of states, as revealed through the regression model, also may result from understatement of the true (perceived) risks of execution in states classified as "zero" execution risk states. A fuller analysis of the differences in crime levels across these classes and of the variations in execution policy across states and over time must await future research.

Hopefully, the main contribution of this research lies in the suggestion that the basic economic and econometric frameworks used by economists to explain behavior in the marketplace can also be applied in explaining criminal and perhaps some other behavior traditionally labeled as "deviant." The regularities uncovered in connection with movements in crime rates and law enforcement activities pose a challenge for future research. The economic approach might prove useful in analyzing recidivism by offenders, the impact of legitimate employment and training opportunities, apparent racial and sex differences in participation in specific crimes, international variations in crime rates, and public and private protection against crime. As to the policy implications emanating from the new findings, however, basic theoretical and methodological questions remain unanswered because of the complexity of the range of choices available and the difficulties associated with quantifying basic parameters affecting the social costs from offenses and other targets of social policy (see n. 33). Estimates of the restraining effect of the risk of execution in terms of the implied trade-offs between lives sacrificed and lives saved, though apparently not negligible, must be viewed as tentative and imprecise also because they may not represent the relevant *marginal* trade-offs. But even if the estimates were accurate, they simply might indicate the extent of the full social costs associated with sacrifices of the lives of convicted persons for the lives òf potential victims, assuming that the actual policy toward capital punishment has reflected a local social optimum. Perhaps the main policy implication of the present study lies in the support it lends to the general deterrence hypothesis. Indeed, if punishment did not deter offenders, then incapacitation and reformation of those apprehended and convicted would become the sole means of crime control. Not only would such means be of limited usefulness because of the small fraction of potential offenders who would be incapacitated or reformed at a point in time given the relevant costs, but incapacitating penalties are intrinsically inefficient modes of taxing illegitimate behavior from a social point of view. In contrast, if offenders do respond to incentives, punishment and law enforcement become more expedient means of crime control independently of any incapacitating or reformatory benefits of sanctions. Indeed, incapacitation and related "cruel" punishment, in principle, can be replaced by more "humane" penalties involving smaller deadweight losses. Moreover, crime control could be achieved through an optimal balance between both negative and positive incentives.

Appendix A

An Analysis of Transformations

Assuming that the correct functional form of the supply-of-offenses function belongs to the following single-parameter class of "power transformations" involving all the variables of relevance, one may write that function

$$q_i^{(\lambda)} = \alpha + \beta_1 Pc_i^{(\lambda)} + \beta_2 Pe|c_i^{(\lambda)} + \cdots + u_i, \tag{A1}$$

where the operator (λ) associated with any variable X_i is defined by $(X_i^{\lambda} - 1)/\lambda$. The $\lambda = 1$ defines the simple linear transformation with all variables represented by their natural values, and $\lambda = 0$ defines the logarithmic-linear transformation. A search for an optimal transformation can be pursued via direct application of the Box and Cox analysis of transformations (1964).

In applying the Box and Cox analysis it is assumed that for some unknown λ that $u_i \sim N(0, \sigma^2)$ and that the variables on the right-hand side of (A1) are uncorrelated with the error term. The determination of an optimal specification is then achieved by first calculating the maximized log likelihood function (excluding constant terms) for alternative values of λ:

$$L_{\text{max}}(\lambda) = -\frac{n}{2} \ln \hat{\sigma}^2(\lambda) + (\lambda - 1) \sum_{i=1}^{n} \ln q_i. \tag{A2}$$

After determining the maximizing value $\hat{\lambda}$, alternative values of λ can be rejected, using large sample maximum-likelihood theory, by testing whether they belong outside of an approximate $100(1 - \alpha)$ percent confidence interval obtained from:

$$2[L_{\text{max}}(\hat{\lambda}) - L_{\text{max}}(\lambda)] < \chi_1^2(\alpha), \tag{A3}$$

where $\chi_1^2(\alpha)$ denotes the χ^2 statistic with 1 df. It can easily be shown through an application of Box and Cox's analysis that in the case of weighted regressions, equation (A2) becomes:

$$L_{\text{max}}(\lambda) = -\frac{n}{2} \ln \hat{\sigma}'^2(\lambda) + (\lambda - 1) \sum_{i=1}^{n} \ln q_i + \frac{1}{2} \sum_{i=1}^{n} \ln N_i, \tag{A4}$$

where $\hat{\sigma}'^2(\lambda)$ denotes the maximum-likelihood estimate of residual variance calculated from the weighted regressions and the $N_i^{1/2}$ denote the weights. Since tests for homoscedasticity reported in Appendix B show that the error terms in equation (A1) are not homoscedastic, and the analysis of residuals suggests optimal weights for obtaining GLS estimates of equation (A1), both equations (A2) and (A4) are utilized in the pursuant empirical investigation to calculate the relevant log-likelihood functions.

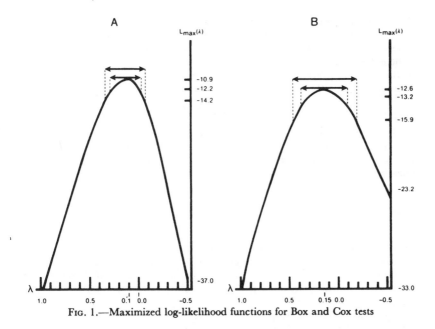

Fig. 1.—Maximized log-likelihood functions for Box and Cox tests

These tests for optimal transformations have been repeatedly applied against data relating to both subsets of states with positive executions and to the full samples of states in both 1940 and 1950. The regression models used in the computation of equations (A2) and (A4) are those underlying equations (5) and (6) in the text, and the tests were conducted with alternative weighting factors and with different estimates of execution risk. A sample of results for selected transformations is reported in table 4, parts A and B. In each table detailed regression results are reported for transformations by $\lambda = 1$ (the simple linear forms), $\lambda = 0.001$ (the approximate log-linear transformation used in connection with the full-observation set), and by $\hat{\lambda}$ (the maximizing value of $L_{max}[\lambda]$). Figure 1 depicts the maximized log-likelihood functions derived from an analysis of one subset of executing states and one full-observation set and indicates the approximate 95 percent and 99 percent confidence intervals associated with λ.

The implications of the Box and Cox tests are rather decisive. Without exception, the tests conducted show that the simple linear form must be rejected as an optimal transformation. The value of L_{max} ($\lambda = 1$) lies far outside the 99 percent confidence interval around $\hat{\lambda}$. In contrast, in all of the tests performed, the log-likelihood function evaluated at $\lambda = 0$ (in executing subsets) or $\lambda = 0.001$ lies within the relevant 95 percent or the 99 percent confidence intervals.

Furthermore, the same unequivocal results are found in tests of transformations related to regression equations where the pair $(P^o c, P^o e | c)$ is replaced by either $(P^o c, P^o e)$ or by $(P^o m, P^o e)$—the basic "prices" of the model (see the discussion in Sections IA and IC). The regression results derived via the latter specification also are found to be consistent with the theoretical expectations. The effects of both Pc and Pe or Pm and Pe are negative and statistically significant. Moreover, the relative magnitudes of the various deterrent effects estimated via the alternative models are found to be the same as those expected from analysis of equation (1).

The preceding analysis indicates the relative superiority of the logarithmic over the simple linear functional form within the class of transformations (A1) which includes both forms as special cases. In view of the discussion in Section IC and the evidence developed in this Appendix, it also is of interest to evaluate the logarithmic transformation within an alternative class of transformations that includes a semilogarithmic functional form as a special case. That class is given by

$$\ln q = \alpha + \beta_1 Pc^{(\lambda)} + \beta_2 Pe|c^{(\lambda)} + \cdots + u. \tag{A5}$$

Here $\lambda = 1$ defines the conventional semilogarithmic specifications and $\lambda = 0$ defines the logarithmic form. By invoking the assumptions made in the preceding discussion, an analysis of transformations can be pursued through a similar application of the Box and Cox approach. The maximized log likelihood, for fixed λ, is here, except for constant terms

$$L_{\max}(\lambda) = -\frac{n}{2} \ln \hat{\sigma}'^2(\lambda). \tag{A6}$$

In the tests conducted in connection with equation (A5), the value of λ that maximizes equation (6), $\hat{\lambda}$, is much closer to $\lambda = 0$ than to $\lambda = 1$. More important, the 99 percent confidence interval around λ always includes $\lambda = 0$, whereas $\lambda = 1$ is always far outside that interval and must therefore be rejected as an optimal transformation.

The general conclusion emerging from these analyses is that under the assumptions concerning the distribution of the disturbance terms, the logarithmic transformation cannot be rejected as an optimal transformation within the classes of "power transformations" considered in this analysis.

Appendix B

The Estimation Procedure and Variables Used

1. *The Estimation Procedure*

The implicit assumption underlying the estimation procedure is that the relative variation in exogenous factors controlling demand-for-enforcement and production-of-deterrence functions is sufficiently greater than that of missing exogenous or stochastic factors controlling supply relationships so that the latter can be "traced out" effectively. Previous research indicates that this assumption is not at odds with findings concerning the effect of conviction risk and imprisonment severity: the relevant estimates derived via OLS and TSLS techniques have been compatible.[36] It should be emphasized that, due to data exigencies,

---

[36] Compare the OLS and TSLS estimates of supply-of-offenses functions in Ehrlich (1970, 1974). Estimates of actual time served in state prisons by prisoners released in sample years have been treated as an exogenous variable even in these earlier analyses partly because of the apparent stability in the distribution of T relative to that of crime rates over periods preceding specific sample years and partly because this variable may in large measure be a true "predetermined" variable in view of the time lag between the date in which offenders are sentenced and their parole eligibility determined and the time of their actual release from prison. Even in the time-series analysis of murder (Ehrlich, 1975a), where no account could be taken of changes in imprisonment severity, the results derived through the simultaneous-equation technique have been found to be quite similar to (unpublished) OLS estimates of the supply-of-offenses functions.

the measure used in this investigation to estimate the length of imprisonment anticipated by potential offenders in 1940 is the actual time served by prisoners released in 1951 rather than in 1940 (T_{50}). Neither the 1940 nor the 1951 measure should necessarily give rise to an important simultaneous-equation bias (see n. 36). But the use of T_{50} as an instrument in the 1940 regressions should practically eliminate biases due to a potentially limiting impact of prison "crowding" on the opportunities to execute long imprisonment sentences in states which experienced unanticipated increases in crime rates in 1940. In contrast, use of T_{50} in the 1940 regressions, in principle, might generate biases due to a potential tendency to mete out relatively long prison sentences in states that experienced relative increases in crime rates in 1940 and because the actual T_{50} figures should be inaccurate measures of the anticipated terms in 1940. The fact that the estimated coefficients of T_{50} as well as of other deterrence variables in the 1940 and the 1950 regressions are found to be statistically indistinguishable (see Section IIB5) lends support to the particular assumption that the instrumental measures of imprisonment terms may be considered "exogenous" or predetermined variables.

A special problem arises in connection with nonexecuting states. In the first place, this class of states, which is at a "corner solution" with respect to use of the death penalty, in practice is found to be an outlier insofar as the rate of crime is concerned. Not only is the murder rate exceptionally low in this class of states, but the rates of robbery and assault there are exceptionally low as well (see table 9). Analysis of optimal defense against murder suggests that declines in the supply of offenses due to exogenous factors would decrease the desire to impose severe sanctions on offenders. Thus, if there were significant shifts in supply functions across subsets of executing and nonexecuting states due to either stochastic factors or to variables not accounted for in the regression analysis, such as medical technology and the degree of social interaction, then these shifts could trace out "demand" rather than "supply" curves (the curves in question relating q to inverse functions of the relevant deterrence variables). Second, and more important, there is a difficulty in assigning quantitative values to the level of execution risk in nonexecuting states. Despite the fact that all states in this class by definition refrain from execution over a substantial period of time, the perceived risk of execution given conviction in these states need not be zero or even identical because of differences in conviction *levels* across states and because of varying expectations concerning future trends. The problem becomes considerably more severe in regressions based on an approximate logarithmic specification: a transformation of $Pe|c = 0$ by the Box and Cox technique with λ set at an arbitrarily small value creates a very large difference between the values of $Pe|c$ in executing and nonexecuting states. Such transformation of the partly null vector of $Pe|c$ measures thus may create the appearance of a significant difference between the constant terms of regressions in the two classes of states where none exist.

A simple remedy is separate estimation of supply curves in the two sets of states and a subsequent test of the equality of the subset of regression coefficients associated with comparable deterrence variables across these sets. Introduction of a dummy variable distinguishing executing and nonexecuting states in the pooled sample of states (i.e., allowance for separate constant terms) as a part of this procedure could account for either "missing variables" in the supply equation or the misspecification of execution risk measures in nonexecuting states and also provide a test for the statistical significance of the *qualitative* effects of these factors. These simple procedures can mitigate but not eliminate the potential simultaneity biases pertaining to estimation of the relationship between the murder rate and the observed risk of execution since they do not address similar difficulties within executing subsets.[37] However, the potential biases that still remain are likely to work against, not in favor of, the theorized deterrent effect of execution.[38]

A second basic problem in the estimation procedure arises from heteroscedasticity in the distribution of error terms. Since the dependent variables are estimates of mean number of offenses per population, their variances are expected to be negatively related to the relevant population base: samples from urban places. Previous cross-sectional studies have shown that the magnitude of squared residuals was negatively related to the relevant population size. In this study the heteroscedasticity postulate has been subjected to a parametric test suggested by Goldfeld and Quandt (1965). The test has been applied by dividing the sample underlying table 8 into high- and low-population states after omitting the middle k states, with k denoting the number of parameters estimated. The results prove decisively contradictory to the hypothesis of homoscedastic errors.[39] In general, the scatter of residuals derived from unweighted regressions strongly indicated the existence of a negative association between residual variances and either state, urban, or (where available) the sample populations: N_S, N_{URB}, and N_{REP}, respectively. The square roots of these population measures were used alternately as weights in deriving GLS estimates of supply functions.

2. *Empirical Counterparts of Theoretical Variables*

The many difficulties associated with use of reported crime rates as measures of the true crime rates in the population have been elaborated upon in previous studies. A problem unique to this investigation is that the reported rates in 1940 and 1950 (q^o) are based on a sample of urban areas, whereas measures of explanatory variables are based on state data. Because consistent measures of all variables could not be obtained, the percentage of the state population residing in urban areas (URB) was introduced as a "correcting factor" in the regression analysis. An independent reason for the introduction of this variable is given in Section IB.

The basic theoretical deterrence variables of interest relate to the mean perceived probabilities of conviction and execution in the population and to the anticipated cost of imprisonment. The respective empirical counterparts of these variables have been estimated via measures of objective risks of conviction and

---

[37] For example, Schuessler's ranking of 41 executing states according to their average homicide rates and execution risks over the period 1937–49 showed that states ranked in the highest quartile by their homicide rates had the second highest measure of unconditional risk of execution (see Schuessler [1952, p. 60]).

[38] The argument can be illustrated unambiguously for the following simplified system. Let

$$\ln q = a + b \ln Pe + u, \tag{I}$$

$$\ln Pe = \alpha + \beta \ln \dot{q} + \gamma \ln Z + v, \tag{II}$$

where Z denotes a vector of exogenous variables. The theory predicts that $b < 0$ and $\beta > 0$. If the disturbance terms u and v are uncorrelated

$$\text{plim } \hat{b} = b + \frac{\beta \text{ Var } (u)(1 - b\beta)}{\beta^2 \text{ Var } (u) + \text{ Var } (v)} > b,$$

where $\hat{b}$ denotes the linear least-squares estimator of b. The analysis is more ambiguous, however, when other endogenous variables are introduced in equation (I).

[39] For example, the F-ratios calculated on the basis of OLS residuals derived from equations 2 and 4 in table 8 and ordered against the urban populations in each state are $F_{39,39} = 5.506$ and $F_{29,29} = 5.125$, respectively, significant even at the 1 percent level.

execution and by the actual length of time served in prison by those released from prison. The construction of each of these measures is discussed in turn.

A desired measure of $Pe|c$ is the ratio of executions to convictions for capital murder in the relevant years. However, inspection of the data reveals that the number of executions per state in a given year was generally small even in 1940 and 1950 and exhibited large percentage changes from year to year. Since these fluctuations amount to severe "sampling errors,"[40] an average ratio of executions to convictions over a number of years would provide a more stable measure. Independent data on convictions are available only in the sample year and only for the category of all murders. Thus, measures have been computed by averaging the number of executions over a number of years preceding and including the sample year in calculating the numerator of $P^o e|c = (\bar{E}^o/C^o)$ (for alternative measures see table 2). Also, alternative measures have been constructed on the basis of executions for all crimes as well as for murder only. The former measure may be relevant because of the possibility that the infrequent executions for other crimes were imposed in connection with crimes where the likelihood of fatal injuries was high. Note that the observed effect of $P^o e|c$ includes, in principle, both deterrence and incapacitating effects. Assessment of the potential incapacitating impact of the death penalty relative to actual imprisonment (see n. 34) shows it to be considerably below even the smallest empirical estimate of the overall impact of $P^o e|c$ that has been derived in the present investigation.

The ratio of all prisoners received in state prisons who were convicted of a specific crime to the number of corresponding crimes known to have occurred in the same state can serve as an index of the unconditional risk of conviction $P^o c = (C^o/Q^o)$.[41] Since in 1940 and 1950 there is only information pertaining to urban crime rates, the absolute number of crimes Q^o is calculated as the product $q^o N_S$ on the assumption that the reported urban rate is an unbiased estimate of the state rate in states with similar rates of urbanization.[42]

[40] It is for this reason and for a generally small variability in the extent of execution across states that data from the year 1960 are not included in this investigation. In that year and in a few earlier and subsequent years, the overall number of executions was about half of the corresponding datum in 1950 and about one-third of that in 1940. Moreover, in 12 out of 20 executing states in 1960 for which complete data were available, only a single execution occurred in that year with the trend in all states clearly leading toward a practical abolition of the death penalty. At such small levels of executions in each state and with an attenuated distribution of execution risk measures, the effects of errors in the estimates of execution risks are likely to dominate the comparisons across states.

[41] Because the numerator of $P^o c$ is an estimate of the total number of persons committed to state prison and the denominator is an estimate of the number of crimes known to have occurred in a given year, their ratio can exceed unity as is the case for two states in 1950 where $P^o c$ for robbery and assault exceeds one. A similar observation applies in one state in 1950 in connection with $P^h c$. For a related reason an estimate of $P^o e|c$ ($PX5$) is found to exceed unity in one state in 1940. The implicit assumption, of course, is that these instrumental measures are proportionally related to the true probabilities.

[42] As has been pointed out elsewhere, estimates of Pc derived by deflating measures of conviction by measures of reported crimes may bias the effect of $P^o c$ on q^o in a negative direction due to the correlation between common error terms, although a spurious correlation in a positive direction is also possible due to the effect of the true levels of Pc on the incentive to report crimes (see n. 43 below). Note, however, that because the numerator of the dependent variable q^o is different from the denominator of $P^o c$ in regressions using FBI crime data, the potential negative spurious correlation is mitigated in this analysis. For further elaboration on issues relating to measurement of $P^o c$ and its estimated effects see Ehrlich (1974, appendix 1 in his section III).

Punishment severity is measured by the median time served in state prisons by prisoners first released from prison, T. Since the relevant theoretical variable is the *cost* of imprisonment m rather than its length, the partial elasticities of offenses with respect to T are expected to be lower than those with respect to m, especially when imprisonment terms are long (see Ehrlich 1974, p. 125). In addition, although an increase in m is expected to reduce the incentive to "enter" a criminal activity by the analysis of Section IA, longer imprisonment terms may also lead to greater rates of recidivism on the part of those released from prisons due to possible adverse effects of imprisonment on relative legitimate employment opportunities. In contrast, imprisonment entails an incapacitating effect on those imprisoned, which operates to reduce the rate of crime independently of the effect of punishment on incentives. In general, the observed effect of T, and consequently also that of P^oc, as measured in the regression analysis, is a mix of all of these effects. (For some calculations of the potential incapacitating effects of imprisonment see Ehrlich [1974, p. 103].)[43] A list of all variables used in the regression analysis is given in table 2.[44]

References

Aday, L. A., and Anderson, R. *Access to Medical Care*. Ann Arbor, Mich.: Health Admin. Press, 1975.

Becker, Gary S. "Crime and Punishment: An Economic Approach." *J.P.E.* 78, no. 2 (March/April 1968): 169–217.

Box, G. E. P., and Cox, D. R. "An Analysis of Transformations." *J. Royal Statis. Soc.* 26, Ser. B (1964): 211–43.

Ehrlich, Isaac. "Participation in Illegitimate Activities: An Economic Analysis." Ph.D. dissertation, Columbia Univ., 1970.

———. "The Deterrent Effect of Capital Punishment: A Question of Life and Death." Working Paper no. 18, Nat. Bur. Econ. Res., 1973.

———. "Participation in Illegitimate Activities: An Economic Analysis." In *Essays in the Economics of Crime and Punishment*, edited by G. S. Becker and W. M. Landes. New York: Columbia Univ. Press, 1974.

———. "The Deterrent Effect of Capital Punishment: A Question of Life and Death." *A.E.R.* 65 (June 1975): 397–417. (*a*)

[43] Data sources not previously cited include U.S. Bureau of the Census, *Prisoners in State and Federal Prisons and Reformatories* (1936–41, 1946) and U.S. Department of Justice (1954) for E^o; U.S. Bureau of the Census, *Prisoners in State and Federal Prisons and Reformatories* (1940) and U.S. Department of Justice (1954) for C_i^o; U.S. Bureau of the Census, *Statistical Abstract of the United States* (1945) and *U.S. Census of the Population: 1950* (1952) for the variables W and X; and U.S. Bureau of the Census, *Statistical Abstract of the United States* (1946, 1953) for N_S, NW, AGE, A_{25-34}, N_{URB}, and URB.

[44] The implicit assumption in the regression analysis is that the proportion of underreported offenses is constant across states. However, the incentive to report a crime is affected by the relevant costs and gains associated with reporting. To the extent that explanatory variables introduced in the regression also affect the incentive to report, their estimated effects would be a mix of their effects on the incentive to commit as well as to report offenses. For example, individuals may be more willing to report an offense if the probability that the offender will be apprehended and punished and the severity of punishment are high. Persons with low opportunity cost of time may be more likely to bear the costs of reporting a crime of given severity, including the costs of filing a complaint and appearing as witnesses in court. The estimated effects of P^oc, T, and X, for example, might therefore be biased in a positive direction and that of W in a negative direction relative to their true effects.

―――. "Deterrence: Evidence and Inference." *Yale Law J.* 85 (December 1975): 209–27. (*b*)

Goldfeld, S. M., and Quandt, R. E. "Some Tests for Homoscedasticity." *J. American Statis. Assoc.* 60 (June 1965): 539–47.

Klebba, A. J. "Homicide Trends in the United States, 1900–74." *Public Health Reports* 90, no. 3 (May–June 1975): 195–204.

Pashigian, B. Peter. "The Hill-Burton Program: The Effects of the Federal Subsidy in Kind on the Hospital Industry." Report no. 7346, Center Math. Studies Bus. and Econ., Univ. Chicago, 1973.

Schuessler, Karl F. "The Deterrent Influence of the Death Penalty." *Ann. American Acad. Polit. and Soc. Sci.* 284 (November 1952): 54–62.

U.S. Bureau of the Census. *Prisoners in State and Federal Prisons and Reformatories.* Washington: Government Printing Office, 1936–41, 1946.

―――. *Vital Statistics of the United States, 1940.* Pt. 1. Washington: Government Printing Office, 1943.

―――. *Statistical Abstract of the United States.* Washington: Government Printing Office, 1945, 1946, 1953.

―――. *U.S. Census of the Population: 1950.* Vol. 2. Washington: Government Printing Office, 1952.

―――. *Historical Statistics of the United States from Colonial Times to 1957.* Washington: Government Printing Office, 1960.

U.S. Department of Health, Education, and Welfare, Public Health Service. *Vital Statistics of the United States, 1950.* Vol. 3. Washington: Government Printing Office, 1953.

―――. *Vital Statistics of the United States, 1971.* Vol. 2. Washington: Government Printing Office, 1975.

U.S. Department of Justice, Bureau of Prisons. *National Prisoner Statistics: Prisoners Released from State and Federal Institutions.* Washington: Government Printing Office, 1951, 1952–53.

―――. *National Prisoner Statistics: Prisoners in State and Federal Institutions, 1950.* Leavenworth, Kans., 1954.

U.S. Department of Justice, Federal Bureau of Investigation. *Uniform Crime Reports.* Washington: Government Printing Office, 1940, 1950–51, 1960, 1970.

Wolfgang, Marvin. "A Sociological Analysis of Criminal Homicides." *Federal Probation* 25 (March 1961): 48–55.

6

DETERRENCE AND INCAPACITATION
Estimating the Effects of Criminal Sanctions on Crime Rates

ALFRED BLUMSTEIN, JACQUELINE COHEN, and
DANIEL NAGIN

This report focuses narrowly on attempts to estimate what are called the "deterrent" and "incapacitative" effects—in terms of crimes averted—of criminal sanctions:

Deterrence is the inhibiting effect of sanctions on the criminal activity of people *other than* the sanctioned offender.

Incapacitation is the effect of isolating an identified offender from the larger society, thereby preventing him or her from committing crimes in that society.

Two aspects of the Panel's task should be emphasized. First, the Panel was not asked to make recommendations to either increase or decrease the use of imprisonment or other sanctions. Any such choice involves weighing the crime-reduction benefits of sanctions against the many costs involved, and the Panel has not attempted to assess those costs; instead, it has focused only on the benefits, in terms of crimes averted, associated with different sanctions. Second, in evaluating the crime-reduction benefits of sanctions, the issue is not whether the Panel believes these benefits to be large or small, but rather the scientific validity of the available evidence.

From Alfred Blumstein, Jacqueline Cohen, and Daniel Nagin (eds.), "Summary," pp. 3-14 in Deterrence and Incapacitation: Estimating the Effects of Criminal Sanctions on Crime Rates. Reprinted by permission of the National Academy of Sciences, Washington, D.C.

ASSESSMENT OF THE EVIDENCE ON DETERRENCE

The hypothesis underlying deterrence derives from the general proposition that human behavior can be influenced by incentives. This leads to the specific prediction that increases in the severity of the penalties or the certainty of their imposition on offenders who are detected will reduce crime by those who are not directly sanctioned. It is argued that, in response to the resulting perceived risk of sanctions, at least part of the population is dissuaded from committing some criminal acts. Thus, all theories of deterrence predict a negative association between aggregate crime rates and sanctions, with levels of sanctions measured either by severity or by risk. The sanction risks usually studied in analyses of deterrence are apprehension, conviction, imprisonment, or execution (all conditional on committing a crime), and sanction severity is usually measured by prison sentence length or time served.

There are three major kinds of research designs for estimating the magnitude and statistical significance of the deterrent effect: experiments, quasi-experiments, and analyses of natural variation. Because of practical, scientific, and ethical constraints, the opportunities for experiments are rare. Quasi-experiments are more common; typically, such studies have examined statutory changes in sanctions (*e.g.*, the abolition of capital punishment) or a clearly defined change in enforcement policy (*e.g.*, a crackdown on speeding violators). The most commonly used approach for measuring deterrent effects is the analysis of the natural variation in crime rates and sanction levels across different units of observation. These analyses interpret a negative association between sanction levels and crime rates (*i.e.*, when sanction levels are high, crime rates are low, and vice versa) as an indication of a possible deterrent effect.

THE EVIDENCE ON NONCAPITAL SANCTIONS: ANALYSES OF NATURAL VARIATION

Taken as a whole, the reported evidence consistently finds a negative association between crime rates and the risks of apprehension, conviction, or imprisonment. The Panel's task is to assess the degree to which the observed association is found *because* the higher sanction levels reduced the amount of crime committed. If the association is found to reflect deterrence, the Panel's task is then to assess the accuracy of the magnitude of the estimated effect.

Sources of Bias

There are three primary obstacles to interpreting the finding of a negative association in analyses of natural variation as valid evidence that sanctions indeed deter crime: (1) the error in measuring crimes; (2) the confounding of incapacitation and deterrence; and (3) the possibility that the level of crime affects sanctions in addition to sanctions deterring crime, which is known as a simultaneous relationship.

Error in Measuring Crimes   The sanction measure most commonly used in studies of deterrence is the risk of being sanctioned for a crime, for example, the risk of apprehension or of imprisonment. In most analyses, these measures are defined as the ratio of the number of times the sanction is imposed to the number of offenses known to the police (*e.g.,* the number of arrests divided by the number of offenses). The number of offenses then appears in both the numerator of the crime rate (offenses per population) and the denominator of the sanction variable.

Data on known offenses are the result of citizens' reports to the police or of the police discovering offenses on their own and of those reports then being recorded in official crime statistics. Because of the way the sanction risk and the crime rate are defined, any variation in the reporting or recording rates in different jurisdictions could cause a negative association, even in the absence of a deterrent effect.

Confounding of Deterrence and Incapacitation   Imprisoning offenders produces an incapacitative effect as well as a deterrent effect. The incapacitation of those offenders who are imprisoned will thereby reduce crime even in the absence of any deterrent effect. For sanctions having incapacitative effects, then, a negative association between crimes and sanctions reflects the combined effects of deterrence and incapacitation, rather than a deterrent effect alone.

Simultaneous Effects   Any negative association between crime and sanctions could also be interpreted as reflecting an inverse causal effect, whereby jurisdictions impose lower sanctions because they have higher crime rates. Such an inverse causal effect of crimes on sanctions may arise because the criminal justice system resources (*e.g.,* police, prosecutors, prisons) become overburdened by the increased amount of crime and hence less able to deal with new offenders. Another explanation for such an inverse effect may be an increased tolerance for criminality in those jurisdictions where crime is more common, as reflected, for example, in a reduction in the average sanctions imposed for a particular type of crime. In either case, crimes and sanctions are then simultaneously related.

The statistical procedures for isolating the deterrent effect in a simultaneous relationship require critical prior assumptions called "identification restrictions." These generally involve assuming that certain factors *do not* influence the crime rate directly, but *do* affect one or more of the other simultaneously related variables (such as sanction levels). If these assumptions are seriously in error, the estimated effect may contain large errors reflecting contamination by the simultaneous effects.

The arguments for and against simultaneity differ appreciably, both in substance and persuasiveness, for different sanctions. Thus, in assessing the evidence, the Panel examined the different sanctions separately and examined each from the perspectives of both the assumption of simultaneity and the assumption of nonsimultaneity. Those assessments involved both the validity of the alternative assumptions and our assessment of the research results under each assumption.

Summary of the Evidence

Analyses of natural variation, with few exceptions, find a negative association between crime rates and noncapital sanction risks, controlling for other presumably causal determinants of crime. Any conclusion that these negative associations reflect a deterrent effect, however, is limited principally by the inability to eliminate other factors that could account for the observed relationship, even in the absence of a deterrent effect.

The most important such factor is the possibility that crime rates influence sanctions as well as vice versa; that is, that there is a simultaneous relationship between crimes and sanctions. If this is so, simultaneous estimation methods are required to isolate the deterrent effect. If simultaneous effects are appreciable, then substantial questions remain about whether the simultaneous analyses have successfully isolated the deterrent effect in the simultaneous relationships.

The extent to which simultaneity is an issue may vary with the kind of sanction employed. The likelihood that sanctions and crime are simultaneously determined is probably greatest for imprisonment, less for conviction, and least for arrest. The extent to which simultaneity does exist has rarely been investigated. Until we have a clearer understanding of simultaneity, however, we believe that caution should be exercised in interpreting the available results as establishing a deterrent effect, and especially so for the sanction of imprisonment.

For those sanctions for which simultaneous effects are probably not appreciable, the deterrence estimates resulting from the nonsimultaneous analyses suffer from the bias introduced by error in measuring crimes; this bias forces a negative association even in the absence of deterrent effects. However, since it is unlikely that the observed negative association can be wholly attributed to measurement error for all crime types, the analyses based on an assumption of nonsimultaneity do offer some credible evidence of the existence of a deterrent effect. The estimates of the magnitude of that effect, however, are likely to be seriously in error because of the bias.

In summary, therefore, we cannot yet assert that the evidence warrants an affirmative conclusion regarding deterrence. We believe scientific caution must be exercised in interpreting the limited validity of the available evidence and the number of competing explanations for the results. Our reluctance to draw stronger conclusions does not imply support for a position that deterrence does not exist, since the evidence certainly favors a proposition supporting deterrence more than it favors one asserting that deterrence is absent. The major challenge for future research is to estimate the magnitude of the effects of different sanctions on various crime types, an issue on which none of the evidence available thus far provides very useful guidance. The research program developed in this report is intended to facilitate these efforts.

THE EVIDENCE ON NONCAPITAL SANCTIONS: EXPERIMENTS AND QUASI-EXPERIMENTS

Controlled experiments are relatively rare; quasi-experiments are far more common, usually taking advantage of abrupt changes in the law or in the actual application of sanctions when these occur. The best examples of controlled experiments in deterrence are the test of the crime-control effectiveness of preventive patrol by police in Kansas City, the San Diego field-interrogation experiment, and the study of the effectiveness of different strategies to reduce income tax evasion. Quasi-experimental studies are available on the effect of changes in penalties for drunk driving, drug use and sales, bad checks, and abortion. The deterrent effects of changes in enforcement or patrol practice have also been examined for speeding, for crime on the subway in New York City, and for crime in general.

The results of the experimental and quasi-experimental studies are mixed: some find evidence of significant deterrent effects and others find no evidence of measurable changes in crime rates. In most cases, however, the research designs suffer from a variety of remediable flaws, which undermine confidence in the results; all too often, other factors can be identified to account for findings of either an effect or of no effect.

When the flaws in a particular study have been identified, that line of research is much more likely to be dropped rather than to be replicated with the flaws corrected. As a result, there is a proliferation of unique studies examining a wide variety of intervention strategies. Because most of the studies are not comparable, the results are usually limited to the specific crime types examined and the specific crime control tactics invoked, and they are often restricted to the particular experimental locale. Therefore, no general conclusions can be drawn from the evidence available at this time from experimental and quasi-experimental studies on deterrence.

THE EVIDENCE ON CAPITAL SANCTIONS: THE DETERRENT EFFECT OF CAPITAL PUNISHMENT ON HOMICIDE

Early empirical efforts to test the deterrence hypothesis for capital punishment typically took three forms: the comparison of the homicide rates in contiguous jurisdictions, some of which had abolished capital punishment; the examination of time-series data on homicide rates within a jurisdiction during the years before and after the abolition of capital punishment; and the comparison of the homicide rates in a jurisdiction just before and after the imposition of a death sentence or an execution. While all these studies failed to find evidence of a deterrent effect, they suffered from a number of methodological weaknesses; the most serious flaw was the general failure to control adequately for the variety of demographic, cultural, and socioeconomic factors that influence homicide rates. Examining "similar" contiguous states or the same jurisdiction over short time periods represents some effort to hold these factors constant; however, when dealing with rare events like homicides and executions (where the numbers are quite small), the crudeness of the controls could mask any effects that may exist. In addition, there were no controls for the effects of noncapital sanctions in reducing homicides.

In contrast, a recent analysis of time-series data for 1933-1969, in which homicides and executions were aggregated for the entire United States, claims to find a deterrent effect for executions. A number of reanalyses of these data have shown those findings to be sensitive to minor technical variations in the analysis, which either reversed the direction of the presumed effect or greatly reduced its magnitude.

The findings of the analysis are particularly sensitive to the time period included and result largely from the fact that, during 1962-1969, executions ceased and homicides increased; however, the increase in homicides was no more than increases in other crimes. Thus, to conclude that a deterrent effect exists, one must assume, first, that the steady rise in homicides over this eight-year period was caused at least in part by the decline in executions and, second, that the two steady trends in executions and homicides were not generated either independently or by some common third cause, which might also account for the rise in other crimes. If one makes those assumptions, then statistical analyses contribute no further information to the test of the deterrence hypothesis.

In summary, the flaws in the earlier analyses finding no effect and the sensitivity of the more recent analysis to minor variations in model specification and the serious temporal instability of the results lead the Panel to conclude that the available studies provide no useful evidence on the deterrent effect of capital punishment.

Our conclusion about the current evidence does not imply that capital punishment should or should not be imposed. The deterrent effectiveness of capital punishment is only one consideration among many in the decision regarding the use of the death penality—and, in that decision, those other considerations are likely to dominate the inevitably crude estimates of the deterrent effect.

ASSESSMENT OF THE EVIDENCE IN INCAPACITATION

Incapacitation involves removing an identified offender from society at large, thereby reducing crime by physically preventing that offender from committing crimes in society. The incapacitative effect of a sanction refers exclusively to that preventive effect and does not include any additional reduction in crime due to deterrence or rehabilitation.

There are fewer problems in inferring the existence of effects from incapacitation than there are in establishing the existence of a deterrent effect. As long as there is a reasonable presumption that offenders who are imprisoned would have continued to commit crimes if they had remained free, there is unquestionably a direct incapacitative effect.

Models exist for estimating the incapacitative effect, but they rest on a number of important, and as yet untested, assumptions. Using the models requires adequate estimates of critical, but largely unknown, parameters that characterize individual criminal careers. The most basic parameters include estimates of individual crime rates and of the length of individual criminal careers as well as of the distribution of both of these parameters across the population of criminals. Because the crimes an individual commits are not directly observable, these parameters are extremely difficult to estimate. Data are also needed on the chance of an individual being sent to prison, which involves the probabilities of apprehension, conviction, and sentence, and on the time actually served in prison; estimates of these variables are more readily determined, and they vary across jurisdictions.

While the currently limited models and parameter estimates cannot be relied on for exact numerical calculation of incapacitative effects, they are useful for relative comparisons. They can be used in this limited way to explore the implications for crime and prison populations of changes from present incapacitation policies. Such explorations reveal that the expected incapacitative effect of any change in imprisonment policy is quite sensitive to the current value of the individual crime rate and to the current value of imprisonment policy variables. When the current rate of imprisonment per crime and the individual crime rate are low, the percentage increase in prison population needed in order to achieve a given percentage reduction in crime is large. Since the high-crime-rate jurisdictions that are most likely to be looking to incapacitation to relieve their crime problems also tend to have relatively lower rates of time served per crime, they can expect to have the largest percentage increases in prison populations to achieve a given percentage reduction in crime.

RECOMMENDATIONS FOR RESEARCH AND PROGRAM MANAGEMENT

RESEARCH ON NONCAPITAL SANCTIONS: ANALYSES OF NATURAL VARIATION

In order to assess the importance of simultaneity, much more attention should be given to establishing which kinds of criminal justice system behaviors are indeed affected by the level of work load. For example, the relationships between the proportion of charges that are dismissed by prosecutors and prosecutorial case load should be examined.

In order to pursue simultaneous analyses, it is important to identify the most important determinants of the sanction variables. These could include police deployment strategies, judicial decisions limiting police discretion, programs oriented at improved prosecutorial management, and legislation prescribing sentences. Those factors that affect sanction levels, without affecting the crime rate directly or being affected by crime rates, are important candidates for use as identification restrictions in simultaneous estimation.

More deterrence analyses should use a time series of cross-sectional data. Analyses of deterrence in the United States have been limited to cross-sectional data because reports of prison commitments and the actual length of imprisonment (*i.e.*, time served) are published sporadically rather than annually. To make time-series analyses possible, data on commitments and time served by crime type should be collected and published on an annual basis. Also, these data should be disaggregated to smaller jurisdictions within states.

Foreign data bases represent potentially rich sources of time-series data on crime rates and sanction levels. In addition to their potential as data sources, analyses of such data will also provide a basis for assessing the generality of results derived solely from United States data.

As an alternative to the aggregate studies that constitute the bulk of the deterrence literature, a fruitful approach might focus on the effects of sanctions on individual criminal behavior. Increased attention should be given to developing both methods and data bases that would make the study of individual criminal behavior possible.

Analyses of more narrowly defined criminal acts should be pursued to provide insight into the deterrability of specific kinds of criminal behavior.

RESEARCH ON NONCAPITAL SANCTIONS: EXPERIMENTS AND QUASI-EXPERIMENTS

Most of the flaws encountered in experimental research on deterrence are remediable through the use of more careful research designs. Since most of the research opportunities in deterrence arise from legislatively or administratively imposed changes in sanctioning, improved designs will often require an increased awareness of changes before they occur. One mechanism for improving the quality of such research would involve creating a panel with both operational and technical expertise to identify opportunities for experiments and advise on the formulation and execution of study designs. We recommend that the National Institute of Law Enforcement and Criminal Justice organize such a panel and support it with internal staff assistance.

The panel should seek out significant changes in policies or operations so that it can act as a clearinghouse to promote studies of these natural experiments as the opportunities arise. Examples of policy changes that might be profitably studied include the variety of career offender programs and the efforts to decriminalize offenses (either legislatively or *de facto* through changes in enforcement).

RESEARCH ON CAPITAL SANCTIONS

A major part of the problem with current knowledge is the extremely broad categories used in studies on capital sanctions. Future research should involve much more intensive analysis of data that are disaggregated into finer categories. Disaggregation should separate the different types of homicide (*e.g.*, those subject to the death penalty from those that are not), find smaller and more homogeneous units of observation (preferably cities), and use time intervals like days or weeks in order to observe the short-term response to capital sentences or executions.

Opportunities for "interrupted time-series" studies of the effect of capital punishment on homicide will be possible if various states reinstitute the death penalty in the wake of recent Supreme Court decisions. If such research is pursued, adequate baseline data establishing the recent trends in capital crimes must be collected. Furthermore, attempts to assess effects should distinguish among the various manifestations of the capital punishment threat, such as the probability of execution for a homicide, the number of capital sentences or executions per year, and the media coverage given to capital sentences or executions.

In undertaking research on the deterrent effects of capital punishment, however, it should be recognized that the strong value content associated with decisions regarding capital punishment and the high risk associated with errors of commission make it likely that any policy use of scientific evidence in this area will impose extremely severe standards of proof; nonexperimental research, to which the study of the deterrent effects of capital punishment is limited, almost certainly will be unable to meet those standards of proof. Thus, the Panel considers that research on the deterrent effects of capital sanctions is not likely to provide results that will or should have much influence on policy makers.

RESEARCH ON INCAPACITATION

Further model development is necessary to reflect more accurately variations in patterns of individual criminal activity. Research should be directed at identifying variations as the offender ages or accumulates a criminal record and any relationships between individuals' crime rates and their likelihood of being apprehended, their career length, and other variables characterizing individual criminal careers. In addition, research on the sequence of crime types committed during a criminal career ("crime-switching") should be pursued in order to determine the degree to which incarcerating a robber also prevents the burglaries that offenders might commit.

It is also important to measure the extent to which offenders' criminal activity persists in the community even after they are incapacitated. This may occur because of replacement of the criminal activity of an imprisoned offender by recruitment from an illegitimate labor market or because of the continued activity of a group of offenders (such as gangs) from which the imprisoned offender was removed. If such patterns are prevalent, they significantly reduce the anticipated incapacitative effect. The patterns of recruitment and persistence for criminal networks should be explored.

Good empirical estimates of the model parameters are essential for reliably estimating the incapacitative effect. The most immediate empirical investigations should be directed at estimating the individual crime rate and the length of a criminal career. These estimates should be disaggregated by crime type and demographic group and should reflect the statistical distribution of the parameters. Two approaches to estimation can be pursued, one involving analysis of recorded arrest histories (police "rap sheets") and the other using self-reports obtained from offenders.

Current estimates of the sanctioning variables can be obtained from criminal justice agency records. These will have to be augmented, however, to reflect the ways the different parts of the criminal justice system respond to changes in their environments. It is necessary to know, for example, to what extent judges and prosecutors increase their use of dismissals when mandatory-sentence laws are passed. Information on the kind and degree of this adaptive response is needed to assess the net incapacitative effect if anticipated gains from increased sanction levels in one part of the system are offset by compensating decreases elsewhere.

This research program will depend critically on securing rich data bases documenting the progress of individual criminal careers, including the crime types and dates of all arrests, convictions, and sentences. Longitudinal samples like the FBI's Careers in Crime file, appropriately augmented by juvenile data and better data on time served, are needed. A survey of self-reported criminality for a subsample of such a file would provide needed data on undetected crimes.

MANAGEMENT AND ORGANIZATION OF A RESEARCH PROGRAM

Common Data Needs

There is a fundamental need for various standard data items that can best be collected centrally. Such common data bases would include two important classes of information. First, cross-sectional, time-series information on crimes and on the processing of suspects, defendants, and offenders by the criminal justice system; these data are important for studies of deterrence. Second, longitudinal information on criminal-career histories of individuals; these data are essential for estimation of incapacitation effects.

To serve these data needs, a central depository of all research data collected by persons undertaking research on the criminal justice system should be maintained by the National Institute of Law Enforcement and Criminal Justice. It should be a condition of federal research support that the data collected be submitted to that depository at a reasonable time after completion of the research projects.

Accessibility of Data

After research findings are published, the need for verification and replication requires open access to the details of the data used. Published results should, as a minimum, report an essential summary of the raw data from which the published results are derived or make the data readily available.

Peer Review

To promote more successful research on crime and the effects of sanctions, the National Institute of Law Enforcement and Criminal Justice should establish a committee of methodological and substantive research experts to review proposals relating to deterrence and incapacitation.

7

HUSTLING
The "Inside" Economy of a Prison

SANDRA E. GLEASON

IN RECENT years economists such as Becker (1968) and Ehrlich (1974) have turned their attention to the study of crime and criminal activities. This research has modeled criminal activities occurring outside the walls of penal institutions. In contrast, this article focuses on illegitimate economic activities or "hustles" occurring inside the State Prison of Southern Michigan.[1] It will be shown that the economic concepts used to explain criminal activities outside the institution also apply in the "inside" economy. The discussion will be developed in three parts: (1) an explanation of why hustling activities develop; (2) an examination of the conditions necessary for hustling to take place; and (3) a discussion of the conditions of production of hustles.

The Need for Hustling Activities

The State Prison of Southern Michigan houses approximately one-half of the inmate population of Michigan; all residents are males ages 23 and older. The prison consists of the maximum security section inside the walls which housed two-thirds of the prison population, or about 3,200 men, in 1975, and the trustee division outside the walls. Less than one-half of the population is white. The prison provides the men's basic needs and a variety of educational and recreational activities at no cost to the residents. In addition, income generating school enrollment[2] or jobs are available for all who are physically and mentally capable, except during periods of overcrowding, to provide the income to purchase goods and services which are not free. Men who are indigent

receive a small monthly stipend. However, some residents find these and other legitimate income sources, such as gifts and government transfer payments, inadequate for their desired consumption, and develop hustling activities to acquire income, goods, and services which would otherwise be unavailable to them.

There are three channels for lawfully acquiring goods and services in the prison. (1) The prison store sells goods for scrip which range from daily hygienic needs to television sets. A limited range of commonly used goods may also be purchased for script at the Jaycees' store if faster service is desired.[3] (2) Purchases inside and outside the in-

* The author gratefully acknowledges the assistance received from several sources. This article was an outgrowth of a dissertation funded by the U.S. Department of Labor. The Michigan Department of Corrections and the staff of the State Prison of Southern Michigan cooperated on all phases of the research. A special word of thanks is owed to the resident clerks at the prison who were interviewed about the "inside" economy. Professors Daniel Hamermesh and Daniel Saks in the Department of Economics and John McNamara in the School of Criminal Justice at Michigan State University provided guidance and encouragement.

[1] The primary data source was interviews with six resident clerks in the prison. These residents ranged in age from the early twenties to the early forties, and included two blacks, three whites, and one Spanish-American. The average interview required six hours.

The men interviewed had served an average of three and one-half years on their current sentences, but four of them had been incarcerated two years or less. Consequently, most of the data referred to the period from 1974-1976. However, since the residents had been incarcerated an average of eight years on both prior and current sentences, references were made to events prior to 1974.

The data about hustling procedures collected in the interviews were included in this article only if one or both of the following sources verified the accuracy of the information: 1) another resident or the prison staff provided the same information about a specified topic, and/or 2) the information was consistent with prior research on prison life. Information about most of the low-risk hustles, including price data, was consistently verified by the six residents. However, the data on high-risk hustles were much less complete; the price data were particularly sketchy. Consequently, the information on the high-risk hustles was often verified by only one additional source.

The use of a small sample of inmates was justified by three considerations. 1) Interviews with a representative sample of the prison population would have identified the information available to the average inmate consumer rather than the details of production and distribution because the typical inmate does not know much about the way the "inside" economy operates. In contrast, the men interviewed were able to provide detailed information due to their relatively long observation of the economic system. In addition the interviewees were shrewd observers of the prison system, partly due to innate intelligence and partly due to their relatively high levels of education. Only one of the six had not completed high school, while three had completed A.A. degrees. 2) A good rapport had been established by the author with the interviewees during previous research activities at the prison. This rapport probably would not have occurred with a larger group which included men who did not know the author. 3) Research on the "inside" economy is a sensitive matter due to the severe penalties associated with the high-risk hustles. Consequently, it was expected that interviews with a small sample rather than a large one were less likely to be perceived by hustlers as a ploy to locate law breakers, and therefore should minimize the risk of bodily harm to the interviewees.

It should be noted that the economic activities discussed in this paper are not unique to the State Prison of Southern Michigan. References to a variety of hustling activities are found in much of the literature about prison life. In addition, the interviewees who had served sentences in other Michigan prisons indicated that a similar range of hustles also were carried out in these prisons with minor variations reflecting institutional differences such as the rules governing gifts from family and friends.

[2] Enrollment in remedial education programs is required by law for inmates who test at less than a sixth grade level of academic competence. Other programs, including high school, G.E.D. preparation, vocational training, and college courses, are voluntary.

[3] The Jaycees' store sells goods to raise money for their activities. Unlike the prison store, which has a waiting line which is usually one to three hours in length, the Jaycees' store provides fast service. This faster service is attractive to men who do not have the time to wait in line because of their jobs and due to personal preference.

From Sandra E. Gleason, "Hustling: The 'Inside' Economy of a Prison," 42(2) Federal Probation 32-40 (June 1978). Copyright 1978 by Federal Probation Quarterly.

stitution may be made by a check written against a man's account. Some restrictions apply to these purchases; for example, only one television set is permitted per man, and contraband items, such as pornography and drugs, may not be purchased. (3) Many goods, such as clothing, may be sent inside as gifts. However, drugs, liquor, pornography, food, and shoes are not permitted as gifts. The one exception is gifts of canned food in December.

The residents estimate that it costs $40-$50 per month to live comfortably inside. The average income received each month from January, 1973 through December, 1975 does fall into this range: $41 in 1973; $47 in 1974; and $50 in 1975.[4] Gifts and government transfer payments represented approximately 75 percent of the average income, and the monthly payroll, approximately 25 percent, during this period. In contrast, expenditures averaged $53 a month in 1973, $59 in 1974, and $62 in 1975. The receipt of scrip during visits explains approximately 58 per cent of the gap between average income and expenditures; the rest of the gap is due to scrip overpayment.[5] However, these data are deceptive since they do not show the great inequality of the income distribution and the seasonal variation in income.

Most of the income is received inside the walls by two groups of men: (1) approximately 600 men employed in the Michigan State Industries earned an average monthly income of wages and bonuses of $63 in 1975, and (2) veterans enrolled in educational programs received approximately $300 a month in educational benefits.[6] Residents whose families helped them financially could have received up to $60 a month in scrip during visits.[7] In contrast, men without visitors or family assistance received no gifts of scrip, and the average monthly income earned by nonemployees of the

Michigan State Industries was about $7. Half-time students earned $3 during a 4-week period; full-time, nonveteran students and the lowest paid institutional jobs, such as kitchen work, $5; and the best paid institutional jobs, including the relatively skilled clerical positions, $15. The only other legitimate income sources available are the production of hobbycraft items or serving as a medical volunteer; the latter may generate an income of $30 a month (Mitford, 1973, p. 65).

Several seasonal variations in the flow of income and expenditures are evident. The major source of the fluctuations in the payroll is the payment of the Michigan State Industry bonus. The bonus is paid in the first month of each quarter, with the largest bonus in July; this causes the third quarter average payroll earnings to be larger than the other quarters. As expected, the average gift increases markedly in the fourth quarter each year for the Christmas season, and then falls in the first quarter of the following year. This appears to be a major factor causing the average income to peak in the fourth quarter. Average expenditures change in the same direction as average income.

The data show that many residents experience a sizeable gap between their average income as compared with even relatively small consumption demands. The only way most residents can increase their income is to develop a hustle. Hustling or dealing consists of selling illegal goods and services wanted by inmates in order to acquire the goods and services, or the media of exchange to buy the goods and services, wanted by the hustler. Hustling provides the hustler with the amenities of life inside, as well as the challenge and satisfaction of "beating the man" (Dixon, 1974). It can be developed to suit each man's needs: Steady and regular production produces a dependable monthly income, while the target marketer may hustle only occasionally to acquire the means to make a specific expenditure and/or to carry him through a period of relatively low income.

The hustler's world of illegal economic activity co-exists with and complements the legal channels of exchange. These activities can best be described as peripheral market activities since the subsistence needs of the residents are provided by other means; if the hustles disappeared it would create inconvenience but no major hardships (Bohannon, 1965, pp. 1-32).

---

[4] The financial records of the residents' accounts are maintained jointly for the prison (inside the walls and the trustee division, including the farm barracks), the Reception and Guidance Center, and the Michigan Parole Camp. Consequently, it is impossible to clearly separate income and expenditures within the walls from those outside the walls. The averages are based on the December 31 population of the prison and the Reception and Guidance Center. The population of the Michigan Parole Camp is not included since it houses some prison trustees in the work-pass program as well as residents from other state correctional facilities who are within 90 days of their parole to a southern Michigan city. The capacity of the parole camp is 140 inmates.

[5] Expenditures include purchases made with scrip and checks written on a man's account. Scrip overpayment is the theft of scrip from the prison store so that the script may be respent on other purchases in the store; it averages approximately $23,000 a month.

[6] This assumes that the men receiving veterans' benefits today are enrolled full-time in educational programs and are comparable in marital status and number of dependents to men admitted in 1969.

[7] The amount of scrip which can be given on each visit was increased from $15 to $20 per visit in mid-1975, and the number of visits was reduced from four to three a month due to overcrowding. A resident may, therefore, receive up to $60 in scrip each month during visits, and is entitled to withdraw $60 a month in scrip from the legitimate earnings and other funds deposited to his account.

Hustling: The Necessary Conditions

Hustling requires some imagination to see the opportunities available, initiative to pursue the opportunities, access to goods and services or working capital, and a willingness to take the necessary risks. Although the risks are largely borne by the hustler, the buyer shares some risks as well.

A hustler must have access to goods and services demanded by other inmates and or access to working capital. For example, a hustle in raw or cooked steaks, yeast, and milk requires employment in a kitchen, the hustle of providing new pressed prison uniforms requires employment in the laundry, while being paid to buy another man's store list requires employment in the prison store. Generally, the more lucrative the hustle, the more highly the job is prized by hustlers; there is competition for such jobs. In contrast, the hustle of gambling, the block storeman, or dope peddling is relatively independent of any job but requires relatively large amounts of working capital; the size of the capital stock constrains the scale of the hustle. The block storeman, for example, may be a small operator handling only a few items in great demand, such as soft drinks and baked goods, or may have a large scale operation and handle goods such as sandwich components as well. The small scale operations have been going out of business, however, because their capital is too limited to keep up with the increases in the prison store prices.

The working capital needed for hustling consists of one of the four media of exchange: cigarettes, green (Federal Reserve notes), scrip, and transfers between men's accounts. The most commonly used media of exchange are cigarettes and green. As Radford (1945) and others have noted,[a] cigarettes are the common denominator for all prices, including the rate of exchange between the media of exchange, since they are readily available to all inmates through purchases in the prison store or by dealing. At the time of this writing, cigarettes sold in the prison store for 39c a pack or $3.77 a carton (10 packs). The basic exchange rate of green to cigarettes is clearly defined: $5 green=25 packs (2½ cartons). Actual rates may vary from these basic rates due to bargaining. Although cigarette store prices have risen over the

last few years, these rates have remained constant and unaffected by transactions of varying sizes. This may reflect the fear of loss in deals, or the scarcity of the supply of green. In contrast, the exchange rate for scrip seems less well defined. It is roughly $3.25 scrip=10 packs (one carton) in block transactions. This suggests that the exchange equation should be $5 green=25 packs= $8.13 scrip, but sources indicate that 25 packs may be worth $7.50 or $10 in scrip. This value range may reflect the lower desirability of scrip relative to the highly prized green.

Six factors affect the choice of a hustle. (1) The more time a man has spent inside, the more knowledgeable he becomes about the available hustles and how to establish himself in the hustle of his choice. (2) The skills which he brings in from outside or acquires while inside will limit his opportunities. For example, there is some evidence that much of the dope peddling is done by men who were associated with drugs on the outside and thus have the necessary contacts and skills to handle the operation inside. This is not surprising when the statistics on 1973-74 commitments are considered. Approximately 6.5 percent of the new commitments were for drug offenses including the possession, sale, manufacture, distribution, and/ or transport of drugs. An average of 16 percent of the new commitments had experimented with drugs and 39 percent indicated occasional or sustained use of, or severe addiction to, drugs; thus a total of roughly 55 percent had some experience with drugs beyond mere street observations of drug activities. There was no reported drug use for about 3.5 percent of the commitments (Michigan Department of Corrections, 1975, 1976). (3) The rules governing gifts affect the potential scope of hustles. For example, the liberalization of the rules governing gifts of clothing undercut the hustle of producing custommade clothing in the garment factory. (4) The effect of increasing the legitimate income by raising pay scales or increasing the amounts of scrip which could be given during visits is uncertain. A larger legitimate income would decrease the need for hustling but would also provide more working capital to expand unlawful activities. Residents make trade-offs between hustling and working conditions, depending on their utility and legal income. For example, a clerk in the academic school receives 75c a day and few hustles are available. However, the working conditions are considered quite pleasant since it is much like

---

[a] Scrip books bear each man's prison identification number; a resident found with another man's scrip should have it confiscated as contraband. However, the residents have found ways of working around the prison rule.
[a] For other examples, see Carroll (1974, p. 166) and Fox (1972, p. 203).

working in an office outside. If a resident is receiving veterans educational benefits or has another good legal income source, he can enjoy a nice job and support himself without hustling. In contrast, work in the kitchen is poorly paid and the conditions are considered to be unpleasant, but the jobs are in demand because of the good hustles in food theft. (5) The stock of competing goods in the prison store and their price, quality, and variety affect the earning power of a hustle. For example, the sale of used watches was a good hustle in the past but was undermined when the prison store began carrying inexpensive digital watches with a manufacturer's guarantee. (6) The hustler's preference for risk determines whether he chooses a relatively safe hustle, such as the small scale theft of steaks from the kitchen, or the more risky hustles, such as dope peddling. The degree of risk is defined as a function of the probability of receiving punishment and the expected punishment.

The probability of receiving punishment depends on four factors. (1) The more frequent a given hustle, or (2) the larger the quantity of goods and services hustled, the more likely it is to be observed. There are limits to how much hustling can occur. Some hustling is tolerated; however, if hustling becomes excessive and raises institutional costs or threatens security, the rules against such activities will be enforced more strictly. This occurred in the past with gambling and the sale of yeast used in the production of spud juice (homemade liquor) : Too much violence resulted, disciplinary problems were created, and the rule enforcement was tightened. As a consequence, the production of spud juice has fallen and its price has increased. (3) The vigilance of the officers varies and thus affects the probability of being caught. This vigilance appears to vary among the different parts of the prison. The honor block guards, for example, are somewhat more tolerant than the guards in other cell blocks since the men living there create few custodial problems. (4) The time a man has spent inside provides him with opportunities to observe and

master good techniques to protect his hustle from discovery. Two facets of self-protection include marking contraband items acquired through hustling with the hustler's identification number,[10] and screening buyers. A deal will be made only if the potential buyer is known to be trustworthy; the care given to the screening depends on the severity of the possible punishment. The net supply price is based on the cost of productive inputs and a discrimination coefficient applied to potential buyers. The discrimination coefficient may vary from a negative coefficient for a "partner" or close buddy to positive infinity for a "stool pigeon" or a buyer considered untrustworthy for other reasons, such as racial difference. The residents prefer to do their hustling within racial groups to avoid potential complications due to racial strife unless there are no alternatives, or the hustler is trying to maximize his immediate dollar gain. The one exception to the use of discrimination coefficients is some commonly exchanged goods, such as freshly made sandwiches, which have very standardized prices.

In addition to the probability of receiving punishment, the hustler is concerned with the type of punishment usually given for each hustle; the risk associated with a hustle is reflected in the return to the hustler. The *Resident Guide Book* clearly defines the economic activities which are unlawful and the two types of charges which may be made in addition to confiscating the contraband items. (a) A major misconduct charge is made for acts that would be felonies under state or federal law, assault or threats of violence, or other serious and potentially disruptive violations of the institutional rules. The more risky hustles, such as the importation of liquor and drugs, gambling, and loan sharking, would be punished as major misconduct; the markup on marihuana and phencyclidine (PCP) is at least 200 percent, while the return to heroin is even greater. (b) A minor misconduct is a rule violation not considered major misconduct. Relatively safe hustles, such as the theft of steaks from the kitchen or the block storeman, would be minor misconduct.[11] As seen in table 1, the average markup on goods sold by the storeman is 100 percent. A man living in the honor block would be removed from this privileged unit for the receipt of either a major or minor misconduct.

The block storeman buys food items from the prison store, or may commission the theft of the items from the store at lower prices than he

---

[10] All items purchased or received as gifts are marked with the resident's identification number; any items with a different number found in his possession during a shakedown for contraband should be confiscated. There is a hustle in changing identification numbers; it is a high-risk activity since the number-marking equipment is closely watched.

[11]a Beef is popular because the mess hall primarily serves pork.

b The punishments for major misconducts are new sentences, detention, confinement to quarters, loss of privileges, payment for property damage, forfeiture of good time or denial of special good time, and suspended sentence if future good behavior occurs. The punishments for minor misconducts are confinement to quarters, loss of privileges, or the assignment of extra duty.

would otherwise pay, and sells them for cigarettes. This is a relatively safe hustle since most of the officers understand the need for this food to break up the daily routine and provide variety in a diet which otherwise would consist entirely of mess hall meals. As a consequence, the storeman's transactions can be relatively frequent and large scale, but the possibility of punishment is offset by the relaxed vigilance of the guards.

Although the data are incomplete, it appears that the more risky the major misconduct hustle, the greater the gain to the hustler. These ventures are severely punished due to the custodial problems which they create: violence associated with nonpayment of debts, theft of money earned or supplies, and threats of personal injury. The following examples illustrate the argument (see table 2) ; the outside price of the high risk hustles averages 25 percent of the inside price. (1) The importation of liquor is a relatively small scale hustle inside. A guard may sell it to the final user, or it may be resold. If the guard earns about $7 for his trouble, the hustler could earn about $5 for his efforts.[12] (2) At least five types of drugs are available inside, although the residents believe that you can buy almost anything inside that is available outside. (a) Probably the most readily available drug is marihuana; relatively little violence is associated with its use so there is less vigilance by the guards about its use. One ounce of marihuana costs $100 to import into the prison, but nets $300-$350 for the hustler. This is in contrast with an average outside street price of about $30 an ounce (*High Times*, 1976, p. 96). The price per cigarette has fallen from roughly one carton in the past to a standard price of five packs due to the same relaxation of attitudes toward marihuana that has occurred outside. (b) PCP, a common animal tranquilizer, earns roughly the same return as marihuana. The price varies with the sophistication of the buyer. (c) Amphetemines and acid (LSD) are available irregularly. No data are available on the rates of return to the hustler. (d) While the data on heroin are incomplete, a rough estimate of the rate of return can be made. Heroin prices fluctuate markedly depending on the available supply, purity, and

quantity purchased; larger purchases reduce risk and therefore are sold at a discount (Brown, 1973, pp. 1 and 28). If one gram sells on the street for $100, it would cost about $350 to import to the prison. The gram could be sold for roughly $1,200, netting the hustler an estimated $850, or twice the return to the importer of PCP and marihuana. (3) Gambling activities are built upon small scale betting; a one pack bet is typical. However, a successful operator may make as much as 200 to 300 cartons a month. If the average return to national government lotteries can be taken as a rough index of the rate of return, the gamblers are making a 50 percent profit (Rubner, 1966, pp. 108-11)[13]; if their rate of return is comparable to that of the outside numbers games, they are making a 40 percent profit. (4) Loan sharking is less of a problem today than in the past since more scrip is available and there is less need for men to go into debt. It is, as a consequence, treated as a less serious offense than in the past since the associated problems have been reduced. However, loan sharking still flourishes. The basic rate appears to be $2 green payment for each $1 green loaned, or two packs for one loaned. However, this rate varies from a ratio of 1.5 for one loaned for close friends to an open ended repayment rate when the debtor fails to repay in the specified time period; under these conditions the creditor can name his own price. In contrast the repayment rate outside is $6 for every $5 borrowed a week for small borrowers (Kaplan, 1968, p. 239). (5) The price of homosexual services ranges from free to ten cartons, or $30, with an average price of roughly one to two cartons, or $3.90 to $7.80. The portion received by the pimp depends on whether a minimum fee is paid to the prostitute and how much the pimp buys for the prostitute to keep him happy.

The demand for hustled goods and services is a function of taste, legitimate and illegitimate money income, the selling price of the commodity, and the prices of related goods available in the store, from other dealers inside, from sellers outside, and receivable as gifts. The net price the buyer is willing to pay is affected by a discrimination coefficient against the seller which reflects the buyer's concern for the trustworthiness of the hustler. The buyer is concerned with the trustworthiness of the hustler for three reasons: (1) the buyer may be implicated in the transaction and therefore subject to punishment or at least confiscation of the contraband item; (2) if the

---

[12] This example and the one given below which estimates the return to heroin sales is based on the assumption that the ratio of net gain to the guard importing the good to the street cost of the good is the same as that for marihuana when the price of marihuana is $30 an ounce, i.e., a ratio of 7:3.
[13] Gambling is the largest source of revenue for organized crime on the outside, and loan sharking is the second highest (President's Commission on Law Enforcement and Administration of Justice, 1967, p. 189).

hustler does not satisfy his part of the deal the buyer has no recourse but strong arming or other forms of pressure; and (3) in some types of purchases, such as the purchase of a used watch, the buyer is concerned that the hustler provides a good quality watch in working condition and guarantees his product for some period of time. Buyers, like hustlers, prefer to deal within their own racial group.

The Conditions of Production

Most hustling consists of relatively small scale, labor intensive, one man operations. This reflects the general attitude of "everyman for himself." Three types of production conditions can be distinguished: (1) no purchased inputs; (2) some inputs are stolen and some are purchased; and (3) all inputs are purchased. There is room for competition,[14] so cut-throat competition is usually avoided due to the violence which might result and the residents' fear of being punished by a transfer to the Marquette prison.[15] There are, however, several exceptions to the prevalent market structure; all are major misconduct and usually require the participation of at least two men cooperating in an organized division of labor. The prices charged by the hustler may be standardized or bargained.

A large proportion of the hustles do not require purchased inputs. Three types can be defined. (1) Institutional supplies may be stolen while on the job and sold without any production; the hustler acts only as a middleman-dealer. Examples include daily milk delivery to customers' cells and the theft of paper from the print shop. (2) A man may use institutional supplies and equipment to produce for his own gain during his free time on the job; this production requires some special skills. Examples include the "jailhouse lawyers," placement on lists for special activities, machine shop workers who produce metal knives and belt buckles, and carpenter shop employees who produce picture frames and television stands from wood scraps and supplies. (3) A man may provide

labor services for other residents, such as the barber giving a manicure.

A second type of hustle entails stealing some raw materials while on the job and combining them with purchased inputs. A common example is the production of sandwiches. Kitchen workers steal steaks or bacon and eggs for sandwich filler, and combine them with bread and sandwich spread bought in the prison store. "Sandwich men" have regular delivery routes in their block. Sandwiches may also be made with purchased fillers such as canned corned beef or tuna.

Some hustles require the purchase of all inputs, including equipment. Examples include the block storeman, hobbycraft production, and the sale of used items. Residents may sell their hobbycraft legitimately to other inmates by receiving money transfers, but some may choose to sell through nonapproved channels instead.[16] Used items may be sold occasionally by any resident, or may be sold by specialists. Specialists are relatively rare; they may concentrate on the sale of used clothing, shoes and boots, pornography, magazines, or other items for which there is enough demand. The specialists have their business undermined by improvements in the stock of items carried in the prison store and the rules regarding gifts.

Although the data are incomplete, it appears that the hustles requiring two or more men are of two types: (1) nonhierarchical organizations, and (2) hierarchical organizations. While both evidence similarities to their counterparts outside, the greatest similarity is found in drug dealing.

The four hustles with a nonhierarchical organization appear to be loosely organized. (1) Protection services are often based on a "con game": One man or several threaten a victim and a third offers to protect the victim from them for a fee of four to six cartons a month. However, if real protection was needed, it would not be provided. These services are attractive to men who fear homosexual rape, or the old or the weak who cannot protect themselves. (2) Yard theft is frequently the theft of purchases being carried by a lone man as he leaves the prison store. The victim is approached by two or more men who grab his bag and run. (3) Cell theft is also a group activity; the items stolen from a cell are normally sold for cigarettes. The extent of cell theft varies: there is less in the honor block than the other cell blocks. The amount of cell theft has decreased since a new locking system

---

[14] For example, each cell block houses about 350 men, and requires at least five or six storemen to provide the needs of the block.
[15] Most residents dislike the prospect of being in the State House of Corrections and Branch Prison in Marquette because of its tighter security, a location which makes visits difficult and telephone calls to family and friends expensive, and fewer jobs are available. There are two exceptions to this: (1) men making hobbycraft items may prefer the location because of lucrative sales to summer tourists, and (2) gamblers believe that gambling tends to be overlooked.
[16] A rare form of production is the specialization by a resident in one type of hobbycraft production, such as leatherwork, instead of holding an institutional job. Their output is sold to an outside distributor through approved channels.

was installed. (4) Some homosexual activity consists of a pimp and his prostitute(s).[17] The usual pattern is that of a black pimp (jocker) and white prostitute (piece). The jocker provides the same services as those provided by the street pimp: he ensures some income for the piece, provides some affection and protection, and arranges assignations. The expenses necessary for the rendezvous, such as callouts and a lookout and location, are paid by the client. The piece, in turn, provides sexual access, affection, and pseudo-feminine services to the jocker.

Gambling and dope peddling are more tightly organized, apparently in a hierarchical organizational scheme. Both require relatively large amounts of capital to finance their operations and yield large profits if successful. The profits are reinvested by the gambler and drug dealer, as well as the storeman, in loan sharking. Since data on gambling are more limited than those on drug peddling, only the latter will be discussed below.

The comparison of the structure of drug dealing inside with that outside reveals five marked similarities. (1) The objective of the hustle is to maximize profits without being caught. (2) The dealer must pay for his supply (the street price plus the cost to have it imported inside), package it, and establish distribution channels. The division of labor is designed to protect the man or men who finance and/or organize these activities by having the actual selling to the final users done by others. (3) Three other functions must be performed at various times: a corrupter ". . . position bribes, buys, intimidates, threatens, negotiates, and sweet-talks himself into a relationship with . . . anyone . . . who might help . . . secure and maintain immunity from . . . punishment"; a corruptee, such as a guard or visitor, must be recruited to import the drugs, and an enforcer ensures that physical, financial, or psychological injury or even death occurs to those threatening the hustle (Cressey, 1972, pp. 36-38). These measures may include robbing new competition of money or supplies, threats of personal injury, punishment for nonpayment of debts, or extorting a percentage of the sales of other deal-

ers in return for permitting them to continue operating. (4) The income earned comes from a number of small transactions. (5) Secrecy is important for security, although the degree of secrecy varies with the submarket: the market for marihuana is fairly accessible to any resident who can pay, and the local suppliers are well known, while information about the market for other drugs is very hard to acquire since it is confined to the "solid cons." In addition, the successful dealer makes infrequent sales and avoids spending his money in ways which will attract attention to his hustle.

The prices charged for hustled goods and services are of two types: standardized and bargained. The greatest standardization is in food items: the psychological, if not the physical need, for the food, the relatively low risk usually associated with food theft, the frequency of the transactions, the low income of most residents, and the ease of entry of new competition create conditions which are not conducive to bargaining. This can be seen in table 1: Inexpensive food items, such as honey buns and soft drinks, are popular since many men can afford them, while expensive food, such as canned corn beef, are bought by the relatively few who can afford it. Most food prices have been standardized as long as the residents can remember; the only deviations occur when an inmate is new to the prison and has not learned the going rates, or when a tough officer is in charge. However, changes in the prison store prices cause a change from one standardized price to another. For example, canned soft drinks were three cans for two packs in the past. The prison store price was raised and a better quality soft drink was stocked, so one can now sells for one pack.

Table 3 gives additional examples of goods and services with standardized prices; their sale would be a legal economic activity outside. The outside prices are greater than the inside prices for all items except sugar and nightly television rentals, and average 305 percent of the inside prices: Prices outside cover all production costs, while prices inside do not.

The prices of goods and services are determined by bargaining when one or more of the following factors must be considered: (1) the reliability of the hustler; (2) the age, condition, and quality of the good; (3) the skill needed to produce the good or service; (4) irregular fluctuations in supply; (5) economics of scale in production; (6)

[17] It is estimated that 60 percent to 90 percent of long term prisoners engage in some homosexual activity while in prison (Mitchell, 1969, p. 68). Three types of homosexual activity can be distinguished. (1) The true homosexual is a small percentage of the prison population, and usually does not sell his services. During 1973-74, roughly 4.5 percent of the commitments were for sexual offenses, but a smaller percentage were for homosexual crimes. Normally heterosexual men or bisexuals oriented toward women become involved in (1) homosexual marriages, or (2) commercial prostitution.

TABLE 1.—*The Storeman's Payments and Receipts*

Item	Prison Store Price	Block Price (packs of cigarettes)	Net Gain*	Gross Margin
Corned Beef (canned)	$ .95	4	$ .61	39%
Potato Chips (large)	.65	3	.52	44%
Honey Buns	.20	1	.19	49%
Soft Drinks (case of 24 cans)	4.50	24	4.86	52%
Tuna (canned)	.65	3	.61	52%
Potato Chips (small)	.15	1	.24	62%

* Dollar equivalent assuming cigarettes are 39c a pack.

TABLE 2.—*High Risk Hustles*

Item	Inside Price (packs of cigarettes)	Inside Price[1]	Outside Price	Outside Price as % of Inside Price
Ahphetemines (1 tablet)	3-10	$1.17—$3.90	10c-$1[2]	9%-26%
PCP (1 tablet)	15-25	$5.85—$9.75	50c-$3	9%-31%
LSD (1 hit)	15-25	$5.85—$9.75	$1-$3[3]	17%-31%
Loan Shark (interest rate)	—	100%	20%	20%
Southern Comfort (1 pint)	—	$10—$15	$3.40	23%-34%
Marihuana (1 cigarette)	5	$1.95	50c-$1	26%-51%

[1] Dollar equivalent assuming cigarettes are 39c a pack.
[2] 1967 prices (President's Commission on Law Enforcement and Administration of Justice, 1967, p. 215).
[3] *High Times*, 1976, p. 96.

TABLE 3.—*Hustles with Standardized Prices*

Item	Inside Price (packs of cigarettes)	Inside Price[1]	Average Outside Price[2]	Outside Price as % of Inside Price
Television Rental (1 night)	5	$1.95	$ .80	41%
Refined Sugar (1 pound)	1	$ .39	$ .27	69%
White Paper (1 ream)	5	$1.95	$4.00	205%
Milk Delivery (daily)[3]	10/month	$3.90	$9.00	239%
Butter (1 pound)	1	$ .39	$1.16	297%
Ground Coffee (1 pound)	1	$ .39	$1.79	459%
Haircut[4]	2	$ .78	$4.00	513%
Steak Sandwich	1	$ .39	$2.40	615%

[1] Dollar equivalent assuming cigarettes are 39c a pack.
[2] The prices given for milk, coffee, sugar, and butter are the lowest average prices in grocery stores.
[3] Milk is delivered in a jar provided by the customer; the average quanity is roughly one and one-half pints. The outside price is the price paid for one pint for thirty days.
[4] Although haircuts are supposed to be free, it is necessary to pay this minimum price to ensure an acceptable haircut. Special cuts require additional payments.

the differential effect of inflation on the prices of purchased inputs; (7) the goods and services are highly personal; (8) the quantity purchased; (9) the desperation of the buyer or seller; (10) the hustling experience of the buyer or seller; (11) risk of the hustle; and (12) the medium of exchange.

Prices are discounted according to the medium of exchange used for payment. The lowest prices (greatest discount) are given for payment in green, while commodities bought with script are priced close to store prices. The preference for a particular medium of exchange depends primarily on where and how it will be used. For example, cigarettes are preferred for daily transactions with the block storeman or to make gambling bets, while green is preferred when a man wants to purchase drugs to be smuggled inside or send money to help his family.

Conclusion

This article has reviewed a number of hustling activities inside the State Prison of Southern Michigan in order to indicate how production occurs and prices and profits are determined. This prison is unusual due to its large size which makes it difficult to tightly control hustling, and therefore may encourage a greater range and scale of hustling activities than would be found in a smaller institution.

The hustles discussed are miniature versions of legal and illegal economic activities taking place outside the prison. The preferred hustles are those yielding the most profit with the minimum risk. Although the data available are limited, they suggest that normal economic forces are in operation in the inside economy. The forces of supply and demand react in the expected ways so that stable markets develop when information is good, and destabilizing forces, such as changes in supply or competing prices, cause market prices to change.

The inside economy will continue to operate as long as the residents have the financial and psychological demand for hustling and access to the resources and jobs which make hustling possible. Enforcement of crackdowns raise the prices of hustled goods and services and increase the potential for profit, while hustling activities which are legalized or undermined by changes in the institutional rules or facilities quickly loose their appeal.

BIBLIOGRAPHY

Becker, Gary S. "Crime and Punishment: An Economic Approach," *J.P.E.*, Vol. 76 (March, 1968).
Bohannon, Paul and Dalton, George. *Markets in Africa: Eight Subsistence Economies in Transition.* Garden City: Anchor Books, 1965.
Brown, George F., Jr. and Silverman, Lester R. "The Retail Price of Heroin: Estimation and Applications." Washington: The Drug Abuse Council, Inc., May, 1973.

Carroll, Leo. *Hacks, Blacks, and Cons: Race Relations in a Maximum Security Prison.* Lexington Books: London, 1974.

Cressey, Donald R. *Criminal Organization: Its Elementary Forms.* London: Heinemann, 1972.

Dixon, George. "Beating the Man" in Spradley, James P. and McCurdy, David W., ed., *Conformity and Conflict: Readings in Cultural Anthropology,* 2nd ed. Boston: Little, Brown, and Co., 1974.

Ehrlich, Isaac. "Participation in Illegitimate Activities: An Economic Analysis," in Becker, Gary S. and Landes, William M., ed., *Essays in the Economics of Crime and Punishment.* New York: National Bureau of Economic Research, 1974.

Fox, Vernon. *Introduction to Corrections.* Englewood Cliffs: Prentice-Hall, Inc., 1972.

Kaplan, Lawrence J. and Matteis, Salvatore. "Economics of Loansharking," *Am. Jour. of Econ. and Soc.,* Vol. 27 (July, 1968).

Michigan Department of Corrections. *Annual Report 1974.* Lansing: Department of Corrections, 1976.

─────────────────────────. *Criminal Statistics 1973.* Lansing: Department of Corrections, 1975.

Mitchell, Roger S. *The Homosexual and the Law.* New York: Arco Publishing Co., 1969.

Mitford, Jessica. "Experiments Behind Bars." *Atlantic Monthly,* Vol. 231 (January, 1973).

President's Commission on Law Enforcement and Administration of Justice. *The Challenge of Crime in a Free Society.* Washington: U.S. Government Printing Office, 1967.

Radford, R.A. "The Economic Organization of a P.O.W. Camp," *Economica,* Vol. 12 (November, 1945).

Rubner, Alex. *The Economics of Gambling.* London: Macmillan, 1966.

"Trans-High Market Quotations," *High Times,* No. 12 (August, 1976).

Part II:

CRIME IN HISTORICAL PERSPECTIVE

In addition to Michael S. Hindus' essay, which was especially prepared for this volume, we have included five articles and one book segment treating crime and crime control in historical perspective. Hindus' essay was prepared without full knowledge of our final selections and, obversely, our selections were made with only partial knowledge of the content of his essay. Nonetheless, as we expected, the selections serve to exemplify many of the conclusions he draws about historical scholarship in this field. We shall comment on this and related matters below. First a word about why we chose to devote a large segment of this volume to historical scholarship.

One obvious reason is that there has been an enormous increase in the amount of historical scholarship on crime and crime control. Any volume attempting to assist criminologists in staying abreast of their field should include such work. Further, there is considerable consensus among criminologists that such work is among the most interesting currently being done. Why it is "interesting" deserves comment, and Hindus' essay was commissioned in part to provide some answers to this question. Finally, work on crime and crime control, perhaps especially that done in historical perspective, is engaging the attention of scholars and others who, earlier, had little interest in this subject matter. We do not mean only that more historians are studying crime. Nor do we mean only that social scientists already interested in crime are more frequently engaging in historical studies. We also mean that the relevance of studies of crime and crime control—particularly, but not only, those done in historical perspective—seems increasingly apparent and noted by scholars, historians, and social scientists alike, whose interests are mainly elsewhere. Because one aim of this and succeeding series volumes is to broaden scholarly interest in criminology, we had a third reason for including historical studies.

Why *are* more historical studies of crime and crime control being done? At one level, the answer is as obvious as the fact that more such studies are being done. Crime and its control have become matters of national concern, as we have already noted. Scholars are not exempt from this concern, their pursuits, without doubt, being partly determined by it. Interest in crime and its suppression is in the air, so to speak, and, again so to speak, scholars breathe that air. Further, scholars need financial support for their labors. Although historical studies have never been high on the agendas of most government and private agencies providing such support, the chances are better that support can be obtained for historical studies of crime and criminal justice agencies, and criminal law too, than for many topics, given the national concern over these matters.

This last, it should at least be said in passing, has its risks or irritations, as well as its potential benefits. One, visible in Hindus' essay, is that those interested in studying crime historically will feel pressed to demonstrate the immediate relevance of their work to current policy dilemmas. While we think that much historical work can be useful to clarifying such dilemmas, we do not think that whether it is or not should be a central criterion in deciding its worthiness, or its supportability. We find ourselves and many others—some of them policy makers—simply hungry for knowledge about our past, hungry to know where we have been. This, arguably, gives us a better sense of where we may be headed which, again arguably, it is necessary to know in order to formulate any policies at all. But even if such knowledge is only minimally helpful in this respect, it helps us in another way: it helps us appreciate more fully the human condition in all its variety, complexity, despair, and hopefulness.

Which brings us to another reason for the burgeoning of historical studies of crime. The post-World War II period has been marked by the discovery, or rediscovery, of many biases in Western scholarship. Hindus mentions the break-up of the "institutional and political synthesis" which governed historical scholarship; Thompson, referring mainly to British historical work, the end of "imperial illusions." Both are taking note, among other things, of the increased interest among historians and others in charting and examining the significance of the experiences of those large segments of the population—indeed, most of us—whose daily lives, or erstwhile activities, have heretofore remained unrecorded and unexplored in scholarly work, or, worse, have been characterized and explained in the gross terms supplied by those with an interest in making little of them. It is a commonplace that history is written by the winners, by those in control; it is also apparent that it is written by those who can write and read, and largely to date from the documents left by those with these competencies. Further, it has usually been written about, as well as from the perspective of, the winning writers and readers. It is the set of biases associated with these facts and conventions that some modern historians have undertaken to reverse or modify. One way of doing so is to explore the experiences of those persons caught up by the criminal justice systems of their time. Incidentally, but importantly, this effort also serves to throw light on the ways in which various policies announced by those who have received historians' attention work out in action, and it throws light as well on the daily lives of those legions of lower officials whose experiences have too seldom been documented.

It should be said, of course, that if one is interested in the experiences of workers, or the poor, or Blacks and other ethnic groups, or women—or, more generally, any of those categories of persons whose histories remain un- or under-written—that documenting and interpreting their law-violating activities, or their brushes with the police, courts, and corrections is only one of the many ways in which it can and should be done. No claim need be made that law-violation and control by legal agencies is the most important part of the experiences of these groupings, only that it is not unimportant. It should also be added that the paper trails left by the police, courts, and corrections frequently turn out to be one of the few remaining sources permitting insight, however limited, into other aspects of the experiences of these neglected categories of persons.

Historical studies of crime and crime control, then, are one way of doing history from the "bottom," to use a current catchword. They permit documentation and interpretation of events involving substantial sectors of the population that have hitherto remained unexamined. Such studies modify our understanding of the past, an understanding typically gained through histories from the "top." This in itself is sufficient justification for doing them and provides one reason for finding them "interesting." They may, and perhaps inevitably do modify our understanding of the present as well—the article by Geoffrey Pearson that follows shows one way this can happen. Pearson is deeply concerned to show that, seen in terms of their situations and traditions, and the understanding of the world that such situations and traditions afford, the "riotous" activities of workers in eighteenth- and early nineteenth-century England were hardly as senseless or purposeless as they have usually been portrayed. Drawing heavily on the work of E. P. Thompson and his associates, he enlarges our understanding of the meaning of the advent of industrialism for all those whom it affected—or perhaps we should say, the meanings of industrialism, for he is especially concerned to portray meaningful experiences that have been forgotten or suppressed. As he points out, such meanings are likely to exist in the present as well—and likely to be unarticulated or suppressed.

Pearson notes that "crime emerges . . . as something central to our understanding of the historical transformation into capitalism." His article argues, as well, that it is something central to our understanding of the maintenance of capitalist relations, and, perhaps, to our grasp of the transformations *of* capitalism, of its changing forms and demands, and the kinds of laws, law-violations, and control measures associated with each. It is this possibility—even more broadly, the possibility that study of crime will help us understand the springs of social change and stability—that makes it "interesting" above all. For this we suppose is one of the master aims of all social science, including history.

Sidney L. Harring, using insights gained from Marx, provides a remarkably detailed analysis of the development and use of criminal law and its administration by the police and courts as an instrument for maintaining capitalist relations during a period of perceived threat. The law in question—New York's "tramp act"—served in the circumstances to criminalize activities (and a state of being) that were part and parcel of a situation associated with the capitalist economic system itself: mass unemployment. The law provided penalties that, if nothing else, served to legitimate removal from the community of unemployed persons feared to be unwilling to accept this situation, and ready to insist on radical changes. Further, fascinating for our time (given as it is to federal subsidization of state crime control, and state subsidization of local crime control), the law helped assure the application of penalties through centralized reimbursement of local costs. Moreover, as Harring illustrates, the law was administered zealously when and as the threat against which it was directed appeared most severe.

Harring undertakes to demonstrate a familiar Marxian contention: that the law and its administration are tools of the ruling class. He certainly succeeds in showing that they can be and that, in Buffalo during the relevant period they functioned in that way, at least in the situation Harring examined. Whether this is always the case is another, thornier, question. Whether Harring has said all that might be said about the criminal law and its administration in Buffalo from 1892-1894, even with respect to the working class and "tramps," is a still further question that might be asked. Presumably E. P. Thompson would ask it (he might ask both), for in the segment we have taken from his remarkable book on the Black Act, Thompson appears to be suggesting that scholars should pay more attention, particularly scholars working in the Marxian tradition, perhaps, to the distinctive contributions that law might make to civilization and civility. Law is, after all, a rather special "instrument" or "tool"—a particular way of ordering social relationships. It is, moreover, in the words of Lon Fuller (1964), an "enterprise," by which he means, in part, itself a system of social relationships, as well as rules, with its own rationalities and demands. Law can be, and has been, studied historically, and it can be seen (as David F. Greenberg notes in passing, in another article in this collection) as something more than "an instrument of class rule." It is pertinent to ask that other functions it performs besides enforcing "class rule," even from a Marxian perspective. And it is pertinent to ask—Thompson's point, we think—what difference it makes for both the ruled and the rulers that the latter choose—if it is a "choice"— to dominate, in part, through law in addition to, or instead of, other "tools."

If it is easy to raise such questions, it is difficult to answer them, and we do not mean to criticize Harring for not answering them in a work directed to another, quite fascinating, end. We do mean to emphasize the potential richness of the study of crime and crime control—again, including the study of criminal law, both substantive and procedural—as a way of throwing light on neglected segments of the population and their experiences, and as a way of expanding our understanding of the dynamics and realities of social change and stability. We think historical studies should continue to be pursued in ever-greater number in this area for reasons already stated, and for additional reasons as well.

Among the additional reasons is that historical studies, almost necessarily, are comparative. This is not to say that historians of crime (or any other subject) need set out to do a comparison between past and present in the way that, say, a sociologist might choose to compare two jurisdictions with quite varied crime rates. Rather, it is the case that given contemporary consciousness—and given, when we are fortunate, studies of comparable contemporary events or institutions—studies of the past will quite unavoidably serve to sharpen our vision of the present, or at least our assumptions about it. Pearson uses this fact explicitly; Harring does so implicitly, inviting us to consider how we now threat the poor and unemployed—migrant workers, for instance. Or what the consequences for influencing police policy of continuing pressures for "professionalization" might bring. Or what the relationship might be currently between those pressing for "reform" and those pressing for greater "repression" (for example, in current "reform" of sentencing laws, with their thrust toward greater "determinancy").

Then, too, historical studies may be directly comparative, contrasting current forms of law administration and seeking the historical roots of these contrasts in the founding circumstances of the organizations utilizing these forms. Wilbur R. Miller compares the circumstances confronting police administrators in London and New York City in the nineteenth century, when both police systems were established. In both cases, as we understand his argument, the task was the same: to win "public" support or, at least, acceptance. London police had, or believed they had to demonstrate relative independence of control by the landed aristocracy still heading the state. This was accomplished by adopting an "impersonal" style, a law- or rule-bound style, affording little discretion to the individual officer. The New York City police, on the other hand, as "representatives" of the governed were able to adopt a more "personal" style, giving more—indeed, much—discretion to the individual officer.

Judgments will differ, surely, as to whether Miller has provided a convincing account of the origins of the differences in discretion still apparently characteristic of the London and New York City police. (Indeed, it is commonly believed that these differences separate the British police forces from substantially all U.S. police forces.) Clearly, however, he has put historical inquiry to good use, using its implicit, probably necessary, comparative possibilities explicitly to explore contemporary differences. (The extent and character of these differences is by no means a settled matter, however. Generally it remains unclear where and how "discretion" is located and controlled in the English and continental legal systems, as compared to U.S. systems. Part of the problem in settling this issue stems from the several uses of the concept of "discretion," as Arthur Rosett makes clear elsewhere in this volume. Another part of the problem stems from the relative absence of comparative studies, historical or contemporary.)

Eric Monkkonen illustrates another use of historical studies of crime and crime control: to generate hypotheses about social change. Somewhat like Millier, Monkkonen is concerned with differences in the organization and activities of the police; unlike Miller, he searches for changes over time and then suggests tentative explanations for these changes. Without detail, Monkkonen supplies a class conflict context for examining the growth of police systems, and for the declining rates of arrests per policeman. The breakdown of previously established, accepted, and understood relations between classes, he suggests, results in perceptions of increasing disorder. Police systems expanded to deal with this disorder. Further, they came to take a "preventative" posture—presumably in contrast to a more purely "responsive" posture maintained by police and their predecessors in the past. Their increased presence provided at least symbolic protection—perhaps established that fabled "thin blue line" between good order and the chaos threatened by the "criminal classes." At the same time, and partly as a result, they could arrest persons less frequently, thereby perhaps avoiding (further) alienation of those making up the "criminal classes" (and thereby dealing at least in part with the problem of acceptance raised by Miller).

We do not want to make the findings of any of the studies we have collected sound more plausible than they seem to us in fact; nor do we want to argue that the studies fully mesh with each other. Hindus' essay does an admirable, if necessarily limited, job of assessing the positive and negative virtues of several important historical studies in criminology, and of teasing out some of the main themes that tie them together. Hindus also makes clear how recently most historians have come to the mass and massive data available in this area, and how recently they have come to conceive of their works as testing (and we would add, generating) hypotheses empircally. (Some sociologists and other social scientists have begun serious historical studies, as Hindus and we have mentioned. Their work, too, lacks full coherence at this point in time, if for different reasons.)

We do find some of the assertions made in the articles we have collected questionable. Monkkonen's speculation that the police, concerned about reducing crime rates by increasing arrests, may have chosen to arrest less strikes us as, well, unrealistic. Perhaps we have misunderstood him: he may rather be saying that if the police had kept up their former pace of arrests, then the crime rates would have been reduced, and then there would have been less justification for expansion of the system. Other studies collected in this volume suggest that the first part of this proposition may be true. Whether a reduced crime rate would have meant more difficulty in expanding police systems is, however, still quite questionable; at least it doesn't seem to have worked that way in the 1970s.

But this is not the place for a lengthy critique of Monkkonen's or others' work. More interesting, we think, are the leads for further and better work that the writings collected here provide. (Further, in every case we believe the strong points of these works outweigh their weak points. And as one of us is fond of pointing out to students, *any* student of even moderate perspicacity can punch holes in even the classic studies in social science and history.)

Monkkonen mentions that the police came to be explected to "prevent" crime rather than merely respond to it. He suggests that one mechanism for appearing to do so has been to identify a "dangerous" class and "harrass" its members. Harring provides evidence that, in some circumstances at least, this is precisely what police did do; he even shows how the law was changed to facilitate this kind of action by broadening the segment of population "legitimately" subject to harrassment, and by increasing the weight of legally permissible penalties. Working class girls, especially those from immigrant families, appear to have been one of the dangerous classes subject to the kinds of preventative harrassment Monkkonen has in view. In many cases, one infers, it was much less what such girls were doing or had done that led to legal attention, than what it was believed they might or were likely to do without such attention—it was this that led to the not-so-tender ministrations of the police, juvenile courts, and probation authorities. Steven Schlossman's and Stephanie Wallach's explanation of this kind of attention to girls during the Progressive Era proceeds at a quite different level from what might be supplied by others more committed to a structural framework for inquiry. But their portrayal of what happened, and the motives of those involved, is not inconsistent with the kind of economy and class-linked explanations the others might provide.

REFERENCE

FULLER, L. L. (1964). The morality of law. New Haven, Conn.: Yale University Press.

8

THE HISTORY OF CRIME
Not Robbed of Its Potential, But Still on Probation

MICHAEL S. HINDUS

INTRODUCTION

The history of crime is a rapidly emerging field of study. Virtually unknown a few years ago except for a small number of older classical works, it now boasts its own journal and international organization. Specialized meetings on the history of crime have been held in the United States and Europe. There is no question that the findings generated by this work are proving of great interest to all scholars in the areas of crime, criminal law, and corrections. But it is less clear why. Is it because of the data generated, the myths shattered? Or is it because historians themselves have contributed new theoretical and methodological insights which social scientists can apply from the historian's example?

As an historian, I should like to argue both points. And, in the course of this essay, I shall try to show why the recent findings are of so much potential value. But as to special insights generated by the historical study itself, I would have to admit serious skepticism. As a discipline, history has no special rules, methodologies, or theoretical assumptions. Historians do have certain skills which may enable them to place a phenomenon or trend into general social context. They share with anthropologists a stance of cultural relativity as well as a search for the integrating interpretation.

But in recent years history and the social sciences (particularly sociology) have been experiencing a shifting of ground. Historical sociology has again been in vogue—whether practiced by historians or sociologists. In the course of this type of scholarship, historians have adopted many of the conceptual modes of the social scientist.

This process has evolved in three distinct stages. The first stage was to reject the institutional and political synthesis of history which had dominated postwar scholarship and to explore in the past some of the staple fields of sociological inquiry, particularly the history of the family, the history of social and geographical mobility, and the history of crime and justice. In so doing, historians concentrated more on social processes, less on finite events.

Historians also found, however, that they were often ill-equipped for this enterprise. As a result, many became trained in quantitative methods. Factor scores and beta values uneasily joined many historians' vocabularies.

More significant than the methodology was the type of sources and data which historians were now using. To understand social process, historians employed different data sources which required new skills to analyze properly. Rather than drawing impressionist conclusions from a sample of literary evidence, historians now collected huge quantities (huge even by social science standards because historians—often with good reason, but occasionally through inordinate skepticism—have avoided much sampling) of data. It became possible for the first time to measure a social phenomenon in the past and compare and contrast it with contemporary observations. This alone may be the most significant single contribution of recent historiography.

The last stage, the inevitable result of the first two, was that historians adopted a more explicit concern with the theoretical implications of their findings. Like social scientists, they began to weave their data into hypotheses. At this point many historians *became* social scientists by rigorously testing theory against data. The classic posture of the historian had once been that of the archaeologist, wandering through the sources with few preconceived notions, reporting on what he or she had found, and interpreting the findings in the context of all that was known about a society in a given period. Of course, it was rare when historians actually maintained that sort of distance from preconceived interpretative ideas. But historians insisted—with considerable justification—that the framework was never explicit, that it was a combination of intuition and chance. Such distance was a casualty of the quantitative revolution, and although hypothesis-testing is still rather novel, it is now a part of the historical inquiry.

It is worth spending some time on this recent transformation of the historians' craft. For one thing, many social scientists have approached historians to see what special skills they could impart, only to find that the cross-pollinization has largely been in the opposite direction. But more importantly, it is impossible to understand much of the impulse behind the study of the history of crime without understanding how the infusion of social science techniques and modes of inquiry has affected the practice of history.

In writing the history of crime (and the history of crime is hardly unique in this regard; indeed, a more classic example would be the history of the family), historians were not, after all, venturing into uncharted territory. There was no shortage of theoretical literature. If the history of crime has seemed obsessed with proving or disproving classic sociological principles, it is only because any discipline in its nascency must test the limits of its knowledge against conventional wisdom.

But there is one more factor which must be kept in mind. By the time a social scientific concept reaches historians, it is probably already on the decline among social scientists. This may be simply because historians typically rely on published works, or simply that when theory is borrowed rather than generated, it is often of a level which is difficult to apply to the historical context. In any event, the historian's use of theory often seems stale and forced.

At this point it may seem that social scientists may gain very little from historians, that the cross-pollinization has been all in one direction and that the hybrid which has resulted has failed to improve the species of scholarship. This fear may seem even more confirmed by my next observation. History is not a policy-making science, and its practitioners do not generally have a voice in social planning. Similarly, until the very recent past, historians have not enjoyed government or foundation largesse. As a result, historians have often taken almost a perverse pleasure in refusing to draw policy implications from their work.

This is hardly the result of the exclusion of historians from policy-making bodies. Rather, this seemingly dispassionate independent stance is a necessary part of the practice of history. At least in theory, the historian is not committed to any particular party line or theory and is able to interpret his evidence with no particular stake in the outcome. There are at least two other reasons why historians may not wish to use their scholarship as the basis for recommending public policy. First of all, they are not trained in this area. Secondly, they do not want to compromise their truth-seeking function by having their work become identified with a policy position which may soon go out of style.

Why historians act in this manner is, of course, of far less significance than the fact that they do. But the fact that historians do not draw policy implications from their work does not mean that those who are better trained to do so cannot use that work for their own policy purposes. Without being too reductionist, it is fair to say that the historian of crime encounters almost every situation with which the contemporary criminologist must contend. Community control of the police, for example, was a burning issue for almost half the nineteenth century. To be sure the issues were drawn somewhat differently, but only somewhat. The clashes were often political, ethnic, and religious, not necessarily racial, but the desire of the working and immigrant classes to be free from the imposition of upper class norms and values was hardly dissimilar from our more contemporary concerns.

Corrections policy provides another example. Employment of the exconvict, the contaminating effect of penal institutions, the demand for community-based corrections, and the merits of different approaches to sentencing were all nineteenth century issues. The problems created by excessive discretion in sentencing were nearly identical to the discontent that has recently led to a return to determinate sentences. On the other hand, the inflexibility of such a system in the nineteenth century led eventually to the indeterminate sentence. Community-based corrections, particularly for juveniles, prostitutes, and other minor offenders, was proposed in the mid-nineteenth century as an alternative to brutalizing, dehumanizing institutions. But such early examples of "diversion" resembled the same foster parent notion which we are now reevaluating.

When the major policy alternatives in the criminal justice area are distilled down to the essentials, almost everything has been tried before. It may take some imagination to recognize probation in the efforts of a Boston bootmaker to keep young offenders out of jail, but his experiences are very germane to today's problems.[1] If an historian analyzes why a particular policy direction succeeded or failed in the past, the social scientist should be able to factor some of those considerations into his own predictive equations. The historian should not have to do this for him.

Moreover, history reveals the human experience in endless variety. This may sound like a cliché, but the historian is conversant with more styles of life, more social dilemmas than any planner can hope to confront in a lifetime. Unlike the policy planner, who can hope at best that his regression equations and simulation models will reduce the risk of some unforeseen monkey wrench destroying his scheme, the historian *knows* the outcome. We know that whipping and branding ceased to be used as punishments (except within penal institutions themselves) in industrializing societies by the mid-nineteenth century; a good historian should be able to indicate why this happened. And a good social scientist should be able to draw his own implications from that analysis, applying that to the aspects of contemporary punishment which are based on shame or pain. A competent social scientist might also recognize in this abolition a far from completely successful attempt to avoid the consequences of labelling.

The irony about the policy maker's complaint is that the history of crime is one of the few areas of history where the policy implications almost jump off the page. Intellectual history is far too abstract; many other potentially useful areas of historical study do not present opportunities for application in modern society. But the criminal justice area presents the same problems as it did 200 years ago, and even the same alternatives are still in the air—centralization or community control, fixed or indeterminate sentences, capital punishment as a deterrent or as a brutalizing force. The social scientist must be able to use this information without jeopardizing the independence which is the mainstay of the historian's craft.

The value of the study of the history of crime, at bottom, is not different from the value of studying *any* form of history. History is dynamic, whether implicitly or explicitly. We see changes over time and can compare the distant past with understandings drawn from more recent explorations. In traditional areas of history, this has been easy—great events or great people dominate and influence future events. But in social history (of which the history of crime and justice is a part) this dynamic is slower, more subtle. The best works in the history of crime help us to understand more clearly our present failures and frustrations by locating their origins and then trying to explain the mindset of those who, for example, "discovered" the asylum, created the juvenile court, or chose a particular model for the police.

This is not to deny that important changes have occurred in crime and criminal justice. However, most of the work which will be discussed in this essay concerns the modern (seventeenth century to the present) context, by which time trial by ordeal was a memory, bodily torture was already on the decline, and the rudiments of the modern adversarial and inquisitorial systems of justice were being erected. Thus, in one sense, the history of crime and justice is comparative and dynamic, offering a cross-sectional and anthropological analysis of enormous import. On the other hand, substantive innovations in criminal justice policy, observable changes in the life patterns of the defendant classes must be detected more subtly.

The history of crime may be termed a new field, akin to recent interest in the history of ordinary people, such as working class, family, and demographic history. But while the interest in this area has burgeoned, the history of crime has its own classics. In 1948 Sir Leon Radzinowicz published the first volume of his *History of the English Criminal Law*.[2] Like the legal history of its era, its focus was largely administrative and political. Recent work in this area, more concerned with behavior, cannot really be said to build on that of this pioneer. Nevertheless, Radzinowicz's work serves as an encyclopedia of detail about every aspect of the criminal justice system in England. Some other major works also preceded the recent interest in the history of crime and justice. One of the best, Rusche and Kircheimer's *Punishment and Social Structure* has become almost a cult classic, not only because of its comparative scope and rigorous analytical framework, but also for its attempt to link punishment with a society's form of economy and production.[3] Although legal historians have largely ignored the history of crime, Leonard Levy's *The Origins of the Fifth Amendment* remains unmatched in its discussion of the historic struggle between the power of the state and the rights of the individual, a struggle played out as much in terms of criminal procedure as in terms of the more visible crusades for freedom of expression.[4]

RECENT WORK IN THE HISTORY OF CRIME

This essay will discuss some of the major findings of the recent work in the history of crime. Although the emphasis is on recent work in American history, older classics which have retained their vitality and works by European scholars which have been unusually influential among American scholars are also considered. The discussion will be thematic, clustered around ideas, theories, and assumptions which underly the research. While the number of potential subjects in the history of crime and justice is vast (encompassing such areas as criminal behavior, law enforcement, punishment, penal codes, and juvenile justice), the number of significant concepts which have played major roles in shaping this research is relatively finite, and helps to give some coherence to the field.

One persistently influential interpretation in the history of crime is what may be termed, despite its reductionism, the social control interpretation. Long a staple in both sociology and history, it has assumed a more complicated dimension in the history of crime.[5] Social control, as used by historians of crime, refers to the imposition of a certain set of dominant, respectable norms onto a class deemed to be deviant to a large extent because of their nonacceptance of these norms. This argument, in all of its variant forms, is a natural one for the history of crime, since the legal system itself provides a formal mechanism for the imposition of the values and norms embodied in statute and case law upon a population which defies or violates those standards. If one assumes that law-making bodies represent a consensus of "respectable society," and that the criminal law proscribes acts clearly beyond the pale, then it becomes almost redundant to think of the interplay between the formal legal system and the defendant as social control.

However, the social control interpretation has rarely fallen prey to this simplistic fallacy. Rather, historians looked at the creation and evolution of components of the criminal justice system and have identified examples of social control in the ways in which certain key choices were made and defended. There are two areas in which this view is most clearly expressed— the history of the penitentiary in America and the evolution of the juvenile justice system.

In the recent spate of interest in the history of crime and justice, perhaps the most influential single work is David Rothman's *The Discovery of the Asylum*.[6] Rothman asks why Americans in the Jacksonian era erected institutions to house the deviant, the poor, and the insane. In the colonial era, by contrast, towns had taken care of their own poor and expelled (in New England through the process of "warning out") those without settlement in a town who were likely to become public charges. Deviance was handled in a variety of ways, ranging from exclusion from the community (through expulsion or execution) to shame (with the expectation that having once been publicly shamed for committing a sin, the individual would return as a fully rehabilitated member of the society).

What accounted for this shift away from what would now be termed outdoor poor relief and community-based corrections (keeping in mind that communities were narrowly defined and that the treatment of those who were not members was harsh by any standards) to a system of institutionalization? Rothman's answer is a complex one, encompassing Jacksonian era fears of social disorder and the extraordinary confidence of those who planned, built, and guided these asylums, prisons, almshouses, and houses of correction and refuge through their formative years. But, essentially, Rothman concludes, no matter how benevolent the spirit which built these institutions, by mid-century all had become virtual storage bins, hiding those people society wished to forget. While the stated goal of reformation seemed to be a failure, incarceration, always an obtainable goal, now seemed to become the primary function of these institutions. And much of this shift from benevolence to incarceration,

Rothman argues, was due to the economic and cultural chasms which separated the idealistic reformers from the inmates and charges which they so vainly (and almost literally) sought to "re-form."

Rothman's book is not, of course, simply a specification of a social control hypothesis. It is majestic in sweep, attempting to describe and interpret a major change in the way in which various marginal and deviant groups in society were treated. Its implications speak to many areas of social policy—not simply the treatment of the insane, poor, criminal, and juvenile (the groups treated specifically in the study), but also areas such as education, family law, medical care, and charitable and public relief. Indeed, for this reason the impact of *Discovery of the Asylum* has perhaps been greater among social scientists and policy planners than among historians.

Again, like any book bold enough to have that sort of impact, *The Discovery of the Asylum* oversimplifies for the sake of clear dichotomies and policy choices. Many years later, these faults do not seem as damning as they once did, and it is impossible for anyone to contemplate these issues without first struggling with the clear issues which Rothman posed. But there are three aspects of the study which should give one pause. First of all, Rothman relates the discovery of the asylum to Jacksonian America, with its entrepreneurial optimism, reformist zeal, and economic, demographic, and social trans-formations. Yet, penitentiaries for reformation as well as confinement were built across the Atlantic, suggesting that a uniquely American interpretation can hardly explain this development.

Secondly, Rothman homogenizes the ideas of those who built and ran these institutions. In fact, not only were there skeptics from the beginning, but at least one of the more notable skeptics, Samuel Gridley Howe, had been one of the earliest and influential promoters of institutionalization. A leader in the Boston prison movement and Director of the Perkins School for the Blind, by midcentury Howe actually opposed the creation of more reformatories for juveniles; believed that a prison sentence could be worse than death; and supported the creation of community-based correctional facilities.[7]

Finally, Rothman can be faulted for a connection which he did not make: the relation between prison and factory is barely mentioned. Obviously, to make much of this resemblance would be to tread on uncertain ground. But both prison and factory developed during the same period. The people who created the factory towns, complete with domitories for operatives, were financial bankers of the prison reform movement, and the goals of the Jacksonian prison and factory were similar. The organization of work in the prison was held to be like a great "manual labor school," similar to Lowell, the prototypical factory town.[8] Both Lowell and the prison attracted visitors from all over the world.

These similarities may be dismissed as superficial, but there are others which seem too essential to the nature of each institution to overlook. The first is organized disciplined labor itself. The prison attempted to replicate the factory in order to instill skills and the value of work into the incorrigible inmates. The second is the profit motive. Of course, the factory was expected to bring a financial return to its owners, but the annual prison reports also reveal an uncanny obsession with profits. Admittedly, proponents of the prison over-optimistically promised profits in return for the huge capital outlays necessary to construct the imposing edifices. Nevertheless, the integration of labor, discipline, and profit might have illuminated some areas of nineteenth-century criminal justice which escaped Rothman's purview. It is no accident that the introduction of the factory was blamed for an increase in crime or that the use of class terminology, particularly with regard to a criminal or laboring class, began to appear during this period.

To explore the connection that Rothman did not make, we must temporarily depart from the analysis of the social control approach to the works of those who draw a more direct relationship between the economic and penal systems.[9] The classic work in this area is Rusche and Kircheimer's *Punishment and Social Structure*, published in America in 1939. Rusche and Kircheimer link punishment to economic and social systems from ancient times to the twentieth century. The fate of convicted offenders (whether criminal by deed or thought) was related to the needs of the economy. Thus, slavery was the punishment in ancient times, and transportation was a common punishment during the age of imperialism, when labor was a scarcity in the farflung colonial outposts. In times of population and labor surplus, they argue, capital punishment was employed on a mass scale. In the industrial era, however, when labor was again a relatively scarce commodity, convict labor (whether within or outside prison walls) replaced the gallows.

Rescued from undeserved obscurity by the renewed interest in the history of crime and justice, *Punishment and Social Structure* is evocative and stim-ulating, rather than empirically definitive. The connection between prison and factory—the obvious link which Rothman refused to explore—has also been probed by the extraordinary work of the French structuralist, Michel Foucault. In *Discipline and Punish*,[10] Foucault describes the historical movement from physical torture to penitentiary discipline. In each case the body was the object of punishment, but the "mere" pain of preindustrial methods of torture was replaced by the more psychological pain of control and confinement in the modern era. Foucault's concern is not explicitly with the relationship between economics, society, and the penal system, but he does connect the strict discipline of the nineteenth century penitentiary with its counterparts in schools, factories, and hospitals. Unlike Rothman, whose reformers merely exemplified misguided benevolence, Foucault concentrated on the growing army of professional disciplinarians, whether they be wardens, doctors, or teachers. Thus, comparing the works of Rothman, Rusche and Kircheimer, and Foucault, we see contrasting views of the same phenomenon: the assertion of control over the prisoner, whether to achieve reformation, labor, or discipline.

The social control approach in *Discovery of the Asylum* helps to explain a subtle shift from benevolence to incarceration. The employment of social control notions in the field of juvenile justice is not quite as subtle. Here we have an unusual three-way debate between two parties, Anthony Platt (1969), and Stephen Schlossman (1976) and Platt again (1977). Modern reevaluation of the Juvenile Court began with a landmark decision in the Supreme Court, *In re Gault*.[11] Platt's *The Child Savers* was the historical equivalent of the Gault decision.[12] In tracing the history of the juvenile court, Platt originally ascribed its flaws and failures to Progressive Era reformers. Platt's "controllers" differed from Rothman's in two major respects. First of all, Rothman's reformers were well-intended innocents whose major failure was their inability to dismantle the institutions once it became abundantly clear that their original functions had become perverted. Platt's reformers, in an age of portending class warfare and increasing xenophobia, were consciously attempting to use the legal system to force recalcitrant youths to conform to middle-class norms. Secondly, while (with the exception of Dorothea Dix) Rothman's reformers were men, many of Platt's were female.

Platt originally employed labelling theory to explain why social workers and middle-level bureaucrats overrode concerns for individual rights in their attempts to railroad incorrigible youths. To Platt, labelling theory explained why the childsavers obliterated the distinction between behavior which was criminally proscribed and that which was merely unsocial, unpleasant, threatening, or nonconforming.

In the introduction to the second edition of *The Child Savers* Platt engages in self-criticism which is perhaps more relevant to the sociology of knowledge from the early 1960s to early 1970s than it is to the history of crime.[13] Platt "confesses" that he originally aimed too low, blaming the repressive qualities of the juvenile justice system on low level functionaries who implicitly used labelling theory in treating or mistreating the children who came before them.

If Platt (1969) aims too low, then Platt (1977) aims too high. The problem with the childsavers, Platt now believes, is that they represented a new capitalist order uncertain of its continued dominance, and determined to employ the new theories of the ascending army of social scientists to ensure their control. The problem with reform, Platt concludes (as if he had just discovered this) is that it altered none of the economic relationships which created the social problems reformers were called upon to solve. Platt sees as essential to understanding this method of domination the class base from which social reformers were recruited. But again, this is a half-hearted beating of a stuffed horse. Historians of all political stripes have long agreed that reformers were not revolutionaries, that they were often tied to, recruited from, and financed by various parts of the established order. Accepting the work of Rusche and Kircheimer (and of Platt's colleagues and students in radical criminology) as if they presented principles as widely accepted as Newton's laws of physics, Platt attempts to graft a doctrinaire Marxian interpretation onto a work solidly critical of liberal history and liberal reform. Platt's revised argument is simplistic and unconvincing for its inability to distinguish between causes and correlations, and for its failure to connect with any more convincing proof than suggesting the economic changes which occurred at the turn of the century and the specific development of the juvenile justice system.

The most recent major work on the history of juvenile justice is Steven L. Schlossman's *Love and the American Delinquent: The Theory and Practice of "Progressive" Juvenile Justice, 1825-1920.*[14] This monograph incorporates both a revisionist view of early ideas on juvenile reform with case studies of the Wisconsin State Reform School and the Milwaukee Juvenile Court. While many of the theoreticians of juvenile reform were from the Northeast, their message was quickly diffused to other parts of the country.

Schlossman forces a reconsideration of the social control interpretation in many ways. In discussing mid-nineteenth century approaches to juvenile corrections, Schlossman reminds us of their heterogeneity, a point which Rothman did not stress. With the family, not the factory, as the model for juvenile corrections, the institutional responses were more flexible. As was the case with the penitentiary, the transatlantic connection proved an important one. But while Europeans flocked to America to study the two major and competing systems of penal confinement, the separate system and the silent system, the direction of influence in the area of juvenile reform went the other way, with Americans copying the German Rauhe Hans and the French Colonie Agricole.[15]

But more significantly, some reformers by midcentury had begun to question the wisdom of institutionalization—especially for juveniles—whether it be in cottages or penitentiary-like reformatories. The intellectual odyssey of Samuel Gridley Howe is particularly revealing, since he was director of an asylum for the deaf, dumb and blind, a staunch supporter of the silent system in the internecine prison reform struggles in Boston in the 1840s, and in general, a person closely associated with institutionalization. By midcentury, though, Howe opposed construction of a juvenile reformatory for girls and by the 1860s, ensconced in the symbolically important but powerless position of Secretary of the Massachusetts Board of State Charities, wrote his famous *Second Annual Report.* In essence, Howe advocated community-based corrections, measures tantamount to diversion, and a reduction in the resort to institutionalization. Moreover, he criticized excessive reliance on institutions, which, he realized took on a life of their own. "So rich endowed," Howe observed, "[they] cannot be got rid of so easily."

The thread of anti-institutional thought is hardly Schlossman's own discovery. But Schlossman carries it through his study, particularly in his discussion of the Milwaukee Juvenile Court, in a way which refines the now admittedly simplistic social control argument by showing that the same ends can be achieved by less obvious means. Although one set of behavioral norms was imposed on groups labelled as deviant for nonconforming but not necessarily criminal behavior, it was not simply a function of class dominance by an all-powerful homogeneous elite. Except for the obvious leaders, those who implemented Progressive reform were usually middle- and lower-middle-class bureaucrats, closer in social status to the defendants than to the elite policy makers.[17] Furthermore, those who were the subject of social control in many respects accepted and encouraged these measures. Parents of incorrigible children actually sought to be relieved of sole responsibility for their offspring.

Finally, Schlossman adds a useful corrective to the institution/anti-institution dichotomy first posed by Rothman. It is clear that Progressive Era reformers invented, borrowed, and implemented a number of alternatives to incarceration. But it is by no means clear that this represented the triumph of an anti-institutional approach to controlling deviance. Schlossman shows that the juvenile court in the Progressive Era was an early promoter of diversion and probation as alternatives to institutionalization. But such alternatives co-existed with houses of refuge and juvenile reformatories. Diversion (for adults as well as juveniles) was also in part a response to the increased demands made on the penal system. What was significant was the degree of control exercised over defendants by parole boards and probation officers, not the specific place in which a sentence was served.

The social control synthesis is not limited to institutionalization. The history of the police in America often involves social control of a more blatant sort. The two major issues in police history concern the relationship between the police and the policed and the organization of police forces with respect to outside political influence and internal discipline and supervision. But the history of the police in America is characterized by a paradox which renders a straightforward social control point of view perilous at best. On the one hand, the characteristic hostility between police and citizen has frequently been blamed on the social gap between these two groups. But an even more significant feature of police history has been the strong ties between the police force and the urban political machine, so that police historically were seen not as the servant of the dominant elite, but as the agent of the bosses. Insofar as the bosses were supported by the ethnic proletariat which apparently also supplied the defendant class, the social control paradigm cannot be easily applied to the police. On the contrary, one explanation of police failure has been patrolmen's persistant reluctance (which applied to the urban machines as well) to enforce various laws against liquor, vice, and various forms of Sunday recreation.

In reality, probably both explanations are true, with the police as political agents more characteristic of the nineteenth century and the police as outside occupier increasingly apparent in the twentieth. To complete the picture, we should go one step further and analyze law enforcement and social control in the colonial era as precursory to the urban police forces of the nineteenth and twentieth centuries.

Law enforcement in colonial America was largely informal and frequently inefficient. Colonial New England towns elected tythingmen who had responsibility for overseeing the morals and behavior of the population. As the strong communitarian impulse which fueled the initial seventeenth-century settlements became more diffuse, as stringent sexual standards began to be violated on an increased scale, some colonies established a more formal system of law enforcement.[18] New York's system, for example, while highly stratified, was extremely inefficient, often commanding little respect from the population.[19]

One way to consider the role of law enforcement in history is to consider the extent to which law enforcement personnel were drawn from the same or similar class as the defendant population or from a distinct and economically or socially superior class. No matter what period in American history, deviance appears to be correlated with certain social characteristics. In *Wayward Puritans*, Kai Eriksen associated criminality with political and religious dissension in the mid-and late seventeenth century.[20] While this analysis may be true for the more visible crimes against church and state (the Salem witch panic being the most obvious example), other research suggests that while colonial deviants may have been more heterogeneous than their more modern counterparts, still deviance was not random. In the extremely critical area of sexual offenses, for example, it seems clear that servants were more likely to be brought into court (because of their inability to ensure child support) than miscreants from other social groups.

In his study of crime and law enforcement in colonial New York, Douglas Greenberg shows that blacks were over-represented in the defendant population, while those of Jewish and Dutch descent were underrepresented.[21] Unfortunately Greenberg offers no conclusive explanation for this observation and is unwilling to consider relative economic status as a cause. In Massachusetts during the era of the American Revolution, William Nelson concludes, criminal defendants were drawn from a variety of social and economic strata.[22]

At first this interpretation of the relative heterogeneity of criminal propensity in the colonial era appears equivocating. But in fact it is a striking mirror of social trends in early America. Admittedly, by almost every measure social stratification increased as the eighteenth century progressed.[23] The distribution of wealth became increasingly skewed and the percentage of the population on the bottom rung of the economic ladder (those without assets who paid no taxes) increased. Yet the pace of social stratification accelerated in the early nineteenth century. So it was with the demography of the criminal population—some concentration among groups clearly seen as deviant (particularly servants and blacks), but the discovery or labelling of the criminal class would await the nineteenth century.

This fact is crucial to understanding the nature of law enforcement. In the relatively closed seventeenth-century communities, everyone had "police power" over each other and shame was an important deterrent. As this moral community became more diffuse, the tythingman was selected to help oversee his equals. As crime and disorder increased in the eighteenth century (and Greenberg's New York provides a good example), law enforcement personnel who were the social equals of the offenders found it difficult to assert their authority.[24]

The notion of a distinct part of the population controlling the behavior of another part—which, to a great extent, is what policing is all about—coincided with and indeed was dependent on the identification and discovery of an urban criminal class in a time of increasing social stratification and disorder.

The two pioneer modern histories of American police departments recount similar stories. In both New York and Boston, a series of riots in the 1830s forced authorities to adopt new methods of controlling a volatile population.[25] Nineteenth-century Americans seemed to experience a collective sense of disorder and, of course, the new modern market economy was extremely susceptible to rioting.[26] Finally, while colonial America, although hardly homogeneous, was still overwhelmingly of English stock, nineteenth-century cities were increasingly and disturbingly heterogeneous. Three major riots in four years triggered the establishment of the Boston police force. The first and last were clear examples of ethnic conflict between Irish Catholics and Yankees and the third may well have been related to antiblack sentiment.[27] In short, at the time police forces were established, America saw the beginning of ethnic conflict and the identification, if not growth, of a criminal or dangerous class.

This brings us back to a central issue in the history of the police in the United States: the relationship between police and population. As Roger Lane shows for Boston, initially the police were drawn from the Yankee population, and no Irish need apply. When the first Irishman was finally admitted to the police force, he was forced to march alone in the annual police parade.[28] While in Boston initially the police were drawn from a different ethnic strata than the policed, in New York this was not the case. The New York police, as James Richardson and Wilbur Miller show, were so reluctant to appear to be too distant from the population that they refused for several years to consider wearing uniforms.[29] Demonstrating an early, if only intuitive sense of community control and accountability, New York required police to reside in the ward which they patrolled.

As I have already indicated, although recruitment patterns would become an important issue in the twentieth century, the more significant issue in the nineteenth century involved the political machines. The police force was more than a ready source of patronage. Laws against vice and liquor were frequently unpopular in ethnic and working class wards. Forced on the urban masses by Republican-controlled state legislators, this legislation could be rendered meaningless by the machine-controlled police through systematic nonenforcement.

Rather than simply an example of social control by elite Protestants over an immigrant, largely Catholic population, what we see in these conflicts over control of the police is another variant of the great battle between urban and rural culture which began in the Jacksonian era and affected so much of American political life until the recent past.[30] More to the point, as both Lane and Richardson show, the urban police were so closely identified with the political machine that their legitimacy was no greater than that of their patron. Bribery and corruption were common facts of police life, political qualifications were the most important criteria for joining the force, and often the purpose of the police seemed more to protect the machine than the populace. Liquor and politics, rather than crime and law enforcement, permeate the early history of the Boston and New York police forces.

Two scholars have attempted recently to add new dimensions to the view that Lane and Richardson expressed. Wilbur Miller, in *Cops and Bobbies*, compares the early years of the New York and Metropolitan London police forces.[31] The second study, Robert Fogelson's *Big City Police*, emphasizes the history of the urban police in the past century.[32] Fogelson's study, in an ironic way, illustrates that even though a major virtue of studying history is the opportunity to observe change, many institutions and policies in the crime and law enforcement area had their fates and histories preordained during their formation. While an impressive and thorough account of successive waves of police reform in major cities in the United States, *Big City Police* often merely rings changes in the litany made familiar by Lane and Richardson. Periodic reform efforts exposed corruption and brutality; results of such investigations often involved a change in the control of the police. While the political machine was the villain in the nineteenth century, professionalization was the panacea in the twentieth. For city after city, Fogelson describes the well-intended search for professional and competent police management, the attempt to upgrade standards for patrolmen, the education and salary questions, and the cosmetic responsiveness to citizen and community concerns.

Yet the result seems to be the same. By the 1960s police reformers were either in charge of or had profoundly influenced every major department, but citizen disaffection was not significantly reduced. Political control of the police, though no longer posed in terms of urban machines against Whiggish state commissions, was still critical. Community control and residency requirements represented attempts to breach the gulf between the police and the policed. Significant strides were made in reducing the disparity between the ethnic distribution of police officers and that of the population of the cities in which they worked. But even as Fogelson describes these accomplishments, he realizes their limitations. Moreover, in terms of the elusive goal of professionalization, police militancy, not greater public appreciation of this goal, has accounted for most of the recent salary gains.

Big City Police, characteristic of the genre, is not about the police itself. Recruitment patterns are reduced to generalizations; there is no systematic analysis of the police-citizen encounter. The sources are mostly investigative reports and the annual reports of police departments and professional groups. Not a study of police per se, then, it is a thorough account of two sustained periods of reform. Of particular interest in Fogelson's analysis of the two most frequently discussed models for the police. The first is the military model, which as Miller shows, was to a great extent the one adopted in England. This model would presumably have tightened up the police command structure while increasing discipline and reducing discretion in the lower ranks (where citizen contact occurs). But the legacy of the nexus between police and politics and the myth of an apolitical military made this model ultimately unattractive.

The second model, associated with the second wave of reform, is the professionalization model. But, as one critic astutely noted, police professionalization was the very antithesis of the concept as used and applied to other professional groups.[33] Rather than permit more discretion (on the assumption that professionals are competent to make independent decisions and are also self-policing), professionalizing the police meant professionalizing the top brass and imposing greater supervision on patrolmen. Ironically, police professionalization is actually closer to the military model previously rejected than to the concept of professionalization used by other occupational groups.

Concentrating on reform, corruption, and institutional history, *Big City Police* is more like a follow-up to the work of Lane and Richardson, not a strikingly original way of conceptualizing the role of the police in America's past. *Cops and Bobbies* takes a completely different tack, using a comparative approach to determine why to Americans, the British bobby has been much better liked, and much more successful than his American counterpart. In the course of answering this question, Wilbur Miller is less concerned with the local political setting of the police and concentrates more on recruitment, police status with relation to the policed, and internal supervision and autonomy.

Police in New York City, according to Miller, represented a form of personal authority appropriate to a democratic society. The individual policeman, not some collective entity, represented law enforcement to the individual citizen. In London, by contrast, the bobby embodied a bureaucratic form of authority. He was not seen as an individual member of society with a special task, but rather as the personal embodiment of the authority of the British crown and Parliament.

This conceptualization, although an oversimplification, becomes for Miller a powerful tool to analyze differences between these two forms of police. Embodying personal authority, the New York cop had more individual discretion on the beat, was less closely supervised, and in many ways appeared to be just an ordinary member of the community. Recruitment reflected the democratic side of this personal authority. New York cops were recruited from ordinary ranks and were not intended to be superior to the population they patrolled and controlled.

In all of these aspects, the London bobby was opposite. As a preprofessional member of a bureacracy in a highly stratified society, the bobby had little of the personal discretion of his New York counterpart. More closely supervised, the bobby was subject to severe internal discipline of a type unknown in New York. And in class-conscious mid-nineteenth-century-London, the bobby, while hardly drawn from the upper strata, was superior socially to the population he patrolled.

The comparative approach has its limitations. Dynamic variation is subordinated to transatlantic contrasts.[34] But Miller's study, by offering a framework for analyzing the police-citizen relationship in these two related cultures, helps explain why Fogelson is ultimately unable to account for the failure of successive waves of reform to transform fundamentally America's police.

One further nontheoretical observation should be made regarding police history. Street crime, as we commonly understand it, plays a minor role in the works of Fogelson, Lane, Richardson, Miller, and Haller. Certainly an assessment of the role of the urban police in dealing with street crime should be an important part of this enterprise. Only Theodore Ferdinand has touched on it, and that in a rudimentary fashion.[35]

We cannot understand the origins of the penitentiary or the police without also considering the nature of the crime and the criminal. Historians have struggled with a number of theories and methods to describe crime in history. The most important historical work on crime and criminals has been statistical. But there are several different ways to interpret data, and there are theories implicit in the various uses historians have made of statistical data on crime in history. Labelling theory is one of the more frequently employed concepts. Labelling theory, as it has been used by historians, assumes that criminal prosecutions were dissociated from actual criminal behavior. A person who falls into one or more of several suspect social categories will be treated as a criminal, not for any specific behavior, but rather for membership in that category. Once so stigmatized, integration into the respectable world may be very difficult. Labelling theory has at least two attractions for the historian. First, by definitionally dissociating prosecution from behavior, the problem of the "dark figure"—the discrepancy between the number of proscribed acts committed and those that come to the attention of the researcher—becomes unimportant. Secondly, labelling theory provides the opportunity for measuring the stigmatizing effect of the criminal justice system.

One recent study of the dangerous class in a nineteenth-century American city is strongly influenced by a labelling perspective.[36] Eric Monkkonen's *The Dangerous Class* is more than a sophisticated application of labelling theory; it is also the most ambitious and systematic attempt to use social science methodology to identify the criminal and dangerous classes and to describe the interaction of these groups with the social welfare and criminal justice apparatus.

Focusing on 25-year period in nineteenth-century Columbus, Ohio, Monkkonen studies 4,514 criminal dockets. Using manuscript censuses and city directories in the matching technique now "de rigueur" in American urban history, Monkkonen identifies the social and demographic characteristics of the defendant population. Although Monkkonen has detailed breakdowns of occupation, nativity, and age by each crime category, his most important conclusions are that certain migrant and immigrant classes were overrepresented (as were rural Ohioans), and the occupational strata of the defendant class was not significantly different from that of the entire population (except for disproportionate numbers of unskilled and farm laborers). Wealth differences, controlled for occupational group, were significant: the defendant class tended to be in more dire financial straits. Monkkonen's conclusions reflect his labelling approach; indeed Monkkonen defines his "main interest . . . [as] the behavior of those *who became defined,* even if momentarily, by the dominant society as criminals [emphasis added]."[37] With some exceptions noted above, Monkkonen concludes that criminals were not especially different "from the noncriminals in their social characteristics." [38] This was the result of the urban society's inability to employ all of its members. Accordingly, some were forced to engage in criminal activities. "And once *labelled criminal* [emphasis added]," Monkkonen concludes, a person had difficulty reintegrating into noncriminal society.[39]

In attempting to determine whether nineteenth-century Columbus differentiated between a criminal class and a dangerous class, Monkkonen carries the analysis one step further by studying the social characteristics of paupers and then matching criminal defendants with paupers. For the 14-year period for which matching is possible, Monkkonen finds that "almost as many criminals were reduced to poverty by their crime as paupers were driven to crime by their poverty." While the criminal and pauper groups did constitute a dangerous class for residents of Columbus, Monkkonen concludes that this class was "not a homogeneous [one] . . . but one with subtle gradations and social mobility."[40] Still, the effect of labelling itself (or as Monkkonen terms it, the "obtrusive nature of our measures—the criminal court and the poorhouse")[41] must be considered.

Monkkonen's book warrants attention not only for its application of labelling theory, but as a sophisticated example of social science methodology. Still, some reservations deserve note. First, the matching technique which is essential to identifying the dangerous class is weakest in picking up members of the marginal and mobile populations.[42] Secondly, the period studied is so short as to provide little more than a snapshot. The historical dynamic is missing. The major value of the work is its massive and relentless assimilation of data. One's view of the book's weaknesses depends on the confidence one places in this type of data to the virtual exclusion of everthing else.

Scholars who study the history of criminal behavior must come to terms with crime statistics. The statistical study of crime is an important part of the historical literature, yet the results are often noncomparable and the methods employed so diverse and eclectic that there are few principles and generalizations which can be drawn from the data.

A classic problem is the extent of a relationship between economic conditions and crime rates. Yet the results of two relatively sophisticated English studies point to opposite conclusions. John Beattie, studying eighteenth-century Surrey, finds crime increased as economic conditions worsened. But Gatrell and Hadden find the opposite was true in the nineteenth century.[43] Needless to say, both studies may well be correct. The difference of a century is not trivial; nineteenth-century criminal statistics reflect the establishment of full time preventive police forces, and the impact of that development on crime statistics is unclear. With a better data base and many more variables at his command, M. Harvey Brenner has found a strong correlation between economic indicators such as high unemployment and increased crime levels.[44] Brenner's study, though limited to the relatively recent past, does provide an empirical confirmation for this longheld assumption.

Another major question is the relationship between crime and urbanization. This issue has two parameters: were the rates of criminal prosecutions higher in cities and did the pattern of prosecutions differ in cities? While this proposition may have seemed self-evident to social scientists, initially it was not clear to historians that urban crime was distinctive. In a surprisingly (given the sparsity of its evidence) influential article, Roger Lane argued that cities actually had a civilizing effect on crime rates.[45] But Lane did not study crime within cities; instead, he looked at aggregate rates for an entire state (Massachusetts) at a time when the urban proportion of the population was increasing. Although a prime example of the ecological fallacy, Lane's argument (perhaps because it suited scholars who wanted to counter the antiurban bias of the fear-ridden 1960s) was widely accepted until historians began looking specifically at urban crime.

Whether the setting be eighteenth-century colonial America (New York City and Newport, R.I.), nineteenth-century France, or nineteenth-century America, crime rates were higher in cities and the distribution of prosecutions had a unique quality.[46] This is hardly surprising; as financial centers, for example, cities had more white collar crime. As geographical specialization began to occur in cities, residences and businesses became separated. Commercial areas, deserted at night, became prime targets for theft. Almost every study has demonstrated higher rates of property-related offenses in cities than for the larger geographical entity.

One influential interpretation of general patterns of criminal prosecutions is by William Nelson.[47] Studying Massachusetts over a 70-year period (1760-1830), Nelson finds a shift in prosecutions from crimes against morality, religion, and authority to crimes against property. He relates this to a general shift within the legal system from ethical unity to the protection of property under the new economic order of postrevolutionary Massachusetts. This is an alluring argument, and at one level is unquestionably valid. Clearly the suppression of fornication, sabbathbreaking, and the like is a product of the colonial era, while crimes against property become a major focus of the criminal justice system in the nineteenth century.

I have discussed elsewhere my differences with Nelson's hypothesis.[48] But there are two conceptual issues which deserve mention here. First, Nelson's hypothesis assumes that the observed changes are explained by internal concerns in the legal system, dissociated from actual behavior. Yet the volume of officially proscribed sexual conduct does fluctuate and 1760, a particularly importune time to begin such an analysis, marked the onset of a sexual revolution in Massachusetts.[49] The subsequent obsession with protection of property was similarly not simply a creation of the legal system; it must be explained in terms of the breakdown of small communities (so that immediate identification of property was no longer automatic) and the growth of a criminal class.

While it is true that prosecutions for sexual offenses declined by 1830, this alone does not indicate that the legal system had turned its attention from morality to property. In fact, throughout the nineteenth century, arrests for property offenses were surpassed by prosecutions for drunkenness and violations of liquor laws. The same urge to control immoral or indulgent behavior persisted from the colonial era to the nineteenth century, but when the breakdown of the old colonial community made the policing of sex more difficult, the legal system shifted its emphasis to the more visible task of rounding up drunks and shutting down taverns.[50] Moral consensus remained at the heart of the criminal justice system, but now was joined by class control.

It is obvious from the theoretical perspectives which have informed the history of crime, that the mere commission of a proscribed act is relatively unimportant. Rather, it serves as a focal point from two separate directions. The first direction might be termed the sociological dimension—what forces act upon the person committing the offense? For this inquiry, labelling theory and a demographic analysis of the defendant population become important analytical tools. But there is a second dimension which encompasses the ranges of acts which are proscribed and the exercise of official authority in ways designed to deter, repress, and punish such conduct. This aspect is represented (or to be precise, underrepresented) by studies of the ways in which the criminal justice system interacts with the defendant from arrest to punishment.

Lurking above are larger questions concerning the nature of law and authority in modern societies. To answer these questions requires a different sort of inquiry, not the behavioral and institutional studies which have already been considered, but rather studies of the legal-political milieu in which both the criminal and penal networks operate. The most important (and in some ways most ambiguous and perplexing) concept in this area might be termed the hegemonic function of law. Obviously, to the doctrinaire Marxist historian, law is an important mechanism for entrenching dominant forces in society. The traditional view saw the law not as an independent basis for legitimacy, but rather just as a tool. When legislators, who enact statutes, do not act in ways which serve this hegemonic end, judges, with their extraordinary discretion, can act to change the law. Given the Anglo-American tradition of judicial independence, opponents of the dominant classes have little opportunity to limit or overturn this power.

In criminal law, we would expect the story to be similar. Those who posed a threat to the politically powerful and propertied classes would be crushed. And, indeed, in Anglo-American legal history, political dissidents have traditionally received harsh treatment by the legal system.[51] When the industrial revolution forced property relations onto a new footing, crimes against property began being punished as severely as political dissension had formerly been.[52] An extraordinary number of new crimes against property were created and made capital in eighteenth-century England, commensurate with the threat posed by a dislocated proletariat to the new forms of landed wealth.

But this is not the most interesting part of the story. In the past few years, a group of English historians, inspired by E. P. Thompson, has revised, specified, and operationalized the concept of the hegemonic function of law.[53] This "restatement of hegemony" appears most clearly in the concluding pages of *Whigs and Hunters* in which Thompson, in the space of eight pages either lays out a brilliant new conception of the relationship between law, legitimacy, and dominance—or quite possibly says nothing very much new at all.[54] Discussing the meaning of legitimacy in criminal law, Thompson concluded that for a legal system to have any authority at all, it must obey its own rules. Even though he believes that the legal system is a major vehicle for ruling class hegemony, he concedes that in order for law to serve this hegemonic function, it not only must appear to be just, sometimes, at least, it must actually *be* just.

Why should this analysis appear to some to be so earth-shattering? In part, Thompson's conclusion is something of a confessional, his concession to liberal society, to those who are such doctrinaire Marxists that anything short of total class domination seems like an underhanded plot. Thompson explains why the legal system can still be the tool of the ruling classes even if it does not use every opportunity to crush and repress dissent and protest. In short, Thompson shows that if the legal system did not follow its rules, its transparency would then rob the law of the legitimacy it needs in order to act as a vehicle for domination.

Thompson's analysis, then, emphasizes the limits which a legal system must observe even as a vehicle for domination. Thus, the legal system is bound to follow its own rules, for that is precisely what cloaks it with legitimacy so that it may be used as a source of power and authority. Again, whether or not this analysis seems redundant will depend on the perspective brought to it by the reader. But Thompson's stress on necessary limitations on the exercise of legal authority permits a more penetrating analysis of the rule of law than most economic determinism had produced.

Thompson's analysis must be considered in the context of his other work in the area of working class history. While showing that the law often acted repressively toward protest and working class movements, Thompson also believed that the basic acceptance of the legitimacy of law by both *protesters and repressers* in effect codified, made part of the law itself, a series of customary rights which were rarely challenged before the dislocating social changes of the eighteenth century.[55] Indeed, the abrogation of those customary rights inspired the protest. In this sense, Thompson's work builds on an older tradition which goes back to the work of George Rude and Charles Tilly on mob behavior.[56]

One of Thompson's associates in the Warwick group, Douglas Hay, has attempted to operationalize his mentor's concepts in a remarkable and stimulating essay, "Property, Authority, and the Criminal Law," an essay in *Albion's Fatal Tree,* the companion volume to *Whigs and Hunters.*[57] In one of the most important essays written in this area, Hay demonstrates how the law, with all its self-imposed and definitional limits, was able to serve as a vehicle for hegemony in eighteenth-century England. Like Foucault, who emphasized the procession to the gallows and the formalities of torture, Hay understands the importance of symbol and ritual in the exercise of legal authority (majesty). Like Thompson, Hay demonstrates that the legal system had to follow its own rules (justice). But an essential and additional component was mercy, exemplified by last minute pardons to those whose convictions seemed unjust, if lawful, or whose death would wound a community more than it would solidify it in support of the law.

For Hay, the use of the criminal law to achieve hegemony helps to explain why eighteenth-century Britain was able to attain a relatively high degree of internal order during a time of great social dislocation and political upheaval, yet did not have to resort to a standing army or permanent police force. In effect, majesty, justice, and mercy in the operation of the criminal law may have well served as counter-revolutionary tactics.

As I have already mentioned, interest in the history of crime is clearly related to new developments in the past decades in the history of working class life. E.P. Thompson's interest in crime exemplified this connection, although in many ways Rude provided the theoretical link between working class activity and perceived deviant or criminal activity.[58] Not surprisingly, the strengths and weaknesses in the literature on the history of crime and justice parallel those of the early work on working class history. Empirical work by American historians, while of increasing technical proficiency, does not permit comparability. Thus, for example, there is no agreement on such obvious questions as the relationship between crime rates and economic trends, the impact of police forces on observable crime rates, and the like.

But a more serious problem is the lack of a strong theoretical perspective. American historians have generally been uncomfortable with the notion of class; when they have written on the subject, they find it easier to deal with elites or with social mobility than with those social groups that the historians of crime and justice must contend with.[59]

More fundamentally, American historians seem to have an extraordinary ambivalence about crime. On the one hand, they realize that the definition of criminal behavior is a relative one; they sense, too, that different subgroups in American society may not share the dominant values of that society (particularly with regard to victimless crimes). But they also feel something should be done about crime, and thus write about the penal and law enforcement systems from a crime control perspective. Furthermore, as a nation founded on rights secured by a written constitution, Americans are unaccustomed to giving much standing to customary rights and feel little sense of outrage when such rights are violated or criminalized. Thus, while there has been some very competent and stimulating work on the history of American crime, there are few works as suggestive as the work of Thompson, Hay and Foucault[60]

Athough American historians are still searching for the proper conceptual frameworks with which to unify the study of the history of crime, the results, although flawed, are nevertheless encouraging. Almost by definition, the history of crime in America cannot be a success story. Instead, it is a story of desperate acts, of repressive or corrupt police, of dehumanizing insitutions, and of a class-based legal system. There are important lessons to be learned from this research, even if they only confirm and echo contemporary skepticism.

In the area of law enforcement for example, it is clear that professionalization of the police is directly at odds (as has always been the case in this country) with the important (or at least politically appealing) notion of keeping the police responsive to the policed community. When the police are seen as an alien or occupying force, violence and hostility result. On the other hand, when police are drawn from the community, it becomes impossible to expect full enforcement of laws which seem only to criminalize popular habits of the community's population. The historical record shows that reconciliation of these two goals is impossible; at the same time, it clarifies the essentially unchanged nature of the conflict and poses the consequences of each alternative in clearest possible terms. Similarly, this dialectical approach can be applied to contemporary issues such as sentencing or incarceration. The dissatisfactions which lead periodically to determinate and then indeterminant sentencing are clear; in the past century and a half, it has been impossible to reconcile the goals sought by proponents of each plan with the inequities which invariably force the switch to the other! Finally, the history of prisons and reformatories for adults and juveniles reveals the incompatibility of the goals of rehabilitation, order, and economy.

As I have indicated, the history of crime, almost by definition, is the history of a series of failures. Throughout the past century and half in America, reforms have promised millennialistic results. Prisons, police forces, the juvenile court, the advent of parole—all were considered not simply aids in controlling crime, but were thought to lead to the eventual eradication of crime as a major social problem. Yet crime will not disappear; we are reduced to taking these messianistic promises and reducing them to recidivism rates. For us, however, the past can serve as a controlled experiment, not as a panacea; a devil's advocate, not a prophet of doom. What is needed is to take the next step—to try to understand through history what is so elusive today: the role of crime and the criminal justice system in society.

NOTES

1. John Augustus, A Report of the Labors of John Augustus for the Last Ten Years in the Aid of the Unfortunate (Boston, 1852). Augustus' volunteer efforts have caused such criminologists as Sheldon Glueck to refer to him as the "pioneer of probation."

2. Sir Leon Radzinowicz, A History of English Criminal Law and Its Administration from 1750 (4v., London, 1948-1968).

3. Georg Rusche and Otto Kircheimer, Punishment and Social Structure (New York, 1939).

4. Leonard W. Levy, Origins of the Fifth Amendment (New York, 1968); other classics include Jerome Hall, Theft, Law, and Society (New York, 1957), and Julius Goebel and T. Raymond McNaughton, Law Enforcement in Colonial New York: A Study in Criminal Procedure, 1664-1776 (New York, 1944). There are also numerous state studies in early American history which were completed in the 1930s, but their value is limited to antiquarian information.

5. The social control interpretation was popularized by Joseph Gusfield, The Symbolic Crusade (New York, 1963), and Michael B. Katz, The Irony of Early School Reform (Boston, 1968).

6. David J. Rothman, The Discovery of the Asylum: Social Order and Disorder in the New Republic (Boston, 1971).

7. On Samuel Gridley Howe, see Michael Stephen Hindus, Prison and Plantation: Crime, Justice, and Authority in Massachusetts and South Carolina, 1767-1878 (Chapel Hill, forthcoming, 1980), Steven L. Schlossman, Love and the American Delinquent: The Theory and Practice of "Progressive" Juvenile Justice, 1825-1920 (Chicago, 1977), and Harold Schwartz, Samuel Gridley Howe, Social Reformer, 1801-1876 (Cambridge, 1956).

8. Francis Gray, Prison Discipline in America (Boston, 1847) and the discussion of this point in Hindus, Prison and Plantation, op. cit.

9. The attempts to find a statistical correlation between observable criminality and economic conditions is discussed elsewhere in this essay.

10. Michel Foucault, Discipline and Punish: The Birth of the Prison (New York, 1977).

11. 387 U.S. 1 (1967).

12. Anthony M. Platt, The Child Savers: The Invention of Delinquency (Chicago, 1969).

13. The second edition, published in 1977, contains the same material as the first with a new introduction and a postscript. The discussion of the second edition concerns only the new introduction.

14. Steven L. Schlossman, Love and the American Delinquent, op. cit.

15. See also the studies of other individual institutions, such as Robert Pickett, House of Refuge (Syracuse, 1969) on New York, and Robert Mennel, Thorns and Thistles (Hanover, N.H., 1973).

16. Distinct but similar discussions of this report can be found in Hindus, Prison and Plantation, and Schlossman, Love and the American Delinquent, op. cit. The quote itself is from Howe's introduction to Massachusetts Board of State Charities, Second Annual Report (Boston, 1866) xli.

17. For another view of Progressive era penal reformers concentrating on female reformatories and female reformers, see Estelle Brenda Freedman, Their Sisters' Keepers: The Origins of Female Corrections in America (unpublished Ph.D. dissertation in history, Columbia University, 1976).

18. See especially George Lee Haskins, Law and Authority in Early Massachusetts: A Study in Tradition and Design (New York, 1960); Goebel and McNaughton, Law Enforcement in Colonial New York, op. cit.; George Athan Billias, ed., Law and Authority in Colonial America: Essays (Barre, Mass., 1965). For a specific example in the area of sexual behavior, see Daniel Scott Smith and Michael S. Hindus, "Premarital Pregnancy in America, 1640-1971: An Overview and Interpretation," Journal of Interdisciplinary History V (1975): 537-570.

19. Douglas Greenberg, Crime and Law Enforcement in the Colony of New York, 1691-1776 (Ithaca, 1976), especially pp. 154-187.

20. Kai Eriksen, Wayward Puritans (New York, 1966).

21. Greenberg, Crime and Law Enforcement, op. cit., 40-49.

22. William E. Nelson, Americanization of the Common Law: The Impact of Legal Change on Massachusetts Society, 1760-1830 (Cambridge, 1976) 40.

23. Studies of social stratification in eighteenth-century Boston include James Henretta, "Economic Development and Social Structure in Colonial Boston," William and Mary Quarterly XXII (1965): 75-92, and Allan Kulikoff, "The Progress of Inequality in Revolutionary Boston," William and Mary Quarterly XXVIII (1971): 375-412.

24. Greenberg, Crime and Law Enforcement, op. cit.

25. The classic studies (albeit less than a dozen years old) are Roger Lane, Policing the City: Boston, 1822-1887 (Cambridge, 1967), and James F. Richardson, The New York Police From Colonial Times to 1901 (New York, 1970). On early nineteenth-century riots in Boston, see Michael S. Hindus, "A City of Mobocrats and Tyrants: Mob Violence in Boston, 1747-1863," Issues in Criminology VI, 2 (1971): 55-83. Of course, as this last article points out, American cities had never been free from collective violence, but that violence seemed to present a greater threat to a seemingly more fragile social order in the Jacksonian period.

26. Karl Polyani, The Great Tranformation: The Political and Economic Origins of Our Time (Boston, 1957) 186.

27. In 1834 Yankee truckmen burned the Ursuline Convent in Charlestown; in 1835 abolitionist leader William Lloyd Garrison was dragged through the streets of Boston with a rope around his waist; in 1837 an estimated fifth of Boston's population participated in the Broad Street Riot, a violent attack on an Irish neighborhood by Yankees. These are described in Lane, Policing the City, and Hindus, "A City of Mobocrats and Tyrants," both op. cit.

28. Lane, Policing the City, op. cit., 75-78.

29. Wilbur Miller, Cops and Bobbies: Police Authority in New York and London, 1830-1870 (Chicago, 1977) 34-37; Richardson, op. cit., 64-65.

30. The requirement in the mid-1960s that state legislatures be apportioned for both houses according to the population ended the longstanding tyranny of rural areas over the cities in many states. Thus, while this conflict may long remain a cultural one, it is unlikely to be settled by minority rule.

31. Wilbur Miller, Cops and Bobbies, op. cit.

32. Robert M. Fogelson, Big City Police (Cambridge, 1977); Mark Haller has also studied police in the late nineteenth and early twentieth centuries, "Historical Roots of Police Behavior: Chicago, 1890-1925," Law and Society Review X (1976): 303-323. However, this article adds little to what was already known about the subject.

33. Egon Bittner, "The Rise and Fall of the Thin Blue Line," Reviews in American History VI (1978): 421-428.

34. This problem is not completely solved in another comparative study in the history of criminal justice, Michael S. Hindus, Prison and Plantation, op. cit.

35. Theodore N. Ferdinand, "The Criminal Patterns of Boston Since 1846." American Journal of Sociology LXXIII (1967): 84-99, and "Politics, the Police, and Arresting Policies in Salem, Massachusetts Since the Civil War," Social Problems XIX (1972): 572-588.

36. Eric H. Monkkonen, The Dangerous Class: Crime and Poverty in Columbus, Ohio, 1860-1885 (Cambridge, 1975).

37. Monkkonen, The Dangerous Class, op. cit., 43.

38. Monkkonen, The Dangerous Class, op. cit., 104.

39. Monkkonen, The Dangerous Class, op. cit., 104.

40. Monkkonen. The Dangerous Class, op. cit., 156. It should be apparent from the quote that this measure is based on a long series of assumptions about causal inferences. While I do not believe that Monkkonen's operating assumptions are uniformly valid, this is a judgement which a trained and interested reader can make for himself. Monkkonen, to his considerable credit, believes in "full disclosure," and all of his hypotheses, including those which did not pan out (and many which, perhaps, did not merit testing) are spelled out in great detail. Monkkonen is also scrupulous about reporting tests of association and statistical significance.

41. Monkkonen, The Dangerous Class, op. cit., 156.

42. For a discussion of this point, See Roger Lane's thoughtful review of The Dangerous Class, "Can You Count on the Down and Out to Stay Down for the Count in Columbus?" Reviews in American History IV (1976): 212-217.

43. John Beattie, "The Pattern of Crime in England, 1660-1800," Past and Present LXII (1974): 47-95; T. Hadden and V.A.C. Gatrell, "Criminal Statistics and their Interpretation," in E.A. Wrigley, ed., Nineteenth-Century Society (Cambridge, 1972): 336-396.

44. M. Harvey Brenner, Estimating the Social Cost of National Economic Policy: Implications for Mental and Physical Health and Criminal Aggression (Report of the Joint Economic Committee, U.S. Congress, 1976).

45. Roger Lane, "Crime and Criminal Statistics in Nineteenth-Century Massachusetts," Journal of Social History II (1968): 156-163.

46. Douglas Greenberg, Crime and Law Enforcement, op. cit., 135-137; Hindus, Prison and Plantation, op. cit.; Abdul Qaiyum Lodhi and Charles Tilly, "Urbanization, Crime and Collective Violence in Nineteenth-Century France," American Journal of Sociology LXXIX (1973): 296-318; Lynne E. Withey, "Crime, Poverty, and Perceptions of Deviance in an Urbanizing Society: The Case of Eighteenth-Century Rhode Island" (paper presented at the International Economic History Congress, Edinburgh).

47. William E. Nelson, "Emerging Notions of Modern Criminal Law in the Revolutionary Era: An Historical Perspective," New York University Law Review XLII (1967): 450-482. This argument appears with greater documentation, but in a more diluted form in Nelson's Americanization of the Common Law, op. cit.

48. Michael S. Hindus, "The Contours of Crime in Massachusetts and South Carolina, 1767-1878," American Journal of Legal History XXI (1977): 212-237.

49. Daniel Scott Smith and Michael S. Hindus, "Premarital Pregnancy in America," op. cit., 538.

50. Michael S. Hindus, Prison and Plantation, op. cit.

51. This was not a feature unique to the Anglo-American system; Foucault describes similar treatment of dissenters in France in Discipline and Punish, op. cit.

52. Douglas Hay, "Property, Authority, and the Criminal Law," in Hay, et al., eds., Albion's Fatal Tree: Crime and Society in Eighteenth-Century England (New York, 1975): 17-63; John Beattie, "The Decline of Capital Punishment in Eighteenth-Century England" (unpublished paper, March 1974).

53. This phrase was first used by Eugene Genovese, Roll, Jordan, Roll: The World the Slaves Made (New York, 1974): 25.

54. E.P. Thompson, Whigs and Hunters (New York, 1975): 262-269.

55. Thompson, Whigs and Hunters, op. cit.; E.P. Thompson, "The Moral Economy of the English Crowd in the Eighteenth Century," Past and Present 50 (1971): 76-136.

56. Although Rude is best known for expressing this viewpoint in The Crowd in History, 1730-1848 (New York, 1964), in many ways the most interesting formulation appears in Wilkes and Liberty: A Social Study of 1763-1774 (Oxford, 1962). The view of the rationality of crowd behavior has come under attack recently, particularly in the work of psychohistorians and the extremely influential writings of historian Bernard Bailyn; see especially Bailyn's The Ordeal of Thomas Hutchinson (Cambridge, 1974).

57. Hay, "Property, Authority, and the Criminal Law," op. cit.

58. E.P. Thompson, The Making of the English Working Class (New York, 1963); George Rude, Wilkes and Liberty, op. cit.

59. Here I am referring to the studies of social mobility which began with Stephen Thernstrom's Poverty and Progress (Cambridge, 1964), and reached a height of statistical sophistication in Thernstrom's The Other Bostonians (Cambridge, 1973). For better or worse, Thernstrom's work has influenced an entire generation of urban historians, who replicated his studies (with their own particular twists, as variations on the theme) for many other cities.

60. It is worth mentioning that Rothman's Discovery of the Asylum is the one book in the history of crime in America to have considerable influence conceptually. Rothman's book has had more influence among social scientists than among historians, undoubtedly because in order to maximize its impact, Rothman oversimplified and dichotomized in ways that historians find hard to accept. Not coincidentally, Rothman's book preceded by only a year or two the recent trends against institutionalization and toward more determinate sentencing. In any event, for whatever the reason, The Discovery of the Asylum is clearly the only work in this area in American history which has had influence comparable to that enjoyed by the works of Hay, Thompson, and Foucault.

9

GOTHS AND VANDALS—CRIME IN HISTORY
GEOFFREY PEARSON

Since the end of the Second World War the understanding of the history of the common people of England has been redrawn, even transformed. In particular, the works of Christopher Hill, Eric Hobsbawm, Raymond Williams and Edward Thompson have illuminated the critical English transition from a predominantly agricultural economy into the world's first urban and industrial nation [1]. It would be wrong to think of these writers as constituting a "School": their work is not marred by that kind of tedious scholastic dogmatism. It also contains within it many shifts of emphasis, and some internal inconsistencies. Nevertheless, these writers do share a common direction which is distinctly socialist. And one of their many accomplishments is that they unearth the experience of the agrarian and industrial revolutions as they were lived and felt "from below" – that is, in terms of the material experience of the common people, rather than "from above" in the committee chambers of high office.

The particular aspect of this work which I will discuss here is its bearing on our understanding of crime. Especially the "senseless" and "irrational" crimes – hooliganism and vandalism, smashing and wrecking – which are thought to be pointless because they do not even submit to the guiding acquisitive principle of theft. Dismissed in a history "from above" as mere "social background" to the allegedly "real" historical events, which are the decisions and opinions of the mighty (judges, manufacturers, rulers etc.), crime emerges in this revitalized social history as something central to our understanding of the historical transformation into capitalism. It is also a body of work which challenges criminology to shake itself out of its ahistorical slumbers, to come to a new understanding of what crime is, an understanding which is concretely situated in real historical time.

> Come all you cotton weavers, your looms you may pull down
> And get employed in factories, in country or in town
> For your cotton masters have found out a wonderful scheme
> These calico goods they weave by hand, they're going to weave by steam.
>
> So, come all you cotton weavers, you must rise up very soon
> For you must work in factories from morning until noon
> You mustn't walk in your gardens for two or three hours a day
> For you must stand at their command, and keep your shuttles in play.
> (19th century weavers' ballad by John Grimshaw of Gorton)

In the winter of 1842 when young Engels came to live in Manchester — hot volcano city of the industrial revolution — he stepped into a world which had already been transformed by the machine. The cotton industry was the spearhead of the English industrial revolution and machinery had been increasingly employed there since the late eighteenth century. The introduction of the power-driven loom, which accelerated from the 1820s, had virtually displaced the handloom weaver. The factory system of labour which accompanied the mechanization of the textile industry had come to rule over and rule out the small-scale domestic economy which had previously been the dominant form of production in the small towns and valleys of Lancashire.

Almost everyone who was anyone, it seems, came to Manchester in the mid-nineteenth century to marvel at the wonders of the new industrial system — Dickens, Disraeli, de Tocqueville, Carlyle [2]. But they usually went home horrified and shocked by the brutality of Manchester. Unless, that is, they were particularly thick-skinned, or blinded by the glitter of wealth which could pour out of the thundering factories. "Manchester is the chimney of the world" is how Major-General Sir Charles James Napier, appointed to command the northern district at a time of massive political disturbances in the manufacturing districts, put the matter. "But who", he added, "wants to live in a chimney?" He might also have mentioned (others did) the stinking, polluted rivers, the excrement piled high in the streets, the squalid cellar homes, or the hordes of unemployed men standing in the streets which greeted Engels' arrival during the depression of 1842.

What is truly extraordinary is that the changes which produced this monstrosity — in Ancoats, a working class district, as few as 35 children out of 100 born would survive until their fifth year — can be described by historians with such calm rhetoric. In a history from above the creation of the factory system is described as the steady erosion of inefficiency by the captains of industry and their new rational methods. It is a history of progress and buoyancy. It tells of the enterprising men — Arkwright,

Crompton, Peel, Hargreaves – whose inventions (mules, carding frames, spinning jennies, etc.) and whose capital was to transform the world.

What a history from above does not tell is that the common people frequently attacked both the machines and their inventors, tore down and burned their mills, and drove these "great heroes" of the industrial revolution out of the locality. If a history from above does mention this opposition at all, it puts it down to ignorance. The story of this bitter resistance, the sense and meaning of riot and vandalism, is reserved for a history from below. A history, that is, which emphasizes the viewpoint of the common people and how the machine contributed to the destruction of their way of life.

Attacks on machines took place from the 1760s when Hargreaves' spinning jenny was repeatedly smashed, and mills which used the jenny were turned over. According to traditional accounts, Hargreaves was chased out of the neighbourhood, and his promotor, the factory owner "Parsley" Peel, retreated from North East Lancashire in disgust, taking his capital to another area where he hoped the work force would be more sensible. Peel's mills near Blackburn and Accrington were completely destroyed, one having been already rebuilt after attacks by machine-smashers only a few years before.

There were many more attacks on machines. One of the most famous periods of disturbance was during the War in Europe when from 1811 to 1813 various kinds of new machines were attacked in Nottinghamshire, Yorkshire and Lancashire. The attackers were known as the "Luddites", and they claimed leadership from a probably fictitious "General Ludd". To mention one more instance, there was a great uprising against the machine in North East Lancashire in 1826 when power-looms were destroyed in the cotton towns. Machine-smashing was not restricted to the textile industry, of course. In 1830 there was an explosion of popular discontent throughout southern and eastern England when the rural poor attacked the hated threshing machines and set fire to hay ricks. Known as the Swing Riots, these rioters attacked the machines in the name of "Captain Swing" [3].

Considerable dispute surrounds the question of how to interpret the activities of the machine-breakers. One dominant traditional form of argument describes these outbreaks of violence as the sporadic, unpredictable and senseless antics of the riff-raff – the mob, "*la canaille*". It asks "Why does the mob riot?". And it answers: "For the fun of it", or simply "Who knows?". There is a powerful line of historical continuity between this response to the "mob" and modern accounts of hooliganism and crime as senseless [4].

Another traditional line of reasoning suggests that loom-breaking, etc. was the desperate action of people pressured and frustrated by the strains of social change into wild and lawless behaviour. This historical form continues, however, to describe the mob as senseless. Its only concession is that machine-breakers are victims of forces outside their control which cause them to behave senselessly and randomly. For example, Smelser in his Parsonian sociological analysis of the industrial revolution in Lancashire points to shifts and alternations in the organization of the economy, factory labour and family life which (he argues) released the bind of steady socializing influence and led to pathological and unsocialized behaviour, e.g. machine-wrecking. He describes it as "a relaxation of the most basic controls over socialized behaviour" and as "violent and bizarre symptoms of disturbance" [5].

In both cases – whether it is the snobbish refusal to allow any meaning whatsoever to mob riot, or the paternalistic response of judging the behaviour as a pathology – the idea that "the mob" represents purposive, rational conduct is banished, out of sight, out of mind. However, these dismissive accounts inevitably fall prey to a contradiction in that while their controlling argument is that machine-breaking is irrational and pointless, it is exceedingly difficult to portray the factory system in anything other than a dark light. And it is precisely this dark aspect of the factory and its machines which guided machine-breaking and gave it its rationality.

Take, as an illustration of this contradiction, some statements by the distinguished historian of the eighteenth century H. J. Plumb. His account of machine-smashing is admittedly schematic, since in the tradition of history from above Plumb is always restless when describing social conditions, anxious to get on with the "real business" of intrigue between the rulers. Nevertheless, his account is plagued with contradiction. At one point he states, for example, how the new machines in textiles "revolutionized the production of yarn and brought to the weaver an age of golden prosperity which was to last for a quarter of a century" [6]. The statement is not so ridiculously wrongheaded as it might at first appear. The earliest phase of mechanization involved the introduction of improved *spinning* machinery which greatly increased the output of yarn and hence the demand for weavers – the weaving looms were as yet unmechanized. The complexities of this early period are best set out in Thompson where he shows that, although the idea of a "golden age" is a myth which overstates the prosperity of the weavers in this period (roughly from the 1780s until the early 1800s) there was, nevertheless, a period of boom in handloom weaving [7]. From then on, however, the condition of the weavers was steadily attacked, so that looking back the earlier period might appear as a "golden age". As Thompson expresses the matter: "The history of the weavers in the nineteenth century is haunted by the legend of better days" [8]. But even in this earlier period of relative prosperity, cotton mills and machines had been attacked, and there is nothing to justify Plumb's rosy optimism of an overall improvement in living standards.

The contradictions deepen in Plumb's account as the antagonistic encounter with the factory system progresses. The worsening conditions are inescapable – the increasing exploitation of children in the mines and factories, the erosion of the more intimate and flexible forms of production which preceded the factory, the repression of working class movements and early trade union organizations, the seven year contracts which bound men to their factory masters at risk of imprisonment, the massive increase in the number of capital statutes which could send men to the gallows for a whole number of newly defined crimes, the destruction of the makeshift economy of the poor which followed from the enclosure of the common land which robbed the common people of their common rights – "rights" which were often redefined as "crimes" (poaching, trespass, wood theft). Plumb mentions most, if not all, of this. He also writes that workmen "viewed with deep suspicion the barrack-like factories whose long and regular hours savoured to them of the prison" [9].. Under the preindustrial systems of production, men had been much more in control of the rhythms of their lives. One should not romanticize this state of affairs – as if every man had been an independent, unalienated and free man – but one should recognize, nevertheless, what was involved in the changes in production systems. Before, the factory workers had customarily observed "Saint Monday" as a day of rest, often taking Tuesday as a holiday as well, then working flat out to finish off the week's work. Factory discipline and factory time changed all that. As Plumb describes the factory:

> The hours of work were fourteen, fifteen, or even sixteen a day, six days a week throughout the year except for Christmas Day and Good Friday. That was the ideal timetable of the industrialists. It was rarely achieved, for the human animal broke down under the burden; and he squandered his time in palliatives – drink, lechery, bloodsports. Or he revolted, burned down the factory, or broke up the machinery, in a pointless, frenzied, industrial *jacquerie* [10].

What is extraordinary is that Plumb, having explicitly set out the grounds for understanding the discontent of the times, continues to describe machine riots as "pointless". The same contradiction is found in other writings on this period. In Bythell's work on the handloom weavers, he writes about the 1826 power-loom smashings: "Their luddism of 1826 was a blind display of hatred against an improved machine which must be destroyed before it took away the old weavers' livelihood", and he refers earlier to these same riots as an "act of blind vandalism" [11]. We must ask, what is blind about an action which strikes out to destroy something which threatens one's own destruction?

What is expressed in these simple contradictions is that it is somehow intolerable to allow rationality to popular resistance and popular violence. It is much more comfortable to write off the machine breakers as a tiny pathological fringe of hot-heads, and to write a cosy history in which the mass of people are said to quietly bear the yoke of the new factory system. That is, as if people understood the superior rationality of the machine, and accepted the injustices which flowed from this superior rationality for the sake of "progress" and "improvement". It is in these ways that historical thought has simply followed the contours of power. Although, as we have seen, even in its language it continued to express – against the will of the author, as it were – the bitter contradictions and struggles which constituted the real history of the period.

What is perhaps an even more fundamental difficulty with these accounts is that we know that within their own community the machine-wreckers often had a heroic status. In striking out at the machine, they were striking out against their oppression within the developing system of factory labour – the relentless monotony of the pace of the machine, the relentless gaze of the factory master and overseer, the relentless tick of the factory clock.

Above all, what must be remembered is that just as the human significance of time [12] was changed by the new rhythms of the factory and the machine, so were many other aspects of culture. In one sense, the arrival of the machine and the factory was the first direct encounter by working people with the *material experience* of hard-headed utilitarian philosophy and political economy. The dominating principle of hard cash, of buying cheap and selling dear, also turned the human relations of the factory into commodity relations and transformed men into objects or cattle. So that when Plumb writes about the "human animal" breaking down under factory conditions, it is necessary to remember that it was precisely the logic of the new systems which reduced men from human to animal status. Language both mirrored and informed these transformations: so that the men and women who worked the machines came to be called, simply, "Hands". The word "common" also underwent a transformation, away from the sense of things "held in common" or a "commonwealth", towards a revaluation of certain (particularly plebeian) practices and customs as "common", meaning "vulgar" [13].

The experience of these transformations should not be underestimated. Resistance to the factory and its logic continued well up into the 1840s, and the Chartist movement in some of the Pennine cotton towns at this time carried as one of its demands that each man should receive, as a birthright, a small-holding of land – they began staking out Pendle Hill for just this purpose.

The logic of the factory and of enclosure worked in an opposite direction. The independence of working men who had access to small patches of land was in utilitarian terms understood as dangerous and wasteful. As late as the Select Committee on Commons Enclosure of 1844 we find the assertion that the enclosure and "improvement" of the land would also bring an "improvement" in the character of the people; and that "the unenclosed commons are invariably nurseries for petty crime" [14]. What is meant by this is that if they had access to land, men would tend their pigs, or their cow, instead of turning into the factory. In the Poor Law Reports of 1834, the culmination of utilitarian principle, there are attempts to calculate how big (or, rather, small) an allotment of land should be given to working men. It was agreed that a small allotment for vegetables provided a working man with an innocent and sober amusement, and, also enabled him to feed his family, thus keeping down the likelihood of wage demands. But the utilitarian logic also dictated that the Poor Law Commissioners should try to calculate what size of an allotment (that is, a garden) would provide amusement and some food without causing the working man to keep away from work, or without causing him to waste too much of his valuable body energy, his labour power, which was the rightful property of the factory owner – and not the man himself. There was a recognition in these Poor Law debates that food (largely potatoes) equals energy, equals improved labour power; but that digging a potato patch spends energy, and workers might find it more enjoyable to spend energy digging the earth to provide food for their family than to rise at the crack of dawn and watch over a noisy and dangerous machine for someone else's benefit [15]. It was a significant moment of illumination of the nature of the contest which was involved in the advancement of the machine and the factory.

It is thus in the nature of this historical transition – which involved profound changes in human values as well as a technological break – that it is utterly impossible to go along with Smelser, for example, and describe the machine-breakers as disorganized and unsocialized beings. Instead we need to ask, "Socialized according to what standards?", and in particular, "Socialized according to *whose* standards?" The machine-smashers were not only courageous and determined in their attacks on the machines, they were also sometimes very discriminating. In early attacks on the spinning jenny during the 1760s, for example, the rioters sometimes spared small machines which had less than twenty spindles – that is, machines which could be operated in small cottages on the established principle of the domestic economy, and which were for this reason regarded as "fair" machines. That is hardly behaviour which could be described as "bizarre", "frenzied", "irrational" or "unsocialized".

The great power-loom smashing of 1826 provides other examples of these kinds of rationality [16]. The outbreak was a particularly determined one which was confined to the cotton towns around Accrington, Blackburn and the Rossendale Valley and which was eventually put down by violent Army reprisals. It is even possible that we should think of it as a general insurrection against the machines in these towns [17]. Be that as it may, the rioters had considerable sympathy within the community. Robert Peel, eventually to become Prime Minister, a man whose fortunes were founded on cotton, found it necessary to rebuke local magistrates for not taking sharp action against the rioters – whether he was motivated as a politician, or as a man with property stakes in the towns, is not clear. The reluctance of magistrates to act decisively was not uncommon, reflecting the fact that local opposition to machinery was so widespread. For example, small masters feared and hated the new machines as much as working people. Without sufficient capital to invest in machinery, the machines threatened to kill their small businesses – a fact which could provide some unexpected alliances of sympathy between the poor and the lower echelons of the owning class. Even before the attacks on the power-looms had started, rioters had been stopped by troops – the most solid embodiment of State power. But when the troops heard the complaints of the weavers, instead of opening fire they opened their knapsacks and gave their food to the rioters. The troops then moved on and the weavers held a meeting amongst themselves to decide whether or not to continue: "Were the power-looms to be broken or not? Yes, it was decided, they must be broken at all costs" [18]. When the first mill was attacked – Sykes Mill at Accrington – the first thing to go, smashed by a woman, was the tyrannical factory clock, the hated symbol of the slave rhythms of factory labour [19]. By nightfall, it is said that there was not a power-loom left standing within six miles of Blackburn. The riots spread to other nearby towns and within three days more than a thousand looms had been destroyed.

It can be argued that 1826 was a year of slump, and that the grievances of the handloom weavers derived from the trade cycle and not from the machine. But, although outbreaks of machine smashing coincided frequently enough with periods of trade recession, I find the argument an unconvincing one which lends itself too easily to a crude economic determinism which ignores the cultural developments which are decisive for an understanding of machine riot.

Nevertheless, it is important to recognize that different outbreaks of machine-breaking could, and did, have different motives. Quite often, for example, what was being contested was not the principle of the machine itself, but the level of wages etc. Attacks on machines provided a way of getting at an employer so as to encourage him to raise wages, improve working conditions, take on more men, or whatever. It is this kind of motive for machine-breaking which Eric Hobsbawm has described as "collective bargaining by riot", a primitive form of trade union struggle.

These "primitive rebels", to use another of Hobsbawm's suggestive phrases, are said to be primitive in the sense that they had not yet found a mature political vocabulary, nor a mature political strategy, within which to phrase their discontent and direct their struggle. This line of thinking urges us to conceive of the Luddites and other machine-breakers as precursors of the mature forms of labour organization.

Hobsbawm's distinctions are important if only because they caution us not to oversimplify machine-smashing, and not to think of it all as direct resistance to machinery as such. It is nevertheless a form of historical reasoning which can in its own way belittle, discredit and misconstrue the motives and actions of the machine-smashers. In claiming machine-breakers for the history of the labour movement, for example, it causes us to compare their frail outbursts with the more "mature" forms of struggle — trade union organization, collective bargaining, the strike, the general strike — which only serves to underline the "primitivity" of the machine-smashers. As working class consciousness emerges, it tells us, men set to one side these infantile forms of resistance to exploitation and "see the light".

It is thus an inherent danger of the concept of "primitive rebellion" that it can lead us to think that the intelligibility of the machine-breakers' struggle only emerges as history unfolds; that its intelligibility is derived only from the subsequent history of the labour movement. As if the intelligibility of the machine-breakers emerges only when they are already dead — when they are dead, then we can come to see them in their "true" historical significance, the vanguard of an emerging proletariat.

The heart of the matter, however, is that the machine-smashers were not a proletariat. On the contrary, they would as often as not be people from the countryside, with its own distinct inherited traditions. People who looked at the factories — shaking and trembling with their violent energy — and who did not like what they saw. It is an important truth that there were some people around at the time of the Luddite disturbances from 1811 to 1813 who were part of the general mood of insurrection which surrounded the period and who expressed more forward-looking political opinions. People who saw in the machines the possibility of liberating men and women from the burden of physical labour, and who could be thought of as early forerunners of a later working class consciousness [20]. But they were the exception rather than the rule. Thompson, with his usual lucidity, expresses the matter thus: "For those who live through it, history is neither 'early' nor 'late'. 'Forerunners' are also inheritors of another past. Men must be judged in their own context" [21]. For this reason, if we are to set machine-breaking in its full context, it is necessary to turn back briefly to some of the inherited traditions of the machine-breakers' world, a world which was entering a rapid eclipse.

The Traditions of the "Crowd" and "Riot"

Farmers taek
nodist form
This time be
fore It is to
let

Be fore
Christ mus
Day sum of
you will be
as Poore as
we if you
Will not seel
Cheper

This is to let you no We have stoel a Sheep, For which the resson Was be Cass you sold your Whet so dear and if you Will not loer pries of your Whet we will Com by night and set fiear to your Barns and Reecks gentleman Farm mers we be in Arnest now and That you will find to your sorrow soon.

(Anonymous letter fixed to the pillory, Salisbury market 1767.) [22]

Luddism and the other machine-breaking riots were not the first burst of a new class anger from an infant proletariat. Rather than being based on the new, emerging traditions of the men of that new class, they were more likely to be based on older traditions. Traditions, that is, which looked back to the domestic economy, to the common lands, and to former traditions of radicalism.

"Riot" and "crime" had been an important feature of the social life of 18th century England. The "crowd", or the "mob" could take as its object the defence of any number of rights and customs – the fair price of food, fair access to the common lands, or smuggling which was so common in England, as in most parts of Europe, to be thought of as a "right" rather than a "crime".

In fact, where one drew the line in 18th century England between what was a "crime" and what was a "customary right" depended very much on one's position in the social order. For example, an activity called "wrecking" was a common occurance in those coastal regions where ships most frequently ran aground and were wrecked [23]. "Wrecking" was a form of coastal plunder in which local people would salvage what they could of wrecked ships and their cargoes for their own use, and it formed an important part of the local economy in some coastal regions. From the point of view of the local people, "wrecking" was an important, even indispensable, part of local life, whereas, to shipping merchants it was a criminal nuisance, and merchants petitioned the government throughout the 18th century to act more severely against wreckers. As a result, an Act of 1753 made "wrecking" a crime punishable by death — although that did not halt the activity.

It is a similar story in relation to a large number of other customary activities of the poor and the common people — taking hares and rabbits from fields; taking gravel and turf; taking fish from streams; collecting wood in the forests. The notorious Black Act of 1723 was one bloodstained piece of legislation, drawn up with extraordinary speed and carelessness by Walpole and his ruling clique, to contain these kinds of offences. The precipitating factors were complex, as Thompson shows in his masterly analysis of the Black Act, involving amongst other things attempts to curry favour with the new Hanoverian monarch whose deer parks at Windsor were in a state of collapse [24]. Local people in that region had begun to reassert their rights in the forest, as opposed to the rights of the deer. Thompson suggests that people may have been looking back to the days of the Commonwealth when "the deer had been slaughtered wholesale, the Great Park turned over to farms, and the foresters had enlarged their 'rights' beyond previous imagining" [25]. Although there was nothing like an insurrection on that scale in the 1720s, the struggle between men and deer had been reengaged — to the disadvantage of the deer. These conflicts should not suggest simply strong feeling against the monarchy. Deer were a damned pest which ate and trampled on crops. Sometimes it is necessary to resurrect very specific details of the local economy in order to understand these struggles. Around Farnham, for example, timber rights were crucial. Farnham was a hop-growing area, depending on a supply of good, strong poles to support the hops, ". . . but if deer cropped ash saplings they grew up bent and unusable for poles" [26]. Men and deer were enemies: unless, that is, the men were privileged men with the right to hunt deer and eat venison.

The Black Act, which was a response to these struggles, made at least fifty distinct offences punishable by death including: going about the countryside armed and in disguised with one's face "blacked" (hence the "Black Act", although the Act was obviously black in other respects too); hunting, wounding or stealing deer; poaching hares, rabbits or fish; damaging fish-ponds; cutting down or damaging trees; maiming cattle; sending anonymous threatening letters; and setting fire to houses, barns, etc. Although it was unprecedented in its venom, the Black Act was just one of many similar enactments in this period: during the 18th century there was an astronomical increase in the number of offences punishable by death [27]. Whereas a history from above might describe this development of Law in 18th century England as the rationalization of property relations, providing a coherent system for the regulation of trade and commerce; "from below" the Law was experienced as the lash of the whip, the threat of transportation, the gallows at Tyburn, and the awful sight of the bodies of convicts swinging in chains. These were the delicate means by which the gentle rulers of Merrie England set out to terrorize the population into conformity with the steady encroachment of the new commercial values and the new property rights.

What precisely did these encroachments involve? To take first the example of land, under a precapitalist arrangement, land was frequently a place where a number of coincident use-rights intersected. This man would have the right to graze cattle here; that man would have the right to take wood from there; this one would have the right to gravel or turf; that one to hares; another would have the right to timber; etc. Sometimes these rights were defined by copyhold – a legal arrangement which might have been established many years before. More commonly perhaps, they were simply honoured as customs which went back, as the people would say, "time out of mind". This messy arrangement of coincident use-rights was anathema to the emerging forms of capitalist ownership through which land was transformed into a commodity:

> During the eighteenth century one legal decision after another signalled that lawyers had become converted to the notions of absolute property ownership, and that . . . the law abhorred the messy complexities of coincident use-right. And capitalist modes transmuted offices, rights and perquisites into round monetary sums, which could be bought and sold like any other property [28].

This was also a period in which the great country houses and country seats of England were being built and Thompson jokes that it was not much fun for those being "sat upon". The volcanic wealth of the new commercial interests – based on stock jobbing, or on the slave trade for example – was unimaginable in a traditional agricultural economy. As these new city spivs exported their city wealth into the countryside, building luxurious mansions and parks local farmers and yeomen were squeezed out. William Cobbett writes in his *Rural Rides*, for example, about Lord Aylesbury's park: he "seems to have tacked park on to park, like so many outworks of a fortified city. I suppose here are 50 to 100 farms of former days swallowed up" [29]. The case was in no sense exceptional. Wealth was beginning to accumulate into lumps, and the land with it. Soon the complaint would be heard, and Cobbett would be one to voice it, that the people were also accumulating into "lumps" or "heaps" in the factories and cities.

It is a vital historical transition surrounded by conflict amounting almost to guerrilla warfare. But often at the centre of this warfare, it was not the very poor; the poor may have had little to do with the struggles which surrounded the Black Act, for example. It was the middle men – the small farmers and yeomen farmers – who often had most to lose, who were at the centre of the disturbances which surround the Black Act, and who were the

"Blacks" who visited the houses and parks of the new rich, who ripped down their fences and attacked their deer:

> We appear to glimpse a declining gentry and yeoman class confronted by incomers with great command of money and of influence, and with a ruthlessness in the use of both . . . [Their] families must have had a rich and tenacious tradition of memories as to rights and customs . . . [But] these farmers had no money from sinecures or killings on the stocks with which to manure their lands, and they remained stationary or declining, with a traditional economy, while the new rich moved in all around [30].

Although in this instance the poor may have been marginal to the disturbances (and even so they were drawn into the conflicts, and labourers figure strongly in the prosecutions brought under the Black Act) there were other areas of resistance where the poor occupied the hot centre. One such form of resistance was the food riot, a persistent interruption in the history of 18th century England. Thompson has shown how the 18th century food riot was no random, hit or miss affair, but an activity tuned to a precise "moral economy" [31]. Precapitalist relations between producers and consumers on the local markets had been hedged about with many regulations and customs which safeguarded the tangible rights of the common people and the poor. For example, corn could not be sold standing in the field to a large buyer; nor was it proper form for farmers to withhold their corn in the hope of rising prices. Corn had to be transported to the local market, and there large buyers were required to delay their deals until common people had made their small purchases. Market bells signalled the restricted period in which the poor could buy first, and weights and measures were also supervized. Most of this regulation of the market was based on custom or common law, although it was sometimes regulated by Statute. For example, "an enactment of Charles II had even given the poor the right to *shake* the measure, so valuable was the poor man's corn that a looseness in the measure might make the difference to him of a day without a loaf" [32].

The regulations were, naturally, constantly evaded and ignored: it is the "natural" privilege of ruling groups to break their own rules without these infractions being called "crimes" and punished with severity. Although, to press the point further, these were not "their own" rules: they were the rules of an older, dying precapitalist formation which the new men, giddy with the prospect of wealth which the new capitalist values promised, had no interest in enforcing. The temptations to break the market customs were many: particularly with the growing demand from the cities and large towns, such as hungry London. Selling in bulk to a large dealer, selling corn as it stood in the field, or hoarding corn in anticipation of a better price — these were also more "rational" market principles which maximized the possibilities of gain for the farmer's labour and investment.

However, another "rational" and "natural" consequence of these rational and natural developments was that the poor did not see eye to eye with the farmers and millers. In times of scarcity, or when prices rose dramatically, "riot" was a common means of restoring the old regulations. These riots were sometimes highly disciplined affairs in which the people attempted to intimidate farmers into selling at a fair price. Commonly enough, the "crowd" engaged in direct action, taking the corn from the farmers by force and distributing it amongst themselves at a fair price (known as "setting the price", similar to the French *"taxation populaire"*) whereupon the money, and in some instances even the sacks, were handed over to the farmer as his rightful due.

"Riot", then, was a well established form of resistance in the 18th century. And, as often as not, simply the threat of riot would be enough to remind magistrates of their obligations to enforce the old customs. Preachers might urge the poor that prayer was the most effective means of surviving food shortages or price rises, but as Thompson remarks, "The nature of gentlefolks being what it is, a thundering good riot in the next parish was more likely to oil the wheels of charity than the sight of Jack Anvil on his knees in church" [33].

Thus, riot or the threat of it formed part of the irregular democracy of the countryside. In his essay "The Crime of Anonymity" Thompson [34] argues that anonymous threatening letters provided a means of dialogue between the "crowd" and the millers, farmers and magistrates. Peter Linebaugh [35] shows, for example, how often a poor man sent to the gallows by a man of means would threaten to haunt his persecutor. The threat seems laughable by modern standards. But it worked often enough to make sense, and the rich man would call off (or buy off) the long arm of the law in order to avoid being troubled by bad spirits, or a bad conscience. At other times the threats were more blood-curdling, "This will all com true . . . kill the over Seeer . . . tom Nottage is a dam Rouge . . . kill him for one there is 4 more we will kill . . . sink your Flour to 2 and 6 a peck set fier tu it and burn it down. Burn up all the Mills . . . Burn up all ever thing an set fier tu the Gurnray" [36]. The threats were nothing if not extravagant, and sometimes they even came in rhyme. The continuity of the tradition can be measured by the fact that during riots against the spinning jenny in Lancashire in the 1760s there were threats to pull down whole towns. It was unlikely that anyone would believe such enormous threats but that was the genre. A claim that an army of men was sworn in and ready to fight and kill and maim was a warning shot from the "crowd" which worked often enough to coerce the local authorities into subsidizing food prices on a local basis, or into enforcing other common rights . . . at least for a time.

However, as far as these forms of popular resistance were concerned, their time was up. So was the time of the forms of social organization from which this resistance claimed its legitimacy. If we once more take the arrival of Engels in Manchester as a datemark, both were by then as good as dead. Population changes spell out the scale of the social changes. In 1773 Manchester had been a town of 24,000 people. In 1801 its population had risen to 70,000; by 1831 the figure was 140,000 with almost a 45 percent increase in the decade from 1821 to 1831. And so it went on. In 1841 there were 217,000 people in Manchester; and by 1851 – the landmark year when the census revealed that now more than half the population of Great Britain were city dwellers – Manchester's population was a quarter of a million [37]. If one takes the whole of the surrounding urban conurbation of Manchester, then the figure is close to half a million people living together in one large "lump".

Even more had changed than just the scale of things. Most importantly there had been the emergence of Chartism demanding a People's Charter involving electoral reform based on universal manhood suffrage which signalled a new kind of consciousness within the working class. The summer of 1842 had also seen a massive industrial and political upheaval throughout the cotton manufacturing districts of Lancashire, with 50,000 workers on strike in Manchester alone. These were the "Plug Riots", so named because striking workers marched into factories and removed the plugs from their boilers and furnaces, thus stopping the factory and enforcing the strike. After considerable political disagreement within their ranks, the Chartist leaders came behind the strike which moved towards a critical political confrontation, demanding the Charter as the condition for returning to work.

The Plug Riots strike was a total failure, involving arrests on a wide scale. When Engels stepped into this transformed world, he was stepping into a world where not only was it reported in some of the industrial towns that ". . . numbers kept themselves alive by collecting nettles and boiling them down" [38], but also 1,500 labour leaders were in prison. The men associated with Chartism and the Plug Riots were different kinds of men with different demands from those who had broken machines. For better or worse, many of them had come to accept the factory, and to resituate their politics accordingly. That is to state the transition too abruptly, however, for as I described earlier, in the smaller outlying cotton towns the Chartists still harked back to the "preindustrial" demand that each man should have a smallholding of land. Perhaps the Plug Riots and the time of Engels' arrival stand as a bridge between two traditions: those of the dying crafts and attitudes of preindustrial England, and the emerging de-skilled factory workers. The political heritage with which Engels came to be associated, of course, turned its back on the old traditions, and embraced the new. This is entirely understandable: to do otherwise at that historical conjuncture would in all probability have meant political suicide. Nevertheless, given the nature of what had been involved, we can perhaps only marvel at the remarkable insensitivity of that well-worn phrase from the *Communist Manifesto* which celebrates the new system as something which ". . . has thus rescued a considerable part of the population from the idiocy of rural life". That, to put the matter bluntly, is not how the machine-breakers would have judged the matter.

The Last Word

. . . a place called Manchester, which has now disappeared
(William Morris, *News from Nowhere*, 1890) [39].

The theme of this essay has been historical, and I have argued that the hooligan behaviour of the machine-breakers is intelligible and rational if one listens to their experience in their own terms – that is "from below". However, the direction of the essay hopefully carries some implications for the ciminological and sociological study of contemporary hooliganism – for example, vandalism, fights between rival gangs of youths, attacks on migrant workers, street crime and mugging, and the powerful ritual violence of football hooliganism. In our historical time we have become all too familiar with the ways in which this trouble, particularly amongst young working class men and boys, is shrugged off as utterly irrational, and is portrayed in the mass media as a series of senseless and mindless spectacles. Although the pace of the mass media has quickened the pulse of these "moral panics" [40] which surround the violent antics of youth, it is true that the machine-breakers were understood in their historical time in much the same way as the hooligans are dismissed in our historical time. There is consequently an urgent requirement on the part of criminologists to ask themselves: How would "our" hooligans appear if they were afforded the same possibilities of rationality and intelligibility, say, as those of Edward Thompson?

A number of directions have already been pointed out [41]. Elsewhere in one, almost certainly too simple an attempt, I have offered a comparative historical account of outbreaks of machine-breaking and hooliganism in the 1960s when migrant workers were attacked by youths in the same Lancashire cotton towns [42]. In the postwar period the British cotton industry entered a rapid decline, involving profound dislocations in the working class life of the cotton towns. Migrant workers – principally from India and Pakistan – were employed in increasing numbers in the textile industry in order to facilitate the technological changeover to more intensive forms of shift-working which were introduced to fight off competition from foreign cotton imports. Ironically, these low-cost cotton imports often came from the same countries as the low-cost migrant labour. Intense conflicts and rivalries emerged between local people and the migrant workers over housing, jobs and – as far as young working class men were concerned – girls. The phenomenon of "paki-bashing" as it was called, which was condemned on all sides as an irrational hooliganism, emerges as a rational (if primitive) form of resistance to the dislocations within the cotton towns when it is set in its social and historical context. "From below" the migrant workers appeared to be the cause of much of the distress in the cotton towns in the late 1950s and 1960s; just as the machines appeared as the enemy of working people in the earlier historical dislocation of the industrial revolution. I have argued that it is much more useful to think of "paki-bashers" in these terms, rather than to conjure with such dubious criminological ephemera as "criminal psychopath" or "chromosome defect" or "unsocialized youth" who are allegedly the products of "broken homes". It is necessary, in other words, to reconnect the fractured political and historical contexts of criminology where it is customary to make an unnecessarily severe distinction between "crime" on the one hand and "politics" on the other [43].

In attempting such an enquiry into the motives of contemporary
• hooliganisms, the criminologist must confront deeply embedded cultural bans which deny any intelligibility to hooligan conduct, a profound line of historical continuity between our own historical time and the apparently remote historical conjuncture of the machine-smashers. In their day also, the powerful ruling elites of landowners and factory owners afforded supreme rationality to their own actions, and were blind to any others. Who could object to the building of the rational factory? Who could object to the dissemination of the rational machine? Who could object to the rational enclosure and improvement of the land? Indeed, when great men built their great country houses, sometimes tearing down whole villages simply in order to improve the view, who could object? And the answer bounced back: only rogues, vagabonds, men tainted with criminal folly, hooligans and vandals.

In what must figure as one of the earliest uses of the word "vandal" to shrug off the implications of working class hooliganism, the *Manchester Mercury* in 1812 compared a huge crowd who attacked a cotton mill involving loss of life on their part, with "the very Goths and Vandals of antiquity". It is no longer customary to drag the Goths into the act, but this early use of the term vandal, a word which has now become wholly transformed, carried with it a powerful imagery of barbarian hordes breaking into the precincts of civilization. In that sense, nothing much has changed. When faced with the sometimes desperate energies of young hooligans – and many of the machine-breakers were also young – mainstream criminology, and the culture which throws it up, becomes self-satisfied and witless.

The historical fate of the machine-breakers is an unhappy one. History, it is always said, is written by the side which wins. The machine civilization has proved the machine-breakers wrong and won the day. But, the historical clock has a long spring and, to my own satisfaction at least, the historical fate of the machine-breakers has not yet been finally settled. We may have yet to see the last of the machine-breakers. As the industrial world moves towards the historical possibility of a damaging ecological crisis, the machines could come to be understood once more as the enemy of human society. If the prophets of ecological imbalance and collapse are even remotely correct, then the day will come when men and women will attack the machines again. They will, of course, be condemned by public authorities as "mindless hooligans", enemies of civilized progress – just as the Luddites and the others were condemned in their time. Their motives will be certainly different from those of the power-loom breakers and the men who wrecked the spinning jennies. Nevertheless, their actions will be equally intelligible. It may even come to pass – when our culture and its preoccupations are as dead and as unthinkable as the Luddites sometimes seem in our time – that the machine-breakers will have the last word.

Notes

1 I am not drawing here on all the work of these authors. The most relevant writings are Thompson, E.P. (1967). "Time, Work-Discipline and Industrial Capitalism", *Past and Present* 38, pp. 56–97; Thompson, E.P. (1968). *The Making of the English Working Class.* Harmondsworth: Penguin; Thompson, E.P. (1971). "The Moral Economy of the English Crowd in the Eighteenth Century", *Past and Present* 50, pp. 76–136; Thompson, E.P. (1975). *Whigs and Hunters.* London: Allen Lane; Thompson, E.P. (1975). "The Crime of Anonymity" in D. Hay et al., *Albion's Fatal Tree.* London: Allen Lane; Hobsbawm, E.J. (1964). *Labouring Men.* London: Weidenfield and Nicolson; Hobsbawm, E.J. (1969). *Industry and Empire.* Harmondsworth: Penguin; Hobsbawm, E.J. (1971). *Primitive Rebels* 3rd Edition, Manchester: Manchester University Press; Hobsbawm, E.J. (1972). *Bandits.* Harmondsworth: Penguin; Hobsbawm, E.J. and Rudé, G. (1973). *Captain Swing.* Harmondsworth: Penguin; Hill, C. (1975). *World Upside Down.* Harmondsworth: Penguin; Williams, R. (1961). *Culture and Society 1780–1950.* Harmondsworth: Penguin; Williams, R. (1973). *The Country and the City.* London: Chatto and Windus; Williams, R. (1976). *Keywords.* London: Fontana. My text and argument relies so heavily on these works that I have not made cumbersome footnotes and references at every point, except in the case of direct quotations. Another crucially important historical work on the early industrial period is Foster, J. (1974). *Class Struggle and the Industrial Revolution.* London: Weidenfield and Nicolson. Finally, although some of their interpretations are now disputed (see Note 17) the list would not be complete without mention of the classical and unprecedented labour history of the Hammonds, in particular Hammond, J.L. and Hammond, B. (1919). *The Skilled Labourer 1760–1832.* London: Longmans, Green, and Co.

2 For a useful account of how Manchester appeared to these distinguished visitors, see Marcus, S. (1974). *Engels, Manchester and the Working Class.* London: Weidenfield and Nicolson, in the chapter entitled "The Town".

3 See Hobsbawm, E.J. and Rudé, G. (1973), op. cit.

4 See Pearson, G. (1975). *The Deviant Imagination*. London: Macmillan, chapter 6.

5 Smelser, N.J. (1959). *Social Change in the Industrial Revolution*. London: Routledge and Kegan Paul, pp. 227, 246.

6 Plumb, H.J. (1950). *England in the Eighteenth Century*. Harmondsworth: Penguin, p. 79.

7 Thompson, E.P. (1968), op. cit., chapter 9.

8 Ibid., p. 297.

9 Plumb, H.J. (1950), op. cit., p. 89.

10 Ibid., p. 150.

11 Bythell, D. (1969). *The Handloom Weavers*. Cambridge: Cambridge University Press, pp. 198, 199.

12 See Thompson, E.P. (1967), op. cit.

13 Williams, R. (1976), op. cit., pp. 61–62.

14 *Report of Select Committee on Commons Inclosure* (1844), vol. 5. London: Her Majesty's Stationery Office, p. 364.

15 *The Poor Law Report on 1834*, edited by Checkland, S.G. and Checkland, E.O.A. (1974). Harmondsworth: Penguin. For example: "The allotment of larger portions of land than ten rods to an individual, has this evil – if the labourer cultivates it himself with only the aid of his family, he over-forces his strength, and brings to his employer's labour a body exhausted by his struggle", Ibid., p. 280. "Nor is this the only evil of the large allotments; a hovel perhaps is erected on the land, and marriage and children follow. In a few years mo̊re, the new generation will want land, and demand will follow demand, until a cottier population similar to that of Ireland is spread over the country, and misery and pauperism are every where increased", Ibid., p. 280. And again: "A farmer of the parish of Guildsfield, in Montgomeryshire, stated that a labourer could not do justice to his master and the land if he had more than half an acre . . . . He added that if he wanted a labourer, and two men, equally strong and equally skilful, were to apply, one of whom had a quarter of an acre, and the other one or two acres of land, he should without hesitation prefer the former", Ibid., p. 282.

16 1826 was a bad year for utilitarianism. In the same year that the textile workers were rebelling against the material embodiment of utilitarian discipline and philosophy, John Stuart Mill at the age of twenty went mad. In his psychic revolt against the utilitarian discipline of his father's educational system, Mill experienced himself as a machine with all feeling drained away from him. See Mill, J.S. (1971). *Autobiography*. London: Oxford University Press, chapter 5. Mill writes that he was cured by reading Wordsworth's poems which he describes as "a medicine for my state of mind", Ibid., p. 89. In a strange premonition of Laingian anti-psychiatry, Mill describes his earlier life under the influence of his father, and then writes of his release through madness: "The time came when I awakened from this [that is, his earlier life] as from a dream", Ibid., p. 80. Elsewhere, in a letter to Carlyle, he describes his "illness" in the following terms: "that period of *recovery* after the petrification of a narrow philosophy" (original emphasis), and also of "my former character, the character I am now throwing off". See, Mineka, F.E. ed. (1963). *The Earlier Letters of John Stuart Mill*. London: Routledge and Kegan Paul, pp. 181, 183. We can only guess at what untold madnesses were produced in the minds of common people by the new forms of discipline. John Stuart Mill's case demonstrates that even the mighty were not exempt from the ill-effects of the emergent petrifying life forms.

17 It is difficult in relation to this and other outbreaks of machine-smashing to fully understand the level of organization of the rioters. It is possible, for example, that the Luddite outbreaks of 1811 to 1813 moved in the direction of an organization for a national uprising of the English people. The case is most forcibly argued in Thompson (1968), op. cit., chapter 14 and passim. One major difficulty is that men who are plotting insurrection leave few traces, especially at a time when labour organizations are legally repressed as they were at the time in England. Most of the evidence for conspiracy, consequently, comes from government spies, informers and *agents provocateurs;* and it is sometimes argued that spies exaggerated the conspiracies in order to impress their paymasters. This is the line of argument in Hammond J.L. and Hammond B. (1919), op. cit. where the idea of an insurrectionary current is dismissed as the product of spies with lurid imaginations. Thompson answers most of these points coherently and, if he is right, then the Luddite

disturbances must certainly be placed in a much broader context of revolutionary agitation than is customary. The case is not settled to everyone's satisfaction, however. Compare, for example, Thomis, M.I. (1970), *The Luddites*. Newton Abbott: David and Charles, who argues, although somewhat unconvincingly, against Thompson. There is a discussion of this conflict in Donnelly, F.K. (1976). "Ideology and Early English Working Class History: Edward Thompson and His Critics", *Social History*, 2, pp. 219–238. As far as the 1826 outbreak is concerned, even less is known. Traditional accounts describe a "mob" travelling from town to town, wrecking looms and mills. If so, it would have had to be a particularly energetic mob. Imagine the energies of Samson which would have been required to destroy more than a thousand looms and several whole mills in just three days, to have successfully evaded troops throughout this period, and all this involving journeys between towns across rough moorland and hills carrying the equipment necessary for loom-breaking. The whole idea is most unlikely. What is at least equally likely is that the insurrection against the power-looms had been planned beforehand; there had certainly been rumours in the air for a few weeks before the first attack took place. For example, a week before the insurrection proper, a country calico weaver recorded in his diary: "There is a great disturbance at Accrington; they break the windows where the steam looms are; the country is all of an uproar for the poor weaver has neither work nor bread", quoted in Bennett, W. (1948). *The History of Burnley 1650–1850*. Burnley: Burnley Corporation, appendix. A third possibility is that it was a fairly spontaneous affair in which people from one town heard that the mills had been attacked in neighbouring towns, thought that it sounded like a good idea, and decided to have a go themselves. What is certain is that the public authorities did not treat the matter lightly. Accounts vary, but several dozen people were charged, about three dozen were imprisoned, and ten men and women were sentenced to hanging, their sentences later commuted to transportation for life. As a response to the riots, turnpike roads were built in the area for easier troop movements, garrisons and prisons were built, and in one instance a factory was defended by cannon and a moat. Whatevery the final outcome to the puzzle (if there is a final outcome) the recent research by John Foster (1974), op. cit. on working class organization in the cotton belt reminds us that we should not underestimate the level or strength of the English working class in the early 19th century.

18 Quoted in Aspin, C. (1969). *Lancashire, the First Industrial Society*. Helmshore: Helmshore Local History Society, p. 48.
19 Hargeaves, B. (1882). *Recollections of Broad Oak*. Accrington: Bowker.
20 See, for example, the letter quoted by Thompson (1968), op. cit., pp. 653–4: "We known that every machine for the abridgement of human labour is a blessing to the great family of which we are a part". The letter was written in May, 1812 at the point when Thompson suggests that Luddism was giving way to revolutionary organization. It was signed "Tom Paine".
21 Ibid., p. 648.
22 From Thompson, "The Crime of Anonymity" in Hay et al. (1975), op. cit., p. 281.
23 For "wrecking", see Rule, J.G. (1975). "Wrecking and Coastal Plunder" in Hay et al., op. cit. For smuggling, see Winslow, C. (1975). "Sussex Smugglers", in Hay et al., Ibid. And for smuggling in France, Hufton, O.H. (1974). *The Poor of Eighteenth Century France*. London: Oxford University Press.
24 Thompson (1975), op. cit. is an extended analysis of the Black Act. There is also a discussion of poaching and the game laws in Hay, D. (1975). "Poaching and the Game Laws on Cannock Chase" in Hay et al., op. cit. The criminalization of the rights of the poor is, of course, reminiscent of Marx's early essay on the debates of the Rhenish Assembly concerning the theft of wood: Marx, K. (1975). "Debates on the Law on Thefts of Wood", *Marx and Engels Collected Works*, vol. 1. London: Lawrence and Wishart. Marx also promised articles on poaching and the game laws which never appeared. For the relationship between Thompson's work and Marx, see Pearson, G. (1976). "Eighteenth Century English Criminal Law", *British Journal of Law and Society*, 3:1, pp. 115–131. For Marx and the question of wood theft as it relates to the situation in Germany, setting the matter in the context of political economy, see Linebaugh, P. (1976). "Karl Marx, the Theft of Wood, and Working Class Composition", *Crime and Social Justice*, Fall-Winter 1976, pp. 5–16.

25 Thompson (1975), *Whigs and Hunters*, op. cit., p. 40.
26 Ibid., p. 131.
27 However, the actual number of convictions did not rise correspondingly and capital sentences were frequently commuted. For a brilliant analysis of how the "rule of law" in 18th century England operated through a blend of terror and mercy, see Douglas Hay's essay, "Property, Authority and the Rule of Law," in Hay et al. (1975), op. cit. There are some ambiguities in Thompson's treatment of the rule of law in *Whigs and Hunters*, op. cit., for which see Pearson (1976), op. cit.
28 Thompson (1975). *Whigs and Hunters*, op. cit., p. 241.
29 Cobbett, W. (1912). *Rural Rides*, vol. 1. London: Dent, p. 17.
30 Thompson (1975). *Whigs and Hunters*, op. cit., pp. 108, 113, 114.
31 In Thompson (1971), op. cit., and Thompson (1968), op. cit., chapter 3.
32 Thompson (1971), op. cit., p. 102.
33 Ibid., p. 126.
34 In Hay et al. (1975), op. cit.
35 Linebaugh, P. (1975), "The Tyburn Riot Against the Surgeons" in Hay et al., op. cit.
36 Thompson (1975), "The Crime of Anonymity" in Hay et al., op. cit., p. 330.
37 Marcus (1974), op. cit., p. 4. What is usually not noted about the 1826 power-loom smashings is that they took place in small, outlying towns which in many essential respects had not yet been drastically changed by the industrial revolution. Towns whose own population explosion belonged to the later period of Victorian buoyancy from the 1850s until the end of the century. Therefore, the rioters were in many ways still "country people". But they were, crucially, country people who lived only twenty miles away from Manchester which was passing through a period of growth more explosive and catastrophic than anything to be witnessed by Engels. The experience of watching, from the sleepy hollows of the Pennine towns, while Manchester – its steam-driven factories, its chimneys, and its slums – grew at such an alarming rate, provides an important inferential clue for reconstructing the motives of the great power-loom smashing of 1826. Significantly, the riots had few repercussions in the much more developed centres of population and industrialization, and although there was a brief period of excitement in some parts of Manchester when power-looms and mills were attacked, the trouble was easily contained. (See Hammond and Hammond (1919), op. cit., pp. 127–8.) The origins of the 1826 riots in the small towns, as opposed to the city, reminds us once again that a simple economic determinism which puts the riots down to "slump" provides an insufficient argument.
38 Fay, C.R. (1920). *Life and Labour in the Nineteenth Century*. Cambridge: Cambridge University Press, p. 178.
39 Morris, W. (1973). *Three Works*. London: Lawrence and Wishart, p. 295.
40 Cohen, S. (1973). *Folk Devils and Moral Panics*. London: Paladin.
41 In particular, Ibid.: Parker, H.J. (1974). *View from the Boys*. Newton Abbott: David and Charles; Mungham, G. and Pearson, G. Eds. (1976). *Working Class Youth Culture*. London: Routledge and Kegan Paul; Hall, S. and Jefferson, T. eds. (1976). *Resistance Through Rituals*. London: Hutchinson; and Taylor, I. (1971). "Soccer, Consciousness and Soccer Hooliganism" in Cohen, S. ed., *Images of Deviance*. Harmondsworth: Penguin. For the role of the mass media in generating concern on the hooligan question, see Cohen (1973), op. cit. on the "Mods and Rockers" disturbances of the mid 1960s; and Hall, S. et al. (eds.) (1978). *Policing the Crisis*. London: Macmillan, on the mugging panic of the early 1970s. For an account of the main lines of critical sociology's approach to hooliganism, see Pearson, G. (1976). "In Defence of Hooliganism: Social Theory and Violence" in Department of Health and Social Security, *Violence* ed. N. Tutt. London: Her Majesty's Stationery Office.
42 Pearson, G. (1976). "Paki-bashing in a North East Lancashire Cotton Town: A Case Study and its History" in Mungham and Pearson eds., op. cit.
43 For example, Horowitz, I.L. and Liebowitz, M. (1968). "Social Deviance and Political Marginality: Notes Towards a Redefinition of the Relation Between Sociology and Politics", *Social Problems* 15:3, pp. 280–296.

10

CLASS CONFLICT AND THE SUPPRESSION OF TRAMPS IN BUFFALO, 1892-1894

SIDNEY L. HARRING

Every workingman is a tramp in embryo. [*Alarm*, October 11, 1884]

The policemen swung their long nightsticks right and left, left and right, and every time they hit a man he fell bleeding like a stuck pig, and whining and moaning like a kicked dog. . . . The horses were pulled up on their hind legs; they pawed the air with their front legs and mowed down the hoboes like grass, tearing their scalps open and bruising and wounding them. [*Buffalo Evening News*, August 25, 1894]

The police in Buffalo, New York, engaged in a prolonged and vicious campaign against tramps during 1893-1894. In those depression years as many as several hundred thousand of the three to four million unemployed workers in the United States "took to the rails" in search of work, thereby exposing themselves to the danger of arrest and six months in prison under the Tramp Acts. The Tramp Acts were part of an increasing tendency of state legislatures to expand the criminal law. These laws, adopted in the 1870s and 1880s in a large number of states, particularly in the Northeast, outlawed travel without visible means of support and subjected a significant proportion of the working class to the threat of months in prison at hard labor. Passing through Buffalo, a major railroad center, was especially risky, for the city's large and disciplined police force had been deployed to catch tramps at the railroad yards. As many as 140 were "pulled" or "vagged" in a single day. At times over 800 were in the Erie County Penitentiary,

The analytical and editorial assistance of Gerda Ray is gratefully acknowledged. Kenneth Kann, Mike Davis, and Drew Humphries made numerous suggestions and criticisms. An earlier version of this paper was presented at the Annual Meeting of the American Sociological Association in New York City, August 30, 1976.

From Sidney L. Harring, "Class Conflict and the Suppression of Tramps in Buffalo, 1892-1894," 11(5) *Law and Society Review* 873-911 (Summer 1977). Copyright 1977 by The Law and Society Association.

where the total number of inmates seldom exceeded 1,000. On at least two occasions nonviolent tramps were shot by the police.[1]

This analysis of the enforcement of the New York Tramp Acts in Buffalo discusses the organization of the police and police decision making in response to a particular crisis. It supports the Marxist contention that the police are not neutral in the class struggle, but rather are an instrument of ruling class domination. Moreover, this police repression was an important factor in the maintenance of class relations, and class struggle, in turn, shaped the development and expansion of the police institution.

The enforcement of the tramp laws also revealed the ways in which reformist and repressive strategies were intermixed within the police apparatus. Bourgeois reformers used police reforms and social work practices to increase the level of repression. Eliminating control of the police by the political machine, another key goal of reformers, was also part of a deliberate strategy to reduce working class influence in the institution.[2] To answer the questions "Why the Tramp Act?" and "Why at this particular time?" requires Marxist analysis of the relationship between the criminal law and class conflict in the late nineteenth century (Hay *et al.*, 1975; Thompson, 1975).

This study will first consider the nature of the Tramp Act in New York State: its origins, scope, and context. Then it will turn to the population most directly affected, the tramps, and their relation to the working class. The next section will analyze the enforcement of the Tramp Act in Buffalo within the context of the characteristics of that community: class composition, ethnicity, working class unrest, and ruling class hegemony. The escalation of strategies to control individual tramps led ultimately to a major confrontation with an "industrial army" of unemployed workers moving through the city.

I. TRAMPING AND THE TRAMP ACT

Tramping in the United States was closely linked with unemployment and the changing nature of the labor market brought about by rapidly developing industrial capitalism. The periodic

---

1. On the general context of the Depression of 1893-94, see Hoffman (1956), Reznick (1953). On Buffalo, see Shelton (1976), who shows clearly that the reformers who dealt with the tramp problem were a ruling elite and used reform measures to serve their class interests; but she does not analyze the repressive nature of their reforms. Ringenbach (1973) describes the tramp problem in this period, but does not adequately consider the class basis of the reformers nor explore the close relationship between violent repression and reform.
2. Hays (1964) and Bernstein *et al.* (1977) deal in detail with the anti-working class nature of progressive reform movements. For a case study of the impact of such reforms on one police department, see Woods (1973).

depressions of the late nineteenth and early twentieth centuries brought on regular peaks in the number of tramps as thousands of workers "took to the rails" in search of work. Moreover, geographical shifts of industry toward the Great Lakes region and beyond, and the existence of "moving" jobs, such as railroad building, mining, crop harvesting, and lumberjacking, meant that travel in search of work was necessary for millions of workers. Unattached immigrant males frequently traveled for a time upon arrival in the country, while looking for a favorable situation. The West attracted sons of Eastern and Midwestern farmers and factory workers, looking either for work or adventure. Finally, some workers resisted the work discipline demanded by factories and preferred to eke out a living from odd-jobs "on the road."[3] Although unemployed workers had traveled in search of work well before the Civil War, it was the large-scale industrial transformation following the war which created a "tramp problem" of major proportions. The large pool of surplus labor characteristic of the capitalist mode of production grew too large and difficult to manage during depressions.

The view that tramping was one mode of working class adaptation to the demands of industrial society is reinforced by an analysis of the tramp population. In 1892-93 J. J. McCook, a sociologist at Trinity College in Hartford, Connecticut, conducted a "tramp census" of 1,349 tramps in fourteen cities, and found that they were nearly indistinguishable from the general working class population in most of their demographic characteristics: 57 percent had trades or professions; 41 percent were unskilled laborers; 56 percent were native born, with those born in Ireland, England, Germany, Canada, and Scandinavia next; 90 percent were literate. Eighty-three percent gave the fact that they were "out of work" as their reason for tramping. Only 11 percent admitted ever having been inmates of almshouses. Sixty-seven percent were not teetotalers, and 39 percent had been convicted of drunkenness. When asked how they got their food, 27 percent said they worked for it, 38 percent that they paid for it, 20 percent that they begged, and 9 percent that they worked and begged. These characteristics are not strikingly different from those of the lower paid half of the male working class population, except for the unusually large proportion of single men (90 percent), the large number of arrests for minor offenses, and the fact that some begged. McCook's survey was conducted by police officers and no doubt contains many inaccuracies, but it compares favorably with another sample consisting of all the patrons of the Baltimore Wayfarers' Lodge during

---

3. There is an extensive literature on tramping, e.g., Ringenbach (1973), Seelye (1963), Tyler (1967), Anderson (1924), Foster (1939).

the first twenty days of February, 1894. Of the nearly 500 questioned, 57 percent were native born, 17 percent Irish, 9 percent German, and 10 percent British. Fifty-five percent were under thirty and 83 percent under 40. Forty percent were in the skilled trades; 8 percent firemen, miners, and sailors; 2 percent bookkeepers and clerks; 2 percent farmers, drivers, or teamsters; and 47 percent general laborers.[4]

There are no good estimates of the size of the tramp population, largely because tramps could not clearly be distinguished from the unemployed. McCook, using a tortured formula derived from his sample, estimated 45,000, but he based this estimate on the number of tramps staying in the police lodgings in Boston in the winter of 1891-92. His estimate is probably low because Boston was off the main tramp circuit, particularly in the winter. Police lodgings housed 39,976 persons in Baltimore alone in 1893, and 1,679 in Buffalo; but these figures include many who were not tramps, as well as an undeterminable number of multiple users, and they exclude the two-thirds of all tramps who, according to McCook's sample, never used such lodgings.[5]

These data locate tramps as solidly working class, not a lumpen proletariat or criminal class who survived by exploiting others. However, Police Chief Pendleton of Lynchburg, Virginia, summarily defined all tramps as criminals, in a manner common at that time:

> . . . They are criminals of the lowest type, who use the time while being helped by kindly disposed persons to spy into those premises and use the information thus acquired to rob those same premises later.
>
> When a man goes to a freight yard with the intention of riding a freight to the next town, he is a thief. He is going to steal a ride, and so even the honest laborer who starts out to "hobo" to the next town in search of work, is morally and actually a thief, and the transition to the old kind of thief is very easy. [Dilworth, 1976:115-16]

Because reformers so often charged tramps with criminality, and used that to legitimate violent repression, it is important to consider the evidence more closely.[6]

---

4. J. J. McCook (1893a, 1893b), who conducted this tramp census, was a professor of sociology at Trinity College in Hartford, Connecticut, and was active in the COS. He carried out numerous elementary surveys for the use of charity reformers (1892a, 1892b). He became interested in tramps when he was chosen by the Hartford Town Meeting to be chairman of a committee on outdoor alms. This led him to a study of tramps as "venal" voters (48 percent voted within a single year) a fact that alarmed McCook, but further supports the argument that tramps were very much like the rest of the working class population in most respects. The Baltimore data are from Gould (1894).
5. McCook (1893b:63-64). The Annual Reports of the police departments in most cities published lodging figures.
6. Two important historical articles emphasize the ways in which the charge of criminality has been misused to artificially separate criminals from the working class to legitimate repression: Linebaugh (1976), Schwendinger and Schwendinger (1976).

The most spectacular form of criminal activity attributed to tramps was train stealing. "Industrial armies" heading East, usually including large numbers of railroad men, "requisitioned" trains, and led great chases, frequently against federal troops.[7] Other train thefts originated in conflicts with hostile train crews. A group of tramps in Medford, New Jersey, stole a train by disconnecting the engine, and ran off with it, leaving a string of cars to serve as housing for 600 workers crowded into Medford to work on the cranberry harvest. Although train stealing was a federal offense, many workers viewed it more prosaically as a means of transportation (*Buffalo Express*, Sept. 13, 1893).

More threatening were occasional reports of violent crimes by tramps. In unrelated incidents near Buffalo during 1894 one railroad conductor was shot and another robbed of his watch and chain by hoboes whom the conductors were trying to throw off trains. A wave of petty "tramp burglaries" was reported along the railroad lines southeast of Buffalo. The wife of a Congressman from upstate New York insisted that he should leave his safe open when he was away from home: "I have seen too many tramps," she said, "to feel at ease, even with dogs running free about the grounds, and would much rather have the silver stolen than be chloroformed by a burglar who could easily drop from one freight train, accomplish the crime, and depart on the next." Police Chief Tillard of Altoona, Pennsylvania, echoed William Pinkerton, famous private detective and strikebreaker, in identifying a class of professional tramp beggars who moved between Bowery hotels in New York and the mining towns of Pennsylvania and Ohio.[8]

While these examples tell us something about the diverse types of tramp crime, McCook's data tell us more about frequency: 6 percent of those he surveyed reported being convicted of a crime, 39 percent reported being convicted of drunkenness, and 2 percent reported stealing part of their food (McCook, 1893a). Even with an allowance for underreporting these proportions are not far out of line with what might be expected for much of the rest of the working class. These is no question that some people who traveled as tramps committed serious crimes, but they could not have been more than a small proportion of all tramps. Petty theft of food and small articles was also often attributed to tramps, and there can be no doubt that hungry people with no work sometimes resorted to such activities. Many tramps, however, insisted on working for

---

7. There are a number of accounts of train stealing in Pollack (1962:chapter 2), McMurry (1970), and Leavitt (1886).
8. For examples of tramp criminal behavior see Leavitt (1886), Rood (1898), Dilworth (1976:117, 123-26), and *Buffalo Express*, September 13, 18, 1893, May 24, 1894.

their food, and major industrial armies set up disciplinary mechanisms to control petty theft.

The efforts of police chiefs, reformers, and newspapers to link all tramps with a few types of criminal behavior is perhaps best understood as an attempt to frighten the "good citizens" who "misguidedly" gave aid to tramps in the belief that they were deserving poor. "There is certainly some reason for this army of lawless bums . . . I believe that the biggest fault is with the people themselves. The American people, as a rule, are too sympathetic and easily worked," was the analysis of Chief Goodrich of Binghampton, New York. "Our people are over and above humane in the handling of tramps," echoed Chief Woods of Erie, Pennsylvania.[9] Unquestionably Goodrich and Woods were correct: working people and small farmers across the country supported the tramp armies, as well as the thousands of individual tramps, with frequent and substantial donations without which it would have been impossible for so many to travel "on the tramp" (Bradshaw, 1896:338).

This discussion of tramp criminality introduces the contradictory meanings of the term "tramp," which require further explanation. Widespread public use óf the term began in the depression of 1873-74, the first major, nationwide industrial economic contraction. The New York Times, for example, first used the term in 1874 to describe the traveling unemployed. During the years that followed it was used almost indiscriminately to describe several different categories of people. "Tramp" came to be applied to those supposedly "work-shy": those who preferred not to work if they could avoid it. This, in the eyes of ruling class reformers, frequently included those unemployed through no fault of their own, a very large proportion of the working class during a depression. The term "hobo," often used in conjunction or even interchangeably with "tramp," properly applied to workers who followed their jobs from place to place. This was most common among harvesters, railroad workers, and lumberjacks in the West. "Vagrants" were distinguished as people who remained within a single community and did not travel, but similar confusion arose over whether vagrants were work-shy or worthy unemployed. "Beggars" were either vagrants or tramps engaged in the particularly reprehensible work of begging on the streets or from house to house. Finally, and intermixed with all the above, were "criminals," a professional criminal class who, according to reformers,

---

9. Dilworth (1976:118-20, 114). Many social scientists of the day linked tramps with crime, e.g., the economist Ely (1893) and the criminologist Lea (1894).

police, and the media, traveled with tramps, used tramping as a cover for their work, and encouraged other tramps to engage in crime, a temptation to which they succumbed all too readily.[10] Thus, the term "tramp" carried with it all these elements, freely confused with each other.[11] Neither reformers nor police usually bothered to make fine distinctions. Criminal images of tramps served to legitimate the high level of repression, but the suppression of crime was not the key motivation behind vigorous tramp control. The police, we shall see, arrested as tramps employed workers, vagrants, disorderly youths, young people traveling in search of work, scabs who refused to work, and local petty criminals.

The large numbers of tramps on the road in the depressions of 1873-1874 and 1877 precipitated the adoption of the Tramp Acts. New Jersey enacted the first American Tramp Act in 1876, followed by a wave of similar acts in northeastern states, including Rhode Island in 1877 and Delaware in 1879. New York's Tramp Act was passed in 1879, in response to the depression and strikes of 1877, and it was revised and strengthened in 1885 as a result of the 1884 depression so that it became a "model" Tramp Act copied by other states (Ringenbach, 1973:22-24; Leavitt, 1886; Hubbard, 1894) (see Appendix). Within twenty years of the first Tramp Act, Harry A. Millis (1898), of the University of Chicago, found that only four of 44 states had no legislation on the subject, although four others left the matter to local option, and three treated tramps as deserving poor, rather than criminals. Five years earlier McCook (1893a) had reported only 21 state Tramp Acts.

The speed with which the acts were adopted, and their timing, require analysis. The major force behind enactment of the law, particularly in the Northeast, was the Charities Organization So-

---

10. The thesis of the "criminalization" of the surplus labor force, particularly the mobile segment, as an instrument of ruling class domination, has been developed most thoroughly for England. R. H. Tawney (1967:275) eloquently set out this issue when writing of the Tudor tramp: "His history is inevitably written by his enemies." Karl Marx (1967:663-67; 713-75) addressed vagrancy and tramping in some detail in *Capital*, especially in the chapters on "The So-Called Primitive Accumulation," and "The Nomad Population." See also Breir (1974). William Chambliss (1964) studied the repression of tramps cross-culturally. The political history of the American tramp has yet to be written. Robert Tyler (1967) looked in some detail at I.W.W. organizing among hoboes, which led to increased police repression. Finally, Caleb Foote (1956) clearly showed that "vagrancy-type" law in Philadelphia in the 1950s operated in the same way.

11. These definitions and confusions of definition come from a reading of articles on tramps, vagrants, beggars, and the unemployed, in *Forum* and *The Charities Review*, two important journals of reformers in the 1890s. E. Lamar Bailey (1898) critized Henry Edward Rood (1898) for failing to make important distinctions where great differences existed, and suggested the basic outline I have used. For discussions of the origin of the term "tramp," see Ringenbach (1973:3-4) and Leonard (1966). For an analysis of the meaning of the term "hobo," see Adams (1902).

ciety (COS). Formed in Buffalo in 1877, and composed primarily of educated members of wealthy bourgeois families, the COS quickly spread across the Northeast. It assumed a major role in the effort to "organize" charities scientifically to prevent indiscriminate almsgiving from demoralizing the working class and encouraging laziness. It emphasized (1) careful investigations to distinguish the worthy poor from the lazy and improvident, (2) forms of charitable assistance designed to put people back to work as soon as possible, and (3) workhouse and prison "rehabilitation" for tramps and other "antisocial" elements who did not adjust to industrial work roles (Lowell, 1894, 1896; Watson, 1922).

Through frequent programs, magazine and newspaper articles, personal contacts, and social events (including opulent charity balls), it sought to organize the bourgeoisie behind its social programs. Some measure of its success is illustrated by its ability to induce the Buffalo mayor to call a meeting of businessmen and COS reformers to raise $100,000 in private contributions for a COS administered relief program (*Buffalo Courier*, Dec. 17, 18, 29, 1893; Jan. 7, 1894). Although the *Express* was the daily paper of Buffalo COS reformers, both the Cleveland Democratic *Courier* and the Republican *Commercial* maintained the same positions on tramps and other social programs. The charitable ideas of the COS and its supporters were rooted in their bourgeois class position and were profoundly violent and anti-working class. The COS advocated starving the children of alcoholics in an attempt to reform their parents, urged unemployed workers in depressions to save for the hard winter months, and criticized public school teachers who fed hungry students (Shelton, 1976: chapter 6; Wilcox, 1895; Almy, 1895).

The COS inspired program also actively promoted the idea that tramps were political troublemakers who incited otherwise well-disciplined local workers to class violence. Particularly after the 1877 railroad strikes, in which dozens of people were killed and hundreds of railroad cars burned, the COS demanded the enactment of Tramp Acts to curb the swelling number of "tramp agitators." Those strikes had involved thousands of railroad and other workers with myriad legitimate grievances; but by blaming them on tramps bent on destruction, the COS and its allies were able to press for the enactment of repressive laws which could then be used against a broad spectrum of the working class (Bruce, 1970; Dacus, 1969).

When working class opposition to the Tramp Acts mounted, particularly during the depression of the 1890s, the COS and its allies recognized that their privileged class position was jeopardized by the impact that tramps had on the rest of the working class, an impact that destabilized existing class relations. Economist Richard T. Ely expressed this fear:

> The greatest danger which threatens a section of the community and in consequence, we may say, the community as a whole, is that a considerable proportion of the unemployed may suffer social shipwreck, and so become part of the "submerged tenth." Recent researches in pauperism and crime make nothing plainer than that there is a section of the wage-earning classes comparatively weak, which in times like these tends to yield to the temptation to become beggars and criminals and prey upon society. [Ely, 1893]

This need to "hold the line" against the erosion of the working class is a major theme of the writings of the COS. Josephine Shaw Lowell emphasized the importance of distinguishing the "genuine worker" from the tramp, and argued that the organizing of charities was necessary to keep relief seekers from permanently degrading themselves and entering the ranks of tramps (Lowell, 1894, 1896).

The Tramp Act significantly expanded the power of the criminal law in controlling the working class in three ways. First, and most important, the focus of the law shifted from beggars and urban vagrants to the most oppressed segment of the working class, the unemployed and the marginally employed, those "living without labor and visible means of support" for at least part of the year. Elbert Hubbard (1894: 593-600) criticizing the Tramp Acts in *Arena* in 1894, described this shift in his analysis of the Delaware Tramp Act. For Hubbard the reason for creating the act was that many workers did not adequately fall within the scope of the vagrancy act because they had money and were looking for work.

Second, the New York Tramp Act, like similar legislation in other states, made what were misdemeanors, if committed by others, felonies if committed by a tramp, thus codifying harsher penalties for traveling unemployed workers: three years at hard labor. This provision alone would have been enough to signal the Tramp Act as a stark example of class justice in a bourgeois legal system that claims to be blind to personal attributes. Although this provision was aimed at the threat of traveling tramp criminals, and focused largely on common kinds of property crime, its effect was to make traveling workers a suspect class with less legal protection than other citizens, since virtually all of them could be legally classified as tramps. Such laws could be used to repress working class labor organizers and political radicals, who were often arrested as tramps.

Finally, the Tramp Act, unlike older vagrancy laws, centralized antitramp policy at the state level by providing that the state reimburse local governments for the cost of jailing tramps. This provision implemented the COS policy of relying on imprisonment to stop the practice of "passing on" tramps to the next town. With a large number of tramps on the road, cost conscious local governments had an incentive to avoid locking them up, but the COS recognized the regional character of the problem, and the inadequacy of ad hoc local practices. State intervention to stop "passing on" provides an early example of the move toward statewide "crime control" measures, paralleling the increase in state control of education, health, and other social services.[12]

These provisions, as repressive as they are, reveal only part of the class oppression of the Tramp Acts, for these laws were enforced by police and judicial actions that often exceeded what the Acts authorized. The development of these enforcement practices in Buffalo, their social foundations, and the functions they served, will be analyzed in the next section.

II.   POLICE REPRESSION OF TRAMPS IN BUFFALO

The harshness of the police repression of tramps in Buffalo in the 1890s was conditioned by the severity of the depression. By 1890, Buffalo was the eleventh largest city in the United States, one of the most important of the Great Lakes centers of transportation, industry, and commerce. Twenty-six railroads served the city, and thousands of ships called annually, making Buffalo a major transshipment point for both Western raw materials and Eastern manufactured goods. The effects of the depression were felt most heavily by the city's working class, which was disproportionately foreign born and employed in manufacturing and unskilled labor. The official estimate of 10,000 unemployed was a gross underestimate: 5,000 were unemployed in the Polish community alone, which represented only 25,000 of the city's total population of 255,664. One out of two railroad workers was reportedly unemployed, and most other industries laid off large numbers of workers as well (Shelton, 1976: chapters 1, 6).

Tramps and the Tramp Act became an important arena of class conflict in Buffalo in the 1890s because of the ties between the local working class and the tramps. This relationship was in turn shaped by the nature of the trade union movement in Buffalo, the organization of a socially conscious ruling class, and the actions of a relatively efficient police department. We will consider the impact of each of these on the enforcement of the Tramp Act.

The Buffalo Central Labor Union (CLU), a confederation of local unions, had become an important local political force since

12. For "passing on" as a focus of reformers, see Ringenbach (1973:20).

its founding in the 1880s. Composed primarily of native born and German skilled workers, it generally favored immigration restriction as a cure for unemployment. There were few Polish or Italian members to resist such a position in the early 1890s. But at the same time the CLU often exhibited class solidarity with nonmember immigrant workers: in April 1894 it passed a resolution criticizing Police Captain Frank Koehler for blocking the holding of a Polish celebration and for forbidding Polish woodworkers to use a meeting hall in order to organize themselves (*Buffalo Express*, April 23, 1894). The CLU support for the immigrant tramp army further demonstrated this working class solidarity. The CLU formed local political alliances with with the Irish Democratic Sheehan machine and the reform right wing of local Republicans, and with the COS on such matters as opposition to child labor and support of the eight-hour day (MacTeggart, 1940; Shelton, 1976: chapter 7).

The CLU was in frequent conflict with conservative Republicans and local Bourbon Democrats, who were most often their employers. CLU unions struck Buffalo industries between four and fifteen times per year and threatened strikes much more often. However, Buffalo unions did not go out on strike in support of the Pullman workers when requested to do so by Eugene Debs. In 1896 they heeded the warnings of Republican manufacturers and those conservative Democratic leaders who defected to McKinley, and voted Republican. In sum, Buffalo's CLU followed a generally conservative trade union policy typical of the era. At times they worked with manufacturers and progressive reformers to gain improved working conditions and higher wages. But when workers were stalemated in conflicts with conservative manufacturers the CLU supported militant strike activities and boycotts.[13] The CLU had some access to the newspapers, where they voiced support for the tramps and criticized the police. However, they lacked the political clout to influence significantly police enforcement of the Tramp Act.

Unlike the hardships for the working class, Buffalo's expanding economy in the 1870s and 1880s had made it a prosperous city for entrepreneurs, many of whom retained personal control over their large local businesses. During the 1890s there were said to be ninety millionaires in the city. And there was a large number of capitalist entrepreneurs, only slightly less wealthy, who dominated the city's economy and were important in the industrial

---

13. John Palmer has analyzed the election of 1896 (1967). The most important local Democratic leaders deserted Bryan for McKinley. MacTeggart (1940) contains accounts of a number of Buffalo strikes and boycotts.

expansion of the entire region (Powell, 1962; Hubbell,1893; Shelton, 1976: chapter 2).

Class conscious and tightly organized, the ruling bourgeoisie had long controlled the political life of the city. They had organized the city government and had served in the most important political positions, including the offices of mayor and police commissioner (Harring, 1975; Shelton, 1976: chapter 4). The economic and political ties of the bourgeoisie were elaborated in their social life. Living in large homes in the center of the city, along Delaware Avenue and its side streets, they knew each other well, were often related by marriage, and met on a regular basis in exclusive clubs (Luhan, 1933).

This ruling class was not monolithic. It was able to accommodate with ward based political machines, as these came to play increasingly important roles. The Irish Democratic Sheehan machine was the largest, but even it never held power. Opposition parties mounted periodic "reform" campaigns, but these carried no political analysis beyond simplistic affirmations of honesty and efficiency (Palmer, 1967; Shelton, 1976: chapter 3).

The decade of the 1890s produced a major bourgeois reform movement in Buffalo, composed of Republicans and Democrats opposed to the corruption and the inefficiency of the traditional machines of both parties. These reformers advocated putting Buffalo's city government on "sound business principles." Ideologically they were committed to the corporate liberal solution of applying new scientific and professional techniques to the amelioration of the worst abuses of industrial capitalism (Shelton, 1976: chapters 1-4; Palmer, 1967). Reformers and more traditional capitalists did not differ over long-term objectives, for both sought a stable capitalist economic system, but only about the best strategy for achieving that goal. Both feared large-scale class conflict, and organized to control it. Often they worked together easily in such areas as police reform and poor relief. The conflict over police reform in this period was predominantly a question of how best to suit the tactics of policing to the rapidly changing practical and ideological aspirations of the bourgeoisie (Bernstein *et al.*, 1977:32-42).

The Buffalo police force was created at the initiative of wealthy Republican businessmen in 1866. The original 100-man force under state control was succeeded by a 200-man municipal force in 1872. After ten stagnant years the force was disciplined, expanded, and reorganized following a serious dock strike and depression in 1884. By 1893 it had grown to 576 men who were well disciplined and reasonably efficient. Although there were occasional charges to the contrary, the Buffalo police built a strong antilabor record for going well beyond the call of duty in breaking strikes. Buffalo's ruling bourgeoisie exerted tight control over the police until well into the twentieth century through a series of businessmen commissioners and a succession of three businessmen superintendents. The CLU and individual unions repeatedly criticized the one-sided use of the police in strikes (Harring, 1975, 1976; Hubbell, 1893).

The enforcement of the Tramp Act in Buffalo began in 1891, when 2,110 arrests were made under that statute, or about 11 percent of the total arrests for the year (see Table). Although we cannot be certain why there were no tramp arrests earlier, several explanations are possible. Throughout this period it is clear that the police had freely arrested people for a wide variety of offenses against the public order, including vagrancy, and many of these arrests may have involved behavior that was charged under the Tramp Act after 1891. For example, there were 1,400 fewer vagrancy arrests in 1891 than in 1890, suggesting that two-thirds of the tramp arrests may have been simply instances of vagrancy. One reason for this shift in categorization may have been that the state paid for persons jailed under the Tramp Act, but not those jailed for vagrancy. Second, 1891 marks the beginning of the administration of Police Chief Daniel Morganstern (1891-1894), a dry goods merchant who served as the first of the businessmen superintendents who administered the force from 1891-1904. This general shift toward more businesslike administration of the force led to a greater number of arrests for two reasons: (1) the class interests of the businessmen exerted more influence over policing measures; as class conflict increased, and the class position of businessmen was threatened, the police became more important as a force of class control; (2) a renewed concern with fiscal efficiency made state financing of imprisonment under the Tramp Act more attractive. The Buffalo police had first engaged in serious strike-breaking activity in 1877. The Great Strike, virtually a general strike in Buffalo, was smashed with a carefully organized club swinging charge. Beginning in the 1884-1886 period Buffalo, like most other cities in the Great Lakes industrial area, greatly strengthened its police force, largely in response to a nationwide wave of strikes calling for the eight-hour day (Commons, 1926: chapter 9). The Buffalo police developed a well-organized, paramilitary antistrike plan that could be implemented on very little notice. And even under normal conditions the Buffalo police functioned as an antilabor force, working closely under the direction of the manufacturers (Harring, 1975, 1976: chapter 6). Finally, the COS was engaged in an intensive drive in Buffalo, and in other cities, to encourage the police to enforce fully the provisions of the Tramp Act. The shift in Buffalo's policy at this time, and the increase by 700 in the aggregate of arrests for tramping and vagrancy, were consistent with this policy.[14]

TABLE

ARRESTS FOR MAJOR PUBLIC ORDER CRIMES BY
SPECIFIC OFFENSE IN BUFFALO: 1886-1900

Year	Total Arrests	Drunkenness	Disorderly Conduct	Vagrancy	Tramps[a]
1886	9,544	2,803	1,876	1,528	0
1887	12,404	4,152	2,513	2,625	0
1888	14,149	5,132	2,572	3,178	0
1889	16,170	5,926	2,532	3,640	0
1890	17,628	6,599	3,210	3,170	0
1891	18,575	6,759	3,160	1,750	2,110
1892	21,383	8,256	3,642	1,779	2,287
1893	19,062	6,144	3,386	1,820	1,925
1894	26,069	6,824	4,014	4,764	4,716
1895	24,889	9,861	3,653	1,690	2,464
1896	22,573	4,139	4,139	1,090	2,423
1897	25,573	10,319	5,085	1,166	3,149
1898	24,489	9,612	4,764	1,118	2,661
1899	23,338	9,971	4,431	1,021	1,622
1900	28,347	12,160	5,121	1,292	1,932

a. Prior to 1891 there were *no* arrests for the offense of being a tramp.
Source: Buffalo Police Department (1886-1900)

Tramp Act enforcement in Buffalo in this early period followed a model familiar in most American cities. Officers were stationed in the railroad yards to arrest tramps, but because of the number of tramps, and the absence of a strong repressive policy, individual police were allowed a great deal of discretion and thousands of tramps got through town safely. But antitramp strategy became consistently more repressive over the next three years, and these tentative and uncoordinated enforcement practices gave way to a strongly stated 1893 policy: all tramps were to be locked up on sight. Arrest statistics record the impact of this policy: by 1894 tramp arrests had more than doubled in three years. Tramping and vagrancy together accounted for 20 percent of the total arrests in Buffalo in 1891 and nearly 40 percent in 1894. Heightened class conflict, beginning with a major railroad strike in 1892 and culminating in a severe depression in 1893-94, led to increased repression of the working class, partly through the Tramp Acts.

The link between the role of the Buffalo police department in class control, particularly strike control, and its vigorous antitramp policies becomes clear through an analysis of the railroad

14. All arrest statistics are from the *Annual Report of the Chief of Police* of the Buffalo Police Department, published from 1873.

switchmen's strike of 1892. The attempt to break the strike quickly merged with an antitramp crackdown: many railroad men went to jail as tramps, along with the itinerant unemployed and workers, who were brought in as scabs but then refused to cross picket lines.

The switchmen's strike, called on August 13, sorely stretched police resources because it was dispersed over miles of railroad lines outside the city limits. On the volatile Polish east side, where most of the tracks were located, Captain Kilroy, the police department's expert in military discipline and strike specialist, spread sixty policemen out along six miles of track. Eighty-five officers were assigned duty at the city limits, sleeping in three cars loaned by the railroad. Brief skirmishes were fought with crowds of strikers and neighborhood supporters, generally ending in club swinging charges by the police. In one such incident Philip Day, a coal and wood dealer, was severely beaten on his own doorstep while watching the police beat Jack Dennison, an engineer returning from the store with groceries.[15]

Crowds of strikers and supporters challenged the police repeatedly around the yards, leading to dozens of incidents. These crowds tried to stop the movement of trains in every way possible while the police tried to keep the tracks open. All in all, the contest was close. A few scab trains were stopped, but others were able to get through. The union charged that police officers were acting as switchmen and assisting in the movement of trains. A delegation went to see Mayor Charles Bishop to register a protest, which was ignored. On the strike front police officers were taunted for scabbing. One crowd of boys, seeing police officers riding on top of boxcars (where brakemen normally ride) called derisively: "Get onto de gay brakemen. Dey's too fat to stand up and dey's so weak dey have to carry brake sticks. I wonder who put up for dey suits" (*Buffalo Express*, August 13-15, 1892).

Suppressing the strike was clearly beyond the capabilities of the Buffalo police. On August 17, the police were augmented by 5,000 State Militia under the command of New York Central Railroad Superintendent Doyle, a General in the Militia, and 200 reserves were hastily recruited by the police and sheriff. "They are there for blood if the lawless element makes a move looking for resistance," warned the reform Republican *Express*. After a few more days of street fighting the strikers capitulated. There were

---

15. Buffalo's 1892 switchmen's strike is well known in labor history, and it is considered one of the major events leading to the formation of the American Railway Union, headed by Eugene Debs, and the Pullman strike of 1894. See Foner (1955:253-54). The events reported here are from the *Buffalo Express*, August 13, 16-17, 1892.

more complaints of militia members throwing switches and helping run trains, which was not unlikely since their leader was an
executive of the railroad. Some militiamen and police reserves
defected while facing striking workers, giving rise to the charge
that there was substantial working class sympathy on the part of
the police.[16] The actions of the regular Buffalo police, however,
contradict this interpretation: the force worked long hours to
break the strike, with a high degree of effectiveness. Their shortcomings appear to have been the result of overextension along
miles of track and the fatigue accumulated from being on the job
for several days. The working class loyalties of individual police
officers were neutralized by a number of factors, including high
salaries, military discipline, and training emphasizing the neutrality of the rule of law. Finally, the ethnic origins of the police
were roughly two-thirds Irish and one-third German, and thus
different from those of much of the working class, particularly the
new immigrant workers. The railroad's charge of inadequate
police protection is more likely to reflect its reactionary demands
for an even higher level of violent repression.[17]

While the strike was in progress, the police engaged in a series
of solidly antiworking class techniques to break it. A mayoral
proclamation forbade congregating on the streets in working class
neighborhoods, and the police enforced the rule. Taverns were
ordered closed in working class districts. Leaflets defending the
strikers were seized, and the distributors arrested. Individual

---

16. *Buffalo Express*, August 17-18, 1892. Foner (1955) asserts that the militia
    and deputies deserted, but not that the police did.
17. The class loyalties of the police in the nineteenth century are the subject
    of much debate. Herbert Gutman, and others following him, emphasize
    the working class social origins of the police and their unreliability as
    agents of bourgeois domination. See, e.g., Gutman (1959a, 1959b, 1964,
    1968a, 1968b). Although Gutman's research is commonly cited in support
    of the "police as workers" hypothesis, it is inadequate for several rea-
    sons: (1) Gutman's work contains as many examples of repressive anti-
    working class behavior; (2) Gutman writes of the period of early industri-
    alization in small to middle sized communities where the bourgeoisie had
    not yet consolidated its control of governmental institutions; (3) Gut-
    man's community studies are highly selective, focusing primarily on
    isolated mining communities with strong working class strike activity.
    Bruce Johnson (1976), argues strongly that the class loyalties of the
    police are with the working class, using in part an historical argument
    similar to Gutman's. He uncritically accepts a few secondary sources
    which do not adequately prove his point, and he totally ignores a large
    body of literature that refutes his position.
       There are a number of accounts of police officers refusing to act
    against strikers, but my examination of many such accounts convinces
    me that they are of questionable validity and that the frequency of such
    displays of working class solidarity on the part of the police is exag-
    gerated. The major source of this error lies in the tendency of bourgeois
    media to reprint, as though they were true, the charges of manufacturers
    and chamber of commerce members, that the police were unreliable.
    Often there were just as many claims by workers that the police were
    scabbing. Where data are available on the deployment of police forces
    during strikes it is often clear that the police were using all means at their
    command to suppress the strike, but the manufacturers still complained
    that this effort was not enough because they wanted to increase the size

strikers and strike leaders were arrested on a number of charges, often fabricated, to get "troublemakers" off the streets. Finally, and most importantly, Chief of Police Daniel Morganstern ordered that the city be cleared of tramps. On August 20, the first day the order was in effect, Buffalo Captain Regan of the first precinct reported that 75 tramps were arrested (*Buffalo Express*, August 19-21, 1892). An *Express* reporter asked Morganstern what the purpose of his order was. The Chief responded:

> The idea is to get as many of these good for nothings as possible out of the way during the present difficulty, as they are apt to hang around with the strikers and incite them, and possibly many do mischief themselves. Besides it reduces the crowds so that it is easier to distinguish the classes of citizens with whom the police and militia have to deal. [*Buffalo Express*, August 21, 1892]

A close examination of these tramp arrests shows that the police could not tell tramps and workers apart. Harry Drew and William Brady, both railroad men, were arrested as tramps and given ten days each. Charles Williams and John Baken were scabs brought in to fill switchmen's jobs, who refused to work when they found there was a strike. They were charged and jailed as tramps, along with six other scabs jailed as vagrants. Drunks, loiterers, stone-throwers, and many more scabs were brought in from the first, second, seventh, and other precincts and given ten- and fifteen-day sentences for tramping. Eventually the newspapers stopped reporting individual arrests and noted simply: "a lot of bums and vagrants collected by the police in first precinct got ten days in the Pen," and "a large number of tramps and vagrants locked up in No. 9" (*Buffalo Express*, August 21-22, 1892).

The switchmen's strike received extensive working class support, which unsettled the Buffalo ruling class. "The whole strike principle is wrong," editorialized the *Express*, "it turns honest men into criminals and upholders of crime" (*Buffalo Express*, August 16, 1892). The idea that "bums and strangers and tramps" were responsible for the violence was attractive to all concerned—including the grand master of the switchmen's union who did not want responsibility for the mass action that was needed to win the union's strike. But no one could distinguish tramps from community residents and railroad men in practice as easily as they did in such statements.[18]

---

of the force, call up the militia, or deputize trusted men as reserve police. Brenda Shelton (1968) argues that the police in this strike were essentially neutral. Evidently this was the case, but that strike was very different from the switchmen's strike of 1892. Both sides were Irish, and the bourgeoisie split over which side to back. Moreover, predominantly Irish police officers were ordered to protect Polish and Italian scabs taking Irish scoopers' jobs, perhaps explaining some of the department's "neutrality." For a fuller discussion of the class position and loyalties of the police, see Bernstein *et al.* (1977).

18. Grand Master McSweeney's statement blaming the violence of the strike on tramps must be understood in the context of the period. Unions were

The increase in the number of workers arrested as tramps and the public clamor for strengthened antitramp measures were an expression of bourgeois perceptions of the tramp as a dangerous troublemaker in local labor relations. Even the grim statistics showing a doubling of tramp arrests in a three-year period do not reveal the full extent to which the criminal justice system was devoted to the repression of workers under the Tramp Acts. During the summers of 1893 and 1894 the Erie County Penitentiary held between 600 and 900 tramps much of the time, out of a prison population seldom exceeding those totals by much. Tramps were routinely given thirty- to ninety-day sentences, and they were virtually never able to pay their fines. Most other offenders were punished with $5 and $10 fines, or ten-day jail sentences. Tramps, then, filled the penitentiary out of proportion to their share of arrests because of the longer sentences they received and their inability to pay fines. They shared the penitentiary with accused awaiting trial, and convicts doing terms, for serious assaults or major property crimes. Not all of these tramps had been arrested in Buffalo, but only a few smaller cities, the largest of which was Niagara Falls, sent prisoners to the Erie County Penitentiary.

These prison statistics still conceal the viciousness of the police in dealing with the victims of unemployment and depression. Much of the violence was committed by police officers, but the overall policies originated with the upper echelon of police officials, the mayor, and local businessmen. Clarence Lucas, for example, a twenty-two-year-old resident of Columbus, Ohio, on his way to Boston where he had been promised a job, was one of six tramps "rolling peaceably into the city on the Lake Shore freight." Two police officers ordered them to drop off and fall in line. Four of them did, but Lucas and another ran, an understandable response given the prospect of a long jail term. The senior police officer, Sergeant Cottrell, opened fire with his revolver and shot Lucas in the calf of his leg (*Buffalo Express*, July 9, 1894).

Local papers encouraged this behavior. "Police in the ninth precinct are furiously in earnest in their attempt to clear their territory of tramps. The morning report to the Sergeant shows 40

---

not strongly established. They were treading a fine line between the need to organize strong mass actions to fight for their members' livelihoods and the class collaborationist AFL policy of seeking respect and recognition from the employers (Felice *et al.*, 1977). Thus while the strike was on, the union actively encouraged mass support by the Buffalo working class, and the working class turned out in great numbers. Since a large number of railroad workers were unemployed, there is no reason to doubt that substantial numbers of tramps were involved in this and other strikes. Thus the characterization of militant strikers as "tramps" probably has an element of truth in it, but it conceals the real issue: tramps were unemployed workers and this use of the term "criminalizes" militant workers and delegitimizes class struggle.

arrests on Saturday and every one of them a tramp." If such publicity was not sufficient to indicate its support, the *Express* a month later celebrated the efforts of Niagara Falls police and directly criticized the Buffalo police for throwing tramps out of town, rather than following orders and jailing them: "Twenty-one tramps were disposed of in Niagara Falls, most given 60-90 days in the penitentiary. Tramps are flowing into the city in generous and unwelcome numbers. The police have orders to gather them in at every turn. A few are sent to jail and others are given walking papers" (*Buffalo Express*, May 14; June 30, 1894).

This accusation of softness on the part of the Buffalo police did not take account of the facts that the population of the county penitentiary was reaching new heights almost daily, and that most of the new inmates were tramps. A contemporary observer visiting the Erie County Penitentiary found a large number of tramps "unloading a canal boat in the hot sun . . . they worked slowly and sullenly and had to be continually hustled by those who had them in charge." The prison was horribly overcrowded: the "Pen," a stone courtyard with two iron gates, held fifty tramps. Eight were packed in a small cell so closely that only the heads nearest the door were visible (*Buffalo Express*, May 31; June 23, 1894). Jack London, who served thirty days in the Erie County Penitentiary on tramp charges during June and July, 1894, described the scene from the inside: "I was forced to toil hard on a diet of bread and water and to march the shameful lock-step with armed guards over me—and for what? What had I done?"[19] London had been taken to the prison in a 16-man chain gang. There he was stripped, bathed, vaccinated, his hair was cropped, and he was clothed in a striped convict suit. Then he was locked in a small, vermin infested

---

19. Jack London was 18 when he was imprisoned in the Erie County Penitentiary. He had left Oakland in April of 1894, trailing Kelley's Army, the largest of the unemployed armies following Coxey's Army toward Washington. London caught up with Kelley near Omaha, marched with it to Hannibal, Missouri, deserting on May 24. By his own account, he refused to accept discipline and often roamed ahead begging for food and keeping the best for himself while the rest of the men went hungry. After deserting he "hoboed" to New York City where he slept, read, and drank ice-cold milk in City Hall Park until he was attacked from behind by a policeman. He fled to Niagara Falls to view the sights, and clumsily ran into a policeman. He was indignant over getting a 30-day sentence without even getting a chance to speak at his trial, and without the judge even going through the formality of finding him guilty. In prison, London quickly became a trusty and, like all the other trusties, used the position to exploit other inmates, engaging in graft for extra food, tobacco, and other minor privileges, such as mailing letters. This required using substantial brute force, since 13 trusties had to maintain their privileged position over 500 inmates in the cellblock: "We could not permit the slightest infraction of the rules, the slightest insolence. If we did we were lost. Our own rule was to hit a man as soon as he opened his mouth—hit him hard, hit him with anything" (London, 1970:110). Upon his release, London begged along the "main-drag" in Buffalo, and spent the money on "shupers" of beer. Later that day he hopped aboard a freight heading south toward Pennsylvania (Foner, 1947:14-21; London, 1970).

cell in a large "hall . . . built out of bricks and rising six stories high, each story a row of cells, say fifty cells in a row. . . . A narrow gallery, with a steel railing [ran] the full length of each tier of cells." Diet consisted of a ration of bread the size of two fists along with water in the form of "coffee" made with burnt bread crusts in the morning, "soup" with grease and salt added at lunch, and as a purplish "tea" at dinner. The work task was to unload huge stay-bolts from canal boats, carrying them over the shoulders like railroad ties, under the watchful eyes of guards with repeating rifles marching on top of the walls (London, 1970: 74-121).

In spite of these inhuman conditions, demands for increased repression contined. Editor George Mathews, a COS member, complained in his *Express*: "The Buffalo police are inactive compared to Niagara Falls. There are hundreds of tramps arriving daily, but the police instead of locking them up attempt to keep them out of town" (*Buffalo Express*, May 31, 1894). The Buffalo police were anything but inactive, but the fact that they were still being prodded illustrates the panic that was seizing the city's ruling bourgeoisie—reformers as well as traditional business leaders.

This panic, and the demand for increased repression of tramps, followed the failure of winter relief measures initiated by the COS in the fall of 1893 in response to the Polish bread riots in the Broadway Market (*Buffalo Express*, August 24-25, 1893). In December, at the request of the COS, Mayor Conrad Diehl invited a number of Buffalo's leading citizens to a meeting. The men agreed to subscribe $50,000 (later raised to $100,000) for a relief fund to pay men for jobs such as stonecutting, at wages fixed low enough not to attract unemployed from out of town. A committee composed largely of COS members, but including other wealthy citizens, was appointed to administer the program (Wilcox, 1895; *Buffalo Express*, December 17, 18, 1893; Shelton, 1976: chapter 6).

The relief program did not work, partly because of the nature of the COS program, and partly because wealthy reformers could not fully grasp the magnitude of the unemployment problem. Over 6,000 applied for relief jobs at 70 cents per day, a figure deliberately set very low so as to constitute the "work test" required by the COS to separate the deserving from the nondeserving poor. The large number who applied were mostly Italians and Poles because Irish, Germans, and Americans "would not work at such low wages" (about one-third the daily rate of a common laborer). Ultimately $64,000 was distributed to 6,277 workers, an average of about $10 each, which was hardly adequate to relieve a family in a Buffalo winter. The COS, refusing to accept its own work test as an adequate measure of who needed relief, began a policy of rigorous investigations to separate the deserving poor willing to work for 70 cents a day from the "frauds" willing to work for such wages although not truly in need. Using police and community informers as investigators they disqualified 2,006 of the first 3,450 enrolled in their relief program, and thereafter enrolled only those who came to them through COS procedures, or who were certified by other proper authority. The Catholic charities, Salvation Army, and working class church groups did not participate in the COS relief program because of its hard line against the poor and its rigid stand against all other "unorganized" forms of charity. COS insistence on investigation in the middle of a cold winter when thousands were obviously hungry, and its disqualification as "frauds" of men willing to work for 70 cents a day on outdoor manual jobs in winter, undermined its position among working class organizations (Shelton, 1976: chapter 6; Wilcox, 1895).

The repressive foundation of COS charity policies emerged very clearly in its analysis of the failure of the winter program. It blamed "imposters," especially among the Poles, and turned more strongly to the police to weed them out, with the support of the rest of the bourgeoisie. A request by the city's poormaster for an additional $30,000 for relief was opposed as unnecessary. The COS turned to increased repression and demand for work and savings that were unrealistic given the depression and high unemployment rate. Frederick Almy, local COS leader, announced that the COS was determined not to repeat the mistakes of the past year. "The system adopted and used last winter did almost as great harm as it did good. It seemed to put a sort of premium on poverty and many were given aid who were perfectly able to take care of themselves." Relief was not the solution. The previous winter had taken many by surprise. Now that summer was coming everyone had time to "practice strict economy" to make ready for the next winter, although the summer of 1894 was to produce even higher levels of unemployment (Shelton, 1976: 148).

The spring of 1894 brought with it conditions that challenged police, charity reformers, and Buffalo's entire bourgeoisie. Large-scale unemployment coupled with increasing labor militancy, particularly the threat of a nationwide railroad strike, made each of these groups more determined than ever to keep Buffalo free from tramps. Yet the number of tramps continued to increase, and editor Mathews saw conspiracy as the only explanation:

> The main cause of the sudden rush to this city appears to be the imminence of a railroad strike hereabouts. Tramps, like all vicious characters, revel in troubled times and a strike is like a picnic to them. Hence it is that whenever a strike is promised the road agents forsake the country and flock to the big cities.

> Much of the damage attributed to strikes is really the work of tramps. In nearly every case when a tramp is arrested in a strike he gives his occupation as a railroad man. [*Buffalo Express*, May 31, 1894]

This hard-line policy emerging from the winter relief program, coupled with a panicky fear among the ruling class of impending conflict brought an immediate response from the police force. Superintendent William S. Bull, a "good businessman" recently installed as a reform police superintendent, ordered the department to increase its repression of tramps. Rather than simply increasing the number of tramps arrested at railroad yards, the new policy called for a large-scale effort requiring the cooperation of the entire city government. The first victims of this new policy were Jeffries' Commonwealth, 350 strong, and "Count" Joseph Rybakowski's "industrial army," made up of 175 Chicago Poles and Bohemians. Both were bound for Washington, D.C.

Jeffries' Commonwealth and Rybakowski's Army were part of a nationwide movement of "industrial armies," closely linked to the Populist political movement (Pollack, 1962: chapter 2). Armies from many parts of the country set out for Washington to demand federally financed public works programs and work for everyone. Coxey's Army, the most famous of these brigades, left Massilon, Ohio, for Washington in March 1893. Coxey was arrested a month later at the Capitol as he presented his demands and was charged with walking on the grass (McMurry, 1970). All told, perhaps 10,000 workers joined these armies at one point or another. They captured the imagination of a large segment of the working class, and were strongly supported by many labor organizations, Populists, and socialists. Populist Governor Lewelling of Kansas issued a widely discussed "tramp circular" defending tramps and ordering the police to cease enforcing the Tramp Act. He carefully outlined the repressive nature of antitramp laws and detailed their adverse impact on the working class. Populist Governor Pennoyer of Oregon carried this one step further when he commented that he "didn't give one whoop" whether federal troops managed to catch tramp train stealers.[20]

Jeffries' Commonwealth had come from Seattle to Duluth by train, and there they had switched to Great Lakes vessels. The Buffalo press reported that they were heading for the city on the towed schooner *Grampian* and described them as "the worst looking freight ever." Two days later an editorial in the *Express* laid

---

20. Pollack (1962: chapter 2). Lawrence Goodwyn, who has written the best analysis of Populism, reprints the entire tramp circular, calling it "properly symbolic of the democratic legacy of Populism (1976:597-99).

out a plan for preventing their arrival, which the police and public officials later adopted:

> We do not want the expense of feeding them, the trouble of sending them to jail, or the difficulty of keeping police surveillance over them. They must be prevented from landing. This is a problem for authorities to solve in the next few days. Perhaps Dr. Wende will discover he has the authority to quarantine them 20 miles from the port unless they consent to sail away quietly. [*Buffalo Express*, July 21 and 23, 1894]

The next day the corporation counsel and the police chief's clerk spent a good deal of time "looking up the law," preparing to advise Superintendent Bull as to his duties. But Dr. Wende, the Commissioner of Health and a COS member, saved the day:

> . . . chances are that all of them will have sore legs if they do give the city a call. It may be that the vaccination (that all hoboes will be given) will not be of the ordinary kind. City Clerk Mark Hubbell has suggested that it might be a good idea to vaccinate them on their legs to prevent them from begging. Commissioner of Health Dr. Wende is seriously considering this suggestion. [*Buffalo Express*, July 24, 1894]

Superintendent Bull had announced that all the tramps would go to the penitentiary, but he was upstaged by the sadistic suggestion of the Health Commissioner. Jeffries' Commonwealth Army landed in Cleveland instead of Buffalo. According to the ship's captain, "they were all mechanics, engineers, sailors, cooks, barbers, all sorts, and a good class of men, clean and intelligent. Victims of the played out boom in Seattle. As trustworthy as any" (*Buffalo Express*, July 23, 26, 1894).

III. POLICE REPRESSION OF COUNT RYBAKOWSKI'S INDUSTRIAL ARMY

Unlike Jeffries' Commonwealth, "Count" Joseph Rybakowski's Army of Polish and Bohemian canal workers from Chicago managed to enter Buffalo, obtaining considerable support in the local Polish community and from organized labor.[21] For a time, the

---

21. Count Joseph Rybakowski was a civil engineer educated in Poland. He was 33 years old in 1894, had "crossed the Atlantic Ocean" several times, was fluent in seven or eight languages, and had worked in both New York City and Chicago. He gave his occupation as "editor of a Polish labor paper" in Chicago, and responded to charges that it was an Anarchist paper by saying that "according to the capitalist press all labor papers are Anarchist papers." Rybakowski had travelled widely in the United States, and knew at least a few members of the Buffalo Polish community. It is not clear whether he really was a count. The Buffalo papers strongly questioned this, but Rybakowski claimed that he was the last member of a noble family. His wife, described as a "young Polish girl" and "the brains of the whole outfit" carried all the cash and travelled ahead of the Army as an advance person, negotiating food and shelter with local officials (*Buffalo Express*, August 16, 17, 21, 28, 1894). There is no evidence that the Countess in fact was the leader of the Army, although her role was important. The charge that she was the "brains" seems best understood as a sexist insult aimed at the Count by the *Express*.

Buffalo bourgeoisie expressed its uneasiness over working class and immigrant challenges to the social order by repressing the tramp army. Rybakowski was a charismatic leader who refused to be bullied by authorities, and he continually mocked the police, the mayor, and other public officials. The tramp army offered a socialist political analysis of tramping which placed responsibility squarely on capitalist exploitation. This boldness was too much for the Buffalo bourgeoisie. By a major feat of personal diplomacy and the threat of massive resistance, the Count managed to delay for four days the execution of Police Superintendent Bull's threat to "vag" his entire 175-man army. Ultimately, however, the army suffered the roughest treatment inflicted on tramps in Buffalo. Two of them were shot by the police with cold-blooded premeditation, twenty were seriously clubbed, and 120 were arrested and jailed for terms of ten days to six months.

The Count's Army was well disciplined and nonviolent. When a farmer near Ashtabula, Ohio, shot one of the members of the Army without cause a number of the men had demanded revenge, but they obeyed the Count's order to march on. When the Army had become involved in a dispute over the use of an old pile of wood near Dunkirk, New York, the Count permitted his arrest by one deputy sheriff in spite of the anger of his men, and he paid for the wood and court costs (*Buffalo Courier*, August 18, 1894).

Upon nearing Buffalo, the Count sent his wife ahead to negotiate with the Mayor and the police. High city officials held a number of meetings to determine how to respond. Superintendent Bull insisted on "vagging" the entire Army, but more moderate voices prevailed. The decision to control and contain the Army, however, ultimately resulted from the Count's defiance of authority and his determination to proceed. When the Army overran a solitary police chief in nearby Hamburg, in the presence of Buffalo Superintendent Bull and Police Commissioner Charles Rupp, it seemed more expedient simply to let them pass through. On the way to Buffalo the Count told a reporter about a stormy meeting in Bull's office. "He made great threats as to what he was going to do with us. He doesn't like our crowd and we don't like or care for him." Another reporter questioned the Count about the prospect of being arrested: "Then the thought of being arrested has no fear for you?" "None whatsoever," responded the Count, "we are traveling in the cause of justice." The Army was met at the city

---

The Army had left Chicago on June 7, 1894. In addition to 175 men, it included two old provision wagons, drawn by old horses, and three banners saying, "Down with Plutocracy," "Fraternity, Equity, Liberty," and "Industrial Independence." The Army had been arrested once before, in Toledo, but had hurriedly been released and sent out of town (*Buffalo Express*, August 21, 1894).

limits by a mounted police patrol and escorted through the south-eastern corner of Buffalo to a farm just beyond the city limits. Although this farm had been loaned to the Army by John Makow-ski, a Polish real estate broker, he apparently did so without au-thority. The farm actually belonged to Father John Pitass, the leader of the Polish Roman Catholics, the Democratic political leader of the Polish community, and a wealthy businessman and real estate speculator. Pitass at once demanded that Police Cap-tain Frank Koehler, the antilabor captain of the eighth precinct, arrest all the tramps for "burning his fence." Koehler responded that the farm was outside of his jurisdiction and that Pitass should see Erie County Sheriff Isaac Taggert (*Buffalo Express*, August 20-21, 1894; *Buffalo Courier*, August 20, 1894; *Buffalo Evening News*, August 21, 1894).

Koehler and Pitass were controversial figures in the Polish community because they were identified with bourgeois efforts to use the police to repress working class unrest. Koehler, of German descent, carried out a disproportionate share of COS investiga-tions since he commanded the largest Polish precinct, and he shared the hard-line COS position. "They are hungry, but have not yet reached the starvation level," was his analysis. After the bread riots of 1893 he dismissed reports that the Poles were starving as "nonsense," pointing out that "almost all of them find enough money to pay their fines" (*Buffalo Express*, August 23-25, 1893; July 11, 1894). Pitass's leadership caused a major split in the Polish community. There were religious riots as parents took their children out of his Catholic schools, and a number of his parishioners left the Roman Catholic Church and formed a Protes-tant denomination. Koehler provided police officers to guard Pit-ass's priests in the saying of mass (Shelton, 1976:7-9).

This division in the Polish community occurred largely along class lines. The Polish neighborhood, located along Broadway on Buffalo's east side, numbered about 25,000 in 1893 and was rapid-ly expanding. Most of the wage earners were common laborers in heavy industry, the docks, and the railroad yards. So severely were the Poles affected by the depression that one newspaper reported that 5,000 were in "imminent danger of starvation." In August of 1893 there had been bread riots in the Broadway Market, followed by an orderly meeting of 5,000 Poles demanding public works jobs (*Buffalo Express*, August 23-25, 28, 1893). By the spring of 1894 the Polish community was even more militant. In June, 500 to 800 Poles marched on the offices of the mayor and the poor depart-ment demanding public works jobs and protesting inadequate poor relief, and had to be dispersed by the police. The editors blamed the disturbances on "anarchists and socialists" who lived among the Poles (*Buffalo Courier*, June 20, 1894; *Buffalo Express*, June 20, 1894). Similar marches followed in July (before the arrival of Rybakowski's Army) and in September (a month after the arrest of the Army). Thus Rybakowski arrived in the midst of an already tense situation, characterized by a high degree of class conflict. This high level of political mobilization occurred outside of existing local political structures. Pitass and Koehler were resented for different reasons: Koehler directed police repression of political meetings and strikes, while Pitass was seen as a wealthy opportunist leading the Polish community for his own selfish ends. Both opposed working class militancy, which Rybakowski effectively tapped (Shelton, 1976: 7-10, 140-48; Obidinski, 1970: chapter 1).

The Polish community strongly backed support of Rybakowski. The Count and his wife paid dozens of calls on community leaders, although some followed Father Pitass and refused to see them. This attention paid off handsomely. Three wagons of clothing and food were collected for the Army in the Polish community, including 400 pounds of sausage, 1,000 loaves of bread, 2 cases of whiskey, 4 kegs of beer, cigars and tobacco. Meetings were held in the Polish community to discuss the social questions raised by the Army. An undetermined number of local men joined; twenty residents of Buffalo were arrested when the Army was crushed, but at least sixty members of the Army escaped arrest, and persons from Buffalo were probably in a better position to do so (*Buffalo Courier*, August 21, 22, 1894).

Captain Koehler denied the existence of such support, repeatedly claiming that the Polish community was through with the tramps, and he harassed local Poles who supported Rybakowski. When a four-person committee was formed to feed the Army, Koehler sought out one of its leaders and found him loading bread into into a wagon at the Broadway Market. "Is that for the hoboes?" he demanded. "It seems to me that food might be distributed to better advantage!" (*Buffalo Evening News*, August 21, 1894). Superintendent Bull prevented the Count from accepting a three-day engagement at a Main Street theater by refusing to permit the speech. Extra police were dispatched to the main roads leading to the hobo camp with orders to prevent them from entering the city. Thirteen tramps who sneaked into the city were arrested, given ten days each, and segregated from other prisoners (*Buffalo Evening News*, August 21-22, 1894).

It was Sheriff Isaac Taggert, however, and not the repressive Superintendent Bull, who went to the hobo camp to investigate the condition of Pitass's fence and found it intact. He talked with the Count, looked at the hands of some of the men and, finding them calloused, announced that the men could stay three days. After leaving the camp Taggert gave a remarkably sympathetic interview.

> I felt a good deal of sympathy and provided them with bread. I thought they needed bread more than bullets. The only crime these fellows are guilty of that I know of is the crime of poverty, and if that is to be regarded as a crime it will come pretty near hitting most of us. When I saw their bruised feet and hands horny from the effects of toil I could not regard them as tramps. They are men out of employment like thousands of others. . . . The Polish people who are helping them are not doing it blindly without looking into the suffering which is at the bottom of the movement. They are really hard working Poles looking for jobs. [*Buffalo Courier*, August 22, 1894]

He sent the Army 300 loaves of bread at his personal expense. Yet despite this he ordered these same people shot, beaten, and arrested three days later.

Sheriff Taggert assumed a critical role in dealing with the Army because it had camped just outside city limits, within his jurisdiction but not that of the Buffalo police. He was the least experienced law enforcement officer involved, having only been in office since May. Taggert was a "dues paying" Democrat with no history of party involvement, who had been appointed to a five-month vacancy in the Sheriff's office when the previous sheriff was removed for vote fraud. He owned two downtown hotels and paid taxes on $100,000 worth of property (*Buffalo Express*, May 30, 1894). As the tramps had approached Buffalo, he had yielded to the demands of a group of wealthy homeowners on Lake Erie south of Buffalo, and deputized them. His friendly relationship with the wealthy lawyers and businessmen on the lake shore was critical in explaining the later attack on Rybakowski's Army. Taggert, who could give 300 loaves of bread to the tramps, could also sympathize with the requests of the wealthy to be sworn in as special deputies to "protect their property" from tramps. Among those sworn in was attorney Henry Ware Sprague, a COS leader who administered a fresh air camp for poor Polish children. While Taggert and others were attempting to arrange the peaceful departure of the tramp army, he was making alternate preparations for repression (*Buffalo Courier*, August 19, 22, 1894; *Buffalo City Directory*). Taggert's deceptively swift change of heart is more comprehensible in light of the change in the overall strategy of the Buffalo bourgeoisie toward Rybakowski's Army. When the Army first arrived, they hoped to speed it along through the city without open conflict. When this did not occur, they prepared the rout Taggert was to lead.

In the meantime the hobo camp was full of activity. There was a major effort to recruit additional members from among the local unemployed. Five hundred Buffalo residents paid 10 cents each for admission to the camp; indeed, since the gatekeepers refused to accept money from "fellow workingmen," the actual number of visitors was much higher. Thirteen tramps were responsible for security, and the entire scene was orderly. Local socialist orators kept the crowd's attention with speeches in Polish, German, and English, and socialist newspapers were distributed free. The Count was invited to an endless round of local meetings (*Buffalo Express*, August 22, 1894; *Buffalo Courier*, August 22, 1894).

The Count and his men were not accustomed to such favorable community response and were somewhat reluctant to leave Buffalo when the sheriff's deputy served them with an eviction notice on the morning of August 24. The previous afternoon it had been announced that the Army was going to move to Woodlawn Beach, a resort area on Lake Erie just south of Buffalo, at the invitation of John Titus, a hotelkeeper frequently charged with selling liquor to minors. Titus's motives are unknown, but his invitation provoked a storm of protest from the wealthy property owners nearby, many of whom had been made deputy sheriffs. William H. S. Otto of the Woodlawn Association announced that the property owners would meet the tramps with shotguns, and went off to see Sheriff Taggert. The series of meetings that followed led to a reversal of Taggert's earlier policy: a decision was made to oust the tramps. The Buffalo police, in consultation with Mayor Bishop, announced that they would carry out the hard line policy they had proclaimed four days earlier. Superintendent Bull warned: "I won't let them set foot in city limits. I am tired of hoboes." Bull, Mayor Bishop, and the city attorney deliberated about using the Buffalo police to dislodge the hoboes from their camp in Cheektowaga, but decided that the police could not legally act outside the city limits. A few hours later the Buffalo police led the charge on the hoboes—outside the city limits. Police officials, city officials, and businessmen jointly made this decision to smash the tramp army. Although notions of legality were strictly observed during discussions, the determination to violate the law by using the Buffalo police for an aggressive attack on a group of peaceable hoboes was also made at the highest level. Three captains leading four companies of officers were dispatched to the city limits. As soon as they arrived, they offered Sheriff Taggert all the support he needed: "I will back you with all my men and I've got enough to kill the whole outfit," promised Captain Killeen, the senior officer present.[22]

The scene immediately preceding the shooting and clubbing is relatively clear. After a deputy served the eviction notice the Count announced that the Army was not ready to leave and would stay as long as it liked. The deputy returned to the Sheriff's office and Taggert, in a fit of rage, announced that he was going to "lock up every damned one of those damned tramps as soon as he could get together a sufficient force of men." The qualification was critical because the Sheriff, unlike the police, did not command a large, disciplined force. His small number of regular deputies had to be augmented by the volunteers who flocked to his office for a chance to participate in the excitement of arresting a large force of tramps. Having failed to recruit private detectives and Buffalo police the Sheriff settled for what he could get: 35 to 40 volunteers, mostly small businessmen armed with their own guns and clubs. This crew, along with an equal contingent of Buffalo police not under Taggert's command, immediately started for the farm in a rented wagon. The half-hour trip was interrupted by a stop at a tavern in the stockyards for "refreshments." Here the Sheriff further incited his men to violence against the peaceful hoboes: "Now understand you're going in there for business. Go right in, don't stop for anything, and take that damned Count dead or alive. Handcuff him first and bring him here at once."

When the deputies arrived at the camp they found a scene of mass confusion. The men were gathered around the Count waiting for some kind of instruction, which was not forthcoming. Some of them picked up clubs from a fallen tree. A Buffalo police officer on horseback rode into the middle of the tramps and announced, "You unwashed dirty devils, you're under arrest, what the hell are you blowing about. Let these boys alone or we'll knock your heads on the other side of the fence." The Count calmed the situation by announcing that he would walk to the court. The men all insisted on standing by the Count and marched off with him (*Buffalo Evening News*, August 19, 24-25, 1894).

Along the way the Count and his men learned what lay in store for them, probably from a reporter. Judge Foster was waiting in his courtroom, a little anteroom off the bar in the roadhouse that he owned in Cheektowaga, 100 feet from the Buffalo line, with a clerk, a city attorney, and a pile of commitment forms that had been completed in advance. In fact, the evening papers had al-

---

22. *Buffalo Express*, August 25, 1894; *Buffalo Commercial*, August 23, 1894; *Buffalo Evening News*, August 24-25, 1894; *Buffalo Courier*, August 25, 1894. The three captains were Killeen, Kress, and Koehler.

ready put out extras announcing that the Count and other tramp leaders had each been given ninety days in the penitentiary and the rank and file ten. This revelation caused a great deal of anger and outrage among the marchers. When they arrived at the court they refused to enter but banded around the Count in a field across the street.

Although the hour walk from Buffalo to Cheektowaga had been uneventful Sheriff Taggert was still preoccupied with violent intentions. Along the road he met John O'Brien, a short stocky Irishman who was returning from hunting with a shotgun over his shoulder. Taggert immediately swore him in as a deputy. "Is that gun loaded?" demanded Taggert. "No Sir," responded O'Brien. "Well, load it," ordered Taggert. O'Brien evidently did not believe the order and did not comply. After a few moments the Sheriff again asked whether or not he had loaded the gun. When O'Brien acknowledged that he had not, Taggert was furious and commanded O'Brien to load the gun right there. It was O'Brien who later fired the first shot at the tramps (*Buffalo Evening News*, August 24-25, 1894; *Buffalo Express*, August 25, 1894).

The Count's refusal to walk inside the court confused the inexperienced Sheriff, who deferred to the Buffalo police. Captain Killeen took command and, mindful of the jurisdictional niceties, ordered the Sheriff to send his men to take the Count, promising to back them with all the Buffalo police present. It is unclear whether a deputy was sent to get the Count, followed immediately by a rush of deputies, mounted Buffalo police, and foot patrolmen, or whether the mounted Buffalo police actually led the charge. In either case, police and deputies beat the tramps for 3 to 5 minutes. The Buffalo Police Department's normal crowd control strategy was a well-disciplined, club-swinging charge, and this time they injured 20 hoboes with clubs, 9 seriously.

The extent of the gun-play is hard to determine. The newspapers, which all had reporters on the scene, reported that "bullets flew like hail." This account may be exaggerated, but it indicated some shotgun and pistol fire. It is clear that most of the shots were fired by Sheriff Taggert's deputies, who were largely small businessmen. It is questionable whether any of the hoboes fired weapons. All of the papers except one reported that they saw a "few" revolvers concealed in the hands of the tramps. A bullet grazed the head of a deputy, and the tramp who reportedly fired the shot suffered a shotgun blast in his leg. That exchange, however, occurred in the middle of a barrage of shooting by the deputies. If the tramps fired at all, they fired only a few times and then only after they had been fired upon by O'Brien in the initial confusion.

It was reported that as one of Taggert's deputies was about to murder the Count in cold blood, Captain Killeen reportedly saved his life by knocking the gun out of the deputy's hand (*Buffalo Evening News*, August 25, 1894; *Buffalo Express*, August 25, 1894; *Buffalo Commercial*, August 24, 1894).

In spite of all the injuries no one called an ambulance for twenty minutes. In the meantime a reporter described what he called the "Battle of Hobo Run":

> The level green field looked like a place of battle. Groaning men with blood streaming from heads and bodies lay prostrate on the field and the grass was dyed with blood. Miraculous no one killed—a score wounded, ten seriously. [*Buffalo Express*, August 25, 1894]

The sympathetic account above belies the hostility of the daily papers. They praised the police action and described the tramps in the worst terms they could muster:

> The hobo army of embryo Anarchists scattered like sheep after being shot and clubbed and the haughty Count became a cringing coward and begged for his life, crouching on his knees like a whipped cur. [*Buffalo Evening News*, August 25, 1894]

Within minutes Count Rybakowski's Industrial Army had been crushed by the Buffalo police and Taggert's deputies. No sooner had the ambulances cleared the scene than the remaining hoboes were lined up and hauled before the judge. The battle had caused a great deal of confusion, and it complicated the commitment process. Because longer sentences were now in order the judge had to fill out the commitment forms again. It took less than two hours to try all 70 men. The Count and ten other leaders received the longest hearing, and were finally bound over for felony indictments for assault, and committed to jail pending indictment.

The sentences of the others ranged from six months (the maximum under the Tramp Act) to discharge. As the *Express* reported: "It was a puzzle to discover the basis for discrimination in sentencing." The key variables appeared to be (1) whether or not the accused had a family; (2) length of "tramphood"; and (3) degree of dirtiness or raggedness. But these guidelines were followed erratically. About ten were discharged without punishment; most of these were from Buffalo and had just joined the Army, though a few were family men from Cleveland and Detroit. Other Buffalo residents were given jail terms, sentences which were illegal because the Tramp Act only applied to people outside their county of residence. The lengths of the sentences were deliberately staggered so that the men would be released and thrown out of town at different times to prevent regrouping. Much of the difference in sentence lengths was purely arbitrary.

By the time the judge had finished with the first 70 tramps, the police brought in 20 more picked up in a massive search of the area. These were also sentenced on the spot. It was now nightfall and the sheer number of prisoners made it impossible to take them to the penitentiary. Besides, Judge Foster did not have the commitment papers ready. The 90 men were held for the night in a nearby barn loaned for the purpose by George Urban, the flour magnate and one of Buffalo's leading citizens.

Judge Foster turned out to be more lenient than Judge King, whose court the next morning "looked like a hospital" as he tried eight of the most seriously injured hoboes who had been arrested after being treated at Fitch Hospital. King gave each a lecture and three months in the penitentiary:

> Why didn't you get work instead of going around with a horde of tramps. Your camp was a school for thieves and burglars and all of you will soon graduate as full fledged crooks. You would just as soon put a knife through a person as to look at him. [*Buffalo Commercial*, August 25, 1894]

The judge, like the press, the police, and the bourgeoisie, glibly defined unemployed workingmen without known criminal records as potential murderers so as to justify more severe punishment. To emphasize his point Judge King asked a reporter as he left court: "Did you have any trouble with them? You ought to have shot a few of them" (*Buffalo Express*, August 25, 1894).

By now almost 100 men had been transported to the penitentiary where the scene was one of mass confusion. They were kept in a large warehouse while prison officials waited for commitment forms. When these arrived the men were processed in small groups. They were bathed and clothed in prison stripes. The women's section was cleared and the tramps were locked eight to a cell on that block. Others were kept in a courtyard under conditions of terrible overcrowding with no place to sleep. A reporter for the conservative *Commercial* visited the prison and managed to use the inhumanity he witnessed to revile the inmates who were its victims. "Not an eye gleamed with intelligence or reflected a human soul," he wrote (*Buffalo Express*, August 26, 1894; *Buffalo Commercial*, August 25, 1894).

There remained the problem of the Count and ten other leaders held in jail awaiting charges. Three days later the district attorney decided not to seek felony indictments. He reasoned that an assault charge would not stand up in court because there was no evidence that the accused had assaulted anyone, and because no jury would convict given the Count's popularity with local workers. They were therefore taken back to Judge Foster's court in Cheektowaga to be tried as tramps. A heavy guard was necessary because the police were fearful that supporters would try to rescue the Count.

These supporters had hired the Count an attorney so that he, unlike the others, had some semblance of a trial. The major witnesses for the prosecution were two deputies who testified that they had seen the Count in the hobo camp and had heard him request more bread from the Sheriff. When the prosecution rested, the Count's attorney made a twenty-minute speech moving for a dismissal on the ground that the prosecution had not proven that any of the accused were tramps. Twenty members of the audience applauded. The motion was denied, and the Count took the stand. He protested that none of them were tramps, arguing that he was employed as a newspaper editor in Chicago and had $45 when he was arrested. Judge Foster convicted him and sentenced him to 90 days. The others got from 10 to 90 days as well, and they were all taken to the Erie County Penitentiary (*Buffalo Express*, August 28, 1894). As their sentences expired each was placed on a train and sent a short distance outside of the county. Every effort was made to get them out of town before winter.

President Reid of the CLU, a machinist who worked for the Lackawanna Railroad, vigorously criticized the police action. His statement reveals the class consciousness of the workers and their solidarity with the tramps:

> When I visited their camp they would not accept admission— wouldn't take money from a workingman. I looked around for the vicious, dirty, bloodthirsty tramps our press has been talking about all week but couldn't find any. I found them ragged but they had tried to improve themselves as much as they could with soap and water. I found that fifty of the men had union cards. The sheriff did good by giving them 300 loaves. How is it that he changed his mind so quickly and gave them bullets instead of bread; treating them like criminals instead of hardworking men? [*Buffalo Express*, August 27, 1894]

Other delegates characterized the sheriff's deputies as "vagrants who hung around city hall," and insisted that "there is not a workingman among them." During 1894 the CLU adopted at least three resolutions attacking the police for repression of working people (*Buffalo Courier*, August 27, 1894; *Buffalo Express*, August 27, 1894). The strongest of these was a response to the suppression of Rybakowski's army:

> Resolved that we the delegates to the CLU in regular meeting assembled do hereby emphatically denounce the said Sheriff Taggert and Superintendent Bull for the flagrant and high handed manner in which they violated the law and treated a body of heroic and self-reliant poor to imprisonment without cause, without reason, and without a semblance of a fair hearing. The indecent haste with which the aforesaid officials acted proves their unworthiness. [*Buffalo Express*, September 10, 1894]

Even such modest support was remarkable considering the danger from the police for working class groups who defended tramps.

Police Superintendent Bull had prevented a public meeting in a hired hall called to explain the purposes of Count Rybakowski's Army. Meetings to organize a joint Buffalo-Rochester contingent to join Coxey's Army had to be held in secret. The police even raided workers' homes in the Polish community looking for the remnants of Rybakowski's Army (*Buffalo Express*, March 28, 1894; August 23, 25-26, 1894). Even within the CLU, however, support for the tramps was not uniform or automatic. At its next meeting a sizable element challenged Reid's presidency, at least in part over his support of the tramps. But he was reelected with over two-thirds of the vote—clear evidence that the workers supported his defense of the rights of tramps.

IV. SUMMARY AND CONCLUSIONS

For three days Count Rybakowski and his "Industrial Army" of Chicago Polish and Bohemian workers were an important part of Buffalo's Polish and working class communities. The support and assistance that Rybakowski received mystified and frightened the ruling bourgeoisie. Mass meetings of up to 5,000 workers demanding jobs, bread riots of 500 or more, community support for striking switchmen so extensive that the police could not suppress it, and well over 1,000 visitors to a "hobo camp," all made it clear that existing class relations were undergoing a strong challenge. Rybakowski, in deciding to stay in Buffalo, posed a serious threat to the privileged position of the bourgeoisie by providing a catalyst for the dissatisfied, local working class. Whether or not Rybakowski's Army, its organizing, and its socialist politics, actually constituted such a threat cannot be known, but the fears of the bourgeoisie were aroused by what they saw: social disorder was frequent and intense. It was conflicts such as this, reproduced throughout the nation in the 1890s, that demonstrated the repressive potential of the Tramp Acts to impose severe sentences on large numbers of workers for trivial offenses.

But the repressive rules of the Tramp Acts are only a part of the story. The pattern of enforcement, both legal and illegal, substantially increased the level of repression. Marginally employed and unemployed workers were seldom able to secure effective redress for wrongs suffered at the hands of police and lower courts. Tramp Act cases were summarily tried before a local justice without a jury, pitting the testimony of a "tramp" against that of a police officer. Strident demands for repression of tramps by local newspapers, businessmen, and frightened citizens encouraged abuses, as did the generally "panicky" atmosphere. The contemporary literature abounds with examples of illegal behavior by police and judges, as well as lawful decisions that produced serious injustice. Often such behavior was lauded as an example of effective local policing. *Forum*, a journal of nineteenth-century reformers, carried an article on the "Rahway Plan," whereby tramps were "arrested on sight and put to hard labor on the streets in chain gangs." This method was supposedly highly successful, but had to be abandoned because it was illegal and "any of the tramps so treated could have sued the city for damages" (Rood, 1898). However, such a suit was not likely since, as a Maryland judge noted, "if these vagabonds do not think the tramp law is constitutional let them raise a fund and carry their case to the appellate" (Hubbard, 1894: 597). The *Express* editorialized against an article on the rights of tramps in *Arena* (a liberal journal of commentary on social issues), saying that "it was more worried about stopping them than in protecting their rights" (*Buffalo Express*, March 26, 1894). Most of the Buffalo victims of the Tramp Act are anonymous. Count Rybakowski and his men were only a few of the 13,502 people locked up as tramps and the 14,973 jailed as vagrants in Buffalo between 1890 and 1895. None of them had any rights in Buffalo, and Buffalo was not atypical.

This analysis of the broad and sweeping power of the state under the Tramp Act parallels Caleb Foote's (1956:603) study of the administration of "vagrancy-type" law in Philadelphia in the 1950s. Such laws serve to secure the banishment of unwanted persons, to harass and control suspicious persons, and to provide a "catchall" criminal statute under which to arrest and punish those who are "otherwise not demonstrably guilty of any crime." Elbert Hubbard noted that the Tramp Act, subjected every member of the working class to arrest and jail for any act that challenged existing class relations:

> . . . this rule of convicting of vagrancy on general principles is to be seen daily in every police court. Prisoners are run in on every conceivable charge, and where the testimony is not sufficient to convict the judge gives the victim thirty days for vagrancy. [Hubbard, 1894: 596-98]

Analysis of reported tramp convictions in the Buffalo press revealed almost every conceivable form of abuse, corroborating Hubbard's analysis. In addition to strikers, scabs, and traveling workers, the Buffalo police also arrested local loiterers, troublemakers, and the husband of a suspected prostitute on tramp charges. Strict legal requirements were ignored: under New York law one could not be a tramp in his own county of residence, but Buffalo residents were convicted as tramps on a number of occasions.

Analysis of the economic, political, and social context of Buffalo's antitramp repression illustrates the class basis of legal repression. A complex network of social relations, shaped by class struggle, determined the antitramp policies that emerged in Buffalo. These social relations extended across the community, involving a half-dozen units of city and county government, traditional commercial and manufacturing interests, reformers, newspapers, and different segments of the Polish community and organized labor. At each stage the impact of changing class relations in a period of intense class conflict had an important impact on the law and on the police.

Class struggle, in a very real sense, accounted for much of the uncertainty and changing policies of those who repressed the tramps. The original plan to stop Rybakowski from entering the city, as Jeffries had been stopped, was blocked by the Army's determination shown in its first confrontation with Superintendent Bull and Police Commissioner Rupp. The Army's reinforcement of the split in the Polish community led to the first public demand that it be repressed. Debate over the charity policies that applied to tramps was reproduced in class struggle over the organization of labor. This analysis of the actual process of decision making underlying the enforcement of criminal law in a community shows that the law is not above class struggle, but another arena in which it occurs.

The class basis of police and charity reform makes inadequate the traditional analysis of "repressors versus reformers." The fundamental purpose of both groups was to preserve the existing class society, and their differences were largely tactical. Moreover, a given person or group moved back and forth between repressive and nonrepressive tactics. By 1893-94, for example, the COS was coming to recognize that unemployment was not effectively controlled by police repression, and it began to organize employment exchanges and other forms of relief. However, heightened class conflict resulted in increasing emphasis on police repression until the immediate crisis abated and the reformers once again had sufficient breathing space to organize less repressive programs. Selection of the most effective tactics for class control depended on the view held by the ruling bourgeoisie of the social context within which it operated, rather than on abstract principles that can easily be labeled "repressive" or "humanitarian."

APPENDIX

AN ACT concerning tramps
(NEW YORK STATUTES, 1885; chapter 490)

passed June 11, 1885

§ 1. Every tramp, upon conviction as such, shall be punished by imprisonment at hard labor in the nearest penitentiary for not more than six months, the expense during such imprisonment not to exceed one dollar a week per capita, to be paid by the state.

§ 2. All persons who rove about from place to place begging, and all vagrants living without labor or visible means of support, who stroll over the country without lawful occupation, shall be held to be tramps within the meaning of this act.

§ 3. Any act of vagrancy by any person not a resident of this state shall be evidence that the person committing the same is a tramp within the meaning of this act.

§ 4. Any tramp who shall enter any building against the will of the owner or occupant thereof, under such circumstances as shall not amount to burglary, or willfully or maliciously injure the person or property of another, which injury under existing law does not amount to a felony, or shall be found carrying any firearms or other dangerous weapon, or a burglars tools, or shall threaten to do any injury to any person or to the real or personal property of another, when such offense is not now punishable by imprisonment in the state prison, shall be deemed guilty of a felony, and on conviction, shall be punished by imprisonment in the state prison at hard labor for not more than three years.

§ 5. Any person being a resident of the town where the offense is committed may, upon view of any offense described in this act, apprehend the offender and take him before a justice of the peace or the competent authority.

§ 6. This act shall not apply to any person under the age of sixteen years, nor to any blind person, nor to any person roving within the limits of the county in which he resides.

§ 7. Any person convicted under this act shall be entitled to the same commutations of sentence as now provided by law for any prisoner committed to the state prison or penitentiary.

§ 8. This act shall take effect immediately.

REFERENCES

ADAMS, Charles Ely (1902) "The Real Hobo: What He Is and How He Lives," 33 *Forum* 438.

ALMY, Frederick (1895) "Excise and Charity in Buffalo," 4 *The Charities Review* 319.

ANDERSON, Nels (1924) *The Hobo.* Chicago: University of Chicago Press.

BAILEY, E. Lamar (1898) "Tramps and Hoboes," 26 *Forum* 217.

BERNSTEIN, Susie, Lynn COOPER, Elliott CURRIE, Jon FRAPPIER, Sidney HARRING, Tony PLATT, Pat POYNER, Gerda RAY, Joy SCRUGGS, and Larry TRUJILLO (1977) *The Iron Fist and the Velvet Glove: An Analysis of the U.S. Police* (2d ed.). Oakland, California: Center for Research on Criminal Justice.

BRADSHAW, J.W. (1896) "The Treatment of Tramps in Small Cities," 7 *The Charities Review* 335.

BREIR, A.L. (1974) "Vagrants and the Social Order in Elizabethan England," 64 *Past and Present* 3.

BRUCE, Robert (1970) *1877: Year of Violence.* Chicago: Quadrangle.

BUFFALO POLICE DEPARTMENT (1873-1900) *Annual Report of the Chief of Police.*

CHAMBLISS, William (1964) "A Sociological Analysis of the Law of Vagrancy," 12 *Social Problems* 69.

CLOSSON, Carlos C. (1894a) "The Unemployed in American Cities," (part I) 7 *Quarterly Journal of Economics* 168.

———(1894b) "The Unemployed in American Cities," (part II) 7 *Quarterly Journal of Economics* 453.

COMMONS, John R. (1926) *History of Labor in the United States* (vol. II). New York: Macmillan.

DACUS, J.A. (1969) *Annals of the Great Strikes.* New York: Arno Press.

DILWORTH, Donald C. (1976) *The Blue and the Brass: American Policing 1890-1910.* Gaithersburg, Md.: International Association of Chiefs of Police.

DUNN, Walter S. (1972) *History of Buffalo and Erie County.* Buffalo: Buffalo and Erie County Historical Society.

ELY, Richard (1893) "The Unemployed" *Harpers Weekly* 845 (September 2).

FELICE, Bill, Nancy STEIN and Jon FRAPPIER. (1977) "Boss and Bureaucrat," 11 *North American Congress on Latin America: Latin America and Empire Report* 5, 3.

FONER, Philip S. (1947) *Jack London: American Rebel.* Secaucus, N.J.: The Citadel Press.

——— (1955) *History of the Labor Movement in the United States* (vol. II). New York: International.

FOOTE, Caleb (1956) "Vagrancy-type Law and Its Administration," 104 *University of Pennsylvania Law Review* 603.

FOSTER, William Z. (1939) *Pages From a Worker's Life.* New York: International.

GOODWYN, Lawrence (1976) *Democratic Promise: The Populist Movement in America.* New York: Oxford University Press.

GOULD, E.R.L. (1894) "How Baltimore Banished Tramps and Helped the Idle," 17 *Forum* 597.

GUTMAN, Herbert (1959a) "An Iron Workers' Strike in the Ohio Valley, 1873-74," 68 *Ohio Historical Quarterly* 353.

——— (1959b) "Two Lockouts in Pennsylvania: 1873-1874," 83 *Pennsylvania Magazine of History and Biography* (July) 307-326.

——— (1964) "The Buena Vista Affair, 1874-75," 88 *Pennsylvania Magazine of History and Biography*, 153.

———(1968a) "The Tompkins Square Riot in New York City on January 13, 1874: A Re-examination of Its Causes and Its Aftermath," 9 *Labor History* 44.

——— (1968b) "Class, Status, and Community Power in Nineteenth Century American Industrial Cities—Paterson, New Jersey: A Case Study," in Frederick Cople Jaher, *The Age of Industrialism in America.* New York: The Free Press.

HARRING, Sidney (1975) "The Buffalo Police: 1872-1900: Labor Unrest, Political Power and the Creation of the Police Institution," 4 *Crime and Social Justice* 5.

——— (1976) *The Buffalo Police—1872-1915: Industrialization, Social Unrest, and the Development of the Police Institution.* Ph.D. Dissertation, Department of Sociology, University of Wisconsin, Madison.

HAY, Douglas, Peter LINEBAUGH, John G. RULE, E.P. THOMPSON and Cal WINSLOW (1975) *Albion's Fatal Tree: Crime and Society in Eighteenth-Century England.* New York: Pantheon.

HAYS, Samuel (1964) "The Politics of Reform in Municipal Government in the Progressive Era," 55 *Pacific Northwest Quarterly* 157.

HOFFMAN, Charles (1956) "The Depression of the Nineties," 16 *Journal of Economic History* 137.

HUBBARD, Elbert (1894) "The Rights of Tramps," 53 *Arena* 593.

HUBBELL, Mark (1893) *Our Police and Our City.* Buffalo: Bensler and Wesley.

JOHNSON, Bruce (1976) "Taking Care of Labor: The Police in American Politics," 3 *Theory and Society* 89.

LEA, Henry Charles (1894) "The Increase of Crime and Positivist Criminology," 17 *Forum* 674.

LEAVITT, Samuel (1886) "The Tramps and the Law," 2 *Forum* 190.

LEONARD, Frank (1966) " 'Helping' the Unemployed in the Nineteenth Century: The Case of the American Tramp," 40 *Social Service Review* 429.

LINEBAUGH, Peter (1976) "Karl Marx, the Theft of Wood, and Working Class Composition: A Contribution to the Current Debate," 6 *Crime and Social Justice* 5.

LONDON, Jack (1970) *The Road.* Santa Barbara, Calif.: Peregrine Publishers.

LOWELL, Josephine Shaw (1894) "Methods of Relief for the Unemployed," 16 *Forum* 659.
—— (1896) "The True Aim of Charity Organization Societies," 21 *Forum* 494.
LUHAN, Mabel Dodge (1933) *Intimate Memories*. New York: Harcourt.
MacTEGGART, Rorie (1940) *A Labor History of Buffalo*. M.A. Thesis, Department of History, Canisus College, Buffalo.
MARX, Karl (1967) *Capital*, (vol. 1). New York: International.
McCOOK, J.J. (1892a) "Some New Phases of the Tramp Problem," 1 *The Charities Review* 355.
—— (1892b) "The Alarming Proportion of Venal Voters," 14 *Forum* 1.
—— (1893a) "A Tramp Census and Its Revelations," 15 *Forum* 753.
—— (1893b) "Tramps," 3 *The Charities Review* 57.
McMURRY, Donald L. (1970) *Coxey's Army*. New York: Arno Press.
MILLIS, Harry A. (1898) "The Law Affecting Immigrants and Tramps," 7 *The Charities Review* 587.
OBIDINSKI, Eugene (1970). *From Ethnic to Status Group: A Study of Polish Americans in Buffalo*. Ph.D. Dissertation, Department of Sociology, State University of New York at Buffalo.
PALMER, John (1967) *Some Antecedents of Progressivism in Buffalo*. Ph.D. Dissertation, Department of History, State University of New York at Buffalo.
POLLACK, Norman (1962) *The Populist Response to Industrial America*. Cambridge, Mass.: Harvard University Press.
POWELL, Elwin H. (1962) "The Evolution of the American City and the Emergence of Anomie: A Culture Case Study of Buffalo, New York, 1810-1910," 13 *British Journal of Sociology* 156.
REZNICK, Samuel (1953) "Unemployment, Unrest and Relief in the United States during the Depression of 1893-97," 61 *Journal of Political Economy* 324.
RINGENBACH, Paul T. (1973) *Tramps and Reformers: The Discovery of Unemployment in New York, 1873-1916*. Westport: Greenwood Press.
ROOD, Henry E. (1898) "The Tramp Problem: A Remedy," 25 *Forum* 90.
SCHWENDINGER, Herman and Julia SCHWENDINGER (1976) "Collective Varieties of Youth," 5 *Crime and Social Justice* 5.
SEELYE, John B. (1963) "The American Tramp: A Version of the Picaresque," 15 *American Quarterly* 535.
SHELTON, Brenda (1968) "The Buffalo Grain Shovellers' Strike of 1899," 9 *Labor History* 210.
—— (1976) *Reformers in Search of Yesterday: Buffalo in the 1890s*. Albany: State University of New York Press.
TAWNEY, Richard Henry (1967) *The Agrarian Problem in the Sixteenth Century*. New York: Harper & Row.
THOMPSON, Edward P. (1975) *Whigs and Hunters: The Origin of the Black Act*. New York: Pantheon.
TYLER, Robert Lawrence (1967) *Rebels of the Woods: The I.W.W. in the Pacific Northwest*. Eugene: University of Oregon Books.
WATSON, Frank Dekker (1922) *The Charity Organization Movement in the United States*. New York: Macmillan.
WILCOX, Ansley (1895) "Concerning Labor Tests," 4 *The Charities Review* 119.
WOODS, Joseph Gerald (1973) *The Progressives and the Police: Urban Police Reform and the Professionalization of the Los Angeles Police*. Ph.D. Dissertation, Department of History, University of California, Los Angeles.

11

THE RULE OF LAW

E. P. THOMPSON

We might be wise to end here. But since readers of this study may be provoked to some general reflections upon the law and upon British traditions, perhaps we may allow ourselves the same indulgence.

From a certain traditional middle ground of national historiography the interest of this theme (the Black Act and its evolution) may be evident. But this middle ground is now being eroded, from at least two directions. On one hand the perspective within which British political and social historians have been accustomed to view their own history is, quite properly, coming under challenge. As the last imperial illusions of the twentieth century fade, so preoccupation with the history and culture of a small island off the coast of Europe becomes open to the charge of narcissism. The culture of constitutionalism which flowered here, under favoured conditions, is an episode too exceptional to carry any universal significance. If we judge it in terms of its own self-sufficient values we are imprisoned within its own parochialism.

Alternative perspectives must diminish the complacency of national historical preoccupation. If we see Britain within the perspective of the

---

1. Paxton's letter of 24 March 1736, SP36.38, fo. 191; Crown briefs in TS11.725.2285 and 11.1122.5824; for case law, Cas. T. Hard. 291-2 and above, p. 210; for Reynolds and his execution, *ON*, 26 July 1736, and (for a slightly different account of his death) P. Linebaugh in *Albion's Fatal Tree*, pp. 103-4.

2. J. H. Plumb, *The Growth of Political Stability in England, 1675-1725*, 1969, *passim* and p. 188.

expansion of European capitalism, then the contest over interior rights and laws will be dwarfed when set beside the exterior record of slave-trading, of the East India Company, of commercial and military imperialism. Or, to take up a bright new conservative perspective, the story of a few lost common rights and of a few deer-stealers strung from the gallows is a paltry affair when set beside the accounts of mass repression of almost any day in the day-book of the twentieth century. Did a few foresters get a rough handling from partisan laws? What is that beside the norms of the Third Reich? Did the villagers of Winkfield lose access to the peat within Swinley Rails? What is that beside the liquidation of the *kulaks*? What is remarkable (we are reminded) is not that the laws were bent but the fact that there was, anywhere in the eighteenth century, a rule of law at all. To ask for greater justice than that is to display mere sentimentalism. In any event, we should adjust our sense of proportion; against the handfuls carried off on the cart to Tyburn (and smaller handfuls than have been carried off in Tudor times) we must see whole legions carried off by plague or dearth.

From these perspectives concern with the rights and wrongs at law of a few men in 1723 is concern with trivia. And the same conclusion may be reached through a different adjustment of perspective, which may coexist with some of the same arguments. This flourishes in the form of a sophisticated, but (ultimately) highly schematic Marxism which, to our surprise, seems to spring up in the footsteps of those of us in an older Marxist tradition. From this standpoint the law is, perhaps more clearly than any other cultural or institutional artifact, by definition a part of a 'superstructure' adapting itself to the necessities of an infrastructure of productive forces and productive relations. As such, it is clearly an instrument of the *de facto* ruling class: it both defines and defends these rulers' claims upon resources and labour-power – it says what shall be property and what shall be crime – and it mediates class relations with a set of appropriate rules and sanctions, all of which, ultimately, confirm and consolidate existing class power. Hence the rule of law is only another mask for the rule of a class. The revolutionary can have no interest in law, unless as a phenomenon of ruling-class power and hypocrisy; it should be his aim simply to overthrow it. And so, once again, to express surprise at the Black Act or at partial judges is – unless as confirmation and illustration of theories which might easily be demonstrated without all this labour – simply to expose one's own naivety.

So the old middle ground of historiography is crumbling on both sides. I stand on a very narrow ledge, watching the tides come up. Or, to be more explicit, I sit here in my study, at the age of fifty, the desk and the floor piled high with five years of notes, xeroxes, rejected drafts, the clock once again moving into the small hours, and see myself, in a lucid instant, as an anachronism. Why have I spent these years trying to find out what could, in its essential structures, have been known without any investigation at all? And does it matter a damn who gave Parson Power his instructions; which forms brought 'Vulcan' Gates to the gallows; or how an obscure Richmond publican managed to evade a death sentence already determined upon by the Law Officers, the First Minister and the King?

I am disposed to think that it does matter; I have a vested interest (in five years of labour) to think it may. But to show this must involve evacuating received assumptions – that narrowing ledge of traditional middle ground – and moving out onto an even narrower theoretical ledge. This would accept, as it must, some part of the Marxist–structural critique; indeed, some parts of this study have confirmed the class-bound and mystifying functions of the law. But it would reject its ulterior reductionism and would modify its typology of superior and inferior (but determining) structures.

First, analysis of the eighteenth century (and perhaps of other centuries) calls in question the validity of separating off the law as a whole and placing it in some typological superstructure. The law when considered as institution (the courts, with their class theatre and class procedures) or as personnel (the judges, the lawyers, the Justices of the Peace) may very easily be assimilated to those of the ruling class. But all that is entailed in 'the law' is not subsumed in these institutions. The law may also be seen as ideology, or as particular rules and sanctions which stand in a definite and active relationship (often a field of conflict) to social norms; and, finally, it may be seen simply in terms of its own logic, rules and procedures – that is, simply *as law*. And it is not possible to conceive of any complex society without law.

We must labour this point, since some theorists today are unable to see the law except in terms of 'the fuzz' setting about inoffensive demonstrators or cannabis-smokers. I am no authority on the twentieth century, but in the eighteenth century matters were more complex than that. To be sure I have tried to show, in the evolution of the Black Act, an expression of the ascendancy of a Whig oligarchy, which created new laws and bent old legal forms in order to legitimize its own property and status; this oligarchy employed the law, both instrumentally and ideologically, very much as a modern structural Marxist should expect it to do. But this is not the same thing as to say that the rulers had need of law, in order to oppress the ruled, while those who were ruled had need of none. What was often at issue was not property, supported by law, against no-property; it was alternative definitions of property-rights: for the landowner, enclosure – for the cottager, common rights; for the forest officialdom, 'preserved grounds' for the deer; for the foresters, the right to take turfs. For as long as it remained possible, the ruled – if they could find a purse and a lawyer – would actually fight for their rights by means of law; occasionally the copyholders, resting upon the precedents of sixteenth-century law, could actually win a case. When it ceased to be possible to continue the fight at law, men still felt a sense of legal wrong: the propertied had obtained their power by illegitimate means.

Moreover, if we look closely into such an agrarian context, the distinction between law, on the one hand, conceived of as an element of 'superstructure', and the actualities of productive forces and relations on the other hand, becomes more and more untenable. For law was often a definition of actual agrarian *practice*, as it had been pursued 'time out of mind'. How can we distinguish between the activity of farming or of quarrying and the rights to this strip of land or to that quarry? The farmer or forester in his daily occupation was moving within visible or invisible structures of law: this merestone which marked the division between strips; that ancient oak – visited by processional on each Rogation Day – which marked the limits of the parish grazing; those other invisible (but potent and sometimes legally enforceable) memories as to which parishes had the right to take turfs in this waste and which parishes had not; this written or unwritten customal which decided how many stints on the common land and for whom – for copyholders and freeholders only, or for all inhabitants?

Hence 'law' was deeply imbricated within the very basis of productive relations, which would have been inoperable without this law. And, in the second place, this law, as definition or as rules (imperfectly enforceable through institutional legal forms), was endorsed by norms, tenaciously transmitted through the community. There were alternative norms; that is a matter of course; this was a place, not of consensus, but of conflict. But we cannot, then, simply separate off all law as ideology, and assimilate this also to the state apparatus of a ruling class. On the contrary, the norms of foresters might reveal themselves as passionately supported values, impelling them upon a course of action which would lead them into bitter conflict – with 'the law'.

So we are back, once again, with *that* law: the institutionalized procedures of the ruling class. This, no doubt, is worth no more of our theoretical attention; we can see it as an instrument of class power *tout court*. But we must take even this formulation, and see whether its crystalline clarity will survive immersion in scepticism. To be sure, we can stand no longer on that traditional ground of liberal academicism, which offers the eighteenth century as a society of consensus, ruled within the parameters of paternalism and deference, and governed by a 'rule of law' which attained (however imperfectly) towards impartiality. That is not the society which we have been examining; we have not observed a society of consensus; and we have seen the law being devised and employed, directly and instrumentally, in the imposition of class power. Nor can we accept a sociological refinement of the old view, which stresses the imperfections and partiality of the law, and its subordination to the functional requirements of socio-economic interest groups. For what we have observed is something more than the law as a pliant medium to be twisted this way and that by whichever interests already possess effective power. Eighteenth-century law was more substantial than that. Over and above its pliant, instrumental functions it existed in its own right, as ideology; as an ideology which not only served, in most respects, but which also legitimized class power. The hegemony of the eighteenth-century gentry and aristocracy was expressed, above all, not in military force, not in the mystifications of a priesthood or of the press, not even in economic coercion, but in the rituals of the study of the Justices of the Peace, in the quarter-sessions, in the pomp of Assizes and in the theatre of Tyburn.

Thus the law (we agree) may be seen instrumentally as mediating and reinforcing existent class relations and, ideologically, as offering to these a legitimation. But we must press our definitions a little further. For if we say that existent class relations were mediated by the law, this is not the same thing as saying that the law was no more than those relations translated into other terms, which masked or mystified the reality. This may, quite often, be true but it is not the whole truth. For class relations were expressed, not in any way one likes, but *through the forms of law*; and the law, like other institutions which from time to time can be seen as mediating (and masking) existent class relations (such as the Church or the media of communication), has its own characteristics, its own independent history and logic of evolution.

Moreover, people are not as stupid as some structuralist philosophers suppose them to be. They will not be mystified by the first man who puts on a wig. It is inherent in the especial character of law, as a body of rules and procedures, that it shall apply logical criteria with reference to standards of universality and equity. It is true that certain categories of person may be excluded from this logic (as children or slaves), that other categories may be debarred from access to parts of the logic (as women or, for many forms of eighteenth-century law, those without certain kinds of property), and that the poor may often be excluded, through penury, from the law's costly procedures. All this, and more, is true. But if too much of this is true, then the consequences are plainly counterproductive. Most men have a strong sense of justice, at least with regard to their own interests. If the law is evidently partial and unjust, then it will mask nothing, legitimize nothing, contribute nothing to any class's hegemony. The essential precondition for the effectiveness of law, in its function as ideology, is that it shall display an independence from gross manipulation and shall seem to be just. It cannot seem to be so without upholding its own logic and criteria of equity; indeed, on occasion, by actually *being* just. And furthermore it is not often the case that a ruling ideology can be dismissed as a mere hypocrisy; even rulers find a need to legitimize their power, to moralize their functions, to feel themselves to be useful and just. In the case of an ancient historical formation like the law, a discipline which requires years of exacting study to master, there will always be some men who actively believe in their own procedures and in the logic of justice. The law may be rhetoric, but it need not be empty rhetoric. Blackstone's *Commentaries* represent an intellectual exercise far more rigorous than could have come from an apologist's pen.

I do not know what transcultural validity these reflections may have. But they are certainly applicable to England in the eighteenth century. Douglas Hay, in a significant essay in *Albion's Fatal Tree*, has argued that the law assumed unusual pre-eminence in that century, as the central legitimizing ideology, displacing the religious authority and sanctions of previous centuries. It gave way, in its turn, to economic sanctions and to the ideology of the free market and of political liberalism in the nineteenth. Turn where you will, the rhetoric of eighteenth-century England is saturated with the notion of law. Royal absolutism was placed behind a high hedge of law; landed estates were tied together with entails and marriage settlements made up of elaborate tissues of law; authority and property punctuated their power by regular 'examples' made upon the public gallows. More than this, immense efforts were made (and Hay has explored the forms of these) to project the image of a ruling class which was itself subject to the rule of law, and whose legitimacy rested upon the equity and universality of those legal forms. And the rulers were, in serious senses, whether willingly or unwillingly, the prisoners of their own rhetoric; they played the games of power according to rules which suited them, but they could not break those rules or the whole game would be thrown away. And, finally, so far from the ruled shrugging off this rhetoric as a hypocrisy, some part of it at least was taken over as part of the rhetoric of the plebeian crowd, of the 'free-born Englishman' with his inviolable privacy, his *habeas corpus*, his equality before the law. If this rhetoric was a mask, it was a mask which John Wilkes was to borrow, at the head of ten thousand masked supporters.

So that in this island and in that century above all one must resist any slide into structural reductionism. What this overlooks, among other things, is the immense capital of human struggle over the previous two centuries against royal absolutism, inherited, in the forms and traditions of the law, by the eighteenth-century gentry. For in the sixteenth and seventeenth centuries the law had been less an instrument of class power than a central arena of conflict. In the course of conflict the law itself had been changed; inherited by the eighteenth-century gentry, this changed law was, literally, central to their whole purchase upon power and upon the means of life. Take law away, and the royal prerogative, or the presumption of the aristocracy, might flood back upon their properties and lives; take law away and the string which tied together their lands and marriages would fall apart. But it was inherent in the very nature of the medium which they had selected for their own self-defence that it could not be reserved for the exclusive use only of their own class. The law, in its forms and traditions, entailed principles of equity and universality which, perforce, had to be extended to all sorts and degrees of men. And since this was of necessity so, ideology could turn necessity to advantage. What had been devised by men of property as a defence against arbitrary power could be turned into service as an apologia for property in the face of the propertyless. And the apologia was serviceable up to a point: for these 'propertyless', as we have seen, comprised multitudes of men and women who themselves enjoyed, in fact, petty property rights or agrarian use-rights whose definition was inconceivable without the forms of law. Hence the ideology of the great struck root in a soil, however shallow, of actuality. And the courts gave substance to the ideology by the scrupulous care with which, on occasion, they adjudged petty rights, and, on all occasions, preserved proprieties and forms.

We reach, then, not a simple conclusion (law = class power) but a complex and contradictory one. On the one hand, it is true that the law did mediate existent class relations to the advantage of the rulers; not only is this so, but as the century advanced the law became a superb instrument by which these rulers were able to impose new definitions of property to their even greater advantage, as in the extinction by law of indefinite agrarian use-rights and in the furtherance of enclosure. On the other hand, the law mediated these class relations through legal forms, which imposed, again and again, inhibitions upon the actions of the rulers. For there is a very large difference, which twentieth-century experience ought to have made clear even to the most exalted thinker, between arbitrary extra-legal power and the rule of law. And not only were the rulers (indeed, the ruling class as a whole) inhibited by their own rules of law against the exercise of direct unmediated force (arbitrary imprisonment, the employment of troops against the crowd, torture, and those other conveniences of power with which we are all conversant), but they also believed enough in these rules, and in their accompanying ideological rhetoric, to allow, in certain limited areas, the law itself to be a genuine forum within which certain kinds of class conflict were fought out. There were even occasions (one recalls John Wilkes and several of the trials of the 1790s) when the Government itself retired from the courts defeated. Such occasions served, paradoxically, to consolidate power, to enhance its legitimacy, and to inhibit revolutionary movements. But, to turn the paradox around, these same occasions served to bring power even further within constitutional controls.

The rhetoric and the rules of a society are something a great deal more than sham. In the same moment they may modify, in profound ways, the behaviour of the powerful, and mystify the powerless. They may disguise the true realities of power, but, at the same time, they may curb that power and check its intrusions. And it is often from within that very rhetoric that a radical critique of the practice of the society is developed: the reformers of the 1790s appeared, first of all, clothed in the rhetoric of Locke and of Blackstone.

These reflections lead me on to conclusions which may be different from those which some readers expect. I have shown in this study a political oligarchy inventing callous and oppressive laws to serve its own interests. I have shown judges who, no less than bishops, were subject to political influence, whose sense of justice was humbug, and whose interpretation of the laws served only to enlarge their inherent class bias. Indeed, I think that this study has shown that for many of England's governing élite the rules of law were a nuisance, to be manipulated and bent in what ways they could; and that the allegiance of such men as Walpole, Hardwicke or Paxton to the rhetoric of law was largely humbug. But I do not conclude from this that the rule of law itself was humbug. On the contrary, the inhibitions upon power imposed by law seem to me a legacy as substantial as any handed down from the struggles of the seventeenth century to the eighteenth, and a true and important cultural achievement of the agrarian and mercantile bourgeoisie, and of their supporting yeomen and artisans.

More than this, the notion of the regulation and reconciliation of conflicts through the rule of law – and the elaboration of rules and procedures which, on occasion, made some approximate approach towards the ideal – seems to me a cultural achievement of universal significance. I do not lay any claim as to the abstract, extra-historical impartiality of these rules. In a context of gross class inequalities, the equity of the law must always be in some part sham. Transplanted as it was to even more inequitable contexts, this law could become an instrument of imperialism. For this law has found its way to a good many parts of the globe. But even here the rules and the rhetoric have imposed some inhibitions upon the imperial power. If the rhetoric was a mask, it was a mask which Gandhi and Nehru were to borrow, at the head of a million masked supporters.

I am not starry-eyed about this at all. This has not been a star-struck book. I am insisting only upon the obvious point, which some modern Marxists have overlooked, that there is a difference between arbitrary power and the rule of law. We ought to expose the shams and inequities which may be concealed beneath this law. But the rule of law itself, the imposing of effective inhibitions upon power and the defence of the citizen from power's all-intrusive claims, seems to me to be an unqualified human good. To deny or belittle this good is, in this dangerous century when the resources and pretentions of power continue to enlarge, a desperate error of intellectual abstraction. More than this, it is a self-fulfilling error, which encourages us to give up the struggle against bad laws and class-bound procedures, and to disarm ourselves before power. It is to throw away a whole inheritance of struggle *about* law, and within the forms of law, whose continuity can never be fractured without bringing men and women into immediate danger.

In all of this I may be wrong. I am told that, just beyond the horizon, new forms of working-class power are about to arise which, being founded upon egalitarian productive relations, will require no inhibition and can dispense with the negative restrictions of bourgeois legalism. A historian is unqualified to pronounce on such utopian projections. All that he knows is that he can bring in support of them no historical evidence whatsoever. His advice might be: watch this new power for a century or two before you cut your hedges down.

I therefore crawl out onto my own precarious ledge. It is true that in history the law can be seen to mediate and to legitimize existent class relations. Its forms and procedures may crystallize those relations and mask ulterior injustice. But this mediation, through the forms of law, is something quite distinct from the exercise of unmediated force. The forms and rhetoric of law acquire a distinct identity which may, on occasion, inhibit power and afford some protection to the powerless. Only to the degree that this is seen to be so can law be of service in its other aspect, as ideology. Moreover, the law in both its aspects, as formal rules and procedures and as ideology, cannot usefully be analysed in the metaphorical terms of a superstructure distinct from an infrastructure. While this comprises a large and self-evident part of the truth, the rules and categories of law penetrate every level of society, effect vertical as well as horizontal definitions of men's rights and status, and contribute to men's self-definition or sense of identity. As such law has not only been imposed *upon* men from above: it has also been a medium within which other social conflicts have been fought out. Productive relations themselves are, in part, only meaningful in terms of their definitions at law: the serf, the free labourer; the cottager with common rights, the inhabitant without; the unfree proletarian, the picket conscious of his rights; the landless labourer who may still sue his employer for assault. And if the actuality of the law's operation in class-divided societies has, again and again, fallen short of its own rhetoric of equity, yet the notion of the rule of law is itself an unqualified good.

This cultural achievement – the attainment towards a universal value – found one origin in Roman jurisprudence. The uncodified English common law offered an alternative notation of law, in some ways more flexible and unprincipled – and therefore more pliant to the 'common sense' of the ruling class – in other ways more available as a medium through which social conflict could find expression, especially where the sense of 'natural justice' of the jury could make itself felt. Since this tradition came to its maturity in eighteenth-century England, its claims should command the historian's interest. And since some part of the inheritance from this cultural moment may still be found, within greatly changed contexts, within the United States or India or certain African countries, it is important to re-examine the pretensions of the imperialist donor.

This is to argue the need for a general revaluation of eighteenth-century law, of which this study offers only a fragment. This study has been centred upon a bad law, drawn by bad legislators, and enlarged by the interpretations of bad judges. No defence, in terms of natural justice, can be offered for anything in the history of the Black Act. But even this study does not prove that all law as such is bad. Even this law bound the rulers to act only in the ways which its forms permitted; they had difficulties with these forms; they could not always override the sense of natural justice of the jurors; and we may imagine how Walpole would have acted, against Jacobites or against disturbers of Richmond Park, if he had been subject to no forms of law at all.

If we suppose that law is no more than a mystifying and pompous way in which class power is registered and executed, then we need not waste our labour in studying its history and forms. One Act would be much the same as another, and all, from the standpoint of the ruled, would be Black. It is because law *matters* that we have bothered with this story at all. And this is also an answer to those universal thinkers, impatient of all except the *longue durée*, who cannot be bothered with cartloads of victims at Tyburn when they set these beside the indices of infant mortality. The victims of smallpox testify only to their own poverty and to the infancy of medical science; the victims of the gallows are exemplars of a conscious and elaborated code, justified in the name of a universal human value. Since we hold this value to be a human good, and one whose usefulness the world has not yet outgrown, the operation of this code deserves our most scrupulous attention. It is only when we follow through the intricacies of its operation that we can show what it was worth, how it was bent, how its proclaimed values were falsified in practice. When we note Walpole harrying John Huntridge, Judge Page handing down his death sentences, Lord Hardwicke wrenching the clauses of his Act from their context and Lord Mansfield compounding his manipulations, we feel contempt for men whose practice belied the resounding rhetoric of the age. But we feel contempt not because we are contemptuous of the notion of a just and equitable law but because this notion has been betrayed by its own professors. The modern sensibility which views this only within the perspectives of our own archipeaagos of *gulags* and of *stalags*, for whose architects the very notion of the rule of law would be a criminal heresy, will find my responses over-fussy. The plebs of eighteenth-century England were provided with a rule of law of some sort, and they ought to have considered themselves lucky. What more could they expect?

In fact, some of them had the impertinence, and the imperfect sense of historical perspective, to expect justice. On the gallows men would actually complain, in their 'last dying words', if they felt that in some particular the due forms of law had not been undergone. (We remember Vulcan Gates complaining that since he was illiterate he could not read his own notice of proclamation; and performing his allotted role at Tyburn only when he had seen the Sheriff's dangling chain.) For the trouble about law and justice, as ideal aspirations, is that they must pretend to absolute validity or they do not exist at all. If I judge the Black Act to be atrocious, this is not only from some standpoint in natural justice, and not only from the standpoint of those whom the Act oppressed, but also according to some ideal notion of the standards to which 'the law', as regulator of human conflicts of interest, ought to attain. For 'the law', as a logic of equity, must always seek to transcend the inequalities of class power which, instrumentally, it is harnessed to serve. And 'the law' as ideology, which pretends to reconcile the interests of all degrees of men, must always come into conflict with the ideological partisanship of class.

We face, then, a paradox. The work of sixteenth- and seventeenth-century jurists, supported by the practical struggles of such men as Hampden and Lilburne, was passed down as a legacy to the eighteenth century, where it gave rise to a vision, in the minds of some men, of an ideal aspiration towards universal values of law. One thinks of Swift or of Goldsmith, or, with more qualifications, of Sir William Blackstone or

Sir Michael Foster. If we today have ideal notions of what law might be, we derive them in some part from that cultural moment. It is, in part, in terms of that age's own aspiration that we judge the Black Act and find it deficient. But at the same time this same century, governed as it was by the forms of law, provides a text-book illustration of the employment of law, as instrument and as ideology, in serving the interests of the ruling class. The oligarchs and the great gentry were content to be subject to the rule of law only because this law was serviceable and afforded to their hegemony the rhetoric of legitimacy. This paradox has been at the heart of this study. It was also at the heart of eighteenth-century society. But it was also a paradox which that society could not in the end transcend, for the paradox was held in equipoise upon an ulterior equilibrium of class forces. When the struggles of 1790–1832 signalled that this equilibrium had changed, the rulers of England were faced with alarming alternatives. They could either dispense with the rule of law, dismantle their elaborate constitutional structures, countermand their own rhetoric and exercise power by force; or they could submit to their own rules and surrender their hegemony. In the campaign against Paine and the printers, in the Two Acts (1795), the Combination Acts (1799–1800), the repression of Peterloo (1819) and the Six Acts (1820) they took halting steps in the first direction. But in the end, rather than shatter their own self-image and repudiate 150 years of constitutional legality, they surrendered to the law. In this surrender they threw retrospective light back on the history of their class, and retrieved for it something of its honour; despite Walpole, despite Paxton, despite Page and Hardwicke, that rhetoric had not been altogether sham.

12

POLICE AUTHORITY IN LONDON AND
NEW YORK CITY 1830-1870

WILBUR R. MILLER

Policemen are a familiar feature of modern urban life, the most conspicuous
representatives of the political and social order. However, until American
society seemed to be falling apart in the mid-1960s, social historians on this
side of the Atlantic gave only a passing nod to the cop on the beat.[1] Like
other institutions which people have taken for granted, the police are products of distinct historical circumstances, the complex process of social
discipline and resistance fostered by the industrial revolution. As Allan
Silver points out, the police represented an unprecedented extension of the
government into the lives of ordinary citizens.[2] Some people welcomed and
others resented this extension, while at the same time its nature and degree
varied in different societies. A comparison of the mid-nineteenth-century
London police — the first modern full-time patrol force, created in 1829 —
and the New York City police — the second such force outside of the British
Empire, created in 1845 — reveals how different political and social developments influenced the principles and practices of police authority.

I

The statutes which established London and New York's police forces provided only a skeleton around which a definition of authority and a public
image of the police could develop. Consequently London's Metropolitan
Police owed much to Charles Rowan and Richard Mayne, the army officer
and lawyer whom Sir Robert Peel appointed to head his new force, while
the New York police were formed and reformed by a succession of elected
and appointed officials throughout the mid-nineteenth century.[3] However
much individuals may be credited or blamed for various aspects of the police,
they worked within a social context which encouraged some responses and
discouraged others. To understand the nature of police authority one must
examine the societies which produced the forces.

Although the British metropolis was a much larger city than the "metropolis of the New World," both were heterogeneous cities marked by gulfs
between wealth and poverty and recurrent social conflict. Michael Banton,
to whom I am indebted for much of the conceptualization later in this
article, argues that police authority reflects the degree of heterogeneity in
modern societies. He finds that the stability of Scottish police authority
reflects a culturally homogeneous society with widely shared expectations,
while the instability of American police authority reflects a culturally heterogeneous society with few shared expectations.[4] However, it is difficult to
maintain that nineteenth-century London was more homogeneous than

From Wilbur R. Miller, "Police Authority in London and New York City 1830-1870," *The Journal
of Social History* 81-101 (Winter 1975). Copyright 1974 by Peter N. Stearns.

contemporary New York. Disraeli spoke of England's "two nations, the rich and the poor" despite their ethnic homogeneity, and social conflict in London had more serious political implications than ethnic squabbles in New York. An examination of the *quality* of conflict in the two cities seems more promising for understanding the nature of police authority than an effort to measure their relative degrees of heterogeneity.

Formed in response to political violence and ordinary crimes against property,[5] the London force took to the streets amidst England's constitutional crisis over parliamentary representation for disenfranchised middle-class citizens. The politically-dominant landed aristocracy met the challenge from the industrial and commercial middle classes, backed by a reserve of working-class anger and violent protest, by tying them to the existing order through the electoral reform of 1832. The next challenge, fended off rather than co-opted, arose from various working-class groups dissatisfied with selecting "one or two wealthy men to carry out the schemes of one or two wealthy associations," the political parties under the new system of representation.[6] Culminating in Chartism, which included demands for universal suffrage, annually elected Parliaments and abolition of the property qualifications for M.P.s among its demands, working-class protest was defeated largely by the middle-class commitment to the social order. After a lull during the prosperous fifties and early sixties, working-class groups again demanded the franchise. Reflecting the increased economic power of workers organized into trade unions, the reform of 1867, another co-optive measure, gave urban workers the vote without altering the balance of social and economic power.[7]

Recurrent political crises were of profound importance to the police force charged with upholding the social order and controlling a turbulent population in the national capital, to which people looked with hope or apprehension in difficult times. Since disenfranchised protestors could have impact on Parliament only "out of doors" — demonstrations in the streets — policemen inevitable collided with them. Would these confrontations feed the fire of social conflict? Would the police be identified as the cutting edge of the ruling minority's oppression? Since their role was fundamentally political amidst challenges to the legitimacy of the government, the commanders of the force had to devise a strategy for containing conflict if they expected the new police to survive the Tory government which created them.

The New York police worked within a different context than their London brethren. New York was not a metropolis in the European sense, the seat of national government as well as center of culture and commerce. Except in the spectacular draft riots of 1863, Americans did not look to New York for the nation's political fate as Englishmen looked to London.[8]

New York did have its own local disorder, the ethnic conflicts which punctuated the era. While not as portentious as London's political disturbances, they did have consequences for the nature of police authority. The presence of large groups of immigrants in American cities gave a distinct tone to class conflict. Antagonism between skilled and unskilled urban workers increased with the filling of the unskilled ranks by immigrants, especially Irish, in the mid-nineteenth century. Native-born workers, concerned about the degradation of their trades by industrialization, regarded the unskilled Irishman, willing to work for longer hours and lower wages, as an economic and social threat. This rivalry between elements of the working class under-cut their sense of common interest against the employers. In fact, the native-born skilled workers who dominated American trade unions accepted the existing political system of representative democracy, believing that it gave all men an equal chance to rise in the world. The rowdy Irishman threatened to disrupt cherished institutions. Organized labor joined the propertied classes in denouncing the Irish draft rioters. While George T. Strong "would like to see war made on Irish scum as in 1688," the leading labor newspaper pictured them as "thieving rascals . . . who have never done a day's work in their lives."[9] The paper remarked, "The people have too much at stake to tolerate any action beyond the pale of the law. . . . No improvement can be made by popular outbursts upon the great superstructure created by the wisdom of our fathers."[10] In England such rhetoric was rarely embraced by working-men; America's propertied and working classes alike saw a political order they valued threatened by irresponsible foreigners who did not appreciate democracy.

Since the New York police upheld the political institutions of representa-tive democracy which most Americans valued, there was little pressure for them to transcend social conflict to ensure their own survival. Instead of supporting the rule of a small elite which was challenged by the majority of London's population, the police supported a political order threatened by an alien minority. Thus to a great extent the police were free to treat a large group of the community as outsiders with little fear for the consequences as long as their actions coincided with most people's expectations.

What sort of police authority emerged from the different social circum-stances of London and New York? In both cities pure repression was un-acceptable, in London because of past failures and tendency to promote more violence, and in New York because it was unacceptable to American democracy.[11] In societies with representative governments, whether aristo-cratic like England or democratic like America, the police ultimately depend on the voluntary compliance of most citizens with their authority. As Edwin Chadwick said, "A police force . . . must owe its real efficiency to the sym-pathies and concurrent action of the great body of the people."[12] The commanders of the two forces had to define the institution to win this public support.

London's Police Commissioners, Rowan and Mayne, had an especially difficult task: they had to develop a force sufficiently strong to maintain order but also restrained enough to soothe widespread fears of police oppres-sion. The combination of strength and restraint became the foundation of the

London Bobby's public image. To achieve acceptance the Commissioners sought to identify the police force with the legal system, which embodied the strength of national sovereignty and the restraint of procedural regularity and guarantees of civil liberties. While the laws of England were hardly a pure realm of justice above contemporary social inequality, they were the broadest available source of external legitimation for the police.

Definition of the force as agents of the legal system made their authority *impersonal*, derived from legal powers and restraints instead of from the local community's informal expectations or the directives of the dominant political party.[13] Amid social conflict the Commissioners, in their own words, "endeavoured to prevent the slightest practical feeling or bias, being shewn or felt by the police."[14] With varying levels of success during their long terms of office Rowan and Mayne determined that "the force should not only be, in fact, but be believed to be impartial in action, and should act on principle."[15]

Behind this commitment to impersonal authority was the strength the police gained from being an independent agency of the national government. The Metropolitan Police, created by Act of Parliament, had no links with London's local government, and the Commissioners, appointed for life, were responsible to the Home Secretary who exercised only a broad authority over them. As a national institution the police could draw upon a reservoir of symbolic as well as physical power. "Power derived from Parliament," said a contemporary observer, " . . . carries with it a weight and energy that can never be infused by parish legislation; and in respect of an establishment for general security, it is doubly advantageous, by striking terror into the depredator, and arming the officer with augmented confidence and authority."[16] Similarly, "the mob quails before the simple baton of the police officer, and flies before it, well knowing the moral as well as physical force of the Nation, whose will, as embodied in law, it represents."[17] Although both the strength and moral authority of the police required several years to develop, impersonal authority proved to be a secure foundation of police legitimacy.

Rowan and Mayne's notion of impersonality extended into many aspects of their force's structure and practice. They made the police into a tightly-disciplined body of professionals divorced from the localities they served. The men were kept out of partisan politics (Bobbies could not vote until 1885) and were often recruited from outside of London. They wore a blue uniform which further separated them from ordinary citizens. The Commissioners inculcated loyalty and obedience, enforced by quick dismissal for infractions, expecting the men to be models of good conduct by subordinating their impulses to the requirements of discipline and the legal system they represented. An observer of the 1850s vividly captured the police image: "P.C. X 59 stalks along, an *institution* rather than a man. We seem to have no more hold of his personality than we could possibly get of his coat buttoned up to the throttling point."[18]

The New York policeman was less thoroughly molded than his London brother, but he did embody a distinct image which reflected conscious efforts as well as circumstantial results. His authority was *personal*, resting on closeness to the citizens and their informal expectations of his power instead of formal bureaucratic or legal standards.[19] Instead of having to rise above social conflict by indentification with the legal system, New York officials created a force which conformed to pre-existing, widely accepted patterns of democratic government. Survival of the new police depended originally on its ability to incorporate ideals of democracy in which authority was not only supposed to serve the people but also be the people. Until 1857, when the state government took over the force, it was directly controlled by popularly-elected local officials and policemen were recruited from the population of the district they patrolled. They did not wear a distinguishing blue uniform until 1853. As representatives of municipal instead of national government, the New York policeman did not have the symbolic authority his London colleague could invoke. Nor did he have the same reserve of physical force to back up his power: he was much more alone on the streets than his London colleague (New York always had fewer patrolmen in proportion to the citizens than London) and his effectiveness depended more on his personal strength than on broader institutional authority.[20]

New Yorkers rejected many important features of the London police as too authoritarian for democratic America. In the late fifties, the *Times* and Mayor Fernando Wood agreed that New York policemen were not as disciplined and efficient as their London brethren, but this was a necessary price of America's healthy social mobility and its citizens' independent spirit.[21] The New York patrolman was more a man than an institution because democracy suspected formal institutional power and professional public officials.[22] Paradoxically, lack of institutional power also meant lack of institutional restraints, and the personal New York policeman often ended up with more awesome power than his impersonal London counterpart.

II

The most important element of the distinction between the impersonal and personal approach is the amount of discretionary authority the patrolman exercised. Every policeman has to exercise personal discretion in his duties — decisions about when and how to act, whom to suspect and whom to arrest. Such choices are the most important part of his work, distinguishing the policeman from the soldier who does not act without direct orders.[23] Nevertheless, the commanders of the force and the judiciary set wide or narrow boundaries to discretion, and various public reactions to the police often center around the degree of discretion people think patrolmen should exercise. Consistent with his image of impersonal authority derived from the powers and restraints of the legal system, the London Bobby's personal discretion was more regulated than that of his New York colleague. Not as closely bound by the legal system, the New York patrolman often acted in the context of official and public toleration of unchecked discretionary power. The London policeman upholding an aristocratic, hierarchical society had more limits on his personal power than the democratic New York policeman.

The patrolman's most formidable discretionary power is his ability to use force to maintain his authority. The commanders of both the London and New York police warned their men to use lethal violence only for self-defense and prescribed punishments for violators of this essential principle.[24] In practice, however, the New York policeman's use of force was much less carefully monitored than in London.

As is well known, the London Commissioners carefully supervised Bobbies' use of force. They inculcated coolness and restraint, restricting the police arsenal to the truncheon. Except in unusually dangerous circumstances, London patrolmen never carried firearms. The Peelers could rely on muscle and blunt weapons partly because their antagonists were not usually more formidably armed, although revolvers seemed to be spreading in the underworld in the late sixties. There was some escalation of weaponry and incidents of unwarranted police violence did occur, but the Commissioners punished men who flouted their rule that restraint was the best way to win public acceptance of the force.[35]

New York's locally-controlled Municipal Police carried only clubs, but when the state government took over the force in 1857 — prompted by a mixture of reform and partisan motives — many New Yorkers violently expressed their hostility to the new Metropolitan force and the police replied in kind. Individual Captains encouraged their men to carry revolvers for self-protection against a heavily-armed underworld.[26] By the end of the 1860s, revolvers were standard equipment, although they were never formally authorized.[27] Guns seemed to be popping throughout the city, the civilians uncontrolled by effective legislation and the police unchecked by their superiors. The New York *Times* complained that shooting was becoming a substitute for arrest and described the patrolman as "an absolute monarch, within his beat, with complete power of life and death over all within his range . . . without the forms of trial or legal inquiry of any kind."[28] Amidst a vicious cycle of criminal and police violence, the patrolman was free to exercise much greater physical force than his London colleague.

Whether he made his arrest violently or quietly the New York patrolman consistently exercised broader personal discretion than the London Bobby. In both cities policemen had wide power to arrest people on suspicion of criminal intent, from stopping and searching people in the street to taking them to a magistrate for examination. Such arrests were more carefully scrutinized by police and judicial officials in London than in New York.

The London Commissioners reduced (although they did not eliminate) complaints of arbitrary arrest by warning their men to be extremely careful about whom they detained, directing that they pay attention to external indicators of social class as a guide to their suspicions.[29] These guidelines did not lift police scrutiny from workers in middle- and upper-class neighborhoods and Parliament endorsed this use of police authority and later expanded stop-and-search and arrest powers.[30] However, the judiciary contributed to control of police discretion by carefully checking patrolmen's grounds for arrest, and higher courts directed that people could be detained without formal trial and charges for only five days in normal circumstances or a maximum of two weeks in unusual cases.[31] Generally magistrates' committals of suspects for jury trial did not keep pace with London's population growth during the 1830-70 period, possibly reflecting declining crime or the shift of many petty offenses to Justice of the Peace's summary jurisdiction from 1847 to 1861.[32] However, since the conviction rate in higher courts in proportion to magistrates' committals *increased* during the period, and higher court convictions in proportion to policemens' arrests also increased, it is quite likely that policemen were arresting and magistrates committing people on grounds that were increasingly firm over the years.[33]

Contemporary American observers testified to London's cautious use of arrest on suspicion when they mistakenly reported that Bobbies could arrest only for overt acts.[34] George W. Walling, who joined the New York force in 1848, said that "A New York police officer knows he has been sworn in to 'keep the peace,' and he keeps it. There's no 'shilly-shallying' with him; he doesn't consider himself half-patrolman and half Supreme Court judge." He did not hesitate to arrest on suspicion even if it were "often a case of 'giving a dog a bad name and then hanging him,' — men being arrested merely because they are know to have been lawbreakers or persons of bad character."[35] Moreover, the Police Justices (elected Justices of the Peace) did not check this aggressiveness. Judges in over-crowded courts did not take time to investigate police charges, tacitly encouraging hasty or arbitrary arrests on suspicion by accepting police testimony without oath or corroboration, refusing prisoners the opportunity of defending themselves, and failing to inform them of their rights or frightening them into confessions.[36] People arrested on suspicion were usually held in the Tombs, but the magistrates also allowed the police to confine them in the station house while they "worked up a case" against them.[37] There was no time limit for detention on suspicion until a reforming judge instituted the English practice in the early 1850s. This seems to have satisfied the New York Prison Association, which had led a public outcry against abuses of detention on suspicion, but it did not attempt to change other practices.[38]

Discretion played an important part in arrests for overt acts as well as on suspicion. Checks could help prevent arbitrary arrests because sometimes both London and New York patrolmen charged people with disorderly conduct when their offense was merely unruliness or disrespect for the officer's authority.[39]

Rowan and Mayne warned Bobbies that "No Constable is justified in depriving any one of his liberty for words only and language however violent towards the P.C. himself is not to be noticed . . .; a Constable who allows himself to be irritated by any language whatsoever shows that he has not a command of his temper which is absolutely necessary in an officer invested with such extensive powers by the law."[40] They put teeth into the warning by forbidding desk officers to discharge people arrested for disorderly conduct who promised to behave in the future. Thus they prevented policemen from using the disorderly conduct charge to scare people into respecting them without having to bring a weak case before the magistrate. The only grounds for station house discharge was false arrest, which had to be reported immediately to Scotland Yard.[41] Although they never eliminated arbitrary disorderly conduct arrests (an epidemic of them broke out in the sixties), the Commissioners kept them in check.[42]

The commanders of the New York force also expected their men to be calm under provocation, and a high official said that disorderly conduct arrests were covered by "a good many rules."[43] However, there is little to suggest that such arrests were limited in practice. A journalist contended that they usually depended "exclusively upon the fancy of the policeman," who had "a discretionary power that few use discreetly."[44] New York patrolmen made many more disorderly conduct arrests than their London brethren. In 1851 they made one for each 109 people; London officers made one for each 380 people. In 1868-69, New York's absolute number of disorderly conduct arrests was greater than London's: 14,935 compared to only 2,616 in the much larger British metropolis.[45] Although there is plenty of evidence that New York was more rowdy than London,[46] the great discrepancy probably reflects London's discouragement of disorderly conduct charges. The heads of the New York force left disposition of patrolmen's charges, without any special checks on disorderly conduct arrests, up to station-house desk officers.[47]

New York patrolmen's free hand for disorderly conduct arrest may illustrate the use of personal action to compensate for lack of institutional authority. Patrolmen could not arrest for assault without a warrant unless they had seen the attack or the victim was visibly wounded. London policemen labored under a similar restriction until they were granted full powers in 1839. In New York, arrests for disorderly conduct may have compensated for limitations of arrest for assault.[48]

After arrest and lock-up came police interrogation and evidence-gathering. Earlier discussion of arrest on suspicion revealed that in New York there was little regulation of these practices. Judges readily accepted police evidence with little concern about how they obtained it. Moreover, the police had no scruples about obtaining confessions by entrapment or "strategem."[49]

In London all levels of the criminal justice system scrutinized interrogation and evidence-collection. With judges and high officials looking over their shoulders, the Commissioners reiterated warnings against false incrimination or distortion of evidence in the courtroom.[50] Repetition of such warnings suggests that policemen engaged in improper practices, but the men at the top were determined to keep them in line.

Until the 1850s, English courts were extremely sensitive about police interrogation, especially inducement of prisoners' confessions by promises or threats. Their concern may have been a carry-over from the days of a harsh penal code when confession of even minor crimes brought death or transportation for life.[51] The Commissioners' directives to their men reflected this sensitivity.[52] Sometimes Bobbies took such cautiousness too much to heart, preventing voluntary confessions because they feared criticism from judges and defense counsel.[53] Following a Court of Queens' Bench decision in 1852, judges began to relax their restrictions on confessions, increasingly accepting prisoners' statements as evidence against them. Nevertheless the Attorney General of England and the Police Commissioners were concerned that patrolmen not carry this too far by presenting all incriminating statements as confessions.[54] The courts seem to have returned to earlier strict interpretations in a case of 1865, and the police fell into line.[55]

Official concern was important because of the power of the police within the criminal justice system of England — they served as public prosecutors, taking charge of serious cases in the higher courts with jury trial as well as petty cases before magistrates. In New York, serious cases left police hands after arrest and became the popularly-elected District Attorney's responsibility. He decided whom to prosecute and how to conduct the case. Critics charged that he was lenient towards his constituents and abused "plea bargaining," which allowed criminals to escape deserved punishment by pleading guilty to lesser offenses.[56] New York policemen, with greater leeway in arrest and interrogation practices than their London brethren, had less power over the outcome of serious cases. Because of the police role in the courtroom, the London Commissioners realized that suspicion of deceit or prosecutorial bias would undermine public acceptance of the force. Watchfulness at all levels of the criminal justice system satisfied a Parliamentary inquiry that England did not need a public prosecutor like the American District Attorney.[57]

The trial is the last stage of police participation in the administration of criminal justice. Police-judicial relations are important for understanding patrolmen's attitudes toward discretionary power and procedural regularity. From their viewpoint, their most significant relationship with judges is how many arrests are rewarded with convictions. A vital element of the policeman's psychology, convictions make the officer feel that his job is worthwhile, giving meaning to his work by validating his judgment to arrest a person. Having made a quick decision, he finds it hard to admit error.[58] Low convictions in proportion to arrests can make policemen into frustrated antagonists of the judiciary, ready to substitute street-corner justice for procedural regularity.

London Bobbies often criticized judicial decisions, but the Commissioners insisted that they keep their comments to themselves and required strict decorum and impartiality in the courtroom.[59] Perhaps more significant, convictions for all crimes in the higher and lower courts increased relative to arrests during the mid-nineteenth century. Averaging about 45 percent of arrests during the 1830s and 1840s, convictions rose to around 55 percent of arrests during the 1860s.[60] Bad in the early years of the force, police-judicial relations improved after 1839, with settlement of a jurisdictional dispute between the Commissioners and magistrates.[61] Increasing convictions suggest that police and judicial standards of proper procedure were moving toward each other.

Although judges in New York made few procedural demands on policemen, from the early days of the force and increasingly after state takeover of the police in 1857, police officials complained of bad relations with the judiciary and charged judges with leniency toward major and minor offenders alike.[62] Lacking statistics comparable to those of London, it is difficult to evaluate these accusations. Available information indicates high conviction rates for drunkenness and vagrancy, slightly fewer convictions for petty larceny compared to arrests than in London, very few assault and battery convictions and in more serious crimes during the 1860s about one conviction for every three arrests.[63] Judges seem to have been more lenient toward serious than petty offenders, whereas in London conviction rates were generally higher for serious crimes.[64] Paradoxically, judges seemed to have overlooked arbitrary arrest practices but let many offenders off. This may have been a last-minute effort to regulate the police — Police Justice Michael Connolly was a crusader against brutality[65] — but the absence of clear guidelines for the police made patrolmen and judges into adversaries.[66] They never moved toward a single standard of conduct.

III

Looking back over the survey of police practices, we have seen the London patrolman's impersonal authority resting on control of discretionary power through the legal system and the directives of the judiciary and heads of the force. In contrast, the New York policeman's personal authority rested on unregulated discretion and less concern for working within legal restraints. The two forces did not develop their images in isolation. As part of the societies which created them, public perceptions of crime and the role of the police were important underpinnings of their authority.

Recognizing that various classes or groups would react differntially to the police, the London Commissioners hoped that the new force had "conciliated the populace and obtained the goodwill of all respectable persons."[67] On the whole they achieved this goal, although antagonism to the force remained in 1870.

"Respectable persons" were not always middle-class, but the Victorian middle classes did see themselves as custodians of respectability. Although hardly united in interest and outlook, the groups composing the middle classes would have shared suspicion of a police too closely linked to the landed aristocracy. They accepted aristocratic domination of politics as long as it was not oppressive. They were always ready to criticize arbitrary policemen, but as their own political influence consolidated over the years, they came to see Bobbies mainly as useful servants for coping with the various unpleasantries of urban life. Rowan and Mayne noticed that predominantly middle-class complaints against the police shifted from oppressiveness to inefficiency during the 1830s. They had to remind complainants that policemen lacked legal power to do many of the things that were expected of them.[68]

The middle classes came to depend for protection and peace and quiet upon an institution which fostered social stability by the restrained exercise of power. Karl Polanyi's argument that the fragility of the industrial and commercial economy tied to the stock market made riotous disorder intolerable in the nineteenth century applies to repressive violence as well. "A shooting affray in the streets of the metropolis might destroy a substantial part of the nominal national capital . . . , stocks collapsed and there was no bottom in prices."[69] In England the military, not the mob, had done the shooting in the past. A police force which contained disorder with a minimum of violence increased people's sense of security and contributed to economic stability. Generally, London's propertied classes believed that public order was steadily improving in the metropolis. Commentators recognized that police restraint as well as power contributed to this orderliness.[70] In the Sunday trading riots of 1855 in Hyde Park, when policemen got out of hand and brutalized innocent spectators as well as participants, the London *Times* joined radical working-class papers in condemning police excesses. The lesson was clear: respectable citizens as well as the populace expected restraint.[71] The middle classes, seeing themselves as the repository of such virtues, usually took pride in a police force with a reputation for respectability and "habitual discretion and moderation of conduct."[72]

During the sixties, a period of economic uncertainty and working-class unrest, "respectable" fear of crime and disorder mounted. The garotting or mugging scare of 1862, the reform riot of 1866 and increasingly violent robberies along with hunger riots in the winters of the late sixties made Londoners question police efficiency. Significantly complaints focused on lack of manpower and the declining quality of recruits, poor administrative methods and excessive bureaucratization and militarization, instead of demands for arming the police or allowing them broader discretion than the law defined.[73] Parliament's response was tougher laws for the police to enforce rather than a redefinition of the force's impersonal authority. Alan Harding is right in calling some of the harsher provisions of the Habitual Criminals Act of 1869 (aimed at the paroled convicts whom most people blamed for the crime wave) "positively medieval," but the act was a precise administrative control which judges interpreted strictly, continuing to monitor police discretionary power.[74] The new law expanded authority but also defined its limits. The police themselves recruited more men, reformed administrative procedures and after Mayne's death in 1868, expanded the detective division which he had always distrusted.[75] They did not resort to violence or unregulated discretionary power. Although strained by a crime wave, impersonal authority was still viable.

Having obtained and retained the "good will" of at least most "respectable persons," could the police achieve the more formidable goal of conciliating "the populace?" Although working-class reaction to the police was as varied as the often conflicting and competing groups which made up the proletariat, generally a working man or woman was more likely to see the police (whom they preferred to call "crushers" instead of "Bobbies") as masters instead of servants. Subordination of the force to the legal system simply meant that it was part of the apparatus which upheld "one law for the rich, another law for the poor." This view that the scales of justice were weighted in favor of the rich and powerful, and only slightly less so toward the middle classes, was the most common theme of working-class social criticism.[76] The Commissioners' concern for the rights of "respectable" Londoners meant that social class was often the basis of police treatment of citizens. Although the Bobby was expected to be polite to "all people of every rank and class," a writer friendly to the police could say, "although well-dressed people always meet with civility . . . it is possible that the ragged and the outcaste may occasionally meet with the hasty word or unnecessary force from the constable, who is for them the despot of the streets."[77] The other side of the coin is that some workers felt that the police were ignoring their neighborhoods, allowing disorder they would not tolerate in "respectable" areas.[78] This partly reflected the dangerousness of some rookeries and dockland slums, but also the Commissioners' policy of "watching St. James's while watching St. Giles's" — patrolling slum areas not to protect the inhabitants from each other, but to keep them from infiltrating nearby prosperous neighborhoods.[79] Workers could complain of both too much and too little police power. Their feelings came out in the popular music-hall songs of the sixties, such as "The Model Peeler," an off-color account of police oppression and dereliction. "Oh, I'm the chap to make a hit,/No matter where I goes it," runs the chorus; "I'm quite a credit to the force,/And jolly well they knows it./I take folks up, knock others down,/None do the thing genteeler,/I'm number 14, double X,/ And called the Model Peeler."[80] Impersonal authority, like so much else in Victorian England, seemed reserved for "respectable" people.

Nevertheless, the force does seem to have worked toward conciliating "the populace." Except among persistently antagonistic groups like the coster-mongers,[81] the police did achieve at least a grumbling working-class acqui-escence to their authority. By the 1860s, there was more violence against

them in the music halls than on the streets.[82] Partly this acquiescence reflected the clearly-established power of the force — "People feel that
resistance is useless," Mayne declared. However, the police also made some
effort to reduce working-class antagonism. Their concern for restraint in
handling political demonstrations was one (imperfectly achieved) aspect.
They also deliberately stayed as much as possible away from the enforcement of Sunday blue laws, which working-class Londoners bitterly resented
as middle-class dictation of their life style. This was not a case of failure to
enforce existing laws, for that would undermine police subordination to the
legal system, but of successfully lobbying in Parliament against new measures
which evangelical Sabbatarians sought in the Victorian era.[83] Upholding a
hierarchical social order, the police never won the "good will" of the working
classes, but because they rejected pure repression the Commissioners achieved
at least acquiescence to police authority. The force had authority, not mere
power.

Across the Atlantic the reactions of both middle- and working-class New
Yorkers to the police were more ambivalent than in London. By limiting the
force's institutional power but tolerating broad personal discretion, New
York's officials revealed a distrust of institutions but great trust in men.
Alexis de Tocqueville argued that democratic Americans impowered their
officials with broad discretion because they elected them, being able to
remove them if they were dissatisfied. In aristocracies like England, on the
other hand, appointed officials independent of both rulers and ruled had to
have more formal checks on their discretion to prevent oppression.[84] Although New York policemen were never themselves elected, they were at first
directly and after 1853 indirectly accountable to elected officials and the
broad directives of public opinion remained their guidelines instead of formal
limitations of their personal power.

Turning from theory to public reactions to the police, Tocqueville's
notion is complicated by the institutional rivalry of the police and judiciary.
"Respectable" New Yorkers, although they criticized democracy's immersion
of the force in partisan politics and sought to move it closer to London's
independent professionalism,[85] usually sided with the police in their controversy with the judiciary, which often owed its position to local, in many
cases working-class Irish, constituencies. This taking of sides was most pronounced after state (Republican) take-over of the police in 1857, while the
Police Justices remained in the unclean (Democratic) hands of local politicians who courted the votes of ignorant and impoverished immigrants. Thus,
to a great extent, the propertied classes formed the constituency of the police
force, while the propertyless made up the support of the lower levels of the
judiciary, the Police Justices. Recurrent quarrels between police officials and
judges were contests, to some extent before but especially after 1857,
between representatives of different class and ethnic constituencies. Such
battle lines had been occasionally drawn in the early years of the London

force, but rarely later on.

Since respectable citizens did not expect justice from the courts, they turned to policemen, tolerating their broad personal authority in the war against crime. Although one's view of the police often depended on one's politics, this toleration frequently transcended partisanship. If to put down crime, said the Democratic *Herald* in 1856,"it were necessary for us to have a Turk as Chief of Police, we, for our own parts, would go for the Turk, turban, Koran and all."[86]

A later journalist remarked of John A. Kennedy, the tough Republican General Superintendent of the Metropolitan Police, that although called "king Kennedy" among "the masses," respectable citizens regarded him more highly. "He has often exceeded his power, and has committed acts that smack strongly of petty tyranny; but there can be no doubt of the fact that he has earnestly and faithfully labored for the cause of law and order."[87]

A little petty tyranny was acceptable in the interests of law and order, especially in light of "a general, and perfectly natural feeling in the community, that it is a postive godsend to get rid of one of the many scoundrels who infest our streets, by any means and through any agency possible" when people lacked faith in "the capacity or common honesty of our legal tribunals."[88] New York was a violent city, whose disorder seemed to be steadily outstripping a police force plagued with manpower shortages and disciplinary problems. Citizens worried about the well-armed politically influential lumpenproletarian "volcano under the city."[89] Violence and distrust of the courts placed a premium on physical force and personal authority instead of London's restrained impersonal authority. Democratic ideology and disorder combined to create a policeman who often seemed more authoritarian than aristocratic England's London policeman.

How did New York's largely Irish immigrant "masses" view the police? James Richardson suggests that they had fewer grievances against the locally-controlled Municipal Police than the state-controlled Metropolitan Police. Nevertheless, the large number of Irish patrolmen in Irish wards, because of the Municipal force's local residency requirement, did not guarantee smooth relations with the working-class Irish public. Irish officers often arrested their countrymen for petty offenses, and complaints of violence or improper arrest, averaging some 29 a year between 1846 and 1854, were not much fewer when Irish officers confronted their countrymen than when WASP policemen dealt with Irish citizens.[90] Common ethnicity may not have been sufficient to overcome class antagonism – policemen seem to have been recruited from skilled workers while the people they arrested were predominantly unskilled laborers.[91] Relations worsened under the state-controlled Metropolitan Police, despite a proportion of Irish patrolmen similar to the levels of the old force.[92] Hatred of the new force, often politically motivated, underlay much of the draft rioters' ferocity, to which Irish policemen replied, in kind, earning the gratitude of respectable New Yorkers.[93] Irish Democrats' antagonism to the Republican state force, roused by judicial and journalistic champions, resembled London radicals' hatred of the police in the 1830s. The anger was as much against whom the police represented as what they did.

The Metropolitan Police do not seem to have made efforts to reduce Irish working-class hostility. Their enforcement of Sunday laws, as bitterly resented by immigrants in New York as by London workers, increased hostility to the force. The old Municipal Police had ignored blue laws except under sporadic Sabbatarian pressures; the Metropolitans, responding to sustained Sabbatarian influence, enforced strict new measures which roused the opposition and evasion of normally peaceful Germans as well as the volatile Irish. The police could not claim impartiality when they enforced laws passed by one group against another's customs and amusements. Eventually enforcement of the blue laws broke down, becoming a convenient tool for Boss Tweed to keep saloon keepers in line and a lucrative source of pay-offs for all levels of the police force. Such corruption seems only to have increased "respectable" criticism without significantly improving relations with the working classes.[94]

IV

Although she wrote before the creation of New York's force, Harriet Martineau captured the difference between London and New York's police. She identified the English police as "agents of a representative government, appointed by responsible rulers for the public good," and the American police as "servants of a self-governing people, chosen by those among whom their work lies."[95] The London policeman represented the "public good" as defined by the governing classes' concern to maintain an unequal social order with a minimum of violence and oppression. The result was impersonal authority. The New York policeman represented "a self-governing people" as a product of that self-government's conceptions of power and the ethnic conflicts which divided that people. The result was personal authority.

This article is a revised and enlarged version of a paper presented at the American Historical Association convention in New York, December 1971.

NOTES

1.   Notable exceptions are Selden D. Bacon's unpublished Ph.D. dissertation (Yale, 1939), "The Early Development of American Municipal Police," and James F. Richardson's dissertation (New York University, 1961), "The History of Police Protection in New York City, 1800-1870," which was not published until 1970 as part of his book, *The New York Police: Colonial Times to 1901* (New York, 1970).
2.   Allan Silver, "The Demand for Order in Civil Society: A Review of Some Themes in the History of Urban Crime, Police and Riot," in David J. Bordua, ed., *The Police: Six Sociological Essays* (New York, c. 1967), 12-14.
3.   For Rowan and Mayne, see Charles Reith, *A New Study of Police History* (Edinburgh, 1956) and Belton Cobb, *The First Detectives and the Early Career of Richard Mayne, Commissioner of Police* (London, 1957), both *passim*. Rowan served 20 years (1829-50), Mayne almost 40 years (1829-68). For the administrative history of the New York Police, see Richardson, *N. Y. Police*, chs. 2-7.
4.   Michael Banton, *The Policeman in the Community* (New York, 1964), esp. ch. 8.
5.   For background on the London police, see Charles Reith, *The Police Idea: Its History and Evolution in England in the Eighteenth Century and After* (London, 1938) and Leon Radzinowicz, *A History of English Criminal Law and its Administration from 1750*, 4 vols. (London, 1948-68), vol. IV.
6.   Walter Bagehot, *The English Constitution* (New York, n.d., first pub. 1868), 14 (quotation).
7.   For English political history see, e.g., Asa Briggs, *The Making of Modern England, 1784-1867: the Age of Improvement* (New York, 1965), chs. 5-10.
8.   For the significance of America's federal system in violence and its control, see David J. Bordua, "Police," in David L. Sills, ed., *International Encyclopedia of the Social Sciences*, 17 vols. (New York, c. 1968), XI, 175-76; Richard Hofstadter, "Reflections on Violence in the United States," in Hofstadter and Michael Wallace, eds., *American Violence* (New York, 1971), 10.
9.   George Templeton Strong, *Diary*, quoted by Richardson, *N. Y. Police*, 141-42; *Fincher's Trades Review*, July 25, 1863, quoted by David Montgomery, *Beyond Equality: Labor and the Radical Republicans 1862-1872* (New York, 1967), 106-07.
10.   *Fincher's Trades Review, loc. cit.*
11.   F. C. Mather, *Public Order in the Age of the Chartists* (Manchester, c. 1959), chs. I, III; Richardson, *N. Y. Police*, ch. 2.
12.   Edwin Chadwick, "On the Consolidation of the Police Force, and the Prevention of Crime," *Fraser's Magazine* 67 (Jan., 1868), 16. Full discussion of the consensual basis of police power is in Silver, "Demand for Order," 6-15.
13.   My contrast between impersonal and personal authority (discussed below) is my distillation of several writers' ideas, most importantly from Banton, *Policeman in the Community*. See also James Q. Wilson, *Varieties of Police Behavior: the Management of Law and Order in Eight Communities* (Cambridge, Mass., 1968), chs. 4-6, and Jerome Skolnick, *Justice without Trial: Law Enforcement in Democratic Society* (New York, c. 1966), 42-70. The impersonal and personal models are meant to be a rough guide, not precise definitions.
14.   Commissioners to J. Scanlon, March 2, 1842, Metropolitan Police Records, Public

Record Office 1/41, letter 88301 (hereafter cited as Mepol).
15.   Parliamentary Papers 1839, XIX, First Report, Constabulary Force Commissioners (hereafter cited as PP), 324. Rowan was one of the authors.
16.   Anon., "Principles of Police, and Their Application to the Metropolis," *Fraser's Magazine* 16 (Aug., 1837), 170.
17.   Anon., "The Police of London," *London Quarterly Review* (July 1870), 48, quoted by Silver, "Demand for Order," 14.
18.   A. Wynter, "The Police and the Thieves," *Quarterly Review* 99 (June 1856), 171; also quoted by Silver, "Demand for Order," 13-14. The writer goes on to say that off-duty, one sees the men as human beings: their public and private roles are separated. For the various features of the London police mentioned in this paragraph, see, e.g., Reith, *New Study*, chs. X-XIII.
19.   See note 13 above.
20.   In 1856, New York had one policeman per 812 citizens, London one per 351 (N. Y. City Board of Aldermen Documents, 1856, XXIII no. 10, Mayor's Annual Message, 35) (hereafter cited as BAD). For later complaints of shortages, see N. Y. State Assembly Documents, 1859, II no. 63, Metro Police Annual Report 1858, 6-7 (here-after cited as AD), and Edward Crapsey, *The Netherside of New York: or, the Vice, Crime, and Poverty of the Great Metropolis* (New York, 1872), 12. For the features of the police mentioned in this paragraph, see Richardson, *N. Y. Police*, chs. 3-5.
21.   N. Y. *Times*, Dec. 9, 1857, 4; BAD 1856, XXIII no. 10, Mayor's Annual Message, 33-34.
22.   For the general mid-nineteenth-century suspicion of expertise, see Daniel Calhoun *Professional Lives in America: Structure and Aspiration 1750-1850* (Cambridge. Mass., 1965), 4-15, 193-94; also Andrew Jackson's famous fears that professional officials would lose touch with the people and threaten the democracy in which "the duties of public officers are, or at least admit of being made, so plain and simple that men of intelligence may readily qualify themselves for their performance" (James D. Richardson, comp., *A Compilation of the Messages and Papers of the Presidents*, 22 vols. [New York, c. 1897, ed. of 1915], III, 1012).
23.   Among the most important discussions of police discretion are Banton, *Police-man*, 127-46; Skolnick, *Justice*, ch. 4; Wayne R. LaFave, *Arrest: the Decision to Take a Suspect into Custody* (Boston, 1965), *passim*; and Joseph Goldstein, "Police Discretion not to Invoke the Legal Process: Low Visibility Decisions in the Administration of Justice," *Yale Law Journal* 69 (1960), 543-94.
24.   Wynter, "Police and Thieves," 170; Police Orders (London) Sept. 6, 1832 (here-after cited as PO), Mepol 7/2, folio 93; Aug. 21, 1830, Mepol 7/1, ff. 95-96. For New York, *Rules and Regulations for Day and Night Police of the City of New-York; with Instructions as to the Legal Powers and Duties of Policemen* (New York, 1846), 6; *Ibid.*, 1851, 6-7; *Manual for the Government of the Police Force of the Metropolitan Police District of the State of New York* (in AD 1860, II no. 88), 90.
25.   Charles Reith, *British Police and the Democratic Ideal* (London, 1943), 36; PP 1834, XVI, Metro. Police, test. Rowan, 12, q. 180; Kellow Chesney, *The Victorian Underworld* (London, 1970), 111, 119; [Thomas Wontner], *Old Bailey Experience* (London, 1833), 338; *Lloyd's Weekly Newspaper*, May 10, 1868, 6.
26.   Richardson, "History of Police Protection," 305-08; N. Y. *Herald*, July 14, 1857, 1; July 15, 1857, 1. Apparently some Municipal Policemen had carried pistols on dangerous assignments. William Bell, ms. *Journal* 1850-51 (New York Historical Society) describes an all-out battle with some rescuers of his prisoner. He intimidated them with his pistol, but in the ensuing affray the gun miraculously never went off. In 1857 one Captain told a reporter that George W. Matsell, Chief of the Municipal Police, had "made it a standing rule to look upon every man as a coward and unfit to be put a second time on duty, where he had descended to the use of a pistol" (*Herald*, July 15, 1857, 1).

27.   James D. MacCabe, *The Secrets of the Great City: A Work Descriptive of the Virtues and the Vices, the Mysteries, Miseries and Crimes of New York City* (Philadelphia, 1868), 72.
28.   *Times*, May 10, 1867, 4; Nov. 18, 1858, 4 (quotation).
29.   PO March 8, 1830, Mepol 7/1, f. 243; April 9, 1831, *Ibid.*, f. 193; Aug. 4, 1831, Mepol 7/2, f. 20; PP 1837, Third Report, Criminal Law Commissioners, App. I, test. Mayne, 20.
30.   In the Metropolitan Police Act of 1839, and the Habitual Criminals Act of 1869. There were enough fears of police power, however, that the 1839 Act's stop-and-search provisions were not adopted outside of London. See Delmar Karlen, Geoffrey Sawer, Edward M. Wise, *Anglo-American Criminal Justice* (New York, 1967), 116.
31.   PO March 1, 1843, Mepol 7/8, f. 259; PP 1871, XXVIII, Metro. Police Annual Report 1870, 8; N. Y. State Senate Documents, 1856, II no. 97, Police Investigation (hereafter cited as SD) test. J. W. Edmonds, 166.
32.   J. J. Tobias, *Crime and Industrial Society in the 19th Century* (London, 1967), 227-28. Contemporaries often used declining committals to verify their belief in declining crime, but modern students agree with Edwin Chadwick that committals reflect the reporting and prosecution of crime more than its actual occurrence. Chadwick, "Preventive Police," *London Review* 1 (Feb. 1829), 260-62.
33.   The basis of this conclusion is the committal and conviction figures in the Parliamentary *Returns of Criminal Offenders* before 1855 and the *Judicial Statistics*, 1856 on. See also sources cited in note 60 below.
34.   M. H. Smith, *Sunshine and Shadow in New York* (Hartford, 1868), 180-81; George W. Walling, *Recollections of a New York Chief of Police* (New York, 1887), 196.
35.   Walling, *loc. cit.*
36.   SD 1856, II no. 97, Police Investigation Report, 3; test. Abraham Beal, General Agent New York Prison Association, 103-04; test. Police Justice Daniel Clark, 43; AD 1849, VI no. 243, Annual Report, N.Y. Prison Association 1848, 59 (hereafter cited as NYPA); AD 1850, VIII no. 198, NYPA 1849, 25-26.
37.   SD 1856, II no. 97, Police Investigation, test. Police Justice G. W. Pearcey, 15, 23-24; test. Capt. G. W. Walling, 91-92; test. ex-Police Justice W.J. Roome, 34; SD 1861, II no. 71, test. Metro. Police Supt. J. A. Kennedy, 6-9.
38.   For criticisms see AD 1849, VI no. 243, NYPA 1848, 44; AD 1850, VIII no. 198, NYPA 1849, 25-26. The NYPA dropped its attacks after the early fifties.
39.   "Necessity is the mother of invention," *Punch* quipped, "so when you find it necessary to make a charge against somebody you have locked up, invent one." *Punch's Almanack for 1854*, 4, in *Punch's 20 Almanacks 1842-1861* (London, 1862?). Paul Chevigny, *Police Power: Police Abuses in New York City* (New York, c. 1969), ch. 8, discusses "cover charges" like disorderly conduct in the modern context.
40.   PO June 3, 1830, Mepol 7/1, ff. 63-64.
41.   PO July 13, 1833, Mepol 7/2, f. 152.
42.   See PO Jan 4, 1863, Mepol 7/24, 12; Sept. 30, 1865, Mepol 7/26, 275; Sept. 12, 1866, Mepol 7/27, 287.
43.   *Rules and Regulations*, 1851, 38; *Manual*, 1860, 90; SD 1861, II no. 71, Police Investigation, test. Metro. Comm. T. C. Acton, 29 (quotation).
44.   Crapsey, *Netherside*, 27; SD 1861, II no. 71, Police Investigation, test. Police Justice J. H. Welch, 14.
45.   1851 figures: PP 1852-53, LXXXI, Arrest Statistics, 290; BAD 1856, XIII no. 16, Chief's Semi-Annual Report, 12-13. I computed the ratios from London's estimated population, 1851, in the above source and New York's 1851 population in Joseph Shannon, comp., *Mannual of the Corporation of the City of New York 1868* (New York, 1869), 215. London 1869 figures are in PP 1870, XXXVI, Metro. Police Annual Report 1869, table 5, 18 (listing "disorderly characters" which I have assumed to be the same as disorderly conduct). N. Y. figures are in AD 1870, II no. 16, Metro. Police

Annual Report 1869, 74. The disparity of these latter figures is all the more impressive considering that London was over twice as populous as New York.

46.   See below, note 89.

47.   SD 1861, II no. 71, Police Investigation, test. Comm. T. C. Acton, 25.

48.   The policy is set forth in *Rules and Regulations*, 1846, 39; and *Ibid.*, 1851, 55. The phrasing is verbatim from London's PO June 25, 1833, Mepol 7/2, f. 14. The *Manual*, 1860 is silent on assault powers.

49.   SD 1856, II no. 97, Police Investigation, test. Capt. J. Dowling, 149; Walling, *Recollections*, 38-39.

50.   PO July 26, 1851, Mepol 7/15, f. 290; Feb 26, 1869, Mepol 7/31, 58; Memo of 1854 by Mayne, Mepol 2/28, loose.

51.   For judicial sensitivity, see the case of *Regina v. Furley*, Central Criminal Court 1844, in *1 Cox's Criminal Law Cases* 76. The court construed the policeman's traditional warning to suspects that what they say may be held against them as a threat or inducement to confession. For possible impact of old harsh laws, see PP 1845, XIV, Eighth Report, Criminal Law Commissioners, App. A, letter of H. W. Woolrych, 281.

52.   PO Nov. 3, 1837, Mepol 7/5, f. 284.

53.   PO May 15, 1844, Mepol 7/9, f. 245; PP 1845, XIV, Eighth Report, Criminal Law Commissioners, App. A, letter of Lord Chief Justice Denman, 211; William Forsyth, "Criminal Procedure in Scotland and England" (1851) in *Essays Critical and Narrative* (London, 1874), 41-42.

54.   The case is *Regina v. Baldry*, Court of Queen's Bench 1852, in *2 Dennison's Crown Cases Reserved* 430. See also James Fitzjames Stephen, *A History of the Criminal Law of England*, 3 vols. (London, 1883), I, 447. For Commissioners' views, Mayne's 1854 memo, Mepol 2/28; the views of Attorney General A. J. A. Cockburn are in PP 1854-55, XII. Public Prosecutors, 186, q. 2396.

55.   PO Sept. 22, 1865, Mepol 7/26, 268; Jan. 2, 1866, Mepol 7/27, 13.

56.   AD 1866, III no. 50, NYPA 1865, 128, 134, 150; AD 1865, III no 62, NYPA 1864, 222; Alexander Callow, *The Tweed Ring* (New York, c. 1965), 148.

57.   See PP 1854-55, XII, Public Prosecutors, report and testimony.

58.   William A. Westley, *Violence and the Police: A Sociological Study of Law, Custom, and Morality* (Cambridge, Mass., c. 1970), 81-82; Albert J. Reiss, Jr., *The Police and the Public* (New Haven, 1971), 134-38.

59.   PP 1837-38, XV, Police Offices, test. Rowan, 101, q. 1078; PO Nov 29, 1829, Mepol 7/1, f. 241; Nov 5, 1830, Mepol 7/1, f. 130; July 9, 1834, Mepol 7/3, f. 45; Sept 27, 1837, Mepol 7/5, f. 279; July 26, 1851, Mepol 7/15, f. 290; Memo of 1854, Mepol 2/28, loose; PO May 13, 1865, Mepol 7/26, 138.

60.   I have computed these approximate percentages from statistics in Anon., "The Police System of London," *Edinburgh Review* 96 (July 1852), 22 (1831-41); Joseph Fletcher, "Statistical Account of the Police of the Metropolis," *Journal of the Statistical Society* 13 (1850), 258 (1842-48); PP 1871, XXVIII, Metro. Police Ann. Report 1870, 21 (1850-70).

61.   See Reith, *New Study*, 150-51; Radzinowicz, English *Criminal Law*, IV, 172ff.

62.   BAD 1852, XIX pt 1 no. 7, Chief's Semi-Annual Report, 107; SD 1856, II no. 97, test. Capt. J. W. Hartt, 101; Capt. J. Dowling, 157; AD 1861, I no. 27, Metro. Police Ann. Report 1860, 6; AD 1867, VII no. 220, Metro. Police Ann. Report 1866, 11-12.

63.   Tenth Precinct Blotter, May 25-Aug. 27, 1855; July 27-Aug. 26, 1856, Ms, N. Y. City Municipal Archives; SD 1861, II no. 71, Police Investigation, test. Comm. T. C. Acton, 27; J.W. Edmonds, 163-64. Arrest figures for assault and battery and petty · larceny are found in the police annual reports. They can be compared with convictions for these offenses in the Court of Special Sessions published in Shannon, comp., *Manual* 1868, 178. Convictions for "simple larceny" in London were 54 percent of arrests in 1868; for petty larceny in New York 29 percent of arrests in 1868-69. Convictions for

"common assault" in London in 1869 were 55 percent of arrests compared to New York's 8 percent for assault and battery in 1868-69. (See AD 1870, II no. 17, Metro. Police Ann. Report 1869, 24 [arrests]; AD 1870, VI no. 108, Ann. Report of the Secretary of State on Criminal Statistics 1869, 144-46 [convictions]; PP 1870, XXXVI, Metro. Police Annual Report 1869, table 5, 18). Comparison of N. Y. felony arrests and convictions is in AD 1867, VII no. 20, Metro. Police Annual Report, 1866, 11-12.

64. This is based on a comparison of the proportion of convictions in indictable offenses and offenses summarily tried by a magistrate in the Parliamentary *Judicial Statistics*, 1856-70.

65. See N. Y. *Times*, April 14, 1867, 5; N. Y. *World*, Feb. 11, 1867, 4.

66. For this remark I am indebted to a letter from James Richardson, commenting on an earlier draft of this paper.

67. PO Oct. 15, 1831, Mepol 7/2, f. 41.

68. See statement (of which I could not locate the original) quoted in Reith, *British Police*, 183, and Comms. to Home Office Jan 6, 1835, Mepol 1/17, letter 27751. By 1835 complaints in the Mepol letter books are overwhelmingly of alleged neglect of duty. Later Mayne wrote to H. Fitzroy, Sept. 29, 1853: "The public now expect to see a constable at all places at every moment that he may be required." (Mepol 1/46, n.p.).

69. Karl Polanyi, *The Great Transformation* (New York, 1944), 186-87, phrase order rearranged.

70. Some contemporary comment on orderliness in the 1850s includes Charles Dickens, "The Sunday Screw," *Household Words* 1 (June 22, 1850), 291-92; *Illustrated London News* 18 (May 31, 1851), 501 and June 28, 1851, 606, on working-class orderliness at the Great Exhibition; Wynter, "Police and Thieves," 173. On the police role, see Frederic Hill, *Crime: Its Amount, Causes, and Remedies* (London, 1853), 6-7; Anon., *The Great Metropolis*, 2 vols., 2nd ed. (London, 1837), I, 11; PP 1837-38, XV, Police Offices, test. Rowan and Mayne, 183-85, qq. 2091, 2094, 2102; PP 1854-55, X, Sale of Beer, test. Mayne, 86, q. 1138. See also Silver, "Demand for Order," 5.

71. London *Times*, July 3, 1855, 8; *Reynolds's Newspaper*, July 29, 1855, 8; *Lloyd's Weekly Newspaper*, July 8, 1855, 6. According to the *Times*, July 16, 1855, 12, overt antagonism to the police was short-lived. The riots are discussed by Brian Harrison, "The Sunday Trading Riots of 1855," *Historical Journal* 7 (1965), 219-45.

72. Anon., "The Metropolitan Police and What Is Paid Them," *Chambers's Magazine* 41 (July 2, 1864), 424.

73. Good accounts of complaints and the state of the force are in the *Times*, Dec 29. 1868, and in "Custos," *The Police Force of the Metropolis in 1868* (London, 1868).

74. Alan Harding, *A Social History of English Law* (Baltimore, 1966), 366; W. L. Burn, *The Age of Equipoise: A Study of the Mid-Victorian Generation* (New York, c. 1965), 176-94.

75. J. F. Moylan, *Scotland Yard and the Metropolitan Police* (London, 1929) 150-57. For Mayne's distrust of detectives, see, e.g., Memo to Superintendents, Jan. 23, 1854, Mepol 2/28, loose. Mayne did turn more to detection in the sixties than earlier, but his successor as Commissioner, Col. E. Y. W. Henderson, considerably expanded the detective force. See PP 1870, XXXVI, Metro. Police Ann. Report 1869, 3-4.

76. For expressions of this grievance, see *Illustrated London News* 3 (Dec. 23, 1843), 406; see also *Reynolds's Newspaper*, May 2, 1852, 8; July 25, 1858, 9; Aug. 17, 1862, 4; April 5, 1863, 4; Feb.9, 1868, 4; *Lloyd's Weekly Newspaper*, July 5, 1863, 1; Thomas Wright, *Our New Masters* (London, 1969, first pub. 1873), 155-56.

77. PP 1830, XXIII, Instructions to Metro. Police, 11; Anon., "Metropolitan Police," 426. Cf. Mrs J. C. Byrne, *Undercurrents Overlooked*, 2 vols. (London, 1860), I, 51, 54-55.

78. *East London Observer*, June 6, 1868, 5; July 4, 1868, 4; Dec. 5, 1868, 4.

79. For danger, Chesney, *Victorian Underworld*, 92-93; Byrne, *Undercurrents*, I,

78-79; James Greenwood, *The Wilds of London* (London, 1874), 1, 56. For police policy, PP 1834, XVI, Metro. Police, test. Rowan, 11, qq. 165-67; *Hansard's Parliamentary Debates* 1830, n.s. vol. 25, col. 358; and Anon., "Police System of London" (1852), 9. Study of the distribution of the London police reveals the most policemen usually in neighborhoods where poverty rubbed shoulders with wealth.
80.   "The Model Peeler" by C. P. Cove, *Diprose's Music-Hall Song-Book* (London, 1862), 50. Cf. the number Mrs Byrne heard in 1860 in *Undercurrents*, I, 256-57.
81.   For the costermongers, see Henry Mayhew, *London Labour and the London Poor*, 4 vols. (2nd. ed., 1862-64), I, 22.
82.   For workers as leaders of the early opposition, see *Hansard's Parliamentary Debates* 1833, 3rd. ser. vol. 16, col. 1139; PP 1833, Cold Bath Fields Meeting, test. Supt. Baker, C Division, 159, qq. 3914, 3917; J. Grant, *Sketches in London* (London, 1838), 391.
83.   Mayne states his outlook on this problem succinctly in PP 1867-68, XIV, Sunday Closing, 8, qq. 127-28.
84.   Alexis de Tocqueville in Francis Bowen, ed., *Democracy in America*, 2 vols. (2nd ed., Cambridge, Mass., 1863; first pub. in U.S. 1835-40), I, 265-68.
85.   See Richardson, *N. Y. Police*, chs. 3-5, 7.
86.   N. Y. *Herald*, March 25, 1856, 4.
87.   MacCabe, *Secrets*, 70-71. The *Herald*, however, did not like the Republican Superintendent, calling him "Mr. Fouche' Kennedy" (Dec. 22, 1860, 6).
88.   *Times*, Nov. 18, 1858, 4, editorializing on the first killing of an offender by a patrolman.
89.   William O. Stoddard's *The Volcano under the City* (New York, 1887) is an account of the draft riots which reminds its readers that the volcano is still simmering. For similar imagery see Samuel B. Halliday, *The Lost and Found: or, Life among the Poor* (New York, 1860), 332; and Junius Henri Browne, *The Great Metropolis: A Mirror of New York* (Hartford, 1869), 74. On New York's violence, see Richardson, "History," 393ff.; *Times*, May 10, 1855, 4; AD 1859, II no. 63, Metro. Police Ann. Report 1858, 14; AD 1865, II no. 35, Metro. Police Ann. Report 1864, 11-13; Crapsey, *Netherside*, 29-30; and especially Charles Loring Brace, *The Dangerous Classes of New York, and Twenty Years' Work among Them* (New York, 1872), arguing that New York could claim "elements of the population even more dangerous than the worst of London" (p. 25).
90.   The figures are rough calculations based on the surnames of officers and complainants in the Complaints against Policemen, 1846-1854, City Clerk Papers, N. Y. C. Municipal Archives.
91.   This conclusion rests on fragmentary records, the Applications for Positions as Policemen 1855, Boxes 3209-10, City Clerk Papers, N. Y. C. Municipal Archives. Of 43 successful applicants, only 3 were unskilled laborers and 7 drivers or other transport workers. Twenty-two were various sorts of skilled workers, one a mechanic, five shopkeepers, five clerks or other white-collar workers. The arrest statistics in the police reports reveal the overwhelming preponderance of unskilled offenders.
92.   For the increase of Irish officers in the Metropolitan Police after a decline in 1857-58, I counted Irish surnames in the lists in D. T. Valentine, comp., *Manual of the Corporation of the City of New York* (New York, 1848-68) for 1856 (last year of the old force), 1858 and 1861 (the last year policemen's names are listed).
93.   See AD 1864, III no. 28, Metro. Police Ann. Report 1863, 13. Joel Tyler Headley, *The Great Riots of New York 1712-1873* (New York, 1873), 305-06, and MacCabe, *Secrets*, 70-71, praise the Irish policemen.
94.   See Richardson, *N. Y. Police*, 52, 57, 110, 154-56, 182-85.
95.   Harriet Martineau, *Morals and Manners* (Philadelphia, 1838), 192. Here "police" refers to the old constabulary and night watch system which preceded modern forces in America.

13

TOWARD A DYNAMIC THEORY OF CRIME AND THE POLICE
A Criminal Justice System Perspective

ERIC MONKKONEN

In the middle of the nineteenth century American cities went through a permanent and significant institutional development that created one of the most visible identifiers of modern urban life—the uniformed police. Police systems modeled after the Metropolitan Police of London, created in 1829, were established in every major American city between about 1840 and 1870. In the past decade, urban historians have produced a dozen full-length studies of these police departments documenting the details of a modern urban institution now a little over a century old.[1] These studies paint a picture of police forces struggling with inadequate pay, corruption, public demands for law and order, conflicts between cities and states for control over the departments, and, someplace in the hazy background, the police fight against crime.

The police became the only agency to which the public could turn for repression of crime and for information concerning it. After traditional means of social control such as constables, their catchers, and the watch had been abandoned, they seemed far too archaic to re-establish. Throughout the nineteenth century, crime was perceived to be on the rise and most contemporary journals periodically printed articles on the increase in criminal incidents. Crime was thought to be the product of the "dangerous class—the poor, the unemployed, and criminals—a rapidly-growing fixture of the expanding cities. Cities grew, the dangerous class in them grew, and the police became ever more important in controlling the perceived criminal concomitant of urbanization.

There is one modern criminological perspective on the relationship of crime and the police that is quite different from that of nineteenth-century observers or twentieth-century scholars like James Q. Wilson, who believe in the simple rule that more police will result in less crime.[2] Opposed to this "crime control" perspective, the "labelling" theorists like Howard Becker, David Matza, and Richard Quinney feel that crime is created by society acting through the agency of the police. They argue that deviant behavior becomes a criminal offense only when it has been labeled and acted upon. Crime is a social act with reality only in its social context.[3]

By moving from the nineteenth-century position that crime is a product of the danger-ous class to one that sees crime as the result of an interaction between the police and the offender, we are alerted to an inherent irony in the criminal justice system. Information about the amount of crime comes through the arrest process, the adjudication process, and the penal system. The more efficient the police and courts are in processing crime, the more crime there appears to be. The better the police get, the less effective they become.[4]

Let us consider an additional irony: as a bureaucracy which, among other things, is concerned with its own survival and growth, police need crime. They thrive when crime increases, finding more opportunities for advancement, larger budgets, more specialists, and more supervisory positions. Thus, the bureaucratic needs of the police require more arrests to create a rising crime rate.[5]

These ironies built into the structure of the criminal justice system should make us aware of the difficulties inherent in the study of police or crime in the past, for the police are not an autonomous social institution; but only one part of the complex system. Unfor-tunately, few studies of the nineteenth-century police have shown any awareness of the subtleties of this system. This problem is serious. As anyone who has attended police history sessions at recent conventions knows, what should be intellectual dynamite all too often turns out to be soporific. There is no generalizing to the larger society, no dealing with the major issues of urban history, and no differentiation between the police and other institu-tions, whether business, social welfare, or political.

The purely narrative orientation of police history has presented the emergence of sig-nificant issues. To correct this, I here pose three important questions concerning the intro-duction and growth of the police in the nineteenth century: first, why did the police system grow; second, what did it do; and, third, how did the dangerous class relate to the new institution of the uniformed urban police? A criminal justice system perspective can help formulate tentative answers to these questions. This perspective always sees the police as agents of the society, creating criminals through the arrest process, dependent on social financing, and caught in the measurement dilemma of arrest rates. Most important, it forces us to write police history from the "bottom up": we simply cannot ignore the roles of the criminal offenders themselves. Most recent work in the history of crime, however, has ignored this approach. Historians can only cite Roger Lane's article published nine years ago in the *Journal of Social History*. This interesting article deals with crime in Massachusetts between 1834 and 1900, but only a miniscule amount of data is presented, showing total court cases and imprisonments for the years 1840, 1860, and 1900.[6]

Why in this age of cliometrics is there so little statistical work on crime? Crime was one of the first topics to be studied by the use of social statistics. The first publications of the American Statistical Association in the late nineteenth century had major articles on crime rates; the 1890 U.S. Census contained one volume devoted to the dangerous class; in Europe, Fregier published *Les classes dangereuses de la population dans les grandes villes, et des moyens des les rendre meillures* in 1840. Historians have data on the wholesale price index in the West before 1860, but not on crime rates. Just because the data "are in some cases unreliable and in most, incomplete,"[7] do we throw up our hands, write more institu-tional histories, and reassert the age-old claim that crime was rising?

The three basic statistics that allow us to establish the crude parameters of the criminal justice system are arrests per thousand, the number of police per capita, and the number of arrests per police officer.[8] For the twentieth century, information can be taken from the *Uniform Crime Reports* of the FBI. Although the reporting base varied greatly between 1934 and 1970, the FBI shows sample size so that per capita data may be calculated (see Table 1). For data prior to 1930, annual mayors' reports usually published the reports of the chief of police, which detailed number and kinds of arrests, size of the police depart-ment, and other information. Although at this time the data are incomplete, the implica-tions of the relationships found are dramatic.

Table 1
Arrests per Police Officer and Officers per 10,000 Persons,
United States: 1934, 1970

	Arrests	Officers
1934	19.1	16.0
1970	24.2	20.4

Source: *Crime in the United States: Uniform Crime Reports, 1970* (Washington, D.C., 1971); *Uniform Crime Reports*, VI, 3 (October, 1935) and VII, 1 (April, 1936).

Figure 1 graphs the arrests per capita and Figure 2 drunkenness rates, while Figure 3 shows the police officers per capita compared to arrests per officer, all for San Francisco from 1863-1917. While the overall arrests do not give a neat line graph, it appears that there are three periods of differing arrest behavior: the first from 1863 to 1875, the second from 1876 to 1900, and the third from 1900 to 1917. Of most interest is the overall decline through the last quarter of the nineteenth century, a decline accompanied by a rising proportion of arrests for drunkenness.

As the police established themselves and became legitimized, their per capita ratio increased despite brief declines, such as the drop between 1882 and 1890. The police per capita figure is important, for it maps the size of the population that a policeman had to survey; the closer the surveillance, the more opportunity an officer presumably had to observe an arrestable offense. Thus, as the size of the individual police officer's universe of potential offenders became smaller, we could predict that the number of arrests per policeman would increase. This is, in fact, the relationship today, for if we compare the arrests per policeman to the police per capita between the 1930s and 1970, we see that both are rising (see Table 1).[9]

But what about the nineteenth century? Here the situation is the inverse, for as the police per capita increase, the arrests per policeman decrease, a startling indication that the nineteenth-century criminal justice system functioned quite differently from the modern one. What were all of the new departments doing? Why was there an obviously different relationship between police and criminals?

Let me suggest an explanation that links the *raison d'être* of the new uniformed, para-military police and the concept of a dangerous class to the changing arrest behavior. We must remember that although the police were a new institution, offenders had been arrested before the police were created. The criminal justice system before the police was *not* a system of informal community sanctions.[10] Rather, it consisted of a diverse set of civil institutions—sheriffs, constables, the night watch, and thief catchers, in addition to occasional citizen action. This system operated as a crisis-oriented public service, not unlike attorneys, coroners, doctors, and fire departments—all of whom respond during or after a crisis. When a need arose, there was a social mechanism available for assistance; the "hue and cry" reflected this pragmatic attitude of crisis-oriented crime control. When a theft occurred, the hue and cry required all who heard to pursue the thief until caught; there was no thought of prevention of the offense.

But the concept of prevention became a major rationale behind the establishment of a permanent, uniformed police, first in England, then in New York and Boston. A moment's reflection reveals that prevention as a social policy involves a shift in emphasis from the offense to the offender, focusing energy on the potential offender. The problem is, of course, that one cannot arrest potential offenders, and arrest after an offense occurs no longer constitues prevention. The concept of the dangerous class provided a solution to this police burden, for if one assumes that an identifiable class of people produces the crime, then prevention can be accomplished by cordoning off this class from society and generating arrest activity within it. The kind of arrest is of little concern, for what counts is who gets arrested. As an institution created to prevent crime, the police were specifically designed to control the dangerous class. Crime prevention in the nineteenth century could mean only one thing: harassment of this group.[11]

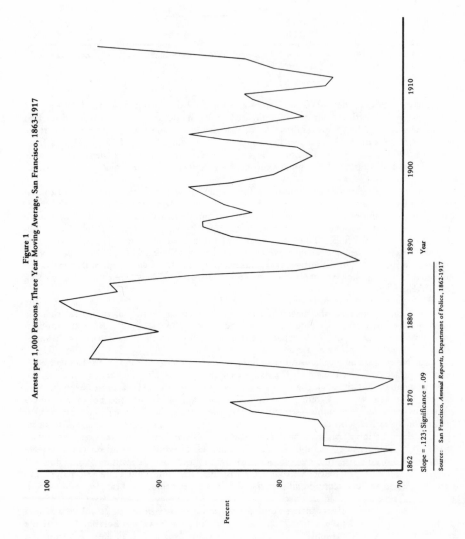

Figure 1

Arrests per 1,000 Persons, Three Year Moving Average, San Francisco, 1863-1917

Slope = .123; Significance = .09

Source: San Francisco, *Annual Reports*, Department of Police, 1862-1917

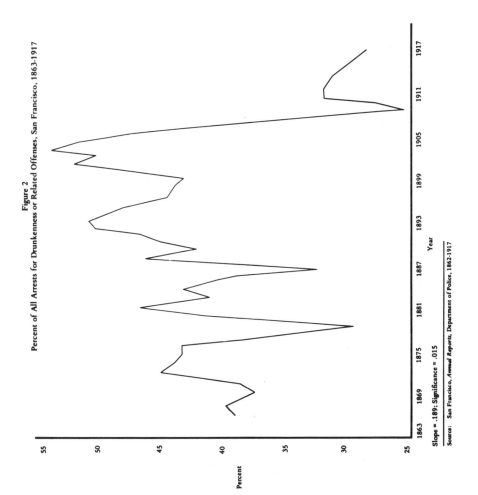

Figure 2
Percent of All Arrests for Drunkenness or Related Offenses, San Francisco, 1863-1917

Slope = .189; Significance = .015

Source: San Francisco, *Annual Reports*, Department of Police, 1862-1917

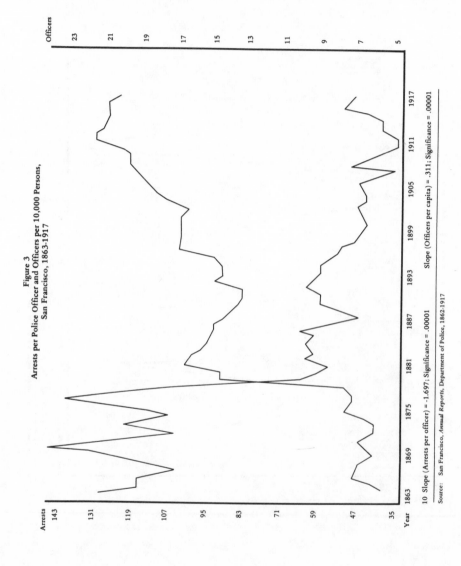

Figure 3
Arrests per Police Officer and Officers per 10,000 Persons,
San Francisco, 1863-1917

10 Slope (Arrests per officer) = -1.697; Significance = .00001   Slope (Officers per capita) = .311; Significance = .00001

Source: San Francisco, *Annual Reports*, Department of Police, 1862-1917

It should be noted that in the highly stratified society of eighteenth- and early nineteenth-century America, even social disorder had had its place. Mobs and rioters engaged in what Eric Hobsbawn has called "pre-political" violence, and a "grammar of dissent" existed between urban rioters and the authorities who controlled them. "General" Ebenezer Mackintosh conducted and coordinated New York mob actions in a " 'most regular Manner." Elites understood this, and they understood the nature of other crime as well. The eighteenth-century world was a place with class-shared perceptions on the meaning and place of disorder.[12] Industrialization and urbanization upset this perceptual ordering and produced cities with increasingly visible, yet anonymous, dangerous classes. From the elite perspective, violence seemed increasingly incoherent and unconnected to political motivation—after all, most men had the vote, so why should mob violence have persisted? Increasing residential segregation ensured that social class distances were paralleled by physical distances: the "grammar" shared by the dangerous class and the elites disappeared; urban violence, which had been perceived as a part of the social order, became disruptive to society.[13]

An additional social effect of industrialization and urbanization increased the demand for police through a change in the dangerous class. Tramps, especially in the post-Civil War era, became a major part of the American social landscape. While not perceived as a threat before the depression of 1873 when thousands of homeless workers roamed the country in search of jobs, tramps gave the concept of a dangerous class even more dramatic meaning. They were especially mobile, and, it was thought by the dominant society, this gave them an increased opportunity to rape, rob, and plunder. The magazine literature of the time ceased to discuss the "Children of the Summer," as the tramps had been patronizingly referred to. Instead, articles appeared offering solutions to the "Tramp Evil." Tramps epitomized the social disorder of the urban-industrial nation; their mere existence ensured that the urban police would continue to grow and be supported by the nondangerous classes of urban society.

The newly created police departments thus had irreconcilable demands placed upon them. They were being asked to end the perceived disorder created by urban-industrial society. This disorder violated the boundaries of social behavior acceptable to the dominant society, but the boundaries were no longer defined or enforced by members of society acting from the stimulus of a real situation. That is, the constables, night watch, neighbors, or bystanders were not called out to catch a thief after a theft had been observed or experienced. Instead, the actual behavioral boundaries were expected to coincide with the *ideal* boundaries. For the first time, socially ideal behavior could be *demanded*, whether feasible or not. Probably the best example of the conflict between social demands placed upon the police and a real situation where they were expected to define boundaries occurred in the enforcement of various Sunday liquor laws. The dominant society could demand that liquor not be dispensed on Sundays, but such enforcement went against the accepted behavior of many working-class neighborhoods, and the police were unable to enforce the law.[14]

The police, in being asked to prevent criminal behavior, were caught on the horns of two dilemmas. First, they faced the problem of arrest rates: the more arrests they made, the more measured crime increased. Assuming that arrests served as a deterrent, the police would be faced with declining crime rates and arrests, thereby decreasing their utility. The second dilemma, equally serious, was that police were being asked to enforce the behavioral boundaries of decorum defined by one class on another, the intended purpose being the prevention of crime. Such boundary definition did not come out of a broad social consensus and was exacerbated by fear of class conflict. Further, enforcement was impossibly difficult, nor was it clear that the goal of prevention had been attained.

The nineteenth century saw clever solutions to these dilemmas. If we refer to our data on arrests per policeman and policemen per capita, we see that the police were increasing in proportion to the population, but their productivity (arrest rates) was decreasing.[15] Further, we see that the measure of crime in society, arrests per thousand, was decreasing in the late nineteenth century. The nineteenth-century criminal justice system was, therefore, characterized by an increasing amount of symbolic order through the increased visibility of the uniformed police and a decreasing amount of actual arrest behavior or boundary enforcement. Everyone had their cake and ate it too. The police bureaucracy satisfied its need for growth and the policemen did less arresting. The dangerous class was actually less harassed and the dominant class saw more symbols of public order and a decreasing crime rate.

This paper has suggested tentative answers to the three questions raised at the beginning, but much more work is needed. We must have sophisticated analyses of what the police did, what pressures created and fostered the growth of the departments, and how the actual behavior of police compared with the ideal behavior. Further, we need to know what kind of people became police officers and how this affected their day-to-day discretion in boundary definition. What did they do on the street? How did they handle the dangerous class? Was "Clubber" Williams voicing the attitude of the average policeman when he claimed, "There is more law in the end of a policeman's nightstick than in a decision of the Supreme Court"?[16]

More important, we need much more work on crime statistics, the dangerous class, and the role of tramps. Far too little is known about the bottom of nineteenth-century society, and there is no excuse for this. The source material is overwhelmingly rich: for example, almost every state has annual reports of court cases by type of offense and county. Original court dockets are also available so that crime rates may be reconstructed even more accurately. I have a project underway to establish a comprehensive statistical series from annual city reports using arrest rates rather than court trials as the base. And there is much more available. The real question is why this material has been ignored. The answer, I think, is the same as that stated by Jesse Lemisch in 1966—most historians continue to be trained to ignore all but society's elites. Traditionally, the police have not been thought of as a particularly glamorous urban bureaucracy in the nineteenth century, and the average offenders are even less fascinating. Moreover, since the study of such groups requires statistical skills and sophisticated questioning, most historians persist in asking other questions. But exciting historical research lies in the linking of criminal statistics to the structure and behavior of criminal justice institutions.

NOTES

1. Roger Lane, *Policing the City: Boston, 1822-1905* (Cambridge, Mass., 1967); James F. Richardson, *The New York Police: Colonial Times to 1901* (New York, 1970); George A. Ketcham, "Municipal Police Reform: A Comparative Study of Law Enforcement in Cincinnati, Chicago, New Orleans, New York, and St. Louis, 1844-1877" (Ph.D. diss., University of Missouri, 1967); John K. Maniha, "The Mobility of Elites in a Bureaucratizing Organization: The St. Louis Police Department, 1861-1961" (Ph.D. diss., University of Michigan, 1970); Jerald E. Levine, "Police, Parties, and Polity: The Bureaucratization, Unionization, and Professionalization of the New York City Police, 1870-1917" (Ph.D. diss., University of Wisconsin, 1971); Eugene F. Rider, "The Denver Police Department: An Administrative, Organizational, and Operational History, 1858-1905" (Ph.D. diss., University of Denver, 1971); David R. Johnson, "The Search for an Urban Discipline: Police Reform as a Response to Crime in American Cities, 1800-1875" (Ph.D. diss., University of Chicago, 1972); Kenneth G. Alfers, "The Washington Police: A History, 1800-1886" (Ph.D. diss., George Washington University, 1975); Louis Cei, "Law Enforcement in Richmond: A History of Police-Community Relations, 1737-1974" (Ph.D. diss., Florida State University, 1975); Allan E. Levett, "Centralization of City Police in the Nineteenth-Century United States" (Ph.D. diss., University of Michigan, 1975); and Louis Marchiafara, "Institutional and Legal Aspects of the Growth of Professional Police Service: The Houston Experience, 1878-1948" (Ph.D. diss., Rice University, 1976). Johnson, Ketcham, Levett, and Miller all bring more than one city into their analyses.

2. See, for instance, Wilson's article, "Lock 'Em up and Other Thoughts on Crime," in the *New York Times Magazine* 9 March 1975), pp. 5 ff, and the replies (13 April 1975), pp. 60-71.

3. David Matza, *Becoming Deviant* (Englewood Cliffs, N.J., 1969) has a good summary and analysis of labelling theory. See also, Howard Becker, *Outsiders: Studies in the Sociology of Deviance* (New York, 1973); and Richard Quinney, *The Social Reality of Crime* (Boston, 1970).

4. Unless, of course, one accepts the deterrence theory of the crime-control perspective. George L. Kelling et al., *The Kansas City Preventive Patrol Experiment: A Summary Report* (Washington, 1974), is an interesting and provocative study of the failure of heavy patrol to have any deterrent effects.

5. Consider the major federal response to urban rioting in the late sixties, which provided massive aid to law enforcement agencies.

6. Roger Lane, "Crime and Criminal Statistics in Nineteenth-Century Massachusetts," *Journal of Social History*, 2 (Winter 1968): 156-63. A large amount of research is needed to determine the validity of Lane's assertion that serious crimes declined because of urbanization.

7. Lane, *Policing the City*, p. 225.

8. It is important to establish these parameters before more complex disaggregation is attempted. See Eric Monkkonen, *The Dangerous Class: Crime and Poverty in Columbus, Ohio, 1860-85* (Cambridge, Mass., 1975), Ch. 2, for a disaggregated, multivariate, causal analysis of crime in one state. Disaggregation requires a carefully thought-out strategy that is sensitive to the nature of the questions being asked and to the arrest process for the different offenses. While a dichotomy like misdemeanor *v.* felony or property *v.* person has an instant appeal, these are not very good schemes unless logically related to the analysis. Crime is a social phenomenon, and the historian should accept society's definitions for the purpose of analysis. There are two primary considerations in disaggregating arrest data, each requiring an understanding of the creation of the data. First, did the offense involve a victim, or did it depend on police aggression? Second, if the offense did have a victim, was its nature such that the victim or a witness could identify the offender, thus making an arrest probable? These considerations must be given priority over any others. My future research strategy includes the disaggregation of the major victimless offenses—public drunkenness, disorderly conduct, vagrancy, loitering, and suspicious persons —mainly as a measure of police behavior, and murder as an indicator of serious felonious offenses. While other procedures are feasible, they must be sensitve to the process that created the data and not automatically assume isomorphism between indicators and behavior.

9. See Wilbur R. Miller, *Cops and Bobbies: Police Authority in New York and London, 1830-1870* (Chicago, 1977), for an interesting discussion of the legitimization question.

10. For an intriguing if erroneous argument that pre-policed society *did* have community-based law enforcement, see Evelyn L. Parks, "From Constabulary to Police Society: Implications for Social Control," *Catalyst* (Summer 1970), 76-97.

11. "Harassment" may be an unfair and inappropriate term, for the police dealt with the dangerous class as administrators of welfare as well as arrestors. Police services ranged from providing soup and coal during hard winters to supplying overnight accommodations for the homeless.

12. See Pauline Maier, *From Resistance to Revolution: Colonial Radicals and the Development of American Opposition to Britain, 1765-1776* (New York, 1972). Also, Eric Hobsbawn, *Primitive Rebels* (Manchester, 1959).

13. See Allan Silver, "The Demand for Order in Civil Society: A Review of Some Themes in the History of Urban Crime, Police, and Riot," in David J. Bordua, ed., *The Police: Six Sociological Essays* (New York, 1967), for a provocative discussion of this aspect of nineteenth-century policing. Silver sees the need to control mobs as the major reason for creating police.

14. Wilbur R. Miller, "Police Authority in London and New York City, 1830-1870," *Journal of Social History* (Winter 1975), 81-101, deals with this issue.

15. For San Francisco (with 49 cases), r = -.743, significant at .001. For Philadelphia (with only 20 cases), r = -.89, significant at .001.

16. Cited by Herbert Asbury, *The Gangs of New York: An Informal History of the Underworld* (New York, 1927), p. 237.

14

THE CRIME OF PRECOCIOUS SEXUALITY
Female Juvenile Delinquency in the Progressive Era

STEVEN SCHLOSSMAN and STEPHANIE WALLACH

The juvenile justice system's discrimination against poor and minority children has been well documented, but the system's discrimination on the basis of gender has been less widely recognized. Drawing on neglected court records and secondary sources, Steven Schlossman and Stephanie Wallach show how girls bore a disproportionate share of the burden of juvenile justice in the Progressive era. The authors note that during the Progressive era female juvenile delinquents often received more severe punishments than males, even though boys usually were charged with more serious crimes. Schlossman and Wallach conclude that the discriminatory treatment of female delinquents in the early twentieth century resulted from racial prejudice, new theories of adolescence, and Progressive-era movements to purify society.

This essay is an historical inquiry into the practice of sexual discrimination against female juvenile delinquents. Although American public policy toward girl offenders first took shape in the middle decades of the nineteenth century—the Victorian era—we have decided to focus on the Progressive era of the early twentieth century. During this latter period scientific and popular literature on female delinquency expanded enormously, and most states adopted the main components

The authors would like to thank Nancy Pottishman Weiss, Merle Borrowman, Geraldine Joncich Clifford, and Sheldon Messinger for their helpful suggestions on earlier drafts of this essay. A portion of the research for this essay was supported by the Spencer Foundation, to which we extend our sincere thanks. Responsibility for errors in fact or interpretation is, of course, our own.

of modern correctional machinery. Our essay spotlights the differences between stated intentions, revealed preferences, and actual outcomes.[1] Although we attempt to develop a broad interpretation, we must emphasize the selectivity of our historical research. We do not pretend to have exhausted available sources, to have explored all possible interpretations of our evidence, or, certainly, to have written the definitive account. Instead, we offer a preliminary synthesis of untapped sources in an effort to call attention to a neglected subject, to encourage additional research on it, and to suggest ways of integrating the topic of female delinquency into the rapidly growing fields of women's history and the history of corrections.

Our essay speaks only indirectly to modern-day issues in juvenile justice. Continuities between past and present will often be apparent, to be sure, but we dare not draw them too explicitly for the simple reason that social scientists know very little about the theory and practice of female juvenile justice between the 1920s and the 1960s.[2] Nonetheless, we do believe it is possible to use history as a force for social change by laying bare the roots and assumptions of anachronistic policies—policies, in this instance, that lag behind our current attitudes toward female sexuality and equal justice for women. Given our reformist goals, it may be useful to explain in advance why we focus on sexual discrimination as opposed to other equally blatant injustices in the correctional system.

Like other critics of American juvenile justice, we decry practices that lead to unwarranted labeling and incarceration of children and that discriminate against poor, minority youth, regardless of sex.[3] We consider it indisputable that, from the early nineteenth century to the present, the juvenile justice system has systematically singled out lower-class children for punishment and ignored middle- and upper-class youth.[4] In this essay, however, our main concern is not with class, ethnic, racial, or age bias, for we believe those themes have been adequately treated elsewhere. Rather, what most interests us now is how, in a correctional system that discriminates consistently against poor, minority children as a whole, females carry a disproportionate share of the burden of injustice.

Discussion of female delinquency is conspicuously absent from most scholarly writing on criminal justice. Despite a persistent hue and cry during the last decade

---

1 See Lawrence Cremin, "Foreword," in *American Education and Vocationalism*, eds. Marvin Lazerson and W. Norton Grubb (New York: Teachers College Press, 1974), p. ix.

2 One reason for the lack of scholarly attention to girl offenders in this period was the emphasis on gang delinquency, in which girls participated very little. There is, however, Paul Tappan's classic *Delinquent Girls in Court* (Montclair, N.J.: Patterson Smith, 1969), originally published in 1947.

3 See, for example, Lois Forer, *"No One Will Lissen"* (New York: Grosset and Dunlap, 1970); Patrick Murphy, *Our Kindly Parent . . . The State* (New York: Viking, 1974); Lisa Richette, *The Throwaway Children* (New York: Dell, 1969); and Ken Wooden, *Weeping in the Playtime of Others* (New York: McGraw-Hill, 1976).

4 See, for example, Michael Katz, *The Irony of Early School Reform* (Cambridge, Mass.: Harvard University Press, 1968); Anthony Platt, *The Child Savers* (Chicago: University of Chicago Press, 1969); Alexander Liazos, "Class Oppression: The Functions of Juvenile Justice," *The Insurgent Sociologist*, Fall 1974, 1, 2–24; and Steven Schlossman, *Love and the American Delinquent* (Chicago: University of Chicago Press, 1977).

about spiraling rates of delinquency, despite mounting evidence demonstrating the ineffectiveness of correctional programs, and despite the women's rights movement, girl offenders are largely ignored. Even as the number of females processed through the juvenile courts climbs steadily, an implicit consensus remains that the male teenager defines the delinquency problem in modern America and suffers most egregiously from correctional injustices.[5]

We suggest two main reasons why girl delinquents receive so little attention. First, girls are accused primarily of so-called victimless crimes, that is, offenses that do not involve clear-cut damage to persons or property. If committed by adults, these actions would not be legally punishable; if committed by boys, the same acts would be interpreted less seriously and punished less severely. Thus, rather ironically, the plight of female delinquents receives little scrutiny because they are accused of committing less flagrant violations of legal codes. Second, traditional stereotypes of women as the weaker and more dependent sex rationalize, indeed even legitimate, discriminatory correctional practices in the name of humanitarianism. As the half-century struggle to enact the Equal Rights Amendment makes abundantly clear, one of the most tenacious beliefs in our society is that women require more comprehensive legal protection than do men. Society justifies "preventive" intervention into the lives of antisocial girls under the rationale that they are especially vulnerable to evil forces and temptations. This so-called chivalrous attitude leads to earlier intervention and longer periods of supervision for delinquent girls than delinquent boys.

The sparse historical writing about female delinquency concentrates on reformatories, especially the pioneering nineteenth-century institutions, rather than on the juvenile justice system as a whole.[6] Furthermore, several of the studies are uncritical and Whiggish in their interpretations, seeing a benign humanitarian spirit

---

[5] For exceptions see Don Gibbons, *Delinquent Behavior* (Englewood Cliffs, N.J.: Prentice-Hall, 1976), 2nd ed., pp. 169–189; William Sanders, *Juvenile Delinquency* (New York: Praeger, 1976), pp. 64–83; Rose Giallombardo, *The Social World of Delinquent Girls* (New York: Wiley, 1974); Meda Chesney-Lind, "Juvenile Delinquency: The Sexualization of Female Crime," *Psychology Today*, July 1974, 8, 43–46; Meda Chesney-Lind, "Judicial Enforcement of the Female Sex Role: The Family Court and the Female Delinquent," *Issues in Criminology*, Fall 1973, 8, 51–69; Kristine Rogers, "'For Her Own Protection . . .': Conditions of Incarceration for Female Juvenile Offenders in the State of Connecticut," *Law and Society Review*, 1972, 7, 223–246; Sarah Gold, "Equal Protection for Juvenile Girls in Need of Supervision in New York State," *New York Law Forum*, 1971, 17, 570–598; Robert Terry, "Discrimination in the Handling of Juvenile Offenders by Social Control Agencies," in *Becoming Delinquent*, eds. Peter Garabedian and Don Gibbons (Chicago: Aldine, 1970), pp. 78–92; Freda Adler, *Sisters in Crime* (New York: McGraw-Hill, 1975), chap. 4; *Crime and Delinquency*, 1977, 23 (issue theme: "Criminal Justice to Women: Not Fair!"); and Paul Katzeff, "Equal Crime," *Boston Magazine*, December 1977, 107–108, 206, 208–210. For an estimate that girls now form nearly one-quarter of the juvenile court clientele, see Rosemary Sarri and Robert Vintner, "Justice for Whom? Varieties of Correctional Approaches," in *The Juvenile Justice System*, ed. Malcolm Klein, v (New York: Russell Sage, 1975), p. 171.

[6] See the pioneering studies by Barbara Brenzel, "Lancaster Industrial School for Girls: A Social Portrait of a Nineteenth Century Reform School for Girls," *Feminist Studies*, Fall 1975, 3, 40–53; and by Estelle Freedman, "Their Sisters' Keepers: The Origins of Female Corrections in America," Dissertation, Columbia University, 1976.

behind early twentieth-century correctional innovations for girls. Margaret Reeves, for example, conducted an exhaustive survey of girls' reformatory programs in the 1920s and concluded, with few reservations, that they embodied the triumph of social conscience in America and the onward march of correctional science.[7] Recently, Robert Mennel, in his ambitious survey of juvenile correctional history, described Progressive-era policies as "the first sign of a more sympathetic attitude toward female delinquents."[8]

On the basis of our research, we consider the traditional interpretation to be lacking in four principal respects: it offers little empirical evidence of benign or effective treatment of girl offenders; it generally blurs the distinction between the stated intentions of correctional reformers and the actual outcomes of their efforts; it deals inadequately with the fears and prejudices underlying benevolent programs for poor, immigrant children; and it does little to illuminate, even obliquely, the practice of sexual discrimination in the juvenile justice system today. We do not quarrel with historians who emphasize the humanitarian spirit that guided such famous juvenile reformers as Jane Addams, Sophonisba Breckinridge, and Edith Abbott, or such lesser figures as Augusta Bronner, Mabel Elliott, Emma Lundberg, and Edith Burleigh.[9] But we do believe that the humanitarian schemes were often quite repressive in design and even more so in outcome.

Our main arguments can be sketched as follows. Although public response to female delinquency emerged in the Victorian era, not until the Progressive period was female delinquency widely perceived as a social problem requiring extensive governmental intervention. In the Progressive period the abundant literature on delinquency was riddled with stereotypical assumptions about women and, in particular, about immigrant women. These stereotypes laid a basis for more punitive treatment of delinquent girls than delinquent boys. Girls were prosecuted almost exclusively for "immoral" conduct, a very broad category that defined all sexual exploration as fundamentally perverse and predictive of future promiscuity, perhaps even prostitution. But while girls, unlike boys, were almost never accused of violating criminal statutes, they received stiffer legal penalties.

Discriminatory treatment of female delinquents was consistent with racial prejudices in the Progressive period. Ethnic girls—immigrants or daughters of immigrants—were seen as inherently more predisposed to immoral conduct than Yankee girls—daughters of native-born parents. Discriminatory correctional practices also embodied the new wisdom of the behavioral sciences, particularly the theories of adolescence generated by such pioneer psychologists as G. Stanley Hall. Finally, the practice of female juvenile justice reflected the quasi-utopian, but ultimately repressive, pursuit of Progressive-era reformers for a more "pure" society, as revealed in the eugenics, antiprostitution, and sex-education campaigns.

[7] Margaret Reeves, *Training Schools for Delinquent Girls* (New York: Russell Sage, 1929).

[8] Robert Mennel, *Thorns and Thistles* (Hanover, N.H.: University Press of New England, 1973), p. 172.

[9] See especially Robert Bremner, *From the Depths* (New York: New York University Press, 1956); and Walter Trattner, *Crusade for the Children* (Chicago: Quadrangle, 1970).

Female Delinquency: The Emergence of a Social Problem

Public response to female delinquency can be traced at least as far back as the Jacksonian period, although the traditional date of origin is 1856, when Massachusetts opened the nation's first reform school for girls. Well known in the latter half of the century, the Massachusetts example inspired emulation by diverse philanthropic organizations in the East and Midwest. Several state governments responded to the wishes of these organizations and built reformatories for girls. Compared to the huge reformatories for boys erected in the nineteenth century— by the 1850s the New York House of Refuge held over one thousand inmates—the institutions for girls were generally small and makeshift, often consisting of two or three converted farmhouses. Several of the girls' facilities were little more than receiving stations; their primary purpose was to facilitate the smooth operation of boys' reformatories after attempts to house both sexes in the same buildings had proved embarrassing failures.[10]

The female reformatories incorporated the evangelical spirit of Victorian religious revivalism. Until the end of the nineteenth century the image of the female delinquent remained mainly that of the individual "fallen woman."[11] This image contrasted sharply with that of the male delinquent, who was described less as a sinner than as a carefully nurtured young criminal.[12] To be sure, boys' delinquencies were roundly condemned but were rarely, as was often the case with girls', regarded as indications of innate moral perversity.

Nineteenth-century authors of crime literature wrote endlessly about delinquency —the classic presentation being Charles Loring Brace's *The Dangerous Classes of New York and Twenty Years' Work among Them*[13]—but they paid very little attention to female delinquents. The "dangerous classes" against whom the reformers warned and about whom newspapers printed sensational stories were overwhelmingly male.[14] When the girl offender did appear in the literature, she was treated mainly as a footnote to the problem of boy delinquency. But early in the twentieth century—especially in the decade preceding the First World War— female delinquency began to attract increasing attention as a separate and pressing social problem.

The heightened public awareness of and growing governmental response to female delinquency in the Progressive era are well documented. Articles on girl

---

[10] Brenzel, "Lancaster"; Mennel, *Thorns and Thistles*, chap. 4; Freedman, "Their Sisters' Keepers," chaps. 3 and 4.

[11] On the image of the "fallen woman,' see Freedman, "Their Sisters' Keepers," chap. 2; for the emphasis on environmental causes behind male criminality, see David Rothman, *The Discovery of the Asylum* (Boston: Little, Brown, 1971).

[12] Schlossman, *Love*, chaps. 2, 3, and 5.

[13] Charles Loring Brace, *The Dangerous Classes of New York and Twenty Years' Work among Them* (New York: Wynkoop and Hallenbeck, 1872).

[14] Miriam Langsam, *Children West* (Madison, Wis.: State Historical Society of Wisconsin, 1964); Thomas Bender, *Toward an Urban Vision* (Lexington, Ky.: University Press of Kentucky, 1975); and Steven Schlossman, "The 'Culture of Poverty' in Ante-Bellum Social Thought," *Science and Society*, 1974, **38**, 150–166.

offenders appeared in a wide range of popular and scholarly journals. The prestigious philanthropic organization, the National Conference of Charities and Correction, began to discuss female delinquency regularly for the first time since the organization's founding in the early 1870s. Several books were devoted in whole or in part to female criminality. While the mass media continued to emphasize the "boy problem," many civic groups began giving equal attention to the "girl problem." Local organizations such as PTAs, juvenile protective associations, women's clubs, and settlement houses sponsored lectures and discussions on the causes and cures of girls' delinquency; they also led campaigns to garner funds for such innovations as girls' clubs, YWCA summer camps, and, to a lesser extent, Girl Scouts.[15]

Governmental investment in the custody and treatment of female delinquents increased dramatically in the Progressive era. The decade between 1910 and 1920 was an especially prolific period for the creation of publicly sponsored reformatories for girls. Whereas between 1850 and 1910 an average of fewer than five new reformatories were created per decade, twenty-three new facilities opened between 1910 and 1920. Furthermore, older ninteenth-century reformatories were expanded in size, staff, and clientele in this decade. Equally important, a number of states took over private girls' reformatories.[16] In short, the involvement of government with female delinquency grew sharply in the Progressive period, reflecting the expanded discussion of the subject in the literature on juvenile crime.

The Practice of Sexual Discrimination

Before trying to explain the rising interest in female delinquency in the Progressive era, it is necessary to demonstrate that girls received discriminatory treatment in juvenile courts and reformatories. The historical sources for such an empirical study are vast but have never been tapped. We have examined the sources selectively and have chosen for close analysis those we believe are representative of three bodies of evidence.

First, we briefly analyze scattered statistical data to demonstrate that juvenile courts treated female delinquents more harshly than male delinquents. Second, we present an overview of cases in a single juvenile court to evoke the actual decision-making process and thereby show that sentimental notions of the "good girl" and conventional ideals of domesticity prefigured punitive treatment for girl delinquents. Third, we look synoptically at the rehabilitative goals and methods of female reformatories to illuminate further the discriminatory nature of treatment. Our goal is to provide empirical evidence for the contention, developed later in

[15] These observations draw upon Schlossman's study of social-reform groups in Milwaukee and of parent-education organizations throughout the country. See Schlossman, *Love*, chap. 7, and "Before Home Start: Notes Toward a History of Parent Education in America, 1897–1929," *Harvard Educational Review*, 1976, **46**, 436–467. Also useful is David McLeod, "Good Boys Made Better: The Boy Scouts of America, Boys' Brigades, and YMCA Boys' Work, 1880–1920," Dissertation, University of Wisconsin, 1973.

[16] Reeves, *Training Schools*, pp. 39ff; and Mennel, *Thorns and Thistles*, pp. 171–179.

this essay, that the practice of female juvenile justice coincided with the ideology of treatment. Discrimination on the basis of sex was no accident, we believe, but rather was integral to both the theory and practice of Progressive-era juvenile justice.

The first body of evidence was derived from court records in Chicago, San Francisco, Milwaukee, and New Haven. Several points stand out most prominently from these data: the vast majority of delinquents, boys and girls alike, were poor, ghetto-dwelling children of recent immigrants; however, unlike males, females were brought to court almost exclusively for alleged early sexual exploration; and female offenders were treated more punitively than males.

The ethnic origins of both boy and girl delinquents are revealing. In Milwaukee, for example, more than 90 percent of the children brought into court were the offspring of European immigrants. Of these, three out of four were either German or Polish. In Chicago, San Francisco, and New Haven the ethnic background of delinquents was similar, although southeastern European countries were more frequently represented, reflecting the different patterns of immigrant settlement in these cities.[17]

That the delinquents were predominantly poor is evident in a number of ways. Although it is impossible to compare the incomes of families of delinquent and nondelinquent children or to assess the contributions of different family members to total income, we do have periodic salary data for the fathers of delinquent youth in Milwaukee. These data suggest the truth of the popular impression that delinquents were primarily from the working class. Their fathers' salaries were low, generally reported to be less than ten dollars per week. Moreover, the salaries were highly irregular: many fathers moved frequently from job to job; many were unemployed for long periods because of seasonal hiring, debilitating illnesses (particularly tuberculosis), and drinking bouts. In addition, an analysis of the occupations of delinquents' fathers, using city directories and addresses supplied in court to distinguish individuals with the same names, indicates that the majority were working class or lower on the economic scale, the single largest category being that of "laborer."[18] A further indication that delinquents came mainly from poor, ghetto families is their residence patterns. The majority of Milwaukee delinquents lived in the poorest immigrant neighborhoods surrounding the city's scattered railway network.

Although similar in their social and cultural backgrounds, girl and boy delinquents were treated very differently in court. Consider the types of crimes for which boys and girls made their first courtroom appearances. The majority of boys were charged with offenses that fell under the adult criminal code. In Chicago, for

---

[17] For data on Milwaukee see Schlossman, *Love*, appendix 2, table 6. Our main source for Chicago is Sophonisba Breckinridge and Edith Abbott, *The Delinquent Child and the Home* (New York: Russell Sage, 1912); for San Francisco, Emily Huntington, Leona Jones, Donna Moses, and Ruth Turner, "The Juvenile Court," Bachelor of Arts Thesis, University of California at Berkeley, 1917; and for New Haven, Mabel Wiley, *A Study of the Problem of Girl Delinquency in New Haven* (New Haven, Conn.: Civic Federation of New Haven, 1915).

[18] Schlossman, *Love*, pp. 143–144.

example, stealing accounted for more than half of the reported crimes.[19] The charges against girls were of an entirely different nature. The majority were charged under the loose heading of "immorality";[20] however, a charge of "immorality" did not mean that a girl had had intercourse or performed some other mature sexual act. Rather, a girl only had to show "signs" in her appearance, conversation, and bearing that she had probably had intercourse in the past or might do so in the near future. These criteria naturally opened the way to invidious judgments, especially because the delinquents were mainly daughters of immigrants, who were, according to contemporary racial mythology, instinctively emotional and lacking in self-restraint. Thus judges and probation officers would see precocious sexual activity where it did not exist, would prematurely regard unfamiliar cultural patterns of behavior and expression as signs of advanced sexual experience, and would be more pessimistic about the implications of sexual exploration by ethnic than by Yankee girls.

In practice, an extraordinarily wide range of conduct was included under the label of immorality: staying away from home, associating with persons of dubious character, going to dance houses, fornicating, coming home late at night, masturbating, using obscene language, riding at night in automobiles without a chaperone, strutting about in a lascivious manner, and so forth. To the courts, being "on the road to ruin" was but one short step from being "ruined"; hence, so-called predelinquents were treated much like those who actually engaged in mature sexual relations. The ostensible purposes behind such a loose definition of crime were to root out the underlying causes of misconduct as soon as they became evident and to instruct ethnic girls that their Yankee counterparts upheld higher standards of sexual propriety than their own parents practiced or condoned.[21]

The different treatment of boy and girl delinquents was even more apparent in the disposition of cases. Far more frequently than girls, boys received the relatively noncoercive sanction of probation—supervision in the child's own home or in a surrogate home approved by the court. In Chicago, for instance, 59 percent of the boys who appeared in court between 1899 and 1909 were placed on probation, as compared to only 37 percent of the girls. Conversely, significantly higher proportions of girls than boys were incarcerated in reformatories for sentences that could last several years. In Milwaukee twice as many girls as boys were committed, and in Chicago one-half of the girl delinquents, as contrasted with one-fifth of the

19 Breckinridge and Abbott, *The Delinquent Child*, pp. 28–35. See also Huntington et al., "The Juvenile Court," appendix.

20 Breckinridge and Abbott, *The Delinquent Child*, pp. 38–40; Huntington et al., "The Juvenile Court," appendix; Alida Bowler, "A Study of Seventy-Five Delinquent Girls," *Journal of Delinquency*, 1917, **2**, 157; Mabel Elliott, *Correctional Education and the Delinquent Girl* (Harrisburg, Pa.: Commonwealth of Pennsylvania Department of Welfare, 1928), pp. 34–35; Louise Ordahl and George Ordahl, "A Study of Delinquent and Dependent Girls," *Journal of Delinquency*, 1918, **3**, 34–35; and Wiley, *A Study of the Problem*, p. 11.

21 Bowler, "A Study of Seventy-Five Delinquent Girls," p. 159; Breckinridge and Abbott, *The Delinquent Child*, pp. 35–39; Elliott, *Correctional Education*, pp. 34–35; Ordahl and Ordahl, "A Study of Delinquent and Dependent Girls," pp. 55–59; and Wiley, *A Study of the Problem*, p. 9.

boy delinquents, were sent to reformatories.[22] In sum, girls appeared in juvenile court on noncriminal charges far more frequently than boys; nonetheless, girls received more punitive dispositions.[23]

We turn now to another body of evidence: the day-to-day experiences of girls in juvenile court. From the archival records of the Milwaukee Children's Court we have chosen several cases from between 1901 and 1920 for examination. Transcripts from actual hearings, we believe, provide the most vivid and dramatic demonstration of the assumptions that shaped the definition and treatment of female delinquency in the Progressive era.[24]

Alleged girl delinquents in Milwaukee had their private lives probed in fine detail so that judges and probation officers could assess the underlying causes of misbehavior. Whenever it could be demonstrated that a girl had used vile language, masturbated, or indulged in lascivious thoughts, the court freely employed some type of intervention, usually probation. Consider the case of Annagret Schmitt. Neither the hearing transcript nor the accompanying records provides a precise reason why Annagret was brought into court—a common occurrence, since it was assumed that some form of aberrant sexual expression was behind any specific accusation. Thus Annagret, like every girl who appeared in court, was subjected to a vaginal examination. The only proof of virginity was an intact hymen. To his own surprise the examing doctor concluded that Annagret was still a virgin, but he informed the court that irritation in her clitoral area indicated she was a regular masturbator. The probation officer, a woman, analyzed the situation as follows: "She masturbates, and she has somewhat injured herself in that way, and probably this is the cause of her conduct at home, and says things [sic] that are not true. . . . [Annagret] most likely is trying to imagine things, and then believes everything is true." Thus, according to the court, Annagret's masturbatory habits explained her penchant for fantasy and justified labeling her a delinquent and placing her under supervision.

In cases of advanced sexual misconduct, the court usually explored the circumstances in excruciating detail. The ostensible goals were to procure evidence

---

[22] Breckinridge and Abbott, *The Delinquent Child*, p. 41; and Schlossman, *Love*, appendix 2, table 3.

[23] In arguing that girls received more punitive treatment, we assume that incarceration is, by its very nature, a harsher form of punishment than probation. We are *not* saying, however, that the treatment of girls in reformatories was harsher than that of boys in reformatories.

[24] These cases derive from Schlossman's sample of 1,200 cases in Milwaukee (10 percent of the total heard in this period). To the best of our knowledge, the Milwaukee court is the only one to have opened its early records for historical investigation; it is consequently impossible to say whether they are strictly representative of experiences in courts elsewhere. Although selected with an eye toward the exemplary and archetypal, each case was necessarily idiosyncratic because, obviously, no two children or their parents were exactly alike. The cases that follow should be appreciated much like opera highlights, as suggestive of a larger drama and of characteristic patterns of interaction among protagonists. To protect client anonymity we have changed the names of children and parents who appeared in court, although we have tried to retain their particular ethnic origins. For the same reason we have not cited the specific dates or docket numbers of individual cases.

against the male or males involved and to evaluate the girls' attitudes toward men and sex. At times, though, the immediate goal seemed to be nothing other than sheer titillation, much like the famous vice reports in this period. Such reports offered, in the names of science and social reform, pornographic scenes that would have been censored in the commercial media. In court, girls were required to recount, with some attempt to recreate the atmosphere, the steps that led to their sexual encounters, their physical experiences ("How far did he go into you; what did you feel; did you bleed?"), and their later subjective reactions. In pursuing this line of questioning the court's assumptions were transparent; it presumed that a girl's moral condition and potential for rehabilitation depended on just how much of her biological purity had been preserved and on how morally revolted she was by her experiences.

At the same time that the court avidly investigated the girls' sex lives, it preached a conventional code of Victorian morality, highlighting especially the virtues of chastity and the joys of marriage. With all good intentions the court lectured sexually precocious girls on how their behavior was endangering their later salability as wives. Without doubt many of the sexually active girls who appeared in juvenile court were immature and would have benefited from intelligent advice about sex. But the advice the court proffered must have struck these girls as naive and irrelevant to their current needs and past experiences. Consider, for example, one judge's advice to a girl who had contracted venereal disease:

> By and by, three or four years from now, some nice fellow will come along, and you love him, and he will love you, and you will get married, and live right. That ought to be the aim of a girl like you, to look forward to the time you have a good home and a good man.

Quaint moral admonitions like these were the court's main antidote to sexual precocity among girls and, if nothing else, reveal the cultural stereotypes that shaped the legal processing of female delinquents.

As observed earlier, juvenile courts did not distinguish between actual delinquency and predelinquency because they saw their mission as the treatment of underlying causes. The courts aimed to "save" girls once it became apparent they were "on the road to ruin." Consider the case of Sara Wadrewski. Sara's father had brought her into court on a charge of disobedience, alleging that she had refused to work, stayed out late, and gone to parties where the girls dressed like boys. As often happened, a probation officer was on hand to supplement the parents' charges by relating neighborhood gossip. Sara, he intimated, probably had had intercourse with several boys because she was seen lying on the grass with them in a local park. A group of neighbors made similar accusations. To the judge's question, "In what way is she a bad girl?" one neighbor responded, "Why, for the reason that she bums around and doesn't work, and doesn't bring no money home, and runs to parties, and then calls names, calls her brother names, he is a cripple." Sara roundly denied most of the allegations, particularly the charges that she had had group sex, or indeed, that she had ever had "connection." But her protestations of virginity were to no avail; shortly after the initial hearing she was committed to the local Catholic reformatory.

Juvenile court sessions were often like scenes from a Kafka novel. One could never be sure that the disposition of a case would be on the basis of the accusations or on the quality of evidence. Despite these uncertainties it was almost guaranteed that a girl would be sent to a reformatory if either she or her parents, especially her mother, were not blushingly contrite about the girl's sexual adventures. A classic case is that of fifteen-year-old Deborah Horwitz, who freely admitted staying out late at night with many boys and who casually flaunted her sexual desires. In addition to Deborah's self-incriminating testimony, efficient snooping by a proba- tion officer into Deborah's bedroom bureau turned up even more incriminating evidence: five self-photos that the court considered racy (although Deborah got no more racy than opening the top button of her high-necked blouse and removing her hat); and a remarkably candid series of letters to a sailor friend that left no doubt about her initiation into the joys of sex.

In such cases the court's custom was to blame the mother for her daughter's actions. Mrs. Horwitz, however, would not stand for it: "I got lots of trouble with the other girl, she needs an operation, and I got lots of trouble with the other children." Nor would Deborah accept the court's harsh evaluation of her behavior. Thus the judge intoned:

> Well, Deborah, this is a very serious matter. If you would live a good life you would be a good woman, and be useful to society, but you have started out very bad. There is only one way to reform you and this is to send you to an institution. I cannot let you go home to your parents. . . . How is it, can't you stop?

Deborah responded, "I can stop, of course I can." "Why don't you behave yourself, then?" the judge rejoined. "These boys tell me that you just coax them." "I never coaxed anybody," Deborah maintained. But to no effect. Precocious sexuality in a girl who would not at least feign repentance and whose parents would not at least feign shock was intolerable to the court. Deborah was committed forthwith to the state reformatory for girls.

As these excerpts reveal, the court defined female delinquency wholly in sexual terms and responded to girls on the basis of Victorian views of women's social role and sexuality. We shall have more to say later about the persistence of these Victor- ian assumptions in the Progressive period. For the present we will extend our study of actual treatment by examining the female reformatories, which, as noted earlier, expanded rapidly in the early twentieth century. Like the juvenile courts, the reformatories operationalized prevailing cultural stereotypes about women and transformed these stereotypes into tools for punishment and rehabilitation.

Female reformatories in the Progressive era had four principal goals. The basic one was the isolation from males of sexually precocious females, preferably in bucolic settings. Elaborate efforts were made to keep all men away from the institu- tions or, indeed, from anywhere near the girls. In California, for example, sponsors of the female reformatory concluded that the mile separating the male from the female institution was inadequate. A new facility far removed from males was essential to eliminate "the influences that mysteriously emanate from the proximity of the sexes."[25] The mere act of isolating delinquent girls came to be seen as a rehabilitative tool. As such, it served an important, latent economic function by rationalizing a minimal public investment in other, more positive, methods of treatment.

Not only were the institutions situated so as to eliminate sexual temptation, but they were also designed to serve a second long-range function. Safe custody was considered a spur to later marriage. By incarcerating delinquent girls the reformatories removed them from the unregulated sexual marketplace of ghetto streets and forced them to save their sexual favors, moral reputations, and health until they were of marriageable age. Most inmates of female reformatories were fifteen or sixteen years old, too young to marry in most states. A minimal stay of two to three years was therefore considered essential; upon release the girls would be of marriageable age and could seek legitimate gratification for their pent-up sexual energies. The institutions further promoted marriageability by placing the girls, after release, in new social settings where their moral improprieties were not common knowledge and where they could search anew for companionship.[26] Like the isolation of inmates from all contacts with men, the assumption that custodial care could have long-term therapeutic value underlay the marital goals of the reformatories. Thus, it could seriously be argued that custody in female reformatories was itself a form of treatment.[27]

[25] Adina Mitchell, *Special Report on the Whittier State School* (Sacramento, Calif.: State Printing Office, 1896), p. 11. See also Mary Berry, "The State's Duty to the Delinquent Girl," National Conference on the Education of Truant, Backward, Dependent and Delinquent Children. *Proceedings* (1918), pp. 82–83; Mrs. Jennie Griffith, "The Training of Delinquent Girls," Conference of the National Committee on Prisons and Prison Labor, *Proceedings* (1919), pp. 15, 17; Miriam Van Waters, "Where Girls Go Right," *Survey Graphic*, 1922, 1, 365; and Maine Industrial School for Girls, *Annual Report* (Waterville, Me.: Sentinel Publishing Co., 1909), pp. 7–8.

[26] Breckinridge and Abbott, *The Delinquent Child*, p. 8; Huntington et al., "The Juvenile Court," appendix; Olga Bridgman, "An Experimental Study of Abnormal Children, with Special Reference to the Problems of Dependency and Delinquency," University of California, *Publications in Psychology*, 1918, 3, 8; Berry, "The State's Duty," p. 87; Edith Burleigh and Frances Harris, *The Delinquent Girl* (New York: New York School of Social Work, 1923), pp. 32, 38–43; Mary Dewson, "Probation and Institutional Care of Girls," in *The Child in the City*, ed. Sophonisba Breckinridge (Chicago: Chicago School of Civics and Philanthropy, 1912), pp. 360–362; Martha Falconer, "Work of the Girls' Department, House of Refuge, Philadelphia," National Conference of Charities and Correction, *Proceedings* (1908), p. 393; and National Conference of Charities and Correction, *Proceedings* (1903), p. 517. Elliott's *Correctional Education*, a follow-up study of ex-inmates from the Sleighton Farms reformatory in Pennsylvania, left no doubt that marriage was the most important variable in explaining postrelease behavior.

[27] This argument was rarely advanced about the boys' reformatories. In fact, although historians have yet to provide adequate documentation, male reformatories apparently experimented with a variety of new correctional ideas in the Progressive era and participated tangentially in the "progressive education" movement. Elaborate vocational-training programs at a few of the larger reformatories became the envy of "progressive" educators such as David Snedden. In addition, many public reformatories experimented with self-government programs designed loosely along the lines suggested by William George in his famous Junior Republics; many adopted new forms of recreational and military training to improve health and discipline and upgraded their academic

Female reformatories did employ nominally rehabilitative programs, if only to give the girls something to do while their virtue was being protected. These programs embodied traditional stereotypes about women. The institutions attempted to instill in inmates the ideology of domesticity and the minimal skills necessary for its practice. According to correctional administrators, a girl's delinquency alone revealed that she had not learned to revere domestic pursuits. Instruction in domesticity was allied with the reformatories' marital goals: inmates would become so devoted to and skillful at domestic chores that they would easily attract husbands. It was as if, in the moral calculus of the juvenile reformers, a rigorous pursuit of domesticity would compensate for the girls' previous immoralities. Moreover, even if the girls failed to find mates shortly after release, they would at least be trained as domestics and so could support themselves while working in upright, middle-class households.[28]

Inmates were expected to take care of their reformatory cottages with the same pride that middle-class women lavished on their homes. Ideally, the girls would assimilate middle-class domestic values and lower-class domestic skills.[29] In each reformatory cottage, the matron served as the domestic educator, teaching girls both proper attitudes and skills. To increase public regard for the vocational-training programs, reformatory superintendents described them as if they were part of the larger home-economics movement that swept the country in the Progressive era.[30] Actually, the training rarely went beyond the chores necessary for personal hygiene and cottage upkeep, with a cooking class or two added for good measure. As one superintendent blithely argued,

---

offerings for older inmates. Of course we do not believe that these newer correctional programs necessarily rehabilitated inmates. Our point is simply that levels of interest and public investment in rehabilitative programs were greater in boys' than girls' reformatories. For background on the relation between "progressive education" and juvenile corrections, see Walter Drost, *David Snedden* (Madison, Wis.: University of Wisconsin Press, 1967); and Jack Holl, *Juvenile Reform in the Progressive Era* (Ithaca, N.Y.: Cornell University Press, 1971).

[28] A widely discussed social "problem" in the Progressive era was the declining availability of trained domestic help; hence it can be argued that the reformatories' emphasis on domestic training was economically functional for the girls. It was also recognized, though, that domestics received wages so low that some were tempted to turn to prostitution for supplementary income.

[29] Mary Berry, "Co-Ordination of Industrial and Vocational Work with Parole Administration," National Conference on the Education of Truant, Backward, Dependent and Delinquent Children, *Proceedings* (1920), pp. 52–60; Bowler, "A Study of Seventy-Five Delinquent Girls," pp. 156–157; Burleigh and Harris, *The Delinquent Child*, pp. 8–9; William Fairbanks, "Girls' Reformatories and Their Inherent Characteristics," National Conference of Charities and Correction, *Proceedings* (1901), pp. 254–262; Miss Mary Hinkley, "Problems of Administration: The Responsibilities of a School Toward Its Girls," National Conference on the Education of Truant, Backward, Dependent and Delinquent Children, *Proceedings* (1920), pp. 20–23; Maine Industrial School for Girls, *Annual Report* (1909), p. 15; Griffith, "The Training of Delinquent Girls," p. 17; and Miss Elizabeth Mansell, "An Institution Program for Delinquent Girls," National Conference on the Education of Truant, Backward, Dependent and Delinquent Children, *Proceedings* (1917), p. 35.

[30] See Emma Weigley, "It Might Have Been Euthenics: The Lake Placid Conference and the Home Economics Movement," *American Quarterly*, 1974, 26, 79–96; and Barbara Ehrenreich and Deidre English, "The Manufacture of Housework," *Socialist Revolution*, October–December, 1975, 5, 5–40.

We never have taught typewriting and stenography. I find that in our community you can get about a dozen girls, who want to use a typewriter to one that wants to use a scrubbing brush. It seems to me that if you can get girls to understand that to be a homemaker is about the best thing that can come into the life of a woman, this is almost the best education they can have at the present time.[31]

Another superintendent was candid enough to admit what must often have been true in other reformatories that boasted "scientific" courses in home economics: "We teach the girls in practical cooking, as few are mentally capable of appreciating food values as taught in regular domestic science courses."[32]

The fourth and final goal of the female reformatories, surely their most ambitious, is implicit in the previous remark on inmates' mental limitations. The female reformatories were expected to play a central role in fulfilling the objectives of the eugenics movement, which achieved its greatest popularity at precisely the same time that governmental investment in female corrections significantly expanded.[33]

Eugenicists in the Progressive era sought to improve the "genetic fund" of the American population by discouraging and, if possible, forcibly preventing propagation by individuals considered innately inferior in culture and intellect. Almost by definition, the eugenicists identified recent immigrants from southeastern Europe as inferior. Relying on the rediscovery of Mendelian genetic theory in 1900, the eugenicists presented several key arguments: social conditions, such as poverty, and personality traits, such as laziness and courage, were discrete "unit characters" transmitted through heredity; unit characters were immutable; race was the primary determinant of human capacities; in some races socially undesirable unit characters predominated; and social legislation was necessary to encourage breeding of the racially fit and discourage breeding of the unfit. According to the eugenicists, persistent immorality among children was a sign of their genetic inferiority or racial degeneracy. To keep these degenerates from further diluting the nation's "genetic fund" and to prevent the nation from committing "race suicide," eugenicists insisted that permanent institutionalization and, if possible, sterilization were essential. The hereditarily degenerate threatened the eugenicists' vision of a more perfect and efficient world devoid of crime, poverty, and disease—a world quite consistent with the vision of many well-known reformers who outwardly were not eugenicists themselves.

Male and female reformatories were to play a special role in the larger eugenics campaign, as early detectors of innate criminality. In this role, however, the reformatories faced a unique problem: from a clientele composed mainly of chil-

[31] National Conference of Charities and Correction, *Proceedings* (1901), p. 258.

[32] California School for Girls, *Biennial Report* (Sacramento, Calif.: State Printing Office, 1918), p. 9.

[33] For background on the eugenics movement we have relied especially on Mark Haller, *Eugenics* (New Brunswick, N.J.: Rutgers University Press, 1963); Donald Pickens, *Eugenics and the Progressive Era* (Nashville, Tenn.: Vanderbilt University Press, 1968); Rudolph Vecoli, "Sterilization: A Progressive Measure?" *Wisconsin Magazine of History*, 1960, **48**, 190–203; Peter Tyor, "Segregation or Surgery: The Mentally Retarded in America, 1850–1920," Dissertation, Northwestern University, 1972; and Allan Chase, *The Legacy of Malthus* (New York: Knopf, 1976).

dren of racially inferior immigrants, how were they to identify those whose inheritance was so inferior as to warrant permanent incarceration or sterilization? By the 1910s the principal method of detection became mental testing, which rapidly evolved through a bewildering variety of forms, culminating in the 1916 Stanford revision of the Binet test—the intelligence quotient (IQ) test. With a seemingly precise instrument like the Stanford-Binet test in hand, psychologists and their helpers administered mental tests with virtual abandon to captive inmate populations. The tests were purported to identify those delinquents whose innate intelligence was so low that, in the judgment of the psychologists, they could never learn to control their instincts and become civilized members of society. These defective delinquents, as they were commonly called, were to be transferred from the reformatories and incarcerated, if facilities permitted, in homes for feeble-minded children— institutions that proliferated in the Progressive era. In sum, the newly devised mental test legitimated eugenic goals by providing a scientific instrument for weeding out from the delinquent population those children whose antisocial behavior was inbred.[34]

Eugenic goals, as we noted, applied equally to male and female reformatories, and IQ and other mental tests were freely administered in both. But the literature on delinquency discussed feeble-mindedness among girls with a special urgency. In part this was because delinquent girls appeared at first to test at somewhat lower levels than delinquent boys.[35] More important, though, were the two widely held beliefs that women bore the primary moral responsibility for determining whether to have children and that women lacked the sexual drives of men. From

---

[34] *The Journal of Delinquency*, published in California, provided the principal forum for discussing this use of mental tests. Its articles were written mainly by psychologists, physicians, psychiatrists, and correctional workers. The *Journal* came especially under the influence of Lewis Terman and several of his students at Stanford, although other prominent members of its editorial board included William Healy, founder of the Juvenile Psychopathic Clinic in Chicago, and Arnold Gesell, the developmental psychologist from Yale.

[35] See, for example, C. S. Bluemel, "Binet Tests on Two Hundred Juvenile Delinquents," *Training School Bulletin*, 1915, 12, 191. Of all the drawbacks of the early IQ tests administered to delinquents, the most basic one was the leeway given to the examiner. The tests left much room for interpretation; often there was no clear-cut right or wrong answer. In such instances the examiners frequently came to dubious conclusions about inmates' mental ages. Consider the following example from Bluemel (p. 187), in which the examiner asked:

> "What is the difference between pride and pretension?" The first replies: "If you have too much pride, you go to certain places—cafes and dance halls. Some pretend to be proud but are poor." The second replies: "Pride means to be proud, and pretension means to pretend to be something that you are not." The third replies: "Pride is something in you that makes you—if you have enough of it—hold yourself a little above people that are without pride. Pretension is false pride." Obviously, these answers indicate that the three girls are at different mental levels. This fact is also attested by their answers to the other questions; and the answers in their totality permit one to make a fair estimate of their mental ages.

See also Ordahl and Ordahl, "A Study of Delinquent and Dependent Girls," pp. 41–73; and Jean Walker, "Factors Contributing to the Delinquency of Defective Girls," University of California, *Publications in Psychology*, 1925, 3, 147–207.

this perspective, sexually precocious girls were morally and biologically perverse. When this view was joined with the belief that delinquent girls' intelligence was so far below normal that they could never learn to control their instincts, it becomes clear why the specter of female delinquency haunted the eugenics movement and why delinquent girls were more frequently incarcerated than delinquent boys.

Sexual Precocity and the Social Order in the Progressive Era

Having sketched the main elements of female juvenile justice in the Progressive era, we return to our earlier questions: why did public interest and investment in female delinquency burgeon so noticeably in this period, and why were girls treated more punitively than boys?

Perhaps the most obvious explanation of the rising interest in female delinquency in the Progressive period would be that the incidence of female delinquency grew until it simply could not be ignored. Much evidence could be marshaled to sustain this argument. One could turn, for example, to the remarkable data on family breakdown, cultural disintegration, and crime in urban immigrant communities documented in Thomas and Znaniecki's 1927 classic, *The Polish Peasant in America*.[36] Equally familiar are Jane Addams's poignant commentaries on the tensions and communication gulfs between mothers and daughters in *Democracy and Social Ethics* and *The Spirit of Youth and the City Streets*.[37] Similarly, one could assess the moral consequences of growing female participation in the work force. Did the increasingly familiar, "promiscuous" social relations of young men and women at work, mainly in the factory, encourage early sexual experimentation, as many contemporaries feared?[38] Finally, one could point to the pervasive image of the white-slave trade, as embodied in the work of the Chicago Vice Commission or Jane Addams's *A New Conscience and an Ancient Evil*.[39] The image of the white-slave trader fueled the era's antiprostitution campaigns and expressed metaphorically the common view that impoverished women were vulnerable to unscrupulous entrepreneurs. In short, the rising public investment in and sensitivity to female delinquency could be seen as a pragmatic response to a real and growing social problem.

Although this argument is appealing, two serious limitations, one methodological and the other conceptual, persuade us, while not ignoring or denying it, to focus our attention elsewhere. First, the argument encounters the methodological difficulties common to all attempts to calculate the actual incidence of crime, whether in the present or, especially, in the past. We agree with modern-day sociologists and criminologists that official crime data and popular impressions of

36 William Thomas and Florian Znaniecki, *The Polish Peasant in America*, 2 vols. (New York: Knopf, 1927).

37 Jane Addams, *Democracy and Social Ethics* (New York: Macmillan, 1902); and *The Spirit of Youth and the City Streets* (New York: Macmillan, 1909).

38 For example, see "Are Low Wages Responsible for Women's Immorality?," *Current Opinion*, May 1913, 54, 402.

39 Jane Addams, *A New Conscience and an Ancient Evil* (New York: Macmillan, 1913).

crime waves are unreliable indices of illegal activity in any period.[40] Second, as Edwin Schur and others have argued, the traditional foci in criminological research on the incidence of crime and the personal characteristics of offenders have often obscured the fact that crime is a social and legal artifact.[41] Crime does not exist in the abstract; certain activities become illegal only when so labeled. This holds true particularly for juvenile delinquency because, as we have seen, its legal definition is extremely broad and imprecise.

To reiterate, we do not deny the possibility that rates of female delinquency were actually on the rise in the Progressive era, although it would be nearly impossible, given the broad definition of delinquency, to determine how to measure its incidence. Rather, our point is simply that the public agencies responsible for defining, prosecuting, and punishing antisocial behavior invariably shape a society's awareness of criminal conduct at any moment. Therefore, whatever the actual incidence of delinquency, it is essential to examine the cultural context in which delinquency was defined and the legal and penal context in which codes were enforced.[42]

We believe the heightened sensitivity to female delinquency and the growing governmental investment in correctional institutions can be best understood in relation to three developments that directly and indirectly affected social policies —eugenic solutions to social problems, increasing popularity of theories of adolescence, and the movement for "social purity." We have already dealt with the first development, the pervasive appeal of eugenics,[43] and so will proceed to the second development, the growing popularity of theories of adolescence.

---

[40] The previously cited texts of Gibbons and Sanders (see footnote 5) are especially sensitive to this difficulty. See also the essays collected under the heading, "The Data of Delinquency: Problems of Definition and Measurement," in *Juvenile Delinquency*, ed. Rose Giallombardo (New York: Wiley, 1966).

[41] Edwin Schur, *Radical Non-Intervention* (Englewood Cliffs, N.J.: Prentice-Hall, 1973).

[42] See especially Platt, *The Child Savers;* and Leon Radzinowicz, *Ideology and Crime* (New York: Columbia University Press, 1966).

[43] The theories and policies proposed in the eugenics movement drew upon several long-term preoccupations of American social reformers. Hereditarian thinking and racial mythologies were staples of American social thought throughout the nineteenth century, existing before the influence of Social Darwinism. Similarly, anti-immigrant hostility was common from the early nineteenth century onward, particularly in the large cities of the Northeast. We believe, nonetheless, that racial mythologies and anti-immigrant prejudice attained, in tandem, a new degree of legitimacy after the rediscovery in 1900 of Mendel's ideas, especially after these were popularized, and distorted, by social scientists whose influence on social policy grew enormously in the Progressive period. For example, Henry Goddard, one of the leading applied social scientists in the country and the first person to translate and adapt the Binet-Simon intelligence tests to American needs, wrote the best-selling bible of the eugenics movement, *The Kallikak Family* (New York: Macmillan, 1912) and led campaigns for literacy tests, restrictive marriage covenants, sterilization laws, and immigration restrictions. Even Jane Addams, a quintessential environmentalist, could endorse "the new science of eugenics" and "its recently appointed university professors" (*A New Conscience*, pp. 130–131). See Charles Rosenberg, "The Bitter Fruit: Heredity, Disease, and Social Thought," *Perspectives in American History*, 1974, **8**, 189–235; Ray Billington, *The Protestant Crusade, 1800–1860* (New York: Macmillan, 1938); and Oscar Handlin, *Boston's*

Differential treatment of boy and girl delinquents did not represent a failure in implementation, we believe, but rather was an inevitable outcome of the sexually biased social-science theories of adolescence that matured in the Progressive era.[44] These theories gave the imprimatur of science to traditional Victorian views of women as weak, impressionable, emotional, and yet erotically impassive.[45] Moreover, these theories helped shape juvenile justice in two major ways: they invalidated the most optimistic features of the juvenile court movement as applied to girls, and they legitimated the creation of new reformatories for girls just when institutional care for boys was being widely challenged.

The central role of Clark University president G. Stanley Hall in developing and popularizing new ideas about adolescence has been well documented.[46] Following Hall's lead, reformers of various hues portrayed adolescence as at once the most malleable and the most problematic time of development. Adolescence represented a new stage of life: anything was possible, for better or for worse. Most important, during adolescence a child's permanent character took shape. Jane Addams captured the common viewpoint most poignantly in her paean to the "spirit of youth": in adolescence the human spirit bursts forth anew in unsuspecting children, enthralling them with the enchantment of life, confusing them with the rush of passion and idealism.[47] During this stage of life, the reformers admonished, children required especially solicitous parental care and creative social planning to help them cope safely with the potentials of adolescence.

Not surprisingly, most commentators believed that the female youngsters of poor immigrant families were particularly vulnerable. They grew up in slums, came from inferior racial stock, and were scarred by cultural norms that sanctioned the open display of male sexual interest. However, this concern for the vulnerability of ethnic girls did not lead to extensive social programs for them. The many organizations developed for children in the Progressive era, such as day and evening clubs, scouts, and summer camps, were promoted much less vigorously

---

Immigrants (Cambridge, Mass.: Harvard University Press, 1941). On the growing role of social scientists, see Julius Weinberg, *Edward Alsworth Ross and the Sociology of Progressivism* (Madison, Wis.: State Historical Society of Wisconsin, 1972); Barry Karl, *Charles E. Merriam and the Study of Politics* (Chicago: University of Chicago Press, 1974); Julia and Herman Schwendinger, *Sociologists of the Chair* (New York: Basic Books, 1974); and Chase, *The Legacy of Malthus,* pt. 2.

[44] Although such theories were not nearly as new as their proponents claimed, they did exert considerable influence on Progressive-era social reformers. See Joseph Kett, *Rites of Passage* (New York: Basic Books, 1977), chap. 8; and Steven Schlossman, "G. Stanley Hall and the Boys' Club: Conservative Applications of Recapitulation Theory," *Journal of the History of the Behavioral Sciences,* 1973, **9**, 140–147.

[45] Two articles that advance the same argument as it applies to formal criminological theory are Doris Klein, "The Etiology of Female Crime: A Review of the Literature," *Issues in Criminology,* Fall 1973, **8**, 3–30; and Dale Hoffman-Bustamante, "The Nature of Female Criminality," *Issues in Criminology,* Fall 1973, **8**, 117–136.

[46] See Dorothy Ross, *G. Stanley Hall* (Chicago: University of Chicago Press, 1972); Kett, *Rites of Passage,* chap. 8; and Schlossman, "G. Stanley Hall and the Boys' Club."

[47] Addams, *The Spirit of Youth.*

for girls than for boys.[48] This resulted, in part, because boys were a much more immediate social threat: their delinquencies posed a clear and present danger, whereas girls' delinquencies engendered more long-term fears. But the best explanation, we believe, lies in the fact that adolescent girls were considered much less malleable than adolescent boys. Institutions like girls' clubs and Girl Scouts received less support than their male counterparts because adolescence in girls, as a life stage, was regarded as a much less promising period for reshaping character. Rather than a new beginning, adolescence in girls was the time when character traits instilled earlier were put to the test. Most writers assumed that by the time girls reached puberty the most promising time for shaping their character had long since passed.[49] Thus, while the psychological theories of adolescence provided a new source of "scientific" optimism for preventing delinquency among boys, they gave no such hope for aiding girls.[50]

For similar reasons, we believe, the promise of the juvenile court movement was less widely acclaimed for girls than for boys. As Schlossman argues in his history of

[48] On boys' clubs, see Schlossman, "G. Stanley Hall and the Boys' Club"; on camps, see McLeod, "Good Boys Made Better"; on Boy Scouts, see Jeffrey Hantover, "Sex Role, Sexuality, and Social Status: The Early Years of the Boy Scouts of America," Dissertation, University of Chicago, 1976; and Peter Schmitt, *Back to Nature* (New York: Oxford University Press, 1969), chap. 10. For a more comprehensive synthesis of these and other organizations aimed at youth, see Kett, *Rites of Passage*, chaps. 7 and 8.

[49] In reaching this conclusion we have relied especially upon: Augusta Bronner, "Effect of Adolescent Instability on Conduct," *Psychological Clinic*, 1915, 7, 249–265; Burleigh and Harris, *The Delinquent Girl*; Mary Paddon, "A Study of Fifty Feeble-Minded Prostitutes," *Journal of Delinquency*, 1918, 3, 1–11; Maude Miner, "The Woman Delinquent," New York City Conference of Charities and Correction, *Proceedings* (1911), pp. 152–165; Rheta Dorr, "Reclaiming the Wayward Girl," *Hampton's Magazine*, January 1911, 26, 67–78; Bridgman, "An Experimental Study of Abnormal Children"; Mary Moxcey, *Girlhood and Character* (New York: Abingdon, 1916); Winifred Richmond, *The Adolescent Girl* (New York: Macmillan, 1926); Ruth True, "The Neglected Girl," in *West Side Studies*, ed. Pauline Goldmark (New York: Survey Associates, 1914), pp. 1–134; Emily Lamb, "A Study of Thirty-Five Delinquent Girls," *Journal of Delinquency*, 1919, 4, 75–85; Ordahl and Ordahl, "A Study of Delinquent and Dependent Girls"; Merritt Pinkney, "The Delinquent Girl and the Juvenile Court," in *The Child in the City*, ed. Breckinridge, pp. 349–354; Breckinridge and Abbott, *The Delinquent Child*; Wiley, *A Study of the Problem;* William Thomas, *The Unadjusted Girl* (Boston: Little, Brown, 1923); Miriam Van Waters, "Causes and Cure" and "The True Value of Correctional Education," in the Miriam Van Waters Papers, Box 11, Schlesinger Library, Radcliffe College; Falconer, "Work of the Girls' Department"; Elliott, *Correctional Education;* Huntington et al., "The Juvenile Court"; Walker, "Factors Contributing to the Delinquency of Defective Girls"; Miss Vida Francis, "The Delinquent Girl," National Conference of Charities and Correction, *Proceedings* (1906), pp. 138–145; and Jane Rippin, "Social Readjustment as the Function of the Judge," Conference of the National Committee on Prisons and Prison Labor, *Proceedings* (1919), pp. 25–31.

[50] We quote from Kett, *Rites of Passage*, p. 224: "Hall, moreover, had written very little about girls, a bias fully reflected in both the literature on boys-work after 1900 and in the masculine orientation and sexual segregation of scouting. . . . It was a boy's world, not a girl's and not a man's, a fact which prompted H. W. Gibson, a YMCA tractarian and boys-worker, to reduce all of adolescent psychology to something called 'boyology.' " A very useful compendium which nicely captures the differences in the theories is *Boy Training*, ed. John Alexander (New York: Association Press, 1915).

"progressive" juvenile corrections, the main rehabilitative tool of the court movement was probation.[51] Ideally, probation was to be a means of family education. Probation officers were to function less as agents of law enforcement than as visiting teachers who would instruct parents and children on how to eliminate family stress and how to use community resources to increase economic security and recreational enjoyment. The theory of probation was built firmly on the assumptions that most children became delinquent during their adolescent years, that adolescents were especially malleable, and that the successful rechanneling of youthful energies into lawful pursuits would motivate parents to modify their behavior toward their children and eliminate delinquency-producing conditions in the home. Probation epitomized the belief that adolescents merited several chances to become upright citizens.

Not so—or at least markedly less so—with erring adolescent girls.[52] Writers on female delinquency argued that, while a female's delinquencies were less criminally culpable, they were also less amenable to change through a relatively informal means of supervision like probation. Girls also received probation less frequently than boys because of the greater tendency to blame parents of delinquent girls. Unlike boys, it was argued, girls did not have places other than their homes in which to spend free time safely. Although writers on delinquency recognized that immigrant mothers and youth entered the work force because of poverty, they nonetheless held that rearing a girl imposed special moral responsibilities. Thus all mothers, regardless of economic circumstances, were obliged to keep their girls at home, when not in school or church, and to transform homes into refuges for protecting female virtue. This tendency to hold mothers more directly responsible for the behavior of girl delinquents than of boy delinquents further diminished the likelihood of probation for girls. If the female delinquent was considered less redeemable than her male counterpart, so too was her mother.

As probation was devalued for girl offenders, incarceration was judged more suitable. Earlier we examined the main rationales for female reformatories; here we will present additional justifications that illuminate why girl and boy delinquents were treated differently. One was the belief that girl delinquents, unlike boys, were not at all childlike in their behavior. By usurping the ultimate adult prerogative—sexual intercourse—female delinquents forfeited their right to be regarded merely as innocent, curious children. Moreover, precocious sexual exploration by girls threatened society's attempt to keep children innocent, chaste, and dependent until marriageable age. Female delinquents thereby subverted family government and had to be removed from their natural homes for the protection of neighborhood youth. Finally, imprisonment was seen as a boon to rehabilitation because of the speed with which neighborhood grapevines disseminated the repu-

---

[51] Schlossman, *Love*, chap. 4.

[52] The citations in note 49 are all relevant here, especially Breckinridge and Abbott, *The Delinquent Child*, pp. 35–38, 72–73, 169; Ordahl and Ordahl, "A Study of Delinquent and Dependent Girls," pp. 60–61; Van Waters, "Causes and Cure," p. 5; Paddon, "A Study of Fifty Feeble-Minded Prostitutes," p. 10; and True, "The Neglected Girl," p. 19.

tations of "bad girls." One writer summed up these diverse rationales for more frequent incarceration of delinquent girls:

> And suppose a boy does bolt? He can try again. Suppose he "goes bad" a second or a third time, either through animal spirits or bad companions? He can begin all over again. Suppose he even stays out nights, and goes into lower forms of degradation? Even then if he can pull himself together physically and morally, he has not lost the chance for a decent manhood and a square deal. But is it so with any delinquent girl? No, a thousand times no! By the publicity of even the appearance in Court her reputation is tarnished, and with her reputation in question, her chance to retrieve herself in the same environment is very small. And in that eighty percent of crimes against the person, does my girl get a fair chance to "try again?" No, the world is against her, evil men are ready to tempt her further, the industrial situation helps to put her at their mercy, and even nature herself gives a last push towards the downward path when she physically handicaps herself. No! My girl who has once become delinquent finds it a 1000 times more difficult to straighten herself than the boy. The delinquent girl must be preserved against the *opportunities* of temptation which are inevitably more fatal to her than to the boy.[53]

Clearly, then, the juvenile reformatory was the best possible place to treat delinquent girls—to protect society from them and them from society.

The third and final development behind growing awareness of female delinquency in the Progressive era was the movement for "social purity." More particularly, we want to analyze the relation of the purity ideal to what several historians have described as the "sexual revolution" of the Progressive era or the beginnings of "the modernization of sex." We believe that changes in sexual mores provided the cultural foundation for the burgeoning interest in female delinquency, the expansion of female reformatories, and the differential treatment of boy and girl delinquents. To explicate our position, we will first examine changing sexual mores in the Progressive era and then point up how they shaped new policies toward female delinquents.[54]

[53] Francis, "The Delinquent Girl," p. 140.

[54] In the 1950s and 1960s the most common historical approach to the subject of morals and sex in the Progressive era was to emphasize its puritanical features. This approach flowed from the interpretation of social-reform movements epitomized by the work of Richard Hofstadter, especially *The Age of Reform* (New York: Knopf, 1955). In the past few years a different historical interpretation has emerged that stresses the loosening grip of Victorian morality on sexual attitudes and holds that "modern" attitudes toward sex first emerged in the Progressive era rather than, as is more commonly thought, in the 1920s. This view rests on several sources of evidence: the work of historical demographers, who argue that rates of premarital pregnancy rose markedly in this period; self-report studies, which indicate that dramatic increases in premarital intercourse occurred; and reexamination of literary sources, which suggests that social discourse in the Progressive era was a good deal less prudish than had been thought. As examples, see Linda Gordon, *Woman's Body, Woman's Right* (New York: Grossman, 1976), pt. 2; Paul Robinson, *The Modernization of Sex* (New York: Harper & Row, 1976); John Burnham, "The Progressive-Era Revolution in American Attitudes Toward Sex," *Journal of American History*, 1973, 59, 885–908; James McGovern, "The American Woman's Pre-World War I Freedom in Manners and Morals," *Journal of American History*, 1968, 55, 315–333; and Carl Degler, "What Ought To Be and

Increasing investment in reformatories for sexually precocious girls reflected a widespread revulsion against the growing frequency and legitimacy of sex as an everyday topic of discussion.[55] The expansion of the government's capacity to punish sexual promiscuity formed one phase of what we term a "sexual counter-revolution." The men and women who led this counterrevolution were, by and large, the same types of middle-class, nonethnic individuals who participated in the better-known political and social reforms of the period. For these men and women, the sexual counterrevolution represented a moral analogue to the cleansing of corruption in the political and economic arenas.[56]

To the counterrevolutionists the public's fascination with sex was inherently dangerous because it threatened the maintenance of conventional family life. They were particularly troubled by many recent changes: the flagrant commercialization of sex in the press; the demystification of sex by doctors, psychologists, and intellectuals; the increasingly open propaganda for dissemination of birth-control devices; and the moral dangers inherent in the discovery of new medical remedies for venereal disease. The counterrevolutionists urged that new strategies were essential to revitalize older sexual ideals, neutralize overstimulated sexual appetites, and purify social discourse on sex. If reticence was no longer possible, purity was.[57]

The counterrevolutionists engaged in three major "reform" campaigns: the wholesale destruction of prostitution; the widespread dissemination of sex educa-

---

What Was: Women's Sexuality in the Nineteenth Century," *American Historical Review*, 1974, 79, 1467–1490.

While we agree with the historians who argue that the early twentieth century witnessed a marked increase in the public's willingness to discuss sex openly, we are uneasy about the tendency to locate the origins of sexual modernity in the Progressive era. This approach, we feel, exaggerates indications of the new morality and plays down evidence of older Victorian thinking. Most important for the history of female juvenile justice, this interpretation shifts attention away from major efforts in this period to reaffirm Victorian moral and sexual standards as well as to recast older religious commands into new secular, scientific language. Thus we both agree and disagree with the new interpretation.

55 On the scholarly side, the psychologist Helen Thompson Woolley noted that between 1910 and 1914 "the number of experimental investigations in the field [psychology of sex] has increased to such an extent that whereas it was difficult at that time [1910] to find anything to review, it is now impossible to review all that I could find" ("The Psychology of Sex," *The Psychological Bulletin*, 1914, 11, 353). If scholars were having a field day with sex, so was the American public: "A wave of sex hysteria seems to have invaded this country," wrote the anonymous author of a piece which has since become an historical classic. "Our former reticence on matters of sex is giving way to a frankness that would even startle Paris." ("Sex O'Clock in America," *Current Opinion*, August 1913, 55, 113).

56 This is our impression from reading the literature; we have not conducted empirical research on the social origins of the counterrevolutionists. Certainly Theodore Roosevelt was the most prominent of the individuals who engaged as fervidly in moral as in political reform. Roosevelt popularized the notion of "race suicide" and boasted that one of his greatest achievements was to have exercised enough will power to remain a virgin until marriage (William Harbaugh, *The Life and Times of Theodore Roosevelt* [New York: Oxford University Press, 1975], p. 15).

57 For general background see David Pivar, *Purity Crusade* (Westport, Conn.: Greenwood, 1973); and David Kennedy, *Birth Control in America* (New Haven, Conn.: Yale University Press, 1970).

tion; and, our main subject, the punishment of sexually precocious girls. Each campaign had a number of concrete, functional goals, but each needs to be seen symbolically as well. Together, the campaigns represented a ritualistic protest against cultural change, a spirited reaffirmation of older moral ideals, and an urgent call for creative new strategies to realize them.

The campaign against prostitution was, ironically, both a contribution to and a sharp reaction against what one author wittily called the arrival of "sex o'clock" in America.[58] Prostitution had been a widespread and fairly well-accepted part of American urban life. To be sure, moralists of many kinds had periodically remonstrated against the easy acceptance of prostitution and were probably responsible for insuring that only one brief effort was made, in St. Louis, to experiment with European methods of regulation.[59] By and large, though, prostitutes sold their services with little interference, and, all evidence indicates, remarkably large percentages of American males used them.[60]

In the Victorian years prostitution was silently tolerated for three principal reasons. For one, prostitutes thrived mainly in the poorer, immigrant neighborhoods, and the feeling was, then as now, that as long as prostitutes remained in the slums, more respectable communities need not worry unduly about them. Second, nineteenth-century popular opinion sanctioned the view that men possessed superabundant sexual energies that required frequent release for mental and physical health. We must be careful not to exaggerate here; for opposite beliefs on male sexuality were also held in the Victorian period. Several reformers argued, for example, that sexual indulgence destroyed men's bodies and minds and that men should be continent in their sexual expression.[61] In retrospect, though, what is remarkable is how easily these contradictory sentiments coexisted—the latter as ideology for public consumption, the former as an "underground" precept guiding actual behavior.[62]

[58] "Sex O'Clock in America."

[59] John Burnham, "Medical Inspection of Prostitutes in Nineteenth Century America—The St. Louis Experiment and Its Sequel," *Bulletin of the History of Medicine*, 1971, **45**, 203–218.

[60] See Roy Lubove, "The Progressives and the Prostitute," *Historian*, 1962, **24**, 308–330; Robert Riegel, "Changing American Attitudes toward Prostitution (1800–1920)," *Journal of the History of Ideas*, 1968, **29**, 437–452; Keith Thomas, "The Double Standard," *Journal of the History of Ideas*, 1959, **20**, 195–216; Egal Feldman, "Prostitution, the Alien Woman and the Progressive Imagination, 1910–1915," *American Quarterly*, 1967, **19**, 192–206; Eric Anderson, "Prostitution and Social Justice: Chicago, 1910–15," *Social Service Review*, 1974, **48**, 203–228; Claudia Johnson, "That Guilty Third Tier: Prostitution in Nineteenth-Century American Theaters," in *Victorian America*, ed. Daniel Howe (Philadelphia: University of Pennsylvania Press, 1976), pp. 111–120; and James Wunsch, "Prostitution and Public Policy: From Regulation to Suppression, 1858–1920," Dissertation, University of Chicago, 1976.

[61] A very useful introduction to the ideals and practices of sex in the Victorian period is *Primers for Prudery*, ed. Ronald Walters (Englewood Cliffs, N.J.: Prentice-Hall, 1974). See also Gordon, *Woman's Body*, chaps. 4 and 8; and Patricia Vertinsky, "Education for Sexual Morality: Moral Reform and the Regulation of American Sexual Behavior in the Nineteenth Century," Dissertation, University of British Columbia, 1974, sect. 2.

[62] We borrow the term "underground" from Bryan Strong, who writes of the attempt in the early twentieth century "to counteract the underground belief in what was called the 'sexual

The third reason for toleration of prostitution was the Victorian sentimentalization of womanhood.[63] "Respectable" women—the only kind men dared marry—were placed gingerly upon a pedestal and viewed as rarefied creatures without sexual motivation. By nature they were so innocent and gentle that it would have been cruel for husbands to impose their sexual lusts upon them. This viewpoint obviously facilitated public acceptance of prostitution: the practice was rationalized as a protection of the home and domestic life through the absorption of men's excess sexual energies.

In the reform campaigns of the Progressive era, the ambivalences and contradictions of Victorian sexual thinking gave way to the unyielding pursuit of purity and innocence. Under the leadership of the counterrevolutionists, city after city conducted elaborate studies of prostitution, revealing how openly prostitution flourished. Estimates varied, but it was conservatively calculated that well over half of American males from all social classes used or had used prostitutes and that many had contracted some form of venereal disease. Using these facts to support their position, the counterrevolutionists attacked regulation or even the toleration of prostitution as blasphemy. The wholesale destruction of prostitution became their goal, and, to a remarkable extent, they succeeded in wiping out many of the nation's most famous red-light districts in the years before the First World War.[64]

The metaphor of the white-slave trade fueled the antiprostitution campaign, but the extent to which prostitution was centrally organized was always uncertain.[65] Two other well-publicized arguments, though, helped sustain the fight against prostitution. The first resulted from several major scientific advances in detection and treatment of venereal disease. The counterrevolutionists drew grave moral implications from these scientific developments. On the one hand, they insisted, the physical devastation and easy communicability of venereal disease demanded rapid elimination of prostitution to safeguard family health. On the other hand, they asserted, the discovery of effective cures for venereal disease required quick destruction of prostitution, lest men be tempted to greater vice by the knowledge that they need not fear infection.[66]

The second rationale for destroying prostitution also drew upon medical opin-

---

necessity,' which declared that men must exercise their sexual power lest their organs weaken or atrophy for want of use. Belief in a 'sexual necessity,' of course, was inconsistent with the ideal of chastity and continence" ("Ideas of the Early Sex Education Movement in America, 1890–1920," *History of Education Quarterly*, 1972, 12, 145).

[63] See, for example, Anne Scott, *The Southern Lady* (Chicago: University of Chicago Press, 1970); and Barbara Welter, "The Cult of True Womanhood: 1820–1860," *American Quarterly*, 1966, 18, 151–174.

[64] See Gordon, *Woman's Body*, p. 204. While we find her argument intriguing, we do not believe there is sufficient evidence to support Gordon's cause-effect contention that "the basis for the weakening of prostitution between 1910 and 1920 was not the conversion of men to purity; it was the conversion of women to 'indulgence' " (p. 192).

[65] For example, see Clifford Roe, *The Prodigal Daughter: The White Slave Evil and the Remedy* (Chicago: L. W. Walter, 1911); and *War on the White Slave Trade*, ed. Ernest Bell (Chicago: Charles C. Thompson, 1909).

[66] The principal medical spokesperson and organizational leader of the counterrevolutionists

ion, although in this instance it was more a medical assertion than a demonstrable advance in scientific knowledge. The counterrevolutionists contended that a single standard of sexual behavior—that of continence—should prevail for men and women.[67] This ideal, as we observed, also had its supporters in the Victorian era. The twentieth-century proponents of continence did little to challenge the underground Victorian view that men's sexual appetites were ravenous. Instead, they emphatically urged continence as part of the larger Progressive-era moral revival, which included such other popular displays of conscience as the prohibition movement and the campaigns against child labor, dime novels, cheap movies, and the easy availability of narcotic drugs. Furthermore, the counterrevolutionists now gained the concerted support of powerful medical organizations against the underground doctrine of "sexual necessity." Three hundred of the nation's leading physicians, for example, issued a much-publicized manifesto in favor of male continence, which declared in part:

> In view of the individual and social dangers which spring from the widespread belief that continence may be detrimental to health, and of the fact that municipal toleration of prostitution is sometimes defended on the ground that sexual indulgence is necessary, we, the undersigned, members of the medical profession, testify to our belief that continence has not been shown to be detrimental to health or virility; that there is no evidence of its being inconsistent with the highest physical, mental, and moral efficiency; and that it offers the only sure reliance for sexual health outside of marriage.[68]

In sum, the counterrevolutionists, who led the antiprostitution campaign, relied heavily on medical opinion to persuade the American public that Victorian sexual liberties were sinful and unhealthy and that continence was possible through moral exertion and the removal of temptation. Paradoxically, then, at the very time when sex was becoming an accepted part of social discourse, a surprisingly effective campaign was led to eliminate one of the most common figures of nineteenth-century society, the prostitute.

Like the antiprostitution crusade, the sex-education movement drew heavily on medical science. Proponents of sex education saw themselves as progressive, fearlessly attacking the Victorian "conspiracy of silence" about sex. On closer inspection, though, sex education appears to have been anything but a modernizing influence. The sex educators fought mainly against imaginary adversaries, for sex was already an everyday topic of conversation. Moreover, the movement's rhetoric was largely puritanical, revealing deep fears about the moral impact of cultural change.[69]

---

was Dr. Prince Morrow, whose activities are well treated in Burnham, "The Progressive Era Revolution."

[67] See especially Thomas, *The Unadjusted Girl*; and Strong, "Ideas of the Early Sex Education Movement."

[68] Quoted in Maurice Bigelow, *Sex-Education* (New York: Macmillan, 1918), p. 161.

[69] We are especially indebted to the works of Pivar, Strong, and Vertinsky, "Education for Sexual Morality." The best primary sources, in our estimation, are *The Social Emergency*, ed. William

The main goals of sex education were to purify discourse on sex, particularly in the popular press and among children, and to instill moral inhibitions against sexual gratification now that effective birth control and cures for venereal disease were becoming widely available. The sex educators were moral crusaders marching under the banners of medical and pedagogical science. They sought to develop instructional techniques for innocently conveying new medical knowledge about sex to children and, at the same time, imbuing sex with older spiritual meanings. Sex education was a means of pedagogical warfare against the purveyors of sexual titillation. Far from encouraging freer discussion of sex, the sex educators wanted to discipline lust and channel it to conventional moral ends.[70]

While the sex educators claimed to bring discussion of sex into the open, their pedagogical approach was so indirect as to be obscurantist. About the only form of open sexual discussion they could tolerate, in fact, involved the mating of plants. The copulation of pistils and stamens served as a model for teaching children acceptable sexual emotion and was much preferred to analogies between human and animal sexuality.[71] To the extent that sex educators actually discussed human sex, it was always as a form of spiritual communion; intercourse was mainly a melding of chaste minds. The sex-education movement, then, is best conceived as part of a new strategy for realizing Victorian moral ideals in an era growing increasingly comfortable with sex. If adults in the Progressive period had become unduly attracted to sex, their children need not be.[72]

How is the sexual counterrevolution related to our main subject—female juvenile justice in the Progressive era? We believe the sentiments that motivated the antiprostitution and sex-education campaigns also inspired punitive treatment of female delinquents. The expansion of female reformatories was especially significant, for they played important instrumental and symbolic roles in the sexual counterrevolution. First, and most pragmatically, the female reformatories

---

Foster (Boston: Houghton-Mifflin, 1914); Bigelow, *Sex-Education*; and National Society for the Scientific Study of Education, *Education with Reference to Sex* (Chicago: University of Chicago Press, 1909).

70 Although the sex educators, by and large, wanted nothing to do with Freud, they were advocating a form of creative repression akin to the goals of the early conservative champions of Freud in America. See Nathan Hale, *Freud and the Americans* (New York: Oxford University Press, 1971).

71 For example, Bigelow writes in *Sex-Education*: "Like eating, [sex] is a necessary function inherited from animals; but there has been an evolution of greater significance. In the animal world, sexual activity has only one function, reproduction; but human life at its highest has superadded psychical and social meaning to sexual relationships, and the result has been affection and the human family. If we reject this higher view of the double significance of sexuality in human life, and insist that only the necessary propagative function is worthy of recognition, it is almost inevitable that most people will continue to accept the hopeless view that human sexuality is on the same vulgar plane as that of the animals; in short, that it is only an animal function. This, I insist, is a depressing interpretation that will never help overcome the prevailing vulgar attitude toward sex" (p. 74).

72 For assessments of the influence of the sex-education movement, see Strong, "Ideas of the Early Sex Education Movement," pp. 152–153; and Vertinsky, "Education for Sexual Morality," chap. 9.

assisted in the medical effort to eliminate venereal disease. They isolated those girls who were assumed most likely to become disease carriers. If the girls were already carriers, the reformatories prevented them from spreading disease and made treatment possible. Second, and most presumptuously, the incarceration of sexually promiscuous girls was thought to facilitate the moral ideal of male continence. By removing from view a prime source of sexual temptation, the reformatories, it was earnestly hoped, would also eliminate a stimulant of sexual desire in ghetto communities, especially for teenage boys. Third, and most urgently, the reformatories took sexually active girls off the street during the age range when prostitutes were most commonly recruited.[73] Hence reformatories, aided by the juvenile courts' punitive attitude toward sexual precocity among girls, would contribute to the attack on prostitution by cutting off a likely supply of new recruits.

Finally, and most idealistically, the reformatories assumed a special symbolic role in the sexual counterrevolution. In an era becoming increasingly fascinated by all things sexual, reformatories offered a warning that society would still not tolerate girls who showed the same interest in sex as boys and reinforced the traditional belief that "normal" girls were sexually impassive. These sentiments seem to us to have represented, to a large extent, a rearguard defense against emerging modern views on the reality of female sexual desire. But if, in fact, the counterrevolutionists lost the war, they were a powerful enough force in the Progressive era to win important battles. We should not gauge their significance in the early twentieth century by their long-term defeat in the battle for sexual liberation.

In sum, we believe that female juvenile justice in the Progressive era was closely tied to the evolution of sexual mores. In an era of shifting cultural norms, new social policies emerged to defend older moral ideals. As we noted earlier, we do not deny the possibility that there may have been a real increase in female delinquency in the early twentieth century. But we insist that, whether the increase was real or imagined, the public response to female delinquency formed part of a larger cultural reaction, an attempt to revitalize Victorian morality and to punish women —prostitutes and sexually precocious girls alike—who impeded attainment of that goal.

Conclusion

We promised earlier not to draw glib comparisons between past and present because of the incomplete nature of our historical research. But our research unequivocally demonstrates that the roots of sexual discrimination in juvenile

---

[73] According to Jane Addams, "it has been estimated that at any given moment the majority of girls utilized by the trade are under twenty years of age and that most of them were procured when younger . . . the average age of recruits to prostitution is between sixteen and eighteen years. . . . All the recent investigations have certainly made clear that the bulk of the entire traffic is conducted with the youth of the community, and that the social evil, ancient though it may be, must be renewed in our generation through its younger members. The knowledge of the youth of its victims doubtless in a measure accounts for the new sense of compunction which fills the community." *A New Conscience*, pp. 52, 112.

justice are deep indeed. Despite radically different attitudes today toward the social role and sexual desires of women, our correctional policies share many of the assumptions common in the nineteenth and early twentieth centuries.[74] Perhaps mainstream ideas about the proper role of women and of female sexuality have not changed as much as some may think;[75] perhaps correctional policies always lag behind changes in cultural perception; perhaps we as a society are trying unconsciously to relieve guilt about the passing of older moral standards by continuing to punish the most vulnerable group of females—poor, minority children who today, as in the past, predominate among incarcerated girls. We do not have a ready answer, but we do believe that there is an intimate relation between a society's correctional system and its deepest values and beliefs. And without doubt the values and beliefs that shaped a discriminatory system of juvenile justice in the Victorian and Progressive eras still dominate the administration of female juvenile justice today.

[74] Richard Flaste, "Is Juvenile Justice Tougher on Girls Than on Boys?" *New York Times*, 6 September 1977, p. 48, cols. 1–4.

[75] The classic argument, of course, is presented in Betty Friedan, *The Feminine Mystique* (New York: Norton, 1963). In addition to previously cited books and articles, the following historical works shed much light on continuities between past and present: Charles Rosenberg, "Sexuality, Class, and Role," *American Quarterly*, 1973, **25**, 131–153; Charles Rosenberg and Carroll Smith-Rosenberg, "The Female Animal: Medical and Biological Views of Women," *Journal of American History*, 1973, **60**, 332–356; Rosalind Rosenberg, "The Dissent from Darwin, 1890–1930: The New View of Woman among American Social Scientists," Dissertation, Stanford University, 1974; and Paula Fass, *The Damned and the Beautiful* (New York: Oxford University Press, 1977).

A Guide to Additional Primary-Source Materials on Female Juvenile Delinquency in the Early Twentieth Century

Bowen, Mrs. Joseph. "The Delinquent Child of Immigrant Parents." National Conference of Charities and Correction, *Proceedings* (1909), pp. 255–261.

Bridgman, Olga. "An Experimental Study of Abnormal Children, with Special Reference to the Problems of Dependency and Delinquency." University of California, *Publications in Psychology*, 1918, 3, 2–59.

Bronner, Augusta. *A Comparative Study of the Intelligence of Girls*. New York: Teachers College Press, 1914.

Burleigh, Edith. "The Advantage of Parole Under a Separate Superintendent." National Conference on the Education of Truant, Backward, Dependent and Delinquent Children, *Proceedings* (1916), pp. 80–83.

Burleigh, Edith. "Some Principles for Parole for Girls." National Conference of Charities and Correction, *Proceedings* (1918), pp. 147–154.

DeBolt, Mrs. L. N. "Industrial Employment as a Factor in the Reformation of Girls." National Conference of Charities and Correction, *Proceedings* (1900), pp. 214–220.

Dummer, Mrs. W. F. "Introduction to Roundtable Discussion on the Delinquent Girl." The American Sociological Society, *Publications*, 1921, **16**, 185–186.

Dye, Charlotte. "The Defective Delinquent." National Conference on the Education of Truant, Backward, Dependent and Delinquent Children, *Proceedings* (1917), pp. 78–82.

Falconer, Martha. "The Culture of Family Life Versus Reformatory Treatment." National Conference of Charities and Correction, *Proceedings* (1914), pp. 108–110.

Falconer, Martha. "Reformatory Treatment for Women." National Conference of Charities and Correction, *Proceedings* (1914), pp. 253–256.

Goddard, Henry. "The Treatment of the Mental Defective Who Is Also Delinquent." National Conference of Charities and Correction, *Proceedings* (1911), pp. 64–65.

Hamilton, Dr. Alice. "Venereal Disease in Institutions for Women and Girls." National Conference of Charities and Correction, *Proceedings* (1910), pp. 53–56.

Harris, Dr. Mary. "Preparing Delinquent Women for the New Citizenship." Conference of the National Committee on Prisons and Prison Labor, *Proceedings* (1919), pp. 6–14.

Harris, Dr. Mary. *I Knew Them in Prison.* New York: Viking, 1936.

Hoag, Dr. Ernest, and Dr. Edward Williams. *Crime, Abnormal Minds and the Law.* Indianapolis, Ind.: Bobbs-Merrill, 1923.

Hodder, Jessie. "The Next Step in the Treatment of Girls and Women Offenders." National Conference of Charities and Correction, *Proceedings* (1918), pp. 117–121.

Holsopple, Francis. "Social Non-Conformity: An Analysis of 420 Delinquent Girls and Women." Dissertation, University of Pennsylvania, 1919.

Kauffman, Reginald. *The Girl That Goes Wrong.* New York: Macaulay, 1911.

Kenworthy, Dr. Marion. "The Logic of Delinquency." The American Sociological Society, *Publications,* 1921, 16, 197–204.

Lundberg, Emma. "The Child-Mother as a Delinquency Problem." National Conference of Charities and Correction, *Proceedings* (1920), pp. 167–168.

Miner, Maude. *Slavery of Prostitution.* New York: Macmillan, 1916.

Miner, Maude. "The Individual Method of Dealing with Girls and Women Awaiting Court Action." Congress of the American Prison Association, *Proceedings* (1921), pp. 8–12.

Montgomery, Miss Sarah. "Discipline and Training of Girls in Industrial Schools." National Conference of Charities and Correction, *Proceedings* (1908), pp. 198–201.

Morrow, Dr. Louis, and Dr. Olga Bridgman. "Delinquent Girls Tested by the Binet Scale." *Training School Bulletin,* 1912, 9, 33–36.

Morse, Mrs. Frannie. "The Methods Most Helpful to Girls." National Conference of Charities and Correction, *Proceedings* (1904), pp. 306–311.

Murray, Virginia. "The Runaway Girl and the Stranded Girl." National Conference of Charities and Correction, *Proceedings* (1920), pp. 175–180.

National Conference on the Education of Truant, Backward, Dependent and Delinquent Children, *Proceedings* (1915), pp. 49–53, and (1917), pp. 36–41, 82–90.

Renz, Emile. "The Intelligence of Delinquents and the Eugenic Significance of Mental Defect." *Training School Bulletin,* 1914, 11, 37–39.

Rippin, Jane. "Municipal Detention for Women." National Conference of Charities and Correction, *Proceedings* (1918), pp. 132–139.

Sessions, Dr. Kenosha. "Some Deductions from the Wasserman Test." National Conference on the Education of Truant, Backward, Dependent and Delinquent Children, *Proceedings* (1915), pp. 47–49.

Sessions, Dr. Kenosha. "The Delinquent Girls as a Community Problem." National Conference on the Education of Truant, Backward, Dependent and Delinquent Children, *Proceedings* (1918), pp. 76–78.

Smith, Dr. Carrie. "The Unadjusted Girl." National Conference of Charities and Correction, *Proceedings* (1920), pp. 180–183.

Taft, Jessie. "Some Problems in Delinquency—Where Do They Belong?" The American Sociological Society, *Publications,* 1921, 16, 186–196.

Van Waters, Miriam. "Juvenile Court Procedure as a Factor in Diagnosis." The American Sociological Society, *Publications,* 1921, 16, 209–217.

Wald, Mrs. Lillian. "The Immigrant Young Girl." National Conference of Charities and Correction, *Proceedings* (1909), pp. 261–266.

Wilson, Otto. *Fifty Years' Work with Girls, 1883–1933.* Alexandria, Va.: National Florence Crittendon Mission, 1933.

Worthington, George, and Ruth Topping. *Specialized Courts Dealing with Sex Delinquency.* New York: Frederick H. Hitchcock, 1925.

Part III:

DISCRETION IN CRIMINAL JUSTICE

Because all recent discussion of discretion treats it as a condition upon which some repairs are urgently due, it is well to be reminded that its presence in the administration of justice is not the product of some inadvertence. It is an essential element of legal orders like ours—rather than simply a practical necessity—because no final dispositions of legal questions are conceivable that do not involve the exercise of human judgment. To be sure, it may be claiming too much for some instances of legal disposition to say that they involved the exercise of "judgment." Still, no matter how foregone a conclusion, it does not become a fact till announced by someone entitled to announce it. Of course, judges sometimes say they had no choice, and legislators try to pass laws intended to leave judges no choices. But the absence of choice does not work in the way that adding a column of numbers compels one and only one correct sum, where it would make no sense to say that the sum actually arrived at is an officially authorized sum. Finding sums and finding answers to legal questions are not the same thing, obviously! The point is that they are not the same thing even in those instances of legal inference that appear to be as algorithmic as algebra.

One might imagine that we exclude the mechanical application of legal norms because the aim of law is justice. And justice is too elusive a catch for a mere network of norms. In our world justice probably cannot be caught without norms, but there is need for "discretion . . . to know through law what is just" (10 Coke's English King's Bench Reports, 140). Law alone would yield greater certainty, but the quest for justice forces us to settle for mere "reasonable regularity" which, Professor Llewellyn (1960: 217) assured us, would come close to "drying up the bubbling flood of words about rule and discretion." Reasonable regularity seems like a modest standard, but judging by what one reads in our times even this has eluded us by quite a wide margin. Of course, "reasonable regularity" is a vague notion. What people expect of it is probably affected by the fact that we do not live comfortably with discretion. Other societies are (and were) more accepting of it. Both traditional precapitalist and revolutionary postcapitalist societies administer justice in a more summary and less standardized manner than we do. This is so, Weber (1954: 301-321) taught, because the tendency toward highly formalized and rationalized legality is closely linked with the ascendance of modern capitalism. We cherish a legal order comprised of generalized and explicit legal norms through which all members of society are treated as formally equal with little regard for substantive differences between them (Balbus, 1977). With such a start it should come as no surprise that we would find existing discretion excessive, or that we would be alert to injustices resulting from its exercise.

Recent attention to discretion in law enforcement and administration of justice brought forth a spate of discoveries and concerns in a manner somewhat reminiscent of the experience of a man who after losing hair for some time realizes that he has become bald. The meaning and import of the concept is, of course, not unambiguous. It has been used to refer to an aspect of legality and it has been used as meaning something distinct from and even opposed to legality. Arthur Rosett's stimulating essay provides us with a review of judicial usage. Though he does not raise the question, one might ask whether the scope of usage discretion has received in recent judicial expressions could not be reduced quite substantially by separating discretionary actions in the sphere of legality proper from discretionary actions in matters merely related to legality. At the very least, an attempt in this direction might address again the question whether there is anything under the sun about which the law is not and could not be dispositive.

In preliterate legal systems the law pertains potentially to everything, but municipal legal orders tend to specify limits to possible legal regulation. Under the "rule of law" only specifically authorized official actions enjoy the status of legal actions, with all others constituting abridgements of the civil liberties of citizens. This formulation neither excludes nor solves the problems encountered when a sphere of competence is authorized, rather than explicitly formulated procedures. These and such problems become distinctly academic, however, when confronted with some simple observations about the functioning of discretion in criminal justice. One need not invoke the philosophy of law to realize that there is something wrong when "only about three or four persons in 100 arrested on a felony charge go to prison, and those who do are not obviously distinguishable from those who do not," as Rosett notes. There must be something amiss in a situation where the norm that is supposed to govern it is found applicable in less than one out of twenty cases!

While we are startled and dismayed by the observation that in the administration of criminal justice the rule has become the exception, most of us are probably not surprised that the penal provisions of various regulatory laws are enforced only in aggravated cases of violation. Donald I. Baker, for example, indicates that in his view no criminal prosecution in price-fixing and market-allocation cases should be undertaken where there exists "confusion caused by past prosecutorial decisions." If this principle were to be adopted in prosecutorial discretion relative to crimes of the ordinary kind, then it would be difficult to imagine how any complaints of any kind could ever be filed. But this is only one of the four principles of discretionary dispensation Baker advances. And he advances them despite his professed belief that "criminal sanctions, particularly substantial individual jail sentences, best deter antitrust crimes." But officials entrusted with the implementation of penal provisions of regulatory laws often believe that resorting to prosecution is generally unwise and they pass up countless opportunities for prosecution over protracted periods of time (Silbey, 1978).

While the presence of illegality in and the modest level of prosecution of business firms has been the target of increasing attention, the condemnation of the liberal attitudes in this area has not reached anywhere near the pitch and universality with which liberalism in criminal law enforcement is condemned. Albert W. Alschuler evaluates the overall effect of legislation that was intended as a measure to eliminate some and to reduce the rest of discretionary freedom in the administration of criminal justice in California. While the California Determinate Sentencing Statute essentially eliminated parole board decision-making powers, and reduced judicial sentencing discretion significantly, Alschuler finds that the "sentencing statute seems to create a bargainer's paradise." That is, the mighty struggle to do away with discretion resulted merely in its displacement into the hands of prosecutors where it is probably even less subject to public scrutiny.

While prosecutorial and judicial discretion concerns—at least in principle—matters of just deserts, discretion in the correctional context deals mainly with what might be called diagnostic decisions and planning based on those assessments. But as Robert M. Garber and Christina Maslach, and Stephen Pfohl, demonstrate in their papers, the agents entrusted with decisions to predict dangerousness and to determine readiness for parole appear to act not on the basis of what one would regard as carefully considered criteria and procedures, but rather in ways that are apt to scandalize even a seasoned observer of the prison scene. They are, in fact, quite unable to make reasoned judgments because, according to Garber and Maslach, "it is impossible to predict with any accuracy who will be dangerous and . . . the best predication is that any individual, regardless of background, will not pose a threat to others." Nevertheless, these trusted agents of society pretend to exercise professional judgment, thereby shielding their decisions from the kind of public scrutiny to which legal-political acts are common exposed. On the basis of these findings one is almost inclined to recommend that the study of rule-governed disposition and discretionary disposition be augmented by a new category under which would be subsumed all those processes involving instinctive or intuitive decision-making. With this in the open, one could then select decision makers of suitable character and temperament, who could be trusted to use common sense soberly and with an open mind. At the very least, the impact of the decision makers' own career contingencies would be eliminated, or reduced.

The disclosure that some decisions in the criminal justice system are not made for any reasons connected with a case at hand, regardless of whether such reasons would be acceptable as proper or rejected as improper, is most difficult to present but the most interesting from a sociological perspective. What comes into play here is neither wisdom nor folly, neither prejudice nor impartiality, neither resoluteness nor intemperateness, nor anything else that may represent the official's correct or incorrect assessment. Instead, what matters are considerations that arise out of the officials' own circumstances, such as, for example, that the case came up as a task close to quitting time. Richard McCleary shows that certain record-keeping requirements are apt to determine the manner and the likelihood of parole officers taking cognizance of the misdeeds of their charges. It is rather important that the reader resist the temptation to focus on the revelations of what might be seen as extreme instances of professional irresponsibility on the part of parole officers. These illustrations merely highlight a much more pervasive aspect of discretionary practices, namely that every decision must be viewed as in some measure related to the circumstances of its occurrence. People who are required to make decisions as part of a vocation or gainful occupation cannot be expected to do so without regard for the organized character of the setting within which they discharge their responsibilities and within which they must find the fulfillment of their own needs and aspirations. One consequence of ignoring these matters is that in not recognizing considerations of practicality and in not knowing where to draw the line that separates them from that form of excessive self-interest that tends to be connected with venality, we end up accepting more corruption as inevitable than we might otherwise.

John Hagan's paper dispels certain presumptions or, at least, reopens the question about the impact of bureaucratization of certain aspects of the administration of justice on fairness and justice. Though his findings cannot be regarded as conclusive for all sorts of settings, he shows that the bureaucratic method is not invariably the bane it is thought to be. It does succeed, as in fact Weber expected it would, in enhancing the chances of equal treatment of traditionally oppressed and disadvantaged minorities when their treatment in bureaucratized settings is compared with the treatment they receive in rural and more personalized jurisdictions.

The topic of discretion in criminal justice is obviously not exhausted in the several discussions presented in this section. Indeed, limitations of space compelled neglecting some prominent aspects of it, of which discretion in police work is a prominent example. But the problem is pervasive and it is difficult to read long about any area of criminal law administration without encountering it in more or less explicit form. Hence, the reader of this volume may expect to find the problem of discretion discussed outside the section bearing this title.

REFERENCES

BALBUS, I. B. (1977). "Commodity form and legal form." Law and Society Review, 11: 571-588.
LLEWELLYN, K. (1960). The common law tradition. Boston: Little, Brown.
SILBEY, S. S. (1978). "Consumer justice: The Massachusetts Attorney General's Office of Consumer Protection 1970-1974." Unpublished Ph.D. dissertation, University of Chicago.
WEBER, M. (1954). On law in economy and society. Cambridge: Harvard University Press.

15

CONNOTATIONS OF DISCRETION
ARTHUR ROSETT

There has been a marked change over the past dozen years in those aspects of the criminal law which attract the greatest attention from lawyers. During the 1950s and early 1960s lawyers were predominantly concerned with matters of structure and definition in the criminal law. Important statutes, judicial opinions, and scholarly articles analyzed the substantive elements of particular offenses. They provided a refined rationale for the law of homicide and theft. The mental elements of crime were delineated by clearer definition of *mens rea,* intent, insanity, inchoate crimes, and conspiracy. Legislative attention to the cognate problems of immaturity produced restructured juvenile court laws in California, Illinois, and New York. The number of constitutional claims raised in criminal cases increased dramatically, but the new rules announced by the appellate courts concentrated primarily on the process due in the formal trial of criminal charges and the admission of evidence at trial. The crowning achievement of this period was the production of a monumental Model Penal Code, which recapitulates and carries forward these structural and definitional tasks. During these years, penal code reform was undertaken in a majority of the states.

In contrast, during the past dozen years the major emphasis has shifted to those processes of the criminal law that are not found in the penal code: how policemen exercise their power to bring people into the criminal process; how prosecutors decide which of the possible charges to file and how they encourage defendants to plead quilty without a trial; how judges and juries exercise their broad sentencing powers; how correctional authorities decide when to release convicts by parole and how offenders are controlled under supervision in institutions and in the community. In short, attention has shifted from formal structure and definition to the informal discretionary aspects of the process. Lawyers have come to recognize that most criminal charges are decided by the exercise of discretion, rather than through the application of a legal rule.

The emphasis on the importance of discretion gained momentum from the American Bar Foundation studies; which supplied the legal community with important observational data and drew together a remarkable group of legal and social scientist scholars (LaFave, 1965; Tiffany et al., 1967; Newman, 1966; Dawson, 1969; Miller, 1969). The work of Remington (1958),Goldstein (1960), LaFave (1965), Newman (1966), Skolnick (1966), et al. made it clear that the criminal courthouse did not operate the way the codes and judicial opinions had led us to think it did. The changing perspective became dominant in 1967 when the National Crime Commission (the President's Commission on Law Enforcement and Administration of Justice) led off its Task Force Report on the Courts with a chapter entitled "Disposition Without Trial," and did not get around to discussing the structural problems of court proceedings and code reform until Chapters 4 and 8 respectively.

During the dozen years that now separate us from the National Crime Commission, its approach has been accepted by the legal community in most of the varied roles lawyers play in the administration of criminal justice, as administrators, judges, legislators, advocates, and scholars. For example, state legislatures have become less sympathetic to the benevolent pretentions of programs providing care and custody for delinquent and dependent children, the mentally ill, and addicts. A major motivation of the resulting code revision has been to circumscribe more narrowly the discretionary power of case workers, judges, doctors, hospitals, and agencies and to restrict decisions on confinement, release, and conditions of treatment with stricter legal standards. Greater procedural safeguards and fuller opportunity for administrative and judicial review have been created.

Legislatures have also devoted greater attention to the sentencing, confinement and aftercare of adult criminal offenders. The stylish idea of the moment, determinate sentencing, has carried legislatures in directions parallel to those taken with juveniles and the mentally disabled. The movement toward determinate sentencing is tied both to the politically conservative urge to get tough with criminals by restricting the dispensing power available to softhearted and soft-headed judges and to liberal suspicion of the discretionary power judges, prosecutors, and parole boards have over convicts.

During the 1970s the sensitivity of legal administrators to problems of discretion has increased greatly. The heads of two of the largest district attorney's offices in the nation have promulgated regulations restricting "plea bargaining" by their deputies and seeking to bring the exercise of discretion regarding the filing of criminal charges under firmer office policy control. Correctional authorities have for the first time been called upon to promulgate rules limiting the discretion of wardens to control the conditions of confinement and discipline of inmates. In a number of departments, police administration has given greater attention to controlling the exercise of authority by the officer in the field. The importance of departmental regulations to channel the exercise of police discretion has been supported both by professional groups such as the Police Foundation and the International Association of Chiefs of Police and by the legal establishment, particularly in the American Law Institute's Model Code of Pre-Arraignment Procedure (1965).

The operation of discretion also has been a dominant concern for the legal scholarly community. The empiricists and observational students have built on the original American Bar Foundation studies and now a substantial number of informative studies of police prosecutors and correctional authorities are available. Academic social scientists have been joined by the researchers from centers of operations research, such as the Rand Corporation, which have applied computer-based systems analysis to the operations of district attorneys and detectives with informative results (Greenwood, 1976).

Scholars have approached the problem of discretion from a variety of directions on a more philosophic level. The moralists and legal philosophers seek to resolve the tension between rule and discretion in a positivistic legal framework. Ronald Dworkin (1972) asks us to take rights seriously and continues his critique of H.L.A. Hart's concept of law (1961), while the brothers Kadish (1973) have joined law and philosophy in an effort to legitimate discretion and rule departure in a legal universe.

For at least a generation the Supreme Court of the United States has avoided considering the constitutional dimensions of discretion in the criminal law, particularly the guilty plea processes by which the bulk of convictions are obtained, the wide sentencing discretion of judge and jury, and the virtually unlimited control of correctional authorities over convicts. The Court has become heavily involved in every one of these areas during the past dozen years. In each situation, the more activist court led by Chief Justice Warren gave initial indications that constitutional considerations severely limit the ambit of official discretion, but a more cautious court in recent years has backed off to a position generally supportive of, if somewhat uncomfortable with, wide discretionary power.

In this essay I want to explore some of the connotations lawyers give the term "discretion" because our thinking about discretion has been hampered by the very slipperiness of the concept. Lawyers occupying varied professional roles describe discretion in the criminal justice process differently. Like the nine blind men, they grab different parts of a very shaggy elephant and react accordingly. Legal philosophers, particularly the positivists, seem to treat discretion as the aether of the jurisprudential universe, the stuff that occupies the empty spaces and fills the gaps that are an inevitable part of any attempt to apply general principles to specific situations. Discretion describes the supplemental authority to define, interpret, and apply rules which is an inevitable part of a legal regime. Constitutionalists sometimes equate discretion with the threat of arbitrary power, and read the term as an antonym of due process of law. Legislators see discretion as a synonym for delegation and are concerned with the careful definition of derivative power. Judges, on the other hand, often see discretion as the equivalent of "give in the joints," that lubricating, dispensing opportunity which is to avoid the silly literal application of a sensible general rule. Understandably, administrators treasure the discretion they exercise, for it gives them the capacity to flex law to serve institutional ends. Discretion enables the administrator to make intake and release decisions that avoid three inmates in a bed or embarrassingly empty wards. It helps them to balance the standards of individual decisions with the desire to make the totality of decisions propel a smoothly sailing ship.

The Oxford English Dictionary carries the comforting message that contemporary uncertainties in defining discretion are not novel. From medieval times the word has carried at least three distinct strands of meaning, two of which seem divergent, if not inconsistent. On the one hand, the Latin root suggests that discrete means bounded, distinct, discontinuous, or consisting of separate parts. Yet from the 1300s on, the term has suggested uncontrolled power of disposal, authority unlimited, liberty to cross the boundaries of rules. Most discussion of discretion in the criminal law has played with these two meanings. Discretion is either an uncontrolled delegation of power, in which the delegate is free from effective supervision, or discretion is the defined ambit within which officials are allowed to operate.

But the dictionary reminds us that there is a third, equally ancient meaning of the term that too often gets lost in the debate between those who see discretion as interstitial dispensation and those who see it as a form of arbitrary, unbounded power in opposition to legality. To possess discretion is to have the faculty of discerning judgment, to be discrete, prudent, sagacious, circumspect, to be capable of wise, sound judgment. This connotation of the term is less concerned with the process of decision, whether it is bounded or free of rules. It focuses on the quality of result that gives it immediate human appeal. Significantly, it focuses on a perceived characteristic of the decision maker which gives us particular confidence that the resulting choice will be wise in the circumstances, that it will take account of the situational context and reflect the decider's appreciation of its overall significance. To understand discretion and respond to its pervasive presence and potential for abuse is an important part of our research agenda. To gain that understanding we must sort out some of the conflicting strands of meaning the concept has absorbed.

The diversity of approach taken by lawyers occupying different roles is not surprising; perspective shapes perception. More remarkable has been the consensus among elements of the community as each has become more conscious of discretion; dissatisfaction with the operation of the criminal law is pervasive and the dominance of discretion is seen as a crucial source of the problem. There is a common disappointment that the system in operation departs so widely from expectations. We have become sensitive to the harshness which is consequent on being stigmatized as a convict, inmate, patient, or ward of a state institution. The "system" is very hard on those subject to its control and the harshness goes beyond the punishment, the measured adverse experience intended as a consequence of misbehavior. It is often unrelated to any rationally justified, functional program. Once inmate status has been applied, it tends to become a permanent stigma, because the "system" resists erasing it. The legal community has had its nose rubbed in the fact that the criminal process treats individuals drawn into it in very disparate ways. Some people are arrested in circumstances that others will not be. A third or more of the individuals arrested are dropped from the process before charges are filed and those charged are likely to be convicted of a variety of offenses of widely differing seriousness. The level of sentences actually imposed often bears little resemblance to those which are provided in the codes. Most of those caught by the police on felony charges are treated mildly, but a small portion of the group is subjected to great harshness. Only about three or four persons in 100 arrested on a felony charge go to prison, and those who do are not obviously distinguishable from those who do not. The process often appears to impose great harshness in a random fashion.

Discretion produces sloppy results, it produces disparate, unfair, unsound, and potentially corrupt results, and it is especially subject to manipulation and the limitations of the individuals who run the apparatus of criminal justice. The reactions of judges, legislatures, administrators, and scholars have been parallel—something has to be done to restrict discretion in the criminal process.

DISCRETION AND THE SUPREME COURT

In the course of sketching this essay I began to collect a list of the salient ways the term is used. I was helped in this enterprise by the availability of the Lexis computer program, which simplified the search for instances in which judges have used the term. In the Supreme Court of the United States alone my initial search uncovered 574 instances in which the Court has referred to discretion in its decisions since 1970. From July 1975 to August 1977, a period including two of the most recent terms of court, 141 references were reported. Very few of these turned out to be insignificant or casual uses of the word. In about 40% of the cases decided with written opinion by the Court over this two-year period a substantial issue for decision was described by the Justices as involving a matter of discretion.

Discretion is an issue in a broad range of important cases brought for judicial consideration and is by no means limited to the criminal law. Less than one-quarter of the cases involved the discretion of judges, juries, and prosecutors in criminal cases and police and correctional agents. More frequently, some sort of discretionary power gave rise to an issue in the work of civil trial and appellate judges, administrative and executive officials, and private individuals (parents, doctors, school principals, church officials, marketing executives, union agents).

It is remarkable how many situations present what the Court sees as a question whether the official possessed discretion to act as he or she did. A political scientist could have a field day comparing the attitudes of different justices or contrasting the same justice's approval of the discretion of judges with his obvious hostility to administrative agencies or policemen. A philologist would have fun with the strange and surprising use made of the word in different settings.

The presidential tapes and papers case, *Nixon v. Administrator of General Services* 433 U.S. 425 (1977), gives some idea of the variety of possible connotations of discretion. This litigation concerned the constitutionality of Title I of the Presidential Recordings and Materials Preservation Act of 1974 (44 USC 2107) passed by Congress shortly after President Nixon's resignation and pardon. The controversy over the custody of President Nixon's papers and tapes raised a number of substantial constitutional claims which produced seven divergent opinions from the nine justices. These opinions use the term discretion to describe various powers of the President, Congress, the General Services Administrator, and the Archivists who work under the Administrator. In addition, the case presents issues involving the discretion of the lower courts and of the Supreme Court although they are not explicitly described with that term. More specifically, the discretion of the President is used to describe: (a) the autonomy of the executive branch of government from Congressional or Judicial control under the doctrine of separation of powers (433 U.S. at 441-445, 500-501, 507-508); (b) the free choice of the President when supervising internal operations within the executive branch (433 U.S. at 514, 548-550); (c) the unreviewable latitude of the President when discharging his enumerated powers under the Constitution (particularly foreign relations and war powers) (433 U.S. at 548-550); and the prudence of the President and his advisers in keeping confidential secret communications between them (433 U.S. At 555-556). Similarly the Court uses the term discretion to describe Congressional actions within constitutionally enumerated powers (433 U.S. at 500), and as a pejorative term to describe the danger of broad and undefined power to interfere with the President's associational and political First Admendment rights (433 U.S. at 467, nt. 29). This lawsuit involved the constitutionality of the statute "on its face," but the Justices differ as to the significance of the Congressional mandate to the Administrator to issue regulations regarding the preservation and access to presidential papers and how the administrator will exercise his rule-making discretion (433 U.S. 496-497, 534-536). The archivists operating under the statute and regulations of course will have to exercise discretionary judgment in deciding whether particular documents are personal or governmental property, whether they are public or private papers. But the majority of Justices are not worried that in exercising that discretion the archivists will imprudently breach the President's privilege and privacy, for these professional archivists are discreet and have a reputation for discretion in handling sensitive matters. (Compare 433 U.S. 452 with 536 and 554). This litigation was quite complex and consisted of at least three different lawsuits (433 U.S. at 430, nt. 1), but the Supreme Court does not deal explicitly with the procedural tangles because it is apparently satisfied with the way the special three-judge District Court and the Court of Appeals exercised their discretion to give priority to one suit and defer consideration of the issues in the others until this matter is settled (433 U.S. at 429-433, nts. 1-3). Finally, this case was heard by the Supreme Court on appeal and therefore the Court lacked the discretion it normally has to decide whether to hear a case. At the root of the matter dividing the Justices is the appropriate use of the Court's power to declare unconstitutional the acts of Congress and the Executive. The dissenting judges feel that the independence of the President should be given greater respect and that the Court in framing the issues and declaring rights should exercise its discretion so as not to interfere with the privileges of this coordinate branch of government.

What ties these connotations together and what makes the Court's opinions a useful place to look for meaning is that these decisions define discretion in terms of the relation between choice or freedom of decision and a commitment to legality. Legal decisions are those made solely by the application of standards, process and the opportunity for review. In some of its uses discretion seems to mean the absence of legality, in others it is an interstitial supplement to a legal regime. In a number of cases the term discretion is clearly being used pejoratively to mean not just the absence, but the opposite, of legality; while in an important number of instances discretion indicates a special kind of legality. The following discussion of the meanings of discretion is organized by the tension between discretion and legality. The categories obviously overlap and the examples are not all drawn from the criminal law. But conflicts between discretion and legality are not notably different in criminal cases and the categories are offered less for their analytical rigor than for what they may suggest for the agenda of researchers and reformers.

Discretion as a Legal Void.

When a decision is said to be within the discretion of the decider it sometimes is implied that the decision is made without prestated governing substantive rules, formal procedures, or an opportunity for review. In an extreme form, discretion is equated with normlessness, procedural informality (particularly the absence of evidence rules and a specific occasion for hearing proof), and unreviewability. In most instances, however, if a vacuum exists it is a weak one, for in almost every case discretionary choice is subject to some standards, some procedure, some review. Often these are complex and formal. For example, the substantive discretion exercised by administrative agencies in making rules and granting licenses occurs in a highly structured setting in which the legislative policies and standards are articulated, the procedural niceties of the Administrative Procedure Act apply, and the decision is subject to extensive judicial scrutiny. Similarly, the discretion of the trial judge to order the conduct of the trial as he or she thinks best occurs against the backdrop of the multivolumed corpus of adjective law, in the rigid and potentially suffocating procedures of the courtroom, and subject to appellate oversight. The jury, as a third example, has broad discretion in reaching a verdict, but does so only after exhaustive instruction on the details of legal rules by the judge, within the charming procedural medievalisms of the jury system, and subject to more frequent reversal on motions for a new trial or on appeal than the system likes to acknowledge.

It may be appropriate to think about discretion as being a legal void, not because the trappings of legality are absent, but because they are largely irrelevant to what is going on. Sometimes there is a legal vacuum because the decision is a private one, not an official or legal one. Sometimes it is an official who is making the choice, but it is clear that nonlegal values or expertise are so dominant in the decision that the legal dimensions lose significance. Two cases in which the Court reviewed technical aspects of environmental protection plans provide good examples, *Union Electric v. EPA* 427 U.S. 246 (1976) and *Kleppe v. Sierra Club,* 427 U.S. 390 (1976). In commenting on the weight a reviewing court should give the administrator's plan, the Court in *Kleppe* observed: "Resolving these issues requires a high level of technical expertise and is properly left to the informed discretion of the responsible federal agencies. . . . Absent a showing of arbitrary action, we must assume that the agencies have exercised this discretion appropriately" 427 U.S. at 412.

The interplay of expertise and legal considerations is also illustrated by the Court's decisions involving the discretion of wardens and correctional officials to limit prisoner's unions, provide legal libraries for prisoners, admit news media to the institution, transfer prisoners among institutions, and control the procedures at disciplinary hearings. "Such considerations are peculiarly within the province and professional expertise of correctional officials and . . . courts should ordinarily defer to their expert judgment in such matters." *Jones v. North Carolina Prisoner's Union,* 433 U.S. 119 (1977).

Discretion may appear to occur in the absence of legality when the context of the particular decision, the time, place, and urgency with which it must be made, place the official beyond effective legal control.

Many of the recent Court decisions involving law enforcement agencies have concerned the activity of individual agents in the field, who operate in a context in which the officer is beyond effective legal control. The decision to stop, frisk, question, arrest, or search can be reviewed after the fact, but discretion is inevitable because it is not possible to anticipate by rule the circumstances encountered on the spot in the middle of the night. The recent cases involving agents enforcing administrative health and safety regulations raise the question whether these noncriminal intrusions should be controlled and channelled by the requirements of a warrant or left to the agent's free judgment. Similarly the conflict among the Justices in *Zucker v. Stanford Daily,*—U.S.—(1978) boils down to a choice between search warrants and subpoenas. The major distinction between these two ways to produce evidence legally is the degree to which the warrant gives broad discretion to the agent executing it, while the subpoena relies on compliance by the person served and formal judicial enforcement.

If discretion is seen as the absence of law, the appropriate response for research and reform is clear when the extent of discretion becomes a problem.

Find a way to fill the void with the familiar incidents of legality:

(a) require standards for the exercise of choice;
(b) require procedural formality by demanding that the decision be made after an adversary trial-like hearing at which conflicting interests are heard and represented by counsel;
(c) require the decider to state the reasons or explain the decision; and
(d) provide review of the decision by someone else.

This approach is typical of administrative lawyers, a number of whom have examined the police, prosecutor and parole board and decided they are just a variety of the common species, administrative agency. Two books by the doyen of administrative law scholars, Kenneth Culp Davis, urge essentially that the solution to the problems of discretion in the criminal law is to apply the sound principles of the Administrative Procedures Act (Davis; 1969, 1975). This approach provides a handy prescription for those who want a neat solution to the problems of discretion. It seems to be that diagnosis provided by the administrative lawyers is incomplete because persons confronted by an arresting policeman in the street or by an overeager prosecutor are not likely to possess the attractiveness, opportunities, or incentives of a businessman denied a license or a certificate of public convenience and necessity. In the context of business regulation those affected by the official action will have the resources, sophistication, and power to assert their interests and make the system give account. The incentive and power structure and the economics of the enforcement of the criminal law usually cut in the opposite direction.

The puzzles of criminal sentencing illustrate the uses and limits of the strategy of responding to discretion as a legal cavity that calls for filling with the amalgam of legality. In most states the sentencing judge or jury possesses very broad discretion under the penal code to impose sentences for serious felonies ranging from a suspended sentence or a small fine to probation, jail, or imprisonment for a period greater than an adult's remaining vigorous years. No meaningful standards are generally provided for the exercise of these wide choices. The Model Penal Code sought to structure the discretion by announcing standards and policy factors to be considered in aggravation or mitigation of punishment (American Law Institute, 1962: 7.01-7.04). More recently, the Supreme Court has adopted a similar approach to the problem of standards for capital punishment, requiring the states to indicate mitigating and aggravating factors for the imposition of death sentences. While some specific factors have been identified, these attempts usually degenerate to the vague and the horatory, in large part because we simply cannot gain general agreement on what punishments are just or why and when they should be imposed on particular people and at what level of severity. The Federal Code revisors recently finessed this problem by delegating the standard setting function to a commission, following the ancient path of wisdom—when faced with an unanswerable question, name a committee.

Another strategy to deal with uncertainty is: when we cannot state standards for the exercise of choice, eliminate the choice. In sentencing, this response is seen in the periodic adoption of mandatory minimum sentences. This approach is used in a political context in which mandatory sentences are almost always severe sentences. The universal consequence is the creation of pressures to use discretion at another point in the process to avoid imposing harsh mandatory sentences. Prosecutors simply stop charging and judges and juries nullify the mandatory rule when they stop convicting for the offense carrying the mandatory sentence. The legislature's intent in providing the mandatory punishment is not accomplished, but it can be said that armed robbers, nighttime burglars of dwelling houses, and professional sellers of narcotics disappear from the courts or at least are magically converted into simple robbers, burglars and sellers.

Most efforts at penal law reform adopt a related approach, seeking to reduce, if they cannot eliminate, the range of discretionary sentencing choice. The Model Penal Code tried to reduce all offense into a few general classifications, eliminating most of the idiosyncratic and senseless differences in punishment that exist for each offense (American Law Institute; 1962: 6.01-6.03). The revision of the California Sentencing Act comparably sought to narrow the choices formerly open to the sentencing judge and correctional authorities by providing determinate sentences for each offense (Ch 1139,California Law of 1976). Experiments with presumptive sentencing and parole grant in the federal system also deal with the range of discretionary choice by narrowing it.

Few recent sentencing reform efforts have emphasized the possibility of reducing the problems of sentencing by reducing the severity of sentences overall, and thereby the potential for abusive discretionary harshness. The new codes adopted in recent years continue to provide extravagantly long prison terms, although few persons in fact are forced to serve them. Not since the Model Sentencing Act was proposed in 1955 has there been a serious proposal to eliminate the potential for lengthy imprisonment (beyond 3-5 years) in most common unaggravated felonies.

Since dealing with sentencing discretion by requiring standards has not been successful, lawyers have turned to the second strategy, procedural formality. There are ancient roots for procedural formality in sentencing. The right of allocution, the defendant's right to be heard and plead regarding sentencing, was one of the first resurrected by the Supreme Court and its origins go back at least to 1689. A constitutional right to counsel now is recognized in all serious criminal cases and its application to sentencing has led to inevitable increases in procedural formality. Yet the character of the sentencing hearing has primarily grown by statute and rule, rather than constitutional court decision. Almost every state encourages a presentence investigation to provide a factual basis for the exercise of sentencing discretion and in most jurisdictions the report is available to the defendant, who has an opportunity to comment and respond to it.

Despite the emphasis on formality, in most courts the sentencing process continues to proceed simultaneously on two levels. At the formal level, reports are prepared, disclosed, and commented on; hearings are public and the entire process seems to occur openly. At the same time, in virtually all courthouses, another parallel network of communication exists between the advocates, the probation officer, and judge. The judge may refuse to be present at these informal discussions, but since the lawyers negotiate with the probation officer, and, in practice, the judge follows the probation officer's recommendation more than nine times out of ten, this informal network subtly shapes the outcome in the final process. As was the case with standards, the procedural safeguards on discretion more often displace the discretionary decision making than replace it.

The third strategy calls for discretion to be controlled by requiring that the decider give reasons for a decision even if there are no prestated standards or formal hearing. The recent California and federal sentencing law revisions and the Court's approach in capital punishment cases all demand such explanations after the fact from discretionary decision makers. The hope is that criteria and standards will grow from the accretion of experience and that sound and cautious decisions will be encouraged by requiring the decider to pause and state coherently what is on his mind. In practice, every attempt to require such explanations leads to the development of a few handy-dandy catchall explanations such as "the interests of justice" which explain nothing and come to be used in the majority of cases.

In most states there has been little, if any, appellate review of sentence, as long as the penalty imposed is within the broad statutory range. Proposals for broader appellate review of sentences have been heard for more than a generation, but only a few states have embraced them. More significantly the impact of appellate review in Connecticut and Alaska, where it exists, does not appear to have been earthshaking (Samuelson, 1977). In those jurisdictions without appellate review of sentences, its function has been absorbed by other informal practices. Sentences are reconsidered, reconciled, reduced, and made less disparate by diagnostic commitments with early release, the early release of inmates by prison administrators through manipulation of good time, furlough, and work release and halfway house programs, and the adjustment of parole release time by administrative parole boards. Ironically, these discretionary decision points, which were largely devices created to alleviate abuse at another discretionary decision point, themselves have become the object of criticism. Now determinate sentencing reformers see the abolition of parole with its excessive grant of discretion to correctional authorities as a major target (Von Hirsch and Hanrahan, 1978).

This description of the response to discretion in criminal sentencing could be reproduced for each of the most significant problem areas in criminal justice: police behavior in the community; prosecutorial charge discretion and related negotiated plea bargaining; the treatment of inmates in prisons and on parole; the care and custody of juveniles, the mentally disabled, and addicted. The problem areas seem diverse in nature and origin but, once reformers see the problem as the absence of legality, the differences shrink and are replaced by a common analysis and response based on the assumption that the appropriate way to deal with the excesses of discretion is to inject a healthy dose of familiar legal structure: standards, process, review. Every lawyer, whatever his or her specific role, is familiar and comfortable with such solutions. This is the patented solution of the wonderful folks who brought you due process of law; who can doubt their rightness?

Yet when we look back on the last dozen years of experience, how pleased can we be with the results? We can be certain that if such reforms are adopted, they will increase the expense and resources needed for decision, that technicalities, procedures, delay, and lawyer's work will multiply, and that the trappings of fairness will be draped over the courtroom. But in most cases the decisions will continue to be made by exercise of at least as great a degree of discretion as before. As mentioned earlier, this sort of reform has had the ability to displace discretion, but not to replace it with formal legality. The formal play is acted out, but the decisions are moved off-stage to be made elsewhere.

This would all be harmless enough if our worries about discretionary processes were just a matter of appearances. These are troublesome because they seem arbitrary, potentially corrupt, governed by whim and stereotype of the decision maker. But we also worry about the substantive content of these decisions. They are troubling because we fear the decisions made are poor ones and too many of them are cruel ones. In this connection procedure reforms are most disturbing in their underachievement. What reason do we have to think that the decisions made under newly formalized legal processes are superior in substance, fairer or wiser than those made previously? Perhaps we are misunderstanding the phenomenon of discretion, erroneously identifying its troubles and therefore misdirecting our efforts to make things better.

Discretion in Opposition to Law

Discretion in recent usage sometimes suggests behavior that is antithetical to law. The term discretion is used as the equivalent of arbitrary whim. For that special breed of American legal moralist, the constitutionalist, the problems of discretion in the criminal law have been particularly troubling. The discretion of police and prosecutors is seen as an insidious threat of official abuse by law. They challenge the legitimacy of discretion in criminal process, claiming that the absence of standards, procedure, and review violates the demands of due process of law.

To understand this use of discretion, it may help to return to some first principles concerning the relation between discretion and legality, which has different constitutional implications when dealing with official, as opposed to private behavior.

The concept of delegated power is central to the concept of official legality. Officials may legally do only what they are granted power to do. When they exceed their delegated power, they are stripped of the protective authority of law. Not only may the overreaching official be forbidden to act by a judicial order *quo warranto*, or its modern equivalent, but the individual aggrieved by the excess of authority is entitled to compensation. The logic regarding official behavior can be summed up by the phrase, "that which is not expressly permitted is forbidden." Law fills the entire universe; it tells the official every action he may do and all other actions are forbidden.

This view casts discretion into a shadow, because discretionary official behavior operates pursuant to a general grant of power in which it is not stated specifically what the official shall do. The more general the grant of power becomes, the more worrisome it becomes to those suspicious of governmental power. As economic, health, and safety regulations became more common during the early part of this century, the law became more tolerant of broad delegations of power, at least when sufficient standards are articulated by the legislature and opportunities for hearing, record, and review allow the official behavior to be measured against the purposes and policies to be pursued. But an important part of insistence on due process of law remains the requirement that the official be prepared to demonstrate the authority to do what was done in the circumstances. When standards, hearing record, and review are absent, it appears that the official is beyond the power to have his or her authority checked by law. These fears are seen most dramatically in the criminal law and other afflictive or confining programs which operate directly on the status and liberty of the individual.

In contrast, when dealing with private behavior the notion of discretion is tied to the concept of residual freedom and individual autonomy. This is the other side of the coin from the concept of delegated power that applies to officials. Now the notion is that law does not fill the entire universe. The individual is free to do as he will as long as specific prohibition of law is not transgressed. The logic of private behavior can be summed up as: "that which is not expressly forbidden is permitted." It is reflected in the criminal law maxim *nulla poena sine lege* that there cannot be a penalty unless the individual's behavior is specifically prohibited by law. The potential and actual disparity in the treatment of comparably situated offenders by police, prosecutors, jurors, judges, wardens, and parole boards leaves those subject to such a process with the sense that it is basically unjust to so vaguely define the forbidden and its consequences. From the individual's perspective, official discretion represents a nonspecific limitation on residual autonomy that provides no clear warning of liability and enlarges the circle of dangerous behavior. Official discretion has a "chilling effect" on the individual's residual freedom of action. The discretion of the individual is residual, it is that which is not delegated or granted to public control and legal rule.

The discretion of the official and the autonomy of the individual are thus related values. The official is not free to treat the individual arbitrarily. The limits placed on official power imply a reciprocal individual right. The opportunity for the official to cheat is reduced and he is kept to the rules of the game by a requirement that the basis for afflictive action be stated in advance, that it be undertaken only upon open and fair demonstration of cause, and that the act be subject to objective review for its compliance with norm and procedure.

This constitutional view of discretion as opposed to legality has had important implications for research and reform. First, it elevates formal bureaucratic compliance with procedure to an all consuming constitutional importance. The experience of the past decade demonstrates that this has been politically expensive. Public support for legality and reform have been sapped by the reversal of convictions of apparently guilty defendants because of procedural irregularities. Perhaps even more expensive have been the lost opportunities for substantive reform that have been deflected because of a felt need to make the case on procedural constitutional grounds. This inappropriate insistence on procedural vices can be seen in debate over capital punishment, plea bargaining, and the institutional treatment of offenders. The substantive dimensions of the prohibition of cruel and unusual punishment emerged briefly from behind the clouds, only to be eclipsed again by concerns for standards, hearings, and the like. Moreover, a constitutional approach to discretion places reformers at the mercy of the constitutional oracle. One problem for the constitutionalists is that in practical terms the Due Process Clause means what the Supreme Court (or perhaps Congress and the Court) says it does. Unfortunately, for the constitutional critics of discretion their position has been harder to sustain after the Court's recent decisions, particularly those regarding capital punishment and the guilty plea.

Discretion as Relief from Law

Any reasonably permanent system of rules must build in the opportunity to escape from the inappropriate application of its own logic, the capacity to compensate for the imperfections in any human system by an occasional individual adjustment, which leaves the basic rule in place, but liberates from excessive unrelieved pressure. Justice and an opportunity for mercy go together. Every civilized legal system, no matter how rigid its pretensions, has built into it some mechanism for dispensation, an allowance for those cases in which we do not want to do what we say we generally want to do. Historically, alongside the common law courts arose a parallel body of jurisprudence and courts to do equity. Over a century ago the courts of law and equity were merged in England and most American states, but the two bodies of substantive rules remained distinct. Today no one would suggest that the Chancellor's power to do equity is not part of the legal system, that it is either a legal void, merely interstitial, or in opposition to law. Flexible dispensation is part of the notion of legality and this is a core meaning of discretion, particularly when it is used, as it so often is by the courts, in juxtaposition with the adjective, "equitable. Equitable discretion is the power of the official to be fair in the face of the rules. When common law judges assumed the powers of the Equity courts, they inherited the Chancellor's discretion to do substantial justice free of the technicalities of the forms of action.

Other formal institutions of legality are designed in a way that allows for dispensation in their application, for example the discretion of juries in reaching a verdict in criminal cases and the power of sentencing judges. There is a hesitance to allow further review or to permit easy reversal of instances in which the power of relief has been exercised. The system's decision rules are slanted in favor of dispensation in the criminal process. This can be seen in the unreviewability of a jury's acquittal, or a judge's dismissal after jeopardy attaches, and the slowness to adopt proposals for appellate review of sentences that call for a symmetrical power of prosecution appeal with potential enhancement, as well as reduction, of penalties.

The desire for relief from legal rules blends into the first connotation discussed, that discretion is the absence of legality. Sometimes legal factors are not sufficient considerations in the decision; some discretion allows other factors to be considered alongside the rules. By recognizing discretionary leeway in the choice, administrative, organizational, political, or budgetary considerations also can be considered. Police and prosecutors are charged with vigorous enforcement of the law, but many offenders are not arrested or charged because of a discretionary decision recognizing that the community no longer supports vigorous enforcement of that particular law, because personnel and budgetary resources are already overcommitted beyond the point where the serious cases can be effectively prosecuted, or because priorities must be established among the possible cases. It is an open secret that in bail and parole release decisions, the exercise of discretion is affected by the practical circumstance when the number of prisoners already confined has increased to the point that dangerous overcrowding exists. To take another example, the latitude allowed juries in reaching a verdict reconciles the demands of legal rules with the sensibilities of the community. Not that the legal rules are irrelevant, because the jury is instructed as to them in detail, but by filtering the rules' application through a body of community representatives, there can be a greater degree of confidence in the political acceptability of the results. This maintains the community's sense of commitment to the law and reduces the number of burned down courthouses.

Our response to discretion also depends on whether the discretionary decision is seen as dispensation of a harsh rule, or an arbitrary deprivation of individual right. When an individual's basic interests—life, liberty, or property —are taken away, we are most disturbed. In contrast, when there is a remission of a sentence or prison term, when a district attorney decides honestly not to charge, or a policeman decided on the basis of his sense of the situation not to arrest, we are less concerned.

Several layers of confusion complicate the use of discretion as dispensation versus discretion as deprivation. First, this approach works only as long as we see the transaction as being between an individual and a state official. But often state action is arbitral, establishing the conflicting rights of adverse individual interests. Then one person's dispensation is the other's deprivation. When the judge exercises discretion to allow the plaintiff additional time to file a pleading, it is a deprivation of the defendant's right to be free of poorly pled, dilatory lawsuits. Similarly, discretionary deference to the expert judgment of the environmental administrator is a deprivation of the claimant's rights to use its property, e.g., to run its steelmill as it will.

This dispensation versus deprivation distinction can become confused and understood to mean that an official can give individuals things they are not entitled to without the trappings of legality, but officials cannot take things away without due process. Or that the official can decline to act without deciding in a due process hearing not to act, but cannot act without appropriate process. In practice both alternatives open to the official are likely to involve some kind of action and the labelling of one as positive and the other negative, one as action and the other as withholding action, can become a word game. The Chancellor rarely exercises his equitable discretion in a mandatory way requiring affirmative action by a respondent. The traditional form of equitable relief is a negative injunction, which forbids the respondent to act in certain ways, but clever chancellors always find a way to put their positive orders in negative form.

A more serious problem with the dispensation-deprivation distinction is that the more general dispensation becomes, the greater the deprivation when it is withheld. This is dramatically seen in the criminal justice process, where almost every defendant is the beneficiary of some from of discretionary dispensation. Many potential convicts are not arrested; and of those who are, a large portion are not charged; of those charged, few are charged with every possible offense at the maximum level of seriousness; of those, a large portion are convicted of lesser offenses; of those, few are sentenced to the full penalties provided by law; and fewer still serve the full term of punishment before remission of their sentence. In such a setting, to follow the rules as written is a great deprivation of dispensation, more inimical to the interests of the defendant than virtually any other decision that can be made in the process. Then the decision to withhold discretionary dispensation itself becomes suspect.

General dispensation is troubling because it leads to tolerance for a level of formal severity that otherwise would be unacceptable. With all their potential severity the penal codes remain in force because they are so rarely invoked to their full potential. If they were regularly and generally applied as written, how many conscientious individuals would remain part of the enforcement machinery? As the stakes go up and the possibilities become more severe, it becomes harder to do without discretionary escape and ironically it becomes harder to accept discretionary choice. The power of the official with dispensatory discretion becomes overpowering. The Supreme Court decisions on capital punishment reflect this tension. The members of the Supreme Court are so divided on this issue that it is hard to speak simply and accurately about what a particular decision stands for; each is likely to consist of half a dozen divergent opinions. But the sequence of decisions runs something like this: first, in *McGautha v. California* 402 U.S. 18 (1971), the Court narrowly rejected the argument that the imposition of capital punishment is a deprivation of due process when the decision to impose the death penalty is made without objective standards governing the choice. Shortly thereafter, however, in *Furman v. Georgia* 408 U.S. 238 (1972), the Court held that a system in which the death penalty decision was left to standardless jury discretion constitutes cruel and unusual punishment. "Furman mandates that where discretion is afforded a sentencing body on a matter so grave as the determination of whether a human life should be taken or spared, that discretion must be suitably directed and limited so as to minimize the risk of wholly arbitrary and capricious action" (*Gregg v. Georgia*, 428 U.S. 153 1———). Then in 1976 the Court rejected several statutes enacted in response to *Furman* which removed all jury discretion and made the death sentence mandatory in all convictions of capital crime. The absence of any opportunity for discretionary dispensation was seen as a threat of harsh punishment as unacceptable as the grant of uncontrolled power of dispensation. Moreover, as the mandatory death cases made clear, removing jury discretion did not eliminate discretion. On the contrary, it merely made the prosecutor's uncontrolled discretionary decision whether to file capital charges all the more important. Discretion was displaced, but not reduced overall.

The sequence of cases is instructive, for the Court first rejects standards in place of discretion, then rejects discretion without standards, and then rejects mandatory death sentences without opportunity for discretionary dispensation.

A final problem with the dispensation-deprivation distinction is that dispensation often becomes the cover for impermissible deprivations. This is perhaps most clearly seen in the cases involving the negotiation of a guilty plea in return for promised concessions by the prosecutor. These concessions may be in terms of release on bail, level or numbers of charges to be filed, level of conviction or sentence. It is hard to think of an example where the lawyer's responses to the abuses of discretion have proved as inadequate as they have with regard to the guilty plea.

For a long time the Court avoided confronting the guilty plea problems in any form. When it did, about a decade ago, its initial concern was with the defendant's plea itself, not the official behavior or exercise of discretion which motivated the plea. A guilty plea in our system permits a criminal charge to proceed to judgment without the legality of trial. The departure from the rules concerning the process of conviction is justified by the consent of the accused, the person with the greatest apparent interest in asserting those rights. If by an autonomous act of consent the individual foregoes those protections, the system feels confident in dispensing with them. The early constitutional guilty plea cases emphasized the capacity of the defendant, whether the plea was a knowing act of will because it was made with the assistance of counsel and information as to consequences, and voluntary, that is, whether there was real choice. When the Court was satisfied in these respects, it even upheld guilty pleas by persons who persisted in claiming their innocence in fact (*North Carolina v. Alford* 400 U.S. 25 (1970). The emphasis on voluntariness overwhelmed a second possible basis for accepting guilty pleas—the high liklihood of factual accuracy. A voluntary plea is acceptable even if not accurate.

Soon the Court's attention was directed to the corollary prosecutorial actions that motivate so many guilty pleas. In the guilty plea trilogy of cases, the Court became more aware of the reciprocal pressures prosecutor and defendant can exert on each other (*McMann v. Richardson,* 397 U.S. 759 (1970); *Brady v. U.S.*, 397 U.S. 742; *Parker v. North Carolina* 397 U.S. 790 (1970). Since it is the defendant who is in personal jeopardy, the prosecutor's pressures can be great indeed. Talk about consent has a hollow ring when it describes acts taken under such pressures. Now the Court talks about the "give and take" of plea bargaining in which there is no element of punishment or retaliation as long as the accused is free to accept or reject the prosecutor's offer. While confronting a defendant with the risk of more severe punishment clearly may have a "discouraging effect on the defendant's assertion of his trial rights, the imposition of these difficult choices (is) an inevitable"—and permissible—"attribute of any legitimate system which tolerates and encourages the negotiation of pleas." The only limits on this power would appear to be when the prosecutor's decision is corrupt or vindictive or the prosecutor fails to keep the bargain once made. The obvious problem is that, as conceived by the Court, the permissible "give and take" of negotiation is now so broad that it is hard to see how "vindictiveness" or corruption would be revealed. There is no room in the mesh of rules to allow investigation of the prosecutor's motive or purpose in exercising his discretion. Yet discretion is most obviously contrary to legality when it is used for ulterior or impermissible purposes, when its exercise is not the honest exercise of judgment.

Discretion as Interstitial or Supplementary to Law

Instead of looking at discretion as the absence of legality, or as a dispensing relief from law, it can be seen as the connective tissue that enables a legal system to work. Something must occupy the gap between the abstract words of a rule and the specific application of the rule to a real situation. The process of interpretation gives the words of legal commands concrete meaning and always involves choices based on the sensibilities of the interpreter. At the point of decision someone must decide what the rule means and how it applies; even in the most rule-governed situations this is a matter of individual judgment, definition, and interpretation.

No rulemaker can foresee all the circumstances that will arise in the future. There will always be cases in which the rule seems to apply, but no sensible person would consider it right to do so. These situations become more common the more general the terms of the rule. Does the rule, "he who sheds blood shall surely die" require capital punishment for barbers?

If a general rule requires discretion in its application, how much more care is needed with a specific rule. Often the number of relevant factors is simply too great for any single rule to take into account without exception and the words of rules are too slippery and ambiguous when applied to specific situations. Each section of a statute could become book length if every contingency were explicitly provided for. As the statute is made more detailed to be specific, loopholes are created and tricky questions of interpretation arise concerning inclusion and exclusion from defined classes. When detail is carried to extremes the commands of law become unintelligible. The law comes to resemble the Internal Revenue Code, which is understandable only through the mediation of that special class of magician-priests called tax lawyers.

Discretion is needed to find facts as well as to apply rules. Despite the impressive trappings of trial and the impression lawyers try to create that procedures can find the "truth," factfinding is an uncertain business. To try a lawsuit generally requires the retrospective construction of historic reality. No mechanical process can do this, particularly when the circumstances are complex and include subtle nuances, fine shadings, and inherently indeterminate issues of mental state, intent, motive, purpose, knowledge. Such issues are not subject to simple demonstration or analysis in a formal hearing. The discerning judgment of a knowledgeable decision maker is a necessary precondition of the capacity of a formal trial to produce a satisfying result.

A third interstitial connotation of discretion occurs in the fashioning of judicial remedies. Once basic rights and liabilities have been found in a lawsuit and the purpose or end to be accomplished by judicial intervention has been defined, flexibility is needed to design the specifics of relief. Should damages be awarded and, if so, how widely should the compensible harm be defined? Is mandatory or injunctive relief called for, and if so, who should be ordered to do what and how should compliance be supervised? More specifically, in seeking to remedy demonstrated discrimination on grounds of race, sex, or age, how should the judge go about remedying the situation? In devising means to the end, the official must be granted leeway to find an effective solution. Remedial discretion is a practical necessity to enable the law to accomplish its purposes. This connotation of discretion is closely related to the power to act purposefully and rationally, to exercise judgment in a complex situation within an express legal grant of power.

Discretion is also used interstitially when a matter is not ripe for formal legal decision, either because too little is known about the situation to state standards and define relevant evidence or because the matter is a minor or preliminary matter, which for an efficient decision must be quickly and simply decided. Mr. Justice Marshall, in an opinion in chambers, declined to stay the opening of bids in the Baltimore Canyon oil drilling controversy, because the decision involved no "irreversible commitment of resources," it could always be corrected later on without permanent damage and therefore it was best left to the unreviewed discretion of the lower court (*New York v. Klepper* 429 U.S. 1307 (1976). On such interim matters the commitment to discretion is primarily an economic consideration because the bother and expense of full legal review does not make sense in the situation. An efficient judgment cannot be one that costs more to make than is at stake or one which takes so long to make that it interferes with the capacity of the process to conclude the dispute. If too much time and energy is invested in preliminary skirmishes and appeals from them, the likelihood of ever being able to carry the dispute itself to resolution is reduced.

For related reasons, discretion is needed to allow officials to act promptly on the spot without fear of second guessing. In baseball the strike zone is defined by rule, the umpire is placed at a strategic vantage point and is expected to be fair, wise, and right most of the time. But for close calls a margin of error must be allowed to the umpire on the field, whose decisions will not be disturbed, except in egregious cases. Indeed, it is unlikely that the net sum of good decisions would be increased by allowing appeals to the commissioner, replays of video tape, and a case-based jurisprudence defining the location of the batter's knees. A more likely result would be a loss in confidence in the basic sense of the game and dropoff in attendance. In this way discretion allows the official on the scenes a margin of error, as the Court appeared to do when it considered the correctness of the trial judge's refusal to grant a permanent injunction in *Piper v. Chris-Craft* 430 U.S. 1 (1977), or more affirmatively when it allowed the judge on the scene to play through situations as they develop. The last sense is what Chief Justice Burger seems to mean in *Gedders v. United States* 425 U.S. 80, 86-87 (1976):

> The trial judge must meet situations as they arise and to do this must have broad power to cope with the complexities and contingencies inherent in the adversary process. To this end, he may determine generally the order in which parties will adduce proof; his determination will be reviewed only for abuse of discretion. . . . Within limits, the judge may control the scope of rebuttal testimony, . . . may refuse to allow cumulative, repetitive or irrelevant testimony, . . . and may control the scope of examination of witnesses. . . . If truth and fairness are not to be sacrificed, the judge must exert substantial control over the proceedings.

The same aspects of the legal situation that support the view that discretion is supplemental and interstitial also suggest that it is inevitable. The need to interpret, to make the general and abstract specific and concrete, the demand for flexibility on the spot to meet immediate situations, the instrumental requirements of remedial pliability to accomplish the laws' aims—all are persistent and universal. When seen this way the implication is less that discretion should be replaced by legality or abolished. Instead of trying to control the decision process itself, interstitial and supplemental discretion is limited by strategies that try to restrict its undesirable consequences. Prestated rules and procedures are of little help, but the potential for bad results can be kept within bounds by limiting discretion to decisions that are of lesser import. If the policeman in the field is not easily controlled, the potential abuse of the power of the police to confine citizens can be limited by rules requiring the prompt presentation of arrested persons in court (Federal Rules of Criminal

Procedure 5(a)). Interstitial interpretative discretion cannot be limited in this way, for the weighty as well as the minor requires interpretation. But interpretative discretion usually can be limited by review after the fact by opportunities for amelioration, correction, and revision and by legislative oversight.

Discretion as a Form of Law

So far, we have seen that discretion may connote the absence of legality, the supplementary cement that holds a legal system together, the dispensing escape from legality and the antonym of legality. Each of these views contrasts discretion with legality and this has three unhappy consequences. It leads to the dispensation-versus-deprivation dichotomy and to formalistic word games. The permissible withholding of ameliorative discretion is indistinguishable from deprivation of right in a system in which almost everyone is the beneficiary of discretionary dispensation. Second, efforts to deal with the tension between discretion and legality run into the sand, in part because the statement of the problem suggests the solution. The solution is counsel, hearing, rules, and review. But this solution rarely eliminates discretion. As the capital punishment cases suggest, it more often merely moves the discretionary choice to another point in the system and perhaps to another actor, and probably in the course of the move it increases the importance of discretion. The ironic result is that attempts to eliminate discretion this way actually increase its importance. But the most important weakness of this way of looking at discretion is that it reinforces preoccupation with traditional lawyers' concerns, process, rules and review, rather than results. The substance and quality of the decision becomes submerged in this preoccupation. But the linguistic roots of the word suggest a fifth connotation of discretion, one which emphasizes the centrality in the discretionary style of decision of the personality of the decider. As was noted at the beginning of this essay, to possess discretion also means that a person has a faculty for discerning judgment, is prudent, sagacious, circumspect, and capable of wise, sound judgment. This connotation suggests the reason why the law creates and protects discretionary power. Discretion is granted because of some belief that the delegate possesses a characteristic that will enhance the quality of decision. It implies a desire to give prominent attention in the decision to something that is not captured by rules and standards, analytical procedures of investigation and proof, something which cannot be replicated in a record for appellate review. It is the decider who is centrally important; the legal structure, typically embodied in rules, norms, procedures, adjective standards and the opportunity for review, diminish in significance and may be deemphasized almost to the vanishing point.

It is hard to be precise in describing just what it is that the decider brings to the decision. Definitions of wisdom and justice have always been a puzzle, but that has not diminished the value of the qualities imperfectly described. One part of the notion is the decider's ability to see the uniqueness of situations, to establish the priorities among the conflicting values, each of which is partially right in this particular case. We value deciders who look at problems contextually, who can discern patterns that are not just the conventional ordering, but fit the special circumstances of this situation. What is important about the individual decision maker that leads us to delegate discretion is an expectation that the quality of decision will be improved, that both the process and its results will show greater sensitivity to the personality of the individuals acted upon. In a sense the choice to downplay general standards and uniform process and review suggests that we want to focus on individual specialness, and the circumstantial elements of their situation, not only on their relation to some abstract characteristics.

A discretionary style of decision also suggests something about the perceived difficulty of the decisions to be made and how much is known about making them well. Easy jobs can be assigned to clerks whose work is wholly structured by rules, policies, and bureaucratic supervision and review. In recent times many of such choices can be programmed into a sophisticated machine and processed by computer. Tougher jobs are not so easily structured. Finding facts or managing enterprises cannot be contained so easily in a manual of rules and operations. Then it becomes more important to develop personnel policies and qualifications for the job. Managers may be guided by established procedures within which they get their job done, but for the substance of their work, wise leaders can say what the goals are, but not how to accomplish them. Clerks and privates are told when to move their left foot, when their right, when to salute. But managers and leaders are merely told to be successful and are expected to devise, for themselves, the best means to the end.

The toughest jobs, and doing justice is certainly one of these, contain even greater uncertainties, for now we not only do not know what operations will produce justice, we are likely to be uncertain precisely what the end consists of or what means best produce it. Faced with the persistent imponderables of the task and the difficulty in gaining social agreement on its content, we must do the best we can. That often means picking the best people for the job by a variety of guides—professional competence, political acceptability, proven success in various endeavors, representativeness of the community as a whole, motivation, and sense of moral calling. Once such people are picked, we try to help them along and hope they will do well often.

To make judicious decisions is to deal with uncertainty. The response of legality to uncertainty is analytical. By defining standards, ordering the facts, and constructing a syllogistic proposition leading from uncertainty to persuasion, lawyers think they can bridge the problematic. Lawyers love the logical form of analysis, for it serves the inner needs that led them to dedicate their lives to seeking legal order. The logical style can be persuasive and serves the advocative bent of lawyers. Yet often the logical form serves only as a cover for unarticulated factors that determine decision. Almost a century has passed since Holmes let a group of law students in on the secret (The Path of the Law, 10 Harv. L. Rev. 457 (1897)):

> The training of lawyers is a training in logic. The processes of analogy, discrimination, and deduction are those in which they are most at home. The language of judicial decision is mainly the language of logic. And the logical method and form flatter the longing for certainty and for repose which is in every human mind. But certainty generally is illusion and repose is not the destiny of man. Behind the logical form lies a judgment as to the relative worth and importance of competing legislative grounds, of an inarticulate and unconscious judgment it is true, and yet the root and nerve of the whole proceeding. You can give any conclusion a logical form. You can always imply a condition in a contract. But why do you imply it? It is because of some belief as to the practices of the community or of a class, or because of some attitude of yours upon a matter not capable of founding exact logical conclusions.

Important schools of thought in American jurisprudence in this century, including scepticism, legal realism, and pragmatism, have been dubious about problem solving by formal logic and making important decisions by syllogism alone. The sceptic starts from doubt, dividing the known from the problematic. The common law advocate thinks in terms of trial, "What shall I be able to prove or defend against in court?" Unless a doubtful matter of fact or value is the center of attention, the trial is an uninteresting and largely worthless event. A trial is not a scientific experiment that determines the certain regularity of natural law. It is an attempt to persuade and to relieve doubt regarding the problematic. When we think about the trial we are more likely to recall the cross-examination, the clever scepticism which casts doubt, than we are to remember the often painful building of an affirmative case.

The point is that the habits of lawyers' thinking about how quality decisions are made can lead them to emphasize the importance of uniform application of rules in a logical way, the rigorous analysis of evidence in search of objective truth, and the articulation of results in a way that demonstrates and validates the inner consistency of the process of decision. Yet when important human decisions must be made in a legal setting, we almost always prefer a process of decision that permits greater emphasis on the discerning, wise, contextual appreciation of the overall significance of a situation.

The perception and assessment of reality always is made through the eyes and mind of an individual. A human process of judgment must accept, if it cannot celebrate, the differences of perception, mind-set, and value of those who make public decisions. It follows that a range of variation in judgment is legitimate and must be recognized as the consequence of asking this person at this time to consider this situation. Perfect uniformity and comparability of result may characterize the ideal of justice, but their importance diminishes when we consider that they are purchased only at the price of desiccating the law. In removing from the process an allowance for the personality of the judge, we limit law's capacity to recognize the humanity of the judged.

A major reason why decisional discretion is committed to a person or a group is because of some collective confidence that such a mode of decision will improve the outcome. Only occasionally do we choose discretion because we affirmatively wish to be free of rules or standards, hearing processes or reviews. More often the choice is made because we prefer decisions that show a sensitivity to context and discerning sagacity, an appreciation of the conflicting complexities of reality that is lost in analytical reductionism. If these are the qualities that are valued, then the subject of study ought to be how to enhance the competence of discretionary decision makers to provide these qualities, not how to reconcile their work with the positivistic assumptions of popular jurisprudence. A positivistic jurisprudence is easy to state and understand initially, although as soon as a lawyer says that the essence of justice is nonsyllogistic and nonanalytical, the left side of his brain cries out with complaints that it cannot evaluate this murky, intuitive stuff, that it all sounds too mystical and idiosyncratic. Yet is is hard to find an important legal process which does not reserve a place for just such special judgment, for the exercise of discretion—a degree of freedom to do what is felt to be appropriate, even if it does not appear to be the logical application of a rule or standard or the calculated gathering and weighing of evidence and even if the process of decision cannot be reconstructed for review.

When discretion is seen this way, not as the opposite or absence or supplement to legality, but as another form of legality, serving the same ends and with just as honored a history, as a preferred means for judgment, then a new agenda for study opens up. What needs to be learned is the process of choosing and socializing and supporting discretionary decision makers so that the qualities we value will be maximized in their decisions. All methods for organizing human activity are subject to the hazard of being ruined by fools and knaves. Some systems, most notably hierarchical bureaucracies, pay a heavy price to reduce the risk of bad people in power. I was taught that the military in which I served was "a system devised by a genius to be run by idiots." Such systems are barely able to tolerate talent; there is little room in the military organization for a Rickover or a De Gaulle. In the criminal justice system tricky issues of qualifications of decision makers are avoided in this country by emphasizing the partisan political dimensions of the selection process. Judges, prosecutors, police chiefs and, to a lesser extent, correctional administrators are chosen in a way that emphasizes their political links to a local community, but is less explicit about their personal character. The agenda for needed research includes study of those qualities that enable an individual to do a superior job of making decisions. To what extent can such people be identified by selection, how can they be trained to be wise, what sorts of supports must be built into the organizations in which they work to strengthen and motivate their performance?

When a system becomes preoccupied by its fear of fools and knaves it distrusts the discretion of all decision makers. In restricting all discretion to avoid the depredations of bad persons the system loses the capacity to fully realize the virtues of good people in power. Harnessing talent, increasing responsiveness, improving the content of decisions are all aims that justify taking risks. To reconcile the prevalence of discretion in the criminal law, we must find ways to limit the risks of discretion to an acceptable level without eliminating the opportunity for wise decision.

REFERENCES

American Law Institute (1965). A Model Code of Pre-Arrangement Procedure, Proposed Appeal Draft. Philadelphia: Author.

_____(1962). Model Penal Code. Proposed Appeal Draft. Philadelphia: Author.

DAVIS, K.C. (1969). Discretionary Justice: A Preliminary Inquiry. Baton Rouge: Louisiana State University Press.

_____(1975). Police Discretion. St. Paul: West.

DAWSON, R. (1969). Sentencing: The Decision as to Type, Length and Conditions. Boston: Little, Brown.

DWORKIN, R. (1977). Taking Rights Seriously. Cambridge: Harvard University Press.

GOLDSTEIN, J. (1960). Police Discretion Not To Invoke the Criminal Process: Law Visibility Decisions in the Administration of Criminal Justice, 69 Yale Law Journal 543.

GREENWOOD, P. et al. (1976) Prosecution of Adult Felony Defendants. Lexington, Heath.

HART, H.L.A. (1961). The Concept of Law. Oxford: Clarendon.

KADISH, M., and KADISH, S. (1973). Discretion To Disobey: A Study of Lawful Departures from Legal Rules. Palo Alto: Stanford University Press.

LaFAVE, W. (1965). Arrest: The Decision To Take a Suspect Into Custody. Boston: Little, Brown.

MILLER, F. (1969). Prosecution: The Decision To Charge a Suspect with Crime. Boston: Little Brown.

NEWMAN, D. (1966). Conviction: The Determination of Guilt or Innocence Without Trial. Boston: Little, Brown.

Presidents Commission on Law Enforcement and Administration of Justice (1967). Task Force Report: The Courts, Washington, D.C.: U.S. Government Printing Office.

REMINGTON, F., and OHLIN, L. (1958). Sentencing Structure: Its Effect on Systems for Administration, 23 Law and Contemporary Problems 495.

SAMUELSON, P. (1977). Sentence Review and Sentence Disparity: A Case Study of the Connecticut Sentence Review Division, 10 Connecticut Law Review 5-89.

SKOLNICK, J. (1966). Justice Without Trial: Law Enforcement in Democratic Society. New York: John Wiley.

TIFFANY, L., McINTYRE, D., and ROTENBERG, D. (1967). Detection of Crime: Stopping and Questioning, Search and Seizure, Encouragement and Entrapment. Boston: Little, Brown.

VONHIRSCH, A., and HANRAHAN, K. (1978) Abolish Parole? Cambridge: Ballinger.

16

TO INDICT OR NOT TO INDICT
Prosecutorial Discretion in Sherman Act Enforcement

DONALD I. BAKER

The Sherman Act is indeed "the Magna Carta of free enterprise"[1]—a statute famed for its breadth and brevity. The recent removal of the "fair trade" provisos[2] restored section 1 to its original simplicity: "Every contract, combination in the form of trust or otherwise, or conspiracy, in restraint of trade or commerce among the several States, or with foreign nations, is declared to be illegal."[3]

Despite its brevity, section 1 in fact functions as two statutes. One is a criminal statute dealing with hard-core violations—price fixing, market allocation, and similar conduct—complete with a set of strengthened felony sanctions added in 1974.[4] The second statute—the other section 1—is a civil statute of extraordinary breadth and flexibility; it invites the judiciary to develop creative equitable remedies responsive to changing restraints in a changing economy.[5]

---

* This Article is based on a speech made by the author before the Antitrust Law Briefing Conference on February 28, 1977. Professor Baker gratefully acknowledges the assistance of his former Special Assistant, Barbara A. Reeves of the California Bar, in preparing the original speech. © Copyright 1978, Donald I. Baker.

† Professor of Law, Cornell University. A.B. 1957, Princeton University; B.A. in Law 1959, Cambridge University; LL.B. 1961, Harvard University. From August 1976 to May 1977 the author served as Assistant Attorney General in Charge of the Antitrust Division, United States Department of Justice.

[1] United States v. Topco Assocs., 405 U.S. 596, 610 (1972).

[2] *See* Consumer Goods Pricing Act of 1975, Pub. L. No. 94-145, § 2, 89 Stat. 801 (codified at 15 U.S.C. § 1 (Supp. V 1975)).

[3] 15 U.S.C. § 1 (1970 & Supp. V 1975).

[4] Antitrust Procedures and Penalties Act, Pub. L. No. 93-528, § 3, 88 Stat. 1708 (1974) (codified at 15 U.S.C. § 1 (Supp. V 1975)).

[5] As a charter of freedom, the [Sherman] Act has a generality and adaptability comparable to that found to be desirable in constitutional provisions. It does not go into detailed definitions which might either work injury to legitimate enterprise or through particularization defeat its purposes by providing loopholes for escape. The restrictions the Act imposes are not mechanical or artificial. Its general phrases, interpreted to attain its fundamental objects, set up the essential standard of reasonableness.

Appalachian Coals, Inc. v. United States, 288 U.S. 344, 359-60 (1933).

From Donald I. Baker, "To Indict or Not To Indict: Prosecutorial Discretion in Sherman Act Enforcement," 63(3) Cornell Law Review 405-418 (March 1978). Copyright 1978 by Cornell University.

This Article focuses on the line dividing the two statutes—the line that determines when the Antitrust Division brings only a civil case and when it brings a criminal case.[6] As Justice Holmes was so fond of noting, whenever a legal distinction is made between two extremes, a line must be drawn to mark where the change takes place.[7] However, as Justice Frankfurter was equally fond of pointing out, "the fact that a line has to be drawn somewhere does not justify its being drawn anywhere."[8] This Article identifies where the line between criminal indictment and civil complaint was drawn while I headed the Justice Department's Antitrust Division and explains why I think it should be drawn there.[9]

We all know what a plain, old-fashioned criminal case looks like. When competitors meet in a smoke-filled hotel room and agree on prices for future sales, they run foursquare into the Sherman Act's clear criminal prohibition of horizontal price fixing.[10] There is nothing new about either price fixing or its per se status. Adam Smith observed in 1776 that most meetings of businessmen end up by their reaching agreement on prices.[11] The

---

[6] The Antitrust Division normally files a companion civil case with any indictment against conduct which has not clearly terminated. Such civil cases seldom have great practical importance because they lead only to an injunction restating the per se rule in the context of the particular industry. What the Antitrust Division does not do is file a civil case, without obtaining a criminal indictment, against hard-core conduct (such as price fixing) where the Government's evidence is weak. In other words, the Division has no intermediate category for cases where it can prove its case by a "preponderance of the evidence," but not "beyond a reasonable doubt." If it does not think it can meet the "proof beyond a reasonable doubt" standard for hard-core conduct, the Justice Department simply does not bring the case.

[7] "Where are you going to draw the line?—as if all life were not the marking of grades between black and white." 1 HOLMES-LASKI LETTERS 331 (M. Howe ed. 1953).

[8] Pearce v. Commissioner, 315 U.S. 543, 558 (1942) (dissenting opinion, Frankfurter, J.). Justice Holmes himself made essentially the same point many years earlier:

I am the last man in the world to quarrel with a distinction simply because it is one of degree. Most distinctions, in my opinion, are of that sort, and are none the worse for it. But the line which is drawn must be justified by the fact that it is a little nearer than the nearest opposing case to one pole of an admitted antithesis.

Haddock v. Haddock, 201 U.S. 562, 631-32 (1906) (dissenting opinion).

[9] My standards for drawing the line appear to be substantially the same as those of my predecessor, Thomas E. Kauper, and those of my successor, John H. Shenefield. Accordingly, I believe this Article describes the modern practice in the Antitrust Division generally, rather than just what occurred during my relatively brief tenure.

[10] "Under the Sherman Act a combination formed for the purpose and with the effect of raising, depressing, fixing, pegging, or stabilizing the price of a commodity in interstate or foreign commerce is illegal *per se*." United States v. Socony-Vacuum Oil Co., 310 U.S. 150, 223 (1940). This message has been repeatedly re-emphasized. *See, e.g.*, Citizen Publishing Co. v. United States, 394 U.S. 131, 135 (1969); United States v. Masonite Corp., 316 U.S. 265, 276 (1942).

[11] *See* A. SMITH, WEALTH OF NATIONS 59 (4th ed. 1850).

Sherman Act was passed 114 years later to deal with price fixing and other offenses. Thirty-seven years after its enactment, the famous *Trenton Potteries* case[12] resolved any doubt as to the per se illegality of price fixing.

We also know what a typical Sherman Act section 1 civil case looks like: a case against restrictive membership rules,[13] a merger case,[14] a case against a patent pool or patent misuse,[15] a tie-in case,[16] a territorial case,[17] or a case against information exchanges that restrict competition.[18] Such cases may involve a full factual inquiry under the rule of reason,[19] or may be subject to one of the "soft core" per se rules (such as the tie-in prohibition or the non-coercive boycott rule).[20] What differentiates civil cases from crimi-

---

[12] United States v. Trenton Potteries Co., 273 U.S. 392 (1927). The Supreme Court's decision in Appalachian Coals, Inc. v. United States, 288 U.S. 344 (1933), created some confusion concerning the continued vitality of *Trenton Potteries*. The distressed conditions of the Great Depression, however, obviously influenced the result in *Appalachian Coals*. Seven years later, in United States v. Socony-Vacuum Oil Co., 310 U.S. 150 (1940), the Court fully reestablished the *Trenton Potteries* rule.

[13] *See, e.g.*, Associated Press v. United States, 326 U.S. 1 (1945).

[14] *See, e.g.*, United States v. First Nat'l Bank & Trust Co., 376 U.S. 665 (1964).

[15] *See, e.g.*, United States v. Line Material Co., 333 U.S. 287 (1948); Mercoid Corp. v. Minneapolis-Honeywell Regulator Co., 320 U.S. 680 (1944).

[16] *See, e.g.*, Northern Pac. Ry. v. United States, 356 U.S. 1 (1958).

[17] *See, e.g.*, Continental T.V., Inc. v. GTE Sylvania Inc., 433 U.S. 36 (1977); White Motor Co. v. United States, 372 U.S. 253 (1963).

[18] *See, e.g.*, United States v. Container Corp. of America, 393 U.S. 333 (1969).

[19] The true test of legality is whether the restraint imposed is such as merely regulates and perhaps thereby promotes competition or whether it is such as may suppress or even destroy competition. To determine that question the court must ordinarily consider the facts peculiar to the business to which the restraint is applied; its condition before and after the restraint was imposed; the nature of the restraint and its effect, actual or probable. The history of the restraint, the evil believed to exist, the reason for adopting the particular remedy, the purpose or end sought to be attained, are all relevant facts.

Chicago Bd. of Trade v. United States, 246 U.S. 231, 238 (1918). *See also* Continental T.V., Inc. v. GTE Sylvania Inc., 433 U.S. 36, 59 (1977).

[20] Under the traditional Sherman Act learning, two categories of cases exist: (1) those involving per se prohibitions, applied without regard to surrounding facts; and (2) those involving "rule of reason" inquiries which require a complete examination of all relevant surrounding facts. The Supreme Court has greatly expanded the number of situations to which the per se label applies. *See* Northern Pac. Ry. v. United States, 356 U.S. 1, 5 (1958). This has created a practical problem for the courts, as per se rules have been extended to conduct which at least *sometimes* enhances competition.

As a result, I suggest, the courts have in fact recognized three working categories. The first I call "hard core" per se cases—involving straight price fixing and market allocations. Here the per se concept applies strictly, creating a bright-line prohibition against the activity without regard to surrounding circumstances. *See, e.g.*, United States v. Socony-Vacuum Oil Co., 310 U.S. 150 (1940). The second category includes what I call "soft core" per se cases. Here the court takes a general look at the conduct nominally subject to a per se prohibition *and* its surrounding circumstances. If it finds the scheme anti-competitive, it

nal cases is that in civil cases the challenged conduct generally has less serious competitive impact, does not involve outright predation, and sometimes is subject to more flexible legal standards.

Of course the two statutes overlap. Some conduct is close enough to the hard-core area that one prosecutor might responsibly prosecute it as criminal, while another would seek only a civil remedy. Similarly, there are long unchallenged categories of conduct that, although properly regarded as "criminal," may warrant only a civil suit initially because of the need to provide fair notice to those affected. How the Department of Justice proceeds in this middle area—the area of overlap between the civil and criminal statutes—is important to the public and challenging to the decisionmakers.

Decisions of the Antitrust Division regarding the proper form of proceeding have been criticized as arbitrary. But in my experience they are not, except in the sense that many honest judgment calls are inevitably so when the question posed is very close.[21] At

---

pronounces the conduct illegal per se. *See, e.g.*, Fortner Enterprises v. United States Steel Corp., 394 U.S. 495 (1969). Courts tend to apply "soft core" per se rules to various vertical arrangements and noncoercive boycotts, and to various aspects of joint ventures. Where the court finds the challenged arrangement to be pro-competitive or potentially pro-competitive, it will tend to define the conduct out of the per se category so as to subject it to a "rule of reason" inquiry. *See, e.g.*, Worthern Bank & Trust Co. v. National Bank-Americard Inc., 485 F.2d 119 (8th Cir. 1973) (reversing district court holding that joint venture membership restriction constituted "boycott" and hence per se illegal). The third general category comprises traditional "rule of reason" cases, in which all facts are relevant. *See, e.g.*, Continental T.V., Inc. v. GTE Sylvania Inc., 433 U.S. 36 (1977).

The Supreme Court seems to have rejected any attempt to create an explicit middle category. In United States v. Arnold, Schwinn & Co., 388 U.S. 365 (1967), the government argued for a rule of "presumptive illegality" for certain types of vertical territorial restrictions, comparable to existing categorizations in the merger area. Brief for the United States at 41, United States v. Arnold, Schwinn & Co., 388 U.S. 365 (1967). The Court rejected this argument because it had not been argued below (388 U.S. at 374 n.5) and imposed a per se prohibition on territorial restrictions in sale-resale arrangements. Ten years later the Court reversed its position on the per se illegality of territorial restraints. Continental T.V., Inc. v. GTE Sylvania Inc., 433 U.S. 36 (1977). *See generally* Baker, *Vertical Restraints in Times of Change: From White to Schwinn to Where?*, 44 ANTITRUST L.J. 537, 543-49 (1975).

[21] In each case, the decision to bring an indictment on a civil case is based on an elaborate memorandum (normally running several hundred pages) prepared by the trial staff in conjunction with their section chief and recommending a particular course of conduct. The memorandum and recommendation are reviewed by the Office of Operation (*see* note 39 *infra*). That office prepares its own recommendation (normally in a memorandum of 10-20 pages) and makes appropriate provisions in the draft proceedings. This material is then reviewed in detail by the Chief Deputy Assistant Attorney General who in turn makes a recommendation to the Assistant Attorney General. Thus the decision to bring a criminal or civil case is based on an extensive analysis of the issues and the facts by both junior and senior officials in the Antitrust Division.

any rate, the area of overlap is small: most criminal antitrust cases involve hard-core price fixing and market allocations in which the defendants have clear notice and the Department has no responsible choice except to proceed by criminal indictment (or information in a misdemeanor case).[22] Those are the cases that Congress surely had in mind when it provided for expanded fines and jail sanctions for Sherman Act violations.

Several key points that emerged during the last twenty years accentuate the dual nature of the Sherman Act. First, the generality of the "civil" Sherman Act today raises serious questions concerning its constitutionality as a criminal statute.[23] Second, the Department of Justice has in recent years enforced the "criminal" Sherman Act so as to give defendants due notice of what it regards as within the Act's criminal prohibitions. And third, a criminal case against a clear civil violation (such as a noncoercive tie-in) would, in my opinion, be subject to criticism as an abuse of prosecutorial discretion.[24] All these facts point to the same conclusion: through the exercise of prosecutorial discretion and implicit judicial recognition of two different sets of rules, the single statute passed by Congress in 1890 has come to function as two statutes. Congress recently emphasized the Sherman Act's dual role by making "criminal" violations felonies and thereby introducing realistic deterrents to hard-core business restraints.[25]

---

[22] The new felony standards (*see* note 4 *supra*) came into effect on December 21, 1974. The Antitrust Division's practice is to indict for felony any individual or corporation involved significantly in a conspiracy after that date. If the particular defendant's conspiratorial activities occurred entirely in the pre-December 21, 1974 period, the Antitrust Division will return a misdemeanor indictment or information. It is therefore plausible that a given investigation of multiple parties will result in both felony and misdemeanor prosecutions.

[23] *See, e.g.*, Papachristou v. City of Jacksonville, 405 U.S. 156 (1972); Coates v. City of Cincinnati, 402 U.S. 611 (1971); Palmer v. City of Euclid, 402 U.S. 544 (1971). In 1913, the Supreme Court upheld the constitutionality of the Sherman Act's misdemeanor provisions in the face of a "void for vagueness" challenge. Nash v. United States, 229 U.S. 373, 376-78 (1913). The same challenge has recently been renewed in the context of the offense being upgraded to a felony; again the vagueness argument was rejected. United States v. Jack Foley Realty, Inc., [1977-2] TRADE CAS. (CCH) ¶ 61,678 (D. Md. July 29, 1977). Both *Nash* and *Jack Foley* dealt with price-fixing situations where the Sherman Act prohibition is not realistically vulnerable to vagueness challenges.

[24] Public confidence is vital to the law enforcement process. Where prosecutorial decisions appear random and erratic, the public is more likely to regard prosecution as a game rather than a serious undertaking. Even if an Assistant Attorney General could obtain a felony indictment against a noncoercive tie-in, and this exercise of discretion could not be overturned as a mattter of law, such a decision would surely deserve public criticism as a flagrant abuse of the responsibility entrusted to the Department of Justice.

[25] The prior $50,000 fine was increased to $1 million for corporations and $100,000 for other persons. The maximum jail sentence was increased from one year to three years.

I

PATTERNS OF PROSECUTORIAL PRACTICE

Over the years, the Sherman Act has been viewed alternatively as primarily a civil or criminal statute. This checkered history accounts in large part for the current prosecutorial practice of using section 1 in both criminal and civil actions.

Originally, the Department of Justice viewed the statute as essentially civil, and, except in a handful of labor cases involving violence, used section 1 to obtain equitable relief.[26] Thus, from 1890 to 1903 the Justice Department instituted sixteen civil cases and only seven criminal cases under section 1.[27]

Fifty years after its enactment, the Sherman Act assumed a new role. Under Thurman Arnold's leadership, the Antitrust Division used section 1 primarily to pursue criminal prosecutions. This shift in focus reflected Arnold's philosophy:

> As a deterrent, criminal prosecution is the only effective instrument under existing statutes. . . . [I]f there were teeth in the civil remedy, it might be a deterrent. But for this purpose the civil injunction is little more than a form of unemployment relief for lawyers since it carries no penalties.
>
> The civil suit has a useful place as a supplement to the criminal proceeding—not as a substitute.[28]

Thus, between 1938 and 1943 the Antitrust Division, under Arnold, brought approximately 340 section 1 cases, 231 of which were criminal prosecutions.[29] Although some of these cases involved simple, old-fashioned price-fixing conspiracies, others raised novel issues concerning industries generally thought exempt from the antitrust laws. *United States v. South-Eastern Underwriters Association*,[30] for example, was originally brought as a criminal case, despite considerable question as to whether the insurance transactions chal-

Antitrust Procedures and Penalties Act, Pub. L. No. 93-528, § 3, 88 Stat. 1708 (1974) (amending 15 U.S.C. § 1 (1970)).

[26] *See* H. THORELLI, THE FEDERAL ANTITRUST POLICY: ORIGINATION OF AN AMERICAN TRADITION 596-97 (1955). *See generally* Letwin, *The First Decade of the Sherman Act: Early Administration*, 68 YALE L.J. 464 (1959).

[27] Posner, *A Statistical Study of Antitrust Enforcement*, 13 J.L. & ECON. 365, 385 (1970).

[28] Arnold, *Antitrust Law Enforcement, Past and Future*, 7 LAW & CONTEMP. PROB. 5, 16 (1940).

[29] These figures were compiled from CCH, THE FEDERAL ANTITRUST LAWS WITH SUMMARY OF CASES INSTITUTED BY THE UNITED STATES 1890-1951, at 179-307 (1952). *See generally* Posner, *supra* note 27, at 385.

[30] 322 U.S. 533 (1944).

lenged were in interstate commerce or even subject to the antitrust laws.[31]

Thurman Arnold clearly went beyond present standards of due process. His actions invited criticism that businesses were branded as criminals on the basis of uncertain conduct and unpredictable rules. The Attorney General's National Committee to Study the Antitrust Laws addressed this very point in 1955, emphasizing the complexity of the modern economy:

> Thus, it may be difficult for today's businessman to tell in advance whether projected actions will run afoul of the Sherman Act's criminal strictures. With this hazard in mind, we believe that criminal process should be used only where the law is clear and the facts reveal a flagrant offense and plain intent unreasonably to restrain trade.[32]

Arnold's standard goes too far in one direction, but this statement goes too far in the other. Criminal prosecution should not be limited to "a flagrant offense" or require "plain intent."

In 1955, the Antitrust Division drew the line somewhere between the two views expressed above:

> In general, the following types of offenses are prosecuted criminally: (1) price fixing; (2) other violations of the Sherman Act where there is proof of a specific intent to restrain trade or to monopolize; (3) a less easily defined category of cases which might generally be described as involving proof of use of predatory practices (boycotts, for example) to accomplish the objective of the combination or conspiracy; (4) the fact that a defendant has previously been convicted of or adjudged to have been, violating the antitrust laws may warrant indictment for a second offense. There are other factors taken into account in determining whether to seek an indictment in cases that may not fall precisely in any of these categories. The Division feels free to seek an indictment in any case where a prospective defendant has knowledge that practices similar to those in which he is engaging have been held to be in violation of the Sherman Act in a prior civil suit against other persons.[33]

---

[31] *Cf.* Paul v. Virginia, 75 U.S. (8 Wall.) 168, 183 (1869) (issuing insurance policy not transaction in interstate commerce).

[32] REPORT OF THE ATTORNEY GENERAL'S NATIONAL COMMITTEE TO STUDY THE ANTITRUST LAWS 349 (1955).

[33] *Id.* at 350 (statement of Stanley N. Barnes, Ass't Att'y Gen. in Charge of Antitrust Div.).

Far less than a complete and detailed explanation, this statement provided little guidance in close cases. Fortunately, the criminal enforcement versus civil enforcement issue was of limited practical importance during the 1950's and 1960's when the Antitrust Division's criminal enforcement program was less extensive than it is now. The Antitrust Division, however, continued to ponder the dual nature of the Sherman Act and in 1967 once again summarized its position:

> The solution of the Antitrust Division to this problem of potential unfairness has been to lay down the firm rule that criminal prosecutions will be recommended to the Attorney General only against willful violations of the law, and that one of two conditions must appear to be shown to establish willfulness. First, if the rules of law alleged to have been violated are clear and established—describing *per se* offenses—willfulness will be presumed. The most common criminal violation of the antitrust laws is price fixing; upwards of 80 percent of the criminal cases filed charge conspiracies to fix prices. The Supreme Court held more than 30 years ago that price fixing was a *per se* violation of the law—one for which no justification or defense could be offered. . . . Second, if the acts of the defendants show intentional violations—if through circumstantial evidence or direct testimony it appears that the defendants knew they were violating the law or were acting with flagrant disregard for the legality of their conduct—willfulness will be presumed.[34]

I find that statement still fair and useful today.

II

WHERE WE STAND TODAY

The criminal-versus-civil issue has increased in importance in the last few years. The Antitrust Division now devotes a larger share of its resources to criminal enforcement than it has at any time since Thurman Arnold's administration.[35] It applies a more

---

[34] THE PRESIDENT'S COMMISSION ON LAW ENFORCEMENT AND ADMINISTRATION OF JUSTICE, TASK FORCE REPORT: CRIME AND ITS IMPACT—AN ASSESSMENT 110 (1967) (footnote omitted).

[35] On May 5, 1977, while still Assistant Attorney General, I reported to Congress:
[T]he Division has over 100 grand jury investigations in progress. This is an affirmative choice, designed to make maximum use of the increased deterrent impact of the Sherman Act felony sanctions enacted by Congress in December 1974. Consequently, there has been a 30 percent increase in the number of pending

liberal policy for initiating grand juries than it did a decade ago,[36] and now has well over one hundred grand jury investigations pending.

The decision to open a grand jury is not a determination that all cases recommended for prosecution by the grand jury will be treated as criminal cases. The Division initiates a grand jury investigation when there is *some* reason to believe that a criminal violation *may* have taken place. Such a standard inevitably results in authorization of grand jury investigations which in fact lead to civil suits rather than criminal prosecutions. The ultimate decision to proceed criminally, civilly, or not at all must await the conclusion of each investigation. The broad powers of civil discovery granted the Antitrust Division under the Antitrust Improvements Act of 1976,[37] remove any need or temptation to convene grand juries to promote civil investigations.[38] The decision to authorize a grand jury investigation is made primarily by the Office of Operations,[39] based upon what it already knows and what it expects to discover about a given case.

---

antitrust grand juries over the pre-felony period. In fiscal year 1976, almost 2,000 attorney-days were spent in grand jury investigations.
Oversight of Antitrust Enforcement: Hearings Before the Subcomm. on Antitrust and Monopoly of the Senate Comm. on the Judiciary, 95th Cong., 1st Sess. 340 (1977) (statement of Donald I. Baker, Ass't Att'y Gen. in Charge of Antitrust Div.) [hereinafter cited as *Oversight Hearings*].

[36] The standard today is whether a potential investigation *might* result in a criminal indictment; if so, the grand jury investigation is usually used and the final decision whether to bring a criminal or civil case is left until the completion of the investigation. In the 1960's, the standard was whether the investigation *probably would* produce a criminal indictment.

[37] Hart-Scott-Rodino Antitrust Improvements Act of 1976, Pub. L. No. 95-435, §§ 101-106, 90 Stat. 1383 (1976) (codified at 15 U.S.C.A. §§ 1311-1314 (West Supp. 1977)).

[38] *Cf.* United States v. Proctor & Gamble Co., 356 U.S. 677 (1958) (grand jury not "short cut to goals otherwise barred or more difficult to reach").

[39] *The Office of Operations* . . . is the focal point of review of all the Division's investigations and litigation. It consists of two senior people—the Director of Operations and his Deputy—supported by three assistants and a small support staff. This office supervises the assignment, opening and closing of investigations. It conducts [the Antitrust Division's] liaison activities with the FTC under the clearance procedure. It reviews every proposal [*sic*] civil and criminal case recommended by any section . . . . Operations is the key reviewer of immunity orders and CID's, both of which must be ultimately signed by the AAG [Assistant Attorney General].
Oversight Hearings, supra note 35, at 336. The Director of Operations is traditionally the highest career official in the Division and he directly supervises the operations of the five main litigating sections in Washington, the eight field offices spread around the country, and the various smaller litigation units.

The Assistant Attorney General must ultimately decide whether to bring a criminal prosecution. He bases that choice in part upon articulated principles, in part upon intuition gained from experience, and ultimately upon the facts of the particular case.

Let me tell you how I made that decision during my tenure as Assistant Attorney General. I believe, as Thurman Arnold believed, that criminal sanctions provide the best mechanism for dealing with price fixing, market allocation, and clearly predatory conduct. Criminal sanctions, particularly substantial individual jail sentences, best deter antitrust crimes.[40] Accordingly, I opted for criminal prosecutions in price-fixing and market-allocation cases, absent any of four special mitigating factors: (1) confusion of the law; (2) truly novel issues of law or fact; (3) confusion caused by past prosecutorial decisions; or (4) clear evidence that the defendants did not appreciate the consequences of their actions.

A. *Confusion of the Law*

In various areas of the economy, there is collusive conduct that would be clearly illegal—and indeed criminal—but for the presence of government regulation or some other arguable antitrust exemption. Where some form of regulatory umbrella exists, I generally believe we should test the scope of any exemption it may provide by civil rather than criminal enforcement. Such an approach is both fairer to the defendant and more conducive to reasoned analysis by the courts. In other words, I would not do what Thurman Arnold did in *South-Eastern Underwriters*—test a long-assumed Sherman Act exemption by bringing a criminal case.

The Antitrust Division has followed such a policy in recent years in "regulatory" and "state action" cases. For example, the New York Stock Exchange fixed commission system was an ancient and classic form of cartel rate making. When the Antitrust Division first focused on this practice in 1968, fixed rates had been in effect for more than 170 years, at least thirty of them under the benevolent eye of the Securities and Exchange Commission. We believed that the practice was illegal under the antitrust laws because it did not satisfy the standard for exemption announced in *Silver v. New York Stock Exchange*.[41] The Antitrust Division chose to proceed against

---

[40] *See* Baker, To Make the Penalty Fit the Crime: How To Sentence Antitrust Felons (Nov. 20, 1976) (remarks before the Tenth New England Antitrust Conference, Boston, Mass.), *reprinted in* [1976] ANTITRUST & TRADE REG. REP. NO. 790, at D-1 (Nov. 23, 1976).

[41] 373 U.S. 341 (1963).

the fixed rates by triggering SEC hearings[42] and by intervening in a private treble-damage case which was about to go to trial under a favorable Court of Appeals mandate.[43] We did not consider—and I would not consider—a criminal prosecution in that situation.

Of course, once the scope of the exemption is defined, a criminal case would be appropriate. Today brokerage rate fixing is clearly illegal under the Securities and Exchange Act Amendments of 1975;[44] it is therefore per se illegal under the antitrust laws. It would now be appropriate to proceed by grand jury investigation and to bring indictments against anybody engaged in such rate fixing.

B. *Truly Novel Issues of Law and Fact*

Criminal proceedings seem less appropriate where the Department's theory of antitrust liability is entirely new. Criminal indictments, particularly felony indictments, in such cases raise important issues of fairness which in turn may affect the likelihood of obtaining a conviction. The recently filed amendments to the *General Electric* and *Westinghouse* consent decrees[45] illustrate the considerations raised by cases posing new issues. The government alleged that GE and Westinghouse engaged in indirect price communication and signaling.[46] Information was communicated in public which established a body of data sufficient to enable each firm to identify the price that the other firm would quote on any given turbine generator. At the same time, the companies adopted policy

---

[42] See Comments of the United States Department of Justice (Apr. 1, 1968), *reprinted in* 1 J. Grossman & S. Glendon, Securities Market Regulation: A Chronology of Events and. Selected Documents 105 (1975), which led to the Commission's opening of *In re* Commission Rate Structure of Registered Nat'l Sec. Exch., SEC File No. 44-144 (1968). The Department's position was amplified and its evidence summarized in the Memorandum of the United States Dep't of Justice on the Fixed Minimum Commission Rates Structure (Jan. 17, 1969), *reprinted in* J. Grossman & S. Glendon, *supra* at 222.

[43] Thill Sec. Corp. v. New York Stock Exch., 433 F.2d 264 (7th Cir. 1970), *cert. denied*, 401 U.S. 994 (1971).

[44] Securities Acts Amendments of 1975, Pub. L. No. 94-29, § 6(e)(1), 89 Stat. 97 (codified at 15 U.S.C. § 78(e) (Supp. V 1975)).

[45] United States v. General Elec. Co., [1977-2] Trade Cas. (CCH) ¶ 61,660 (E.D. Pa. Sept. 19, 1977), *modifying* [1962] Trade Cas. (CCH) ¶ 70,488 (E.D. Pa.); United States v. Westinghouse Elec. Corp., [1977-2] Trade Cas. (CCH) ¶ 61,661 (E.D. Pa. Sept. 19, 1977), *modifying* [1962] Trade Cas. (CCH) ¶ 70,503 (E.D. Pa.).

[46] Plaintiff's Memorandum in Support of a Proposed Modification of the Final Judgment Entered on October 1, 1962 Against Each Defendant, United States v. General Elec. Co., [1977-2] Trade Cas. (CCH) ¶ 61,660 (Sept. 19, 1977); United States v. Westinghouse Elec. Corp., [1977-2] Trade Cas. (CCH) ¶ 61,661 (Sept. 19, 1977), *reprinted in* 42 Fed. Reg. 17,004, 17,006-07 (1977).

positions that had the effect, and allegedly the purpose, of assuring each seller that the other would adhere to the formula price. The government viewed this as a case of "avoidable cooperation,"[47] rather than simply unavoidable "conscious parallelism."[48]

Given the unusual nature of that case, I did not and would not choose to proceed criminally. As far as I know, criminal prosecution was never considered in the course of this investigation—either during my tenure or during that of my predecessor. That the conduct involved might be labeled "price fixing" is not determinative of the mode of proceeding where the case involves novel conduct. In fact, the best remedy I saw for this particular phenomenon was an injunctive order preventing the firms from continuing their pattern of price signaling and response. The relief, originally included in a draft civil complaint, was ultimately implemented as a modification of outstanding consent decrees for reasons explained in the government's memorandum.[49]

C. *Confusion Caused by Prior Prosecutorial Action*

The third situation in which a civil action may provide the appropriate enforcement procedure for what might be regarded as criminal conduct occurs when a proposed case represents a departure from past practices of the Department of Justice. For example, I would not feel bound by a prior Business Review letter[50]— especially an old one—when the letter was based on what now would be regarded as incorrect analysis or policy. Yet such a changed position should not be unveiled in a criminal indictment. Rather a civil suit should be brought to "fire a shot across their bow." Having made its new position clear, the Department could proceed criminally in the future.

Years of prosecutorial acquiescence in longstanding open conduct may create a similar situation. For example, the Antitrust Division long tolerated "recommended" fee schedules by bar associations, although such schedules had the clear purpose and necessary effect of stabilizing prices for legal services. When the Division decided to prosecute such schedules as illegal, it initiated a

---

[47] *Id.* at 17,006-09.

[48] *Id.* at 17,007.

[49] *Id.* at 17,009.

[50] The Antitrust Division's Business Review Procedure is set forth in 28 C.F.R. § 50.6 (1976). Generally, it provides that an applicant can obtain a statement of the government's "present endorsement intention" with respect to a particular live transaction fully disclosed to the government. Normally, the request for such a ruling, the ruling itself, and the supporting documentation are made public. *See id.*

civil suit against the Oregon State Bar.[51] This suit was followed by the Supreme Court's decision holding such fee schedules illegal under the antitrust laws.[52] Having once given the professions full and adequate warning, the Justice Department may now take a more aggressive posture. In the future, it would be appropriate to proceed criminally against this type of scheme.

D. *Clear Evidence the Defendants Did Not Appreciate the Consequences of Their Actions*

Occasionally defendants engage in per se price fixing, but their conduct clearly indicates that they had no idea they were violating the antitrust laws. There may, for instance, have been open and widely advertised public meetings among a group of naive businessmen without an antitrust counsel. An illustrative case arose a few years ago when a group of local gasoline dealers in a western state made public announcements calling for meetings to stabilize prices and eliminate price wars. I would normally regard such conduct as entirely indictable.[53] Yet the naive innocence of the exceptionally unsophisticated may deserve some weight in prosecutorial judgment. Although a showing of specific intent is not required to establish a price-fixing violation,[54] prosecutors recog-

---

[51] United States v. Oregon State Bar, 385 F. Supp. 507 (D. Ore. 1974).

[52] Goldfarb v. Virginia State Bar, 421 U.S. 773 (1975).

[53] *See, e.g.*, United States v. Wholesale Tobacco Distribs., Inc., No. 77 Cr. 131 (S.D.N.Y., filed Feb. 17, 1977) (allegedly illegal conduct took place at publicly announced association meetings). I reject the suggestion that the Antitrust Division should proceed civilly in price-fixing conspiracies of limited economic impact, such as those involving a small industry or local market. Resources are limited, and the Department of Justice cannot discover, investigate, and prosecute every small, local price fixer. But once the decision to proceed against a local price-fixing conspiracy has been made, the same standards should apply as would be applicable to a larger conspiracy. I firmly believe that price fixing by a local service firm is as much a criminal violation as price fixing by a national manufacturer. *See* Baker, Antitrust Enforcement in the Service Sector (Sept. 15, 1976) (remarks to Wash. State Bar Ass'n, Antitrust Section) (on file at the *Cornell Law Review*). The service sector today accounts for one-third of the United States' GNP. The Antitrust Division is currently putting more resources into antitrust enforcement in the service sector to match changes in the economy, and criminal indictments should be used against price fixing and other hard-core restraints by local service firms. *See, e.g.*, United States v. Jack Foley Realty, Inc., [1977-2] Trade Cas. (CCH) ¶ 61,678 (D. Md. July 29, 1977) (indictment of Montgomery County, Md. real estate brokers).

[54] Normally it is stated that "[u]nder the Sherman Act a combination formed for the purpose *and* with the effect of raising, depressing, fixing, pegging, or stabilizing the price of a commodity in interstate or foreign commerce is illegal *per se*." United States v. Socony-Vacuum Oil Co., 310 U.S. 150, 223 (1943) (emphasis added). However, in fact, "[p]urpose and effect are disjunctively linked in antitrust analysis, both under the rule of reason and in the application of the *per se* doctrine. If the purpose or (assuming a very different and in-

nize that a judge or jury might be disinclined to convict under such circumstances. The violator's naiveté is, however, a much less compelling consideration than the other three I have mentioned.

Conclusion

The Antitrust Division's increased use of grand jury investigations makes its choice of whether to proceed against violators with civil or criminal actions a matter of growing practical importance to the business community and the bar. Close cases will remain close and they will not go away. It necessarily follows that with *very close* cases decisions could go either way. Articulation and consistent application of principles for deciding the form of proceeding give parties some notice of the standards to which their conduct will be held. Ultimately, however, these hard choices require judgment calls by the Assistant Attorney General. All we can ask is that in making such calls he be fair, candid, and dispassionate. Only then can he hope to maintain public confidence in the integrity of the antitrust enforcement process.

---

nocent purpose) if the predictable effect of conduct is to fix prices (or achieve anything else held *per se* unlawful) the conduct runs afoul of the *per se* rule. Similarly, if either the purpose or effect of a practice evaluated under the rule of reason is sufficiently adverse to competition to outweigh any benefits, the conduct is deemed unreasonable." L. SULLIVAN, HANDBOOK OF THE LAW OF ANTITRUST § 71, at 194 (1977).

17

SENTENCING REFORM AND PROSECUTORIAL POWER
A Critique of Recent Proposals for "Fixed" and "Presumptive" Sentencing

ALBERT W. ALSCHULER

In the American system of criminal justice, power over punishment is allocated primarily among four types of governmental decision-makers — legislatures, prosecutors' offices, courts, and correctional agencies (including, most notably, parole boards).[1] The thrust of many recent proposals for sentencing reform has been to reduce or elminate the discretion of both courts and correctional agencies and to increase the extent to which legislatures specify criminal penalties in advance.[2] In "fixed" sentencing schemes, statutes specify the exact penalty that will follow conviction for each offense; in systems of "presumptive" sentencing, statutes specify a "normal" sentence for each offense but permit limited departures from the norm in atypical cases. Although prosecutors' offices have in practice probably had a greater influence on sentencing than any of the other agencies (not excluding state legislatures), the call for sentencing reform has largely ignored this extensive prosecutorial power. In my view, fixed and presumptive sentencing schemes of the sort commonly advocated today (and of the sort enacted in California[3]) are unlikely to achieve their objectives so long as they leave the prosecutor's power to formulate charges and to bargain for guilty pleas unchecked. Indeed, this sort of reform is likely to produce its antithesis — to yield a system every bit as lawless as the current sentencing regime but one in which discretion is concentrated in an inappropriate agency and in which the benefits of this discretion are made available only to defendants who sacrifice their constitutional rights.

Before turning to this thesis, I want to set the stage by analyzing the problem of sentencing reform in more traditional terms and by trying to separate a number of issues from one another.

From Albert W. Alschuler, "Sentencing Reform and Prosecutorial Power: A Critique of Recent Proposals for "Fixed" and "Presumptive" Sentencing," pp. 59-88 in Determinate Sentencing: Reform or Regression? (which was supported by a grant from the National Institute of Law Enforcement and Criminal Justice, Law Enforcement Assistance Administration, U.S. Department of Justice).

The central concern of most recent discussion of sentencing issues has been how much sentencing discretion criminal justice officials should have, but an equally important question may be where sentencing discretion should reside. This paper will consider three separate decision points in the criminal justice system — parole, the judicial determination of sentence, and prosecutorial plea negotiation. It will briefly examine the different purposes, both legitimate and illegitimate, that are likely to be served by vesting discretion at these distinct points, and it will explore some functional interrelationships among them. Because a number of recent reform proposals have apparently disregarded obvious features of our criminal justice system, the emphasis of many of these remarks will be on the simple rather than the sophisticated.

I

THE DISCRETION OF
PAROLE BOARDS

Of the various components of the call for sentencing reform, academic observers have probably been most receptive to proposals for the drastic restriction or elimination of the powers of parole boards. These extensive powers reflect a reformative jurisprudence implemented, for the most part, in the early Twentieth Century as a concomitant of the Progressive Movement.[4] The asserted justification for the parole board's sentencing powers is essentially that expert penologists, who can evaluate an offender's conduct and his response to treatment in prison, can best determine the appropriate moment for his release.

That I and many other academics adhered in large part to this reformative viewpoint only a decade or so ago seems almost incredible to most of us today. To probe a person's psyche and to predict his future behavior is always an awesome task, and the optimistic belief that one can discern a person's general propensity for law observance from his regimented conduct in a prison now seems remarkably naive. Although not all of us are ready simply to abandon rehabilitation as one objective of the criminal process (at least not in every circumstance), we have become far less ambitious in pursuing this goal than we were a few years ago when we encouraged our state legislatures to adopt some variation of the Model Penal Code's sentencing scheme. Our general disillusionment stems from both jurisprudential and pragmatic considerations. Even if the state could achieve its rehabilitative objectives far more often than it does, we have become doubtful that an offender's wrongdoing justifies a broad assumption of governmental power over his personality. Moreover, we have tried almost everything, and almost nothing seems to work.[5] The sad fact is that, so far as we can tell, most prisoners are not perfectable victims of social ills who will respond to one kind of treatment or another. Some — an undetermined number — may draw a lesson from the unpleasant experience of being arrested, convicted and punished; but apart from this "specific deterrence," only two personal experiences, aging and religious conversion, seem likely to work dramatic changes.

The principal practical effect of our emphasis on "cure" has been to encourage convicts to view their time in prison as an exercise in theatre.[6] They "volunteer" for group therapy and other rehabilitative programs, say the right things about the help that they have received, and even find Christ and become guinea pigs for medical experimentation in hypocritical efforts to curry favor with parole boards. In addition, we have become increasingly aware that the very indeterminacy of indeterminate sentences is a form of psychological torture.[7]

Even if parole boards do not effectively serve their intended function, they are probably not utterly useless. As a statewide agency, a parole board can sometimes exercise its power in such a manner as to reduce the disparities in sentencing created by the varying outlooks of local judges and prosecutors. In addition, as an agency somewhat removed from local pressures and emotions and as an agency whose decisions are removed in time from the adjudication of guilt, a parole board can sometimes counteract the untoward vindictiveness of local sentencing officials.[8] (It seems worth noting that the concept of parole as a period of supervised release halfway between confinement and freedom can be retained even if the sentencing powers of parole boards are eliminated. Parole release has been criticised on the ground that it constitutes merely a gratuitous "hold" over former prisoners rather than a meaningful aid to reintegration or a worthwhile form of policing,[9] but if a supervised period of transition from prison to the streets does seem desirable, it can become a regular feature of every prison sentence rather than a subject of the parole board's discretion.[10])

In America's regime of guilty plea bargaining, an offender who has exercised the right to trial is likely to receive a much more severe sentence than an otherwise identical offender who has pleaded guilty.[11] The available evidence suggests that parole boards have used their sentencing powers to reduce this disparity, albeit to a limited extent.[12] Reduction of the sentence differential between guilty plea and trial defendants may be another worthwhile "incidental" function of parole boards, and when the ability of parole boards to perform this function is reduced or eliminated, the power of bargaining prosecutors is likely to be increased. With the restriction of the parole board's discretion, a defendant who is considering whether to accept a proposed plea agreement need not fear that parole practices may, to some extent, deprive him of the apparent benefit of his bargain. Equally, a defendant who is considering whether to stand trial cannot hope that parole practices will ameliorate the penalty that our system of criminal justice threatens for this exercise of a constitutional right.

Nevertheless, the desirability of restricting the powers of parole boards is not necessarily much affected by the institution of plea bargaining, for a great deal depends on what happens next. The powers currently exercised by parole boards can be assumed by legislatures or transferred to judges to be exercised following an offender's conviction, or they can be transformed into additional levers for prosecutors to use in inducing pleas of guilty. In California, the sentencing power of the Adult Authority has been so extensive that most practitioners have seen little point in plea bargaining when an offender seemed certain to be sentenced to state prison in any event.[13] With the recent elimination of the Adult Authority as part of California's sentencing reform, bargains affecting the length of an offender's stay in state prison will undoubtedly become commonplace.[14] Much of the Adult Authority's power will, in other words, be transferred to the prosecutor's office.[15] Moreover, when the benefits of discretion become available *only* through the plea bargaining process, the concentration of abusive power in the hands of a single agency is especially to be feared. I therefore turn to proposals to restrict the discretion of trial judges.

II

JUDICIAL SENTENCING DISCRETION

The advocates of fixed and presumptive sentencing commonly argue that judicial sentencing discretion stands on about the same discredited footing as the discretion of parole boards. For example, Andrew von Hirsch has written, "Wide discretion in sentencing has been sustained by the traditional assumptions about rehabilitation and predictive restraint. Once these assumptions are abandoned, the basis for such broad discretion crumbles."[16] Unlike the discretion of parole boards, however, judicial sentencing discretion is not an outgrowth of the optimism of the Progressive Era.[17] Judges have had broad sentencing powers for as long as prisons have been used to punish, and indeed longer. I recently discovered an old volume of Tennessee and North Carolina statutes that contains some illustrations, including the following provision on horse stealing enacted by the Tennessee General Assembly in 1807:

> Be it enacted, that every person who shall feloniously steal, take and carry away, any horse, mare or gelding, the property of another person, the person so offending, shall, for the first offense be adjudged and sentenced by the court before whom convicted, to receive on his or her bare back, a number of lashes, *not exceeding thirty-nine,* be imprisoned *at the discretion of the court, not less than six months, and not exceeding two years,* shall sit in the pillory two hours on three different days, and shall be rendered infamous . . . and shall be branded with the letters H. T. *in such manner and on such part of his person as the court shall direct;* and on the second conviction shall suffer death without benefit of clergy. [Emphasis added][18]

Still more interesting, from my perspective, is a North Carolina statute on suborning perjury that was enacted in 1777 — 13 years before the establishment of the Walnut Street Jail in Philadelphia, the event commonly viewed as inaugurating the use of imprisonment as a penal sanction in America. This statute provided that a convicted offender should "stand in the pillory one hour, have his or her right ear nailed thereunto, *and be further punished by fine and imprisonment at the discretion of the court.*"[19]

The North Carolina Legislature of 1777 would probably have agreed with the position adopted by the California Legislature 200 years later: "[T]he purpose of imprisonment for crime is punishment."[20] Rather than establish a system of fixed sentences, however, the North Carolina Legislature chose the opposite extreme; it imposed no limitations whatever upon the trial judge's power to determine the length of an offender's confinement. This bit of history suggests that the medical model of rehabilitation has not been the exclusive or the primary impetus for the grant of judicial sentencing discretion in America.

Simply in terms of blameworthiness or desert, criminal cases are different from one another in ways that legislatures cannot anticipate, and limitations of language prevent the precise description of differences that can be anticipated. One need not adopt grandoise rehabilitative goals to think that it should sometimes make a difference whether an armed robbery was committed with a machine gun, a revolver, a baseball bat, a toy gun or a finger-in-the-pocket. Perhaps it should also make a difference whether the crime was motivated by a desperate family financial situation or merely a desire for excitement, whether the robber wielded a firearm himself or simply drove the getaway car, whether the victim of the crime was a blind newstand operator whom the robber did not know or a person against whom the robber had legitimate grievances, whether the robber took five cents, $100,000 or a treasured keepsake that the victim begged to retain, whether the crime occurred at noon on a crowded streetcorner or at 1:00 a.m. in an alley, whether the robber walked voluntarily into a police station to confess or desperately resisted capture, and whether the robber was emotionally disturbed and or a calculating member of an ongoing criminal organization.

The principal function of judicial sentencing discretion has probably been to permit a detailed consideration of differences of this sort in culpability — a consideration that legislatures have historically recognized their own inability to provide. When, in recent years, a judge has sentenced one of several co-felons to a term of probation and the others to imprisonment, he was likely to remark that the defendant placed on probation had exhibited greater rehabilitative potential than the others. The judge may have meant nothing more, however, than that the favored defendant was young, had participated in the crime in a relatively minor way, had been induced to participate through some beguilement on the part of his confederates, and therefore seemed substantially less blameworthy than his fellows. Even when our rhetoric has emphasized reformation, the dominant reality may have been "just deserts."

The varieties of human behavior are, in short, so great that a legislative definition of crime must usually encompass acts of substantially differing culpability. Even more importantly, the personal characteristics of offenders may remain as important in a sentencing regime based on desert as in a regime based in part on the goals of rehabilitation and predictive restraint. Our past optimism concerning criminal justice issues apparently accorded with our view of history as progress and of America as the new-found land: "Did someone rob a bank? If so, this person must never have had a chance. We will give him that chance. We will teach him how to be a welder, and he will not rob banks any more." Recently, however, America has experienced Vietnam, Watergate and, in the criminal justice area, a series of studies that seem to demonstrate the naivete of our earlier rehabilitative ambitions. Some Americans have apparently become weary and disillusioned in general and tired of thinking of offenders as individuals in particular. Although a corrective for the undue optimism of the past was undoubtedly in order, the corrective may be carried too far. We may find ourselves thinking, "Don't tell us that a robber was retarded. We don't care about his problems. We don't know what to *do* about his problems, and we are no longer interested in listening to a criminal's sob stories. The most important thing about this robber is simply that he *is* a robber. He committed the same crime as Bonnie and Clyde." Should this sort of sentiment prevail, I believe that we will have lost something, not in terms of the effectiveness of the criminal justice system, but as human beings. One need not know what to do about an offender's problems to regard those problems as highly relevant to the punishment that he should receive.

Sentencing reformers typically object to the instrumental use of human beings to accomplish generalized social objectives. It seems to them more consistent with individual dignity to punish an offender because he "deserves" it than to punish him for the sake of society at large. Nevertheless, treating defendants of differing culpability alike for the sake of certainty in sentencing seems to involve greater instrumentalism than our current sentencing regime. In a system of fixed or presumptive sentencing, cases may arise in which the legislative "tariff" will prove unjust, but the reformers do not seem to worry very much about the problem. Their apparent attitude is that one who commits a crime must always expect to pay the price. This punishment may be deserved only in the sense that it was specified in advance. Nevertheless, "the law must keep its promises."[21]

The intellectual progenitor of today's fixed-sentencing movement, Cesare Beccaria, wrote in 1764, "[C]rimes are only to be mesaured by the injury done to society. They err, therefore, who imagine that a crime is greater or less according to the intention of the person by whom it is committed."[22] If we were to adhere to Beccaria's remarkably primitive concept of blame, the formulation of a workable fixed-sentencing scheme might not be too difficult a task. Nevertheless, reformers in the last quarter of the Twentieth Century are not in fact so inhumane. As von Hirsch has observed, "[The seriousness of a crime] depends both on the harm done (or risked) by the act and on the degree of the actor's culpability."[23] It seems noteworthy that Beccaria himself recognized that a consideration of factors other than social harm would require individualized sentencing: "[I]t would be necessary to form, not only a particular code for every individual, but a new penal law for every crime."[24]

Most of today's reformers recognize the need for some small amount of judicial discretion to take account of variations in culpability within single offense categories. Their proposals typically provide for variations of plus-or-minus 20 percent or plus-or-minus one year in the presumptive prison sentence for each offense. A basic question, of course, is whether this limited degree of flexibility is enough.[25] In addition, California's recently revised penal code, like the Fogel-Walker proposal in Illinois, leaves the most important component of the sentencing decision — the choice between prison and probation — to the same lawless discretion as in the past.[26] The seemingly ludicrous result is that a judge may have an unfettered choice between probation and a specified prison term but no power to reach an intermediate judgment. Whatever the logic of their demands for certainty, some liberal reformers seem unwilling to advocate the "mandatory minimum sentences" that they have previously condemned and unwilling to take any step that will obviously be disadvantageous to defendants. Hence their retention of probation on the same discretionary terms as in the past.

Some of today's reformers also recognize that a more precise definition of substantive crimes will be necessary before a scheme of presumptive sentencing can be fair, and the Twentieth Century Fund Task Force on Criminal Sentencing has drafted an "illustrative presumptive sentencing statute for armed robbery" to demonstrate the feasibility of the task. The statute seems, however, to demonstrate the opposite. It divides the crime of armed robbery into six degrees and yet takes account of only two variables, the sort of weapon used and the amount of physical violence threatened. Even the attempt to rationalize these two variables is somewhat crude; for example, robbery with a Tommy gun is treated no differently from robbery with a .22 target pistol. More importantly, variables such as the amount of money taken, the number and character of the victims, the motivation for the crime, and any special disabilities of the offender are relegated to a list of aggravating and mitigating circumstances that may sometimes justify a departure from the presumptive sentence.

The Task Force's effort to provide an "exclusive" list of aggravating and mitigating factors itself seems troublesome. For example, under the Task Force proposal, a judge would apparently be expected to disregard the fact that a particular offender was seized with remorse, turned himself in, and provided information that led to the arrest and conviction of a half-dozen violent criminals. Perhaps the Task Force did not make a focused decision that this sort of post-crime conduct is irrelevant to the punishment that an offender should receive. The authors may instead not have thought very much about the issue, and therein lies the danger of attempting to specify all relevant sentencing factors in advance.[27] More importantly, a general, unweighted list of aggravating and mitigating factors does not do much to confine discretion. If every significant variable were domesticated in the same manner that the draft domesticates a few, and if each variable were then cross-tabulated with every other variable, the resulting armed robbery statute would probably exhibit about the same prolixity as an entire penal code today. Armed robbery in the 161st degree might be the taking of property worth between ten and 50 dollars from a single victim without special vulnerabilities by a mentally retarded offender acting alone and using a loaded firearm.[28]

A more promising approach is currently being developed by Leslie Wilkins, Jack Kress and their associates in the city of Denver and state of Vermont,[29] and by Judge Sam Callan and the other criminal district court judges in El Paso, Texas.[30] In essence, these scholars and court officials have been working to evolve a "point system" under which a sentencing judge assigns values to a number of recurring sentencing factors in the cases that come before him. When an offender has been convicted of a

Class 2 felony under the local penal code, for example, the judge might start with a base score of six points. Then he might add two points because the offender carried a firearm during the crime, add another two points because he fired this weapon, add still another point because the offender was convicted of a serious misdemeanor within the past year, subtract two points because the offender cooperated in the prosecution of other offenders, and so on. The final score is translated into a presumptive sentence which the judge may disregard (and not just within a limited range of plus-or-minus 20 percent or plus-or-minus one year), provided he articulates his reasons for doing so.[31]

The development of judicial guidelines of this sort seems worthwhile but is probably not enough. A narrowing of the range of statutory penalties, coupled in some instances with a more precise definition of substantive offenses, does seem desirable in virtually every American jurisdiction. I have emphasized that discretion has its uses even in a sentencing regime based on just desert, but of course discretion also has a darker side. Whenever discretion is granted, it will be abused. In some instances, individual differences in culpability will be less important than differences in race, class, lifestyle and other irrelevancies. Even when officials consider only what they should, moreover, they will do so in differing ways, and troublesome inequalities will result. Despite my criticism of fixed sentencing proposals, the question today is probably how much we should move in the direction of fixed sentences, not whether we should do so.

III

PROSECUTORIAL PLEA BARGAINING

Any sentencing reform, whether great or small and whether in the form of fixed sentences, presumptive sentences or sentencing guidelines, can be undercut by the practice of plea bargaining, and the advocates of dramatic change in our system of criminal punishment have dutifully noted that prosecutors do, in effect, make sentencing decisions in formulating charges[32] and in negotiating pleas of guilty. They have even proclaimed, "There can be no practical understanding of any sentencing system without an appreciation of the role played by plea bargaining."[33] Sometimes after these brief glances in the direction of reality, however, and sometimes without them,[34] the reformers have for the most part ignored the dominant reality of prosecutorial sentencing power. They have usually sought to leave this power as they have found it, and they have not paused to consider what effect a still-unchecked power to bargain might have on the achievement of their objectives.

It seems unlikely that today's reformers are truly content with the regime of prosecutorial power as it is. There is hardly any objection to judicial sentencing discretion that does not apply in full measure to prosecutorial sentencing discretion — a discretion which has been, in practice, every bit as broad and broader.[35] As much as judicial discretion, the discretion of American prosecutors lends itself to inequalities and disparities based on disagreements concerning issues of sentencing policy; it permits at least the occasional dominance of illegitimate considerations such as race and personal or political influence; and it may lead to a general perception of arbitrariness and uncertainty, contribute to a sense of unfairness, and even undercut the deterrent force of the criminal law.

There are additional objections to prosecutorial sentencing discretion that do not apply with nearly so much force to judicial discretion. The exercise of prosecutorial discretion is more frequently made contingent upon a waiver of constitutional rights; it is generally exercised less openly; it is more likely to be influenced by considerations of friendship and by reciprocal favors of a dubious character; it is commonly exercised for the purpose of obtaining convictions in cases in which guilt could not be proven at trial; it is usually exercised by people of less experience and less objectivity than judges; it is commonly exercised on the basis of less information than judges possess; and, indeed, its exercise may depend less upon considerations of desert, deterrence and reformation than upon a desire to avoid the hard work of preparing and trying cases. The discretion of American prosecutors, in short, has the same faults as the discretion of American judges and more.

The *laissez faire* attitude of sentencing reformers toward this concentration of governmental power in prosecutors' offices is probably not the product of blindness or indifference. It is probably best explained by a pervasive sense that, for one reason or another, the institution of plea bargaining is impregnable. The reformers may have accepted the claim that trial courts would be swamped if the power to bargain for guilty pleas were substantially restricted, or they may have nodded at assurances that efforts to restrict the bargaining process would merely drive it underground. Moreover, the reformers probably have little desire to engage in what they see as a fruitless political battle. They may sense that sentencing reform will have a rough enough time in the political arena without a hopeless charge at the prosecutor's well-entrenched — and very comfortable — ways of doing business. The Twentieth Century Fund Task Force has put it this way: "The propriety of plea bargaining — whether it is desirable to eliminate it, if this is a practical possibility — will continue to be debated. But sentencing reform cannot be held in abeyance until the debate is resolved, if it ever is."[36] In other words, discussions of plea bargaining may be interesting, but we have the world's work to do.

I am not at all persuaded that our society is too impoverished to give its criminal defendants their day in court. Most nations of the world, including many far poorer than ours, do manage to resolve their criminal cases without bargaining. Nor do I accept the "boys-will-be-boys" theory that plea bargaining is inevitable, a theory that depends on the cynical view that prosecutors and defense attorneys will work to undercut even a clear and authoritative legal condemnation of bargaining in its various forms. Moreover, I believe that the political battle could be won if those who recognize the injustice of our current regime of prosecutorial power would simply fight the fight. The only public opinion poll on plea bargaining of which I am aware reports that an overwhelming and growing majority of Americans oppose the practice.[37] Nevertheless, I shall not pursue these issues in this paper. I shall merely contend that if the reformers are correct — if the practice of plea bargaining is indeed invulnerable — this circumstance argues strongly against the reformers' proposals. The asserted resiliency of plea bargaining militates as forcefully against the various changes that the reformers have sought as it does against the changes that they have foregone. Indeed, from my perspective, the worthwhile goal of sentencing reform might almost as well be forgotten if plea bargaining cannot be restricted.

The reformers themselves, of course, do not see it this way. They vaguely argue that their proposals would rationalize the plea bargaining process, and some of them also suggest — usually in private — that these proposals might constitute the first step toward an eventually more substantial restriction of prosecutorial sentencing power. One must always start somewhere, they maintain, and not necessarily with the most pernicious manifestation of the evil.

Consider, however, a criminal code in which offenses have been defined in great detail and in which the legislature has attached a single fixed sentence to each offense. Suppose, in other words, that not an ounce of discretion remains in the hands of trial judges and parole boards — and then suppose that prosecutors retain an unchecked power to substitute one charge for another in the plea bargaining process. It seems doubtful that even Ray Bradbury or Franz Kafka could devise a more bizarre system of criminal justice than this one. Despite the reformers' talk of certainty, the lawlessness of our system of criminal justice would probably not be reduced in this new regime. The persistence of plea bargaining would yield the same disparity of outcomes, the same racism and classism, the same gamesmanship, and the same uncertainty. The unchecked discretion over sentencing that has apparently distinguished our nation from all others would continue, but it would reside, not just predominantly, but exclusively in the prosecutor's office. The benefits of this discretion would, moreover, usually be available only to defendants who sacrificed the right to trial, and the pressure to plead guilty would therefore be likely to increase. We would have abandoned our old discretionary regime — a regime in which mercy could be given — and substituted a new discretionary regime in which mercy would only be sold.

The defenders of plea bargaining sometimes debate whether the bargaining process should focus on the number and level of the charges against a defendant or instead on specific sentence recommendations. Plea bargaining in a world of fixed sentencing, however, would combine the worst features of both forms of negotiation. In our current system of criminal justice, the principal advantage of charge bargaining is that it involves a measure of shared discretion and tends to intrude less dramatically upon the judicial sentencing function. Even after a charge-reduction bargain has been fully effected, a trial judge is likely to retain a significant choice in the sentence to be imposed, and he may exercise this choice without undercutting the credibility of the prosecutor who struck the bargain. When plea negotiations focus on prosecutorial sentence recommendations, by contrast, judges usually follow the course of least resistance and simply ratify the prosecutors' sentencing decisions.[38] The advantage that charge bargaining exhibits in our current system of criminal justice would plainly disappear in a system of fixed sentences. In such a system, bargaining about the charge would *be* bargaining about the sentence. A nonjudicial officer would determine the exact outcome of every guilty plea case, and every defendant who secured an offer from a prosecutor in the plea bargaining process would be informed that his conviction at trial would yield a sentence of precisely X years while his conviction by plea would yield a sentence of precisely Y.[39]

Although plea negotiation in a system of fixed sentencing would not have the same advantages as charge bargaining today, it would retain the same defects. The principal virtue of sentence-recommendation bargaining in our current system of justice is that it permits a reasonably precise adjustment of the concessions that a guilty-plea defendant will receive. Charge bargaining, by contrast, must proceed by leaps from one charge to another. In one case, replacing the offense that has been charged with the next available offense may result only in the substitution of a slightly less serious felony. In another case, "going down to count 2" may result in a midsdemeanor conviction. In still another case, there may be no lesser offense that seems at all related to the defendant's conduct. A prosecutor may often be forced to choose between withholding any concession and granting one that seems too generous, and he may sometimes find that penal code draftsmen have failed to provide a lesser offense that he can properly substitute for the offense initially charged. Because plea bargaining in a system of fixed sentencing would similarly require the substitution of one charge for another, accidents of spacing in the drafting of penal codes would assume substantial importance. In addition, prosecutors would face the same temptations for overcharging that they face in systems of charge bargaining today, and criminal conduct would be mislabeled as defendants pleaded guilty to offenses less serious than those that they apparently committed.[40]

In short, a system of fixed sentencing would not "rationalize" the plea bargaining process. Not only would plea negotiation assume a greater importance in this system than in our current sentencing regime, but this negotiation would take an even less desirable form — a form that would exhibit neither the shared discretion of today's charge bargaining nor the flexibility and honesty in the labeling of offenses of today's sentence bargaining. Plea bargaining would probably be more frequent; its effect would be more conclusive; and it would be bargaining of the least desirable type.

Of course I have spoken in terms of a simplified model — a "pure" fixed-sentencing system that none of today's reformers, to my knowledge, have advocated. The evaluation of detailed "real world" proposals becomes more complicated and the prediction of results more perilous. For one thing, many of today's reformers couple their proposals for increased certainty in sentencing with proposals for a substantial reduction in the severity of criminal punishments.[41] To the extent that the reformers accomplish this second objective, the plea bargaining leverage of prosecutors is likely to be reduced. A prosecutor who can threaten only a penalty of three years following a defendant's conviction at trial plainly has less bargaining power than a prosecutor who can threaten a sentence of twenty-five years.[42] Nevertheless, a caveat of Professor Franklin Zimring is worth repeating: "Once a determinate sentencing bill is before a legislative body, it takes only an eraser and pencil to make a one-year 'presumptive sentence' into a six-year sentence for the same offense."[43] Political forces may push sentencing reform away from the humanitarian objectives of its authors and toward a sterner model. Even when liberal reformers succeed initially in securing a reduction in penalties, cases in which a legislatively specified penalty seems too lenient will probably attract more attention than cases in which the penalty seems too severe. Politicians who cannot find any other issue on which to campaign can always propose an increase in the penalty for whatever crime is currently in the public eye.[44]

Individual prosecutors may, of course, respond to legislative reform in differing ways. Even when their bargaining powers are unrestricted, some prosecutors may sense that the exercise of these powers would be inconsistent with the legislature's desire for certainty. These prosecutors might try to "play it straight;" if the legislature thought that a person with one prior felony conviction who stabbed another person in the shoulder deserved four years' imprisonment, they might refuse to undercut this democratic judgment by "omitting the prior conviction" in exchange for a plea of guilty. Other prosecutors, however, might take a more flexible view, and county-by-county variations (or disparities) might result.

In the main, the new California sentencing statute seems to create a bargainer's paradise. The statute authorizes extended prison terms for offenders who have been previously sentenced to prison for other crimes, for offenders who were armed or who used firearms during the commission of their crimes, for offenders who deprived their victims of extraordinarily large amounts of property, and for offenders who inflicted personal injury while committing their crimes. In each instance, a prosecutor can apparently foreclose the additional punishment simply by failing to allege the relevant aggravating circumstance, and the prosecutor's decision can, of course, become the subject of a trade. The principal practical use of habitual offender and other statutory provisions for enhanced punishment in most states has, in fact, been to provide plea bargaining leverage; these provisions have been very rarely invoked except when defendants have asserted the right to trial. In addition, although the authorized sentences for felonies are commonly stated in terms of a three-year range — three, four or five years, for example — the trial judge is not authorized to select the most severe of these options unless the prosecutor has filed a motion alleging some aggravating circumstance (not a circumstance specified by the statute — *any* aggravating circumstance that strikes the prosecutor's fancy). Whether such a motion will be filed seems likely to become a frequent topic of discussion during plea negotiations, and of course a prosecutor can also agree not to oppose a defense attorney's efforts to obtain the least severe of the authorized terms. (A prosecutor might, indeed, add some sweetener to a bargain by agreeing to file a motion in mitigation of the defendant's punishment himself.) As I have noted, bargains for an award of probation are not limited by the new California statute. Finally and perhaps most importantly, the statute does not restrict the prosecutor's ability to substitute one charge for another in the plea bargaining process. Under this statute, some of the powers formerly exercised by the California Adult Authority will have been assumed by the legislature through its narrowing of the range of authorized penalties, and judges will also have slightly greater powers than in the past. The big winners, however, are the prosecutors.

The California statute does exhibit some countervailing tendencies. Formerly, the reduction of a first-degree murder charge to second-degree murder in California did not deprive the Adult Authority of the power to hold an offender in prison for the rest of his life. Under the new statute, a reduction to second-degree murder will make the difference between a sentence of death or life imprisonment (with or without the possibility of parole) and a term of five, six or seven years. In this offense area, the prosecutor's plea bargaining leverage — the value of a charge-reduction to second-degree murder — may have been increased.

Under the old code, however, a prosecutor could threaten an armed robber with a potential life sentence if he were convicted at trial. The offer of a probated sentence conditioned upon serving a county jail term of one year or less was therefore a very powerful lever. Under the new code, the maximum sentence for armed robbery when no injury has been inflicted and when a weapon has not been fired is five years (two, three or four years for the crime of robbery itself plus an additional year for being armed). In this offense area, although an offer of probation remains remarkably coercive, the prosecutor's bargaining leverage may have been reduced.[45] (Note, however, that a prosecutor can restore the prospect of life sentence if he can charge the defendant with kidnapping for the purpose of committing a robbery.)

As I have suggested, one consequence of the California Adult Authority's broad sentencing powers was that defense attorneys usually saw little point in plea bargaining when acceptance of the prosecutor's best offer would lead to a state prison sentence. Because prosecutors will now be able to bargain more specifically about the length of an offender's penitentiary confinement, the guilty-plea rate is very serious — or "automatic prison" — cases seems likely to increase. A second consequence of the Adult Authority's broad powers, however, was that prosecutors usually sought ways to avoid prison sentences when felony defendants were willing to plead guilty. Even in a relatively aggravated case, a prosecutor was likely to offer a charge-reduction to a misdemeanor or a "wobbler" (an offense that the court could treat either as a felony or as a misdemeanor) or to recommend an award of probation on the condition that the defendant serve a county jail term.

Bargaining patterns established in response to California's distinctive regime of indeterminate sentences may not change dramatically with the implementation of the new sentencing law. Perhaps the offer of county jail sentences even in rape and armed robbery cases became common because of the perceived necessities of the plea bargaining process when the Adult Authority reigned supreme. Nevertheless, the view that this sort of offer is appropriate may now have become internalized. Prosecutors may have persuaded themselves that their offers of county jail time in serious felony cases are just, or they may simply not pause to reconsider this established way of inducing guilty pleas merely because the new statute has been enacted. Under the new law, however, prosecutors will gain the power to make "intermediate" offers of relatively short prison sentences.

With this newfound power, the extraordinarily favorable (and extraordinarily coercive) offers of the past may gradually become less frequent. Of course a defendant who would have pleaded guilty in exchange for a county jail sentence followed by a term of probation may refuse to plead guilty in exchange for a two-year reduction in his prison term. Thus, although the guilty-plea rate in "automatic prison" cases may increase, the guilty-plea rate in other sorts of cases may decline. Prosecutors may, in other words, begin to offer only prison sentences in cases in which, for the sake of obtaining what was formerly the only available sort of bargain, they would have agreed to non-prison sentences in the past. One consequence may be an increase — perhaps even a dramatic increase — in the population of California's state prisons.

Although Chief Justice Burger has suggested that legislation affecting the work of the courts ought to be accompanied by a "judicial impact statement,"[46] the preparation of such a statement for California's new sentencing law is beyond my competence. There will be pulls in different directions, and much will depend upon the idiosyncratic responses of individual prosecutors in what will remain a highly discretionary regime. The persistence of unchecked prosecutorial power itself, however, is a dominant and probably fatal aspect of the California reform. In California as elsewhere, the proponents of sweeping change in our sentencing laws have ignored the ways in which our system of criminal justice is a system.[47]

Of course, in terms of doing its job, the machinery of criminal justice is sometimes not much of a system at all; the allegation that ours is a non-system whose left hand does not know or care what its right hand is doing may very often be accurate.[48] In terms of protecting its bureaucratic ways of processing criminal cases, however, the American system of criminal justice is indeed a system, and the effect of suppressing an injustice at one point in the criminal process may be to cause a comparable injustice to appear at some other point.[49] Reform of our amorphous regime of criminal justice is not impossible, but it is feasible only when one begins with a will to see it through. Without this commitment, the principal effect of sentencing reform will be to push the evils of excessive discretion toward an easy instrument of accommodation, the practice of plea bargaining.

Plea bargaining can be retained in a system of fixed or presumptive sentencing without undercutting the reformers' objectives, but only if its form is substantially altered. In place of the prosecutor's sentencing power, the legislature must specify the reward that will follow the entry of a plea of guilty. Just as a sentencing statute can treat the carrying of a firearm as an aggravating factor leading to an additional year's imprisonment, it can treat the entry of a plea of guilty as a mitigating factor leading to a specified reduction in penalty. Under such a statute — coupled, of course, with the elimination of plea bargaining by prosecutors — the "break" that follows the entry of a guilty plea would not depend upon the prosecutor's whim. It would not be affected by a prosecutor's feelings of friendship for particular defense attorneys, by his desire to go home early on an especially busy day, by his apparent inability to establish a defendant's guilt at trial, by his (or the trial judge's) unusually vindictive attitude toward a defendant's exercise of the right to trial, by the race, wealth or bail status of the defendant, by a defense attorney's success in threatening the court's or the prosecutor's time with dilatory motions, by the publicity that a case has generated, or by any of a number of other factors — irrelevant to the goals of the criminal process — that commonly influence plea bargaining today.[50]

The principal objection to a legislative regularization of the sentence differential between guilty-plea and trial defendants is probably that it would make the penalty that our system imposes for the exercise of a constitutional right so painfully apparent. Open articulation of the principle that makes our system of plea bargaining effective should indeed cause us to blush. Nevertheless, if sentencing reformers are unwilling to go this far toward channeling and controlling the plea bargaining process, perhaps they should abandon the reform effort. Determinate sentencing statues may not always make things worse, but without a major restriction of prosecutorial power, the reformers plainly will not accomplish the goal of more certain sentencing that they have sought so earnestly and, to a considerable extent, so rightly.

Some sentencing reformers may believe that prosecutorial discretion is more valuable than judicial discretion, and if so, they have things topsy-turvy. The reformers have levelled their attack — a basically well-founded if somewhat one-sided attack — on the form of discretion that is most frequently exercised "on the merits" of criminal cases for the purpose of taking differences in culpability into account. They have disregarded the form of discretion that is most frequently bent, manipulated, twisted and perverted in order to gain convictions when guilt cannot be proven, make the work of participants in the criminal justice system more comfortable, and save the money that might otherwise be required to implement the right to trial. If the reformers hope to do more than reallocate today's lawless sentencing power in such a way as to give prosecutors an even heavier club, they must exhibit greater courage. They must view the criminal justice system as a system, recognize that their belief in equal justice is currently challenged more by the practices of prosecutors than by those of trial judges, and bite the bullet on the question of plea bargaining.

DISCUSSION

U.S. Circuit Court Judge David Bazelon was invited to the podium to make a few remarks.

Bazelon opened with the reminder that one type of crime, street crimes of violence, had prompted the current interest in sentencing. "That's why we're here," he said. "Yet in this conference, and in most conferences, we don't talk about the kinds of crimes that brought us here."

He went on to remind the audience that such street crimes almost invariably were tied to the disadvantaged in society. "Let's not kid ourselves: there is social injustice," he said. "And we'd better start looking to see how that social injustice is connected to the crimes that frighten us."

"It's said that like crimes should be treated with like sentences," he continued. "Yet I must, I will, I still cling to the ideal of individualized justice. Others have recognized that in abandoning individualization here we make it progressively easier to abandon it elsewhere. I fear that if we shift from concern with the individual to mechanical principles of fairness, we may cease trying to learn as much as possible about the circumstances of life that may have brought the particular offender to the bar of justice."

A member of the audience then made several points. First, he said, he did not agree that the idea of determinate sentencing had swept the country as extensively as some speakers had implied. Secondly, he said that while rehabilitation was a central purpose of imprisonment in the rhetoric of the last 50 years, it had not been carried out in practice. Also, the purpose of a central sentencing authority such as a parole board could be to modify disparity, rather than to increase it.

Professor Alschuler replied that a centralized sentencing

agency might well be desirable. But he said centralization was a distinct issue from the timing of the sentencing decision. Current parole practices could be justified, he added, only if a prisoner's adjustment to institutional life and response to treatment programs were genuinely relevant to the amount of time he should be required to serve.

A prosecutor objected to Professor Alschuler's characterization of the prosecutor's role. Increased power for prosecutors was not a bad thing, he said. In California, he thought it necessary because in recent years imprisonment rates had been too low for violent crimes.

Another participant observed that there was evidence indicating that appellate review of sentencing had been avoided in the past by appellate courts because judges preferred to rely upon parole boards to reduce inequities.

One member of the audience asked Professor Alschuler what specific suggestions he had for controlling plea bargaining. What, he asked, about setting standards?

Professor Alschuler replied that he could not advocate standards for a process he would like to see eliminated. □

FOOTNOTES

1. In addition, governors exercise the power of executive clemency, and police officers sometimes make "stationhouse adjustments" that effectively impose penal sanctions.

2. See A. von Hirsch, *Doing Justice: The Choice of Punishments* (1976); *Fair And Certain Punishment: Report of the Twentieth Century Fund Task Force on Criminal Sentencing* (1976); D. Fogel, ". . . *We Are The Living Proof* . . .": *The Justice Model For Corrections* (1975); M. Frankel, *Criminal Sentences: Law Without Order* (1972). See also *Struggle For Justice: A Report on Crime and Punishment in America*, prepared for the American Friends Service Committee (1971); J. Mitford, *Kind and Usual Punishment: The Prison Business* (Vintage ed. 1974); *New York Times*, Dec. 6, 1975, p. 29, col. 1 (Senator Kennedy); *New York Times*, Feb. 3, 1976, p. 13, col. 1 (Attorney General Levi); *New York Times*, April 26, 1976, p. 1, col. 1 (President Ford).

3. See California Senate Bill No. 42, approved by the Governor, Sept. 20, 1976, filed with the Secretary of State, Sept. 21, 1976.

4. D. Rothman, Address to the Advisory Committee of the National Institute of Law Enforcement and Criminal Justice, Washington, D.C., Feb. 1976 (unpublished). Professor Alan M. Dershowitz prepared a short history of sentencing reform in America for the Twentieth Century Fund Task Force on

Criminal Sentencing. He noted that as early as 1787 Dr. Benjamin Rush proposed a system of indeterminate sentencing in which an offender's release from prison would depend upon his progress toward rehabilitation. In 1847, S. J. May argued against judicial sentencing on the ground that every offender should be held in prison "until the evil disposition is removed from his heart." The first indeterminate sentencing law in the United States, providing a three-year sentence for "common prostitutes" which could be terminated at any time by the inspectors of the Detroit House of Correction, was enacted at the behest of Zebulon R. Brockway in 1869. The following year, the National Prison Congress endorsed indeterminate sentencing with a religious fervor that persisted among prison officials in the decades that followed. Dershowitz, *Background Paper*, in *Fair and Certain Punishment, supra* note 2; see D. Fogel, *supra* note 2, at 1-64. Despite some noteworthy intellectual precursors dating back at least to Dr. Rush's proposal in the Eighteenth Century, the flowering of indeterminate sentencing has been a relatively recent phenomenon.

5. See, e.g., Martinson, "What Works? — Questions and Answers About Prison Reform," *The Public Interest,* Spring 1974, p. 22.

6. See N. Morris, *The Future of Imprisonment* (1974).

7. See, e.g., Ramsey, Book Review, 24 *Stanford Law Review* 965 (1972).

8. See, e.g., N. Morris, *supra* note 6, at 48.

9. J. Mitford, *supra* note 2, at 236-48.

10. See Calif. Penal Code §3000(a) (at the expiration of an inmate's determinate sentence less whatever "good time" credit he has earned, he "shall be released on parole for a period not exceeding one year, unless the board for good cause waives parole and discharges the inmate from custody. . . .").

11. E.g., Administrative Office of the United States Courts, "Federal Offenders in the United States District Courts 1971," Exhibit VII, at 13; Alschuler, "The Trial Judge's Role in Plea Bargaining, Part I," 76 *Columbia Law Review* 1059, 1085-86 n. 89 (1976).

12. See, Shin, "Do Lesser Pleas Pay?: Accommodations in the Sentencing and Parole Processes," 1 *Journal of Criminal Justice* 27 (1973).

13. Alschuler, "The Prosecutor's Role in Plea Bargaining," 36 *University of Chicago Law Review* 50, 101-03 & n. 29 (1968).

14. See pp. 20-24 *infra.*

15. Professor Phillip E. Johnson read a draft of this paper and commented that it was somewhat misleading to speak of the transfer of power to the prosecutor's office. Because defense attorneys are active participants in the negotiating process, Professor Johnson suggested that one might better refer to the enhanced power of *both* the prosecutor and his adversary. Of course defense attorneys do have a significant voice in the formulation of plea agreements. Nevertheless, after a defense attorney has made his arguments and exerted whatever plea bargaining leverage he can, a prosecutor must still determine what punishment is acceptable to the state before entering a plea agreement. In this sense, the input provided by the defense attorney can be viewed as one important influence on an official sentencing decision made by the prosecutor. Professor Johnson is certainly correct that a prosecutor's sentencing power is likely to be constrained by a variety of circumstances, and although I have continued to refer to prosecutorial power, I hope that my language does not convey too imperial an image.

16. A. von Hirsch, *supra* note 2, at 98.

17. Professor Dershowitz wrote that penal code revisions between 1790 and 1830 "reflected the views that certainty of punishment is more important than

severity of punishment," yet the statute that he cited to illustrate this proposition, a Massachusetts statute on maiming enacted in 1804, gave trial judges discretion to select any term of solitary imprisonment not exceeding ten years. Dershowitz, Background Paper, in *Fair and Certain Punishment, supra* note 2, at 85 & 134 n.6. Professor Dershowitz also quoted a 1750 Massachusetts statute which provided "that where there shall appear any circumstances to mitigate or alleviate any of the offenses against this act. . . it shall and may be lawful for the judges . . . to abate the whole of the punishment of whipping or such part thereof as they shall judge proper," and a 1676 Pennsylvania law which empowered judges to sentence offenders who were unable to pay a fine to "Corporal punishment not exceeding twenty Stripes, or do Service to Expiate the Crime." *Id.* at 133 n.2 & 134 n.5.

18. An Act Defining the Punishment to be Inflicted on Persons Guilty of the Crimes and Offenses Therein Mentioned, §4, Tenn., Dec. 3, 1807, in 1 E. Scott, "Laws of the State of Tennessee Including Those of North Carolina" 1056 (1821).

19. "An Act for the Punishment of Such Persons as Shall Procure or Commit Any Wilful Perjury," N. Car., April 8, 1777, in 1 E. Scott, *supra* note 20, at 155-56 (emphasis added). Many of the early Nineteenth Century statutes included in Scott's interesting volume provided for punishments such as a fine of not less than 50 or more than 1,000 dollars, imprisonment for not less than one nor more than 12 months, and whipping "on the bare back with a whip or cow-skin, with not less than ten nor more than 39 lashes." Later in the Nineteenth Century, terms of imprisonment became longer as state penitentiaries replaced local jails and as both capital and corporal punishment fell into disfavor, yet broad judicial sentencing discretion remained the norm. See e.g., "Revised Statutes of the Territory of Colorado," ch. 22, §44 (1868) ("Every person convicted of the crime of rape, shall be punished by confinement in the penitentiary for a term not less than one year, and such imprisonment may extend to life").

20. Calif. Penal Code §1170 (a) (1).

21. See Holmes-Laski Letters 806 (Howe ed. 1953).

22. C. Beccaria-Bonesana, "An Essay on Crimes and Punishment" 33 (Academic Reprints ed. 1953).

23. A. von Hirsch, *supra* note 2, at 69.

24. C. Beccaria-Bonesana, *supra* note 22, at 33.

25. Fixed and presumptive sentencing schemes have focused primarily on the sentence to be imposed for a single crime. Before being apprehended, however, an offender commonly will have committed five armed robberies, or will have made 150 fraudulent entries in his employer's books, or will have sold 1,000 counterfeit lottery tickets. To multiply a legislatively fixed or presumptive sentence five or 150 or 1,000 times in this situation seems manifestly unjust, yet simply to disregard the defendant's "additional" crimes seems at least equally improper. None of today's reformers have devised a non-discretionary formula for weighing multiple crimes that seems equitable in all situations.

The approach of the new California statute toward this problem is better than most. When a judge imposes consecutive sentences for multiple felonies, the aggregate sentence is limited to "the greatest term of imprisonment imposed by the judge for any of the crimes, including any enhancements . . . plus one-third of the middle term of imprisonment prescribed for each other felony conviction for which a consecutive term of imprisonment is imposed without such enhancements." Calif. Penal Code §1170.1a (a). In addition, the aggregate sentence imposed for crimes other than the "base" offense cannot exceed five years. Id. §1170.1a(e). The decision whether to impose consecutive sentences, however, is left to the judge's discretion. In multiple-crime situations, this discretion seems necessary, and indeed, more discretion might well be desirable.

Of course, under the new California statute, additional crimes can lead to additional punishment only when they are alleged and proven; neither the trial judge nor correctional authorities can take additional crimes into account informally to any great extent in determining the sentence for a single offense. Although this reform will promote procedural fairness in sentencing, it may, in some instances, lead to more complicated trials. In the past, a prosecutor might have decided to charge only a few offenses in a particular case, knowing that conviction of these offenses would give the sentencing authority sufficient power to punish uncharged offenses as well.

26. The new statute does direct the California Judicial Council to adopt rules to promote uniformity in the grant or denial of probation as well as to promote uniformity in resolving other sentencing problems, such as whether to impose consecutive or concurrent sentences. Calif. Penal Code §1170.3.

27. Additional illustrations are provided by the "guided discretion" capital punishment statutes favored by the Supreme Court in *Greg v. Georgia,* 428 U.S. 153 (1976), and its companion cases. A defendant convicted of capital murder might wish to make the following speech to the jury about to consider whether capital punishment should be imposed: "I am deeply sorry for my crime, which I recognize was about as bad as any that can be imagined. I did, in fact, go to the police station shortly after the killing to surrender and make a full confession. Although I have done some terrible things in my life, you may wish to know, before deciding whether I should live or die, that I have also done some good. I once risked my life in combat to save five comrades — an action for which I was awarded the Silver Star — and for the last 10 years I have personally cared for my invalid mother while supporting five younger brothers and sisters." The mitigating factors listed in today's capital punishment statutes are sometimes quite general, but none that I have seen in any statute would permit a jury to consider any of the circumstances mentioned in this defendant's speech (or, for that matter, any other evidence of pre-crime virtue or post-crime remorse). Apparently the Florida statue upheld in *Proffitt v. Florida,* 428 U.S. 242 (1976), would not; yet the Supreme Court pluarlity, seemingly oblivious to the statute's limitations, declared in a companion case, "A jury must be allowed to consider on the basis of all relevant evidence not only why a death sentence should be imposed, but also why it should not be imposed." *Jurek v. Texas,* 428 U.S. 262, 271 (1976).

28. In addition to its illustrative armed robbery statute, the Twentieth Century Fund Task Force provided a brief description of how it might treat a number of other crimes. This description is forcefully dissected in Zimring, "Making the Punishment Fit the Crime: A Consumer's Guide to Sentencing Reform," *Hastings Center Report,* Dec. 1976, p. 13.

29. See L. Wilkins, J. Kress, D. Gottfredson, J. Calpin & A. Gelman, Sentencing Guidelines: Structuring Judicial Discretion: Final Report of the Feasibility Study (1976).

30. See "Memorandum to Members of the El Paso County Bar From Judges of the Criminal District Courts," Dec. 16, 1975 (unpublished). The El Paso "point system for sentencing" is substantially less sophisticated than that which Wilkins, Kress and their associates are developing. Without the aid of a computer, an LEAA grant, or a detailed study of past sentencing practices,

Judge Callan devised it one day while sitting in a bathtub. El Paso's sentencing reform is especially interesting, however, because the district court judges coupled it with a prohibition of prosecutorial plea bargaining (a prohibition that seems to have been entirely effective). I intend to describe and evaluate the El Paso experiment in a forthcoming article.

31. A similarly promising approach is incorporated in S. 1437, the compromise proposal for a revised federal criminal code introduced by Senators McClellan and Kennedy. This bill would establish a United States Sentencing Commission and direct it to prescribe a "suggested sentencing range . . . for each category of offense involving each category of defendant." A federal judge who imposed a sentence outside the suggested range would be required to state his reasons, and the sentence that he imposed would ordinarily be subject to appellate review. S. 1437, 95th Cong., 1st Sess. (1977).

32. In practice, the initial formulation of charges by a prosecutor's office is a substantially less important component of the sentencing process than plea bargaining. Indeed, prosecutors may generally exercise too little sentencing discretion at the charge-formulation stage rather than too much. One vice of the plea bargaining system is that it encourages prosecutors mechanically to charge "the highest and the most" at the outset and to withhold the exercise of any equitable discretion until they can receive something in return. (Of course this analysis refers only to the formulation of charges in cases that prosecutors have tentatively decided to pursue to conviction. Prosecutorial "diversion," like plea bargaining, is commonly a device for securing a restriction of liberty without the bother and expense of trial, and this form of prosecutorial sentencing should be analyzed in similar terms.)

33. Dershowtiz, Background Paper, in *Fair and Certain Punishment, supra* note 2, at 81.

34. Judge Frankel, for example, briefly mentioned that "the great majority (ranging in some jurisdictions to around 90 percent) of those formally charged with crimes plead guilty," but Judge Frankel did not consider the bargaining process that lies behind this lopsided figure and its substantial impact on sentencing. See M. Frankel, *supra* note 2, at vii.

35. A trial judge's sentencing discretion is ordinarily limited by the range of penalties that the legislature has provided for a particular offense, but a prosecutor who is dissatisfied with the range of penalties authorized for one offense can frequently use his charging power to substitute another.

36. *Fair and Certain Punishment, supra* note 2, at 26-27.

37. D. Fogel, *supra* note 2, app. III at 300 (70 per cent disapproval; 21 per cent approval; 9 per cent "don't know").

38. Alschuler, *supra* note 11, at 1063-67.

39. This form of bargaining would be even more explicit, and even less subject to judicial review, than today's sentence bargaining. A defendant who is offered a specific sentence recommendation today in exchange for a plea of guilty can usually be almost certain that the recommended sentence will be imposed, but there remains some chance that the trial judge will reject the prosecutor's proposal. Moreover, the sentence that would follow a conviction at trial is rarely made explicit in sentence bargaining today. The greater explicitness of the plea bargaining process in a system of fixed sentencing would, of course, have its advantages, particularly in terms of letting each defendant know the consequences of his choice of plea, but it would make the coercive character of the guilty plea system all the more apparent.

40. See Alschuler, *supra* note 11, at 1136-46.

41. Von Hirsch, for example, recommends adoption of "a [sentencing] scale whose highest penalty (save, perhaps, for the offense of murder) is five years — with sparing use made of sentences of imprisonment for more than three years." A. von Hirsch, *supra* note 2, at 136. At least in an aggravated murder case involving an Eichmann, a Speck, or a Manson, the public will undoubtedly insist — as I confess that I think it should — on the power to hold the offender in prison for the rest of his life; and if life sentences have an appropriate place in a scheme of penalties for murder, it may attach too much importance to the results of criminal conduct (for example, whether an offender has killed or has merely turned his victim into a comatose "vegetable") to limit the penalty for all other crimes to five years' imprisonment.

Consider a not very unusual case that recently arose in my jurisdiction. Two young men entered a small liquor store owned by an elderly couple. One of the men took a bottle of Scotch from the shelf and brought it down hard on the head of the male store owner. He then gouged and twisted the jagged neck of the bottle into the store owner's neck, causing several deep wounds. At this point, the woman store owner emerged from a back room. The second robber hit her in the face with his fist and then administered a brutal and disfiguring beating while she lay helpless on the floor. Police photographs of the victims' wounds were more than enough to inflame even relatively hardened passions.

Von Hirsch proposes a two-dimensional sentencing "grid" with 20 different penalty levels determined by (1) the seriousness of the crime and (2) the offender's prior criminal record. If one assumes that the robbers in this case had no significant prior records, they would not be eligible for the "top," five-year penalty but only for some unspecified penalty four or five notches down the scale. This penalty — apparently "somewhere between 18 months and three years" — seems to me inadequate. I have read about "false positives" and the dangers of prediction, but I would not want to meet these violent offenders on the street or in a liquor store until they were at least a decade older than they are today. If past experience is any guide, moreover, my orientation is probably less punitive than that of most state legislators. The chance that the von Hirsch proposal would prove politically acceptable may therefore be small, and an evaluation of the likely effects of sentencing reform should probably not proceed on the assumption that this kind of change in penalty levels can be effected.

Von Hirsch's proposal suggests another possible defect of fixed-sentencing schemes, for it would make warning and unconditional release "the prescribed penalty for the least serious offenses." So minimal penalty may be appropriate in many cases, but whether it should be advertised in advance as the *only* possible sanction for certain crimes is a somewhat different question. Presumably behavior should not be made criminal at all unless it involves a significant departure from community standards of morality, and when an offender knows that he does not risk even so much as a fine if apprehended, he may conclude that he has a "license" to engage in criminal behavior. (Forgive me if I sound like the former prosecutor I am.) A degree of uncertainty concerning the community's response to crime may have deterrent virtue, and although the sanctions that we threaten as well as those that we impose should be limited by considerations of just desert, it does not seem inconsistent with this principle to bark a bit harder than we will probably want to bite in the "typical" case.

42. See A. von Hirsch, *supra* note 2, at 104-05. In one sense, prosecutorial power may also be restricted when a fixed or presumptive sentencing scheme

does not reduce the aggregate severity of criminal penalties but merely "evens out disparities" by limiting departures from a previously established "norm." This sort of sentencing scheme can best be viewed as having two countervailing components. First, it limits the ability of prosecutors to threaten unusually harsh, "exemplary" penalties for defendants who stand trial and in that sense reduces prosecutorial bargaining power. Second, this scheme effectively establishes mandatory minimum sentences for offenses and thus gives prosecutors the kind of bargaining leverage commonly observed today when mandatory penalties have been enacted.

43. Zimring, *supra* note 28, at 17.

44. This danger cannot necessarily be eliminated by assigning the task of setting presumptive sentences to a commission or other nonlegislative body. Once a commission has established a seemingly lenient presumptive sentence for a particular offense, the pressure for legislative revision is likely to be much greater than when the legislature has established a broad range of sentences for that offense and when judges have imposed a variety of sentences within this range (even if the average judicial sentence is every bit as lenient as the presumptive sentence that a commission would approve).

Of course our system of discretionary sentencing cannot reasonbly be defended on the ground that it enables criminal justice officials to fool most of the people most of the time. If the popular will favors more severe sentences than judges in fact impose, the popular will should probably prevail. Nevertheless, the imperfections of the democratic process seem especially pronounced in the criminal justice area, and I suspect that the popular will is sometimes misperceived. In the course of working on a state penal code revision, for example, I was struck by the manner in which "liberal" proposals were abandoned or defeated although almost no one seemed to oppose them on the merits. The first modification of a proposal was likely to occur when it was presented to a reporters' group composed primarily of academics. Some reporters would explain that they favored the proposal as drafted but that the state bar committee on the revision of the penal code would not and that it was necessary to be "realistic." The proposal would be further modified by the state bar committee on the ground that, although most committee members favored it, the board of directors of the state bar would not. Then the board of directors would repeat the process, noting that the proposal could not be "sold" to the legislature in its current form. Finally, individual legislators would explain that they had no personal quarrel with the draft submitted by the state bar but that it would be unacceptable to their constituents. In talking with a constituent or two on the next seat of the Greyhound Bus, however, I usually found that they were not the yahoos that had been depicted and that they favored the proposal as it had first been presented to the reporters' group.

Apart from the general tendency to perceive the rest of the world as less progressive than oneself, there is a difference between making sentencing decisions "in the large" and making them "in the specific." People may sound vindictive in conversations about criminal justice issues with pollsters (a phenomenon that may be attributable in part to the kind of leadership that politicians often provide in this area), yet the same people may be decent and humane when confronted with specific cases. In El Paso, Texas, a few years ago, District Attorney Steve Simmons announced a policy of opposing probated sentences in burglary cases, even those involving first offenders. Simmons had apparently concluded that this policy would be popular, and indeed it probably was. After some resistance, El Paso's district judges decided that they could not withstand the political pressure exerted by the District Attorney's office, and as a result, virtually all burglary defendants exercised the option of being sentenced by juries. In at least 90 percent of all first-offense burglary cases, juries — composed of people who may well have nodded their general approval of the District Attorney's policy when they read about it in the newspapers — awarded probated sentences. Similarly, Governor James R. Thompson of Illinois recently proposed that fondling should be included in a group of "X-rated felonies" carrying severe mandatory penalties. Governor Thompson is an astute political leader, and his proposal probably did not run counter to the sentiment of the times. In observing the treatment of a number of fondling cases in court and in the plea bargaining process, however, I have been impressed by the magnanimity that the families of the victims generally seem to exhibit. Typically, a defendant has inflicted substantial psychic injury upon a young child, and the child's parents appear in court in a distraught condition. More often than not, however, these parents agree that the appropriate social response to the crime is merely to provide psychiatric assistance to the offender, and with the parents' consent many fondling cases are "diverted" from the criminal justice system prior to conviction.

This analysis does not suggest that if popular sentiment truly favors tougher sentences, that sentiment should be defeated through manipulation or deception. It does suggest that "the people" themselves and their representatives should consider whether sentencing decisions cannot best be made "in the specfiic." It is consistent with democratic values for popularly elected legislatures and for the public to recognize the dangers of excessive severity that are likely to arise when sentencing decisions are made on too abstract a basis.

45. The authors of the new California statute apparently determined the presumptive penalties for particular felonies primarily by examining the amount of time that the Adult Authority had required offenders to serve for those felonies in the past. It might therefore seem that a reduction of one charge to another should have about the same effect under the new statute as under the old. Under the old statute, however, defendants and defense attorneys undoubtedly have less complete knowledge of the Adult Authority's sentencing practices than they did of the range of legislatively authorized penalties, and they probably responded more to the latter than to the former. In addition, even a defendant with detailed knowledge of the Adult Authority's practices was likely to be a "risk-averter" and concerned about the danger that he might receive a more severe sentence than the norm. Most importantly, a defendant who had been charged initially with a more serious crime than that to which he had pleaded guilty was very likely to be treated more severely by the Adult Authority than other defendants in the same conviction category. See Alschuler, *supra* note 16, at 96 ("San Francisco defense attorney Benjamin M. Davis adds, 'All the charges against a defendant may be dismissed except one. But if the defendant is sentenced to the penitentiary and comes before the Adult Authority, those super-judges will want to know all about the ten robberies' "); J. Mitford, *supra* note 5, at 101 ("The Adult Authority's official orientation booklet states: 'The offense for which a man is committed is only one of the factors that the AA considers when making a decision.' Other factors may be (and often are) crimes for which the prisoner was arrested but never brought to trial. . . .").

46. Burger, "The State of the Federal Judiciary — 1972," 58 A.B.A.J. 1049, 1050 (1972); see Chief Justice Burger's 1977 report to the American Bar Association, 63 A.B.A.J. 504 (1977).

47. At the conference at which this paper was initially presented, Professor Raymond I. Parnas, one of the principal authors of the new California statute, protested that he and his colleagues had indeed considered the relationship between this statute and prosecutorial sentencing power. Professor Parnas did not, however, deny that the California statute would substantially augment the bargaining power of prosecutors, nor did he argue that this enhanced prosecutorial power was either desirable or consistent with the professed objectives of the statute. By contrast, D. Lowell Jensen, the District Attorney of Alameda County, did argue that enhanced prosecutorial discretion was desirable. He observed that many prosecutors had supported enactment of the California statute for exactly this reason.

48. Consider, for example, the case of a friend of mine who recently received a ticket for careless driving and who was convinced that she was innocent. With some indignation, she went to the courthouse to tell her story to the judge. Prior to trial, a city prosecutor approached and offered various concessions in exchange for a plea of guilty, but my friend resisted his efforts. The prosecutor finally said, "What about a dismissal? Would you agree to take a defensive driving course if I dropped the charge?" My friend, still reluctant, was willing at least to consider the possibility. "Is it a good course," she asked, "or just some sanctimonious Mickey Mouse?" "Lady," the prosecutor said, "I don't know anything about the course. Do you want the dismissal or don't you?" In this incident, the prosecutor used the powers of his office to pressure a possibly innocent defendant into a program whose content he did not know and whose utility he had never considered.

49. See D. Oaks & W. Lehman, A *Criminal Justice System and the Indigent* 178-96 (1968).

50. The use of administrative rule-making procedures and the formulation of internal guidelines for prosecutorial decision making might help to reduce the influence of these extraneous factors. See, e.g., Vorenberg, "Narrowing the Discretion of Criminal Justice Officials," 1976 *Duke Law Journal* 651, 681-83. I am not convinced, however, that guidelines could domesticate prosecutorial sentencing power to such an extent that plea bargaining by prosecutors would become compatible with the objectives of today's sentencing reformers.

First, just as it is difficult or impossible for legislatures to specify all relevant sentencing factors in advance, it is difficult or impossible for prosecutors to do so. Guidelines may tend to be so general as to provide only minimal constraints on a prosecutor's discretion. Of course it is hard to quarrel in the abstract with the ideal of the rule of law. When a governmental decision-making process can be reduced to a formula that will yield justice in a substantial majority of cases, the development of rules and guidelines usually does seem worthwhile. Nevertheless, the test of the pudding is in the eating; the problem of balancing justice in the individual case against the desirability of legal rules cannot be resolved without regard to the specific problem at hand; and rather than call for less discretion and more rules in an abstract way, it would be desirable for the scholars currently enamored of this approach actually to try their hands at drafting some useful guidelines.

Second, even reasonably specific guidelines may prove delusive in practice. Prosecutorial guidelines seem to be frequently honored in the breach, see, e.g., Georgetown University Law Center Institute of Criminal Law and Procedure, "Plea Bargaining in the United States: Phase I Report" 33, 124 (1977), and indeed these guidelines may sometimes be intended more for show than for implementation. In Houston, Texas, the District Attorney once announced a policy against recommending less than a ten-year sentence in any case of robbery by firearm, yet a number of Houston defense attorneys told me of cases in which their skillful bargaining had led to less severe prosecutorial sentence recommendations for their clients. Most of these defense attorneys seemed unaware that other attorneys were achieving the same success, and it gradually became apparent that the District Attorney's announced policy serviced in practice as a sales device comparable to that of some Maxwell Street clothing merchants: "Our usual price in a case of robbery by firearm is ten years, but for *you* . . . ." Partly because plea bargaining policies are usually subject to ill-defined exceptions for "weak cases," this sort of evasion does seem common. In addition, prosecutors frequently subvert office policies by taking "unofficial" positions "off the record" and by agreeing "not to oppose" actions that they cannot affirmatively recommend. Dale Tooley, the District Attorney in Denver, commented that his office had developed guidelines for a variety of prosecutorial decisions and had generally found them useful. He added, however, "I have yet to see the policy that an assistant district attorney couldn't get around when he wanted to." Personal interview, July 11, 1977. Although one might of course provide for judicial review at the behest of disgruntled citizens (or perhaps some other device for enforcing prosecutorial rules at least on occasion), it is far from clear that this mechanism would yield beneficial results as often as it proved burdensome and oppressive.

18

THE PAROLE HEARING
Decision or Justification

ROBERT M. GARBER and CHRISTINA MASLACH

A detailed content analysis of tape-recordings of 100 randomly selected California parole hearings revealed that these hearings take the form of short, unstructured diagnostic interviews in which the hearing officers ask questions of the prisoners who respond in a very minimal way. Different patterns of questioning and prisoner response occurred for hearings where the eventual decision was to grant parole as opposed to deny parole, and this decision outcome could be predicted with a high degree of accuracy by discriminant function analyses. In general, the hearing officers made their own psychological assessments of the prisoners, even though they lacked knowledge and training in this diagnostic skill. According to the results of this study, the parole decision-making process appears to be a reliable one, but nevertheless its validity is questionable.

INTRODUCTION

Many decisions cannot be made easily, given that they require the rejection of one or more plausible courses of action. However, they become especially difficult when they: (1) are based on minimal information; (2) involve ambiguous standards or criteria; or (3) result in serious consequences (such as life or death). When all of these factors are present, there is very little basis for arriving at a reasonable decision with any degree of confidence. And yet, this is precisely the type of situation that exists in the parole hearing, where decisions must be made continually about whether or not a prisoner is to be released from prison. Information is minimal because the hearing lasts only a matter of minutes. The concepts of "rehabilitation" and "good parole

*This research was prepared as expert testimony for *Van Geldern v. Kerr,* Civil No. C-72-2088 SAW, at the request of Sidney Wolinsky of Public Advocates, Inc., San Francisco, attorney for the plaintiffs. Preparation of this manuscript was funded by Biomedical Sciences Support Grant 3-S05-RR-07006-08S1 to the junior author. We wish to thank Paula Flamm and Desdemona Cardoza for their help in the coding phase of the research, and Rick Jacobs and Curtis Hardyck for their assistance in the data analysis.
†Department of Psychology, University of California at Berkeley.

risk" are extremely ambiguous, and there are no clear guidelines as to what behavioral objectives are required for parole. Finally, the consequences of the decision are obviously serious since, from the prisoner's viewpoint, it could mean freedom or another year behind bars, while from the hearing officer's perspective, it could mean sending back to the community either a rehabilitated citizen who has paid his dues or a person who will further prey on society by committing more crimes.

THE PAROLE SYSTEM IN CALIFORNIA

Indeterminate sentencing has been viewed as a tool for treatment and rehabilitation. Its goal is to allow offenders to be kept in custody as long as necessary in order to effect the desired changes in their individual character and to ensure that they will not be released until they no longer present a threat to the community — either economic or physical. When this desired rehabilitation has been accomplished, the prisoner is placed on parole, a limited freedom where he is released to the community under the supervision of a parole officer. For male felons in California, the decision to release an inmate from prison prior to the final expiration of his sentence has been a responsibility delegated exclusively to an administrative board called the California Adult Authority. The decisions are made within the wide-ranging minimum and maximum terms for specified crimes (e.g., five years to life for first-degree robbery) which are set by the state legislature and are applied by trial judges.[1]

In theory, the parole decision is a "balanced scientific decision made by experts, at a comparatively leisurely pace, upon ample and accurate information accumulated in the real-life, post-conviction milieu" (Parsons-Lewis, 1972, p. 1523). Traditionally these decision-makers have been considered skilled experts in human behavior, capable of weighing all relevant data fairly and knowingly. In practice, however, this is not the case. The decision to grant or deny parole is made following a brief hearing conducted by two members of the Adult Authority staff (usually career corrections personnel) with the prisoner present. Such a hearing is generally held only once a year for each prisoner who is eligible for parole.

In conducting this hearing, the policy priorities considered by the Adult Authority in their decision to grant or deny parole are, according to their 1973 policy statement: (1) protection of society, (2) punishment of the offender, (3) deterrence of crime, and (4) rehabilitation of the criminal. There are, however, no specific guidelines beyond these general priorities, since the Adult Authority purposely has no formal published criteria for its decisions. Instead of applying a set standard of protection and punishment, the Adult Authority operates on the assumption that no two

---

[1]Subsequent to the completion of this research and its presentation as expert evidence by the authors in the July 1976 court hearing of Van Geldern v. Kerr, the California State Legislature enacted a new sentencing law which took effect July 1, 1977. The new law abolished the existing indeterminate sentencing system (which had been in effect for 60 years) and replaced it with a determinate sentencing system. Under this new system, there are fixed sentences for various crimes (as set by the legislature), and thus there is no need for a system in which the decision to release a prisoner is continually under review. In spite of this change in the California parole system, the current research is still important for the understanding it provides of the previous California system and for similar decision-making institutions elsewhere.

prisoners are alike, and "therefore, no specific criteria can be developed which will apply to all cases" (Kerr, 1972, p. 8). On the one hand, this flexible policy reflects a stated concern for the unique and individual qualities of each prisoner being considered for parole. But, on the other, it creates a serious problem of ambiguity and a lack of objective, standardized procedures for both the hearing officers and the prisoners. Without common practices yielding comparable decisions in similar cases, such decision-making suffers from injustices that are a source of considerable frustration and hostility among inmates.

Research on Parole Decision-Making

Although the decision to grant or deny parole is central to the concepts of indeterminate sentencing and individual treatment, there presently exists relatively little empirical research on the topic. In addition, researchers have traditionally focused on inmates in studies of parole success and recidivism instead of on the decision-makers themselves and the bases for their decisions. One reason for this apparent emphasis on outcome rather than process has been the assumption that the decision-makers are skilled experts. However, this assumption, along with others about the parole system, has recently begun to be challenged.

Over the past few years in California, questions about the operation of the parole and sentencing system have been raised through efforts in the State Legislature towards modification of the indeterminate sentencing laws. In preparation for this new legislation, several committees undertook studies of sentencing and parole decision-making. The results of these investigations, which relied primarily on unsystematic interviews with parole policy-makers, have portrayed the parole bureaucracy in a very uncomplimentary light. Both the report of the California Assembly Criminal Procedure Committee (1968) and the report of the California Assembly Select Committee on the Administration of Justice (1970) stated that the criteria for parole decisions had no rationally justified basis and were arbitrary and unscientific. More recently, a report by the California State Bar Association (1975) reached similar conclusions and recommended the abolition of the Adult Authority and a procedure for release review hearings in which the prisoner was entitled to procedural due process, representation by counsel, and the right to call and cross-examine relevant witnesses.

On several occasions, parole decision-makers have reported their own views of the parole process in systematic surveys. In the most extensive study of this kind (Gottfredson & Ballard, 1965), questionnaires were completed by employees of the Youth and Adult Corrections Agency, which included all members of the Adult Authority as well as the Board of Trustees of the California Institution for Women. These questionnaires were designed to assess the institutional goals (as viewed by the respondent) and the factors used in making a parole decision. Of the 25 goals listed, only two were rated as very important: "protect the public" and "release inmates at the optimal time for most probable success on parole." One factor was rated as very important in parole decisions — "past record of assaultive offenses." In a more recent study (Aitken, 1975), where Adult Authority members were questioned about the factors they considered in parole decisions, the factors that predominated were: (1) original crime, (2) behavior in prison, (3) attitude of the inmate, and (4) outside influences (e.g., political climate; letters from prosecutors, judges, or victims). While such studies provide some interesting insights into the beliefs of hearing officers, it is important to note that these self-reports leave unanswered questions of how and to what extent these allegedly important factors actually influence decision-making in the parole hearing.

An alternative approach has been simulations of the parole decision process. One recent simulation study conducted by Wilkins, Gottfredson, Robison, and Sadowsky (1973) was designed to evaluate what information about the convict makes up the basic core relevant to the parole decision. To do this, Wilkins et al. asked their subjects, who included staff from the United States Parole Board, to consider 50 bits of information on 26 "typical" cases selected from actual case files. They found that, on the average, subjects used 40% of the information available to them in order to arrive at a final decision. The bits of information most often selected were: (1) the official version of the commitment offense, (2) the inmate's version of the same offense, (3) the time already served, (4) the type of prior offenses by the inmate, and (5) the age of the offender.

Over-all, although patterns did emerge with regard to the bits of information used to reach a decision, the results failed to reveal any detailed basis for these decisions which would discriminate cases paroled from those denied. Instead, Wilkins et al. found considerable disparity in the information selected by different decision-makers in the course of making their decision. This finding leads to the conclusion that the same decision by different decision-makers is often reached in widely different ways — and different parole decisions reached by similar routes. The researchers hypothesize that the major element in the parole decision is the decision-maker's own view of making the continued punishment fit the original crime.

Other simulation studies of the parole decision process lend further support to this hypothesis. Takagi (1967), in his study of the California parole agency, showed that parole outcome can be viewed largely as a function of the parole agent (agents who supervise ex-convicts already released on parole) and organizational orientation (also see Takagi & Robison, 1969). Kingsnorth (1969) found similar biases in the way individual agents differ in the types of information they choose to report and in the impact of that information on their decisions. Kingsnorth concluded that "decisions are made on an intuitive basis so that discharge from parole is dependent on circumstances of time and place rather than on any systematic assessment of relevant data" (p. 217).

The potential impact of this "hunch" approach to decision-making is highlighted in an earlier study by Hakeem (1961). The purpose was to see if experienced parole officers could accurately predict parole outcomes. To do this, Hakeem compiled case summaries of 200 former parolees, half of whom violated parole and half of whom completed parole successfully and were discharged. He then asked a group of experienced parole agents to read and classify the case summaries according to which parolees would succeed or fail on parole. In addition, he asked a group of accountants to do the same thing. The results of this study indicated that the parole officers were slightly worse judges of parole outcome than the accountants, but that neither group made better predictions than would have resulted from chance alone. Furthermore, the parole agents showed a systematic bias in the direction of predicting failure even though the case summaries were evenly divided between success and failure.

Over-all, the available research on parole decision-making (of which the above is a limited review) paints a rather confused and conflicting picture. While individual decision-makers convey to investigators a process delineated by clearly ordered priorities and decision-making criteria, the impression given by the various committee reports and simulation studies is one of an arbitrary decision process which is based on subjective factors and infused with the individual bias of the decision-maker. In weighing the importance of these conclusions, the limitations of the various research approaches must be taken into account. Clearly, the studies of decision-makers and decision-making practices are of questionable validity when the conclusions are based entirely on self-reports and obvious post hoc simulations of the actual process. Some major questions that need to be addressed concern the actual operation of the parole decision-making system. How are the principles of rehabilitation and indeterminate sentencing applied in the practice of parole decisions? What is the correspondence between the self-reports of the decision-makers and their actual behavior in parole hearings? What variables operating in the interaction between hearing officer and inmate predict the likelihood of a given parole decision? And finally, what is the contribution, if any, of the prisoners to this parole decision-making process?

CURRENT RESEARCH

The present research evolved from the recently generated public interest in the administration and practice of parole decision-making. In addition to new laws, one result of this concern was the instigation of numerous legal actions in both state and federal courts. One of these legal actions, the federal lawsuit of Van Geldern v. Kerr, Civil No. C-72-2088 SAW, provided the data for the present study. Van Geldern is a class-action lawsuit which was heard before Judge Stanley Weigel of San Francisco in July, 1976.[2] It was brought by prisoners in California in an attempt to challenge existing parole procedures by asking for constitutional due process safeguards in the administration of parole hearings. These hearings are ordinarily not recorded or open to the public, but it was necessary to gain access to them in order to present the case for trial to the court. The needed access was obtained through a court order allowing the attorneys to tape-record these previously closed Adult Authority proceedings. The current research utilized the tape-recordings generated by the discovery order and was designed to provide a content analysis of these parole hearings for use by the court.

The main goals of this exploratory analysis were threefold. First, the study attempted to provide a valid and systematic assessment of parole hearings in operation, describing the form and content of the interactions that normally take place behind closed doors. Second, the study tried to deduce the decision-making rules used by the hearing officers to either grant or deny parole. Finally, the third goal was to assess the congruity between the principles of the individual treatment model and their implementation into the parole decisions that were actually made.

---

[2]As of this writing (September 1977), the court has yet to make a ruling.

METHOD

Subjects

The subjects in this study were the hearing officers and prisoners present at 100 parole hearings of the California Adult Authority during the months of September and October 1974. This sample of hearings was randomly selected from an available pool of over 300 tape-recorded hearings. The hearings took place at San Quentin and Vacaville prisons where permission to tape-record parole hearings had been granted for discovery in the case of Van Geldern v. Kerr. The actual tape-recording of the hearings was directed and supervised by the law firm of Public Advocates, Inc. which represented the plaintiffs.[3]

Coding Instruments

Three independent content analyses were developed for scoring the Van Geldern tapes. The first analysis coded the variety and frequency of topics discussed by the hearing officers, as well as the manner in which they were raised (Adult Authority Content Analysis). The second analysis coded the variety and frequency of the comments made by the prisoners and the responses of the hearing officers to these comments (Prisoners' Response Content Analysis). The third analysis coded certain topic patterns and a series of legal questions pertaining specifically to the objectives of the lawsuit itself (Legal Analysis). An analysis was also made of several time-related variables.

Adult Authority Content Analysis. The Adult Authority coding instrument was a two-dimensional matrix comprised of 18 subject categories and four process categories (for a total of 72 cells). The subject categories were the content topics generally discussed during the course of parole hearings. They included: prior life style of the prisoner (before incarceration), prior criminal behavior, paroles and revocations, commitment offense, legal records, prison custody (classification and discipline record), prison rehabilitation, prison associations (activities other than rehabilitation), prior parole hearings, current parole hearing and criteria for parole, psychological assessment (hearing officer's reference to the prisoner's psychological state), psychological reports (psychological assessment of the prisoner made by the prison psychological staff), prisoner's health, medical evaluation, prisoner's physical appearance, post-release activities, post-release support (prisoner's future contact with parole officer, or use of psychological or medical care), and unscored content.

---

[3]The court order required that prisoners be informed of the purpose of the tape-recording and that they have the option to refuse such recording of their hearing. A written consent form was presented to each prisoner prior to his hearing, and he indicated whether he did or did not consent to the tape-recording. This signed consent form was reviewed orally by the hearing officer at the start of the hearing in order to ensure that the prisoner understood the options available to him. Ninety-four percent of the prisoners who had hearings during the sample period gave their consent for tape-recordings, while 6% exercised their option to refuse. The written consent of the hearing officers was not required by the court order since they were acting in their role as public officials. Special measures were taken during the coding of the tapes to mask identifying information so that the responses of both prisoners and hearing officers were anonymous and confidential.

The process categories referred to the manner in which the various subject categories were raised during the hearing. They included: question, informational statement, judgment (evaluation of prisoner in terms of hearing officer's personal judgment), and advice. Each content unit was scored by checking the appropriate one of the 72 subject × process cells of the scoring matrix.

Prisoners' Response Content Analysis. The prisoners' response coding instrument was a two-dimensional matrix comprised of 20 prisoner behavior categories and four hearing officer response categories (for a total of 80 cells). The prisoner behavior categories represented the content and style of the prisoner's self-presentation to the hearing officers. These categories included: asks question or shows confusion; general complaints; complaints about prison programs or facilities; complaints about legal issues or fairness of the hearing; minimal responses (responses which show little initiative by the prisoner to go beyond a recitation of details to answer a question) about general topics; minimal responses about the prisoner's past (prior record, prior life style, parole revocation, commitment offense); minimal responses about institutional experiences (prison conduct, prison programs, prisoner's physical condition); minimal responses about the prisoner's future (parole program, outside living, outside activities, outside employment); minimal responses about the prisoner's present psychological state; general defensive statements (statements which assess psychological, as opposed to legal, responsibility); defensive statements which blame oneself for prison behavior; defensive statements which blame the situation for prison behavior; defensive statements which deny guilt; general affirmative statements (statements where prisoner takes the initiative to raise topics that he wants to talk about); affirmative statements about the prisoner's past; affirmative statements about institutional experiences; affirmative statements about the prisoner's future; affirmative statements about the prisoner's present psychological state.

The hearing officer response categories represent the manner in which the hearing officer reacted to the prisoner's statement. They included: accepted (either supportive acceptance or minimal acknowledgment), validity or importance questioned (hearing officer challenges truth of prisoner's statement), interrupted, and ignored (lack of obvious response to prisoner's statement, or change of topic). Each content unit was scored by checking the appropriate one of the 80 prisoner behavior × hearing officer response cells of the scoring matrix. In contrast to the Adult Authority content analysis, which focused exclusively on the individual hearing officer, the prisoners' response content analysis focused on the interaction between prisoner and hearing officer (although the emphasis was on the prisoner).

Legal Analysis. The legal analysis coding instrument consisted of two separate sets of categories. One of these was a set of instances where the presence of an attorney would have been helpful to a prisoner in presenting his case or protecting his rights.[4] A category was checked if the particular instance occurred at least once during the hearing. The second set of categories referred to certain pattern characteristics of the topics that were discussed. The content of the first topic to be raised and of the topic that dominated the hearing (as determined by time spent on the topic or repeated

---

[4]Since the legal issues do not bear directly on the goals of this study, these categories and the resulting data will not be presented in this article.

returns to it) was scored by checking the appropriate one of 16 subject categories (which were similar to the Adult Authority content analysis categories).

Timing Analysis. An indirect measure of the importance of various aspects of the parole hearing was the amount of time spent on each one. These time factors were scored by coders who listened to the tapes and recorded the various times with the aid of a digital clock calibrated in 100ths of a minute. Time scores were also recorded for the duration of the hearing, measured from the hearing officer's initial greeting of the prisoner to the final statement made. In addition, the length of the hearing officers' deliberations was measured from the first statement after the prisoner had left the room to the final statement about the case.

Coding Procedure[6]

A team of four to six coders, all students at the University of California at Berkeley, was organized for each of the three content analyses and the timing analysis. The coding team for the legal analysis was composed of law students from Boalt Hall Law School, while the remaining teams were made up of advanced undergraduates with various social science majors (i.e., psychology, criminology, and sociology). These teams met separately several times a week over a period of nearly two months to practice using the coding instruments until a high degree of reliability was achieved (the interrater coefficients of reliability ranged from .82 to .92).

The actual coding of tapes (which took about four weeks) was done in listening sessions where pairs of coders worked together. In all cases, coders were blind to the outcome of the parole hearing since the decisions occurred after the hearing was completed. For both the Adult Authority and the prisoners' response content analyses, two coders from the same analysis team worked together. While one coder scored the hearing content, the other simply listened. These roles were alternated for each subsequent hearing. The use of two coders from the same analysis team reduced fatigue and provided a source of feedback about potentially ambiguous passages. If a coder was uncertain about how to score a particular content unit, he or she could consult with the other coder. For the timing and legal analyses, the pairs of coders were made up of one member each from the timing and legal analysis teams, thus allowing the two analyses to be scored simultaneously. The pairs of coders were changed throughout the coding so that no systematic biases occurred as a result of two coders always working together.

RESULTS

The data from this study will be presented in two parts. First, there will be a description of the timing and content patterns of the parole hearings. Next, the relationship of these factors to the decision-making process will be explored through several detailed statistical analyses.

---

[6]Copies of the coding forms and the coding manuals are contained in Garber (1976).

A Descriptive Summary of Parole Hearings

Of the 100 parole hearings sampled, 39% resulted in a decision to grant parole and 61% resulted in denial. On the average these parole consideration hearings lasted 16.2 minutes, although they ranged from some that lasted less than 5 minutes to one that was 40 minutes in length. The length of the hearing officers' deliberations to reach their decisions ranged from less than 30 seconds to 10 minutes, with the average deliberation lasting 1.5 minutes. Almost a third of the deliberations took less than 30 seconds, and in nearly three fourths of the cases, the final decision process took less than 2 minutes. The outcome of the deliberation was related to its length, with decisions to grant parole taking longer (2.1 minutes) than decisions to deny parole (1.2 minutes). This difference of less than a minute is, nevertheless, statistically significant ($F = 7.69$, $df = 1/98$, $p < .006$).

Topic Pattern

As the parole hearings generally operate, one of the hearing officers reviews a prisoner's central file immediately prior to his being interviewed. By noting the first topic raised in the hearing, inferences could be made about what the hearing officer considered salient from the file and viewed as of primary importance for the hearing. In addition, this first line of questioning could be seen as setting the tone for the remainder of the hearing. The results show that "psychological assessment" is most often this first topic (19%). Furthermore, when we examine the first four topics discussed, "psychological assessment" appears in 56% of the cases. To reiterate, this category refers to the use of psychological terms or psychologically probing questions or statements by the hearing officers (such as saying that a "psychosexual problem" exists or that the prisoner is "really together"). It does *not* include any references to the "psych. reports" prepared by the institutional staff.

After "psychological assessment," the next most frequent opening topics were the commitment offense (12%), prison discipline (10%), and prison rehabilitation (10%). The category of "parole plans" was the first topic raised in only three of the 100 hearings, but in each instance the prisoner was granted a parole. When the first four topics are considered, "parole plans" is among them only 15% of the time; however, its presence suggests that the prisoner is significantly more likely to be granted parole ($\chi_c^2 = 4.39$, $df = 1$, $p < .03$).

A most striking result is that the category of "psychological assessment" is not only first but foremost as well. In addition to being raised first most often, it is also rated as the dominant topic in 52% of the hearings scored. No other topic is even a close second to this overriding psychological emphasis. It should be noted that this topic coding was done by the legal analysis coders who were law students, and not by psychology students (who might be more inclined to view the world along psychological dimensions).

Adult Authority Content Analysis. "Psychological assessment" is the major topic discussed by the hearing officers during the course of the parole hearing — a finding which is consistent with the previous results from the topic pattern analysis. "Psychological assessment" accounts for nearly a quarter of the hearing officer content (22.3%) and is almost twice that of the next most frequently discussed topic. A second feature of this analysis is the emphasis on discussion of prison behavior. Two categories, "prison custody" (12.5%) and "prison rehabilitation" (10.7%), together account for almost a second quarter of the hearing officer content. These categories cover the areas of rule infractions and prison training and therapy programs. Following these two categories in terms of frequency was discussion of the commitment offense (10%). A third point in this analysis is the apparent lack of future-oriented discussion. References to parole plans in terms of "post-release activity" (5.2%) and "post-release support" (1.1%) account for little more than 6% of the hearing officer content. From this seemingly minor emphasis on future plans, compared to previous criminal and present prison behavior, we may infer the relative weight given by hearing officers to past, present, and future behavior in determining a prisoner's parole readiness.[6]

The Adult Authority content analysis also recorded the manner in which the content areas were broached. The results show that the topics were raised most often in the form of questions posed to the prisoner (54%). The next most frequent category was "informational statements" (40%), followed by "judgments" (6%). "Advice" was rarely given.

Prisoners' Response Content Analysis. The most striking aspect of this analysis is the dominant use of the "minimal response" categories, with 62% of the prisoners' responses characterized as such. This means that prisoners respond by providing a minimum of information to the hearing officers. For example, when a prisoner is asked how he is doing in the institution, a minimal response would be "ok" or "fine." In contrast, an affirmative response to the same question would go beyond the minimal answer and give further information about what the prisoner is doing that makes him "fine" or "ok." This prevalence of minimal responses is particularly noteworthy since the parole hearing is the major (if not only) opportunity for inmates to add to or refute information contained in their central file. This lack of initiating behaviors is further substantiated by the fact that "affirmative statements" account for only 20% of the total responses made by prisoners and that questions and complaints are relatively scarce (approximately 6% each). In addition, it is worth noting the relative absence of denial and defensive statements in the prisoners' verbal behavior (a total of only 4%).

The hearing officers' most frequent response to the statements of the prisoner is one of general acceptance (78%). This is not to say that they necessarily believe or support any statement by the prisoner, but rather that they do not challenge or confront him directly. The remaining hearing officer response categories of "validity questioned" (11%), "interrupted" (9%), and "ignored" (1%) occurred relatively infrequently, but constitute a serious challenge to the inmate's self-presentation.

An Analysis of Parole Decision-Making

From the descriptive data presented thus far, it is possible to characterize parole hearings as short, unstructured interview sessions where the hearing officers typically

---

[6]While it would have been useful to code the positive or negative value of a topic in addition to its frequency (e.g., was the prisoner's behavior in prison evaluated as good or bad by the hearing officer), in practice it was very difficult for the coders to do so with any degree of reliability.

ask psychologically oriented questions and the prisoners respond passively in a minimally informative, nonaffirmative manner. This description of the content and style of the interaction says little about the decision-making strategies involved, other than to generally suggest what information is available to the decision-makers. The general hypothesis being investigated in this study is whether or not any relationship exists between the content of the parole hearing and the decision to grant or deny parole. This next section reports the results of several statistical analyses in an attempt to understand how the factors that characterize the parole hearing contribute to the decision-making process.

Method of Analysis. The principal analytical tool used here is the method of discriminant function analysis (Overall & Klett, 1972). Discriminant function analysis (DFA) is used to classify individuals into two or more mutually exclusive groups on the basis of their scores on a number of independent or predictor variables. In essence, DFA utilizes multiple regression procedures in cases where the criterion variable is nominal (the mutually exclusive groups). After first determining the maximum amount of variation that can be associated with differences between the groups, DFA procedures then develop equations to predict that difference. In the two-group situation, the prediction equation derived from a DFA is almost identical to a multiple regression equation where the criterion is a dichotomous variable. The only difference is that the beta weights from multiple regression are reported as standardized discriminant function coefficients in the DFA. These coefficients are interpretable as the relative contribution of its associated variable to the discriminant function, and the sign ($+$ or $-$) indicates whether the variable is making a positive or negative contribution. In the case where classification is the primary objective, DFA has a distinct advantage over multiple regression in that most DFA computing programs go beyond simply generating the prediction equation and actually apply it, predicting group membership for each individual case.

In each analysis to be reported here, the criterion variable was the outcome of the parole hearing (parole v. denial), and the predictors were the various content categories scored in the Adult Authority and prisoners' response content analyses. Since individual hearings varied with respect to time and content units, all category frequencies were standardized by being transformed to proportions. The differences between these proportions for the paroled and denied groups were also tested for statistical significance.

Adult Authority Content Analysis. The first set of analyses focused on the subject categories of the Adult Authority content analysis. Prisoners who were paroled had hearings in which there was a significantly greater proportion of discussion about post-release activities ($F = 22.75$, $df = 1/98$, $p < .001$), post-release support ($F = 7.94$, $df = 1/98$, $p < .01$), and prior parole hearings ($F = 5.76$, $df = 1/98$, $p < .05$). Prisoners who were denied parole had hearings in which there was a significantly greater proportion of discussion about prison rehabilitation ($F = 8.24$, $df = 1/98$, $p < .01$) and prison custody ($F = 4.54$, $df = 1/98$, $p < .05$).

The DFA considered how well the subject categories were able to discriminate between prisoners who were paroled and prisoners who were denied parole. When 15 predictors were included in the analysis, 46% of the criterion group variation was accounted for by variation in the predictors. This proportion of accountable variation is derived from a highly significant canonical correlation of .68 ($F = 4.34$, $df = 16/83$,

Table 1. Standardized Discriminant Function Coefficients in the Adult Authority Analysis Prediction Equation[a]

	Coefficient
Post-release activities	.72
Psychological assessment	.56
Post-release support	.43
Paroles and revocations	.41
Physical appearance	−.31
Prison rehabilitation	−.30
Current hearing/criteria	−.29
Commitment offense	−.21
"Psych" reports	−.18
Prior hearings	.17
Unclassified content	.17
Prior life style	.13
Legal records	.09
Prisoner's health	.07
Prison associations	−.06

[a]A positive coefficient indicates the variable is making a contribution in favor of granting parole and a negative coefficient indicates a contribution toward denial.

$p < .001$). Using this prediction equation, it was then possible to correctly classify 83% of the hearings into paroled or denied groups ($\chi_c^2 = 43.56$, $df = 1$, $p < .001$). This high degree of predictability indicates that there are systematic decision-making strategies shared by many of the hearing officers in these 100 different hearings.

The standardized discriminant function coefficients from this first analysis are presented in Table 1. Clearly the best prediction of a parole outcome is the proportion of time spent in a hearing discussing the future plans of the prisoner relative to the time spent discussing other topics. The relative presence of psychological assessment topics also appears to strongly predict a parole outcome. On the other hand, high proportional frequencies of questions or statements relating to the prisoner's appearance, prison rehabilitation programs, commitment offense, or to the criteria for parole predict a denial decision by the hearing officers. It should be noted that the weight or importance of a variable in predicting hearing outcome, as indicated by its discriminant function coefficient, is not tied to the absolute frequency with which that variable occurs in hearings. This is best illustrated by the fact that although the categories of "post-release activities" and "post-release support" combined account for little more than 6% of the hearing content, they are the best predictors of its outcome.

Prisoners' Response Content Analysis. The second set of analyses used the prisoner behavior categories of the prisoners' response content analysis. Prisoners who were paroled spoke a greater proportion of the time about the future than did prisoners who were denied parole, both in terms of minimal responses ($F = 21.01$, $df = 1/98$, $p < .001$) and affirmative statements ($F = 7.38$, $df = 1/98$, $p < .01$).

Table 2. Standardized Discriminant Function Coefficients in the Prisoners' Response Analysis Prediction Equation[a]

	Coefficient
Minimal response re: future	.89
Affirmative statement re: future	.58
Minimal responses re: institution	.50
Minimal responses re: past	.48
Defensive statements	.48
Affirmative statements re: psychological state	−.34
Denial of legal guilt	−.31
Situation blame re: prior behavior	−.30
Self-blame re: prison behavior	.26
Affirmative statements re: past	.21
Complaints re: legal issues	−.20
Question/confusion	−.15
Affirmative statements re: general	.13
Situation blame re: prison behavior	.08
Minimal response re: general	.05
Complaints re: general	−.05
Affirmative statement re: institution	−.03
Self-blame re: prior behavior	−.03

[a]Positive coefficients indicate variable operates in favor of parole and negative coefficients indicate a contribution toward denial.

Prisoners who were denied parole had a greater proportion of complaints about legal issues ($F = 9.30$, $df = 1/98$, $p < .01$), complaints about prison programs or facilities ($F = 5.61$, $df = 1/98$, $p < .05$), questions or signs of confusion ($F = 6.76$, $df = 1/98$, $p < .05$), and denial of legal guilt ($F = 4.65$, $df = 1/98$, $p < .05$).

The second DFA attempted to determine which prisoner behaviors contributed most to the outcome of the hearing. The results of this analysis again yielded a highly significant canonical correlation between predictors and criterion of .66 ($F = 3.44$, $df = 18/81$, $p < .001$). This correlation indicates that the combination of the 18 prisoner behavior categories was able to account for approximately 44% of the criterion group variability. The effectiveness of this prediction equation is demonstrated by the fact that 79% of the hearings were correctly classified into the appropriate hearing outcome group ($\chi_c^2 = 33.64$, $df = 1$, $p < .001$).

The standardized discriminant function coefficients for this second analysis are presented in Table 2. Consistent with the results of the previous DFA, the presence of a high proportion of statements and minimal responses by the prisoner about future events is the best predictor of an outcome decision to grant parole. In addition, the presence of minimal responses about the prison and the prisoner's past, defensive statements, and statements blaming oneself for one's prison behavior are also predictive of a parole outcome. In contrast, high proportional frequencies of affirmative statements about one's psychological state, denials of legal guilt, and statements blaming the situation for one's prior behavior appear to predict a denial outcome.

Behaviors Initiated by Prisoners. A third DFA sought to separate out from the entire hearing the unique contribution of the prisoner to the parole decision-making

Table 3. Standardized Discriminant Function Coefficients in the Prisoners' Initiated Behaviors Prediction Equation[a]

	Coefficient
Affirmative statement re: future	.56
Complaints re: legal issues	−.51
Affirmative statement re: institution	−.39
Question/confusion	−.39
Affirmative statement re: past	−.28
Complaints re: program/facilities	−.28
Affirmative statement re: psychological state	−.23
Complaints re: general	−.17
Affirmative statement re: general	−.05

[a]Positive coefficients indicate variable operates in favor of parole and negative coefficients indicate a contribution toward denial.

process. In other words, what impact did prisoner-initiated behaviors have on the outcome of the hearing? Table 3 presents the standardized discriminant function coefficients for the nine variables used in this analysis. The canonical correlation was .50 ($F = 3.87$, $df = 9/90$, $p < .005$), which meant that 25% of the criterion group variation was accounted for by variation in the predictor variables. Using the prediction equation, 70% of the hearings were correctly classified into the paroled and denied outcome groups ($\chi_c^2 = 16.00$, $df = 1$, $p < .001$). It is noteworthy that of the nine prisoner-initiated behaviors, only one of them has a positive discriminant function coefficient in the direction of predicting a parole outcome. That is, the larger the proportion of a prisoner's affirmative statements about the future, the greater the likelihood that he will be granted a parole. However, for the other eight behaviors, the negative coefficients all predict denial outcomes. This suggests that in most instances, prisoner-initiated behaviors are counterproductive in gaining a decision granting parole. Thus, the low profile of most inmates during parole hearings is justified by the data. If they initiate too much, they are likely to be denied parole — except when they bring up future plans.

DISCUSSION

The results of the data analyses present an over-all picture of the parole hearing as a relatively short, diagnostic interview session which places a heavy emphasis on psychological assessment. The hearing officers generally ask questions of the prisoners and acknowledge their answers in a noncommittal way. For their part, the prisoners typically make minimal responses to the questions and add little to present a case of their own. In hearings where the eventual outcome is parole, the hearing officers focus more attention on the prisoner's parole plans, his prior experiences on parole, and his psychological state. The prisoner generally responds minimally on these topics, but also makes affirmative statements about his future behavior. In contrast, in hearings which result in a denial of parole, the hearing officers direct their questions toward the prisoner's current disciplinary problems and rehabilitation activities. In response the prisoners generally deny their guilt, complain about the legal issues surrounding their incarceration and about their treatment in prison, and ask questions about their parole status. Over-all, the form and content of the hearing is largely determined by the hearing officers. Although the prisoners occasionally contribute new information, such self-initiated behavior usually results in denial of parole.

Three major issues emerge from these findings. The first of these is the purpose and utility of the parole hearing for the decision-makers. A second concern is the role of the prisoner and his contribution to the decision-making process. The third issue of reliability and validity in parole decision-making points to the more general question of the fit between the theory and the practice of parole decision-making.

The Purpose of Parole Hearings

Some of the evidence from the content analyses suggests that the decisions which follow parole hearings are made prior to the hearing or, at the most, within the first few minutes. The fact that the hearings averaged only 16 minutes in length supports the conclusion that the decision being made does not rest entirely on information uncovered in the hearings. Considering the potential impact of the decision (keeping a man in prison for another full year or granting him his date for freedom), it is unlikely that the necessary information could be assessed accurately in such a short time. Furthermore, the brevity of the deliberations (1½ minutes on the average) also suggests that the hearing interview is not the primary source of data for parole decision-making.

If the parole decision is actually made at the beginning of the hearing, rather than afterwards, then two possibilities come to mind. First, it may be that the decision is based solely on information in the prisoner's central file. This file is quickly reviewed by the hearing officer in the few minutes before the hearing begins. It is conceivable that the hearing officer arrives at a decision of parole or denial on the basis of this review and then pursues one or another line of questioning according to that prehearing decision. Support for this hypothesis comes from research on the employment interview situation, which finds that such interviews are characterized by brevity, stereotyping of applicants, and the tendency for interviewers to make up their minds beforehand on the basis of a résumé and to then discount any interview information that does not confirm their prior expectations (Webster, 1964).

A second possibility is that the hearing officers have become so skilled in identifying various "types" of prisoners that they are immediately able to classify individuals in terms of those who are ready for parole and those who are not. The results of the present study, which found that the "psychological assessment" category was judged as the dominant topic in over half the hearings, suggest that the hearing officers use the hearing (and/or the central file) for this diagnostic purpose. Once having identified some psychological problem on the part of the prisoner, the hearing officers need no further time to consider other information since the obvious decision is to keep the prisoner in the institution for further treatment of the problem.

If the decision to grant or deny parole is indeed made prior to the parole interview, then what purpose does the hearing serve for the decision-makers? First of all, the hearing may actually be of no use whatsoever. It is quite possible that the hearing officers would arrive at the same decisions in the absence of any face-to-face interaction with the prisoner. In fact, one could argue that the only effect of the hearings is a detrimental one for most inmates. Since the hearings are conducted throughout the state, they require the hearing officers to be on the road for weeks at a time, away from family and friends, in the rather remote communities where most of the prisons are located. This isolated life style may take its toll in the hearing itself. This would be especially true if the hearing officers believed that they would be able to make the same decisions from some home base without conducting on-the-spot interviews with the prisoners around the state.

A second hypothesis is that the hearing may be used to justify a decision that has already been made. As mentioned before, the decision to release a man from prison or keep him there is one of considerable weight and importance. Therefore, it seems reasonable to suggest that the hearing serves as an opportunity for the hearing officer to verify (at least in his own mind) that he has made the correct decision. This hypothesis is supported by the results of the discriminant function analyses, which showed that different patterns of questioning took place in hearings where the outcome was a granting of parole, rather than a denial. In hearings resulting in a decision to grant parole, the hearing officers focused their attention on the plans developed by the prisoner for his release. A prisoner's well-laid parole plans could be seen as validating the prior decision to release him. This is especially significant since all prisoners who appear before the hearing officers are legally eligible for parole and therefore could all have made appropriate plans for their release. Whether or not these plans are actually discussed in the hearing depends primarily on whether or not the hearing officer chooses to ask about them. In contrast to parole-granting hearings, hearings where a denial was the outcome decision were characterized by different lines of questioning. The hearing officers were more concerned about factors that could indicate that the prisoner is not ready for release (i.e., prison disciplinary problems and rehabilitation programs). The emphasis on these factors could be interpreted as evidence that the hearing officers had already made a decision to deny parole and were attempting to support and justify their position in the hearing.[7]

At this point, no final conclusions can be formed about the utility of the hearing for the hearing officers. In principle, if the hearing does indeed serve no decision-making function, then it occupies the position of a "legal fiction." That is, its sole purpose is to present an illusion of legally responsible, rationally determined, and just decisions in a system where that may not be the case.

The Role of the Prisoner in Parole Decisions

A second issue that emerges from the present study is the impact of the prisoner's role in the decision-making process. From the results of the prisoners' response content analysis, it is easy to picture a quiet and obsequious prisoner responding rather passively to the line of questioning set by the hearing officers. This passive style of

---

[7]Even if this were the typical pattern of parole decision-making, it is conceivable that in some cases the hearing officer would find his initial judgment disconfirmed during the hearing and would change his ultimate decision. If so, an analysis of the data by time periods might shed some light on what factors would make the verbal content of the hearing a more crucial aspect of the parole decision.

self-presentation may serve several functions for the prisoner. First of all, it may reflect an adaptive response to the prison system. Prisoners may believe that, since anything they say can be used against them, it is best to remain relatively silent and to avoid calling undue attention to themselves. Such a belief would appear to be an accurate assessment of the situation, since the present data analysis showed that almost all of a prisoner's self-initiated behaviors were weighted heavily in the direction of a denial of parole.

The nonparticipatory role of a prisoner may also reflect his feelings of inferiority or helplessness when confronting the authority of the parole board. The passivity of prisoners in these hearings could be their reaction to a situation where someone else has all the power and they have none. An analogous situation was created experimentally by Zimbardo and his colleagues (Zimbardo, Haney, Banks, & Jaffe, 1973) when they constructed a simulated prison environment. To staff their prison, Zimbardo et al. used a homogeneous population of college males and randomly assigned half of them to be prisoners and half of them to be guards. In so doing, they created a situation in which there were two comparable groups, with one group having all the power (the guards) and the other group having none (the prisoners). Zimbardo et al. found that the mock prisoners reacted strongly to this experimental manipulation of power. The typical behavioral syndrome that they exhibited was one of passivity, dependency, depression, helplessness, and self-deprecation. In many ways, the syndrome exhibited by the mock prisoners parallels the behavior of real prisoners appearing for parole consideration. It is possible that some sort of redistribution of power (such as allowing attorneys to represent prisoners at the hearings) could reduce the detrimental effect that the current parole system appears to have on the prisoner.

A third explanation of the prisoner's passive role in the parole hearings is that the prisoner lacks the necessary competence to effectively present himself and his case for parole consideration. First of all, he may be unable to recall, on the spot, the critical arguments in his favor, or he may be unable to express his views articulately. Secondly, he may disagree with the hearing officers about the facts of his case and yet find it difficult to persuade them that his version is the "correct" one and not an excuse or false alibi. According to the legal analysis (reported in Garber, 1976), some type of factual conflict occurred in 39% of the hearings.

If the prisoner is not skilled in making a positive self-presentation, he may also be viewed as less likeable as a person, and this in turn may affect his chances for obtaining parole. Such a relationship between liking and decision outcomes has been demonstrated in research on jury decision-making behavior. Mitchell and Byrne (1973) found that jurors liked defendants with attitudes similar to theirs and that this liking influenced their judgments. In addition, juror decisions are affected by the defendant's social status (Landy & Aronson, 1969) and physical attractiveness (Efran, 1974). If one extrapolates from these findings on juror decisions, it becomes clear that the prisoner has several factors operating against his being liked by the hearing officers. The prisoner is of lower status than the hearing officers and does not typically share their attitudes (especially with regard to prison issues). Even the physical attractiveness variable is salient here in light of the fact that the hearing officers' references to "physical appearance" were predictive of parole denial. From our observations, the hearing officers were very well groomed, in suits and ties, and were generally about 20 years older than the inmates who were in their prison uniforms. If, in addition, the prisoner has difficulty in presenting a competent, affirmative case for himself, then it appears unlikely that he would be able to win over the hearing officers in his brief appearance before them.

The Reliability and Validity of Parole Decision-Making

The underlying philosophy of the parole system is that each individual offender can be treated and rehabilitated while in prison and that, once rehabilitated, he can be released since he no longer poses a threat to society. In order to implement this philosophy, several assumptions have to be made. One is that the prisoner's "problems" can be diagnosed accurately and appropriate treatment provided. Another is that accurate assessments can be made of a prisoner's degree of rehabilitation and of his future behavior in society as a free man. While the first assumption rests on the abilities of judges and correctional personnel, the second rests on the competence of the hearing officers. The question to be asked of the hearing officers is, can they indeed make these assessments of rehabilitation and these predictions of future dangerousness? If they cannot, then the validity of the parole system is seriously undermined.

To rephrase the question being raised here, is the parole decision-making process a reliable one and a valid one? Reliability refers to the consistency, across hearings, in the manner in which hearing officers arrive at their decisions. If the process is reliable, it means that all of the hearing officers use the same method of integrating information and that different officers would arrive at the same decision on any one case. According to the results of the present study, the parole decision-making process is indeed a reliable one. Whatever the criteria being used by the hearing officers, they were applied in a fairly consistent or reliable fashion (as indicated by the highly significant canonical correlations of the discriminant function analyses). This evidence of decision-making reliability might appear to contradict the findings of Wilkins, Gottfredson, Robison, and Sadowsky (1973), which revealed a marked variability in the information used by decision-makers. However, an alternative explanation is that the current results and those of Wilkins et al. are not in conflict because they are about different stages in the parole process. That is, it is possible that hearing officers may differ in how they evaluate the prisoners' central files but that once they make that evaluation about a parole applicant, they are consistent in adopting a line of questioning based on (and perhaps justifying) that hypothesis.

If the parole decision-making process is reliable, is it also valid? Validity refers to whether or not the decisions truly reflect the goal set for them. Given the Adult Authority's stated policy aim of public protection, the goal of the parole hearing is to distinguish between those prisoners who will and who will not behave in a dangerous or criminal manner at some time in the future. If the decision-making process is valid, it means that all the hearing officers can assess accurately the potential dangerousness of any prisoner.

However, the inference to be drawn from the present study and related research is that this process is *not* a valid one. Research conducted on psychological predictions, using trained mental health professionals, has found that such predictions are usually unreliable and, as a result, invalid (Ennis & Litwack, 1974; Meehl, 1971; Rosenhan, 1973). Furthermore, a study by Pogrebin (1974) found that psychiatric evaluations were of little use in predicting parole success. In their appraisal of the prediction of dangerousness, Wenk, Robison, and Smith (1972) conclude that it is impossible to predict with any accuracy who will be dangerous and that, in fact, the best prediction is that any individual, regardless of background, will not pose a threat to others.

If mental health professionals cannot make reliable and valid psychological evaluations and predictions of dangerousness, then it seems highly unlikely that untrained hearing officers could succeed in so formidable a task. In their testimony in Van Geldern v. Kerr, the hearing officers indicated that they had very little, if any, background in psychology, and they were often unable to correctly identify basic definitions of various types of mental illness. Despite this lack of formal training and basic knowledge, the evidence in our study is that the hearing officers' personal evaluations of psychological factors played a major role in their decision-making. The category of "psychological assessment" was usually the dominant topic in the hearing and was an influential variable in predicting the hearings' outcomes. Furthermore, in an analysis of the written reasons given by hearing officers for denial decisions (presented as evidence in Van Geldern v. Kerr), Levy (1975) found that they cited "psychiatric reasons" most frequently as justification for denying parole.

Thus, although the hearing officers have no demonstrated skills in making psychological evaluations, such evaluations underlie their decisions to grant or deny parole. Clearly, there is no evidence that they can make valid psychological assessments and predictions of dangerousness, and this diagnostic invalidity constitutes a major source of arbitrariness in the parole system.[8] Any decision based on unreliable and invalid psychological dimensions can hardly be valid itself. As a result, there is an apparent lack of correspondence between the goals of the parole system (treatment, rehabilitation, and release) and the abilities of the decision-maker to identify them.

CONCLUSION

This study represents an important first in research on parole decisions because its analysis centers on the processes taking place in actual (rather than simulated or self-reported) parole hearings. It utilizes content analysis, which is a fairly simple and straightforward methodological approach that is shown to generate some very powerful data. Because of the reliance on tape-recordings, the analysis was limited to verbal data (i.e., what people said during the hearing). Use of these data alone led to some very good predictions of decision outcome, but it is quite possible that the remaining unexplained variance could be accounted for by the influence of various nonverbal behaviors. For example, a prisoner who entered the hearing room with a swagger or a hostile expression on his face may have had a negative impact on the hearing officer, which might bias the type of opening questions and in turn make denial of parole more likely. In addition to nonverbal behavior, specific information in the prisoner's file could have also influenced the parole decision, but it was not possible in this study to assess either of these. It should also be noted that what one says is not necessarily

---

[8]Additional evidence of the invalidity of this process lies in the ability of outside factors to influence the percentage of paroles granted. According to testimony presented in Van Geldern v. Kerr, the parole rate in California has varied widely over the years in response to policy statements from the governor and the legislature. Obviously, if parole decisions vary in response to political pressures, they can hardly be regarded as accurate assessments of the individual prisoners.

what one thinks and that the decision-making process going on in the mind of the hearing officer may not be completely represented by the content of what he says during the hearing. Even with these limitations on the source of data, the study reveals some interesting and significant patterns in the factors that predict decision outcome.

REFERENCES

Adult Authority Policy Statement #24. *Functions and Priorities for Term Setting and Revocation of Parole.* March 1973.

Aitken, R. The Adult Authority. California State Bar Committee *Report and Recommendations on Sentencing and Prison Reform,* Los Angeles, 1975.

California Assembly Criminal Procedure Committee. *The Deterrent Effects of Criminal Sanctions.* Sacramento, 1968.

California Assembly Select Committee on the Administration of Justice. *Parole Board Reform in California: Order Out of Chaos.* Sacramento, 1970.

California State Bar Association. *Report and Recommendations on Sentencing and Prison Reform.* Los Angeles, 1975.

Efran, M. G. The effect of physical appearance on the judgment of guilt, interpersonal attraction, and severity of recommended punishment in a simulated jury task. *Journal of Research in Personality,* 1974, **8,** 45–54.

Ennis, B. J., & Litwack, T. R. Psychiatry and the presumption of expertise: Flipping coins in the courtroom. *California Law Review,* 1974, **62,** 693–752.

Garber, R. M. *An Exploration and Analysis of Parole Decision-Making in California.* Unpublished master's thesis, University of California, Berkeley, 1976.

*Gottfredson, D., & Ballard, K. *Prison and Parole Decisions: A Strategy for Study.* Unpublished manuscript, Institute for the Study of Crime and Delinquency, California Medical Facility, Vacaville, 1965.

Hakeem, M. Prediction of parole outcome from summaries of case histories. *Journal of Criminal Law, Criminology, and Police Science,* 1961, **52,** 145–155.

Kerr, H. *Standards Used for Determining Eligibility for Parole.* A Report to the California State Legislature, January 1972.

Kingsnorth, R. Decision-making in a parole bureaucracy. *Journal of Research in Crime and Delinquency,* 1969, **6,** 210–218.

Landy, D., & Aronson, E. The influence of the character of the criminal and his victim on the decisions of simulated jurors. *Journal of Experimental Social Psychology,* 1969, **5,** 141–152.

Levy, L. Personal communication, 1975.

Meehl, P. E. Law and the fireside inductions: Some reflections of a clinical psychologist. *Journal of Social Issues,* 1971, **27,** 148.

Mitchell, H. E., & Bryne, D. The defendant's dilemma: Effects of jurors' attitudes and authoritarianism. *Journal of Personality and Social Psychology,* 1973, **25,** 123–129.

Overall, J., & Klett, C. *Applied Multivariate Analysis.* New York: McGraw-Hill, 1972.

Parsons-Lewis, H. S. Due process in parole-release decisions. *California Law Review,* 1972, **60,** 1518–1556.

Pogrebin, M. Is the use of a psychiatric facility for parole evaluation justifiable? *International Journal of Offender Therapy and Comparative Criminology,* 1974, **18,** 270–274.

Rosenhan, D. On being sane in insane places. *Science,* 1973, **179,** 250–258.

Takagi, P. *Evaluation Systems and Adaptations in a Formal Organization: A Case Study of a Parole Agency.* Unpublished doctoral dissertation, University of California, Berkeley, 1967.

Takagi, P., & Robison, J. The parole violator: An organizational reject. *Journal of Research in Crime and Delinquency,* 1969, **6,** 78–86.

Webster, E. *Decision-Making in the Employment Interview.* Montreal: McGill University Press, 1964.

Wenk, E. A., Robison, J. O., & Smith, G. W. Can violence be predicted? *Crime and Delinquency,* October 1972.

Wilkins, L. T., Gottfredson, D. M., Robison, J. O., & Sadowsky, C. A. Information selection and use in parole decision-making. *Parole Decision-Making Supplementary Report V,* National Council on Crime and Delinquency, 1973.

Zimbardo, P., Haney, C., Banks, C., & Jaffe, D. The mind is a formidable jailer: A Pirandellian prison. *The New York Times Magazine,* April 8, 1973, 38*ff.*

19

THE PSYCHIATRIC ASSESSMENT OF DANGEROUSNESS
Practical Problems and Political Implications

STEPHEN PFOHL

In September 1974, a federal district court in Toledo issued an interim order in major "right-to-treatment" litigation on behalf of the 700 patients at Ohio's maximum security hospital for the "criminally insane."[1] A major section of this interim order required the state to seek the diagnostic services of independent mental health professionals to re-evaluate the status of each patient at Lima State Hospital.[2] These specially contracted psychiatric decision-makers were grouped into twelve multidisciplinary review teams. Each team consisted of a psychiatrist, a clinical psychologist, and a psychiatric social worker. Teams were required to decide whether a patient was mentally ill or a psychopathic offender dangerous to self and others and in need of placement in a maximum security facility. Patients would continue to be confined in Lima State Hospital only if they were "immediately dangerous" and needed maximum security or if they were "psychopathic offenders" requiring further treatment.[3]

The work of the patient review teams was important for two reasons. First, their decisions significantly affected the lives and life chances of patient-inmates for years to come. Second, these decisions represented an example of a process widely advocated as a determinant for the use of imprisonment: the assessment and prediction of dangerousness. Indeed, the criterion of dangerousness "has been accepted by two national commissions, by the American Law Institute, by the American Bar Association, by the National Council on Crime and Delinquency in its Model Sentencing Act and its policy statements, by many commentators and in many criminal codes."[4]

Those who favor the psychiatric predictions of dangerousness as justification for confinement in a maximum security facility often refer to the process as if its realiability were objectively verified. Those who carry it out are viewed as expert technicians. These special teams of clinical diagnosticians were accepted as such by criminal justice and mental health officials and by advocates for patients' rights as well. Participants in the litigation leading to the patient reviews were optimistic about the success of psychiatric prediction. Legal advocates representing the patient-plaintiffs were confident that the clinicians recruited for these reviews were the state's "leading experts." According to a

This project was developed in conjunction with a larger study of the methods of psychiatric diagnosticians. It is sponsored, in part, by a grant from the Ohio Division of Mental Health. The author acknowledges the critical and constructive readership of Simon Dinitz, Ron Kramer, Gisela Hinkle, Clyde Franklin, and Diane Vaughan.

Justice Department attorney participating in the case, "The most distinctive part of the order was [that] the Court required people at Lima to be evaluated against some sort of valid standard for commitment to see if all patients really belonged there."[5]

Despite the optimism of those who favor its use, psychiatric prediction finds little empirical support. Research on the prediction of violent behavior does not instill confidence in its reliability. Existing literature consistently reveals very low rates of prognostic accuracy. Whether one develops "predictor scales" based on as many as 100 variables,[6] employs the results of psychological testing, or relies on the judgments of experienced diagnosticians, prediction rates rise no higher than two wrong judgments for every one right judgment.[9] A recent review article on this subject has gone so far as to refer to the prediction process as "flipping coins in the courtroom."[10]

Clearly the predictive process is unreliable. What is at least as serious is its consistent tendency to overpredict failure. "They tend to predict antisocial conduct in many instances where it would not, in fact, occur. Indeed . . . research suggests that for every correct psychiatric prediction of violence, there are numerous erroneous predictions. That is, among every group . . . presently confined on the basis of psychiatric predictions of violence, there are only a few who would, and many more who would not, actually engage in such conduct if released."[11] It is the documentation of such overprediction that led Norval Morris to conclude: "The concept of dangerousness for sentencing purposes is an equivocal principle that leads to gross injustice."[12]

In the wake of considerable doubt about the validity of psychiatric predictions, one cannot view lightly the work of the specially contracted Lima patient review teams. They were asked to do what research suggested they could not have the expertise to do. By considering an individual's past record and assessing present performance, they were to determine whether a patient needed confinement in a maximum security institution. Of what did their considerations and assessments consist? To what degree were decisions reflective of certain "political interests" and diagnosticians' class- or culture-based assumptions? These are the questions with which we are concerned here. If the validity of the prediction of dangerousness is in question, clearly its political significance is not. After all, the essence of such decisions is that the power of the state will be invoked to restrict the future options of those who are considered harmful to the interests of others.

Methodology

Our assessment of the political interests displayed in making decisions about dangerousness and the need for maximum security is derived from a field study of the diagnostic process. To study this process, a group of seven researchers observed the work of the twelve teams of psychiatric professionals in 130 diagnostic sessions. After obtaining informed consents, observers situated themselves as unobtrusively as possible in order to note relevant features of social interaction before, during, and after the evaluation team's interviews of patients. In addition to observers' descriptions of this process, tape recordings and transcripts were made of these selected evaluation sessions.

Furthermore, each participating psychiatric professional was subsequently interviewed regarding his or her impressions, opinions, and reflections of both the patient reviews and the presence of the researcher-observers. An analysis of these materials provides the basis for our interpretation of the political interests involved in predicting dangerousness and the need for maximum security confinement.

Social Characteristics of Psychiatric Professionals Studied

Thirty-seven clinicians participated in the patient review process. Eleven were psychiatrists, thirteen were psychologists, and thirteen were social workers. All were "outside" professionals who were neither employees of Lima State Hospital nor of any other state agency. Some were in private practice. Others worked in community mental health or forensic clinics. Several were affiliated with universities. Nearly all psychiatrists had been recruited directly by the Ohio Commissioner for Forensic Psychiatry, while nearly all the social workers had been recruited by colleagues or by legal advocates for the patient-plaintiffs. Psychologists, who were recruited by either the Forensic Commission or by colleagues, shared with the psychiatrists "considerable past experiences" with patients similar to those they diagnosed at Lima. Most social workers, however, had no past experience with such "maximum security" individuals. In terms of professional orientation, half the clinicians described themselves as "eclectics," and nearly one-third stated that they were "psychoanalytically" oriented. Eight of thirty-seven clinicians were women, of whom seven were social workers. All psychiatrists were male. Five of the diagnosticians were blacks. Of these, two were psychiatrists and three were social workers.

How the Predictive Review Teams Viewed Their Own Work

The diagnostic review teams saw their work in a "professional" rather than a political context. Their assessments were viewed in terms of an applied clinical science. They did not regard themselves as judicial arbiters of freedom. Their definition of their work is revealed in the following set of observations.

"Discovery" Versus the Court's Work of "Decision-Making"

The findings of the patient review teams were presented to the federal court, which in principle made the final decision about which patients were to be released, transferred, or retained. In practice, the court, with few exceptions, followed the recommendations of the psychiatric professionals. Nonetheless, the review team members constantly reminded themselves that it was the court that was really deciding on a patient's fate. They were only "discovering" what a patient was really like. This separation between a team's discoveries and a judge's decision is illustrated in the following excerpt.

Excerpt 1. From a Transcript of a Patient Review. (The team is discussing its work in relation to the court's expectations.)

Psychologist: Are we supposed to go for that label or not? Say whether or not they are now psychopathic offenders?
Psychiatrist: I guess so. . . .
Psychologist: If they're a psychopathic offender they're going to stay here?
Psychiatrist: Yes. . . .
Social worker: He said they're all going back to court anyway.
Psychologist: All of these people, whether we label them psychopathic offender or not, are going back to the court anyway?
Psychiatrist: Yes.
Social worker: The're all going back?
Psychologist: What's the difference. . . . Here's a man labeled psychopathic offender and he goes back to court. And a man we say is not a psychopathic offender, and he goes back to court too? Then what?
Social worker: It's not for us to determine where they go.
Psychologist: That's right. The court makes the final ruling—whether he stays here, goes to jail or whatever.

Through conversation, such as that just presented, teams constructed definition of their work as professional discovery and not judicial decision-making. Nonetheless, teams were frequently observed carefully constructing their diagnostic language in terms of what they thought the court needed to hear so that a particular recommendation would be accepted. For instance, one team thought that a particular patient could benefit from staying for further treatment even though he was not believed to be a "psychopathic offender." This team decided to call him a psychopathic offender to obtain treatment for him, although clinically they agreed that this label was inappropriate. Another team thought that a patient was truly a "psychopathic offender," but believed that such persons cannot be treated. They thought that it would be wasteful to hold such an individual in a maximum security hospital when his "psychopathy" could as easily "burn out" in a restricted penal setting. On this basis, they withheld the label "psychopathic offender" and simply recommended that the individual no longer needed the special custody and care of the maximum security setting at Lima.

The careful wording ɔ. reports and evaluation statements to secure desired legal outcomes suggests tʰɛt teams were adjudicating as much as they were discovering psychiatric realities. On the surface this appears to contradict the psychiatric professionals' deíinitions of themselves as neutral interpreters of data who render expert opinions but do not structure legal decisions. Teams protected themselves from perceiving this contradiction by reinterpreting possible inconsistencies in terms of other "facts" that preserved the "discovery" aspects of their work. For instance, the team that classified a patient as a psychopath in order to get treatment for him introduced a technical distinction between legal and psychiatric psychopathy. Although the label was psychiatrically untrue, the team suggested that it was legally acceptable. As one psychiatrist put it: "In the psychiatric-psychological sense [this] is a little different than it is in the legal sense." Hence the team could give a patient a label that was psychiatrically invalid without explicitly recognizing that they were playing with terminology in order to expedite a particular legal adjudication. It was suggested that "legally" this was their only alternative.

The use of psychiatrically untrue but legally acceptable labels produced legal outcomes compatible with clinical opinions about the need for treatment. In the long run, however, this practice creates two additional problems. First, it places an "untrue" label on a particular patient, a label that then becomes an official part of his diagnostic record. Second, the practice is highly unstandardized. Not all teams used "untrue" labels to get what they wanted; some teams simply avoided imposing any label. One team was concerned that if a patient were called a psychopath, he would have to remain incarcerated. A member of the team said: "I think we could simply waive the psychopathic offender bit and not even say he's recovered or not, just go on and say he doesn't need care, custody, et cetera." This team may include a certain diagnostic term and another may not, but either way there is no telling whether the team thought the term was clinically valid. In reading final reports, it is impossible to discern what a team really had in mind.

Liberal or "Reform-Oriented" Work

Patient-reviewers viewed Lima State Hospital in generally negative terms. Indeed, the public image of this maximum security institution was formed by reports of abuse and neglect. In 1971 the *Cleveland Plain Dealer* condemned the hospital as "a chamber of horrors" because of reports of violence against patients. Against this unfavorable assessment of the hospital as a whole, members spoke of their own work in reformist terms. They frequently expressed the opinion that many Lima patients did not really belong there. They believed that their work would help to release such persons. Moreover, they generally felt that their assessments of patients were liberal or even lenient and that only the most dramatic or overwhelming evidence prompted recommendations for continued maximum security.

Excerpt 2. From Psychiatrist Interview

We didn't recommend many (for) maximum security or dangerousness. . . . Generally we gave, kind of gave, people a chance if they had a fairly reasonable explanation of things and seemed to know where they were going and where they were heading, had some organization to things. Unless the evidence was overwhelmingly against them. If anything, we tended to be more lenient than restrictive. . . . We recommended a lot of them, didn't have to be there. A great percentage. At least 75 percent of them.

"Protecting the Community"

Although members generally saw their work as part of a liberal reform effort, they also thought they were protecting society from potentially harmful criminals. While they believed that many patients had been previously misclassified, they also believed that a 'sizable portion of the hospital population represented a genuine danger to the public. When the members believed that they had discovered such persons, they had no qualms about recommending confinement. As one member put it, "There are those I would lock up for thirty years at age sixteen."

The psychiatric teams thus assumed that certain patients were clearly dangerous and needed to be isolated from the community. Moreover, dangerous people were perceived to fall into two general categories: those whose "mental disturbances" prevented them from following society's rules and those who had not internalized society's rules in the first place. The first group would simply be labeled "dangerous." The second were considered "psychopathic offenders." For our purposes we shall refer to the first group as characterized by "psychiatric dangerousness" and the second by "psychopathic dangerousness." The criteria by which teams "discovered" each type are discussed below.

Reliance on Life-Threatening Behaviors, Histories of Violence, Assessment of Personal Control, and Certain Idiosyncratic Themes

In considering dangerousness, review teams were instructed to determine whether a patient was extremely likely to do immediate harm to self or others. Several assumptions added specificity to this criterion. The first of these assumptions narrowed the definition of harm. Only behaviors that were considered as "harmful to life" were assumed to be dangerous.

Excerpt 3. From Psychologist Interview

Dangerousness is danger to life. . . . My personal definition of snatching a purse or you know maybe minor physical hurt—I would not consider that real dangerousness. That could happen if a person loses his temper. But when the life is threatened or a very serious physical injury, I would consider that dangerous. Even, I think, in my definition, probably raping I would not consider that very dangerous. Its bad, but I don't consider this dangerous to life.

The restriction of the idea of dangerousness to life-threatening behaviors was typical of the definitions of nearly all team members. Several mentioned forcible rape, along with murder, as an example of dangerous behaviors. Most commonly, however, members believed that sexual assaults that were not accompanied by serious physical injury were not to be categorized as dangerous. This assumption is revealed in the following final evaluation statements. In noting this definitional restriction, it should be remembered that most "sex offenders" were hospitalized as "sexual psychopaths" and (when believed dangerous) could be retained in a maximum security setting by stating that they were still in need of treatment in the hospital's special psychopath unit. In other words, such "psychopathically dangerous" individuals could be retained without being technically designated as dangerous.

Excerpt 4. From Final Evaluation Report

He is considered to have the capability for repeating, almost immediately, the sexual offenses for which he was charged [sexual molestation of young girls]. But he is not considered to be dangerously assaultive, in that it is not felt that he would be likely to kill. It is therefore the opinion of this examining team that this patient is not in need of continued hospitalization in a maximum security facility.

Excerpt 5. From Final Evaluation Report

Even though he does not present immediate danger either to himself or to others, there is a possibility that . . . he may act out violently, especially if provoked and/or in a situation of some seductive maneuver by a member of the female sex. There was some evidence in his record that the patient allegedly molested some female patients while in Dayton State Hospital.

A second assumption about dangerousness involved the criteria teams used to recognize the likelihood for inflicting immediate harm. In nearly all cases, a past history of violence was an assumed prerequisite for viewing a patient as dangerous.

Excerpt 6. From Social Worker Interview

In terms of what occurred between the three of us, I think it's accurate to say that a person would have had to act in a violent fashion, where he would have had to physically harm someone for us to think of him in terms of being dangerous. If that hadn't happened in the past we didn't blame him as such.

A past history of violence was generally constructed from a survey of a patient's record. Team members cited a number of elements within that record that were routinely examined for signs of dangerousness. These included the description of criminal offenses, the record of fights or assaultive incidents within the hospital, and the record of times that a patient was placed in seclusion or in restraint. Also considered was a noted shift in a patient's behavior resulting from shifts in medication.

The prerequisite of a history of violent behavior was modified by two considerations. First, most teams assigned more significance to recent violence than to occurrences in the distant past. Just how distant that past had to be was a judgment that varied across teams and between patients. One team considered that a previous manslaughter incident was unimportant because for the last twenty years the patient had manifested no violence. Another used a ten-year period as a yardstick; still another thought that a patient's ward behavior for the previous two years was the best indicator of potential dangerousness.

A second qualifier to the criterion of past violence occurred in cases where teams noted the presence of "dangerous delusions." Such delusions were most frequently said to represent paranoid constructions in which patients had much self-investment. It was believed that patients who manifested these psychotic symptoms were likely to act out violently to defend their rigid worlds of "unreality." As indicated in the following excerpt, such delusions were often assumed to be predictive of dangerousness despite the absence of any history of violent acts.

Excerpt 7. From Final Evaluation Report

She believes that the Mafia, as well as her mother, brother, and sister-in-law are out to kill her by the use of odorless and tasteless poison. Indeed, she states that these people have gotten to the attendants who then tried to kill her by overdosing her on medicine. . . .
    In summary, [the patient] is actively delusional at this time and the previous diagnosis of schizophrenia, paranoid type, still holds. . . . In reference to the question of dangerousness to others, [the patient] has never been assaultive to anyone although she is often argumentative. . . . However, the investment of her delusional system is seen as so great that she might strike out at anybody who tries to disrupt it. . . . This is a mentally ill woman [paranoid schizophrenia] who has the potential of being dangerous to others. It is suggested that she be retained in Lima.

"Recency" and "dangerous delusions" thus modify recorded past violence as a criterion for predicting dangerousness. In general, past violence was treated as a necessary but not sufficient condition in the determination of dangerousness.

Teams also made a fourth assumption: that the truly dangerous individual would reveal his "lack of control" or "lack of ego strength" in the course of an interview. Of course, the manifestation of what was often called "uncontrolled impulsivity" could be inferred from a record of repeated violent offenses. In fact, one team frequently appeared to rely almost exclusively on the past record, even in cases where patients appeared to be presently cooperative and intact and had not evidenced violent or disruptive behaviors for an extended period. Most teams, however, recognized that records were occasionally incomplete or inaccurate and that they gave only an abstract account of incidents that sometimes originated in social situations. Teams thus relied on patients' own explanations for their violence as key elements in assessing the likelihood of immediate dangerousness. The following excerpt describes the process of comparing the patient's own account with the record of what he had done.

Excerpt 8. From Social Worker Interview

We looked at past behaviors. We looked at what it was he did that was called dangerous. . . . Then [in the interview] we asked the patient direct questions about possible harm he's done to himself or others, and if he ever thought about anything like this. . . . How does the person handle it when he gets angry; what does he do; what thoughts and fantasies does he have; what were the circumstances if he did strike out at someone? We always got the patient's point of view on the past behavior.

The assessment of a patient's self-control was assumed to be the central element in an interview to determine dangerousness. In the stress of rapid questioning about past and future violence, it was believed that patients would reveal the degree to which they were in control of any aggressive impulses. Often, teams applied deliberate pressure and provocation through an aggressive interview technique referred to as "stressing." As one psychiatrist indicated, this technique is believed to uncover whether "the individual is so mentally affected that he cannot use restraints." The assumed importance of this aspect of interviewing is documented in the following quotations excerpted from team member interviews.

Excerpt 9. From Psychiatrist Interview

. . . the thing is . . . the amount of control they have in the interview. . . . We did stress them. We thought that was definitely necessary. We guys would shoot questions from the side and occasionally some buts, you know, a few of the fellows would jump up and, you know, some of the crazier ones would go: "I know karate, and you better watch it. I can kill."

The three assumptions discussed so far (that dangerousness meant life threatening behavior, that dangerousness required a past history of violence, and that dangerousness is revealed in the stress of interviewing) were common to each of the review teams. Teams did differ in making more specialized or idiosyncratic assumptions. As already mentioned, one team appeared to place a greater emphasis on the past record. Another team focused more on a patient's ability to express insight into past deeds of violence. Another paid more attention to a patient's verbalization of his or her dreams and fantasies. Another believed the results of psychological testing were very helpful and complained that these were not uniformly available for all patients. Still another team paid considerable attention to signs of dangerousness that it believed to be present in a patient's "repressed anger." According to that team's psychologist, a patient who "could not express anger" was assumed to be "potentially dangerous and explosive." This member cited a case in which the team asked a patient "what it felt like to be a bastard." The patient's passive, nonemotive response ("I don't like it") was assumed to be a cue that anger and potential violence were simmering within. This assumption was also expressed by another member of the same review team, who stated that "I have a feeling if people, if they lash out with very, very little provocation that there must be so much anger that they are likely to murder somebody or kill somebody, or do very real harm."

Another rather idiosyncratic approach to the diagnosis of dangerousness was expressed by one psychiatrist in the following excerpt.

Excerpt 10. From Psychiatrist Interview

I have a feeling we pretty much adhered to our own concept of what we thought would be dangerous. I think we thought in terms of how likely is this man to do something very violent almost immediately after he's turned loose. And another criteria we used was "How would I feel having this man as my next-door neighbor?"

This approach was not common to all teams, but it demonstrates the significance of team members' operating definitions of dangerousness.

Reliance on "Excuse-Making" and
"Rationalizing" Behaviors

A history of life-threatening behaviors was not a necessary criterion in assessing "psychopathic dangerousness." Nonetheless, psychopathic individuals were frequently viewed as even more dangerous than those who had in fact murdered or perpetrated violent assaults in the past. It was reasoned that there was "no telling" what these individuals, without the guidance of a social conscience, would do. They were characterized by one team as "a bunch of scary boys" and by another as "lacking the very quality of humanness." They were generally viewed as "manipulators" and "con artists" who were concerned only with themselves, and from whom society definitely needed protection. Whereas team members relied on cues concerning "lack of control" during interviews to predict dangerousness, signs of "excuse-making" and "rationalizing" were viewed as the most important indicators of the "psychopathic offender." Once diagnosed, custodial recommendations were made to protect society from these persons whom one member described "as more dangerous and definitely with a more guarded prognosis."[13]

Difficult Predictions About the Need for Maximum Security

For most reviewers, predictions about who should remain confined in a maximum security environment were seen as the most difficult type of psychiatric assessment. When there was disagreement among team members, it arose in cases of assessing dangerousness or need for confinement. Assessments of such matters as "mental illness" or "incompetency to stand trial" were viewed as "easy" by comparison. According to one psychologist, a prediction regarding "extreme likelihood of immediate danger" was a "tough point because it was a situational diagnosis." In the words of another clinician, recommendations about the need for maximum security were difficult because "very often a patient described as potentially dangerous [in the record] did not impress us as such during the interview." At other times teams believed that patients were potentially more dangerous than the record suggested. This, too, was said to make predictions more difficult.

Excerpt 11. From Social Worker Interview

Dangerousness, I think, is a word that covers all kinds of grey matter. Depending on certain acts, we really are in the dark as to what kind of history defines dangerousness. In a lot of cases there was very little to document that a guy was dangerous. Now he may have been much more dangerous than what was in the record. In a few cases we found, for example, a newspaper clipping, which kind of clarified why the guy was at Lima State. In those cases you had a piece of journalism which in some ways informed you a lot better than the admission note or the psychiatric history of the guy.

Not all members thought that predictions regarding dangerousness and the need for maximum security were difficult. Some clinicians appeared ready to let a past record "speak for itself." One psychiatrist stated, "Our team found no difficulty in determining dangerousness. Dangerousness was seen in the record, by looking at past performances." According to another, "the patient himself has determined the degree of dangerousness through a history of repeated acts." In general, however, most team members did believe that their predictive tasks were difficult. This difficulty was summed up by a psychiatrist who stated: "I don't think we were able to spell out what exactly they mean by dangerousness. I think that's so difficult."

Confidence in the Accuracy of Predictions

Despite the perceived difficulty of their task, twenty-six of thirty-two clinicians questioned stated that they were confident of the accuracy of their predictions concerning dangerousness and the need for maximum security. Indeed, eleven stated that they were "very confident." The few who were unsure cited knowledge of research and doubts about the accuracy of past records as reasons for being less confident. On the other hand, those who were confident generally trusted both official reports and their own clinical skills. The fact that other team members shared in the same recommendations was also frequently cited as a basis for members' confidence.

Excerpt 12. From Psychiatrist Interview

Yeah, I think we felt confident. . . . We all felt, none of us were new at this, all of us had many years of experience, so that we felt that we could make a diagnosis as well as anybody. And so none of us felt at all backward or had any feelings of serious inferiority, feelings about our capacity to make it. And, as I said, we were able to check each other, support each other, as needed in our decision making. So when we got through, when we came upon a decision, we felt fairly comfortable.

Images of Deviance Produced by the Predictive Review Teams

Review teams were ordered to make predictions about patients' future behaviors and future needs for confinement. In doing so, they produced particular images of dangerous deviants and the way they can best be controlled. These images have obvious implications for the operation of the criminal justice system. They are summarized in the following observations.

Individualistic Explanations for Deviant Behavior

Review teams did not simply categorize patients: They provided them with clinical identities that "explained" (or at least told a story about) why they were dangerous and in need of maximum security confinement or why they might be safely released as harmless. A full discussion of the various interactional strategies through which diagnosticians arrived at identities for patients is beyond the scope of this chapter. Suffice it to say that in reviewing patients' past records, in inducing patients to talk about their "own" problems, and in collectively arriving at formulations of patients' psychological conditions, teams worked hard at fitting patients into individualized theories of deviance.[14] Teams searched extensively and negotiated constantly for the traumatic event, the distorted fantasy, the disrupted relationship that produced an image of the patient. This psychiatric accounting was often constructed after a team had already arrived at its conclusion about a patient. Sometimes knowledge of the past record or a brief "first impression" of the patient was enough to generate explanatory accounts. Much theorizing about a patient's deviant identity took place after a "gut-level" decision by clinicians about his disposition. The theorizing was "reconstructed logic" explaining why clinicians thought what they thought after they thought it.

Teams' early summary judgments about patients are typically illustrated in the following excerpts. These conversations occurred before teams interviewed patients. In such instances, interviews and post-interview discussions are designed to arrive at conclusions about a patient's real identity.[15]

Excerpt 13. From Transcript of Patient Review. (The team is trying to decide whether the patient is a "psychopathic offender" and needs continued custody and care in maximum security.)

Psychologist: The record started when he was thirteen. He's only twenty-two. Nowhere near burning out yet. What else does he have? Does it say? Breaking and entering, that kind of bit?

Psychiatrist: He served time. . . .

Psychologist: He's been around a couple of them. . . .

Psychiatrist: Now most of these people also have in their records . . . a history of broken homes, trouble beginning when they're kids.

Social Worker: It says that he took this with a lesser charge.

Psychologist: What was the first charge?

Social Worker: The original charge was kidnapping. . . . He committed this offense right after he came off parole.

Psychologist: Yeah.

Psychiatrist: Yeah, two days later, I think. . . . He timed it so he wouldn't break parole.

Psychologist: Another stone.

Social Worker: (laugh) Who do you say? He's going to be stoned in the interview.

Psychologist: Stone cold psychopath. [Team then digresses for a few exchanges, making comparisons between psychopaths and other patients. The psychiatrist then "refocuses" the conversation to the topic of patient 421.]

Psychiatrist: Well, I hate to admit this, but my mind is made up on these people even before we see them.

Psychologist: Well, there is wh . . . we do have to, its a matter of degree here.

Social Worker: Its a matter of degree in terms of whether they stay here now or go back to court right away.

Psychiatrist: Yeah.

Psychologist: Well, I'll admit I'm a little prejudiced, but I'm going to withhold my judgment. Basically what this guy is—what twenty-two years of age. Its not just that he's into it. He's a psychopathic offender and he should stay here a longer time. Well, I don't know. . . . Twenty is just a bad age to be working on these guys.

Social Worker: Yeah, they haven't learned.

Psychologist: The twenties is the worst decade to be a psychopath.

In the previous excerpt, such things as a patient's age, the timing of his last offense, and the repetitive nature of offenses are used to construct a theory about the patient as a particular clinical type—the "stone cold psychopath." In the process of interviewing, such theory-building continues. Teams use patients' responses and their own clinical observational skills to document the individual roots of pathology. In the following excerpt, a psychologist "explains" the meaning of a "rather long look" that a patient gave to a research observer. The researcher believed that the patient was just being inquisitive about what he was writing down. The psychologist, equipped with his special clinical skills and with an emerging theory that the patient's past violence was related to his homosexuality, was able to "see" far more. He was able to ascertain a "certain lack of control."

Excerpt 14. From Transcript of Patient Review

Psychologist: I'm bothered by his inability to remember all these things he has been, or his inability to admit remembering. These things that he's done in the past that are associated with homosexuality, and us just. . . .

Psychiatrist: An arbitrary enough homosexual. . . . I guess he's afraid that we'll decide against him, because he's—uh—homosexual. He feels some persecution about being judged a homosexual. And—uh—when he was talking about who he was attracted to—uh—I forgot the question that preceded it, whether or not you asked if he was homosexual or what. I noticed he gave a rather long look to our observer here, and—uh—I don't think that means anything much more than what we all suspect.

Psychologist: Yeah.

Psychiatrist: But—uh—I think it suggests a certain—uh—lack of control, perhaps—uh—in that—uh—or lack of judgment. [As] if he was trying to cover his homosexuality, which he seemed to be doing.

Two other recurrent methods of "theory-building" during interviews include the "offering of individual motives" through the phrasing of questions and the "offering of explanatory commentary" following a patient's response to some questi⊙... Sometimes this explanatory commentary, although it is about the patient (i.e., "Now you can see the paranoid defenses in this type of answer"), is addre ;ed exclusively to other team members. It is as if an aside is being made in a p y and the patient cannot hear it. An example of the method of "offering motives" is presented below. The clinician suggests that the patient validate an individualized interpretation of his problems.

Excerpt 15. From Transcript of Patient Review. (In this exchange the clinician is pursuing documentation for his theory regarding the patient's poor self-concept and his exaggerated need to impress others.)

Social Worker: Well, so if you got picked up as many times as the other guys that made you as good as the others?
Patient: Not really.
Social Worker: Well, I mean—uh—sort of a prestige thing—uh—that everybody's doing it, getting arrested and somebody who doesn't might be looked down on?
Patient: Well, it might in a sense. A person that might be tougher than everybody.
Social Worker: Everybody was boasting about getting arrested and thrown in jail and so on, or if it was a stolen car?
Patient: Mmmmm, yes.

Excerpt 16. From Transcript of Patient Review. (In this excerpt team members theorize both through asking questions and through offering explanatory commentaries.)

Psychiatrist: Do you like to tell jokes? Can you think of any jokes?
Patient: I don't really know (pause). I hear a lot of Polack jokes from Mr. _____, one of the attendants.
Psychiatrist: Can you think of one?
Patient: Yeah. I can. You want to hear it? (*laugh*) This is funny. This Polack bought this bird dog and took it out one day and came back and took it out again and one Polack said to the other that if that dog don't fly tomorrow, I'm going to shoot him right on the ground. So much for the Polack joke. Hope none of you are Polish.
Psychologist: Would it matter? How much would it matter?
Patient: Well, I don't want to hurt nobody's feelings.
Psychologist: Well you didn't ask first though. You asked later.
Patient: That's another thing I do. You know, sometimes I say something and stop and think that wasn't a very good thing to say.
Psychologist: Feel embarrassed now? Your ears are turning a little red.
Patient: No, not embarrassed, a little idiotic that you wanted me to tell these jokes. But I guess you're just trying to make me feel comfortable.
Psychologist: No. I'm not trying to make you feel comfortable. People, uh, the kind of jokes that people think or tell or enjoy helps me to know something about them. . . . (*pause*) The joke that you told has

something to do with the way you feel about yourself. The dumb Polack joke. You refer to yourself as a dumb hillbilly?

In post-interview discussions, teams solidify their theorizing about the roots of an individual patient's pathology. Often as soon as a patient leaves the room, team members make statements such as, "Well, it's obvious to me . . ." or "It's pretty clear that the patient is. . . ." Sometimes a final theory awaits negotiations and compromises among team members. In any event, the situational basis for a particular diagnosis is dropped off in the formulation of a final theory about the patient's individual problems. For instance, in the case of the individual whose pathology was indexed by his "dumb Polack" joke, the logic that governed team members' assessments is discarded in favor of a professionalized "reconstructed logic." In discussing a final recommendation, the psychologist inquires of the psychiatrist, "What would you say. Inadequate personality?" The psychiatrist responds: "Why, certainly I would weigh that adult stress reaction. And I would say inept personality. And then the sexual deviation is explaining the act he committed." In the case of the individual theoretically cast as being overdependent on others, the team drew on a previous entry in the patient's record to suggest evidence of "emotional immaturity and group delinquency reaction of adolescence." The "uncontrolled look" by the individual allegedly denying his homosexuality was transformed into a statement that "he shows apparent personality disorder, with paranoid schizoid elements." The diagnosticians succeeded in constructing (or fitting patients into) theories about individual deviance. These theories accompany and justify recommendations for release or retention.

Sustaining the "Impression" that Deviance Can Be Identified and Managed at the Level of Individual Psychopathology

In constructing individual theories of deviance, diagnosticians fix the blame for violent, harmful, or dangerous behavior on the psychiatric realities of "psychopathology" of patients. Such practical theorizing preserves the professional identity of psychiatric diagnosticians. It also denigrates patients' attempts to "socially account" for psychiatric problems.

The professional identity of diagnosticians is preserved (or situationally accomplished) through the specialized language and style of their reports about patients. As mentioned previously, the empirical basis for these reports (i.e. the joke, the "long look," the response to a "motive loaded" question) is discarded in favor of abstract professional terminology depicting "syndromes" and "symptoms." This display of professional theorizing and expert language was an important part of team members' interactions with one another. It functioned to sustain in the diagnostic dialogue their identities as experts in what they were doing. Yet, as important as it was to maintain professional appearances before each other, it was equally important to establish the appearance of expertise before the legal audience to which they reported. Feelings were transformed into findings, perceived states of affairs into expert opinions. As illustrated below, displays of uncertainty or confusion were eliminated from final reports.

Excerpt 17. From Transcript of Patient Review. (The team is making its final recommendations. It has spent considerable time trying to make sense out of a patient's jumbled legal record.)

Social Worker: *[Dictating the report.]* This team is confused and unable to determine the present legal status of. . . .
Psychologist: No. Don't say we're confused, even if we are. . . .
Social Worker: Oh. Okay. What if I say we were unable, from the record, to determine the basis.
Psychologist: Right. It's the legal record that's the problem.

The maintenance of an expert identity requires teams to disguise ambivalence and confusion. It also requires that cautious phrasing be used in cases where teams may, in fact, be skeptical of the predicative consequences implied by their apparently expert pronouncements. The use of such "discretionary vagueness" is explained in the following statement.

Excerpt 18. From Psychiatrist Interview.

If a patient is in the hospital, he is medicated. He's improved and so on, fine. He might act out two or three days later again. But today, if you interview and find no, I'm not saying this individual is dangerous. We never do this. We say he is potentially dangerous, although controlled at this time. You know, you never leave the door that wide open. Not with these cases.

Through the careful use of professional language, psychiatric diagnosticians manage a professional identity of themselves as technically proficient predictors of dangerousness. Theorizing about the individual or psychopathological basis for patients' problems also serves to deny the validity of social accounts for patients' present situations. Specifically, it requires clinicians to discount explanations that may have little to do with "psychiatric reality" but a lot to do with cultural, class, or political reality. For instance, a patient may come from a cultural setting in which much of the world is interpreted through the notions of "fate" or "chance." He may have lived in a lower-class setting in which violence was construed as a "normal" response to personal affronts. He may now live in a setting where his "disruptive behaviors" are frequently provoked by the discriminatory or abusive actions of those "in charge." Actually, most Lima State patients come from, have lived in, and presently dwell in all three such settings. Nonetheless, accounts concerning their behaviors using fatalistic cultural notions, lower-class definitions of violence, or a political analysis of hospital pressures are routinely interpreted as evidence of delusional thinking, denials of responsibility, and paranoid reactions. In this way, attempts to fit patients into theories about psychiatric realities function to obscure the other realities by which patients ordinarily live.

Our suggestion that psychiatric theorizing denigrates social accounts does not imply that diagnosticians never consider cultural, class, or political variables. At various points, clinicians were observed making statements such as "Well, we can't be shocked. We have to consider that this (incest) is more common among these (mountain) people. It doesn't have the same moral meaning." "Boy, I'll tell you. He comes from a part of Cleveland, mmmmm, [where] I'd carry a gun around." "You know, the first-degree murder thing, it was because he killed a white man. If it was a black it would have been different."

At first glance, the statements appear to widen the understanding of a patient's troubles, opening the door to other social accounts for his "deviance." But this is not how such statements are used in practical psychiatric theorizing. These statements can represent a sympathetic viewing of a patient, but they are not allowed to pass as theoretical accounts for personal troubles. They may help a team "see" that the patient is a cooperative and honest person. They will not help explain why the patient did what he did, however. An illustration of this contention is found in the case of a young black male who was paralyzed from the waist down from a shooting incident several years ago. He was charged with carrying a concealed weapon. His parents, who believed he was acting "too wild" and disturbed around the house, reported him to the police. Their testimony in court was apparently a key element in his commitment to Lima State Hospital until he was restored to reason. During the interview, the patient was composed, but he stated that he would probably continue to carry a weapon to protect his property and that he had refused to take his medication because it made him sick.

After the patient left the room, the psychologist discussed signs of paranoid schizophrenia and expressed concern over the patient's intent to carry a gun, his almost "unnatural fear" of someone taking his property, and his "perceived emnity or hostility towards his family." The psychiatrist elaborated upon this, stating: "This is abnormal. You don't carry a knife around to stab someone becauese you feel you'll get stabbed. This man was disturbed." The social worker initially seemed less sure of this line of theorizing. Shouldn't the case be seen in relation to a social-cultural milieu in which gun-carrying would be seen as "normal"? The psychiatrist responded by pointing out that while these broader issues were important, they were really not the patient's problem. His problem was psychiatrically refocused at the individual level. His disturbed behavior at home was the "real" issue. The social worker accepted this "insight" and returned to theorizing about the patient's individualized trouble. Late in the interview, even the social worker theorized entirely at the level of individualistic psychiatric reality. The patient's disturbed behavior was discussed as a form of compensation for his physical disability. Social accountings were discarded in favor of individualized psychiatric explanations.

The preoccupation of psychiatric diagnosticians with individualistic explanations for deviance has definite political implications. As agents of social control, these professionals represent the state's power to hospitalize its citizens involuntarily. By emphasizing the importance of one explanatory framework (psychiatric) to the near exclusion of another (social), psychiatric assessments of dangerousness function to control the acceptability of certain "realities" as well as behaviors. Often this inattention to other than individualistic psychiatric themes seems sociologically naive. In one case a team asked a lower-class male patient what he would do if he were on a public bus and someone came up and started calling him obscene names. The patient stated that it depended on whether the person was a male or a female. If it was a male, he said that the person deserved to get punched. Such an answer is probably to be expected from the perspective of a culture and class, in which the possibility of violence and rigid distinctions between expectations for males and females are taken as commonplace. From the vantage point of psychiatric diagnosticians, however, the situation looked quite different. Team members noted the distinction between males and females "as if" it were evidence of the patient's ambivalence toward women and saw the fact that the event may precipitate violence as indicative that "his judgment remains impulsive."

In another case, a patient's story about being victimized by a "crackpot psychiatrist," by staff discrimination, and by the lack of treatment in Lima State Hospital and at a home for delinquents—which he described as more a jail than a school—were taken as evidence of his need to rationalize and drive to manipulate. One woman's story of sexual abuse at the hospital was taken as evidence of delusions and projections of her homosexual identity to others, although she had previously testified at public hearings about this incident. As the team suggested in formulating its final opinion, "some of this goes on but mostly it's just her delusions."

The preceding examples were presented as illustrations of a prevailing pattern.[16] Potentially plausible cultural, class, and political accounts are struck down in favor of explanations that favor a focus on the individual roots of social deviance. This practice has important implications, not only for the diagnostic fate of individual patients, but for the system of social control as a whole. The present system of criminal justice is, after all, constructed on an individualistic model of deviance. It is the individual offender who is held culpable for violations against the sociolegal order of things. The work of diagnostic professionals reinforces the operation of that system. Their work in "discovering" the individual roots of dangerousness and need for maximum security, and their disregard of cultural, class, and political accounts regarding these matters underscores the belief that violent crimes are best explained in terms of troublesome or pathological individuals. Thus while achieving a sense of expert identity, diagnosticians simultaneously further the interests of the existing mechanisms of social control.

Summary Remarks

The psychiatric assessment of dangerousness and need for maximum security is a political act because through it the state's power is invoked to restrict citizens' freedoms. Insofar as we have observed that diagnosticians favor individualized psychiatric accounts to the exclusion of social explanations for deviance, their acts are political in a second sense as well. They play a "gatekeeping" function whereby a certain version of human reality—that which explains troublesome behavior at the individual or psychopathological level—is rewarded, and other versions—those that explain behavior in terms of cultural, class, or political accounts—are punished. Past, present, or possibly future behaviors are wrenched from their social context. They are interpretively converted by psychiatric diagnosticians into theories of personal pathology. Moreover, the empirical basis for judgments about the psychogenic roots of deviance is transformed or obscured by the use of an abstract professional language. The management of this language helps to secure an expert identity for its users. It also serves to mask essentially moral or political judgments in the logic and rhetoric of psychiatric expertise. The whole process of psychiatric determination of the needs to be confined supports a criminal justice system that emphasizes individuals rather than collectivities as the real perpetrators of violence and harm.

In observing the political implications of the prediction process, it is not suggested that psychiatric diagnosticians consciously victimize anyone, deliberately denigrate other versions of reality, or intentionally participate in the maintenance of a particular system of social control. These things happen. The perspective of the diagnosticians themselves is best characterized by the term "false consciousness." They are sincere in viewing their work as discovery. They appear capable of simultaneously supporting ideals of reform and social control.

Despite the "good" intentions of the psychiatric professionals, however, psychiatric predictions of need for confinement have "bad" consequences and should be abandoned, for such predictions have not proved better than decisions by mere chance. They have produced high rates of false positives as well as depreciating the social realities. Worst of all, they have reinforced an assumption within the criminal justice system that systematically prevents the realization of social justice: the assumption that violent or dangerous behavior can best be explained at the individual or psychogenic level. This assumption reifies an individualistic view of the world while discrediting the conception that human potentials, possibilities, and practices are intricately related to the fates of the collectivities in which they live and find both meaning and existence.[17] Through almost exclusive adherence to this principle, the criminal justice system can isolate violence in the acts of individuals. Ignored are social meanings of such acts. These meanings may vary greatly in terms of self-consciousness or reflective awareness. Certainly the violence of the political terrorist and the violence of the youth defending his "rep" in the street fight or the husband his "masculinity" in the bedroom are not to be equated. Yet each may express the problems of power and privilege or the experience of their absence. The meaning of such violence represents a range of human action considerably wider than the restrictive scope of psychiatric reality.[18]

Let us make a suggestion for a modest improvement in psychiatric predictions. We have argued that decisions about who needs to be confined in maximum security are inherently political. Hence, if these decisions must be made (as they will be in the forseeable future), they should be rendered in a more explicitly political forum such as that of a jury hearing in a formal court setting. We have also argued that psychiatric predictions are not particularly accurate in sorting out dangerous persons or psychopathic individuals; they are expert only in the careful management of their user's professional identities. These careful management practices should be discarded and the work of psychiatric professionals should be displayed as but one input within the context of advocacy and cross-examination. If this is done, the usefulness of psychiatric judgments can be preserved, without treating these judgments as the objective products of expert technologies. Psychiatric professionals can be queried about the bases for their opinions. Decision-makers can be exposed to their inferential logic-in-use as well as their justificatory logic of professional resonstruction.

The suggestion of a juried hearing is based on observations of several of the few cases in which Lima State patients appealed the recommendations set forth by psychiatric review teams. Legal advocates debated the issue of a patient's dangerousness and need for confinement and interrogated the "experts" involved in a decision. In one case the psychiatric team had concluded that a patient was "a creature of pure impulse, with no controls whatsoever, no conscience, and no feelings of remorse or sensibility" and that he was "considered to be immediately dangerous to others and in continued need of hospitalization in a maximum security facility." During the hearing, legal advocates produced evidence that the patient "had not shown aggressiveness or assaultiveness" during his stay at the hospital. Testimony by hospital staff indicated that "the patient could be adequately cared for outside a maximum security institution." In the light of this additional evidence, the court reversed the recommendation of the "experts" and decided that the patient did not need maximum security. The court was informed by more than psychiatric predictions, and rightly so. We conclude that the professional prediction of dangerousness should be replaced by public adjudication. This would ensure that judgments regarding involuntary confinement remain in the explicitly political arena to which they belong.

The institutionalization of mandatory adjudication may devaluate the expertise of psychiatric decision-makers, which will elicit considerable opposition from psychiatric professionals themselves. As Brodsky has observed, the well-versed cross-examiner can create "an 'expert witness' nightmare." While the adversary system "provides a base of common challenge points," it may, for the uncertain witness, precipitate a discrediting experience.[19] Nonetheless, our consistent discovery of inconsistency, disguised as professional caution, indicates that the adversary situation is required for fairness to the individual whose fortunes turn on these professional perceptions.

Throughout this chapter we have been concerned with the processes by which "expert psychiatric knowledge" is assembled about patients and "expert status" accorded to its creators. We have been led to certain moral and political reservations about the present status of psychiatric contributions to decisions about dangerousness. We have concluded that psychiatric knowledge is a well-managed "appearance of objectivity" rather than a set of "objective facts." Its factual authenticity must not be taken for granted. It counts—and counts heavily—in the lives of patients whose psychological and social realities are assessed in terms of their dangerousness and need for maximum security.

Because of the serious consequences of psychiatric decision-making, we believe that the basis for its "authority," and its dependence on a process of negotiated social interaction, should be displayed for public scrutiny. We hope that the presentation of our findings represents a step in this direction. We are confident that the public adjudication of each attempt to confine someone as dangerous (or in need of maximum security) will represent another more permanent advance. This step will realize the spirit of Judge David Bazelon's ruling in the case of *Covington* v. *Cameron*,[20] which stated that it was the court's responsibility to see that psychiatric decision-makers reach "reasoned" and not "unreasonable" conclusions, employ "proper criteria," and "do not overlook anything of substantial relevance." To bring decision-makers out of the mystic shelter of expertise and into the public scrutiny of the courtroom should advance these goals. We conclude by agreeing with Judge Bazelon that "to do less would abandon the interests affected to the absolute power of administrative officials."[21]

Notes

1. Actually, although Lima State Hospital has been traditionally referred to as a hospital for the "criminally insane," only a small proportion of its nearly

700 patients were technically "not guilty by reason of insanity." About one-third of its patients were "mentally ill offenders" transferred from penal settings. Another third were classified as "incompetent" and still waiting to stand trial, while about one-fifth of the patients were "psychopathic offenders," hospitalized under Ohio's version of a "sexual psychopath statute." The remaining patients were split between those "not guilty by reason of insanity," those transferred (as behavior problems) from civil mental hospitals, and those believed to have incurred mental problems while on probation or parole.

2. Other results of this "right to treatment" ruling involved the setting of minimum standards for treatment. For a fuller discussion of this case and others, see Stephen J. Pfohl, *Right to Treatment Litigation: A Consideration of Judicial Intervention Into Mental Health Policy* (Columbus, Ohio: Ohio Division of Mental Health, 1975).

3. Technically, decisions about "dangerousness" (i.e., the extreme likelihood of inflicting immediate harm) and those regarding "psychopathic offenders" (i.e., needing the continued custody and care of Lima State Hospital) were different. The practical consequences, however, were the same: continued confinement. For our present purposes, we are less concerned with what technically embodies a decision than we are with the assumptions and interests of the decision-makers. As such, both categories of decisions about continued confinement will be considered simultaneously.

4. Norval Morris, *The Future of Imprisonment* (Chicago: University of Chicago Press, 1974), pp. 62-63.

5. Pfohl, p. 24.

6. Ernst Wenk, J. Robison, and G. Smith, "Can Violence Be Predicted?" *Crime and Delinquency* 18 (1972): 393-402.

7. Edwin Megargee, "The Prediction of Violence with Psychological Tests," in C. Speilberger (ed.), *Current Topics in Clinical and Community Psychology* (New York: Academic Press, 1970), pp. 98-156.

8. Harry Kozol, R. Boucher, and R. Garofalo, "The Diagnosis and Treatment of Dangerousness," *Crime and Delinquency* (1972): vol. 18:371-392, 1972; Henry Steadman and Joseph Cocozza, *Careers of the Criminally Insane* (Lexington, Mass.: Lexington Books, D.C. Heath, 1974).

9. Actually, rates are usually considerably lower. The "maximum rate" referred to here would entail the retention of all "criminally insane" or "forensic" patients under age fifty, while still incurring a 2:1 ratio of false positive predictions (see Steadman and Cocozza). Other studies (such as Wenk, Robison, and Smith) have found the false prediction rate to be as high as 95 percent.

10. Bruce J. Ennis and Thomas R. Litwack, "Psychiatry and the Presumption of Expertise: Flipping the Coins in the Courtroom," *California Law Review* 62 (May 1974): 693-752.

11. Alan Dershowitz, "Psychiatrists' Power in Civil Commitment," *Psychology Today* 2 (February 1969): 47.

12. Morris, p. 63.

13. In addition to their belief that "psychopathic offenders" were among the most dangerous of patients, some teams also believed that they were "untreatable." Their model for understanding these persons assumed that psychopaths cannot learn from experience and that their antisocial personalities can "burn out" only with age. As such, some psychopathic offenders were recommended for release from a maximum security "treatment" setting and transfer to a penal setting where they simply pass time (something that was assumed to be the only effective solution for their "psychopathy"). Other teams that assumed that psychopaths could be treated recommended that similar individuals be kept in the maximum security hospital where they truly belonged.

14. Teams generally searched for evidence to confirm "theories" that were being developed about patients, but this does not mean that patients had no impact on the outcomes of psychiatric decisions. Interviews with selected patients convinced us that patients often tried to manage a particular identity in front of team members. Sometimes patients' "resistance" clearly altered the direction of diagnosticians theorizing. So did the occasional resistance of team members to each other. In such cases, where theories were modified or compromised, teams appeared to display an additional show of reconstructed logic, in demonstrating wither "that's what we were saying all along anyway" or "it's only different because of 'new evidence,' not better theorizing."

15. Teams all worked to construct "individualized theories" during their final post-interview discussions. Not all teams "theorized" to the same extent in reviewing records and interviewing patients. For instance, three of eleven teams observed showed little evidence of "theory construction" before talking with patients. Two of these had actually decided not to review records until after talking with patients. Only two teams out of eleven displayed no evidence of theorizing about patients in their actual interviewing procedures.

16. Of the eleven teams observed, only one seemed particularly open to accounts other than the "psychiatric." It should be noted, however, that an occasional display of "sociological" knowledge was employed as a disclaimer in the promotion of more individualized theorizing. For instance, a psychiatric explanation was sometimes prefaced by the lead-in phrase: "Well, of course this does happen and it could be the case, *but. . . .*"

17. The suggestion that human conduct is intricately related to, rather than determined by, the socioeconomic forces that shape the fate of collectivities is quite deliberate. We are here presenting a "critical analysis" that envisions individual actions as restrained, but not caused by infrastructural variables.

18. There is no attempt here to romanticize "proletarian violence." The relation between the meaning of violence for the actor and the experience of

relative powerlessness has been mapped out in numerous investigations. See Lynn Curtis, *Violence, Race, and Culture* (Lexington, Mass.: Lexington Books, D.C. Heath, 1975).

19. Stanley L. Brodsky, *Psychologists in the Criminal Justice System* (Carbondale, Ill.: Admark, 1972), p. 95.

20. See *Covington* v. *Cameron*, 419 F.2d 617 (D.C. Cir. 1969).

21. Bazelon is here excerpted in Jonas Robitscher, "The Right to Treatment: A Social-Legal Approach to the Plight of the State Hospital Patient," *Villanova Law Review*, 18 (November 1972): 19.

20

HOW PAROLE OFFICERS USE RECORDS
RICHARD McCLEARY

INTRODUCTION

A parole bureaucracy uses its records to classify and process men released from prison. Assuming only this internal use, parole records should give an accurate description of parolee behavior according to the classification criteria. In fact, parole records are more likely to reflect the needs and problems of parole officers (*POs*). I attribute this bureaucratic dysfunction to the discretion allowed POs gathering and reporting information. In most cases, the PO himself decides what information will actually go into the official record. By exercising editorial discretion, the PO can suppress information that might make his job difficult or include information that might facilitate work goals or objectives. This is how POs use their records.

Traditional studies of the PO's work environment divide it into halves, the PO-parolee interaction and the PO-bureaucracy interaction. Glaser's (1964; See also Irwin, 1970) view of the PO-parolee interaction is typical in that it emphasizes control; a successful PO is one who can control his clients. Takagi (1967) has noted that within this context, a successful PO must also balance and satisfy certain explicit and implicit demands of the bureaucracy. The factor common to these halves of the PO's work environment is record-keeping. The data presented here[1] will show that a successful PO is one who knows how to manipulate his

---

[1] I have been collecting the participant/interview data presented here since 1974. The initial phase of data collection lasted six months and consisted of interviews and in-office observation. Over fifty parole officers (*POs*), supervisors, and Department of Corrections (DC) officials were interviewed at least once. In-office observation during this period was relatively informal and aimed at gaining a working knowledge of the routine in each branch office. The second phase of data collection also lasted six months but consisted primarily of field observation. On an average of two days (or nights) per week, I accompanied POs on "house call" rounds. Notes made during this period make direct reference to twenty-two POs interacting with clients. The final ongoing phase of data collection uses informants to track theoretically interesting cases. These data are validated through multiple informants and records. As presented, the data have been "contaminated" to disguise incidents or episodes and their actors. A detailed description of methods appears in an earlier report of this study (McCleary, 1975).

The bureaucracy studied here is a metropolitan division of a state parole agency. About fifty POs work out of half a dozen branch offices, each run by a supervisor. "DC officials" are all management employees above the rank of supervisor. This includes both line managers and technical support managers who are not involved in direct line functions.

*The substance of this paper was shaped by a seminar in social psychology ("Bureaucracy, social experimentation, and evaluation") conducted by Donald Campbell, Nancy Cochrane, and Andy Gordon. I am indebted to Howard Becker, Dick and Sarah F. Berk, Arlene Daniels, David McDowall, James Pitts, Marshall Shumsky, and Carol A. B. Warren for critical assistance.

From Richard McCleary, "How Parole Officers Use Records," 24(5) *Social Problems* 576-589 (June 1977). Copyright 1977 by the Society for the Study of Social Problems, Inc.

records, though this is not a simple task. Straightforward record-keeping entails costs that the PO must weigh against potential benefits.

A note on the unique historical determinants of record-keeping in the parole bureaucracy will be followed by an outline of the practical costs of record-keeping. A PO will not report minor crimes, incidents, or violations he observes in his caseload. When a PO does report an incident, he is creating records to accomplish an end, with benefits expected to outweigh the practical costs of reporting the incident. The inescapable implication is that parole records do not reflect the behavior of parolees, but the many problems arising in the PO's work environment. Three general problems lead to the most common forms of manipulating records: (1) records created to threaten parolees, (2) records created to get rid of troublesome parolees, and (3) records created to protect the PO and his superiors.

HISTORY

Many of the phenomena described here arise from recent changes in the law, particularly the U.S. Supreme Court decision in Morrissey *versus* Brewer, extending the Constitutional protection of due process to parolees. Prior to 1972, a PO could detain a parolee in County Jail for weeks without filing charges; parolees could be returned to prison on the basis of the PO's determination that the parolee had a "bad attitude" or was making a "poor adjustment to parole." After 1972, POs were required for the first time to file specific charges before ordering a parolee's detention. Furthermore, parolees received the right to a quasi-judicial hearing on all charges the PO might file. The parolee or his or her attorney had the right to cross-examine the PO and the verdict of the hearing could be appealed to the courts.

The effect of *Morrissey* on the PO's work environment was traumatic. POs lost much of their strategic advantage in the PO-parolee interaction. Because specific charges provable in hearings were required, it became difficult to re-imprison parolees on the basis of catch-all charges. Post-*Morrissey*, POs no longer had absolute control over their parolees.

More important, *Morrissey* introduced a new set of bureaucratic demands. Before 1972, the bureaucracy used its records internally to classify and process men released from prison. After 1972, the bureaucracy increased use of its records externally to justify classification decisions to outside agencies such as the courts. It was only after 1972, that the Department of Corrections (*DC*) began to use electronic data processing equipment for cataloging and retrieving parole records. This abrupt change introduced accountability and decision costs into the PO's work environment. One veteran PO described the change this way:

> It used to be 'the' records, now it's 'my' records. If I recall correctly, in the old days, I never signed my monthly reports. If I forget to sign one now, Terry sends it back to me. Nothing gets out of this (branch) office without a signature. That's so they know who to come back to if there's any trouble.

Routine Organization: Incentives for Underreporting

As far as the DC is concerned, a PO has two major duties. First, the PO must survey, and if necessary, service a given number of parolees. Surveying and servicing are not well defined. But as a rule of thumb, the DC would expect a PO to "know what's going on" in his caseload.

The PO's second major duty is to write records the DC requires to discharge its statutory obligations. Most of the records are monthly reports. Every month a PO must contact each of his parolees at least once. In theory, any new information the PO gleans will appear in the reports. In practice this seldom happens.

When things are going smoothly[2] between a PO and his parolees, the monthly reports are

---

[2] The interaction of PO and parolee is an equilibrium system (Irwin, 1970), which can be disrupted

dull and uninformative. Reports are submitted to the branch office supervisor who approves them with his signature and forwards them to the DC. At the end of a month, the supervisor receives a computerized summary of all the records written by his POs. The summary serves as a ledger, telling the supervisor how many reports his POs owed and how many they remitted. If a PO has neglected to file a report on one of his parolees, the omission is highlighted in the summary. Thus, monthly reports are ordinarily used as a minimal check on the PO's job performance.

When relations are poor between a PO and his parolees, the monthly reports will contain information relating to a crime, incident, or violation of the parole contract. If the PO receives this information from another criminal justice agency he simply acts as an information conduit. More commonly, the PO independently discovers crimes, incidents, or violations. While the PO is legally bound to report this information, practical considerations counter this directive. Practical considerations, generating incentives for underreporting, fall into five major categories of cost.

(1) *Full reporting cuts into the PO's "free" time.* When asked what facet of their job is the most attractive, POs invariably mention the flexible schedule. For example:

> My wife and I have a restaurant and this job gives me a lot of free time for the business. I spend two half-days a week here and then take care of my fieldwork in the evenings. When you have an arrangement like I have, you have to handle things off the record. If the cops catch one of my men shooting up, I go through the motions of requesting a warrant. But if I catch the man myself, I handle it my own way. My way accomplishes the same thing and only takes one tenth the time. I've got my own style. If I went by the book, they'd have me down here six days a week writing reports.
>
> Half the POs on this side of town are full-time students. This job doesn't pay much and it doesn't offer much of a future. But if you're going to school, it's perfect because the hours aren't set. If I can do my job in twenty hours, that's my business.

Since most POs moonlight at other pursuits requiring a flexible schedule, underreporting crimes, incidents, and violations maximizes the PO's "free" time.[3]

(2) *Full reporting places the PO in jeopardy.* Whenever the PO reports an incident, he runs the risk of a hearing. A DC superior reading the report may pressure the PO to request a warrant. The warrant must go to hearing, and as POs see it, this is a risk:

> When you go into that hearing, you're the one on trial . . . If you lose the hearing, the DC people never let you forget it. They don't tell you up front, but they expect you to perjure yourself if the hearing gets close. I won't do that. I'll tell you how ridiculous it is. When I catch a parolee in violation, I handle it myself. If I reported it, somebody would get after me to file a warrant and I don't need that headache.

POs routinely speak of "winning" or "losing" revocation hearings. During the course of this

---

by either actor or by external forces such as the DC or other criminal justice agencies. Smooth going, or equilibrium is the normal state of the system and it is understood that neither the PO or the parolee need be at fault when equilibrium is disrupted.

[3] Weber's fifth characteristic of a bureaucracy provides a counterpoint here. According to Gerth and Mills (1958: 198), "When the office is fully developed, official activity demands the full working capacity of the official . . . Formerly, in all cases, the normal state of affairs was reversed: official business was discharged as a secondary activity." A majority of the POs, in contrast, see official duties as a sideline. Over thirty percent of the POs are full time students, for example; one PO actually completed a Ph.D. while a full time employee of the DC. The DC is aware of this situation unofficially. One high DC official estimated that POs spend no more than fifteen hours per week attending to official business. Toleration here is viewed as a fringe benefit by both sides; illuminating the paradox of the bureaucrat who chooses a career largely because it is *not* a career. The DC then defines loyalty as something other than "the full working capacity of the official." So long as the PO satisfies these other demands, his "free" time is his own.

study, nearly all revocation warrants were based on information developed by the police or prosecutor, not on information developed by POs. While this trend permits a number of plausible interpretations, it is fully consistent with the claim made here: POs ignore violations that they might be required to "prove" in hearing.

(3) *POs believe that the DC evaluates their performance favorably on the basis of low case-load return-to-prison rates.* An incident becomes actionable only after the PO reports it. Thus, the more crimes, incidents, or violations the PO reports, the higher his return-to-prison statistic. A branch office supervisor explained:

> New POs always ask me how many revocations the DC wants them to have in a year. I always answer that we don't have quotas but I don't think they believe me. It's funny the way they ask too—like it's a company secret. Then they go away mad because I won't trust them with the secret number . . . Most POs have a quota mentality of some sort.

This supervisor's impression is accurate. POs place a great emphasis on their caseload return statistic:

> I don't think it's a secret around here that the POs with the lowest return rates get all the goodies . . . I have the lowest return rate in this office and it generates a lot of malice . . . No, I don't try to meet a quota. It's simply a result of my work style. I'm effective. The quickest way to get your books audited is to come up with too many revocations. I've seen that happen to a lot of POs.

There are no data to suggest that the DC evaluates its POs on the basis of this or any other statistic[4] yet most POs operate under a "quota mentality" that leads to underreporting.

(4) *Full reporting may result in "busy work" for the PO.* To a PO, much of the work assigned by his supervisor is considered "busy work," that is, work that is not only time consuming but also unnecessary. In fact, a supervisor can punish a PO informally by creating "busy work." How this factor leads to underreporting is illustrated in the special case of missing or AWOL parolees. A supervisor described the general situation this way:

> When a PO can't find a parolee, he submits an AWOL report. Thirty days later, the DC issues an apprehension warrant. When the parolee is apprehended, he gets a hearing and is sent back to prison. Of course, it's not that cut and dried. For one thing, I suspect that many of my POs make informal arrangements with their parolees. So if one of my POs comes in here with an AWOL report, I want him to be damn sure that the parolee's not attending his mother's funeral or something like that. The parolee might have thought that his PO didn't care about leaving the district for that sort of thing. Also, it's well known that POs have tricked their parolees into violation by giving them verbal permission to leave the district. I believe that's called 'bagging a man.' Well, sir, those things don't happen in my office because I make it difficult for my POs to file an AWOL report. I require a great deal of hard work before I (counter) sign one. In that way, I can satisfy myself that a report is basically honest and that it will stand up in hearing.

So in most cases, POs will not promptly report AWOL parolees:

> You got to be stupid to report a dude AWOL. That's a lot of work. If you wait a few weeks, the dude will probably show up with some jive excuse. Otherwise he'll get busted ripping off. Either way, you saved yourself a lot of trouble by not reporting the dude AWOL.

---

[4] There is so little variance in this statistic that it could not be used to evaluate performance. The POs who were "promoted" during the course of this study had neither high nor low return-to-prison rates. POs nevertheless emphasize this statistic. Many POs can recite their return-to-prison rates to the third digit, and when POs have exaggerated their statistics to me, the exaggeration has always been an underestimation.

(5) *A PO may restrict his options by reporting a violation.* Some POs have stated explicitly that reporting incidents is not part of their "real" job:

> It's not part of my job to catch clients in violation. When I do, I want to counsel the client and I can't do that if I work through the system. Once I report a violation, I lose my freedom to act as a professional.

This attitude is typical of the POs who view themselves as counselors or therapists. In a more general sense, reporting a violation restricts such options as "giving the man a second chance" or "giving a break" to a client deemed worthy:

> What a PO can do is dispense justice. The system can't do that because of the regulations. When I see a client who deserves a break, I can give it to him as long as no one knows about it. I like helping parolees and sometimes that's the only way I can help.

Most POs value this discretionary power greatly and thus underreport incidents for this reason alone.

SUMMARY

These five specific cost categories can be generalized to time, effort, freedom, and jeopardy. Generally, whenever the PO reports an incident discovered in his caseload, he risks paying a practical cost. Consequently, the PO will not report an incident unless the resulting record is practically useful to him in some way, with potential benefits of recording the incident outweighing potential costs. Underreporting is the expected mode of behavior, reinforced by the organizational contingencies outlined. But there are three general sets of circumstances inclining POs to break away from the expected mode. These circumstances offer a counterbalancing incentive; by reporting an incident, the PO creates a useful record. The circumstances include situations where the PO can (1) initate a record to threaten or coerce a parolee, (2) initiate a record to eliminate a troublesome parolee, or (3) initiate a record that will protect himself and his DC superiors.

1. Using Records to Threaten a Parolee

When things go badly between the PO and one of his clients, the fault may be with the PO, the DC, or with some outside agency. But if the parolee is at fault, the PO can use his records to threaten, persuade, or coerce his client "back into line." The alternative mechanism of control, returning the troublesome client to prison, entails the risk of a warrant hearing.

To understand this phenomenon, consider what an official record or document means to the parolee. Throughout his prison career, social workers and security personnel thumbed through dossiers while making decisions that affected the inmate's life. Institutional assignments, assignments to rehabilitative programs, privileges, punishments, and eventually parole itself were all decided on the basis of papers kept in a manila folder. In the end, this ominous dossier follows the inmate out of prison.

During a group therapy session, a parolee described a routine visit to see his PO. The parolee's description of this episode is revealing:

> I go in to see him and he's acting real funny. You know, like I done something–but I didn't. I'm clean now. He asked me some funny questions about my job, like how I was getting along with my boss and how I liked the work. Everytime I answered a question, he looked in my file to see if I was telling the truth. I think he had a snitch sheet on me. I hope I answered all the questions right.

Perhaps the PO was initiating a friendly off-the record conversation during which he absent-mindedly picked up a dossier and began to page through it. Yet the parolee's interpretation of this episode has a basis in fact. Experienced POs are sensitive to the threatening aspects of dossiers and usually take some precautions to put their clients at ease. For example, I observed one PO writing a report in the presence of a client. The PO showed his client both the standardized form and an official document referred to in the report. The PO explained what each was and then asked the parolee if he had any questions. The PO later told me:

> I try not to do any writing while the man's in my office. If I have to, I always explain what I'm writing and why I have to write it. I show the man all the forms I have to use. This may sound funny, but a lot of parolees are like rabbits. They scare easily. I don't want a man to do something rash because he misunderstands something I'm doing. When I say 'something rash,' of course, I mean absconding.

Most POs will show clients routine documents to put the client at ease. For the same reason, most POs will answer any simple questions a client might ask about his dossier. But no PO would "absent-mindedly" page through a dossier in the presence of a client. This action has an unambiguous meaning to the PO and to the parolee. Just as a PO can physically manipulate files to intimidate, or alternatively, to relax a parolee, a PO may write reports under certain conditions for no other reason but intimidation. Before the 1972 *Morrissey* decision, the PO was able to back up his threats in a very tangible way. One veteran PO described this situation:

> In the old days, you'd give a man a warning. If he didn't listen to you, you'd issue a "detain for investigation" warrant. He'd sit in jail for a few weeks while you "investigated," and believe me, that did the trick usually. Of course, if it didn't, well, then you had to send the man back to the joint. But at least you gave him two chances first. Nowadays you either ignore the violation or you send the man back to the joint. There's no in-betweens.

The difference is that the PO can no longer support threats with swift, sure sanctions. This restructuring of the PO-parolee interaction has led directly to a number of novel ways to use records. This statement of a younger PO suggests how clients can be threatened:

> In an average case, I'd start by giving the client a friendly warning. If that didn't work, I'd write an official warning. If the official warning didn't work, I'd try to place the client in a special caseload where he could receive individualized treatment. If there were no individualized treatment available, I might request a warrant. Then I'd try to reason with the client, and if we could work something out, I'd drop the warrant. If not, I'd still get one more chance to work something out at the hearing. One possibility might be an order that increased my revocation powers. Now that's about a half-dozen steps, right? It's a six-step escalation that I can stop at any time. What it does is it puts psychological pressure on the client. It shifts the burden of revocation back to him. He's forced to grow up or go back to jail.

The process amounts to a war of nerves between the PO and his client, each trying to dominate the other. Of course, the process was less necessary when POs had more effective weapons at their disposal.

The six-step escalation process has a number of by-product records, one of which is the "final, offical warning." One PO discribed that record this way:

> These guys are misleading you with their talk about official warnings. There's no such thing. It's something they made up. I'll tell you what they mean. When you write the report, you say, 'Gave client warning about such-and-such.' Then you show that to the client to scare him. But it doesn't mean anything. If you really want to scare him, you send him his offical warning by mail. One time I had this junkie—a white kid. His mother was causing problems for him. She didn't have any respect for me or for the job I was trying to do.

Well, I finally gave him an official warning and mailed a copy to his mother. I never had any trouble with him after that. His mother kicked his ass everytime he got out of line. But an official warning isn't *official*. The DC won't take any action on it. It's just something you use to bring a client back into line.

This PO was not entirely correct. Offical warnings do have other uses:

Of course, if you warn a man about something, and later on if it goes to revocation, you've protected yourself. The Public Defender is going to question your charges. So what you do is go back in your files and bring out the warning. The fact that the man didn't raise any objections at that time means that he's admitting to the basics of the warning, and by implication, the basics of the charge against him. So warnings have two uses. They let a man know you mean business—put the fear of God into him—and they protect you if you have to go after a warrant.

The revocation process itself has become largely a psychological weapon. A warrant will usually not be issued for a single violation complaint, but even if issued, it is not likely to be upheld in hearing. Warrants are still effective if used properly, however:

The trick to requesting warrants is finesse. You've got to rely on your reputation (with the supervisor) to get a warrant in the first place and then you've got to rely on your wits so it doesn't blow up in your face. A warrant is only good if you *don't* use it. Let me explain that. One time this dude cuts out to St. Louis to visit his family. I forgot where his family lived, so I reported him AWOL. When he got back to town, there was a warrant out on him. Now that was just sloppy work on my part. The warrant would have been thrown out in hearing and I would have looked like a chump. I think I gave him permission to cut out but then forgot to write it down. I should have called his mother before reporting him AWOL anyway. Well, I visited this dude in jail and told him I'd drop the warrant if he stayed out of trouble. The dude was so grateful that he broke down and cried. Later it occurred to me that that's the only way to use a warrant. The dude's got to be ignorant. You get a jailhouse lawyer or some smart gangbanger and he's going to laugh right in your face. Those dudes are too tough to scare. But if you've got a tired dude or a scared dude, you can break him with a warrant.

The PO's motives in this connection are obvious. In an earlier report of this study (McCleary, 1975), the concepts of *competence* and *realism* implied a certain amount of control; a competent, realistic PO appears to control his clients. Formal or official methods of control can be costly to the PO, while informal methods, often as effective, may be less costly. Moreover, as the cost of formal control is born by the bureaucracy itself, the informal methods such as manipulating records have become an accepted mode of operation. This is apparent in the typical comment of a branch office supervisor:

There's something final about the written word. A PO can talk himself blue in the face and get no response from the parolee. If he puts it down on paper, though, he gets results. Parolees know that once something gets written down, it's final. I encourage my POs to utilize their reports that way.

While a PO ignores incidents to minimize his risk and costs, the DC expects the PO to control his parolees. So POs will report incidents as a means to establish or reassert control over troublesome parolees.

2. Using Records to Get Rid of a Parolee

What is the PO to do when threats prove ineffectual? Psychological coercion is always the preferred means of control; reimprisonment, as the potentially most costly alternative, is the least preferred. One intermediate option is to eliminate the troublesome parolee by reporting incidents that suggest a pathology requiring treatment. The DC maintains a number of special programs to provide services for unusual parolee-types. To place a client in one of these programs, the PO must first report one or more incidents in support of a pathological theory. These reports can serve double duty as threats. The PO, for example, can give the client a "final, official warning" about a pathological behavior. If the threat works, the PO has accomplished his goal. If not, the PO applies for an administrative order to transfer the troublesome client out of the caseload and into a special program. The administrative order must be approved by the PO's supervisor and often by higher DC officials. As this procedure amounts to considerable extra work for the PO, the motivating circumstances must be strong.

In one case, a parolee was accused of beating his wife. The police were called but took no action because the wife refused to make an official complaint. The police notified the DC, however, and the PO in charge of the case was asked to investigate the situation:

> There wasn't too much to report. She didn't have any bruises, so it couldn't have been too bad. I think she just gets hysterical and goes overboard. There's nothing I can do in this case except warn the man and hope it doesn't happen again.

But it did happen again, and as before, the wife refused to make an official complaint. This time the PO was reprimanded for his "inaction."

> I don't know what they want me to do. She doesn't have any marks on her and she won't press a charge. He denies even touching her. If I went after a revocation on this, they'd throw it out and accuse me of overreacting. They want me to do something but they won't tell me what. If this happens again and she gets hurt or something, they're going to blame me for it.

The PO resolved this problem by transferring the parolee to a special treatment caseload for "violent offenders." But the PO was candid about his motives:

> I felt like a fool arguing that he was violent. Violence had nothing to do with what was going on there. And I don't think the violent offender PO will be able to help. But it's not my problem now. I'm just happy to get rid of that case.

This case was unusual in a number of respects. The PO was a novice, and because he had not commented on his client's "violent" nature before this incident, the transfer was not as smooth as it might have been. Experienced POs will usually get rid of a case before the situation gets this far out of hand.

The general attitude among POs is that the special treatment programs are an alternative to reimprisonment. This statement is typical:

> In most cases, I'm going to have more freedom if my client is an addict. The reason for that is that we know how to deal with the problem. We've got special programs for addicts. If you take some other client whose problem is just that he's a thief, well, we don't have a special program for thieves. Maybe someday we will. But right now, if an addict and a thief are busted for petty theft, the thief's going back to prison. The addict will be transferred to a special program and continued on parole. He gets a second chance that he wouldn't have had before we started the special program.

And most POs acknowledge the practical differences between placing clients in special programs and returning clients to prison:

> Well, it's just easier. It's easier to get it okayed by your supervisor for one thing. Usually you can even get your client to "volunteer." I don't believe that any of these special treatments are going to work but what else can I do? I want to avoid revocations because they're messy and time consuming. Placing your client for treatment is the easiest way to do that sometimes.

POs are also aware of the political considerations involved in getting rid of clients:

> Write up a new parole plan and then get your supervisor to sign it. For some programs,

you need Mr. Chaseham's signature but that's not hard to get if you know the ropes. When you get his okay, no program can turn your client down.

Social workers employed by the special treatment programs are aware of the PO's motives for sending clients to the programs. For example, a social worker associated with a narcotic offender program complained:

A lot of POs have the idea that this is a last-chance program, and of course, it's not. They're sending us parolees who should have been returned to prison instead. There aren't many treatable addicts here now, just screw-ups. The addicts who could benefit from our program can't get in because there's not enough room and because their POs don't want to send them here until there's no other choice. I do my best to stop these abuses but it's nearly impossible. A PO who knows how to write a persuasive case and who perhaps has some clout with the politicians can get a parolee past me very easily. I turn down a lot of applicants and then get overruled by the people upstairs. Of course, anyone recommended by Chaseham gets in. He doesn't understand the problems we have here.

The DC administration seems to be aware of the ways POs use the special treatment programs. An administrator connected with the narcotic offender program backed up this social worker's complaint:

POs think of our program as a dumping ground. They send us only the cases that are untreatable. It's a convenient way for them to get rid of the cases that cause them trouble.

And referring to another treatment program, a DC official said:

This program appeals to everyone. We are dangerously understaffed and it gave us a chance to hire more POs. It gives our research people something to evaluate. It gives our young turks work that they see as meaningful. And last but not least, it gives all the POs a chance to get rid of their troublemakers. I'd anticipated a morale problem because the POs assigned to this program are set up an élite unit. But the other POs don't seem to mind too much. The program gives them a chance to weed their caseloads.

Special treatment programs are ordinarily implemented as "pilot projects" and are then institutionalized if it appears that the program fills a need. This depends on the number of parolees serviced by the program, and no special treatment program has ever been phased out for lack of business.

Finally, when threats fail and there are no available treatment programs, the PO may reluctantly decide to return a parolee to prison. Returning the parolee to prison entails the known risk of seeking a revocation warrant and defending it in hearing. Not returning the parolee to prison entails a potentially greater risk. The PO can resolve this dilemma by "building a case" against the parolee. This process consists of creating a dossier that incorporates only incidents compatible with the qualities of "dangerous," revocable "criminality." When the PO builds a strong case, he minimizes his chances of "losing" the revocation hearing.

There is a unity here which summarizes the manipulation of records discussed up to this point. POs will not report incidents because of costs in time, effort, security, and freedom. However, the DC expects its POs to control their clients, and when a parolee cannot be controlled, the PO must use his records to reassert himself. The PO will first initiate records meant to threaten the parolee. Second, the PO will initiate records suggesting a treatable pathology. Usually the PO can use these records to get rid of the troublesome parolee through a special treatment program. Finally, when threats have failed, and when no special treatment program is available, the PO will initiate records to "build a case" against the parolee. In all of these processes, the PO's motive is the control of his clients.

3. *Using Records as Protection*

So far, only the PO-parolee interaction has been considered. An equally important facet of the PO's work environment is the system of informal demands made upon him by the bureaucracy. To satisfy these demands, the PO will often "use" his records to protect himself, his supervisor, and higher DC officials.

Protection is best illustrated by an example. In early 1975, reporters from two newspapers began an investigation of alleged mismanagement in the DC. A few disgruntled POs served as press informants and thus learned of the planned series of articles. Rumors caused panic in more than one branch office as POs hurried to clean up their files. The series turned out to be more limited and less sensational than expected, however, and within a few weeks the only residual effect was an epidemic of writer's cramp in the branch offices. One PO described the episode this way:

> That's the only time I ever saw all nine POs in the office at the same time. We wrote a lot of paper that week. When the story hit, we were all protected. The funny thing is that the story didn't say anything bad about anyone in our office. It was a false alarm, I guess. A week later, everything was back to normal.

This incident typifies protection. Under most circumstances, POs report little or no information to the DC. But from time to time, a PO will suddenly "go by the book," reporting every incident he observes regardless of the cost. The PO is protecting himself and his superiors from some potential threat such as, in this illustration, adverse publicity.

Other researchers (E.g., Takagi, 1967; Irwin, 1970) have defined protection as the writing of records so as to demonstrate *absolute* compliance with *minimal* rules in *every* case. If the PO has a model checklist, for example, he will develop a report format which includes every item on the checklist but nothing else. When trouble arises, this format protects the PO by demonstrating his *literal* compliance with rules and regulations. The theory of protection presented here, however, defines this use of records as something that happens only in special cases. I will develop this theory in a round about way, working from the circumstances and conditions that lead to the *need* for protection. First, the data suggest that in every case, protection can be defined strictly in terms of certain types of parolees. For example:

> The rule of thumb in my caseload is that any man can miss one report period *gratis*. I'll take that back. I've got one or two men I'd report AWOL if they were five minutes late for an appointment. They're basically dangerous men.

POs often speak of "dangerous" men, but generally mean "troublesome". In this respect, a supervisor's comment is more revealing:

> Sometimes a violation is important because of who the parolee is. If you take your average parolee, he can get arrested on a drunk charge and that won't be too important. But suppose the parolee's a convicted cop killer. Well, for him, that's going to be an important violation. If nothing else, it's going to get in the newspapers because of who he is. Any violation that makes the papers is important. We did have a cop killer on parole out of this office once and that man couldn't sneeze without two reporters showing up here.[5]

---

[5] See Emerson (1969) for a discussion of how assessments of moral character affect juvenile court decisions. Schur (1971) discusses this aspect of decision-making from a broad theoretical foundation.

The *need* for protection also arises when a PO is fired or resigns. The PO assuming the case-load has no idea where protection is needed, so he takes no chances:

> When I took this caseload over, the records were in pretty bad shape. I couldn't decipher them. The first thing I did was report eight clients AWOL. The second thing I did was to complete a dozen visitations that looked fishy to me. I wrote up two warnings out of the twelve. The records are in good shape now, so I can take it easy. That may sound like overreaction to you but it's not. The same thing would happen if somebody took this caseload over from me tomorrow. You've got to protect yourself, You never know what kind of work the PO who had the district before you did. You don't want to get blamed for his mistakes. Also, you don't know why the last PO left. He may have been fired. If that's the case, the people downtown are going to be expecting you to come up with a lot of unreported violations. If you don't find that stuff, they're going to think that you're just as sloppy as the PO they fired.

There is a fairly consistent turnover rate among newly hired POs which generates bursts of incident reports. The important point is that the *need* for protection arises because someone *expects* the PO to discover incidents in his caseload.

Examples of the conjunction of these two factors the occurrence of special parolee-types and the expectations of others are found by examining the peculiar relationship of the DC to the parole board. As this parole board is filled by executive appointment, board members often have religious, academic, labor, or political backgrounds and no particular allegiance to the bureaucracy. Nevertheless, the DC is subordinated to the parole board in many respects. This relationship results in a muted board-bureaucracy antagonism that can be sensed in the branch offices. A supervisor told me, for example:

> The parole board could release (a murderer) and if he killed (again), we'd be the scape-goats. They cover their mistakes with *special board orders*. If they let (a murderer) go, they'd write a special order that says, 'Hey, watch this guy. He's dangerous.' Then afterwards they'd say, 'Why didn't you watch this guy like we told you to?' They don't get blamed for releasing dangerous men. We get blamed for not following their special board orders.

This supervisor has exaggerated the problem somewhat. A *special board order* is simply a codicil to the standard parole contract which places special restrictions on the parolee. For example, an inmate might be paroled on the condition that he live in a halfway house for narcotic offenders or that he submit to psychiatric outpatient care. Nevertheless, POs, supervisors, and higher DC officials view the special order as a "red flag," warning not about the special problems of the parolee but about the *post hoc* attention likely to be paid the parolee. In other words, the parole board expects something to happen and their expectation presents the PO with a dilemma:

> Some of these special board orders are just for the record. An order will say that a client has to report twice weekly, say, but being realistic, they can't expect me *or* the client to follow that order. What happens is that I follow the order for the first month and then I slack off. Maybe after six months I can write a request to lift the order. They'll usually grant my request but there's a catch. If I lift the order and the client screws up, my neck is on the chopping block. The thing you have to learn is which special orders are for the record and which ones are for real.

The statement of the dilemma is typical; most POs solve it be taking no chances whatsoever:

> I had a "sexually dangerous" client once. After maybe a month, I called his home at curfew and there was no answer. I reported it. Maybe that's not fair to the client but at least I'm protected. Once I report it, it's out of my hands. They can do whatever they want to but they can't come back to me six months later and ask why I wasn't doing my

job. All I have to do is bring out my report and ask them why they didn't revoke the client six months earlier. Those cases are like ping-pong matches. They set me up by issuing the special order and I set them up by following it to the letter. It goes back and forth like that unitl they get tired. Then they'll change the order or transfer the client to a special caseload or something like that.

The practical cost of reporting such incidents is the loss of freedom. This may be a desired end in some cases, however. The loss of freedom will also limit the PO's personal liability for a "bad" decision.

The relationship between the DC and the parole board, and the subsequent *need* for protection, is actually a special case of a general phenomenon. Whenever the DC deals regularly with other bureaucracies, the interaction generates a number of demands and expectations.[6] The effects of the interaction at the lower levels of the DC are predictable. Regarding the prosecutor's office, for example, a supervisor complained:

Auslander phones my POs all the time and I don't like that. He's supposed to go through me when he has a complaint. It's not a good idea to let a PO know that the prosecutor doesn't like a parolee. Some POs are intimidated and they start harrassing the parolee.

And also with regards to the prosecutor's office, a PO commented:

You get pressure from all the agencies. Auslander's the worst because he's sneaky. If he asks about a client, you know he's checking up on you. It's like they're using that one case to judge your overall performance. What you do, of course, is interpret the rules strictly on that case. Then you're doing your job and nobody can complain.

POs have made similar statements about the courts:

Judge Kraft is hard on POs. He'll take you in his chambers and tell you how he wants you to handle the parolee. If that's not bad enough, he checks up on you later. I advise my clients to file for a change of judges when they go in front of Kraft.

The need for protection arises when POs deal with other bureaucracies. This includes the press, the parole board, the prosecutor, and the courts. The bureaucrats in these agencies have rigid, formal notions of how POs should handle their jobs. POs cannot routinely live up to these standards. But from time to time, a PO will become aware that he is handling a special case, of interest to some other agency. This means to the PO that the outside agency will scrutinize his handling of the special case, and will form an opinion of his general ability solely on the basis of his performance in the special case. To protect himself, the PO "goes by the book."

The DC will, in this circumstance, demand protection from its POs. The DC comes into contact with (and perhaps, is accountable to), outside agencies only in special cases, so the political image of the DC rests on the behavior of its POs in these cases. Protection is the normal manipulation of records. POs who do not protect themselves risk being labeled incompetent or unrealistic, with consequences implied by those labels.

CONCLUSION

The phenomena described here have two implications. First, parole records do not accurately reflect the behavior of parolees. This is not a novel finding, however. Bittner

---

[6] There is a distinction here between agencies that deal routinely with the DC, the police, for example, and agencies that do not. Expectations and demands arise only in the former case. See Sudnow (1965) for a discussion of how routine dealings between a public defender and prosecutor result in normal crimes. Normal crimes emerge precisely because these two offices interact routinely and frequently.

and Garfinkel (1967) have shown that even where record-keeping is strictly regulated, the practical costs charged to the record writer amount to "good reasons for bad records." Zimmerman's (1969: 1970) studies of public aid intake offices also note that the practicalities of bureaucratic work shape the records produced by the office. In the area of parole itself, Prus and Stratton (1976) have specified a number of mundane considerations determining the PO's case decisions.[7]

A second, more important implication concerns the role of the bureaucracy in the various uses of records. Career contingencies in the DC are such that POs are rewarded for producing "bad" records and punished for producing "good" records. The DC realizes some political benefit from the dynamic operation of these contingencies but it does so at the price of a straightforward loss of data. That the DC can classify and process men released from prison even in a total information vaccum suggests that the DC *per se* makes no decisions of any consequence. Classification decisions are instead left up to the street-level bureaucrat, that is, to the PO, and to other criminal justice agencies.

The organizational outcomes or labels that emerge from this process appear to have little bearing on the statutory goals of the DC. The first outcome, "success," can be described as a stochastic process. If a parolee can survive for two years without coming into contact with other criminal justice agencies, he is discharged as a "success." POs may discover behavior that is inconsistent with this outcome but career contingencies encourage the POs to supress reports of it. The second outcome, "failure," is defined as the complement of the first and is likewise nearly stochastic. If a parolee cannot survive for two years without coming into contact with other criminal justice agencies, he is returned to prison as a "failure."

The two deterministic exceptions to this process are "treatable" cases and special cases. "Treatable" cases can be viewed as incipient "failures" because the PO is likely to discover a pathology only after the parolee has had an initial contact with a criminal justice agency. If it appears that further contacts will occur, the PO is encouraged to use his records to get rid of the parolee.[8] Finally, in special cases, the PO must report whatever behavior he observes, or in the extreme, is expected to observe. In special cases, the PO is acting as an agent of some other bureaucracy, and is collecting information that is useful not to the DC, but to the outside agency. Classification and processing is left up to the outside agency. By abrogating authority in these cases, inter-agency squabbles are avoided, and in that sense at least, the PO has protected himself and his DC superiors.

REFERENCES

Bittner, Egon and Harold Garfinkel
  1967 " 'Good' organizational reasons for 'bad' clinical records," *in* H. Garfinkel, Studies in Ethnomethodology. Englewood Cliffs, N.J.: Prentice-Hall.
Emerson, Robert M.
  1969 Judging Delinquents. Chicago: Aldine.
Gerth Hans H. and C. Wright Mills
  1958 From Max Weber: Essays in Sociology. New York, Oxford University Press.

---

[7] These concerns are most critical in the area of program evaluation. McDowall (1976) has reviewed a number of bureaucratic case studies, concluding that program evaluation is not impossible even with "bad" records, if the evaluator is aware of the record-keeping contingencies. Most evaluators ignore the intervening variables, treating records as if they were a direct function of the program goals. In this sense, an evaluation is not "only as good as the records" upon which it is based, but rather, will be optimally valid when based on site-specific knowledge.

[8] I am not implying that the treatment programs serve no function at all except this one. The DC derives substantial funds through the programs and this resource would be lost if POs transferred clients to the programs only under these circumstances. The many parolees who are obviously in need of special treatment are transferred to the programs directly, either by the parole board or by the PO himself after his initial contacts with the parolee. When a parolee is transferred to a program after a substantial period of time in a caseload, however, it is invariably a case where the PO wants to get rid of the parolee.

Glaser, Daniel T.
   1964   The Effectiveness of a Prison and a Parole System. Indianapolis: Bobbs-Merrill.
Irwin, John
   1970   The Felon. Englewood Cliffs, N.J.: Prentice-Hall.
McCleary, Richard
   1975   "How structural variables constrain the parole officer's use of discretionary power," *Social Problems*: 23(2).
McDowall, David
   1976   "Notes on the use of official records," Mimeo, Evaluation Research Program, Department of Psychology, Northwestern University.
Prus, Robert and John Stratton
   1976   "Parole revocation and decision-making: private typings and official designations," Federal Probation: 40(1).
Schur, Edwin M.
   1971   Labeling Deviant Behavior. New York: Harper and Row.
Sudnow, David
   1965   "Normal crimes: sociological features of the penal code in a public defender office," *Social Problems*: 12(2).
Takagi, Paul T.
   1967   Evaluation Systems and Deviations in a Parole Agency. Stanford University: Unpublished Ph.D. Dissertation.
Zimmerman, Don
   1969   "Record-keeping and the intake process in a public welfare agency," in S. Wheeler (ed.), On Record. New York: Russell Sage Foundation.
   1970   "The Practicalities of Rule Use," in J. Douglas (ed.), Understanding Everyday Life. Chicago: Aldine.

21

CRIMINAL JUSTICE IN RURAL AND URBAN COMMUNITIES
A Study of the Bureaucratization of Justice

JOHN HAGAN

Urbanization is a standard explanatory theme in the sociological literature on the environmental causes of crime (Clinard; Glaser; Wolfgang). However, attention is rarely given to the influence of urbanization in determining official modes of response to crime (see Blumberg; Skolnick).[1] The current research departs from tradition in providing a comparative analysis of rural and urban sentencing patterns. The analysis is intended as a case study of the effects of urbanization, and its close correlate, bureaucratization, on institutionalized decision-making.

URBANIZATION, BUREAUCRATIZATION, AND THE COURTS

For the courts at least, to urbanize means to bureaucratize. Sociologists are agreed about this correlation, but disagreed about its consequences. Thus Tepperman finds, in a study of 72 juvenile courts, a succession of strong relationships between the population of a court jurisdiction, the number of juveniles handled, and the number of judges, probation officers, and clinic staff associated with a court. Tepperman then follows Weberian ideal-type assumptions in arguing that increases in court size will lead to a pattern of bureaucratization characterized by: (1) the establishment and communication of universalistic standards of decision-making; (2) specific, rather than diffuse, orientations to the objects of decision-making; and (3) the reduction in importance of statuses ascribed to "clients" as criteria upon which decisions are made (347).[2] To Tepperman's displeasure, these hypotheses are confirmed as applied to the sentencing of male and female offenders in the 72 courts studied. His concern is that male and female adolescents have differing sorts of

From John Hagan, "Criminal Justice in Rural and Urban Communities: A Study of the Bureaucratization of Justice," 55(3) *Social Forces* 597-612 (March 1977). Copyright 1977 by The University of North Carolina Press.

problems that are ignored in an impersonal bureaucracy whose organizational priority is efficiency.

A contrasting view of the consequences of court bureaucratization is found in Reiss's discussion of the abuses of discretionary justice. Reiss notes that "The bureacratization of . . . justice . . . presumably should guarantee the distributive property of justice, since a property of bureaucracies is the universalistic application of standards according to rules" (693). The problem, according to Reiss, is that the discretion given to agents of the law opens the door to unequal treatment, particularly when the limits of discretionary power are unclear. This problem is intensified by the judicial tendency to focus on decision-making in the particular case rather than on the distributive effect of decisions in the aggregate of cases. Reiss concludes that "Since the system of criminal justice both permits considerable authorized discretion by officials in making decisions and fails generally to monitor the unauthorized use of discretion in making decisions, it has contributed further to a variability in the standards of justice and the equity of their administration" (694).

Reiss does not specifically indicate whether the variability of bureaucratized justice is differentially targeted at minority group offenders. However, Chambliss and Seidman do. These authors begin with the assumption that, ". . . the tendency and necessity to bureaucratize is far and away the single most important variable in determining the actual day to day functioning of the legal system. . . ." (468). It is then argued that,

. . . the large number of persons brought before *municipal* courts for minor transgressions of the law leads to an almost completely automatic sentence for certain types of offenders. Furthermore, even for more serious offenses the pressure to make the decision expeditiously (which is in large part a carry-over from the heavy burden created by the large number of minor offenders handled) leads to the judges relying heavily on the advice of 'specialists'—in this case probation and parole officers who make pre-sentencing reports on offenders before the court for sentencing (468, emphasis added).

We will consider Chambliss and Seidman's argument in more detail later. For the moment, we will simply note their conclusion that, "Under these circumstances, institutionalized patterns of discrimination against the poor are inevitable" (469).

Austin Turk provides a final view of the court bureacracy that brings us full circle to predictions much like those initially indicated by Tepperman. Turk argues that the important court-related advantages of socially dominant groups derive from the definition of their own proscribed behaviors as legally less serious than the prohibited behaviors common to socially subordinate groups. Building from this assumption, Turk notes that a strict judicial observance of these preferential laws is sufficient to allow the collective advantage of those in whose favor the laws were initially constructed. The implication is that a sophisticated court bureaucracy would not employ differential sentencing tactics. In this context, Turk concludes that, ". . . discrimination is not only in principle unnecessary but is likely to be counterproductive in contributing to the demystification of the structure of legal control."

We have reviewed to this point a variety of good reasons why sentencing disparities *may or may not* occur in urban court bureaucracies. Combined with these conflicting arguments is a consensual view that *either* outcome is undesirable. Thus, Albert Reiss predicts a variability in bureaucratized justice that Chambliss and Seidman argue is discriminatory, while Tepperman and Turk predict a uniformity in sentencing that on the one hand is seen as impersonal, and on the other as deflecting attention from the disadvantaging character of the laws themselves. The apparent irony of this situation is that we seem agreed that the consequences of bureaucratization are bad, but disagreed about what the consequences actually are.

These disparate views of the effects of urbanization and bureaucratization are disturbing, but not necessarily surprising. Weber reminds us that, ". . . bureaucracy as such is a precision instrument which can put itself at the disposal of quite varied . . . interests. . . ." (Gerth and Mills, 231). The instruction that follows from this warning is that, ". . . in every individual historical case, one must observe in what special direction bureaucratization has developed" (232). One way of heeding this advice is to consider more carefully the specific referents of Chambliss and Seidman's conclusions.

Chambliss and Seidman construct their remarks with particular reference to two types of criminal offenders who are handled in distinctively different ways by the court system: (1) minor offenders who often are sentenced peremptorily to either fine payment or prison, and (2) more serious offenders whose sentencing is delayed during the preparation of pre-sentencing reports by probation officers. Two studies (Hagan, b, c) offer a backdrop for Chambliss and Seidman's concern. First, a study of 1,000 offenders admitted to five prisons in a western Canadian province reveals that Indian and Metis[3] persons are nearly twice as likely as whites to be incarcerated in default of fine payments (Hagan, b). Second, a study of 765 offenders for whom pre-sentence reports were prepared indicates that probation officer's recommendations for sentence are a source of unfavorable treatment for Indian and Metis offenders (Hagan, c). The current study extends analysis of these two data sets into urban and rural contexts. The purpose is to determine what the consequences of urbanization and bureaucratization actually are for the judicial treatment of minority group offenders.

THE DATA

The data for this analysis were gathered in the Province of Alberta (Canada). The first sample of 974 offenders consists of persons admitted to the five largest prisons in the Province over a two-month period, from February 15 to April 15, 1973. The second sample consists of 507 questionnaires, based on pre-sentence reports, completed by probation officers in all offices of the Adult Probation Department, during a four-month period from February 1 to June 1, 1973.[4] Each sample provides coverage of all jurisdictions in the Province.

The analysis began with an attempt to develop measures of urbanization and bureaucratization. It quickly became apparent, however, that this approach ignored a fundamental polarization between Alberta's two large cities on the one hand, and the remainder of the Province on the other. Calgary and Edmonton each have a population of over 400,000 persons. Both of these cities have felt the full effects of urbanization and bureaucratization. This situation is reflected in various court statistics. For example, 60 percent of the cases ($N = 206,306$), 53 percent of the judges ($N = 62$), and 51 percent of the probation officers ($N = 76$) in the Province are located in Edmonton and Calgary. The remainder of the Province is distinctively rural in character, with court resources spread thinly over a vast, but sparsely populated, land area. Thus, the next largest jurisdiction, Lethbridge, covers a large geographical area with only 3 percent of the cases, .6 percent of the judges, and 6 percent of the probation officers in the Province.

It further can be noted that the urban and rural court jurisdictions represent widely varying levels of bureaucratization. Judges in the two urban jurisdictions operate in extremely crowded court settings, with considerations of time and space a constant problem. Most judges in the urban jurisdictions have law degrees (82%). The situation in the rural setting is quite different. Judges in these jurisdictions travel extensively, frequently hearing their cases in storefront court-rooms. Far fewer of the judges in the rural jurisdictions have law degrees (34%), with many of the non-legally trained judges having police backgrounds. Similar patterns are found in the probation department. Urban offices, in addition to their size, are staffed primarily by trained social workers, and are hierarchically organized from a chief probation officer, through senior probation officers, to junior level probation officers. Rural offices are small, often without a senior probation officer, and again are often staffed with persons of police background. With reference to the Alberta court system, then, it seems fair to repeat the initial point of this section, that urbanization is closely correlated with bureaucratization.

Taking advantage of the polarized court settings we have described, the analysis in this paper is based on case dispositions in Edmonton and Calgary, as compared with those in the other rural jurisdictions of the Province.

THE METHODOLOGY AND THE VARIABLES

The analysis proceeds in two stages. In the first stage, the pre-sentencing data are analyzed using the techniques of path analysis.[5] The variables included in this phase of the analysis follow in an assumed logical–temporal sequence: the offender's ethnic background (X_1); his prior record (X_2); the statuatory seriousness of his most serious offense (X_3); the number of charges against him (X_4); the probation officer's perception of the offender's demeanor (X_5);[6] his evaluation of the offender's success prospects (X_6); the probation officer's recommendation for sentence (X_7); and, the final disposition imposed (X_8). The codings for each variable are indicated in the top part of Table 1. The analysis proceeds *within* urban and rural samples, with unstandardized regression coefficients used in comparisons between samples. Direct and indirect effects within the two path models are then systematically "decomposed" to further clarify the causal linkages involved (Alwin and Hauser).

The second stage of the analysis focuses on the prison sample. Because the variables in this data set are dichotomized, and because a preceding tabular analysis suggested interaction effects, the technique applied in this part of the study is Goodman's "modified multiple regression approach to the analysis of dichotomous variables." The variables considered in this phase of the analysis include: the offender's ethnic background (X_a); the type of jurisdiction where sentenced (X_b); the offender's level of alcohol use[7] (X_c); and the type of disposition imposed (X_d). The dichotomized codings for each of these variables is indicated in the bottom part of Table 1.

Table 1. THE VARIABLES

Notation	Variable	Scale				
A.	**The Pre-Sentencing Data**					
X_1	ethnic background	white	(1)	Indian & metis	(2)	
X_2	prior convictions	number equals scale				
X_3	Offense seriousness (measured as maximum statuatory sentence)	6 months	(1)	7 years	(6)	
		18 months	(2)	10 years	(7)	
		2 years	(3)	14 years	(8)	
		3 years	(4)	life or	(9)	
		5 years	(5)	death		
X_4	number of charges	number equals scale				
X_5	Perception of demeanor (5-item Guttman scale)	scored on Likert scale of favorableness, from one to five				
X_6	Evaluation of prospects for success on probation	scored on Likert scale of favorableness, from one to five				
X_7	recommendation	absolute discharge				(1)
		conditional discharge or fine				(2)
		probation				(3)
		prison				(4)
X_8	final disposition	as above				
B.	**The Prison Data**					
X_a	ethnic background	white	(1)	indian & metis	(2)	
X_b	type of jurisdiction	Urban	(1)	rural	(2)	
X_c	level of alcohol use	temperate	(1)	intemperate	(2)	
X_d	disposition	no fine option	(1)	fine option	(2)	

THE ANALYSIS

STAGE ONE

The first step in the analysis of the pre-sentencing data was to calculate the correlation (r_{ij}) and path (p_{ij}) coefficients presented in Table 2. On the basis of this table, regression equations were then rewritten with those paths retained that were statistically significant at the .001 level and explained more than one percent of the variation in the dependent variable.[8] The results are presented in path models of the pre-sentencing process in rural (Figure 1) and urban (Figure 2) communities. In both of these models, all effects of the offender's ethnic background are mediated by the probation officer's recommendation. Thus, our primary interest is in discussing the links between the offender's ethnic background and the formation of the recommendation for sentence.

Figure 1 presents the path model of the pre-sentencing process in rural communities. Here ethnic background has both direct and indirect effects on the formation of recommendations. The direct effect of ethnic background on recommendation (p_{71}) is .15. Beyond this, the offender's prior record and the probation officer's evaluation of his success prospects both interpret the relationship between ethnicity and recommendation. Thus, ethnic background has an indirect effect through the offender's prior record ($p_{72}p_{21} = .04$), through the offender's success prospects ($p_{76}p_{61} = .08$), and through prior record and success prospects ($p_{76}p_{62}p_{21} = .03$) combined. Of this, all but the effects through prior record can be called "extra-legal"—in the sense that this impact of the offender's ethnic background is not attributable to the operation of correlated legal variables. This "total extra-legal effect" ($p_{71} + p_{76}p_{61}$) is .23.

Figure 2 presents the path model of the pre-sentencing process in urban areas. The most notable feature of this model is the part played by prior record as the mediator of the effects of ethnic background, and the absence of extra-legal links between ethnicity and recommendation. The link between ethnic background and prior record (p_{21}) increases here to .30. In turn, prior record is linked both directly and indirectly (through offense, number of current charges, and success prospects) to the probation officer's recommendation for sentence. Mediated by these links, the "total legal effect" of ethnic background on recommendation ($p_{76}p_{62}p_{21} + p_{72}p_{21} + p_{74}p_{42} + p_{73}p_{32}p_{21}$) is .10.

To this point, we have discussed the effect of ethnic background *within* each of the two samples. We have noted that ethnicity has an extra-legal effect on probation officers' recommendations in rural areas, while no evidence of this effect was found in urban areas. To make comparisons between samples, we turn next to the unstandardized regression coefficients (see Blalock). Thus, unstandardized coefficients (b_{ij}) are used in Table 3 to decompose the effects of ethnic background on recommendation in the two samples.[9] The method of constructing this table was to compute the full series of reduced form equations for the dependent variable, recommendation. This series began with the equation containing the single ex-

Table 2. CORRELATION AND PATH COEFFICIENTS IN RURAL AND URBAN SAMPLES*

	X_{1A}	X_{1B}	X_{2A}	X_{2B}	X_{3A}	X_{3B}	X_{4A}	X_{4B}	X_{5A}	X_{5B}	X_{6A}	X_{6B}	X_{7A}	X_{7B}	X_{8A}	X_{8B}
X_1			.22	.30	-.05	.05	-.15	-.01	.02	.16	.30	.22	.29	.16	.23	.16
X_2	.22*	.30*			-.01	.22	.06	.25	.03	.13	.38	.36	.34	.37	.30	.33
X_3	-.05	-.02	.01	.23*			.11	.27	-.02	-.03	.03	.28	.19	.42	.20	.41
X_4	-.16*	-.09	.09	.23*	.10	.23*			.03	-.05	.13	.11	.15	.26	.17	.27
X_5	.02	.13	.02	.12	-.03	-.04	.04	-.06			.31	.46	.03	.23	.06	.20
X_6	.25*	.07	.31*	.23*	.04	.23*	.14*	.01	.29*	.43*			.49	.53	.46	.42
X_7	.16*	.02	.15*	.13*	.17*	.25*	.10	.11*	-.11	.05	.40*	.38*			.73	.71
X_8	.01	.04	.04	.05	.07	.12*	.05	.07	.00	.06	.13*	.01	.63*	.59*		

aSub-script "A" indicates rural sample (N=265), while sub-script "B" indicates urban sample (N=241). Correlation coefficients are listed to the right of the diagonal, with the dependent variables indicated by column. Path coefficients are listed to the left of the diagonal, with the dependent variables indicated by row.

*Path coefficients that are statistically significant at the .001 level and explain more than one percent of the variation in the endogenous variable.

Figure 1. PATH MODEL OF THE PRE-SENTENCING PROCESS IN RURAL COMMUNITITES

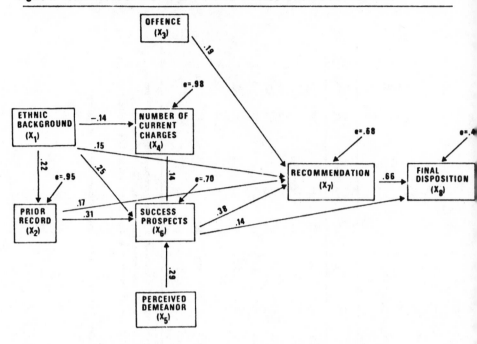

Figure 2. PATH MODEL OF THE PRE-SENTENCING PROCESS IN URBAN COMMUNITIES

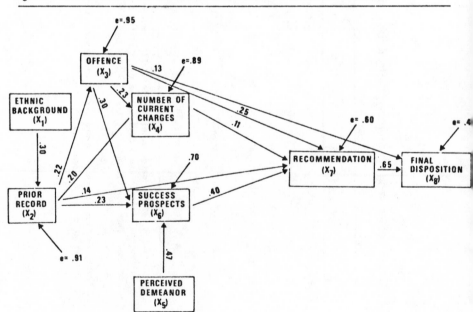

ogenous variable, ethnicity; variables which intervene were then successively added, proceeding in sequence from cause to effect until the intervening variables were exhausted.

Turning to the results of this process recorded in Table 3, we see that the total effects of ethnic background in the urban (.38) and rural (.41) samples are similar. The difference lies in the way these effects are imposed. In the urban sample, 66 percent of the effect of ethnic background on recommendation is mediated by prior record ($b_{71} - b_{71.2} = .25$). In the rural sample, prior record accounts for only 22 percent of this effect. In contrast, 53 percent of the effect of ethnic background on recommendation is direct ($b_{71} - b_{71.23456} = .22$) in the rural sample, while the comparable figure in the urban sample is only 11 percent. In sum, the urban sample seems to represent a rather legalistic pattern of decision-making, while the rural sample does not.

Table 3. DECOMPOSITION OF THE EFFECTS OF ETHNIC BACKGROUND (X_1) ON RECOMMENDATION (X_7) IN URBAN AND RURAL MODELS OF THE PRE-SENTENCING PROCESS*

Equation Number	Unstandardized Coefficients (b)		Mediating Variable	Indirect Effects	
	Urban	Rural		Urban	Rural
1	.38	.41	--	--	--
2	.13	.32	X_2	.25	.09
3	.14	.33	X_3	-.01	-.01
4	.17	.37	X_4	-.03	-.04
5	.10	.37	X_5	.07	.00
6	.04	.22	X_6	.06	.15
-	--	--	direct effects	.04	.22
-	--	--	total effects	.38	.41

*See text for a discussion of the reduced form and structural equations used in the construction of this table. Use of standardized and unstandardized regression coefficients in this table yields similar results. These calculations are available, on request, from the author.

STAGE TWO

In the second stage of the analysis, we are concerned with four dichotomized variables, in a sample of offenders admitted to the five largest prisons in the Province. Offenders go to prison in two principal ways: (1) they are sentenced there directly, or (2) they are incarcerated in default of fine payment. In the Province under study, incarceration of Indians for public drunkenness, under the default provision, is so frequent that the involved sections of the criminal code have earned the folk designation of "Indian offenses." Our interest is in determining variation in this pattern by urban and rural communities.

To determine how the dependent variable [(d) disposition] is related to the other three variables [(a) ethnic background, (b) type of jurisdiction, and (c) level of alcohol use], we begin with the four-way table presented in Table 4. For a complete understanding of the methodology that follows, the reader is directed to Goodman's work. However, the discussion is phrased in terms of parameters that describe the main effects of variables A, B, and C, and certain interaction effects among these variables, in a manner analogous to corresponding effects in the conventional analysis of variance model. The basic idea is to determine the significance of differences between the observed and expected "odds" of getting a particular disposition under various hypothesized main and interaction effects.

Table 4. CROSS-CLASSIFICATION OF INCARCERATED OFFENDERS WITH RESPECT TO FOUR DICHOTOMIZED VARIABLES: (A) ETHNIC BACKGROUND, (B) TYPE OF JURISDICTION, (C) LEVEL OF ALCOHOL USE, AND (D) DISPOSITION

Variable A	Variable B	Variable C	Variable D	
			No Fine	Fine
Ethnicity	Jurisdiction	Alcohol Use	Option	Option
White	Urban	Temperate	199	117
Indian	Urban	Temperate	31	31
White	Rural	Temperate	81	50
Indian	Rural	Temperate	41	100
White	Urban	Intemperate	78	30
Indian	Urban	Intemperate	32	15
White	Rural	Intemperate	24	9
Indian	Rural	Intemperate	32	104

The first step is to examine the fully saturated model that includes all possible main and interaction effects. This model is presented in Table 5 with estimated parameters (λ) and their corresponding standardized values. The strongest of the effect parameters listed is that linking ethnic background to disposition ($\lambda^{A\bar{D}_1} = .26$), indicating that Indian and Metis persons are much more likely than whites to go to jail in default of fine options. The next largest parameters link rural jurisdiction to incarceration by default ($\lambda^{BD_1} = .18$), and indicate that the link between ethnicity and disposition is reduced in urban areas, and increased in rural

Table 5. ESTIMATE OF THE MAIN AND
INTERACTION EFFECTS OF THE THREE VARIABLES
(A, B, C) PERTAINING TO VARIABLE D IN TABLE 4
UNDER THE SATURATED MODEL

Variable	λ	Standardized Value
D	.10	2.36
AD	.26	6.14
BD	.18	4.11
CD	-.09	-2.01
ABD	-.18	-4.04
ACD	-.03	-.65
BCD	-.06	-1.40
ABCD	.07	1.61

areas ($\lambda^{AB\bar{D}}{}_{11} = -.18$). In other words, the problem of native people going to jail in lieu of fines is most acute in rural areas.

The remaining relationships of interest involve the third variable, level of alcohol use, as this is indicated by classification officers in the criminal justice system. Perhaps surprisingly, the effect parameter CD is negative ($\lambda^{C\bar{D}}{}_1 = -.09$), indicating that "temperate" offenders are slightly more likely than "intemperates" to go to jail in default of fines. This finding may suggest a moderately successful effort to keep revolving door drunks out of the prison system. However, the ACD and BCD parameters ($\lambda^{AC\bar{D}}{}_{11} = -.65$ and $\lambda^{BC\bar{D}}{}_{11} = -1.40$) reveal that such success may be more prevalent among whites, and in urban communities.

Using the size of the standardized values in Table 5 it is possible to estimate which parameters in the saturated model are of negligible consequence. Using this criterion, five new models (H_1, H_2, H_3, H_4, H_5) are presented in Table 6. A sixth model (H_6) is also generated to determine the total amount of variation due to the main and interaction effects of variables A, B, and C. The inclusion of an ABC term in each of these models establishes D (disposition) as the dependent variable.

The first model presented in Table 6 includes only the main effects of variables A, B, and C. The fact that the value of p for this model is statistically significant at the .001 level reveals that the expected and observed frequencies for the marginal tables are significantly different, thus indicating that the main effects of A, B, and C do not sufficiently account for variation in dispositions. However, addition of the interaction term ABD in model two produces the desired statistical nonsignificance, indicating that this model *does* adequately fit the observed data. For our purposes, adding the ABD term indicates the importance of the finding that Indians are most likely to be incarcerated in default of fine payments in *rural* areas. Model three retains the ABD interaction effect, but removes the CD effect of alcohol

Table 6. CHI-SQUARE VALUES FOR SOME MODELS PERTAINING TO TABLE 4

Model	Fitted Marginals	Degrees of Freedom	Likelihood Ratio Chi-square	P	Parameters Included in the Model
H_1	ABC, AD, BD, CD	4	25.26	.00	D, AD, BD, CD
H_2	ABC, ABD, CD	3	6.33	.10	D, AD, BD, CD, ABD
H_3	ABC, ABD	4	9.25	.06	D, AD, BD, ABD
H_4	ABC, ABD, BCD	2	2.96	.22	D, AD, BD, CD, ABD, BCD
H_5	ABC, ABD, BCD, ACD	1	2.64	.10	D, AD, BD, CD, ABD, BCD, ACD
H_6	ABC, D	7	126.04	--	D

use on disposition. Subtraction of the chi-square value of H_2 from the chi-square value of H_3 reveals that the *CD* parameter does not have a statistically significant effect $[X^2(H_3) - X^2(H_2) = 2.92$, with 1 degree of freedom and $.05 < p < .10]$. At the same time, model three, without this *CD* effect, maintains the desired statistical *non*significance ($p = .06$).

Model four adds the *BCD* interaction term, involving the tendency for intemperate offenders to be more frequently incarcerated in lieu of fine payment in rural areas. Comparison of models four and two reveals that the *BCD* interaction term $[X^2(H_2) - X^2(H_4) = 3.37$, with 1 degree of freedom, $.05 < p < .10]$ just misses statistical signficance at the .05 level. Finally, model five adds the *ACD* effect, but the addition of this effect is of negligible significance $[X^2(H_4) - X^2(H_5) = .32$, with 1 degree of freedom, p is statistically nonsignificant]. Thus, model three is the most parsimonious one that fits the data, although the addition of the *BCD* term in model four comes very close to being a statistically significant improvement over model three. Both of these models illustrate the problems of criminal justice, particularly for native people, in rural areas.

DISCUSSION AND CONCLUSIONS

We began with an empirical question: What are the consequences of urbanization and bureaucratization for the judicial treatment of minority group offenders? Past discussion and research on this issue produce consensus that the bureaucratization of criminal justice is bad, but little agreement on exactly what the consequences of this process actually are for minority offenders. In search of an answer to this question, a study was designed to compare judicial sentencing of Indian and white offenders in urban and rural communities of a Canadian province.

Communities in the province chosen for study are bipolarized in their characteristics. Each of the two largest cities in the province has a population of over 400,000 persons, while the rest of the province is distinctively rural in character. This urban–rural dichotomy is paralleled in indicators of bureaucratization: the two urban jurisdictions are heavy in their caseloads, large and well-trained in their staff, and hierarchical in their organization. The rural jurisdictions rank far lower on each of these dimensions. The results of our analysis are thus viewed as relevant to both the problems of urbanization *and* bureaucratization.

Although our research cannot completely vindicate the urban court bureaucracy, it does at least demonstrate the persistent, and relatively more serious, problems of rural jurisdictions. Probation officers in rural areas, as contrasted with those in urban communities, sentence Indian and Metis offenders severely, without the justification of correlated legal variables (i.e., prior record, offense seriousness, and number of charges). In addition, native offenders are more likely to be sent to jail in default of fine payments in rural, than in urban jurisdictions. These findings indicate serious and enduring problems in the less bureaucratic criminal justice systems of rural communities. At the same time, the fears of Chambliss and Seidman that the use of judicial discretion would encourage sentencing disparities in crowded urban court settings are not supported. Rather, as Turk and Tepperman suggest, the trend is toward uniformity in the urban bureaucratized context.

In interpreting the trend toward equal treatment in urban communities, it is important to note that concern for equal application of a law is a separate issue from the justness or fairness of the law itself. Turk's point was that equality in sentencing can deflect attention from the tendency of dominant groups to define the proscribed acts of subordinate groups as more serious than their own. In the current context, the penal response to public drunkenness serves as a useful example. Indians more frequently than whites drink and recover in public. There are differences in access to, and preferences for, privacy in drinking. Given the resulting group-linked differences in behavior, equal treatment of those who violate public drinking norms cannot produce an equality of legal outcomes. Indians, and other subordinate groups, will continue to populate, disproportionately, our prisons until surrogate institutions of privacy (e.g., overnight detoxification centers) are developed as alternatives to incarceration.

Some further cautions are called for before the findings of this research are generalized, or any final inferences are drawn. First, it deserves note that Canada differs substantially from the United States in important population patterns. Native people in Canada live in their largest numbers in rural areas, while blacks in the United States live with much greater frequency in the cities. These varying patterns may influence the urban development of court bureaucracies within and between both countries.

Second, we should also note that native persons characteristically migrate in Canada *from* rural *to* urban areas. It will be recalled that in urban settings, probation officers focused on native offenders' prior records in assigning them more severe sentences than whites. Since in many cases these prior records will presumably derive from experiences in rural communities, it is plausible that rural patterns of differential treatment may lead to urban sentencing decisions that perpetuate the initial inequities. These decisions would, of course, be justifiable in terms of the immediate information available to the decision-makers involved. It is only in a larger processual view of the record-keeping process that such problems become apparent. Thus, a fuller understanding of the bureaucratization of justice will probably await the availability of new types of longitudinal data on the judicial process.

NOTES

1. Although there are occasional studies of rural jurisdictions (Brakel and South; Esselstyn; Willcox and Bloustein), most criminal justice research focuses on individual urban communities (e.g., Dolbeare; Levin), with few (if any) attempts at comparison. With Klonoski, ". . . our concern . . . is that community variations do in fact exist and are only now coming under scrutiny by social scientists (75; see also Goldman; Wilson).

2. A fourth factor discussed by Tepperman is the "displacement of organizational goals by procedural and exigent organizational concerns" (347). The main thrust of his paper is to examine deviation of organizational practice from an anti-bureaucratic or "individualized" ideal in the treatment of juvenile offenders. We consider this point only in passing, since our interest in Tepperman's data is concentrated on more traditional concerns about equality before the law and the intrusion of extralegal variables into judicial decision-making.

3. The term Metis refers to a person of mixed, in this case Indian and white, ancestry.

4. The prison sample included all 1,000 persons admitted to the five prisons over the two-month period; inadequate information on one or more variables resulted in dropping 26 offenders from the analysis. The second sample is drawn from 765 questionnaires completed simultaneously with pre-sentence reports over a four-month period. The 765 questionnaires represent a response rate of over 76 percent. From these questionnaires, all 507 cases involving a judicial request for a probation officer's recommendation for sentence were selected for analysis. For a more detailed discussion of the sampling procedures applied, see Hagan (a).

5. Several of the variables used in the analysis can be considered no more than ordinal in their level of measurement. However, following arguments presented by Bohrnstedt and Carter, Boyle and Labovitz (a, b), the measures used in this analysis are treated as interval scales, and parametric statistics are applied. To assure that this strategy did not distort our conclusions, a test of the ordinal-treated-as-interval assumption was applied, using a program adapted for ordinal path analysis (Smith). The results, indicating minimal discrepancies, are available on request from the author.

6. Perceived demeanor is measured on the basis of a five-item Guttman Scale that asks the probation officer to evaluate whether the offender: (1) understands the charges, (2) is polite, (3) is cooperative, (4) acknowledges his guilt, and (5) indicates remorse. The scale results in a coefficient of reproducibility of .99 and a coefficient of scalability of .91.

7. Each offender incarcerated in a provincial institution is ranked on admission by a classification officer as either "temperate" or "intemperate" in his use of alcohol. Although this measure may be biased in the direction of underestimation, it is assumed that the error involved is uncorrelated with other variables relevant to this analysis, and that therefore the measure is sufficient for our purposes.

8. For a discussion of the liabilities of using significance tests alone as the criterion for selecting causal paths, see Heise (61).

9. The use of standardized coefficients in these calculations leads to identical substantive conclusions. These results are available on request from the author.

REFERENCES

Alwin, D., and R. Hauser. 1975. "The Decomposition of Effects in Path Analysis." *American Sociological Review* 40(February):37–47.

Blalock, H. 1967. "Path Coefficients Versus Regression Coefficients." *American Journal of Sociology* 72(May):675–6.

Blumberg, Abraham. 1967. *Criminal Justice*. Chicago: Quadrangle Books.

Bohrnstedt, G., and T. M. Carter. 1971. "Robustness in Regression Analysis." In Herbert L. Costner (ed.), *Sociological Methodology 1971*. San Francisco: Jossey-Bass.

Boyle, R. P. 1970. "Path Analysis and Ordinal Data." *American Journal of Sociology* 75(January):461–80.

Brakel, S., and G. South. 1969. "Diversion from the Criminal Process in the Rural Community." *American Criminal Law Quarterly* 7(Spring):122–73.

Chambliss, William, and Robert Seidman. 1971. *Law, Order, and Power*. Reading, Mass.: Addison-Wesley.

Clinard, Marshall. 1966. *Slums and Community Development: Experiments in Self-Help*. New York: Free Press.

Dolbeare, Kenneth. 1967. *Trial Courts in Urban Politics*. New York: Wiley.

Esselstyn, T. C. 1953. "The Social Role of the County Sheriff." *Journal of Criminal Law, Criminology, and Police Science* 44(July–August):177–84.

Gerth, Hans, and C. Wright Mills. 1968. *From Max Weber*. New York: Oxford University Press.

Glaser, Daniel (ed.). 1970. *Crime in the City*. New York: Harper & Row.

Goldman, Nathan, 1963. *The Differential Selection of Juveniles for Court Appearance*. National Research and Information Center, National Council on Crime and Delinquency.

Goodman, L. 1972. "A Modified Multiple Regression Approach to the Analysis of Dichotomous Variables." *American Sociological Review* 37(February):28–46.

Hagan, John. a:1974. "Criminal Justice in a Canadian Province." Unpublished Ph.D. dissertation, University of Alberta.

———. b:1974. "Criminal Justice and Native People: A Study of Incarceration in a Canadian Province." *Canadian Review of Sociology & Anthropology* (August)220–36.

———. c:1975. "The Social and Legal Construction of Criminal Justice: A Study of the Pre-Sentencing Process." *Social Problems* 22(5):620–37.

Heise, D. R. 1969. "Problems in Path Analysis and Causal Inference." In Edgar F. Borgatta (ed.). *Sociological Methodology 1969*. San Francisco: Jossey-Bass.

Klonoski, James, and Robert Mendelsohn (eds.), 1970. *The Politics of Local Justice*. Boston: Little, Brown.

Labovitz, S. a:1967. "Some Observations on Measurement and Statistics." *Social Forces* 46(December):151–60.

———. b:1970. "The Assignment of Numbers to Rank Order Categories." *American Sociological Review* 35:515–24.

Levin, M. 1972. "Urban Politics and Judicial Behavior." *The Journal of Legal Studies* 1:193–221.

Reiss, A. J. 1974. "Discretionary Justice." In Daniel Glaser (ed.), *Handbook of Criminology*, Chicago: Rand McNally.

Skolnick, Jerome. 1966. *Justice without Trial*. New York: Wiley.

Smith, R. B. 1972. "Neighborhood Context and College Plans: An Ordinal Path Analysis." *Social Forces* 51(December):199–217.

Tepperman, L. 1973. "The Effects of Court Size on Organization and Procedure." *Canadian Review of Sociology & Anthropology* 10(4):346–65.

Turk, A. 1976. "Law, Conflict, and Order: From Theorizing Toward Theories." *Canadian Review of Sociology & Anthropology*, forthcoming.

Wilcox, B., and E. Bloustein. 1968. "Account of a Field Study in a Rural Area of the Representation of Indigents Accused of Crime." In Rita J. Simon (ed.). *The Sociology of Law*. San Francisco: Chandler.

Wilson, J. Q. 1968. "The Police and the Delinquent in Two Cities." In Stanton Wheeler (ed.). *Controlling Delinquents*. New York: Wiley.

Wolfgang, M. 1968. "Urban Crime." In James Q. Wilson (ed.), *The Metropolitan Enigma*. Cambridge: Harvard University Press.

Part IV:

ORGANIZATIONAL CRIMINALITY

Traditionally, criminological theory and criminal law have focused on individuals. Theoretically, criminal phenomena have been conceived as the products of individuals; legally, their responsibility. One result is that we are unable to think (or write) very clearly about criminal phenomena that are not in any simple sense, at least, perpetrated by individuals. Another result is that the law has difficulty in dealing with them.

Edwin H. Sutherland's notion of "white collar crime" helped turn the attention of criminologists to some of the sorts of phenomena at issue: violations of laws regarding restraint of trade; misrepresentation in advertising; patent infringements; illegal rebates; unfair labor practices. His work, however, mainly emphasized the ways in which such phenomena are similar to those conventionally perceived and treated as criminal, rather than highlighting differences that would force criminologists to reconceptualize the field. (One exception is that Sutherland was interested in pointing to the high status of persons engaged in white collar crimes. This served his purpose of challenging theories relating all crime to poverty and other "pathologies.")

For example, Sutherland passionately argued that the law violations of corporations are properly considered "crimes," rather than dispassionately dissecting the reasons why, and implications of the fact that, portions of the public and the law choose to treat them differently. In some cases, as he reasoned, the difference may be due mainly to the influence of those perpetrating the "acts" in question. But this may be neither all nor theoretically the most interesting difference, it being somewhat unclear whether it makes sense to think of phenomena like the manufacture of unsafe vehicles, or widespread violations of food purity laws, as "acts" in the ordinary sense. At the very least, to do so runs the risk of missing their complex, cooperative nature, and also their intimate ties to valued phenomena—such as the manufacture of vehicles per se, and the production of food. Further, partly as a result of his focus on individuals, but for other reasons as well, Sutherland developed a "cultural" explanation of such phenomena, by and large, neglecting their broader, "structural" sources. Like other criminals, he argued, white collar criminals learn to commit their white collar crimes, and they do so as a result of association with others favoring such activities. In one sense (and to the extent that criminal acts, perpetrated by individuals, are in question), this is probably so, but not too helpful, for it fails to help us grasp the larger sources of the values and attitudes in question. When "organizational criminality" is at issue, most of all such a posture may fail to direct thought sufficiently to the context of the *organization*.

We have collected four readings in this section dealing with what we have termed "organizational criminality." We do not intend to close any options by using this term, but instead to open some. Roughly we intend to focus attention on criminal phenomena that are not easily conceived as the acts of individuals; they are, instead, associated with, even perpetrated by, large-scale, complex organizations. The readings deal variously with these phenomena, which are, we think, both analytically fascinating, and of great and increasing social importance. We are not alone in these judgments. The articles reprinted here, as well as the much larger array of articles and books we could not reprint, show this. Clearly more work is going on in this area, and we think more, much more, should go on.

Analytically, as already noted, we need to become clearer about what it means to talk or write about "deviant acts by complex organizations," "organizational deviance," criminogenic and quasi-legal behaviors" within and between the "multiple tiers" of an industry, and "corporate misconduct"—some of the several terms and phrases used by our authors. Although there is a long tradition in sociology, especially, of talking and writing about "organizational behavior," the meaning of the term remains somewhat cloudly. The cloudiness is even thicker when one is referring to crime. The articles reprinted here may do less to dispel the clouds than point to the need for conceptualizing designed to do so.

The social importance of this area needs little comment. All of us everywhere are increasingly affected by phenomena produced by, or associated with, large-scale, complex organizations, for good and ill. Indeed, much of the lives of most of us are spent "within" such organizations, private and public. Perhaps all we need say is that the work of criminologists would benefit from more explicit acknowledgment of this fact. It is not only that criminal phenomena of vast import are associated with large-scale organizations, crime control phenomena are as well. More careful consideration of the relevance of existing varieties of organizational theories, developed in sociology and public administration, among other disciplines, for criminology is long overdue. Happily, it seems to be happening.

M. David Ermann and Richard J. Lundman draw on organizational theory to bring some order to the study of "deviant action" by an organization and of efforts to control such actions by organizations. Whether their definitional and classificatory efforts will prove useful remains to be seen, of course. But one theoretical gain, potentially, is in drawing attention to relations between organizations and their environments. These environments consist in some important part of other organizations, and not, of course, only organizations advertently designed to control them. Ermann and Lundman appreciate this fact.

Norman K. Denzin focuses on a single "industry"—liquor distilling and distribution—and explores the ways in which it various "tiers" or levels engage in, or press other levels to engage in, criminal and quasi-criminal phenomena. Studies of the relations *among* organizations is one of Ermann's and Lundman's recommendations. Denzin makes clear one of the senses in which such relations act as "controls" that is not fully explicit in their typology.

Christopher D. Stone turns to some of the dilemmas facing the legal enterprise in the control of "corporate misconduct," emphasizing what he takes to be a trend toward prescribing "organizational adjustment measures" designed to influence the ways decisions are made in organizations. He contrasts these measures with traditional means of dealing with organizational misconduct: providing negative incentives for the organizations, and holding individuals liable for corporate misconduct. A third measure, somewhat more distant from a traditional criminal law response, has been to establish regulatory agencies, which, in turn, promulgate rules and standards. All have their difficulties, particularly if the aim is conceived to be preventing the misconduct in the first place, but even (for reasons Ermann and Lundman suggest too) if all that is wanted is early, but permanent, cessation of the offensive phenomena. So, Stone suggests, the legal enterprise is sometimes, perhaps more frequently, moving to require corporations to structure themselves in certain ways designed to prevent, or provide early detection and correction, of, offensive phenomena. Stone is not particularly sanguine about the likelihood that such measures will prove effective, but he certainly thinks them worth a try. From a criminological standpoint, they deserve the closest study.

Ivan Light deals not with a large-scale complex organization that is incidentally involved in criminal phenomena, but with one that exists to profit from them. (It can be argued that this is a distinction easily made conceptually, but difficult to apply empirically!) It makes, we think, a nice complement to the other articles collected in this section. They consider the protocriminal or criminal phenomena associated with organizations considered "legitimate"; Light considers some of the functions usually performed by legitimate organizations carried out, however haphazardly or wastefully, by an "illegitimate" organization. The other authors explicitly or implicitly consider ways of limiting the criminal phenomena associated with large-scale complex legitimate organizations, ways that would avoid destroying their legitimate outputs. Light's article implicitly raises the question of how the positive functions of illegitimate organizations might be preserved.

Light contributes to a debate of long standing in criminology between the cultural and the structural determinists, to put it too simply but not inaccurately. (Ruth Rosner Kornhauser's contribution to this volume explicitly analyzes versions of these positions.) He also treats another related issue that runs through a number of articles. Is numbers gambling "irrational" or might it be seen, if viewed in full context, as "rational"? Without strain, and without holding that numbers gambling is the most rational (in the sense of "beneficial") way of dealing with "small change" that could be adopted, Light makes quite clear that, in the circumstances, the activity is fully understandable, linked to quite ordinary "economic" motives, and perhaps even beneficial for the individuals participating in it, as well as for the community sustaining it.

22

DEVIANT ACTS BY COMPLEX ORGANIZATIONS
Deviance and Social Control at the
Organizational Level of Analysis

M. DAVID ERMANN and RICHARD J. LUNDMAN

Only recently has there been sociological recognition that many of the discomforts characteristic of the contemporary experience are traceable to the actions of large-scale organizations. C. Wright Mills (1956; 1959) was among the first to raise this issue and call for its systematic sociological study. He argued (1959:176) that social scientists should illustrate for the powerless the ways in which their personal troubles relate to the actions of large-scale organizations. More recently others have expanded upon Mills' argument, isolating the distorted perceptions of deviance available in nearly all deviance texts, readers, and classroom lectures, and asking where studies of organizationally structured racism, poverty, and war-making are to be found (Gouldner, 1968; Liazos, 1972; Thio, 1973).

There also appears to be increasing governmental and public interest in such issues. During the last decade, but particularly since Watergate, there has been a seemingly endless series of reports of improper actions by large-scale organizations. These include corporate avoidance of tax payments (Vanick, 1975), corporate bribery of foreign officials (Martz, Thomas and Krishner, 1976), prison misuse and abuse of inmates (Sage, 1974), domestic spying by the Central Intelligence Agency (President's Commission, 1975), and abuse of children by public schools (Kozol, 1967), to name but a few. As a consequence, Spencer (1973:91) observed that "there is growing unrest that our major societal

[1] An earlier version of this paper was presented at the annual meeting of the American Sociological Association, San Francisco, August, 1975. The authors are grateful to two anonymous reviewers for their suggestions. We shared equally in this work and the order of our names could just as easily have been reversed. They are merely listed alphabetically.

[2] Large-scale organizations hereafter will be referred to as organizations. This analysis refers specifically to hierarchically-ordered organizations.

From M. David Ermann and Richard J. Lundman, "Deviant Acts by Complex Organizations: Deviance and Social Control at the Organizational Level of Analysis," 19(1) *The Sociological Quarterly* 55-67 (Winter 1978). Copyright 1978 by The Midwest Sociological Society.

institutions are not serving the public interest and that these institutions must somehow be made more visible and accountable to the public at large."

Associated with increased awareness of the problems posed by large-scale organizations has been the tendency to attribute responsibility to persons within those organizations.[2] Reminiscent of the social pathologists of an earlier era (cf. Mills, 1943), contemporary students of organizational misconduct generally attempt to identify the types of persons most likely to engage in deviant actions (cf. Rogow and Lasswell, 1963). Thus, the Watergate investigators as social control agents sought to determine which of the president's men were responsible: the paradoxical conclusion was "all the president's men" (Bernstein and Woodward, 1974).

On those occasions when social control of organizations (as opposed to control of persons within organizations) has been addressed, it typically has been conceptualized as occurring inadvertently in situations where the power of the interacting organizations is approximately equal. Thus, Thompson and McEwen (1958) focused on competition, bargaining, cooperation, and coalition in their analysis of control. Aiken and Hage (1968) applied an exchange perspective in their analysis of organizational interdependence among health and welfare organizations; and Levine and White (1961) and Jacobs (1974) used this perspective to suggest how organizations are constrained through exchange relationships. Control thus has been conceptualized as informal, reciprocal, and not the manifest reason for interorganizational relationships. And attempts to control organizations have been viewed as incidental by-products of other interactions.[3]

The aim of the present study, is to suggest the sociology of deviance be expanded to recognize (1) organizations, not just individuals, commit deviant acts, and (2) other organizations have formal responsibilities and power to control the deviant acts of organizations. This paper will provide a framework for analyzing deviance in light of these suggestions.

The Sociology of Organizational Deviance

There have been recurrent efforts to direct sociologists toward the development of an organizational deviance perspective. Sutherland's (1949) analysis of white collar crime led him to conclude that "white collar crime is organized crime." Reiss (1966) called upon students of social deviance to shift attention to organizational deviance. Coleman (1974) traced a history of the emergence of "juristic" actors, noting that they are now more powerful than individual persons and suggesting that it is necessary to search for ways to constrict their power (cf. also, Stone, 1975). Wheeler (1976:532), finally, called for the development of an organizational deviance perspective, observing that:

It was just about a quarter century ago that the late Edwin H. Sutherland published his little book on white collar crime, so it is hardly an original idea to return to the topic and

[3] For exceptions see: Ermann et al., 1976; Leavitt et al., 1973:248-67; and Zald and Davis Hair, 1972.

related issues. . . . But it is essential because so little has happened in the intervening years. It is necessary to urge that we redirect our attention from the petty thief to the corporate executive, from the offender who haunts the streets and alleys to those who inhabit the finer restaurants, and from the police to the FTC, SEC, and IRS.

Particularly in recent years, there has also begun to emerge an empirical organizational deviance literature. There have been studies of corporate deviance (Clinard, 1952; Geis, 1967; Lane, 1953; Hay and Kelley, 1974; Farberman, 1975), governmental deviance (Senate Select Committee, 1976; Roebuck and Barker, 1974; Kobler, 1975; Sage, 1974), and the social control of such deviance (Stone, 1975; Zald and Davis Hair, 1972; Jacobs, 1974). There has also been attention given to organizational responses to attempts at social control (Ermann et al., 1976; Molotch and Lester, 1975).[4]

As a consequence of this research, we can now attempt to anticipate certain of the elements necessary for a viable organizational deviance framework. Specifically, four conditions appear to be needed for an action to become defined as organizationally deviant.

First, to become deviant an action must be contrary to norms maintained by actors external to the subject organization. All large organizations exist in complex normative environments that prescribe and proscribe selected actions. For our purposes, the most important normative expectations of those environments define the rewards that intended beneficiaries of organizational actions should receive. Expectations regarding these beneficiaries are often diffuse, always subject to change, and occasionally contradictory. Nevertheless, it is possible to identify a temporally specific consensus. Thus, American businesses currently are expected to serve owners, labor unions are expected to serve members, hospitals are expected to serve patients, and police departments are expected to serve their communities. Violation of these temporally specific normative expectations constitutes the first element of organizational deviance.

Second, the action must find support in the norms of a given level or division of the organization. Police brutality, for example, qualifies as organizational deviance since it generally is supported by patrol level norms emphasizing solidarity and secrecy (Lundman, 1977). Acts of embezzlement, by contrast, are not organizationally deviant, because the norms of the embezzler's peer group are not supportive of this action (Cressey, 1971).

Third, the action must be known to and supported by the dominant administrative coalition of the organization. Such knowledge and support may be active (as when members of the coalition encourage, cover up, or ignore an action), or passive (as when they fail, for whatever reason, to take reasonable precautions to assure compliance with external expectations).[5] Thus, the actions of supervisors who discriminate on the basis of sex without the knowledge of their superiors, or those of faculty members who give all students 'A' grades while being protected by tenure from sanctioning by their dean, do not constitute

---

[4]See Ermann and Lundman (1978) for a sociological perspective on corporate and governmental deviance, and attempts to control these actions.

[5]In this latter instance we suggest application of the legal notion of the "reasonable man."

organizational deviance. Elite knowledge and support of these behaviors, however, would transform them into instances of organizational deviance.

Fourth, because organizational deviance is organizationally specific, new members must be socialized to participate in it. For an action to be organizationally deviant, therefore, it is necessary that socialization of new members include inculcation of norms and rationalizations supportive of such an action.

Organizational deviance, in sum, refers to action attributed to an organization which is labeled deviant because it violates the normative expectations surrounding the organization. Moreover, the action is peer and elite supported. What we are speaking of, for instance, are the predictable deaths of chemical workers who die of cancer, the actions of charities which spend all their incomes on fund-raising and administration, and the domestic spying of the CIA. This definition emphasizes the organizational rather than individual components of these deviant actions.

Types of Organizational Deviance

As noted, imputing deviance to an organization occurs in a complex normative environment. Blau and Scott (1962:45-54), however, provide a *cui bono* taxonomy that can be adapted in order to reduce some of the complexity of extra-organizational expectations. Using their taxonomy, we posit the existence of a temporally specific consensus external to an organization. This consensus specifies the priorities of claims that can be made by competing actors upon the organization. Four categories of actors can make claims: (1) members, (2) owners and managers, (3) publics-in-contact, and (4) the public-at-large. At any one time, however, only one type of claimant *normatively* is the main beneficiary for a particular organization. In their words, "although all parties benefit, the benefits to one party furnish the reason for the organization's existing while the benefits to others are essentially a cost" (1962:43). That one party is termed the "prime beneficiary."

Four types of organizations follow from application of the *cui bono* criterion. First are mutual benefit associations, such as labor unions, where prime beneficiaries are the members. Second are business concerns, intended to make a profit, where the prime beneficiaries are owners. Third are service organizations such as social work agencies where prime beneficiaries are clients; and finally are commonweal organizations such as police and fire departments where the prime beneficiary is the public-at-large.

Each of the four types of organization poses its own instances of organizational deviance. That is, what is deviant in one type of organization often is acceptable for the others. Mutual benefit organizations may be labeled deviant if they fail to maintain internal democratic control by, or benefit to, the membership. On the other hand, American business concerns currently are not labeled deviant if they lack internal employee democracy, but may be so identified if they fail to survive or earn sufficient profit for their owners. Service organizers, with clients unable to judge the adequacy of service received, pose problems if they betray the trust of their vulnerable clients. In general, failure to maintain internal democracy or earn a profit does not make service organizations deviant. Finally, commonweal organizations may be labeled deviant if they cannot be subjected to external democratic control.

Because of the normative diversity that exists, however, actors other than prime beneficiaries expect to benefit from the organization. In addition to serving the public at large, for example, commonweal organizations such as police departments also are obliged to provide members with adequate training, protect the rights of arrested citizens, and be accountable to their governmental jurisdictions. Similarly, business concerns, in addition to serving owners, are expected to be responsive to employees, customers, and the public-at-large. Each organization, then, has normatively defined secondary beneficiaries. Failure to serve their interests constitutes an additional type of organizational deviance.

In sum, organizational deviance refers to actions that interfere with the flow of benefits to actors consensually recognized as having legitimate claims upon an organization. The protection of such recognized claims is mandated to organizations whose functions are to control organizational behavior.

Controller Organizations

Most organizations constantly interact with other organizations that have responsibilities and powers for labeling and controlling their deviance.[6] On the federal level, governmental controller organizations include the Civil Aeronautics Board, Federal Aviation Agency, Environmental Protection Agency, Federal Trade Commission, and the Interstate Commerce Commission. Nationwide private organizations such as Common Cause, Consumers Union, the various groups inspired by Ralph Nader, and the Sierra Club also have attempted to assume control responsibilities. A host of state and local social control organizations, such as county level economic crime units and Better Business Bureaus, complete this partial inventory.

What distinguishes these controllers from other organizations is that their *manifest* purpose is to control other organizations. Unlike businesses, for example, wherein the manifest purpose is profit, the public reason for the existence of controller organizations is control.

Each controller organization is mandated to protect certain social actors from specified deviant actions by given types of organizations. Business controllers concerned with loss of financial viability or failure to serve owners, for instance, are expected to be attentive to actions that deny shareholders a voice in decision making. They thus may establish rules for stockholders meetings and procedures for expressing stockholder dissatisfaction. Other controllers of business organizations, however, are expected to be attentive to socially dysfunctional outputs that threaten to injure the public-at-large (e.g., pollution), and may attempt to establish specific output criteria. The Securities and Exchange Commission is an example of the former, while the Environmental Protection Agency illustrates the latter.

---

[6]The extent of these controls is illustrated by the General Motors estimate that 1.3 billion dollars are spent annually to comply with government regulations (Porter, 1976).

As shown in Figure 1, a maximum of sixteen types of controller organizations are potentially derivable by relating the four types of organizations (mutual benefit association, business concern, etc.) to the four types of deviance (breakdown of internal democracy, loss of financial viability, etc.) Columns in the figure indicate the type of organization to be controlled with these organizations defined by their primary beneficiaries. Rows indicate types of deviance (and hence the need for control) posed by organizations. Deviance is defined by the injury to a primary or secondary beneficiary. Thus, in cell 6 are controller organizations responsible for loss of financial viability in business organizations (e.g., Securities and Exchange Commission); and in cell 12 are controller organizations concerned with preventing commonweal organizations from violating the rights of vulnerable clients (e.g., American Civil Liberties Union).

Available descriptions of controller organizations suggest that a major distinction should be made between those concerned with promoting the interests of prime beneficiaries and those concerned with secondary beneficiaries. In the case of protecting prime beneficiaries, represented by cells along the diagonal (cells 1, 6, 11, and 16), there exists a congruence between the prime beneficiary of the organization and the deviance that is the concern of the controller. The Joint Commission on Accreditation of Hospitals and local police civilian review boards, for example, are both concerned with protecting the interests of prime beneficiaries.

In the cells not along the diagonal, however, the actors who would be victimized by the deviant acts are not the prime beneficiaries. The Environmental Protection Agency, for example, protects the public-at-large from the actions of business organizations. Similarly, the American Civil Liberties Union protects arrested citizens from the action of police organizations charged with serving the interests of the public-at-large. In both of these instances, there is a lack of congruence between the normative prime beneficiary of the organization being controlled and the concern of the controller organization.

This distinction between congruent and non-congruent cells suggests the following hypothesis: *controller organizations located in non-congruent cells will be limited in protecting the interests of secondary beneficiaries because they are required to minimize their interference with the interests of primary beneficiaries.* That is, the efforts of control organizations located in non-congruent cells will tend to be compromised (cf., Perrow, 1961:865). Controller organizations concerned with the industrial pollution thus frequently have been forced to lower standards because of claims of severe financial losses, and auto makers have successfully lobbied against EPA emission requirements. Similarly, police organizations have successfully argued that the Supreme Court's Miranda decision and other procedural safeguards reduce their ability to protect the public-at-large from crime.

We suggest, therefore, that the assigned functions of controller organizations may be more important than usually assumed. We believe that addressing the problem in this way is necessary for the development of a sociology, as

Figure 1. A Typology of Controllers of Organizations

Type of Deviance	Types of Organizations Being Controlled				
	Mutual Benefit (e.g., local labor union)	Business	Service (e.g., hospitals)	Commonweal (e.g., police)	'Victims' of deviance
Breakdown of internal due process	National Labor Relations Board (1)	Fair Employment Practices Commission (2)	Employee Union (3)	Civil Service Commission (4)	*Participants*
Loss of financial viability	'Parent' Union (5)	Securities and Exchange Commission (6)	State Rate Setting Commission (7)	City Auditor (8)	*Owners*
Betrayal of vulnerable actors	The Courts (9)	Better Business Bureau (10)	Joint Commission on Accreditation of Hospitals (11)	American Civil Liberties Union (12)	*Public-in-contact*
Erosion of external control, or socially dysfunctional output	U.S. Department of Justice (13)	Environmental Protection Agency (14)	Common Cause (15)	Civilian Review Board (16)	*Public-at-large*
Primary Beneficiary	*Participants*	*Owners*	*Public-in-contact*	*Public-at-large*	

opposed to a social psychology, of the social control of organizational deviance. It is this issue which occupies our attention in the following section.

Labeling and Sanctioning Organizational Deviance

As labeling-oriented students of individual social deviance have shown, labeling and sanctioning are not automatic nor even frequent reactions to normatively proscribed acts (Becker, 1963; Scheff, 1966). Indeed, it appears that most such acts go undetected (Short and Nye, 1958). When detected by lay persons most are not reported to professional labelers (Gold, 1966), and if reported, most deviant actors are not formally processed (Black and Reiss, 1970). Complete and formal processing of individual social deviance, then, is the exception rather than the rule.

It appears that complete and formal processing also is an exception for organizational deviance, but for reasons other than the psychological and social psychological statements typically offered as explanations for the infrequent processing of individual deviance.[7] Rather, a number of structural contingencies combine to limit the labeling and sanctioning of organizational deviance. First, because the deviance is organizational, it would appear that bureaucratic structure impedes discovery by individuals of the organizational sources of their personal troubles. Mayhew (1968), for instance, found that there were significant problems in dealing with organizational racial discrimination when the stimulus for control was a complaint system. Similarly, Ennis (1967:40) reported that only 10 percent of consumer fraud victimizations were ever reported. Finally, it is unlikely that individual customers at local Sears stores could have discovered that the small appliance "bait and switch" policies they experienced were part of a nationwide Sears policy. It is suggested, therefore, that because these actions are organizational in nature, the source of the stimulus which initiates control is an important determinant of labeling. Specifically, controller organizations which rely primarily upon complaint systems are likely to be less effective than organizations which also seek out instances of organizational deviance on their own.

Our second observation is that once an instance of organizational deviance has been identified, delegation of control power and the consequent creation of countervailing force are more effective than the retention of power by the controller. This is the case, in part, because the relations between controlled and controller organizations are generally more protracted than those which occur in the context of individual deviance. As a consequence, organizations such as General Motors and the Environmental Protection Agency tend to develop accommodative relations (Coleman, 1974; Friedman, 1962). Delegation of power is disruptive of this tendency toward accommodation.

In addition, the vested bureaucratic interests of controller organizations tend to interfere with effective responses to organizational deviance. This is especially the case for controllers charged with protecting the interests of

---

[7] See, for example, Ennis (1967) for a discussion of the personal reasons why individuals elect not to report their criminal victimization to the police.

secondary beneficiaries. These controller organizations because they are located in non-congruent cells may temper their efforts because of a concern not to interfere with the flow of primary benefits. Protectors of secondary beneficiaries, therefore, seek to protect and promote their own organizational interests by ignoring troublesome but important deviance in favor of less troublesome misconduct. Thus, in the aftermath of the recent oil spill off Cape Cod the Coast Guard indicated that the ship responsible has been involved in, and on occasion cited for, 18 minor mishaps during the last 12 years. The Coast Guard also indicated, however, that it did not intend to push for the requirement that tankers have double hulls which would help prevent spills, since that design would result in higher oil prices and shortages of oil.[8]

Similarly, in the context of organizationally supported but legally unjustified police violence (Reiss, 1971), both the American Civil Liberties Union and the Civil Rights Division of the U.S. Justice Department have protected their own organizational interests by carefully choosing occasions for public intervention. If there had been a delegation of power so that victims had sufficient resources to protect themselves collectively, such organizational considerations would have been unimportant. It is our hypothesis, therefore, that controller organizations that delegate power (in effect, creating a set of countervailing forces) are more likely than others to create effective control, particularly when they are mandated to protect secondary beneficiaries.

Third, the timing of the control may reduce labeling and sanctioning effectiveness. Timing may be prospective, processual, or retrospective. Prospective controls exist when control is attempted before a deviant act can occur. They typically seek to assure that an organization is capable of performing nondeviantly; they cannot determine that the organization will act nondeviantly, only that it can do so. For instance, the periodic safety inspections of coal mines produce shows of conformity by the operators, and minimal penalties for violations. Activities then tend to revert to normal levels of violation as inspectors and licensors depart. Inspectors may have checked the availability of masks, fans, and detector devices, but they cannot determine if these will be used. Thus, reliance upon prospective controls invites cycles of renewal and deterioration, which coincide with the periodicity of licensing and inspection procedures.

Processual controls, which are relatively uncommon, exist for instance in the presence of U.S. Department of Agriculture inspectors at meat packing plants. These inspectors control actual behavior rather than capability, and have the authority to close plants or reject meat that fails to meet standards. But they are vulnerable to co-optation because of their long periods of contact with those they are intended to control. In decisions such as theirs, where many cases could reasonably lead to differing judgments, the prime beneficiary (management) is present, while the secondary beneficiaries (consumers) are abstractions, and their interests may suffer as a result. Processual controls, nevertheless, may be effective relative to others, but they often are prohibitively expensive.

[8]Reported on the CBS Evening News, December 21, 1976.

Retrospective controls occur after the fact of deviance, when a controller or a victim recognizes that beneficiary rights have been violated and seeks some form of sanction. Such controls typically depend on the existence of a victim who knows of, and formally complains about, the deviance, or a controller that seeks out instances of deviance. As noted previously, however, many individuals elect not to pursue their rights.

Because of the limitations associated with each technique, effective control often may be greatest when a combination of techniques is used. For instance, the Better Business Bureau's failures to control (Ajemian, 1971) may be related to its reliance on a retrospective (complaint) system. On the other hand, the Securities and Exchange Commission's relative effectiveness (Green, 1972:216-23) may be related to its combined use of retrospective and prospective controls. The advantages of multiple techniques flow from the observation that all organizations seek to protect their interests by maintaining organizational secrets (Weber, 1967:247). When deviance is among these secrets, penetration by any one technique alone is likely to be relatively difficult. Thus, it would appear that multiple techniques relative to timing are likely to be more effective than any single technique.

Fourth, it would appear that the certainty and severity of sanction relates to effectiveness. In many instances of individual deviance, acts are spontaneous or emotional and, therefore, the possibility of detection and punishment are not among the factors present during construction and release of the action (Wolfgang, 1958). Moreover, there is evidence that most individuals do not possess the information necessary to calculate accurately the probabilities of being detected or punished (Miller et al., 1971).

In most instances of organizational deviance, by contrast, actions are deliberate, so the possibility of detection or punishment can be among the factors considered (Sutherland, 1949; Geis, 1973). Moreover, organizations possess sufficient information to make relatively rational decisions regarding the benefits and costs of a particular action. Thus, business concerns have regularly engaged in price fixing (e.g., Lane, 1953) under the correct assumption that the benefits outweigh the costs. Similarly, the CIA and FBI have continued to engage in illegal activities for which the assumption was that rewards would exceed "flap potential." Finally, police organizations routinely violate rights of arrested citizens (Reiss, 1971) correctly assuming that the possibility of detection and sanctioning is extremely low (Kobler, 1975). Because organizational deviance is thus calculated, we hypothesize that increases in the certainty and severity of punishment are related directly to decreases in the incidence of such deviance. Stated alternatively, as the costs of organizational deviance exceed the benefits, the incidence of these actions should decline.

Fifth, the legitimacy of the controller organization, as reflected in its control of its domain, relates to effectiveness of control. Legitimacy can be operationally-defined as the number of controller organizations competing for the same control activity. In the case of business organizations, for example, the SEC is the single control organization in its sphere of activity and it is quite powerful. By contrast, a large number of organizations compete for the right to protect the interests of persons in contact with business organizations, including various Nader groups, Consumers Union, and the Better Business Bureaus. As a consequence, no one group speaks as effectively as it might for consumers because attention, interest, and power all are spread across a variety of organizations. We, therefore, hypothesize that the greater the legitimacy of the controller organization, the greater the probability of effective control.

Finally, the relative resource deficiencies of controller as compared to controlled organizations reduces their power. Controlled organizations often are powerful actors possessing great wealth, a monopoly of skill, and greater longevity than individuals. In order to label and sanction them effectively, controller organizations must possess comparable resources. We agree with the common sense assumption, therefore, that great disproportions in wealth and skilled personnel produce weak controls.

In this section, we have specified elements we believe central to an analysis of the labeling and sanctioning of organizational deviance. These elements suggest the importance of studying social control of organizational deviance at the organizational level of analysis.

Summary and Conclusion

Our purpose has been to provide a framework for the analysis of a neglected area of research: *organizational* deviance and its control. We have defined the phenomenon, suggested several reasons for studying it, provided a framework for its analysis, and illustrated application of the framework.

In conclusion we would emphasize the anticipatory[9] nature of the present analysis, since the organizational deviance literature is not yet well developed. It must be recognized, however, that organizational deviance and control are increasingly important phenomena in contemporary society, with continual disclosures of abuses by business, mutual benefit, social service, and governmental organizations. These actions often represent episodes of organizational rather than individual deviance. As a consequence, we suggest that a concern with organizational deviance should be among the theoretical, empirical, and methodological interests of an increasing number of contemporary sociologists. The final aim of the present study has been to stimulate these interests.

---

[9] For a discussion of theoretical anticipation see: Merton, 1967:13ff.

REFERENCES

Aiken, Michael and Jerald Hage. 1968. "Organizational interdependence and intraorganizational structure." American Sociological Review 33:912-30.

Ajemian, James. 1971. "The Unrepresented Citizen in a Bureaucratic Society: A Comparative Analysis of Three Citizen Complaint Organizations." Unpublished doctoral dissertation, University of Michigan, Ann Arbor.

Becker, Howard S. 1963. Outsiders; Studies in the Sociology of Deviance. New York: Free Press.

Bernstein, Carl and Bob Woodward. 1974. All the President's Men. New York: Warner.

Black, Donald and Albert J. Reiss, Jr. 1970. "Police control of juveniles." American Sociological Review 35:63-77.

Blau, Peter M. and W. Richard Scott. 1962. Formal Organizations. San Francisco: Chandler.

Clinard, Marshall B. 1952. The Black Market. New York: Holt, Rinehart & Winston.

Coleman, James S. 1974. Power and the Structure of Society. Philadelphia: University of Pennsylvania Press.

Cressey, Donald R. 1971. Other People's Money. Belmont, Calif.: Wadsworth.

Ennis, Phillip H. 1967. "Crime, victims and the police." Trans-Action 4:36-44.

Ermann, M. David, Alan M. Horowitz and William B. Waegel. 1976. Accounts offered in response to imputations of deviance to the CIA: 1947-1975. Paper presented at the annual meeting of the Society for the Study of Social Problems, New York (August).

Ermann, M. David and Richard J. Lundman. 1978. Corporate & Governmental Deviance: Social Problem of Organizational Behavior. New York: Oxford.

Farberman, Harvey. 1975. "A criminogenic market structure: the automobile industry." Sociological Quarterly 16:438-57.

Friedman, Milton. 1962. Capitalism and Freedom. Chicago: University of Chicago Press.

Geis, Gilbert. 1967. "White collar crime: the heavy electrical antitrust cases of 1961." Pp. 139-51 in Marshall B. Clinard and Richard Quinney (eds.), Criminal Behavior Systems: A Typology. New York: Holt, Rinehart & Winston.

———. 1973. "Deterring corporate crime." Pp. 246-58 in Ralph Nader and Mark Green (eds.), Corporate Power in America. New York: Viking.

Gold, Martin. 1966. "Undetected delinquent behavior." Journal of Research in Crime and Delinquency 3:27-46.

Gouldner, Alvin W. 1968. "The sociologist as partisan: sociology and the welfare state." American Sociologist 3:103-16.

Green, Mark J. 1972. The Closed Enterprise System. New York: Grossman.

Hay, George A. and Daniel Kelley. 1974. "An empirical survey of price fixing conspiracies." Journal of Law and Economics 17:13-39.

Jacobs, David. 1974. "Dependency and vulnerability: an exchange approach to the control of organizations." Administrative Science Quarterly 19:45-59.

Kobler, Arthur. 1975. "Police homicide in a democracy." Journal of Social Issues 31:136-84.

Kozol, Jonathan. 1967. Death At An Early Age. New York: Houghton Mifflin.

Lane, Robert E. 1953. "Why business men violate the law." Journal of Criminal Law, Criminology, and Police Science 44:151-65.

Leavitt, Harold J., William R. Dill and Henry B. Eyring. 1973. The Organizational World. New York: Harcourt, Brace, Jovanovich.

Levine, Sol and Paul E. White. 1961. "Exchange as a conceptual framework for the study of interorganizational relationships." Administrative Science Quarterly 5:583-601.

Liazos, Alexander. 1972. "The poverty of the sociology of deviance: nuts, sluts, and 'preverts'." Social Problems 20:103-20.

Lundman, Richard. 1977. Police misconduct as organizational deviance. Paper presented at the annual meeting of the American Sociological Association, Chicago (September).

Martz, Larry, Rich Thomas, and Bernard Krishner. 1976. "The $7 million man in Tokyo." Newsweek, February 16:60.

Mayhew, Leon. 1968. Law and Equal Opportunity. Cambridge: Harvard University Press.

Merton, Robert K. 1967. Theoretical Sociology. New York: The Free Press.

Miller, Dorothy, Ann Rosenthal, Don Miller, and Sheryl Ruzek. 1971. "Public knowledge of criminal penalties: a research report." Pp. 205-26 in Stanley Grupp (ed.), Theories of Punishment. Bloomington: Indiana University Press.

Mills, C. Wright. 1943. "The professional ideology of social pathologists." American Journal of Sociology 49:165-80.

———. 1956. The Power Elite. New York: Oxford.

———. 1959. The Sociological Imagination. New York: Grove.

Molotch, Harvey and Marilyn Lester. 1975. "Accidental news: the great oil spill as local occurrence and national event." American Journal of Sociology 81:235-59.

Perrow, Charles. 1961. "Goals in complex organizations." American Sociological Review 26:854-65.

Porter, Sylvia. 1976. "Do U.S. regulations work." The Morning News. Wilmington, Del., November 30:22.

President's Commission. 1975. Report to the president by the commission on CIA activities within the United States. Washington: U.S. Government Printing Office.

Reiss, Albert J., Jr. 1966. "The study of deviant behavior: where the action is." Ohio Valley Sociologist 32:1-12.

———. 1971. "Police brutality: answers to key questions," Pp. 225-38 in Richard Knudten (ed.), Crime, Criminology, and Contemporary Society. Homewood, Ill.: Dorsey.

Roebuck, Julian B. and Thomas Barker. 1974. "A typology of police corruption." Social Problems 21:423-37.

Rogow, Arnold A., and Harold D. Lasswell. 1963. Power, Corruption, and Rectitude. Englewood Cliffs, N.J.: Prentice-Hall.

Sage, Wayne. 1974. "Crime and the clockwork lemon," Human Behavior 3:16-23.

Scheff, Thomas. 1966. Being Mentally Ill. Chicago: Aldine.

Senate Select Committee to Study Governmental Operations with Respect to Intelligence Activities. 1976. Intelligence Activities and the Rights of Americans. Washington, D.C.: Government Printing Office.

Short, James and F. Ivan Nye. 1958. "Extent of unrecorded delinquency—tentative conclusions." Journal of Criminal Law, Criminology and Police Science 48:296-302.

Spencer, Gary. 1973. "Methodological issues in the study of bureaucratic elites: a case study of West Point." Social Problems 21:90-103.

Stone, Christopher D. 1975. Where the Law Ends: Social Control of Corporate Behavior. New York: Harper & Row.

Sutherland, Edwin H. 1949. White Collar Crime. New York: Dryden.

Thio, Alex. 1973. "Class bias in the sociology of deviance." American Sociologist 8:1-12.

Thompson, James D. and William J. McEwen. 1958. "Organizational goals and environment." American Sociological Review 23:23-31.

Vanick, Charles. 1975. "Corporate tax study, 1974." The Congressional Record, 94th Congress, First Session (Tuesday, October 7):1-6.

Weber, Max. 1967. From Max Weber. Hans N. Gerth and Wright Mills (eds. and trans.). New York: Oxford.

Wheeler, Stanton. 1976. "Trends and problems in the sociological study of crime." Social Problems 23:525-34.

Wolfgang, Marvin. 1958. Patterns of Criminal Homicide. Philadelphia: University of Pennsylvania Press.

Zald, Mayer and Feather Davis Hair. 1972. "The social control of general hospitals." Pp. 51-81 in Basil Georgopoulos (ed.), Organizational Research on Health Organizations. Ann Arbor, Michigan: Institute for Social Research, University of Michigan.

23

NOTES ON THE CRIMINOGENIC HYPOTHESIS
A Case Study of the American Liquor Industry

NORMAN K. DENZIN

Whiskey and alcoholic beverages have been produced in the United States since 1640 and have been taxed intermittently by the federal and state governments since 1791. The 18th Amendment and the Volstead Act of 1919 stopped the growth of the industry and made the production of alcoholic beverages (except for medicinal, sacramental or scientific research purposes) illegal. While a few distillers remained in production under strict governmental control, the majority of distillers were driven out of business to be replaced by bootleggers (Sinclair, 1964; Gusfield, 1963; Kane, 1965).

OVERVIEW

In this article I wish to examine, from a symbolic interactionist perspective, the organizational development of the American liquor industry since Prohibition.

* I wish to thank Patricia T. Clough for her assistance in this research. Graduate students in Sociology 414–416 at the University of Illinois gathered ethnographic data on the public drinking establishments discussed in the text. Portions of this research were supported by the Graduate College Research Board and the Department of Sociology of the University of Illinois. The comments of Evelyn K. Denzin, Sidney J. Kronus, William Cockerham, Stanley Cross and Julian Simon were particularly helpful. Finally, I wish to thank Catherine Daubard for her assistance in the ordering and reconceptualization of the entire research question.

Blumer's (1969) proposals for the foundations of a theory of organizations suggest that the interactionist examines and stresses the informal, as opposed to the formal attributes of any organizational complex. Rather than viewing organizations in rigid, static terms, the interactionist sees organizations as living, changing forms which may outlive the lives of their respective members and, as such, take on histories that transcend individuals, conditions and specific situations. Rather than focusing on formal structural attributes, the interactionist focuses on organizations as *negotiated* productions that differentially constrain their members; they are seen as moving patterns of accomodative adjustment among organized parties. Although organizations create formal structures, every organization in its day-to-day activities is produced and created by individuals, individuals who are subject to and constrained by the vagaries and inconsistencies of the human form. Organizations ((including the licensed alcoholic-beverage industry) are best conceptualized as complex, shifting networks of social relationships. The sum total of these relationships—whether real or only symbolized, whether assumed and taken for granted or problematic and troublesome—constitute the organization as it is sensed, experienced, and acted upon by the individual or relational

From Norman K. Denzin, "Notes on the Criminogenic Hypothesis: A Case Study of the American Liquor Industry," 42(6) *American Sociological Review* 905-920 (December 1977). Copyright 1977 by the American Sociological Association.

member. Power, control, coercion and deception become central commodities of negotiation in those arenas that make up the organization.

Hamilton et al.'s (1938:3–4) image of an industry is well-suited to this analysis of the liquor industry. They remark:

In a literal sense, there is no such thing as an industry. . . . Instead . . . there is only a host of individuals . . . engaged in a varied assortment of personal activities—the digging of coal, the smelting of ore, the advancement of personal fortunes. . . . They are human beings who engage in human activities. . . . It is amid this babble of tongues, this confusion of purposes, this drama of divergent dramas that industry is to be found. . . . Yet industry is a name for what is at best a loose aggregate of business units engaged in performing a single service or producing a single commodity. . . . An industry is like an individual . . . it has a character, a structure, a system of habits of its own. Its pattern is out of accord with a normative design; its activities conform very imperfectly with a charted course of industrial events.

This investigation, starting from such assumptions, utilizes a case study method and focuses upon interactions and negotiations among members of this industry. Data have been drawn from all levels of the industry, but in particular the state of Illinois and the twin cities of Champaign-Urbana. The attention to negotiations among organizational members led directly and immediately to the consideration of criminogenic activities. I shall examine the extent to which criminogenic and quasi-legal behaviors have served the interests of the members of this industrial complex (see Bell, 1960; Gross, forthcoming). I hope to show that this criminogenic tendency (that is, the intended and unintended violation of the legal code) is present at all levels of the industry and can be traced to the historical context of the industry's development, to its present structure, and to the relational patterns which exist within what appears to be a single economic enterprise. Basic to the analysis which follows is the assumption that the organizational structure of any industry involves multiple tiers, levels or social worlds of interaction. Taken together, these multiple segments constitute the organization as its members know it (Hamilton et al., 1938). Five such tiers, manufacturers, distributors, retailers, the legal order and drinkers, will be identified. Criminogenic activity evolves as a result of interaction among (as well as within) each of these tiers.

As one moves from the local level to the state, regional and national levels of the industry, the actual drinking transaction and the drinking act become less problematic. What emerges as problematic is the production, distribution and sale of a single product—the alcoholic beverage. This product—however bottled, branded, endorsed, packaged, priced or displayed—must somehow reenter the system where its last contender exited, be this the storeroom of the wholesaler, the shelves of the retailer or the refrigerator of the consumer. These two objects—one an actor (the drinker-consumer), the other a product (the alcoholic beverage)—emerge as central to the American liquor industry. They must be brought together, over and over again, and American society has given the liquor industry the license and mandate to join these two commodities in any of a variety of ways (Abrahamson, 1938:395–429).

HISTORICAL CONTEXTS

The interlocking effects of Prohibition and Repeal set the historical context for the post-1934 expansion of the liquor industry, and their enactment served to make the liquor industry a unique enterprise within the American marketplace.

Perhaps the most striking effect of Prohibition/Repeal was the concentration of alcohol manufacture in the hands of four large distillers—(1) Distillers Corporation (Seagrams, Ltd.), (2) Schenley Distillers Corporation, (3) National Distillers Products Corporation and (4) Walker (Gooderham & Worts, Ltd.). By the mid-1920s the Big Four had absorbed some 60 distillers in Illinois, Indiana and Kentucky (East, 1952; Oxenfeldt, 1951). The Big Four, unlike many of their smaller competitors, were able to survive Prohibition because, concomitant with their cushion of capital, (1) they were able to establish or maintain Canadian bases of operation and/or (2) they were able to receive government sanction for the production of alcohol for legal uses (Oxenfeldt, 1951).

Prohibition and the public furor accompanying it convinced the large distillers that, if the production of liquor was to be not merely legal but also profitable, the public image of the liquor industry (and of alcohol consumption) must be transformed. This attempt at dramaturgical management took two directions: (1) to transform the image of the distilling industry itself which had been tainted by the violence and corruption of bootleg production and (2) to transform the act of alcohol consumption to a socially-approved act. The latter was especially important because temperance forces and anti-saloon sentiment among large segments of the population did not immediately dissipate with Repeal. The following statement well illustrates the tactic used by distillers to create a more favorable image for alcohol consumption:

> In order to forestall attacks from various dry organizations, which the WTCU spearheaded, we emphasized one of the basic principles of the Distilled Spirits Institute [DSI]: moderation, moderate drinking. Don't over-sell, don't over-drink. [Frank Schwengel, retired brigadier-general and marketing advisor for Seagrams]. (Durrell, 1967:3)

A concomitant technique was to disassociate the distilling industry from tavern consumption. According to a prominent legal consultant for DSI (field interview, July 1975), after Repeal, distillers shifted from a saloon concept of consumption to a carry-home model. Distillers turned their economic efforts to the construction of a "rational," non-tavern, retail-outlet sales program.[1] By separating themselves from taverns, the distillers placated the anti-saloon-league advocates and succeeded in placing the blame for alcohol misuse upon the saloon drinker.

---

[1] Brewers were given taverns, or so it appears. As one distilling executive remarked, "There are only ten bars in Chicago where I want our product sold" (field interview, June, 1975). Today, approximately 75% of all alcoholic beverages are consumed in off-premise locales.

The passage of Repeal was proposed, of course, under the condition that not only would the production and sale of alcohol be legalized, but also that government regulation and taxation would be imposed. Much of the propaganda extolling government regulation and taxation (and, thereby, gaining support for Repeal) was financed by large distillers and brewers (Dobyns, 1940:6). For some groups, the economic benefit of alcohol taxation held sway. Much publicity stressed the loss of tax monies from liquor sales combined with the high cost of attempting to enforce Prohibition. Business, chafing under the taxation burden of World War I, was particularly susceptible to this argument and threw support behind the Repeal movement. Propaganda, supported by the large corporations (particularly DuPont), went so far as to promise that the recent and unpopular income tax could be eliminated by the use of tax monies from alcohol. Other groups, even some sincere temperance groups, were influenced by the supposed benefits of government regulation. The argument was emphasized that Prohibition bred more social ills than it cured and that the bootleg trade was far more detrimental than would be a well-regulated, legal industry (Dobyns, 1940:19–27).

It was hoped that a conciliatory attitude toward regulation and taxation by the distilling industry would pay off in the long run by moderating public opinion of the industry itself and of alcohol use. In the meantime, the liquor industry encouraged government control as the price it was willing to pay for legalization.

As it turned out, government regulation never proved to be much of an inhibition to profits. One reason for this was that the liquor industry itself helped to write the rules. Within ten days of ratification of the 21st Amendment, a Code Authority was created, consisting of the top executives from the large distillers. President Roosevelt directed the Code Authority to draw up a set of guidelines for the federal regulation of their industry. Owsley Brown (president of Brown-Foreman Distillers), L. S. Rosensteil (Schenley's) and Frank Thompson (Seagram's) created the Distilled Spirits Institute (DSI). In the immediate post-Repeal days, the industry, through DSI, worked closely with the federal government—a government-industry relationship which may be without precedent in American history (Durrell, 1967).

DSI encouraged high government regulation and taxation as a cover behind which to hide and reform their collective self-image. While appearing to meekly accept a weak position, they learned from their industrial counterparts in oil, railroads and automobiles how to cover their ever-expanding behaviors through the newly emerging and complex antitrust laws. The liquor corporations kept a low profile, concentrated on dramaturgical management, and busied themselves behind the scenes in the direction of vertical and horizontal integration. Furthermore, Repeal put a great deal of the responsibility for regulation of the liquor industry upon state and local officials (as well as national officials). This placed liquor corporation representatives in a situation where they could corrupt the very persons who were intended to control them.

A final consequence of Prohibition/ Repeal was that government regulation introduced what came to be termed the *three-tier system* of distribution in the wine and spirits industry. Under this system,

> the three levels of supplier, wholesaler and retailer must be maintained separate and independent of each other, and the supplier must sell only to the wholesaler, and the latter only to the retailer. The wholesaler, therefore, stands between the retailer and the manufacturer. (Switzer, 1975:5)

Hidden in the above language is one basic point which had been the touchstone of the Anti-Saloon League; namely, that distillers and brewers owned, or staked tavernkeepers, imposed quotas upon them and forced them to take money out of the pockets of family men (Sinclair, 1964; Gusfield, 1966). "Tied taverns" or "tied houses," as they were called, permitted outside interests to control the politics, moralities and drinking patterns of local communities. By placing the wholesaler between the manufacturer and the retailer, the state and federal governments attempted to break the tied-tavern relationship—at least on the surface.

OBDURATE REALITIES

At the national level, Repeal produced a complex set of laws and procedures unique to every state in the United States (see Distilled Spirits Council, 1974). These procedures include tax and its collection procedures, size of retail containers, local option rulings on retail sales and license permits for distillers' representatives. Also at the national level, antitrust laws and federal tax statutes[2] set boundaries for corporate activity.

At the state level, each State Liquor Commission sets the regulations and modifications of the three-tier system of distiller, distributor and retailer. There are two state models. *Monopoly states* permit the sale of bottled distilled spirits only in state-owned stores. *License states* are states where distilled spirits are sold under a licensed, private enterprise system. This system operates with three variations. For example, in Illinois distributors are given territorial monopolistic rights for the distribution of a particular brand-name product. In addition, licensed resident manufacturers (rectifiers) may sell beverages manufactured within the state directly to retailers (Switzer, 1975).

States also set minimum age limits for consumption of alcoholic beverages and, in some states, this may be differentiated between hard liquor and beer or wine.

At the local level, local liquor commissions (which in Illinois are headed by the mayor) set laws regulating the number of and fees for liquor licenses, decide who receives liquor licenses, and define operating procedures for retail establishments (i.e., hours of operation). Local communities also may set limits such as

---

[2] Government taxation and regulation created a dual effect upon the current system. Liquor taxation is the most expensive factor in producing every gallon of distilled alcohol. Federal taxation is $10.50 per gallon, state tax may be as high as $2.50, and some communities impose a local option tax. This situation causes distillers to comment that the cheapest product in their industry is the alcoholic beverage. Because federal and state taxes must be paid by the distiller before the product leaves his warehouse (i.e., before payment of account), the liquor industry is a high capital, low-labor business—a characteristic which discourages competition from small-scale entrepreneurs.

minimum age for consumption of alcoholic beverages and impose a local excise tax on alcoholic beverages.

These legal procedures, variably enforced and understood, influence the operation of this industry at every tier-level. Such codes also define the circumstances for criminogenic behavior at each level. Members of one tier may be unaware of, or only partially understand the laws which apply to any other tier. In addition, they may be unaware of, or misunderstand those laws and regulations which apply to their own level (field interviews, 1975).

FIVE-TIER STRUCTURE OF THE AMERICAN LIQUOR INDUSTRY

As Hamilton et al. (1938:3–4) observed, there is no such thing as a single industry. At least five different tiers resolve into distinct social worlds which constitute those collective realities that make up this particular industry. The 21st Amendment recognized the three tiers of distiller, distributor and retailer. Closer inspection reveals the presence of two additional tiers: first, drinkers themselves and second, those individuals and agencies committed to the enforcement of the liquor laws— state and local liquor commissions, the police, the FBI, the Treasury Department, and the Bureau of Alcohol, Firearms and Tobacco (BAFT).

Distillers

At the executive level of rival distilling firms, hostile, not cordial or congenial relationships appear to be the pattern, although these participants will seldom permit personal animosities to enter into profitmaking decisions. Oxenfeldt (1951:478) notes that the executive offices of the large distillers are all located in New York City, within a short radius of one another. (There has been a recent regional shift to Chicago.) The executives meet often and know one another well. With few exceptions, they belong to the same organizations and clubs, including DSI and the Licensed Beverage Industries Institute. They also contribute to the same

charities, all in the collective name of the industry. Oxenfeldt (1951:478) states:

> There is no close personal friendship between the top executives of the major distilling corporations . . . their relations vary somewhere between friendly rivalry and intense personal antagonism.

Conversely, separate distillers tend to be tightly bound through kin relationships. Of the four major whiskey producers, all but one are family controlled, with control extending into pre-Prohibition days. (For an illustration of one such family, see Gaines, 1975.) The same pattern appears to hold for brewers and wineries, at least until quite recently (see Horowitz and Horowitz, 1965).

Two highly visible phenomena at the distilling level are the emphases placed upon in-house legal advice, and upon advertising. Every major distiller, brewer and vintner employs a legal staff. Its chief function is to monitor the changing laws within each state, to keep in touch with relevant legal representatives of the industry, and to represent the best interests of the industry to local, state and national political entities. They ensure that their corporations do not grossly violate any stature or ruling that would inhibit the sale of their products. These staffs also enter into negotiations with distributors when territorial contracts are reviewed annually and new quotas set (see Distributor section).

The respective advertising arms of the industry bid against one another at the agency level to capture ever-larger drinking audiences (Bretzfield, 1955; Simon, 1969). Advertising points to perhaps the largest and most heterogeneous sector of the liquor world: the drinker, the ultimate point of contact for all the interactions that make up this world. The drinker can make or break new programs. His purchasing patterns determine package programs and advertising campaigns, and his shifting moods—regarding taste, product and brand—enter into the long-range planning programs of the distiller, distributor and retailer.[3]

---

[3] One example will serve to highlight the centrality of the drinker-consumer in this process (but also see

Distillers also engage in product promotion within their own ranks. One distiller gives its corporate executives a "Friday package" which consists of a bottle of gin, vodka and blended whiskey. This is expected to last one week, and they are expected to display these products when they host social occasions. Each Friday afternoon at 4:00 PM these executives leave their offices with their gifts wrapped in brown paper bags. Their corporate identity is maintained, although the price of their gift is hidden (field interview, July, 1975).

The most striking characteristic of the distiller level is that such activity is a huge and complex concern, national and even multi-national in nature. Large corporations view themselves as Big Business and define their activity as modern, "rational" promotion of a product similar to any other product. The attitude of the modern corporate executive toward his product equates the sale of whiskey, beer and wine with the marketing of standard grocery items. The vice-president of sales for a large corporation which holds sole United States rights to import one of the four top scotches in the world remarked, "Scotch is no harder to sell than shoestrings or overalls. It's a matter of marketing, promotion and packaging" (field interview, July, 1975).

Distributors

As in the distilling tier, family ties bind many of the distributorships in the area studied. Eight of the ten wholesalers in the

---

the discussion of street salesmen in the Distributor section). After eight years of planning, testing and field experimentation, Heublein, Inc., in the fall of 1975, introduced a new product named "Hereford Cow" which comes in chocolate, mocha and strawberry flavors. Aimed at youth, it was introduced simultaneously in two test cities, Champaign-Urbana and the South Side of Chicago. Hereford Cow was forced onto the shelves of all the bars served by the local distributor (see discussion of off-invoicing). Within four weeks it was rejected by all bars. While its initial sales in South Side Chicago of 150,000 cases in two weeks far surpassed expectations, it has since dropped off in sales. Heublein is searching for a new product for this particular audience (field interviews, August, 1975).

seventeen-county area under consideration (downstate Illinois) are related either through marriage or direct kin lineage.

The most important advertising commodity or medium for the distributor is the street salesman. He or she links the distributor to the retailer and thereby connects the customer to the distiller. Distributors (through street salesmen) must court retailers to maintain a clientele, and this courting process takes the form of special attention, extra visits and other favors. Distributors are required, at the same time, to conform with state regulations. For instance, the state of Illinois demands that all beer be paid for upon delivery and gives 30 days for all other alcoholic products. If a retailer or tavern owner fails to meet a payment deadline he or she goes on a delinquent payment list that is filed in the state capitol each Wednesday. No distributor can legally deliver to a retailer whose name is on the delinquent list.

In Illinois, distributors typically receive a territory for the sale of a particular distiller's products. Wholesalers cannot sell outside of their territories, but the agreement is that only one contract will be awarded per territory. Territories, however, are not always clearly boundaried, and wholesalers often find themselves in a situation where a particular distiller has "dualed" their territory (such a move may also be a threat or attempt to force the distributor to meet higher quotas of product sales). This means that two wholesale houses are in fierce competition to sell the same product to the same retail outlets. "Dualing" leads to deals in an attempt to control territories.

At the state level, the distiller is supposed to verify his territorial commitment to specific distributors by annually filing a list of accredited distributors who can sell his products. Typically, in order to obtain such a territorial monopoly contract, distributors must meet quotas. When contracts are terminated, termination is generally initiated by the distiller, who will argue that the distributor has not given his product sufficient attention over the last sales period. Since the distributor depends on distiller contracts, he must move a certain amount of the product to survive. He must convince retailers to stock a certain amount of that distiller's products. At the same time, if the retailer feels that he is being overloaded with unsaleable products, he is likely to take his business elsewhere. In this way, the street salesman must help the retailer to please his customers. However, the distributor can be caught between the public and the distiller. One example comes from a street salesman who serves small racial and ethnic retail liquor outlets in South Chicago. The drinkers in this area prefer to purchase (in pint-sized quantities) only the most prestigious scotches, bourbons, gins and vodkas. However, they change their taste patterns almost weekly, leaving the salesman either understocked or overstocked for his outlets. (This drinker, who comprises over 50% of the drinking population in Washington, D.C., Chicago and New York City, is particularly problematic for the distilling industry [see Liquor Handbook, 1975].)

Some distillers do, however, attempt to establish distributor loyalty to their prime items. One major distillery has an exclusive club to which only presidents of distributorships can belong. Membership in the club is passed on from father to son; hence, the name "Happy Sperm Club." Should a father fail to produce a son, he must marry his daughter to a male who is willing to enter the business. Once the male heir assumes control, the father relinquishes his membership in the club. A common practice of this club is to schedule a two-week vacation in some exotic resort area for distributors. Such notables as Gloria Steinem, Tom Hayden, Huey Newton, Merle Miller, Walter Hinkle, Bill Cosby and Don Rickles have lectured and entertained at these functions.

Distributors represent the weakest link in the three-tier model. They can be rejected by retailers or find themselves either "dualed" or without a contract from the distiller. They are in a poor bargaining position and are under constant pressure from the distiller to meet new quotas. Retailers can turn elsewhere; without distiller contracts, franchises and retail accounts, the distributor is out of business.

Retailers

Retailers include both package outlets and on-premise sales (taverns). In 1944, 34 families controlled 60 of the 80 local taverns in Champaign-Urbana. Since then, the number of taverns has more than doubled and the same families control a large proportion of these enterprises. One family controls all but one of the six local retail sales outlets (excluding grocery stores and drugstore chains). That family now has a virtual monopoly on retail sales. Family control typically extends through three generations. Intense family loyalty is engendered and a kind of entrepreneurial pride characterizes these industries. For instance, one of the principal liquor retailers in Champaign-Urbana, when asked to comment on his chief competitor, stated, "It is my goal to drive that SOB out of the business. Even if I have to lose money on a particular deal, I will make a fool out of him." Retailers also disrespect outsiders who rely upon chain-store assistance in the sale of alcoholic products. A large up-state retailer remarked,

I started in 1934 with a corner shop and couldn't even get a sign in the door. I paid $200 a month rent. I paid off the bootleggers, the police; I kept up my bills. I didn't let the outsiders drive me out. What do these people in the chain stores, the grocery stores and drug stores think they can do? They don't know the business. They'll never drive me out. (field interview, June 1975)

The modern retailer reads the Liquor Store Magazine (1974). He permits the distiller to rent shelf space in his store for prominent display of products. He thinks in terms of more efficient ways to increase profits.

The retailer must renew his license annually. When licenses are renewed (they cost from $1,250 to $1,500), the applicant is fingerprinted; local liquor commissioners use this occasion to remind the applicant that it is a special privilege to hold such a license. Licenses can be suspended from two to thirty days, typically for serving underage drinkers; and holders of liquor licenses cannot hold elected public office in the state of Illinois.

The local retailer feels a resentment

toward the legal order, feeling that it deprives him of his political and economic rights. They resent the outside chain-store entry into their market. (Between 1967 and 1975, the number of retail licenses in Champaign-Urbana doubled, especially those for the off-premise consumption of beer, wine and distilled products. All but two of the new permits went to grocery and drugstore chains.)

While retailers must maintain a cordial relationship with the local legal structure, the nature of their business often demands that they engender a regular clientele. These two demands can conflict with each other, as when drinkers resent being asked to show proof of age or to wait in line while others do so. Bars or taverns often find that they must create a unique social world within their establishments to produce patron loyalty. One means for doing this is to adopt or manipulate the relevant social objects or symbols of the clientele they wish to attract. This can include the display of fraternity mugs and paddles, holding "playboy bunny" nights, sponsoring intramural football teams and, in some cases, hiring university football players as bar bouncers. This serves, in part, to connect the bar with the university's athletic department.

Drinkers are often regarded by bar owners as fickle. One local bar which had been existence for 25 years changed hands in the summer of 1975. The new owner, whose father had in fact owned the property, completely changed the decor and pinball arrangements in the "new bar." He immediately lost a regular crowd that had roots going back 25 years. He is still in the process of regaining that lost crowd.

The retail level connects most directly with the drinker. The retailer must, however, negotiate with all other tiers in the industry. It is the most conspicuous, yet perhaps the most complicated tier of all.

The Drinker

The drinker is the presence behind every other tier. Studied, courted, deceived, he keeps the system going. As we shall show later, distillers, distributors and retailers routinely violate or challenge the civil-legal code, yet are seldom taken to court. It is the drinker who receives the most direct scrutiny by law enforcement officials and who is the most likely participant in the system to bear the legal burden of illegal production, distribution, sale and consumption. The drinker's use and misuse of alcoholic beverages serve as a reminder that the object called alcohol is consumed and acted upon under a variety of social definitions and circumstances, some of which lead to unlawful behavior.

The Legal Order

The legal order consists, at the *local level*, of liquor commissions, the police and the courts. Retailers and drinkers receive the closest surveillance at this level. At the *state level*, state liquor commissions monitor the conduct of retailers, distributors and distillers. At the *national level*, BAFT, the FCC and FTC, and the Treasury Department (more generally) are responsible for locating illegal liquor transactions.

The federal and state monitoring of liquor laws and liquor violations is weak. In Illinois, at the state level a six-person Liquor Control Commission, consisting of a president, secretary and director plus three adjunct members, oversees the operation of the state's liquor code. This commission is reappointed after each gubernatorial election. and has a nine-member investigative team that covers the entire state. The federal government, except through the understaffed operations of the BAFT and FTC, is also in a weak position to monitor violations of the liquor codes. The failure of the state and federal governments to cooperate has led to a situation that currently is being exploited by organized crime (Cecil, 1974:2).

At the local level, at least in theory, the administration of the civil-legal code is much more intense. The fact that all enforcement branches (liquor commissions, police and courts) may be intertwined politically potentially can mediate and distort the function they are intended to fulfill.

At the legal level, the liquor industry is a very loosely-monitored, semi-understood and taken-for-granted system, as the following interview with the previous president of the Illinois Liquor Control Commission reveals. When asked about Regulation 6, Article 4, which requires that all distillers place on file the territories wherein they have granted distributors exclusive sales rights, he remarked, "I have never heard of the rule; if it was important I would know about it" (field interview, June, 1975). A prominent legal consultant for the distilling tier confessed that often members of the state liquor commission call *him* when they have questions concerning the meaning of the law. Certainly, few drinkers are aware of the laws that limit the number of retail outlets in any city, nor are the prices of licenses commonly known. Additional complexity is introduced when multinational corporations buy up specific distillers and purchase exclusive sales rights to specific brands. One retailer remarked, "You never know from day to day who owns these damned corporations or what their policies are" (field interview, August, 1975).

TIERS: COOPERATION, COMPETITION AND CRIMINOGENIC ACTIVITIES

The present research focused on the organizational development since Repeal of the five tiers of the industry, with special attention given to criminogenic activity, be these behaviors of omission, comission, evasion or outright illegality. We shall examine such behaviors within each tier as well as those which emerge from the interrelationships among tiers.

Repeal opened the way for a small group of distillers at the national level to capitalize on a relatively new and ambiguous situation. Not only did they have to redefine themselves for the federal government, but they also had to formulate a collective image of self that could be sold to the public. The following discussion of each tier suggests that the industry has succeeded in becoming an institutionalized American economic industry. Gross instances of corruption and illegal behavior became clouded behind complicated corporate laws and local statutes. In the end, drinkers, tavern owners, retailers, wholesalers, manufacturers and

the legal structure all profited. Deception and illusion became marketable commodities. Bootleg liquor gradually disappeared and up-graded alcoholic products appeared on the market. A normalized system that assumed a taken-for-granted nature emerged, was solidified and, gradually, became institutionalized into local, state and national laws.

The multi-tiered liquor industry in the mid-1970s appears to be a highly stable enterprise. However, hidden behind its interactional structure are a variety of criminogenic activities, usually quite deliberately calculated, which economically benefit one or more participant or tier in the system. The economic benefits are not confined just to profit margins on the stock market, nor to the dollars produced by a single bar or retail outlet at the end of a year. Rather, the economics of the liquor industry translate into private, personal economies of style, career, prestige, power, collegiality and friendship. At each tier, different economies are battled over. This produces different criminogenic activities at each level. Often clouded behind elaborate symbolic campaigns and structures—e.g., a new drink for the young urban sophisticate—the industry and its participants enhance their own positions at someone else's expense. The competitive interactions that tie tier members together encourage intra-industry exploitation and criminogenic conduct (Benson, 1975; Gross, forthcoming). We shall present evidence in support of this argument, beginning with the distiller who is the most powerful force within the industry.

Distillers

Distillers violate as well as challenge antitrust laws. Large corporations can hide behind complicated corporate structures which allow them to gain major holdings in competing lines or to diversify within the same product line.

A case in point is offered by the history of Heublein, Inc., which produces vodka, mixed cocktails, dry gin, cordials, beer, rum, table wines, sherries, and all wines sold under the names of Italian Swiss Colony, Inglenook, Lejon Petri and Gambarelli & Davito. Subsidiaries of Heublein, Inc. include Allied Grape Groups (82% controlled), United Vintners, Inc., Kentucky Fried Chicken Corporation, Heublein (Canada, Inc.), Heublein International Ltd. and Smirnoff Beverage & Import Company. The 1968 acquisition of controlling interest in United Vintner's Inc. led the FTC to issue a complaint that Heublein's was in violation of the Clayton Anti-Trust Act. Heublein's denied the charge, asserting that its interest in United Vintner's gave California grape growers a marketing edge to meet industry competition. The FTC dropped its charges.

Major distillers, such as Heublein's, flirt with antitrust laws. They are seldom brought to court, and when they are, high-ranking corporation executives often profit by relinquishing their shares in a competing corporation for a handsome profit.[4]

Distillers often negotiate with one another over the relative prices they will set for their respective products. Federal law requires that no distiller market a product at a price lower than the price he lists at a designated time in an affirmation state. Deceit, deception, misrepresentation and "unintended leaks" of information abound at these times. At least one large scotch manufacturer is now under suit for his latest filing procedures. Lax monitoring at the state and national levels leads members of the industry to sue one another over pricing procedures and pricing violations. In this sense, they police themselves.

Not only do manufacturers violate antitrust laws but they also exert excessive pressure to meet quotas upon distributors

---

[4] A former president of a major United States distillery gave the following information in an interview, July, 1975.

In 1934, his brother joined forces with a Canadian distiller and they profited greatly in post-Prohibition days. In the 1950s, the brother joined another firm which acquired the rights to a particular brand of scotch. At that time, the firm held controlling shares in the three top-selling scotches in the world. In 1968, the FTC brought an antitrust suit against his firm. The antitrust suit was tied up in the courts for six years. The FTC won and forced him to sell his shares in the company. He sold his shares for a 50% profit. The result of the FTC's suit was to make profits for the offender.

who, in turn, pass this pressure along to the retailer. In response to such pressures, retailers often deceive the customer into believing that he is getting a good buy on a particular product. A specific problem that ties the distiller to the wholesaler and to the retailer is the *off-invoice strategy* which arises from competition among wholesalers. Distillers put pressure on wholesalers to move a particular product by threatening to withold supplies of a top-selling item. They demand that wholesalers buy more of this product than they can normally move in a month's time. To get his money out of the unnecessary inventory, the wholesaler will give retailers extra liquor, off the invoice, as long as the retailer buys a portion of the premium liquor. This violates several laws. The retailer may make the sale, not ring it up on his cash register and, thereby, avoid federal and state taxes. The wholesaler, who has paid the proper taxes on the products he has received, violates federal and state laws by keeping a second set of books which falsify his invoice orders to the retailer (see Farberman, 1975, for a similar instance in the auto industry).

A third form of distiller-manufacturer behavior, which does not violate any specific laws but which deceives the customer, is the practice of *multiple branding*. Abrahamson (1938) reports that distillers believe that consumers have only the haziest notions of the differences between whiskeys. Accordingly, the more brands a distiller can offer, the greater the likelihood that he can capture a broader sector of the market. In 1951, it was estimated that there were over 30,000 rival brands of whiskey on the national liquor market which were controlled by less than 40 separate distillers. Single companies may have as many as 50–100 different brands. National Distillers markets ten brands of bourbons, each appealing to a different audience, each marketed by the same distiller. Immediately after Prohibition, when the stock of aged whiskey was at an all-time low, blended whiskeys came on the market. In order to encourage the purchase of their products, distillers prefaced all their labels with the word "old"—thus, Old Taylor, Old Rip Van Winkle, Old Charter, etc. (Abrahamson, 1938:414).

Branding produces product identification, which is intended to produce self-identification on the part of the drinker. The distiller endeavors to cultivate drinkers who will purchase only prestige items. The distiller manipulates the drinker and attempts to maintain the illusion that certain brands are still distilled by the same families that originated the product. Most, if not all, original scotches and bourbons initially tied to specific families have long since been purchased by large-scale corporations who simply maintain the original brand name and label.

Quasi-tied houses represent a third form of distiller-brewer manipulation of the legal code. While the three-tier model prohibits the intervention of the distiller-brewer in the actual sale of his product, informal agreements arise which tie taverns to manufacturers. This tie is made through the wholesaler (who himself may be tied to a particular distiller or brewer) who does favors for tavern owners. Wholesalers make special runs. They stop by up to three times a week to chat with tavern owners and managers. They fill special orders and make special deals to favored customers. A *norm of reciprocity* (Gouldner, 1959) is expected to operate. In return for special services, the tavern owner is expected not to solicit or to indulge in the services of another distributor, even if his "tied" distributor cannot deliver the products he needs. This norm locks the tavern owner into a compromising and, at times, uneasy relationship with the wholesaler.

Distributors

As noted earlier, distributors are prohibited from selling outside their prescribed territories. However, *territorial violations,* in which distributors cross one another's territory and make illegal sales, represent a frequent form of illegal behavior on the part of the distributor. A *norm of silence* operates; one will not tell on another wholesaler if that one will not tell on him. Similarly, retailers who can make profit purchases are not about to report that they bought from a wholesaler outside their territory. (In Illinois, there is

the famous rumor of a 4,000-case purchase of a Canadian blended whiskey by a retailer from a distributor who was 200 miles outside his territory. The retailer, one of the largest in the state, could laugh about the matter and the wholesaler in question could deny it. The case was never investigated.)

Distributors can negotiate with one another. In Champaign-Urbana, in response to a recent labor strike at the Anheuser-Busch factory in St. Louis, the local distributor holding the sole rights to Busch products found himself out of stock. He began selling what he termed "brand X" which, upon inspection, was found to be Old Style beer. The local Old Style distributor denied selling it to the Anheuser-Busch distributor. The matter came under brief investigation by the Executive Director of the State Liquor Commission but nothing came of it (Weiss, 1976). Some distributors agree to ignore infractions and permit each other to serve old customers, usually family friends, who reside in another's territory (field interview, September, 1975). Such agreements engender goodwill and lead distributors to help one another out when they find themselves short of some needed product.

Distributors must negotiate the payments they receive for delivered goods to retailers. As mentioned before, all beer must be paid for upon delivery and all other alcoholic products within 30 days or the retailer goes on a delinquent payment list. No wholesaler legally can distribute to a retailer whose name is on the delinquent list. However, *delinquent list manipulation,* in which a distributor withholds a name from his delinquent list, constitutes another semi-illegal act on the distributor's part. Variations include rebuying overstocked products with kickback funds or extending illegal credit to a retailer by doctoring the invoice books.

The *Wall Street Journal* featured an article noting that distributor kickbacks to retail stores seem common in New York City (Kwitny, 1975). The author notes that at the wholesale level: (1) salesmen carry cash from store to store to give kickbacks to retailers; (2) wholesalers ship free loads of whiskey to retailers and account for the missing merchandise by reporting a warehouse theft; (3) distributorships list salespersons who receive high commissions which actually go to retailers who patronize certain houses; (4) some wholesale houses print lists indicating the amount of kickback money that is available when a retailer purchases certain products.

Distributors also can make agreements with specific retailers or tavern owners to supply them with specific goods or services, any or all of which may be illegal or semi-illegal. In 1944, the Illinois Liquor Control Commission Code made it illegal for any distributor to provide a tavern owner with walk-in coolers, free glasses, free calendars, clocks, bar equipment, mirrors or outside display signs. The economic slump of 1971–1974 led distributors to begin enforcing this law informally, telling their favorite tavern owners that "the feds had come down on them and they could no longer provide these services" (field interview, August, 1975).

Retailers

The retailer is the most entrepreneurlike and independent operator in the system and is, thereby, most free to manipulate, deal and negotiate agreements that are in his own best interests. Retailers who achieve sufficient size are in an enviable position for they can control wholesalers and exert pressures through wholesalers back to the manufacturer. Some retailers bypass distributors and deal directly with the distiller—a direct violation of the 21st Amendment. Retailers can manipulate distilling corporations into making special deals with them simply because they can move large volumes of a particular product. In some situations, a retailer can make arrangements to be served by a distributor who actually resides in another territory. In these instances, the size and power of the retailer lead him to take take control over the local market distribution of a particular product. In one instance, a retailer virtually controls both a wholesale house and a distilling house. He buys outside his territory and refuses to permit his major distillers to deal with his chief local competitor. If they deal with that individual, he threatens to cancel all contracts with the house in question.

Such illegal and semilegal behaviors enable community retailers to amass the power necessary to control local competition. A retailer bent on running a competitor out of business can, through deals, buy a product in sufficiently large quantity to systematically undersell his competitor.

Retailers can negotiate with one another, i.e., they may agree to set a bottom price on a certain product. Groups of tavern owners may agree to take a hard or soft line on the enforcement of the legal drinking-age law and they may or may not cooperate in the organization of a communication network that warns fellow bar owners of an impending police raid. Retailers can agree to cater only to certain drinking audiences and in a campus town such agreements often flow along the organizational lines of housing units, sororities and fraternities. On the other hand, outright battles may occur when a new bar owner enters the public drinking arena and attempts to take stable patrons from other bars.

Many tavern owners violate the laws every day. They serve underage drinkers and they fail to meet local building, sanitation and wiring codes. Bribes to building inspectors are not uncommon, nor are bribes to the local political structure. Tavern owners' violations come under the direct scrutiny of local liquor commissions, and they are frequently monitored by police departments through raids and periodic checks. Retailers are in a direct position to receive kickbacks from distillers and wholesalers as well as being the beneficiaries of delinquent-list manipulations. In a similar fashion, tavern owners and retailers give preferred customers charge accounts and reduced prices on certain beverages. Both practices are prohibited by local statutes.

The Legal Order

The political administration of local statutes can permit preferred citizens to obtain liquor licenses when others are denied such privileges. Blocks of votes can be purchased when local, state and national politicians take stands on expanded liquor-licensing or increases in the tax on alcoholic products (see Henderson, 1934; Anderson, 1976).

Rubenstein (1973:420) has made the following observations (based on his field work with the Philadelphia Police Department from 1968 to 1971) on the politics of liquor control:

> The state monopoly over liquor licensing has converted the right to drink into a source of political capital—cash and favors—which is exploited by state and city governments and their agents, the police, to assure compliance with their interests. Politicians exact enormous fees for selling and transferring lucrative licenses, and the police are obliged to maintain the efficacy of the system by harrassing those who do not adhere and protecting those in favor.

Rubenstein could be describing several cities in the state of Illinois. Consider the following on the shakedown of tavern owners in the city of Chicago:

> Former County Board Chairman —— was found guilty on two charges that he shook down tavern owners in exchange for issuing or renewing their liquor licenses. . . . —— has been accused of extorting $17,500 from [two tavern owners] in exchange for helping [tavern owner] obtain a liquor license. (Fisher, 1976)

In Champaign-Urbana, the prices for liquor licenses, which nominally cost between $1,250 and $1,500 depending on the class of liquor type, were reported to range from $500 to $20,000 (field interviews, June-August, 1975). One individual reportedly received a second tavern with a renewed license in return for giving up a license. One applicant told interviewers he had been assured he would receive his license and proceeded to engage in expensive modifications of his new drinking establishment. Well into the project, he was informed that his license application was problematic and he would have to "speak to" certain persons about his proposed license (field interview, June, 1975).

At the local level, corruption, payoffs and conflicts of interest can be observed in any of the following areas: (1) license applications, (2) license renewals, (3) protection of licenses, (4) protection against raids and (5) alterations of zoning laws so

"dry" areas can be converted into "wet" areas where new licenses can be awarded.

At least two tavern owners over the last 30 years purportedly were driven out of business because they refused to "protect" their licenses. In another report, a dry township was converted into a wet township (as negotiations were underway to establish a large out-of-town shopping center) by the movement of a construction worker into the dry township for one month. A construction firm set up a house trailer for him and paid all his expenses. At the end of the month he called for a referendum to vote the township wet. Since he was the only resident in the township, the vote carried. The owner of the construction firm was a local politician.

The Drinker

Space prohibits any detailed discussion of the drinker as a separate tier within the American liquor industry (for a recent review of the drinking pattern of Americans, see Liquor Handbook, 1975). Observations gathered from distributors, retailers, tavern owners, distillers, importers and brewers do, however, support the following conclusions. First, the American drinker is a willing supporter of the industry that produces the alcoholic beverages they consume. That is, they purchase what is offered to them. Second, they are somewhat cynical, if uninformed, about the products they purchase. Third, the everyday drinker has little knowledge of the complex interactions that bind bar owners, retailers, distributors, distillers and the legal order to one another. Drinkers assume that the products they desire will be present when they want them. Laws, codes, liquor commissions, territorial boundaries and tied houses are not relevant realities for the drinker. The complex social structure that brings a particular brand of bourbon into the hands of a drinker is unknown or only barely glimpsed. Yet that structure exists because the drinker *qua* buyer assumes it will exist. The success of the industry has been, and continues to be based on the actualization of this assumption (see Cavan, 1967; LeMasters, 1975; Roebuck and Frese, 1975).

SOME NOTES ON
CRIMINOGENIC BEHAVIOR WITHIN
THE AMERICAN LIQUOR INDUSTRY

This case study of a single economic enterprise, stressing a symbolic interactionist perspective, has examined the five tiers that makeup the American liquor industry. Consistent with the interactionist method, attention was given to the relationships and actions that make up the world of this social structure. The alcoholic beverage and the drinker-consumer relationship constituted a basic focus of attention from level to level, tier to tier.

Any discussion of criminogenic behavior is complicated by the fact that there is no clear-cut theoretical consensus of what constitutes a criminogenic act. It can be assumed, however, that in order for a criminogenic act to be produced, an individual or corporate structure must (1) be in a situation wherein they have the *opportunity* to produce such an act, (2) have the *means* at their disposal for producing that act and (3) possess a *motive* or explanation to account for that behavior. Although a discrete theory of the emergence of criminogenic behavior within a complex organization is beyond the scope of this paper, a few tentative observations which fall within the schema suggested above can be made.

Opportunity

Concealment, by secrecy or ignorance or both, appears to be a factor in some illegal and semilegal acts whose existence depends upon being hidden, either from other tiers or from the general public. Multiple branding, price fixing, or conflicts of interest are examples of behaviors which would not bear close scrutiny. The family bonds within the tiers of distiller, distributor and retailer probably facilitate concealment.

Perhaps the most striking characteristic of the liquor industry is *complaisance* on the part of the drinker-consumer. The drinker, although cynical, appears to find the convenient delivery into his hands of the desired alcoholic beverage to be the most relevant reality. Throughout the industry, although most participants assume

that the legal code is broken, few individuals care to pursue the matter. This may be particularly true for within-industry behaviors such as territorial violations, but it also appears to hold true for such illegalities as sale to minors, complicity of the political system and protection of licenses. Like organized crime, the liquor industry depends upon delivery of a product whose procurement is desired and whose price does not exceed what the customer is willing to pay (Vold, 1958:227). The liquor industry, as Al Capone suggested, is a "legitimate racket" (Sutherland, 1940:12). Although complaisance appears to contradict the role of concealment, this may be only a superficial paradox. The rule of the game appears to be that participants will close their eyes to all but the most obvious of indiscretions.

The complaisant and taken-for-granted attitude, both within and without the industry, taken toward criminogenic activities suggests that below the articulated legal structure there exists an *informal structure*, one which often contradicts or supersedes the formal structure. The informal structure may define as "legal" activities which are defined as "illegal" by the formal structure. The taken-for-granted reality of the former legal order is, perhaps, more illusory than it is concrete.

Means

The efficacy of many regulations depends upon accurate *self-reporting* by levels within the industry itself. Distillers supply figures for tax accounts, distributors are responsible for delinquent-list reporting, and retailers share in accounting for invoice figures. *Scarcity of penalties* and *weak enforcement* of laws often allow the industry to operate unmolested. *Structural ties between the political order and enforcement agencies* (such as those between local liquor commissions and the police) belie separation of power between legislation and implementation. Such ties collapse into one unit—the liquor industry—the essential ingredients of power, control and corruption. Bribery of officials (or shakedown of retailers, depending on the viewpoint), protection of licenses, and alteration of zoning laws are particularly applicable in this category.

Motive

The multi-tier nature of the liquor industry seems to be linked to both crimes of competition and crimes of cooperation. Obdurate realities for each tier appear to be quite distinct and to create problems unique to participants within the same level. Individuals within each level often referred to themselves as "we" and definitionally aligned themselves with other members of the same tier. This *quasi group solidarity* may produce cooperational crimes such as price fixing, mutual concealmeant of violations and warnings of police raids.

Alienation from the law (usually the feeling that laws are unfair or unrealistic) also appears to be linked to crimes of cooperation, especially those which require cooperation between tiers to circumvent the law. Consensual definition of regulatory codes as "out-of-date" or "crazy" was used, directly or indirectly, as an *a priori* justification for breaking or bending the law (field interviews, 1975). Further, the widespread attitude among all levels that the liquor industry has a virtual mandate from the public (i.e., the passage of Repeal) provides the rationalization that many of the regulatory codes (defined as holdovers from Prohibition) are superseded by the "higher law" of Repeal.

Although the frequency of criminogenic behaviors and their significance for the industry overall awaits further studies, field interviews found the assumption of such behaviors to be common talk among all levels. This produces a *callousness of attitude* which crosscuts all tiers and appears to be a factor in crimes of competition. The assumption that other participants have few scruples fosters the belief that survival in such an arena depends upon adoption of the same attitude. This belief becomes the *sine qua non* for the presence of criminogenic activity in any organizational complex.

Clearly, the opportunities to engage in criminogenic activities are not problematic for the participants in the American liquor industry. Indeed, in large part, they structure the situations, engender the motive and produce the means which allow them to engage in such activities.

It is not clear whether governmental control of such substances as alcoholic beverages engenders the kinds of industry-initiated criminogenic activities observed in the several tiers of the liquor industry. Bribery, kickbacks, antitrust violations, payoffs and the circumvention of legal codes may or may not be specific to this industry. It awaits further case studies of an historical and observational nature to determine whether or not criminogenic conduct is basic to the survival, growth and success of American economic enterprises. Until such studies are available, we can only conclude with the following observation of a high-ranking official in one American distilling firm:

> We break the laws everyday. If you think I go to bed at night worrying about it, you're crazy. Everybody breaks the law. The liquor laws are insane anyway. (field interview, August, 1975)

REFERENCES

Abrahamson, Albert
1938 "Whiskey—incidence of public tolerance in price policy." Pp. 395–429 in Walton Hamilton, Mark Adams, Albert Abrahamson, Helen Everett Meiklejohn, Irene Till and George Marshall (eds.), Price and Price Policies. New York: McGraw-Hill.
Anderson, Jack
1976 "How the liquor industry gets its political favors." Chicago Daily News, November 5.
Bell, Daniel
1960 The End of Ideology: On the Exhaustion of Political Ideas in the Fifties. New York: Free Press.
Benson, J. Kenneth
1975 "The interorganizational network as a political economy." Administrative Science Quarterly 20:229–49.
Blumer, Herbert
1969 Symbolic Interactionism. Englewood Cliffs, N. J.: Prentice-Hall.
Bretzfield, Henry
1955 Liquor Marketing and Liquor Advertising: A Guide for Executives and Their Staffs in Management, Sales and Advertising. New York: Abelard-Schuman.
Cavan, Sheri
1966 Liquor License. Chicago: Aldine.

Cecil, E. J.
1974   "Washington report." Liquor Store Magazine 81(1):2.
Distilled Spirits Council of the United States, Inc.
1974   Summary of State Laws and Regulations Relating to Distilled Spirits, 21st edition. Washington, D.C.: Distilled Spirits Council.
Dobyns, Fletcher
1940   The Amazing Story of Repeal: An Exposé of the Power of Propaganda. Chicago-New York: Willett, Clark.
Durrell, Raymond
1967   "The story of DSI: part 1: Repeal and the blue eagle hatch the DSI." Beverage Executive, April 1:1–4.
East, Ernest E.
1952   "The distillers' and cattle feeders' trust, 1887–1895." Illinois State Historical Society Journal 45:101–23.
Farberman, Harvey A.
1975   "A criminogenic market structure: the automobile industry." Sociological Quarterly 16:438–57.
Fisher, Dennis D.
1976   "Coles found guilty of tavern owner shakedowns." Chicago Sun-Times, March 27:8.
Gaines, James
1975   "Rise of the house of Seagram." Newsweek, August 25:16–7.
Gouldner, Alvin
1959   "Reciprocity and autonomy in functional theory." Pp. 241–70 in L. Gross (ed.), Symposium in Social Theory. Evanston, Il.: Harper and Row.
Gross, Edward
Forth-   Organizational sources of crime: a theoreti-
coming   cal perspective." In Norman K. Denzin (ed.), Studies in Symbolic Interaction, Vol. 1. Greenwich, Ct.: JAI Press.
Gusfield, Joseph R.
1966   Symbolic Crusade: Status Politics and the American Temperance Movement. Urbana, Il.: University of Illinois Press.
Hamilton, Walton, Mark Adams, Albert Abrahamson, Helen Everett Meiklejohn, Irene Till and George Marshall
1938   Price and Price Policies. New York: McGraw-Hill.
Henderson, Yandell
1934   A New Deal for Liquor: A Plea for Dilution. Garden City, N.Y.: Doubleday, Doran.

Horowitz, Ira and Ann R. Horowitz
1965   "Firms in a declining market: the brewing case." Journal of Industrial Economics 14:129–53.
Kane, Frank
1965   Anatomy of the Whiskey Business. Manhasset, N.Y.: Lake House Press.
Kwitny, Jonathon
1975   "Booze business: liquor and corruption are drinking buddies." Wall Street Journal 55(103): 1–18.
LeMasters, E.E.
1975   Blue-Collar Aristocrats: Life-Styles at a Working Class Tavern. Madison, Wi.: University of Wisconsin Press.
Liquor Handbook
1975   New York: Gavin-Jobson Associates.
Liquor Store Magazine
1974   81(1). New York: Gavin-Jobson Associates.
Oxenfeldt, Alfred R.
1951   Industrial Pricing and Market Practices. New York: Prentice-Hall.
Roebuck, Julian B. and Wolfgang Frese
1975   The Rendevezous: A Case Study of an After-Hours Club. New York: Free Press.
Rubenstein, Jonathon
1973   City Police. New York: Farrar, Straus and Giroux.
Simon, Julian L.
1969   "The effect of advertising on liquor brand sales." Journal of Marketing Research 6:301–13.
Sinclair, Andrew
1964   Era of Excess: A Social History of the Prohibition Movement. New York: Harper and Row.
Sutherland, Edwin H.
1940   "White-collar criminality." American Sociological Review 5:1–12.
Switzer, Frederick M.
1975   The Three-Tier System of Distribution in the Wine and Spirits Industry. St. Louis, Mo.: Wine and Spirits Wholesalers of America, Inc.
Vold, George B.
1958   Theoretical Criminology. New York: Oxford University Press.
Weiss, Bob
1976   "State probes beer delivery." Daily Illini 105(129):1.

24

CONTROLLING CORPORATE MISCONDUCT
CHRISTOPHER D. STONE

THE control of corporate misconduct has become one of the most significant challenges the society faces. This should be apparent even to those who regard as extravagant some of the charges directed against corporations—that the energy crisis is simply a corporate contrivance, or that the corporations are run by evil people, indifferent to the poisoning of our environment. What has not been exaggerated is the increasing importance of corporations in our lives. More and more, it is they who invent, invest, produce, distribute, and farm. As a result, a large measure of wrongdoing is inevitably corporate.

Indeed, we would do well to understand the term "corporation" in its original and most comprehensive sense, as comprising not merely businesses but all the other large-scale organizations of a modern society. A mismanaged pension fund can sadden as many lives as a mismanaged assembly line. Genetic research at universities may pose as great a threat as the toxic by-products of the chemical industry. The investors who bought New York City municipal bonds, misled as to the City's true financial plight, are as put

From Christopher D. Stone, "Controlling Corporate Misconduct," 48 *The Public Interest* 55-71 (Summer 1977). Copyright 1977 by National Affairs, Inc.

out as any victim of stock fraud (but apparently lack any legal recourse).

This preeminence of corporations in social activity is a state of affairs that the law inherited, but unfortunately did not plan for. When much of the law and political theory was taking shape, there were indentifiable humans, operating independently of complex institutional frameworks, who did the things that it is the job of the law to prevent. The law responded with rules and concepts concerning what motivated people, and what was possible, just, and appropriate toward them. There were, of course, all manner of corporations—churches, municipalities, guilds, universities—during the years the law was forming. But the courts were rarely pressed to consider whether the rules they were developing might be inappropriate or ineffective to deal with this new breed of social actor. Some of the reasons were doctrinal: There were doubts whether a corporation, a *persona ficta*, could be liable for wrongful acts. Others were practical: The size and structure of the early corporations were so unprepossessing that when a wrong was done, it was usually not hard to locate a responsible individual—a "culprit"—and apply the sanctions of the law to him.

The industrial revolution gave corporations a prominence, size, and complexity that made further disregard impossible. But only in a few ways did the law account for the corporation as a special sort of actor demanding the attention of specially adapted laws. The exceptions were almost entirely in shareholder-management relations, where the problems that arose were unique to corporations and where there were thus no preexisting rules to accommodate each emerging situation: How many directors did a corporation need? On what grounds could dividends be compelled? To deal with such questions, the law, unfettered by precedent, often ventured directly inside the organization itself, laying down express requirements on the structure of management and the decision process. The directors could vest some of their power in a management committee, but certain decisions (the declaration of dividends, for example) could not be delegated; the corporate officers could make day-to-day decisions (such as how many units to produce), but major organic changes (the sale of assets, or a merger) had to be submitted to the shareholders for two-thirds approval.

But such meddlings with the corporations' internal governance were almost always designed to protect and define in advance the increasingly complex interests of the investor—not those of the corporation's customers, its neighbors, or its fellow citizens. Where the corporation was performing acts that, in theory, the ordinary person could perform—polluting the environment, producing harmful goods, committing crimes (in other words, where it was dealing with the "outside world" rather than with its shareholders)—there already existed a network of rules addressed to "persons." The most economical solution was simply to fit the corporation into this pre-existing body of law. Nothing was required except to ignore, one by one, the earlier qualms about whether the corporation ("that invisible, intangible, and artificial being," according to Chief Justice Marshall) could be regarded as a person—a wrongdoer in its own right.

Applying existing law to corporations without distinction was the simplest but not necessarily the best course of action. Had the law considered the problem afresh, it might better have taken into account the special institutional features that render corporations, as a concern of the law, distinct from individuals. Instead, we found ourselves confronting corporations with two basic strategies that had evolved in dealing with ordinary people.

Counterorganizational measures

Since the corporation itself cannot be imprisoned, the primary counterorganizational measure is simply to confront it, as we do the man in the street, with a negative profit contingency (a civil judgment, a criminal fine), if it should wander outside the law—in other words, to threaten its pocketbook. The punishment must "fit the crime," so that a good bookkeeper would recognize that, when the likely gains are balanced against the likely losses, the organization will find the prohibited activity a "bad bargain."

The likelihood that this sort of threat will succeed obviously depends on a corporation's sensitivity to profits, the subject of a debate that has suffered some unfortunate exaggerations on both sides. For example, the supposition that corporations seek to maximize profits is not undermined merely because other goals seem to attract them as well—prestige, expansion, etc. As Alfred D. Chandler has observed, "these other goals also take money . . . profits provide it." The more precise question is whether the pursuit of profit is ever subordinated to the realization of other aims; I think the answer to this is: Yes—but not ordinarily, and not in large measure. Thus, at least as far as the profit-making organizations are concerned, it makes sense to use profit threats as the foundation of our corporate-control strategies. The government communicates to the firms—through law—the price tag for failing to meet society's standards, and then allows each company to make the necessary changes to avoid the penalty in whatever way it can most economically and fittingly devise. This doesn't work badly in the typical situations. Indeed, the law is often less successful in controlling the not-for-profit corporations, such as municipalities and hospitals, whose motives are less easy to identify and grasp.

The problem is that the law must deal with the aberrant as well as the average; thus I think we should be cautious before presuming that the modern business corporation presents nothing more complex than Economic Man writ large. To begin with, the individual actors at each level of corporate activity (shareholders, directors, middle management, ·workers) are subject to constraints that are often incongruent with the profit of "the corporation" as a whole. In fact, the absence of identity between the shareholders' interests and those of "the corporation" is the very idea behind two of the most basic notions of corporate and commercial activity: limited liability and bankruptcy. The shareholders of a tanker company, for example, are not indifferent if one of its ships runs aground. But if there is a wreck, the shareholders know that, except in rare cases, they cannot be sued as individuals by the injured parties to recover any damages the corporation cannot satisfy. What this means (assuming perfect economic rationality) is that in deciding such matters as routes and how much money to spend on hulls and safety devices (and, indeed, how much money to put into the company), the investors' calculations are skewed toward letting the company impose high risks on society. If no accident results, the shareholders will reap the profits of skimping on safety measures. If a ship runs aground, they will be shielded from full responsibility for the harm they have helped to cause.

Incongruities of this sort are no less troublesome when we turn to the giant "public" corporations that are effectively under the direction of hired managers rather than shareholders. Threats to the corporate treasury do not necessarily intimidate the top executives, whose tenure and salary almost inevitably survive lawsuits untouched; the burden falls on the shareholders. (In fact, an ironic twist of this reasoning has led some courts to treat corporate wrongdoers less severely than individuals, lest the "innocent shareholders" —or, in the case of municipalities, "innocent taxpayers"—suffer). And the vast majority of workers are even more insulated. The farther down the operational ladder, the more the "profit goal" of the total organization (so far as there is one) takes the form of targets and objectives for the shop, the department, and the plant; these "immediate" subgoals and objectives determine the horizons and interests of the employees. The potential for future corporate penalties—the possibility that the controller of the corporation someday might have to write a check in payment of a penalty (perhaps five or six years in the future, given the delays of litigation)—is at most a distant and abstract part of the subgroup's reality.

And to the extent that the individual managers or the organization as a whole are not "rational"—to the extent they do subordinate profit to prestige, or to the excitement of carrying out technology to its logical and dramatic limits—the money threats of the law are oblique, at best.

None of this means that the law's counterorganizational threats are fundamentally misplaced. My concern is rather that there can exist—even within business corporations and more commonly in other organizations—pockets of activity (in the boardroom, or in the plant) that are relatively impervious, for certain periods of time, to the law. However atypical and however limited these pockets may be, we should be concerned that they may exist often enough, and may be of significant enough magnitude, to warrant adopting alternative measures.

Counterpersonnel measures

The classic alternative—the second basic approach—has been for the law to hold employees individually liable through fines, damages, and even imprisonment. These counterpersonnel measures are undeniably a valuable supplement. But they are less effective than one might suppose, and in some ways may even do more harm than good.

I know this sounds odd, especially to followers of the business press, who are regularly forewarned of the increased vulnerability —if not the imminent imprisonment—of the managerial class. Still, the real risk of personal liability ought to be put in perspective. For willful, self-serving wrongdoing, such as stock swindling (which can be identified with a particular hand and mind), the threat of personal legal liability is certainly real. But for other kinds of corporate misbehavior—e.g., when the employee and his company are unleashing a toxic substance into the community, or allowing distribution of a faulty product—the law's bite is not half as bad as its bark.

Why should this be so? To begin with, when an employee injures others by acting on his own account (as, for example, in many self-benefiting securities violations), he will be the sole target of legal action. But in the more ordinary cases, where an employee is acting on his company's behalf, the corporation, as his principal, will be liable as well. The practical effect is that in most situations a plaintiff proceeds against the corporation, rather than troubling to identify and collect from a particular employee.

Moreover, even when someone—a diligent prosecutor, for example—tries to pursue some accountable flesh, it is not easy to do so. If there really was someone clearly responsible, the organizational underbrush may be too thick to find him. (Did the malfeasance occur during the morning shift, or at night?) More frustrating, the division of tasks may be so extensive that responsibility is impossible to assign, even using the term in its ordinary, moral sense; settling *legal* responsibility is all the more difficult, especially in criminal actions, since the law is reluctant to impose liability without proof of actual knowledge, and the burden of proof favors the defense.

These considerations make it particularly hard for the law to pressure top-level corporate managers, who wield the most power to keep the corporation steered within the law, but who can also claim with considerable justification that they "didn't know" what was going on in the bowels of their organizations, where so much of the trouble is brewing. It is also fairly common that in prosecuting corporate employees (particularly those at the top of their organizations) the law runs into a series of socially ordained hurdles; the prosecution finds itself trying to convict well-spoken, well-dressed, church-going, white community leaders—persons not likely to be judged harshly. Prison sentences are rare, reserved for the headline-grabbing crimes only.

Fines and civil judgments are invoked against corporate employees more liberally than imprisonment. But one should not assume that the individual executive really bears the final brunt. Under the corporation codes of the major states, when an employee suffers a judgment or fine for actions undertaken on behalf of the corporation, he can often get reimbursement (indemnification) from corporate funds; the arrow of whatever law he has broken is obligingly deflected to the corporation itself, and passed through it to the shareholders, and perhaps the consumers and creditors. In other cases, the director or officer may be protected by liability insurance, a coverage provided by perhaps 85 per cent of major American corporations. And even in cases of conduct so willful and unlawful that neither indemnification nor insurance is available, it is almost impossible to prevent a corporation from reimbursing its errant officer (or "good soldier") in other ways—by "bonuses," a delayed raise, or a sweet "consulting" contract.

Some general problems

There are additional difficulties rooted in the complexity of modern commerce and technology—the sort of society corporations make possible. The legal system evolved around, and responds to, a simpler set of difficulties than the most critical problems we now face.

Consider, for example, the law of negligence, which is at the heart of private legal "repair." A model negligence case is one in which Smith, who is walking across the street, is accidentally but negligently hit by Jones' carriage. Note that 1) Smith knows *that* he has been injured; 2) Smith knows *who* has caused the injury; 3) it is possible to assess fairly well the *nature and extent* of his injuries; and 4) the *technical inquiry* involved in analyzing what happened is not too complex—i.e., simple laws of physics are involved, within commonsense experience. (The model also assumes that if the legal damages can be lain at the feet of the responsible actor, he is likely to change his behavior in the future; as we have already seen, this assumption is problematic when a corporation is involved.)

But contrast this model case with the situations that are increasingly of concern in society today. The food we will eat tonight (grown, handled, packaged, and distributed by various corporations) may contain chemicals that are slowly killing us. But while we may have misgivings in principle, we cannot know with certainty *that* we are being injured by any particular product, or *who* might be injuring us. We would also have a difficult time proving the *nature and extent* of our injuries (even more so proving the extent attributable to any particular source). Finally, the evidence to be evaluated is far more complex and technical than in the model case—perhaps so much so that the courts or even agencies cannot realistically be expected to unravel it, especially after the fact. Worst of all, by the time we discover what is happening—for example, that teenage girls are developing vaginal cancer because of medication their mothers took before they were born—it is often too late.

Moreover, at some point the costs associated with the law's traditional approaches transcend the benefits. Some rules are clear enough, and command enough respect, that they are ordinarily self-enforced. But the less the sense that the law is right, the greater the costs of policing. Some of the costs are obvious: administering and staffing

court systems and administrative agencies. There are costs of care-
fulness: Keeping harmful drugs off the market is a valuable goal,
but the result may be a delay in getting valuable medicine to patients who need it. There is overkill: injunctions that shut down factories to obviate what would have been a lesser harm to the community. There are the costs of outright error: We command less
flammability in children's sleepware, only to discover later that the
"remedy"—a flame retardant—is carcinogenic. And there are the
subtle costs of delay: By the time we comprehend the dangers posed
by polyvinyl chloride and asbestos, huge investments and even patterns of life have built up around them, making changes "unrealistic."

Invading the corporate structure

It is against these drawbacks that we should evaluate the emergence of a new approach to the control of corporate misconduct.
The harbingers are so unheralded, and on such scattered frontiers,
that few people have yet recognized it as a distinct new legal genus,
and one of considerable significance.

Traditionally, the legal efforts to control corporate misconduct
have taken two tacks. The first has been to allow a firm a great deal
of autonomy in its planning and implementation, but to subject it to
penalties if its choices turn out badly. If a manufacturer's product
is substandard and causes injury, the company (under the counterorganizational strategies) or sometimes select employees (under the
counterpersonnel strategies) may be held answerable. The second
approach (which can be viewed as evolving from perceived shortcomings in the first approach), has been to displace the judgment
of the firms with the judgment of public agencies regarding certain
product, service, or more recently, work-place qualities. Department
of Transportation regulations, for example, require that autos include seatbelts; the Occupational Safety and Health Administration
(OSHA) requires that certain guard rails be 42 inches high.

By contrast, in the developing style of corporate control, the law
neither stands aside until harm has been done, nor does it impose
inflexible standards. The idea, instead, is to decrease the likelihood
of harmful behavior through direct legal requirements regarding
corporate *management structure* and *decision processes*. This is not
a wholly new approach, but it has been used in the past only
sparingly and, as I observed earlier, ordinarily in the interests of the
investor. As a condition of enjoying corporate privileges, a business
must establish a board of directors (usually with at least three mem-

bers), a president, and (varying from state to state) perhaps a secretary and a treasurer. But traditional law has not gone beyond that to insist upon designated medium-level and lower-level management positions. We allow a company handling explosives to decide, wholly on its own, whether to have an executive in charge of safety, and if so, to determine his powers and level in the management structure.

In the past few years, however, there have been indications that this historical reluctance to invade the corporate management structure is fading. In 1973, a consent decree settling numerous charges of discrimination against women and racial minorities directed the Bell companies to establish compliance officers whose duties—mostly monitoring of hiring, firing, and advancement—were spelled out in detail. The current regulations of the Food and Drug Administration (FDA) require the drug companies to establish quality-control units, many of whose powers and obligations are prescribed by the government—i.e., withdrawn from the sole discretion of the companies. In 1974, in settling a civil fraud action against Mattel, Inc. (growing out of improper financial reporting), the Securities and Exchange Commission (SEC) forced the giant toy manufacturer to establish two special committees of the board—one on financial control and audit, the other on litigations and claims. The functions of the committees are not left for the corporation to establish—as is traditional—but are spelled out in the order of the court.

Such recent "invasions" of organizational autonomy have not been limited to establishing new posts and committees. In several areas, the "outside world" has begun to prescribe criteria concerning who may hold, and who may be disqualified from holding, certain corporate jobs. Requirements have been imposed on corporate internal information systems, with provisions that data of a specified sort must be gathered by firms, and considered by designated officers for action. The recent FDA regulations, for example, require that responsible corporate officials be notified in writing of possible drug-products defects, so they will not be able to claim later that they "knew nothing about it."

In other areas, the managerial level at which decisions of a certain kind must be made is no longer solely a matter of company discretion: The Federal Communications Commission allows radio broadcasters the final say on playing records that glorify illegal drugs, but insists that "someone in a responsible position [i.e., "a management-level executive at the station"] know the content of the lyrics." Internal lines of authority have been specified, by law, those who audit a quality-assurance program at a nuclear plant must be independent of the areas being audited.

Perhaps most intrusively of all, the "outside world" is increasingly taking a hand in the selection process by which key corporate slots are filled: Directors and special counsels have been "negotiated" into corporations, with court, agency, and/or plaintiff-shareholder approval. Such actions are appearing mostly in response to securities-law violations. But at least one federal judge has warned a recidivist corporate polluter that if it did not mend its ways, the court would send its own designate into the company—as a sort of in-house "probation officer"—to take over the pollution-control activities of corporate officers who might be interfering with the process of rehabilitation.

It is not just the profit-making corporations that have been subject to these developments. Within the past few years mental hospitals, prison systems, and school systems have been placed in "receivership," as it were, by federal and state judges, with the courts appointing trustees or their equivalents and occasionally ordering some restructuring of internal organization and procedures. Recent reports on the CIA and FBI have urged bureaucratic restructuring as a means toward tighter control. And the National Institute of Mental Health is laying down guidelines for genetic research (primarily in universities and research institutions) that detail critical features of internal management.

Organizational-adjustment measures

All these forms of control can be classified as what I call "organizational-adjustment measures." Unlike the traditional approaches, their focus is not so much on what the organizations *do*, but on the ways that the organizations *decide*. In general, the strengths of these new approaches are almost point for point the drawbacks of the traditional measures. The traditional measures are oriented remedially. The organizational-adjustment measures focus on prevention. The traditional measures undeniably have a prospective element insofar as they raise threats of future liability. But as we saw, there are reasons to doubt that threats to organizations or their employees will induce the most appropriate changes in information systems, role definitions, authority structures, technical programs, etc. By contrast, the new measures prescribe the presumably appropriate changes directly.

The traditional approaches, insofar as they are based on administrative or legislative rule-making, have an even more fundamental drawback: the inevitable lag between the identification of a problem and the institution of a rule to cover it. Are employees who work with asbestos being subjected to high risks of cancer? What psychological and physical dangers lurk in various forms of manufacturing processes? What are the dangers of various forms of pesticides to field workers, consumers, and the environment? Tragically, these are all problems that corporations were anticipating (or could have anticipated, given adequate adjustments) long before the lawmakers got wind of them. It is the company doctors who first treat the injuries, company chemists who live with and first test the new compounds, and company health records in which data gathers. One of the virtues of the organizational-adjustment measures is that by requiring corporations to pinpoint areas in which rule-making may be needed, organizations are, in effect, brought into the law-making process.

Now, of course, nothing the law does is ever so one-sidedly good, and I cannot deny that these organizational-adjustment measures, like much else that emanates from our vast governmental bureaucracy, will have their own costs and complications. Requiring special personnel and tasks imposes expenses that can, from case to case, exceed the most optimistically anticipated benefits. Other measures risk politicizing corporate policies and personnel selection, with unforseeable but troublesome implications. And there is a toll these measures could exact in organizational innovation and efficiency. Universities aim to educate; armies, to fight; hospitals, to treat and cure. These goals provide a context in which commands are interpreted and actions synchronized. The more the intrusions reinforce aims that seem inconsistent or discordant—or are just plain stupid— the more energy will be wasted, in resistance and bad feelings.

The true costs

All these costs concern me, but I think they must be kept in perspective. Sometimes the true costs seem rather low on any scale of measurement. Consider the Nuclear Regulatory Commission's decision that a licensee establish a security organization and "maintain and follow written procedures which document its structure and . . . detail the duties of . . . individuals responsible for security." Such an approach, which leaves it up to the licensee to supply the details of organizational responsibility, can hardly be faulted as either expensive or stultifying. Yet it has the virtue of forcing the company to think through problems and relationships that it might not otherwise come to grips with, and to clarify what is expected of each individual. From the point of view of costs, one wonders what real objections there can be, other than that it increases the accountability of persons who would rather remain anonymous.[1]

We should also keep in mind that in many situations the organizational-adjustment measures may prove a lot less costly and less stultifying than the most likely alternatives—such as an outright injunction against production, or a product recall, or increased government authority over the most minute details of operation. In one of the first occasions when the courts and the SEC became involved in the appointment of a special outside director, the idea came not from the government but from one of the corporation's own defense lawyers—the alternative would have been to plunge the company into receivership. Similarly, although Mattel had to spend many thousands of dollars to implement the settlement mentioned above, the arrangement may have been a relatively inexpensive way to restore consumer, creditor, and investor confidence in a scandal-rocked company. Indeed, Mattel has not split apart—as some might have predicted—from the divergent forces of all those special directors, committees, and counsel, but has recently turned a profit.

Sometimes, it is true, the costs of internal invasions will prove large and nagging—such as with the extensive pre-market testing required under the new Toxic Substance Control Act. But even then, who can say that the benefits may not be greater still? Two chemical spills alone—of kepone into the James River and PCB into the Hudson—have caused losses running perhaps into the hundreds of millions of dollars, and considerable human suffering. The long-range effects of aerosols on the atmosphere are still unknown, but potentially beyond measure.

I do not mean to suggest that the organizational-adjustment measures are foolproof or that—had they been in operation—they would have nipped all these problems in the bud. But in so many of the commercial tragedies of recent years, it is striking how many clues of danger there were, which were not acted upon because of institutional weaknesses.

---

[1] Increased accountability need not rest only on moral and psychological grounds. Nonperformance of a specified obligation can be made to require immediate discharge of an employee; the legal system can make an individual who failed to abide by his job description answerable to anyone who is injured by a product that passed through his control, whether or not the injured party can prove negligence. It would also be possible to attach criminal sanctions for nonperformance in certain circumstances.

Some general guidelines

I draw several conclusions from all this. Society will, and in my view should, increasingly explore organizational-adjustment measures as a means of preventing corporate misconduct. Such measures are, however, fraught with risks; before we see their wholesale employment, considerable thought must be given to the sorts of situations that might initially warrant their employment on an experimental basis, as we try to learn more about their strengths and weaknesses.

It is probably easiest to justify the use of the measures when the agency or group desiring the internal adjustments has access simply to bargain for the changes—for example, when the government is contracting for the development of a relatively unique product (e.g., a weapons system) and wants the contractor to provide an acceptable quality-control system, to accept on-site military representatives, etc. The contractor does not want to surrender managerial autonomy freely, but to the government such concessions are a form of performance "insurance," for which it is prepared to pay as part of the contract package.

In many respects, demands by unions to participate in management are of the same character. Traditional union demands have involved fixed targets (wages, hours) rather than an ongoing involvement in the decision process. But at some point, the employees' marginal welfare will dictate a shift in focus. For example, the Oil, Chemical, and Atomic Workers have increasingly sought representation on the company committees that establish health and safety standards. Rather than to discourage such demands or rule them out of order as "invasions of management prerogative," such practices should be encouraged, to see if they might be molded into practical alternatives to some of the externally imposed mechanisms of, e.g., OSHA, which are less subject to cost-benefit constraints.

A similar situation involves the settlement of shareholder derivative actions, suits brought on the company's behalf against directors and top officers for losses caused by their negligence or willful mismanagement. Such actions have traditionally been settled by payment of a generous bounty to the plaintiffs' attorney, a modest reimbursement by the defendants, and some cheap promises to be more careful in the future. Recently, however, at least one public-interest law firm has insisted on settlements that reconstitute the company's managerial structure as a means of preventing the recurrence of the wrong; other settlements have included establishing new board committees, the appointment of special independent directors, changes in board size, amendment of bylaws, etc. It is easy to see that, in part, these concessions are being granted by those who run the companies in exchange for smaller personal payments than they otherwise would have to make. But if the settlement is approved by the shareholders, there is no reason to discourage such trade-offs; an organization may stand to benefit more from a moderate reconstruction of its management than from the classic but perfunctory cash payment.

There are other situations in which several companies in an industry—ordinarily the more responsible and financially stable—will favor a particular measure (an extra degree of pre-market testing, say), but will be reluctant to adopt it unilaterally, fearing a competitive disadvantage. In this case, a government-"mandated" organizational change is nothing more than a way of implementing broadly accepted minimum standards. As a result, resistance is likely to be minimal, and success high. Such changes do have one interesting drawback (in common with a good deal of legislation): Since the costs are more readily borne by the larger companies, the extra protection of the organizational-adjustment measures may clash with some of the values that underlie the antitrust laws—such as preserving competition.

Beyond these areas in which the organizational adjustments are negotiated or generally acceptable, justification becomes more difficult. The strongest argument for intercession is that an organization has already broken the law or caused serious injury, and the internal adjustments are demanded as a condition of probation. Corporate probation is a notion that has received surprisingly scant attention, especially considering the unavailability of other remedies used in dealing with individuals—e.g., imprisonment, or psychotherapy as a condition of release. Under a model corporate rehabilitation bill that I have drafted, when a company has been convicted of a criminal offense or subjected to a civil judgment in an amount greater than $250,000, the court may hold a hearing to determine whether the conduct giving rise to the judgment arose from an uncorrected pattern of company policies, practices, or procedures, and whether the company might reasonably be demanded to make changes in them after considering costs and benefits.

If the court so found, it could order the company to report in a "proposed rehabilitation agenda" why, in its opinion, the wrongful conduct had occurred, what measures it proposed to prevent a recurrence, and which officers would be responsible for carrying out the agenda. (If the company believed that no special rehabilitative measures were necessary or feasible in the circumstances, it would so state and explain.) When an agenda acceptable to the court and interested parties was arrived at, its terms would be, in effect, a probation order. I doubt that there would be widespread need for the courts to exercise such powers, but they would be important to have on hand, especially to deal with corporate recidivists—the chronic price-fixers, polluters, etc.

The non-profit organizations are another area in which the case for extending these measures seems especially strong. In many ways, non-profits are the most undaunted by present law, sometimes through the special immunities they enjoy, sometimes because of judicial sympathy, and sometimes because their management is further removed from profit constraints than the management of business corporations (although the differences are not nearly so striking as the terminological distinction between "for-profit" and "not-for-profit" would suggest). For example, the financial management of non-profits is notoriously bad; all the reasons for requiring, say, independent audit committees on corporations listed on the stock exchanges would seem to apply all the more forcefully to some of our giant charities. I have no doubt that municipal corporations and other governmental agencies are peculiarly suited to being brought under internal requirements of various sorts, but here one must be particularly sensitive to the blurring of political lines of authority.

Finally, there is a range of situations—unfortunately, the broadest —that possesses none of the simplifying features of the cases discussed above. Where our concern is with staving off damage from toxic substances or dangerous drugs, for example, the interests involved cannot as satisfactorily be brought into negotiation, the risks of allowing "one bite of the apple" may seem too large, and some of the measures the society might propose (e.g., intensive pre-market testing) may lie well beyond the minimum standards the organizations will accept as appropriate. Each case will have to be judged on its own merits, and one can only hope that some sense of proportion will be maintained. How serious, in terms of magnitude and irreversibility, is the harm we are trying to prevent? Are the existing measures for coping with the problem really inadequate, and are there alternative methods available? What costs will the contemplated organizational-adjustment measures impose? And if they are implemented, what is the likelihood that they will succeed? Are there procedural "ground rules" we can establish to allay the conflicts and confusions?

Restoring cooperation

How well organizational-adjustment measures will work, I cannot say; the answers will obviously vary from case to case. But in spite of my own reservations, I think that in many areas such measures are going to spread—and spread successfully—precisely because the corporations will come to recognize that, as a way of dealing with a significant range of problems, the idea has something in it for them, as well as for the public.

This may sound odd. But what is most evidently missing in our corporate/social relations today, and needs to be restored, is a measure of mutual trust and respect. As things stand, we are settling into a self-defeating cycle in which the anti-corporate sentiment is increasingly shrill and ill-informed, and the corporate response is too often self-defensive, unheeding, and unconstructive. When the evidence suggests a possible problem—like work-related cancer—governmental agencies, distrustful of what is going on within the corporation's walls, will be inclined to slap together a battery of regulations without adequate information, if only to protect themselves from criticism.

In such circumstances, some systematic integration of the "inside" with the "outside" could lead—and may be the only way to lead—to new, more productive patterns of cooperation. From the point of view of corporate management, it seems no great hardship to provide assurances that internal regulations (for example, quality control) are being carried out effectively and in good faith—and to identify those now-anonymous employees who will be accountable if they are not.

In any event, such an arrangement is a lot less intrusive than having Washington take over a growing number of decisions on the most minute details of operations, or being forced to collect and hand over ream upon ream of undigested raw data. From the point of view of the regulator, there are also several advantages. It is far less costly for the government to send a single inspector to certify a quality-control system, than to try to oversee each and every detail of operation. Similarly, to contain bribery, it makes sense to conscript the firms themselves into enforcement service, by requiring them to institute appropriate internal accounting procedures—if only because there are simply not enough federal auditors, thank goodness, to go around. To regulate behavior in this fashion, with some degree of irreducible "self-policing," involves a larger measure of trust than the most outspoken corporate critics may be prepared to allow. But they should realize that when the law tries to overextend its reach, there is inevitably a tendency for the organizations increasingly to wink at violations that are not likely to be detected, and to comply only begrudgingly, when it is prudent to do so. (Resistance to law need not always take the form of foot-dragging or fudging data; one of the most effective ways for a corporation to keep "those idiots" off its back is to answer their requests with truckloads of data.)

All these measures will undeniably bring along their own red tape. My hope is that as a sort of historical quid pro quo, there will be a reduction elsewhere in the inevitable and unnecessary paperwork that results when the government has to second-guess the corporations from a distance, or fire shotguns—when a less suspicious and more cooperative effort might do every bit as well.

25

NUMBERS GAMBLING AMONG BLACKS
A Financial Institution

IVAN LIGHT

CULTURAL AND INSTITUTIONAL EXPLANATIONS OF POVERTY

The literature on poverty conventionally distinguishes institutional and cultural explanations (Light and Wong, 1975; Elesh, 1977). The distinction hangs upon whether an explanation identifies social institutions or the culturally-induced behavior of the poor as the cause of poverty. Although this taxonomy satisfactorily encompasses the structures of explanation, two intervening processes always precipitate poverty. These two are low income and wasteful and/or destructive consumption.

Low income is the most obvious cause of poverty, but the balance between income and consumption is always the technical issue. Even where disposable family incomes are above the poverty level, wasteful or destructive expenditures may deplete a family's reserve until income is no longer adequate. In this case, wasteful consumption—not low income—actually caused a family's poverty. Naturally, when incomes are inadequate, low income becomes the immediate cause of poverty but, even here, wasteful or destructive consumption can exacerbate it.

The intervening processes of low income and wasteful/destructive consumption are compatible in principle with either institutional or cultural explanations of poverty. For example, institutional explanations of income-induced poverty have stressed external barriers imposed by racial discrimination, structural unemployment, minimum wage laws, labor exploitation, the split labor market, and so forth. Cultural explanations of low income-induced poverty have stressed unfavorable work habits (absenteeism, soldiering, tardiness) which reduced employability, attributing these variously to the lack of a Protestant ethic, or the presence of employment and earning-inhibiting cultural residues (Banfield, 1974).

On the neglected consumption side, cultural explanations have emphasized the adverse consequences of wasteful/destructive consumption habits allegedly characteristic of the "disreputable poor" (Matza, 1966). For example, in the decades of temperance agitation preceding the Prohibition Era in the United States, much social research concerned insobriety among the working class and the putative connection of drinking and pauperism (Koren, 1899: 64–99). Many other consumption habits have been linked to poverty, among them: unsophisticated shopping, purchase of luxuries, big families, unhealthy diet, excessive use of installment purchase, failure to save and gambling (Glazer and Moynihan, 1970: 33; Foxall, 1974).

* The author gratefully acknowledges a grant from the University of California Academic Senate, Los Angeles Division. The American Bankers Association permitted inspection and reproduction of their unpublished research findings. The author also wishes to thank Oscar Grusky, Robert Herman, Joan Huber and Lynne Zucker for advice.

From Ivan Light, "Numbers Gambling Among Blacks: A Financial Institution," 42(6) *American Sociological Review* 892-904 (December 1977). Copyright 1977 by the American Sociological Association.

One institutional response to this catalogue of wasteful consumption practices has been to question the scope of culturally-induced consumption differences between the poor and nonpoor. This issue produced a complex and contradictory literature which permits no easy encapsulation (Alexis, 1962; Nixon, 1963; Simon and Simon, 1968; Stafford et al., 1968; Sturdivant, 1969; Cicarelli, 1974). In some cases, undeniable income-linked differences have appeared—for example, lower rates of life insurance purchase by the poor. Even here, institutional writers have insisted that poverty produces situational pressures which require the poor to seek irregular and often more expensive alternatives to those prevailing elsewhere in the market (Light, 1972: 152–69; Ferman and Ferman, 1973; Wong, 1977). In a memorable phrase, Caplovitz (1963) observed that "the poor pay more" because the retail stores of the slum compel it. Similarly, successive studies of pawnbrokers and loan sharks have concluded that poor people turn to high-priced lenders because they are unable to obtain credit in cheaper institutions (Forman, 1906: 622; Seidl, 1968: 88–9). In all of these cases, the poor are making unwise, destructive or wasteful purchases, but circumstances rather than improvidence necessitates the waste.

The ideological implications of any simply cultural or simply institutional explanation of poverty are mutually repugnant (see Huber, 1974), and a spirit of dogmatism often has characterized social science discussion as a result. The source of this dogmatism is the insistence that cultural and institutional theories of poverty must exclude one another. This insistence is fallacious because cultural and institutional explanations can produce poverty jointly as well as singly. Recognizing this possibility of conjoint causality, Valentine (1968: 117) nonetheless condemned it as "eclectic," and social scientists have been dismayingly willing to accept this unwarranted constraint.

The treatment of Lewis' (1968) "culture of poverty" thesis is a case in point. Lewis' detractors as well as his defenders accepted the premise that his thesis is a cultural theory (Leacock, 1971). Yet, the premise is strictly untrue for, in Lewis' view, historic institutions gave rise to contemporary cultures of poverty. His total explanation actually included both institutional and cultural components so it was never a purely institutional nor a purely cultural explanation. The controversial Moynihan report was only a specific application of Lewis' formula to American blacks (Rainwater, 1967). Moynihan asserted that slavery, a bygone institution, had engendered a matriarchal cultural tradition among blacks. The female-headed family, a cultural survival of the bygone institution, had become the principal cause of poverty among American blacks today. Moynihan's thesis contained cultural and institutional components; it was never a purely cultural explanation.

True, a purely cultural phase succeeded a purely institutional phase in both the Lewis and Moynihan versions. (The sequence might, in principle, have been reversed.) On the other hand, no barrier prevents institutional-income and/or institutional-consumption causes from coexisting in time with cultural-income and/or cultural-consumption causes. Numbers gambling offers empirical confirmation of this logical possibility. Numbers gambling is a wasteful consumption practice of the poor. Existing literature attributes this wasteful consumption to cultural causes. This cultural-consumption orthodoxy is simplistic. Actually, numbers gambling combines institutional and cultural causes in the same time span. Therefore, this empirical case supports the conclusion that institutional and cultural causes of poverty may operate conjointly in a situation, and that empirical determination of preponderance is necessary in every case.

NUMBERS GAMBLING: A FINANCIAL INSTITUTION

In the late nineteenth century and until roughly 1940, policy wheels were the prevailing type of lottery among urban blacks and whites of the lower class. Although policy gambling persisted in Chicago and Detroit until 1940, numbers gambling by now has replaced policy in all major American cities. In numbers gambling, a "gig" bettor stakes a small sum on three digits, 000 to 999. Instead of a wheel or drum, the house takes its winning number from published numbers such as bank clearing totals, volume on the New York Stock Exchange, or parimutuel totals. The published figures eliminate the possibility of a rigged outcome, a decisive technical advantage over the policy format (Light, 1974). Beale and Goldman (1974: 541; cf. Roebuck, 1967: 136; Black Enterprise, 1973: 12) estimate that numbers gamblers in the United States wagered 2.5 billion dollars in 1973, roughly ten percent of all illegal gambling revenue.

Discursive evidence claims that blacks were overrepresented among policy gamblers, but the implications of these statements are unclear (Crapsey, 1872: 104; Martin, 1868: 517; Du Bois, 1899: 265). There is no evidence that blacks were overrepresented relative to poor nonblacks; in addition, white ethnics commonly had their own lotteries which may have been functional equivalents of policy gambling (Ianni, 1972: 67; Carlson, 1940: 24). However, Caribbean blacks invented and popularized numbers in this country during the 1920s. As a result, numbers gambling was still 60 percent black in 1934 (Light, 1974: 55). Carlson (1940: 3-4; see also Caldwell, 1940:2) noted that although "white people of the lower economic classes" had begun to bet on numbers, this form of gambling remained "predominantly an urban negro [sic] activity." Currently, Marcum and Rowen (1974: 31) observe that numbers gambling is "concentrated among blacks and ethnic groups in the older cities, especially in the East and Midwest." The Fund for the City of New York (1972) found that blacks represented 30 percent of numbers bettors, but only 20 percent of the city's population. This progression indicates that numbers began as an exclusively black lottery, but diffused to nonblacks.

Studies of lottery gambling, even those most sympathetic to blacks, have always regarded the betting as superstitious nonsense justifying a prodigal waste of money (Riis, 1892: 155; Peterson, 1952: 194; Drake and Cayton, 1962: II, 491). The amount wasted is substantial. Drake and

Cayton (1962: II, 481; cf. Warner and Junker, 1941: 19) concluded that the policy syndicate on Chicago's South Side employed 5,000 persons and grossed at least 18 million dollars in 1938. This sum would represent $64 for every black person in Chicago and $256 for a family of four. The median income of all families in Chicago was $1,463 in 1940, so numbers gambling of blacks accounted for about 17.5 percent of family income. More recently, the Fund for the City of New York (1972: 9) concluded that New Yorkers wagered 600 million dollars a year on numbers bets. Blacks represented 30 percent of New York's numbers bettors, so the city's black population presumably laid 180 million dollars on numbers in that year. This sum represents $87 for every black person in New York City. Since the median family income of blacks in New York was $7,309 in 1969, nearly five percent of black family income went for numbers gambling. This estimate is conservative. Director of Political Affairs for the Congress of Racial Equality, Ed Brown (1973) has claimed that in Harlem alone blacks wager "at least" 300 to 500 million dollars a year on numbers. If only 300 million dollars were wagered yearly, this betting gross would represent about $300 for every black person in Harlem or 16 percent of family income. In the 94 percent black Bedford-Stuyvesant section of Brooklyn, Lasswell and McKenna (1972: 55-62) examined numbers gambling between 1963 and 1970. Their estimates are the most reliable of any. They found that impoverished residents spent between 2.5 and 5.1 percent of per capita income on numbers bets. Admittedly, these estimates of betting volume are crude and vary widely. Nonetheless, even the lower estimates indicate that numbers betting represents a significant waste of money by poor people.

Why do poor blacks waste money on numbers? The sociological literature on gambling is scanty (Scimecca, 1971: 56; Tec, 1964: 105) and it offers only two efforts to explain numbers gambling as opposed to gambling in general, the usual focus. The two offer exclusively cultural explanations. Carlson (1940) called attention to "the culture complex" underlying the numbers gambling of Detroit blacks. This complex included dream interpretation, folklore and music, social roles, spiritualism, ceremonial festivities, fad and fashion in playing style, and an extensive gambling jargon. McCall (1963) stressed the "symbiotic" relationship between spiritualist cults and numbers gambling, claiming that the superstitions mutually reinforced each other. The cultural source of the superstition McCall identified as animistic religions of West Africa and Caribbean "hoodoo." In view of the heavy folklore surrounding the numbers complex, cultural explanations have an undeniable plausibility. Moreover, the metropolitan black press continues to depict numbers gambling as a "soul" preoccupation (E. Brown, 1973) while reminding readers that blacks invented the game. In all cases, what is evoked is a specifically black cultural heritage rather than a generalized "culture of poverty." Nonetheless, the prevailing cultural interpretation of numbers gambling among blacks comes down to a cultural-consumption interpretation of poverty among this group.

The evidence supporting the cultural side of black numbers gambling is too strong to deny, but a close look at numbers gambling turns up three telling anomalies. First, of cultural theories of gambling in general, the preeminent is Devereaux (1968; see also Thurner, 1956) who stresses the incompatibility between gambling and the Protestant work ethic. The obvious difficulty is that black numbers gamblers are predominantly Protestant fundamentalists whose gambling can only occur despite the restraint of this religious tradition. Hence, the cultural baggage of blacks does not provide unmixed support for numbers gambling. Second, a cultural explanation of black numbers gambling cannot account for the 70–80 percent of numbers gamblers who are now nonblack. This objection was less serious when numbers was an exclusively black preoccupation, but the subsequent diffusion of the game to nonblacks compels the conclusion that cultural continuities originating in the black heritage cannot give the whole explanation. The supposed improvidence of the lower class offers a class cultural explanation for numbers gambling by the black and nonblack poor. However, the actual distribution of gambling among social classes lends little evidentiary support. Li and Smith (1976) reported national survey data which show that the propensity to gamble is positively associated with socioeconomic status, a result repugnant to any class cultural theory. The best evidence cited in support of a negative relationship between socioeconomic status and gambling is Tec (1964; see also Newman, 1972: 85). However, Tec concentrated only on football pool gambling, an admitted preoccupation of the working class. Numerous studies (Bloch, 1951: 218; Commission, 1975: 13) report that identifiable social groups have favorite gambling activities. For example, the Fund for the City of New York (1972) reported that low-income gamblers preferred numbers, but high-income gamblers preferred casino games; at middle-income levels, sports and race track betting prevailed. This mosaic of gambling preferences implies that the correlation between social-economic status and gambling depends upon which gambling game is under scrutiny.

Third, a fundamental assumption of any cultural theory of gambling is the expectation that rates should remain stable over long periods of time in reflection of cultural divergences. But the history of lottery gambling in general (Light, 1974: 52–3) and numbers gambling in particular (Carlson, 1940: 4, 138, 158; Caldwell, 1940: 30) shows abrupt shifts in participation: lottery gambling increases in frequency in economic hard times and declines in periods of prosperity. Cultural theory cannot account for cyclical fluctuation.

On the other hand, the increase in numbers gambling in periods of business depression immediately suggests the anomie theory (Durkheim, 1951: 241–46). Merton (1957: 149) also identifies the numbers gambling of blacks as a form of "innovative deviance." Big prize lotteries offer the possibility of immense wealth to winners, and sociological treatments of these have commonly asserted that working-class bettors hope to strike it rich (Stocking, 1932: 558; Marcum and Rowen, 1974: 30; Ianni, 1974: 110), a conclusion congenial to anomie theory (Tec, 1964: 62; Zetterberg, 1962: 122). A related view has developed in economics since the analysis of Friedman and Savage (1948) reversed the economists' long-standing belief that gambling is always irrational. Even the enemies of gambling within the economics profession now acknowledge that gambling is "rational when a person's wish to obtain an otherwise unattainable large prize is very large" (Rubner, 1966: 52). Eadington (1972: 24; see also Off Track Betting Corporation, 1973: II) assumes that numbers gambling satisfies this condition and, thus, justifies its economic rationality.

Anomie theory fits big prize lotteries, but it does not fit numbers gambling because numbers bettors do not expect to change life-style when they win. On an average bet of one dollar, a numbers winner receives a pot which may range from $500 to $600. Players are expected to tip the runner ten percent of winnings, a practice which reduces net gain to $450–$540. In the depressed Bedford-Stuyvesant sector of Brooklyn, slum dwellers averaged only 50 cents a numbers wager, so their expected return was only $225 to $270 in 1970. These calcualtions exaggerate expected return because the game permits less radical bets than the three-digit gig. In "single action," for example, a bettor selects only one digit at odds of 10 to 1. The maximum return in this popular bet is only $6, less the runner's tip. These returns fall far short of riches permitting a change in life-style.

Personal Saving

Sellin (1963:19; see also Ianni, 1974; 110) supposes that numbers gambling thrives because a "segment of the population enjoys betting" and does not regard it as harmful. But the entertainment theory does not correspond with the bettors' understanding of the numbers game. On the contrary, they vigorously disclaim betting for the thrill, fun or sport of it. Numbers gamblers view the game as a rational economic activity and characteristically

refer to their numbers bets as "investments" (Carlson, 1940: 138–9).

Most gamblers understand their numbers betting as a means of personal saving. This ubiquitous self-justification is the crucial prop for the entire gambling order (Eadington, 1972: 29; Ianni, 1974: 78). The bettor's justification for this seemingly preposterous misconception arises from unsatisfactory experiences with depository savings techniques. Once a numbers collector has a man's quarter, they aver, there is no getting it back in a moment of weakness. If, on the other hand, the quarter were stashed at home, a saver would have to live with the continuing clamor of unmet needs. In a moment of weakness, he might spend the quarter. Therefore, in the bettor's view, the most providential employment of small change is to bet it on a number (Grow, 1939: 213; see also Whyte, 1943: 41). "The dime or quarter which one bets is scarcely missed," writes R. Brown (1973), "but when one 'hits' the payoff is a chunk of money large enough to be really useful to the winner." Bettors do win (Johnson, 1971: 42). On an average day, the betting public receives back in "hits" fifty percent of its total wager. From the bettors' perspective, numbers gambling is a means of converting change into lump sums; in effect, a savings method (see Samuelson, 1973: 423; Commission, 1975: 17).

The methodical style of numbers gambling also indicates that bettors have adopted a long-range perspective, suggesting a rational savings strategy. The Fund for the City of New York (1972: Appendix 15) found that 72 percent of numbers bettors placed a bet "two or three times a week" and 42 percent bet every day. The Off Track Betting Corporation (1973) concluded that: "The typical numbers player currently wagers on the game between 2 and 4 times a week." Even more strikingly, the Fund for the City of New York (1972: Appendix 25) found that 41 percent of numbers bettors had been betting on the game for ten years or more, and 59 percent for six to ten years. Indeed, the largest bettors were those who had been playing the longest. The frequency of wagering and the decades-long perseverance of numbers gamblers outlines an average playing career which encompasses 1,300 trials. In a decade of gambling at this rate, a gambler confidently can expect to hit at least once (for $550) against his total investment of $1,300. Viewed from a decade's perspective, the expected return of a numbers gambling career approaches the expected value of the game (Ignatin and Smith, 1976; Ianni, 1974: 78; Eadington, 1972: 205).

Numbers games attract funds which would not otherwise be saved in depository accounts (cf. Rubner, 1966: 36). First, numbers gambling is convenient. Numbers runners make a regular circuit of their customers who thus do not have to go out of their way to bet. In addition, numbers stations are located in newsstands, pool halls, cigar stores and groceries which people visit on an average day. Therefore, even people who have savings accounts find it convenient to lay a dollar on a number while at the barber shop rather than risk making no "investment" at all in the day. The fund for the City of New York (1972: 57; see also Haller, 1970: 623) concluded that a legalized numbers game would require seven to ten thousand outlets to compete with the illegal game in convenience. In 1970, Bedford-Stuyvesant alone contained 1,345 numbers runners whose business was making it easy to bet (Lasswell and McKenna, 1972: 111).

The friendly atmosphere of numbers gambling encourages "saving." People choose to deal with a numbers runner whom they trust and like (McKay, 1940: 112–3). Therefore, interactions with this person are enjoyable. An established numbers station is usually operated in a small grocery store, candy shop or beauty parlor. Stores of this sort often serve as neighborhood hangouts as well as retail outlets (cf. Whyte, 1943: 143; Firey, 1947: 190). When placing a bet, a gambler has an opportunity for a few moments of sociable interaction with whomever is hanging around. The sociable atmosphere of a numbers station thus stimulates to "saving" these persons who would otherwise simply have spent all small change.

Numbers gambling also appeals to the race pride and community spirit of the ghetto public. The real extent of altruistic motivations is unclear, but the experience of state lotteries suggests that altruistic motives do induce some people to gamble. When asked why they purchased Connecticut state lottery tickets, 82 percent of bettors mentioned financial reasons and 33 percent the benefit to the state.[1] In some cases, blacks have actually gotten together in order to set up an unemployed friend as their numbers runner (McKay, 1940: 112–3). However, even in cases where the direct support of a friend is not involved, blacks understand their numbers gambling as a local form of work-relief (Drake and Cayton, 1962: II, 493; Ottley, 1943: 155; Black Enterprise, 1973: 44; Ofari, 1970: 44–5). Numbers gambling syndicates do provide a lot of employment in black communities. Lasswell and McKenna (1972: 168) found that numbers gambling syndicates were the largest employers in the slum, second only to the federal government. Numbers collectors frequently double as town criers and fund raisers on their rounds. One black informant, an experienced collector in Detroit, observes that passing the hat for hard-luck cases was a regular function of his daily rounds. In this manner, the people who regularly dealt with him put themselves into a loose federation for mutual assistance in time of need.

Consumer Credit

In addition to drawing savings out of an impoverished population which finds saving difficult, numbers-gambling banks also make credit available to poor people who would otherwise be unable to obtain it (Dominguez, 1976: 38). The capital fund from which this credit derives is the gambling play of the neighborhood. The methods by which this capital returns as credit to the local economy are sometimes circuitous and sometimes direct.

Numbers runners make direct loans to customers. These direct loans are of two sorts. First, numbers runners sometimes permit the needy to borrow the where-

---

[1] I am grateful to John T. Macdonald and Fillis W. Stober, State of Connecticut, Commission on Special Revenue, for showing me these unpublished tabulations.

withal to bet. Eighteen percent of numbers players in New York City acknowledged placing bets on credit (Fund for the City of New York, 1972: Appendix 29). Among those who bet a dollar or more per day, this percentage increased to 23. Second, some runners lend cash to steady customers. Nine percent of numbers players in New York City had borrowed cash from their numbers runner for some purpose other than betting. Among persons who usually bet a dollar or more per day, this percentage increased to 15 percent. These percentages are modest, and there is no indication of how recourse to credit varies with income or color. On the other hand, a 1970 sample of California households (Day and Brandt, 1972: Table 6.2) found that eight percent of white and 15 percent of minority households with annual incomes less than $7,500 reported borrowing money from a credit union. Therefore, the direct credit service of numbers gamblers is roughly comparable to credit unions in a low income population.

A wider credit conduit is the return to the local community of numbers gambling profits as loan shark's capital. This return is the standard underworld employment of numbers gambling profits (Seidl, 1968: 32-3; Kaplan and Matteis, 1968). Consumers and small businessmen are the principal customers of slum loan sharks who actually frequent banks in order to approach disappointed loan applicants, sometimes being waved or pointed out to these by the platform official (Seidl, 1968: 16-7; 109-19, 139; Congressional Record, 1967). In many cases, numbers gamblers and loan sharks are the same individual, who simply transfers money from one pocket to another when he changes roles (Anderson, 1974: 25, 127, 130-1; Ianni, 1974: 80, 136; Knudten, 1970: 140).

Business Investment

Numbers racketeers have been the largest investors in black-owned business or ghetto real estate and the chief source of business capital in the ghetto (Roebuck, 1967: 142; Drake and Cayton, 1962: II, 487; Caldwell, 1940: 153; Strong, 1940: 133; see also Whyte, 1943: 145; cf. Ofari, 1970: 46). In addition, numbers bankers have been virtually the only sources of business capitalization available to local blacks lacking collateral or credit rating (Cook, 1971). As a result of these loans, black-owned businesses not actually owned by numbers bankers were often in debt to them (Drake and Cayton, 1962: II, 469). Finally, numbers bankers have been leading philanthropists in depressed black neighborhoods, making donations to churches and athletic teams, and providing Christmas and Easter baskets for the poor (cf. Perucci, 1969; Whyte, 1943: 142-5).

MAINSTREAM FINANCIAL INSTITUTIONS: MALFUNCTION

One way to appraise the importance of numbers gambling in the financial life of the slum is to compare this subterranean financial system with the saving and investment services of mainstream financial institutions, such as banks. Even a casual review of relevant literature proves that mainstream institutions do not now, nor have they ever in the past (U.S. Immigration Commission, 1911: 216) been able to provide the same standard of financial service in depressed communities which they routinely provide in affluent ones (Hiltz, 1971; Dominguez, 1976: 18). The chronic malfunction of mainstream financial institutions in the slum leaves an enormous service gap in which a diversity of popular financial institutions—including the numbers racket—plausibly may flourish.

Saving

Poor people in general and nonwhites in particular make less use of banks for savings or checking accounts than do nonpoor (Lewis, 1968: 190-2; Irons, 1971: 420). Low income is the most obvious cause: the less money people earn, the less they have to deposit in banks. National survey data confirm this expectation (see Table 1). The consumption of banking services declines as income declines. Of those who own no savings account, 75 percent (1972) and 80 percent (1970) explained that lack of "money left over" after paying bills was the reason

Table 1. Usage of Banking Services by Color and Family Income, 1966 and 1972

	Have a Savings Account (%)		Have a Regular Checking Account (%)	
	1966	1972	1966	1972
All Persons	52	73	56	76
Family Income:				
$15,000 & over	} 74	84	} 84 [a]	85
10–14,999		81		83
6–9,999	68	72	78 [a]	76
4–5,999	47	} 58	63 [a]	} 62
Under 4,000	28		38 [a]	
Color:				
White	60	74	71 [a]	80
Nonwhite	30	61	23 [a]	48

Sources: Opinion Research, 1966: 33, 71; Harris, 1972: 49, 55.
[a] Regular and/or special checking account.

(Harris, 1972: 73; Opinion Research, 1966: 39). Among those who had no checking account, 45 percent (1962) and 46 percent (1966) blamed lack of money, the modal explanation.

Investment

A result of nondepositing in banks is noncreation of capital funds in them. This shortage begins the "capital gap" in the inner city, a condition which strangles consumer, mortgage and business credit alike (Garvin, 1971: 445). Moreover, such funds as do make their way into deposit accounts in low-income areas do not, in general, find local investment outlets. Because they lack collateral and have irregular and low income, poor residents make bad risks for bank loans (King, 1929: 18–9; Neifeld, 1939: 169; Dominguez, 1976: 19). In addition, the sums poor people borrow are normally too small to permit profitable lending (U.S. Senate, 1970: 89, 160; 1968: 404). Even credit unions require federal subsidies to offer loans to the poor at legally permissible rates of interest (Cargill, 1973). Therefore, consumer finance companies, like banks, also avoid poor families (Booth, 1973: 71).

Small business loans in poverty areas are more risky than investments in corporate or government securities (Cross, 1969: 45, 46; U.S. Senate, 1970: 148). Adverse profit considerations also have shaped mortgage lending policies in inner cities. Savings and loan associations routinely refuse to issue mortgages in "red-lined" areas deemed to be in deterioration (U.S. Senate, 1975). The undesirability of consumer, business or mortgage investment opportunities has resulted in a flight of capital from the inner city to more profitable suburban locations (see Orren, 1974: 145–78). A source of interracial tension, this flight of capital owes more to economic calculation than to color prejudice. In 1971, for example, all U.S. banks had 13 percent of total assets in government securities whereas the nation's 20 black-owned banks had 30 percent of their assets so invested. The ultra-conservative investment policies of the black-owned banks led Brimmer (1971) to observe that the black banks were "diverting resources from the black community into the financing of the national debt." This investment policy contributes to the "almost total void of low cost credit and capital" in the inner city (U.S. Senate, 1968: 408).

Bank-Community Relations

Nonfinancial barriers to the normal operation of depository institutions arise from the mutual lack of sympathy of bankers and the poor. The cultural ethos of a bourgeois society provides bankers with no basis for an indulgent view of poor people, and the problem is more acute when the poor are also nonwhite. Blacks have complained for over 200 years that white bankers discriminate against them (Light, 1972: 19). This persistent complaint turned up in Harris' (1972: 94) research for the banking industry. In this survey, 43 percent of nonwhites but only 18 percent of whites agreed that banks made it "too difficult" for nonwhites to obtain loans.

Banking industry research (Harris, 1970: 97-8) confirms that the loan turndown rate "has been highest among lower income groups and nonwhites." Bankers also have acknowledged the interpersonal problems which arise when white credit managers refuse nonwhite customers (U.S. Senate, 1970: 195-6). However, banking industry spokesmen have denied that bankers' race prejudices were the source of the problem (Haugen, 1968: 103; U.S. Senate, 1970: 160; see also Marsh, 1971). The practical line between prejudice and an adverse but impartial bank decision is difficult to draw because of the connection of color characteristics with economic marginality. A U.S. Senate (1968) investigation addressed allegations that the racism of white bankers was responsible for the inner city financial gap. However, the extensive hearings provided no evidence of more than a clash of cultural standards; and subsequent research also has unearthed no evidence that the color antipathies of bankers distort their business judgment.

Nonetheless, poor minorities fervently believe that bankers discriminate against them and discourage their patronage (Day and Brandt, 1972: 102). This belief nourishes the antipathy of these people to banks (Cross, 1969: 51, 54, 66; Kurtz, 1973: 55). Banking industry research shows a decline of confidence in banks as family income declines (Harris, 1972: 28; 1970: 46), but color makes an autonomous contribution. Black people are more alienated from banks than would be expected on the basis of income or educational attainment alone (Root, 1966: 65). Selby and Lindley (1973) found that Atlanta blacks were less prone than whites to maintain a checking account, even holding constant the blacks' generally lower income and educational level. Similarly, banking industry research (Harris, 1972: 49) found that among families

with incomes under $6,000 a year, the poorest class, 62 percent had checking accounts but only 48 percent of nonwhites did (Table 1). More generally, surveys record a level of disenchantment with business and banks which is higher among nonwhites than among the poor. For example, Harris (1972: 131) found that among families with annual incomes less than $6,000, 37 percent rated banks "very high" in their concern for helping the local community, but only 28 percent of nonwhites agreed. Harris (1970: 130) also found that among families with annual incomes less than $6,000, 34 percent perceived bankers as "highly concerned" with helping their community, but only 16 percent of nonwhites made this friendly rating.

Naturally, many expressions of mistrust reflect hostile stereotypes rather than harsh experience. Harris (1970: 46; also Hiltz, 1971: 996) reported that nonwhites indicated less familiarity than whites with every type of financial institution except the sales finance company. Ignorance and public image in principle are open to change through "education" which bankers now view as the key to extending their market in black and low-income areas. The banks' record of recent extensions in response to "advertising and promotional activities" proves that poor people's unfavorable attitudes are open to suasion (Opinion Research, 1966: 74).

However, the malfunction of mainstream service in inner cities is neither epiphenomenal, nor easily rectified within a profit system. To extend service markets in low-income neighborhoods, depository institutions must surmount the barriers posed by the residents' poverty as well as their ignorance of and antipathy toward banks. Although the record of recent extensions proves these barriers are not insuperable, the dollar costs of attracting new bank customers increase as the income of the new customers decreases, but marginal revenues decline. Hence, profit-making institutions cannot provide normal service levels in poverty areas. As a result, the private burden of supporting the savings-investment cycle in such localities falls upon whatever financial institutions the poor improvise.

CONCLUSIONS

Banks combine the savings of depositors to create a capital fund for business, mortgage and consumer investments. Numbers banks mimic this rhythm, first taking in the "savings" of the poor, then returning capital to the poor community in the form of usurious loans, free loans, philanthropy and direct business investments by racketeers. Therefore, numbers gambling banks are an irregular financial institution.

Prevailing economic conditions in black neighborhoods mutely suggest that numbers banks have not provided a level of financial service sufficient to sustain economic development, even though they helped to close a gap left by the chronic malfunction of mainstream financial institutions. Numbers banking did not, therefore, represent a "sensible, strong, and adequate response to environment" (Glazer, 1971: 42). From the point of view of local economic development and collective social mobility, the numbers-loan shark system is less efficient than rotating credit associations, another financial improvisation of urban blacks (Light, 1972; Bonnett, 1976).

This explanation extends and amplifies the strictly cultural view of numbers gambling which has hitherto prevailed in sociological literature. Numbers gambling of blacks actually reflects the conjoint influence of institutional as well as cultural causes. On the institutional side, the malfunction of mainstream financial communities in low-income communities creates a financial problem. Residents reach into their cultural repertoires for solutions. The solutions they extract have consequences for the rate and character of local economic development.

The case of numbers gambling suggests that cultural and institutional causes may operate in tandem, and their segregation in sequential all-cultural or all-institutional historical phases is not an adequate resolution of their tension. Cultural repertoires offer whole or partial solutions for institutionally-induced disabilities. Therefore, the institutional disability and the cultural solution coexist. When institutions obstruct, victims cope. There is no reason to suppose that all victims' cultural repertoires contain the same remedies nor that all remedies have identical consequences. True, numbers gambling is a remedy, but a wasteful one; and the chronic malfunction of financial institutions which encouraged this remedy does not render numbers gambling a fully satisfactory alternative.

REFERENCES

Alexis, M.
1962 "Some Negro-white differences in consumption." American Journal of Economics and Sociology:11–28.
Anderson, Annelise G.
1974 The Economics of Organized Crime. Ph.D. dissertation, Columbia University.
Banfield, Edward
1974 The Unheavenly City Revisited. Boston and Toronto: Little, Brown.
Beale, David and Clifford Goldman
1974 "Background paper." Pp. 27–88 in Easy Money: Report of the Task Force on Legalized Gambling. New York: Twentieth Century Fund.
Black Enterprise
1973 "Legalized numbers." 3 (April): 41–5.
Bonnett, Aubrey W.
1976 Rotating Credit Associations among Black West Indian Immigrants in Brooklyn: An Exploratory Study. Ph.D. dissertation, City University of New York.
Booth, S. Lees (ed.)
1973 1973 Finance Facts Year Book. Washington, D.C.: National Consumer Finance Association.
Bloch, Herbert A.
1951 "The sociology of gambling." American Journal of Sociology 57:215–21.
Brimmer, Andrew F.
1971 "Small business and economic development in the Negro community." Pp. 164–72 in R. Bailey (ed.), Black Business Enterprise. New York: Basic Books.
Brown, Ed
1973 "CORE warns Harlem: beware of OTB and Howard Samuels." N. Y. Amsterdam News (March 31): A-5.
Brown, Robert
1973 "A black economist looks at the proposal." N. Y. Amsterdam News (March 31): A-5.
Caldwell, Lewis A. H.
1940 The Policy Game in Chicago. M. A. thesis, Northwestern University.
Caplovitz, David
1963 The Poor Pay More. Glencoe, Il.: Free Press.
Cargill, Thomas
1973 "Credit unions and the low-income consumer." The Journal of Consumer Affairs 7: 69–76.

Carlson, Gustav G.
1940   Number Gambling: A Study of a Culture Complex. Ph.D. dissertation, University of Michigan.

Cicarelli, James
1974   "On income, race, and consumer behavior." American Journal of Economics and Sociology 33:243–7.

Commission on the Review of National Policy toward Gambling
1975   First Interim Report. Washington, D.C.: U.S. Government Printing Office.

Congressional Record
1967   "Study of organized crime and the urban poor." 113: 24460–4.

Cook, Fred J.
1971   "The black mafia moves into the numbers racket." New York Times Magazine (April 4): 26ff.

Crapsey, Edward
1872   The Nether Side of New York. New York: Sheldon.

Cross, Theodore
1969   Black Capitalism. New York: Atheneum.

Day, George S. and William K. Brandt
1972   A Study of Consumer Credit Decisions: Implications for Present and Prospective Legislation. National Commission on Consumer Finance, Technical Studies, Vol. I.

Devereaux, Edward C., Jr.
1968   "Gambling." International Encyclopedia of the Social Sciences 6:53–62.

Dominguez, John R.
1976   Capital Flows in Minority Areas. Lexington, Ma.: Heath.

Drake, St. Clair and Horace R. Cayton
1962   Black Metropolis, 2nd ed. New York: Harper and Row, Harper Torchbooks.

Du Bois, W. E. B.
1899   The Philadelphia Negro. Philadelphia: University of Pennsylvania Publications, Series in Political Economy and Public Law.

Durkheim, Emile
[1897]   Suicide. Glencoe, Il.: Free Press.
1951

Eadington, William R.
1972   The Economics of Gambling Behavior: An Economic Analysis of Nevada's Tourist Industry. PhD. dissertation, Claremont Graduate School.

Elesh, David
1977   "Poverty theory and income maintenance: validity and policy relevance." Pp. 156–71 in Maurice Zeitlin (ed.), American Society, Inc. (2nd ed.). Chicago: Rand McNally

Ferman, Patricia R. and Louis A. Ferman
1973   "The structural underpinnings of the irregular economy." Poverty and Human Resources Abstracts 8:3–17.

Firey, Walter
1947   Land Use in Central Boston. Cambridge, Ma.: Harvard University Press.

Forman, S. E.
1906   "Conditions of living among the poor." U.S. Bureau of Labor Bulletin 64:593–698.

Foxall, G. R.
1974   "Sociology and the study of consumer behavior." American Journal of Economics and Sociology 33:127–36.

Friedman, Milton and Leonard J. Savage
1948   "The utility analysis of choices involving risk." Journal of Political Economy 16:279–304.

Fund for the City of New York
1972   Legal Gambling in New York: Discussion of Numbers and Sports Betting. New York: Fund for the City of New York.

Garvin, W. J.
1971   "The small business capital gap: the special case of minority enterprise." Journal of Finance 26:445–57.

Glazer, Nathan
1971   "The culture of poverty: the view from New York City." In J. Alan Winter (ed.), The Poor: A Culture of Poverty or a Poverty of Culture? Grand Rapids, Mi.: William B. Eerdamns.

Glazer, Nathan and Daniel P. Moynihan
1970   Beyond the Melting Pot, 2nd ed. (rev.). Cambridge: Massachusetts Institute of Technology Press.

Grow, Raymond
1939   "De king is daid." American Mercury 48:212–5.

Haller, Mark H.
1970   "Urban crime and criminal justice: the Chicago case." Journal of American History 57: 619–35.

Harris, Louis and Associates, Inc.
1970   The American Public's View of Banks and Bankers in 1970: The Findings of a Survey Conducted for the Foundation for Full Service Banks. Unpublished manuscript, Library of the Federal Deposit Insurance Corporation, Washington, D.C.
1972   The American Public's and Community Opinion Leaders' Views of Banks and Bankers in 1972. Philadelphia: Foundation for Full Service Banks.

Haugen, Carl E.
1968   "Short term financing." Pp. 95–105 in Eli Ginzberg (ed.), Business Leadership in the Negro Crisis. New York: McGraw-Hill.

Hiltz, S. Roxanne
1971   "Black and white in the consumer financial system." American Journal of Sociology 76:987–98.

Huber, Joan
1974   "Poverty, stratification, and ideology." Pp. 1–16 in Joan Huber and Peter Chalfant (eds.), The Sociology of American Poverty. Cambridge: Schenkman.

Ianni, Francis A. J.
1972   A Family Business. New York: Russell Sage.
1974   Black Mafia. New York: Simon and Schuster.

Ignatin, George and Robert Smith.
1976   "Economics of gambling." Pp. 69–91 in William Eadington (ed.), Gambling and Society. Springfield, Il.: Thomas.

Irons, Edward D.
1971 "Black banking—problems and prospects." Journal of Finance 26:407–25.

Johnson, Thomas A.
1971 "Numbers called Harlem's balm." New York Times (March 1): 1.

Kaplan, Lawrence J. and Salvatore Matteis
1968 "The economics of loan sharking." American Journal of Economics and Sociology 27:239–52.

King, Willford Isbell
1929 The Small Loan Situation in New Jersey in 1929. Trenton: New Jersey Industrial Lenders' Association.

Knudten, Richard D.
1970 Crime in a Complex Society. Homewood, Il.: Dorsey.

Koren, John
1899 Economic Aspects of the Liquor Problem. Boston and New York: Houghton Mifflin.

Kurtz, Donald V.
1973 "The rotating credit association: an adaptation to poverty." Human Organization 32:49–58.

Lasswell, Harold D. and Jeremiah B. McKenna
1972 The Impact of Organized Crime on an Inner City. Springfield, Va.: U.S. Department of Commerce, National Technical Information Service.

Leacock, Eleanor B. (ed.)
1971 The Culture of Poverty: A Critique. New York: Simon and Schuster.

Lewis, Oscar
1968 "The culture of poverty." Pp. 187–200 in Daniel P. Moynihan (ed.), On Understanding Poverty. New York: Basic Books.

Li, Wen Lang and Martin H. Smith
1976 "The propensity to gamble: some structural determinants." Pp. 189–206 in William Eadington (ed.), Gambling and Society. Springfield, Il.: Thomas.

Light, Ivan
1972 Ethnic Enterprise in America. Berkeley and Los Angeles: University of California Press.
1974 Number and Policy Gambling in New York City, 1872–1973: Guide to New York Times with Annotations. Monticello, Il.: Council of Planning Librarians.

Light, Ivan and Charles Wong
1975 "Protest or work: dilemmas of the tourist industry in American Chinatowns." American Journal of Sociology 80: 1342–68.

McCall, George J.
1963 "Symbiosis: the case of hoodoo and the numbers racket." Social Problems 10:361–7.

McKay, Claude
1940 Harlem: Negro Metropolis. New York: Dutton.

Marcum, Jess and Henry Rowen
1974 "How many games in town? The pros and cons of legalized gambling." The Public Interest 36:25–54.

Marsh, James
1971 "Viewing the loss experience in minority enterprise loans." The Bankers' Magazine 154:84–7.

Martin, Edward Winslow (James McCabe, pseud.)
1868 The Secrets of the Great City. Philadelphia: n.p.

Matza, David
1966 "The disreputable poor." Pp. 289–302 in Reinhard Bendix and Seymour Martin Lipset (eds.), Class, Status, and Power, 2nd ed. New York: Free Press.

Merton, Robert K.
1957 Social Theory and Social Structure (rev. ed.). New York: Free Press.

Neifeld, M. R.
1939 Personal Finance Comes of Age. New York and London: Harper.

Newman, Otto
1972 Gambling: Hazard and Reward. London: Athlone Press.

Nixon, Julian H.
1963 "The changing status of the Negro—some implications for savings and life insurance." The American Behavioral Scientist 6:80–2.

Ofari, Earl
1970 The Myth of Black Capitalism. New York: Monthly Review Press.

Off Track Betting Corporation (N.Y.)
1973 Legalized Numbers: A Plan to Operate a Legal Numbers Game Now. New York: Off Track Betting Corporation.

Opinion Research Corporation
1966 New Dimensions in Full Service Banking. Princeton: Foundation for Commercial Banks.

Orren, Karen
1974 Corporate Power and Social Change. Baltimore: Johns Hopkins University Press.

Ottley, Roi
1943 New World A-Coming. New York: World.

Perucci, Robert
1969 "The neighborhood 'Bookmaker': entrepreneur and mobility model." Pp. 302–11 in Paul Meadows and Ephraim H. Mizruchi (eds.), Urbanism, Urbanization, and Change: Comparative Perspectives. Reading, Ma.: Addison-Wesley.

Peterson, Virgil W.
1952 Barbarians in Our Midst. Boston: Little, Brown.

Rainwater, Lee
1967 The Moynihan Report and the Politics of Controversy. Cambridge: Masachusetts Institute of Technology Press.

Riis, Jacob A.
1892 How the Other Half Lives. New York: Scribner's.

Roebuck, Julian B.
1967 Criminal Typology. Springfield, Il.: Thomas.

Root, Anthony
1966 "On banking the social conscience." The Bankers' Magazine 155:64–6.

Rubner, Alex
1966 The Economics of Gambling. London: Macmillan.

Samuelson, Paul A.
1973   Economics. 95th ed. New York: McGraw-Hill.
Scimecca, Joseph A.
1971   "A typology of the gambler." International Journal of Contemporary Sociology 8:56–72.
Seidl, John
1968   Upon The Hip—A Study of the Criminal Loan Shark Industry. Ph.D. dissertation, Harvard University.
Selby, Edward B. and James T. Lindley
1973   "Black customers—hidden market potential." The Bankers' Magazine 156:84–7.
Sellin, Thorsten
1963   "Organized crime: a business enterprise." Annals of the American Academy of Political and Social Science 347:12–9.
Simon, Julian and Rita Simon
1968   "Class, status, and savings of Negroes." American Sociologist 3:218–9.
Stafford, James, Keith Cox and James Higginbotham
1968   "Some consumption pattern differences between urban whites and Negroes." Social Science Quarterly 49:619–30.
Stocking, Collis
1932   "Gambling." Encyclopedia of the Social Sciences, Vol. 6. London: Macmillan.
Strong, Samuel M.
1940   Social Types of the Negro Community of Chicago: An Example of the Social Type Method. Ph.D. dissertation, University of Chicago.
Sturdivant, Frederick D. (ed.)
1969   The Ghetto Marketplace. New York: Free Press.
Tec, Nechama
1964   Gambling in Sweden. Totowa, N.J.: Bedminster.

Thurner, Isidore
1956   "Ascetic Protestantism, gambling and the one-price system." American Journal of Economics and Sociology 15:161–72.
U.S. Immigration Commission
1911   Reports of the Immigration Commission. U.S. Senate, 61st Congress, 2nd Session, Document 753. Immigrant Banks. Vol. 37. Washington, D.C.: U.S. Government Printing Office.
U.S. Senate, Ninetieth Congress, 2nd Session. Committee on Banking and Currency
1968   Financial Institutions and the Urban Crisis. Washington, D.C.: U.S. Government Printing Office.
1970   Credit in Low-Income Areas. Washington, D. C.: U.S. Government Printing Office.
U.S. Senate, Ninety-Fourth Congress, 1st Session. Committee on Banking, Housing, and Urban Affairs
1975   Home Mortgage Disclosure Act of 1975, Parts 1 and 2. Washington, D.C.: U.S. Government Printing Office.
Valentine, Charles A.
1968   Culture and Poverty. Chicago: University of Chicago Press.
Warner, W. Lloyd and Buford H. Junker
1941   Color and Human Nature. Washington, D. C.: American Council on Education.
Whyte, William Foote
1943   Street Corner Society. Chicago: University of Chicago Press.
Wong, Charles
1977   "Black and Chinese grocery stores in Los Angeles' black ghetto." Urban Life 5:439 - 64.
Zetterberg, Hans
1962   Social Theory and Social Practice. New York: Bedminster.

Part V:

DELINQUENCY THEORY

Other readings in this collection treat theories of crime causation, but sociological theories are the special concern of the three in this section. Moreover, particular attention is paid to sociological theories attempting to account for the law-violating activities of young persons. David F. Greenberg shows how considering increased exclusion of young persons from the labor market, characteristic of industrial societies, helps elaborate and further specify received sociological theories about the distribution and forms of such activities. Travis Hirschi and Michael J. Hindelang test textbook claims about the lack of relation between intelligence, as measured by "IQ" schedules, and delinquency. They find these claims unfounded and further find, to their surprise, that theories of juvenile delinquency have been unaffected by the claims or, in some cases, have taken note of the ways in which intelligence may affect delinquency. Hirschi and Hindelang then show how more explicit consideration of the relationship between intelligence and delinquency, especially as mediated by school experiences, can enrich existing theories. In the portion of her book reprinted here, Ruth Rosner Kornhauser examines the assumptions about human nature, culture, society, and delinquent conduct itself underlying several of the received theories that Greenberg and Hirschi and Hindelang have elaborated.

Besides its other virtues, Greenberg's article is especially interesting in its effort to bring a macroscopic and historical perspective to bear on delinquency theories. He points to Marx as the source of this perspective, particulary, we suppose, in its emphasis on attempting to tease out the implications of the shifting situation of young persons with respect to "relations of production." As he points out, most Marxian work in criminology has either not been concerned with etiology, or has been critical of causal theories formulated in other traditions. Or, even more troublesome, it has gone little beyond asserting the importance of a larger, historically sensitive view for understanding crime and delinquency, without demonstrating how such a view might in fact enhance understanding, and without, as Greenberg especially notes, reformulating the broader view to bring it to bear on the specific subject matter at hand. While Greenberg, too, is critical of received theories, his criticism is mostly implicit, and his article consists for the most part in demonstrating how taking account of the changed position of young persons in the productive process, and the consequences of this changed position for the everyday lives of young persons, can expand theories formulated in narrower, and often less dynamic, terms.

Hirschi and Hindelang write in a different tradition; we do not mean to be perjorative in calling it the "positivist" tradition. Those familiar with recent work in criminology written from a Marxian point of view—whether called "new," "critical," or "radical"—will recognize that positivism has been its particular, self-designated anathema. It may be surprising then, at least to some of those writing in the Marxian tradition (but presumably not to Greenberg), how well what Hirschi and Hindelang find, and how they interpret what they find, about the correlations between intelligence and delinquency fits with what Greenberg says about the criminogenic qualities of school experiences for young persons. Greenberg argues that school experiences may exacerbate the already considerable problems of youth, moving them to certain forms of delinquency. Hirschi and Hindelang help specify which sectors of the youthful population may be particularly vulnerable to experiencing such problems and, implicitly at least, particularly invulnerable to such controls as exist to prevent or contain delinquent solutions to them.

Insofar as the articles by Greenberg and by Hirschi and Hindelang are representative of current work on delinquency theory, that work may be said to be in a phase of revision and refinement. One strong urge is to make it more macroscopic (to use an ugly but useful term again): to see delinquency in societal and historical perspective; to tie what is asserted about individuals and their immediate contexts such as families and schools to what can be asserted about broader contexts, such as relations between whole categories of persons, the young and the old, the rich and the poor, and the work and marketplaces that condition the formation and experiences of the persons in these categories. Another strong urge is to assemble and analyze large masses of data, something now easier with computers at hand, or to bring the results of such empirical analyses to bear on theories, if not to overturn them, then to modify and articulate them more finely. Cutting across both trends or part of them is the urge to clarify the assumptions underpinning theoretical assertions.

It will doubtless be apparent to readers that Kornhauser finds theories of delinquency employing the network of assumptions she calls the "cultural deviance model" less attractive than those founded on the assumptions of the "social disorganization model." If doubt remains, it will be dispelled by reading the rest of her quite remarkable book—which we urge readers to do. Assuming that she has correctly characterized these assumptions, it is difficult seriously to disagree with her. But we do want to register some thoughts that were generated by reflecting on her analysis. These may or may not add up to a disagreement.

Theories founded on the assumptions of the disorganization model, especially in what Kornhauser calls its "control" version, emphasize constraints on persons and the weakening of constraints. Too simply, they turn attention to forces moving persons *not* to engage in delinquent or criminal conduct. This may not be a necessary consequence of employing such theories, but we think it is a common one. Theories of the sort utilizing notions of "cultural deviance," on the other hand, turn attention to forces moving persons *to* engage in delinquent or criminal conduct; put somewhat differently, they move the analyst to consider what the delinquent or criminal is attempting to achieve; or said still another way, what the person's conduct *means* as he or she (and, indeed, as others) sees it. This may well be a necessary consequence of employing a theory based on a cultural deviance model, and in any case is, in our judgment, a useful one.

It is not clear how Kornhauser would classify the work of Greenberg (she mentions in passing that she does not deal with work in the Marxian tradition) or the work of Hirschi and Hindelang. However this may be, in both cases it is arguable that more than a little concern is given to the meaning of the conduct to be accounted for, and that this meaning, in part, is discovered by searching for norms generated by the particular, historically conditioned structural positions of the persons whose conduct is at issue. Whether these norms add up to a "culture" or a "subculture" is questionable, of course, and partly depends on what one chooses to make of these terms. Some parts of Kornhauser's work that are not reprinted here explore this question brilliantly.

The study of the delinquent activities of young persons has been a fruitful one for the development of sociological theories of law violation—more fruitful, in many ways, than the study of the criminal activities of adults. An important reason may be that, dealing with a class of persons sharing a more or less common set of experiences, sociologists have been able to do better what many are best at doing—namely, inferring what a meaningful—a human—response would be to such a set of experiences. Robert Merton's well-known theory of "anomie" is the result of just such an enterprise at a very high level of abstraction. Albert K. Cohen's deservedly famous theory of delinquency carries on that work at a more specific level, as does the work of the other theorists noted in the articles collected here. We think it is work well worth continuing and should not like to see it discarded along with less sophisticated "cultural deviance" work.

26

DELINQUENCY AND THE
AGE STRUCTURE OF SOCIETY

DAVID F. GREENBERG

Much attention has been paid in research on the causes of delinquency to the role of such variables as class, sex, and race. By comparison, the relationship between age and criminality or delinquency, though noted in passing in many studies, has received little systematic attention. This paper will present a theoretical analysis of the age distribution of criminal involvement. In particular, I will attempt to show that the increasingly disproportionate involvement of juveniles in major crime categories, though not readily explained by current sociological theories of delinquency, can be understood as a consequence of the historically changing position of juveniles in industrial societies. This changing position, I will argue, has its origin, at least in Europe and the United States, in the long term tendencies of a capitalist economic system. Although the conceptual framework for this analysis is Marxist, the approach taken appropriates Marxian theory for criminology in a way that departs from earlier Marxist writings on crime. The nature of this departure will be spelled out explicitly in the concluding section.

Age and Criminal Involvement

As can be seen from Table 1, crime-specific arrest rates in the United States show substantial variation with age. For 1970, per capita arrest rates for vandalism and property crimes not involving confrontation with a person (burglary, grand larceny, auto theft) peak at age 15–16, fall to half their peak values in two to four years, and continue to decline rapidly. Arrest rates for narcotics violations and offenses involving confrontation with a person (homicide, forcible rape, aggravated assault, robbery) peak at age 19–21 and also decline with age, but less rapidly.

Studies of recidivism show that rearrest rates for those officially labeled as offenders also decline with age [1].

From David F. Greenberg, "Delinquency and the Age Structure of Society," 1 *Contemporary Crises* 189-223 (April 1977). Copyright 1977 by Elsevier Scientific Publishing Company.

TABLE I

1970 Arrests Per 100,000 Population by Age*

OFFENSE	13 14	15	16	17	18	19	20	21	22	23	24	25–29	30–34	% under 18	% under 21
Murder and non-negligent manslaughter	3.5	13.2	20.1	25.2	35.8	35.5	35.2	*40.2*	35.3	36.6	37.8	30.7	24.4	10.2	24.5
Forcible rape	12.5	32.5	43.2	54.3	61.8	*64.7*	60.6	60.4	54.3	52.6	50.6	36.1	22.9	20.6	41.6
Robbery	164	274	340	373	393	*394*	358	346	293	250	250	154	82.5	32.2	55.3
Aggravated assault	109	189	243	272	309	317	320	*347*	328	316	*355*	284	240	17.6	30.5
Burglary	979	979	*1463*	1302	1176	968	788	697	585	527	505	320	191	50.9	69.8
Larceny over $50	2178	*2741*	*2740*	2408	2183	1788	1460	1309	1100	953	936	631	463	50.4	66.4
Auto theft	397	898	*965*	759	556	436	344	295	236	197	193	119	69.1	52.9	71.6
Vandalism	570	*613*	514	375	238	191	141	134	111	76.4	97.1	69	50.6	71.6	80.8
Narcotic drug laws	215	665	1169	1585	1971	*2073*	1187	1763	1447	1199	1039	587	312	22.0	52.2

*Arrests are based on I.B.I. statistics for 1970, population is number of males recorded in the 1970 census. The peak age in each offense category is set in italic type.

The risks in using agency-generated data to draw conclusions about group differences in rates of criminal involvement have been underscored repeatedly [2]. However, field and self-reporting studies of delinquency confirm that delinquents do abandon crime in late adolescence [3,4]. West, for example, found the average career length of his "serious thieves" to be about two years in his field study [5]. Evidence that declining arrest rates cannot be attributed to improved ability to escape apprehension is provided by Wilson [6], who found that self-reported participation in crime declined after age 15, with no relationship between age and probability of apprehension.

There is also evidence from self-reporting studies that recruitment to delinquency declines with age [7].

Already in nineteenth century United States, it had been noted that criminal involvement tended to decline with age [8], but fragmentary evidence suggests that the peak was higher than at present, and the decline gradual [9]. Tabulations of prosecutions, convictions and imprisonments for nineteenth century Europe show higher peak ages in agrarian nations like France, Italy and Austria than in industrialized nations like England [10]. The shift in arrest toward younger age brackets in recent decades in a number of other countries [11] is also suggestive of a relationship between the age distribution of crime and economic development.

In terms of delinquency theory, systematic variation in delinquent involvement with age requires explanation no less than other systematic differences. Indeed, age variation may help to test delinquency theories constructed to explain other sources of variation, such as class or sex. Since these other sources of variation can be explained in many ways, the adequacy with which rival theories explain age variation may help us to distinguish among them.

At a practical level, the rising volume of juvenile crime is creating public clamor for less lenient treatment of juvenile offenders. Intelligent response to this development requires an understanding of the social forces that have led to the increase.

Delinquency Theory and the Age Distribution of Crime

Since neither infants nor the elderly possess the prowess and agility required for some forms of crime, *some* association between age and criminal involvement can be expected on biological grounds alone. It is equally evident that the strong variation with age shown in Table 1 cannot be explained in these terms alone. Biological explanations based on other correlates of age than physical ability are equally weak. The Gluecks' proposal that delinquency may be caused by delayed maturation [12] is inconsistent with the absence of any difference in physical maturity between delinquent and non-delinquent boys of the same age [13]. Moreover, any explanation of age variation in criminality based on psychological reactions to physiological changes accompanying adolescence would be difficult to reconcile with the great variation in delinquent involvement among juveniles as well as the lateness of peak involvement in violence offenses. If age is relevant to criminality, the link should lie primarily in its social significance.

Yet contemporary sociological theories of delinquency shed little light on the relationship between crime and age. If, for example, lower class male gang delinquence is simply a manifestation of a lower class subculture as Miller [14] has maintained, it would be mysterious why 21-year-olds act in conformity with the norms of their subculture so much *less* often than their siblings just a few years younger – unless the norms themselves were age-specific. While age-specific expectations may contribute to desistance from some forms of delinquent play, such as vandalism and throwing snowballs at cars, as Clark and Haurek [15] suggest, there is no social class in which felony, theft and violence receive general *approval* for persons of any age. Moreover, adult residents of high crime areas often live in fear of being attacked by teenagers, suggesting that if delinquency is subcultural community does not form the basis of the subculture.

The difficulty of accounting for "maturational reform" within the framework of the motivational theories of Cloward and Ohlin [16] and Cohen [17] has already been noted by Matza [18]. In both theories, male delinquents cope with the problems arising from lower class status by entering into and internalizing the norms of a subculture which repudiates conventional rules of conduct and *requires* participation in crime. As with other subcultural theories, it is not at all clear why most subculture carriers abandon activities that are so highly prized within the subculture with such haste.

This desistance is doubly perplexing in anomie or opportunity theories [19] because the problem assumed to cause delinquency, namely the anticipation of failure in achieving socially inculcated success goals through legitimate means, does not disappear at the end of adolescence. At the onset of adulthood, few lower and working class youths are close to conventionally defined "success," and realization that opportunities for upward mobility are drastically limited can only be more acute. Students can perhaps entertain fantasies about their future prospects, but graduates or dropouts must come to terms with their chances. It is true that they can do this by reducing their aspirations and thus lessening anomie, but this seems to happen only slowly. According to Bachman [20], high school drop-outs' aspirations decline by about half a standard deviation over a four-year period, not fast enough to account for the rapid decline in theft involvement with age.

Cloward and Ohlin do note that many delinquents desist, but explain this in *ad hoc* terms unrelated to the main body of their theory. Writing of neighborhoods where violence is common, they assert,

> As adolescents near adulthood, excellence in the manipulation of violence no longer brings status. Quite the contrary, it generally evokes extremely negative sanctions. What was defined as permissible or tolerable behavior during adolescence tends to be sharply proscribed in adulthood. New expectations are imposed, expectations of "growing up," of taking on adult responsibilities in the economic, familial, and community spheres. The effectiveness with which these definitions are imposed is attested by the tendency among fighting gangs to decide that conflict is, in the final analysis, simply "kid stuff." . . . In other words, powerful community expectations emerge which have the consequence of closing off access to previously useful means of overcoming status deprivation [21].

In view of Cloward and Ohlin's characterization of neighborhoods where gang violence is prevalent as so disorganized that no informal social controls limiting violence can be exercised [22], one can only wonder whose age-specific expectations are being described. Cloward and Ohlin do not say. This explanation, for which Cloward and Ohlin produce no supporting evidence, is inconsistent with their own larger theory of delinquent subcultures. In addition, it seems inconsistent with the *slowness* of the decline in the violence offense categories. Since recent panel studies [23] find no support for opportunity theory, the failure of the theory to explain the age distribution of crime is not surprising.

In a departure from the emphasis placed on social class membership in most motivational theories of delinquency, Bloch and Niederhoffer [24] interpret such forms of delinquency as adolescent drinking, sexual experimentation, and "wild automobile rides" as responses to the age status problems of adolescence. Denied the prerogatives of adulthood, but encouraged to aspire to adulthood and told to "act like adults," teenagers find in these activities a symbolic substitute which presumably is abandoned as soon as the genuine article is available. As an explanation for joy-riding and some status offenses, this explanation has manifest plausibility. For other categories it is more problemmatic, since it assumes that delinquents interpret activities behaviorally associated largely with adolescence as evidence of adult stature. When Bloch and Niederhoffer turn to more serious teenage crime, their explanations are vague and difficult to interpret, but in any event seem to depend less on the structural position of the juvenile.

In *Delinquency and Drift*, Matza [25] provides an alternative approach to the explanation of desistance. His assumption that many delinquents fully embrace neither delinquent nor conventional norms and values, but instead allow themselves to be easily influenced without deep commitment, makes desistance possible when the delinquent discovers that his companions are no more committed to delinquency than he is. This discovery is facilitated by a reduction in masculinity anxiety that accompanies the attainment of adulthood. There are valuable insights in this account, but unresolved questions as well. Insofar as the discovery of a shared misunderstanding depends on chance events, as Matza suggests [26], *systematic* differences in desistance remain unexplained (I will cite evidence for such systematic differences below). Why does desistance from violence offenses occur later and more slowly than for theft offenses? Why are some juveniles so much more extensively involved in delinquency than others? Matza's remarkable presentation of the subjective elements in delinquency must be supple- mented by an analysis of more "objective," structural elements in causation if such questions are to be answered.

That is the approach I will take. Working within the tradition established by Bloch and Niederhoffer, I will present an analysis of the structural position of juveniles in American society and elaborate the implications of that position for juvenile involvement in crime. Because the focus will be on age differences, no attempt will be made to address unresolved issues in delinquency theory that have no obvious relationship to age differences (e.g. does association with delinquents follow or precede delinquent acts); however, when the theory does predict variations in delinquency *within* an age-cohort, these will be noted and compared with the available empirical data.

The theory to be presented will have two major components. The first, a theory of motivation, locates sources of motivation toward criminal involvement in the structural position of juveniles in American society. The second, derived from a control theory perspective, suggests that the willingness to act on the basis of criminal motivation is distributed unequally among age groups because the costs of apprehension are different for persons of different ages. Although some of the theoretical ideas (e.g. control theory) on which I will be drawing have already appeared in the delinquency literature, each by itself is inadequate as a full theory of delinquence. When put together with some new ideas, however, a very plausible account of age and other systematic sources of variation in delinquent involvement emerges.

Anomie and the Juvenile Labor Market

Robert Merton's discussion of anomie [27] has provided a framework for a large volume of research on the etiology of crime. Although Merton observed that a disjunction between socially inculcated goals and legitimate means available for attaining them would produce a strain toward deviance *whatever the goal* [28], specific application of the perspective to delinquency has been restricted to an assessment of the contribution to delinquency causation of the one cultural goal Merton considered in depth, namely occupational success. Cloward and Ohlin [29], for example, attribute lower class male delinquency to the anticipation of failure in achieving occupational success goals as adults. Their involvement in theft is interpreted as a strategy for gaining admission to professional theft and organized crime circles, that is, a way of obtaining the tutelage and organizational affiliations necessary for the successful pursuit of *career* crime, rather than for immediate financial return. Crime is thus seen as a means toward the attainment of *future* goals rather than *present* goals.

The assumption that delinquency is instrumentally related to the attainment of adult goals is plausible only for limited categories of delinquency, e.g. students who cheat on exams in the face of keen competition for admission to college or graduate school [30], and youths who save what they earn as pimps [31] or drug merchants [32] to capitalize investment in conventional business enterprises.

For other forms of delinquency this assumption is less tenable. Delinquents would have to be stupid indeed to suppose that shoplifting, joy-riding, burglary, robbery or drug use could bring the prestige or pecuniary rewards associated with high status lawful occupations. Nor is there evidence that most delinquents seek careers in professional theft or organized crime. In the face of Cohen's characterization of delinquents as short-run hedonists [33] and the difficulty parents and teachers encounter in attempting to engage delinquent youths in activities which could improve chances of occupational success (like school homework), the future orientation assumed in opportunity theory is especially farfetched.

The potential explanatory power of anomie theory, is, however, not exhausted by Cloward and Ohlin's formulation, because delinquency can be a response to a discrepancy between aspirations and expectations for the attainment of goals other than occupational ones. Most people have a multiplicity of goals, and only some of them are occupational. As the salience of different life goals can vary with stage of the life-cycle, our understanding of delinquency may be advanced more by an examination of those goals given a high priority by adolescents than by considering the importance attached to different goals in American culture generally.

The literature on youth reports a consensus that the transition from childhood to adolescence is marked by a heightened sensitivity to the expectations of peers, and concommitantly, a reduced concern with the fulfillment of parental expectations [34]. High value comes to be attached to popularity with peers, and exclusion from the most popular cliques becomes the occasion for acute psychological distress.

Adolescent peer groups and orientation to the expectations of peers are found in many societies [35]. In American society, the natural tendency of those who share common experiences and problems to prefer one another's company is accentuated by the importance parents and school attach to popularity and to the development of the social skills they believe will be necessary for later occupational success [36]. In addition, the exclusion of young people from adult work and leisure activity forces adolescents into virtually exclusive association with one another, cutting them off from alternative sources of validation for the self (as well as reducing the degree of adult supervision). A long run trend toward increased age segregation created by changing patterns of work and education has increased the vulnerability of teenagers to the expectations and evaluations of their peers [37].

This dependence on peers for approval is not itself criminogenic. In many tribal societies, age-homogeneous bands of youths are functionally integrated into the economic and social life of the tribe and are not considered deviant [38]. In America, too, many teenage clubs and cliques are not delinquent. Participation in teenage social life, however, requires resources. In addition to personal assets and skills (having an attractive appearance and "good personality," being a skilled conversationalist, being able to memorize song lyrics and learn dance steps, and in some circles, being able to fight), money is needed to purchase clothing, cosmetics, cigarettes, alcoholic beverages, narcotics, phonograph records, transistor radios, gasoline for cars and motorcycles, tickets to films and concerts, meals in restaurants [39], and for gambling. The progressive detachment of teenage social life from that of the family and the emergence of advertising directed toward a teenage market (this being a creation of postwar affluence for major sections of the population and the "baby boom") have increased the importance of these goods to teenagers and hence have inflated the costs of their social activities.

When parents are unable or unwilling to subsidize their children's social life at the level required by local convention, when children want to prevent their parents from learning of their expenditures, or when they are reluctant to incur the obligations created by taking money from their parents, alternative sources of funds must be sought. Full or part-time employment once constituted such an alternative.

The long-run, persistent decline in teenage employment and labor force participation has progressively eliminated this alternative. During the period from 1870 to 1920, many states passed laws restricting child labor and establishing compulsory education. Despite a quadrupling of the "gainfully employed" population from 1870 to 1930, the number of gainfully employed workers in the 10–15 year-old age bracket *declined*. The Great

Depression resulted in a further contraction of the teenage labor force and increased the school-leaving age [40]. Only in 1940 did the U.S. government stop counting all persons over the age of 10 as part of the labor force [41]. In recent years, teenage labor market deterioration has been experienced mainly by black teenagers. From 1950 to 1973, black teenage labor force participation declined from 67.8% to 34.7%, while white teenage labor force participation remained stable at about 63%. The current recession has increased teenage unemployment in the 16–19 year old age bracket to about 20%, with the rate for black teenagers being twice as high [42].

This process has left teenagers less and less capable of financing an increasingly costly social life whose importance is enhanced as the age segregation of society grows. Adolescent theft then occurs as a response to the disjunction between the desire to participate in social activities with peers and the absence of legitimate sources of funds needed to finance this participation.

Qualitative evidence supporting this explanation of adolescent theft is found in those delinquency studies that describe the social life of delinquent groups. Sherif and Sherif noted in their study of adolescent groups that theft was often instrumentally related to the group's leisure time social activities.

> In several groups. . . , stealing was not the incidental activity that it was in others. It was regarded as an acceptable and necessary means of getting needed possessions, or, more usually, cash. Members of the aforementioned groups frequently engaged in theft when they were broke, usually selling articles other than clothing, and *often using the money for group entertainment and treats* [43].

Carl Werthman reports that among San Francisco delinquents:

> Shoplifting . . . was viewed as a more instrumental activity, as was the practice of stealing coin changers from temporarily evacuated buses parked in a nearby public depot. In the case of shoplifting, most of the boys wanted and wore the various items of clothing they stole; and when buses were robbed, either the money was divided among the boys, or it was used to buy supplies for a party being given by the club [44].

Studies of urban delinquent gangs or individuals in England [45], Israel [46], Sweden [47], Taiwan [48] Holland [49] and Argentina [50] present a uniform picture: unemployed or employed but poorly paid male youths steal to support their leisure-time, group-centered social activities.

Joseph Weis' study of middle class delinquency using self-reports [51] is also consistent with the interpretation of adolescent theft presented here. Using key cluster analysis, Weis extracted three distinct factors from the correlation matrix for involvement in different forms of delinquency for the males in the sample. These oblique factors could be characterized as social, property, and aggression. The analysis for girls produced two factors: there was no aggression factor, while the other two factors were very similar to the social and property factors among the boys. For both boys and girls, the correlation between the oblique factor domains for social offenses (drinking, marijuana use, curfew violations, gambling use of false I.D. cards, drag racing, and similar offenses) and for property offenses (theft, burglary, shoplifting, etc.) was positive and moderately strong, as would be predicted if thefts are undertaken to finance peer-related social activities.

On the reasoning presented here, strain should be experienced most acutely by teenagers who are unable to achieve popularity on the basis of personal attributes and who lack alternative sources of self-esteem (e.g. school success or warm relationships with parents). Indeed, teenagers in this position may attempt to win friends by spending money on them [52]. Evidence that unpopular boys are more likely to become delinquent [53], and that delinquents tend to have unsatisfactory relations with peers [54] and parents [55] is consistent with my argument.

Where parents subsidize their children adequately, the incentive to steal is obviously reduced. Because the cost of social life can increase with class position, a strong correlation between social class membership and involvement in theft is not necessarily predicted. Insofar as self-reporting studies suggest that the correlation between participation in nonviolent forms of property acquisition and parental socio-economic status is not very high [56], this may be a strong point for my theory. By contrast the theories of Cohen, Miller, and Cloward and Ohlin all clash with the self-reporting studies.

In view of recent suggestions that increases in female crime and delinquency are linked with changing gender roles (of which the women's liberation movement is taken either as a cause or a manifestation), it is of interest to note that the explanation of adolescent theft presented here is applicable to boys and girls, and in particular, allows for female delinquency in support of *traditional* gender roles related to peer involvement.

Weis' work is consistent with this interpretation, as are differences in the forms of theft boys and girls undertake. Boys, who traditionally have paid girls' expenses on dates and therefore have a greater need for cash, are more likely to rob or to burglarize homes and stores, taking items for resale, while girls more often steal items (such as clothing and cosmetics) for personal use.

Increases in female crime which have occurred largely in those forms of theft in which female involvement has traditionally been high [57] are thus more plausibly attributed to the same deteriorating economic position in the face of escalating costs of social life that males confront. than to changes in gender role.

As teenagers get older. their vulnerability to the expectations of peers is reduced by institutional involvements that provide alternative sources of self-esteem: moreover. opportunities for acquiring money legitimately expand. Both processes reduce the motivation to engage in acquisitive forms of delinquent behavior. Consequently. involvement in theft should fall off rapidly with age. and it does.

Delinquency and the School

My explanation of juvenile theft in terms of structural obstacles to legitimate sources of funds at a time when peer-oriented leisure activities require access to financial resources implicitly characterizes this form of delinquency as instrumentally rational: the theory assumes that money and goods are stolen because they are useful. Acts of vandalism. thefts in which stolen objects are abandoned or destroyed. and interpersonal violence not necessary to accomplish a theft cannot be explained in this way. These are the activities that led Albert Cohen to maintain that much delinquency is "malicious" and "non-utilitarian" [58] and to argue that the content of the delinquent subculture arose in the lower class male's reaction to failure in schools run according to middle class standards.

Although Cohen can be criticized for not indicating the criteria used for assessing rationality – indeed. for failure to find out from delinquents themselves what they perceived the goals of their destructive acts to be – and though details of Cohen's theory (to be noted below) appear to be inaccurate. his observation that delinquency may be a response to school problems need not be abandoned. Indeed. the literature proposing a connection between one or another aspect of school and delinquency is voluminous [59]. I will concentrate on two features of the school experience. its denial of student autonomy and its subjection of some students to the embarrassment of public degradation ceremonies.

In all spheres of life outside the school. and particularly within the family. children more or less steadily acquire larger measures of personal autonomy as they mature. Over time. the "democratization" of the family has reduced the age at which given levels of autonomy are acquired. The gradual extension of freedom that normally takes place in the family (not without struggle!) is not accompanied by parallel deregulation at school. Authoritarian styles of teaching. and rules concerning such matters as smoking, hair styles. manner of dress, going to the bathroom, and attendance, come into conflict with expectations students derive from the relaxation of controls in the family [60]. The delegitimation of hierarchical authority structures accomplished by the radical movements of the 1960s has sharpened student awareness of this contradiction.

The symbolic significance attached to autonomy exacerbates the inherently onerous burden of school restrictions. Parents and other adults invest age-specific rights and expectations with moral significance by disapproving "childish" behavior and by using privileges to reward behavior they label "mature." Because of this association. the deprivation of autonomy is experienced as "being treated like a baby." that is, as a member of a disvalued age-status.

All students are exposed to these restrictions. and to some degree, all probably resent them. For students who are at least moderately successful at their schoolwork. who excel at sports. participate in extra-curricular school activities. or who are members of popular cliques, this resentment is likely to be more than compensated by rewards associated with school attendance. These students tend to conform to school regulations most of the time. rarely collide with school officials. and are unlikely to feel overtly hostile to school or teachers. Students who are unpopular, and whose academic record, whether from inability or disinterest, is poor, receive no comparable compensation. For them, school can only be a frustrating experience: it brings no current gratification and no promise of future pay-off. Why then should they put up with these restrictions? These students often get into trouble, and feel intense hostility to the school.

Social class differences must of course be taken into account. Pre-adolescent and early adolescent middle and upper class children are supervised more closely than their working class counterparts. and thus come to expect and accept adult authority, while working class youths, who enter an unsupervised street life among peers at an early age have more autonomy to protect. and guard their prerogatives jealously [61]. To the extent that they see in the school's denial of their autonomy preparation for a future in occupations that also deny autonomy, and see in their parents' lives the psychic costs of that denial. they may be more prone to rebel than middle-class students, who can generally anticipate entering jobs that allow more discretion and autonomy.

Middle class youths also have more to gain by accepting adult authority than their working class counterparts. Comparatively affluent parents can control their children better because they have more resources they can withhold, and are in a better position to secure advantages for their children. Likewise, children who believe that their future chances depend on school success may conform regardless of whether they reject close regulation intellectually. Where returns on school success are reduced by class or racial discrimination, the school loses this source of social control. It similarly loses control over upper class children, whose inherited class position frees them from the necessity of doing well in school to guarantee their future economic status.

Only a few decades ago, few working class youths – or school failures with middle class family backgrounds – would have been exposed to a contradiction between their expectations of autonomy and the school's attempts to control them because a high proportion of students, especially working class students, left school at an early age. However, compulsory school attendance, low wages and high unemployment rates for teenagers, and increased educational requirements for entry-level jobs have greatly reduced dropout rates. Thus in 1920, 16.8% of the 17 year-old population were high school graduates; and in 1956, 62.3% [62]. In consequence, a greater proportion of students, especially those who benefit least from school, is exposed to this contradiction.

Common psychological responses to the irritation of the school's denial of autonomy range from affective disengagement to the school ("tuning out" the teacher) to smouldering resentment, and at the behavioral level from truancy to self-assertion through the flouting of rules. Such activities as getting drunk, using drugs, joy-riding, truanting, and adopting eccentric styles of dress, apart from any intrinsic gratification these activities may provide, can be seen as forms of what Gouldner has called "conflictual validation of the self" [63]. By helping students establish independence from authority (school, parental, etc.), these activities contribute to self-regard. Their attraction lies in their being forbidden.

As a status system, the school makes further contributions to the causation of delinquency. Almost by definition, status systems embody invidious distinctions. Where standards of evaluation are shared, and position is believed to reflect personal merit, occupants of lower statuses are likely to encounter problems in maintaining self-esteem [64]. The problem is somewhat alleviated by a strong tendency to restrict intimate association to persons of similar status. If one's associates are at roughly the same level as oneself, they provide the standards for self-evaluation [65]. In addition, "democratic" norms of modesty discourage the flaunting of success and boasting of personal merit, thereby insulating the less successful from an implied attribution of their failures to their own deficiencies.

These norms are not, however, universal in applicability. In our society, certification as a full-fledged social member is provided those whose commitment to the value of work and family is documented by spouse, home, car and job (for women, children have traditionally substituted for job). Institutional affiliations are thus taken as a mark of virtue, or positive stigma. Those who meet these moral tests are accorded standards of respect in face-to-face interaction not similarly accorded members of unworthy or suspect categories – e.g. prison and psychiatric hospital inmates, skid row bums, the mentally retarded, and unaccompanied women on the streets of New York. In particular, members are permitted to sustain self-presentations as dignified, worthy persons, regardless of what may be thought or said of them in private [66]. Students, however, especially failing students and those with lower class or minority origins, are accorded no comparable degree of respect. As they lack the appropriate institutional affiliations, their moral commitment to dominant institutions of society is suspect. In this sense, they are social strangers; we don't quite know what we can expect from them. They are, moreover, relatively powerless. In consequence, they are exposed to evaluations from which adults are ordinarily shielded.

This is especially true at school, where school personnel continuously communicate their evaluations of students through grades, honor rolls, track positions, privileges, and praise for academic achievement and proper deportment. On occasion, the negative evaluation of students conveyed by the school's ranking systems is supplemented by explicit criticism and denunciation on the part of teachers who act as if the academic performance of failing students could be elevated by telling them they are stupid, or lazy, or both. Only the most extreme failures in the adult world are subjected to degradation ceremonies of this kind.

The feelings of students subjected to this form of status derogation are well captured by a high school student describing a conversation with his school principal.

> I told him that the teacher was always trying to "put me down" in front of the class. I told him that the teacher knew I didn't like math so why did he keep calling on me just to "put me down," to make me look bad. I'm not as dumb as he thinks so I "turned it around" on him and got the class to laugh at him. See how he likes being the fool. The principal said I was a wise guy, thought I was a "smart alec." He said that what I needed was a good old-fashioned talk behind the wood shed. I told him "Who're you going get to do it; better not try or somebody is going to get hurt, bad!" Man he turned white and started to shake. "You're suspended for threatening a school official." That's good, I said, this school, this school ain't worth a shit anyway [67].

Cohen [68] has argued that working class youths faced with this situation protect their self-esteem by rejecting conventional norms and values. Seeking out one another for mutual support, they create a delinquent subculture of opposition to middle-class norms in which they can achieve status. This subculture is seen as supporting the non-utilitarian acts of destructiveness that alleviate frustration.

There is little difficulty in finding evidence of adolescent destructiveness, however the choice of target may be more rational than Cohen allows. The large and growing volume of school vandalism and assaults on teachers indicate that delinquents often do see the school in antagonistic terms. Other targets, too may be chosen for clear reasons. In his study of gang violence, Miller found that,

> Little of the deliberately inflicted property damage represented a diffuse outpouring of accumulated hostility against arbitrary objects; in most cases the gang members injured the possession of properties of particular persons who had angered them, as a concrete expression of that anger (defacing automobile of mother responsible for having gang member committed to correctional institution; breaking windows of settlement house after eviction therefrom). There was thus little evidence of 'senseless' destruction; most property damage was directed and repressive [69].

Other targets may be chosen because of their symbolic value, e.g. membership in a despised racial group or class stratum, or in the adult world, which represents repressive authority. It is not unlikely that an unanticipated consequence of recent black nationalist movements has been an increase in crimes by minority group members that victimize whites.

Empirical research suggests the need for revision of other components of Cohen's theory as well. Delinquents do not necessarily reject conventional values or career goals except when in the presence of their peers [70]. A modern society contains numerous status systems that are not in competition with one another; acceptance of one need not require repudiation of others. In particular, students who do not reject the value system endorsed by parents and school officials but who do not succeed in its terms can nevertheless accept the value system of a subculture of delinquency (in the sense of Matza [71]) as a "second best" alternative on pragmatic grounds.

Self-reporting studies of delinquency indicate the association between class and most forms of delinquency to be weaker than Cohen supposed. School failure, though class-linked, is not the monopoly of any class, and the self-esteem problems of middle class youths who fail are not necessarily any less than those of working class schoolmates. Since parental expectations for academic achievement may be higher in middle class families, and since school failure may auger downward mobility, these problems could conceivably be worse. If delinquency restores self esteem lost through school failure, it may serve this function for students of all class backgrounds.

The impact of school degradation ceremonies is not limited to their effect on students' self-esteem. When a student is humiliated by a teacher the student's attempt to present a favorable self to schoolmates is undercut. Even students whose prior psychological disengagement from the value system of the school leaves their self-esteem untouched by a teacher's disparagement may react with anger at being embarrassed before peers. The high school student quoted earlier complained of being ridiculed *in front of his class*. It is the situation of being in the company of others whose approval is needed for self-esteem that makes it difficult* for teenagers to ignore humiliation that older individuals, with alternative sources of self-esteem, could readily ignore.

Visible displays of independence from, or rejections of authority can be understood as attempts to re-establish moral character in the face of affronts. This can be accomplished by direct attacks on teachers or school, or through daring illegal performances elsewhere. These responses may or may not reflect anger at treatment perceived to be unjust, may or may not defend the student against threats to self-esteem, may or may not reflect a repudiation of conventional conduct norms. What is crucial is that these activities *demonstrate* retaliation for injury and the rejection of official values to an audience whose own resentment of constituted authority causes it to be appreciative of rebels whom it would not necessarily dare to imitate. Secret delinquency and acts that entailed no risk would not serve this function.

Field research on the interaction between teachers ,and delinquent students [72] and responses of delinquent gangs and individuals to challenges to honor [73] support this dramaturgical interpretation of delinquency. Most gang violence seems not to erupt spontaneously out of anger, but is chosen and manipulated for its ability to impress others. Nonutilitarian forms of theft, property destruction and violence may well be understood as quite utilitarian if their purpose is the establishment or preservation of the claim to be a certain sort of person, rather than the acquisition of property.

Goffman [74] has called attention to the common features of activities in which participants establish moral character through risk-taking. Such activities as dueling, bull fighting, sky diving, mountain climbing, big game hunting, and gambling for high stakes are undertaken for the opportunity they provide to carve out a valued social identity by exhibiting courage, daring, pluck and composure.

These qualities are those the industrial system (factory and school) tend to disvalue or ignore: the concept of seeking out risks and "showing off" is antithetical to the traditional ethos of capitalism, where the emphasis has been placed on minimizing risk, using time productively, and suppressing the self to demonstrate moral character. Consequently, participants In action systems based on displays of risk-taking have traditionally been drawn primarily from classes not subject to the discipline and self-denial of industrial production, e.g. the European nobility, bohemian populations, and the unemployed poor.

More recently, as production has come to require less sacrifice and self-denial from large sectors of the work force, and to require the steady expansion of stimulated consumption for its growth, the more affluent sectors of the labor force are increasingly encouraged to seek an escape from the routinicity of daily life through mild forms of risk-taking (e.g. gambling and skiing) as well as through the leisure use of drugs and sex.

The similarity between the subculture of delinquency and that of the leisurely affluent [75] makes sense in view of the position of the delinquent *vis à vis* the school. Like the factory, the school frequently requires monotonous and meaningless work. Regimentation is the rule. Expressions of originality and spontaneity are not only discouraged, but may be punished [76]. Students who reap no present rewards from school work or anticipate only the most limited occupational rewards in return for subordinating themselves to the discipline of the school are free to cultivate the self-expressive traits which the school fails to reward. As Downes [77] has pointed out, they may come to regard adults who work as defeated and lifeless because of their subordination to a routine that necessitates self-suppression, and hence try to avoid work because of the cost in self-alienation.

Traditionally this has been especially true of students with lower class backgrounds; Finestone [78] has described their adaptation and Rainwater [79] has interpreted the expressive features of lower class black male urban culture in these terms. However, when the political and occupational sectors of society lose their legitimacy, students of other classes may find the prospect of entering conventional careers in those sectors so repugnant that they lose the motivation to achieve in school, and also cultivate life styles based on self-expression or politically motivated risk-taking. The bright hippies and radicals from white middle-class backgrounds in the late 1960s are a case in point.

The similarity between delinquent and non-criminal recreational risk-taking warns us that the pursuit of status through risk-taking need not *necessarily* arise from problems in self-esteem. Once a status system rewarding delinquent activity exists, students may act with reference to it in order to *increase* prestige in the group, not only to prevent prestige from falling. Thus teachers may be provoked [80], gang rivals taunted, and daring thefts and assaults perpetrated, even in the absence of humiliation.

When students drop out or graduate from high school, they enter a world that, while sometimes inhospitable, does not restrict their autonomy and assault their dignity in the same way the school does. The need to engage in crime to establish a sense of an autonomous self, and to preserve moral character through risk-taking is thus reduced. In addition, the sympathetic audience of other students of the same age is taken away. Thus school-leaving eliminates major sources of motivation toward delinquency.

In this respect, it is especially ironic that delinquency prevention programs have involved campaigns to extend the duration of schooling. American panel studies indicate that the self-esteem of dropouts rises after leaving school [81] and that dropping out produces an immediate decline in delinquency [82]. In England, when the school-leaving age was raised by one year, the peak age for delinquency also rose simultaneously by one year [83].

Despite this evidence that the school contributes to delinquency, it is hardly necessary. In Cordoba, Argentina, patterns of delinquency are fairly similar to those in the United States even though the school-leaving age for working-class children is 10, and delinquents report generally favorable attitudes toward school [84]. Unsatisfactory school experiences simply add to the economic motivations created by the exclusion of juveniles from the labor market.

Masculine Status Anxiety and Delinquency

Many observers have remarked on the disproportionate involvement of males in delinquent activity and the exaggerated masculine posturing that characterizes much male delinquency. Though sex differences in delinquency are not as pronounced in self-report studies as in arrest reports, and seem to be gradually narrowing, they nevertheless remain considerable, especially in the violence offense categories. Theoretical explanations for these differences not based on innate sex differences have alternatively emphasized differences in the socialization of boys and girls, which lead to differences in gender role [85], and "masculine protest" against maternal domination and identification [86]. especially in the female-based households of the lower class [87]. In such households, the argument goes, boys will tend to identify with the mother, and hence will experience uncertainty and anxiety in later years in connection with their identification as a male. To allay this anxiety, they reject the "good" values of the mother and engage in "masculine" forms of delinquency.

Application of the theory to delinquency in the United States has not been entirely successful. Male delinquency does appear to be associated with what has been interpreted as anxiety over masculinity, but is independent of whether the household in which the child is raised lacked an adult male [88].

This finding points to the need for a revision in the argument.

Hannerz [89] has pointed out that children raised in homes without fathers may still have alternative male role models. Indeed, children raised in a community where adult male unemployment rates are high may spend more of their time in the company of adult males who could serve as role models than their middle class peers. I would argue, in addition, that Miller's adherence to the psycho-analytic framework blinds him to important sources of anxiety connected with masculinity that are unrelated to the family configuration in early childhood. Males who are not in doubt about their identity as males may nevertheless feel anxiety in connection with anticipated or actual inability to fulfill traditional sex role expectations concerning work and support of family. This masculine *status* anxiety can be generated by a father who is present but ineffectual, and by living in a neighborhood where, for social-structural reasons, many men are unemployed — regardless of whether one's own father is present in the household.

Men who experience such anxiety because they are prevented from fulfilling conventional male role expectations may attempt to alleviate their anxiety by exaggerating those traditionally male traits that *can* be expressed. Attempts to dominate women (including rape) and patterns of interpersonal violence can be seen in these terms. In other words, crime can be a response to masculine status anxiety no less than to anxiety over male identity; it can provide a sense of potency that is expected and desired but not achieved in other spheres of life.

In this interpretation, a compulsive concern with toughness and masculinity arises not from a hermetically sealed lower-class subculture "with an integrity of its own" nor from the psychodynamics of a female-headed household [90] but as a response to a contradiction between structural constraints on male status attainment imposed by the larger economic and political order, and the cultural expectations for men that permeate American society. The role of the subculture Miller describes is to make available the behavioral adaptations that previous generations have developed in response to this contradiction, and thus to shape those responses. We should therefore expect persons suffering from masculine status anxiety who were members of groups in which the structural sources of masculine status anxiety have been common and long-standing to develop more coherent and stereotyped adaptations than individuals who were not members of such groups, e.g. in lower class blacks as compared with recently unemployed white collar employees [91]. We should also expect those adaptations to attenuate in groups that ceased to encounter such contradictions, either because structural constraints to the fulfillment of traditional role expectations had been eliminated, or because expectations for men in the larger society had changed.

If I am correct in assuming that delinquents in the last years of elementary school and early years of high school are not excessively preoccupied with their occupational prospects, but become more concerned with their futures toward the end of high school — and there is some qualitative evidence to support this assumption [92] — then masculine anxiety during these early years must stem from other sources. One plausible source lies in the contradiction between the school's expectations of docility and submission to authority, and more widely communicated social expectations of masculinity. While the school represses both boys and girls, the message that girls get is consistent; the message boys receive is contradictory. This difference would help to explain sex differences in delinquency in early adolescence.

Most of the behavior that can be explained plausibly in this way — smoking, sexual conquests, joy-riding, vandalism, fighting between boys — is fairly trivial, and either becomes legal in mid to late adolescence, or abates rapidly. Anxiety over inability to fulfill traditional male occupational roles would show up late in adolescence. If I am correct in holding that such anxiety is an important source of criminal violations, the ratio of male to female participation should increase with age during adolescence, and there is evidence from self-reports that it does, at least among middle class youths [93].

One would expect masculine status anxiety to appear with greatest intensity and to decline most slowly in those segments of the population in which adult male unemployment is exceptionally high. This conforms to the general pattern of arrests for violence offenses such as homicide, forcible rape and assaults — offenses often unconnected with the pursuit of material gain, and hence most plausibly interpreted as a response to masculine status anxiety. Rates of arrest for these offenses peak in the immediate post-high school age brackets (several years later than for the property offenses) and the decline is slower than for property offenses. Moreover, blacks are over-represented in violence offense arrests to a much greater degree than in arrests for property offenses. Thus in 1973, the ratio of black to white arrests for burglary, larceny and auto theft was 0.45; for non-negligent homicide, forcible rape and aggravated assault, 0.85; for robbery, 1.79 [94]. This relative over-representation of blacks is confirmed in victimization studies [95] and in self-reporting studies of delinquency [96] and thus cannot be explained as a manifestation of racial differences in risk of apprehension.

Costs of Delinquency

So far some possible sources of variation with age in motivation to participate in common forms of criminal activity have been identified, but this is only half the story, for one may wish to engage in some form of behavior but nevertheless decide not to do so because the potential costs of participation are deemed unacceptably high. Costs can be a consequence of delinquency, and must be taken into account. Control theorists have begun to do so [97].

Costs can originate with internal or external sources of control. Superego restraints and favorable self-concepts and ideals exemplify internal sources of control [98]; they threaten the potential delinquent with guilt and shame. External costs can include parental disapproval and loss of privileges, school-imposed sanctions (ranging from teacher's disapproval to suspension or expulsion), loss of job and reduced prospects for future employment, acquisition of a police or juvenile court record, and deprivation of freedom through a reformatory sentence. Although external costs are actually imposed only on those who are caught, fear of incurring costs can inhibit potential delinquents and lead actual delinquents to desist.

To what extent can internal or external costs contribute to the age distribution of criminality? With the exception of those forms of minor delinquency considered far more discrediting to adults than to juveniles [99], it is unlikely that *internal* controls play a major role in generating age *differences* in criminal involvement, for it seems unlikely that moral inhibitions substantially increase from mid to late adolescence. Indeed, we generally expect people to take a more pragmatic view of morality as they get older.

External costs, however, are likely to vary with age. In early adolescence the potential costs of all but the most serious forms of delinquency are relatively slight. Parents and teachers are generally willing to write off a certain amount of misbehavior as "childish mischief," while enormous caseloads have forced juvenile courts in large cities to adopt a policy that comes very close to what Schur [100] has called "radical nonintervention" for all but the most serious cases. Moreover, the confidentiality of juvenile court records reduces the extent to which prospects are jeopardized by an arrest.

Given the slight risk of apprehension for any single delinquent act, the prevalence of motivations to violate the law, and the low costs of lesser violations, we should expect minor infractions to be common among juveniles, and the self-reporting studies generally suggest that they are. Where the risk of incurring costs does procure abstention, we should suppose fear of parental disapproval would be the most salient. Teenagers who have good relationships with parents would presumably be the most concerned with incurring their disapproval, and they do have lower rates of involvement in delinquency [101].

As teenagers get older, the potential costs of apprehension increase: victims may be more prone to file a complaint, and police to make an arrest.

Juvenile court judges are more likely to take a serious view of an older offender, especially one with a prior record. Older offenders risk prosecution in criminal court, where penalties tend to be harsher, and where an official record will have more serious consequences for later job opportunities.

Delinquents are acutely sensitive to these considerations. According to several youthful offenders testifying before the New York State Select Committee at a hearing on assault and robbery against the elderly,

> If you're 15 and under you won't go to jail ... That's why when we do a "Rush and Crib" – which means you rush the victim and push him or her into their apartment, you let the youngest member do any beatings. See, we know if they arrest him, he'll be back on the street in no time [102].

In interviews, former delinquents often attribute their own desistance to their unwillingness to risk the stiffer penalties they would receive if arrested and tried as adults [103]. Thus the leniency of the juvenile court contributes to high levels of juvenile crime.

Just as the costs of crime are escalating, new opportunities in the form of jobs, marriage, or enlistment in the armed forces create stakes in conformity and as Matza points out [104], may also relieve problems of masculine status anxiety. Toward the end of high school, when student concern about the future increases, the anticipation of new opportunities is manifested in desistance from delinquency and avoidance of those who do not similarly desist. Consistent with this interpretation is the fact that in both England and the United States, the peak year for delinquent involvement is the year *before* school-leaving.

Labeling theorists have tended to emphasize the role that apprehension and official processing of delinquents may play in increasing their subsequent delinquent involvement, either through the effect of labeling on self-concept and attitudes [105] or because prospects for legitimate employment are jeopardized through stigmatization [106]. The evidence available does not suggest that this happens to any great extent [107]. This is not necessarily surprising. As Schur [108] has pointed out, children may develop psychological defenses that serve to neutralize the discrediting imputations of others. When the negative label is applied by adults who are perceived as antagonists (police, judges, jailers) it should not be difficult to avoid being deeply influenced by their evaluations. Moreover, the confidentiality of juvenile court records helps to shield delinquents from later stigma.

Those whose opportunities for lucrative employment are limited by obstacles associated with racial and/or class membership will have far less reason to desist from illegal activity than those whose careers are not similarly blocked. The kinds of jobs available to young members of the lower strata of the working class tend to be tedious and financially unrewarding (when they are available at all). Marriage may appear less appealing to young men whose limited prospects promise inability to fulfill traditional male expectations as breadwinner. Even an army career may be precluded by an arrest record, low intelligence test scores, physical disability, or illiteracy. Thus the legitimate opportunity structure, even if relatively useless for understanding entrance into delinquency, may still be helpful in understanding patterns of desistance.

The same may be said of the illegal opportunity structure. Those few delinquents who are recruited into organized crime or professional theft face larger rewards and less risk of serious penalty than those not so recruited, and their personal relationships with partners may be more satisfying. They should be less likely to desist from crime, but their offense patterns can be expected to change.

This reasoning suggests that the association between criminal involvement on the one hand and race and class on the other should be stronger for adults than for juveniles. If this is so, arrest rates in a given offense category should decline more rapidly for whites and youths with middle class backgrounds than for blacks and youths with working class and lower class backgrounds. In the male birth cohort studied by Wolfgang, Figlio and Sellin, whites were more likely to desist after an offense [109]. F.B.I. crime career data also suggest higher rearrest rates for blacks than for whites [110] and a number of studies of recidivism of released prisoners have found somewhat higher recidivism among black ex-prisoners than among white ex-prisoners. Though based on small samples, Chambliss' field study of delinquency [111] does indicate a much higher desistance rate for middle class delinquents.

If, as is often suggested, crimes of violence involve less reflection and deliberation than crimes of acquisition, violence offenses should respond less elastically to increased external costs than property offenses. For this reason, we should expect violence crime rates to decline less rapidly with age than property crime rates, and this prediction is verified (see Table I).

Delinquency and the Social Construction of the Juvenile

Among the structural sources of adolescent crime identified here, the exclusion of juveniles from the world of adult work plays a crucial role. It is this exclusion that simultaneously exaggerates teenagers' dependence on peers for approval and eliminates the possibility of their obtaining funds to support their intensive, leisure-time social activities. The disrespectful treatment students receive in school depends on their low social status, which in turn reflects their lack of employment. In late adolescence and early adulthood, their fear that this lack of employment will persist into adulthood evokes anxiety over achievement of traditional male gender role expectations, especially among males in the lower levels of the working class, thus contributing to a high level of violence.

Institutionalized leniency to juvenile offenders, which reduces the potential costs of delinquency, stems from the belief that teenagers are not as responsible for their actions as adults [112]. The conception of juveniles as impulsive and irresponsible gained currency around the turn of the century (see for example, Hall [113]) when organized labor and Progressive reformers campaigned for child labor laws to save jobs for adults, a goal given high priority after the Depression of 1893. This conception was, in a sense, self-fulfilling. Freed from ties to conventional institutions, teenagers *have* become more impulsive and irresponsible.

The exclusion of teenagers from serious work is not characteristic of all societies. Peasant and tribal societies could not afford to keep their young idle as long as we do. In such societies, juvenile crime rates were low. Under feudalism, too, children participated in farming and handicraft production as part of the family unit beginning at a very early age.

In depriving masses of serfs and tenant farmers of access to the means of production (land), European capitalism in its early stages of development generated a great deal of crime, but in a manner that cut across age boundaries. Little of the literature on crime in Elizabethan and Tudor England singles out juveniles as a special category.

The industrial revolution in the first half of the nineteenth century similarly brought with it a great deal of misery, but its effect on crime was not restricted to juveniles. Children of the working class in that period held jobs at an early age and in some sectors of the economy were given preference. Only middle and upper class children were exempt from the need to work, and they were supervised much more closely than they are nowadays. As far as can be judged, juvenile crime in that period was a much smaller fraction of the total than at present, and was more confined to the lower classes than it is now [114].

In modern capitalist societies, children of all classes share, for a limited period, a common relationship to the means of production (namely exclusion) which is distinct from that of most adults, and they respond to their common structural position in fairly similar ways. Although there are class differences in the extent and nature of delinquency, especially violent delinquency, these are less pronounced than for adults, for whom occupational differentiation is much sharper.

The deteriorating position of juveniles in the labor market in recent years has been ascribed to a variety of causes, among them the inclusion of juveniles under minimum wage laws, changes in the structure of the economy (less farm employment), teenage preference for part-time work (to permit longer periods of education) which makes teenage labor less attractive to employers, and the explosion in the teenage labor supply created by the baby boom at a time when women were entering the labor market in substantial numbers [115]. Whatever contribution these circumstances may have made to shifting teenage employment patterns in the short-run, the exclusion of juveniles from the labor market has been going on for more than a century, and may more plausibly be explained in terms of the failure of the oligopoly-capitalist economy to generate sufficient demand for labor; than to these recent developments [116].

In both the United States and England, the prolongation of education has historically been associated with the contraction of the labor market [117], casting doubt on the view that more education is something that the general population has wanted for its own sake. Had this been true, the school leaving age would have jumped upward in periods of prosperity, when a larger proportion of the population could afford more education, not during depressions. Moreover, the functionalist argument that increased education is necessary as technology becomes more complex would apply at best to a small minority of students, and rests on the dubious assumption that full-time schooling is pedagogically superior to alternative modes of organizing the education of adolescents.

The present social organization of education, which I have argued contributes to delinquency, has also been plausibly attributed to the functional requirement of a capitalist economy for a docile, disciplined and stratified labor force [118], as well as to the need to keep juveniles out of the labor market.

Thus the high and increasing level of juvenile crime we are seeing in present-day United States and in other Western countries orginates in the structural position of juveniles in an advanced capitalist economy.

Delinquency is not, however, a problem of capitalism alone. Although there are many differences between crime patterns in the United States and the Soviet Union, the limited information available indicates that delinquency in the Soviet Union is often associated with leisure-time consumption activities on the part of youths who are academic failures, and who are either not working or studying, or are working at or preparing for unrewarding jobs [119]. This suggests that some of the processes described here may be at work in the Soviet Union. Since Soviet society is based on hierarchical domination and requires a docile, disciplined and stratified labor force, this parallel is not surprising.

One might, in fact, generalize from this analysis, to conclude that any society that excluded juveniles from the world of adult work for long periods and imposed mandatory attendance at schools organized like ours would have a substantial amount of delinquency.

Criminology and Marxist Theory

For the first time in many decades, criminologists are again drawing on Marxian social theory. The small corpus of literature in this vein has thus far been devoted primarily to the analysis of criminal law and criminal justice administration [120], the criticism of liberal reform proposals [121], and the critique of non-Marxist contributions to the theory of crime causation [122].

Until recently, the only positive contribution this literature made to the theory of crime causation was the assertion that under capitalism crime is not pathological but rational [123]. The limitations of such an approach are manifest. When the mechanisms by which capitalism causes crime are left unspecified, only True Believers are likely to be persuaded of the connection, especially in the face of the persistence of crime in non-capitalist societies. In addition, other important questions about causation (why is there such variability in criminal behavior on the part of those who live in capitalist societies? Why does the amount and nature of crime undergo historical change?) are left unanswered.

However, several developments are leading radical criminologists to a new interest in questions of etiology. The prominence crime has assumed as a political issue has made it difficult for radicals trying to organize working class constituencies to dismiss the continuing rise in street crime by pointing out that crime is merely a "social construction" (feminist agitation over rape has had a similar effect), or by changing the subject to government and corporate crime. Within the discipline, the current reassessment of labeling theory is redirecting theoretical interest from secondary deviation resulting from labeling by law enforcement agencies to social structural sources of primary deviance [124]. Moreover, the recent Marxist critiques of phenomenology, existential sociology and symbolic interactionism as excessively voluntaristic, ahistorical and astructural [125] (paralleling the collapse of a New Left that emphasized voluntarism and subjectivity) has made radical criminologists more receptive to causal explanations of criminal behavior than has been the case in the recent past.

This paper has attempted to develop a Marxian perspective on the causation of crimes commonly committed by juveniles — for other recent Marxian work on causation see [126]. I have assumed throughout that there is no necessary contradiction between such traditional criminological concerns as the causal role of such institutions as family and school or psychological concepts like self-esteem and anxiety on the one hand, and Marxist theory on the other (although I have criticized elements in non-Marxist theories of delinquency, many of the points of criticism concern elements that are not crucial from the point of view of Marxism). Rather, Marxism compliments these traditional concerns by placing them in a larger framework.

Although not so fully developed that it can simply be "applied" to problems at hand, Marxism directs our attention to the manner in which changing modes and relations of production lead to historically changing criminogenic contradictions [127] within or between particular institutions. The analysis of these contradictions can only be carried out concretely, for particular historical epochs and particular forms of criminality. The same approach can be brought to the sociology of criminal law (which from this perspective need not be seen *solely* as an instrument of class rule), and can be of value in studying crime in non-capitalist as well as in capitalist societies. To leave off analysis with the statement that crime is rational and creative under capitalism is to fail to draw on the richness of the Marxist legacy.

From the point of view of theory, Marxism can serve to integrate criminology with questions central to macrosociological theory. The viewpoint I am recommending constitutes an implicit reproach to both consensus and conflict models in criminology. The conflict model, embraced by many radical criminologists in the 1960s in the face of massive social conflicts in American society (major statements of the conflict perspective can be found in [128]) fails to specify the lines along which conflicts appear, and where cooperation can be located. In that any society has elements of both consensus and dissensus, cooperation and conflict, varying historically in degree and form, both points of view distort social reality by omission, and by portraying a uniformity where diversity exists. Historical materialism provides the conceptual tools for investigating the degree of conflict present in a society and the forms it takes.

At the level of practice, the Marxist perspective exposes the limitations of liberal meliorism. For decades, criminologists have proposed such reforms as the elimination of poverty and racial discrimination in order to reduce crime, as if these social problems were mere oversights, little snags in a generally beneficial social order. Marxist theorists tend to see these problems largely as produced by and insoluble within the framework of a class society. My analysis of delinquency suggests that most proposed "solutions" to the delinquency problem would have little impact. A thorough integration of teenagers into the labor force would require a major restructuring of work and education, and this is hardly to be expected in the foreseeable future.

Although I have argued for the general compatibility between Marxist and non-Marxist approaches to crime causation, there are points of tension which must be mentioned. Unlike positivists, Marxists have been concerned with the dynamic interplay between objective conditions and subjective consciousness. Responses to objective conditions – including criminal responses – are contingent on the level of group awareness of the origins of oppressive objective conditions in class dynamics and of the possibilities for engaging in collective action to change these conditions. My analysis of delinquency is implicitly predicated on the low level of such consciousness now present among most American teenagers. That could change, though the prospects of change in the immediate future do not appear especially bright.

Marxists have also approached the question of class differently from non-Marxists. In this essay, I have used the term "class" in the very imprecise manner of non-Marxist criminologists, to refer to position on a ranked scale. In applications to delinquency this usage is ordinarily extended to juveniles by assigning them to the class of their parents. This approach has been relatively unsuccessful in explaining delinquency; class, thus defined, is a poor predictor of delinquency.

Marxian theorists take class to be defined by relationship to the means of production [129], but have conceptualized such relationships too narrowly. Feminist theorists have pointed out the unique relationship to production of the housewife in a capitalist economy (for a summary of the major statements on this question, see Fee [130]) and here I have argued that juveniles in an advanced capitalist economy have a common, if temporary, relationship to the means of production, characterized by exclusion during a period of mandatory training for entry into the labor force. In Marxian terms, this means that juveniles can no more be assigned the class of their parents than housewives can be assigned the class of their husbands. The high rate of juvenile crime is largely a response to the conditions imposed on this class under conditions of weak class consciousness.

In this instance, at least, the Marxian perspective yielded insights into the nature of delinquency that non-Marxian approaches to class have failed to provide. It is not necessarily true, however, that all forms of crime originate *directly* in the problems confronting a particular class, even if class is defined in the flexible manner I propose. The dynamic functioning of a class society leads to social differentiation along many lines other than class, and the resulting differences in experiences, opportunities and costs may have great relevance for criminal involvement. The contribution of Marxism is to view such differentiation as the product of relations of production and reproduction, rather than as an *a priori* given.

Acknowledgements

I am grateful to Ava Baron, Eliot Freidson, Daniel Glaser, Irwin Goffman, Drew Humphreys, Caroline Persell, Edwin Schur and James Q. Wilson for helpful discussions and suggestions.

NOTES

1 Wolfgang, M.E., R.M. Figlio and T. Sellin (1972). *Delinquency in a Birth Cohort*. Chicago: University of Chicago Press; Glueck, S. and E. Glueck (1937). *Later Criminal Careers*. New York: The Commonwealth Fund; Glaser, D. (1964). *The Effectiveness of a Prison and Parole System*. Indianapolis: Bobbs-Merrill, 469–474.

2 Beattie, R.H. (1955). "Problems of Criminal Statistics in the United States," *Journal of Criminal Law, Criminology and Police Science* 55: 359–369; Kitsuse, J.I. and A.V. Cicourel (1963). "A Note on the Uses of Official Statistics." *Social Problems* 11: 131–139; Wolfgang, M.E. (1963). "Uniform Crime Reports: A Critical Appraisal," *University of Pennsylvania Law Review* 111: 708–738; Robinson, S.M. (1966). "A Critical View of Uniform Crime Reports," *Michigan Law Review* 64: 1031–1054; Wheeler, S. (1967). "Criminal Statistics: A Reformulation of the Problem," *Journal of Criminal Law, Criminology and Police Science* 58: 317–324.

3 Baittle, B. (1961). "Psychiatric Aspects of the Development of a Street Corner Group: An Exploratory Study," *American Journal of Orthopsychiatry* 31: 703–712; Miller, W.B. (1966). "Violent Crime in City Gangs," *Annals of the American Academy of Political and Social Science* 364: 96–112; Gold, M. (1970). *Delinquent Behavior in an American City*. Belmont, Cal.: Brooks Cole; Hindelang, M.J. (1971). "Age, Sex, and the Versatility of Delinquent Involvements," *Social Problems* 18: 522–535;

4 Offer, D. (1969). *The Psychological World of the Teenager: A Study of Normal Adolescent Boys*. New York: Basic Books.

5 West W.G. (1976). "Serious Thieves: Lower Class Adolescent Males in a Short-Term Deviant Occupation." Unpublished paper.

6 Wilson, N.K. (1972). *Risk Ratios in Juvenile Delinquency*. Ann Arbor: University Microfilms.

7 Private communication from Patricia Miller.

8 Michigan State Prison (1878). *Annual Report*.

9 Monkkonen. E. (1975). *The Dangerous Class: Crime and Poverty in Columbus Ohio 1860–1884*. Cambridge: Harvard University Press.

10 Neison, F.G.P. (1857). *Contributions to Vital Statistics*. Third Edition. Quoted in J.J. Tobias, *Nineteenth Century Crime: Prevention and Punishment*. Newton Abbott: David and Charles. Quetelet, A.J. (1831). *Recherches sur le Penchant au Crime aux Différents Ages*. Brussels: Académie Royale; Lombroso C. (1968). *Crime: Its Causes and Remedies*. Montclair, N.J.: Patterson Smith 175–177.

11 Normandeau A. (1968). *Trends and Patterns of Robbery*. Unpublished Ph. D. Dissertation University of Pennsylvania; McClintock. F.H.. N.H. Avison and G.N.G. Rose (1968). *Crime in England and Wales* London: Heinemann Educational Books 179; Lopez-Rey. M. (1970). *Crime: An Analytical Approach*. New York: Praeger; Schichor. D. and A. Kirschenbaum (1975). "Juvenile Delinquency and New Towns: The Case of Israel." Paper presented to the American Society of Criminology.

12 Glueck, S. and E. Glueck (1968). *Delinquents and Non-delinquents in Perspective*. Cambridge: Harvard University Press 169–171.

13 Ferracuti F.. S. Dinitz and A. Esperanza (1975). *Delinquents and Nondelinquents in the Puerto Rican Slum Culture*. Columbus: Ohio State University Press.

14 Miller W B. (1958), "Lower Class Subculture as a Generating Milieu of Gang Delinquency " *Journal of Social Issues* 14: 5–19.

15 Clark J.P. and E.W. Haurek (1966). "Age and Sex Roles of Adolescents and their Involvement in Misconduct: A Reappraisal." *Sociology and Social Research* 50: 495–503

16 Cloward, R A. and L.E Ohlin (1960). *Delinquency and Opportunity: A Theory of Delinquent Gangs.* New York: Free Press.

17 Cohen, A.K. (1955). *Delinquent Boys.* New York: Free Press.

18 Matza, D. (1964). *Delinquency and Drift.* New York: Wiley 24–27.

19 Merton, R.K. (1957). *Social Theory and Social Structure.* Revised Edition. New York: Free Press; Cloward R. and L. Ohlin (1960), op cit.

20 Bachman, J.G., S. Green and I. Wirtanen (1972). *Dropping Out   Problem or Symptom.* Ann Arbor: Institute for Social Research.

21 Cloward, R. and L. Ohlin (1960). op. cit.

22 Ibid., 174–175.

23 Elliot, D.S. and H.L. Voss (1974). *Delinquency and Dropout.* Lexington, Mass.: Lexington Books; Quicker, J. (1974). "The Effect of Goal Discrepancy on Delinquency" *Social Problems* 22: 76–86; Lalli, M. and W. Roberts (1974). "The Strain Theory of Delinquency " Unpublished paper University of Pennsylvania.

24 Bloch, H.A. and A. Niederhoffer (1958). *The Gang.* New York: Philosophical Library 29–30.

25 Matza, D. (1964). Op. cit.

26 Ibid. 54–58.

27 Merton, R. (1957). Op. cit., 131   194

28 Ibid., 166

29 Cloward, R. and L. Ohlin (1960). op. cit.

30 Perlin, L.I., M.R. Yarrow and H.A. Scarr (1967). "Unintended Effects of Parental Aspirations: The Case of Children's Cheating " *American Journal of Sociology* 73: 73–83. Bergman, D. (1974). "The Absence of Guilt in Cheating." Unpublished paper presented to the American Anthropological Association; Barnes, B. (1975). "School's Honor Code Gets an F." *New York Post* (September 24): 18.

31 Milner, R and C. Milner (1972). *Black Players: The Secret World of Black Pimps.* Boston: Little Brown, Ianni, F. (1974). *The Black Mafia.* New York: Simon and Schuster.

32 Woodley, R. (1972). *Dealer: Portrait of a Cocaine Merchant.* New York: Warner Paperback Library.

33 Cohen, A. (1955). Op.cit. 25.

34 Blos, P. (1941). *The Adolescent Personality: A Study of Individual Behavior.* New York: Appleton; Bowerman C.E. and J.W. Kinch (1959). "Changes in Family and Peer Orientation of Children between the Fourth and Tenth Grades," *Social Forces* 37: 206. Tuma, E. and N. Livson (1960). "Family Socioeconomic Status and Attitudes toward Authority," *Child Development* 31: 387; Conger, J.J. (1971). "A World They Never Knew: The Family and Social Change," *Daedalus* 100: 1105–1138; (1973). *Adolescence and Youth.* New York: Harper & Row 286–292.

35 Eisenstadt, S.N. (1956). *From Generation to Generation: Age Groups and Social Structure.* New York: Free Press; Bloch and Niederhoffer (1958), op. cit.

36 Mussen, P H., J.J. Conger and J. Kagan (1969). *Child Development and Personality.* New York: Harper & Row.

37 Panel on Youth of the President's Science Advisory Committee (1974). *Youth: Transition to Adulthood.* Chicago: University of Chicago.

38 Mead, M. (1939). *From the South Seas: Part III. Sex and Temperament in Three Primitive Societies.* New York: Morrow; Eisenstadt, S.N. (1956), op. cit., 56–92; Minturn, L. and W.W. Lambert (1964). *Mothers in Six Cultures: Antecedents of Child Rearing.* New York: Wiley.

39 Insofar as meals are not served regularly in some lower class families, biological and social needs here converge. Mertonian theory implicitly but erroneously assumes that the welfare state functions well enough to meet basic biological needs.

40 Panel on Youth (1974), op. cit., 36–38.

41 Tomson, B. and E.R. Fiedler (1975). "Gangs: A Response to the Urban World (Part II)," in Desmond S. Cartwright, Barbara Tomson and Herschey Schwartz (eds.), *Gang Delinquency.* Monterey, Cal.: Brooks/Cole.

42 Raskin, A.H. (1975). "The Teenage Worker is Hardest Hit," *New York Times* (May 4): F3.

43 Sherif, M. and C.W. Sherif (1964). *Reference Groups: Exploration into Conformity and Deviation of Adolescents.* New York: Harper & Row, 174.

44 Werthman, C. (1967). "The Function of Social Definitions in the Development of Delinquent Careers," in *Task Force Report: Juvenile Delinquency.* Washington, D.C.: Government Printing Office, 157.

45 Fyvel, T.R. (1962). *Troublemakers.* New York: Schocken Books; Parker, H.J. (1974), op. cit.

46 Toby, J. (1967), op. cit., 136–137.

47 Ibid., 137–138.

48 Lin, T. (1959), op. cit., 259.

49 Bauer, E.J. (1964). "The Trend of Juvenile Offenses in the Netherlands and the United States," *Journal of Criminal Law, Criminology and Police Science* 55: 359–369.

50 DeFleur, L. (1970), op. cit.

51 Weis, J. (1976). "Liberation and Crime: The Invention of the New Female Criminal." *Crime and Social Justice* 6: 17–27.

52 Parker, H.H. (1974), op. cit.; Toby (1967), op. cit., 137.

53 Rolf, M. and S.B. Sells (1968). "Juvenile Delinquency in Relation to peer Acceptance-Rejection and Socioeconomic Status." *Psychology in the Schools* 5: 3–18; West, D. (1973). "Are Delinquents Different?" *New Society* 26 (November 22): 456.

54 Rothstein, E. (1962). "Attributes Related to High Social Status: A Comparison of the Perceptions of Delinquents and Non-Delinquent Boys," *Social Problems* 10: 75–83; Short, J.F., Jr. and F.L. Strodtbeck (1965). *Group Process and Gang Delinquency.* Chicago: University of Chicago Press, 243–244; Hirschi, T. (1969). *The Causes of Delinquency.* Berkeley: University of California Press, 145–161.

55 Nye, F.I. (1958). *Family Relationships and Delinquent Behavior.* New York: Wiley, ch. 8; Hirschi, T. (1969), op. cit., 83–109.

56 Short, J.F., Jr. and F.I. Nye (1958). "Extent of Unrecorded Delinquency: Tentative Conclusions." *Journal of Criminal Law, Criminology and Police Science* 49: 296–302; Reiss, A.J., Jr. and A.L. Rhodes (1961). "The Distribution of Juvenile Delinquency in the Social Class Structure," *American Sociological Review* 26: 730–732; Dentler, R. and L.J. Monroe (1961). "Early Adolescent Theft," *American Sociological Review* 26: 733–743; Clark, J.P. and E.P. Wenninger (1962). "Socio-Economic Class and Area as Correlates of Illegal Behavior Among Juveniles," *American Sociological Review* 27: 826–834; Akers, R.L. (1964). "Socio-Economic Status and Delinquent Behavior: A Retest," *Journal of Research in Crime and Delinquency* 1: 38–46; Hirschi, T. (1969), op. cit., pp. 66–82.

57 Simon, R.J. (1975). *Women and Crime.* Lexington, Mass.: Lexington Books.

58 Cohen, A. (1955), op. cit., p. 25.

59 Schafer, W.E. and K. Polk (1967). "Delinquency and the Schools," in *Task Force Report: Juvenile Delinquency and Youth Crime.* Washington, D.C.: Government Printing Office; Polk, K. and W.E. Schafer (1972). *Schools and Delinquency.* Englewood Cliffs, N.J. Prentice-Hall.

60 These expectations are derived from young peoples' knowledge of family arrangements in our society generally, not only from their own family circumstances. When controls in their own family are not relaxed, this can provide an additional source of conflict.

61 Psathas, G. (1957). "Ethnicity, Social Class, and Adolescent Independence from Parental Control," *American Sociological Review* 22: 415–423. Kobrin, S. (1962). "The Impact of Cultural Factors in Selected Problems of Adolescent Development in the Middle and Lower Class," *American Journal of Orthopsychiatry* 33: 387–390; Werthman, C. (1967), op. cit.: Rainwater, L. (1970). *Behind Ghetto Walls.* Chicago: Aldine, 211–234; Ladner, J. (1971). *Tomorrow's Tomorrow: The Black Woman.* Garden City: Doubleday, 61–63; Elder, G. (1974). *Children of the Great Depression: Social Change in Life Experience.* Chicago: University of Chicago Press.

62 Toby, J. (1967), op. cit., 141.

63 Gouldner, A. (1970). *The Coming Crisis in Western Sociology.* New York: Basic Books, 221–222.

64 Cohen, A. (1955), op. cit., 112–113; Sennett, R. and J. Cobb (1972), *The Hidden Injuries of Class*. New York: Alfred A. Knopf.

65 Hyman, H.H. (1968). "The Psychology of Status," in H.H. Hyman and E. Singer (eds.), *Readings in Reference Group Theory and Research*. New York: Free Press, 147–168.

66 Goffman, E. (1955). "On Face-Work: An Analysis of Ritual Elements in Social Interaction," *Psychiatry* 18: 213–231.

67 Ellis, H.G. and S.M. Newman (1972). "The Greaser is a 'Bad Ass'; The Gowster is a 'Muthah'; An Analysis of Two Urban Youth Roles," in Thomas Kochman (ed.), *Rappin' and Stylin' Out: Communication in Black America*. Urbana: University of Illinois Press, 375–376.

68 Cohen, A. (1955), op. cit., 121–137.

69 Miller, W.B. (1966). "Violent Crime in City Gangs," *Annals of the American Academy of Political and Social Science* 364: 96–112.

70 Matza, D. (1964), op. cit., 33–68; Short, J.F., Jr. and F.L. Strodtbeck (1965), op.cit., 47–75.

71 Matza, D. (1964), op. cit., 33.

72 Werthman, C. (1967), op. cit.

73 Short, J.F., Jr. and F.L. Strodtbeck (1965), op. cit., 185–216, Horowitz, R. and G. Schwartz (1974). "Honor, Normative Ambiguity and Gang Violence," *American Sociological Review* 39: 238–251.

74 Goffman, E. (1974). "Where the Action Is," in *Interaction Ritual*. Garden City: Anchor Books, 149–270.

75 Matza, D. and G.M. Sykes (1961), "Juvenile Delinquency and Subterranean Values," *American Sociological Review* 26: 712–719.

76 Dennison, G. (1969). *The Lives of Children: The Story of the First Street School*. New York: Random House; Friedenberg, E.Z. (1964). *The Vanishing Adolescent*. Boston: Beacon Press; (1965). *Coming of Age in America: Growth and Acquiescence*. New York: Random House; Goodman, P. (1964). *Compulsory Miseducation*. New York: Horizon Press; Greene, M.F. and O. Ryan (1965). *The School Children: Growing Up in the Slums*. New York: Pantheon; Hargreaves, D.H. (1972). *Interpersonal Relations and Education*. London: Routledge and Kegan Paul; Hentoff, N. (1966). *Our Children Are Dying*. New York: Viking Press; Herndon, J. (1968). *The Way It Spozed to Be*. New York: Simon and Schuster; Jackson, P.W. (1968). *Life in Classrooms*. New York: Holt Rinehart and Winston; Kohl, H. (1967). *36 Children*. New York: New American Library; Nordstrom, C., E.Z. Friedenberg and H.A. Gold (1967). *Society's Children: A Study of Ressentiment in the Secondary School*. New York: Random House; Roberts, J.I. (1970). *Scene of the Battle: Group Behavior in Urban Classrooms*. Garden City: Doubleday; Webb, J. (1962). "The Sociology of a School," *British Journal of Sociology* 13: 264–272.

77 Downes, D.M. (1966). *The Delinquent Solution: A Study in Subcultural Theory*. New York: Free Press.

78 Finestone, H. (1957). "Cats, Kicks and Color," *Social Problems* 5: 3–13.

79 Rainwater, L. (1970), op. cit.

80 Werthman, C. (1967), op. cit.

81 Bachman, J.G., S. Green and I. Wirtanen (1972). *Dropping Out — Problem or Symptom*. Ann Arbor: Institute for Social Research.

82 Elliot, D.S. and H.L. Voss (1974). *Delinquency and Dropout*. Lexington, Mass.: Lexington Books, 115–122; Mukherjee, S.K. (1971). *A Typological Study of School Status and Delinquency*. Ann Arbor: University Microfilms.

83 McClean, J.D. and J.C. Wood (1969), op. cit.

84 DeFleur (1970), op. cit.

85 Grosser, G. (1952). *Juvenile Delinquency and Contemporary American Sex Roles*. Unpublished Ph.D. Dissertation, Harvard University.

86 Parsons, T. (1947). "Certain Primary Sources and Patterns of Aggression in the Social Structure of the Western World," *Psychiatry* 10: 167–181; Cohen, A. (1955), op. cit., 162–169.

87 Miller, W.B. (1958), op. cit.

88 Tennyson, R.A. (1967). "Family Structure and Delinquent Behavior," in M.W. Klein (ed.), *Juvenile Gangs in Context*. Englewood Cliffs, N.J.: Prentice-Hall; Monahan, T.P. (1957). "Family Status and the Delinquent Child: A Reappraisal and Some New Findings," *Social Forces* 35:

251–258; Rosen, L. (1969). "Matriarchy and Lower Class Negro Male Delinquency," *Social Problems* 17: 175–189.

89 Hannerz, U. (1969). *Soulside: Inquiries into Ghetto Culture*. New York: Columbia University Press.

90 Miller, W.B. (1958) op. cit.

91 A similar perspective on subcultures of violence and their relationship to masculinity has been developed by Curtis, L. (1975). *Violence, Race and Culture*. Lexington, Mass.: Lexington Books.

92 Werthman, C. (1967), op. cit.

93 Weis, J. (1967), op. cit.

94 Federal Bureau of Investigation (1974). *Crime in the United States. Uniform Crime Reports – 1973.* Washington, D.C.: Government Printing Office, 133.

95 Task Force Report (1967). *The Assessment of Crime*. Washington, D.C.: Government Printing Office.

96 Puntil, J.E. (n.d.). "Youth Survey Marginals." Chicago: Institute for Juvenile Research.

97 Briar, S. and I. Piliavin (1965). "Delinquency, Situational Inducements, and Commitment to Conformity," *Social Problems* 13: 35–45; Piliavin, I.M., A.C. Vadum and J.A. Hardyck (1969). "Delinquency, Personal Costs and Parental Treatment: A Test of a Reward-Cost Model of Juvenile Criminality," *Journal of Criminal Law, Criminology and Police Science* 60: 165–172; Hirschi, T. (1969), op. cit.; Ehrlich, I. (1973). "Participation in Illegitimate Activities: A Theoretical and Empirical Investigation," *Journal of Political Economy* 81: 521–565.

98 Reckless, W.C., S. Dinitz and E. Murray (1956). "Self Concept as an Insulator against Delinquency." *American Sociological Review* 21: 744–746.

99 Clark, J.P. and E.W. Haurek (1966), op. cit.

100 Schur, E.M. (1973). *Radical Nonintervention: Rethinking the Delinquency Problem*. Englewood Cliffs, N.J.: Prentice-Hall.

101 Hirschi, T. (1969), op. cit., 81–109.

102 Williams, L. (1976). "Three Youths Call Mugging the Elderly Profitable and Safe," *New York Times* (December 8): B2.

103 I have discussed the question of desistance with male juveniles on probation in Manhattan for theft offenses, and with a number of my students who have been involved in various forms of theft. The latter group includes both apprehended and unapprehended former thieves. No claim is made for the representativeness of this small sample.

104 Matza, D. (1964), op. cit., 55.

105 Tannenbaum, F. (1938). *Crime in the Community*. New York: Columbia University Press, 19–20.

106 Schwartz, R.D. and J.H. Skolnick (1962). "Two Studies of Legal Stigma," *Social Problems* 10: 133–142.

107 Hirschi, T. (1975). "Labelling Theory and Juvenile Delinquency: An Assessment of the Evidence," in Walter R. Gove (ed.), *Labeling of Deviance: Evaluating a Perspective*. New York: Halsted Press; Tittle, C.R. (1975). "Labelling and Crime: An Empirical Evaluation," in Walter R. Gove (ed.), *The Labelling of Deviance: Evaluating a Perspective*. New York: Halsted Press; Mahoney, A.R. (1974). "The Effect of Labeling upon Youths in the Juvenile Justice System: A Review of the Evidence," *Law and Society Review*, 8: 583–614.

108 Schur, E.M. (1973), op. cit., 125.

109 Wolfgang, M.E., R.M. Figlio and T. Sellin (1972), op. cit., 201.

110 Federal Bureau of Investigation (1972). *Crime in the United States. Uniform Crime Reports – 1971.* Washington D.C.: Government Printing Office, 138.

111 Chambliss, W.J. (1973). "The Saints and the Roughnecks," *Society* 11: 24–31.

112 This leniency has increased over the past decade, partly in response to the arguments of labeling theorists such as Schur, E.M. (1973), op. cit., that punishment of delinquents would be counter-rehabilitative, and because of the state's growing fiscal inability to cope with the social problems engendered by a deteriorating capitalist economy and polity, described by O'Connor, J. (1973). *The Fiscal Crisis of the State*. New York: St. Martin's Press. Scull, A. (1977). *Decarceration: Community Treatment and the Deviant – A Radical View*. Englewood Cliffs, N.J.: Prentice Hall, explicitly discusses the community corrections movement in these terms.

113 Hall, G.S. (1904). *Adolescence: Its Psychology and Its Relations to Physiology, Anthropology, Sociology, Sex, Crime, Religion, and Education.* New York: Appleton.

114 In nineteenth century England, juveniles were over-represented in crime statistics by comparison with the continent not because the social position of juveniles was very different, but because the age distribution of the English population was skewed toward the younger age brackets by the rapid growth in the English population during the nineteenth century. In the latter half of the century, juveniles were under-represented by comparison with their numbers in the English population, despite the high percentages of offenders who were juveniles; see, e.g. Lombroso, C. (1968), op. cit., 176; Tobias, J.J. (1972). *Urban Crime in Victorian England.* New York: Schocken Books, 78, 167.

115 Kalacheck, E. (1973). "The Changing Economic Status of the Young," *Journal of Youth and Adolescence* 2: 125-132.

116 Carson, R.B. (1972). "Youthful Labor Surplus in Disaccumulationist Capitalism," *Socialist Revolution* 9: 15-44; Bowers, N. (1975). "Youth and the Crisis of Monopoly Capitalism," in *Radical Perspectives on the Economic Crisis of Monopoly Capitalism.* New York: Union of Radical Political Economy.

117 Musgrove, F. (1965). *Youth and the Social Order.* Bloomington: Indiana University Press.

118 Cohen, D.K. and M. Lazerson (1972). "Education and the Corporate Order," *Socialist Revolution* 8: 47-72; Gorz, A. (1972). "Technologie, Techniker und Klassenkampf," in A. Gorz, *Schule and Fabrik.* Quoted in Gero Lenhardt, "On the Relationship between the Education System and Capitalist Work Organization." *Kapitalistate* 3: 128-146; Bowles S. and H. Gintis (1975). *Schooling in Capitalist America: Educational Reform and the Contradictions of Economic Life.* New York: Basic Books.

118 Connor, W. (1970). *Deviance in Soviet Society.* New York: Columbia University Press; Polk, K. (1972). "Social Class and the Bureaucratic Response to Youthful Deviance." Paper presented to the American Sociological Association.

120 Quinney, R. (1974). *Criminal Justice in America: A Critical Understanding.* Boston: Little, Brown; Quinney (1974). *Critique of Legal Order: Crime Control in Capitalist Society.* Boston: Little, Brown.

121 Platt, T. (1974). "Prospects for a Radical Criminology in the United States," *Crime and Social Justice: A Journal of Radical Criminology* 1: 2-10.

122 Taylor, I., P. Walton and J. Young (1973). *The New Criminology.* London: Routledge, Kegan Paul; Manders, D. (1975). "Labelling Theory and Social Reality: A Marxist Critique," *The Insurgent Sociologist* 6: 53-66.

123 Gordon, D. (1971). "Class and the Economics of Crime," *Review of Radical Political Economics* 3: 51-75; Taylor, I., P. Walton and J. Young (1973), op. cit.

124 Mankoff, M. (1971). "Societal Reaction and Career Deviance: A Critical Analysis.", *Sociological Quarterly* 12: 204-218; Taylor, I., P. Walton and J. Young (1973), op. cit.; Manders, D. (1975), op. cit.

125 Lichtman, R. (1970). "Symbolic Interactionism and Social Reality: Some Marxist Queries." *Berkeley Journal of Sociology* 15: 75-94; McNall, S.G. and J.C.M. Johnson (1975). "The New Conservatives: Ethnomethodologists, Phenomenologists, and Symbolic Interactionists," *The Insurgent Sociologist* 5: 49-55; Grabiner, G. (1975). "The Situational Sociologies: A Theoretical Note." *The Insurgent Sociologist* 5: 80-81.

126 Seppilli, T. and G.G. Abbozzo. "The State of Research into Social Control and Deviance in Italy in the Post-War Period (1945-1973)," in Herman Bianchi, Mario Simoni and Ian Taylor (eds.), *Deviance and Control in Europe.* New York: Wiley, Pearce, F. (1975). *Crimes of the Powerful: Marxism, Crime and Deviance.* London: Pluto Press; Schwendinger, H. and J.R. Schwendinger (1976). "Delinquency and the Collective Varieties of Youth," *Crime and Social Justice* 5: 7-25.

127 I use this word, with some reservations, to indicate that steps taken to produce or reproduce social domination may be responded to in ways that interfere with that production or reproduction. Students may not be "cooled out" by low grades; they may rebel. Reservations are necessary because a Marxian contradiction has, at least potentially, the capability of overturning its source, not merely of being somewhat dysfunctional. The conventional sorts of crime

discussed in this paper do not have that capability; if anything, they tend to stabilize existing social arrangements, though in a manner that is disadvantageous for much of the population Only if the nature of the crimes were to change drastically would criminality be a manifestation of contradiction in the strict sense of the word. In that case we would be talking about a revolutionary movement.

128 Chambliss, W.J. (1976). "Functional and Conflict Theories of Crime: The Heritage of Emile Durkheim and Karl Marx," in William J. Chambliss and Milton Mankoff (eds), *Whose Law, What Order?* New York: Wiley; Denisoff, R.S. and C. McCaghy (1973). *Deviance, Conflict and Criminology.* Rand McNally.

129 Stolzman, J. and H. Gamberg (1973–1974). "Marxist Class Analysis versus Stratification Analysis as General Approaches to Social Inequality," *Berkely Journal of Sociology* 18: 105–126.

130 Fee. T. (1976). "Domestic Labor: An Analysis of Housework and Its Relation to the Production Process," *Review of Radical Political Economics* 8: 1–8.

27

INTELLIGENCE AND DELINQUENCY
A Revisionist Review

TRAVIS HIRSCHI and MICHAEL J. HINDELANG

Recent research on intelligence and delinquency suggests that (1) the relation is at least as strong as the relation of either class or race to official delinquency; (2) the relation is stronger than the relation of either class or race to self-reported delinquency. In an analysis of the history of the research on the IQ-delinquency relation, we trace the developments leading to the current textbook position that IQ is not an important factor in delinquency. This position, which came into vogue about forty years ago and is still held by many sociologists, has its roots in: (1) a medical to sociological paradigm shift in this century; (2) the failure of subsequent research to substantiate the early exorbitant claims that low IQ was a necessary and sufficient condition for illegal behavior; (3) early negative reviews of research on this question by Sutherland and others; (4) reservations about the validity of the measurement of both IQ and delinquency; (5) erroneous interpretation of research findings; (6) speculation regarding factors which might account for the relation. It is noted that many currently prominent sociological theories of delinquency implicitly or explicitly use IQ as a crucial theoretical element. We show that IQ has an effect on delinquency independent of class and race, and we argue that this effect is mediated through a host of school variables.

Few groups in American society have been defended more diligently by sociologists against allegations of difference than ordinary delinquents. From the beginning, the thrust of sociological theory has been to deny the relevance of individual differences to an explanation of delinquency, and the thrust of sociological criticism has been to discount research findings apparently to the contrary. "Devastating" reviews of the research literature typically meet with uncritical acceptance or even applause, and new theories and "new criminologies" are con-

From Travis Hirschi and Michael J. Hindelang, "Intelligence and Delinquency: A Revisionist Review," 42(4) *American Sociological Review* 571-587 (August 1977). Copyright 1977 by the American Sociological Association.

structed in a research vacuum, a vacuum that may itself claim research support.

A major source of this stance toward individual differences is the notion widely held in the field of deviance that "kinds of people" theories are non- or even anti-sociological. Most of the major theorists in the area (Sutherland, Merton, Cohen, Becker) have more or less explicitly argued this point, and efforts to bring criminology "up-to-date" with the rest of sociology frequently imply that interest in individual differences is an outmoded relic of the field's positivistic past (e.g., Matza, 1964; Taylor et al, 1973). Another source of this stance toward difference is frankly moral. According to Liazos (1972), who provides extensive documentation, sociologists repeatedly assert that deviants are "at least as good as anyone else." If Liazos' analysis is any guide, we may assume it is easy to confuse the moral-evaluative "as good as" with the empirical "the same as." For example, Liazos goes on to argue that the repeated assertion that " 'deviants' are *not different* may raise the very doubts we want to dispel." Sociologists have observed for some time that, "always and everywhere, *difference* is the occasion and excuse for ignoring the equal claims of others" (Ross, 1901:25). They therefore feel duty-bound, it seems, to protect delinquents from those who would justify abusing them on these grounds.

Among the many possible individual differences between delinquents and nondelinquents, none is apparently more threatening to the integrity of the field and to its moral commitments than IQ. To the standard list of scientific and moral arguments against IQ, the sociological student of crime and delinquency can add the weight of a half-century struggle against biological theories and the predatory social ethic they are alleged to foster. In fact, the single argument against IQ developed within criminology is sufficiently simple and persuasive that the standard list need not be invoked. At the time criminology became a subfield of sociology, marked differences in IQ between delinquents and nondelinquents were pretty much taken for granted, and a major task confronting those wishing to

claim the field for the sociological perspective was to call these alleged differences into question. This task was successfully accomplished. IQ, it was confidently suggested, doesn't matter (see Sutherland, 1924:108). Today, textbooks in crime and delinquency ignore IQ or impatiently explain to the reader that IQ is no longer taken seriously by knowledgeable students simply because no differences worth considering have been revealed by research.

As we shall show, the textbooks are wrong.[1] IQ is an important correlate of delinquency. It is at least as important as social class or race. This fact has straightforward implications for sociological theorizing and research, most of which has taken place within the context of official denial of IQ differences. Its implications for social policy are variably straightforward and are, in any event, strictly irrelevant to questions of the current impact of IQ on delinquency: the actual relation between IQ and delinquency must be the standard against which all arguments, including our own, are judged.

The Current Textbook View

Many textbooks do not even mention IQ (e.g., Gibbons, 1970; Bloch and Geis, 1962). Most, however, introduce the subject and then argue against its significance. The basic position is that there are no differences in IQ between delinquents and nondelinquents. The research and reviews most frequently cited in support of this conclusion are now over forty years old (e.g., Murchison, 1926; Sutherland, 1931; Zeleny, 1933). The tendency to rely on summaries provided by other textbooks, especially, in this case, those written by psychologists, is much in evidence.

Despite the selectivity of textbook summaries of the evidence, most of them leave the reader with the distinct impression that IQ may be a very important

---

[1] In a more general treatment of the measurement and correlates of delinquency, Gordon (1976) independently reaches conclusions about the importance of IQ that are very close to those reported here.

cause of delinquency after all. Few textbook writers seem able to resist additional arguments that have the effect of undercutting their basic position:

> It is now generally recognized that so-called intelligence tests tend to measure the degree to which the individual has assimilated and internalized middle-class values rather than intelligence.

> We could anticipate that a feeble-minded individual would be more readily incarcerated than other individuals. (Haskell and Yablonsky, 1974:216)

> It is not mental deficiency per se which results in crime; rather the inability of a mentally deficient person to make adequate social adjustments. . . . (Johnson, 1968:173)

> Although a higher percentage of delinquent children come from the ranks of the mental defective, particularly from those of borderline intelligence, it is not the mental deficiency per se but the inability of the child to make adequate school or social adjustments that usually results in delinquency. (Sutherland and Cressey, 1974:174, quoting Coleman, 1950)

> The great proportion of persons with low intelligence scores undoubtedly are nondeviants, whereas there are large numbers of persons with above normal intelligence who are. (Clinard, 1968:170)

All of these arguments take for granted a negative correlation between IQ and delinquency. The "middle-class values" interpretation of IQ tests suggests that scores on these tests may well be the strongest predictor of delinquency available. The "not per se" argument asserts that the relation is, in fact, causal in the usual meaning of the term—i.e., nonspurious. The "more readily incarcerated" view contradicts the "not per se" argument by suggesting a direct link between IQ and, at least, official delinquency. And the "great proportion" argument asserts only that the relation is not perfect. Still, the current view, simply stated, is that IQ makes no difference. This view is not supported by the results of research.

Recent Research on Official Delinquency

At least half a dozen recent studies permit examination of the effects of IQ on official delinquency. These studies have been conducted in diverse settings, they rely on a variety of measures of IQ and of delinquency, and they all employ some measure of control for the effects of such variables as social class and race. All of them show IQ to be an important predictor of official delinquency.[2]

How strong is this effect? Since social class and race are considered important correlates of official delinquency by almost everyone, they should provide a sufficiently stringent criterion and be available for comparison. Further, since both class and race are frequently used to discount the effects of IQ, this comparison will provide evidence relative to the common argument that IQ effects are merely a by-product of race and class effects.

IQ, Social Class and Official Delinquency

Reiss and Rhodes (1961) examined the juvenile court records of more than 9,200 in-school *white* boys in Davidson County, Tennessee. Using three-category divisions on occupational status of the head of household and on IQ, they found that the rate (per 100) of court adjudication ranged from 5.7 in the high to 9.6 in the low status groups, and from 4.8 in the high to 10.3 in the low IQ groups. In other words, the rate of adjudication in the lowest occupational group was 1.7 times that of the highest occupational group, while the rate of the adjudication in the lowest IQ group was 2.1 times that of the highest IQ group.[3] Since the distributions of occupational status and IQ were roughly comparable, in the Davidson County data IQ is more important than social class as a predictor of official delinquency among white boys.

Hirschi (1969) examined the police rec-

---

[2] Unless otherwise noted, all references to "the relation between IQ and delinquency" assume an inverse correlation.

[3] When father's occupational status was dichotomized and IQ trichotomized, the two variables were shown to have independent effects, with some tendency toward interaction: the effects of occupational status were more marked as IQ decreased, which also says that the effects of IQ were more marked for blue-collar than for white-collar boys.

ords of over 3,600 boys in Contra Costa County, California. Since previously published analyses do not directly compare the effects of social class and IQ, we have reanalyzed these data, with the results shown in Tables 1 and 2 (for details of data collection, see Hirschi, 1969:35–46).

In these data, the effect of IQ on official delinquency is stronger than that of father's education. Among whites, the gamma for the relationship between IQ and delinquency is −.31, while the comparable gamma for father's education is −.20; among blacks, the gammas are −.16 and −.05, respectively. Although the data are not shown, a composite measure of family status which includes employment and welfare status, presence of the father, and education and occupation of the parents shows results comparable to those for father's education in both racial categories. For whites, the gamma is −.18; for blacks, it is −.09. When the effects of this measure of family status and IQ are examined *simultaneously* within racial groups, the results are consistent with the zero-order relations. Both family status and IQ are independently related to official delinquency; the superiority of IQ in comparison with family status, however measured, is especially noticeable among blacks.

Wolfgang et al. (1972) obtained IQ scores on 8,700 of the 10,000 boys in their Philadelphia cohort. They do not present measures of association for these IQ scores and delinquency, nor do they show tabular material in which IQ is treated as an independent variable. They do, however, present average IQ scores by

Table 1. Percent Committing Two or More Official Delinquent Acts by IQ (Stanford Binet) and Race[a]

	IQ				
	0–19	20–39	40–59	60–79	80–99
White males	22.6 (204)	25.6 (282)	14.6 (309)	8.4 (341)	6.2 (403)
Black males	38.2 (429)	36.2 (273)	26.2 (158)	19.7 (71)	19.0 (42)

[a] IQ scores are shown as percentiles. Gammas, calculated on the entire range of delinquency scores (0–4), are −.31 for whites and −.16 for blacks.

number of contacts with the police in groups homogeneous on class and race. The differences in average scores between chronic offenders and nondelinquents range from nine IQ points among high socioeconomic status nonwhites to fourteen IQ points among low socioeconomic status whites (Wolfgang et al., 1972:62, 93). Again, although no direct comparison with social class is possible, the Philadelphia data reveal a strong relation between IQ and delinquency independent of class.[4]

West (1973:84) followed 411 London boys over a ten-year period and "compared the delinquent and non-delinquent groups on the prevalence of low IQ in just the same way [he] compared them on other factors such as poverty, large families, or criminal parents." The relation between IQ and delinquency in West's data is substantial. While one-quarter of those with IQ scores of 110 or more had a police record, the same was true of one-half of those with IQ scores of 90 or less. Even more impressively, while only one in fifty boys with an IQ of 110 or more was a recidivist, one in five of those with an IQ of 90 or less fell in this category. West (1973:84–5) concludes from his thorough analysis that "low IQ was a significant precursor of delinquency to much the same extent as other major factors." Although he reports a stronger relation between family income and delinquency than that typically reported in American studies, IQ was able to compete with it on equal terms and to survive when family income and several other measures of family culture were controlled by a matching procedure.

It should be noted that the striking differences in delinquency produced by IQ in West's data reflect a difference in IQ of about 12 points between nondelinquents and recidivists—a difference that falls within the range of the race- and SES-specific differences calculated from the Wolfgang et al. data. West's data agree with those of Wolfgang et al. that the IQ effect is largely attributable to multiple offenders (recidivists), which may explain

4 Wolfgang et al. used the Philadelphia Verbal Ability Test. The typical IQ test has a standard deviation of 15.

Table 2. Percent Committing Two or More Official Delinquent Acts by Father's Education and Race[a]

Race	Father's Education				
	Less than High School Grad.	High School Graduate	Trade or Business	Some College	College Graduate
White Males	17.7 (356)	14.3 (485)	13.4 (82)	8.0 (201)	7.8 (306)
Black Males	33.8 (343)	34.4 (209)	42.1 (57)	30.8 (123)	19.1 (84)

[a] Gammas, calculated on the entire range of delinquency scores (0–4), are −.20 for whites and −.05 for blacks.

the relatively weak performance of IQ in studies of self-reported delinquency.

IQ, Race and Official Delinquency

Comparison of the effects of race and IQ is more difficult than the class-IQ comparison because of a greater paucity of data or, at least, of appropriately analyzed data. There can be no doubt that IQ is related to delinquency within race categories. All of the studies mentioned are consistent on this point. The relative strength of the two variables is, however, open to question.

The multiple regression analysis using number of offenses as the dependent variable presented by Wolfgang et al. (1972:275–9) includes both race and IQ. Unfortunately for present purposes, it also includes highest grade completed and number of school moves, variables which account for the bulk of the explained variance in this measure of delinquency. Thus, the fact that race places third behind these school variables and IQ accounts for virtually nothing cannot be taken as direct evidence of their relative importance. We know that IQ is strongly related to delinquency in the Wolfgang

Table 3. Percent Committing Two or More Official Delinquent Acts by IQ and Race[a]

Race	IQ	
	Low	High
White males	24.3 (486)	9.4 (1053)
Black males	37.6 (702)	23.3 (266)

[a] IQ scores dichotomized at the 40th percentile.

data independent of race. We know, too, that IQ is strongly related to the school variables (r=.468 for highest grade completed) that, in variance terms, do most of the work. Therefore, we know that if these intervening variables were excluded from the analysis, the proportion of variance accounted for by IQ would increase substantially.

In the Contra Costa data, IQ and race have virtually identical effects on official delinquency. For illustration, we compare a dichotomous measure of IQ with the two categories of race in Table 3.

Measures of association between IQ and delinquency and between race and delinquency reflect the percentage differences in Table 3: race and IQ are virtually identical in their ability to predict delinquency. For race, r=.26; for IQ, r=.27.

The findings of McCord and McCord (1959:66, 203) from the Cambridge-Sommerville Youth Study are sometimes cited (e.g., West, 1973:91) as showing "no connection between low IQ and delinquency." Although in the McCords' data those in the lowest IQ group (80 or below) did have an intermediate rate of conviction during the follow-up period,[5] within the normal range of IQ scores (above 80) there was a monotonic decrease in rates of conviction from almost one-half in the 81–90 IQ group to one-quarter in the 110 or more IQ group. Because those in the lowest IQ group are only ten percent of

[5] Our figures are for the experimental and control groups combined (McCord and McCord, 1959:66, 203). Strictly speaking, the McCord data apply to adult criminality as well as juvenile delinquency, since the average age of their subjects was 27 at the time data on convictions were obtained.

the sample, the McCords' data, too, show an inverse relation between IQ and official misconduct.

Such problems of interpretation do not arise in Short and Strodtbeck's (1965) study of gang delinquency in Chicago. They report that gang boys scored lower on "all six intelligence measures" than non-gang boys in the same (lower) class; this difference held for white and black respondents alike.

Toby and Toby (1961) found "intellectual status" to be a significant forerunner of delinquency independent of socioeconomic status. And Reckless and Dinitz (1972) found that their teacher-nominated "good" boys had IQs from 8 to 12 points higher than their teacher-nominated "bad" boys in a class-homogeneous area.[6]

All in all, it seems reasonable to conclude on the basis of currently available data that IQ is related to official delinquency and that, in fact, it is as important in predicting official delinquency as social class or race. We know of no current research findings contrary to this conclusion.

Self-Reported Delinquency

A significant consequence of the no-IQ-difference position was that it helped set the stage for extensive use of self-report methods of measuring delinquent behavior. This position explicitly asserts that delinquents are as likely as others to possess the various skills reflected by IQ tests. If, however, the assumption of equal ability is unfounded, the measurement of delinquent behavior by the self-report method may be confounded with IQ, i.e., those most likely to commit delinquent acts may be least able to report adequately on their behavior. The self-report method, especially questionnaires,[7]

---

[6] The Toby-Toby and Reckless-Dinitz studies may be marginal to the question of IQ effects. However, this concern would carry greater weight if their results were contrary to research focusing directly on the IQ question.

[7] Early warnings that the questionnaire method is especially limited by the high rates of illiteracy among delinquents (Erickson and Empey, 1963) have gone essentially unheeded.

therefore does not provide an unambiguous test of the hypothesis that IQ is related to delinquent behavior.

In any event, most studies do find a relation between IQ and self-reported delinquency, but this relation is less robust than that found in official data. At one extreme, West (1973:158) found that 28.4 percent of the worst quarter of his sample on self-reported delinquency had low IQs, as compared to 16.6 percent in the remaining three-quarters—a difference only slightly smaller than his finding for official delinquency.

Weis (1973), too, found differences as strong as those typically reported when delinquency is measured by official data. In his study in a white upper-middle-class community near San Francisco, Weis collected Wechsler-Bellevue IQ scores and self-reports of delinquency for 255 male and female eleventh-grade students. One of the clusters emerging from his analysis was a property deviance scale that included items on theft, burglary, shoplifting and vandalism. When these scores were trichotomized, Weis found that 27 percent of those with IQ scores of less than 110, and 49 percent of those with IQ scores of 110 or more, had low scores on the property deviance scale. He found a similar difference (23% versus 41%) on a social deviance scale that included items on marijuana, alcohol and gambling.[8]

More typical of self-report studies, however, are the relations from the Contra Costa data shown in Table 4. Among white males, twice the proportion in the lowest as in the highest IQ group report involvement in two or more of a possible six delinquent acts; among black males the comparable ratio is 3:2.

Whatever the strength of the relations in Table 4, we believe they should be evaluated by comparison with social class and race. As Table 4 shows, race has no impact on self-reported delinquency—a finding consistent with much of the self-report literature (e.g., Williams and Gold, 1972). The same literature has consistently re-

---

[8] For details of data collection, see Weis (1973). The data reported in the text cannot be found in Weis' dissertation. We are grateful to him for making them available to us.

Table 4. Percent Committing Two or More Self-Reported Delinquent Acts by IQ and Race [a]

Race	Low IQ				High IQ
White males	24	26	20	19	12
	(196)	(270)	(302)	(336)	(396)
Black males	27	26	19	19	18
	(393)	(257)	(149)	(68)	(39)

[a] IQ scores are grouped in percentiles as in Table 1. Gammas, calculated on the entire range of delinquency scores (0–6), are –.15 for whites and –.07 for blacks.

vealed a weaker relation of social class (e.g., Nye et al., 1958; Akers, 1964) to self-reported delinquency than that found in Table 4. The weight of the evidence is that IQ is more important than race and social class. The voluminous criticisms advanced against self-report delinquency research—with an eye to rescuing social class—presumably would have the same or even greater consequences for IQ. For example, the heavy reliance on in-school populations, the overabundance of minor offenders, and the dependence on subject cooperation may work to attenuate the relationship between social class and delinquency. If so, there is reason to believe that these factors would also depress the relation between self-reported delinquency and IQ. In fact, Hirschi (1969:46) reports that among those with the highest grades in English who had no police records, 79 percent cooperated with the self-report survey, while among those with the lowest grades in English who had police records, only 38 percent cooperated. More importantly, not only did grades in English and official delinquency substantially affect cooperation with the self-report survey, the two factors were found to interact: low ability boys with police records were disproportionately unlikely to appear in the self-report sample. Since official delinquents are likely to be "self-report" delinquents (if sampled), the number of self-reported delinquents in the sample is considerably depressed, especially at the low end of the ability scale.

In short, however delinquency is measured, IQ is able to compete on at least equal terms with class and race, the major

bases of most sociological theories of delinquency. At the same time, a relation between IQ and delinquency is routinely denied in sociological textbooks.

Implications for Theory

Our original purpose in introducing theory was frankly argumentive: we expected to find theorists struggling with a conflict between their own logic and the erroneous "results of research" on IQ. In short, we expected to find that they had often been led astray by the anti-IQ climate of criminology.

Actual examination of currently influential theories required revision of our plans. In most cases, theorists were not paying all that much attention to the "results of research." We had been led astray by the naive textbook assumption that theory organizes research and research tests and modifies theory. In the case of IQ, however, it would be more accurate to say that theory opposes research and research ignores theory.

Theories from the period (Merton, 1938; Sutherland and Cressey, 1974) when most researchers considered low IQ a strong correlate of delinquency ignore this variable,[9] while theories from the period when IQ was almost universally considered irrelevant predict either very strong negative (Cohen, 1955) or weak but important positive relations (Cloward and Ohlin, 1960) with delinquency. And a theoretical tradition (labeling) spanning both periods has managed to take a position opposite to research in both of them. Although all of these theories have been heavily researched, investigators have paid little or no attention to their views regarding IQ.

Since it is difficult to argue with those who agree, we will briefly show that resistence to consideration or inclusion of IQ does not characterize any current theory; that, on the contrary, several important theories require a relation between IQ and delinquency. Explicit recognition of this

[9] The Gluecks reported periodically throughout the thirties that their delinquents were "burdened with feeblemindedness" (e.g., Glueck and Glueck, 1934).

fact would only increase their scope, the plausibility of their claims, and their consistency with research findings.

The best example is Cohen's (1955) effort to relate social class to delinquency by way of differential experience in the educational system. In Cohen's theory, children differentially prepared or qualified encounter a school system that treats all comers alike. Children inadequately "prepared" for success in school find the experience painful and are likely, as a consequence, to turn to delinquency. The place of IQ in this process would seem obvious and, in fact, Cohen (1955:102–3) could not be more explicit on this question:

> It may be taken as established that ability, as measured by performance in conventional tests of intelligence, varies directly with social class. . . . The conventional tests do test for abilities that are highly prized by middle-class people, that are fostered by middle-class socialization, and that are especially important for further achievement in the academic world and in middle-class society. In short, *the results of these tests are one important index of the ability of the child to meet middle-class expectations*, to do the kinds of things that bring rewards in the middle-class world. (emphasis added)

In Cohen's theory, intelligence intervenes between social class and delinquency or it is at least an important indicator of the social class of the *child*. In either case, IQ should be more strongly related to delinquency than such indirect measures of the ability of the child to meet middle-class expectations as *"father's* occupation."

Cohen's views on the interchangeability of IQ and class illustrate how the former could have been used to extend the scope of his theory beyond the confines of "lower-class delinquency." The situation facing the middle-class child with low IQ may not be all that different from the situation facing the lower-class child and, if such a situation explains the delinquency of one of them, it may explain the delinquency of the other as well. If both lower- and middle-class delinquency can be explained by the same mechanism, Cohen's reliance on a separate mechanism for middle-class boys (Cohen, 1955:162–9) is

inexplicable or is, at the very least, theoretically and empirically inelegant.

If a zero relation between IQ and delinquency would falsify Cohen's theory, it would virtually falsify the theory of Cloward and Ohlin (1960) as well, but for quite different reasons. Cloward and Ohlin (1960:111) suggest a positive relation between intelligence and delinquency:

> Some persons who have experienced a marked discrepancy between aspirations and achievements may look outward, attributing their failure to the existence of unjust or arbitrary institutional arrangements which keep men of ability and ambition from rising in the social structure. Such persons do not view their failure as a reflection of personal inadequacy but instead blame a cultural and social system that encourages everyone to reach for success while differentially restricting access to the success-goals. In contrast to this group there are individuals who attribute failure to their own inadequacies—to a lack of discipline, zeal, intelligence, persistence, or other personal quality.

In other words, the lower-class boy with a high IQ whose talents go unrecognized and unrewarded is a prime candidate for delinquency.

On the basis of available evidence, Cloward and Ohlin are wrong. For present purposes, however, the point is that their theory requires research on the IQ of juvenile offenders and is enduring testimony to the dangers in the view that IQ need be "no longer seriously considered" by criminologists.[10]

At first glance, labeling theory would seem to be an exception to our argument that IQ is important, since this theory puts no stock in the notion that individual differences may act as causes of delinquent behavior. In one of the first efforts by a labeling theorist to neutralize individual-difference research, Tannenbaum (1938:6) focused special attention on IQ, arguing that "whatever 'intelligence' is, it has no demonstrated relationship to crime." As labeling theory has "progressed," how-

---

[10] Although Merton (1938) ignores IQ and its "success" implications, IQ is obviously relevant to any opportunity theory.

ever, as it has become more closely associated with the conflict perspective according to which "society organizes itself for the protection of the ruling classes against the socially inferior" (Doleschal and Klapmuts, 1973:622), it has tended more and more to recognize that it too is dependent on individual differences. The generally low IQ of official delinquents is now accepted by labeling theorists and is used as evidence *for* their view that the system discriminates against or creates the disadvantaged (Doleschal and Klapmuts, 1973:612, 616; Polk and Schafer, 1972:34–54).

If labeling theorists argue that discrimination produces the relation between IQ and delinquency, then the mechanism that connects IQ to delinquency is the bone of contention between labeling and conventional theories—not the fact of a relation itself. We will return to the mechanism question.

Perhaps the only major theory strictly silent on the question of IQ is Sutherland's "differential association" (Sutherland and Cressey, 1974:75–7). Sutherland (1931) played a major role in constructing the current position of criminology on IQ. He rejoiced in its alleged failure to discriminate between delinquents and nondelinquents, and his influential text continues to belittle "mental testers" to the present day. Even so, differential association has nothing to fear from intelligence. This theory faintly suggests a positive association among those exposed to the delinquent culture (as does any theory that emphasizes the need to learn crime), but it really cannot be used to predict even the sign of the relation in the general population. If the theory cannot predict the sign of this relation, it is, nonetheless, capable of accounting for any relation between IQ and delinquency that might be revealed by research.

A final set of theories might be grouped under the heading of "social control" (for a convenient summary, see Nettler, 1974). These theories focus on a broad range of causal variables, and they are relatively open to individual differences, to the idea that "in learning to conduct ourselves, some of us need more lessons than others" (Nettler, 1974:232). Although none of them may now consider IQ of central importance, most suggest a negative association, and none would have difficulty absorbing this variable. In fact, for those sociologically-oriented control theories that emphasize "stakes in conformity" (e.g., Toby, 1957), IQ is of obvious importance.

Most sociological theories, then, have been saying for some time that IQ should be related to delinquency for the same reason that social class is, or should be related to it. Given the theoretical overlap of IQ and social class, the contrast in how the research community has reacted to their varying fates would be hard for an outsider to understand.

The finding that social class was unrelated to self-reported delinquency produced a large volume of follow-up research. The "finding" that IQ was unrelated to any measure of delinquency was, in contrast, accepted without so much as a murmur of protest. The literature on IQ contains none of the "what may have gone wrong"* kinds of methodological critiques so often encountered in efforts to save social class. Instead, it is marked by considerable speculative ingenuity directed against an established relation. The extent to which this relation has been established may be revealed by a review of the history of IQ testing as it applies to delinquency and crime.

History

As a cause of delinquency, IQ got off to a very strong start in the first years of this century. The notion that "imbeciles" and "idiots" would be unable to resist criminal impulses or, for that matter, even to distinguish right from wrong, was a straightforward extension of Lombroso's then prestigious theory of the born or biologically defective criminal. Initial research did nothing to dampen enthusiasm for this idea. Goring (1972:255) in Great Britain reported that criminals "as a class, are highly differentiated mentally from the law abiding classes," and Goddard (1914:7) in the United States concluded that "probably from 25% to 50% of the people in our prisons are mentally defective and incapable of managing their affairs with ordinary prudence." In the period 1910–1914, the "percentage feebleminded" in fifty studies of institutionalized delinquents had a median value of 51 (Sutherland, 1931:358). Since it was then assumed that the proportion feebleminded in the general population was less than one percent (Goring used an estimate of .46 percent), the conclusion that faulty intelligence was the "single most important cause of crime" followed, or at least seemed to follow directly from the evidence.

If we follow the fate of IQ through mainstream criminology, we discover that its day was very brief. Less than two decades after Goring estimated .6553 as a "minimum value" for the correlation between mental defectiveness and crime, Sutherland (1931) was poking fun at the absurdities of the "mental testers."[11] His negative review of their research was so influential that the "modern" or "recent" position on IQ described by today's textbooks appears to have been firmly established at that time, i:e., forty-five years ago.

Sutherland's stance is not difficult to understand. As Savitz (1972:xviii) has reminded us, the medical profession seized power in criminology before the end of the nineteenth century and still maintained a preeminent position in the early days of intelligence testing—both Goring and Goddard were physicians. A short time later, however, criminology had become a subfield of sociology. Given this shift in disciplinary dominance, an equivalent

---

[11] Sutherland summarized about 350 studies conducted between 1910 and 1928 noting downward trends in the proportion feebleminded in delinquent and criminal groups, as well as inconsistencies in the results. "In those early days of mental testing the influence of Goddard was very great; he had asserted that the more expert the mental tester the larger the proportion of delinquents he would find to be feebleminded. Many of the testers attempted to demonstrate their superiority in that manner." "Consequently a report regarding the proportion of a delinquent group feebleminded is of primary significance in locating the mental tester upon a scale of mental testing methods. In this sense the psychometric tests of delinquents throw more light upon the intelligence of the mental testers than upon the intelligence of delinquents." (Sutherland, 1931:358–62).

paradigm shift is now pretty much accepted as a logical necessity. "Intelligence" was a central element of the "old" paradigm. It just had to go. And go it did.

The history of IQ in research findings is not so quickly or easily told. The initial claims about the proportion of feebleminded delinquents were excessively high because—as Merrill (1947:159) has pointed out—researchers were basing their cutting point on children in institutions for the mentally deficient. The logic of this procedure went something like this: if no child in an institution for the feebleminded has a mental age in excess of twelve, then a mental age of twelve or less is sufficient to classify a person feebleminded. There was nothing especially silly about this procedure, it merely made the mistake of assuming that the same procedure would not also classify a large portion of the general population feebleminded. As it became apparent that a too-large portion of the general population would be classified feebleminded, the mental age requirement was first abruptly and then gradually lowered, with the result that the proportion feebleminded among delinquents also first abruptly and then gradually declined. Sutherland (1931) called attention to this twenty-year trend—which, in fact, continued for another 30 years (Woodward, 1955; Caplan, 1965)—and allowed his readers to conclude that it would continue until the initial claims of difference between delinquents and nondelinquents had no foundation in fact.

The most direct evidence against an IQ difference resulted from the extensive testing of the draft army in World War I. Murchison (1926) and Tulchin (1939) reported that the distribution of intelligence in the draft army was virtually identical to the distribution among adult prisoners. Without including details of the investigation, Murchison also reported that the prisoners in a certain midwestern institution were more intelligent than the guards, an anecdotal fact even now more widely quoted than the results of many carefully conducted studies showing important differences in favor of the intelligence hypothesis. Although Sutherland (1931:364) acknowledged that "serious questions have been raised regarding the validity of these tests and the validity of using the draft army as a sample of the general population,'' he carefully noted that "the consistency in results is a fact that cannot be overlooked.''

By the late 1920s and early 1930s, the evidence was sufficiently mixed that summaries of the research literature were arriving at variant conclusions. Thomas and Thomas (1928:365) concluded from their review of the same literature examined by Sutherland that important differences between delinquents and non-delinquents on IQ were "beyond question.'' They reached this conclusion by focusing on the many studies reporting such differences and by discounting the draft-army research as being so clearly out of line as to be suspect. In 1935, Chassell published an extensive review of research on this question. Her general conclusion, based on nearly 300 studies:

> Undoubtedly the relation between morality and intellect in the general population is considerably higher than usually found in restricted groups. Nevertheless, it is hardly probable that this relation is high. Expressed in correlational terms, the relation in the general population may therefore be expected to fall below .70. (Chassell, 1935:470)[12]

As IQ tests improved, the average score of samples of delinquents also improved until, with the advent of the Revised Stanford Binet and the Wechsler-Bellevue scales in the late 1930s, they were obtaining an average IQ of about 92 (Merrill, 1947; Woodward, 1955; Caplan, 1965). With the advent of these improved tests about 35 years ago, the marked trends and occasional fluctuations of earlier research apparently came to an end. Since that time, it has been reasonable to expect that samples of delinquents would differ from the general population by about eight IQ points. This conclusion has been accepted by Woodward (1955) and Caplan (1965) in

major reviews of the literature and is generally consistent with the more recent research reviewed in this paper.

The question, then, is how a reliable eight IQ point difference was converted to the no-difference conclusion of the textbooks. One possibility is that an eight IQ point difference was not seen as theoretically or practically important. This possibility is easily disputed: no modern reviewer has questioned the importance of a difference of this magnitude.[13] Assuming that ten percent of the population is delinquent, this difference would produce a correlation (Yule's Q) between IQ and delinquency of about −.4.

The neglect of IQ after a reliable and important difference had been established may be traced to the initial plausibility of an unusual number of counter-arguments. These arguments are so numerous and diverse that we can hope to deal with them only generally and briefly.

The Spuriousness Argument

Scholarly reviews of the literature have made much of the hypothesis that the low IQs of delinquents are a spurious consequence of differences in class or culture. Against the estimated eight IQ point difference between delinquents and non-delinquents, Woodward (1955) assembles a good deal of material suggesting the possibility that cultural factors are at work: the children of professionals differ from those of unskilled manual workers by about 20 IQ points; average IQ scores are low in *areas* with high delinquency rates;[14] children in large families have low IQ scores and are more likely to be delinquent; overcrowding is related both to low IQ and to delinquency; finally, studies based on sib-sib comparisons (such as Healy and Bronner, 1936) and on other methods of control for cultural factors

---

[12] Present-day researchers would not be so modest about a correlation of .70! Chassell's caution may be indicative of the standards against which empirical relations were judged in the early days of quantitative research. These standards may account for the ease with which reviewers were able to reject IQ as a "significant" causal variable (see also footnote 1).

[13] Caplan (1965:104) refers to this eight-point difference as a "first class" relationship. As noted below, however, he cautions the reader that cultural factors be taken into account before it is accepted as genuine.

[14] This is an example of what might be called the reverse ecological fallacy: because IQ and delinquency are related at the ecological level, it is *unlikely* that they are related at the individual level.

"tend to support the contention that complete control *would* eliminate the difference between delinquents and nondelinquents" (Woodward, 1955:289; emphasis added).[15] As we have seen, the evidence says otherwise. Differences by class and race do not account for IQ differences between delinquents and nondelinquents. These differences remain pronounced within groups homogeneous on these variables. If there exists a cultural correlate of both IQ and delinquency strong enough to account for the relation between them, it has not yet been identified.

Ten years after Woodward's influential review (see Wootten, 1959:302), Caplan (1965) was unable to find additional research material bearing directly on her cultural hypothesis. His conclusions about the effects of IQ are, however, if anything, more skeptical than Woodward's, because he is able to cite an additional source of concern.

Arguments Focusing on the Measurement of Delinquency

The advent of the self-report method helped Caplan (1965:120–1) call into question the measures of delinquency upon

---

[15] Healy and Bronner (1936) controlled cultural factors by matching 105 delinquents with their same sex, nondelinquent sib nearest in age and then comparing IQ test scores. Although they found an IQ difference in favor of the nondelinquents, this difference was not statistically significant and was not interpreted as practically or theoretically significant by them. (Thirty-four percent of the delinquents and 26 percent of the nondelinquents had IQs under 90.)

The difficulty with this widely cited study (e.g., Wootton, 1959) is that its design makes the outcome a statistical necessity. Pushing the logic of Healy and Bronner's matching procedure one step further, we would compare identical twins raised together, only one of whom was delinquent. Since the correlation between the IQs of identical twins raised together is about .87, a figure "nearly as high . . . the correlation between two parallel tests for the same individual" (Eckland, 1967:177), we would be asking whether errors in IQ measurement are related to delinquency. By the same token, knowing that the "control" is a brother or sister reared in the same household tells us a good deal about what to expect in the way of IQ (in most studies the sib-sib correlation is in the neighborhood of .55), and there is little reason to expect the original relation to survive with anything like its "natural" magnitude.

which the original findings of IQ differences were based. Once again, the evidence against IQ was inferential rather than direct: if official data measure delinquency imperfectly, then imperfections in measurement rather than the phenomenon itself may account for the observed relation. And, indeed, few have been able to resist ascribing IQ differences between officially identified delinquents and nondelinquents to the ability of the bright delinquent to avoid detection or to differential response of officials to high and low IQ adolescents (e.g., Sutherland, 1931; Doleschal and Klapmuts, 1973; Stark, 1975).

Both the differential detection and differential reaction hypotheses require that IQ have a direct or independent effect on official delinquency.[16] Such direct effect hypotheses compete with intervening variable hypotheses and may be directly tested when the latter are available. A competing hypothesis widely mentioned in the literature (e.g., Short and Strodtbeck, 1965:238; West, 1973:44) is that IQ affects delinquency through school performance. If IQ has the direct effect suggested by the differential detection and reaction hypotheses, nothing consequent to IQ can explain the zero-order relation. Two studies bear on this question. When Wolfgang et al. removed by statistical adjustment the effects of such intervening variables as highest grade completed, the relation between IQ and such "detection" measures as number of offenses virtually vanished (Wolfgang et al., 1972:275–9). (We have replicated this finding with the Contra Costa County data.) Taking a somewhat different approach, West (1973:217) also was able to reduce the relation between IQ and official delinquency below the significant level by matching on peer and teacher ratings on "troublesomeness." These ratings were made at ages eight and ten, well before the delinquent acts recorded by officials. Once again, then, *the*

---

[16] Contrary to the "intelligence per se is not a cause . . . " arguments with which it is often paired, the differential detection argument suggests that, in fact, intelligence per se *is* a cause of delinquency— when delinquency is measured by official records.

differential ability to avoid detection and the differential official reaction on the basis of IQ arguments are not supported by available evidence. (The tests of the official reaction hypothesis are limited by available data to reactions by the police.)

Tests of these and related direct effect hypotheses[17] at the same time identify the mechanism linking IQ to delinquency. This mechanism, the data suggest, is performance in and attitudes toward the school. That school variables are strong enough to account for the impact of IQ should come as no surprise. Their significance for delinquency is nowhere in dispute and is, in fact, one of the oldest and most consistent findings of delinquency research (e.g., Thrasher, 1963; Gold, 1970; Hindelang, 1973; Weis, 1973). What should come as a surprise is the easy acceptance of the no-difference-on-IQ conclusion, since the consequences of IQ differences are generally accepted as major predictors of delinquency. This brings us to the most troublesome of the arguments against IQ effects.

Arguments Focusing on the Measurement or Meaning of IQ

The facts we have presented compete with a wide variety of counter-arguments that focus on the meaning or measurement of IQ: "anybody can learn anything" (Eckland, 1967:174–5, quoting Faris, 1961:838), "it is impossible to make intelligence part of any respectable theory" (ASR referee, 1975), "so-called intelligence tests measure only 'test intelligence' and not innate intelligence" (Clinard, 1968:170), and "mainly they [IQ tests] measure the socioeconomic status of the respondent" (Chambliss and Ryther, 1975:373). Excellent discussions of many of these issues are available in the sociological literature (Eckland, 1967;

---

[17] Other very old direct effect hypotheses are that IQ differences stem from (1) the inability of the unintelligent to understand distinctions between right and wrong or (2) their inability to foresee and appreciate the consequences of their acts. These hypotheses assume that low IQ children are more likely to be delinquent, regardless of the social consequences (e.g., school difficulties) of their lack of IQ. Again, current data do not appear to support hypotheses of this form.

Gordon, 1975). We will deal only with those counter-hypotheses that have a direct bearing on the relation between IQ and delinquency and that can be addressed to some extent using data already presented.

The cultural bias of IQ tests. The argument against IQ tests most frequently encountered in the sociological literature is that these tests are biased against low-income and minority group children. Specific test items (e.g., "What color are rubies?") are often presented to show the obviousness of this bias (Chambliss and Ryther, 1975:373). Since the groups said to be discriminated against by IQ tests are the same groups with high rates of delinquency, the cultural bias hypothesis is certainly plausible. In form, it is identical to the traditional cultural hypothesis previously encountered and may be tested using the same data. These data show that the bias hypothesis is inadequate: important differences in IQ between delinquents and nondelinquents *within* race and class categories cannot be explained by argument or evidence that these tests are biased in favor of middle-class whites.

The stability of test scores. To the extent that IQ test scores are unstable and subject to subtle social influence, the meaning of a correlation between IQ and delinquency is open to question. It may be that reaction to the misbehavior of the child influences his IQ, that the low IQ child today may be the high IQ child tomorrow, and so on. These possibilities are summarized in assertions that "the scores are highly unstable through time" (Polk and Schafer, 1972:195). Unfortunately for such assertions, they are not consistent with the evidence: the IQs of children at four or five years of age have a correlation of about .7 with their IQs at age 17 (Bloom, 1964); after age ten, test-retest correlations (regardless of the number of years between the tests) fall between the test's reliability and the square of its reliability (Jensen, 1969:18). For that matter, the ability of IQ tests to predict delinquency at some period far removed from their administration is inconsistent with the gross implications of the instability argument.

A fall-back position for those who

would argue instability is that these scores *could be* manipulated by simple and straightforward shifts in the environment of the child:

We may treat people differently out of ignorance or prejudice, but the result is the same as if the supposed differences were real. Studies have shown that school children seen as liable to be educationally backward become educationally backward and that, vice versa, children seen as educationally capable become educationally capable. (Taylor et al., 1973:142; see also Polk and Schafer, 1972:46; Schur, 1973:164)

The study cited in support of such arguments is Rosenthal and Jacobson, *Pygmalion in the Classroom* (1968). In this study, students in grades K through 5 in one elementary school were given group-administered IQ tests at the end of the 1964 academic year. The following fall, a random 20 percent of the students were identified to their teachers as students expected to show unusual intellectual gains during the academic year. In May, 1965, all students were re-tested on the same IQ test. Although both the experimental and the control subjects showed IQ gains, the experimental group showed a 3.8 point greater gain, with the bulk of this gain coming in the first and second grades. On the basis of these results, Rosenthal and Jacobson (1968:98) conclude that favorable expectations of teachers "can be responsible for gains in their pupils' IQ's and, for the lower grades, that these gains can be quite dramatic."

Unfortunately, *Pygmalion* has problems. Snow (1969:197) asserts that the study "stands as a casebook example of many of Darrell Huff's (*How to Lie with Statistics*) admonitions to data analysts" and that it "fails to come close to providing an adequate demonstration of the phenomenon" (the effects of teacher expectations on IQ scores). Thorndike (1968:708) begins his similarly negative review with what has turned out to be a prophetic statement:

In spite of anything I can say, I am sure it (*Pygmalion in the Classroom*) will become a classic—widely referred to and rarely examined critically. Alas, it is so defective technically that one can only regret that it ever

got beyond the eyes of the original investigators!

Thorndike concludes that "the basic data . . . are so untrustworthy that any conclusions based upon them must be suspect." And, indeed, this too was prophetic. Elashoff and Snow (1971) report that *none of nine attempts to replicate the effects of teacher expectations on IQ scores has been successful.* One would think that this would be enough to put an end to the "Rosenthal effect." However, Beeghley and Butler (1974:750) still maintain that the effects of teacher expectations on IQ "have been forcefully demonstrated by Rosenthal and Jacobson," and they muddy the waters by citing two "replications" of *Pygmalion.* In the first, "changes in intellectual functioning were not expected" by the investigators themselves (Meichenbaum et al., 1969:307) and in fact, as far as we can determine, IQ was not even a variable in the study. In the second, the author summarizes a variety of research results and concludes the findings do not "provide any direct proof that teacher expectations can influence pupil performance" (Pidgeon, 1970:126). Ironically—for a study which Beeghley and Butler purport to be a replication of *Pygmalion*—Pidgeon (1970:126) notes that the Rosenthal and Jacobson study "would bear repetition, providing conditions could be found for employing a more satisfactory research design." As of now, it is clear that no labeling or expectation effects of the sort alleged by Rosenthal and Jacobson (and widely cited in the crime and delinquency literature) have been established.

Conclusions

The assertion that IQ affects the likelihood of delinquent behavior through its effect on school performance is consistent with available data. The corollary descriptive assertion that delinquents have lower IQs than nondelinquents is firmly established. Both of these assertions are inconsistent with the "no-IQ-difference" view of the textbooks. They are clearly inconsistent with the image of the delinquent in much sociological writing on the subject, and those planning prevention and treatment programs would do well to take them into account.[18]

Interestingly enough, most modern theories of delinquency assume (and some explicitly state) that IQ affects delinquency. That their views have been ignored by researchers testing them speaks to the depth of the concern that individual differences are both non-sociological and positively dangerous. In this sense, IQ is doubly significant in that it represents an entire class of variables traditionally ignored by sociological students of crime and delinquency. Variables in this large residual category (virtually everything beyond class, culture, and official processing) will not lose their status as alternative hypotheses simply by being ignored, and they will continue to restrict and even embarrass sociological theory until some effort is made to incorporate them.

For that matter, IQ is a poor example of a variable that may require modification of sociological perspectives. As of now, there is no evidence that IQ has a direct impact on delinquency. The police bias, differential ability to avoid detection, and inability to appreciate moral distinctions hypotheses are not consistent with current data. If the mechanism linking IQ to delinquency is school performance and adjustment, then IQ does not lead away from the arena in which sociological theories have focused their quest for the antecedents of delinquency; rather, it helps illuminate the social processes occurring there.

REFERENCES

Akers, Ronald L.
1964 "Socio-economic status and delinquent behavior: a retest." Journal of Research on Crime and Delinquency 1:38–46.
Beeghley, Leonard and Edgar W. Butler
1974 "The consequences of intelligence testing in public schools before and after desegregation." Social Problems 21:740–54.

[18] See Nettler (1974:162–5). The range of treatment programs affected by these differences is considerably broader than is usually imagined: "The frequent mental dullness . . . and reading and writing disabilities of a larger proportion of delinquents *make them poor risks for industrial training* (Shulman, 1951:781, emphasis added).

Bloch, Herbert A. and Gilbert Geis
1962 Man, Crime and Society. New York: Random House.
Bloom, B.A.
1964 Stability and Change in Human Characteristics. New York: Wiley.
Caplan, Nathan S.
1965 "Intellectual functioning" Pp. 100–38 in Herbert C. Quay (ed.), Juvenile Delinquency. Princeton: Van Nostrand.
Chambliss, William J. and Thomas E. Ryther
1975 Sociology: The Discipline and Its Direction. New York: McGraw-Hill.
Chassell, Clara F.
1935 The Relation between Morality and Intellect. New York: Teachers College, Columbia University.
Clinard, Marshall B.
1968 Sociology of Deviant Behavior. New York: Holt, Rinehart and Winston.
Cloward, Richard E. and Lloyd E. Ohlin
1960 Delinquency and Opportunity. New York: Free Press.
Cohen, Albert K.
1955 Delinquent Boys: The Culture of the Gang. New York: Free Press.
Coleman, James C.
1950 Abnormal Psychology and Modern Life, Glenview, Il.: Scott, Foresman.
Doleschal, Eugene and Nora Klapmuts
1973 "Toward a new criminology." Crime and Delinquency Literature: 607–26.
Eckland, Bruce K.
1967 "Genetics and sociology: a reconsideration." American Sociological Review 32:193–4.
Elashoff, J. and R. Snow
1971 Pygmalion Reconsidered. Worthington, Oh.: Jones
Erickson, Maynard L. and LaMar T. Empey
1963 "Court records, undetected delinquency and decision-making." Journal of Criminal Law, Criminology and Police Science 54:456–69.
Faris, Robert E. L.
1961 "The ability dimension in human society." American Sociological Review 26:835–43.
Gibbons, Don C.
1970 Delinquent Behavior. Englewood Cliffs, N.J.: Prentice-Hall.
Glueck, Sheldon and Eleanor Glueck
1934 Five Hundred Delinquent Women. New York: Knopf.
Goddard, Henry H.
1914 Feeble-Mindedness: Its Causes and Consequences. New York: Macmillan.
Gold, Martin
1970 Delinquent Behavior in an American City. Belmont, Ca.: Brooks/Cole.
Gordon, Robert A.
1975 "Examining labeling theory: the case of mental retardation." Pp. 83–146 in Walter Gove (ed.), The Labelling of Deviance. New York: Wiley.
1976 "Prevalence: the rare datum in delinquency measurement and its implications for the theory of delinquency." Pp. 201–84 in Mal-

colm W. Klein (ed.), The Juvenile Justice System. Beverly Hills, Ca.: Sage.

Goring, Charles
[1913] The English Convict. Montclair, N.J.: Pat-
1972   terson Smith

Haskell, Martin R. and Lewis Yablonsky
1974   Crime and Delinquency. Chicago: Rand McNally

Healy, William and Augusta F. Bronner
1936   New Light on Delinquency and Its Treatment. New Haven: Yale University Press.

Hindelang, Michael J.
1973   "Causes of delinquency: a partial replication and extension." Social Problems 20:471–87.

Hirschi, Travis
1969   Causes of Delinquency. Berkeley: University of California Press.

Jensen, A. R.
1969   "How much can we boost I.Q. and scholastic achievement?" Harvard Educational Review 39:1–123.

Johnson, Elmer
1968   Crime, Correction and Society. Homewood, Il.: Dorsey Press.

Liazos, Alexander
1972   "The poverty of the sociology of deviance: nuts, sluts, and preverts." Social Problems 20:103–20.

McCord, William and Joan McCord
1959   Origins of Crime: A New Evaluation of the Cambridge-Somerville Study. New York: Columbia Press.

Matza, David
1964   Delinquency and Drift. New York: Wiley.

Meichanbaum, Donald H., Kenneth S. Bowers and Robert R. Ross
1969   "A behavioral analysis of teacher expectancy effect." Journal of Personality and Social Psychology 13:306–16.

Merrill, Maud A.
1947   Problems of Child Delinquency. Boston: Houghton Mifflin.

Merton, Robert K.
1938   "Social structure and anomie." American Sociological Review 3:672–82.

Murchison, Carl
1926   Criminal Intelligence. Worcester, Ma.: Clark University Press.

Nettler, Gwynn
1974   Explaining Crime. New York: McGraw-Hill.

Nye, F. Ivan, James F. Short, Jr. and Virgil J. Olson
1958   "Socio-economic status and delinquent behavior." American Journal of Sociology 63:381–9.

Pidgeon, Douglas
1970   Expectation and Pupil Performance. London: National Foundation for Educational Research in England and Wales.

Polk, Kenneth and Walter E. Schafer
1972   Schools and Delinquency. Englewood Cliffs, N.J.: Prentice-Hall.

Reckless, Walter C. and Simon Dinitz
1972   The Prevention of Delinquency. Columbus: Ohio State University Press.

Reiss, Albert J. and Albert L. Rhodes
1961   "The distribution of juvenile delinquency in the social class structure." American Sociological Review 26:720–32.

Rosenthal, R. and Lenore Jacobson
1968   Pygmalion in the Classroom. New York: Holt, Rinehart and Winston.

Ross, Edward A.
1901   Social Control. New York: Macmillan.

Savitz, Leonard D.
1972   "Introduction." Pp. v–xx in Gina Lombroso-Ferrero, Criminal Man. Montclair, N.J.: Patterson Smith.

Schur, Edwin M.
1973   Radical Non-Intervention: Rethinking the Delinquency Problem. Englewood Cliffs, N.J.: Prentice-Hall.

Short, James F., Jr. and Fred L. Strodtbeck
1965   Group Process and Gang Delinquency. Chicago: University of Chicago Press.

Shulman, Harry M.
1951   "Intelligence and delinquency." Journal of Criminal Law and Criminology 41:763–81.

Snow, R.
1969   "Unfinished Pygmalion." Contemporary Psychology 14:197–9.

Stark, Rodney
1975   Social Problems. New York: CRM/Random House.

Sutherland, Edwin H.
1924   Criminology. Philadelphia: Lippincott.
1931   "Mental deficiency and crime," Pp. 357–75 in Kimball Young (ed.), Social Attitudes. New York: Holt, Rinehart and Winston.

Sutherland, Edwin H. and Donald R. Cressey
[1939] Principles of Criminology. Philadelphia: Lip-
1974   pincott

Tannenbaum, Frank
1938   Crime and the Community. Boston: Ginn.

Taylor, Ian, Paul Walton and Jock Young
1973   The New Criminology. New York: Harper.

Thomas, William I. and Dorothy Swaine Thomas
1928   The Child in America. New York: Knopf.

Thorndike, R. L.
1968   "Review of R. Rosenthal and L. Jacobson, 'Pygmalion in the Classroom.' " American Educational Research Journal 5:708–11.

Thrasher, F.
[1927] The Gang. Chicago: University of Chicago
1963   press.

Toby, Jackson
1957   "Social disorganization and stake in conformity: complementary factors in the predatory behavior of hoodlums." Journal of Criminal Law, Criminology and Police Science 48:12–7.

Toby, Jackson and Marcia L. Toby
1961   Low School Status as a Predisposing Factor in Subcultural Delinquency. New Brunswick, N.J.: Rutgers University. Mimeo.

Tulchin, Simon H.
1939   Intelligence and Crime. Chicago: University of Chicago Press.

Weis, Joseph
1973   Delinquency among the Well-to-Do. Un-

published Ph.D. dissertation. University of California, Berkeley.

West, D. J.
1973 Who Becomes Delinquent? London: Heinemann.

Williams, Jay and Martin Gold
1972 "From delinquent behavior to official delinquency." Social Problems 20:209–29.

Wolfgang, Marvin, Robert M. Figlio and Thorsten Sellin
1972 Delinquency as a Birth Cohort. Chicago: University of Chicago Press.

Woodward, Mary
1955 "The role of low intelligence in delinquency." British Journal of Delinquency 5:281–303.

Wootton, Barbara
1959 Social Science and Social Pathology. New York: Macmillan.

Zeleny, Leslie D.
1933 "Feeblemindedness and criminal conduct." American Journal of Sociology 38:564–78.

28

UNDERLYING ASSUMPTIONS OF BASIC MODELS OF DELINQUENCY THEORIES

RUTH ROSNER KORNHAUSER

Origins of Delinquency Theories

At the heart of the various sociological approaches to delinquency are two contrasting analytic models: one locates the causes of delinquency in social disorganization, the other, in cultural deviance. Social disorganization refers to the relative lack of articulation of values within culture as well as between culture and social structure. Cultural deviance refers to conduct which reflects socialization to subcultural values and derivative norms that conflict with law. Cultural deviance models, two variants of social disorganization theory (strain and control models), and the combination of either of these cultural deviance models in mixed models of delinquent subculture together yield four causal models that encompass the principal current sociological explanations of delinquency.

These models were intended to account for crime as well as delinquency. Some subsequently constructed theories, not all of which fit into the foregoing categories, have been applied primarily to adult crime or to all deviance, and are not examined here. Among the most influential of these is Lemert's account (1972, chap. 1) of the societal reaction to deviance; he has taken care to dissociate his approach from labeling theory, with which it is often grouped. His is a control model; labeling theory, to the extent that it implies an explanation of the causes of deviance rather than the reactions of others to it, is most akin to a cultural deviance model (see Becker, 1963). What is sometimes called conflict theory, as represented in various statements of a neo-Marxian perspective, emphasizes structurally determined conflicts of interest, rather than value conflict. While it can be considered as a type of social disorganization theory, it is not readily assimilated to any of the specific models analyzed herein.

The first control versions of social disorganization theory were developed by Thrasher and by Shaw and McKay, and the first strain version by Merton. Shaw and McKay were responsible for the first effort to combine social disorganization and cultural deviance theories in a model of delinquent subculture; Sutherland elaborated the first pure cultural deviance model. Except for strain models, delinquency theory originated at the University of Chicago and was part of the output of the "Chicago School."

The concepts and direction of contemporary sociological thought were founded in efforts to comprehend the genesis and development of modern

From Ruth Rosner Kornhauser, "Underlying Assumptions of Basic Models of Delinquency Theories," pp. 21-50 in Social Sources of Delinquency: An Appraisal of Analytic Models. Copyright 1978 by the University of Chicago.

societies in their encounters with urbanization, industrialization, migration, and mobility. From the series of contrasting and often polar types of society that emerged in these analyses are derived most of the terms by which culture and social structure are characterized today. The two major models of delinquency theory are rooted in different legacies of the classic analyses of social change.

With a conception of the distinctiveness and variable importance of culture, some. of the classic writers—notably Marx, Durkheim, Thomas, and Park—were able to contemplate with relative equanimity the secularization of culture and the decline of community as they chronicled new structural developments. Functional differentiation necessitates exchange relationships which, when beneficial, generate the interests and sentiments that bind people to each other and to the fulfillment of reciprocal obligations. Hierarchical differentiation supplies leadership and coordination. Its structures of authority and power provide the coercive controls that back up the internal controls attempted in socialization, as well as the indirect controls implicit in role reciprocities. In the increased scope and novel forms of functional interdependence and hierarchical ordering these writers found unifying types and levels of social relationships to provide the foundations of both social integration and social order. Moreover, while all levels of culture are weakened by the attenuation of sacred legitimacy, the rapidity of social change, and the complexity of social differentiation, the unifying structures of modern societies nevertheless provide a foundation for a common culture. However weakened by the loss of its grounding in an immutable moral order, and however confined to broad generality by virtue of the diversity of its constituency, modern culture thus draws some strengths from sources unavailable to subcultures, partly compensating in scope and adaptability for what it lacks in depth and certainty of an unequivocal ordering of values in a hierarchy of moral priority.

Social disorganization theorists draw on the foregoing aspects of the classic tradition. In social disorganization models, culture, social structure, and situation are conceptually distinct, and each is construed as a variable. Thus no society or subunit is ever perfectly organized or totally disorganized. Modern society is not, therefore, the very paradigm of social disorganization, nor is a high degree of social organization automatically attributed either to the subunits of modern society or to premodern societies. On the contrary, modern society is seen as having certain relatively effective bases of structural and cultural unity. The sources of delinquency are sought in distinctive cultural flaws and specific structural inadequacies, some forms of which are present in all societies. In short the social distribution of delinquency is accounted for by the differential distribution of situationally rooted forms of social disorganization.

In cultural deviance models, by contrast, social structure and situation are either subsumed under culture or miscellaneously absorbed in it, with the result that their independent influences cannot be identified. Ignoring the lesson of social change analysis—that culture, social structure, and situation need not necessarily stand in isomorphic relation to each other— cultural deviance theorists retained an inclusive conception of culture as equivalent to the totality of the social. Sustained by allegiance to cultural relativism, they adopted the view that cultures or subcultures differ only in their content; each is equally viable, equally the object of deep commitment, and equally capable of producing perfectly socialized persons. Culture is neither conceptually distinct from other social phenomena nor variable in its strength.

Nevertheless, cultural deviance models also bear the marks of their origin in the formative analyses of social change. Like the classic tradition of which it was a part, the Chicago school was not unified. Some polarities that emerged in social change analyses, especially those presented by Tönnies and Redfield, seemed to portray modern society as permanently disorganized, and barren of culture and strong social bonds. Cultural deviance models are heir to this portion of the legacy of the classic tradition. Construing what were ideal typical constructs as accurate representations of empirical reality, Sutherland concluded that value consensus was the exclusive property of simple, homogeneous societies. Convinced that modern society lacks a common culture, but possessed of no other concept with which to understand the social, cultural deviance theorists were compelled to locate culture somewhere, or else behavior had no social cause they could identify. This problem they solved by endowing subculture with the formidable power attributed to a culture before it was stripped of its homogeneous social base, its sacred roots, and its unchanging environment. In the myriad of vigorous subcultures that allegedly flourish everywhere, while culture fails, they located the source of perfect order. In the conflicting subcultures that define the void of societal culture, they located the source of complete disorder and its manifestation in high delinquency and crime rates.

Classification of Major Models

Social disorganization models (Thrasher, Shaw and McKay, Merton) assume consensus on certain basic values codified in criminal law and view delinquency as infraction of legal norms resulting from weakened commitment to conformity. Since neither man nor society is perfect or wholly perfectible, the causes of delinquency lie in malfunctioning social structures, malintegrated cultures, or faulty links between the two. Commitment to deviant subcultural values and norms is not a necessary and rarely a sufficient condition of delinquency. The intervening causes of delinquency are in varying pressures (strains) or varying constraints (controls) resulting from varying degrees of social disorganization. Candidates for delinquency are socially selected from incumbents of social positions burdened with undue strain, or from those isolated from controlling social bonds.

Social disorganization theory contains two variants: strain models and control models. *Strain models* focus on the consequences of social disorganization for the production of pressures to engage in delinquency. Strain is defined as the frustration of needs or wants and is indicated by a discrepancy between aspiration and expectation. Delinquent acts are motivated by the frustrated wants they gratify. Strain is a product of universally distributed human needs or uniformly distributed cultural values in a context of structured inequality of access to them. Delinquency releases the tension generated by the discrepancy between aspiration and expectation while it provides the means for achieving valued goals. Controls are implicitly treated as constant across persons and situations and are therefore ignored.

Control models assume that strain is relatively constant across persons, for wants can be gratified only at the cost of foregoing the gratification of other wants, so that everyone has unfulfilled wants. Since nonnormative means usually provide quicker and easier routes to such gratification, everyone has sufficient motivation to delinquency. Hence delinquency is an omnipresent vulnerability, the resort to which is a function not of frustrated wants but of the ratio of its costs to its benefits. Thus differential vulnerability to delinquency is determined by variation in the strength of social controls, the sum of which account for the net costs of delinquency.

Social controls are actual or potential rewards and punishments that accrue from conformity to or deviation from norms. Controls may be internal, invoked by the self, or external, enforced by others. Direct controls originate in purposeful efforts to forestall or limit deviance, while indirect controls emerge as by-products of role relationships established for other purposes and are components of role reciprocities. (1) Direct internal controls are manifested in guilt and shame, the products of effective socialization, which varies across persons and over the lifetime of a person. (2) Direct external controls are the products of scrutiny, supervision, and surveillance, designed to preclude, deter, or detect deviance, upon threat or imposition of specified penalties. (3) Indirect internal controls are represented in the self by stakes in conformity, which consist of (*a*) the rational awareness of interests and (*b*) sentiments of attachment, both products of rewarding social relationships. (4) Indirect external controls are enforced by others in sustaining role relationships; they are the products of (*a*) the saliency of the rewards dispensed by others and (*b*) the form and composition of role networks. Social units that command the most salient rewards have the most power to enforce role obligations and thus engender the highest costs of deviance. Social bonds vary in depth, scope, multiplicity, and degree of articulation with each other. Unified role networks, in which multiple social bonds of substantial depth and scope pyramid upon or encircle the person, multiply the costs of deviance, for deviance in any one domain simultaneously jeopardizes interests and attachments formed in all interlocked social relationships.

From the perspective of control theory, need gratification, which provides the motive force to delinquency in strain models, is but a condition of the effectiveness of social controls. Frustrated needs, however pressing, do not cause delinquency unless they also weaken controls. Strong social bonds exist to the extent that social units mediate gratifications for each other. Apart from the costs imposed in direct controls, such as the pangs of conscience or the pains of imprisonment, it is the cost of foregoing these gratifications that constrains delinquency. Of principal interest are the youth's bonds to family, school, and community, which affect or embody the main social controls that account for the costs of delinquency.

In *cultural deviance models* (Sutherland, Sellin, Miller), delinquency is always normative. Except for the mentally disabled who cannot be fully socialized, the uniform outcome of socialization is perfect conformity. The cause of delinquency thus lies in the plethora of conflicting subcultures among the constituent subgroups of highly differentiated societies. The intervening cause, both necessary and sufficient, of delinquency is socialization to subcultural values condoning as right conduct what the controlling legal system defines as crime. Delinquents are conformists to autonomous subcultures whose values are judged deviant by alien systems of law imposed by agents of another, more powerful cultural order. Apart from membership in or contact with relatively powerless subgroups whose values endorse illegal conduct, there is no social selection for delinquency.

Although these theories have been more commonly known as "culture conflict" or "cultural transmission" theories, I have preferred the term "cultural deviance" to emphasize (1) that in this approach subcultures are deviant, individuals never; and (2) that culture conflict here refers *not* to the effects of *all* value differences between cultures, but rather to the belief that the cause of delinquency lies in subcultures that differ in their very definitions of crime. The older terms are inappropriate in this analysis, for not all kinds of "culture conflict" theories need entail an explanation of delinquency that ties it to value differences in the definition of delinquency itself. For example, culture conflict may be thought to cause delinquency not because one of the contending cultures positively endorses conduct condemned in the criminal law, but because culture conflict results in disintegration of parental control in the subordinate group, or tensions between the conflicting groups that weaken community controls, or reduced commitment to any system of values. Such theories would not qualify under the rubric of cultural deviance models. According to Sutherland, originator of the pure cultural deviance model, the basic paradigm of this approach is given by the fabled "criminal tribes of India," whose culture mandates crimes abhorred in the so-called legal culture (1956, p. 20).

Mixed models (Shaw and McKay, Cohen, Cloward and Ohlin) combine strain or control variants of social disorganization models with cultural deviance models to explain an alleged delinquent subculture. Like social disorganization theories, they maintain that most delinquents are selected for delinquency on the basis of experienced strain or weak controls. Like cultural deviance theorists, they maintain that delinquency will not ensue for most youths, no matter how severely strained or inadequately controlled, without the endorsement of a delinquent subculture. These are nonrecursive models that locate a degree of social disorganization in the larger community or society, but find order and coherence in the structure and culture of the delinquent subgroup. Initially a dependent variable fully explained by social disorganization, the delinquent subculture is transformed into a partially autonomous cause of delinquency by virtue of its stability over time, its regulation of an alternative structure of status and opportunity, the numbers of its constituents, and the strength of their commitment to delinquent subcultural values. As an independent variable, it explains additional variance in delinquency, over and above whatever aspects of social disorganization contribute to its origin and persistence. The delinquent structure and culture also feed back into and become components of social disorganization.

Although strain and control models differ in certain crucial respects, in this chapter I shall be mainly concerned with contrasting social disorganization theory, all of whose versions share certain basic assumptions with cultural deviance theory. I shall ignore mixed models, for these introduce no additional underlying assumptions. Insofar as they treat the delinquent subculture as an independent variable capable of generating delinquency on the basis of internal processes of socialization, they operate with the assumptions of cultural deviance models. Insofar as they treat the delinquent subculture as a dependent variable, capable of surviving only in a context of social disorganization and dependent for a supply of recruits upon exogenous selective processes, they operate with the assumptions of social disorganization models. The evaluation of mixed models depends upon the empirical validity of their separate components and the logical validity of combining models with such contrasting presuppositions.

The ensuing discussion is based on the classification of theories, not theorists. The same theorist may incorporate a variety of theoretical models in his work, as do Shaw and McKay, so that the underlying logic of each approach is obscured. In addition, both models emerged at the University of Chicago at the same time, so that each is permeated with the outlook of the other, which has further obscured the opposition of the two. Thrasher published *The Gang* in 1927; Shaw and his collaborators published *Delinquency Areas* in 1929; although he did not develop his distinctive culture conflict theory until the mid thirties, Sutherland published the first edition of *Principles of Criminology* in 1924.

Since these men are all considered to be representatives of the Chicago school, the differences among them have not usually been appreciated. The enduring popularity of delinquent subculture theories, in which the two major models are seemingly merged, has also tended to blur awareness of the fundamentally opposed presuppositions of social disorganization and cultural deviance models. Yet Thrasher, who uses a control model, and Merton, who uses a strain model, present relatively pure disorganization theories, uncontaminated by the notion of delinquent or delinquency-inducing subcultures. Shaw and McKay, however, were not consistently loyal to the postulates of social disorganization theory. They vacillated between developing a pure control model and incorporating elements of a cultural deviance model into their theory, eventually joining the two to form the first mixed model of delinquent subculture.

Sutherland and Sellin, who present pure cultural deviance models, have an image of modern society as permanently disorganized in consequence of its alleged lack of common values. Yet disorganization is not a cause of delinquency in their work, for delinquency is always normative. The very idea of social disorganization was eventually rejected by Sutherland as "ethnocentric." He substituted the notion of culture conflict, which places all cultures on an equal footing. Since "culture conflict" is also a prominent feature of Shaw and McKay's approach, and to a lesser extent of Thrasher's, their approaches are easily confounded with that of Sutherland. In their work, however, culture conflict refers to the heterogeneity of conventional cultures. It is a component of social disorganization, for it prevents the development of effective controls. All ethnic subcultures are assumed to share conventional attitudes about law.

Though they influenced each other, Sutherland represents a different facet of the diverse Chicago tradition from that of Thrasher and Shaw and McKay. The latter were heavily indebted to Thomas and Park, mentors of the Chicago school. From Thomas came the idea of social disorganization resulting from the consequences of massive migrations in industrializing societies; from Park came the idea of ecological processes in the development of the city, particularly segregation and succession as a source of disorganization, and the important idea of *variation* in the degree of disorganization, depending upon the different social characteristics of populations aggregated in their appropriate niches of the urban environment. For Thomas it was not culture conflict in the sense of opposing subcultural values that caused disorganization; rather it was the erosion of subcultures formed in small peasant communities as they encountered an urban, industrial environment to which they were ill adapted. The ethnic subculture could then not serve as an effective guide to action, and the ethnic community could not serve as an agency of social control. Furthermore, neither Thomas nor Park had an image of modern society as a chaos of warring subcultures. Social disorganization was followed by reorganization; both men, especially Park, noted the development of new integrating mechanisms appropriate to the urban society, such as the associational structure and the mass media of communication (see, e.g., Janowitz 1966; Thomas 1966, pp. 3–10).

Sutherland appears to have been less influenced by Park and Thomas. He completed his doctorate in 1913, before Park came to Chicago and before Thomas, then a professor at Chicago, had finished his work on *The Polish Peasant in Europe and America* (the first volumes were published in 1918). From then until 1930, when he returned to Chicago as a professor of sociology, his work seems to have been eclectic. His early work in criminology shows little sign of the theory he later made famous; it was concerned mainly with the heredity-environment controversy and espoused what he called the "multiple-factor theory" of crime causation. Yet Sutherland was influenced by some aspects of the Chicago tradition. In the 1934 edition of his text appeared the first statement, only a few paragraphs long, that culture conflict, in the specific sense of conflict about legal rules, was the only cause of crime. Not until the 1939 edition did a formal statement of his so-called differential association theory appear. He reports that during his five years of teaching at Chicago he was strongly influenced by Wirth, from whom he adopted the view that the culture conflicts presumed to be rampant in heterogeneous urbanized society are the sole cause of crime; and he also temporarily adopted Shaw and McKay's concept of social disorganization (Sutherland 1956, pp. 14–17, 21). An additional influence at this time was Sellin, a non-Chicagoan, with whom he worked on *Culture Conflict and Crime*, the other classic of the cultural deviance approach.

Actually, he seems to have taken over Shaw and McKay's concept of the delinquent-criminal culture, and, influenced by Wirth and Sellin, generalized it, and transformed its meaning. For Shaw and McKay the delinquent-criminal culture is the *sole* prodelinquent culture; *all* others are conventional. For them, its self-maintaining mechanisms are limited, its locus confined to the disorganized slum upon which it is dependent for a supply of recruits and to which it owes its persistence, as a parasite upon a helpless host. Repudiating their characterization of the delinquent subculture as a sign and consequence of social disorganization, Sutherland retained their characterization of it as a reversal of conventional values, akin to the culture of the "criminal tribes of India," and assimilated to this model his explanation of all subgroup differences in crime rates. In so doing he created a theory very different from theirs.

In the chapters that follow, I shall examine the major models of delinquency theory in greater detail. In this chapter I will attempt to show the presuppositions on which they are based. Despite the interpenetration, both apparent and real, of the two models, the underlying assumptions about man, society, and deviance that characterize social disorganization and cultural deviance theories are fundamentally opposed. These assumptions are, for the most part, unacknowledged; yet fidelity to their logical implications would yield more consistent causal models, more strictly differentiated from each other, and more amenable to empirical verification.

Cultural Deviance versus Social Disorganization Definitions of Delinquency

CULTURAL DEVIANCE MODELS

In cultural deviance models there is no such thing as deviance in the ordinary meaning of that word. If conformity is defined as obedience to the norms of one's culture and deviance as violation of those norms, then human beings apparently lack the capacity for deviance. Except for the idiot and the insane, who cannot know what they are about, the universal experience of mankind is conformity to the norms of the groups into which they have been socialized and to which they owe allegiance. People never violate the norms of their *own* groups, only the norms of other groups. What appears to be deviance is simply a label applied by an outgroup to the conforming behavior endorsed in one's own subculture.

Delinquency is the same as any other kind of deviance. Delinquency is the enactment of permitted or, more usually, required subcultural roles and rules in jurisdictions where they are forbidden. *Within* a society with a unified value system there is no delinquency or crime. Highly complex modern societies do not qualify as unified by common values. Recent writers in this tradition have emphasized a few cultural divisions, such as classes (Miller). But for the originators of the cultural deviance approach, culture conflict is virtually unlimited. They see modern societies as composed of multitudes of subsocieties, each with its own subcultures—not simply classes, racial and ethnic groups, age grades, regions, and divisions by sex and size of community, but countless other subcultures formed inexorably along the lines of complex structural differentiation—each of which has its own definition of lawful conduct, binding, with total efficiency, on the "in-group" (Sutherland 1956, p. 20; Sellin 1938, pp. 29–30). The problem of delinquency arises because some subgroups are more powerful than others and succeed in incorporating into law their ideas, for example, that theft or homicide or littering is wrong, which automatically makes criminals of those members of less powerful subgroups who are piously thieving, killing, and littering in accordance with *their* norms. From this perspective delinquency is piety toward subcultural norms; and delinquents are the seeming victims of the agents of a foreign power, members of another subculture who, by virtue of superior force and trickery, have gained control of the state and its legal machinery.

SOCIAL DISORGANIZATION MODELS

Social disorganization theories do not imply a *general* theory of deviance, for the logic of this model does not imply that deviance is a unitary phenomenon. Nor does it imply that deviance is a matter of definition, a judgment rendered from the standpoint of alien norms. Social disorganization theories assume not only that people frequently violate the norms of their own groups but also that they frequently violate norms whose moral validity they do not deny and against which they do not seek to construct a set of oppositional values. Undoubtedly some deviance follows from commitment to alternative values, either individually or subculturally elaborated. But much, if not most, deviance involves the breach of consensual values.

Social disorganization theories assume, then, that the definition of delinquency is uniform for all constituent subgroups of the society. Delinquency is infraction of law, is caused not by commitment to different norms, but by indifference to, or weakness of, shared norms. "Many persons," Hirschi (1969, p. 25) contends, from a control perspective, "do not have an attitude of respect toward the rules of society; many persons feel no moral obligation to conform regardless of personal advantage." According to Merton's (1957, p. 157) strain model, a protracted period of social disorganization results in "a situation in which calculations of personal advantage and fear of punishment are the only regulating agencies." Delinquents are impious toward the law, not pious toward a counterformulation of law. Not variation in the *content* of values defining what is morally valid, but variation in the *strength of commitment* to values of unopposed moral validity, is the cause of delinquency. The objective of social disorganization theory is to uncover the social sources of that variation.

The idea of a delinquency-inducing subculture, either in the subunits of ordinary society, or in the interstitial formations of gangs, is not present in Thrasher's work. He was not ignorant of the idea of subculture, for the conception of a delinquent-criminal subculture was being vigorously developed by his colleagues and contemporaries, Shaw and McKay. Rather, his theory was different from and more consistent than theirs. Delinquents were demoralized under the conditions of deregulation that weak social controls imply. They were not born into or captured by groups having opposing moralities. For Shaw and McKay, insofar as they remain within the confines of their control model, much delinquency is explained without reference to socialization to an oppositional delinquent subculture. Social disorganization produces weak institutional controls, which loosen the constraints on deviating from conventional values. Social disorganization also results in defective socialization, when conventional values have not been adequately internalized. Reiss (1951) follows in this tradition. For Merton, anomie or normlessness is the precursor of delinquency. In the more recent formulations of Nye (1958), Matza (1964), Briar and Piliavin (1965), and Hirschi (1969), the *content* of moral values is not a significant source of variation in delinquency (although these writers differ among themselves about the relation between values and delinquency).

Social disorganization theorists have also tended to assume that delinquents themselves acknowledge the moral validity of the laws they violate. This is only in part a factual issue. If true, it supports the view that normlessness, rather than prior socialization to a deviant subculture, precedes delinquency. But, given that delinquency is intermittent even among the most delinquent youth, that it is very widespread in the youthful population, and that a large proportion of delinquent acts are not very serious, it seems unnecessary to assume that most delinquents need take a stand on the moral validity of their actions. If they hardly need construct an elaborate oppositional system, they scarcely need stop to consider whether they affirm their society's values either.

Empirical questions aside, it seems that the *logic* of social disorganization theory does not require an unequivocal answer to the question of delinquents' values. It is not inconsistent with the theory to assume that some *individual* delinquents may indeed deny the moral validity of the laws they violate. Extreme forms of social and psychological pathology may well produce inhuman or cynical perspectives. The logic of social disorganization theory does imply about delinquents' beliefs the following presumptions: (1) Whether or not delinquents themselves have delinquent values, the subgroups from which they are disproportionately drawn do not have values condoning delinquency. (2) If, in certain social locations, there is such a thing as a delinquent subculture, delinquency is not caused by inadvertent socialization to its norms; delinquents are selected for incorporation into it on the basis of their prior condition of normlessness resulting from either severe strains or weak controls. (3) To remain true to their definition of delinquency, social disorganization theorists would predict what Matza asserts as fact: that the "subculture of delinquency . . . is not a delinquent subculture" (1964, p. 33). If delinquency is *viola-*

tion of generally *agreed upon* legal norms, breached for *personal advantage*, then the subculture of delinquents should consist, not of oppositional values that deny the moral validity of laws, but of beliefs that rationalize public values to make easier the pursuit of private gain.

Human Nature, Socialization, and Cultural Variability

The temper of modern sociology is hostile to the assertion of a human nature or of cultural universals based on man's nature. This hostility crosses ideological lines. Though most modern sociologists deny to man a human nature, they regularly endow him with a nature in their writings, albeit rarely in open acknowledgment. Dennis Wrong (1961) has ably exposed the "oversocialized conception of man" prevalent in current sociological thought, especially in the variously termed "order," "consensus," or "integration" models of Parsons and his followers, and has called for the purposeful development of a more complex statement of human nature, one that recognizes man's desires for material and sensual gratification and his striving for power. The prospects of such an endeavor are poor, however, because the idea of a human nature is distasteful to sociologists of all persuasions, not least to the opposing "conflict" theorists.

Today, when the relativist perspective marches under the banners of science and positivism, any assertion of a specific human proclivity is likely to be labeled "dubious," and the modern writer is quick to demonstrate his scientific orthodoxy. Ralf Dahrendorf, a hardy exponent of the conflict school, presents himself as a relativist when he criticizes the functional interpretation of stratification because "every such explanation is bound . . . to have recourse to dubious assumptions about human nature," and argues that it is "plausible to assume that the . . . values capable of regulating human behavior . . . are unlimited" (1970, pp. 17, 20). But Dahrendorf is not a relativist; in his view structures of authority are required (are a "functional necessity") in all societies, in order to impose the sanctions by which norms are enforced. The power, thus inevitably distributed unequally, creates dominating and dominated classes, with natural conflicts of interest. Conflict rather than consensus is one outcome; another is that the established norms are those of the ruling class (1970, p. 26; 1959). Surely this universal structural feature of societies implies *some* limits to cultural variability—for example, obedience must be a value in every society: the ruling class will see to that.

Further, his "constraint" theory of social order involves as concrete—and even less sanguine—a conception of human nature as that of his opponents. Dahrendorf's strictures about human nature refer to Davis and Moore's contention that an incentive structure of unequal rewards is required to motivate human beings, recalcitrant in their sloth but alert to their self-interest, to fill difficult but socially necessary positions for which long training is required (Davis and Moore, 1945). Evidently internalization of norms and the desire for approval from their fellows are insufficient to accomplish that end. Yet Dahrendorf, in opposing Parsons's view that both social order and social integration are ensured by normative consensus, adopts the Hobbesian position that conformity is enforced by organized sanctions. The structure of authority through which sanctions are exercised accounts for social order, social integration, and the existence of stratification. Men are motivated by the fear of concrete punishment and the hope of concrete ·reward, not by a socialized need for approval from their fellows or by the particular cultural values supposedly internalized during the process of socialization. Self-interest—the desire to gain positive and avoid negative sanctions rather more tangible than the diffuse sanction of approval-disapproval—accounts for conformity. (For the distinction between diffuse and organized sanctions, see Radcliffe-Brown 1934, pp. 531–34.) This assertion about the nature of human nature is as vigorous as and indeed very similar to Davis and Moore's conception.

In this same debate about the causes and consequences of stratification, Tumin (1953, 1955, 1963), like Dahrendorf, criticizes the Davis-Moore thesis for its neglect of the dysfunctions of stratification and for its assumption of constancy in human nature. The values that can be instituted in a society are various, and primacy in the human motivational repertoire is determined by cultural emphases. Unlike Dahrendorf, Tumin denies the inevitability of stratification, claiming that unequal rewards are unnecessary to ensure the performance of functionally critical tasks. Socialization to values different from those that now prevail would suffice, for whatever the norms of a society, men are socialized to seek approval by conforming to them.

Moore has replied that such an "extremely relativistic view of cultural values and social institutions . . . is empirically unwarranted and theoretically doubtful. . . . Cultural relativism and . . . [the] notion that anything is possible through socialization represent a kind of denial of orderly and reliable generalizations about human societies . . . [that is not] immoral . . . [but] just wrong." Their differences, Moore concludes, confirm that "assumptions regarding human nature underlie most if not all structural propositions of substantial generality" (Moore 1963, pp. 27, 28).

Ideologies and theories do not always neatly coincide, as contemporary partisans of the conflict perspective are wont to assume (Horton 1966). Even Marx, hero of the conflict school, envisioned some constancy in human nature. The achievement of utopia, where man is free to realize the full potential of his human nature, requires the abolition of private property; its reinstitution would guarantee a return to the dominance of material self-interest and class interest, which must be among the primary expressions of human nature if their supremacy cannot be nullified except in a situation where their pursuit brings no rewards. Assumptions about human nature are likely to be found in any theory about the behavior of human beings, despite the denials of their authors.

Cultural Deviance Models

Given the current climate of opinion, cultural deviance theories have enjoyed a certain cachet because they seem to insist that man has no human nature. Ostensibly, cultural deviance theorists proceed from three premises: man has no nature, socialization is perfectly successful, and cultural variability is unlimited. They remain faithful, however, only to the last two of these, for fidelity to the second premise is logically incompatible with constancy to the first.

From the cultural deviance perspective, man has no human nature, only a social nature. That man has no human nature is allegedly attested by cultural variability, which is startling and obvious, and which could not occur in the first place if man had a human nature. If there are human needs or impulses or drives, these are unknown or unknowable, for none can possibly survive the socialization process sufficiently intact to allow their recognition. None in fact has: man never acts except in conformity to the norms of his culture, and the men of different cultures act in marvelously diverse ways. Man is wholly a creature of his culture.

Man's behavior is thus testimony to and product of the perfection of human socialization. People cannot commit delinquent or criminal acts unless these acts have first been defined as proper or desirable by the groups to which they owe allegiance. Their conceptions of right and wrong are initially determined by the groups that socialize them. Apart from the preemptive process of socialization, there is nothing else; people are unable to do things they have learned to believe are wrong. According to Sutherland and Sellin, they never do, unless they are mentally disabled. Only middle-class delinquency violates cultural norms, and it should be called psychopathology rather than delinquency (Kvaraceus and Miller 1959, p. 86). The only *real* delinquency is normative. Between total cultural indoctrination, on the one hand, and psychopathology and biology, on the other, there is nothing that could possibly induce people to violate norms. Psychological or biological incapacity of this severity is very rare, however, and therefore inconsequential in delinquency causation.

Wrong (1961, p. 187) has noted that in the "oversocialized" view of human nature, the concept of internalization has been reduced in meaning to "learning" or "habit-formation." This is certainly true in cultural deviance theory, in which man learns right from wrong in the same manner and with the same efficiency as Pavlov's dogs learned to salivate at the sound of a bell. In addition, the experience of socialization itself creates an overriding need for group approval. The social man thus experiences a degree of socialized terror so overwhelming that he will not ordinarily risk violating the norms of his group. No matter how strong the strains toward deviance, how weak and ineffectual the controls on deviance, they will not, for the normal individual, produce delinquent acts until those acts have group approval. But an individual cannot create group approval of a delinquent act; only a group can create a culture defining that act as nondelinquent. An individual or group under stress or freed from controls may or may not—the theory fails to specify if, when, or why groups will develop oppositional values—come to evaluate some acts as nondelinquent which more favored persons or groups evaluate as delinquent. Unless and until the *group* does so, the stresses or opportunities experienced by group members cannot produce delinquency. The sole cause of group differences in rates of delinquency must always lie in different subcultural definitions of delinquency: in no other way can the effects of socialization be nullified.

Social disorganization, then, is not in any way a cause of delinquency: it cannot by itself undo the effects of socialization. Its impact, when it has one, is purely accidental. The youth under stress is not searching for delinquent solutions; the youth freed from controls is not contemplating delinquent actions and searching for delinquent companions with whom to commit them. They must *learn* that delinquent solutions are possible and desirable. If stress and availability *happen* to increase their exposure to delinquent subcultures, delinquency will result from their socialization to delinquent patterns. Otherwise, delinquency is unthinkable for the socialized human being.

It should be apparent that, despite disavowal of the concept of human nature, cultural deviance theory contains a hidden and benign conception of human nature. According to a current sociology text, the leaders in the field have demonstrated once and for all the logical and empirical untenability of the idea that there are forces in man "resistant to socialization . . . because it assumes some universal biological drive system distinctly separate from socialization and social context—a basic and intransigent human nature" (quoted in Hirschi 1969, p. 18). Now it is one thing to say that human nature is unknown and unknowable. It is quite another to say that there are *no* impulses in man resistant to socialization. That *is* a very definite assertion of human nature that is simply the reverse of the assertion that there are such forces. When such a presumption is contained in a theory that also denies to man the capability of violating norms without a culture behind him, we have a vision of human nature in which original sin has been replaced with original virtue. To become the automaton conformist of cultural deviance theory, man must have a nature that is wholly passive, docile, tractable, and plastic in all other ways: he must be wantless, with muted drives of infinite mutability. How else could he turn out to be so good? He must *learn* to be willful, greedy, and cruel.

Cultural deviance theory assumes that there is unlimited variability in cultural and subcultural values. This premise is the keystone of the entire theory, for without dissensus concerning the constitutive rules of society, the explanation of delinquency provided by this approach collapses. Cultural deviance theorists provide little justification or documentation of this assumption, because they consider it to be an obvious fact. Sellin (1938, p. 23) asserts that the limitless variability of legal norms is a generalization securely backed by science. There is boundless diversity of values not only between societies, but within modern societies as well. Apart from the juxtaposition of different cultures resulting from conquest and migration, the complexity of social differentiation in modern societies attests to the presence of many subcultures containing values of limitless variety.

Besides their belief in unlimited cultural variability as fact, why do cultural deviance theorists deny that there is any *necessary* basis for at least *some* uniformity of values? Competing theories see some uniformity in legal norms between or within societies and trace it to three sources: universal cultural values are derived from universal human needs, or the requirements of all societies, or the characteristics of a particular type of society. The first two explanations are viewed as invalid by cultural deviance theorists, because the first directly and the second indirectly is based on a conception of human nature—and man has no discernible nature. It may be that self-preservation is the first law of nature, but man is not a part of nature; he exists only in society. And in society, Sutherland (1956, p. 103) assures us, some subcultures value life, and others do not: life itself is an "ethnocentric" value. The third explanation, insofar as it applies to modern societies, is false: modern societies necessarily produce diversity, not uniformity.

Within a society, social differentiation is the inevitable source of value diversity. Modern societies are highly differentiated; they are above all the locus of crime. In homogeneous societies there is complete value consensus and little or no crime. When theorists fail to distinguish culture from social structure, structural differentiation *is* cultural differentiation. Cressey, for example, implies that "culture conflict" is simply another name for structural differentiation (1968, pp. 50, 51–52). In this formulation the differentiated society itself is responsible for dissensus. Structural differentiation means here that *society* defines different conduct for different positions. But the same society whose culture delineates its social structure according to differentiated norms contradicts itself by laying down laws of universal applicability, thereby ensuring culture conflict (which thus becomes synonymous with social structure). There is a double confusion, of concepts and of content. First, there is the familiar equation of culture, social structure, and culture conflict. Second, the classes of actions regulated in law for everyone are assumed to be the same actions differentially regulated by position, but there *is* no overlapping content, there is no "culture conflict." Are people who are required to wear dresses exempted from stopping at red lights? Are the recipients of deference allowed to assault those who must defer? Laws regulate the citizen, a status all share. Anatole France complained that the law impartially forbids rich and poor alike to sleep under bridges, but it can hardly be claimed that society's *moral* norms define sleeping under bridges as appropriate for the poor, while its *legal* norms define it as inappropriate for all. People may not be equal before the law or after it, but their inequality stems from the unequal resources differentially distributed to positions in a social structure, not from conflict in different sets of societal norms. However, to distinguish norm conflicts from conflicts of interest, one must first distinguish culture from social structure.

Most writers in the cultural deviance tradition, including Cressey himself in other formulations, attribute norm conflict to subcultural formation. There is no basis for normative uniformity in modern societies because subcultures form inexorably along the lines of complex social differentiation. All structurally differentiated units *are* subcultures. The norms of these autonomous subcultures differ ineluctably in their conceptions of right conduct. Modern societies do not break down parochial loyalties or smash subcultures into a dead level of conformity, as some have claimed Neither do they incorporate all comers into their nationwide economic and political structures, as more sanguine commentators suggest. On the contrary, the complexity of social differentiation offers unparalleled opportunities for the development of myriads of insulated subcultures. The encapsulation of subgroups, not their incorporation into the larger society, is the primary fact of our time.

The value differences originating in the highly differentiated society extend even to those values that lie at the root of human and social existence. Like the "criminal tribes of India," each subgroup has its own definition of what is lawful. In the inevitable conflicts between subcultural definitions of lawful conduct lies the cause of crime. In Sutherland's words (1956, p. 20):

> Culture relating to criminal law is not uniform or homogeneous in any modern society. This lack of homogeneity is illustrated . . . in the criminal tribes of India. Two cultures are in sharp conflict there. One is the tribal culture which prescribes certain types of assault on persons outside the tribe, in some cases with religious compulsions. The other is the legal culture as stated by the Indian . . . governments. . . . When members of the tribe commit crimes, they act in accordance with one code and in opposition to the other. According to my theory, the same

principle or process exists in all criminal behavior. . . . Culture conflict in this sense is the basic principle in the explanation of crime. This culture conflict was interpreted as relating specifically to law and crime; and as not including conflict in relation to religion, politics, standard of living, or other things. At an earlier date I had used the concept of culture conflict in this broader sense on the assumption that any kind of culture conflict caused crime. . . . [Then] I restricted the concept to the area of law and crime. This may be called the principle of specificity in culture conflict.

Since there is no basis for establishing agreement on values, law reflects the values of powerful groups. An instrument of dominant groups, the state serves their special interests, for there is no common interest.

SOCIAL DISORGANIZATION MODELS

In social disorganization theory, man has a human nature, socialization can never be perfect, and cultural variability has some limits.

Although early social disorganization theorists presented a list of universal human needs, such efforts have gone out of style. The image of man common to all social disorganization theorists must be inferred from their estimates of the effectiveness of socialization in preventing deviance.

The early control models were heavily influenced by the thinking of Park and Thomas. For them, socialization could never be perfect because man's imperfection meant that society could never be perfectible. Park, whose article on community organization and juvenile delinquency prefigured the themes developed by Thrasher and Shaw and McKay, remarks on "how utterly unfitted by nature man is for life in society." He learns to "accommodate, but not wholly reconcile, himself" to the social order (Park 1952, pp. 52–53). From Thomas, Thrasher and Shaw and McKay adopted the idea of a set of universal human needs— Thomas's four wishes (the desires for new experience, security, response, and recognition). For Thomas too, man's native endowment accounted for tension between the individual and society. Man's desires were too strong ever wholly to find expression in acceptable ways (1967, p. 42). "There is . . . always a rivalry between the spontaneous definitions of the situations made by the member of an organized society and the definitions which his society has provided for him. The individual tends to a hedonistic selection of activity, pleasure first; and society to a utilitarian selection, safety first." Thrasher and Shaw and McKay thus sought in weakened controls the conditions under which men's needs escaped from regulation to find fulfillment in the ways, legal or illegal, that were least costly. While the contemporary control theorist has stopped trying to catalog the human motivational repertoire, he nevertheless still finds plausible the assumption that socialization does not blunt or eradicate the energy with which men seek gratification of their needs (see Nye 1958, pp. 3, 5).

Strain models, too, are based on the belief that the strength of instigation to need gratification is so powerful that needs, themselves the product of successful socialization to cultural values, will, when frustrated, evade the attempts of socialization to ensure their conventional mode of fulfillment. While strain models ignore variation in the effectiveness of socialization, the theory presupposes it.

Unlike cultural deviance models, social disorganization models assume that socialization is a variable, not a constant, characteristic of men. It is always more or less effective, never perfect: first, because man is an active participant in socialization, which allows him to offer some resistance to it; and second, because social disorganization is present to some degree in all societies, which cannot therefore provide the conditions of perfect socialization.

Implied is a view of human nature in which man is active, moved to gratify strong wants, and receptive to efforts to socialize him primarily as they relate to the gratification of wants. Whether wants are biologically or psychologically derived, or culturally specific, the means available to gratify them are always scarce relative to the wants. Since all wants can never be wholly or simultaneously gratified, socialization does not blunt the energy with which men seek to maximize their gratifications. From among the experiences available to him, man chooses to learn that which appears to gratify his needs or wants best. There is no guarantee that his choice will coincide with the intentions of those who socialize him. That man is potentially unruly is thus given in the human condition.

Furthermore, in all societies the means by which needs are gratified are unequally distributed—another source of variation in the effectiveness of socialization. Nor is society ever so completely integrated and ordered that efforts to socialize are free of discontinuities. Hence socialization is never so complete that human beings can resist the pressures to deviate arising from undue strain or the opportunity to deviate arising from weak external and indirect controls.

Man does not require culture to give him permission before he can violate norms. Though all men are raised in groups and experience socialization, the process of socialization can never produce so perfect an articulation between man and society that men are impervious to frustration or immune to temptation. Man and society are something of a problem to each other.

Social disorganization theory also assumes that there are limits to cultural variability, at least within a society, especially with respect to the values the criminal law protects, and that all subgroups evaluate and define most crimes in similar ways. Like their opposite numbers, social disorganization theorists provide little justification for this belief, because they consider its truth to be obvious. What is the foundation of their certainty?

1. A belief in universal human needs can serve as the basis for assuming a common core of value agreement among the members of a society. Equipped with Thomas's four wishes, Thrasher and Shaw and McKay readily assumed that economic sufficiency, health, safety, and the like were valued by all subgroups. Especially when security is one of those basic needs, it is easy to believe that similarly constituted human beings will not find it difficult to agree on what actions are a threat to their security.

2. Of far greater importance, and common to all social disorganization theories (though explicit in none), is the postulate that within any entity sufficiently knit to be called a society (or a group in it), there are some minimum rules required for its mere existence. The definition of a group —a number of people capable of concerted action for common ends— implies *some* consensus. No human group could come into existence, let alone survive, that tolerated uncontrolled theft, assault, or murder. The protection of its members from force and fraud, and their agreement about what constitutes force and fraud, are minimum requirements of all collectivities. Indeed, there is the further presumption that these minimal requirements will result in the institutionalization of *some* similar cultural values between all societies, as well as in all subgroups within them. These pan-human "rules of the game"—rules about the safety of the person and his possessions, rules without which sustained social interaction cannot occur—are everywhere and always embodied in law.

This postulate is not peculiar to social disorganization theory; it is widespread in the history of social thought. What is peculiar is its denial in cultural deviance theory. It is not the private property of a particular ideology; it is present in competing ideologies. Delinquency theories do not fit into the gross molds supplied for them by contemporary radical partisans. Cultural deviance theories are not "conflict" models because they postulate total dissensus; nor are social disorganization theories "order" models because they postulate a minimum of consensus. The consensus presumed in social disorganization theory and in the most vigorous conflict theory is a prudential consensus. It is not derived from a particular cultural value system, nor does it imply that there is additional basis for consensus within a society or that value consensus is the basis of social order. Yet cultural deviance theory, despite its dissensus assumption, is wedded to a consensus model of social order (see Ellis 1971; and the discussion of social order below).

Ideological classifications of delinquency theories are a poor guide to understanding them. A classification that places Marx, Mills, and other heroes on one side, and a globally conceived social disorganization theory on the opposing side, denies their common assumptions (cf. Horton 1966). Marx and Mills analyzed social disorganization with some of the same presuppositions and conclusions as social disorganization theorists, and neither of these writers found the roots of social conflict in different subcultural definitions of delinquency and crime. Even the most truculent conflict theorist, from Hobbes to Marx to Mills, has not assumed that what people are fighting about is the right to burglarize someone's house or injure anyone at will. The conflicts that rend a society are not the ones presumed in cultural deviance theory. They are conflicts of interest that stem from inequality in the distribution of resources, or conflicts of value about the meaning and importance of freedom and equality. Most writers from all traditions have assumed that men were similar enough to arrive at a prudential consensus concerning the prerequisites, not for a stable group life, but for *any* group life. Rules protecting the integrity of the person and possessions, whether private or collective, are such a prerequisite. For Thomas (1967, p. 43), as for all social disorganization theorists, most of the rules in the criminal code were thus not at issue within a society.

If a universal requirement of group life is a prudently stipulated agreement about the rules that make it *possible*, then a minimal consensus should undergird most of the rules restricting the use of force and fraud embodied in criminal law. Such agreement neither generates nor guarantees orderly social relationships, nor does it preclude conflicts of value or of interest. These rules make group life possible; they do not make it just, happy, rewarding, equitable, or stable. About these values, no consensus is required or implied.

Hence, however much the criminal law may reflect the special privileges of powerful groups, it always has some core of prudently stipulated consensual norms; however much the state may be the vehicle of particular interests, it will always to some degree represent the common interest. White-collar crimes—engaging in sharp business practices or evading taxes —are often cited as prototypical examples of special interest legislation embodied in the criminal law. Since juveniles cannot commit such crimes, social disorganization theories of delinquency have not been faced with the problem of separating the universal from the particular components in the criminal law. Juvenile status offenses (such as truancy, running away, ungovernability) constitute a sizable proportion of officially processed juvenile offenses, but they pose no special problem for social disorganization theorists. There is no evidence that the specific prohibitions enacted in these laws are any less offensive to the powerless than to the powerful: the poor more than the rich turn in their own children under these entitlements (Sutherland and Cressey 1955, pp. 177–78).

Social disorganization theory does not deny that law serves the powerful more effectively. than the powerless. Inferences from the theory suggest the circumstances under which the more a society is disorganized—the more discordant its culture, the less integrated its structure—the more inequitable will be its laws, in conception and in execution. But these are not the laws that, by and large, affect juveniles.

3. Social disorganization theory differs from cultural deviance theory in its diagnosis of the distinctive features of modern societies. The processes at work in modern society are viewed as undermining subcultures rather than encouraging their development. In cultural deviance theory the processes that weaken culture strengthen subcultures; in social disorganization theory many of the same processes weaken both culture and subcultures, while others strengthen culture at the expense of subcultures.

In Thrasher's and Shaw and McKay's views, the vast movement of peoples characteristic of the urban-industrial society breaks down subcultures by uprooting them from the rural-agrarian habitats to which they were adapted. The ensuing heterogeneity of populations with different heritages attenuates commitment to each separate subculture even as it prevents the formation of a common culture in the most heterogeneous locales. The potential of unprecedented differentiation for producing and sustaining subcultures is more than counteracted by the equally unprecedented centralization of economic and political institutions. Incorporation into nationwide labor and consumer markets and national electorate destroys the social insulation required for the sustenance of subcultures with truly distinctive values, while it provides a structural base for a single culture. The mass media present styles and standards that simultaneously disparage parochial subcultures and serve as the foundation for a common culture. The prospects for a strong common culture are not especially bright, and the prospects for strong subcultures are even dimmer; but only very strong subcultures could develop perspectives denying the moral validity of the primitive norms encased in the core of the criminal law.

In Merton's view the distinctive features of class-stratified societies contrast with those based on ascriptive status criteria, such as an estate system. Where achievement predominates, both in structure through substantial mobility and in culture through its high valuation and its linkage to the value of equality of opportunity, strong class subcultures cannot survive. Egalitarian cultural values do not tolerate, nor fluid social structures permit, the development of insulated subcultural perspectives.

For all social disorganization theorists, the incorporation of subgroups into the larger society, rather than their encapsulation from it, is the primary fact of our time. The basis for dissensus about legal rules is unlikely to emerge from *subculturally* generated values. The conflicts of interest that follow the lines of structural cleavage are usually contests for possession of similar values, or, more rarely, contests over the principle of distributive inequality. In either case the norms defining force and fraud, which regulate these contests, are unlikely to be at issue.

Society

THEORIES OF SOCIAL ORDER

What is the basis of social order? Any theory of society must identify the sources of social control. Desmond Ellis calls the three answers to this question the normative, coercive, and exchange solutions. He (1971, p. 692) phrases the problem in Hobbes's terms: given the scarcity of means relative to strongly instigated wants, "How can one establish a society in which force and fraud are not routinely used in satisfying wants?"

In the normative solution, most closely identified with Parsons, order is ensured by value consensus and by the individual's need to win approval by conforming to shared norms, whatever his self-interest. Socialization simultaneously produces both outcomes; it results in the internalization of shared norms, in the process of which the norms themselves and a "need-disposition" to conform become constitutive parts of the personality (Parsons 1951, pp. 36–45).

In Hobbes's coercive solution, prudence dictates that, to avoid the war of all against all, men agree to set up norms that bar the use of force and fraud. The legitimacy of those norms is based on the mutual agreement of the members of a society; conformity to them is ensured by a strong sanctioning system. The state and its laws exist to protect men from one another.

In the exchange solution, functional interdependence creates mutually beneficial reciprocity relations that would be jeopardized by the imprudent use of force and fraud (Ellis 1971, p. 694). Sentiments of attachment may form around stable exchange relations that provide for the satisfaction of wants. The affective bonds between participants thus become an additional component of the cost-benefit ratio to be reckoned by those who would rupture the relationship.

Each perspective identifies norms, exchange, or coercion as a basis of social order in *all* societies, rather than identifying each with a particular type of society, as Durkheim does. For Durkheim organic solidarity was the product of exchange relations in a complex division of labor; with a simple division of labor, mechanical solidarity (norms) ruled. Durkheim's classification of polar types of society is superior to some others developed in social change analysis, such as the folk-urban and Gemeinschaft-Gesellschaft polarities, because it does not equate modern society with social disorganization. Modern societies are both integrated (solid) and ordered (controlled) by the interdependencies created by a complex division of labor. But his formula misjudges the strength of interdependency in a simple division of labor and contributes, as do the folk and Gemeinschaft classifications, to the idea that primitive societies are held together solely by their uniform sacred cultures. But those primitive people alleged to be so securely linked with their society by their sacred common culture are often even more securely locked into it by their dependence on their fellows.

Ellis draws his examples of the exchange solution from primitive societies. In one instance the establishment of peaceful relations among previously hostile groups is explained by the herdsmen's need in dry seasons for water supplies located in enemy territory. Subsequently developed kinship and ritual ties between the groups are founded on an initially expedient interchange adapted to economic necessity.

CULTURAL DEVIANCE MODELS

Part of the ideological appeal of the cultural deviance model of delinquency lies in the notion that it embraces the currently popular coercive theory of social order. It is an easy conclusion to draw from a theory that makes so much of value conflict, views law as the codification of the cultural norms of powerful groups, and sees in court and prison the only social controls available in modern society.

In truth, cultural deviance models rely wholly on the normative solution to the problem of social order. Cultural deviance theory asserts that *only* value consensus produces social order; where there is no consensus there is no basis for social order. Coercive theory holds that men refrain from violating laws for fear of punishment. Cultural deviance theory denies that men ever violate norms out of considerations of reward and punishment. On the contrary, in the little societies in which men have their being, securely tucked away from the surrounding society, people never violate norms. There are no crimes against subcultures. In the larger society, the locus of warring subcultures, dissensus prevails; thus there is no basis for social order, and crime abounds. Its jails do not deter crime; they simply contain the prisoners who commit crimes as socialized members of subcultures.

Since cultural deviance theory affirms that total consensus is the sole basis of order and denies that there is any consensus, especially about law, in modern societies, the theory cannot identify or explain order in modern society. This failure stems in part from the polar typology of societies in which modern society is by definition disordered; but it also stems from the inability to distinguish culture from social structure. In this theory either culture is the blueprint for social structure, or social structure finds its sole expression in culture: they are the same. To make use of the coercive and exchange approaches to social order, it is necessary to consider the effects of social structure apart from culture.

Cultural deviance theorists acknowledge that there is *some* consensus in modern societies; it may be that they rely on that insubstantial basis for the small amount of order that presumably does exist. With only the culture concept at their disposal, they have no other choice. Sellin assumes that there are some common norms but does not name them (1938, p. 84). Miller allows that an interest in cars, sports, and family life extends across otherwise disparate class cultures, but how can these few common concerns serve as the foundation of social order? He also states (Kvaraceus and Miller 1959, p. 71; Miller 1959, 1969) that the same lower-class culture that produces delinquency is "functional" in industrial societies. It soothes the masses who have to do the dirty work, by encouraging them to booze, brawl, fornicate, and steal. Everything balances, with just a little inconvenience left over. They get the fun and toil; we get the money and worry. Delinquency is a small price to pay for the smooth functioning of the industrial machine. We can conclude that subculture, cannily guided by the invisible hand, produces disorder and a larger order.

Even Sutherland identifies an element of common culture in modern American society, "an individualistic ideology which has been logically and intellectually harmonious with a criminalistic ideology" (Sutherland and Cressey 1955, p. 85). From colonial times to the present, in public and private, at the top and bottom of society, vast numbers of crimes have been committed, for "opposition to law has been a tradition in the United States" (p. 38). Perhaps this is what limits variation in the subcultural definitions of crime. Each subgroup does not define as victims members of other groups. The rich do not steal only from the poor, or the poor only from the rich. All are busy stealing everyone else blind. In violent crimes each man's hand is raised against his brother. Thus modern man avoids Hobbesian chaos: he joins the war of all against all; his culture endorses it. All are socialized to preserve that society to which they are bound by their common complicity in crime. Thus disorder caused by culture is order, war is peace, Orwell notwithstanding.

Social Disorganization Models

Implied in social disorganization theory is the use of all three models to explicate the bases of social order in *all* societies. In distinguishing culture from social structure, social disorganization theory is equipped to examine the effects of each separately.

Control models rely heavily on the exchange explanation of social order. The strength of social bonds is the foundation of social control; its variability accounts for delinquency. It is not the only source of controls, but the web of social relationships is their most important source in the community at large. Where culture is thin, the web of interdependency is sometimes dense. Control models are also congenial to the coercive explanation of order. Although "direct controls" by formal agencies of social control have not received much attention in most control theories, supervision and surveillance in family, school, and other institutions are accorded importance.

Finally, control models grant to the normative solution substantial explanatory power. The nonmoral norms built up prudentially in exchange (or coercive) relations are usually assumed to have reached the status of cultural norms, at least under stable conditions. The weakness of culture in early control theories, and defective socialization to cultural values in all control theories, are causes of delinquency, thereby attesting to the importance of shared norms in accounting for social order. It is evident that exchange, coercion, and shared norms undergird one or more of the four types of control described earlier that are distinguished in control models.

Strain models appear initially to emphasize the normative solution, since they assume a broader range of consensus and assign a more or less uniformly successful outcome to the socialization process. But strain theory itself argues strongly against the adequacy of the normative explanation of social order. Consensus about success goals *produces* disorder (the resort to illegal means) because it increases competition for scarce values. Strain theory therefore falls back (implicitly) on the exchange solution. The web of interdependency is weak where unequal exchanges prevail. The inability of some actors to enter exchange relationships on terms deemed sufficiently beneficial to them is the source of disorder. It follows (in logic if not in fact) that a more secure social order might be based on greater mutuality (less inequality) in exchange, with normative controls supported by controls emanating from a satisfactory system of exchange relationships.

As for coercive controls, it is unclear to me what the logic of strain theory implies. On this the extant strain model in delinquency theory is silent, which suggests a negative judgment of the effectiveness of such controls.

Strains versus Controls

The strain and the control variants of social disorganization theory are very different, but they do not begin from such opposed premises that their combination is precluded. Such a synthesis may be easier to desire than to accomplish. Why cannot delinquency be conceived to result from *both* strong strains and weak controls?

Strain and control models are distinguished by what each omits from its explanation of delinquency. Strain models ignore variations in internal and external controls; control models ignore variations in the strength of motivation to delinquency. Strain is defined as the discrepancy between aspiration and expectation. Strain models, especially when the frustrated wants are socially derived, as in the reigning strain model, assume that all children have been equally well socialized, have equally strong ties to family and other social units, and have the same culturally defined wants. The very effectiveness of their socialization and the strength of their cultural commitments are the source of their problems, for goal achievement is not equally accessible to all. What differs is their structurally determined capacity to fulfill those wants, and nothing else.

This presupposition disturbs control theorists, who contend that strain theory assumes constancy where there is considerable variation. Not all children are equally well socialized or have equally strong attachments to family, school, or community. Therefore, says the control theorist, not all children are equally committed to conformity; and not all milieus are equally effective units of social control.

Theories that generate strain from the frustration of culturally induced goals are indeed in difficulty. If the child is sufficiently socialized to have a strong desire for conventional goals, he should be well enough socialized also to have the internalized values governing the conventional means of achieving them. If he is so strongly committed to conventional goals as to persist in his pursuit of them in the face of great difficulty, he should also be strongly enough attached to conventional persons and institutions to resist the temptation to use nonnormative means. How, then, can strain models avoid assuming a constancy in controls that is contrary to fact?

If it were conceded that controls do indeed vary, it would still not satisfy the control theorist. Control theory claims that only controls vary; strain does not. There is always ample motivation for anyone to deviate, for the scarcity of means relative to wants makes unfulfilled desires inevitable for everyone. Since need frustration is a chronic condition of humanity, there is always the temptation to use nonnormative means.

The great diversity of wants resists categorization. Wants have no fixed point at which satiety is reached. To infer strain by comparing resources with needs is unsatisfactory, for need levels cannot be meaningfully specified. Compare a millionaire with a strong need to make his second million fast to a struggling clerk with a strong need to find a few thousand dollars for a down payment on a house. Whose need is greater? Who is more strained? Would comparing the magnitude of their discrepancy scores (money desired minus money expected) yield a meaningful measure of the frustration experienced by each?

The strain theorist rightly protests that the motivation to deviate is not in fact the same for everyone. It is, I think, plausible to assume that strain is a variable, and it is not logically necessary for control theory to assume otherwise. The gratification-deprivation balance cannot really be identical for all.

Neither is need frustration wholly unmeasurable. *Felt* frustration can be measured, and such a measure may be related both to discrepant goal orientation and to delinquency.

Finally, if there are no natural limits to the gratification of needs or wants, there are social limits. The variable effectiveness of socially imposed limits and their variable acceptance by the person ensure that strain will vary among persons and situations. Durkheim argues that "nothing appears in man's organic nor in his psychological constitution which sets a limit to [insatiable needs]," and therefore "it is not human nature which can assign the variable limits necessary to our needs"; however, "society . . . can play this moderating role." Because cultural norms specify the rewards appropriate to different positions, when rapid social change invalidates the customary standards, "a new scale cannot be immediately improvised," and men's aspirations know no limit. Durkheim's explanation of anomic suicide suggests that cultural norms effectively geared to existential conditions can limit desire (Durkheim 1951, pp. 247, 249, 250, 252–53).

Hirschi, who approvingly concedes that "control theorists have always assumed . . . [that] the motivation to crime . . . is constant across persons," uses as headnote for the explication of his own control theory the following quotation from Durkheim. "The more weakened the groups to which [the individual] belongs, *the less he depends on them,* the more he consequently depends only on himself and recognizes no other rules of conduct than what are founded on his private interests" (1969, p. 16; italics added). Interdependency creates the conditions under which men are controlled by group rules. But strong social bonds set limits to aspiration, because interdependency is created and sustained by the mutual gratification of wants. A thoughtful effort to distinguish social integration (solidarity, cohesion) from social order (social control) defines integration in precisely these terms: "Social integration exists to the degree to which Ego and Alter are interdependent, i.e., mediate gratifications and deprivations for each other" (Ellis 1971, p. 696).

Effective (i.e., well established and highly relevant) cultural norms and effective (highly integrated) social structures do not merely supply controls; they also set limits to wants, thereby affecting strain levels. Some men, in some social situations, are satisfied with less than others.

Where does this leave control theory?

1. Control theory must, I think, grant that strain is a variable, not a constant.

2. If it is reasonable to assume, however, as control theory does, the truth of the following propositions, then the control theorist can still ignore variation in strain. *(a)* Human beings are strongly motivated to satisfy their needs or wants. *(b)* Compared with the strength of instigation to want gratification, socially induced self-limitations on wants are weak and pre-

carious. Socialization is not a final process in which internalized norms set ultimate limits to aspiration and fix forever the strength of internalized prohibitions on the use of nonnormative means. Limits change with changing individual and social circumstances. Even limited wants press strongly for gratification. All human beings, even the least strained, are subject to considerable strain. *(c)* Means are always scarce relative to wants, even for those with relatively limited wants. *(d)* Nonnormative means often provide the quicker and easier route to gratification of needs and wants. *(e)* Both acceptance of limits and commitment to normative means of achieving goals are variable across persons and over the lifetime of each person. Continuing commitment to conformity is dependent on the continuing gratification it provides. Conversely, the resort to nonnormative means is dependent on its costs. The costs of delinquency are largely a function of the extent to which the individual is involved in rewarding social relationships that would be jeopardized by nonconformity. The strength of controlling social bonds varies over time and space. Compared with strain, which markedly afflicts all persons, controls have a much wider range of variation. Given *relatively* limited variation in strain, resort to illegal means is mainly a function of the greater variation in controls.

3. There is another, more compelling reason that control models can ignore strain. Strain will not cause delinquency unless it simultaneously weakens controls. Extreme frustration of sexual desire is unlikely to cause rape if conscience is strong, or if the penalty is death, or if strong attachments to loved ones are jeopardized. Yet controls affect delinquency in part independent of a high prior level of some specific strain, for controls impose high strain levels on those who would use nonnormative means. The sum of social controls sets the relative costs of enduring alternative strains. The would-be rapist refrains from rape not because his level of sexual frustration is necessarily lower than the rapist's, but because his net costs of facing alternative strains are higher. He is more committed to life, or more involved in rewarding social relationships, or more subject to a punishing conscience.

Strain affects delinquency to the extent that need gratification is a condition of the effectiveness of controls. The child whose needs are frustrated by a person or institution cannot be effectively socialized by them, nor will he be strongly attached to them. The child "strained" by unmet needs does not respond well to his family's efforts to socialize or supervise him (Reiss 1951, p. 198).

Must strain *always* be accompanied by weakened controls before it results in crime? Consider the following case from the archives of anthropological jurisprudence. Quijuk, an Eskimo, whose wife had died, stole a neighbor's wife with his brothers' help. Survival in the exigent Arctic environment requires at least two cooperating people. The wronged husband then killed Quijuk and his brother. The Eskimo community, which normally executes murderers, exercised no sanctions against Quijuk's killer (Bohannon 1964). Was not Quijuk's crime an example of pure strain at work? His survival depended on his having a wife: his need could not have been greater. In fact, however, Quijuk's desperate need cut him off from his fellows. His brothers, who helped in the abduction, did not offer him one of *their* wives. Neither did anyone else in the community, which also refused to avenge his death. Quijuk's bonds to his community were broken. No one would help him. He had nothing to lose by his crime.

Is it true, on the other hand, that a change in the effectiveness of controls can cause an increase in crime without a prior increase in the level of strain? A critic (Ellis 1971, p. 697n) of the normative theory of social order calls attention to the following incident:

> The precariousness of social order is well illustrated in the nature of events which followed the strike of policemen in Montreal. These events suggest that it would be more profitable for sociologists to take the Hobbesian view that governmental institutions exist to protect men from other men than to view them as monuments to consensus.

It can hardly be claimed that the effect of the policemen's strike depended upon the antecedent strain level of Montreal residents. The strike *did* remove policemen from the streets; and crime rates soared.

In conclusion, the prospects for the synthesis of strain and control models are not very good. The differences between the two models are not irreconcilable, but they are not easily bridged. The control theorists can safely ignore strain because its effect on delinquency is registered in weak controls or none at all. But the effect of controls on delinquency is partly independent of prior strain level. The strain theorist cannot ignore controls because they determine the relative tolerability of all relevant types and levels of strain.

Part VI:

PREVENTION, TREATMENT, AND CONTROL

Robert Martinson's (1974) well-written, widely reprinted article[1] on the results of treatment efforts 1945-1967 obviously struck a responsive chord. Preventive and correctional treatment had been under suspicion for a long time; Martinson and his colleagues summed-up various trials that found it guilty of failing to produce desired effects on delinquency and crime—if not beyond doubt, then at least by a preponderance of the evidence.

Why this summing-up should have occasioned so much response—and we think it did—is worth at least a lengthy essay. Whatever the reasons, responses have not ceased. Treatment efforts are continuing to receive close scrutiny. It is not at all clear, we think, that they are being abandoned, although some have interpreted abandonment as the appropriate next step. Instead, we think, treatment practitioners are being harder pressed to justify investment in their programs by presenting assurance beforehand that afterward some rational assessment of these efforts will be possible. As other surveys of reports on treatment have shown, three that follow show that this has typically been difficult.

Richard J. Lundman and Frank R. Scarpitti present recommendations designed, in the main, to remedy this difficulty. Having conducted a thorough search for information on the many delinquency prevention projects rumored or known to have been conducted, they found but 40 reports that in some degree permitted independent assessment of the nature and results of such projects. All were directed at asserted causes of delinquency, usually through group or individual casework. Most did not permit a fully confident assessment of results. Those that did—projects that approximated experimental designs and used objective measures of delinquency—showed that such projects failed to produce significantly less delinquency among members of experimental groups.

These authors' nine recommendations are worth serious consideration, both by those who propose and implement delinquency prevention projects and by those who fund them. Several of the recommendations in effect suggest a more rigorous scientific posture toward such projects, one that will help assure cumulation of knowledge so that past mistakes and failures will not be endlessly repeated under new labels. We should like to add two recommendations that are consistent with theirs but not made explicitly: namely, much more attention should be given to the character of the "treatment" experimental subjects receive, and to whether there is good reason to suppose that they did, and the control subjects did not, receive this "treatment."

These are perhaps two ways of making the same point—that even some of the best-designed projects leave us in the dark about *what happened*. One way in which this takes place is through failure explicitly to explore the operational implications of the "treatment" being applied: what it is that is supposed to happen and have effect, and whether what is supposed to happen happens. We are reminded of a point made by Charles E. Silberman in an informal talk some years ago. Silberman was studying schools. A persistent finding, which puzzled him, was that within wide limits variations in the number of students per teacher seemed to make little difference in teacher effectiveness. He went on to say that a few days' observation in classrooms suggested why this might be so: teachers with few students did not do anything much different from those with many. The point can and should be applied to criminological experimentation. It is persistently found, for example, that, within wide limits, the sizes of the case loads served by probation and parole officers have little affect on their ability to reduce recidivism (or, though here the data are less consistent, to detect recidivists). What is seldom shown, however, is that officers with small case loads act differently than those with large ones. And, presumably, the variable of interest is not size of case load, but how it may affect officer-offender interactions; it is the latter that needs close attention.

What is perhaps another version of the same difficulty can be seen in the suggestive article by Joan McCord, reprinted in this volume. McCord's 30-year follow-up of the Cambridge-Somerville Youth Study appears to show that the treatment methods employed did not prevent delinquency. Why "appears," given the almost classic experimental design and the multiple objective measures, both in accordance with the recommendations of Lundman and Scarpitti? The treatment program, according to her brief description, consisted of tutoring, medical and psychiatry attention, participation in summer camp and other community programs, and friendly counsel for some of the experimental subjects (and members of their families). What we do not learn, however, is whether members of the control group *also* had such services, possibly in like amounts, from sources other than the Cambridge-Somerville Youth Study. It is possible that other documentation of this famous study supplies the crucial facts in this matter. We only want to insist that these facts *are* crucial, because the "experimental" quality of the study consists largely in the application of "treatment" to one group and the nonapplication, presumably, of the "treatment" to a matched control group. It is impossible to tell from McCord's report alone whether this condition was met.

McCord's follow-up has great value in any case, for she undertook to explore possible unanticipated, negative "side effects" of treatment: its effects upon subjects' health, occupational, and other experiences. While the same reservation holds about whether these are side affects of the "treatment," the study is unusual in even considering them. It is also unusual in demonstrating why "subjective" measures of project effectiveness are not properly interpreted as an indication that, in fact, a project has reduced delinquency, a point strongly made by Lundman and Scarpitti.

Robert R. Ross and H. Bryan McKay provide an informative and witty resume and assessment of the results of introducing "behavior modification" programs into the correctional scene. One hypothesis that might be drawn from their review is that those who operate treatment programs in prisons (and other "total institutions") will inevitably be pressed to turn their skills to dealing with persons who create trouble *in* prisons. A related hypothesis, clearly implicit in the article, is that treatment programs will be acceptable to prison administrators to the extent that they hold out promise of dealing with such trouble-makers. One way of doing so is by presenting programs that in fact, or apparently, employ the incentive systems already in place in prisons. These are mainly directed toward maintaining peace in prisons.

Ross and McKay hold that the evidence for the effectiveness of behavioral modification programs in reducing institutional troublemaking is fairly substantial—but they do not present evidence for this conclusion. We are more skeptical than they appear to be. Almost every treatment program introduced into prisons and other total institutions has been initially justified by its promise to reduce the relevant form of "recidivism" after release. When programs have been shown to be less effective for this purpose than advertised, a second justification has usually been put forward: that the program reduced institutional trouble. One might speculate about a "natural history" of justifications for prison treatment programs along these lines.

We strongly agree with the propositions set out by Ross and McKay about correctional treatment generally. They suggest, summarily, that research on correctional treatment is of insufficient quality to justify either abandonment of treatment efforts or research on them. As we have already noted, we do not believe treatment efforts are in fact being abandoned. We hope that the same is true with respect to research on them.

The final reading might have been placed in other sections. Some of the findings have clear implications for the use of arrest rates in the economic model; discretionary decisions are discussed throughout; and many police organizations are large and complex, suggesting, again, the relevance of organizational theories for criminology. We have placed the article by Jan. M. Chaiken, Peter W. Greenwood, and Joan Petersilia here to underline what may be their main point: the criminal investigation process, as currently organized, arguably contributes little to the control of crime through the identification of offenders or the preparation of cases against those identified. Nor do investigators appear to do a very adequate job of public relations by assuring victims that those offending against them are being pursued.

These findings, first made available in 1975,[2] have sparked considerable controversy,[3] even though, it is our impression, the authors' findings about how investigators spend their time, how most perpetrators are identified, and the vagaries of police-prosecutor relations could have come as no surprise to most police administrators. Notwithstanding this fact, if it is one, officially the effectiveness of investigators has seldom been questioned, and of course this is what Chaiken, Greenwood and Petersilia do. They draw the inferences there to be drawn. They are even so bold as to suggest that reorganization of police departments, presumably radically reducing the proportion of conventional investigators, might be cost-effective. Whether this will happen, and if so, how, might well be an important topic for inquiry.

We cannot conclude these remarks without mentioning the frequently heard argument that starts with "a nation that could place a man on the moon should be able. . . ." The point, of course, is that if we only tried harder we could succeed in putting a stop to crime. This is an attractive but naive thought. A people who succeed by trying hard in one area can only be counted on to try hard in others, not to succeed. Indeed, they can probably be expected to try too hard and regardless of the promise of success. Even before the sad and sobering observations of the critics of treatment could be absorbed, we were summoned to new attempts, if the return to punishment should be called "new." This eager activism is, as many have noted, characteristically American; we must always do something and we are quite certain that doing something is always better than doing nothing. Just how deeply the expectation of action is among us is revealingly illustrated by considering what might happen if one drew a straightforward business-like conclusion from the findings of Chaiken, Greenwood, and Petersilia. While detectives spend virtually no time on solving run-of-the-mill property crimes, they do report dutifully to the scene of a reported crime, spend time surveying the locale, interviewing victims and possible witnesses, and writing up reports on these activities and the gathered information. These reports are filed and, for all intents and purposes, forgotten. We consider it unimaginable that police dispatchers could tell callers who report that their residences have been burglarized the unvarnished truth; the impression has to be conveyed that something is being done. Yet, would it not be wiser to forget the 90% non-promising cases and to allocate the saved time to the clearance of the promising ones?

As we indicated earlier, we do not think treatment will be abandoned—nor do we think it should be abandoned. But we do recommend that it be continued with a somewhat less anxious faith that there is never any harm in trying. And we do not mind going on record by recommending the same advice to those who wish to replace treatment with punishment.

NOTES

1. This article is based on the less widely known volume by Lipton et al. (1975). A later survey, with results similar to Martinson's, examines studies through 1975: Greenberg (1977).

2. Three volumes were published: Greenwood and Petersilia, 1975; Chaiken, 1975; and Greenwood et al., 1975.

3. See the U.S. Department of Justice's publication entitled *The Criminal Investigation Process,* which contains "An Evaluation of the Rand Corporation's Analysis of the Criminal Investigation Process" by Daryl F. Gates and Lyle Knowles, originally published in the July 1976 issue of *The*

Police Chief, as well as a response by Greenwood, Chaiken, and Petersilia to this critique. The article we have reprinted takes account of certain of the criticisms made by Gates and Knowles, mainly resulting in some clarifications of language.

REFERENCES

CHAIKEN, J. M. (1975). The investigative process, volume II: Survey of municipal and county police departments. Santa Monica, Cal.: Rand.

GREENBERG, D. F. (1977). "The correctional effects of corrections: A survey of evaluations." In D. F. Greenberg (ed), Corrections and Punishment. Beverly Hills, Cal.: Sage.

GREENWOOD, P. W. and PETERSILIA, J. (1975). The criminal investigation process, volume I: Summary and policy implications. Santa Monica, Cal.: Rand.

GREENWOOD, P. W., CHAIKEN, J. M., PETERSILIA, J., and PRUSOFF, L. (1975). The criminal investigation process, volume III: Observations and analysis. Santa Monica, Cal.: Rand.

LIPTON, D., MARTINSON, R., and WILKS, J. (1975). The effectiveness of correctional treatment: A survey of treatment evaluation studies. New York: Praeger.

MARTINSON, R. (1974). "What works?—Questions and answers about prison reform." Public Interest, 35: 22-54.

U.S. Department of Justice, Law Enforcement Assistance Administration, National Institute of Law Enforcement and Criminal Justice (1977). The criminal investigation process: A dialogue on research findings. Washington, D.C.: U.S. Government Printing Office.

29

DELINQUENCY PREVENTION
Recommendations for Future Projects

RICHARD J. LUNDMAN and FRANK R. SCARPITTI

The criminal deviance of juveniles is one of the major problems confronting contemporary society. Slightly less than half the persons arrested for serious offenses are under eighteen years of age.[1] Arrests of young people have doubled over the last decade, as compared to relatively minor increases for those eighteen and over.[2] And recent self-report studies suggest that the social and demographic correlates of delinquency are expanding to include female, middle-class, majority, and rural juveniles as well as male, lower-class, minority, and urban youths.[3] Thus, the contemporary crime problem is largely attributable to the actions of juveniles.

Public concern with the phenomenon of juvenile crime has produced a multitude of programs aiming to control and prevent delinquency. It has been estimated that, since 1965 alone, over 6,500 different attempts at prevention have been launched.[4]

RICHARD J. LUNDMAN is Associate Professor, Department of Sociology, Ohio State University. **FRANK R. SCARPITTI** is Professor and Chair, Department of Sociology, University of Delaware.

1. See, for example, S. T. Reid, *Crime and Criminology* (Hinsdale, Ill.: Dryden Press, 1976), p. 58.

2. See, for example, R. D. Knudten, *Crime in a Complex Society* (Homewood, Ill.: Dorsey Press, 1970), p. 724.

3. See, for example, J. R. Williams and M. Gold, "From Delinquent Behavior to Official Delinquency," *Social Problems*, Fall 1972, pp. 209−29.

4. M. Dixon, *Juvenile Delinquency Prevention Programs* (Washington, D.C.: National Science Foundation, 1974).

From Richard J. Lundman and Frank R. Scarpitti, "Delinquency Prevention: Recommendations for Future Projects," 24(2) *Crime & Delinquency* 207-220 (April 1978). Copyright 1978 by National Council on Crime and Delinquency.

The results of these projects have not been particularly encouraging. Indeed, our own research and the research of others lead to the nearly inescapable conclusion that few, if any, of these efforts successfully prevented delinquency.[5] As a consequence, many people have been tempted to ignore previous efforts in an understandable haste to discover new prevention strategies.[6]

We believe it likely, however, that a careful study of previous attempts at prevention will prove to be crucial in increasing the probability of success of future projects. The study of earlier efforts will assist in eliminating unnecessary errors and will reduce the replication of unsuccessful techniques among stereotyped populations of youths. The purpose of this paper is to determine what can be learned from the study of past delinquency prevention attempts. The paper begins with a brief review of previous efforts; a series of nine recommendations for future projects are then advanced and discussed.

DELINQUENCY PREVENTION: A REVIEW

Method

Our search for attempts at delinquency prevention was limited to those professionally published or, in the case of continuing projects, to those for which a preliminary report was available. Our search was also limited by a self-imposed requirement that a report contain independently interpretable information on both the nature and results of the project.

We proceeded by examining a variety of general and specific indexes thought likely to include references to delinquency prevention projects. Thus, we examined the *Monthly Catalog of United States Government Publications* (1958–73); *Crime and Delinquency Abstracts* (1969–71); *The Challenge of Crime in a Free Society* (1967); Social Science & Humanities Index (1952–74); and *National Criminal Justice Reference Service/Juvenile Delinquency Prevention* (an LEAA computerized bibliographic service).

Of nearly 1,000 citations, 127 were more closely examined in light of the above requirements. We found that 25 previous efforts[7] and 15 continuing

5. R. J. Lundman, P. T. McFarlane, and F. R. Scarpitti, "Delinquency Prevention: A Description and Assessment of Projects Reported in the Professional Literature," *Crime & Delinquency*, July 1976, pp. 297–308; and Ibid.

6. For a discussion of the "newism" characteristic of the field of delinquency prevention, see J. Stratton and R. Terry, *Prevention of Juvenile Delinquency* (New York: Macmillan, 1968).

7. R. Baron, F. Feeney, and W. Thornton, "Preventing Delinquency through Diversion: The Sacramento County Diversion Project," *Federal Probation*, March 1973, pp. 13–19; L. Berkowitz and J. Chwast, "A Community Center Program for the Prevention of School Dropouts," *Federal Probation*, December 1967, pp. 36–40; C. Berleman and T. W. Steinburn, "The Execution and

projects[8] contained information on the nature and results of the prevention venture.

Evaluation of a Delinquency Prevention Program," *Social Problems*, Spring 1967, pp. 413–23; P. Bowman, "Effects of a Revised School Program on Potential Delinquents," *The Annals of the American Academy of Political and Social Science*, March 1959, pp. 53–61; D. Braxton, "Family Casework and Juvenile First Offenders," *Social Casework*, February 1966, pp. 87–92; R. Brown and D. Dodson, "The Effectiveness of a Boys' Club in Reducing Delinquency," *The Annals*, March 1959, pp. 47–52; B. Demsch and J. Garth, "Truancy Prevention: A First Step in Curtailing Delinquency Proneness," *Federal Probation*, December 1968, pp. 31–37; R. Downing, "A Co-Operative Project of an Elementary School and a Family Agency," *Social Casework*, November 1959, pp. 499–504; A. Franklin, "The All-Day Neighborhood Schools," *The Annals*, March 1959, pp. 62–68; M. Friedman and E. Chone, "Delinquency, Employment, and Youth Development," *Federal Probation*, December 1962, pp. 45–49; A. Fried, "A Work Camp Program for Potential Delinquents," *The Annals*, March 1959, pp. 39–46; J. Gandy, "Preventive Work with Street Corner Groups," *The Annals*, March 1959, pp. 107–16; G. Jereczeck, "Gangs Need Not Be Delinquent," *Federal Probation*, March 1962, pp. 49–54; C. Kaufman, "Community Service Volunteers: A British Approach," *Federal Probation*, December 1973, pp. 35–41; S. Kobrin, "The Chicago Area Project—A 25 Year Assessment," *The Annals*, March 1959, pp. 19–29; G. Konopka, "Co-ordination of Services as a Means of Delinquency Prevention," *The Annals*, March 1959, pp. 30–37; H. Meyer, E. Borgotta, and W. Jones, *Girls at Vocational High* (New York: Russell Ságe, 1965); G. Penner, "An Experiment in Police and Social Agency Co-operation," *The Annals*, March 1959, pp. 79–88; H. Poorkaj and C. Bockelman, "Impact of Community Volunteers and Delinquency Prevention," *Sociology and Social Research*, April 1973, pp. 335–41; E. Powers and H. Witmer, *An Experiment in the Prevention of Delinquency* (New York: Columbia University Press, 1951); W. Reckless and S. Dinitz, *The Prevention of Juvenile Delinquency* (Columbus, Ohio: Ohio State University Press, 1972); E. Shanus and C. Dunning, *Recreation and Delinquency* (Chicago: Chicago Recreation Commission, 1942); M. Stranahan and C. Schwartsman, "An Experiment in Reaching Asocial Adolescents through Group Therapy," *The Annals*, March 1959, pp. 47–52; R. Tefferteller, "Delinquency Prevention through Revitalizing Parent-Child Relations," *The Annals*,, March 1959, pp. 69–78; and F. Thrasher, "The Boys' Club and Juvenile Delinquency," *American Journal of Sociology*, 1936, pp. 50–66.

8. These continuing projects are N. Beale, "Edison Project," Potter School, Fourth and Clearfield Streets, Philadelphia, Pa. 19133; J. Beasley, "Project VIII—Focus on Dropouts in a New Design," Paducah Public Schools, 10th and Clark Streets, Paducah, Ky. 42001; J. K. Butler, *Albuquerque Bernadillo County Youth—Related Property Crime Reduction Program Evaluation Design* (Albuquerque, N.M.: University of New Mexico Press, 1973); J. E. Carter, "Project Arise, Macon County Board of Education, P.O. Box 90, Tuskegee, Ala. 36083; M. Filogram, "Texarkana Dropout Prevention Program," 223 E. Short Tenth Street, Texarkana, Ark. 75501; R. J. Gemignani, "Youth Service Systems," *Federal Probation*, December 1972; D. Graham and R. Wurzburger, "Planning for Diversion: A Case Example," in *Back on the Street*, R. Carter and M. Klein, eds. (Englewood Cliffs, N.J.: Prentice-Hall, 1976), pp. 234–39; D. E. Henley, "Project Outreach," Sheridan School District No. 2, P.O. Box 1198, Englewood, Colo. 80110; A. Holley, "Northeastern Accelerated Learning Achievement Center," Northeastern High School, 3840 Grandy, Detroit, Mich. 43207; P. Hunsicker, "Police Help Youth," *Delinquency Prevention Reporter* (Washington, D.C.: U.S. Govt. Printing Office, March-April, 1972); W. H. Katz, "Project MAS—More Alternatives for Students," Thomas J. Quirk Middle School, 85 Edwards Street, Hartford, Conn. 06120; O. G. Lee, "Project Cadre," Seattle Public Schools, 1729 17th Avenue, Seattle, Wash. 98122; A. Maron, "The Juvenile Diversion System in Action," *Crime & Delinquency*, October 1976, pp. 461–69; and P. Pritchess, "Law Enforcement Screening for Diversion," *Youth Authority Quarterly*, Winter 1974, pp. 49–64.

Summary of Findings[9]

All of the past projects we encountered involved attempts to correct the pre-sumed causes of delinquency, usually through group or individual casework. Psychotherapy, counseling, and detached gang workers were also frequently used as prevention techniques. The youths involved in these efforts were gen-erally inner-city, working- or lower-class males, and they were frequently from minority groups. Most were subjects in projects with preexperimental research designs, thereby making reliable assessment of results difficult. A minority of the projects, however, used experimental or quasi-experimental designs, permitting more reliable assessment of results.

In attempting to assess projects, we found several factors to be crucial. As a consequence of preexperimental rather than quasi-experimental research de-signs, subjective measurement techniques, or concern with dependent vari-ables other than delinquency, most projects reported in the professional liter-ature did not permit reliable assessment of results. And those projects with experimental designs and objective measurement of delinquent behavior had not successfully prevented delinquency.

The continuing programs we examined revealed similar problems: preex-perimental designs, subjective measurement techniques, and objective meas-urement of actions other than delinquency. We found little reason to believe that a major breakthrough in delinquency prevention is forthcoming.

DELINQUENCY PREVENTION: RECOMMENDATIONS

As a consequence of our review of these programs, we believe that a number of recommendations for future projects are in order. Certain of these recom-mendations are intended to assist in the avoidance of unnecessary errors while others are intended to encourage diversification in the characteristics of future projects.

Recommendation One

Researchers Should Expect Future Projects to Be Unsuccessful. As has been indicated here and elsewhere, there is little reason to believe that past attempts at delinquency prevention have been successful. Even projects with the best intentions, designs, and methods of evaluation[10] have failed to demonstrate differences between their experimental and control groups. Newer programs, such as those involving diversion, are likely to meet with similar success.[11]

Thus, it appears to us that persons about to start a delinquency prevention

9. For an expanded discussion of these findings, see Lundman et al., "Delinquency Preven-tion."

10. See, for example, Reckless and Dinitz, *Prevention of Juvenile Delinquency.*

11. See, for example, R. J. Lundman, "Will Diversion Reduce Recidivism?" *Crime & Delin-quency*, October 1976, pp. 428–37.

program should do so with the expectation that the project will not be successful. This is not to suggest that delinquency prevention projects should not be undertaken or, if undertaken, should not be pursued in earnest. However, such an expectation would be realistic, in view of past attempts at delinquency prevention. And maintaining this attitude throughout the course of a project would have important—positive—effects.

First, this expectation might decrease researchers' tendency to suppress the results of unsuccessful projects. During the course of our research, we encountered an article reporting the beginning of an attempt to assess the accuracy of the Glueck delinquency prediction scale.[12] No results were included since the purposes of the paper were to describe the research design and, ostensibly, to alert professionals to this crucial test of the Glueck instrument.

After reading the article, we attempted to find a paper or papers reporting the results of the study. No papers had appeared in professional journals. Jackson Toby apparently had the same concern and contacted the New York City Youth Board (NYCYB) to determine why the results of the study had not been published.[13] He reports that NYCYB did not make the data public because they did not validate the accuracy of the Glueck instrument. According to C. Ray and Ina Jeffery—who apparently succeeded in gaining access to the unpublished data—publication was suppressed because the prediction error rate in the Glueck instrument was found to be 84 percent.[14]

Recent statements indicate that suppression is relatively common.

Dixon, for instance, reports that extensive search procedures uncovered 6,500 attempts at delinquency prevention since 1965 alone. Only 350 resulted in generally available reports, and slightly less than 100 of these reports were judged worthy of evaluation. Dixon suspects, and we concur, that a large proportion of projects were not reported because the projects were unsuccessful.[15] If researchers expected their projects to be unsuccessful, we believe there would be less hesitation to report the results of all research—negative or positive.

Further, if researchers adhered to this expectation and regularly sent reports of unsuccessful projects to professional journals, it is possible that the publication policies of professional journals might change. Journals do not routinely publish the results of unsuccessful projects. Given the present state of the art, we believe that this policy should be changed since identification of questionable hypotheses is at least as important as confirmation of useful techniques.

12. R. Whelan, "An Experiment in Predicting Delinquency," *Journal of Criminal Law, Criminology and Police Science*, November-December 1954, pp. 432—41.

13. J. Toby, "An Evaluation of Early Identification and Intensive Treatment Programs for Predelinquents," *Social Problems*, Fall 1965, pp. 160—75.

14. C. Jeffery and I. Jeffery, "Prevention through the Family," in *Delinquency Prevention*, W. Amos and C. Wellford, eds. (Englewood Cliffs, N.J.: Prentice-Hall, 1967).

15. Dixon, *Juvenile Delinquency Prevention Programs*.

Recommendation Two

Researchers Should Publish the Results of All Projects. The reasons for this second recommendation are straightforward and have already been given. Therefore, we will restrict our comments to the implications of this recommendation.

First, we believe that researchers should not be funded unless it is clear in the proposal that every effort will be made to publish the results of the research. Publication of all research findings should be readily available in most large library systems. As our own research and that of Dixon indicate, it is very difficult at present to determine what has been done in delinquency prevention.

Second, editors of.professional journals, university presses, and even commercial publishing houses must be convinced that reports of unsuccessful projects should be available. If publication of professional manuscripts and monographs through existing outlets continues to be difficult, funding agencies and agents must take responsibility for publication. At the minimum, this implies regular collection, publication, and distribution of reasonably detailed abstracts of continuing and completed projects. Ideally, professional journals would be created by all federal agencies involved in delinquency prevention research. These journals should be easily available to anyone interested in the field.

Manuscripts or monographs accepted for publication must be of professional quality. Projects must be carefully designed, and funding agents should determine, *as a condition of funding*, that the researchers can produce publishable materials.

Finally, reliable reporting demands that implementation and evaluation be conducted independently.[16] Moreover, evaluation by independent professionals increases the probability that the research results will be published. Independent evaluators are less tied to the success of the project and are thus more likely to make the results of *all* projects public.

Recommendation Three

Future Delinquency Prevention Programs Must Be Sensitive to and Protect the Rights of the Juvenile Subjects Involved. Most juvenile subjects involved in delinquency prevention programs have not been adjudicated delinquent. Because so little is known about what causes delinquency—and even less is known about how to prevent it—it is crucial that all future projects be

---

16. By this we do not mean that implementors should not have contact with social science researchers. Indeed, intimate contact in the context of theorizing and research design is crucial. We do suggest, however, that evaluation be undertaken by individuals other than those involved in the implementation of a project.

sensitive to and protect the rights of the juvenile subjects. Even though these juveniles have been identified or labeled "predelinquent" or "delinquency prone," they are entitled to the same rights as any other juvenile.

During the course of our research we did not encounter any projects which suggested overt violation of the rights of the juvenile subjects. Apparently, none of the youths involved had sustained either social or emotional injury. However, the *potential* for injury must be recognized. Any prevention project, writes Tony Tripodi, can conceivably injure the participants.[17] His basic concern is with the negative effects of early identification and subsequent segregation, which may set in motion "delinquency fulfilling prophecies." As a consequence, the probability of delinquent behavior may actually increase rather than decrease.

We agree that this possibility exists, although the efforts we examined struck us as largely benign. This is not the case, however, with all projects. For example, Georgetown psychologist Juan B. Cortes[18] has proposed a delinquency prevention project based upon the early—and largely unsupported—theories about the relationship between body type and delinquency.[19] Cortes suggested that the following delinquency prevention program be instituted in Washington's "wickedest precinct":

> In the area selected, determine all those families who have children under 7 years of age. A preventive program should begin in families whose eldest children are not yet over 7 years of age and in those recently married or about to have children. Families with already delinquent children should be excluded from this particular stage of the project.
>
> From among these families with children under 7, determine those who are *potentially delinquent* families. This selection can be accomplished with a minimum of difficulty by using such an instrument as the Gluecks' Social Prediction Table.
>
> Study individually the "delinquent" families thus selected (quite probably they will not exceed 10—20 percent of the homes with children under 7) and classify them in two main groups: (a) those with parent(s) *who would not or could not cooperate*, and (b) those with parent(s) *who would and could cooperate*.
>
> Develop techniques for tactfully and helpfully informing and training the parents of the second group in the necessary modifications of their child-rearing practices and in their relationships with each other. Both cooperative and uncooperative families should be helped.

Considering the prediction error rate in the Glueck delinquency prediction scale, mentioned earlier, it is certain that such a project would be unsuc-

17. T. Tripodi, Book Review of *The Prevention of Juvenile Delinquency* by W. Reckless and S. Dinitz, *Social Work*, January 1974, pp. 119—20.

18. J. Cortes, *Delinquency and Crime: A Biophysical Approach* (New York: Seminar Press, 1972).

19. See, for example, W. Sheldon, *Varieties of Delinquent Youth: An Introduction to Constitutional Psychiatry* (New York: Harper, 1949).

cessful. And it might well violate the rights of the subjects involved. Such a project might set in motion delinquency-fulfilling prophecies and focus atten- ion on only disadvantaged juveniles. In the words of a reviewer of Cortes's b ok, proposals such as this

> are a clear demonstration that environmental or labelling theories are not univer- sally accepted among informed members of the community and . . . they demon- strate the possibility of elitist and racist experimental proposals in crime prevention.[20]

To avoi⁻¹ ʰese and other problems, the design and implementation of pre- vention ⸝ᵣ ⸝grams must be approached cautiously.

Recommendation Four

The Theoretical Foundations of Future Delinquency Prevention Programs Should Be Expanded to Include Sociological as Well as Psychological Under- standings of the Causes of Delinquency. With but a few exceptions, we found that previous delinquency prevention efforts reflected psychological understandings of the causes of juvenile delinquency. As a consequence, at- tention has been directed toward treatment of individuals.

Given the history of failure in prevention, researchers should begin to com- bine individual treatment[21] with sociological and social psychological per- spectives on the causes of juvenile delinquency. In their emphasis on the structural correlates of delinquency, the sociological and social psychological perspectives may complement and enrich traditional causal imageries which focus on differences among persons.[22]

David Matza, for example, places primary emphasis upon the group nature of delinquency and the shared misunderstandings of delinquent commitment maintained in "situations of company."[23] Projects based on this type of theo- rizing would logically concentrate on dispelling these shared misunderstand- ings. Robert Merton argues that delinquency and other forms of juvenile de- viance emerge when juveniles are denied access to legitimate means of reach- ing cultural goals.[24] The prevention implication here is that potential delin- quents should be provided legitimate means.

20. R. Block, Book Review of *Delinquency and Crime: A Biophysical Approach* by Juan B. Cortes, *Contemporary Sociology*, July 1973, p. 429.

21. For a discussion of the individual treatment perspective, see E. Schur, *Radical Noninterven- tion* (Englewood Cliffs, N.J.: Prentice-Hall, 1973).

22. A. Cohen argues that psychological theories of deviance emphasize differences among persons. For an expanded discussion of this point, see *Deviance and Control* (Englewood Cliffs, N.J.: Prentice-Hall, 1966).

23. D. Matza, *Delinquency and Drift* (New York: Wiley, 1964).

24. R. Merton's initial statement of anomie theory was "Social Structure and Anomie," *Ameri- can Sociological Review*, October 1938, pp. 672–82.

Our intent in this paper is not to advocate integration of any one of these viewpoints with existing individual treatment perspectives. We do propose that researchers begin to broaden their attack on delinquency.

Recommendation Five

Future Delinquency Prevention Programs Should Focus Primary Attention on Preventing Delinquent Behavior.   Too many of the projects ostensibly concerned with the prevention of delinquency failed to determine whether delinquency had actually been prevented. In some cases researchers apparently assumed that if the program had been an operational success, then delinquency had been prevented. Solomon Kobrin's assessment of the Chicago Area Project illustrates this type of reasoning:

> In all probability these achievements have reduced delinquency in the program areas, as any substantial improvement in the social climate of a community must. *However, the extent of the reduction is not subject to precise measurement. In the final analysis, therefore, the Area Project Program must rest its case on logical and analytical grounds.*[25]

Operating on this assumption, researchers did not undertake to examine actual changes in rates of delinquent behavior.

Other projects concentrated on behaviors or attitudes thought to be predictive of future delinquency, such as truancy or dropping out of school. Change in these behaviors was seen to reflect a corresponding change in the rate of delinquent behavior. Ruth Tefferteller argued that because "effective bridges were built between children and their parents," delinquency had been prevented.[26] Again, actual changes in rates of delinquent behavior were not examined.

The problem here is that both assumptions are without empirical support. We are not aware of any evidence indicating that an improvement in the community environment or a change in behaviors other than delinquency leads to a reduction in rates of delinquent behavior. In fact, independent assessment of projects such as these has provided a convincing demonstration of their failure to reduce delinquency.[27]

Researchers should continue to describe the operational problems encountered, since these descriptions alert others to potential problems, and activities

---

25. Kobrin, "The Chicago Area Project."

26. Tefferteller, "Delinquency Prevention through Revitalizing Parent-Child Relations."

27. For example, C. Berleman and T. Steinburn, "The Execution and Evaluation of a Delinquency Prevention Program," *Social Problems*, Spring 1967, pp. 413–32; W. McCord and J. McCord, *Origins of Crime: A New Evaluation of the Cambridge-Somerville Youth Study* (Montclair, N.J.: Patterson Smith, 1959); Powers and Witmer, *An Experiment in the Prevention of Delinquency*; and Reckless and Dinitz, *Prevention of Juvenile Delinquency*.

designed to reduce truancy or change self-concepts can assist the juveniles involved in a project. However, the incidence of delinquency today demands that assessment of changes in delinquent behavior be given primary attention.

Recommendation Six

In All Future Delinquency Prevention Programs, Delinquency and Other Indicators of Prevention Effect Should Be Objectively Measured. Most of the projects we examined relied upon subjective assessments of effectiveness. In certain projects, administrators assessed the results, while other programs relied on the subjects' statements and perceptions. Clearly, perceptions such as these are liable to distortion. Project administrators generally have a vested interest in the success of their projects, and it is likely that these interests bias perception. Participants' viewpoints are equally liable to distortion as subjects seek to rationalize involvement in a program.

Both juveniles and role-model teachers involved in the Walter Reckless and Simon Dinitz project evaluated the program highly.[28] The juvenile subjects were "overwhelmingly favorable to the program," thought they had benefited from it, and believed their friends could also benefit from exposure to such a program. The teachers perceived significant improvement in the school performance of the experimental subjects and enthusiastically proclaimed the positive effects of their efforts. Based upon subjective evaluations, then, there was every reason to believe that the project had been a success.

The objective data, however, do not support these positive subjective evaluations. Although there was some indication of experimental improvement in intervening variables, there were no statistically significant differences in any of the objective criteria. Specifically, there were no differences between the experimental and control subjects in arrest, drop-out, attendance, grades, school achievement, and self-perception.

In general, then, subjective evaluations of preventive effect are unreliable when compared with objective measures. Therefore, we recommend that all indicators of preventive effect be objectively measured.

Recommendation Seven

Researchers Involved in Future Deliquency Prevention Programs Should Explore the Possibility of Employing Additional and More Sensitive Indicators or Measures of Delinquent Behavior. Of those projects which involved objective measurement of delinquent behavior, all relied upon official police or court statistics as indicators or measures of delinquency.[29] The problem here is that these statistics are notoriously unreliable since changes in rates of de-

28. Reckless and Dinitz, *Prevention of Juvenile Delinquency.*
29. See, for example, Powers and Witmer, *An Experiment in the Prevention of Delinquency.*

linquency may occur for reasons that have little or nothing to do with the existence of a prevention project. For example, among the variables which influence the release versus referral decisions of police officers and intake personnel is the amount of residential space available in local detention centers.[30] If a detention facility is at or near capacity, arrest or referral occurs only in the context of the most serious offenses. The result is a temporary decrease in the overall delinquency rate. If, on the other hand, residential space is available, arrests and referrals temporarily increase, thereby forcing the researcher to the uncomfortable conclusion that the prevention project actually increased rates of delinquency.

In addition, it appears that the decisions made by members of the juvenile justice system are biased in that male, minority, inner-city, and working-class juveniles are disproportionately represented in official delinquency populations. Although this overrepresentation may be a function of real behavioral differences,[31] we know it is also traceable to a process of selection based upon these very same extralegal characteristics.[32] Since subjects involved in most prevention projects are typically inner-city, working-class, minority males, it is not unreasonable to suggest that among the many reasons for the projects' failure with such juveniles is the tendency for police officers to be less lenient with them than with other youths. Stated alternatively, police arrest practices may mask a reduction in the *total* frequency or seriousness of delinquency.

Finally, diversion from the juvenile justice system is an old practice.[33] Police officers routinely release many more juveniles than they arrest,[34] and intake personnel frequently use informal probation as an alternative to formal processing.[35] At the very least, reliance upon official statistics results in a severe distortion of the total volume of delinquency.

For these reasons, we suggest use of additional, *but not alternative*, indicators or measures of delinquent behavior. We recommend use of self-reported delinquency as another indicator of delinquent behavior. This recommendation involves certain methodological problems, but these difficulties are assessable, if not largely resolvable, using existing techniques. In 1966, Martin Gold proposed a combination card sort-interview technique which

---

30. See, for example, Matza, *Delinquency and Drift.*

31. See, for example, Williams and Gold, "From Delinquent Behavior to Official Delinquency."

32. Ibid.

33. R. Smith, "Diversion: New Label—Old Practice," in *Criminal Justice Monograph: New Approaches to Diversion and Treatment of Juvenile Offenders,* P. Lejins, ed. (Washington, D.C.: U.S. Govt. Printing Office, 1973), p. 39.

34. See, for example: R. Lundman, R. Sykes, and J. Clark, "Police Control of Juveniles: A Replication" (Paper presented at the annual meeting of the American Society of Criminology, November 1975).

35. See, for example, D. Cressey, *Diversion from the Juvenile Justice System* (Washington, D.C.: U.S. Govt. Printing Office, 1974), p. 17.

permits validation of self-reported delinquencies.[36] Researchers contemplating future delinquency prevention programs should consider this technique or other, comparable instruments.[37] We also recommend that future measures of delinquency be made more sensitive by eliminating status offenses and victimless crimes. These offenses do not distinguish juveniles likely to be seriously and frequently delinquent in the future from others likely to be marginally delinquent, since nearly all juveniles report a high rate of involvement in such behavior.[38] Inclusion of these offenses inflates delinquency rates and may hide the impact of prevention efforts. Thus, analysis should be restricted to those offenses which would be criminal if committed by an adult.

Recommendation Eight

Researchers Involved in Future Delinquency Prevention Programs Should Consider Using Different Types of Subjects in the Projects. Recent research involving self-reported delinquency has revealed that the differences reflected in official delinquency statistics between male and female, majority and minority, and urban and rural juveniles are significantly reduced when unreported delinquency is examined.[39] Stated simply, it now appears that serious and frequent delinquency is female, middle class, and rural as well as male, lower class, and urban. Involvement of female, majority, or rural juveniles as subjects is important for at least two reasons. First, it would appear that recent, dramatic increases in overall delinquency rates are partially a function of expansion of the social and demographic correlates of delinquent behavior. In any attempt to reduce overall delinquency rates, attention must be directed toward juveniles formerly excluded from prevention efforts.

Second, involvement of other types of juveniles would show whether certain intervention techniques are effective with some juveniles and not with others. We now know that casework, group work, and community organization are generally ineffective with inner-city, working-class, minority males. It is possible that these techniques might be more effective with other types of juvenile subjects.

36. M. Gold, "Undetected Delinquent Behavior," *Journal of Research in Crime and Delinquency*, January 1966, pp. 27–46; and M. Gold, *Delinquent Behavior in an American City* (Belmont, Calif.: Brooks/Cole, 1970). See also J. Williams and M. Gold, "From Delinquent Behavior to Official Delinquency."

37. Foster et al. have utilized a similar technique. See J. Foster, S. Dinitz, and W. Reckless, "Perceptions of Stigma Following Public Intervention for Delinquent Behavior," *Social Problems*, Fall 1972, pp. 202–09.

38. A. Cohen, *Delinquent Boys: The Culture of the Gang* (Glencoe, Ill.: Free Press, 1955); W. Miller, "Lower Class Culture as a Generating Milieu of Gang Delinquency," *Journal of Social Issues*, November 1958, pp. 5–19; and J. Scott and E. Vaz, "A Perspective on Middle-Class Delinquency," *Canadian Journal of Economics and Political Science*, August 1963, pp. 324–34.

39. Support for this observation can be found in Gold, "Undetected Delinquent Behavior," and in Williams and Gold, "From Delinquent Behavior to Official Delinquency."

Recommendation Nine

All Future Delinquency Prevention Projects Should Be Experimental in Design. Most of the studies we examined were preexperimental in design.[40] Typically, a single group of juveniles was first exposed to some type of treatment and then followed to determine whether the treatment had been effective.

Numerous problems are associated with this type of design, and they prevent reliable assessment of results. It is impossible to determine whether the changes in the dependent variable are a result of exposure to an independent variable or the result of the influence of uncontrolled, extraneous variables such as history or maturation. As a consequence, we believe that projects based upon preexperimental designs are futile and should not be proposed, much less funded.

Experimental designs make more reliable assessment of results possible. The use of sample selection techniques involving some form of random choice for both experimental and control groups permits control or assessment of extraneous variables. Other issues, including the generalizability of the results, remain problematic, but they do not relate to the problem of distinguishing the effects of the experimental treatment from the effects of other variables. We strongly suggest that experimental designs be used in all future delinquency prevention projects.

Quasi-experimental designs represent a useful, but less satisfactory, alternative in situations where experimental designs are not possible. Although numerous variations exist, the primary characteristics of quasi-experimental designs are the use of some nonrandom assignment technique and the resulting sacrifice of certain of the controls characteristic of experimental designs. Matching is typically used in assigning subjects to treatment and control groups. Rarely, even with a large sample, can subjects be matched on more than a few important dimensions. Thus, the effects of unmatched differences in the subjects assigned to the experimental and control groups often intrude, making it difficult to distinguish treatment effects from uncontrolled differences. Roscoe Brown and Dan Dodson sought to determine whether the presence of a Boys' Club prevents delinquency.[41] An area served by a Boys' Club was matched with two other areas in terms of income, rental costs, education, and population, and a significantly lower rate of official delinquency was reported for the area served by the Boys' Club. However, the Boys' Club area was 2 percent black while the other areas were 11 percent and 9 percent black. It is difficult to reliably determine whether the Boy's Club,

40. D. Campbell and J. Stanley, *Experimental and Quasi-Experimental Designs for Research* (Chicago: Rand McNally, 1963), pp. 6ff. All materials on experimental designs are derived from this source.
41. Brown and Dodson, "The Effectiveness of a Boys' Club in Reducing Delinquency."

unmatched differences, or some combination of both accounted for differences in rates of official delinquency.

Certainly, quasi-experimental designs are superior to one-shot case studies since they generally permit greater control of the extraneous variables that plague pre-experimental designs. We believe that they should be used in situations where experimental designs are not possible.

SUMMARY AND CONCLUSIONS

Official statistics indicate that delinquent behavior is increasing in total volume and that different types of juveniles are becoming involved in delinquency. The public concern over this unhappy situation will undoubtedly result in continued attempts to prevent delinquent behavior.

However, delinquency is an enormously complex phenomenon. Few prevention efforts give any indication of having successfully prevented youngsters from engaging in law violation. Moreover, we know little about why particular projects failed to prevent delinquency. If researchers and practitioners were more realistic and expected future projects to be unsuccessful, if the results of all projects were made public, and if the implementation-evaluation components of all future projects were separate, we would certainly learn much more about strategies for prevention.

Too often, it has been impossible to assess the results of delinquency programs. We find little reason for endlessly replicating the same tired techniques among stereotyped populations of youths. Instead researchers should broaden their attack on delinquency. Juveniles demographically different from those involved in past attempts should be among the subjects in future projects. Additional measures of delinquency, experimental designs, and objective evaluation should also be incorporated in future projects.

However, as new prevention programs are developed and implemented, practitioners and researchers must recognize that their juvenile subjects deserve special protections. Generally, these subjects have not been found guilty of anything beyond possession of characteristics or behaviors which someone believes are predictive of delinquency. In our zeal to help, we must not lose sight of the fact that juveniles who have not been adjudicated delinquent have the right to refuse that help.

30

A THIRTY-YEAR FOLLOW-UP OF
TREATMENT EFFECTS
JOAN McCORD

ABSTRACT: *Over 500 men, half of whom had been randomly assigned to a treatment program that lasted approximately 5 years, were traced 30 years after termination of the project. Although subjective evaluations of the program by those who received its benefits would suggest that the intervention had been helpful, comparisons between the treatment and control groups indicate that the program had negative side effects as measured by criminal behavior, death, disease, occupational status, and job satisfaction. Several possible processes are suggested in explanation of these findings.*

In 1935, Richard Clark Cabot instigated one of the most imaginative and exciting programs ever designed in hopes of preventing delinquency. A social philosopher as well as physician, Dr. Cabot established a program that both avoided stigmatizing participants and permitted follow-up evaluation.

Several hundred boys from densely populated, factory-dominated areas of eastern Massachusetts were included in the project, known as the Cambridge–Somerville Youth Study. Schools, welfare agencies, churches, and the police recommended both "difficult" and "average" youngsters to the program. These boys and their families were given physical examinations and were interviewed by social workers who then rated each boy in such a way as to allow a selection committee to designate delinquency-prediction scores. In addition to giving delinquency-prediction scores, the selection committee studied each boy's records in order to identify pairs who were similar in age, delinquency-prone histories, family background, and home environments. By the toss of a coin, one member of each pair was assigned to the group that would receive treatment.[1]

The treatment program began in 1939, when the boys were between 5 and 13 years old. Their median age was 10½. Except for those dropped from the program because of a counselor shortage in 1941, treatment continued for an average of 5 years. Counselors assigned to each family visited, on the average, twice a month. They encouraged families to call on the program for assistance. Family problems became the focus of attention for ap-

proximately one third of the treatment group. Over half of the boys were tutored in academic subjects; over 100 received medical or psychiatric attention; one fourth were sent to summer camps; and most were brought into contact with the Boy Scouts, the YMCA, and other community programs. The control group, meanwhile, participated only through providing information about themselves. Both groups, it should be remembered, contained boys referred as "average" and boys considered "difficult."

The present study compares the 253 men who had been in the treatment program after 1942 with the 253 "matched mates" assigned to the control group.

Method

Official records and personal contacts were used to obtain information about the long-term effects of the Cambridge–Somerville Youth Study.[2] In 1975 and 1976, the 506 former members of the program were traced through court records, mental hospital

This study was supported by U.S. Public Health Service Research Grant No. 5 R01 MH26779, National Institute of Mental Health (Center for Studies of Crime and Delinquency). It was conducted jointly with the Department of Probation of the Commonwealth of Massachusetts.

An earlier version of this paper was presented at the 28th annual meeting of the American Association of Psychiatric Services for Children, San Francisco, California, November 10–14, 1976.

The author wishes to express appreciation to the Division of Alcoholism, to the Cambridge & Somerville Program for Alcoholism Rehabilitation, to the National Institute of Law Enforcement (through Grant NI 74-0038 to Ron Geddes), to the Massachusetts Departments of Mental Health, Motor Vehicles, and Correction, and to the many individuals who contributed to this research.

Requests for reprints should be sent to Joan McCord, 1279 Montgomery Avenue, Wynnewood, Pennsylvania 19096.

[1] An exception to assignment by chance was made if brothers were in the program; all brothers were assigned to that group which was the assignment of the first brother matched. See Powers and Witmer (1951) for details of the matching procedure.

[2] A sample of 200 men had been retraced in 1948 (Powers & Witmer, 1951), and official records had been traced in 1956 (McCord & McCord, 1959a, 1959b).

From Joan McCord, "A Thirty-Year Follow-Up of Treatment Effects," 33(3) *American Psychologist* 284–289 (March 1978). Copyright 1978 by the American Psychological Association, Inc.

records, records from alcoholic treatment centers, and vital statistics in Massachusetts. Telephone calls, city directories, motor-vehicle registrations, marriage and death records, and lucky hunches were used to find the men themselves.

Four hundred eighty men (95%) were located; among these, 48 (9%) had died and 340 (79%) were living in Massachusetts.[3] Questionnaires were mailed to 208 men from the treatment group and 202 men from the control group. The questionnaire elicited information about marriage, children, occupations, drinking, health, and attitudes. Former members of the treatment group were asked how (if at all) the treatment program had been helpful to them.

Responses to the questionnaire were received from 113 men in the treatment group (54%) and 122 men in the control group (60%). These responses overrepresent men living outside of Massachusetts, $\chi^2(1) = 10.97$, $p < .001$.[4] Official records, on the other hand, provide more complete information about those men living in Massachusetts.

Comparison of Criminal Behavior

The treatment and control groups were compared on a variety of measures for criminal behavior. With the exception of Crime Prevention Bureau records for unofficial crimes committed by juveniles, court convictions serve as the standard by which criminal behavior was assessed. Although official court records may be biased, there is no reason to believe that these biases would affect a comparison between the matched groups of control and treatment subjects.

Almost equal numbers in the treatment and control groups had committed crimes as juveniles—whether measured by official or by unofficial records (see Table 1).

It seemed possible that the program might have benefited those referred as "difficult" while damaging those referred as "average." The evidence,

TABLE 2

Juvenile Delinquency and Adult Criminal Records

Record	Treatment group	Control group
Official juvenile record		
No adult record	14	15
Only minor adult record	33	27
Serious crimes as adults	25	25
No official juvenile record		
No adult record	71	.70
Only minor adult record	86	99
Serious crimes as adults	24	17
Total	253	253

however, failed to support this hypothesis. Among those referred as "difficult," 34% from the treatment group and 30% from the control group had official juvenile records; an additional 20% from the treatment group and 21% from the control group had unofficial records. Nor were there differences between the groups for those who had been referred as "average."[5]

As adults, equal numbers (168) had been convicted for some crime. Among men who had been in the treatment group, 119 committed only relatively minor crimes (against ordinances or order), but 49 had committed serious crimes against property (including burglary, larceny, and auto theft) or against persons (including assault, rape, and attempted homicide). Among men from the control group, 126 had committed only relatively minor crimes; 42 had committed serious property crimes or crimes against persons. Twenty-nine men from the treatment group and 25 men from the control group committed serious crimes after the age of 25.

Reasoning that the Youth Study project may have been differentially effective for those who did and did not have records as delinquents, it seemed advisable to compare adult criminal records while holding this background information constant.

TABLE 1

Juvenile Records

Record	Treatment group	Control group
No record for delinquency	136	140
Only unofficial crimes	45	46
Official crimes	72	67
Total	253	253

[3] Two hundred forty-one men from the treatment group and 239 men from the control group were found; 173 from the treatment group and 167 from the control group were living in Massachusetts.
[4] Among those sent the questionnaire, the response rate for men living in Massachusetts was 53%; for men living outside Massachusetts, the response rate was 74%. A similar bias appeared for both groups.
[5] For the treatment group, 18% had official records and an additional 13% had unofficial records. For the control-group "average" referrals, the figures were 19% and 13%, respectively.

Again, there was no evidence that the treatment program had deflected people from committing crimes (see Table 2).

The treatment and control groups were compared to see whether there were differences (a) in the number of serious crimes committed, (b) in age when a first crime was committed, (c) in age when committing a first serious crime, and (d) in age after which no serious crime was committed. None of these measures showed reliable differences.

Benefits from the treatment program did not appear when delinquency-prediction scores were controlled or when seriousness of juvenile record and juvenile incarceration were controlled. Unexpectedly, however, a higher proportion of criminals from the treatment group than of criminals from the control group committed more than one crime, $\chi^2(1) = 5.36$, $p < .05$. Among the 182 men with criminal records from the treatment group, 78% committed at least two crimes; among the 183 men with criminal records from the control group, 67% committed at least two crimes.

Comparison of Health

Signs of alcoholism, mental illness, stress-related diseases, and early death were used to evaluate possible impact of the treatment program on health.

A search through records from alcoholic treatment centers and mental hospitals in Massachusetts showed that almost equal numbers of men from the treatment and the control groups had been treated for alcoholism (7% and 8%, respectively).

The questionnaire asked respondents to note their drinking habits and to respond to four questions about drinking embedded in questions about smoking. The four questions, known as the CAGE test (Ewing & Rouse, Note 1), asked whether the respondent had ever taken a morning eye-opener, felt the need to cut down on drinking, felt annoyed by criticism of his drinking, or felt guilty about drinking.[6] The treatment group mentioned that they were alcoholic or responded *yes* more frequently, as do alcoholics, to at least three of the CAGE questions: 17% compared with 7%, $\chi^2(1) = 4.98$, $p < .05$.

Twenty-one members of each group had received treatment in mental hospitals for disorders other than alcoholism.[7] A majority of those from the treatment group (71%) received diagnoses as manic-depressive or schizophrenic, whereas a majority of those from the control group (67%) received less serious diagnoses such as "personality disorder" or "psychoneurotic," $\chi^2(1) = 4.68$, $p < .05$.

Twenty-four men from each group are known to have died. Although the groups were not distinguishable by causes of death, among those who died, men from the treatment group tended to die at younger ages, $t(94) = 2.19$, $p < .05$.[8]

The questionnaire requested information about nine stress-related diseases: arthritis, gout, emphysema, depression, ulcers, asthma, allergies, high blood pressure, and heart trouble. Men from the treatment group were more likely to report having had at least one of these diseases, $\chi^2(1) = 4.39$, $p < .05$.[9] In particular, symptoms of stress in the circulatory system were more prevalent among men from the treatment group: 21%, as compared with 11% in the control group, reported having had high blood pressure or heart trouble, $\chi^2(1) = 4.95$, $p < .05$.

Comparison of Family, Work, and Leisure Time

A majority of the men who responded to the questionnaire were married: 61% of the treatment group and 68% of the control group. An additional 15% of the treatment group and 10% of the control group noted that they were remarried. Fourteen percent of the treatment-group and 9% of the control-group respondents had never married. The remaining 10% of the treatment group and 13% of the control group were separated, divorced, or widowed. Among those ever married, 93% of each group had children. The median number of children for both sets of respondents was three.

About equal proportions of the treatment- and the control-group respondents were unskilled workers (29% and 27%, respectively). At the upper end of the socioeconomic scale, however, the con-

---

[6] This test was validated by comparing the responses of 58 acknowledged alcoholics in an alcoholism rehabilitation center with those of 68 nonalcoholic patients in a general hospital: 95% of the former and none of the latter answered *yes* to more than two of the four questions (Ewing & Rouse, Note 1). Additional information related to alcoholism is being gathered through interviews.

[7] An additional five men from the treatment group and three men from the control group had been institutionalized as retarded.

[8] The average age at death for the treatment group was 32 years ($SD = 9.4$) and for the control group, 38 years ($SD = 7.5$).

[9] Thirty-six percent of those in the treatment group and 24% of those in the control group reported having had at least one of these diseases.

trol group had an advantage: 43% from the control group, compared with 29% from the treatment group, were white-collar workers or professionals, $\chi^2(2) = 4.58$, $p < .05$. For those whose occupations could be classified according to National Opinion Research Center (NORC) ranks, comparison indicated that the control-group men were working in positions having higher prestige, $z = 2.07$, $p < .05$ (Mann-Whitney U test).

The questionnaire inquired whether the men found their work, in general, to be satisfying. Almost all of the men who held white-collar or professional positions (97%) reported that their work was satisfying. Among blue-collar workers, those in the treatment group were less likely to report that their work was generally satisfying (80%, compared with 95% among the control group), $\chi^2(1) = 6.60$, $p < .02$.

The men described how they used their spare time. These descriptions were grouped to compare the proportions who reported reading, traveling, doing things with their families, liking sports (as spectators or participants), working around the house, watching television, enjoying music or theater or photography, doing service work, enjoying crafts or tinkering, and participating in organized group activities. The treatment and control groups did not differ in their reported uses of leisure time.

Comparison of Beliefs and Attitudes

The men were asked to evaluate their satisfaction with how their lives were turning out, their chances for living the kinds of lives they'd like to have, and whether they were able to plan ahead.[10] Men from the treatment and the control groups did not differ in their responses to these questions.

A short form of the F scale (Adorno, Frenkel-Brunswik, Levinson, & Sanford, 1950) developed by Sanford and Older (Note 2) was included in the questionnaire. Men were asked whether they agreed or disagreed with the following statements: "Human nature being what it is, there must always be war and conflict. The most important thing a child should learn is obedience to his parents. A few strong leaders could make this country better than all the laws and talk. Most people who don't get ahead just don't have enough willpower. Women should stay out of politics. An insult to your honor should not be forgotten. In general, people can be trusted."

Despite diversity in opinions, neither answers to particular questions nor to the total scale suggested that treatment and control groups differed in authoritarianism. Both groups selected an average of 2.9 authoritarian answers; the standard deviation for each group was 1.7.

Each man was asked to describe his political orientation. About one fifth considered themselves liberals, two fifths considered themselves conservatives, and two fifths considered themselves as middle-of-the-road. No one considered himself a radical. Treatment and control groups did not differ reliably.

The men also identified the best periods of their lives, and, again, there was little difference between control and treatment groups.

Subjective Evaluation of the Program

Former members of the treatment group were asked, "In what ways (if any) was the Cambridge–Someville project helpful to you?"

Only 11 men failed to comment about this item. Thirteen noted that they could not remember the project. An additional 13 stated that the project had not been helpful—though several of these men amplified their judgments by mentioning that they had fond memories of their counselors or their activities in the project.

Two thirds of the men stated that the program had been helpful to them. Some wrote that, by providing interesting activities, the project kept them off the streets and out of trouble. Many believed that the project improved their lives through providing guidance or teaching them how to get along with others. The questionnaires were sprinkled with such comments as "helped me to have faith and trust in other people"; "I was put on the right road"; "helped prepare me for manhood"; "to overcome my prejudices"; "provided an initial grasp of our complex society outside of the ghetto"; and "better insight on life in general."

A few men believed that the project was responsible for their becoming law-abiding citizens. Such men wrote that, had it not been for their particular counselors, "I probably would be in jail"; "My life would have gone the other way"; or "I think I would have ended up in a life of crime."

More than a score requested information about their counselors and expressed the intention of communicating with them.

---

[10] This set of questions was developed at the University of Michigan Survey Research Center as a measure of self-competence. It has an index of reproducibility as a Guttman Scale of .94 (see Douvan & Walker, 1956).

Summary and Discussion

This study of long-term effects of the Cambridge–Somerville Youth Study was based on the tracing of over 500 men, half of whom were randomly assigned to a treatment program. Those receiving treatment had (in varying degrees) been tutored, provided with medical assistance, and given friendly counsel for an extended period of time.

Thirty years after termination of the program, many of the men remembered their counselors—sometimes recalling particular acts of kindness and sometimes noting the general support they felt in having someone available with whom to discuss their problems. There seems to be little doubt that many of the men developed emotional ties to their counselors.

Were the Youth Study program to be assessed by the subjective judgment of its value as perceived by those who received its services, it would rate high marks. To the enormous credit of those who dedicated years of work to the project, it is possible to use objective criteria to evaluate the long-term impact of this program, which seems to have been successful in achieving the short-term goals of establishing rapport between social workers and teenage clients.

Despite the large number of comparisons between treatment and control groups, none of the objective measures confirmed hopes that treatment had improved the lives of those in the treatment group. Fifteen comparisons regarding criminal behavior were made; one was significant with alpha less than .05. Fifteen comparisons for health indicated four —from three different record sources—favoring the control group. Thirteen comparisons of family, work, and leisure time yielded two that favored the control group. Fourteen comparisons of beliefs and attitudes failed to indicate reliable differences between the groups.

The objective evidence presents a disturbing picture. The program seems not only to have failed to prevent its clients from committing crimes—thus corroborating studies of other projects (see, e.g., Craig & Furst, 1965; Empey, 1972; Hackler, 1966; Miller, 1962; Robin, 1969)—but also to have produced negative side effects. As compared with the control group,

1. Men who had been in the treatment program were more likely to commit (at least) a second crime.

2. Men who had been in the treatment program were more likely to evidence signs of alcoholism.

3. Men from the treatment group more commonly manifested signs of serious mental illness.

4. Among men who had died, those from the treatment group died younger.

5. Men from the treatment group were more likely to report having had at least one stress-related disease; in particular, they were more likely to have experienced high blood pressure or heart trouble.

6. Men from the treatment group tended to have occupations with lower prestige.

7. Men from the treatment group tended more often to report their work as not satisfying.

It should be noted that the side effects that seem to have resulted from treatment were subtle. There is no reason to believe that treatment increased the probability of committing a first crime, although treatment may have increased the likelihood that those who committed a first crime would commit additional crimes. Although treatment may have increased the likelihood of alcoholism, the treatment group was not more likely to have appeared in clinics or hospitals. There was no difference between the groups in the number of men who had died before the age of 50, although men from the treatment group had been younger at the age of death. Almost equal proportions of the two groups of men had remained at the lowest rungs of the occupational structure, although men from the treatment group were less likely to be satisfied with their jobs and fewer men from the treatment group had become white-collar workers.

The probability of obtaining 7 reliably different comparisons among 57, with an alpha of .05, is less than 2%. The probability that, by chance, 7 of 57 comparisons would favor the control group is less than 1 in 10,000.[11]

At this juncture, it seems appropriate to suggest several possible interpretations of the subtle effects of treatment. Interaction with adults whose values are different from those of the family milieu may produce later internal conflicts that manifest themselves in disease and/or dissatisfaction.[12] Agency intervention may create dependency upon outside

---

[11] This estimate is conservative. The count of 57 comparisons includes comparisons that are not independent (e.g., adult criminal record and crimes after the age of 25), but only 7 independent significant relationships have been counted. If comparisons for any stress-related disease, for NORC ranking of occupation, and for job satisfaction without controlling work status are counted, 10 out of 60 comparisons were significant.

[12] Such conflicts seem to have been aroused by intervention in the lives of hard-core unemployables (Padfield & Williams, 1973).

assistance. When this assistance is no longer available, the individual may experience symptoms of dependency and resentment. The treatment program may have generated such high expectations that subsequent experiences tended to produce symptoms of deprivation. Or finally, through receiving the services of a "welfare project," those in the treatment program may have justified the help they received by perceiving themselves as requiring help.

There were many variations to treatment. Some of these may have been beneficial. Overall, however, the message seems clear: Intervention programs risk damaging the individuals they are designed to assist. These findings may be taken by some as grounds for cessation of social-action programs. I believe that would be a mistake. In my opinion, new programs ought to be developed. We should, however, address the problems of potential damage through the use of pilot projects with mandatory evaluations.

REFERENCE NOTES

1. Ewing, J. A., & Rouse, B. A. *Identifying the "hidden alcoholic."* Paper presented at the 29th International Congress on Alcohol and Drug Dependence, Sydney, New South Wales, Australia, February 3, 1970.
2. Sanford, F. H., & Older, J. J. *A short authoritarian-equalitarian scale* (Progress Report No. 6, Series A).

Philadelphia, Pa.: Institute for Research in Human Relations, 1950.

REFERENCES

Adorno, T. W., Frenkel-Brunswik, E., Levinson, D. J., & Sanford, R. N. *The authoritarian personality.* New York: Harper, 1950.

Craig, M. M., & Furst, P. W. What happens after treatment? A study of potentially delinquent boys. *Social Service Review,* 1965, *39,* 165-171.

Douvan, E., & Walker, A. M. The sense of effectiveness in public affairs. *Psychological Monographs,* 1956, *70*(22, Whole No. 429).

Empey, L. T., & Ericson, M. L. *The provo experiment: Evaluating community control of delinquency.* Lexington, Mass.: Lexington Books, 1972.

Hackler, J. C. Boys, blisters, and behavior: The impact of a work program in an urban central area. *Journal of Research in Crime and Delinquency,* 1966, *12,* 155-164.

McCord, J., & McCord, W. A follow-up report on the Cambridge-Somerville youth study. *Annals of the American Academy of Political and Social Science,* 1959, *322,* 89-96. (a)

McCord, W., & McCord, J. *Origins of crime.* New York: Columbia University Press, 1959. (b)

Miller, W. B. The impact of a "total community" delinquency control project. *Social Problems,* 1962, *10,* 168-191.

Padfield, H., & Williams, R. *Stay where you were: A study of unemployables in industry.* Philadelphia, Pa.: Lippincott, 1973.

Powers, E., & Witmer, H. *An experiment in the prevention of delinquency: The Cambridge-Somerville youth study.* New York: Columbia University Press, 1951.

Robin, G. R. Anti-poverty programs and delinquency. *Journal of Criminal Law, Criminology, and Police Science,* 1969, *60,* 323-331.

31

BEHAVIOURAL APPROACHES TO TREATMENT IN CORRECTIONS
Requiem for a Panacea

ROBERT R. ROSS and H. BRYAN McKAY

Les auteurs analysent un mode particulier de traitement, la modification du comportement; ceci à la lumière des critiques récentes formulees a l'endroit du traitement dans le domaine correctionnel. Quand on fait trop de promesses au sujet de programmes presentés comme une panacée, le désenchantement inévitable qui en resulte pousse à les rejeter dans leur ensemble sans en faire une bonne appréciation critique. Le fait de ne pas analyser adéquatement la modification du comportement pourrait conduire à en oublier les possibilités pour ce qui est des programmes axés sur la collectivité et pour la gestion des établissements correctionnels.

Every person who has reason to believe that a deceased person died, . . . as a result of, . . . misadventure, negligence, misconduct or malpractice; by unfair means; . . . under such circumstances as may require investigation, shall immediately notify a coroner of the facts and circumstances relating to the death. [Coroners Act, R.S.O. 1970, ch. 87, s. 7.]

It has become fashionable to adopt the position that treatment in corrections is dead. Martinson, the funeral director, may have signed the death certificate for treatment through his critical review of the published research on treatment in corrections. [Lipton et al., 1975; Wilks and Martinson, 1976] In spite of opposing opinions [Palmer, 1975] there seems to be a widespread acceptance of the view that treatment has been tried and found wanting. The rush to "bury the remains" is reminiscent of an Agatha Christie novel. The apparent tacit agreement to leave stones unturned, the collective sigh of relief at the funeral director's words of reassurance, the haste to inter the remains are familiar grist for the mystery writer's scenarios.

A coroner may at any time during an investigation or inquest issue his warrant for a *post-mortem* examination of the body . . . or such other examination or analysis as the circumstances warrant. [R.S.O. 1970, ch. 87, s. 24(1)]

After a death it is sometimes profitable to conduct an autopsy before the funeral. Our failure to do a careful autopsy on treatment in corrections will, we contend, lead to four erroneous conclusions:

From Robert R. Ross and H. Bryan McKay, "Behavioural Approaches to Treatment in Corrections: Requiem for a Panacea," 20(3) *Canadian Journal of Criminology and Corrections* 279-295 (July 1978). Copyright 1978 by the Canadian Criminology and Corrections Association.

1. The quality of correctional research is sufficiently good to make possible an adequate assessment of the efficacy of correctional treatment. It is not.
2. The treatment employed in corrections is an adequate reflection of the variety and quality of treatment more broadly available in the mental health field. It is not.
3. There are no treatment programs which have been shown through adequate research to be efficacious. There are.
4. The "failure" of treatment reflects simply the inadequacy of the treatment and not the inadequacy of the environment in which the treatment is applied. It does not.

> . . . he shall issue his warrant to take possession of the body and shall view the body and make such further investigation as is required to enable him to determine whether or not an inquest is necessary. R.S.O. 1970, ch. 87, s. 12(1)

Clearly, there is not a plethora of evidence that the programs in corrections which were engendered by the mental health movement lead to improved rehabilitation or a reduction in the rate of crime.

One might argue that the "treatment approach" has done little more than modify our language, aid in the documentation of the failure of corrections, engender major role conflict for criminal justice personnel and increase the cost of preparing the offender to recidivate to his correctional home. In fact, a case could be made to the effect that some treatment approaches have made our "patient" worse. Stuart, 1970; Ross and McKay, 1976 However, the failure needs to be brought into perspective before we complete the funeral arrangements. We ought to identify what we are burying. Often in corrections new treatment techniques are adopted both wholeheartedly and foolhardily; at times exclusively, and often with little question as to their applicability to the population in the field. Often, too, once they are accepted they are modified so much by the pressures of the correctional environment that their similarity to the actual techniques is apparent but hardly real. More regrettable, perhaps, is the characteristic acceptance by correctional staff of new techniques *in name only*. Whereas psychology has often been characterized by radicalism, corrections too frequently suffers from euphemism. McKay, 1976 Offenders are often remarkably (albeit negatively) affected by their entry into the criminal justice system. So are treatment programs.

> Where a person dies while in the custody of an officer of a correctional institution or lock-up or while a ward of a training school, the officer in charge thereof shall immediately give notice of the death to a coroner and the coroner shall issue his warrant and hold an inquest upon the body R.S.O. 1970, ch. 87, s. 23

In the present paper we will provide an autopsy of behavioural approaches to the treatment of the offender.

The advent of behaviour modification in corrections was heralded with considerable excitement, enthusiasm, and optimism. Tremendous sums of money were poured into the new strategy. It quickly pervaded the field of corrections and often completely replaced established and apparently progressive programs in institutions. For example, we discovered through a survey conducted in 1968[Ross, 1968; Ross and McKay, 1974; Ross and McConkey, 1975] that sixty-three correctional settings in the United States and Canada had been involved in projects which were labelled as "behaviour modification programs", and that in at least sixty per cent of these cases behaviour modification programs were viewed by the officials of the correctional jurisdiction as core elements in their criminal justice system. When one considers that operant was first introduced to corrections in other than short-term experimental projects not before the early 1960's one can see how rapidly this "new" technique was adopted in corrections.

Yet operant was a relatively untried treatment modality. Correctional settings were adopting this technique more on promise than accomplishment. Lavish praise had been heaped on the efficacy of the method in other areas, particularly in mental hospitals and institutions for retarded children. However, seldom could one find any solid evidence that the technique brought improvement to the success of these institutions in discharging or rehabilitating their patients.

Operant; Treatment of Choice

> The men who rush into undertakings of vast change usually feel they are in possession of some irresistible power.[Hoffer, 1951, p. 17]

The reasons for corrections' adoption of operant with such enthusiasm and alacrity deserves some scrutiny. One of the reasons for the ready acceptance of operant was that it was relatively new. In corrections novelty frequently serves as a substitute for efficacy. It was not new in the sense that it departed in a major way from the goals of the traditional correctional program it was to supplant. Its intended accomplishment was almost isomorphic with the goal of many correctional programs: behavioural control. There are, in fact, many apparent similarities between what is standard fare in a correctional institution and the characteristics of an operant program. The emphasis on consequences for behaviour has a key position in both, although the type of consequence and the type of behaviour in question might differ. The treatment intervention is in the form of environmental manipulation — clearly characteristic of penological approaches for decades. In many ways the new operant could be perceived by the administrators as just fancy, socially acceptable, professional, "treatment appearing" versions of what generations of wardens had been providing for ages — incentive programs. The new operant did much to bolster the ego strength of many correctional administrators by showing that there was an empirical base for what they viewed as their creations. It would be comforting, in a sense, to feel that one of the reasons that operant was adopted so eagerly was that it was founded on laboratory evidence and appealed to the wardens as a logical common-sense system. In truth, it was a reinforcer for their efforts; a way for them to rapidly elevate their status through making them equal to the professionals who often before had stolen their glory. Science had finally discovered what they had known all along. No wonder it was adopted; it made their common-sense into scientific enterprise. The administrators immediately became experts in the field that so long had bothered them — treatment.

Few correctional administrators would venture into a new field unless they were prepared to withstand the criticism they might expect to receive as they usually do when they break with tradition. Operant posed little threat in this regard — they could bring innumerable "experts" to testify with clear statements as to the success of these programs elsewhere. One of the characteristics of reinforcement therapists may be that they become so versed in dispensing reinforcement that they develop strong habits of making highly reinforcing statements about their own efforts. Praise for the success of operant abounds. It is a little more difficult to find the justification for such praise.

The mental health movement is very prone to fads. Often treatment of choice is determined not by what is therapeutic but by what is fashionable. [Ross, 1976] The behaviour modification movement, once it got rolling, very quickly achieved the peak of fashion. New journals for this "discipline" sprang up; "behaviour mod." clubs became active; a large number of new books were published; training centres, workshops, internships and whole departments were established in a phenomenally short time. One cannot be sure, of course, to what extent the popularity and social acceptance of the movement determined its rapid adoption by corrections but it seems, in retrospect, that it was more than just the promise of success that appealed to corrections officials. It is customary for new movements to be acclaimed through statements of their underlying principles which, too often, are simple generalizations, trite verbiage, or emotionally laden truisms whose basis is frequently evangelical zeal rather than objectivity. The chants of the behaviour modifiers, however, had great appeal; theirs was the song of science.

> Proselytizing is more a passionate search for something not yet found than a desire to bestow upon the world something we already have. . . The creed whose legitimacy is most easily challenged is likely to develop the strongest proselytizing impulse. [Hoffer, 1951, p. 102]

The proponents of behaviour modification programs generally made three claims in selling their product:

1. The treatment strategy was rigorously derived from laboratory based empirical research with animal and human subjects. The claim of scientific respectability had considerable appeal to corrections officials and not just because it provided a strong defence against political critics. Corrections in the sixties was being taken to task for basing its programs on tradition,

administrative expediency and rationalism rather than on scientific enquiry. The introduction of operant coincided with the introduction of many correctional research departments, increased correctional research grant support, and heightened criminological research activity in the universities. The time was ripe, then, for the advent of an empirically based treatment program.

2. The time was particularly ripe for a treatment strategy that, its adherents claimed, was not only based on research but was itself eminently researchable. In a field where almost no adequate data were available regarding program efficacy (a source of considerable embarrassment) here was a new form of intervention which purported to make the assessment of success not only simple, possible and desirable, but essential. No program based so solidly on science could do otherwise. Now that they had the behaviourists they could find out how well "we" (the officials) were doing or how badly "they" (the offenders) were doing. Moreover, they got two birds with one stone — a "window-dressing" psychologist and a researcher who could do what they should have been doing for years. Finally, their critics would not only be reluctant, but would have serious difficulty arguing down scientific objectivity.

3. A major feature of operant programs is their apparent simplicity. The principles are few in number; easy to understand and recall; and simple to express and explain. Operant principles are not shrouded in a mystique of intellectual loftiness; they are stated in common, everyday language easily grasped by academician or layman; the jargon which characterizes so many treatment methods is almost nonexistent in operant; one does not need to have a bachelor's degree as a prerequisite to understanding the approach and, more important, one does not need years of graduate training to be an effective practitioner. Correctional administrators could readily become competent in this approach — the administrator who had a couple of undergraduate credits in psychology through extension courses could view himself as an authority on the subject. Correctional officers and "even" inmates could thoroughly understand the major principles after several courses of instruction and implement a program after some twelve weeks of training. Or so it appeared. Operant was decidedly not "professional" as that term is misunderstood in the correctional field, and was common-sensical rather than mystical. It dealt with things one could see (behaviour) rather than with things one had to be a member of the cult to understand.

Administrators accepted operant because they were sure they understood it and, thus, could control it and the people who used it. They accepted it because it was something their own people could do — in fact, they *were* doing it only not as intensively as they ought, or as systematically. They "bought it" because their "professionals" would now be busy intensifying, systematizing, and researching what the corrections people had been doing instead of rocking the boat.

The new breed of "professional", the behaviour modifier, seemed a delightful contrast to many others of their ilk whom corrections officials had encountered. Too often the "professionals" had engendered improvements in the standard of care in the correctional setting but at considerable cost and for questionable goals.

> (As The Riot progresses a newly acquired psychologist begins the role as liaison between the few hard core prisoners responsible for it and the outside authorities.)
>
> Wiping a hairy forearm across his face, Kelley sat back on his heels. "What's goin' on out there? Fletcher still runnin' the show?"
>
> "Yeah, him and the headshrinker. The headshrinker got into the act."
>
> "How'd that happen?"
>
> "Remember when you saw him leavin' the kitchen? Well, he was goin' out front. Skinny Burns drew up a petition, and Fletcher wouldn't take it out there. So Skinny saddled up the headshrinker."
>
> "Whose side is he on?"
>
> "The headshrinker?"
>
> "Yeah."
>
> "Ours, man. He's more on our side than we are. I guess you'd hav'ta call him a ring-leader. Been out front three, four times already. Acts like he's really getting his kicks. Got on the radio and said he agrees with what we're askin' for?"
>
> "What we askin for?"[Elli, 1968, p. 111]

With this new treatment modality the institution did not have to become a hospital. One did not have to view the inmate as a poor sick patient who needed treatment and tender love and care and warmth and empathy. The administrators did not have to transfer their authority to the part-time medical staff; they just gave it to the psychologist who actually behaved more like an administrator than the administrators. The psychologist promised to make the institution more efficient and the staff's work easier. They even seemed to relish making out forms! No more would the administrator have to live with the excessive molly-coddling or the explaining away of the inmate's behaviour as a result of some mysterious inner compulsions — notions which were thought to characterize "traditional" professional programs — nor would he have to revert to rigid and regimented discipline and aversive controls. Operant was a happy medium in the treatment of offenders; it promised equity — clear-cut predictable consequences for one's behaviour delivered neither sympathetically nor harshly, just matter-of-factly, objectively, unemotionally but fairly, and on the basis of clear-cut criteria: more just than the system of justice that sent them.

Another reason for the willing acceptance of operant by corrections officials was the eagerness of the practitioners to work with the most difficult patients. Psychotherapists are often accused of working most with those who need treatment the least. They often work with only a highly selected type of patient; often those who evidence the YAVIS syndrome (young, attractive, verbal, intelligent, successful).[Schoffield, 1964] Frequently the poorly motivated, behaviourally disordered, inarticulate, negativistic inmate is seen as "unlikely to benefit from treatment". Many superintendents report the experience of having most of their "problem" inmates referred back to them as "not amenable to therapy at this time" while many of their "good" inmates were being saturated with treatment. A pleasant contrast it was, indeed, when, with the advent of operant they were invited to send their worst inmates for treatment. Many behaviour modifiers extended this invitation as their initial step in convincing the administration to adopt the behaviour modification approach. Nor were these merely extravagant claims for the power of the method; the claims were backed up by action; frequently with very dramatic effects. Here, the administrators thought, is a treatment that not only will satisfy our needs for window-dressing, but may also help us — and, as an afterthought, it might even work. These practitioners also appeared to be interested not just in altering the "psyche" of the offenders (not of much interest to an administrator if the behaviour problems didn't change, as was usually the case); they were interested in changing his *behaviour* — in ameliorating his antisocial acts and fostering his prosocial behaviour. It appeared, in short, that they seemed intent on reducing management problems, and on helping the offenders conform. Surely, this is a new breed of professionals — they speak our language, copy our methods, and even share our goals.

Finally, operant promised to be an economically feasible treatment endeavour which would be administratively efficient, cheap and quick. It would be efficient both because the approach is highly systematic and because almost all matters requiring decisions and action would be handled according to clear principles in the form of contingencies that were easily and clearly communicated, automatically enacted and relatively fixed. Discussions were required for very few decisions; logistical matters and problems would be minimal in comparison with other treatment endeavours. In most instances rather lavish grants could be obtained by the treatment staff through outside agencies to finance the project — for professional salaries, technical help, bookkeeping, and equipment and materials. The beauty of it, of course, was that the warden would not have to obtain monies for salaries for a large number of "professionals" — they would not be needed. These programs would utilize the facilities and the staff already available. Although the program fitted to some extent the educational rehabilitation model (in contrast to the treatment model) one did not have to wait for long periods of time until the inmate's scholastic level or internal dynamics had improved sufficiently before he might be expected to behave better. Operant promised to deliver behaviour change very quickly; attitude change and educational achievement would come about later, fostered by the inmate's new behaviour.

In sum: the psychologist with operant could do things other than those that didn't seem to work; could do so without blowing up the established system; could be expected to bring great success with major problems, and do so economically, justly, efficiently, and quickly. The new professional supported the administrator's goals and elevated his status; emphasized control of behaviour and was admirably scientific and easy to understand, and, perhaps, just perhaps, he might rehabilitate a few offenders.

The behaviour modifiers who dubbed themselves "environmental engineers" prided themselves on their ability to modify people's behaviour — including administrators. After all that is what their techniques purported to do. They used all of their techniques, as well as most of the foregoing arguments to sell their method. It was bought very quickly; it was easy to sell and its acceptance probably reflects not at all on the special skills of the psychologists who sold it. Yet the wardens who "bought it" felt that they were the ones who sold their program to the psychologists! Surely a reflection of the genuine skills of the psychologists. Or was it?

> The coroner shall summon such persons to attend an inquest as he considers advisable. . . .R.S.O. 1970, ch. 87, s. 26(1)

Our survey of the use of behaviour modification in corrections both impressed and dismayed us. We learned of a considerable number of "operant conditioning" programs being conducted not just by psychologists but by a variety of practitioners from probation officers to prison wardens. Operant was being employed throughout the range of correctional settings — from community programs for pre-delinquents to maximum security hospital programs for the criminally insane. We learned of an operant program which was designed to increase the yield of milk in a prison dairy farm[2] and a complex token economy designed and administered by a prison inmate. We received an impressive quantity of information on correctional operant programs in the form of letters, pamphlets, brochures, manuals, journal articles, technical notes and the like. Much of the material was unpublished, and some was classified as "confidential". Many of the "operant" programs were operant in name only — they were a masquerade.

> When a youth it assigned to CHAPS, he is counseled in reference to the rules and regulations of the Arizona State Industrial School and the CHAPS Project. The student is played a tape that explains the CHAPS project and our Behavior Modification Program. . . Our Behavior Modification Program is a system that places more emphasis in rewarding adaptive behavior rather than punishing maladaptive behavior. It was, however, felt that for this program to succeed some forms of sanctions are needed. Cochise Hall Accelerated Services Project: CHAPS, cited in: Ross and McKay, 1974

Some CHAPS "sanctions": march 1-5 hours, Cochise meditation 1-15 days, transfer to Miles meditation.[Ross and McKay, 1974]

Beginning with the early 1960's and up until 1974 it became almost customary to affix the label "behaviour modification" to corrections programs, particularly incentive programs, which had been in existence for decades before the beginning of laboratory investigations of operant conditioning. Unfortunately, the label was also applied to many programs which were exclusively punitive. The label was used at times as an euphemism for tyranny.[Ross and McKay, 1974; Ross, 1975; Ross and Price, 1976] In one correctional jurisdiction the reduced diet which is used as a punishment for inmates already being punished by segregation was re-labelled "behaviour mod. meat loaf".

Bastardizing therapy techniques, we would argue, is characteristic of correctional treatment. The adverse effect in the case of behaviour modification was seen in 1974 when two significant events occurred.

1. The United States Bureau of Prisons halted all behaviour modification programs under way in their institutions; and

2. The L.E.A.A. withdrew funding for behaviour modification programs in corrections.[Bailey, 1975a]

Interestingly one year after the United States Bureau of Prisons halted those programs, the G.A.O. (the auditing agency for Congress) condemned behaviour modification programs in three prisons: Leavenworth, El Reno, and Marion.[Bailey, 1975b] The institutions' spokesman, in response, declared they were not using behaviour modification programs — what they were doing was the same but the label was dropped.

Our review of the published literature made it quite clear that as a rehabilitative tool the kind of behaviour modification programs used in correctional institutions (typically token economy, programmed learning, contingency management) was singularly unimpressive. There are twenty-four programs described in the literature which have been conducted in institutional settings which adequately qualify as behaviour modification programs.

As can be seen from Table 1 only a small number of these programs present any outcome data related to rehabilitation. Of those that do provide outcome data (see Table 2) the adequacy of the research is, in most cases, questionable.

Our review leads us to essential agreement with that of Braukman et al.[1975] which concluded:

In general, when program comparison between these behaviorally oriented programs and comparison programs have been possible, little or no differences in outcome have been reported.[p. 311]

In fact, there is evidence that with female adolescent offenders increased

TABLE 1

INSTITUTIONAL PROGRAMS

Senior Author	Subjects	Target Behaviours	Control Group	Follow-up
Staats (1965)	Case study	Reading problem	Case study	No
Tyler (1967)	Case study	School grades	Case study	No
Tyler and Brown (1968)	Juvenile males n = 15	Knowledge of current events	Yes	No
Meichenbaum (1968)	Juvenile females n = 10	Classroom behaviour	Yes	No
Bednar (1970)	Juvenile males n = 32	Academic achievement and behaviour	Yes	No
Clements (1968)	Adult males n = 16	School work	Yes	No
Jesness and DeRisi (1973)	Juvenile males n = 15	Classroom behaviour	Yes	No
Fineman (1968)	Juvenile males n = 20	Rule compliance	No	No
Rice (1970)	Juvenile males n = 20	Rule compliance	No	No
Burchard (1972)	Juvenile males n = 11	Aggressive behaviour	No	No
Pavlott (1971)	Juvenile females n = 60	Rule compliance	Yes	No
Krueger· (1971)	Juvenile males n = 18	Positive comments	Yes	No
Burchard (1965)	Juvenile males n = 12	School behaviours	Yes	No
Tyler (1967)	Juvenile males n = 15	Institutional behaviours	Yes	No
Burchard (1972)	Case study	Aggressive behaviour	Case study	No
Wetzel (1966)·	Case study	Stealing	Case study	Yes
Brown (1968)	Case study	Aggressive behaviour	Case study	No
Horton (1970)	Juvenile males n = 6	Aggressive behaviour in card-playing	No	No
Fodor (1972)	Juvenile females n = 8	A.W.O.L.	No	No
Cohen (1971)	Juvenile males n = 41	Academic and social behaviour	Yes	Yes
Jesness (1972)	Several hundred	Token economy various behaviours	Yes	Yes
McKee (1971)	Adult males n = 29	Cellblock token economy and staff training	Yes	Yes
Ross (1976)	Juvenile females n = 200	Various behaviours	Yes	Yes
Petrock (1971)	Adult males n = ?	Token economy various behaviours	No	No

TABLE 2

INSTITUTIONAL PROGRAMS WITH FOLLOW-UP

Senior Author	Subjects	Program	Control group	Major results
Cohen (1971)	Juvenile males n = 27	Programmed Learning Token economy	Questionable Control Group	Less recidivism at 1 and 2 year follow-up but = at 3 years
McKee (1975)	Adult males n = 29	Cellblock Token economy	3 control groups (n = 113) 1. Occupational training 2. Trade School 3. Regular institutional program Not matched Not randomly assigned	18 month follow-up 28% convicted of criminal offence vs 1. 47% 2. 32% 3. 37%
Jesness (1972)	Several hundred	Token economy contingency management	3 control groups: 1. Former inmates 2. Other institutions 3. T.A. Questionable adequacy	12 month follow-up Parole violations less than controls
Ross (1976)	Juvenile females n = 25	Token economy contingency management	Matched controls	12 month follow-up increased recidivism increased negative reports

recidivism has been fostered by ''behaviour modification''[Ross, 1968; McKay and Ross, 1973; Ross and McKay, 1974; Ross, 1974; Ross, 1975; Ross and McKay, 1976] Perhaps too much was promised. In spite of the limitations of the research both in quality and quantity, we can conclude with confidence that behaviour modification is not the panacea it was touted as when it was introduced to corrections.

Rehabilitation of the offender, however, is only one goal of corrections (perhaps an unrealistic one); institutional management is another. In this regard there is rather impressive evidence that behaviour modification is worthwhile. In each of the programs presented in Table 1 a behavioural approach was found to be successful in either reducing anti-social behaviour in the institution or in enhancing the offenders' academic achievement or industrial productivity. Again, unfortunately, the adequacy of the available research is often poor, but there is sufficient evidence to support the conclusion that behaviour modification can be effective in institutional management and in the academic and vocational training of the offender. We should note that there now are established standards to safeguard the right of offenders in behaviour modification programs.[A.P.A., 1974]

The efficacy of behaviour modification programs in community-based programs has been quite clearly demonstrated, particularly through the pioneering street-corner work of Schwitzgebel,[1964] the Achievement Place group home programs of Hoefler,[1975] family management programs of

TABLE 3

COMMUNITY-BASED PROGRAMS

Senior Author	Setting	Subjects	Target Behaviour	Control Group	Follow-up
Bailey (1970)	Group home	Pre-delinquents n = 5	Classroom behaviour	No	No
Miller (1971)	School	Pre-delinquents n = 40	English classwork	No	No
Phillips (1968)	Group home	Pre-delinquents n = 3	Aggressive statements	No	No
Phillips (1971)	Group home	Pre-delinquents n = 4	Punctuality	No	No
Schwitzgebel (1964)	Street-corner	17 years 8 previous arrests n = 2	Talking to a tape recorder	Yes	Yes
Schwitzgebel (1964)	Street-corner	17 years n = 20	Interview attendance	Yes	Yes
Tharp and Wetzel (1969)	Probation	Delinquents n = 89	Various	No	Yes
Ross (1970)	Probation	Delinquents n = ?	Various	No	No
Alvord (1971)	Family behaviour management	Delinquents n = 28	Child management	No	No
Stuart (1971)	Home	Pre-delinquent n = 1	Curfew, chores	No	No
Alexander (1973)	Home	Families n = 46	Family training management	Yes	Yes
Kirigin (1975)	Group home	Pre-delinquent n = ?	Homework	No	No
Jeffrey and Jeffrey (1970)	Slum project	16-21 years n – 50	Social and academic behaviours	No	Yes
Doctor (1973)	Probation	Adults n = 24	Attending meetings; positive behaviours	No	Yes
Braukman (1974)	Group home	Pre-delinquents n = 6	Job interview skills	No	No
Weathers and Liberman (1975)	Probation	Delinquents n = 6	Family management	Yes	Yes
Wener et al. (1975)	Group home	Pre-delinquents n = 6	Interaction with police	No	No

Alexander and Parsons,[1974] and the behavioural consulting work of Tharp and Wetzel[1969] in probation.

Table 3 presents an overview of the published programs in community-based behaviour modification in corrections. Table 4 presents those programs which do provide follow-up data within an adequate research framework. Clearly, there is evidence of success.

TABLE 4

COMMUNITY PROGRAMS WITH FOLLOW-UP

Senior Author	Subjects	Target Behaviours	Control Group	Major Results
Schwitzgebel (1964)	Males 17 years $\bar{X}$ = 8 arrests n = 20	Interview attendance and performance	Matched controls (street-corner B. Mod.)	(3 years follow-up) — fewer arrests — less "time"
Tharp and Wetzel (1969)	Males probationers n = 89	Various social and academic behaviours	Own control: A-B-A (behavioural consulting to parents, teachers)	(18 month follow-up) 1. decline in offences 2. increase in grades 3. improved behaviour ratings
Jeffrey and Jeffrey (1970)	Males delinquents n = 50	Appropriate social and academic behaviours	No controls (Slums of Washington)	Increased anti-social behaviour
Doctor and Palakow (1973)	Adults probationers n = 26	Meeting attendance: contingency management re: new positive behaviour	No control group "Baseline"	Employed time 45%→77% $\bar{X}$ prob. viol. 1.7→1.5 yr. $\bar{X}$ new arrests 2.0→0.15 yr.
Phillips (1971)	Males Pre-delinquents n = 16	Group home behaviour program	Achievement Place 2 control groups	(1 year follow-up) 19% committed to instit. vs 53%-54% controls
Kirigin *et al* (1975)	Males pre-delinquents n = 18	Group home behaviour program	Achievement Place Institution controls matched (matched by P. O. as "comparable")	(2 year follow-up) — 22% vs 47% controls committed to instit. — 56% vs 33% in school
Alexander and Parsons (1973)	Families court-referred n = 46	Behavioural family management	Controls: 1. Rogerian group 2. Psychodynamic group therapy 3. No intervention	(6.8 month follow-up) — less referral to juvenile court
Weathers and Liberman (1975)	Juvenile males probationers n = 6	Behavioural family management	Untreated control	(3 month follow-up) No effect on: curfew viol., school attendance; number of anti-social incidents or grades

However, not all programs either in institutions or community are successful in offender management or rehabilitation. When we examined the paramenters in these behaviour modification programs we found three factors which seem to differentiate the successful programs from the failures:

1. The successful programs were not *imposed* on the offenders in authoritarian fashion but *involved* the offenders in program planning.

2. In successful programs the target behaviours were not anti-social behaviour. They sought to strengthen prosocial behaviours rather than attempting directly to reduce the frequency of inappropriate or anti-social acts. They thus avoided the pitfall of strengthening anti-social behaviour by giving it undue attention and avoided generating expectancies for anti-social behaviour.[3]

3. They neutralized or mobilized the offender's peer group.

Clearly behaviour modification has considerable potential for corrections, but it is no panacea. If one looks only at recidivism data one gets a gloomy picture. It is only by a close examination that one can obtain an adequate understanding of the limitations and the value of behaviour modification. If we adopt the position that treatment should be buried because nothing works across the board we are indeed throwing the baby out with the bath-water.

On the other hand there are those who would blame not the treatment but the environment — the correctional institution — and would have us discard not only the baby and the bath-water but the entire plumbing system!

We should never have promised panaceas.

Footnotes

1. We are grateful to the Research Services Division of the Ontario Ministry of Correctional Services for the support and encouragement which they provided throughout our research programs. We are particularly appreciative of the helpful suggestions of A.C. Birkenmayer and R. E. Smith.

2. *Correctional Industries*, Department of Public Institutions, State of Nebraska.

3. For elaboration of these pitfalls, see Ross and Price.[1976]

References

ALEXANDER, J. F. and PARSONS, B. V. ''Short-term Behavioral Intervention with Delinquent Families: Impact on Family Process and Recidivism.'' *Journal of Abnormal Psychology*, 1973, *81*, 219-225.

ALVORD, J. R. ''The Home Token Economy: A Motivational System for the Home.'' *Corrective Psychiatry and Journal of Social Therapy*, 1971, *17*, 6-13.

A.P.A. MONITOR, ''Psychology briefs . . . START . . . unconstitutional'', 1974, *12*, 5 (November).

BAILEY, J. S., WOLF, M. A. and PHILLIPS, E. L. ''Home-Based Reinforcement and the Modification of Pre-delinquents' Classroom Behavior.'' *Journal of Applied Behavior Analysis*, 1970, 3, 223-233.

BAILEY, C. A. (Ed.) *Corrections Digest*, 1975(a), July, 6, 3.

BAILEY, C. A. (Ed.) *Corrections Digest*, 1975(b), August, 6, No. 17, 1.

BEDNAR, R. I., ZELHART, P. F., GREATHOUSE, L. and WEINBERG, S. ''Operant Conditioning Principles in the Treatment of Learning and Behavior Problems with Delinquent Boys.'' *Journal of Counseling Psychology*, 1970, *17*, 492-497.

BRAUKMAN, C. J., MALONEY, D. M., FIXSEN, D. L., PHILLIPS, E. L. and WOLF, M. M. ''Analysis of a Selection Interview Training Package for Pre-delinquents at Achievement Place.'' *Criminal Justice and Behavior*, 1974, *1*, 30-42.

BRAUKMAN, C. J., FIXSEN, D. L., PHILLIPS, E. L. and WOLF, M. M. ''Behavioral Approaches to Treatment in the Crime and Delinquency Field.'' *Criminology*, 1975, *13*, 299-331.

BROWN, G. D. and TYLER, V. O. ''Time Out From Reinforcement: A Technique for Dethroning the 'duke' of an Institutionalized Delinquent Group.'' *Journal of Child Psychology and Psychiatry*, 1968, 9, 203-211.

BURCHARD, J. D. and BARRERA, F. "An Analysis of Time Out and Response Cost in a Programmed Environment." *Journal of Applied Behavior Analysis*, 1972, *5*, 271-282.

BURCHARD, J. D. and TYLER, V. "The Modification of Delinquent Behavior Through Operant Conditioning." *Behavior Research and Therapy*, 1965, *2*, 245-250.

CLEMENTS, C. B. and McKEE, J. M. "Programmed Instruction for Institutionalized Offenders: Contingency Management and Performance Contracts." *Psychological Reports*, 1968, *22*, 957-964.

COHEN, H. L. and PHILIPCZAK, J. *A New Learning Environment*. San Francisco: Jossey-Bass, 1971.

CORONERS ACT. R.S.O. 1970.

DOCTOR, R. M. and POLAKOW, R. L. *A Behavior Modification Program for Adult Probationers*. Presented at American Psychological Association Convention, 1973.

ELLI, F. *The Riot*. New York: Avon, 1966.

FINEMAN, K. R. "An Operant Conditioning Program in a Juvenile Detention Facility." *Psychological Reports*, 1968, *22*, 119-1120.

FODOR, I. E. "The Use of Behavior Modification Techniques with Female Delinquents." *Child Welfare*, 1972, *51*, 93-101.

GRISWOLD, H. J., MISENHEIMER, M., POWERS, A., and TROMANHAUSER, E. *"An Eye for An Eye."* New York: Holt, Rinehart and Winston, 1970.

HOEFLER, S. A. "Achievement Place: An Evaluative Review." *Criminal Justice and Behavior*, 1975, *2*(2), 146-168.

HOFFER, E. *The True Believer*. New York: Harper and Row, 1951.

HORTON, L. E. "Generalization of Aggressive Behavior in Adolescent Delinquent Boys." *Journal of Applied Behavior Analysis*, 1970, *3*, 205-211.

JEFFREY, C. R. and JEFFREY, I. A. "Delinquents and Drop-Outs: An Experimental Program in Behaviour Change." *Canadian Journal of Corrections*, 1970, 12, 1-12.

JESNESS, C. F. and DeRISI, W. J. "Some Variations in Techniques of Contingency Management in a School for Delinquents." In J. STUMPHAUSER (Ed.), *Behavior Therapy With Delinquents*. Springfield, Ill.: Thomas, 1973.

JESNESS, C. F., DeRISI, W. J., McCORMICK, P. M. and WEDGE, R. F. *The Youth Center Research Project*. Sacramento: California Youth Authority, July 1972.

KIRIGIN, K. A., PHILLIPS, E. L., TIMBERS, G. A., FIXSEN, D. L. and WOLF, M. M. "Achievement Place." In ETZEL, B., LeBLANC, J. M. and BAER, D. M. (Eds.) *New Developments in Behavioral Research: Theory, Method, and Application*. Trenton, N. J.: Lawrence Erlbaum Associates, 1975.

KRUEGER, D. E. "Operant Group Therapy with Delinquent Boys Using Therapist's Versus Peer's Reinforcement." Doctoral dissertation, University of Miami, 1971.

LIPTON, D., MARTINSON, R. and WILKS, J. *The Effectiveness of Correctional Treatment Evaluation Studies*. New York: Praeger, 1975.

McKAY, H. B. and ROSS, R. R. *Token Gestures for Offenders*. Presented at Canadian Psychological Association Meeting, Victoria, B.C., 1973.

McKAY, H. B. "Desperate Diseases Require Desperate Remedies." *Crime and/et Justice*, *4*, 1, 1976.

McKEE, J-M. and CLEMENTS, C. B. "A Behavioral Approach to Learning: the Draper Model." In H. C. Rickard (ed.) *Behavioral Intervention in Human Problems*. New York: Pergamon Press, 1971.

MEICHENBAUM, D., BOWERS, K. and ROSS, R. R. "Modification of Classroom Behavior of Institutionalized Female Adolescent Offenders." *Journal of Behavior Therapy and Research*, 1968, *6*, 343-353.

MILLER, L. J. "Effects of Tokens and Tokens with Backup Reinforcers on the Academic Performance of Juvenile Delinquents." Unpublished doctoral dissertation, University of Kansas, 1971.

PALMER, T. "Martinson Revisited." *Journal of Research in Crime and Delinquency*, 1975, *12*(2), 133-152.

PAVLOTT, J. "Effects of Reinforcement Procedures on Negative Behaviors in Delinquent Girls." Unpublished doctoral dissertation, University of Pittsburgh, 1971.

PETROCK, F. and YEARGAN, C. "Readjustment Unit Project: A Behavior Modification/Therapeutic Community in a Maximum Security Correctional Setting." Unpublished manuscript, Youth Reception Centre, Yardsville, New Jersey, 1971.

PHILLIPS, E. L. "Achievement Place: Token Economy Reinforcement Procedures in a Home-style Rehabilitation Setting for 'Pre-Delinquent' Boys." *Journal of Applied Behavior Analysis*, 1968, *1*, 213-223.

PHILLIPS, E. L. "Achievement Place: Token Economy Reinforcement Procedures in a Home Style Rehabilitation Setting for Pre-Delinquent Boys." *Journal of Applied Behavior Analysis*, 1971, *4*, 45-49.

RICE, P. R. "Educo-Therapy: A New Approach to Delinquent Behavior." *Journal of Learning Disabilities*, 1970, *3*, 16-23.

ROSE, D. S., SUNDEL, M., DeLANGE, J., CORWIN, L. and PALUMBO, A. "The Hartwig Project: A Behavioral Approach to the Treatment of Juvenile Offenders." In R. ULRICH, R. STACHNIK and J. MABRY (Eds.), *Control of Human Behavior. 2*, New York: Scott, Foreman, 1970.

ROSS, R. R. *Problems in Applying the Operant Model to Treating Delinquency*. Paper presented at Clarke Institute of Psychiatry, University of Toronto. July 1968.

ROSS, R. R. and McKAY, H. B. *Token Gestures for Offenders*. Paper presented at Annual meeting of Canadian Psychological Association, Victoria, 1973.

ROSS, R. R. and McKAY, H. B. *Rewards for Offenders: Modifying the Correctional Environment*. Unpublished manuscript, University of Waterloo, 1974.

ROSS, R. R. *Treatment of Adolescent Offenders: Some New Findings*. Presentation at Conference on Research in Corrections, Parliament Buildings, Toronto, 1974.

ROSS, R. R. *The Effectiveness of Behavioral Treatment Programs for Female Delinquents in a Correctional Institution*. Paper presented at Symposium: "New trends in Criminology", Simon Fraser University, Vancouver, B.C., April 1975.

ROSS, R. R. and McKAY, H. B. *Behavior Modification and the Offender Therapist: Are They Compatible?* Paper presented at annual meeting of the Canadian Psychological Association, Quebec City, June 1975.

ROSS, R. R. and McCONKEY, N. "Behavior Modification With the Offender: An Annotated Bibliography." *Canadian Journal of Criminology and Corrections*, 1975 (Special Supplement).

ROSS, R. R. and PRICE, M. J. Behavior Modification in Corrections: Autopsy Before Mortification." *International Journal of Criminology and Penology*, 1976, *4*, 305-315.

ROSS, R. R. and McKAY, H. B. "A Study of Institutional Treatment Programs." *International Journal of Offender Therapy and Comparative Criminology*, 1976, *20*, 165-173.

ROSS, R. R. *Behavior Modification in the Control and Treatment of the Offender*. Presented at Criminology Colloquium, University of Ottawa, 1976.

SCHOFFIELD, W. *Psychotherapy: The Purchase of Friendship.* Englewood Cliffs, New Jersey: Prentice-Hall, 1964.

SCHWITZGEBEL, R. L. and KOLB, D. A. "Inducing Behavior Change in Adolescent Delinquents". *Behavior Research and Therapy,* 1964, *1*, 297-304.

SCHWITZGEBEL, R. L. *Street Corner Research: An Experimental Approach to the Juvenile Delinquent.* Cambridge: Harvard University Press, 1964:

STAATS, A. W. and BUTTERFIELD, W. H. "Treatment of Nonreading in a Culturally Deprived Delinquent: An Application of Reinforcement Principles." *Child Development,* 1965, *36,* 925-942.

STUART, R. B. "Behavioral Contracting within the Families of Delinquents." *Journal of Behavior Therapy and Experimental Psychiatry,* 1971, *2,* 1-11.

STUART, R. B. *Trick or Treatment: How and When Psychotherapy Fails.* Champaign, Illinois: Research Press, 1970.

THARP, R. G. and WETZEL, R. J. *Behavior Modification in the Natural Environment.* New York: Academic Press, 1969.

TYLER, V. O. "Application of Operant Token Reinforcement to Academic Performance of an Institutionalized Delinquent." *Psychological Reports,* 1967, 21, 249-260.

TYLER, V. O. and BROWN, G. D. "The Use of Swift, Brief Isolation as a Group Control Device for Institutionalized Delinquents." *Behavior Research and Therapy,* 1967, *5,* 1-9.

WEATHERS, L. and LIBERMAN, R. P. "Contingency Contracting with Families of Delinquent Adolescents." *Behavior Therapy,* 1975.

WERNER, J. S., MINKIN, N., MINKIN, B. L., FIXSEN, D. L., PHILLIPS, E. L. and WOLF, M. M. " 'Intervention Package': An Analysis to Prepare Juvenile Delinquents for Encounters with Police Officers." *Criminal Justice and Behavior,* 1975, *2*: 55-83.

WETZEL, R. "Use of Behavioral Techniques in a Case of Compulsive Stealing." *Journal of Consulting Psychology,* 1966, *30,* 367-374.

WILKS, J. and MARTINSON, R. "Is the Treatment of Criminal Offenders Really Necessary?" *Federal Probation,* 1976, March, 3-9.

32

THE CRIMINAL INVESTIGATION PROCESS
A Summary Report

JAN M. CHAIKEN, PETER W. GREENWOOD, and
JOAN PETERSILIA

Criminal investigation is one of the more important functions of municipal and county police departments. Yet many police administrators know little about the nature or effectiveness of their own department's investigative operations and even less about the situation in other departments.

At the request of the National Institute of Law Enforcement and Criminal Justice, the Rand Corporation undertook a nationwide study to fill some of these gaps in knowledge.[1] The objectives of the two-year study were—

1. This article summarizes the work of all the Rand researchers engaged in the study. In addition to the authors, they are: Robert Castro, Konrad Kellen, Eugene Poggio, Linda Prusoff, and Sorrel Wildhorn. The study was performed under Grant 73–NI–99–0037–G from the National Institute of Law Enforcement and Criminal Justice, Law Enforcement Assistance Administration, Department of Justice. The points of view or opinions stated here do not necessarily represent the official position or policies of the Department of Justice. The latest version of the complete study is Peter W. Greenwood et al., *The Criminal Investigation Process* (Lexington, Mass.: D. C. Heath, 1977).

From Jan M. Chaiken, Peter W. Greenwood, and Joan Petersilia, "The Criminal Investigation Process: A Summary Report," 3(2) *Policy Analysis* 187-217 (Spring 1977). Copyright 1977 by The Regents of the University of California.

- to describe, on a national scale, current investigative organization and practice;
- to assess the contribution of police investigation to the achievement of criminal justice goals;
- to ascertain the effectiveness of new technology and systems that are being adopted to enhance investigative performance;
- to determine how investigative effectiveness is related to differences in organizational form, staffing, procedures, and so forth.

While the objectives were broad, many questions of potential interest had to be excluded from consideration in order to have a study of manageable size. In particular, the study focused on Part I crimes,[2] thereby excluding analysis of how misdemeanors and vice, narcotics, and gambling offenses are investigated. Also, little attention was paid to personnel practices such as selection, promotion, and motivation of investigators.

DESIGN OF THE STUDY

Several principles guided our study design. First, the research had to be conducted with the participation and oversight of experienced police officials from around the country. Second, information had to be collected from many police departments: single-city studies had already been conducted, and their lack of persuasiveness stemmed from the possibility that the host department was unique in some way. Third, in as many departments as possible, information had to be obtained through direct on-site interviews and observations.

We secured the participation of the law enforcement community by appointing a suitable advisory board,[3] retaining a prosecutor and retired federal and local investigators as consultants,[4] and assembling a panel of currently working investigators. The advisory board reviewed and vigorously criticized our research approach, data-

2. Part I crimes are criminal homicide, forcible rape, robbery, aggravated assault, burglary, larceny, and auto theft. Except in the case of homicide, the FBI definitions of these crimes include attempts.

3. The advisory board consisted of Cornelius (Neil) J. Behan (New York City Police Department); James Fisk (member of the Los Angeles Police Commission); Thomas Hastings (Rochester, New York, Police Department); Jerry Wilson (former Chief of the Washington, D.C., Police Department); and Eugene Zoglio (professor, Prince George's Community College).

4. Consultants were Sydney Cooper, Carmine Motto, Albert Seedman, Seymour Silver, and Raymond Sinetar.

collection instruments, findings, and interpretations of the findings. The consultants assisted in designing data instruments and participated with Rand staff in on-site interviews in many locations. The panel of working investigators commented on the validity of our observations in other cities, by comparing them with their own daily experiences, and highlighted important issues that could not be captured by numerical data.

We collected data from a large number of departments by developing a comprehensive survey questionnaire and distributing it to all municipal or county law enforcement departments that had 150 or more full-time employees or that served a jurisdiction whose 1970 population exceeded 100,000. This survey produced extensive information from 153 jurisdictions (of the 300 solicited) on such topics as departmental characteristics, investigators' deployment, investigators' training and status, use of evidence technicians, nature of specialization, evaluation criteria, police-prosecutor interaction, case assignment, use of computer files, and crime, clearance, and arrest rates.[5] For example, the number of officers assigned to investigative units was found to average 17.3 percent of the police force. Thus, the investigative function in the United States costs about $1 billion per year—about the same as the cost of the entire court system.[6]

On-site interviews were conducted in more than 25 of the 153 police agencies. Many of these were selected because they were known to have implemented novel investigative practices that were reportedly successful; others were selected on the basis of their survey responses indicating interesting programs or data resources and a desire to participate. Project staff and consultants visited each of these departments, observing and participating in the operations of the investigative units and discussing their procedures with personnel at various departmental levels. In some cities, Rand staff monitored individual investigators and their supervisors continu-

5. The complete results of the Rand survey are reported in Jan M. Chaiken, *The Criminal Investigation Process: Volume II. Survey of Municipal and County Police Departments,* R–1777–DOJ (Santa Monica, Calif.: The Rand Corporation, October 1975).

6. See, for example, National Criminal Justice Information and Statistics Service, "Expenditure and Employment Data for the Criminal Justice System" (Washington, D.C.: U.S. Government Printing Office, updated annually).

ously over a period of several days to obtain realistic profiles of their activities.

Some departments gave us previously prepared written evaluations of their investigative programs. In addition, several departments cooperated closely with the Rand staff and provided access to data that were subsequently used in one of the component studies.

One useful data source, located and made available during the course of the survey, was the Kansas City (Missouri) Detective Case Assignment File, which had been maintained since 1971. This unique computer file contained daily information submitted by individual detectives, permitting us to determine, for each investigator and each investigative unit, the time spent on various activities, the number of cases handled, and the number of arrests and clearances produced. The file greatly facilitated our analyses of how detectives spend their time and to what purposes and effects.

Additional sources of information included a computer-readable file of 1972 Uniform Crime Reporting data provided by the FBI and a limited telephone survey of robbery and burglary victims.

FINDINGS

Arrest and Clearance Rates

Several earlier studies, each conducted in a single city or in a small number of neighboring cities, had shown that *department-wide clearance*[7] *and arrest statistics are not suitable measures of the effectiveness of investigative operations.* Our own study, using data from cities across the country, confirmed this observation in several different ways. The implication is that measures of effectiveness related to solving crimes must be defined carefully and can only be interpreted in conjunction with other information related to prosecution of arrestees, public satisfaction with the police, deterrence effects, and so forth.

In a study in New York City, published in 1970, Greenwood found that the average number of clearances claimed for each burglary arrest varied from 1 to 20 across the city's precincts, depending primarily on how frequently clearances were credited on

7. A crime is *cleared* when a perpetrator is apprehended or is identified as unapprehendable. The latter possibility is intended to apply in "exceptional" circumstances, such as when the perpetrator is dead.

the basis of *modus operandi* only.[8] Similarly, Greenberg's 1972 study in six California departments found wide variation in clearance rates because of differences among departments in the strictness with which FBI "exceptional clearance" guidelines were applied.[9] Our own study[10] using 1972 data from all departments with 150 or more employees, showed that the average number of clearances claimed for each arrest for a Part I crime ranged from a low of 0.38 to a high of 4.04, a factor of over 10. The ratio from high to low was even larger for each individual crime type, such as robbery or auto theft. Some departments claim a clearance for an auto theft whenever the vehicle is recovered, while others will not claim a clearance unless the perpetrator is arrested and charged for the instant offense. Clearance statistics are also affected by the amount of effort devoted to classifying reported crimes as "unfounded" when the police find no evidence that a crime was actually committed. This practice both reduces reported crime rates and increases reported clearance rates.

With administrative discretion playing such a large role in determining a department's clearance rates, any attempt to compare effectiveness among departments using clearance rates is evidently meaningless. Even comparisons over time within a single department are unreliable unless steps are taken to assure that no change occurs in administrative practices concerning clearances and classification of crimes. Arrest rates, too, are unreliable measures of effectiveness, since arrests can be made without resulting in any clearance.[11] The frequency of such events can be judged from the

8. Peter W. Greenwood, *An Analysis of the Apprehension Activities of the New York City Police Department*, R–529–NYC (New York: New York City-Rand Institute, September 1970). For the reader unfamiliar with this field, let us explain that more than one clearance can be claimed for a single arrest if the person arrested for a specific crime is then charged with, or admits to, crimes he committed elsewhere.

9. Bernard Greenberg et al., *Enhancement of the Investigative Function, Volume I: Analysis and Conclusions; Volume III: Investigative Procedures— Selected Task Evaluation; Volume IV: Burglary Investigative Checklist and Handbook* (Menlo Park, Calif.: Stanford Research Institute, 1972). (Volume II is not available.)

10. Chaiken, *Criminal Investigation Process: Volume II*, pp. 36, 37.

11. In some jurisdictions, persons may be arrested "for investigation" without a crime being charged. In all jurisdictions, persons are occasionally arrested by error and are subsequently released by a prosecutor or magistrate without any clearance being claimed by the police.

fact that, in half of all departments, the number of arrests for Part I crimes exceeds the number of clearances.[12]

Quite apart from their unreliability is the fact that arrest and clearance rates reflect activities of patrol officers and members of the public more than they reflect activities of investigators. Isaacs,[13] Conklin,[14] and our own study showed that approximately 30 percent of all clearances are the result of pickup arrests by patrol officers responding to the scene of the crime.[15] In roughly another 50 percent of cleared crimes (less for homicide and auto theft), the perpetrator is known when the crime report is first taken, and the main jobs for the investigator are to locate the perpetrator, take him or her into custody, and assemble the facts needed to present charges in court (see table 1). This means that around 20 percent of cleared crimes could possibly be attributed to investigative work, but our own study showed that most of these were also solved by patrol officers, or by members of the public who spontaneously provided further information, or by routine investigative practices that could also have been followed by clerical personnel.[16]

In fact, we estimate that no more than 2.7 percent of all Part I crime clearances can be attributed to special techniques used by investigators. (These are called "special action cases" in table 2.)

12. Instances in which several perpetrators are arrested for a single crime may also explain an arrest/clearance ratio of over 1.

13. Herbert H. Isaacs, "A Study of Communications, Crimes, and Arrests in a Metropolitan Police Department," Appendix B of Institute of Defense Analyses, *Task Force Report: Science and Technology*, A Report to the President's Commission on Law Enforcement and Administration of Justice (Washington, D.C.: U.S. Government Printing Office, 1967).

14. John Conklin, *Robbery and the Criminal Justice System* (Philadelphia, Pa.: J. B. Lippincott Co., 1972).

15. After initial publication of the Rand study, this finding was further confirmed by a Police Foundation study, "Managing Investigations: The Rochester System," by Peter B. Bloch and James Bell (Washington, D.C., 1976). While that study was intended primarily to compare team policing with nonteam policing, the report presents data that make it possible to calculate the ratio of on-scene arrests to all clearances by arrest for three crimes. The data show that, in Rochester, 31.7 percent of burglary clearances by arrest, 31.1 percent of robbery clearances by arrest, and 28.7 percent of larceny clearances by arrest were the result of on-scene arrests.

16. See Peter W. Greenwood, Jan M. Chaiken, Joan Petersilia, Linda Prusoff, Bob Castro, Konrad Kellen, Eugene Poggio, and Sorrel Wildhorn, *The Criminal Investigation Process: Volume III. Observations and Analysis*, R–1778–DOJ (Santa Monica, Calif.: The Rand Corporation, October 1975), chap. 6.

TABLE 1. CLEARED CASES HAVING INITIAL IDENTIFICATION OF PERPETRATOR
(AS A PERCENTAGE OF ALL CLEARED CASES)

Crime Type	Kansas City				Total Initial ID from Five Other Departments[c]
	Arrest at Scene	Complete ID by Victim or Witness	Uniquely Linking Evidence[a]	Total Initial ID[b]	
Forgery/fraud	30.6	20.0	39.7	90.3	90.9
Auto theft	38.5	12.7	<7.8	>51.2[a]	47.4
Theft	48.4	8.6	17.2	74.2	70.0
Commercial burglary	24.4	16.9	16.9	58.2	80.0
Residential burglary	26.7	42.7	<6.2	>81.7[a]	80.0
Robbery	28.4	20.9	10.6	59.9	53.4
Felony morals	25.8	27.8	27.8	81.4	72.8
Aggravated assault	28.6	63.4	7.9	>94.1[a]	100.0
Homicide	28.3	34.8	10.9	74.0	42.9

NOTE: Numbers may not add to total because of rounding errors.

[a] If no cases of uniquely linking evidence were found in the sample, or if there were no cases other than those with initial identification, 95 percent confidence points are shown.

[b] I.e., the sum of the three preceding columns.

[c] Berkeley, Long Beach, and Los Angeles, California; Miami, Florida; and Washington, D.C.

TABLE 2. SPECIAL ACTION CASES (PERCENTAGE OF ALL CLEARED CASES)

Crime Type	Kansas City		Five Other Departments[a]	
	Sample Estimate	Maximum Estimate at 95% Confidence	Sample Estimate	Maximum Estimate at 95% Confidence
Forgery/fraud	0	5.7	0	12.7
Auto theft	0	6.9	0	14.6
Theft	0	3.2	0	25.9
Commercial burglary	4.9	12.4	10	39.4
Residential burglary	0	3.5	0	13.9
Robbery	7.1	16.6	9.5	15.6
Felony morals	0	14.5	9.1	36.4
Aggravated assault	0	5.9	0	25.9
Homicide	10.2	37.3	0	34.8
All types[b]	1.3	2.7		

[a] Berkeley, Long Beach and Los Angeles, California; Miami, Florida; and Washington, D.C.

[b] This figure is shown for Kansas City only and reflects the relative numbers of cleared cases of each type in that city. The maximum estimate for the total is lower than the estimate for any single crime type, because the sample size is larger.

The remaining 97.3 percent of cleared crimes will be cleared no matter what the investigators do, so long as the obvious routine follow-up steps are taken. Of course, included in the 2.7 percent are the most interesting and publicly visible crimes reported to the department, especially homicides and commercial burglaries. But the thrust of our analysis is that all the time spent by investigators on difficult cases where the perpetrator is unknown results in only 2.7 percent of the clearances.

This finding has now been established for enough departments to leave little doubt of its general correctness, with some variation, for all departments. By establishing a restricted interpretation of what constitutes "routine processing," a department might find that investigative skill or "special action" contributes to as many as 10 percent of all its clearances. Even so, the basic conclusion remains the same. Only in cases of homicide, robbery, and commercial theft did we find that the quality of investigative effort could affect the clearance rate to any substantial extent. Conversely, the contribution of victims, witnesses, and patrol officers is most important to the identification and apprehension of criminal offenders.

Variations with Departmental Characteristics

Once the nature of investigators' contributions to arrest and clearance rates is understood, it must be anticipated that variations in these rates among departments will be explained primarily by characteristics that have nothing to do with the organization and deployment of investigators. This is in fact what we found from our survey data.[17] The three most important determinants of a department's arrest and clearance rates are the department's size, the region of the country it is located in, and its crime workload.

Large departments (measured by number of employees, budget, or population of the jurisdiction) claim more clearances per arrest in all crime categories than do smaller departments. However, the arrest rates of large and small departments do not differ.

Departments in the South Central states claim higher clearance rates than those in other regions, which follow in the order of North Central, South Atlantic, Northeast, and West. However, arrest rates vary in almost exactly the reverse order. Evidently, these differences

17. See Chaiken, *Criminal Investigation Process: Volume II*, pp. 38–47.

reflect administrative practices or patterns of crime commission rather than differences in effectiveness.

In regard to crime workload, we found that departments having a large number of reported crimes per police officer have lower arrest rates than other departments. This relationship works in the following way: The annual number of arrests per police officer rises nearly (but not quite) in direct proportion to the number of reported crimes per police officer until a certain threshold is reached. Beyond this threshold, increasing workload is associated with very small increases in the number of arrests per police officer. The thresholds are at approximately 35 Part I crimes per police officer per year and 3.5 crimes against persons per police officer per year. These thresholds are fairly high, as only about 20 percent of departments have greater workload levels.[18]

These findings are consistent with the assumption that a city can increase its number of arrests or decrease the number of crimes (or both) by increasing the size of its police force, but the effect of added resources would be greatest for cities above the threshold.

In regard to clearance rates, the data showed that departments with high crime workloads tend to claim more clearances per arrest than cities with low crime workloads. As a result, clearance rates are less sensitive to workload than arrest rates are. Although clearance rates for every crime type were found to decrease with increasing workload, the decreases were not significant for some types of crimes.

These workload relationships apply to all police officers, not just investigators. Although investigators are known to make more arrests per year than patrol officers, and our data confirmed this, the effect is small: we could not find a significant variation in arrest or clearance rates according to the fraction of the force in investigative units. In other words, if the total number of officers in a department is kept fixed, switching some officers into or out of investigative units is not likely to have a substantial effect on arrest or clearance rates.

18. The 1972 data revealed a linear relationship between arrests per officer and crime workload, up to the threshold, but the intercept of the straight line fit was at a positive value of arrests per officer. After 1972, crime rates in the United States generally increased. Since we did not perform any longitudinal analyses, we do not know whether the thresholds also increased or remained at the same levels.

Aside from the effects of size, region of country, and workload on clearance and arrest rates, we did find a few smaller effects of possible interest. Departments that assign a major investigative role to patrolmen have lower clearance rates, but not lower arrest rates, than other departments. This appears to reflect the fact that patrolmen cannot carry files around with them and therefore do not clear old crimes with new arrests. Departments with specialized units (concentrating on a single crime, such as robbery) were found to have lower arrest rates, but not lower clearance rates, for the types of crimes in which they specialize, as compared with departments having generalist investigators. Departments in which investigators work in pairs had lower numbers of arrests per officer than those in which they work singly. Since we did not collect data permitting a comparison of the quality of arrests produced by solo and paired investigators, this finding must be interpreted with caution. Still, the practice of pairing investigators, which is common only in the Northeast, is brought into sufficient question to warrant further research.

Most other characteristics of investigators were found to be unrelated to arrest and clearance rates. These include the nature and extent of the investigators' training, their civil service rank or rate of pay, and the nature of their interactions with prosecutors. However, the lack of correlation probably indicates more about the inadequacies of arrest and clearance rates as measures of effectiveness than about the inherent value of training and other characteristics.

How the Investigator's Time Is Spent

From an analysis of the Kansas City (Missouri) computer-readable case assignment file, and from observations during site visits, we determined that, although a large proportion of reported crimes are assigned to an investigator, many of these receive no more attention than the reading of the initial crime incident report. That is, many cases are suspended at once. The data show that homicide, rape, and suicide invariably result in investigative activity, and that at least 60 percent of all other serious types of cases receive significant attention (at least half an hour of a detective's time). Overall, however, less than half of all reported crimes receive any serious consideration by an investigator, and the great majority of cases that are actively investigated receive less than one day's attention. Table 3 shows,

TABLE 3. PERCENTAGE OF REPORTED CASES THAT DETECTIVES WORKED ON

Type of Incident	Percentage
Homicide	100.0
Rape	100.0
Suicide	100.0
Forgery/counterfeit	90.4
Kidnapping	73.3
Arson	70.4
Auto theft	65.5
Aggravated assault	64.4
Robbery	62.6
Fraud/embezzlement	59.6
Felony sex crimes	59.0
Common assault	41.8
Nonresidential burglary	36.3
Dead body	35.7
Residential burglary	30.0
Larceny	18.4
Vandalism	6.8
Lost property	0.9
All above types together	32.4

SOURCE: Kansas City Case Assignment File; cases reported from May through November 1973.

for several crime types, the percentage of cases that detectives worked on during the study period (1 May 1973 to 30 April 1974).

The net result is that the average detective does not actually work on a large number of cases each month, even though he may have a backlog of hundreds or thousands of cases that were assigned to him at some time in the past and are still theoretically his responsibility. Table 4 shows the number of worked-on cases per detective per month in the various units of the Kansas City Police Department.[19] Except in the case of the Missing Persons Unit, the number of worked-on cases per detective is generally under one per day. If we imagine that each case is assigned to a particular investigator as his responsibility, the table shows the average number of cases that an investigator would be responsible for and work on in a month.

19. "Worked-on" means that at least half an hour was spent on the case. The types of cases assigned to each unit are described in Greenwood et al., *Criminal Investigation Process: Volume III*, pp. 53–55. For example, the homicide unit handles not only homicides but also suicides and unattended deaths from natural causes.

TABLE 4. AVERAGE NUMBER OF WORKED–ON CASES
PER DETECTIVE PER MONTH

Unit	No. of Cases
Crimes against persons	9.2
Homicide	11.2
Robbery	7.7
Sex Crimes	6.2
Crimes against property	16.9
Auto theft	19.5
Nonresidential burglary	9.4
Residential burglary/larceny	22.9
General assignment	18.6
Incendiary	7.8
Forgery/fraud/bunco	10.4
Shoplifting/pickpocket	20.9
Youth and women's	26.0
Missing persons	88.4

SOURCE: Kansas City Case Assignment File.

Our data revealed that most of an investigator's casework time is consumed in reviewing reports, documenting files, and attempting to locate and interview victims. For cases that are solved (that is, where a suspect is identified), an investigator spends more time in postclearance processing than in identifying the perpetrator.

For Kansas City, we found the following breakdown of investigators' time. About 45 percent is spent on activities not attributable to individual cases—doing administrative assignments, making speeches, traveling, reading teletypes, making general surveillances (of junkyards, pawnshops, gathering spots for juveniles, and the like), and occupying slack time (for example, in a unit that is on duty at night to respond to robberies and homicides). The remaining 55 percent of the time is spent on casework. Of this, 40 percent (or 22 percent of the total) is spent investigating crimes that are never solved; just over 12 percent (7 percent of the total) is spent investigating crimes that are eventually solved; and nearly 48 percent (26 percent of the total) is spent on cleared cases after they have been solved.[20] These figures, of course, apply only to Kansas City. But after reviewing them (and more detailed tabulations) with investiga-

20. Activities after the case is cleared can include processing the arrestees, vouchering property, meeting with prosecutors, appearing in court, contacting victims, and completing paperwork.

tors from other cities, and after comparing them with our observational notes, we concluded that they are approximately correct for other cities, with variations primarily in the areas of slack time (if investigators are not on duty at night) and time spent in conference with prosecutors.

Thus, investigators spend about 93 percent of their time on activities that do not lead directly to solving previously reported crimes. How are they to be judged on the quality of these activities? The time they spend on cases after they have been cleared serves the important purpose of preparing cases for court: this activity will be discussed below. The time they spend on noncasework activities serves a general support function for casework and therefore may be useful in ways that are difficult to quantify. The time they spend on crimes that are never solved can only be judged in terms of its public relations value and possible deterrent value, because most of these crimes can be easily recognized at the start. (They are primarily the ones where no positive identification of the perpetrator is available at the scene of the crime.) Police administrators must ask themselves whether the efforts devoted to investigating crimes that are initially unsolved are justified by either the small number of solutions they produce or the associated public relations benefits.

Collecting and Processing Physical Evidence

A police agency's ability to collect and process physical evidence at the scene of a crime is thought to be an important component of the criminal investigation process. In our study, however, we analyzed only one aspect of the collection and processing of physical evidence—their role in contributing to the *solution* of crimes, as distinguished from their value in proving guilt once the crime is solved.

Earlier studies have shown that evidence technicians are asked to process the crime scene in only a small number of felony offenses.[21] And, even when the crime scene is processed, a significant portion of the available evidence may not be retrieved.[22] Police administrators,

21. See Brian Parker and Joseph Peterson, "Physical Evidence Utilization in the Administration of Criminal Justice" (Berkeley, Calif.: School of Criminology, University of California, 1972).

22. President's Commission on Crime in the District of Columbia, *Report of the President's Commission on Crime in the District of Columbia* (Washington, D.C.: U.S. Government Printing Office, 1966).

aware of these deficiencies, have begun to experiment with a variety of organizational changes designed to increase the number of crime sites processed for physical evidence.

Our analysis of the collection and processing of physical evidence in six police departments that employ different procedures[23] confirmed that a department can achieve a relatively high rate of recovery of latent prints from crime scenes by investing sufficiently in evidence technicians and by routinely dispatching these technicians to the scene of felonies. The latent print recovery rate is also increased by processing the crime scene immediately after the incident has been reported, rather than at a later time. Some of our data supporting these conclusions are shown (for burglary cases) in the first three lines of table 5.

TABLE 5. PRODUCTIVITY OF CRIME SCENE PROCESSING FOR FINGERPRINTS, RESIDENTIAL BURGLARY SAMPLE[a]

Item	Long Beach	Berkeley	Richmond
Percentage of cases where technicians were requested	58.0	76.6	87.6
Cases where prints were recovered, as percentage of cases where a technician was requested	50.8	42.0	69.1
Cases where prints were recovered, as percentage of total cases	29.4	32.2	60.5
Cases where perpetrator was identified as a result of lifted prints, as percentage of total cases	1.5	1.1	1.2

[a] The sample comprises 200 randomly selected residential burglary cases (cleared and uncleared) from each of three departments.

The last line of table 5, however, shows that the rate at which fingerprints are used to identify the perpetrator of a burglary is essentially unrelated to the print recovery rate. From 1 to 2 percent of the burglary cases in each of three departments were cleared by identification from a latent print, despite substantial differences in operating procedures. In Richmond, evidence technicians are dispatched to nearly 90 percent of the reported burglaries and recover prints from 70 percent of the scenes they process, but the fraction

23. The six departments are those in Berkeley, Long Beach, Los Angeles, and Richmond, California; in Miami, Florida; and in Washington, D.C. For further details, see Greenwood et al., *Criminal Investigation Process: Volume III*, chap. 7.

of burglaries solved by fingerprints is about the same as in Long Beach or Berkeley, where evidence technicians are dispatched to the scene less frequently and lift prints less often.

Why does lifting more prints not result in a higher rate of identification? The most plausible explanation seems to be that police departments are severely limited in their capability for searching fingerprint files. If a suspect is known, there is little difficulty in comparing his prints with latent prints that have been collected. Thus, latent prints may help to confirm a suspect's identification obtained in other ways. But in the absence of an effective means of performing "cold searches" for matching prints (where the suspect is unknown), the availability of a latent print cannot help solve the crime.

From a comparison of the fingerprint identification sections in Washington, Los Angeles, Miami, and Richmond, we determined that, for all these departments, from 4 to 9 percent of all retrieved prints are eventually matched with those of a known suspect. However, the number of "cold-search" matches produced per man-year differed substantially among departments, according to the size of their inked print files and the attention devoted to this activity. In some departments, technicians performing cold searches produced far more case solutions per man-year than investigators.

We infer that an improved fingerprint *identification* capability will be more productive of identifications than a more intensive print *collection* effort. Although some techniques and equipment currently available to police departments were found to enhance identification capability, the technology needed to match single latent prints to inked prints is not fully developed and appears to us to be of high priority for research.

Preparing the Case for Prosecution

Police investigation, whether or not it can be regarded as contributing significantly to the *identification* of perpetrators, is a necessary police function because it is the principal means by which all relevant evidence is gathered and presented to the court so that a criminal prosecution can be made. Thus, police investigators can be viewed as serving a support function for prosecutors.

Prosecutors frequently contend that a high rate of case dismissals, excessive plea bargaining, and overly lenient sentences are common consequences of inadequate police investigation. The police, in response, often claim that even when they conduct thorough investigations, case dispositions are not significantly affected. We undertook a study to illuminate the issues surrounding this controversy about responsibility for prosecutorial failure.

On the basis of discussions with prosecutors, detectives, and police supervisors, we developed a data form containing 39 questions that a prosecutor might want the police to address in conducting a robbery investigation. When we used this form to analyze the completeness of robbery investigations in two California prosecutors' offices, chosen to reflect contrasting prosecutorial practices in felony case screening but similar workload and case characteristics,[24] we found that the department confronted by a stringent prosecutorial filing policy ("Jurisdiction A") was significantly more thorough in reporting follow-on investigative work than the department whose cases were more permissively filed ("Jurisdiction B"). Yet, even the former department fell short of supplying the prosecutor with all the information he desired: each of 39 evidentiary questions that prosecutors consider necessary for effective case presentation was, on the average, covered in 45 percent of the cases in Jurisdiction A. Twenty-six percent were addressed by the department in Jurisdiction B. (Table 6 lists the 39 questions. The summary entries indicate the percentage of cases where a question could be answered from information in the documents provided by the police to the prosecutor.)

We then determined whether the degree of thorough documentation of the police investigation was related to the disposition of cases, specifically to the rate of dismissals, the heaviness of plea bargaining, and the type of sentence imposed. Our analysis showed differences between the two jurisdictions. For example, none of the sampled cases was dismissed in Jurisdiction A; furthermore, 60 percent of the defendants pled guilty to the charges as filed. By comparison, in Jurisdiction B about one-quarter of the sampled cases were dismissed after filing, and only one-third of the defendants pled guilty to the charges as filed.

24. Peter W. Greenwood et al., *Prosecution of Adult Felony Defendants in Los Angeles County: A Policy Perspective*, R–1127–DOJ (Santa Monica, Calif.: The Rand Corporation, March 1973) led us to expect significant differences in police investigative effort and prosecutorial posture between the two selected jurisdictions.

A comparison of the two offices' heaviness of plea bargaining is shown in table 7. Although plea bargaining appears to be lighter in Jurisdiction A, this may simply reflect that the gravity of criminal conduct was less in the A than the B cases; that is, special allegations were considerably more frequent to begin with in B. One cannot conclude that only the quality of documentation of the police investigation accounted for the difference.

A similar conclusion applies to the type of sentence imposed: while there were differences in sentencing, the variations in other case characteristics indicate that these differences might not necessarily be related to thoroughness of documentation. This analysis

TABLE 6. PRESENCE OF INFORMATION IN POLICE REPORTS (IN PERCENTAGES)

Case Information Desirable for Prosecution	Jurisdiction A[a] Information from at Least One Source[b]		Jurisdiction B[a] Information from at Least One Source[b]	
1. What INTERVIEWS were conducted?	100.0		100.0	
Offense				
2. Is there a verbatim report of the instant OFFENSE?	90.4		95.2	
3. Is there a verbatim report of the FORCE USED?	95.2		36.5	
4. What was the PHYSICAL HARM to the victim?	47.6	57.5%	18.5	36.2%
5. Is there a detailed description of the PROPERTY taken?	90.4		27.2	
6. What was the method of S(uspect)'s ESCAPE?	71.4		45.4	
7. What type of VEHICLE was used by S?	38.0		45.4	
8. What type of WEAPON was used by S?	85.7		63.6	
9. If a gun was used, was it LOADED?	19.0		13.5	
10. If a gun was used, when was it ACQUIRED?	28.4		.0	
11. Where is the LOCATION of the weapon now?	9.5		18.1	
Suspect				
12. Was S UNDER THE INFLUENCE of alcohol or drugs?	42.8		22.7	
13. What are the details of S's DEFENSE?	18.9		.0	
14. What is S's ECONOMIC STATUS?	14.2	39.3%	4.5	14.0
15. Was S advised of CONSTITUTIONAL RIGHTS?	100.0		63.6	
16 If multiple suspects, what is their RELATIONSHIP?	42.7		.0	
17. Is there evidence of PRIOR OFFENSES by S?	66.6		9.0	
18. Is there evidence of S's MOTIVES?	47.6		18.1	
19. Is there evidence of past PSYCHIATRIC TREATMENT of S?	9.5		4.5	
20. What is S's PAROLE OR PROBATION status?	37.8		18.1	
21. Does S have an alcohol or drug ABUSE HISTORY?	23.8		9.0	
22. Where is S EMPLOYED?	28.5		4.5	

TABLE 6.—*Continued*

Case Information Desirable for Prosecution	*Jurisdiction A*[a] Information from at Least One Source[b]		*Jurisdiction B*[a] Information from at Least One Source[b]	
Victim/Witnesses				
23. What is the RELATIONSHIP between S and V(ictim)?	4.7		9.0	
24. What is the CREDIBILITY of the W(itnesses)?	9.5		.0	
25. Can the W make a CONTRIBUTION to the case prosecution?	23.8	31.1%	13.5	3.4%
26. Were MUG SHOTS shown to V or W?	51.7		4.5	
27. If shown, are the PROCEDURES and RESULTS adequately described?	30.0		.0	
28. Was a LINE-UP conducted?	53.0		.0	
29. If conducted, are the PROCEDURES and RESULTS adequately described?	40.0		.0	
30. Was an effort made to LIFT FINGERPRINTS at the scene?	41.0		4.5	
31. If made, were USABLE FINGERPRINTS OBTAINED?	59.0		9.0	
32. Were PHOTOS TAKEN at the crime scene?	35.0		4.5	
33. Is the EXACT LOCATION from where the photos and prints were taken given?	29.0		.0	
34. Did V VERIFY his statements in the crime report?	24.0		.0	
35. Did V have IMPROPER MOTIVES in reporting the offense?	4.7		.0	
Arrest				
36. What was the legal BASIS FOR SEARCH AND SEIZURE?	23.8		36.3	
37. How was the LOCATION OF EVIDENCE learned?	33.3		32.0	
38. How was the LOCATION OF S learned?	66.6	52.3%	68.1	52.2%
39. How was the ARREST OF S made?	85.7		72.7	
Overall	45.0%		26.4%	

NOTE: The percentages within the matrix refer only to the presence of information the police chose to record; they may not represent a complete picture of the information gathered by the police in the course of the investigation. It is possible that certain police officers record only "positive" information and assume that an omission of information automatically implies that the information is either not applicable or inappropriate in a specific case.

[a] Twenty-one robbery cases in each sample.

[b] Percentage of cases that presented this information from at least one source.

leads us to suggest that the failure of police to document a case investigation thoroughly *may* contribute to a higher case dismissal rate and a weakening of the prosecutor's plea bargaining position.

TABLE 7. A COMPARISON BETWEEN A AND B OF DISPOSITIONS
BY PLEAS OF GUILTY

Disposition	Percentage in Jurisdiction A	Percentage in Jurisdiction B
Plea of guilty to original charges	61.1	31.8
Plea of guilty to original charges but with special allegations stricken or not considered	27.7	22.7
Plea of guilty to 2d degree robbery reduced from 1st degree robbery	5.5	18.1
Plea of guilty to other lesser offense	5.5	4.5
Cases dismissed	—	22.7

NOTE: Because of rounding, columns do not add to 100 percent.

Relations between Victims and Police

Many investigators, as well as top-ranking police officials, have defended the investigative function, not because it contributes significantly to the identification of perpetrators, but because it is one of the principal contacts the police maintain with the victims of serious crimes. But, despite these verbal espousals of the public service function as an important part of the investigative role, our observations in departments across the country indicate that most police merely respond initially to the crime scene and file a cursory report; rarely do they subsequently contact the victims about the progress of the case. This is understandable, given the rising number of reported crimes and relatively constant police budgets.

While it seems reasonable to suggest that local police departments might win more public confidence by notifying the victim when the perpetrator has been identified, such a policy of routine feedback could be self-defeating. For example, if the police were to inform a victim that the perpetrator of his crime had been apprehended and was not being charged with his offense but being prosecuted on another, the victim, rather than feeling more confident in the police or the criminal justice system, might in fact become disillusioned. And a resentful victim could become highly vocal about his dissatisfactions and cause other citizens to be negative about police performance.

How much information to give the victim and when to give it were the questions behind a telephone survey we made of robbery and burglary victims. This study must be regarded as exploratory; the survey was conducted simply as an initial attempt to explore victims' feelings about receiving information feedback and about which types of information are most important.

The inquiry summarized by table 8 was accompanied by two pairs

TABLE 8. KIND OF INFORMATION WANTED BY VICTIMS

Survey Question: As a Victim, Did You Want the Police to Inform You?	Yes	No	Indiff-erent	If Your Answer Was "Yes," How Important Was It to You to Be Informed?	
				Very	Somewhat
If your case was solved?	32 (89%)	1 (3%)	3 (8%)	26	6
If a suspect was arrested?	30 (83%)	5 (14%)	1 (3%)	22	8
If a defendant was tried?	27 (75%)	4 (11%)	5 (14%)	15	12
If a defendant was sentenced?	27 (75%)	4 (11%)	5 (14%)	16	11
What sentence was imposed?	27 (75%)	4 (11%)	5 (14%)	16	11
If the defendant was re-leased from custody?	18 (50%)	11 (31%)	7 (19%)	11	7

of questions, with the first question of each pair addressing the victim's desire to have feedback on a specific matter and the second eliciting his probable reaction if the feedback occurred. Table 9

TABLE 9. RESPONDENT'S DESIRE TO BE TOLD OF POLICE DECISION TO SUSPEND INVESTIGATION OF HIS CASE

Victim's Response	Burglary	Robbery	Total
Yes	16	10	26 (72%)
No	3	4	7 (19%)
Indifferent or no answer	1	2	3 (8%)
Total	20	16	36 (100%)

displays the responses on whether or not the victim wanted to be told of a police decision to suspend or drop investigative effort on his case if such a decision were made: these responses suggest a consistent preference for knowledge about this police decision, but with an observable tendency to the contrary in cleared robbery cases (which involve a relatively small segment of the underlying population). Table 10 exhibits the victims' responses to the question of what their reactions would be if they were told that no further investigation was intended on their cases. We note that approximately one-third of our sample would react negatively to unfavorable feedback (and the proportion would be higher if the data were weighted to reflect the relative numbers of each crime type).

TABLE 10. VICTIM'S PREDICTED REACTION TO INFORMATION THAT POLICE
WILL SUSPEND INVESTIGATION OF HIS CASE

Victim's Prediction of His Own Reaction	Burglary	Robbery	Total
Appreciative of being told and agreeable to police decision	3	1	4 (12%)
Understanding and resigned	11	7	18 (53%)
Disturbed and resistant	4	1	5 (15%)
Angry and resentful	2	5	7 (21%)
			34ª (100%)

ª Two victims were omitted: the response of one was not applicable, and the other declined to answer.

To the extent that our survey results may reach beyond the confines of our small sample, they broadly support the belief that there is a strong market for information feedback to victims from the police. But they also tend to confirm the view that some victims, if given unfavorable information, will develop undesirable attitudes toward the police. Finally, our results suggest that other repercussions from information feedback, of which the police are sometimes apprehensive, are of slight significance. Few victims, no matter how distressed by information coming from the police, indicated that they would act inimically to police interests.

Proactive Investigation Methods

In a departure from the typically reactive mode (so called, because the investigator does not focus on the case until after a crime has occurred) of most investigators assigned to Part I crimes, some police departments have shifted a small number of their investigators to more proactive investigation tactics. Proactive units usually deal with a particular type of offender, such as known burglars, robbery teams, or active fences. A number of such units have been supported on an experimental basis with funds from the Law Enforcement Assistance Administration.[25]

The proactive team members often work quite closely with other investigators, but, unlike regular investigators, they are not assigned a caseload of reported crimes. Instead, they are expected to generate other sources of information to identify serious offenders. These

25. For a description of five antirobbery units of this type, see Richard H. Ward et al., *Police Robbery Control Manual* (Washington, D.C.: National Institute of Law Enforcement and Criminal Justice, 1975).

other sources may include informants they have cultivated, their own surveillance activities, or undercover fencing operations operated by the police themselves.

The primary objective in establishing these units is to reduce the incidence of the target crime. The reduction is supposed to result from the containment achieved by successfully arresting and prosecuting offenders and from the deterrent effect on others of the publicity given the proactive programs. Therefore, the arrest rates of these units are typically used as a measure of their primary effect; and changes in the rate of incidence of the target crime are also cited. The chief problem in using these two measures is the difficulty of isolating the unique effects of the proactive unit from other activities of the police department and from external factors affecting crime or arrest rates.

In the course of our study, we looked at several such units by either examining evaluation reports or making direct observations. In general, they all seemed to produce a much higher number of arrests for the officers assigned than did other types of patrol or investigative activities. Consistent effects on targeted crime rates could not be identified.

In order to determine which activities of these units actually resulted in arrests, we examined in considerable detail a sample of cases from two units, the Miami Stop Robbery unit and the Long Beach (California) Suppression of Burglary unit.

From the sample of robbery cases in Miami, we determined that, although the Stop officers averaged 4 arrests per man-month, half of which were for robbery, in 10 out of 11 of these arrests the Stop officer was simply executing a warrant obtained by some other unit or accompanying another officer to make the arrest. In Long Beach, the Suppression of Burglary officers averaged 2.4 arrests per man-month, half of which were for burglary or for receiving stolen property. An analysis of 27 of the arrests disclosed that just half (13) resulted from the unit's own work; the remaining arrests were by referral or were the result of routine investigation that could have been handled by any other unit.

Our general conclusion was that proactive techniques can be productive in making arrests, particularly for burglary and fencing. To be effective, however, the units must be staffed with highly motivated and innovative personnel. And the officers' efforts must be carefully monitored to preclude their diversion to making arrests for other units and to ensure that their tactics do not become so aggressive as to infringe on individual liberties.

We have identified several distinguishable functions performed by investigators: preparing cases for prosecution after the suspects are in custody; apprehending known suspects; performing certain routine tasks that may lead to identifying unknown suspects; engaging in intensive investigations when there are no suspects or when it is not clear that a crime has been committed; and conducting proactive investigations. In addition, investigators engage in various administrative tasks and paperwork related to these functions.

We have enough information about the effectiveness of each function to begin asking whether the function should be performed at all and, if so, who should do it. The notion that all these functions must be performed by a single individual, or by officers having similar ranks or capabilities, does not stand up to scrutiny; in fact, many police departments have begun to assign distinguishable functions to separate units. Our own suggestions, to be presented below, support this development and extend it in certain ways. If a function now assigned to investigators can be performed as well or better, but at lower cost, by patrol officers, clerical personnel, or information systems, it should be removed from the investigators; if it serves the objectives of the prosecutor, then it should be responsive to the needs of the prosecutor; and, if especially competent investigators are required, the function should be assigned to a unit composed of such officers.

In this section we describe the implications of our findings for changes in the organization of the investigative function, the processing of physical evidence, and the role of the public.[26]

26. For an expanded discussion of the policy implications, see Peter W. Greenwood and Joan Petersilia, *The Criminal Investigation Process: Volume I. Summary and Policy Implications*, R–1776–DOJ (Santa Monica, Calif.: The Rand Corporation, October 1975).

Preparing Cases for Prosecution

Postarrest investigative activity—not only important for prosecution but also one of the major activities now performed by investigators—can perhaps be done in a less costly or more effective manner.

Our observations indicate that the current coordination, or lack thereof, between the police and prosecutorial agencies does not support a healthy working relationship. It allows for a situation in which each can blame the other for outcomes in court that it views as unfavorable.

Most prosecutors do not have investigators on their staff. If they do, these investigators are usually occupied with "white-collar" offenses rather than street crimes. Generally, then, the prosecutor relies on police investigators to provide the evidence needed to prosecute and convict arrestees. But inherent in this situation is a conflict between prosecutor and police. An arrest is justified by *probable cause*—that is, by an articulable, reasonable belief that a crime was committed and that the arrestee was the offender. Often, the police are satisfied to document the justification for the arrest rather than expend further investigative effort to strengthen the evidence in the case. The prosecutor, on the other hand, may be reluctant to file the charges preferred by the police, or to file at all, if he believes the evidence would not suffice for a conviction, that is, as *proof beyond a reasonable doubt.* Many cases appear to be affected by the conflicting incentives of police and prosecutor, as reflected in failures to file and in lenient filing, early dismissals, or imbalanced bargaining.

One way of ameliorating this problem is to make explicit the types of information that the prosecutor and police agree are appropriate to collect and document, given the nature of the crime. The form we designed for robbery cases (summarized in table 6) gives an example of how such information can be made explicit. Each jurisdiction should develop appropriate forms for major categories of crimes. Such written documents would assist the police in becoming more knowledgeable about the type and amount of information that a prosecutor requires to establish guilt for each type of offense and in allocating their investigative efforts to provide this information.[27]

27. Alternatives that might accomplish some similar aims include having the prosecutor provide the investigators with periodic evaluations of their case preparation efforts; training new investigators in case preparation; or having on-call attorneys assist in the preparation of serious cases.

We observed that the prosecutor's strictness with respect to filing decisions can affect the thoroughness of case preparation. In turn, the thoroughness of documentation may affect the percentage of cases subsequently dismissed and the degree of plea bargaining. We suggest, therefore, that prosecutors be mindful of the level of investigative documentation in their jurisdictions, especially in offices where the officer presenting the case may not have participated in the investigation.

One rationale advanced in some police departments for minimizing the factual content of formal investigative reports is that these reports are subject to discovery by defense counsel and thereby facilitate the impeachment of prosecution witnesses, including policemen. Such departments believe that the results of detailed investigations are better communicated orally to the prosecutor's office. The results of our research, while not conclusive, tend to refute this argument. In the jurisdiction ("A") where detailed documentation is prepared, no such negative consequences were noted; but in the jurisdiction ("B") having less information in the documentation, oral communication failed in some instances to reach all the prosecutors involved in the case.

Above and beyond merely improving coordination between police and prosecutors, it is worthy of experimentation to assign the prosecutor responsibility for certain investigative efforts. We feel that a promising approach would be to place nearly all postarrest investigations under the authority of the prosecutor, either by assigning police officers to his office or by making investigators an integral part of his staff, depending on the local situation. A test of this arrangement would show whether it is an effective way of assuring that the evidentiary needs for a successful prosecution are met.

Apprehending Known Suspects

We have noted that, in a substantial fraction of the cases ultimately cleared, the perpetrator is known from information available at the scene of the crime. If he or she is already in custody, the case becomes a matter for postarrest processing, as discussed above. If the perpetrator is not in custody, it is important for the responding officer(s), whether from investigative or patrol units, to obtain and make a record of the evidence identifying the suspect. This requires that the responding officers be permitted adequate time to conduct an initial investigation, including the interviewing of possible witnesses, and that the crime-reporting form be designed in such a way that the presence of information identifying a suspect is unmistakably recorded.

Apprehending a known suspect may or may not be difficult. Assigning all such apprehension to investigators does not appear to be cost-effective, especially if the investigators are headquartered at some distance from the suspect's location and a patrol officer is nearby. We believe that certain patrol officers, whom we shall call generalist-investigators, could be trained to handle this function in such a way that the arrests are legally proper and a minimum number of innocent persons are brought in for questioning. Only when apprehension proves difficult should investigative units become involved.

Routine Investigative Actions

For crimes without initial identification of a suspect, we found that many of those eventually cleared are solved by routine investigative actions—for example, listing a stolen automobile in the "hot car" file, asking the victim to view a previously assembled collection of mug shots for the crime in question, checking pawnshop slips, awaiting phone calls from the public, and tracing ownership of a weapon.

One implication of this finding is that any steps a police department can take to convert investigative tasks into routine actions will increase the number of crimes solved. Technological improvements, especially in information systems, produced many of the clearances we identified as "routine." In the absence of good information systems, such clearances might never have occurred or might have been difficult to achieve. The ability of patrol officers to check rapidly whether a vehicle is stolen or, more important, whether the owner is wanted for questioning produced numerous case solutions in our samples. Well-organized and maintained mug-shot, *modus operandi,* or pawn-slip files also led to clearances.

A second implication is that it may not be necessary for *investigators,* who are usually paid more than patrol officers or clerks, to perform the functions that lead to routine clearances. We believe that an experiment should be conducted to determine the cost and effectiveness of having lower-paid personnel perform these tasks.

Once clerical processing is complete, some action by a police officer may still be needed; for example, the suspect may still have to be apprehended. Such action should be assigned to generalist-investigators.

Investigating Crimes without Suspects

Two basic objectives are served by taking more than routine investigative action when the suspect is unknown. One objective is to solve the crime; the other is to demonstrate that the police care about the crime and the victim. The latter objective can be carried out by generalist-investigators who are responsible to a local commander concerned with all aspects of police-community relations. This type of investigative duty does not require specialized skills or centralized coordination. The officers performing it could readily shift between patrol and investigative duties. In departments with team policing, such investigations could be a task rotated among team members.

If the objective is actually to solve the crime, police departments must realize that the results will rarely be commensurate with the effort involved. An explicit decision must be made that the nature of the crime itself or public concern about the crime warrants a full follow-up investigation. A significant reduction in investigative efforts would be appropriate for all but the most serious offenses. If, in a less serious offense, a thorough preliminary investigation fails to establish a suspect's identity, then the victim should be notified that active investigation is being suspended until new leads appear (as a result, for example, of an arrest in another matter).

Serious crimes (homicide, rape, assault with great bodily injury, robbery, or first-degree burglary) warrant special investigative efforts. These efforts can best be provided by a Major Offenses Unit, manned by investigators who are well trained and experienced in examining crime scenes, interpreting physical evidence, and interrogating hostile suspects and fearful witnesses, and who are aided by modern information systems. One reason for establishing such a unit is to identify the investigative positions that require special skills and training and that demand knowledge of citywide crime patterns and developments. Our observations suggest, by way of contrast, that current staffing patterns rarely allow most investigators to see these highly serious cases. Therefore, when such cases arise, the investigators are frequently ill equipped to cope with them and unduly distracted by the burden of paperwork on their routine cases.

A Major Offenses Unit would concentrate its efforts on a few *unsolved* serious felonies. The team would consist of a relatively small number of experienced investigators closely supervised by a team commander. From our observations, it appears that the most serious impediment to high-quality investigative work is the traditional method of case assignment and supervision. In nearly every department, a case is normally assigned to an individual investigator as his sole responsibility, whether he is a generalist, specialist, or engaged in team policing. Supervisors do not normally review the decisions he makes on how to pursue the investigation, and his decisions are largely unrecorded in the case file. Consequently, the relative priority an investigator gives to the tasks on a given case assigned to him depends largely on the number and nature of his other case assignments and on his personal predilections and biases. Caseload conflicts and personal predilections frequently lead an investigator to postpone unduly or perform improperly the critical tasks of a particular case assignment.

Assigning cases to investigative teams rather than to individuals could eliminate this problem. For effective operations, the team should include approximately six men and be led by a senior investigator knowledgeable about the local crime situation, criminal law, and police mangement. The leader's primary responsibility would be to keep informed of progress on the cases assigned to his team and to make the broad tactical decisions on the team's expenditure of effort. Each day the subordinate investigators would perform individually assigned tasks. A clerk delegated to the team would prepare progress reports to document the daily accomplishment on open cases and to assist the leader in making the allocation for the following day. These reports would also help the leader identify which of his men were most effective at which tasks. Such an approach should assure that significant steps in an investigation are objectively directed by an experienced senior investigator.

Proactive Investigations

Our research into proactive units—let us call them "strike forces" —leads us to conclude that they can be relatively productive. In instances where such units were successful, they were manned by motivated and innovative personnel. The gain in employing them becomes illusory when mere quantity of arrests is emphasized, for then their efforts tend to be diverted into making arrests that are not the result of unique capabilities. We feel that departments should employ strike forces selectively and judiciously. The operation of strike forces necessitates careful procedural and legal planning to protect the officers involved and to ensure that the defendants they identify can be successfully prosecuted. These units also require close monitoring by senior officers to ensure that they do not become overly aggressive and infringe on individual privacy.

In all likelihood, the relative advantage of strike force operations in a particular department will not persist over a long period of time. The department must accustom itself to creating and then terminating strike forces, as circumstances dictate.

Processing Physical Evidence

Most police departments collect far more evidence (primarily fingerprints) than they can productively process. Our work shows that cold searches of inked fingerprint files could be far more effective than routine follow-up investigations in increasing the apprehension rate.

Fingerprint-processing capabilities should be strengthened as follows. First, the reference print files should be organized by geographic area, with a fingerprint specialist assigned to each area; no area should have more than 5,000 sets of inked prints. Second, to assure a large number of "request searches," which imply a cooperative effort between investigator and fingerprint specialist, some communication links should be devised to help motivate and facilitate the reciprocal exchange of information between these two parties. Third, the fingerprint specialists should be highly trained, highly motivated, and not overloaded with other tasks that might detract from their primary function.

Several existing systems for storing and retrieving inked prints with specified characteristics (of the latent print or the offender) appear useful and were widely praised by departments that have them. However, further research might contribute a major technological improvement in the capability of police departments to match latent prints with inked prints.

Role of the Public

Our research persuaded us that actions by members of the public can strongly influence the outcome of cases. Sometimes private citizens hold the perpetrator at the scene of the crime. Sometimes they recognize the suspect or stolen property at a later time and call the investigator. Sometimes the victim or his relatives conduct a full-scale investigation on their own and eventually present the investigator with a solution. Collectively, these types of citizen involvement account for a sizable fraction of cleared cases.

Police departments should initiate programs designed to enhance the victim's desire to cooperate fully with the police. Such programs might both increase apprehension rates and improve the quality of prosecutions. Specifically, when major crimes are solved, police departments should announce the particular contribution of members of the public (respecting, of course, any person's desire for anonymity). A realistic picture of how crimes are solved will help eliminate the public's distorted image of detectives and will impress on them the importance of cooperating with police.

Reallocation of Investigative Resources

Ultimately, our suggestions imply a substantial shift of police resources from investigative to other units. However, such reallocations cannot be justified on the basis of current knowledge alone; they must await testing and evaluation of each of our recommendations. If we prove correct, most initial investigations would be assigned to patrol units under the direction of local commanders. To improve the quality of initial investigations, the patrol force would have to be augmented with a large number of generalist-investigators. These officers would also perform certain follow-up work, such as apprehending known suspects and improving communications with victims and witnesses of crimes. The resources needed to field generalist-investigators would be obtained by reducing the number of investigators.

Additional major reallocations of resources away from "traditional" reactive investigative units are implied by our suggestions to have clerical personnel and generalist-investigators perform routine processing of cases, to increase the use of information systems, to enhance capabilities for processing physical evidence, to increase the number of proactive investigative units, and to assign investigative personnel to the prosecutor for postarrest preparation of cases. If all these changes were made, the only remaining investigative units concerned with Part I crimes would be the Major Offenses Units. The number of investigators assigned to such units would ordinarily be well under half the current number of investigators in most departments.

In no way does our study suggest that total police resources be reduced. On the contrary, our analysis of FBI data suggests that such a reduction might lower arrest and clearance rates. Reallocating resources might lead to somewhat increased arrest and clearance rates, but our suggestions are intended primarily for the more successful prosecution of arrestees and for improved public relations.

We know that most of the changes we advocate are practical, because we observed them in operation in one or more departments. For example, a number of departments have recently introduced "case screening," whereby each crime report is examined to determine whether or not a follow-up investigation should be conducted. Our findings indicate that the decision rule for case screening can be quite simple. If a suspect is known, the case should be pursued; if no suspect is known after a thorough preliminary investigation, the case should be assigned for routine clerical processing unless it is serious enough to be assigned to the appropriate Major Offenses Unit. The definition of "serious" must be determined individually by each department, since it is essentially a political decision.

Another current innovation is "team policing," in which investigators are assigned to work with patrol officers who cover a specified geographical area. While there are many organizational variations of team policing,[28] most forms would permit the introduction of generalist-investigators having the functions we describe, and some already include such personnel.

We know of no jurisdiction in which the prosecutor currently administers postarrest investigations, although investigators have been assigned to several prosecutors' offices (for example, in Boston, New Orleans, and San Diego) to facilitate interactions with the police. Only a careful experiment will determine the feasibility and effectiveness of making the prosecutor responsible for postarrest investigations.

The National Institute of Law Enforcement and Criminal Justice has funded the introduction of revised investigative procedures in five jurisdictions. The experimental changes, which are based partly on the findings of our study, will be carefully evaluated to determine whether, to what extent, and under what circumstances they actually lead to improved effectiveness.

28. See, for example, Peter B. Bloch and David Specht, *Neighborhood Team Policing* (Washington, D.C.: National Institute of Law Enforcement and Criminal Justice, December 1973).

Part VII:

CRIME AND CRIMINALS IN
THE UNITED STATES IN THE 1970s:
STATISTICAL APPENDIX

JOSEPH G. WEIS

JAMES HENNEY

This appendix provides a brief overview of crime and criminals in the United States during the 1970s. Data have been selected which follow crime from the point of becoming known to the police, to arrest, prosecution, incarceration, and parole. Victimization data include findings on the fear of becoming a victim, rates of victimization by offense from 1973 to 1977, and the characteristics of personal and household victimizations. A final section includes data on two current issues in criminology—the female offender and deterrence.

Some information was acquired from original sources. We should like to acknowledge the assistance of Michael J. Hindelang and Ann L. Pastore, the Director and Information Specialist of the *Sourcebook of Criminal Justice Statistics,* for providing data on victimization which will appear in the 1978 version of the *Sourcebook.* Other data on victimization and death sentences were provided by Marilyn Marbrook, Statistics Division of the National Criminal Justice Information and Statistics Service, Law Enforcement Assistance Administration.

CRIMINAL ACTIVITY IN THE UNITED STATES
DURING THE 1970s

Known Offenses, Arrests, and Prosecutions

The data presented in Table 1 represent a compilation of Federal Bureau of Investigation statistics on criminal activity in the United States during the 1970s. The data are restricted to the seven major "index" crimes—murder, forcible rape, robbery, aggravated assault, burglary, larceny-theft, and motor vehicle theft. The figures on arrests and prosecutions are further broken down into adult and juvenile categories. The rates of arrest of prosecution for a particular age grouping have been computed on the basis of the size of that age-specific population in the United States, not on the total population.

Several interesting trends emerge from the table. First, it is apparent that the level of criminal activity has not diminished over the past eight years. The rate of arrest for index crimes has increased by almost 27%. The major portion of this increase occurred between 1973 and 1974 when the index offense rate rose by about 17%. However, it should be noted that starting in 1976 the rate of offenses showed some very small declines.

Arrests for both adults and juveniles have reached increasingly higher levels throughout the decade. Adult arrest rates have risen by 21% and juvenile rates have increased by 22%. While the size of the arrested population continues to grow, the disproportionate concentration of juveniles in this population has not changed. By 1977 the arrest rate for juveniles was 65% greater than that for adults. This represents only a two percentage point increase in the juvenile/adult ratio from 1970. As was the case with offenses known to the police, the sharpest rise in adult and juvenile arrests occurred between 1973 and 1974.

Turning to the prosecution data, we once again see that activity has increased during the 1970s. Probably the most noteworthy finding is the difference over time between the rates of prosecution for adults and the rates of referral to juvenile court. From 1970 to 1977 adult prosecutions rose about 9%. Meanwhile, juvenile court referrals increased by 36%. Thus, while adult prosecution rates have not kept up with increases in adult arests, the increases in juvenile prosecutions have outdistanced the increases in juvenile arrests. In short, the probability of arrest followed by prosecution is greater for a juvenile in 1977 than it was in 1970, but this is not true for adults. Finally, as was true for offenses known to the police and arrests, the sharpest rise in prosecutions occurred between 1973 and 1974 and by 1976 small reductions in the rates were evident.

Criminals Under Correctional Supervision

Between 1971 and 1977 there has been a 40.7% increase in the number of adult felons incarcerated in state and federal institutions in the United States. From the low of 196,092 in 1972, there has been a steady increase in the number of persons locked-up in prison, to an estimated high of 278,600 in 1977. During this same time period, the incarceration rate, as measured by prisoners on hand in these institutions at year end, has increased from a low in 1972 of 94.7 to a high in 1977 of 129.0. This means that we are keeping more and more people in prison at any given point in time as we move through the decade.[1]

These changes are attributable to increases in the number of both men and women imprisoned, although the percentage increases have been larger for women than men. The percentage increase between 1971 and 1977 among women prisoners is 76.1%, while among men it is 39.5%. During this time period, the sex ratio of male to female prisoners has decreased from approxi-

Table 1: Trends in adult and juvenile index crimes for the 1970s[a]

Year	Index Crimes Known to the Police Rate[d]	Arrests Adults N[c]	Arrests Adults Rate[e]	Arrests Juveniles N[c]	Arrests Juveniles Rate[f]	Prosecutions[b] Adults N[c]	Prosecutions[b] Adults Rate[e]	Prosecutions[b] Juveniles N[c]	Prosecutions[b] Juveniles Rate[f]
1970	3,984.5	687,126	692	586,657	1132	270,621	597	181,922	787
1971	4,164.7	764,756	742	632,548	1206	250,575	591	156,864	724
1972	3,961.4	786,664	734	630,451	1184	209,385	590	119,554	684
1973	4,154.4	758,396	725	613,824	1219	235,751	627	165,869	901
1974	4,850.4	810,138	886	664,289	1558	203,228	713	141,226	1050
1975	5,281.7	1,082,250	877	819,561	1471	187,036	708	136,556	1145
1976	5,266.4	1,045,206	855	741,900	1388	160,378	669	105,148	1008
1977	5,055.1	1,113,381	840	818,994	1386	169,488	649	116,809	1069

a. Index Crimes include murder, forcible rape, robbery, aggravated assault, burglary, larceny, theft, and motor vehicle theft. Adults are 18 or older, juveniles are 10 to 17 years old.

b. A referral to juvenile court is considered a prosecution.

c. Changes in absolute frequencies from year to year may reflect changes in the proportion of the population included in FBI census areas and may not precisely reflect true changes in criminal activity.

d. Rate per 100,000 population of the resident population of the United States, adjusted by year.

e. Rate per 100,000 adult population.

f. Rate per 100,000 juvenile population.

Source: U.S. Department of Justice, Federal Bureau of Investigation, Uniform Crime Reports, 1970:114,126, 1971:110,122, 1972:133,126, 1973:116,128, 1974:174-186, 1975:174,188, 1976:181,217

Table 2: Sentenced prisoners by sex, and rate of incarceration, in state and federal institutions[a]

Year	Male	Female	Total	Incarceration Rate Per 100,000 Population
		Sex		
1971	191,732	6,329	198,061	96.4
% Change 71-72	(−1.0)	(−1.0)	(−0.9)	
1972	189,823	6,269	196,092	94.7
% Change 72-73	(+4.0)	(+6.6)	(+4.2)	
1973	197,527	6,684	204,211	97.8
% Change 73-74	(+6.7)	(+9.5)	(+6.9)	
1974	210,881	7,324	218,205	103.6
% Change 74-75	(+10.9)	(+20.8)	(+11.1)	
1975	233,900	8,850	242,750	113.0
% Change 75-76	(+8.3)	(+12.8)	(+8.5)	
1976	253,308	9,983	263,291	123.0
% Change 76-77	(+5.6)	(+11.6)	(+5.8)	
1977	267,456[c]	11,144[c]	278,600[b]	129.0[d]
% Change 71-77	(+39.5)	(+76.1)	(+40.7)	

a. Derived from "Prisoners in State and Federal Institutions," Numbers 1, 2, 3, and 4, National Prisoner Statistics Bulletin, Law Enforcement Assistance Administration, tables "Sentenced Prisoners in State and Federal Institutions, by Region and State," "Prisoners in State and Federal Institutions by Sex," and "Rate of Incarceration in State and Federal Institutions, by Region and Jurisdiction"; and from Sourcebook; and 1977 estimate from "Trends in Adult Parole Population and Adult Prison Population, State and Federal" (p. 37) in "Parole in the United States: 1976 and 1977," Uniform Parole Reports, National Council on Crime and Delinquency. This series of data began in 1971.

b. Estimate from Uniform Parole Reports cited above.

c. Estimate computed as .96 male, .04 female.

d. Estimated rate per 100,000 resident population in United States.

mately 30:1 in 1971 to approximately 23:1 in 1977. More women are being incarcerated and a higher proportion of prisoners are women.

The number of prisoners released to parole has also increased every year, although as a proportion of the number imprisoned there has been little change. Approximately 30% of sentenced prisoners in state and federal institutions are released to parole each year. Parole remains the favored method of release,

Table 3: Conditional and unconditional releases of sentenced prisoners in state and federal institutions by sex and year[a]

Year	Total	Conditional Release[b]			Total			Uncondi-tional Release[c]
		Parole Male	Female	Total	Total Male	Female		
1970	56,979[f]	54,130[e]	2,849[e]	66,254[g]	62,941[e]	3,313[e]		22,526[h]
1971	61,859[f]	58,766[e]	3,093[e]	71,929[g]	68,333[e]	3,596[e]		24,455[h]
1972	67,982[d]	64,582[e]	3,400[e]	79,049	75,375	3,674		28,465
1973	67,305[d]	63,939[e]	3,366[e]	78,262	74,507	3,755		26,782
1974	65,962	62,594	3,368	77,038	73,238	3,800		25,109
1975	78,724	74,862	3,862	89,808	85,469	4,339		30,694
1976	77,181	73,028	4,153	89,253	84,529	4,724		29,938
1977	87,384[i]	83,015[e]	4,369[e]	101,609[g]	96,529[e]	5,080[e]		34,547[h]

a. Derived from "Prisoners in State and Federal Institutions," Numbers 1, 2, 3, and 4, National Prisoner Statistics Bulletin, Law Enforcement Assistance Administration, tables "Selected Departures of Sentenced Prisoners in Federal and State Institutions," "Movement of Sentenced Prisoners in State and Federal Institutions by Region and State," and "Number and Type of Conditional and Unconditional Releases for Sentenced Prisoners in State and Federal Institutions by Region and State" and from the Sourcebook, 1977, table "Adult Felons Released and Paroled from State Prisons and Reformatories, U.S. 1965-1974."

b. Includes parole, probation, suspended release, and other.

c. Includes expiration of sentence, commutation, and other.

d. Estimate computed as .86 of total conditional releases.

e. Estimate computed as .95 male, .05 female.

f. Estimate computed as adults paroled from state institutions divided by .93, the proportion of state to total paroles.

g. Estimate computed as estimated paroles divided by .86, the proportion of parole to total conditional releases.

h. Estimate computed as .34 of total releases.

i. Estimate based on reported increase of 13.5% over 1976 of releases to parole (pp. 12-13) and estimates reported in "Estimated Adult Prison Releases and Parole Entries, State and Federal, 1965-1976" (pp. 54-55), in "Parole in the United States: 1976 and 1977," Uniform Parole Reports, National Council on Crime and Delinquency.

with other conditional releases (e.g., probation, supervised release) and unconditional releases (e.g., expiration of sentence, commutation) being used less often.[2]

Contrary to the rising incarceration rate among adult offenders, the institutionalization of juveniles has become a less-favored correctional alternative in the 1970s, due primarily to probation subsidy programs, deinstitutionalization of status offenders, community treatment programs, youth service bureaus, and changes in juvenile justice policy (e.g., the Juvenile Justice and Delinquency Prevention Act of 1974) which support noninstitutional alternatives to incarceration. Between 1971 and 1975 there was a decrease of 14.2% in the number of boys and girls in public detention and correctional facilities. Again, the changes among females are most dramatic—there is a 30.1% decrease in the number of girls institutionalized, compared to a 9.3% decrease for boys. This trend of decarceration of juvenile offenders may continue through the 1970s, particularly because of the renewed commitment to deinstitutionalization in the 1977 Amendments to the Juvenile Justice and Delinquency Prevention Act and the efforts of the federal government to extend decarceration to less serious juvenile delinquents. But this outcome is far from certain.

Table 4: Juveniles in public detention and correctional facilities by sex and year[a]

Year	Male	Female	Total
1971	41,781	12,948	54,729
% Change 71-73	(−16.1)	(−17.8)	(−16.6)
1973	35,057	10,637	45,694
% Change 73-74	(−0.8)	(−4.7)	(−1.7)
1974	34,783	10,139	44,922
% Change 74-75	(+9.0)	(−10.7)	(+4.6)
1975	37,926	9,054	46,980
% Change 71-75	(−9.3)	(−31.0)	(−14.2)

a. Derived from "Children in Custody: Juvenile Detention and Correctional Facility Census," 1971, 72-73, 74, and 75, Law Enforcement Assistance Administration, tables "Juveniles in Public Juvenile Detention and Correctional Facilities, by Sex, for Regions and States," "Selected Characteristics of Public Juvenile Detention and Correctional Facilities," and "Number of Juveniles in Public Detention and Correctional Facilities for Juveniles by Sex for the United States, Regions, and States." There are no 1972 data available in this census series, and data from years subsequent to the 1975 census are not yet published.

VICTIMIZATION

The use of victimization surveys—asking people whether and how they have been victimized—has increased the potential to measure accurately the nature of crime and criminals. It has also allowed researchers to better understand the public's attitudes toward and fears of being the victim of a crime.

The Fear of Crime

It is clear that the fear of becoming the victim of a crime is pervasive, although there are, as one might expect, some differences in the fear of victimization by type of offense and characteristics of the victim. When asked how much they "worried about" becoming a victim of a variety of crimes (burglary, robbery, rape, heroin sales, corporate crime, governmental crime), a majority of a nationwide sample of adults stratified by sex and race were afraid of becoming a crime victim. More than one-half (52%) worry ("a lot" or "a little") about the possibility of being victimized by government officials, but more than three-fourths (79%) worry about the sale of heroin in their neighborhood and more than two-thirds (71%) worry about the prospect of their home being burglarized. Apparently, people are more concerned about victimization by individuals than by corporate bodies such as business corporations or governmental bureaucracies—the possibility of direct confrontation with the offender instills more fear than being the indirect victim of a white collar criminal.

Except for the offense of rape, where 56% of the males but 73% of the females worry about victimization (of self or someone in the family), there are virtually no sex differences in the likelihood of being afraid of victimization. However, there are important race differences—in general, a higher proportion of blacks than whites worry about being victimized, as well as higher proportions who worry "a lot" about becoming a victim. Otherwise put, blacks are more likely to worry and their fears are more salient. For example, 76.5% of blacks and 64.7% of whites are afraid of becoming a victim, while 49.3% of blacks but only 29.8% of whites worry "a lot" about this prospect.

Trends in Victimization

Reports of actual *personal* and *household* victimization allow an assessment of the relationship between the subjective experience of victimization anxiety and real probabilities of victimization. Table 6 shows the number and rates of both personal and household victimizations between 1973 and 1977. (The data began in 1973, when the National Crime Survey was initiated by the Law Enforcement Assistance Administration and the U.S. Bureau of the Census.) There are big differences in the rates of victimization by category of offenses and by particular crimes. Among *personal* victimizations in 1977 the rate for crimes of theft (97.3) is almost three times as large as that for crimes of violence (33.9). The highest victimization rate for violent crimes is for assault and the lowest is for rape. Simple larceny with no contact between the victim and offender constitutes the bulk of thefts from persons and has, by far, the highest rate (94.6) among personal victimizations. Household larceny has the highest rate (123.3) for *household* victimizations, followed by burglary and motor vehicle theft.

The rank order of victimization rates among all of the crimes has remained the same over the past five years, and the rate for each offense has remained relatively stable, although there have been small but statistically significant increases and decreases in rates for some offenses. Over the entire five-year period, all of the major crimes except rape and robbery increased significantly, while motor vehicle theft declined by more than 10% and the rate of household burglary showed a steady decrease. 1974 was a high mark for a number of offenses, with gradual declines thereafter (e.g., robbery, aggravated assault, burglary). In short, the probability of becoming a victim of a crime is highest for simple larceny and household larceny, with the likelihood of victimization probably not changing very much given the relative stability of victimization rates over the past five years.

Personal Victimization

Of course, not everyone has an equal chance of becoming a victim—different categories of people have different probabilities of becoming the victim of different offenses. Tables 7 and 8 present data on the extent of personal victimization in 1976 by sex, race, economic status, and age.

Table 5: Fear of victimization, by type of victimization, race, and sex, United States, 1977

Question: "How much do you worry about being the victim of each of the crimes I am going to read you? Do you worry a lot, a little, or not at all about (READ LIST)?"

| | Total | | | | Race | | | | Sex | | | |
| | | | | | Black | | White | | Male | | Female | |
	A lot	A little	Not at all	No opinion	A lot	A little	A lot	A little	A lot	A little	A lot	A little
A person forcing his way into your home and stealing some of your possessions	27	44	27	1	52	32	23	47	24	44	30	45
A person pointing a gun at you on the street and robbing you	25	33	41	2	46	31	21	33	25	32	25	34
A man raping (you or) someone in your family	37	33	28	2	58	22	34	35	32	24	41	32

A person selling heroin to youngsters in your neighbor-hood	54	25	19	2	66	17	52	26	53	26	55	24
Being cheated by corporations	30	35	32	3	46	29	28	36	32	33	28	37
A government official illegally tapping telephones or opening mail	22	30	45	2	28	32	21	31	23	30	22	31

NOTE: These data were derived from a nationwide random telephone survey of 1,447 adults conducted in July 1977. ''Not at all'' and ''No opinion'' were not presented by race and sex. Percents may not add to 100 because of rounding.

Source: Sourcebook, 1978, Table 2.5

Table 6: Personal and household crimes: Number of victimizations and victimization rates, by type of crime, 1973-1977

Type of Crime	1973	(Rate per 1,000) 1974	1975	1976	1977
Personal victimizations					
Crimes of violence					
Number	5,351,000	5,510,000	5,573,000	5,599,000	5,902,000
Rate	32.6	33.0	32.8	32.6	33.9
Rape					
Number	156,000	163,000	154,000	145,000	154,000
Rate	1.0	1.0	0.9	0.8	0.9
Robbery					
Number	1,108,000	1,199,000	1,147,000	1,111,000	1,083,000
Rate	6.7	7.2	6.8	6.5	6.2
Assault					
Number	4,087,000	4,148,000	4,272,000	4,344,000	4,664,000
Rate	24.9	24.8	25.2	25.3	26.8
Aggravated assault					
Number	1,655,000	1,735,000	1,631,000	1,695,000	1,738,000
Rate	10.1	10.4	9.6	9.9	10.0
Simple assault					
Number	2,432,000	2,413,000	2,641,000	2,648,000	2,926,000
Rate	14.8	14.4	15.6	15.4	16.8

Crimes of theft					
Number	14,971,000	15,889,000	16,294000	16,519,000	16,933,000
Rate	91.1	95.1	96.0	96.1	97.3
Personal larceny with contact					
Number	504,000	520,000	524,000	497,000	461,000
Rate	3.1	3.1	3.1	2.9	2.7
Personal larceny without contact					
Number	14,466,000	15,369,000	15,770,000	16,022,000	16,472,000
Rate	88.0	92.0	92.9	93.2	94.6
Total population age 12 and over	164,363,000	167,058,000	169,671,000	171,901,000	174,093,000
Household victimizations					
Household burglary					
Number	6,458,700	6,720,700	6,743,700	6,663,400	6,764,900
Rate	91.7	93.1	91.7	88.9	88.5
Household larceny					
Number	7,537,300	8,933,100	9,223,000	9,300,900	9,418,300
Rate	107.0	123.8	125.4	124.1	123.3
Motor vehicle theft					
Number	1,343,900	1,358,400	1,433,000	1,234,600	1,296,800
Rate	19.1	18.8	19.5	16.5	17.0
Total number of households	70,442,400	72,162,900	73,559,600	74,956,100	76,412,300

Note: May not add to total shown because of rounding.

Source: "Criminal Victimization in the U.S.: A Comparison of 1976 and 1977 Findings, Advance Report," National Criminal Justice Information and Statistics Service, Law Enforcement Assistance Administration, November 1978.

Table 7: Estimated rate (per 100,000 persons 12 years of age or older) of personal victimization, by sex, race, and age of victim, and type of victimization, United States, 1976[a]

(Rate per 100,000 12 years of age or older)

Type of victimization and race of victim	Age of victim						
	12 to 15	16 to 19	20 to 24	25 to 34	35 to 49	50 to 64	65 or older
Sex of victim: Male							
Base:							
White	7,037,700	6,985,300	8,109,100	13,808,700	14,808,700	13,655,600	8,151,200
Black and other races	1,300,500	1,206,200	1,201,800	1,797,600	1,894,900	1,468,200	877,100
Rape and attempted rape:							
White	0	21	78	27	0	9	13
Black and other races	B	B	B	B	B	B	B
Robbery:							
White	1,508	1,193	1,135	711	582	409	545
Black and other races	2,375	1,972	2,186	1,772	1,505	2,304	999
Assault:							
White	5,215	7,623	5,918	4,342	1,867	948	681
Black and other races	3,988	5,212	5,712	5,281	1,244	1,282	316
Personal larceny with contact:							
White	356	441	222	155	143	148	180
Black and other races	325	917	1,219	487	306	609	520
Personal larceny without contact:							
White	16,498	15,895	16,347	12,052	8,559	6,263	2,970
Black and other races	10,006	10,759	14,330	11,693	7,448	6,978	2,470

Sex of victim: Female

Base:							
White	6,721,800	7,016,700	8,286,100	13,975,600	15,423,900	14,988,400	11,726,300
Black and other races	1,289,800	1,278,800	1,435,700	2,218,400	2,321,300	1,713,20	1,171,500
Rape and attempted rape:							
White	190	295	402	204	8	0	0
Black and other races	340	965	536	306	0	96	0
Robbery:							
White	332	518	593	350	313	296	141
Black and other races	303	812	1,964	1,068	556	571	458
Assault:							
White	3,103	3,708	3,174	2,075	1,220	505	195
Black and other races	3,221	4,205	3,973	2,980	1,046	1,060	821
Personal larceny with contact:							
White	105	331	355	287	203	308	351
Black and other races	0	174	771	798	663	698	935
Personal larceny without contact:							
White	14,575	14,235	13,148	10,245	7,869	5,078	1,789
Black and other races	9,621	9,108	8,532	9,247	6,413	3,337	2,185

a. Subcategories may not sum to total because of rounding.

Source: Sourcebook, 1978, Table 3.11

755

Table 8: Estimated rate (per 100,000 persons 12 years of age or older) of personal victimization, by race and family income of victim, and type of victimization, United States, 1976[a]

(Rate per 100,000 persons 12 years of age or older)

Type of victimization and race of victim	Under $3,000	Family income						Not ascertained
		$3,000 to $7,499	$7,500 to $9,999	$10,000 to $14,999	$15,000 to $24,999	$25,000 or more		
Base:								
White	8,951,900	27,225,600	14,663,700	35,766,100	36,261,900	14,367,800		13,488,500
Black and other races	3,140,600	6,495,000	2,352,700	3,593,200	2,692,900	862,500		2,038,000
Rape and attempted rape:								
White	196	108	107	58	41	51		37
Black and other races	406	123	195	36	185	B		56
Robbery:								
White	1,384	678	543	430	390	429		649
Black and other races	1,430	1,528	1,338	1,070	1,194	B		1,193
Assault:								
White	3,629	2,689	2,685	2,385	2,209	2,231		2,401
Black	4,170	2,796	1,837	2,867	2,911	B		2,068
Personal larceny with contact:								
White	543	285	251	162	189	240		338
Black and other races	654	627	589	559	573	B		611
Personal larceny without contact:								
White	8,796	7,474	8,658	9,199	10,872	13,336		7,951
Black and other races	5,971	6,298	8,406	9,453	12,196	B		7,938

a. Subcategories may not sum to total because of rounding.

Source: Sourcebook, 1978, Table 3.12.

Sex. The victimization rates are higher for males than females for all offenses except, of course, rape and larceny with contact. The sex difference is greatest for the more serious crimes of violence and is smallest for the less serious property offenses. For robbery and assault the victimization rates among whites are two to five times as high among men as women, while the differences in rates among black males and females, though still significant, are smaller than among whites. For larceny with contact between the victim and offender, the victimization rates are higher for young males of both races, but at age 20 among whites and age 25 among blacks the rate becomes higher for females. The rates for larceny without contact are similar for men and women of both races, with male rates being slightly higher than female rates. It should also be noted that this is the only offense for which black females have a lower victimization rate than white females. The patterns for this offense can probably be attributed to the greater likelihood of anonymous victimization, hence equalizing the chance of victimization by sex and race.

Race. Victimization rates are typically higher for blacks than whites, with some variation by the sex, age, and economic status of the victim. The only offense for which whites show consistently higher rates is larceny without contact. It is higher for whites for all ages except 50-64 years old, for both sexes, and at income levels below $10,000. The victimization rate for tape is higher among black than white women, with the victims of both races being typically young and poor. For robbery, blacks are victimized at higher rates among males and females at all income levels. Assault is more likely among blacks in general, at practically all income levels, but the victimization rate differs among males and females. Among women it is higher for blacks at all ages except 35-49, while among men it is higher for whites at all ages except 25-34 and 50-64. Victimization rates for larceny with contact are also higher for blacks. Among women the rate is higher for young whites, but is higher for blacks 20 years or older.

Income. The poor have higher rates of victimization for all offenses except larceny without contact, an offense which, almost by definition, means that the victim has valuable property to be taken. The poorest of both races are most often the victims of rape, with a steady decrease in the rate as income increases among whites, while among blacks the rate is highest among the poor and fluctuates at other income levels. For both races there is an increase at the higher income levels, which may reflect a higher rate of reporting of this offense among middle class women. Among whites the poorest are the most likely victims of robbery and the wealthier are less likely, while among blacks there is a more steady rate that remains over 1,000 for all income categories. Assault is apparently pervasive at all income levels, although the highest victimization rates are among those with incomes less than $3,000. At all income levels above this, there are relatively steady rates of over 2,000. The poorest also have the highest victimization rates for larceny without contact, with steady decreases as income increases for whites but a more stable rate of about 600 for blacks at all income levels. Larceny without contact again has a different pattern of victimization—the highest victimization rates are among those with incomes greater than $15,000. The rate is higher among whites with incomes less than $10,000 and among blacks with incomes greater than $10,000.

Age. In general, the young are most likely to be victimized. For rape, most victims are under 34 years old, although black women 50-64 years old are being raped while same-age white women apparently are not. The highest victimization rates for robbery are for victims under 24 years old, although among black males 50-64 years old the rate is almost as high as at 12-15 years old. Assault is also an offense of the young, with the highest rates among victims under 24 years old and the lowest rates among the oldest victims. Both larceny with and without contact are predominantly offenses aimed at young victims, with a steady decrease in the victimization rate as age increases.

Household Victimization

Tables 9 and 10 present data on the extend of household victimization in the United States during 1976. The rates of victimization computed for various demographic categories suggest a number of observations.

Race. For two of the three property crimes examined, burglary and auto theft, the rate of victimization is much higher among black than white families. With respect to larceny, racial differences in victimization are not as dramatic, with whites showing a slight tendency to be victimized more often than blacks.

Income. The amount of income a family possesses is also related to the probability of household victimization. Families of low socioeconomic status are much more likely to be burglarized than are those families in higher income brackets. This relationship exists among white families as well as blacks. For example, the rate of burglary victimization among black families with less than $3,000 income is 137.4 per 1,000 households. The comparable rate among blacks with incomes between $15,000 and $25,000 is 98.1 per 1,000 households. It is also interesting to note that the family income level at which burglary victimization rates drop off substantially is much lower ($3,000-$7,499) for whites than it is for blacks ($10,000-$14,999).

Turning to larceny and auto theft, the data show positive associations between family income levels and these two rates of property victimization. Again, these relationships hold up across racial categories. Among white families, those with incomes exceeding $25,000 have the highest rates of larceny and motor vehicle theft. Among blacks, those with incomes between $7,500 and $10,000 are victimized to the greatest extent.

Age. For all three offenses—burglary, larceny, and motor vehicle theft—the younger the head of the household, the greater the probability of victimization. The data presented in Table 10 show that for burglary the rate among families with a head less than 20 years old is four times that among families headed by someone 65 or older. The age differences in victimization rates are similarly great for both larceny and motor vehicle theft. For larceny, the youngest age

Table 9: Estimated rate (per 100,000 households) of household victimization, by family income, race of head of household, and type of victimization, United States, 1976[a]

(Rate per 100,000 households)

Type of victimization and race of head of household	Under $3,000	$3,000 to $7,499	$7,500 to $9,999	Family income $10,000 to $14,999	$15,000 to $24,999	$25,000 or more	Not ascertained
Base:							
White	5,983,570	14,330,910	6,647,900	14,644,710	13,331,800	5,022,630	6,103,510
Black and other races	1,816,530	2,781,940	934,090	1,336,070	926,670	261,600	834,120
Burglary:							
White	11,063	8,709	8,387	7,336	8,169	9,385	7,373
Black and other races	13,744	13,103	13,681	10,573	9,806	B	11,268
Larceny:							
White	9,776	11,276	13,118	13,971	14,046	14,141	9,951
Black and other races	8,266	10,825	13,016	14,161	12,355	B	9,067
Vehicle theft:							
White	941	1,256	1,625	1,813	1,781	2,326	1,415
Black and other races	702	1,902	3,429	3,116	2,690	B	1,455

a. Subcategories may not sum to total because of rounding.

Source: Sourcebook, 1978, Table 3.32.

Table 10: Estimated rate (per 100,000 households) of a household victimization, by age of head of household and type of victimization, United States, 1976[a]

(Rate per 100,000 households)

Type of victimization	12 to 19	20 to 34	Age of head of household 35 to 49	50 to 64	65 or older
Base	1,094,900	22,091,700	13,521,500	18,458,900	14,789,100
Burglary	20,729	12,355	9,280	6,750	5,020
Larceny	17,813	17,187	14,472	9,457	5,954
Vehicle theft	2,741	2,429	1,890	1,233	611

a. Subcategories may not sum to total because of rounding.

Source: Sourcebook, 1978. Table 3.31.

group has a victimization rate that is three times that of the oldest group. For motor vehicle theft the ratio is about four and one-half to one.

CURRENT ISSUES IN CRIMINOLOGY

The Female Offender: Sex and Age Differences in Crime

The 1970s have been declared the decade of female crime. It has been asserted that there are substantial increases in female crime for both serious (violent) and less serious (property) offenses, and that women criminals are becoming more like their male counterparts, much in the same way that "liberated" women in general are behaving more like men. Substantial increases in the kind of crimes available to female white collar employees—e.g., embezzlement—have been predicted as a consequence of the entry of women into occupations previously less available to them. The data, in some cases, suggest these kinds of changes in female crime and, in other cases, they do not.

Table 11 presents 1970 and 1977 arrest rates by sex and age for each of the FBI Index Crimes except rape, plus three other offenses which historically have been considered "female crimes." Overall, the data show that crime is a predominantly male enterprise, among both adults and juveniles. There are substantial differences in the arrest rates, with the largest differences for the serious offenses (murder, robbery, burglary, assault, car theft) and the smallest differences for the less serious offenses (larceny, forgery, fraud, embezzlement).

The arrest rates for *murder* are much higher for males than females, with the highest rates among adults of each sex and male-to-female ratios of arrest rates for juveniles of 13:1 and for adults of 6:1. These rates are relatively stable from 1970 to 1977.

There are also substantial differences in the arrest rates for *robbery*—male arrests outnumber female arrests by from 13:1 among juveniles to 17:1 among adults. There has been a noticeable increase in robbery between 1970 and 1977 among juvenile males; they now have a higher arrest rate (129.03) for robbery than adult males (115.61), as do juvenile females (9.56) over adult females (9.05). During the same time, there was a slight decrease in the adult male rate and a slight increase in the adult and juvenile female rates. Because of the equal but opposite changes in rates among men and women, the sex ratio of robbery arrest rates is significantly smaller in 1977 than 1970, signaling a small but perhaps important move toward parity between the sexes in robbery among adult offenders.

Aggravated assault showed large increases in arrest rates among adult and juvenile males, increases that are five to eight times as large as the increases among females. The sex ratios are approximately 6:1 for juveniles and 7:1 for adults, and they remain stable from 1970 to 1977. Adult males are clearly most violent, followed by juvenile males, adult females, and juvenile females.

The arrest rate for *burglary* is the highest among juvenile males, and between 1970 and 1977 there were large increases in the male arrest rates and smaller

Table 11: Arrest Rates by Offense, Sex and Age[a]

| | Juvenile[b] | | | | Adult | | | |
| | 1970 | | 1977 | | 1970 | | 1977 | |
Offense	Male	Female	Male	Female	Male	Female	Male	Female
Murder	5.28	.39	5.39	.47	20.06	3.76	19.39	3.34
	(13.54)[c]		(11.47)		(5.34)		(5.81)	
Robbery	114.94	8.40	129.03	9.56	117.79	6.84	115.61	9.05
	(13.68)		(13.50)		(17.22)		(12.77)	
Aggravated Assault	73.31	11.57	107.64	18.04	188.32	26.32	239.23	32.73
	(6.34)		(5.97)		(7.16)		(7.31)	
Burglary	568.18	26.38	757.58	45.48	269.54	13.48	303.03	18.93
	(21.53)		(16.66)		(19.99)		(16.01)	
Larceny	943.40	315.46	1075.27	406.50	436.68	184.50	558.66	282.49
	(2.99)		(2.65)		(2.37)		(1.98)	
Car Theft	273.97	14.89	225.73	21.48	111.73	5.45	87.41	6.38
	(18.39)		(10.51)		(20.50)		(13.70)	
Forgery	13.63	4.75	21.20	8.05	61.27	18.13	59.59	24.07
	(2.87)		(2.63)		(3.38)		(2.48)	
Fraud	9.61	2.88	63.01	15.89	103.62	38.07	170.65	96.53
	(3.34)		(3.97)		(2.72)		(1.77)	
Embezzlement	1.02	.32	2.10	.56	12.17	3.94	6.46	1.87
	(3.19)		(3.75)		(3.09)		(3.45)	

a. Derived from Uniform Crime Reports, 1970 and 1977, table "Persons Arrested by Offense, Sex, and Age Group." The rates are calculated per 100,000 population of each sex-age category; adjustments for percentage of population for each year from Resident Population statistics, U.S. Census Bureau.

b. An adult is 18 or older, a juvenile is under 18 years old.

c. Ratio of male to female arrest rate.

increases among females. The sex ration decreased from approximately 20:1 to 16:1 among both adults and juveniles, reflecting higher proportionate rate increases among females, even though the juvenile increase was 10 times greater among males than females and the adult increase was six times greater among males than females.

The sex ratios are much smaller for *larceny*—among juveniles about three boys are arrested for every girl, while approximately twice as many men as women are arrested. The rates for juvenile males are by far the highest, almost twice as high as those among adult males, followed by juvenile females and adult females. Between 1970 and 1977 there are rate increases among all sex and age categories, with increases about 1:5 times as large among males as females, but no significant changes in the sex ratios among adults or juveniles.

Car theft is a young male offense, and the sex ratios of arrest rates are smaller among adults. There were substantial decreases in male arrest rates between 1970 and 1977, especially among juveniles, and slight increases among females, especially among juveniles. These changes in arrest rates, primarily the dramatic decreases in the male arrest rates rather than the increases in the female arrest rates, are responsible for the smaller sex ratios in 1977 than 1970 among both juveniles (from approximately 18:1 to 10:1) and adults (from 20:1 to 14:1).

For non-Index Crimes, the sex differences are less pronounced. The highest arrest rate for *forgery* in 1977 is among adult males (59.59), followed by adult females (24.07). There is an increase in the juvenile male arrest rate, but a slight decrease in the adult male rate, while both women and girls show increases between 1970 and 1977. The consequence is a small decrease in the sex ratio, particularly among adults, from 3:38 in 1970 to 2:48 in 1977.

Fraud shows a similar pattern of sex differences and change over time. The highest arrest rate in 1977 is among adult males (170.65), followed by adult females (96.53). There are large increases between 1970 and 1977 in arrest rates for all sex and age groups, with the largest increase for men, then women, boys, and girls. Among juveniles, the sex ratio increases from 3.34 in 1970 to 3.97 in 1977, while among adults it decreases from 2.72 to 1.7. These small changes suggest that boys and girls are becoming more different in their fraudulent behavior, while that of men and women is converging. The difference in direction of change between juveniles and adults can be attributed to the rate increase being four times as large among boys as girls, while the rate increase among women is almost as large as that among men.

The arrest rates and their changes over time for *embezzlement* do not support predictions of increased female involvement. The arrest rate in 1977 is highest among males (6.46), followed not by adult females as in 1970, but by juvenile males (2.10), then adult (1.87) and juvenile (.56) females. Between 1970 and 1977 there are arrest rate decreases for both men and women, and the sex ratios for both adults and juveniles increase from approximately 3:1 in 1970 to 3.5:1 in 1977, meaning that males and females may be becoming less alike for this crime.

Capital Crimes, Death Sentences, and Race

Deterrence research and theory has renewed the interest in capital crimes, the number of persons sentenced to death, and the role that race plays in both. Table 12 shows the arrest rates and number sentenced to death for the two most significant capital offenses—murder and rape—for whites and blacks from 1970 to 1977.

Examining the arrest rates for *murder,* it is apparent that after a decrease in 1976, the white rate is close to the highest that it has been in the past eight years. For blacks there is also an increase, but the rates for 1976 and 1977 are the lowest since 1970. What is perhaps most striking is the difference in murder arrest rates—the black rate is, on the average, approximately 10 times the white rate, even though the absolute number of murder arrests is similar (1977: white = 7,866; black = 8,731). However, this black-to-white ratio of murder arrest rates has *declined* steadily from a high of 13.87 in 1971 to the low of 8.04 in 1977. This is a result of the rate increases among whites and more substantial decreases among blacks. These data suggest less fatal violence among blacks and more violence among whites as we proceed through the decade of the 1970s.

The number sentenced to death for murder dropped substantially in 1977, from the highs of 1975 and 1976. There were almost 100 fewer sentenced to death in 1977 than 1976. The number of whites (68) and blacks (62) sentenced to death is similar, as are the totals from 1970-1977—whites = 538, blacks = 514. This, of course, is an overrepresentation of blacks as compared to their representation in the general population. On the other hand, the absolute number of black arrests for murder is greater than for whites and so is the rate per 100,000 race category. If one examines the death sentence curve from 1970-1977, the trend is virtually identical for whites and blacks. There is a steady decline from 1970 to the low point of 1973, a dramatic jump to the highs of 1975, and the sharp decrease down to the numbers in 1977 similar to those in 1970. That is, the sentencing trends do not vary by race; changes in sentencing seem to affect convicted murderers of different races in the same way. In fact, based on the number of whites and blacks who are sentenced to death as a proportion of the number arrested for murder, one could argue that whites are disproportionately sentenced to death. Regardless, the data suggest that if there is race discrimination, as is often suggested regarding the use of the death sentence, it occurs either at the point of arrest (hence the large black-white ratio of arrest rates) or in those social, economic, and cultural conditions which are responsible for the behavioral differences.

Examining the arrest rates for *rape,* it is apparent that after a slight decrease in 1976, the white rate is the highest that it has been in the past eight years. For blacks there is also an increase in 1977, among the highest of the decade. Again, there is a large race difference in rape arrest rates—the black rate is, on the average, seven times the white rate, even though the absolute number of rape arrests is similar (1977: white = 12,932; black = 12,156). However, this

Table 12: Arrest rates and persons sentenced to death by offense, race and year[a]

Year	Murder Arrest Rate[b] White	Black	Murder Sentenced to Death White	Black	Rape Arrest Rate White	Black	Rape Sentenced to Death White	Black	Total Sentenced to Death[d]
1970	3.59 (11.77)[c]	42.29	64	52	5.79 (7.60)	44.03	0	9	127
1971	3.70 (13.87)	51.33	45	50	5.79 (8.34)	48.29	3	3	104
1972	3.92 (12.83)	50.30	26	40	6.61 (8.00)	52.88	3	5	75
1973	4.15 (11.30)	46.90	11	22	7.00 (7.19)	50.33	3	4	42
1974	4.53 (11.49)	52.08	67	60	7.09 (7.71)	54.70	4	12	151
1975	4.64 (9.54)	44.31	121	140	7.06 (6.87)	48.57	3	14	285
1976	3.83 (8.63)	33.08	136	88	6.71 (6.60)	44.29	1	4	233
1977	4.59 (8.04)	36.94	68	62	7.55 (6.81)	51.44	1	0	133

a. Derived from Uniform Crime Reports, 1970–1977, table "Total Arrests by Race"; and from National Prisoner Statistics Bulletins entitled "Capital Punishment," table "Prisoners Received from Court Under Sentence of Death, by Race, Offense, Region, and Jurisdiction," as well as directly from the National Criminal Justice Information and Statistics Service when not available in published form.

b. Rate per 100,000 population of race category; adjustments for percentage of population for each year from resident population statistics, U.S. Census Bureau.

c. Ratio of black to white arrest rate.

d. Includes all capital offenses, plus "other" race category; the other offenses and races are inconsequential.

765

black-to-white ratio of rape arrests has *declined* steadily from a high of 8.34 in 1971 to 6.81 in 1977. This is the result of the rate increases among whites and more substantial decreases among blacks. These data suggest that there is more rape being committed by whites and less by blacks or that the apparent increased reporting of rape victimization is occurring at a greater rate among the victims of white rapists (viz. white women).

The number sentenced to death for rape is much smaller than for murder and, like murder, dropped to the fewest in the decade—one white rapist. Unlike death sentences for murder, more blacks (51) than whites (18) have been sentenced to death for rape between 1970 and 1977. Given that the absolute number of rape arrests is similar for blacks and whites, one might expect a more equal number of death sentences. The charge of racial discrimination in death sentences can be more readily defended for rape than murder. If one examines the death sentence curve from 1970-1977, whites have an almost straight line averaging about three per year, while the black curve follows the murder death sentence line, dropping from 1970 to 1973, increasing dramatically in 1974 and 1975, and crashing to the low of zero in 1977.

It is difficult to say what these data tell us about the deterrent potential of the death sentence. Suffice it to say that regardless of the fluctuations in the number of death sentences by year, the murder and rape arrest rates have remained relatively stable compared to other offenses over the years and the differing increases and decreases by race may be difficult to explain as a consequence of the imposition of death sentences unless one assumes or proposes that there is a race and/or offense difference in the deterrent effect of capital punishment.

NOTES

1. If time served in prison is decreasing, the numbers in prison over any span of time—and the incarceration rate measured this way—are increasing even more than these figures suggest. Also, these figures do *not* include prisoners sentenced to jails.

2. On December 31, 1977, there were approximately 181,800 adults under the supervision of U.S. state and and federal parole agencies (173,300 on parole, 8,500 under mandatory release). Source: "Parole in the United States: 1976 and 1977," Uniform Parole Report, National Council on Crime and Delinquency.

ABOUT THE EDITORS

SHELDON L. MESSINGER is Professor of Law at the University of California, Berkeley and continues to be associated with the Center for the Study of Law and Politics there. Formerly, he was Professor and Dean of the School of Criminology at the University of California, Berkeley.

EGON BITTNER received his Ph.D. from the University of California, Los Angeles in 1961. He taught at the University of California, Riverside, and was a Research Social Scientist at the Langley Porter Neuropsychiatric Institute, University of California Medical School, San Francisco. He is presently Harry Coplan Professor in the Social Sciences and Chairman of the Sociology Department at Brandeis University.